THE CHINESE CLASSICS

THE SHOO KING

or

THE BOOK OF HISTORICAL DOCUMENTS

THE CHINESE CLASSICS

*Copyright reissue, in five volumes
by the Hong Kong University Press*

*Reprinted from the last editions of the Oxford University Press. A number of errata listed by
James Legge have been corrected in the text. Added at the front of each volume are Concor-
dance Tables to later translations in English, French and German and to the* SHIH-SAN-CHING
CHU-SHU FU CHIAO-K'AN-CHI 十三經注疏附校勘記, *Shanghai 1935.*

Volume I contains a portrait of Dr James Legge with a BIOGRAPHICAL NOTE *by Dr L. T. Ride,
Vice-Chancellor of the University of Hong Kong. Volume II contains* NOTES ON MENCIUS *by
Dr Arthur Waley, originally published in* ASIA MAJOR, *NS.I, i, 1949.*

THE CHINESE CLASSICS

*with a translation, critical and exegetical
notes, prolegomena, and copious indexes*

by

JAMES LEGGE

IN FIVE VOLUMES

III

THE SHOO KING

*Second edition with minor text corrections
and a Concordance Table*

HONG KONG
HONG KONG UNIVERSITY PRESS
1960

THE OXFORD UNIVERSITY PRESS, AMEN HOUSE, LONDON E.C.4
AND 417 FIFTH AVENUE, NEW YORK 16 ARE EXCLUSIVE
AGENTS FOR ALL COUNTRIES EXCEPT ASIA EAST OF BURMA

Printed by
CATHAY PRESS
153 Island Road at Aberdeen
Hong Kong

HISTORY

CONCORDANCE TABLE TO

Karlgren[1], Couvreur[2] and *Shih-san-ching chu-shu*[3]

No.	尚　書	THE SHOO KING	Legge	Karlgren Tr.	Karlgren Glosses	Cou-vreur	十三經
No.	唐　書	The Book of T'ang					
1	堯　典	The Canon of Yaou	15	1	1–44	1	117
2	舜　典	The Canon of Shun	29	—	—	12	125
3	大　禹　謨	The Counsels of the Great Yu	52	—	—	32	134
4	皋　陶　謨	The Counsels of Kaou-yaou	68	8	1–106	44	138
5	益　稷	Yih and Tseih	76	—	—	49	141
	夏　書	The Books of Hea					
6	禹　貢	The Tribute of Yu	92	12	1–145	61	146
7	甘　誓	The Speech at Kan	152	18	1–167	89	155
8	五子之歌	The Songs of the Five Sons	156	—	—	91	156
9	胤　征	The Punitive Expedition of Yin	162	—	—	95	157
	商　書	The Books of Shang					
10	湯　誓	The Speech of Tang	173	20	1–171	101	160
11	仲虺之誥	The Announcement of Chung-hwuy	177	—	—	103	161
12	湯　誥	The Announcement of T'ang	184	—	—	108	162
13	伊　訓	The Instructions of E	191	—	—	113	162
14	太　甲　上	T'ae Kea, Part i	199	—	—	118	163
15	太　甲　中	T'ae Kea, Part ii	205	—	—	122	164
16	太　甲　下	T'ae Kea, Part iii	209	—	—	124	165
17	咸有一德	Both possessed Pure Virtue	213	—	—	127	165
18	盤　庚　上	Pwan-kang, Part i	220	} 20	} 1–174	132	168
19	盤　庚　中	Pwan-kang, Part ii	233			140	170
20	盤　庚　下	Pwan-kang, Part iii	243			147	171
21	說　命　上	The Charge to Yue, Part i	248	—	—	150	174
22	說　命　中	The Charge to Yue, Part ii	254	—	—	154	175
23	說　命　下	The Charge to Yue, Part iii	259	—	—	158	175
24	高宗肜日	The Day of the Supplementary Sacrifice of Kaou-tsung	264	26	1–214	162	176
25	西伯戡黎	The Chief of the West's Conquest of Le	268	26	1–218	163	176
26	微　子	The Viscount of Wei	273	27	1–220	165	177
	周　書	The Books of Chow					
27	泰　誓　上	The Great Declaration, Part i	281	—	—	171	179
28	泰　誓　中	The Great Declaration, Part ii	289	—	—	176	181
29	泰　誓　下	The Great Declaration, Part iii	294	—	—	180	182
30	牧　誓	The Speech at Muh	300	29	1–228	184	182
31	武　成	The Successful Completion of the War	306	—	—	187	183
32	洪　範	The Great Plan	320	29	1–231	194	187

倘　書		THE SHOO KING	Legge	Karlgren		Cou-vreur	十三經
				Tr.	Glosses		
No.	周　書	The Book of Chow					
33	旅　獒	The Hounds of Leu	345	—	—	209	194
34	金　縢	The Metal-bound Coffer	351	35	1–248	213	195
35	大　誥	The Great Announcement	362	36	1–258	220	197
36	微子之命	The Charge to the Viscount of Wei	376	—	—	229	200
37	康　誥	The Announcement to the Prince of K'ang	381	39	1–278	232	202
38	酒　誥	The Announcement about Drunkenness	399	43	1–296	245	205
39	梓　材	The Timber of the Tsze Tree	413	46	1–307	254	208
40	召　誥	The Announcement of the Duke of Shaou	420	48	2–63	258	211
41	洛　誥	The Announcement concerning Lo	434	51	2–74	269	214
42	多　士	The Numerous Officers	453	55	2–94	281	219
43	無　逸	Against Luxurious Ease	464	56	2–105	290	221
44	君　奭	Prince Shih	474	59	2–114	297	223
45	蔡仲之命	The Charge to Chung of Ts'ae	487	—	—	307	227
46	多　方	Numerous Regions	492	62	2–133	311	227
47	立　政	The Establishment of Government	508	67	2–145	321	230
48	周　官	The Officers of Chow	523	—	—	331	234
49	君　陳	Keun-ch'in	535	—	—	339	236
50	顧　命	The Testamentary Charge	544	70	2–156	344	237
51	康王之誥	The Announcement of King K'ang	562	—	—	358	243
52	畢　命	The Charge to the Duke of Peih	569	—	—	363	244
53	君　牙	Keun-ya	578	—	—	369	246
54	冏　命	The Charge to Keung	583	—	—	372	246
55	呂　刑	The Prince of Leu upon Punishments	588	74	2–174	375	247
56	文侯之命	The Charge to Prince Wan	613	78	2–194	390	253
57	費　誓	The Speech at Pe	621	80	2–198	393	254
58	秦　誓	The Speech of the Duke of Ts'in	626	81	2–200	396	256

[1] Karlgren, Bernard, 'The Book of Documents', The Museum of Far Eastern Antiquities, *Bulletin 22*, p. 1–81. Stockholm 1950.

    Glosses 1, in MFEA, *Bulletin 20*, p. 39–315. Stockholm 1948.

    Glosses 2, in MFEA, *Bulletin 21*, p. 63–206. Stockholm 1949.

[2] Couvreur, S., 書經 *Chou King*. Texte chinois avec une double traduction en français et en latin, des annotations et un vocabulaire. Imprimerie de la Mission Catholique, Ho Kien fou, 1897, in-8, p. 8 + 464. Facsimile reissue by Cathasia, Paris—Leiden, 1950.

    There is also a 1916 Hien Hien edition, without the Latin translation, p. 8 + 334 + 3 folding maps.

[3] 十三經注疏附校勘記 Photographic reproduction of the Yüan 1817 woodblock edition 景印阮刻; in 2 vols. (24 + 2782 p.), Shanghai 1935.

NOTE ALSO

Pelliot, Paul, Le *Chou-King* en caractères anciens et le *Chang Chou che wen*, *Mémoires concernant l'Asie orientale*, II, Paris 1916, p. 123/177, 7 plates.

Legge, James, *The Texts of Confucianism*, Part 1, The Shu King. Sacred Books of the East, Vol. III, p. 1–272, The Clarendon Press, Oxford 1895.

Cordier, Henri, *Bibliotheca Sinica*. Paris 1904–24; col. 1376–80, 1781–2.

Yüan, Tung-li 袁同禮, *China in Western Literature*, a continuation of Cordier's *Bibliotheca Sinica*. Far Eastern Publications, Yale University, New Haven, Conn., 1958, p. 291*f*.

Shang-shu t'ung-chien 尙書通檢. Compiled by Ku Chieh-kang 顧頡剛. Harvard-Yenching Institute, Peiping 1936. Punctuated text with index.

Shih-san-ching so-yin 十三經索引. Compiled by Yeh Shao-chün 葉紹鈞. K'ai-ming shu-tien 開明書店. Shanghai 1934. Sentence Index.

THE CHINESE CLASSICS.

VOL. III.

THE SHOO KING,
OR
THE BOOK OF HISTORICAL DOCUMENTS.

不以文害辭，不以辭害志，以意逆志，是為得之。

Mencius, V. Pt. I. iv. 2.

THE

CHINESE CLASSICS:

WITH

A TRANSLATION CRITICAL AND EXEGETICAL NOTES,
PROLEGOMENA, AND COPIOUS INDEXES.

BY

JAMES LEGGE, D.D.,

OF THE LONDON MISSIONARY SOCIETY.

IN SEVEN VOLUMES.

VOL. III.—PART I.

CONTAINING

THE FIRST PARTS OF THE SHOO-KING.
OR THE BOOKS OF T'ANG; THE BOOKS OF YU; THE BOOKS OF
HEA; THE BOOKS OF SHANG; AND THE PROLEGOMENA.

London:

HENRY FROWDE,

OXFORD UNIVERSITY PRESS WAREHOUSE, AMEN CORNER, E.C.

HONGKONG:

PRINTED AT THE LONDON MISSIONARY SOCIETY'S

PRINTING OFFICE.

PREFACE.

The Author is sorry that so long a time has elapsed between the publication of the Works of Mencius and the appearance of this third volume of his undertaking. He felt it necessary, in 1862, to rest in a great measure from his labours on the Chinese Classics, both to recruit his strength, and to devote himself closely to his directly missionary duties; while certain other tasks were pressed on him by friends, which he could not well decline. In the month of March, 1863, he commenced printing his translation of the Shoo and the accompanying notes; but fresh and unexpected engagements, in connection with his position in Hongkong, interposed many hindrances to the progress of the work; and during the last year he was often laid aside from it by repeated attacks of illness. New views of the text, moreover, and of the various questions considered in the Prolegomena, presented themselves as he proceeded, and in many cases prolonged research and reflection were required before he could make up his mind upon them. He can only hope, now that this portion of his task is done, that the extent and execution of it will be deemed some apology for the delay which has occurred in giving it to the public. He does not anticipate so much delay in the appearance of the volumes that remain. The next will be the *She King*, or the Book of Poetey.

Two translations of the Shoo were already in existence. The older is in French, and was the Work of Father Gaubil, one of the ablest of the many able Jesuit Missionaries of the early part of last century. It was published at Paris in 1,770, under the editorship of M. De Guignes, who interspersed not a few notes of his own among those of the author. besides making other additions to the Work. Gaubil's own manuscript was lost; but the editor had the use of two copies which had been taken of it. He found it necessary, however, he tells us, to review and correct the version by having recourse to the Chinese text; and this is to be deplored. Gaubil may have often paraphrased his original, as M. De Guignes says; but I have no doubt the translation, as written by him, was more correct than as it now appears. The second translation was the work of the late Rev. Dr. Medhurst, and was published by him at Shanghae in 1846. He assigned as his reasons for giving it to the world, that 'Gaubil's translation was too free, and in many respects faulty, and had never been commonly known in England.' It may be doubted, however, whether his version be any improvement on the other. Dr. Medhurst's attainments in Chinese were prodigious. But his work on the Shoo was done hastily. He seems to have consulted no native commentary but that of Ts'ae Ch'in; and his notes are very inferior to those of Gaubil.

The Author ventures to hope that the translation now offered represents the Chinese original much more faithfully than either of those previous ones. When he first wrote it, many years ago, having less confidence in himself than he now has, he made free use both of Gaubil and Medhurst. He wrote it all out again in 1862, seldom, if ever, looking at them; and found it necessary to make many changes in every page. Not a little of it was written out a third time, while the work was going through the press.

The Author has often heard Sinologues speak of the difficulty of understanding the Shoo, and hazard the opinion, that, if we had not the native commentaries, we should not be able to make out the meaning of it at all. He would be far from denying that the book is difficult. His own labour on it has been too toilsome to allow his doing so. At the same time, it is by no means unintelligible. Here and there a passage occurs, which yields no satisfactory result after the most persistent study; but in general, if we had not the native commentaries, we should simply have to study the text as intensely and continuously as the native commentators did. They differ, indeed, very frequently among themselves; but this no more entitles us to say that the meaning of the Shoo cannot be determined than similar discrepancies in the views of interpreters on many texts would justify us in saying that the Bible is unintelligible. In a few places, the Author has been obliged to propound an interpretation quite new. He might have done so in very many more; but he preferred, wherever it was possible, to abide by views that had occurred to some native scholar, rather than start new ones of his own.

The Author is grateful for the kind reception which his two previous volumes have met with from Sinologues both in China and in other countries. One, who of all others has the best right to counsel in such a case, will pardon him for introducing here a suggestion which he offered, and giving his reasons for not attending to it. 'I should have desired,' wrote he, 'that, during the publication of the Four Books, you could have been assisted phrase by phrase, or, so to speak, word by word, by a Chinese scholar perfectly versed in Mandchou. I present this view, that you should not in your following publications deprive yourself of this excellent succour, without which one cannot arrive at an interpretation in conformity with the official (not to say sacramental) sense adopted by the most eminent men of the empire.' Now, before the Author commenced publishing in 1860, the plan thus suggested was considered by him, and he concluded that the advantage to be derived from it would not compensate for the expense and trouble which it would occasion. In the first place, the Manchoos are as dependent as ourselves on the Chinese interpreters. In the second place, the official sense is now very different from what it was before the Sung era; and even in the present dynasty, many of the most distinguished scholars and highest officers do not hesitate to propound and maintain interpretations which are at variance with it. In the third place, the Author hopes, in the course of his labours, to explode not a few of the views about the Classics, which may be pronounced official; believing that, by doing so, he will render the greatest service to the Chinese nation, and facilitate the way for the reception of Christianity by its scholars and people.

Students who read the present volume carefully will find in the annotations little trace of the doubt about the historical genuineness of the first Parts of the Book, and some other points, to which decided expression is given in the Prolegomena. The fact is, that when the earlier notes were written, the doubts in question had not assumed consistency in the Author's mind; and he subsequently thought it the best course to continue his interpretation and criticism of the text on the assumption that the whole was genuine. This would have at least the advantage of enabling the student to understand more readily whatever he might find in native writers.

A great desideratum in the study of the Classics of China is a really good dictionary. The Author is not thinking of the translations or compilations by Morrison, Gonçalves, Medhurst, and others; but the Chinese themselves have no dictionary which gives a satisfactory historical analysis of the characters of the language and traces from the primary meaning of each term its various subsequent applications. When a dictionary shall have been made on true principles, by some one who understands the origin of the characters, and has pursued the history of every one through the various forms which it has assumed, the interpretation of the Classics will be greatly simplified.

The Author's obligations to the Rev. Mr. Chalmers, for the Indexes of Subjects and Proper Names, the Essay on Ancient Chinese Astronomy, printed in the Prolegomena, and for various suggestions and assistance in the progress of the Work, have been great. Nor must he fail to acknowledge gratefully the services rendered to him by Wang T'aou, a graduate of Soo-chow. This scholar, far excelling in classical lore any of his countrymen whom the Author had previously known, came to Hongkong in the end of 1863, and placed at his disposal all the treasures of a large and well-selected library. At the same time, entering with spirit into his labours, now explaining, now arguing, as the case might be, he has not only helped but enlivened many a day of toil.

Mr Frederick Stewart, Head Master of the Government Schools in Hongkong, and Mr. G. M. Bain, of the "China Mail" Office, have very kindly aided in the correction for the press. Few typographical mistakes have escaped their notice. Some errors in Chinese names should have been detected by the Author, but escaped his notice through the pre-occupation of his mind with other matters.

HONGKONG. 12th July. 1865.

CONTENTS.

I. THE PROLEGOMENA.

CHAPTER I.

THE HISTORY OF THE SHOO KING.

CHAPTER II.

ON THE CREDIBILITY OF THE RECORDS IN THE SHOO.

CHAPTER III.

ON THE DETERMINATION OF THE PRINCIPAL ERAS IN THE SHOO.

CHAPTER IV.

THE ANNALS OF THE BAMBOO BOOKS.

CHAPTER V.

THE ANCIENT EMPIRE OF CHINA.

CHAPTER VI.

LIST OF THE PRINCIPAL WORKS WHICH HAVE BEEN CONSULTED IN THE PREPARATION

OF THIS VOLUME.

II. THE BODY OF THE VOLUME.

III. INDEXES.

ERRATA.

I. IN THE CHINESE TEXT.

Page	Column.				Page	Column.			
* 71,	2,	for 采 read 柔.			260,	10,	insert 説.		
* 75,	3,	„ 底 „ 厎			*276,	2,	for 出 read 岀.		

The same alteration elsewhere, except in V., xxii. 16.

*313, 4, „ 祇 „ 祇.

In some other cases, the same change.

* 87,	1,	for 戞 read 戛.			397, *et al.*	3,	for 并 read 并.		
* 141,	3,	„ 刋 „ 刊			*369,	5,	„ 巳 „ 已.		
* 203,	1,	after 彎 insert ○			*558,	6,	„ 王 „ 皇		
* 241,	6,	for 愚 read 遇.							

* PAGE 13,.......Col. 6th.....................after 命 *dele* Comma.
* „ 63,.............4th................... for 從 read 從.
* „ 84, Between 2d and 3d Columns,. for 九 節 „ 八 節.
* „ 99,.............7th................... „ 貞 作 „ 貞, 作.
* „ 168,.............2d................... „ 罰 爾 „ 罰, 爾.
* „ 218, Between 6th and 7th Columns, ...by 鳴 insert 十 節.
* „ 276,.............9th.....................after 2d 畏 insert a Comma.
* „ 390,.............5th................... „ 師 insert a Comma.
* „ 440,.............8th................... „ 繹 *dele* Comma.
* „ 454,.............6th................... for 威. read 威.
* „ 525,.............5th...................after 日 insert a Comma.
* „ 541,.............2d................... for 訓. read 訓.
* „ 558,.............10th................... „ 下. „ 下.
* „ 565,.............5th................... „ 功. „ 功.
* „ 597,.............2d...................by 典 insert 十 一 節.

II. CHINESE CHARACTERS IN THE NOTES.

Page.	Line.	Column.			Page.	Line.	Column.		
* 1,	6,	II,	for 微 read 徵		* 87,	2,	II,	for 戞 read 戛	
* 18,	26,	„	„ 居 „ 宅		*238,	7,	I,	„ 子 „ 于	
* 20,	10,	„	„ 日 „ 夜		*252,	8,	II,	after 眒) insert 眩	
* 30,	55,	I,	„ 記 „ 紀		*310,	25,	I,	for 既 read 哉	
* 51,	1,	II,	„ 且 „ 乃		*482,	17,	„	„ 天 „ 有	
* 66,	17,18,	I,	„ 祇 „ 祇						

III. IN THE PROLEGOMENA.

Page.	Line.		Page.	Line.	
5,	16,	for 82 read 72.	38,	21,	for Shih read Mih.
7,	6, note	tables, read tablets.	40,	4,	„ Sung „ Suy.
11,	8,	11th „ 12th.	68,	8,	„ Y'ang „ T'ang.

* Corrected

IV. IN THE TRANSLATION AND NOTES.

Page.	Line.		Page.	Line.	Column.
128,	In title of Book for II. read I.		* 23,	11,	2, for 于眉 read 于眉.
289,	294, 301, 306, 320, 343, 350, 362, 376,			26,	„ Ching „ Suy.
381,	399,——		33,	7,	2, „ -shing „ Shing.
	for THE BOOKS OF SHANG read THE		35,	25,	2, „ 37 „ 27.
BOOKS OF CHOW.			46,	21,	1, „ 6 „ 1.
6,	11,	for Hëaou read Gaou.	48,	13,	2, „ 80 „ 81.
9,	3,	„ Le „ Leu.	* 64,	24,	1, transpose 是 and 時.
11,	8,	„ Chang „ Chung.	85,	14,	2, for eleven read twelve.
17,	8,	„ Sea „ four Seas.	99,	18,	2, „ 1 „ 12.
90,	11,	af. Emperor ins. bowed, and.	141,	14,	2, ʃaf. waters put a full stop.
128, et al. 3,		for Te read Che.	149,	7,	1, for Han read Chow.
	5,	„ Ta „ T‘ae.	152,	26,	2, „ 2d Yu „ Hoo.
137,	3,	af. Këang ins. and went on to	162,	14,	1, „ XXVI.,p.10 „ XXII.,p.9
		Tung-ling.	223,	11,	1, „ our „ one.
139,	8,	for Urh read Shoo.	224,	16,	2, „ prunasily „ primarily.
195,	4,5,	Transpose elders and relations.	317,	30,	2, „ that „ than.
223,	11,	af. people dele Comma.	372,	15,	2, „ Q „ P.
335,	4,	„ connection ins. a Comma.	388,	23,	1, „ 10 „ 11.
342,	4,	for are like read should examine.			
460,	8,	„ te „ to.			
481,	3,	„ Hwang „ Hung.			
551,	6,	„ screens „ screen.			
553,	1,	„ dele and.			
572,	11,	„ dele that of.			
630,	7,	„ prosperity read calamity.			

* Corrected

PROLEGOMENA.

CHAPTER I.

THE HISTORY OF THE SHOO KING.

SECTION I.

DOWN TO THE BURNING OF THE BOOKS IN B.C. 212.—
THE NAME OF THE SHOO; ITS COMPILATION AND NUMBER OF
BOOKS; ITS SOURCES.

1. I have translated the name Shoo King by 'The Book (or Classic) of Historical Documents.' The term *shoo* shows us by its composition[1] that it denotes 'the pencil speaking;' and hence it is

Name of the Shoo, and its significancy. often used as a general designation for the written characters of the language. In the preface to the Shwŏ Wăn, the oldest extant dictionary of the Chinese, we are told that 'when Ts'ang Kĕĕ first made characters (*shoo*), they were, according to their classes, resemblances of the objects, and therefore called *wăn* (delineations); that afterwards, when the forms and their sounds (or names) were mutually increased, they were called *tsze* (begetters); and that, as set forth on bamboo or silk, they were called *shoo* (writings).'[2] From this use of the term the transition was easy to the employment of it in the sense of writings or books, applicable to any consecutive compositions; and before the time

1 書=聿曰. 聿 means 'an instrument for writing or describing characters,' and 曰 means 'to speak.'   2 蒼頡之初作書蓋依類象形故謂之文, 其後形聲相益即謂之字字者孳乳而寖多也著于竹帛謂之書書者如也. The Shwŏ Wăn (說文) was completed A.D. 100, in the 12th year of the 4th emperor of the Eastern Han dynasty (漢和帝永元十二年). The author's name was Heu Shin (許慎). He is often referred to also by his designation of Shuh-chung (叔重).

of Confucius we find it further specially applied to designate the historical remains of antiquity, in distinction from the poems, the accounts of rites, and other monuments of former times.[3] Not that those other documents might not also be called by the general name of *shoo*.[4] The peculiar significancy of the term, however, was well established, and is retained to the present day. *The* SHOO, in the lips of Confucius, denoted documents concerning the history of his country from the most ancient times to his own ; as spoken of since the Han dynasty, it has denoted a compilation of such documents, believed (whether correctly or not, we shall presently inquire) to have been made by the sage. In the prolegomena to my first volume, p. 1, I have called it 'The Book of History,' and Medhurst styles it 'The Historical Classic, the most authentic record of the Annals of the Chinese Empire ;' but both these designations are calculated to mislead the reader. The Book, even as it is said to have come from the hand of Confucius, never professed to contain a history of China ; and much less are we to look in it for the annals of that history. Its several portions furnish important materials to the historian, but he must grope his way through hundreds of years without any assistance from the Shoo. It is simply a collection of historical memorials, extending over a space of about 1,700 years, but on no connected method, and with great gaps between them. This is the character of the Work, and nothing more is indicated by the name Shoo King.

2.   As to the name 'Shang Shoo,'[1] by which the Classic is very frequently both spoken and written of, it is generally said by scholars that it originated subsequently to. the burning of the Books.

The name Shang Shoo. Thus Maou K'e-ling tells us that 'the Shoo was anciently named simply the Shoo, but that, after the portions of it preserved by Fuh-shang appeared, as they were the Books of highest antiquity, it was named the Shang Shoo.'[2] Maou's statement is

---

3 See the fourth paragraph.   4 An instance quite in point may be referred to in the third and only existing part of Mih-tsze's treatise on Manes (明鬼篇). On the 6th page, he has two quotations from the Shoo King, and one from the She. The latter is introduced by 周書大雅有之, 'We read in the Ta Ya, *one of the Books of Chow.*'

1 尚書.   2 書舊祇名書,自伏書出後,以其爲上古之書,故名尚,見孔氏正義. See the 古文尚書寃詞, Bk. I., p. 10. In explanation of the term 尚, Maou adds—若春秋說題辭尚者上也,上世帝王之遺書也,劉熙釋名 (The 釋名 still remains. Lew He belonged to the closing times of the Han dynasty), 尚者上也,以堯爲上始,而書其時事也. A difficulty occurs in receiving this view from the 28th and 30th of the Books of

based on the authority of K'ung Ying tă, of the T'ang dynasty. It is so far correct,—in saying that the oldest name of the Book was simply the Shoo; but the epithet of *Shang* was in use before the time of Fuh-shang. We find it in the treatise of Mih-tsze referred to above.[3] We may acquiesce in the meaning which is assigned to it. *Shang* may be descriptive of the documents with reference either to their antiquity or to the value set upon them.

3. In the Analects, Confucius and Tsze-chang quote from the Shoo by the simple formula—'The Shoo says.'[1] In the Great Learning, four different Books, all in the classic as we have it now, are mentioned by name.[2] Mencius sometimes uses the same formula as Confucius,[3] and at other times designates particular Books.[4] It is most natural for us to suppose that Confucius, when he spoke of

Did Confucius compile the classic of the Shoo?

'The Shoo,' had in his mind's eye *a collection* of Historical Documents bearing that title,—the same which we still possess in a mutilated condition. But it may not have been so. His language—'The Shoo says'—may mean nothing more than that in one of the ancient documents, come down from former times, well known to many, and open to general research, so and so was to be found written. Such even Chinese critics must allow to have been his meaning, if he used the phrase before he himself made the compilation of the documents which they universally ascribe to him. I propose now to inquire on what authority the sage is believed to have made such a compilation; and, as a specimen of the current tradition on the subject, I may commence by quoting the account in the 'Records of the Suy dynasty' (A.D. 589–617).—'Historical Documents began immediately with the invention of written characters. Confucius inspected the documents in the library of Chow; and having found the records of the four dynasties of Yu, Hea, Shang, and Chow, he preserved the best among them, and rejected the others. Beginning with Yu and

Chow, which belong to the period of what is called the Ch'un-ts'ew; and Maou concludes by saying that as the Books of the Shoo were recovered in the Han dynasty, they then characterised all documents prior to the times of Ts'in as of high antiquity (書 出 漢 代 其 視 奏 以 前 皆 上 古 耳). This conclusion of Maou is overthrown by the use of the term by Mih-tsze.   3 See the 明 鬼 篇 下, p. 7.—故 尚 書 夏 書 其 次 商 周 之 書 語 數 鬼 神 之 有 也.

1 書 云. Ana. II. xxi; XIV. xliii.   2 The Great Learning, Comm. i. 1, 2, 3; ii. 2; ix. 2; x. 11, 14.   3 書 曰. I. Pt. II. iii. 7; xi. 2; III. Pt. I. i. 4; Pt. II. ix. 6; VI. Pt. II. v. 4.   4 I. Pt. I. ii. 4; II. Pt. I. iv. 6; III. Pt. II. v. 6; IV. Pt. I. viii. 5; V. Pt. I. v. 8; VII. Pt. II. iii.

coming down to Chow, he compiled altogether a hundred Books, and made a preface to them.'5

The earliest authority for these statements is that of K'ung Gan-kwŏ, about B.C. 90. When it is said that Confucius compiled the Book of Poetry, substantially as it exists at present, his own language may be adduced in corroboration. He tells us how he reformed the music, and gave the pieces in the Imperial songs and Praise songs all their proper places. He tells us also, in round numbers very nearly approaching the exact calculation, how many the pieces of poetry were.7 But nowhere does he speak of having laboured in a similar way upon the Shoo, or of the number of documents comprehended in the collection. He spoke of them often with his disciples, as he did of the poems; but neither in the Analects nor in Mencius have we a hint of his having selected a hundred pieces from the mass of early historical memoirs, and composed a preface for them.

Gan-kwŏ's testimony is in the preface to his commentary on the Shoo King, enlarged by the additional Books which had been recovered from the wall of Confucius' house,—of which I will speak at length in the next chapter. Recounting the labours of his 'ancestor, Confucius,' on the Music, Rites, Poems, and other remains of ancient literature, he says that 'he examined and arranged the grand monuments and records, deciding to commence with Yaou and Shun, and to come down to the times of Chow. When there was perplexity and confusion, he mowed them. Expressions frothy and unallowable he cut away. What embraced great principles he retained and developed. What were more minute and yet of importance he carefully selected. Of those deserving to be handed down to other ages and to supply permanent lessons, he made in all one hundred Books, consisting of Canons, Counsels, Instructions, Announcements, Speeches, and Charges.'8

5 隋書, 志第二十七, 經籍一.—書之所興, 蓋與文字俱起, 孔子觀書周室, 得虞, 夏, 商, 周四代之典, 刪其善者, 上自虞下至周爲百篇, 編而序之.   6 Ana. IX. xiv.   7 Ana. II. ii.   8 See the 尙書序 in 'The Thirteen King.'—先君孔子........ 討論墳典, 斷自唐虞以下, 訖于周, 芟夷煩亂, 翦截浮辭, 舉其宏綱, 撮其機要, 足以垂世立敎, 典, 謨, 訓, 誥, 誓, 命之文, 凡百篇. In an earlier part of the preface Gan-kwŏ has described the 墳 as 'the Books of Fuh-he, Shin-nung, and Hwang-te,' and the 典 as 'the Books of Shaou-haou, Chuen-heuh, Kaou-sin, Yaou, and Shun.' Of these I shall speak farther on; but we must take 墳典 in this paragraph more generally, or its parts will be very inconsequent. Ying-tă expands 討論墳典 into 討整論理此三墳五典, 幷三代之書也.

4|

Of Confucius having written a preface to the hundred Books which he thus compiled, Gan-kwŏ does not speak distinctly. His language implies that among the remains which came into his charge there was a preface to the Books, which he broke up into its several parts, prefixing to each Book the portion belonging to it; but he does not say that Confucius was the author of it.[9]

Confucius died B.C. 478, and thus nearly 400 years pass by before we find the compilation of the Shoo ascribed to him. I know that the genuineness of Gan-kwŏ's preface—commonly named 'The Great Preface,'[10]—is called in question, though, as I think, on insufficient grounds; but we find the same testimony which has been adduced from it given about the same time by Sze-ma Ts'een, who was acquainted with Gan-kwŏ, and consulted him specially on the subject of the Shoo.[11] Ts'een's 'Historical Records'[12] must have been completed between B C. 103 and 97, and became current in the reign of the emperor Seuen, B.C. 82—48. In them, in the Life of Confucius, we read that the sage, on his return to Loo in his old age, B.C. 483, 'made a preface to the Records of the Shoo, and compiled and arranged them from the times of Yaou and Shun down to duke Muh of Ts'in.'[13] Ts'een speaks more definitely than Gan-kwŏ on the point of the Preface. The fact of the compilation is equally asserted by both. But they cannot be regarded as independent witnesses. Ts'een's information came to him from Gan-kwŏ; and to them are to be traced all the statements on the subject which we find in the chronicles of the Han and subsequent dynasties. It is possible—it is not improbable—that Confucius did compile a hundred ancient documents, which he wished to be regarded as *the Shoo par eminence.* His doing so would have been in harmony with the character which he gave of himself as 'A transmitter and not a maker, believing in and loving the ancients;'[14] and with his labours on the Classic of poetry and on the Ch'un-ts'ew. The Shoo's beginning with

[9] 伏生以舜典合於堯典, 益稷合於皐陶謨, 盤庚三篇合爲一, 康王之誥合於顧命, 復出此篇幷序, 凡五十九篇, 爲四十六卷……書序, 序所以爲作者之意, 昭然義見, 宜相附近, 故引之各冠其篇首, 定五十八篇, [10] 大序   [11] See the 前漢書, 儒林傳, 第五十八, p. 9.—安國爲諫大夫, 授都尉朝, 而司馬遷亦從安國問, 故遷書載堯典, 禹貢, 微子, 洪範, 金藤, 多古文說.   [12] 史記   [13] See the 史記四十七, 孔子世家第十七, p. 12.   [14] Ana. VII. i.

5]

the Canons of Yaou and Shun is also what might have been expected from him of whom it is said in the Doctrine of the Mean that 'He handed down the doctrines of Yaou and Shun as if they had been his ancestors.'15   But however reasonable in itself may be the belief that he compiled the Shoo as it existed at the time when the ambitious emperor of Ts'in issued his edict that the ancient books should be consigned to the flames, I have thought it right to show that the evidence which we have for it is by no means conclusive.   What Gan-kwŏ is supposed to say, and Ts'een says explicitly, about his writing a preface to the compilation, is, it will be presently seen, still more questionable.

4.   Whether Confucius determined that so many of the ancient historical documents of his country were worthy of being preserved, and stamped them with his own authority, so fixing the Canon of the Shoo, or not, the evidence is satisfactory enough that after his time there was current under this name

The Shoo after the time of Confucius was a recognized standard collection of ancient documents.

an acknowledged and authoritative collection of such documents.

It has been pointed out how he used in his quotations the vague formula—'The Shoo says,' which may mean 'An ancient document says,' or 'One of the Books in the Canon of the Shoo says;' and that Mencius often does the same.   The language of the latter philosopher, however, in one place loses much of its force, if we do not understand him to be referring to a definite collection.   'It would be better,' he said, 'to be without the Shoo than to give entire credit to it;' and immediately after, he specifies one of the Books of Chow.—'In the "Completion of the War," I select two or three passages only which I believe.'1   The natural interpretation of the character *Shoo* as here employed is certainly that which I propose.   In my comment upon it, vol. II., p. 355, I have spoken of two or three methods which have been thought of to give it a different meaning.   They are all strained, and designed to escape from what we should call *doctrinal* difficulties.   Mencius speaks with little reverence for the Shoo, and with little reverence for Confucius, if he believed that the Master had compiled it in the way which K'ung Gan-kwŏ describes.   He may have been wrong in doing so,

15 中庸, xxx. 1.

1 Men. VII. Pt. II.—盡信書‧則不如無書。吾於武成‧取＝三策而已矣‧

or he may have been right;—what he did say remains in the record of his Works.

The quotation of particular documents by their names in The Great Learning and in Mencius, which has likewise been pointed out, directs us to the same conclusion. The same thing is often found in the Record of Rites.

In the Commentary of Tso-k'ew Ming on the Ch'un-ts'ew, in Mih-tsze, Seun-tsze, and other writers of the two last centuries of the Chow dynasty, a different style of quotation prevails, which is still more decisive on the point in hand. They not only quote the Shoo as Confucius and Mencius do, but they specify the different parts or divisions of it,—the Books of Yu, of Hea, of Shang, of Chow. I need refer the reader only to the quotation from Mih-tsze given in the third note to par. 2 above.

Whether the Collection of Historical Documents, which was thus current in the closing period of the Chow dynasty, consisted of a hundred different Books, no more and no fewer, is a question on which I find it difficult to give a definite opinion. It was so believed after the Preface to the Shoo was found in the wall of Confucius' house in the reign of the emperor Woo (B.C. 139—86), or earlier.[2] That preface, such as it is, will be seen in this volume, pp. 1—14. Gan-kwŏ assumed that it was complete, and based on it his statement that the Shoo contained the hundred Books mentioned in it. Copies of it were current among the scholars of the Han dynasty, differing a little from that published subsequently as Gan-kwŏ's in the relative order of some of the Books; but we have their testimony as to the entire number in the collection being a hundred.[3]

There are some things, however, which make me hesitate to receive these statements without question. For instance, Sze-ma Ts'een in his Records of the Yin dynasty, when telling us that Woo Heen made the *Heen E*, which is mentioned in the Preface, Not. 22, adds

> Did the Shoo consist of a hundred Books or Documents?

2 I think it more probable that this event took place in the reign of the emperor King (景帝), B.C. 155–140. It is generally said to have happened in the end of Woo's reign. But king Kung of Loo, to enable whom to enlarge his palace the old house of the sage was being pulled down, died, it is said, B.C. 127, more than 40 years before Woo's reign ended. See Yen Jŏ-keu, as quoted in the 尚書後案辨附, p. 29. The different statements which we find on the subject arise from confounding the date of the discovery of the old tables with that of the completion of Gan-kwŏ's commentary.   3 Thus Ch'ing Heuen or Ch'ing K'ang-shing tells us that the Books of Yu and Hea (or the Yu-hea Books) were 20; those of Shang, 40; and those of Chow, 40:—a hundred in all. See K'ang-shing's brief account of the Shoo, given in the 後案卷十三, p. 58.

7]

that he also made the *T'ae-mow*, which has no place in it.[4]   In the Commentary of Tso-k'ew, under the 4th year of duke Ting (B.C. 505), mention is made of the Announcement to the prince of K'ang, which is now the 9th of the Books of Chow, and in the same paragraph of a Charge or Announcement to *Pih-k'in*, on which the Preface is silent.[5]   In the 21st of the Books of the first dynasty of Han, there is a quotation from 'the *Yuĕ Ts'ae*, one of the Books of the Ancient Text,' and on the same page a Book called *Fung Hing* is spoken of, of neither of which do we read elsewhere.[6]

Further, several writers of the Han dynasty speak of 102, and of 120 Books.   It is difficult to explain their language; but it appears inconsistent with the tradition which has since prevailed, that the Canon of the Shoo contained, before the time of Ts'in, only one hundred documents.[7]

Maou K'e-ling endeavours quite unsuccessfully to prove that the phrase, 'A hundred Books,' was older than Gan-kwŏ, and his discovery of the Preface.   He refers first to a passage in Mih-tsze, where it is said that 'the duke of Chow read in the morning 100 Books.'   This can have nothing to do with the subject.   Several of the Books of the Shoo were composed after the time of the duke of Chow.   Mih simply means to commend his industry, as is evident from the sentence which follows, that 'in the evening the duke gave audience to 70 officers.'[8]   He refers also to a sentence in the writings of Yang Heung, that 'those who in former times spoke of the Shoo, arranged (or prefaced) it in 100 Books';[9] but Yang died A.D. 18, being posterior to Gan-kwŏ by nearly a century; and the sequel of the passage shows that he had in mind critics subsequent to that

4 See the 殷記, p. 3.—巫咸治王家有成, 作咸艾作太戊.   5 See the 左傳, 定公四年—命以伯禽, 而封於少皥之虛…… 命以康誥, 而封於殷虛.   6 See the 律曆志第一, 下.—古 文月采篇曰, 云云; 畢命豐刑曰……王命作策豐刑.   7 See the 古文尚書寃詞, 卷二, p 7, and the 經義考, 卷七十三, 書 二, p. 1. Maou gives two ways of explaining these expressions. The first is—Add to the ac- knowledged 100 Books one for the Preface, and one for a different edition of The Great Speech, which somehow was current; thus we have 102. The second refers to the 120.—He adduces a work called 尚書璿璣鈐, where it is said that Confucius found 120 Books; that out of 102 he made the Shang Shoo, and out of 18 the Chung How; and these were the 120 (百兩 篇). I do not know how to interpret Chung How (中候). The explanations do not enlight- en the darkness of the subject.   8 See Mih-tsze, 卷之十二, 貴義 p. 3, 昔者 周公旦朝讀百篇 夕見漆 (=七) 十士.   9 See 楊子法言, 卷四 問神篇 p 4.—昔之說書者序以百.

scholar.—On the one hand, allowing that Gan-kwŏ found the Preface, as it is still current, with the other tablets (which there is no reason to doubt), we cannot be certain that the Canon of the Shoo did not at the end of the Chow dynasty contain more than a hundred Books; nor, on the other hand, can we be certain that the hundred Books mentioned in it were all then existing. Not a few of them may have been lost or cast out before that time. I believe myself that it was so, and will give my reasons for doing so in the next section.

That the Preface, whether it be complete or not, was not written by Confucius, is now the prevailing opinion of scholars throughout the empire. I have shown that Gan-kwŏ himself

The Preface was not written by Confucius. did not ascribe it to the sage. Sze-ma Ts'een did, and was followed by Lew Hin, Pan Koo, Ch'ing Heuen, and other scholars of the Han dynasty. Their doing so proves that they had little of the critical faculty,—unless we are prepared to allow that Confucius was a man of very little discrimination and comprehension of mind. It will be sufficient for me to give here the judgment in the matter of Ts'ae Ch'in, the disciple of Choo He, and whose commentary is now the standard of orthodoxy in the interpretation of the Shoo.—After quoting the opinions of Lew Hin and Pan Koo, he says:—'When we examine the text of the Preface, as it is still preserved, though it is based on the contents of the several Books, the knowledge which it shows is shallow, and the views which it gives are narrow. It sheds light on nothing; and there are things in it at variance with the text of the Classic. On the Books that are lost it is specially servile and brief, affording us not the slightest help. That it is not the work of Confucius is exceedingly plain.'[10]

5. The questions which have thus far been discussed can hardly be regarded as of prime importance. It seemed necessary to give attention to them in a critical introduction to the Shoo; but it matters little to the student that he cannot discern the *imprimatur* of Confucius on the collected Canon;—he has the sage's authority for some Books in it, and he has evidence that after his time there was a Compilation of ancient historical documents acknowledged by the scholars of the empire. And it matters little to him what was the exact number of documents in that Collection;—many of them have been irretrievably lost and we have to do only with those which are now current as having fortunately escaped the flames of Ts'in. There remains, however, at this part of our in-

10 See the 集傳書序

quiries, a question really curious and of great interest.—What were

The sources of the Shoo.

the sources of the Shoo? What proofs have we of the composition in ancient times of such documents as it contains, and of their preservation, so that some of them might be collected in a sort of historical Canon?

To begin with the dynasty of Chow.—We have the Work commonly called 'The Rites of Chow.'[1] It is also and more correctly called 'The Officers of Chow.'[2] Under the several departments into which the administration of the government was divided, it gives the titles of the officers belonging to them, and a description of their duties. I will not vouch for the tradition which ascribes the composition of it to the duke of Chow; but it no doubt contains the institutions and arrangements made by him in completing the establishment of the dynasty.

Under the department of the minister of Religion we find the various officers styled *Sze*,[3] a term which has been translated 'Recorders,'[4] 'Annalists,'[5] 'Historiographers,' and simply 'Clerks.'[6] There are the Grand Recorder, the Assistant Recorder, the Recorder of the Interior, the Recorder of the Exterior, and the Recorder in attendance on the emperor. Arranged under the department of the minister of Religion, they were advisers also of the prime minister of the government, and of Heads of Departments generally, on all subjects which required reference to history and precedent. Among the duties of the Recorder of the Interior were the following:—'In case of any Charge given by the emperor to the prince of a State, to an assistant Grand counsellor, to a minister, or to a great officer, he writes the Charge on tablets;' 'In case of any Memorials on business coming in from the different quarters of the empire, he reads them *to the emperor*;' 'It is his business to write all Charges of the emperor, and to do so in duplicate.'[8] Of the duties of the Re-

---

1 周禮. Biot names it—'Le Tcheou Li, ou Rites de Tcheou.'   2 周官. This is the name in the grand edition ordered by the emperor K'ëen-lung of the present dynasty,— the 欽定周官義疏.   3 史.   4 This is the definition given in the Shwŏ Wăn,—記事者, 'one who records events.' Morrison, Dict., *in voc.*, observes that the character is formed from 'a *hand* seizing the *middle*,' and defines it as 'an impartial narrator of events.' The *hand* holds the pencil, and describes things without swerving to the right or left.

5 Thus Biot renders the term.   6 See my translation of the Analects, VI. xvi.   7

大史, 小史, 內史, 外史, 御史.   8 See the 周官, Ch. xxvi. P. 35, 凡 命諸侯, 及孤, 卿, 大夫, 則策命之; p. 36, 凡四方之事書, 內 史讀之; p. 38, 內史掌書王命遂貳之.

corder of the Exterior it is said :—'He writes all Commands for the exterior domains;' 'He has charge of the Histories of the States in all parts of the empire;' 'He has charge of the Books of the three great sovereigns and the five rulers;' 'It is his business to publish in all parts of the empire the Books and the characters in them.'[9]

These passages show clearly that under the Chow dynasty, from its commencement in the 11th century before our Christian era, there was provision made for the compilation and preservation of imperial charges and ordinances, of records of the operations of the general government, and of histories of the different States; and, moreover, for the preservation and interpretation of documents come down from more ancient times.

The Recorders mentioned in the 'Officers of Chow' belonged of course to the imperial court; but there were similar officers, though not so numerous, at the courts of the various feudal princes. It was of such that Confucius spoke when he said that in his early days a historiographer would leave a blank in his text rather than enter anything of which he had not sufficient evidence.[10] They also were the writers of the Books which Mencius mentions,—' the Shing of Tsin, the Taou-wuh of Ts'oo, and the Ch'un-ts'ew of Loo '[11]

When we ascend from the Chow dynasty to those of Shang and Hea which preceded it, we do not have the same amount of evidence for the existence under them of the class of officers styled Recorders. Chinese critics, indeed, say that it did then exist, and even earlier; my own opinion is, that the institution was in active operation during the dynasties just named:—but the proofs are not adequate. For instance, Ma Twan-lin says, 'The pencil of the recording officers was busy from the time of Hwang-te. Its subsequent operation is clearly seen from what we know of Chung Koo, the Grand Recorder

9 Pp. 39-42 外 史 掌 書 外 令; 掌 四 方 之 志; 掌 三 皇 五 帝 之 書; 掌 達 書 名 於 四 方. Biot translates this last par.—掌 達 書 名 於 四 方 by 'Ils sort chargés de propager les noms écrits, ou les signes de l'écriture, dans les quatre parties de l'empire.' This was the view of Wang Gan-shih of the Sung dynasty, who says—書 名 者 字 也. 書 and 名 are thus taken in apposition, or, at best, as Biot renders,= 'written names,'= characters; which seems to me an unnatural construction. K'ang-shing took 書 名 as meaning simply 'the names of the Books,' as 'The Canon of Yaou,' 'The Tribute of Yu;' which names the Recorder of the Exterior made known throughout the empire. So far as the characters 書 名 are concerned, this interpretation is the likeliest; but it makes the whole passage so weak and frivolous that it cannot be admitted. K'ang-shing mentions, however, that some took 名 in the sense of 字, 'characters,' and made 書 名 = 'the characters in the various Books.' This is nearer to the view which I have taken. 10 Ana. XV. xxv. 11 Men. IV. Pt. II. xxi.

of Hea, and Kaou She, the Grand Recorder of Shang.'[12]   But all that we know of the names mentioned is from the Bamboo Books and from the Ch'un-ts'ew of Leu,—both comparatively recent and insufficient authorities.[13]   I attach more force to what we find in the 10th of the Books of Chow, par. 13, where Fung is told to warn his 'friends, the Grand Recorder and the Recorder of the Interior,' of the dangers of drunkenness.   By the 'Recorder of the Interior' there, it is argued that we must understand the officer who had exercised that function at the imperial court of Shang, and was now living in retirement in the State of Wei after the overthrow of his dynasty.

Independently of the Institution of Recorders, if we may admit the testimony of the Shoo itself, both emperors and ministers were in the habit of committing their ordinances and memorials to writing during the rule of the House of Shang.   Woo-ting, B.C. 1321, is described as making a writing to communicate the dream which he had to his ministers;[14] and, more than 400 years earlier, we have E Yin addressing his remonstrances to the young emperor T'ae-kĕ in a written form.[15]   Going back to the dynasty of Hea, we find that the prince of Yin, during the reign of Chung-k'ang, generally believed to have begun B.C. 2158, in addressing his troops, quotes 'The Statutes of Government,' in a manner which makes us conceive of him as referring to some well-known compilation.[16]   The grandsons of the great Yu, likewise, make mention, in 'The Songs of the Five Sons,' of his 'Lessons,' doing so in language which suggests to us the formula which Mencius was wont to employ when he was referring to the documents acknowledged to be of authority in his day.[17]   There can be no doubt that about 2000 years before our era the art of writing was known in China, and that it was exer-

12 See the 文獻通考 卷五十一, Art. 史官.—史官筆自黃帝有之,自後顯著夏太史終古,高太史商勢. [While this sheet is going through the press, my attention has been called to a Soo-chow edition of Ma Twan-lin's Work, where this passage is read—史官肇自黃帝有之,自後顯者,云云. This reading is, no doubt, preferable to that in the copy in my own possession.]   13 See the 竹書紀年,注箋,卷之四, p. 12, and 卷之六, p. 23.   What Leu says is found, in his Ch'un-ts'ew, 卷第十六 先識覽第四. The 太平御覽卷二百三十五, p. 4, gives the following abstract of his statements:—夏太史令終古,見夏桀惑亂,載其圖法而泣,乃出奔商.商太史高勢見周之迷亂,載其圖法,出之周.   14 Pt. IV. Bk. VIII., Pt. i. 2, 15, Bk. V. Pt. i. 2.   16 Part III. Bk. IV. 4.   17 Bk. III. See particularly 訓有之, in par. 6, and compare it with the 於傳有之, in Men. I. Pt. II. ii. 1, et al.

cised in the composition of Documents of the nature of those which we read in the Shoo King. Whether an institution like that of the Recorders of Chow existed at so early a date does not appear. We can well believe that, as time went on, all written memorials were produced more numerously and frequently. We can well believe also that, in the revolutions and periods of confusion which occurred, many memorials were lost. Mencius complained that in his time the feudal princes destroyed many of the records of antiquity, that they might the better perpetrate their own usurpations and innovations.[18] The same thing would go on during the dynasties of Shang and Hea. Time is at once a producer and a devourer. Many records of Yu and T'ang and their successors had perished before the Canon of the Shoo was compiled, but sufficient must have remained to supply the materials for a larger collection than was made.

Confucius once expressed himself in a manner which throws light on the point which I am now considering.—'I am able,' said he, 'to describe the ceremonies of the Hea dynasty, but K'e cannot sufficiently attest my words. I am able to describe the ceremonies of the Yin dynasty; but Sung cannot sufficiently attest my words. They cannot do so because of the insufficiency of their records and wise men.'[19] The State of K'e was ruled by the descendants of the great Yu, and that of Sung by those of T'ang. The various institutions of Hea and Shang ought to have been preserved in them, and their scholars should have been careful to watch over the literary monuments that could be appealed to in support of their traditions and ordinances. But the scholars had failed in their duty; the monuments were too mutilated and fragmentary to answer their purpose. The Master would not expose himself to the risk of relating or teaching what he could not substantiate by abundant evidence. Where had he got his own knowledge of the ancient times? Some critics tell us that he was born with it;—an affirmation which no foreigner will admit. He must have obtained it by his diligent research, and his reasoning, satisfactory at least to himself, on what facts he was able to ascertain. His words show us that, while in his time there were still existing documents of a high antiquity, they were not very numerous or complete.

6. Before we pass on to the next chapter, it will be well to say something on ' the Books of the three great sovereigns, and the five

18 V. Pt. II. ii. 2.   19 Ana. III. ix.

rulers,' which 'The Officers of Chow,' as quoted on page 11, mentions as being under the charge of the Recorder of the Exterior. Nothing certain or satisfactory, indeed, has ever been ascertained about them ;

The Books of the three Sovereigns and five rulers.
but the amount of discussion to which they have given rise renders it desirable that I should not leave the passage unnoticed.

What were those Books? Gan-kwŏ says in his preface, referred to above on page 4, that 'the Books of Fuh-he, Shin-nung, and Hwang-te were called the *Three Fun*, as containing great doctrines ; and those of Shaou-haou, Chuen-heuh, Kaou-sin, Yaou, and Shun were called the *five Tëen*, as containing standard doctrines.'[1] He was led to this explanation by a passage in the Tso Chuen, the most valued commentary on the Ch'un-Ts'ew. It is there said, under the 12th year of duke Ch'aou (B.C. 530), that E-Seang, a Recorder of the State of Ts'oo, 'could read the three *Fun*, the five *Tëen*, the eight *Sih*, and the nine *K'ew*.'[2] It would appear from this, that in the time of Confucius there were some books current having the names which are given ; but what they were, and whether a portion of them were the same with those mentioned in 'The Officers of Chow,' we cannot tell.   Woo Sze-taou,[3] a scholar of the Yuen dynasty, observes :—'The Recorder of the Exterior had charge of the "Books of the three Hwang ;" nothing is said of the "three Fun." E-seang could read the "three Fun ;" nothing is said in connection with him of the "three Hwang." K'ung Gan-kwŏ thought that the Books of the three Hwang and the three Fun were identical ; but there is no good reason to adopt his conclusion.' Too Yu of the Tsin dynasty, the glossarist of the Tso Chuen, contented himself with saying that Fun, Teen, Sih, and K'ew were all 'the names of ancient Books.' Whatever those Books were, we may safely conclude that they were of little worth. According to Gan-kwŏ's own account, Confucius rejected the three *Fun*, and three out of the five *Teen*, when he was compiling the Shoo ; and by whomsoever the Shoo was compiled, we are well assured that it never contained any document older than the Canon of Yaou. We should be glad if we could have light thrown on the passage in 'The Officers

---

[1] 伏犧 神農 黃帝 之書 謂之 三墳 言大道也. 少昊 顓頊 高辛 唐虞 之書 謂之 五典 言常道也.   [2] 佐史倚相 其能讀三墳五典八索九丘   [3] 吳師道. He is quoted in the 經義考 書一.

of Chow ;' but we must be content, as is so often the case in historical inquiries, to remain in ignorance, and have our curiosity ungratified.[4]

4 I have not thought it worth while to mention in the text a forgery of 'the three Fun,' which was attempted A.D. 1084, when a certain Maou Tsëen (毛漸) pretended to have discovered the ancient Books. The imposition was soon exploded.

SECTION II.

FROM THE BURNING OF THE BOOKS, B.C. 212, TO THE TIME OF CHOO HE, A.D. 1130.

THE RECOVERY OF A PORTION OF THE SHOO BY FUH-SANG, CALLED THE MODERN TEXT; AND OF A SECOND PORTION BY K'UNG GAN-KWO, CALLED THE ANCIENT TEXT. THE GENERAL ACKNOWLEDGMENT OF GAN-KWO'S BOOKS.

1. In the *prolegomena* to vol. I., pp. 6–9, I have given an account of the burning of the books, and of the slaughter of many of the literati, by the first emperor of the Ts'in dynasty. The measures were barbarous and wanton, but the author of them and his advisers adopted them as necessary

The burning of the Books.

to the success of the policy which the new dynasty was initiating. The old feudal system of the empire had been abolished; a new order of administration was being introduced; the China of the future, to be ruled for ever by the House of Ts'in, must be dissevered entirely from the China of the past. In order to this the history of former times, it was thought, should be blotted out, and the names which had been held in reverence for hundreds and thousands of years be made to perish from the memory of men. The course taken was like that ascribed to our Edward I., when in A.D. 1284 he assembled all the bards of Wales, and caused them to be put to death. When the premier Le Sze advised that the books should be burned, he made an exception, according to the account of his speech given us by Sze-ma Ts'een, in favour of the copies in keeping of the Board of Great Scholars; but those must have shared the common fate. If they had not done so, the Shoo would not have been far to seek, when the rule of Ts'in came in so short a time to an end.

The founder of that dynasty, which he fondly thought would last for myriads of years, died in B.C. 209. His second son, who succeeded him, was murdered in 204, and the House of Ts'in passed away.

The dynasty of Han dates from B.C. 201, and in the 4th year of its second emperor, B.C. 190, the edict of Ts'in, making it a capital crime to have the ancient books in one's possession, was repealed. Thus, the Shoo and the other classics (with the exception of the Yih-king) were under the ban for less than a quarter of a century.

2. Among the 'Great Scholars' of Ts'in, there had been one named Fuh Shing,[1] but commonly referred to as 'Fuh-săng,[2] which is equivalent to Mr. Fuh, or the scholar Fuh. He belonged to Tse-nan in Shan-tung; and when the order for the burning of the Shoo

Fuh-săng   went forth, he hid the tablets of the copy which he had in a wall. During the struggle which ensued, after the extinction of the Ts'in dynasty, for the possession of the empire, Fuh-săng was a fugitive in various parts; but when the rule of Han was established, he went to look for his hid treasure. Alas! many of the tablets were perished or gone. He recovered only 29 Books (as he thought) of the Classic. Forthwith he commenced teaching, making those Books the basis of his instructions, and from all parts of Shan-tung scholars resorted to him, and sat at his feet.[3]

In all this time, no copy of the Shoo had reached the court. The emperor Wăn (B.C. 178--156), after ineffectual attempts to find some scholar who could reproduce it, heard at last of Fuh-săng, and sent to call him. Fuh was then more than 90 years old, and could not travel; and an officer, called Ch'aou Ts'ŏ, belonging to the same department as the Recorders mentioned in the last section, was sent to Tse-nan to receive from him what he had of the Shoo. Whether Ts'ŏ got the very tablets which Fuh had hidden and afterwards found again, or whether he only took a copy of them, we are not told. It is most likely that, being an imperial messenger, he would carry away the originals. However this be, those originals were, and his copy, if he made one, would be, in the new form of the characters introduced under Ts'in,—what was then 'the modern text;' and by this name the portion of the Shoo recovered by Fuh-săng is designated to the present day.

The above account is taken from Sze-ma Ts'een. Gan-kwŏ gives a relation of the circumstances materially different. According to

Varying traditions   him, 'Fuh-săng of Tse-nan, being more than 90
about Fuh-săng.   years of age (when the emperor Wăn was seeking for copies), had lost his originals of the text, and was delivering by

[1] 伏勝.   [2] 伏生.   [3] See the 史記 一百二十一, 儒林, 列傳第六十一

16]

word of mouth more than twenty Books to disciples.'[4]   From another passage we gather that he estimated Fuh-săng's Books, with which he was well acquainted, at 28; but he says nothing of the visit to Fuh of Ch'aou Ts'ŏ.   Wei Hwang, of the first century of our era, says that when Ch'aou Ts'ŏ went to him, Fuh-săng, being over 90, was unable to speak plainly, and made use of a (? grand-) daughter to repeat what he said; and that her dialect being different from Ts'ŏ's, he lost 2 or 3 in every ten of her words, supplying them as he best could according to his conception of the meaning.[5]   This last account, as being more marvellous, has become the accepted history of the manner in which so many Books of the Shoo were recovered through Fuh-săng.   Even Regis follows it, as if he had not been aware of the more trustworthy narrative of Sze-ma Ts'een.[6]

3.   The statement of Sze-ma Ts'een, that Fuh-săng found again the tablets containing 29 'p'ëen,'—Books, or parts of Books,—of the Shoo, is repeated by Lew Hin in his list of the Books in the imperial library under his charge, of which I have given some account in the *proleg.* to vol. I. pp. 3–5.   It is there expressly said, moreover, that there were, in the classical department of the library, '29 portions of the text of the Shang Shoo.'[1]   Those Books were:—

The 29 Books of Fuh-săng.   'The Canon of Yaou;' 'The Counsels of Kaou-yaou;' 'The Tribute of Yu;' 'The Speech at Kan;' 'The Speech of T'ang;' 'The Pwan-kăng;' 'The Day of the Supplementary Sacrifice of Kaou-tsung;' 'The Conquest of Le by the Chief of the West;' 'The Viscount of Wei;' 'The Great Speech;' 'The Speech at Muh;' 'The Great Plan;' 'The Metal-bound Coffer;' 'The Great Announcement;' 'The Announcement to K'ang;' 'The Announcement about Drunkenness;' 'The Timber of the Tsze-tree;' 'The Announcement of Shaou;' 'The Announcement about Lŏ;' 'The Numerous Officers;' 'Against Luxurious Ease;' 'Prince Shih;' 'The Numerous Regions;' 'On the Establishment of Government;' 'The Testamentary Charge;' 'Leu on Punishments;' 'The Charge to Prince Wăn;' 'The Speech at Pe;' and 'The Speech of the Duke of Ts'in.'

It was discovered subsequently, that 'The Canon of Shun' was incorporated by Fuh-săng with that of Yaou; the 'Yih and Tseih' with 'The Counsels of Kaou-yaou;' 'The Charge of king K'ang'

4 See Gan-kwŏ's Preface, p. 13 ·   5 See the 古文尚書寃詞 卷一, p. 6.
6 See Y-King, vol. I., pp. 104–106.

1 經二十九卷

with 'The Testamentary Charge;' and that the 'Pwan-kăng,' given by him as one Book, was in reality three Books. Hence it is often said that Fuh-săng's Books amounted to 34,—as was really the case.

But there is a statement very generally accepted,—that Fuh-săng's Books amounted only to 28, which requires some discussion. 'The Great Speech,' as it is now current, forms three Books. In 'the modern text' it formed only one; and it came to be denied, in the time of the Han dynasty, that even that one proceeded from Fuh-săng. Lew Heang says:

Did 'The Great Speech' form one of Fuh-săng's Books?

—'In the end of the reign of the emperor Woo (B.C. 139–86), some one among the people found "The Great Speech" in a wall, and presented it. When it was submitted to the Board of Great Scholars, they were pleased with it, and in a few months all began to teach it.'[2] Ma Yung, Wang Suh, and Ch'ing Heuen, all affirm that 'The Great Speech' was a more recent discovery than the other Books. Wang Ch'ung,[3] towards the end of our first century, wrote: —'In the time of the emperor Seuen (B.C. 72–48), a girl, north of the Ho, among the ruins of an old house, discovered three Books,— one of the Shoo; one of the Le; and one of the Yih. She presented them to the court. The emperor sent them down to the Great Scholars; and from this time the number of the recovered Books of the Shang Shoo came to be fixed at 29.'

All these accounts, attributing to 'The Great Speech' a later origin than to the rest of Fuh-săng's Books, must be set aside. Sze-ma Ts'een's testimony is express as to the number of 29; and, what ought to settle the matter, Fuh-săng himself, in the Introduction which he made to the Shoo, used the language of the Book, as the scholars of the eastern Han read it in the text, the preservation of which they ascribed to 'a girl, north of the Ho.'[4] That text was substantially what I have given in this volume in an appendix (pp. 297–299). We cannot wonder that it should have troubled the scholars. Such a piece of wild extravagance, and having in it nothing of the passages of 'The Great Speech,' quoted by Mencius and others!—this to be going abroad as part of the Shoo of Confucius! They would have done right to cast it out of the classic. They were wrong in denying that it was brought to light, after the fires of Ts'in, by Fuh-săng. We are therefore in this position in regard to him. Among his tablets were some containing that farrago,

2 劉 向 別 錄, quoted in the 古 文 尙 書 寃 詞, 卷 一, p. 7.   3 王 充, Quoted by Se-ho as above.   4 See as above, pp. 8, 9.

and he must have erred in classing them with the others, which were portions of the true Shoo. I have not been able to think of any other explanation which will unravel, so satisfactorily, the perplexities of the case. Fuh-săng gave to the world 29 Books as of the Shoo, but in regard to one of them he was mistaken. The stories of its being a subsequent discovery, due to a girl, were devised to save his reputation.

4. According to what I quoted above, p. 16, from Sze-ma Ts'een, many Scholars resorted to Fuh-săng, and learned from him what he had to teach about the Shoo. His two principal disciples were

Disciples of Fuh-săng; and Schools of the Modern Text. a Gow-yang Ho-pih,[1] commonly designated Gowyang-săng, and a Chang-săng,[2] to whom he delivered his comments on the Shoo in 41 Books,[3] of which some fragments still remain. Each of these became the founder of a school, the professors and writings of which are distinctly traced by the critics down into the dynasty of Tsin. Ho-pih's successor was a distinguished scholar and officer, called E Hwan.[4] His great-grandson, Gow-yang Kaou,[5] published 'The Shang Shoo in paragraphs and sentences, in 31 Books.'[6] From the same school flowed at least two other Works;[7] 'The meaning of the Shang Shoo explained,' in two Books, and 'Decisions on the Shang Shoo,' by Gow-yang Te-yu and others, in 42 Books.'[8] The reputation of 'The School of Gowyang,' was pre-eminent during the dynasty of the eastern Han.

[1] 歐陽生,字和伯.   [2] 張生.   [3] 傳四十一篇. By the time of the Suy dynasty, this work had dwindled away to three *p'een*.   [4] 倪寬.   [5] 歐陽高.   [6] 尙書章句,三十一卷. See the 前漢藝文志, upon the Shoo.   [7] 尙書義說,二篇.   [8] 歐陽氏地餘等尙書議奏. 歐陽學,東京最盛. See the introductory Chapter to Yung-ching's Shoo, 綱領一, pp. 2, 3. The Continuation of Ma Twan-lin's Work (proleg. vol. I., p. 134) gives the following table of the School of Gow-yang.

The school founded by Chang-săng, and which by and by diverged into two branches was not less prolific in Works upon the Shoo. Chang delivered his learning to Hea-how Too-wei a scholar of Loo,[9] from whom it descended to a Hea-how Shing.[10] This Shing was a man of more than ordinary ability and research; and in obedience to an imperial order, he compiled a Work, which appears in Lew Hin's catalogue as 'The Shang Shoo, in paragraphs and sentences, in 29 chapters;'[11] and formed the basis of 'The Greater school of Hea-how.'[12] A nephew of Shing, called Hea-how Këen,[13] published a sequel to Shing's Work, which he called, 'An Explanation of Ancient Views on the Shang Shoo, in 29 Books,' which was also in the imperial library in Lew Hin's time.[14] Këen was looked up to as the founder of 'The Lesser school of Hea-how.'[15] From those two schools proceeded many Works upon the Shoo, the names and authors of which are duly chronicled by Chow E-tsun, in his 'Examination of the meaning of the King.'[16] But the names are all that remain. Not one of the writings survived, in a complete form, the troubles which prevailed during the reign of Hwae, the third emperor of the dynasty of the Western Ts'in.[17]

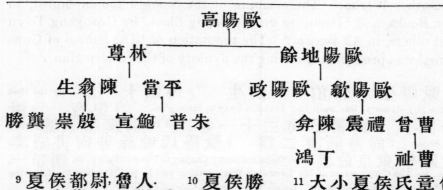

[9] 夏侯都尉魯人. [10] 夏侯勝 [11] 大小夏侯氏章句 二十九卷. [12] 號爲大夏侯氏學. [13] 夏侯建. [14] 大 小夏侯解故二十九篇. [15] 小夏侯氏學. [16] The Hea-how schools are thus exhibited. [17] The reign of the Emperor Hwae (懷) is known by the name of Yang-këa (永嘉). Maou Se-ho says:—及永嘉之亂,歐陽,大小夏侯, 尙書並亡.—The Hea-how Schools are thus represented:—

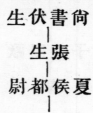

The 'modern text,' therefore, and the views of the scholars who taught it, are now as a whole lost to literature. Under the reign of the emperor Ling, the last but one of the eastern Han, in A.D. 161, Tsae Yung, one of the chief scholars and officers of the time, had 'the modern text' of the Shoo, and the current text of several of the other classics, engraved on stone tablets, and set up with imperial sanction in one of the colleges in Lŏ. Of the tablets of the Shoo there remain only some shattered fragments, containing in all 547 characters.[18] But for the happier fate of the Books discovered about a century after Fuh-săng, of which we have now to speak, there would have remained but a tantalizing record of him, and some sporadic passages of his text gathered from the writings of various scholars. The Shoo had nearly been lost a second time, without any fires of Ts'in, through the natural process of decay, and the convulsions continually occurring in a distracted empire.

5. When the wrath of Ts'in was raging against the Shoo and all who dared to keep it in their possession, there were no doubt several who acted as Fuh-săng did, and hid away their tablets where they hoped to be able to find them and bring them forth at a future time. A descendant of Confucius had done so with the tablets containing the Shoo, the Le, the Classic of Filial Piety, and the Analects, concealing them in a wall of the house where the sage had lived, and which continued to be the home of the K'ung family.[1] But he never reclaimed them. They remained unknown, till towards the latter part of the reign of the emperor Woo. Then, as I have related in the *proleg.*

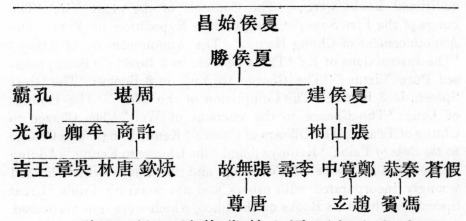

18 See the 隸釋 of 洪适景伯 卷第十四, 石經尙書殘碑.

1 The name of this individual is not known. Sze-ma Ts'een does not give it. Gan-kwŏ simply says he was one of his forefathers. Some make him a 孔鮒; others a 孔騰 (which is most likely); and the Records of Suy say his name was 孔惠.

21]

to vol. I., pp. 12, 13, the king of Loo, a son of the emperor King, known to posterity by the honorary title of Kung, or 'The Respect-ful,'[2] was pulling down the house of the K'ung, to enlarge a palace of his own which was adjacent to it.   In the wall were found the tablets, or what remained of the tablets, which have just been men-tioned; and when the prince went into the hall or principal apartment of the building, he was saluted with strains of music from invisible instruments, which made him give up his purpose of demolition and appropriation.   The chronicling of this marvellous circumstance might lead us to look suspiciously on the whole narrative; but the recovery of the tablets, and the delivery of them by the prince to the K'ung family, are things sufficiently attested.[3]

Discovery of the tablets of the Ancient Text.

The chief of the family at that time was K'ung Gan-kwŏ, one of the 'Great Scholars,' and otherwise an officer of distinction.   The tablets were committed to his care.   He found they were written or engraved in the old form of the characters, which he calls 'tadpole,' and which had long gone into disuse.   By the help of Fuh-sǎng's Books, which were in the modern or current characters of the day, and other resources, he managed, however, to make them out, and found he had got a treasure indeed.—From the tablets of the Shoo he deciphered all the already recovered Books, with the exception of 'The Great Speech,' and of it there was the true copy. In addition he made out other five and twenty Books; and he found a preface containing the names of one hundred Books in all.   The additional Books were:—'The Counsels of the great Yu;' 'The Songs of the Five Sons;' 'The Punitive Expedition of Yin;' 'The Announcement of Chung Hwuy;' 'The Announcement of T'ang;' 'The Instructions of E;' 'The T'ae Këǎ, in 3 Books;' 'Both posses-sed Pure Virtue;' 'The Charge to Yuě, in 3 Books;' 'The Great Speech, in 3 Books;' 'The Completion of the War;' 'The Hounds of Leu;' 'The Charge to the viscount of Wei;' 'The Charge to Chung of Ts'ae;' 'The Officers of Chow;' 'Keun-ch'in;' 'The Charge to *the duke of* Peih;' 'Keun-ya;' and 'the Charge to Keung.' Adding to these the 29 Books of Fuh-sǎng, and the Books which he had wrongly incorporated with others, and not counting Fuh's 'Great Speech,' we have 58 Books of the Shoo, which were now recovered.

K'ung Gan-kwŏ.

[2] 魯王共,景帝子,共(=恭)其謚也.   [3] See 漢藝文志, upon the Shoo; Gan-kwŏ's Preface; and a hundred references in the Books of Han and subsequent dynasties.   [4] 科斗字.

Gan-kwŏ himself reckoned the Preface one Book, and made out the
number to be 59. Being all on the tablets in the old 'tadpole'
characters, Gan-kwŏ's Books were described, in distinction from
Fuh-săng's, as 'the ancient text.'[5]

6. When he had made out to read the tablets in the way which
I have described, Gan-kwŏ presented them to the emperor, in B.C. 96,
with a transcript in the current characters of the time,[1] keeping a
second transcript of them for himself; and he received an order to

Gan-kwŏ's Commentary; and how
it was not immediately made public.

make a commentary upon the whole.[2]
He addressed himself to this work, and
accomplished it, and was about to lay before the emperor the result of
his studies, when troubles occurred at court, which prevented for a
time any attention being paid to literary matters. In B.C. 91, some
high officers became victims to a charge of practising magical arts.
Next year the emperor fell sick, and a charlatan, named Keang Ch'ung,
high in his confidence, and who had a feud with the heir-apparent, declared that the sickness was owing to magical attempts of the prince
to compass his father's death. In preparation for this charge, he
had contrived to hide a wooden image of the emperor in the prince's
palace. An investigation was made. The image was found, and
considered by the weak monarch to be proof positive of his son's
guilt. The prince, indignant, procured the murder of his accuser,
and liberated the felons and others in prison to make head against
a force which was sent by the prime minister against him. Being
defeated, he fled to the lake region in the south, and there killed
himself.[4] The reader will be led by this account to think of the
accounts which we have of diablerie and witchcraft in Europe at a
later period, and will not wonder that Gan-kwŏ's commentary was
neglected amid such scenes, and that the enlarged text which he had
deciphered was not officially put in charge of the 'Great Scholars,' to

5 Gan-kwŏ arranged the 58 Books in 46 *Keuen* (卷) or sections, with reference to the notices
of them in the preface, where two or more Books are sometimes comprehended under one notice.
They are mentioned also in Lew Hin's catalogue as 'the ancient text of the Shang Shoo, in 46
chapters' (尚書古文經四十六卷). They are also subsequently designated as
57 *p'ëen*, the 'Canon of Shun' having been supposed to be lost. Other enumerations are adduced
and explained in the 1st chapter of Maou Se-ho's 'Wrongs of the Ancient Text.'

1 He tells us in his Preface that 'he wrote them moreover on bamboo tablets.' But he must
have made two copies in the current character. If only the 'tadpole' tablets had been deposited
in the imperial library, Lew Heang could not have compared them, as we shall find immediately
that he did, with Fuh-săng's Books.   2 承詔爲五十九篇作傳.

3 江充.   4 See K'ung Ying-tă's notes on Gan-kwŏ's Preface, towards the conclusion;
通鑑綱目, on the 1st and 2d of the years 征和; and Maou's 'Wrongs of the Shoo,'
Ch. 11., pp. 5, 6.

whom had been given in the 5th year of Woo (B.C. 135) the care of the five King.[5]   Soon after, moreover, Gan-kwŏ himself died, and it was long before his commentary obtained the imperial recognition and sanction.

7.   Happily, Gan-kwŏ's commentary, though it was not publicly recognised, was not lost.   The critics have clearly traced its transmission through the hands of various scholars.   The recipient of it from Gan-kwŏ was a Too-wei Chaou,[1] from whom it passed to Yung T'an of Këaou-tung.[2]   A Hoo Chang of Ts'ing-ho[3] obtained it from Yung T'an, and passed it on to Seu Gaou of K'wŏ,[4] who delivered it to two disciples,—Wang Hwang,[5] and T'oo Yun.[6]   From the latter of these it was received by Shing (or Shwang) K'in of Ho-nan.[7]

The editors of Yung-ching's Shoo, having arrived step by step at Shing K'in, then state that, in the close of the western Han, during the usurpation of Mang (A.D. 9–22), the school of 'the ancient text' was established along with that of Fuh-săng, and that Wang Hwang and T'oo Yun were held in great honour.[8]   From this they make a great leap over the dynasties of the Eastern Han, the after Han, and the Western Tsin, to the first reign of the Eastern Tsin (A.D. 317–322), when Mei Tsih of Yu-chang presented to the emperor Yuen a Memorial along with a copy of Gan-kwŏ's commentary.   If it really were so, that we could discover no traces of the commentary during those 300 years, there would be ground both for surprise and suspicion on its unexpected re-appearance.   But the case does not stand so.

Before taking up the transmission of the commentary on through the later dynasties of Han, and that of Tsin, I must say something more on the testimony which we have from Lew Hin as to the existence of the 'ancient text' in the imperial library, and also call attention to the confirmation which he gives of both text and commentary's being current among scholars outside the official Boards. Not only does he give 'the ancient text of the Shang Shoo, in

---

5 This neglect of the ancient text is commonly expressed by—未立于學官. The Books peculiar to it are also called in consequence—逸書, and sometimes 外書.

1 都尉朝.   2 膠東庸譚. Yung is commonly referred to as Yung-săng.
3 清河胡常; Chang was styled 少子. He was a 'Great Scholar,' and rose to higher office.   4 虢徐敖. Gaou was also an officer of distinction (右扶風掾).
5 王璜, a native of 琅邪.   6 塗惲, a native of 平陵, and styled 子眞.
    7 乘 (al. 桑) 欽. styled 君長.   8. See their 綱領, 一, pp. 4, 5.

46 sections,' at the very top of the list of Books upon the Shoo in his catalogue; but he adds in a note, that his father Heang had compared this with the text of the classic taught by the schools of Gow-yang and of the greater and less Hea-how; that he had found one tablet or slip of the 'Announcement about Drunkenness' wanting, and two of the 'Announcement of Shaou;' that more than 700 characters were different from those in Fuh-săng's Books, and that individual characters were missing here and there to the amount of several tens. Further, in the reign of the emperor Gae (B.C. 5– A.D.), Hin proposed that the ancient text of the Shoo, Tso-k'ew's Ch'un Ts'ew, the She of Maou, and certain unrecognized portions of the Le, should all be publicly acknowledged, and taught and studied in the imperial college. The emperor referred the matter to the classical Board, which opposed Hin's wishes. Indignant, he address- ed a letter to the members, which may still be read. It is too long for translation here as a whole; but it contains the following asser- tions important to my purpose;—that the ancient text of the Shoo, Maou's She and the Tso-chuen, were all in the library; that of the three the Shoo was the most important; *that Yung T'an of Keaou- tung had taught among the people a text corresponding to that in the library;* and that they, the appointed conservators and guardians of the monuments of antiquity, were acting very unworthily in not aiding him to place the texts in the position which was due to them. Hin's remonstrances were bitterly resented, and he would have come to serious damage but for the interference of the emperor in his favour.[9] He was obliged to drop his project; but we may conclude that his efforts were not without effect. It was probably owing to him, that, in the succeeding reign and the usurpation of Mang, with which the Former or Western Han terminated, the claims of the ancient text were acknowledged for a short time.[10]

Having thus strengthened the first links in the chain of evidence for the transmission of Gan-kwŏ's commentary, I go on to the times of the Eastern Han, which are a blank in the account given by the editors of Yung Ching's Shoo.

There was a scholar and officer, named Yin Min,[11] whose life ex- tended over the first two reigns of the dynasty (A.D. 25–74). We

9 See the Memoir of Lew Hin in the 前漢書, 楚元王, 傳第六.   10 See Maou's Wrongs of the Shoo, III., p. 9.   11 尹敏. See the account of him in the 後漢 書, 儒林, 列傳第六十九. 尚一初習歐陽上書, 後受古文. 兼善毛詩, 穀梁, 左氏春秋.

read that in his youth he was a follower of the school of Gow-yang, but afterwards obtained and preferred the ancient texts of the Shang Shoo, the She of Maou, and Tso-k'ew's Ch'un-ts'ew.

About the same time lived Chow Fang,[12] who obtained a copy of the ancient text, and composed 'Miscellaneous Records of the Shang Shoo, in 32 Books.'

In the next reign, and extending on to A.D. 124, we meet with a K'ung He,[13] the then chief of the K'ung family, in which, it is said, 'the ancient text had been handed down from Gan-kwŏ, from father to son, without break.'

Contemporary with He, and carrying the line on to nearly A.D. 150, was Yang Lun,[14] who at first, like Yin Min, was a learner in the Gow-yang School, but afterwards addicted himself to the ancient text, established himself somewhere in an island on a 'great marsh,' and gathered around him more than a thousand disciples.

For more than half a century, the Records seem to be silent on the subject of Gan-kwŏ's ancient text and commentary. We come to the period of the 'After Han,' or, as it is often designated, the period of the 'Three Kingdoms.' In the kingdom of Wei, its first scholar was Wang Suh,[15] whose active life extended from A.D. 221 to 256. He wrote 'Discussions on the Shang Shoo,' and 'a Commentary on the Shang Shoo of the Ancient Text,' portions of both of which were in the imperial library under the dynasty of Suy.[16] Suh is often claimed as having belonged to the school of Gan-kwŏ. The evidence for this is not conclusive. Another 'ancient text,' as we shall see presently, had become public. But the evidence is quite sufficient to show that Suh must have seen Gan-kwŏ's commentary, and had his views moulded by it.

Connecting the 'After Han' and the dynasty of Tsin, we have the name of Hwang-p'oo Meih,[17] whose researches into antiquity remain in the 'Chronicle of Emperors and Kings,'[18] which everywhere quotes the 58 Books of Gan-kwŏ's ancient text. Meih, we are told, was guided in his studies by a cousin of the name of Leang Lew;[19]

12 周防. The account of him follows that of Yin Min.—受古文尚書,撰尚書雜記,三十二篇.   13 孔僖. See the same chapter of the 東漢 Records.—自安國以下,世世傳古文不絶.   14 楊倫. His biography follows that of K'ung He.—師事司徒丁鴻,習古文尚書,講學大澤中,弟子至千餘.   15 魏王肅   16 尚書駁議,隋志五卷. 古文尚書注,隋志十一卷.   17 皇甫謐   18 帝王世紀 19 See the account of Meih, in the Books of Tsin, 列傳,第二十一卷.—謐從姑子外弟梁柳.

and this Lew, we know from another source, possessed Gan-kwŏ's text and commentary. The Records of Tsin are now mutilated. They contain no chapter on Books and Literature like those of Han and other dynasties, and are otherwise defective. It was not always so, however. K‘ung Ying-tă quotes a passage, which distinctly traces the ancient text from the time of Wei down to Mei Tsih.[20] ‘Ch‘ing Ch‘ung,’[21] it is said, ‘Grand-guardian of Tsin, delivered the Shang Shoo in the ancient text to Soo Yu of Foo-fung;[22] Soo Yu delivered it to Leang Lew of T‘een-shwuy [this was the cousin of Hwang-p‘oo Meih]; Lëang Lew, who was styled Hung-ke,[23] delivered it to Tsang Ts‘aou of Ching-yang, styled Yen-ch‘e;[24] Ts‘aou delivered it to Mei Tsih of Joo-nan, styled Chung-chin, the chief magistrate of Yu-chang;[25] Tsih presented it to the emperor, and an order was given that it should be made public.’

The records of Suy confirm this account of the coming to light of Gan-kwŏ's text, and the authoritative recognition both of it and his commentary. They tell us that the old tablets (or the copy of them) ‘had been preserved in the imperial library of Tsin, but that there was no commentary on them;’ that ‘in the time of the Eastern Tsin, Mei Tsih, having obtained the commentary of Gan-kwŏ, presented it;’ and that ‘thereupon the text and commentary had their place assigned them in the national college.’[26]

Having brought down thus far the history of Gan-kwŏ's commentary, I must leave it for a short space, to speak of another ancient text, which made its appearance in the time of the Eastern Han, and gave origin to a school which flourished for several centuries.

8. A scholar and officer, named Too Lin,[1] had been a fugitive; having many wonderful escapes, during the usurpation of Mang. While wandering in Se-chow, he discovered a portion of the Shoo

---

20 See Ying-tă's long annotation on the title of the Canon of Yaou, on the last page.   21 鄭冲. He attained the dignity of Grand-guardian in A.D. 254.   22 扶風蘇愉. He was styled Hew-yu (休愉), and had high rank in the period Heen-he (咸熙), A.D. 264, 265.

23 梁柳字洪季.   24 城陽臧曹字彥始.   25 汝南梅賾字仲眞. 眞爲豫章內史遂于前晉奏上其書而施行焉. I have not translated 內史, the name of Tsih's office. I apprehend that at court he was a Recorder of the Interior, and was sent to Yu-chang, the present Keang-se, of which his father appears to have been governor. See the 晉職官志.   26 See 隋志 第二十七 經籍一.—晉世祕府所存有古文尙書經文今無有傳者,…至東晉豫章內史梅賾始得安國之傳奏之,…於是始列國學.

1 杜林. See the account of him in the 後漢書 列傳 第十七卷.

on lacquered tablets in the ancient text,[2] which he so much prized,

Too Lin's lacquered Ancient Text; and the Scholars who commented on it.

that he guarded it as his richest treasure, and amid all his dangers always kept it near his person. Afterwards, when the empire was again settled by the first emperor of the Eastern Han, Lin became acquainted with Wei Wang and other scholars. Showing them his discovery, he said, 'In my wanderings and perils I have been afraid that this text would be lost, but now it will be cared for and transmitted by you, and its lessons will not fall to the ground. The ancient text is not, indeed, at present authorised, but I hope you will not repent of what you learn from me.' Wei Wang, we are told, set great store by the Books he was thus made acquainted with, and he composed his 'Explanations of the Meaning of the Shang Shoo,'[3] which were based on them.

Subsequently to Wei Wang, three most eminent scholars published their labours upon Lin's Books. At the close of the Literary Chronicle of the Eastern Han, Pt. I., it is said, ' Kea K'wei produced his "Explanations" of Lin's Books; Ma Yung, his "Commentary;" and Ch'ing Heuen his "Comments and Explanations." From this time the ancient text of the Shang Shoo became distinguished in the world.'[4]

K'wei's work was soon lost. It was in three sections, was undertaken by order of the emperor Chang[5] (A.D. 76–88), and was designed to show wherein Lin's Books agreed with or differed from those of Fuh-săng.[6] Ma Yung's work was existing—a portion of it at least—in the Suy dynasty, in 11 *Keuen*. Heuen published more than one work on the Shoo. The library of Suy contained ' nine *Keuen* of the Shang Shoo,' and three *Keuen* of a 'Great Commentary on the Shang Shoo.'[7] They must have been existing later, for nearly all that we know of them is through quotations made by K'ung Ying-tă and Luh Tih-ming of the T'ang dynasty;—we find them indeed in the Catalogues of T'ang. They are now lost, and have gone, with scores of other works on the Shoo, whose names

[2] 于西州得漆書古文尙書一卷. There is a difficulty in my mind about Lin's Books being all in one *Keuen*. How are we to understand that term? [3] 尙書訓旨. The memoir of Wang, in the 後漢書, says expressly—從杜林受古文尙書, 爲作訓旨. [4] 杜林得古文尙書, 林同郡賈逵爲之作訓, 馬融作傳, 鄭玄注解, 由是古文遂顯於世. [5] 肅宗孝章皇帝. [6] Its full title was—尙書古文同異. [7] 尙書大傳三卷.

might be picked out in the Han and other chronicles, into the gulf of devouring time.

The 'lacquered' Books, as we learn from Ying-tă,[8] amounted to the same number as Gan-kwŏ's, though they were not all the same as his. They were:—'The Canon of Yaou;' 'The Canon of Shun;' 'The Counsels of the 'Great Yu;' 'The Counsels of Kaou-yaou;' 'The Yih and Tseih;' 'The Tribute of Yu;' 'The Speech at Kan;' 'The Songs of the Five Sons;' 'The Punitive Expedition of Yin;' '*The Kwuh Tsŏ*;' '*The Kew Kung, in nine Books*;' 'The Speech of T'ang;' '*The Teen Paou*;' 'The Announcement of T'ang;' 'Both possessed Pure Virtue;' 'The Instructions of E;' '*The Sze Ming*;' '*The Yuen Ming*;' 'The Pwan-kăng in 3 Books;' 'The Day of the Supplementary Sacrifice of Kaou-tsung;' 'The Conquest of Le by the Chief of the West;' 'The Viscount of Wei;' 'The Great Speech, in 3 Books;' 'The Speech at Muh;' 'The Completion of the War;' 'The Great Plan;' 'The Hounds of Leu;' 'The Metal-bound Coffer;' 'The Great Announcement;' 'The Announcement to K'ang;' 'The Announcement about Drunkenness;' 'The Timber of the Tsze tree;' 'The Announcement of Shaou;' 'The Announcement about Lŏ;' 'The Numerous Officers;' 'Against Luxurious Ease;' 'The Prince Shih;' 'The Numerous Regions;' 'The Establishment of Government;' 'The Testamentary Charge;' 'The Announcement of King K'ang;' 'The Charge to Keung;' 'The Speech at Pe;' 'The Charge to the Prince Wăn;' 'Leu on Punishments;' and 'The Speech of the Duke of Ts'in.'

I have put in italics the Books of Too Lin which were different from those of Gan-kwŏ, amounting to thirteen. An equal number of Gan-kwŏ's were wanting,—'The Announcement,' namely, 'of Chung Hwuy;' 'The T'ae Kĕă, in 3 Books;' 'The Charge to Yuĕ, in 3 Books;' 'The Charge to the Viscount of Wei;' 'The Charge to Chung of Ts'ae, 'The Officers of Chow;' 'The Keun-ch'in;' 'The Charge to Peih;' and 'The Keun-ya.'

Such were the Books of Too Lin, according to Ying Tă;[8] and on them Kea K'wei, Ma Yung and Ch'ing Heuen commented, according to the Records of Han. The authors of the Records of Suy repeat the latter statement, and immediately add:—'But the Books which they commented on, and handed down, were only 29. They mixed up with them, moreover, the modern text. They did not agree

---

8 See his notes at the commencement of the Shoo, in his explanation of the title 虞書.

with the ancient copy of K'ung Gan-kwŏ.'[9]　There is a perplexity here, which I do not know how to disentangle. We hardly have a comment remaining from this Too-lin School on any Books but those of Fuh-săng! It professed to follow an 'ancient text,' and yet with that it mixed up 'the modern text!' Moreover, Ying-tă has preserved a portion of Ch'ing Heuen's preface to his Shoo, in which he professes himself to be a follower of Gan-kwŏ,[10] and yet his text and Books were different from Gan-kwŏ's! I confess that the 'lacquered' Books of Too Lin are a mystery to me, and as the writings of Kea, Ma, and Ch'ing upon the Shoo have all perished, we can never arrive at satisfactory conclusions about them. I will venture one speculation.——Gan-kwŏ tells us in his Preface, that after he had deciphered his 58 Books, there still remained some fragments of tablets, from which he could make out nothing worth preservation. Others may have attempted to do so, however. We know that a Chang Pa[11] pretended to have made out 100 Books. Now in Lew Hin's Catalogue, the last but one entry on the Shoo is——'Books of Chow, 71 *pëen.*' If we add to Gan-kwŏ's 58 Books, the 13 Too Lin, to which I have called attention above, we obtain the exact number of 71. Is it not a 'concatenation accordingly,' that the lacquered Books were a compilation from this collection? Whatever may be thought of this suggestion, it is plain to me that all which we read about Ch'ing Heuen and others does not affect the validity of the argument for the text and commentary first made public through Mei Tsih as the ancient text deciphered by Gan-kwŏ and the commentary upon it composed by him.

9. I resume the history of Gan-kwŏ's text and commentary, which, it has been seen, were at length publicly acknowledged in the reign of

9 然其-賈逵, 馬融, 鄭玄-所傳, 唯二十九篇, 又雜以今文, 非孔舊本.　　10 The passage is not easy of interpretation.-我先師棘下生子安國, 亦好此學, 自世祖興, 後漢衞, 賈, 馬, 二三君子之業, 則雅才好博, 既宣之矣, 歐陽氏失其本義, 今疾此菑冒, 猶疑惑未悛也. The student will see that Ch'ing disowns the schools of the modern text, and claims connection for himself, through Wei Wang, K'wei, and Ma Yung, with Gan-kwŏ. But all these commented on Too Lin's Books. Wang Ming-shing would get out of this difficulty by referring to the account of Kea K'wei in the Records of the Eastern Han, where it is said that 'his father received the ancient text of the Shoo from T'oo Yun,' and that 'K'wei continued to transmit his father's learning.' Thus there is record against record; or it may be that K'wei, like Wei Wang, abandoned his former studies of the Shoo, and addicted himself to Too Lin's Books.　11 張霸　See Maou's 'Wrongs of the Shoo,' Ch. II., p. 7.

the first emperor of the Eastern Tsin (A.D. 317–322).   The schools

History of Gan-kwŏ's commentary resumed.

of the modern text had perished during the troubles of the period A.D. 307–312; there were now in the field only those of Ch'ing Heuen and Gan-kwŏ, and for some time they had nearly an equal course. The line of Tsin terminated in A.D. 420, and during 200 years which followed, the supremary of the empire was swayed by six different Houses. We learn from the Records of Suy, that under the dynasty of Ts'e (A.D. 480–502), the followers of Ch'ing greatly predominated;[1] that under those of Leang (A.D. 503–557) and Ch'in, (A.D. 558–588) 'Kung and Ch'ing walked together,[2] and that the same continued under Suy (A.D. 589–617), the school of Ch'ing waxing smaller and smaller.[3]

An interregnum of a few years ensued, till the authority of T'ang was acknowledged in A.D. 624, and the empire was united as it had not been since the times of Han. The second emperor of T'ang gave orders for a grand edition of the Shoo, under the superintendence of K'ung Ying-tă, assisted by the principal scholars and officers of the time.   They adopted the commentary of Gan-kwŏ, and enriched it with profuse annotations. Their work was ordered to be printed in the 5th year of the third emperor, A.D. 654, and appeared with the title of 'The Correct Meaning of the Shang Shoo, by K'ung Ying-tă and others.'[4] It remains, happily, to the present day. Choo E-tsun gives the titles of about seventy commentaries and other writings upon the Shoo published from the time of Fuh-săng to the T'ang dynasty, of which not one now exists but the commentary of Gan-kwŏ, and it might have disappeared like the rest, if it had not been embodied in the work of Ying-tă. I have indicated my doubts in the former section whether Confucius compiled the Books of the Shoo;—it is certainly to two of his descendants that we are indebted for the recovery and preservation of those of them which are still in our possession.

An important measure with regard to the form of the characters in the text was taken in A.D. 744, by the 6th of the T'ang emperors. Up to that time the text had appeared in the style of the public courts of Han, in which Gan-kwŏ had represented the ancient 'tadpole' characters. The emperor Heaou Ming ordered a Board of Scholars, under the presidency of a Wei Paou,[1] to substitute for

1 齊代唯傳鄭義.   2 梁陳所講, 有孔鄭二家.   3 至
隋孔鄭並行, 而鄭氏甚微.   4 孔氏穎達等尙書正義
1 衞包.

31]

this the form which was current in his day, and there appeared 'The Shang Shoo in the Modern Text,' in 13 *keuen*.'[2] The designation of this edition as 'the modern text' is unfortunate, as the student may be led to confound it with the Books of Fuh-săng.[3] But from this time the distinction between the ancient and the modern texts virtually ceased.   Fuh-săng's Books, with the exception of his 'Great Speech,' were all comprehended among the 58 Books of Gan-kwŏ, which had now got the field entirely to themselves.   All through the T'ang, and on through the period of the 'Five Dynasties' (A.D. 908–974), no scholar doubted but that he had, through the work of Ying-tă, the Books which had been found more than a thousand years before in the wall of Confucius' house.

The sovereignty of the dynasty of Sung dates from A.D. 975, and it lasted for 305 years.   It was a period of great mental activity, a protracted Augustan age of Chinese literature.   The writers of Sung quoted by the editors of Yung-ching's Shoo amount to 110.   The greatest name among them is that of Choo He, who was born in A.D. 1,130.   And he is remarkable in connection with the Shoo, for having doubted the authenticity of the Books and commentary ascribed to Gan-kwŏ.   In the next section, I shall consider the grounds of his doubts.   Up to his time, the authority both of Books and commentary was unchallenged.   If some suspicions were entertained, it can hardly be said that they found articulate expression.[4]

While many of the writings on the Shoo in the first half of this period have perished, there still remain sufficient to prove abundantly the learning and ability which were brought to the illustration of the classic.   There are the Works of Soo Shih,[5] of Lin Che-k'e,[6]

2 唐孝明皇帝今文尙書,十三卷.   3 Ma Twan-lin clearly explains the change which was thus made:—按漢儒林傳,孔氏有古文尙書,孔注 安國以今文讀之,唐藝文志有今文尙書十三卷,注 言玄宗詔集賢學士,備包改古文從今文,然則漢之所 謂古文者,科斗字今文者隸書也,唐之所謂古文者,隸 書,今文者世所通用之俗字也.   4 See last note in the 書經傳 說,綱領—where Ch'in Te (陳第), of the Ming dynasty, is quoted, to the effect that Woo Ts'ae-laou (吳才老) anterior to Choo He, was the first to point out the difference between the style of Gan-kwŏ's Books and the others.   5 蘇軾, styled Tung-po (東坡), *al.* Tsze-chen (子瞻), *al.* Mei-shan (眉山). He published 書傳十三卷.   6 林 之奇, styled Shaou-ying (少穎), and San-san (三山). His 'Collected Explanations of the Shang-shoo' (尙書集解) was in 58 *keuen*. I can speak of its thoroughness, having read and re-read it.

of Ch'ing Tseaou,[7] of Hea Seen,[8] of Leu Tsoo-heen,[9] and of others not a few.

10.   We found above that, taking together the Books of Gan-kwŏ, and 13 others which were in the catalogue of those of Too Lin, we had in all 71 Books of the Shoo, which were recovered nominally (to say the least) after the fires of Ts'in.   There remain 29 Books of

Of the Books of the Shoo which were never even partially recovered. Had they not perished before the Ts'in dynasty?

the hundred mentioned in the Preface spoken of in the last section.   I there suggested (p. 9) that portions might have been cast out or lost from the Collection of Historical Writings before the time of Ts'in.   The titles of those 29 were:—'The Kaou Yu;' 'The Le Kuh;' 'The Le Yuh;' 'The Punitive Expeditions of T'ang;' 'The Joo Kew;' 'The Joo Fang;' 'The Hea Shay;' 'The E Che;' 'The Chin Hoo;' 'The Ming Keu;' 'The Tsoo How;' 'The Yuh-ting;' 'The Heen E, in 4 Books;' 'The E Chih;' 'The Chung-ting;' 'The Ho Tan-keă;' 'The Tsoo-yih;' 'The Instructions of Kaou-tsung;' 'The Fun K'e;' 'The Ch'aou Ming;' 'The Kwei Ho;' 'The Kea Ho;' 'The Government of King Ching;' 'The Tsëang Poo-koo;' 'The Charge to Suh-shin, with Presents;' and 'The Pŏ-koo.'

In regard to these titles, it is to be observed, that, where they are not simply names of emperors or ministers, the information given about them in the notices of the preface is so scanty, that there are several of them which we cannot venture to translate.   Ts'ae Ch'in, as quoted on p. 9, has called attention to this, saying that on the Books which are lost the Preface is so servile and brief that it does not afford us the slightest assistance.   He thence draws the conclusion that the Preface could not be the work of Confucius.   Granted; but I draw a further inference, that whensoever and by whomsoever the Preface was made, the author could not have had those Books entire before him.   If he had, it is inexplicable that he should not have told us as much about them as he has done generally of the others which still remain.   The statement of Gan-kwŏ, that the tablets of the Preface were found with the others in the wall of Confucius' house, is not to be called in question.   It was made therefore before the burning of the Books,—and when it was made, there

---

7 鄭樵, styled Yu-chung (漁仲), and Këä-tse (夾漈).   8 夏㑩 styled Yuen-suh (元肅), and K'o-shan (柯山).   He produced 'Explanations of the Shang Shoo (尚書解),' in 16 *keuen*.   9 呂祖謙, styled Pih-kung (伯恭) and Tung-lae (東萊).   His 'Talkings on the Shoo' (書說) was in 35 chapters.

were existing of many of the *p'een* no more than what now exists—merely the names.

Further, some (seven at least) of the missing Books,—the Heen E, the Kwei Ho, and the Kea Ho—had reference to freaks or prodigies of nature,—'extraordinary things,' of which Confucius did not talk.[1]   We may assume that he would not have introduced such Books into a Canon of Historical Documents; and I argue besides, that they had fallen into deserved neglect before the time of Ts'in.   The good sense of scholars had seen their incongruity with the other documents of the Shoo, and they had been imperceptibly consigned to oblivion.   Add to these considerations, that we have hardly a single sentence in Mencius, the Le, Seun-tsze, or any other writings claiming to be as old as the Chow dynasty, taken from the missing Books, and my conclusion is greatly strengthened, that we have not lost by the fires of Ts'in so much of the Shoo as is commonly supposed.

It is by no means certain that the Canon did not at one time contain more than the hundred Books mentioned in the Preface. It is to me more than probable that it did not contain the whole even of them, when the edict of the Ts'in emperor went forth against it.   Of all that appeared for a time to be lost in consequence of the edict much the larger portion was ultimately recovered.

1 Ana. VII. xx.

SECTION III.

From Choo He to the present day.—

DOUBTS THROWN ON THE BOOKS PECULIAR TO GAN-KWŎ'S TEXT AND ON HIS COMMENTARY; WHICH, HOWEVER, ARE TO BE RECEIVED.

1.   The editors of Yung-ching's Shoo give the names of 115 scholars of the Yuen (A.D. 1,280–1,367) and Ming (A.D. 1,368–1,644) dynasties, of whose labours they make use in their annotations; and

The many Works published on the Shoo, since the time of Choo He.

Choo E-tsun, bringing his researches into the last century, enumerates the titles of more than 350 Works upon the classic, from Choo He downwards.

All these Writings have the whole of the Shoo, or as much as their authors acknowledged to be genuine, for their subject. On particular Books, especially the two Canons, the Tribute of Yu, and the Great Plan, about 200 works have been published during the same time. All this shows how the Shoo continues to hold its place in the minds of the Chinese. Its very difficulties seem to fascinate the scholars, who for the most part repeat one another sadly ; but now and then, we find a commentator who endeavours to shake off the trammels of Choo He, and to look on the ancient document with his own eyes.

2. Choo He did not himself publish a complete commentary on the Shoo. He edited, indeed, a copy of the classic, containing the
Choo He did not himself com-
ment on the Shoo. 58 Books of Gan-kwŏ, and the Preface as a separate *p'ëen.*[1] We have also his 'Remarks upon the Shoo,'[2] collected and published by some of his disciples ; but they are mostly confined to the Canons, the Counsels of Yu, the Announcement of Shaou, the Announcement about Lŏ, and the Metal-bound Coffer. He had come to entertain very serious doubts as to the authenticity of Gan-kwŏ's commentary, and of the Books additional to Fuh-săng's ; and he was painfully impressed with the difficulties of the text even in Fuh-săng's Books,—its errors, transpositions, and deficiencies. He shrank, therefore, from the task of attempting for the Shoo what he had done for the other classics, and in A.D. 1,199, the year before his death, devolved it on Ts'ae Ch'in, one of his favourite disciples, to make 'A Collection of Comments on the Shoo,'[3] instructing him to revive the distinction of 'modern text' and 'ancient text,' and to indicate by those names the relation of each Book to Fuh-săng or to Gan-kwŏ.

Ts'ae Ch'in undertook the labour, and completed it in ten years. His commentary appeared in 1,210, and at once attracted general admira-
The Commentary of Ts'ae. tion. After K'ung Ying-tă's 'Correct Meaning,' it was certainly the most important work which had been produced upon the Shoo. Nor has it been superseded. It remains to the present day the standard of orthodoxy, and is universally studied throughout the empire. To give only one eulogium of it.—Ho K'eaou-sin,[4] of the Ming dynasty, says :—'From the Han downwards, the works upon the Shoo had been many.

---

1 尚書古經. E-tsun says he had not seen this work (未見). It was, no doubt, the text adopted by He's disciple, Ts'ae Ch'in.   2 書說.   3 Ts'ae says in his preface :—慶元已未冬, 先生交公命沈作書集傳.   4 何喬新. See the 經義考, 書十一, p. 4.

But in the comments of Gan-kwŏ there is often much violence done to the text, which the amplifications of Ying-tă labour to sustain. Choo He had a great esteem for the views of Wang Gan-shih,[5] Leu Tsoo-heen, Soo Shih, and Lin Che-k'e; but the first of them errs in forced meanings, the second in excessive ingenuity, the third in summariness, and the fourth in tediousness. When the "Collected Comments" of Ts'ae came forth, distinguishing what Books were peculiar to the modern, and what to the ancient text, and what were common to both, and discussing also the forged prefaces, both the Great one, and the Little, then the grand principles and the grand laws of the two emperors and the three kings were brilliantly displayed to the world.' The scholars of China would deem me but a lukewarm admirer of their model commentator. I have often thought him deficient both in comprehension and discrimination, and prefer to him Lin Che-k'e, tedious as he is said to be. Ts'ae's distinguishing merit is his style, which will often bear comparison, for clearness and grace, with that of Choo He himself.

3. Choo He's doubts about the authenticity of the Books and commentary ascribed to Gan-kwŏ were plainly enough indicated; but his expression of them was not very decided. The suspicion, once given

The Ancient Text and Gan-kwŏ's Commentary still more doubted in the Yuen, Ming, and present dynasties.

out by such an authority, went on to grow. Under the Yuen dynasty, about the beginning of the 14th century, Woo Ch'ing published his 'Digest of Remarks on the Shang Shoo.'[1] The Work, so for as it goes, is well worthy of study. Ch'ing was a bold thinker and a daring critic. He handled the text with a freedom which I have not elsewhere seen. But his Work contains none of the Books which were deciphered by Gan-kwŏ. He rejects also the 'Great Speech' which Fuh-săng gave, believing that it was not originally among his Books, and confines himself to the other 28, which he believes are all of the Shoo that we now have.

Under the Ming dynasty, many critics followed in the wake of Woo Ch'ing. Kwei Yew-kwang,[2] and Shih King,[3] may be particularly

[5] 王安石. He was contemporary with Soo Shih, and, in every respect one of the ablest men of his day. His views were published by his son Wang Fang (王雱). E-tsun gives the work as 王氏安石仔雱, 新經尙書義. It was in 13 *keuen*, and is unfortunately lost.

[1] 尙書纂言. Woo Ch'ing (吳澄) is variously styled,—幼淸, 草廬, and 臨川 [2] 歸有光, styled 熙甫, and 震川 [3] 郝敬, styled 仲輿, and 京山

mentioned.   The former tells us that from his youth he had doubted
'all the talk about modern text and ancient text,' and that, afterwards, having met with some dissertations of Woo Ch'ing, he was
delighted with the agreement of their views, and tried to obtain the
Work of Woo mentioned above.   Disappointed in this, he published
Fuh-săng's Books with his own commentary, and prefixed the dissertations of Woo.[4]   The latter published 'Discussions on and Explanations of the Shang Shoo,'[5] in ten *keuen*.   He does not appear
to have seen Woo Ch'ing's Writings; but he goes beyond him
in his animosity to the ancient text and commentary.   In eight
of his *keuen*, he explains Fuh-săng's Books; the remaining two are
devoted to an exposure (as he thinks) of the falsehood of the ancient
text.   So strongly had the views of these and other critics taken
possession of the scholars of Ming, that in A.D. 1,643 a memorial was
presented to the emperor Chwang-lëĕ,[6] praying that the Books
peculiar to the ancient text might be cast out, and the subjects at
the competitive examinations be taken only from Fuh-săng's.   The
dynasty was in its death-throes.   The poor emperor had his hands
and head more than full with the invading Manchoos; and while
the empire passed from his sway, the ancient text was allowed to
keep its place.

Under the present dynasty, the current of opinion seems to run,
as in the Ming, against the Books, Commentary, and Preface ascribed
to Gan-kwŏ.   The works of Wang Ming-shing and Keang Shing, of
which I have made much use in my notes, speak in almost every
page, in the most unmeasured terms, of 'the false K'ung.'   The ancient
text, however, is not without its defenders.   So far as the government is concerned, things remain as they have been since the T'ang
dynasty.   The editors of Yung-ching's Shoo do not take up the
argument.   They give prominence, indeed, in their Introduction, to
the opinions of Choo He and his followers, but pass no judgment of
their own; and they use equal care in unfolding the meaning of the
suspected portions, and of those which all acknowledge.

4.   I shall conclude this chapter on the history of the Shoo with
an exposition of the grounds on which I cherish for myself a confidence in the authenticity of the ancient text and Gan-kwŏ's commentary on it, and some discussion of the principal arguments
advanced on the other side.   Minor arguments, based on the language

---

4 The title of his Work is 尚書叙錄.   5 尚書辨解.   6 莊烈愍
皇帝, A.D. 1628-1643.   7 See Maou's Wrongs of the Shoo, Ch. I. p. 1.

of particular passages in the Books, have been noticed in the notes upon them in the body of the Work.

[i.] With regard to the Commentary,—the controversy about it has not to a foreigner the interest or importance which it has to a Chinese.   Suppose that it really was not the production of Gan-kwŏ, yet there it was, actually existing in the beginning of our 4th century. No one can tell who composed it. Mei Tsih presented it to the emperor Yuen, and it received the authoritative acknowledgment. Tsih did not claim it as his own. He said it was the commentary of K'ung Gan-kwŏ, which had been handed down from one scholar to another for nearly four hundred years. Once made public, it ere long became the standard explanation of the classic; and its authority was unchallenged for more than eight hundred years. We are indebted to the annotations of the T'ang scholars upon it for most of what we know of the views of Ma Yung, Ch'ing Heuen, and other commentators of the Han dynasties. Whether it was written by the true K'ung, or by a false K'ung, it is a work the value of which cannot be over-estimated.

With regard to the Books themselves,—they are supported largely by the quotations from them which occur in the Analects, Mencius, Shih-tsze, Seun-tsze, and other Writings. I have been careful to point out this in the notes upon the several Books. A considerable portion of some of them is in this way guaranteed to us. The Books of the New Testament are not better attested by the citations from them in the works of the early Christian Fathers.

The opponents of the authenticity explain this by asserting that 'the false K'ung' carefully gathered out all the passages of the Shoo which were anywhere quoted, and wove them, along with the other materials of his own devising, so as to form the present Books. But this is only their hypothesis, and a very clumsy and unlikely hypothesis it is. On the one hand, it makes the forger to have been a scholar of very great learning and research ; so much so, that we are unwilling to believe that such a man could have stooped to a fraudulent attempt. On the other hand, it makes peculiarities, most natural if we admit the Books, to be silly contrivances to avert the suspicion of forgery. For instance, the text of a passage in the Books and of the same passage as quoted by Mencius has certain verbal differences. An easy explanation presents itself. Mencius was not concerned to be verbally accurate. He was sufficiently so for his purpose. It may even have suited him better to quote according to the sense than exactly according to the letter. But the hypothesis of which I am speaking requires a different explanation. The 'false K'ung' quoted from Mencius, and purposely altered his text in order to escape detection! This may be said; but it is unlikely in the highest degree. The Books have been subjected to the severest ordeal of unkindly criticism; and to me it is incomparably easier to believe their authenticity than to admit the arguments advanced against them.

[ii.] 'The Books of K'ung first appeared in the time of the Eastern Tsin. No scholars had seen them before that time. This circumstance is a very strong indication of forgery.' So said Choo He; and his assertions are repeated *ad nauseam* to the present time. But the history of the Books and Commentary which I gave in the last section furnishes a sufficient reply to them.

There were at one time, it is admitted on nearly all hands, both the Books and Commentary;—in the reign of the emperor Woo of the first Han. What is alleged, is that these were not the same as those which were made public by means of Mei Tsih. Well:—as to the Books. When Gan-kwŏ had deciphered them, he presented them to the emperor, and they were placed in the imperial library. There they were nearly a hundred years after, when Lew Hin made his catalogues. Hin's father compared their text with that of Fuh-săng's Books, and noted the differences between them. Hin himself endeavoured to have them made the subject of study equally with the smaller collection of Fuh-săng. They continued in the imperial library on to the time of the Eastern Tsin. They were there when Mei Tsih presented both the Books and the Commentary which he had received from Tsang Ts'aou. So the Records of Suy expressly testify. The Books received permanently the authoritative recognition due to them, and were commanded to be studied in the national college, in the time of the Eastern Tsin; but they had been lying on the shelves of the imperial library from the time of Gan-kwŏ downwards. They were not seen or not studied simply because the Government had not required them to be so. Next:—as to the Commentary. That Gan-kwŏ did write a commentary on his 58 Books is allowed, and its transmission is traced from scholar to scholar on into the Eastern Han. When did it perish? There is no intimation that it ever did so. On the contrary, I have shown above, pp. 25–27, that its existence rises as a fact, here and there, at no great intervals of time, on the surface of the literary history of the empire, till we arrive at Mei Tsih. Tsih received 'The Shang Shoo in the ancient text' from Tsang Ts'aou. That Shang Shoo comprehended both Gan-kwŏ's transcript of the text and his commentary. The Records of Sung are decisive on this point.

'But,' the adverse critics persist in alleging,—'but Ch'ing Heuen and Ma Yung, Ch'aou K'e[1] in his comments on Mencius, Wei Ch'aou on the Kwŏ Joo,[2] and Too Yu on the Tso-chuen, when they have to speak of any of the Books peculiar to the ancient text, call them "Yih Shoo." '[3] And they could not otherwise designate them. They had not seen them themselves. They do not call them "Wang Shoo,"[4] which would mean Lost or Perished Books. All that 'Yih Shoo' denotes, is that the Books were lying concealed, and had no place among the studies in the national college.[5]

It is urged again, 'But if Yin Min, K'ung He, and other scholars, were really in possession of Gan-kwŏ's Books and Commentary, why did they not bring them to the notice of the court, and get them publicly acknowledged before the time of the eastern Tsin?' The argument in this question has been much pressed on me by Wang T'aou, of whom I have spoken in the preface. But there is little weight in it. We know that the attempt of Lew Hin to obtain the recognition both of Books and Commentary was defeated, and he himself obliged, in consequence of it, to retire from court. If we knew all the circumstances of K'ung He and other scholars and of their times, we should probably cease to wonder at their being content to keep their treasures in their own possession. For every event there are in providence the time and the man.

[iii.] 'In the catalogue of Lew Hin, we have the entries:—"Of the Shang Shoo 29 p'een,"[6] and "Of Old King 16 keuen."[7] Those old King were false Books of the Han times, and were distinguished from the true Books of the Shoo by the carefulness of the Han scholars.' So says Kwei Yew-kwang;—by the strangest misreading of his authority. The words of the catalogue are:—'Of the Shang

1 See the proleg. to vol. II., pp. 4-7.   2 韋昭. Both he and Too Yu were of the Western Tsin.   3 逸書.   4 亡書.   5 See Maou K'e-ling on the meaning of the phrase 逸書 in his 'Wrongs of the Shoo,' Ch. III. p. 4.   6 Wang T'aou writes:—漢書有載, 孔僖家有古文尚書, 世世相傳, 亦載僖子季彥, 獨治古義, 不在科第之例, 而世人莫識, 則當肅宗時, 何不上進乎, 何以謹藏于家, 使世不知也.   7 藝文志有尚書二十九篇, 古經十六卷. See Yew-kwang's preface, quoted in the 經義考, 書十八

Shoo in the ancient text 46 *keuen*,' and 'Of *King* 29 *keuen*.'[8] Gan-kwŏ's Books and Fuh-săng's are mentioned in the order and manner exactly the opposite of what the critic asserts. If we were to argue from this (which it would be absurd to do) after his fashion, we should say that the Han scholars indicated their confidence in the Books of the ancient text, and their suspicion of Fuh-săng's.

[iv.] 'As compared with Fuh-săng's Books, those peculiar to Gan-kwŏ are much more easily read.   The style is so different, that even a tyro is conscious of it. This circumstance is sufficient to awaken suspicions of the latter.' This difference of the texts was first noticed particularly by Woo Ts'ae-laou, who said :—'In the additional Books of Gan-kwŏ, the style flows easily and the characters have their natural significations.   It is otherwise with the Books of Fuh-săng, which are so involved and rugged, that it is sometimes not possible to make them out.'[9] Choo He dwelt on the point, and insinuated the conclusion to which it should lead.   He had probably spoken more strongly on the subject than he has written, for Ts'ae Ch'in expresses his opinion against the authenticity of Gan-kwŏ's Books very decidedly.   'Fuh-săng,' says he, 'reciting the text, and crooning it over as in the dark, yet strangely managed to give the difficult Books ; and Gan-kwŏ examining and deciding among his tadpole tablets, all in confusion and mutilated, only made out those which were easy ! This is inexplicable.'[10] Woo Ch'ing and a hundred others follow in a similar strain.

The difference alleged between the texts must be admitted to a considerable extent.   There are differences, however, likewise among the Books of Fuh-săng.   The difficulty of reading and interpreting the Pwan-kang and the Announcements in the Books of Chow cannot be exaggerated.   They have often been to myself an *infandus dolor*.   The Canons, on the other hand, are much easier ; and some of the other Books are hardly more difficult than the Books of Gan-kwŏ.   Nor are *his* Books really easy.   They only appear to be so, where we come to one of them, after toiling through some of the more contorted portions common to both texts.

[8] 尙書古文經,四十六卷;經二十九卷 There is added 傳四十一篇. See above, p. 19.   [9] 安國所增多之書,皆文從字順,非若伏生之書,詰曲聱牙,至有不可讀者   [10] 伏生背文暗誦,乃偏得其所難,而安國考定于科斗古書,錯亂磨滅之餘,反專得其所易,則有不可曉者.

Moreover, the style of the Books differs according to their subjects. The Announcements are the hardest to understand of all. The Charges, Speeches, and Instructions are much simpler; and the Books which we owe to Gan-kwŏ consist principally of those. Perhaps he did polish somewhat in his transcription of them. In making out his tadpole tablets, he was in the first place obliged to make use of Fuh-săng's Books. But for them, which had been engraved happily in the newer form of the characters at a time when the knowledge of the ancient form was still possessed, the tablets from the wall of Confucius' house might have been of little use. That Gan-kwŏ did not servilely follow the 'modern text' we conclude from the readings of the schools of Gow-yang and Hea-how, different from his in many passages, which the industry of critics has gathered up; but as he had to learn from it to read the tablets submitted to him, we can understand how he would generally follow it, and take it often on trust, when he could not well tell what his own authority said. When he came, however, to new Books, which were not in Fuh-săng, the case was different. His aids had ceased. He had to make out the text for himself as he best could. I can conceive that, when he had managed to read the greater portion of a paragraph, and yet there were some stubborn characters which defied him, he completed it with characters of his own. That he was faithful and successful in the main is shown by the many passages of his Books that are found in other writings older than his time. But, however we endeavour to account for the smoother style and readier intelligibility of the portions of the Shoo which we owe to him, those characteristics of them are not, to my mind, sufficient to overthrow their claims on other grounds to be regarded as authentic.

[v.] 'The style of Gan-kwŏ's own preface is not like that in other writings of the Western Han. It resembles more the compositions of the Ts'in dynasty. The Little Preface, moreover, was unknown to Fuh-săng; and it savours of the style of the After Han.' Choo He thus expresses himself. The authenticity of the Books does not depend on that of either of the Prefaces; but the great critic certainly fell into a glaring error in ascribing the Little Preface to the time of the After Han. Nearly every sentence of it is found in the Records of Sze-ma Ts'een, a contemporary of Gan-kwŏ, and who, no doubt, had got it from him! Fuh-săng, indeed, was not possessed of it. He may never have had it. If he did have it before the edict against the Shoo, the tablets of it were lost in the same way as those of all the Shoo which he ever had excepting his 29 Books. 'It savours of the style of the After Han,' and yet we find it in a Work of the First Han, composed fully 300 years before the date which Choo He would assign to it:—this is a striking instance of the little reliance that can be placed on critical judgments, even of the most distinguished scholars, which are based on their taste in the matter of style.

As to the preface of Gan-kwŏ, we must pay the less attention to Choo He's attributing it, on the ground of its style, to the times of Tsin, after finding him so egregiously mistaken in his decision on the same ground about the other. Lew Hin, moreover, in his remarks on the Shoo, prefixed to his list of the Books of it in the imperial library, repeats the most important statements in the Preface, and nearly in its very words.

[vi.] 'Gan-kwŏ says, in his preface, that, when he had finished his commentary, the troubles connected with the practice of magical arts broke out, and he had no opportunity of getting the imperial sanction to his Work. Now all this must be false. We know from the Han Records, that the troubles referred to broke out in B.C. 91.[9] But Sze-ma Ts'een tells us that his Histories came no farther down than the period T'ae-ch'oo (B.C. 103–100).[10] At the conclusion of his account of the K'ung family, he speaks of Gan-kwŏ, saying, "He was one of the Great Scholars under the present reign, and died an early death, after being made guardian of Lin-hwae."[11] It follows that Gan-kwŏ was dead before the year B.C. 100. No troubles, therefore, happening ten years later, could affect him or any of his undertakings.' I do not know who first constructed this argument against the authenticity of Gan-kwŏ's preface, and, by implication, of his commentary; but Maou K'e-ling allows correctly that it displays much ingenuity. And yet there must be a flaw in it.

That the troubles spoken of prevented the recognition of Gan-kwŏ's commentary is asserted repeatedly in the Books of Han. From what source soever it arose, the persuasion that it was so with regard to Gan-kwŏ and his commentary, as his preface represents, has prevailed from the century in which he died down to the present time. If the matter can be decided on the *quod semper, ubique, et ab omnibus*

---

9 漢武帝紀征和元年巫蠱起
至太初而訖.

10 See the last words of Sze-ma Tseen's Preface, placed at the end of his histories.—大史公曰,余述黃帝以來,

11 安國爲今皇帝博士,至臨准大守早卒.

principle, then we must acknowledge the truth of the account given (professedly) by Gan-kwŏ of himself.

With regard to the statement of Sze-ma Ts'een, that his histories were not brought down lower than B.C. 100, there it is, standing out (in a strange way) at the end of the last chapter of his Records, which is a sort of epilogue to the rest. A close study of that chapter, however, has convinced me that he was labouring on his Records for years after B.C. 100, and that his terminating sentence must receive a different interpretation from that commonly put upon it.

In one place, Ts'een tells us that his Records brought the history down from Yaou to the year B.C. 121.[12]

He tells us again, that it was after the defeat sustained by Le Ling at the hands of the Huns, and when he himself endeavoured to appease the anger of the emperor against the unfortunate general, and was therefore put into prison,—that it was then that he addressed himself with redoubled energy to his work of historiography.[13] This date brings us to B.C. 97, three years later than the period T'ae-ch'oo.

Further, in the historical Records, there are various narratives and entries of things posterior to B.C. 100,—even narratives of things growing out of the magical delusions which came to a head in B.C. 91.[14] The statement which I have made, therefore, on p. 5, that Ts'een completed his Work in B.C. 96, though many of the critics so affirm, cannot be correct.

The various conflicting statements in Ts'een's Preface, and the later entries in his Records, may be in a measure reconciled in the following way.—At first it was not his intention to bring his history farther down than B.C. 121, in which case he would probably have done little more, in several divisions of the Records, than edit the materials collected by his father. Subsequently, he resolved to bring the history down to the period T'ae-ch'oo, which he did in his account of the emperor Woo. So long as he lived, moreover, he kept adding to his different memoirs, and hence we have the narrative of events which took place later than the year B.C. 91, when the troubles commenced, which prevented the imperial recognition of Gan-kwŏ's

---

[12] 於是卒述陶唐以來, 至于麟止. See the 太史公自序, p. 6. The emperor Woo fancied that he had found a K'e-lin in B.C. 121, and thereon changed the style of the period from 元朔 to 元狩.   [13] 七年而大史公遭李陵之禍, 幽於縲絏, 乃喟然而歎曰, 云云. See p. 5.   [14] See the Wrongs of the Shoo, pp. 5, 6.

commentary. When he says that Gan-kwŏ died an early death in the reign of the emperor Woo, it does not follow that that event did not take place after the period of *T'ae-ch'oo*.[15]

Whatever may be thought of this suggestion, the statements in the Preface are so directly and repeatedly borne out by the Records of the Han dynasties, that we cannot but admit their verity.

[vii.] 'In the preface to the Shwŏ Wăn, Heu Shin says that his quotations from the Shoo King were taken from K'ung's Books. Yet the passages adduced are all from Fuh-săng's 28 Books, with only one exception. That one is from the Charge to Yuě, Pt. i., p. 8; and as it is given in Mencius, the probability is that Shin took it from him. How is it that the lexicographer could be using Gan-kwŏ's Books, and yet we should find in his Work only one doubtful quotation from all the 25 which were recovered by him additional to those of Fuh-săng?' I do not know who was the author of this difficulty; but a difficulty it certainly is. The Books of Gan-kwŏ were 58. Heu Shin says he used them, and yet he quotes only from the little more than one half of them which were common to the 'modern text.' Was there a copy current in Heu Shin's time of Fuh-săng's Books according to Gan-kwŏ's text, *i.e.*, with the different readings which he had preferred from his tablets? This would be one way of solving the difficulty. There is, however, another, which is on the whole to be preferred. Heu Shin undertook his dictionary, after Kea K'wei had declined the task. But in carrying through the work, he made constant reference to that scholar.[16] K'wei, we have seen, had adopted the Books of Too Lin. They were in an 'ancient text,' though different from that of Gan-kwŏ. Shin must have confounded the two, and supposed that, while he was really quoting from Too Lin, he was quoting from Gan-kwŏ. The Books of Too Lin, though not all the same as Gan-kwŏ's, were the same in number. How, even with them before him, Shin's quotations are only from the same Books as Fuh-săng's,—this still leaves the perplexity which I have pointed out above, in connection with the writings of Kea K'wei, Ma Yung, and Ch'ing Heuen.

5. The question of the authenticity of Gan-kwŏ's Books and commentary has now been sufficiently gone into. It had occurred

---

15 The year of Sze-ma Ts'een's death is disputed. It is often said to have taken place in the end of the emperor Woo's reign. Wang Ming-shing refers it, I think successfully, to the beginning of the next reign,—that of the emperor Ch'aou, B.C. 85-71. See the 十七史商榷, 卷 一, p. 4. 16 See Maou's Wrongs of the Shoo, Ch. VII., p. 7-9.

to myself long ago that a complete copy of the Shoo, as it was before
the time of the Ts'in dynasty, might possibly
be found in Japan.   I am pleased to discover
that the same idea has been entertained at different times by Chinese
scholars.   Very decided expression was given to it in the 11th
century by Gow-yang Sew,[1] from whom we have a song upon a
'Knife of Japan,' which concludes with :—

May the Shoo complete be yet found in Japan?

'When Seu Fuh went across the sea,
The books had not been burned;
And there the hundred p'een remain,
As in the waste inurned.

Strict laws forbid the sending them
Back to our Middle Land;
And thus it is that no one here
The old text has in hand.'[2]

The critics for the most part treat the idea with contempt; and
yet in the year 1697, the 36th of K'ang-he, a petition was presented,
requesting the emperor to appoint a commission to search for the
Shang Shoo, beyond the seas.[3]   Japan is now partially opened.   By
and by, when its language is well known, and access is had to all its
literary stores, this matter will be settled.

1 歐陽修, styled 永叔. He died A.D. 1073.   2 All of the song which I have seen
runs:—傳聞其國居大海,　土壤沃饒風俗好,　前朝
貢獻屢往來,　士人往往工詞藻,　徐福行時書未
焚,　逸書百篇今尚存,　令嚴不許傳中國,　舉
世無人識古文. See the 經義考書二, p. 6.   3 See Wrongs of the
Shoo, Ch. I., pp. 3, 4.

46]

CHAPTER II.

ON THE CREDIBILITY OF THE RECORDS IN THE SHOO.

THE FIRST AND SECOND PARTS ARE LESS RELIABLE THAN
THE OTHER THREE, AND HAVE MUCH OF WHAT IS LEGENDARY IN THEM.
OF YAOU, SHUN, AND YU, THE LAST IS TO BE REGARDED AS THE
FOUNDER OF THE CHINESE EMPIRE. HIS GREAT LABOURS IN REGULATING
THE WATERS AND SURVEYING AND DIVIDING THE LAND.

1.   The conclusion to which I came in the last Chapter was, that
in the 58 Books which now form the *textus receptus* of the Shoo, we
have so much of the classic, as it existed in the end of the Chow
dynasty.   Through Fuh-săng first, and then through K'ung Gan-
kwŏ, all this portion—a larger proportion of the whole than is
generally supposed—was recovered within little more than a century
of the time when the first emperor of Ts'in ordered that the books
should be consigned to the flames, and about a century before our
Christian era.   There were no doubt mutilations and transpositions,
as well as alterations of the ancient text, but they were not so great
as to affect the substantial integrity of the book.   In the subsequent
transmission of the Shoo to the present day, the text has undergone
the corruptions which are unavoidable to literary documents in
their passage over so long a space of time; but the errors which have
in this way crept in are not more, nor of more importance, than
those which it is the object of critical inquiry to eliminate from our
most valuable documents in the West.[1]   There is really nothing
seriously to shake our confidence in the eight and fifty Books of the
Shoo which we have, as being substantially the same with those
which were known to Seun-tsze, Mencius, Mih-tsze, Confucius himself, and others.

1 Not a few eminent Chinese critics have laboured to construct an accurate text.   There is a
large mass of materials in the 古文尙書撰異 of 段玉裁, to which I have made
frequent reference; but it would have added too much to my labour, and not have repaid the time
to gather up the various readings throughout.

We come now to inquire how far the documents of the Shoo can Whether the documents of the Shoo are reliable or not. be relied on as genuine narratives of the events which they profess to relate.   And it may be said at once, in reference to the greater number of them, that there is no reasonable ground on which to call them in question. Allowance must be made, indeed, for the colouring with which the founders of one dynasty set forth the misdeeds of the closing reigns of that which they were superseding.   I have pointed out, moreover, in the notes on 'The Counsels of the Great Yu,' how the failures of a favourite hero may be glossed over, and actual defeat represented as glorious triumph.   But the documents of the Shoo are better en- titled, I conceive, to credit than the memorials which are published at the present time in the Peking Gazette.

The more recent they are, the more of course are they to be relied on.   The Books of Chow were contemporaneous with the events which they describe, and became public property not long after their composition.   Provision was made, we have seen, by the statutes of Chow, for the preservation of the monuments of previous dyn- asties.   But those monuments were at no time very numerous, and they could not but be injured, and were not unlikely to be corrupt- ed, in passing from one dynasty to another.   From the time of T'ang, the Successful, however, commonly placed in the 18th century before Christ, we seem to be able to tread the field of history with a some- what confident step.

2.   Beyond the time of T'ang we cannot be so sure of our way. Our information is comparatively scanty.   It has in itself less of The oldest documents are not to be relied on so much as the others. verisimilitude.   Legend and narrative are confusedly mixed together.   This is more especially apparent in the first and second Parts of the Work.

[i.] 'The Book of T'ang,' known as 'The Canon of Yaou,' and all but one portion (which, indeed, must be classed with the others), of 'The Books of Yu' are, professedly, the compilations of a later time.   They all commence with the words which I have translated —'On examining into antiquity, we find,'———.   If the construction of the paragraphs, which has been generally preferred since the time of Choo He, be adopted, the point on which I am insisting is equally prominent.   We should then have to render.—'When we make a study of the ancient emperor Yaou, the ancient emperor Shun, the ancient Yu, the ancient Kaou-yaou, we find,'———.   On either version the chronicler separates himself from his subject.   He writes from a modern standpoint. Yaou, Shun, Yu, and Kaou-yaou are in the distant vistas of antiquity.

In my notes on the first paragraph of the Canon of Yaou, I have pointed out the absurdity of the interpretations which the scholars of Han—Gan-kwŏ, Ma Yung, and Ch'ing Heuen—gave of the words in question. Possibly, they had some idea of avoiding the conclusion to which the natural reading of them would lead, and therefore put upon them the forced meanings which they did. Morrison would infer from the first character,[2] that 'a considerable part of the Shoo is merely tradition;' but the character is itself uncertain, and, even if it were not so, no inference from it can be extended beyond the document to which it belongs. The scholars of the Sung and more recent dynasties seem never to have been struck with the uncertainty which either of the admissible interpretations attaches to the whole contents of the first two Parts of the classic. Their critical taste and ability made them reject the strained constructions of earlier times, but it never occurred to them to say to themselves,—'Well; but doing this, and taking the language as it ought to be taken, we cannot claim the authority for the records concerning Yaou, Shun, and Yu, which we are accustomed to do. Who compiled the Canons and the Counsels? When did he or they live? Are we not sapping the foundation of some of the commonly received accounts of the most early period of our national history?' Reflections like these do not appear to have occurred to any of the Chinese critics; but I submit it to my readers, whether they might not have justly done so.

At the same time, it is to be admitted, that the compiler of these Parts was possessed of documents more ancient than his own time,— documents which had probably come down from the age of Yaou and Shun. There are three things which to my mind render this admission necessary. First, there are the titles of the high officers about the courts of the two emperors, which we do not meet at a later age. The principal personage, for instance, was styled 'The Four Mountains;' next to him was 'The General Regulator;' and the minister of Religion was 'The Arranger of the Ancestral Temple.' The peculiarity of these designations indicates that the compiler had received them from tradition or from written records (which is more likely), and that they were not invented by himself. Second, the style of these Parts is distinguished, in several paragraphs, from

1 曰若稽古.　2 曰, See the preface to his dictionary, p. viii.

49]

that of the Books of Hea, Shang and Chow. The exclamations, 'Alas!' 'Ah!' and 'Oh!' in particular, are expressed by characters which we do not find elsewhere used in the same way.[3] Third, the directions of Yaou to his astronomers, to determine the equinoxes and solstices by reference to the stars culminating at those seasons, could not be the inventions of a later age. The equinoxes were then in Taurus (Pleiades) and Scorpio, and the solstices in Leo and Aquarius. We shall find in the next chapter how these statements have been employed to ascertain the era of Yaou. No compiler, ignorant of the precession of the equinoxes, which was not known in China till long after the Christian era, could have framed them with such an adjustment to the time of which he was writing.

The two circumstances which I have pointed out in this paragraph may seem to conflict with each other. In the first place, the compilation of the Books of the first and second Parts of the Shoo, at a date long subsequent to that of which they treat, is calculated to lessen our confidence in them; while the admission, again, of ancient documents among their contents may be thought to establish their authority sufficiently. It is my duty, however, to call attention to both the points. They lie equally upon the face of the Books. It may be impossible to separate what is old from what is more recent, —to distinguish what the compilers added of their own from what was universally received before their time. Perhaps no two critics who make the attempt will come to identical conclusions. For my own part, I have no hesitation in adjudging the first two paragraphs in the Canon of Yaou to the compiler, and generally all the narrative portions in the other Books. I think, likewise, that I can trace his hand in various expressions throughout, which make us think of the dominion of the chieftains Yaou and Shun according to our impressions of the empire when it had been consolidated and extended, many hundreds of years subsequent to them.

[ii.] The references to Yaou and Shun in the succeeding Parts of the Shoo are so very scanty as to excite our surprise, and induce

Yaou and Shun do not appear as the sage-heroes of history till the time of the Chow dynasty.

the idea that it was not till the time of the Chow dynasty that they obtained the prominent place in the early history of the empire which is now assigned to them.

In the Books of Hea, Shun is not mentioned at all, and Yaou is mentioned only once. In the third of the 'Songs of the Five Sons,'

3 Consult 吁, 咎, and 都 in Index III.

he appears as 'the prince of T'aou and T'ang, who possessed the country of K'e.' In that description of him we hear the voice of the most early tradition. Yaou is not yet the emperor ruling over 'ten thousand States,' but a prince or chieftain, having his seat north of the Yellow River, and ruling over the land of K'e. We may doubt whether his authority extended over all the territory subsequently known as K'e-chow; but it had not yet reached south of the Ho, and hardly west of it, where it divides the present provinces of Shen-se and Shan-se.

In the Books of Shang, Yaou and Shun are mentioned once, where the language is magniloquent enough; but it is so vague that we can learn nothing from it as to their original position. In the Charge to Yuĕ, (Part. iii., par. 10) E Yin is introduced as having said, 'If I cannot make my sovereign like Yaou and Shun, I shall feel ashamed in my heart as if I were beaten in the market place.' We are then told that Yin, fired with this ambition, so dealt with T'ang the Successful, that he became equal to Great Heaven. By this time Yaou and Shun had become mythical personages, embodying the ideal of a perfect sovereign.

We come to the Books of Chow, and in them we have two references to the ancient heroes. The one is in 'The Officers of Chow,' where Yaou is spoken of under the dynastic name of T'ang, and Shun under that of Yu, and the small number of their officers is contrasted with the multitude of those of Hea and Shang.[4] The second is in 'The Prince of Leu on Punishments,' Ch. II. The passage is very confused; and some critics think that it speaks only of Yaou, while others (with whom I agree) hold that Shun is the subject of it. The traditions of his time (or, it may be, the accounts of them in the Canons) are blended with those of a still earlier date, and we see, as through a mist, the beginnings of the empire, as Shun lays its foundations, now by martial prowess beating down barbarian wickedness, now by humility and benevolence, with the assistance of his chiefs, conciliating the affections of the people.

The above are all the places in the Books of Hea, Shang, and Chow, where Yaou and Shun are referred to. The first of them gives us a simple reminiscence, separated by less than half a century from the year assigned to the death of Shun; and it is very instructive as to the real position which Yaou occupied. From the second we learn nothing valuable; but we find the men growing into larger

4 See Bk. xx., p. 3.—唐虞稽古·建官惟百·

dimensions, as the distance through which they are looked back to lengthens. In the third their original smallness is indicated, though they are said to have secured the repose of the 'ten thousand States.' The fourth is more suggestive, but we know not how to reconcile it with the statements in the Canons of the two first Parts. T'ang is silent about Yaou and Shun, when he is vindicating his overthrow of the Hea dynasty. Woo, in the same way, has nothing to say about them, when he would justify his superseding of the dynasty of Shang. Above all, the duke of Chow, the real establisher of the dynasty of Chow, and the model of Confucius, amid all his appeals to ancient precedents in support of the policy of his House, never mentions them. When we turn to the She King, the book of ancient songs and ballads, no Yaou and Shun are there. It is nearly all, indeed, of the dynasty of Chow, and celebrates the praises of king Wăn and his ancestors; but it is impossible not to be surprised that no inspiration ever fell upon the 'makers' from the chiefs of K'e. They are mentioned once in the Yih King, but it is in the appendix to that Work, which is ascribed to Confucius, and the authenticity of which is much disputed.

Taking all these things into consideration,—the little that is said about Yaou and Shun in the later Parts of the Shoo itself, and the nature of that little; the absolute silence in reference to them of the She; and the one doubtful mention of them in the Yih,—I am brought to the conclusion, that the compilation of the first two Parts was not made till some time after the commencement of the Chow dynasty. Certain it is, that, during this dynasty, Yaou and Shun received a prominence which they did not previously possess. Confucius in particular adopted them as his favourite heroes, and endowed them with all the virtues, which should render them models to sovereigns in all time. Mencius entered into the spirit of his master, and, according to the bolder character of his own mind, pushed the celebration of them farther, and made them models for all mankind. Then, for the first time, under the hands of these two philosophers, they took their place as the greatest of sages. To the compiler, probably, they owed their designation of ' te,'[5] emperor or vicegerent of God, as well as all those descriptions which aid the natural illusion of the mind, and set them before us as ruling over a territory equal to that of the kings of Chow.

3. The accounts of Yaou and Shun, and especially of the connec-

5 帝.

tion between them, are so evidently legendary that it seems strange

The accounts of Yaou and Shun are evidently legendary. how any one can accept them as materials for history. When Yaou has been on the throne for seventy years, finding the cares of government too great for him, he proposes to resign in favour of his principal minister, the 'Four Mountains.' That worthy declares his virtue unequal to the office. Yaou then asks him whom he can recommend for it; be the worthiest individual a noble or a poor man, he will appoint him to the dignity. This brings Shun upon the stage. All the officers about the court can recommend him,—'Shun of Yu,[1] an unmarried man among the lower people.' His father, a blind man, was also obstinately unprincipled: his mother was insincere: his brother was arrogant; and yet Shun had been able by his filial piety to live harmoniously with them, and to bring them to a considerable measure of self-government and good conduct. Yaou was delighted. He had himself heard something of Shun. He resolved to give him a preliminary trial. And a strange trial it was. He gave him his own two daughters in marriage, and declared that he would test his fitness for the throne by seeing his behaviour with his two wives!

We are to suppose that Shun stood this test to which he was subjected. We find him next appointed to be 'General Regulator,' the functions of which office he discharged so successfully, that, after three years, Yaou insisted on his consenting to accept the succession to the throne. They then reigned together for about a quarter of a century, till the death of Yaou, who enjoyed the superior dignity, while Shun took all the toils of government.

To the above incidents there are other two to be added from the Shoo. Yaou was not childless. He had at least one son, mentioned as Choo of Tan; but the father did not feel justified in transmitting the empire to him, in consequence of the unworthiness of his character, so much did concern for the public weal transcend Yaou's regard for the distinction of his own family. In regard to Shun, he appears in one place as a farmer, during the early period of his life, in the neighbourhood of mount Leih, which was not far from Yaou's capital.

1 虞舜. Bunsen, calling these characters Yü-shin, supposes that the 虞 is 禹, the name of Yu the Great, and says that they are 'simply a mythical combination of Yü (禹) and Shin (舜), in order to connect the great deliverer [that is, Yu the Great] with the two old emperors, Yaou and Shin.' This is an instance of the errors into which the subtlest reasoners are liable to fall, when they write 'without book.' See 'Egypt's Place in Universal History,' vol. III., p. 399.

In Sze-ma Ts'een and Mencius these scanty notices are largely added to.[2] We have Shun not only as a farmer, but also as a fisherman, and a potter. His 'insincere' mother is his step-mother, and his 'arrogant' brother but a half-brother. Yaou has nine sons, who are sent with his two daughters, and a host of officers, to serve Shun amid the channeled fields. Even after this, his wicked relatives continue to plot against his life; and on one occasion, when they thought they had accomplished their object, the bad brother, after saying that his parents might have the sheep and oxen, storehouses and granaries, proceeds to Shun's house to appropriate his shield and spear, his bow and lute, and his two wives to himself, when lo! there is Shun sitting calmly on a couch, and playing on his lute!

There are other incongruities. Shun's appearing in the Shoo at first merely as a private man was, according to Ts'een, simply through the reduced circumstances of his family. He proves him to have been of the blood royal, and traces his descent from Hwang-te, or the Yellow emperor. But Yaou was also descended from Hwang-te; and thus Shun is made to marry his own cousins,—a heinous crime in Chinese law, and also in the eyes of Chinese moralists. My readers will probably agree with me that we ought not to speak of the *history* of Yaou and Shun, but of legendary tales which we have about them.

4. Passing on from the connection between Yaou and Shun to that which Yu had with each of them, until he finally succeeded to the

The accounts of the connection of Yu with Yaou and Shun are of the same legendary character.

latter, we find much that is of the same character. Yaou, in what year of his reign we do not know, appears suddenly startled with the ravages of an inundation. The waters were embracing the mountains, and overtopping the hills, and threatening the heavens with their surging fury. Was there a capable man to whom he could assign the correction of the calamity? All the nobles recommend one K'wăn, to whom Yaou, against his own better judgment, delegates the difficult task; and for nine years K'wăn labours, and the work is still unperformed.

For his want of success, and perhaps for other reasons, K'wăn was put to death; and Yu, who was his son, entered into his labours.[1]

2 See the 史記, 卷一, pp. 6, 7; and Mencius, V. Pt. i. ch. II., *et al.*

1 The subject of the connection between K'wăn and Yu, and between their labours, is invested to me with a good deal of difficulty. It is the universal belief of the Chinese that Yu was the son of K'wăn. The Shoo does not tell us so. The language of 'The Great Plan,' p. 3, does not necessarily imply the fact. Sze-ma Ts'een, Ch. II., p. 1, however, affirms it (禹傷先人

We have nothing definite in the Shoo about the year, or the manner of Yu's designation to the work. Some time after the death of Yaou, when Yu is superintendent of Works, Shun compliments him on the success with which he had regulated the water and the land, and appoints him to be 'General Regulator' under him, as he himself had formerly been under Yaou. The measures of Yu in remedying the disasters of the inundation are detailed at length in the first of the Books of Hea, which I shall consider in the sequel. His appointment to be 'General Regulator' may be considered as preliminary to his being called to occupy the throne. The Shoo does not tell us that Shun had a son; but Mencius assumes that such was the case, and that the son was weak or worthless like Choo of Tan, so that the example of Yaou had again to be copied. Three and thirty years after the death of that sovereign, Shun tells Yu that the laborious duties of the government wearied him, being now between ninety and a hundred years old, and summons him to take the leadership of the people. Yu declined the dignity again and again, till Shun waxed peremptory. They then reigned together for about fifteen years, when Shun died, and Yu was left in sole possession of the empire.

This tale of Yu's accession to the throne is not so marvellous as the story of Shun. It is sufficiently so, however, to bear out what I have suggested of there being a legendary element in it. We cannot but be struck with the way in which the more salient points of the previous narrative re-appear. The empire to the worthiest; the common weal before private and family advantage:—these are the lessons for the enforcement of which the accounts of Yaou, Shun, and Yu, in their relations to one another, were framed to the fashion in which they have descended to us.

5. Yu the Great was the founder of the dynasty of Hea. The throne descended in his line, for a period of about four centuries

Yu is the first historical ruler of China.

and a half. This fact sufficiently distinguishes him from Yaou and Shun, and indicates the point of time when the tribe or tribes of the Chinese people passed

鯀功之不成受誅，云云）, and the language of the Le Ke, 祭法, par. 1, is also very strong in support of it (夏后氏亦禘黄帝而郊鯀祖顓頊而宗禹）. Notwithstanding these testimonies, I still query the point in my own mind. We have no certain data as to when Yu entered on his labours. The statements of Mencius, Bk. III., Pt. i, iv. 7, ascribe his appointment to Shun, while Yaou was still alive; and the notice in 'The Great Plan,' makes it subsequent to K'wăn's death. The language there should, probably, make us take the most emphatic meaning given to the term 殛, applied, in the Canon of Shun, and in Mencius, to Shun's dealing with K'wăn.

from the rule of petty chiefs, and began to assume the form of a nation subject to a sovereign sway.   In the time of Mencius there were some who found in the fact merely an evidence of the inferiority of Yu in virtue to the more ancient heroes.   'He made the empire,' it was said, 'a family property, instead of transmitting it, as they did, to the worthiest.'   Mencius of course had his reply.   It was not Yaou who gave the empire to Shun, but Heaven, of whose providence Yaou was only the instrument.   So in the case of Shun and Yu.   Shun assisted Yaou in the government 28 years, and Yu assisted Shun 17 years.   Yih, Yu's prime minister, however, only assisted him 7 years.   Then, moreover, the sons of Yaou and Shun were both bad, while K'e, the son of Yu, was a man of talents and virtue.   These differences or contrasts in the situations were all equally from Heaven; which thus brought it about that the people would have K'e to reign over them, and not Yih.   Mencius winds up his argument with a dictum of Confucius:—'T'ang [Yaou] and Yu [Shun] resigned the throne to their worthy ministers.   The sovereign of Hea [Yu] and the sovereigns of Yin and Chow transmitted it to their sons.   The principle of righteousness was the same in all the cases.'[1]

Confucius and Mencius were obliged to resort to this reasoning by the scheme which they had adopted of the ancient history of their country; but they explicitly affirm the fact to which I am calling attention,—that the empire, such as it then was, first became hereditary in the family of Yu.   This fact constitutes him a historical personage, and requires that we consider him as the first sovereign of the Chinese nation.

6.   Bunsen says:—'Yu the Great is as much an historical king as Charlemagne; and the imperial tribute-roll of his reign in the Shu-king is a contemporary and public document just as certainly as are the capitularies of the king of the Franks.'[1]   That Yu is an historical king is freely admitted; but that the tribute-roll of his reign which we have in the Shoo-king was made by him, or is to be accepted as a genuine record of his labours, must be as freely denied.

What Bunsen calls the tribute-roll of Yu's reign is always edited as the first of the Books of Hea, which form in this volume the third Part of the Shoo.   But all which it details took place, or is imagined to have taken place, before the death of Yaou, not only before Yu

The account of Yu's labours in the Shoo cannot be received as history.

1 Mencius. V., Pt. I., Chh. v., vi.
1 Place of Egypt in Universal History, vol. III., p. 395.

occupied the throne, but when there was no prospect of his ever doing so. The Book belongs to the period of Yaou and Shun, and appears out of its chronological order. Its proper position would be in the first Part; and it must share in the general uncertainty which I have shown to belong to the documents of the oldest portions of the classic.

In my notes upon the Book, p. 93, I have said that the name,— 'The Tribute of Yu'—conveys a very inadequate idea of its contents. It describes generally the labours of Yu in remedying the disasters occasioned by the inundation referred to above, in paragraph 4, as startling Yaou, and his subsequent measures in dividing the land which he had rescued from the waters, and determining and apportioning the revenues to be paid by its different provinces.

To enable us to judge of the credibility of Yu's labours, we must first get before our minds some definite idea of the state of the country when he entered upon them. Mencius thus describes it, giving the picture which he drew to himself from the records of the Shoo:—'In the time of Yaou, when the empire had not yet been reduced to order, the vast waters, flowing out of their channels, made a universal inundation. Vegetation was luxuriant, and birds and beasts swarmed. Grain could not be grown. The birds and beasts pressed upon men. The paths marked by the feet of beasts and prints of birds crossed one another throughout the Middle Kingdom. ......Yu separated the nine different branches of the Ho, cleared the courses of the Tse and T'ă, and led them to the sea. He opened a vent for the Joo and Han, regulated the course of the Hwae and Sze, and led them all to the Keang. When this was done, it was possible for the people of the Middle Kingdom to get food for themselves.'[2] This may seem a sufficiently frightful picture; but it is sketched with colours all too light. Such was the overflow of the waters of the Ho, that Yaou spoke of them, from the point of view in his capital, as embracing the mountains, overtopping the hills, and threatening the heavens. As they proceeded on their eastern course, they separated into a multitude of streams, and formed a delta of part of the present provinces of Chih-le and Shan-tung, where the people were shut up on the elevated grounds. The waters of the Keang required regulating nearly as much. All the affluents of these two mighty rivers, and whatever other streams, like the Hwae, lay between them, were in similar disorder. The mountains where the rivers

2 Mencius, Bk. III., Pt. I. iv. 7.

had their rise, and the chains of which directed their courses, were shaggy with forests, that rose from the marshy jungles which grew around them. If we suppose that when North America began to be colonized from Europe, its rivers, from the St. Lawrence southwards, had all been wildly and destructively flowing abroad, its rolling prairies slimy fens, and its forests pathless, we shall have an unexaggerated idea of what China was, according to the Shoo, in the days of Yu.

Into such a scene of desolation Yu went forth. From beyond the western bounds of the present China proper he is represented as tracking the great rivers, here burning the woods, hewing the rocks, and cutting through the mountains which obstructed their progress, and there deepening their channels, until their waters are brought to flow peacefully into the eastern sea. He forms lakes, and raises mighty embankments, until at length 'the grounds along the waters were everywhere made habitable; the hills were cleared of their superfluous wood; the sources of the streams were cleared; the marshes were well banked; and access to the capital was secured for all within the four seas. A great order was effected in the six magazines *of material wealth;* the different parts of the country were subjected to an exact comparison, so that contribution of revenue could be carefully adjusted according to their resources. The fields were all classified with reference to the three characters of the soil; and the revenues for the Middle Kingdom were established.'

The Shoo does not say what length of time was required to complete so great an achievement; but we can gather from it that it did not extend over very many years. It was *un fait accompli* before the death of Yaou. K'wăn had laboured upon the flooded country for nine years without success; and though it is not expressly said that Yu's appointment was made by Shun after he became co-emperor with Yaou, the presumption is that it was so,—a presumption which might be declared a certainty if we could put confidence in the statements of Mencius. Mencius adds that Yu was eight years away from his home while going backwards and forwards on the work.[3] Sze-ma Ts'een allows Yu thirteen years to put his curb upon the floods; while Ma Yung thought that in three years eight of the provinces were so rectified, that Yaou considered the whole work as good as done, and resigned the administration to Shun.[4]

---

3 See a portion omitted in the quotation from Mencius above.   4 See the concluding note on p. 150.

I have been careful to point out in my notes the indications which we have that Yu was not left single-handed in the enterprise. He had Yih with him to help to open up the woods with fire. He had Tseih to show the people how to cultivate the ground as it was reclaimed from the waters and the jungles. But if we allow that all the resources of the empire (so to speak) were at his disposal, the work which he is said to have accomplished far exceeds all limits of credibility.

I am glad to be sustained in this opinion by the judgment of the late Edward Biot the younger, and will here introduce some sentences from an able article by him in the 'Journal Asiatique' for August and September, 1842. He says:—'The Yellow river, after its entrance into China, has a further course of 560 leagues; the Këang, taken only from the great lake of Hoo-kwang visited by Yu, has a course of nearly 250 leagues; the Han, from its source to its junction with the Këang, is 150 leagues long. These three rivers present a total length of nearly 1,000 leagues; and adding the other rivers [on which Yu laboured], we must extend the 1,000 to 1,500. ......Chinese antiquity has produced one monument of immense labour,—the great wall, which extends over nearly 300 leagues; but the achievement of this gigantic monument required a great number of years. It was commenced in pieces, in the ancient States of Ts'in, Chaou, and Yen, and was then repaired and lengthened by the first emperor of the Ts'in dynasty. Now such a structure, in masonry, is much easier to make than the embankment of enormous streams along an extent of 1,200 or 1,500 leagues. We know, in effect, how much trouble and time are required to bring such works to perfect solidity. We can judge of it from the repeated overflowings of the Rhone, and the lower Rhone is not a fourth of the size of the Ho and the Këang in the lower part of their course. If we are to believe the commentators, Yu will become a supernatural being, who could lead the immense rivers of China as if he had been engaged in regulating the course of feeble streamlets.'[5]

These illustrations of Biot are sufficiently conclusive. I may put the matter before the reader by one of a different character. I have represented the condition of the surface of China when Yu

5 See the number of the 'Journal Asiatique' referred to, pp. 160, 162. Most of this chapter was written before I had an opportunity of seeing it. A sinologue of very extensive research calling in question, in conversation, the views which I told him I was going to propound about the Yu Kung, I was led to make another effort (having made several fruitless ones) to obtain in Hongkong a copy of the 'Journal Asiatique,' that I might find what were Biot's views, and was fortunate enough, among a heap of odd numbers, to discover what I wanted.

entered on his labours by supposing the regions of North America, from the St. Lawrence southwards, to have been found in similar disorder and desolation by the early colonists from Europe in the seventeenth century. Those colonists had not the difficulties to cope with which confronted Yu; but we know how slowly they pushed their way into the country. Gradually growing in numbers, receiving constant accessions from Europe, increasing to a great nation, inferior to no other in the world for intelligence and enterprise, in more than two centuries they have not brought their territory more extensively into cultivation and order than Yu did the inundated regions of China in the space of less than twenty years!

The empire, as it appears in 'The Tribute of Yu,' consisted of nine provinces. On the north and west its boundaries were much

The empire was not so large, nor so organized, in Yu's time as it is represented.

the same as those of China Proper at the present day. On the east it extended to the sea, and even, according to many, across it, so as to embrace the territory of Corea. Its limits on the south are not very well defined. It certainly did not reach beyond the range of mountains which run along the north of Kwang-tung province, stretching into Kwang-se on the west and Fuh-këen on the east. Even though we do not reckon those three provinces in Yaou's dominion, there still remains an immense empire, about three times as large as France, which we are to suppose was ruled over by him, the chief of K'e, and the different regions of which sent their apportioned contributions of grain, and other articles of tribute, to his capital year by year.

But besides this division of the empire, the Book gives us another into five domains, by which it extended 2,500 *le* from the capital on every side, the whole thus constituting a square of 5,000 *le*. We have Yu's own declaration of his services in completing those domains, and in organizing the regions beyond, as far as the borders of the four seas, and placing them under the government of four presidents.[6] It is impossible for us to put credit in this representation. The five domains cannot be put down on the territory of China, ancient or modern. I have shown in my notes, pp. 148, 149, the difficulties which attend the account that we have of them. With reference to a similar but more minute arrangement of domains given in 'The Rites of Chow,' Biot says that 'it is evident that these symmetrical divisions have nothing of reality.'[7] There is not the

6 See the 'Yih and Tseih,' par. 4.   7 Le Tcheou-li, tome II., p. 169.

same difficulty with the division into nine provinces. Their mountains and rivers are, in the main, the same which have existed since the earth received its present form, and which will continue to the end of the world. The difficulty is in believing that Yu dealt with them as he is said to have done, and that there was in his time an empire exercising sway over such an extent of the country. As we must deny, however, the division into domains, for the making of which we have what purport to be Yu's own words, and which occupies six paragraphs in 'The Tribute of Yu,' it may be deemed less presumptuous to question the division into nine regions, which it is nowhere expressly said in the Shoo that he made,—to question it as not having been in existence at all in his time.

The accounts which we have of the empire subsequent to Yu forbid us to allow that it had attained in his day so great a development. The third sovereign of the Hea dynasty, T'ae-k'ang, grandson of Yu, having crossed the Ho on a hunting expedition, found his return obstructed by the chief of K'eung, and was never able to regain his throne. His five brothers had gone with their mother, and were waiting for his return on the banks of the Lŏ, when they heard of the movement against his authority. They then poured out their sorrow in songs, which are given in the Shoo. One of them refers to Yu as 'The sovereign of the myriad States!' while another speaks of Yaou, 'the prince of T'aou and T'ang, who possessed this country of K'e,'—'this country,' which was then held by the representatives of Yu. Nearly a hundred years elapsed, after the expulsion of T'ae-k'ang, before the House of Hea regained sure possession of the throne. This was done, B.C. 2,078, by Shaou-k'ang, whom we find lurking about, not far from the old capital of Yaou, for nearly the first forty years of his life, now herding the cattle of one chief, and anon acting as cook in the establishment of another, who discovers his worthiness, and gives him his two daughters in marriage. All these events transpire, we may say, on the banks of the Ho, and there is no indication of the country elsewhere being interested in them. It is believed that Yu died at Hwuy-k'e in the present Chĕ-këang; but it was not till the last year of Shaou-k'ang that any chief was appointed in that part of the country in the name of the reigning House.

When we come to the dynasty of Shang, B.C. 1,765–1,122, we find it difficult to admit that even then there was a China at all equal to that which Yu is said to have ruled over. The Shoo tells us of its founder T'ang the Successful; and in him and Këĕ, the last sovereign of the line of Yu, we seem merely to have the chief of Shang warring with the chief of Hea. It next gives us some notices of the minority of T'ae-këă, T'ang's successor; and then there is a blank in the history for three hundred years. When the field is occupied again, we meet with Pwan-kăng, the 17th sovereign, in great trouble, engaged in transferring his capital from the north of the Ho to the present district of Yen-sze in Ho-nan, on the south of it. To reconcile the murmuring people to the trouble of the removal, he reminds them that he was only acting after the example of former kings, and that the capital of the dynasty had already been in five different places. The nation, evidently, had still its seat in the neighbourhood of the Ho, and notwithstanding all that Yu is supposed to have done in regulating the waters of that river, its principal settlement had to be frequently changed in consequence of inundations. The accounts are not those of a great people, but of a tribe which had little difficulty in migrating from one spot to another.

Later still, we find a fact which is more conclusive perhaps on the point in hand than any of the considerations which I have yet adduced. The empire of the Chow dynasty consisted, like that of Yaou, of nine provinces. The old province of K'e formed three of them; Seu was absorbed in Ts'ing; and Lëang had disappeared from the empire altogether. Portions of the more eastern parts of it may have been embraced in the provinces of Yu and Yung, but much the greater part was wild barbarian territory, beyond the limits of the Middle Kingdom.[8] The kings of Chow ruled over a territory less than that of Yaou by the present provinces of Sze-ch'uen and Yun-nan! The dominions of Chow were not under-estimated, but the dimensions of the empire in the days of Yu have been greatly exaggerated. We can no more admit that he ruled over the nine provinces ascribed to him, than that he executed the stupendous labours of which he has the glory.

7. What then are we to think of 'The Tribute of Yu,' telling us, as it does, of the nine provinces, and of the labours put forth, The view to be taken of the Book *Yu Kung*. and the contributions imposed upon them by Yu? According to Biot, in the article of the 'Journal Asiatique,' already referred to, we are to find in it 'only the progress of a great colony.' He says further:—'Admitting even that Yu really visited all the points mentioned in the chapter, and

8 See the Chow Le, Bk. xxxiii.

so ran over more than the 1,500 leagues of which I have spoken, we should simply have to regard him as the first explorer of the Chinese world. In his general exploration, he established the posts of the colonists or planters on different points of the territory which he occupied by force, or which he obtained by a friendly arrangement with the natives. He caused the wood around those posts to be cut down, and commenced the cultivation of the soil. He may have commenced also, along with his colonists, certain labours on some rivers, carried off some stagnant waters, or embanked some lakes. At every one of his posts, he examined the productions of the ground, and the articles which they could obtain by barter from the natives. He then determined the nature of the contributions which every new colony should send to the mother colony. Such is still, in our days, the method pursued by the leaders of the pioneers who engage in exploring the deserts of America. They establish posts where they may purchase furs from the natives, and may commence at the same time the clearing of the forests. After Yu, the labours of draining the country and clearing the forests continued during some ages, and the result of all was attributed by Chinese tradition to the first chief.'

The reader cannot fail to be struck with the ingenuity of the above view; and I believe that there is an inkling of the truth in it. It is certainly an improvement on the view previously advanced by Father Cibot in his very learned essay on 'The Antiquity of the Chinese,' which appears under the name of 'Ko a Jesuit,' at the beginning of the 'Memoires sur les Chinois.' Himself of opinion that the territory on which Yu laboured was of small extent, Cibot thinks that this chief, remaining at the centre of his government in K'e-chow, might yet have sent expeditions of discovery, and to fix, on the ground of what he had learned of the other provinces, the imposts to be drawn from them, in the same way as has been done under all the succeeding dynasties, when it has been designed to extend the empire by colonies and the opening up of the country. 'Of how many countries of America,' says he, 'have charts and descriptions been given, before they were peopled, or even on the eve of being so? If what has thus been said of their mines, productions, and curiosities, proves the knowledge of Europeans, what we find in the *Yu Kung* will prove the similar knowledge which Yu had of the territory of China.'[1]

1 See Memoires concernant l'Histoire, &c., des Chinois, vol. I., p. 215.

PROLEGOMENA.] ON THE CREDIBILITY OF THE RECORDS IN THE SHOO. [CH. II.

For myself, I cannot admit that Yu really visited all the points which he is said to have done, nor can I find in the order in which his labours are detailed the steps by which the great Chinese colony actually proceeded to occupy the country. We recognize its primitive seat in the southern parts of the present Shan-se, with the Ho on the west and south of it. Across that stream lay the present Shen-se on the one side, and Ho-nan on the other. Into those portions of the country the subjects of Yu would penetrate long before they reached as far south as the Këang. In point of fact we know that they did do so. His son fought a battle with the prince of Hoo, at a place in the present department of Se-ngan in Shen-se; and the usurper E kept his grandson, T'ae-k'ang, a sort of prisoner at large in a part of Ho-nan. But the country of Ho-nan was in the province of Yu, the 7th in order of Yu's operations; and that of Shen-se was in Yung, the last in order. It is plain, therefore, that we are not to look in the *Yu Kung* for indications of the historical course and progress of the great Chinese colony.

'The Tribute of Yu' describes the country of China as its extent came to be ascertained in the course of the dynasties of Hea and Shang, and as its different parts were gradually occupied by the increasing and enterprising multitudes of the Chinese people, and contributed their various proportions of revenue and tribute to the central government which continued to be in K'e-chow. There were memorials of toils which the great Yu had undergone in making good the first foot-hold of his tribe, and of allotments of territory which he had made to the most distinguished among his followers. The nature of the country, in many places covered with forests and inundated, had caused the colonists much trouble in their advances. It occurred to some historiographer to form a theory as to the way in which the whole country might have been brought to order by the founder of the Hea dynasty, and he thereupon proceeded to glorify Yu by ascribing so grand an achievement to him. About the same time the popular stories of Yu's self-denial, in remaining with his wife only four days after their marriage, in passing thrice by his door regardless of the wailings of his infant son K'e, in flying about over the country, here driving his carriage over the level ground, there forcing his way up the rivers in a boat, now toiling through the marshes in a sledge, and anon stalking along the steep and slippery sides of the hills, with spikes to his shoes, with a measuring line in his left hand and a square and pair of compasses in his left, until his body was wasted to a shadow, and the skin of his hands and feet was callous:—these popular stories found their recognition in the 'Yih and Tseih,' and prompted at once the conception of the romance of the *Yu Kung*, and obtained for it a favourable reception. Then Yu could enter well into association with Yaou and Shun, and form a triad with them at the beginning of the Chinese monarchy. Their wisdom and benevolence appeared in him, combined with a practical devotion to the duties of his position, in which all sovereigns might have a model, that would for ever win them from indolence and self-indulgence, and stimulate them to a painstaking discharge of their responsibilities.

The conclusion to which a careful consideration of 'The Tribute of Yu' has brought me is thus far enough from the opinion of Bunsen, that it was 'a contemporary and public document of his reign.' It is to be regarded on the contrary as *a romance*, of which Yu is the subject, composed long after him,—composed probably after the dynasty which he founded had passed away. Cibot quotes several Chinese authorities, affirming its late composition. Biot seems inclined to attribute the Book, as we now have it, to Confucius. 'It is at least certain,' he says, 'that Confucius brought together in this chapter various *souvenirs* long antecedent to his own epoch;' and he adds, that 'carrying its composition no farther back than this, we should have in it one of the most ancient geographical documents in the world.' But I showed, on pp. 3–6 of these prolegomena, that we have no sufficient reason to believe that Confucius had anything to do with the compilation of the Shoo. We have, moreover, an indication, I think, in the Shoo itself, that the duke of Chow was familiar with this record of Yu's labours. Towards the close of that statesman's counsels to king Ching on the 'Establishment of Government,' we find him saying:—'Have well arranged your military accoutrements and weapons, so that you may go forth beyond the steps of Yu, and be able to travel over all beneath heaven, even to beyond the seas, everywhere meeting with submission.'[2] How was the duke of Chow acquainted with 'the footsteps of Yu?' It must have been either by tradition, or by some written account of them. The latter is the more probable. I have already called attention to the fact, that the large territory included in Yu's province of Lëang did not form a part of the dominions of Chow. It was natural that the duke of Chow, so ambitious and far-reaching as we

2 See Pt. V., Bk. XIX., p. 22.

know him to have been, should be anxious that the sway of his House should not come short of that ascribed to either of the previous dynasties. On another occasion, he summoned the duke of Shaou to go on with him, 'abjuring all idleness, to complete the work of Wǎn, till their empire should entirely overspread the land and from the corners of the seas and the sunrising there should not be one disobedient to their rule.'[3] His reference to 'the steps of Yu' does not prove that Yu really travelled and toiled and subdued the face of nature as the *Yu Kung* reports; it only proves that such was the current belief at the commencement of the Chow dynasty, affording at the same time a presumption that that document was then among the archives of the empire. This is my opinion,—that 'The Tribute of Yu' was among the written monuments of ancient times, which passed from the dynasty of Shang, and came under the care of the Recorders of the Exterior under that of Chow. Then subsequently it was very properly incorporated in the collection of Historical documents now known as the Shoo.

8. The opinion of Bunsen, that 'The Tribute of Yu' was a contemporary and public document of Yu's reign, was mainly grounded on the confidence which he reposed in the genuineness of a stone pillar, with an inscription, said to have been erected by Yu on the top of mount Hǎng, in the present Hoo-nan. He says:—'We have Yu's own unquestionably genuine account of the labour employed upon the great work by which he saved the country in the inundation. After the Egyptian monuments, there is no extant contemporary testimony more authentic, and none so old as the modest and noble inscription of that extraordinary man. It is true that it has now become illegible, but a copy was made of it about 1200 in the time of the Sung, which has been preserved in the high school of Si-an-fu, and in the imperial archives at Pekin. Hager has given a tracing of it. Only those who are unacquainted with the subject can entertain any doubt as to its originality.'[1] Perhaps, if the learned writer had made himself more fully acquainted with the history of this tablet, he would have expressed himself as strongly against its genuineness.

The casting of tripods or vases and of bells is asserted of Yu by very ancient traditions. Nine vases particularly are ascribed to him, each one having on it a chart of one of the nine provinces. Biot

---

3 Pt. V., Bk. XVI., p. 21.
1 See 'Egypt's Place,' &c., vol. III., pp. 394, 395.

says of them :—'The existence of these early sculptured or graved charts appears to me entirely admissible;—they represented the nine regions known to the first Chinese, and were not pictures of the empire of Yu. But after the ages which elapsed, without doubt, between this first chief and the dynasty of Chow, and after the extension of the Chinese rule, the respect of the Chinese for their ancestors became transformed into a veritable rite; the personage of Yu increased in their remembrances, and grew into a sort of demigod, who had reduced the world to order. Then the nine regions traced upon the vases of Yu became the nine provinces of his pretended empire.' That there were in the Chow dynasty nine vases, ascribed to Yu, and looked on as palladia of the empire, is sufficiently attested; but it is by no means clear that they had on them a series of charts of his nine provinces. But this is not the place to enter on any discussion of them. The earliest mention of them will be found in a note below.[2] I have introduced them here, merely to contrast the ancient references to them with the comparatively modern era when the stone tablet on mount Hăng began to be spoken of.

The first writer whose testimony to the existence of this tablet is adduced is Chaou Yih,[3] a Taouist recluse of the Eastern Han, who lived towards the end of the first century

History of the tablet of Yu on mount Hăng. It is all a fable.

of our era. He has left us a 'History of Woo and Yue;'[4] but the Work so abounds in ridiculous stories, of

2 For Biot's remarks, see the article on the *Yu Kung* in the 'Journal Asiatique,' p. 176. The earliest reference to the tripods of Yu, is, I believe, in the Tso Chuen, under the 3d year of duke Seuen (B.C. 605), where a messenger from the emperor Ting appears in colloquy with a general of the State of Ts'oo. The general wished to know the size and weight of the tripods. The answer was :—'The prosperity of the govt. depends on the sovereign's virtue, and not on the tripods. Anciently, when Hea was distinguished for its virtue, they got plans of distant regions, and *remarkable* objects in them. The nine pastors sent in the metal of their provinces, and tripods were cast, with representations on them of those objects. This was done exhaustively, so that the people could recognize the sprites and evil things; and when they went among the rivers, marshes, hills, and forests, they did not meet with misfortune;—yea, the sprites of the hills and waters did not come in their way. Thus a harmony was secured between the high and the low, and all received the blessing of Heaven. When the virtue of Keĕ was all obscured, the tripods passed over to Shang,—for 600 years. In consequence of the cruel tyranny of Chow of Shang, they passed over to Chow. When the virtue is brilliant, the tripods though light are heavy; when it gives place to darkness and disorder, they become light though heavy. Heaven sustains bright virtue :—where that is, its favour rests. King Ching fixed the tripods in Keă-juh (郟鄏; in the pres. Ho-nan), and divined that the dynasty should last 30 generations, and 700 years. This is Heaven's decree, and though the virtue of Chow is decayed, that decree is not changed. You need not ask about the weight of the tripods.' This account of the tripods is not very clear; but it is as clear in the translation as in the original. We should not infer from it that they had on them charts of the nine provinces. Accounts differ as to what became of them,—whether they came into the possession of Ts'in, or were sunk in a river by the last sovereign of Chow, See the 太平御覽,

which I give a specimen below,[5] that we can put little credit in anything which it relates. Among other things stated in it was this:—that 'the spirit-like Yu had left an inscription on the hill of Keu-leu;'[6]—Keu-leu being the name of one of the 72 peaks given to mount Hăng, and indeed, the principal one of them all, so that the names Keu-leu and Hăng are sometimes used interchangeably. In various topographical Works, written between the Han dynasty and that of Y'ang, mention is made of Yu in connection with mount Hăng; but they only reproduce the fables of Chaou Yih, and say nothing definite of the pillar about which we are inquiring.

Under the T'ang dynasty, accounts of it were abundantly rife; but there is no evidence that they were anything more than stories floating about among the people, or that any person of character had seen the interesting relic. On the contrary, the writer who has given us the fullest description of it, tells us that he had himself been unable to find it on the mountain, after the most diligent search. This was the famous Han Yu, among whose poems is the following, on mount Keu-leu:—

> 'Upon the peak of Keu-leu, sure there stands,
> Yu's pillar, fashioned by most cunning hands;
> The stone carnation, characters all green,
> Like tadpoles bent, like leeks invert, are seen;

卷第七百五十六, art. 鼎; and the 格致鏡原, 卷四十三, art. 鼎. 3 趙曄. The catalogue of the imperial libraries calls him, 趙煜 See the 四庫全書目錄 卷六. 4 吳越春秋. 5 Of the accounts of this Book, the reader may take the following specimen:—'K'wăn being thrown into the water, after he was put to death on mount Yu, was changed into a yellow dragon, and became the spirit of abyss of Yu (為羽淵之神). Yu was then appointed to undertake the task of regulating the waters. For seven years he laboured without effect, and, full of heaviness, ascertained from some books of Hwang-te, that among the pillars of heaven, the south-eastern mountains, there was one called Yuen-wei (宛委), where there was a book concealed, in characters of green gem, on tablets of gold, bound together with silver, which would be of use to him. He then went east, ascended mount Hăng, and sacrificed a white horse. Not finding what he sought, he went to the top of the mountain, looked towards heaven, and whistled. There he fell asleep, and dreamed that a boy, in red embroidered clothes, calling himself the messenger of the azure waters, came to him, and told him that if he ascended the Yuen-wei hill, on such and such a day of the third month, he would find the gold tablets. The boy at the same time indicated that this hill was in the east; and thither Yu went, and on the day appointed dug up the gold tablets, with their gem characters, which told him how to proceed to accomplish his mighty work.' See Chaou's Work, 卷四. 6 神禹有岣嶁山銘. See the 鮚埼亭集 外編 卷三十五; and the 曝書亭集 卷四十七, art. 1. I say in the text that there 'was' such a statement in Chaou's Work, because that Work is now mutilated, and I have glanced over the copy to which I have access without finding the statement in question.

68]

With pheasants floating here, the phœnix there,
Tigers and dragons make, between, their lair.
A monument so grave is hidden well,
And imps might pry, and nothing find to tell.
A solitary Taouist saw the stone.
'Twas chance him led.—I came, with many a groan,
And, weeping fast, searched round and searched again;
'Twas labour lost, the quest was all in vain.
The monkeys, 'mid the foliage of the wood,
Seemed sadly to bewail my grieving mood.'[7]

Two important points are established by these lines:—the one, that Han Yu himself, though he searched diligently for the pillar, could not find it; the other, that the voucher in his time for its existence was a solitary Taouist, one of a class which deals in things fantastic and prodigious, whose averment we pronounce, with a justifiable foregone conclusion, is more likely to be false than true.

From the T'ang dynasty we come to Sung. For more than three hundred years after Han Yu, we read nothing about the pillar. Still it was talked about; and in the 12th century, two of the ablest men in China purposely visited mount Hăng to put the question as to its existence at rest by their personal examination. They were Choo He, the most distinguished critic and philosopher of his age, and Chang Nan-hëen, also an eminent scholar. Their search for the stone was as fruitless as that of Han Yu had been; and to my mind the judgment of Choo He that it never had any existence but in Taouist dreams is decisive. Chinese writers account for the failure of him and the other intelligent seekers to find it, by attributing to it a personal intelligence. It was 'a spirit-like thing, which could appear and disappear at pleasure.'[8]

Not very long after the search of Choo He, in the period *Kea-ting* (A.D. 1208–1224) of the 13th emperor of the Sung dynasty, there came to the mountain an officer from Sze-ch'uen, called Ho Che, and was

7 See the Works of Han Yu, 卷三.一岣嶁山尖神禹碑,　字青石
赤形摹奇,　科斗拏身薶倒披.　鸞飄鳳泊拏虎螭,
　事嚴迹秘鬼莫窺,　道人獨上偶見之,　我來咨
嗟涕漣洏,　千搜萬索何處有,　森森綠樹猿猱悲.
Accounts of the pillar, of a similar kind, are found in the 丹鉛總錄卷一, quoted from
徐靈期, and 崔融, both, like Han Wăn-kung, of the T'ang dynasty.　8 斯文
顯晦, 信有神物. See the 丹鉛總錄, referred to above.

conducted by a woodcutter to the peak of Chuh-yung, where he found the monument and took a copy of it, which he had engraved and set up *in the Taouist monastery* of Kwei-mun.[9] Here then was the monument seen at last, and the inscription on it copied,—more than 3,000 years after its erection. So long time it had endured, standing there on the mountain, exposed to all elemental influences! This alone is sufficient to prove the falsehood of it. I have seen monuments in China a thousand years old, and which had been in a measure sheltered from the weather; but in every case the engraving on them was in some parts illegible. The tablet of Yu could not have stood, where it is said to have done, for such a length of time, and been found in the condition in which Ho Che is said to have found it. What was brought to light in the 13th century was a clumsy forgery. I have called attention by italics to the fact of the copy being set up in a Taouist monastery. A Taouist brain first conceived the idea of the monument, and Taouist hands afterwards fashioned it. An ordinary forger would have left gaps in the inscription to tell their own tale of its ancient date; but it was supposed that posterity would believe that this spirit-like thing had bid defiance to the gnawing tooth and effacing fingers of time.

When the discovery was made public, it was not generally credited. We should have thought that so precious a monument would draw many visitors to it, now that its place was known, and that it would even become an object of the public care. No such thing. Even the copy taken by Ho Che would seem to have had the 'spirit-like' quality, attributed to the monument, of making itself either visible or invisible. Under the Sung dynasty, people refused to receive it; and we have to come to the period Ching-tih[10] of the Ming dynasty, in the early part of the 16th century, before we meet with it again. Then, an officer of the province of Hoo-nan, Chang Ke-wǎn,[11] professed to have found the copy engraved by Ho Che, which he transcribed; and since his time it has had its place among the monuments, real or pretended, of Chinese antiquity.

It will occur to the reader to ask whether the stone be still on mount Hǎng. In a copy of the inscription, published in 1666, by a Maou Tsǎng-këen, which is in the possession of the Rev. Mr. Chalmers, the

---

[9] 宋嘉定中, 有蜀士, 何賢艮致, 于祝融峰下, 樵子導 之至碑所, 手摸其文, 刻于虁門觀中。 [10] 正德 It was under this style that the 11th of the Ming emperors (武宗毅皇帝) reigned, A.D. 1506–1521. [11] 張季文

70]

editor speaks of the difficulty of reaching the top of Keu-leu, how ladders are necessary and hooks, and says that he had himself been to the spot and handled the stone. But he says also, that the characters and stone had both been of an immense size, and are now all in fragments, so that the inscription cannot be made out. Let it be granted that there are some fragments of rock on one of the summits of mount Hăng, with old characters cut on them, how is it known that these were ever any tablet of Yu? or how is any verification obtained from them of the inscription, as we have it? Choo He and Chang Nan-hëen, in the 12th century, might very well have seen the remains described by Tsăng-këen, and decided that Yu had never had anything to do with them. Their character shows certainly that Han Yu and the other writers of the T'ang dynasty were only describing an ideal tablet of Yu,—which, indeed, we might conclude on other grounds. The only voucher for the points involved in the above questions is Ho Che, or rather the story which we have of his discovery of the monument in the 13th century.

The review which I have given of the history of the stone sufficiently shows my own opinion, that it is not entitled to the least credit; and I am supported in this view by the great majority of Chinese archæologists, so little ground is there for Bunsen's affirmation that 'only those who are unacquainted with the subject can entertain any doubt as to its originality.' He based his conclusion on a monograph of the inscription, published at Berlin in 1811 by M. Klaproth, which I have not seen. I have read an account of it, however, in the second volume of Remusat's 'Melanges Asiatiques.' Klaproth, it would appear, having become convinced of the genuineness of the monument, addressed himself particularly to show that the 'tadpole' characters have been correctly identified. This might very well be the case, without the arguments which I have urged against it being at all affected. There was nothing to hinder the maker or makers of it, say in the time of the Sung dynasty, from disguising their fraud, by writing it after the model of the most ancient forms of the characters. My friend, Wang T'aou, in a Chinese monograph of it, observes on this point:—'The maker of it was clever in imitating the ancient form of writing; and it was this ability which enabled him to impose on many.' On the next page the reader will find a copy of the inscription, such as it is, taken from the sheet in the possession of the Rev. Mr. Chalmers. The characters were first reduced by a photograph, and then copied for a wooden block to suit the size of my page. By the side of each tadpole character is the modern form which is supposed to have taken its place. I give it simply as a curiosity. In a note below will be found some remarks on Bunsen's attempt to translate it. More than sufficient space has been allowed to it in the text of these prologomena, as my object, in adverting to it at all, was simply to show that an argument could not be constructed from it to invalidate the opinion which I have advanced as to the late origin of the *Yu Kung*.[12]

12 The identification of a few of the characters in the copy of which Bunsen ventured a translation was different from that in the copy here printed. The 丹鉛總錄 gives the inscription thus:— 承帝曰嗟, 翼輔佐卿, 洲渚與登, 鳥獸之門, 參身洪流, 而明發爾興, 久旅忘家, 宿嶽麓庭, 智營形折, 心罔弗辰, 往求平定, 華岳泰衡, 宗疏事裒, 熒餘伸禋 鬱塞昏徙, 南瀆衍亨. 永制食備, 萬國其寧, 竄舞永奔. Now I undertake to say, that of a good deal of this it is not possible to ascertain the meaning with any degree of certainty. Bunsen speaks of a version by Father Amyot, published by Hager, which, he says, is not in the true sense of the word a translation. (This may be seen in Williams' 'Middle Kingdom,' Vol. II., pp. 204, 205.) He acknowledges Klaproth's attempt to be a translation, but not quite accurate in some parts. His own attempt to give an accurate version I will not take the trouble to discuss. He says that those who have any acquaintance with the language will understand, from a literal Latin version of the characters, the philological principle on which his translation is based; but the fact is, that a very moderate acquaintance with the language is sufficient to show that Bunsen knew very little about it. If his interpretation of Egyptian monuments be not better than his interpretation of 'the monument of Yu,' his volumes on 'Egypt's Place in Universal History' are of little value.

If the writer of the inscription knew what he was doing in pencilling his tadpole characters, I do not think they have all been correctly identified. Accepting the identification given in this note, I would propose the following as an approximation to a correct interpretation:—

'I received *the words of* the emperor, saying, "Ah!
Associate helper, aiding noble!
The islands and islets may now be ascended,
That were doors for the birds and beasts.
You devoted your person to the great overflowings,
And with the day-break you rose up.
Long were *you* abroad, forgetting your family;
You lodged at the mountain's foot as in a hall;
Your wisdom schemed; *your* body was broken;
Your heart was all in a tremble.
You went and sought to produce order and settlement.
At Hwa, Yŏ, T'ae, and Hăng.
By adopting the principle of dividing *the waters, your* undertakings
  were completed.
With the remains of a taper, *you* offered your pure sacrifice.
There were entanglement and obstruction, being swamped, and removals.
The southern river flows on in its course;
For ever is the provision of food made sure;
The myriad States enjoy repose;
The beasts and birds are for ever fled away."'

72]

承帝曰咨翼輔佐卿洲渚與登鳥獸

之門參身洪流而明發爾與以旅忘

家宿嶽麓定智營形折心岡弗辰往

來平定華嶽泰衡宗疏事袁勞餘伸

禋鬱塞昏徙南瀆衍亭衣制倉備萬

國其寧竄舞蒸奔

9. From the view which I have taken of the labours of Yu, the reader will understand that I do not identify the deluge of Yaou

Should the deluge of Yaou be identified with that described in the Book of Genesis? with that described by Moses in the Book of Genesis. I am inclined, however, to believe that, in the language of the Shoo-king respecting the terrible nature of the inundation which frightened Yaou and Shun, we have the voice of tradition, affirming the earlier and universal catastrophe,—universal at least in the sense that it involved the destruction of 'all flesh,' all the individuals of our race, excepting those who were preserved with Noah in the ark.

Missionaries,—Protestant missionaries especially,—accepting the labours of Yu as historical, have expressed themselves incautiously on the identity of the two deluges. Dr. Gutzlaff, for instance, wrote: —'We do not doubt but Yaou's was the same flood recorded in sacred history, though we are not able to give the exact date from Chinese history; nor do we hesitate to affirm that China was peopled after the deluge.'[1]

Bunsen has taken occasion from this to express himself with undue severity of 'the confusion and ignorance of the missionaries, believing that Yu's labours referred to the Flood of Noah, which never reached China.'[2] And again:—'The inundation in the reign of Yaou had just as much to do with Noah's flood, as the dams he erected and the canals he dug had to do with the Ark. The learned Jesuit Fathers were well aware of this, but they were prevented by orders from Rome from publishing the truth. The fact of so absurd an idea being accepted by the English and Scotch Missionaries, and even by Morrison himself, is a very melancholy instance of the way in which the sound judgment of learned men may be warped by rabbinical superstition and the intolerant ignorance of their Churches, in the investigation of historical truth.'[3]

Now, Morrison gave his opinion in the matter in very guarded terms; and I do not think that he was farther from the truth than his critic. In the preface to his dictionary, p. xiii., he observes:—'In the Shoo-king mention is made of a great and destructive accumulation of waters upon the face of the earth; whether it be called Inundation or Deluge is immaterial. The removal of the waters, and settling the state of all the various regions then known is understood by the phrase *Yu Kung*. Yu was the person who effected that

1 See 'A Sketch of Chinese History,' &c., vol. I. p. 130. 2 'Place of Egypt,' &c., vol. III. p. 398. 3 See as above, p. 406.

74]

work. This Deluge makes a grand epoch in Chinese History. After a fanciful account of the creation, there follows a period of Chinese civilization, when Fuh-he's successors introduced marriage; government; working in metals; the use of musical instruments; and characters for the division of time. The profligacy and misrule of the monarch Te-chih[4] is noticed, and then follows Yaou's deluge; after which the earth is again represented as overspread by wild uncultivated vegetation, and over-run by savage beasts.....The above is a faithful outline of the picture drawn, by Chinese writers, of the history of the ancient world as known to them. Its similarity to that given by the Jewish Legislator must be observable to every one; and the probability, that both accounts refer to the same remote facts, is not to be overturned by slight anachronisms, or a discordancy in the detail.'

To the same effect are the observations of Dr. Medhurst. He calls the time between Fuh-he and Yaou and Shun the 'traditionary Period' of Chinese history, and adds:—'While we might be unwilling to give full credit to what Chinese writers say of the events of this period, it is not improbable that much of it is drawn by tradition from the correct account of the antediluvian age handed down by Noah to his posterity. The coincidence of ten generations having passed away, the institution of marriage, the invention of music, the rebellion of a portion of the race, and the confused mixture of the divine and human families, closed by the occurrence of the flood in the time of Yaou, might lead us to conclude that in their allusions to this period, the Chinese are merely giving their version of the events that occurred from Adam to Noah. When Yu ascended the throne, the lands were drained, and China became habitable.'[5]

In these representations of two of the most distinguished Protestant missionaries, the traces of 'rabbinical superstition,' and of subjection to 'the intolerant ignorance of their churches,' seem to me hardly discernible. Possibly there may be in the Chinese accounts of Fuh-he and his successors some faint echo of the primitive tradition;—I am not concerned at present to enter upon that subject. What is said in the above quotations about the deluge of Yaou, however, is misleading. The reader is led to suppose that it comes in Chinese history, as caused by the declension and wickedness of the times immediately preceding,—a judgment of Heaven. If it were so,

4 帝摯.   5 China: Its State and Prospects, pp. 5, 6.

the view which they take would be greatly strengthened. But the Shoo is entirely silent on this point. Not a word is said as to the flood's being a punishment of the sins either of ruler or people.

But now, according to the views which I have sought to establish, the labours of Yu are not history, but myth. He did not perform the prodigious achievements on the mountains and rivers which are ascribed to him. That he was the laborious founder of the Chinese empire, and did much within the small space of territory which was then comprehended in its limits, there is no occasion to deny; but the gradual extension of the empire and development of its resources and order, which were the growth and accomplishment of many centuries, have been attributed to him by the Chinese, and their romance has been accepted by missionaries and others. The labours of Yu being denied, no place is left in his time for the deluge of Yaou. The utmost that can be allowed is an inundation of the Ho, destructive enough, no doubt, but altogether unfit to be described in the words put into the mouths of Yaou, Shun and Yu about it. Did the compilers of the first Parts of the Shoo draw upon their fancy for the floods that embraced the mountains and overtopped the hills and assailed the heavens? or did they find them in the tradition of a deluge by which 'all the hills that were under the whole heaven were covered?' I prefer to take the suggestion in the latter question as the fact, and therefore think that in the description of the inundation of Yaou's time we have an imperfect reference to the deluge of Noah.

10. Before leaving the subject of Yu and his labours, it will be well to say something on another point, the commonly received account of which may be urged as inconsistent with the conclusions I have endeavoured to establish. Can the population of China in Yu's time be ascertained, even approximately?

The population of China in the time of Yu.

Two sinologues have touched on this question:—Edward Biot the younger, in articles on 'The Population of China, and its Variations,' in the 'Journal Asiatique' of 1856; and T. Sacharoff, of the Russian Embassy in Peking, in an essay on 'The Rise and Fall of the Chinese Population,' translated into English last year by the Rev. W. Lobscheid.

The articles of Biot were written when his knowledge of Chinese subjects was immature, six years before he published in the same Journal the view of the *Yu Kung*, to which I have had occasion to make frequent reference. Had they been produced at a later date, he would not have accepted the statement of Ma Twan-lin, that the number of the people, on the conclusion of Yu's labours, amounted to 13,553,923 souls;—a number, which he, on certain hypothetical reasonings of his own, increased to 21,415,198.

Sacharoff would reduce the smaller of these estimates to a single million; but his remarks on the subject betray considerable confusion of thought. He says:—'Two censuses were at the disposal of native authors for ascertaining the amount of the population of China, during the happy reigns of Yaou and Shun, the epochs of the highest civilization. These were:—the division of the country for administrative purposes; and the extent of the really cultivated land. The first would, indeed, be a sufficient ground for arriving at a satisfactory conclusion, if the ancient documents stated the number of the principal provinces. If, *e. g.*, we take the nine provinces, into which Yaou divided the empire in the 23d century, then the population must have been very small, and could hardly exceed 100,000 families, or one million individuals. A calculation based on the extent of arable land proves nothing, because the classics scarcely state how many square rods were counted to a family, whilst nothing is said of the total amount of cultivated land, so that by fixing a certain figure, we are obliged to accept an arbitrarily given number of individuals.'[1]

I have endeavoured to find Ma Twan-lin's authority for the assertion, that, when Yu had reduced the empire to order, the inhabitants amounted to 13,553,923; and the oldest writer in whom I have met with it is Hwang-p'oo Meih, who died A.D. 282.[2] The statement, occurring thus, for the first time, about two thousand five hundred years after the date to which it refers, is of no historical value. As given by Meih, indeed, it is merely the result of certain calculations by him from the extent of the empire ruled by Yaou, and does not profess to be grounded on any certain data. So many absurdities are related, moreover, on the same page about Yu and other ancient worthies, that I am surprised the estimate of the population ever obtained any currency.

For instance, Meih begins by referring to the legends about Shin-nung and Hwang-te,—how the empire of the former extended, from

1 The Numerical Relations of the Population of China, &c., p. 10. Hongkong: A Shortrede & Co., 1864. 2 See Meih's Chronicle of Emperors and Kings, quoted by the editor of the Books of the After Han, 志第十九, p. 1.

east to west, a space of 900,000 *le*, and from north to south, 850,000 *le;* and how the latter, after having invented boats and carriages to traverse this mighty territory, determined the position of the different States in it by astronomical calculations. The author thinks that what is said about Shin-nung exceeds belief; but he goes on to quote the authority of Confucius (taken however from the 'Family Sayings,' an apocryphal Book) for the empire of Chuen-heuh, as extending to the Moving Sands on the west, Cochin-china on the south, the Sea on the east, and Yew-ling (north of Chih-le) on the north; and then, he comes to Yaou and Yu. Yu's nine provinces contained, he estimates, 24,308,024 *k'ing*, or nearly 368 million acres, of which 9,208,024 *k'ing*, or 140 million acres, were cultivable. Then comes in the amount of the population, and the further statement that the empire contained at that time 10,000 States. It is added on the authority of the 'Classic of Hills and Seas,' a book full of all sorts of prodigious stories, that Yu made two of his officers—Ta-chang, and Shoo-hae—walk, the one from the extreme east to the extreme west, and the other from the extreme north to the extreme south, and count their paces. The former traversed 223,300 *le*, and 71 paces; the latter 233,500 *le*, and 75 paces; but we must suppose that Mcih was here counting only 100 paces to a *le*.[3] In fact, it is difficult to tell, how he took the terms, for he subjoins that, within the four seas, from east to west were 28,000 *le*, and from north to south 26,000. There were 5,350 famous hills; 467 hills producing copper; and 3,609 producing iron. The writer is evidently writing at random. The estimate of the population is no more to be received than any of all the other notices which he gives.

When Sacharoff says that, if we take the nine provinces, into which Yaou divided the empire, the population could hardly exceed one million individuals, it is difficult to understand what he means. If we could accept 'the nine provinces,' as indeed veritable portions of the empire, and believe that the country was occupied, even thinly, to that extent, we might very well allow a population for them, not of one million, but of twenty millions. But the critical study of the documents of the Shoo forbids us, as I have shown, to think of Yaou and Shun as other than petty chieftains, whose dominions

---

[3] 禹使大章步自東極至於西垂, 二億三萬三千三百 里七十一步, 又使竪亥步南極北盡於北垂, 二億三萬 三千五百里, 七十五步. The thing is differently stated in the copy of the 山 海經, which I have,—printed in 1818, the 23d year of the reign Këa-k'ing.

hardly extended across the Ho; and though Yu was the founder of a dynasty that lasted for more than four centuries, it is doubtful whether the last of his successors ruled over so much as the nine provinces of Yaou. The arguments on which I have maintained these conclusions might have needed reconsideration, if the estimate of thirteen millions and a half of inhabitants in Yu's time had been supported by a tittle of independent evidence; being merely a rough and random calculation at a period long subsequent, on the assumption of such a territory, those arguments are unaffected by it.

The number of one million which Sacharoff would allow for the Chinese of Yu's time is, it seems to me, abundantly large. The population of the country, in the time of king Ching, when the duke of Chow was administering the government, is given as 13,704,923; that is, according to the current accounts, the population had only increased 151,000 in eleven centuries and a half. If we suppose one million of inhabitants in Yu's time, and that they doubled every two hundred years, they ought to have amounted, in the time of the duke of Chow, to about one hundred millions. And yet we may say that there was no increase at all in all that space of time. About 400 years after, in the 13th year of king Chwang, B.C. 683, the population had decreased below what it was in Yu's days, and is given as only 11,941,923. It is evident from these figures, that the accounts of the population of the empire before our era cannot be regarded as approximations even to the truth;—especially it is evident, that assigning to Yu more than thirteen millions is simply of a piece with the assigning to him the achievements of a demigod on the face of the water and the land.

Ma Twan-lin, after Hwang-p'oo Meih and other early writers, calls attention to the decrease in the number of States, composing the empire, under each of the three early dynasties. At a grand *durbar* held by Yu on mount T'oo, 10,000 princes appeared to do him homage;—there were then 10,000 States. When the dynasty of Shang superseded Hea, those 10,000 were reduced to a little over 3000; and according to Meih, there was a corresponding diminution in the number of the people. In the beginning of the 12th century, B.C., when king Woo established the rule of Chow, his princes were only 1,773; and, again adds Meih, the people had dwindled correspondingly. But the people were more, according to Meih himself, in the beginning of the Chow dynasty than they had been in Yu's days, by 151,000 individuals. I say again, that it is evident the 10,000

States, of more than twenty centuries before our era, never had any existence. The state of the country under the successors of Yu, which I have pointed out on p. 61, is altogether inconsistent with the idea of such an empire. The magniloquent style of speech, however, once introduced, subsequent writers adopted it. Confucius himself and Mencius adhered to it, hiding thereby from themselves, their contemporaries, and posterity the truth about their own times, and the small beginnings of their history in the distant past.

11. I will not attempt to question the credibility of the Books of the Shoo lower down than the time of Yu. Those belonging to his dynasty are only three; and each of them is brief. As I said in the first paragraph, from the beginning of the Shang dynasty, we seem to tread the field of history with a somewhat confident step. The Books of Chow are sufficiently to be depended on, for they must have been made public while the memory of many of the things which they describe was still fresh.

The results which I have endeavoured to bring out in this chapter are :—first, that Yu is a historical personage, and was the founder of the Chinese empire, but that nearly all that the Shoo contains of his labours is fantastical exaggeration; and second, that Yaou and Shun were also real men, chiefs of the earliest Chinese immigrants into the country, but that we must divest them of the grand proportions which they have, as seen through the mists of legend and of philosophical romance. It seems folly to attempt to go beyond the Shoo, and push the history centuries farther back to the time of Fuh-he. We have now to inquire in the next chapter whether it be possible, from the Shoo or other sources, to determine with any satisfaction how long before our era we are to place those worthies.

CHAPTER III.

ON THE DETERMINATION OF THE PRINCIPAL
ERAS IN THE SHOO.

THERE IS NO CHRONOLOGY IN THE SHOO; AND IT WAS NOT TILL
THE HAN DYNASTY THAT THE CHINESE BEGAN TO ARRANGE
THEIR ANCIENT HISTORY WITH REFERENCE TO A COMMON ERA.
THE PERIODS OF THE THREE DYNASTIES, AND OF YAOU AND SHUN.
CHINESE HISTORY BEGINS ABOUT 2000 YEARS BEFORE CHRIST.

1.   On my first conception of this chapter, my idea was to designate it 'The Chronology of the Shoo.'   Such is the title of the third
chapter of Gaubil's 'Observations on the Shoo-king,' in which he
has touched, succinctly and ably, on nearly all the points to which I
have to call the attention of the reader.   'The Chronology of the
Shoo,' however, would be a misnomer.   There is no arrangement or

There is no Chronology in the Shoo.   succession of dates in it which can be so described.   We learn from it that the dynasty of
Chow succeeded to that of Shang, and the dynasty of Shang or Yin
to that of Hea; and that prior to Yu, the founder of the Hea, there
were the reigns of Shun and Yaou.   In its present condition, it contains only scanty notices of a few of the sovereigns in the earlier
dynasties, and the length of the reigns of two or three of them is
stated; but even when it was complete, it did not embrace a list of all
the rulers of China, and of the number of years which they reigned
respectively :—and much less did it specify any date as a great era
in the distant past, from which the commencement of the successive
dynasties, and the accessions of the different monarchs in each of
them, should be calculated.   As Gaubil has observed, 'If we had only
the Shoo-king, we should have but confused ideas of the time comprised in the four [five] Parts of the book.'   We need not be surprised
at this.   The chronology of a nation comes to be cultivated as a
science, only after it has long subsisted, and when the necessity is
felt of arranging the events of its history in regular series on the
course of time.

2.   It was in the Han dynasty that it was first attempted to construct a chronological scheme of the history of the empire.   For this purpose its scholars employed the well-known cycle of 60 years,

Chronologising began in the Han dynasty. The cycle of 60 years.   in the 2d year of the 76th revolution of which, according to the commonly received views, I am now writing; and which is with the Chinese what the century is with us.   It was assumed that this cycle had been made in the reign of Hwang-te by Ta-naou, one of his officers; but I need hardly say that the assumption rests on no satisfactory grounds. Believing the views which I have advocated in the last chapter to be correct, I must pronounce Hwang-te to be a fabulous personage, so far as any connection with the Chinese empire is concerned.   If such a man ever lived at all, it was elsewhere than in China; and it is not till we come to the times of Ts'in and Han, more than 2,000 years after the period assigned to him, that we find Ta-naou spoken of at all.[1]   And though the invention of the cycle is then generally ascribed to him, there are writers who give the credit of it to Fuh-he long before.[2]   What is of more importance to observe is, that the cycle, as it is now universally recited and written, was not employed before the end of the Former Han dynasty, *i.e.*, until after the commencement of our Christian era, to chronicle years at all:—its exclusive use was to chronicle the days.   Koo Yen-woo, one of the

The original use of the Keă-tsze cycle was to chronicle days.   ablest scholars of the present dynasty, says expressly on this point:—'The 22 cycle characters [*i.e.*, the 10 stem characters from *kĕă* to *kwei*, and the 12 branch characters from *tsze* to *hae*] were used by the ancients to chronicle the days, and not to chronicle the years.   For chronicling the years there were the 10 stem names of *oh-fung*, &c., down to *twan-mung*, and the 12 branch names of *shĕ-t'e-kih*, &c., down to *juy-han*.   The way of later times, to say that such a year was *kĕă-tsze*, and so on, was not the ancient way.'[3]   Yen-woo then quotes from the preface to the *Wae-ke*,[4] or 'Additional Records,' a supple-

1 See the 事物紀原, 卷一, art. 甲子. We read:—世本曰, 大撓造甲子。呂氏春秋曰, 黃帝師大撓。黃帝內傳曰, 帝旣斬蚩尤, 命大撓造甲子, 正時。月令章句曰, 大撓探五行之情, 占斗剛所建, 于時始作甲乙以名日, 謂之幹, 作子丑, 以名月, 謂之支. 支幹相配, 以成六旬.   2 See the 通鑑綱目, 前編卷之二—伏羲氏作甲歷, 定歲時.   3 See the 顧炎武日知錄卷二十, art. 古人不以甲子名歲.   4 劉恕通鑑外紀目錄序.

ment to the 'General Survey' of History by Sze-ma Kwang,[5] with whom Lew Shoo, its author was associate, the following testimony: —'The years of the sovereigns before (!) and after Fuh-he, down to king Le, are, I apprehend, dark and hardly to be ascertained; and we borrow the names of the *keă-tsze* cycle to chronicle them;' adding himself:—'When did this practice of borrowing the cycle names to chronicle the years commence? It commenced in the time of the usurper Mang' (A.D. 9—22). The statement of this writer, that the ancients chronicled years by the names oh-fung shĕ-t'e-kih, &c., is very questionable; but I must content myself, for the present, with referring to what is said on the subject in the appendix to this chapter, on the 'Astronomy of the ancient Chinese,' with which the Rev. Mr. Chalmers has favoured me. So far as my reading has gone, there cannot be produced a single unchallengeable example of the naming of any year by any cycle characters whatever, previous to the termination of the Chow dynasty.

In the Shoo itself the current cycle is used to chronicle days, and days only. Years are specified according to their order in the reign of the sovereign to whom they are referred. Such specification of years, however, is in our classic exceedingly rare.

There can be no doubt that before the Han dynasty a list of sovereigns, and of the lengths of their several reigns, was the only method

The ancient method of determining the length of Chinese history. The want of documents which could make it available now.

which the Chinese had of determining the duration of their national history. And it would still be a sufficiently satisfactory method, if we had a list of sovereigns and of the years each reigned, that was complete and reliable. We do not have this, however. Even in the early part of the Han dynasty, Sze-ma Ts'een's father and himself were obliged to content themselves with giving simply the names and order of most of the rulers in the dynasties of Shang and Hea. The lengths of the several reigns in

5 Sze-ma Kwang gets the credit of fixing the standard chronology; but let me call the attention of the student to Choo He's account of the matter. He tells us:—'When Kwang first made a Chronological scheme, his earliest date was the 1st year of Wei-lĕĕ (B.C. 424). Afterwards, he extended his dates to the time of Kung and Ho (B.C. 840). After this again, he made his "Examination of Antiquity," beginning with the period of "highest antiquity," but he could give no dates of years earlier than that time of Kung and Ho. It was Shaou K'ang-tsĕĕ who pushed the calculations up to the 1st year of Yaou (溫公初作編年, 起于威烈王, 後又添至共和, 又稽古錄, 始自上古, 然共和已上之年, 已不能推矣, 獨邵康節, 却推至堯元年, 云云). The passage is quoted in Hăng Ch'in-fung's notes on the annals of the Bamboo Books, 卷三, p. 4. Choo He appears to have been fascinated in a measure by the Bamboo Books.

the standard chronology have been determined, mainly, I believe, to make the whole line stretch out to the years which had been fixed on astronomical considerations for the periods of Chung-k'ang of the Hea dynasty and of Yaou.   It will be seen in the sequel, and more fully in the next chapter, how the Bamboo Books contrive to shorten many of the reigns, so that those periods shall be less remote than they are commonly placed by about 200 years.

If in the Four Books, or in any other books of the Chow dynasty, we had a statement of the length of the national history from any given era to that of the writer, the notice would be exceedingly valuable.   Or, if the lengths of the reigns of the sovereigns of Shang and Hea, cursorily mentioned, were given, we should be in a position to make an approximate computation for ourselves.   I do not know, however, of more than two passages in all those books, which are really helpful to us in this point.   Both of them are referred to by Gaubil.   If the reader will turn to the passage translated from the Tso-chuen, in the note on p. 67 above, he will see it there stated that the dynasty of Shang possessed the empire for 600 years. That is one of the passages.   The other is the very last chapter of the Works of Mencius, where that philosopher says that 'from Yaou and Shun to T'ang—a period including all the dynasty of Hea—were 500 years and more; that from T'ang to king Wăn—the period of the Shang dynasty—were 500 years and more; and that from king Wăn to Confucius were 500 years and more.'   Now, we know that the birth of Confucius took place in B.C. 551.   Adding 551 to the 1500 years 'and more,' given by Mencius, we have the era of Yaou and Shun, at 2,100 years before our Saviour, or thereabouts.   The words of Mencius,—'from Yaou and Shun to T'ang,' are, indeed, sadly indefinite.   Does he mean the end of Shun's reign, and the beginning of Yu's? or does he mean the beginning of Yaou's reign? I think it was the latter which he intended.   But vague as his language is, I do not think that with the most painstaking research we can determine anything more definite and precise concerning the length of Chinese history than it conveys.   Mencius knew nothing of rulers before Yaou, nor do I.   What we are told of Yaou and Shun, moreover, is little trustworthy.   About 2,000 years before the Christian era, China, which has since become so large an empire, rises before us, with small beginnings, in the vista of the past.   I do not think that anything more precise than this can be said upon the subject.   Let us see.

3. The last of the kings of the Chow dynasty mentioned in the Shoo is P'ing, the 13th of the line, whose 'Charge to Prince Wăn' of Tsin forms the 28th Book of the 5th Part. His place in history is well ascertained. Confucius' Chronicle of the Ch'un Ts'ew commences in B.C. 721. The 1st of the 36 eclipses mentioned in it took place three years after, on the 14th February (N.S.), B.C. 719; and it is recorded that in the month after king P'ing died.[1] Here, therefore, is a point of time about which there can be no dispute. In the words of Gaubil, 'we know the time of the end of the Shoo-king.' An earlier date in the Chow dynasty is known with the same certainty. The She mentions an eclipse which took place on the 29th August, B.C. 775, in the 6th year of king Yew, who preceded P'ing.[2] Yew reigned 11 years, and his predecessor, king Seuen, 46, whose reign consequently commenced B.C. 826. Up to this date Chinese chronologers agree. To the ten reigns before king Seuen, the received chronology assigns 295 years, making the dynasty begin in B.C. 1,121. The Bamboo Books assign to them only 223, making it commence in B.C. 1,049. In the lengths of five of the reigns the two schemes agree; but whether the longer estimate of the other five or the shorter is to be preferred, I do not see that we have sufficient grounds to determine. Gaubil, reasoning from the cycle names of the days, which are given in several of the Books of Chow (as I have pointed out in my notes on the various passages), would fix the commencement of the dynasty in B.C. 1,111 [or 1,110]. If we suppose that Mencius, as is most likely, in saying that 'from king Wăn to Confucius were 500 years and more,' intended by 'king Wăn' the commencement of the Chow dynasty, we have to conclude that this era must be between B.C. 1,051 and 1,161. The date in the Bamboo Books places it too late; that in the common chronology cannot be far from the truth.

The period of the Chow dynasty.

4. In treating of the period of the Shang dynasty, we cannot fix a single reign with certainty by means of astronomical data. The common chronology assigns to it 28 reigns extending over 644 years, so that its commencement was in B.C. 1,765. The Bamboo Books make the sovereigns to be 30, and the aggregate of their reigns only 508, so that the dynasty began in B.C. 1,557. Pan Koo of the Han made the length of the dynasty 529 years.

The period of the Shang dynasty.

1 三年，春王二月，巳巳，日有食之。三月，庚戌天王崩
2 See the She, Pt. II., Bk. IV., Ode ix.—十月之交，朔日辛卯，日有食之

The difference of two reigns between the schemes of Sze-ma Kwang and the Bamboo Books is unimportant, and, if they otherwise agreed, could only affect the length of the dynasty by 6 years. Some remarks on those reigns will be found in the note on Mencius, V., Pt. I., v. 5. That the number of reigns is not over-estimated we may infer from the statement of Mencius that between T'ang, the founder of the dynasty, and Woo-ting, the 20th (or 22d) sovereign, 'there had been six or seven worthy and sage rulers.'[1] In the 15th of the Books of Chow, the names of three of the sovereigns are given, and the duration of their reigns, to show how Heaven is likely to crown a good king with length of sway :—T'ae-mow, who reigned 75 years; Woo-ting, who reigned 59; and Tsoo-këǎ, who reigned 33. The two schemes which I have mentioned agree in the length of those reigns, and of five others. From the statement in the Tso-chuen, that the Shang dynasty lasted 600 years, and that of Mencius, that 'from T'ang to king Wăn were 500 years and more,' we may judge that the 644 years assigned to the Shang by the standard chronology are too many, and the 508 years of the Bamboo Books too few.

5. According to the common chronology, the dynasty of Hea lasted 439 years; according to the Bamboo Books, it lasted 431. The difference between the two schemes is not great, though they agree exactly in the lengths of three of the reigns only. Mencius' words, that 'from Yaou and Shun to T'ang were 500 years and more,' include the period of Yaou and Shun as well as that of the Hea dynasty; but the years which he assigned to the two early sages, probably, did not differ much, if at all, from the common estimate of the two chronologies.[2] If we add 150 years either to 431 or 439, the sum is under 600 years. The period usually assigned to the Hea dynasty cannot be far from the truth.

The period of the Hea dynasty.

In the 4th of the Books of Hea we have the record of an astronomical fact, which we might hope would enable us to determine the time of its occurrence, with as much certainty as the year of the death of king P'ing of the Chow dynasty is determined. In the reign of Chung-k'ang, the 3d of Yu's successors, there was an eclipse of the sun in the sign Fang. Sze-ma Kwang places the event in Chung-k'ang's 1st year,=B.C. 2,158 (or 2,159); the Bamboo Books place it in his 5th year,=, according to them, B.C. 1,947 (or 1,948). Neither

1 See Mencius, II., Pt. I. i. 8.—由湯至於武丁,賢聖之君,六七作
2 Compare his statements in V. Pt. I., v. and vi.

of these years can be correct.   Such an eclipse could not have taken place in them.

Gaubil tells us that the most famous astronomers of the T'ang dynasty, and subsequently those of the Yuen, determined this eclipse for the year B.C. 2,128 (or 2,127) on the 1st day of the 9th month, which year, moreover, they fixed as the 5th of Chung-k'ang; and that other astronomers of the same dynasties determined it for B.C. 2,155 (or 2,154), which would be the 5th of Chung-k'ang in the common chronology.   He himself adopted and zealously supported the latter determination; but subsequent and more accurate calculations seem to prove that he was in error.   The reader is referred to what I have said on the subject in the body of the Work, pp. 167, 168. The eclipse of B.C. 2,128 may possibly be that mentioned in the Shoo; and yet a different one, or more than one, may be found, within the period of the Hea dynasty, which would satisfy the necessary conditions.   The authenticity of the Book in which we have the statement about the eclipse is called in question; but I have pointed out that that particular passage is guaranteed by its being quoted in the Tso-chuen.   The history or story in connection with which the statement is given is also put down, by Bunsen [3] and others, as nothing better than 'a popular fable;' and neither am I concerned to deny this:—it may very well consist with the reference to the natural phænomenon which actually occurred.   That phænomenon, however, shows that neither of the current chronologies of the time is to be relied on; and it does not by itself enable us to fix the time of the reign of Chung-k'ang.

6.   We come to the earliest period of Chinese history,—that of Yaou and Shun.   The Shoo assigns 50 years of independent reign-ing to Shun: and Sze-ma Kwang and the Bam-

Period of Yaou and Shun.   boo Books adopt the estimate.   It says also that he was on the throne along with Yaou 30 years.   Mencius says these were only 28; but the two additional years may be made out by supposing that they were years of mourning after the death of Yaou.   Yaou had reigned at least 70 years, before he felt the neces-sity of some one to relieve him of the toils of government.[1]   Both Kwang and the Bamboo Books adopt Yaou's 70th year, as the date of Shun's association with him, and so assign to him in all 100 years. Pan Koo gives 70 years to him, and 50 to Shun, thus strangely

3 Egypt's Place in Universal History, vol. III., p. 402.
1 See the Canon of Yaou, p. 12.

allowing the 28 or 30 years of their associate rule to drop altogether out of his chronology.[2] Kwang's standard tables place Yaou's first year in B.C. 2,357, (or 2,356); the Bamboo Books place it in 2,145. There is thus a difference of rather more than 200 years between them. As we found them both wrong in regard to the reign of Chung-k'ang, we must hence conclude that they are wrong also in regard to the period which we are now examining.

It has been generally supposed that Yaou's directions to the astronomers He and Ho, in the first Book of the Shoo, furnished data sufficiently certain to enable us to determine his era. The Shoo does not tell us indeed, in what year of his reign Yaou delivered those instructions, but the chronologers have all assumed that it was in his first year. The remarks of Mr. Chalmers on the point, in the appendix to this chapter, show that the value of Yaou's observations for chronological determinations has been overrated. The emperor tells his officers, that, among other indications which would enable them to fix the exact period of the cardinal points of the year, the vernal equinox might be ascertained by observing the star *neaou;* the summer solstice by observing the star *ho ;* the autumnal equinox by observing the star *heu;* and the winter solstice by observing the star *maou.* It was assumed by the scholars of the Han dynasty that by *neaou* was to be understood the constellation or equatorial space then called *sing,*[3] beginning at α Hydra, and including a space of 2°; and that by *ho* was to be understood *fang,*[4] corresponding to π Scorpio, and including 4°. It was assumed also, that, as the result of the observation (of the manner of which the Shoo says nothing), *sing* would be found to pass the meridian at six o'clock in the evening, at the vernal equinox; and that the other stars mentioned would pass it at the same hour at the seasons to which they were referred.

I do not think there is any reason to call these assumptions in question. The scholars of Han, ignorant of the fact of the procession of the equinoxes, could not have arbitrarily fixed the particular stars to suit their chronological views;—their determination of them must have been in accordance with the voice of accredited tradition. Supposing that the stars were all what it is now believed they were, to what conclusions are we led by them as to the era of Yaou?

Bunsen tells us that Ideler, computing the places of the constellations backwards, fixed the accession of Yaou at B.C. 2,163,[5] which is

---

2 See the 前漢書律歷下, p. 15.　3 星.　4 房.　5 Place of Egypt, &c., III., p. 400.

only 18 years before the date in the Bamboo Books.   On the other hand, J. B. Biot finds in the statements of the Shoo a sufficient confirmation of the date in the received chronology, B.C. 2,357.[6]   Freret was of opinion that the observations left an uncertainty to the extent of 3 degrees, leaving a margin of 210 years.[7]   It seems to myself that it is better not to insist on pressing what Yaou says about the stars of the equinoxes and solstices into the service of chronology at all.   Gaubil, Biot, and the other writers on the subject, all quote Yaou's observations so far as they had astronomical reference ; but they take no notice of other and merely popular indications, which he delivered to his officers to help them to ascertain the seasons. They would know the spring, he tells them, by the pairing of birds and beasts, and by the people's beginning to disperse into the country on their agricultural labours.   Analogous indications are mentioned for summer and autumn ; till in the winter time the people would be found in their cosy corners, and birds and beasts with their coats downy and thick.   Taken as a whole, Yaou's instructions to He and Ho are those of a chief speaking popularly, and not after the manner of a philosopher or astronomer.   We must not look for exactness in his remarks about the cardinal stars.   The mention of them in the earliest portion of the Shoo proves that its compiler, himself, as I showed in the last chapter, of a later date, had traditions or written monuments of a high antiquity at his command ; but Yaou was as likely to be speaking of what he had received from his predecessors as of what he had observed for himself ; and those predecessors may not have lived in China, but in another region from which the Chinese came.   If it were possible to fix the exact century, in which it was first observed that the stars of the equinoxes and solstices were *neaou* and *heu*, *ho* and *maou*, that century may have been anterior to Yaou, and not the one in which he lived.

7.   From the review which I have thus taken of the different periods of Chinese history, documents purporting to belong to which are preserved in the Shoo, it will be seen that the year B.C. 775 is the earliest date which can be said to be determined with certainty.   The exact year in which the Chow dynasty commenced is not known ; and as we ascend the stream of time, the two schemes current among the Chinese themselves diverge more widely from each other, while to neither of them can we accord our credence.   The accession of Yu, the first *sovereign* of the nation, was probably at some time in

6 Etudes sur l'Astronomie Indienne et Chinoise, pp. 361–366.   7 Bunsen, as above ; p. 401.

the nineteenth century before Christ; and previous to him there were the chiefs Shun and Yaou. Twenty centuries before our era the Chinese nation appears, beginning to be. To attempt to carry its early history to a higher antiquity is without any historical justification. There may have been such men as Chinese writers talk of under the appellations of Chuen-heuh, Hwang-te, Shin-nung, Fuh-he, &c.; but they cannot have been rulers of China. They are children of the mist of tradition, if we should not rather place them in the land of phantasy.

For myself, I had adopted the chronology of the Septuagint as nearer the truth than that of our present Hebrew Bibles, more than five-and-twenty years ago, before it was definitely in my plan of life to come to China as a missionary; but the history of China need not seriously embarrass any one who follows the shortest chronology of Scripture. Writers like Bunsen, who follow the will-o'-the-wisps of their own imagination, may launch their shafts against the intolerance of churches, and narrow-mindedness of missionaries. On Chinese ground we can afford to laugh at *their* intolerance. Each bolt they discharge is mere *brutum fulmen;* each shaft, *imbelle telum.*

APPENDIX

ON THE

ASTRONOMY OF THE ANCIENT CHINESE.

By the Rev. John Chalmers, A.M.

1. The Chinese believed the earth to be a plane surface;—"straight, square, and large,"[1] measuring each way about 5,600 *le* (=1,500 miles), and bounded on the

The Earth, the Sun, the Heavens.　　four sides by "the four seas."[2] The North sea and the West sea were of course purely imaginary. The earth was motionless, while the sun and the moon and the starry heavens were continually revolving with great rapidity. This is the fixed belief of the Chinese even at the present day. The sun was estimated to be about 15,000 *le* (=4000 miles) from the earth, and it was supposed that the city of Loh was in "the centre of heaven and earth,"—the middle of the Middle Kingdom.[3] In other places the shadow of a perpendicular gnomon was not due north and south at noonday, or else it was too short

[1] 直, 方, 大, see the Yih-king, 坤卦.　　[2] Shoo, Pt. II. Bk. I. 13.; Pt. III. Bk. I.
Pt. ii. 14—23.　　[3] Shoo, Pt. V. Bk. XII. 14.

90]

or too long; but here it was not found to deviate in either direction, and its length on midsummer-day was to the length of the gnomon as 15 to 80. The distance assigned to the sun is in fact the earth's radius, and was a natural inference from the plane figure of the earth, taken in connection with the different elevation of the sun in different latitudes. From the same premisses it was also inferred that the shadow would be all awry at noon in places far east or far west of Loh;—those on the east being too near the morning sun, and those on the west too near the evening sun. The following legend [4] may be quoted as illustrative of the supposed nearness of the sun to the earth. "There is a country in the far west, in the place of the setting sun, where every evening the sun goes down with a noise like thunder, and the king of the country leads out a thousand men on the city wall to blow horns and beat gongs and drums, as the only means of keeping little children from being frightened to death by the unearthly roaring of the monster." The writers of the early Han dynasty hesitate not to affirm that the experiment to prove the deviation of the shadow at noon was made with all the necessary apparatus,—clepsydras, gnomons, &c., and found successful. But the clepsydra is not mentioned in any authentic writing of earlier date than the Han; and we may safely conclude that this, as well as some other instruments mentioned by interpreters of the classics, and in the Chow-le, was unknown to the ancient Chinese. The clepsydra is described by Aristotle (B.C. 384 —322).

The Chinese have made attempts at various times to calculate the distance of the sidereal heavens. In the History of Tsin [5] the result of a calculation is given with amusing minuteness. It is said :—" By the method of right-angled triangles the distance between heaven and earth was found to be 81,394 le, 30 paces, 5 feet, 3 inches, and 6 tenths !" Another calculator [6] gives 216,781½ le. The diameter of the sun is given by one writer as 1000 le; [7] and he is said to be 7000 le below the heavens (the firmament).

2. "The first calendars of the Greeks were founded on rude observations of the rising and setting of certain stars, as Orion, the Pleiades, Arcturus &c."[1] The same

The Seasons.   may be said of the calendars of the Chinese. Even after Meton and Callippus the Chinese calendar must have been founded on very "rude" observations indeed. During the two centuries and a half embraced by Confucius' History of the later Chow dynasty, the commencement of the year fell back a whole month. This is demonstrable from the dates of the 36 eclipses, of which a list will be found subjoined, and from a variety of references to months, and days of the cycle of 60, which occur throughout the History. It is probable that an error of another month was committed before the fall of the dynasty in the 3d century B.C. The rapid derangement of the months, and consequently of the seasons during this period, however, most probably arose from the adoption of some erroneous system of intercalation, invented to supersede the troublesome observations of the stars from month to month. And the consequence was, that the knowledge of the stars came to be cultivated only for purposes of astrology,—a science in which accuracy is no object. Hence even at the present day, the signs of the zodiac, or the 28 mansions of the moon, are most frequently represented not as they appear now, but as they appeared to Yaou and Shun.[2] The earliest account, which has any claim to authenticity, of the stars employed to mark the cardinal signs of the zodiac, is in the Canon of Yaou. According to

[4] 異域志.   [5] 晉志.   [6] 張揖.   [7] 徐整長歷.
[1] See Smith's Dictionary of Antiquities, Article *Calendar*.   [2] Shoo, Pt. I. Bk. I.

the interpretation of that document, the equinoxes were in Taurus (Pleiades) and Scorpio, and the solstices in Leo and Aquarius in the time of Yaou. No doubt there was a tradition to this effect at the time when the Shoo-king was compiled, for the author knowing nothing of the precession of the equinoxes, could not have adjusted them to the time of which he was writing. His " examination of antiquity " [3] was so far accurate, although the details of his narrative may and even must be mythical. Even Yaou himself may be so. In accordance with Chinese ideas of a sage, Yaou in a few pompous sentences makes it appear that he is perfectly acquainted beforehand with the results of the observations which he orders his astronomers to make :—" You will find the star is in *neaou,*" &c. But did they find the stars as Yaou said they would find them ? We are supposed to believe that they did, of course ; but since we are not told, we claim the liberty to doubt. Suppose, for the sake of argument, that Yaou, before the observations were made, was dependent on tradition for his know- ledge, and that his astronomers were capable of making accurate observations, they would in that case have had to report some failure in the verification of his statements. But apart from this, we are prepared to affirm that three of the men sent to the four borders of China could not have seen the stars, which occupied for the time being the equinoctial and solstitial points, culminating on the evenings named. *E. G.,* the first point of Libra could not be seen culminating at nightfall, when the sun is in the first point of Cancer, for it must culminate at 6h. P.M., whereas the sun would not set in any part of China in midsummer much before 7h. P.M., and the stars would not be visible for half an hour after sunset. This last fact would stand equally in the way, at the equinoxes, of the observers' seeing their stars culminating, unless, indeed, the time of observation was several centuries later than the date usually assigned to Yaou (B.C. 2356—2255), so that the stars to be observed had ceased to be exactly in the solstitial colure. The astronomer who went to the *north in winter* is the only one who would have no difficulty of this kind. He might see his star long before it cul- minated. But unless he had a good clock, he could not tell that it culminated at 6h. P.M. In the course of the long winter evening he would lose his reckoning sadly. The clepsydra also, supposing that he had one, might be ice-bound. The observation could have been made more conveniently in every way at the central station than at the northern border.

The value of the astronomical part of the Canon of Yaou, as a confirmation of the received chronology, has been much overrated. According to the obvious interpreta- tion of the text, Yaou had *reason* to expect the stars he mentioned to be in the equinoctial and solstitial colures. But what his reason was we are left to conjecture. It might be personal observation ; or it might be tradition from his great-grandfather, or from Noah himself.

Scorpio, the *Ho* of Yaou, was considered, even to the end of the Chow dynasty, an important guide to the knowledge of the seasons, as is evident from the frequent references to it in the writings of that time.[4]   An ode in the Book of Poetry, attributed to Chow-kung, begins with the words,[5] "In the seventh month *Ho* passes on,"—that is to say, passes to the westward of the meridian at nightfall. From which it would follow that in the sixth month it was in the meridian at the same hour. This would have been the case if the seventh month had coincided with ours, or with the end of July and part of August, but not if the year had commenced with our December, as

3 First sentence of Canon of Yaou.   4 左傳 國語 &c. ·   5 詩 豳風

the Chinese say the year of the Chow dynasty always did. Here therefore is an argument against the prevailing opinion, which there are other strong reasons for setting aside, that king Woo, when he became emperor, ordered that the year should begin before the winter solstice, while the first month was still absurdly styled the first of spring. The fact is, the months of the year fell into this great disorder afterwards, through neglect, and not on account of an imperial decree. It is probable, however, that even in Chow-kung's time the first month of the year was the last of the winter season, the error of one month passing down from the previous dynasty. As early as B.C. 775, we find the year beginning with our December; and 50 years after, it begins with January again.

The former date, B.C. 775, is very important, as being the earliest which astronomical calculation really confirms. The tenth month of that year commenced on 29th of August (new style)—the 28th day of the cycle of 60—with an eclipse of the sun, which is mentioned in the Book of Poetry.[6] The first month of next year, unless an intercalary month intervened, would begin about the end of November.

The passage in the Tso Chuen,[7] in which Confucius is made to say that in the 12th month of the year, Scorpio was still visible in the west, is not intelligible, for the sun must have passed through Scorpio in October, and the 12th month was certainly not our September.

A very ancient and characteristic method of determining the seasons and months of the year, to which the Chinese are fond of alluding, was by the revolution of Ursa Major. One of its names, of which it has several, is "the Northern Bushel." Under this name it is often confounded with the North Pole, and also with one of the 28 mansions in Sagittarius, which has the same name. Its tail is called the "handle." There is a clear statement of this method of determining the seasons in the writings of Hoh-kwantsze:[8]—"When the tail of the Bear points to the *east* (at nightfall), it is *spring* to all the world. When the tail of the Bear points to the *south*, it is *summer* to all the world. When the tail of the Bear points to the *west*, it is *autumn* to all the world. When the tail of the Bear points to the *north*, it is *winter* to all the world." It is well to keep in mind that the body of the Great Bear was in ancient times considerably nearer to the north pole than it is now, and the tail appeared to move round the pole somewhat like the hand of a clock or watch. The Historical Records say, that the seven stars of the Northern Bushel are spoken of (in the Shoo, Pt. II. Bk. I. p. 5) when it is said, "The pivot and the gem-transverse adjust the seven directors." According to later interpreters, the sun, moon, and five planets are the seven directors, and the pivot, &c., refer to an astronomical instrument. But the ancients knew nothing of the five planets. No reference to them as *five* can be found in the classics. On the contrary, they seem to have supposed, as the Greeks did before Pythagoras, that Lucifer and Hesperus were two stars. Hence in the Book of Poetry we find lines to this effect :—

> "In the east there is Lucifer
> In the west there is Hesper."[9]

And the references to the five planets in the Chow Ritual, and in the three annotated editions of the Chun Ts'ew, are evidence of their later origin. The same may be said of the use of the planet Jupiter for astrological purposes, which belongs to the time of the Contending States, or to the early Han. At that time the period of

6 詩, 小雅. 7 左傳, 哀公十二年. 8 鶡冠子, Sec. V. 9 詩, 小雅.

Jupiter was supposed to be exactly 12 years, so that he gave a year to each sign of the Zodiac, therefore he is always called the *year star*. Considering this exact law of motion in the planet, one Chinese author remarks :—"It must be a spiritual thing without doubt."

The annexed figure will illustrate the use of Ursa Major as a kind of natural clock, whose hand makes one revolution in a year. The earth's surface (square of course) is converted into a dial, and the horizon is divided into 12 parts, making due north the centre of the first division. In theory the time of observation is 6h. P.M. precisely. But it was necessary to wait till the stars were visible. If the tail then pointed due east, it indicated the vernal equinox; but if it pointed due west, as represented in the figure, it was the autumnal equinox.

In this instance, the hand of the clock points a little in advance of the sun in the ecliptic, and to the bright stars in Scorpio, for the tail of the Bear always points to Scorpio. So then we have still Scorpio as the sign of mid-autumn.

This symmetrical position of the Great Bear, or "Northern Bushel," with reference to the seasons, is essential to the Chinese creed; and hence to this day, maugre the precession of the equinoxes, it retains its position in the estimation of almost all Chinese, learned and ignorant. The seasons still arrange themselves round the dial in exactly the same way, Winter going to the north, Spring to the east, Summer to the South, and Autumn to the west.

3. The most common and the earliest division of the ecliptic is that of the 28 mansions. These are of very unequal extent, and consequently very inconvenient for any purpose but that of astrology. The apportioning of 7 of these mansions to each of the cardinal points is also nothing more than an astrological device; but the Chinese student comes in contact with it so frequently, that some explanation of its origin seems very desirable. We must remember that the hour of midnight at the winter solstice is with the Chinese a grand epoch; a sort of repetition of the T'ae-keih or commencement of all things. Let the circle in the annexed figure represent the position of the ecliptic at midnight in mid-winter, in relation to the Chinese earth, represented by a square space in the centre. At the season and hour in question, in the time of Yaou, Leo would be in the meridian, and south of the zenith in the middle of China; Taurus would be in the west, and Scorpio in the east; and it is correctly inferred that Aquarius, though invisible, would be north of the nadir.

The Zodiac.

94]

Accordingly, the seven winter mansions of which Aquarius is the centre are assigned to the north, and the seven summer mansions of which Leo is the centre are assigned to the south. Thus far the arrangement agrees with that already described according to the motion of the Great Bear. But the vernal mansions go to the west, and the autumnal ones to the east, reversing the previous direction of these two seasons, and in opposition to the prevailing notion of the Chinese that spring belongs to the east, &c. This discrepancy does not seem however to trouble their minds at all, and we may safely leave it unexplained.

The angular value of the 28 mansions varies from 1° to 30°, and modern books differ materially from the older ones as to the dimensions of each. Even the four great divisions differ more than 30° one from another. The following are their respective lengths as given in the introduction to Yung-ching's Shoo-king. The circle was divided into $365\frac{1}{4}$ degrees :—

The 7 Northern Constellations embrace			$98\frac{1}{4}$	deg.
,,	Western	,,	80	,,
,,	Southern	,,	112	,,
,,	Eastern	,,	75	,,
		Total	$365\frac{1}{4}$	deg.

This division of the ecliptic is, with some slight variations, common to the Arabians, the Hindoos, and the Chinese ;—a fact which seems to point to the common origin of these races, or to their inter-communication at a period of which history gives us as yet no information.

Besides this inconvenient system of unequal constellations or mansions, the Chinese have, in common with western nations and the Hindoos, the division of the Zodiac into twelve equal parts or signs. This improvement was probably also introduced in the end of the Chow, or the beginning of the Han dynasty. The Sinologue will see a reference to two of these signs in the Tso Chuen,[1] where they are mentioned for an astrological purpose, in connexion with the planet Jupiter. The following is a list of the Chinese signs, with the constellations to which they correspond. The commencement with Aries is optional, as the Chinese usually write them round a circle.

1 大梁 Aries-Taurus.		7 大火 Libra-Scorpio.
2 實沈 Taurus-Gemini.		8 析木 Scorpio-Sagittarius.
3 鶉首 Gemini-Cancer.		9 星紀 Sagittarius-Capricorn.
4 鶉火 Cancer-Leo.		10 玄枵 Capricorn-Aquarius.
5 鶉尾 Leo-Virgo.		11 娵訾 Aquarius-Pisces.
6 壽星 Virgo-Libra.		12 降婁 Pisces-Aries.

The commencement of the first month of spring between the 20th of January and the 19th of February is said to fall always within the 11th of these signs. This ought therefore to coincide with our Aquarius; and the fact that it includes part of Pisces might be taken as indicative of an earlier date than that of our Zodiacal nomenclature; but it seems rather to be an accommodation to the ancient traditions. We do not find that the ancient Chinese made much practical use of the 12 signs; and even to the present day the 28 mansions of the moon have retained their place in preference to the more scientific division.

[1] 左傳襄公二十八年.

4. Slowly and reluctantly did the Chinese astronomer awake to the recognition of the fact that the position of the equinoxes in the ecliptic was shifting from age to age. With the traditions of 2000 years embodied in the classical literature of his country, and engraven on the tablets of his memory, and with the alteration of a whole sign in the position of the equinoctial points staring him in the face, his mind remained sealed against the entrance of the new idea; and went on in its old ruts by sheer *vis-inertiæ*. Hipparchus (B.C. 160—125) discovered the precession of the equinoxes by comparing his own observations with those of Aristyllus and Timocharis, or others who preceded him by not more than two or three centuries; whereas the first man in China who took notice of the precession lived in the 4th century of the Christian era (Comm. on Canon of Yaou, p. 21). He was separated from Yaou by a period of 2600 years !

Precession of the Equinoxes.

5. The invention of the cycle of 60 is ascribed to Hwang-te (B.C. 2,636), and in particular its application to years is affirmed to have commenced in his reign; but this is a mere fiction. It was not applied to years even in the time of Confucius. The Cycle consists of two sets of characters; one set of 10, and one set of 12,—which are combined in couples, odd to odd and even to even, making in all sixty combinations.

The Cycle of 60 ; and its Applications.

The "twelve terrestrial branches," as they are called, were first invented, in all probability, to distinguish the twelve spaces into which the horizon is divided, as described above. Their names and order are as follows:—

Months.

1 子 tsze, 2 丑 ch'ow, 3 寅 yin, 4 卯 maou, 5 辰 shin, 6 巳 sze, 7 午 woo, 8 未 we, 9 申 shin, 10 酉 yew, 11 戌 seuh, 12 亥 hae.

The common mode of expression, 建子, 建丑 &c., "to set up *tsze*," "to set up *ch'ow*," &c., refers to the tail of the Great Bear pointing to *tsze, ch'ow*, and the other ten divisions of the dial. *Tsze*, the first character always indicates due north, and the middle of winter.

It was an easy step, from the original application of the 'twelve branches' to the months, to a duodecimal division of the day; but according to native authorities this was not adopted till the time of Han. It does seem strange that the Chinese should have existed so long without any artificial division of the day; and yet in recording eclipses, where the time of the day is a most important item, it is never mentioned.

Hours.

The application of the cycle to days is undoubtedly a very ancient practice. But it would seem from a passage in the Shoo, Pt. II. Bk. IV., par. 8, that the days were originally arranged in tens *only*, by means of the 10 "celestial stems." These are:—

Days.

1 甲 keă, 2 乙 yih, 3 丙 ping, 4 丁 ting, 5 戊 mow, 6 巳 ke, 7 庚 kăng, 8 辛 sin, 9 壬 jin, 10 癸 kwei.

Yu is made to say, "I remained with my wife only the days *sin, jin, kwei, keă*." These are the last three and the first of the above set of characters, and the natural inference from their use here is that they were invented to divide the month into three equal parts (three decades); and that in course of time they were combined with the twelve branches to make the famous Chinese cycle of *sixty*. The first mention of the

¹ 一 日 十 二 時 始 於 漢, See Morrison's View of China, Chron. Tables.

cyclical name of a day is found in the Shoo, Pt. IV. Bk. IV. p. 1. It is said to have been in the 12th month of the first year of the emperor T'ae-kĕă. The current chronology makes this year to be B.C. 1,752. But the chronology is utterly valueless; and we have no sufficient data by which to verify the day. Moreover, this is the only instance of the use of the cycle which occurs before B.C. 1,121 of the same chronology. In the Books of Chow it is frequently employed.

The state of confusion in which Chinese chronology is found to be, down to the time of the Eastern Chow, and the fact that not a single instance of the application of the cycle to years can be found till after the classical period, are sufficient to satisfy us that this invaluable method of dating years was never used in ancient times. The first attempt to arrange the years in cycles of sixty is found in Sze-ma Ts'een's Historical Records, in a *table* constructed for the purpose of intercalation, and extending over a period of 76 years, the first year being B.C. 103. But instead of using the Chinese cyclical characters, he employs words of two and three syllables, which, considered from a Chinese point of view, must be pronounced barbarous. We give the names applied to the first thirteen years. Perhaps some one acquainted with the ancient language of the Hindoos may hereafter be able to identify them. The second word in each name has some connexion with the motion of the planet Jupiter; and Sze-ma says that *Sheht'e*, part of the first name, means Jupiter. His commentator adds that Jupiter belongs to the east, and is the essence of wood, the spirit of the Green god, *Ling-wei-jang*. This last word is one of six meaningless trisyllables, applied to the the god of the north pole and to the five elemental gods, during the Han dynasty, for which also we must seek a foreign origin. They are given below:—

Names of Years in Sze-ma Ts'een's History, probably of foreign origin.

B.C.						
103	焉	逢	攝	提	格	yenfung shět'ekih.
102	端	蒙	單	關	落	twanmnug tangoh.
101	游	兆	執	徐		yewchaou chiliscu.
100	彊	梧	大	芒		keangwoo tamanglŏh.
99	徒	維	敦	洽	若	t'oowei tuntsang.
98	祝	犂	協	奮		chuhle hĕĕheă.
97	商	橫	赤	噩		shanghung ch'ihfunjŏ.
96	昭	陽	作	茂	獻	ch'aouyang tsŏhgŏh.
95	橫	艾	閹	淵		hunggae yenmow.
94	尙	章	大	敦		shangchang tayuenheen.
93	焉	逢	困	漢		yenfung kw'antun.
92	端	蒙	沇	提	格	twanmung juyhan.
91	游	兆	攝			yewchaou shět'ekih.

Names of gods, probably of foreign origin.

The god of the north pole	北	帝	*Yaou pih paou*	耀 魄 寶	仰 怒 紐.
The Green god (wood)	青	帝	*Ling wei jang*	靈 威	
The Red god (fire)	赤	帝	*Ch'ih p'eaou noo*	赤 熛	
The Yellow god (earth)	黃	帝	*Shay ch'oo new*	含 樞	

The White god (metal)   白帝   *Pih chaou ken*   白招矩.

The Black god (water)   黑帝   *Heih kwang ke*   叶光紀.

Various attempts have been made to analyse the second word *Sheht'ekih*, (in Cantonese *Shipt'ai kak*. Is *Shipt'ai* intended to represent the Hindoo name of Jupiter,—Vrishaspati; and *kak* the Hindoo chacra, or cycle?) applied to the first year of Sze-ma Ts'een's Table; and to determine which of the 12 branches' it ought to be identified with. Sze-ma himself, besides saying that *sheht'e* is Jupiter, explains the term to mean the place of that planet in the ecliptic; and again, with strange inconsistency, he says elsewhere it is the star or constellation to which the tail of Ursa Major points. In a work called the 'Classic of Stars,'[1] *sheht'e* is said to denote a "spiritual instrument of western nations." Now this confusion of words without knowledge is easily accounted for on the supposition that the cycle of 60 years was introduced from the Hindoos, to whom the Chinese were indebted in the time of Sze-ma Ts'een for other things even more important. In justice to Sze-ma, however, or rather to the compilers of the Work that goes by his name, for it is the work of more than one hand, it ought to be stated that they saw that the motion of Jupiter was in the opposite direction to that in which the "12 branches" are reckoned, and would give them in the reverse order. They therefore had recourse again to the Great Bear; and explained that the character belonging to that month of any year when Jupiter rose before the sun in the east was the cyclical character for that year. They then tell us that, in the year B.C. 103, Jupiter rose in the morning during the first month, which is (寅) *yin*, the third of the 12 branches. This ought therefore to be the cyclical character for 103. But future chronologists made it (丑) *ch'ow*, the second. Probably they did this because the History says that Jupiter was in *ch'ow*. But if this was their reason, they overlooked the fact that on the following year the planet is said to be in (子) *tsze*, and again after another year has elapsed, he is in (亥) *hae*, going backwards over the characters. They evidently lighted upon the wrong expression. The original[2] runs thus:—"In the *sheht'ekih* year, the (陰) *yin* of the year, moving to the left, is in (寅) *yin*, and the star of the year (Jupiter) moving, in the opposite direction, to the right, is in *ch'ow*." The word (陰) *yin* here is too vague to be translated. It means any thing which is the reverse of the star, or the counter part of the star. Chinese scholars are fond of using this form of expression:—"The year is in *keah-tsze*;"[3] but probably very few ever reflect on the meaning of the phrase, or know that it has its origin in the above passage from the Historical Records, much less could they say for certain whether it is the *yin* of the year, or the *star* of the year, that they intend to say is "in *keah-tsze*."

The characters before in use for the cycle of 60 days were soon substituted for the longer names: but not without some diversity of opinion as to where the cycle should commence. In the chronological Tables given in the Historical Records the cyclical characters have been supplied by a later hand, from B.C. 840 downwards; but in every case the authority of the scholars of Tsin (A.D. 265-419) is quoted. Seu Kwang[4] seems to be most closely followed; but he was preceded in the same department of labour by Hwangfoo Meih,[5] and perhaps also by the inventor of the so-called Bamboo Books.[6] So then the cycle of 60 years cannot have commenced earlier than the Han,

[1] 星經   [2] 史記天官書   [3] 歲在甲子   [4] 徐廣
[5] 皇甫謐   [6] 竹書紀年.

and owes its present form to the scholars of Tsin; although the Chinese for the most part still glory in the delusion that it was invented by Hwangte, $(60 \times 75 =)$ 4500 years ago.

6. The Chinese month has always been lunar; and as twelve lunations come short of a solar year by nearly 11 days, it is necessary from time to time to insert an extra month to preserve a general correspondence with the solar year.   The

Intercalation. statement of Yaou (Shoo, Pt. I. par. 8), that the year consists of 366 days, was made with a view to facilitate the process of intercalation which he ordered his astronomers to conduct.   But to reckon the solar year at 366 days would occasion an error of a whole month in 40 years; so that in the course of his long reign of 100 years Yaou might have seen great cause to shorten the solar period.   It would seem, however, that neither he nor his successors made any attempt to obtain more accurate numbers, and that in fact their intercalation was regulated by the natural recurrence of the seasons, and rude observations from year to year.   During the Chow dynasty, intercalary months were placed at irregular intervals, but most frequently at the end of the year.

The Chinese seem even then to have had no idea of the proper interval between two intercalations, which is now known to be 32 or 33 months on an average.   The amount of error which they actually committed in the commencement of the year has been already referred to; and we now give a few examples gathered from the "Ch'un Ts'ew" of Confucius.   According to the theory of later writers, the year ought always to have commenced between November 22 and December 22; but on the contrary we find that the year B.C. 719 commenced .... on January   16;

,,	703	,,	,, January	20;
,,	688	,,	,, January	4;
,,	685	,,	,, January	1;
,,	658	,,	,, January	3;
,,	626	,,	,, January	8;
,,	605	,,	on November	18;
,,	583	,,	,, November	16;
,,	556	,,	,, November	17;
,,	540	,,	,, November	19;
,,	529	,,	,, November	18;
,,	526	,,	,, November	15.

For an instance of the intercalary month placed at the end of the year on three successive occasions, the reader is referred to Sze-ma Ts'een's Chronological Tables,—Ts'in dynasty, years 207, 204, & 201, B.C.   Each of these would be separated from the other by 36 lunations instead of 32; and a proportionate amount of error would be caused in the situation of the months.

In the second century before the Christian era, the Chinese made extraordinary efforts to open communication with the West.   They explored due west as far as the

Reform of the calendar. borders of Persia.   Beyond theno madic tribes of Huns and Scythians, their immediate neighbours, the Chinese travellers found nations comparatively civilised, dwelling in cities and towns.   Their horses were far superior to any known in China, and were eagerly coveted by the emperor. They had wine made from grapes, which the rich preserved for many years.   Among other objects of interest unknown in Eastern Asia are mentioned single humped camels (C. Arabicus) and ostrich-eggs.   At the same time they became acquainted with the northern parts of India,—Shindo (Scinde ?), Dahea, &c.[1] Sze-ma Ts‘een, who gives a full history of these discoveries, does not indeed tell us that they became acquainted with the cycle of Callippus, either through the Bactrians or the Hindoos; but there is scarcely a shadow of doubt that this was the case. In no other way can we account for the sudden appearance, in Ts‘een's History, of a method so far in advance of anything known before in China, and one which had been already employed in the West for more than two centuries. The cycle of Callippus is simply this :— $4 \times 19 = 76$ years $= 27759$ days $= 940$ lunations. It must have been well known to Alexander, the pupil of Aristotle, and the conqueror of Sogdiana, Bactria, and the Punjab, B.C. 328—325. The reformation of the Chinese calendar by Sze-ma Ts‘een and others, with the help of these numbers, dates from the winter solstice of the year 104 B.C. In order to make this epoch appear as perfect as possible, they overlooked minor differences, though amounting to a whole day in the case of the solstice, and declared that new moon, and winter, and midnight, all coincided, at the commencement of the first of the cycle. From this remarkable epoch all dates before and after were to be calculated by the new method. In constructing a calendar for short periods, or even for a century or two, the method was invaluable; but with unlimited faith in its perfection, the Chinese scholars of that day proceeded to solve by means of it all difficult problems of ancient chronology; and here of course it led them astray. We can easily see the amount of error which they committed in reckoning back 16 centuries to the first year of T‘ae-keă, or ten centuries to the 13th year of Woo-wang. In round numbers, the error of the Metonic cycle, as modified by Callippus, amounts to one day in the time of new moon for every 300 years, and three days in the time of winter solstice for every 400 years. So then the scholars of Han, in calculating the day of new moon at the commencement of the Chow dynasty, made an error of three days. As Confucius has nowhere told us, and possibly could not tell, how many years the Chow dynasty had lasted up to his own time, the problem the chronologers had to solve was to find a year near the supposed date of Woo-wang, which should commence with the day *sin-maou*. Such a year being found would, according to the Shoo-king, Pt. V. Bk. III. par 1, be the 13th of king Woo. Calculated according to the Metonic cycle from the epoch of Han, the year in question is B.C. 1121. But if we attempt to verify this date by modern methods, we find that the supposed first new moon of 1121 would fall three days later than *sin-maou*, and moreover that the whole lunation would be before the winter solstice, and belong according to the Chinese theory to the preceding year. So then, if we are not prepared to reject all the dates in the Shoo-king as spurious, we have no alternative but to condemn the received chronology. But the chronology of the whole period embraced by the Shoo rests on nothing better than mere conjecture, and imperfect astronomical calculations, made after the reformation of the calendar in the 2nd century B.C. We can have no hesitation therefore in rejecting it.

It may be well to state here one or two additional arguments in favour of the view that the Chinese borrowed their astronomy from the West before the Christian era. It is stated by Sir J. F. Davis, in his work on *The Chinese*, Vol. II. p. 290, that the Hindoo cycle of sixty years "is a cycle of Jupiter, while that of the Chinese is a solar cycle." The learned author does not explain what he understands by "a solar cycle" of 60 years, nor does he give any authority for the statement. We have found, on the

[1] 身毒, 大夏

100]

contrary, that the Chinese cycle, like the Hindoo one, is connected with the period of Jupiter. In the same page of the above work it is said, " Besides the lunar zodiac of twenty-eight mansions, the Hindoos *(unlike the Chinese)* have the solar, including twelve signs." But we have seen that the Chinese have also the twelve signs.

Another proof that the Chinese borrowed from the Hindoos is the use they made of conjunctions of the five planets. The rise of the Han dynasty, it is asserted, was marked by one of those conjunctions. And as the Hindoo era, *cali-yug,* commenced (B.C. 3102) with a conjunction of all the planets, so the Historian of Han places a conjunction of all the planets in the reign of Chuen-heuh (B.C. 2513—2436, mod. chr.), just at the time when that emperor is said to have corrected the calendar, and fixed the commencement of the year in February. The late Baron Bunsen, in his Work on Egypt (Bk. IV. Pt. IV.), has attempted to verify this conjunction of the planets; but this, as well as the credence he gives to the tablet of Yu, only shows his ignorance of the subject; and that he ought to have manifested more of a fellow feeling with the 'ignorant' and 'superstitious' and 'intolerant' missionaries, who mistook the inundation of Yaou for the flood of Noah. These ancient conjunctions of the planets are utterly unworthy of credit. There was a rough approximation to such a conjunction at the commencement of the Han dynasty, in May, 204 B.C. But the only real conjunction of the five on record is that of Sep. 15, 1186 A.D., in the Sung dynasty. The Chinese in this matter seem to have been servile imitators of the Hindoos; and the Hindoos in their turn borrowed from the Greeks. When the expression "ts'eih ching" (七政), "the seven directors," is taken in the sense of sun, moon, and five planets, and applied to days, the idea is obviously and confessedly western.

7. Referring to the Shoo, Pt. III. Bk. IV. parag. 4, we find this sentence :—'On the first day of the last month of autumn the sun and moon did not meet harmoniously in Fang." Upon which there was beating of drums, and a general commotion such as the Chinese usually make on the occasion of an eclipse of the sun. It is evident, from the quotation of the passage in the *Tso-chuen,* that an eclipse of the sun is meant, and also that the record existed in some form or other in the time of *Tso K'en-ming.* On the other hand, it cannot be denied that the genuineness of this part of the Shoo is open to great suspicion, and in particular, that the phrase 辰弗集于房, *lit.* "The heavenly bodies were not harmonious in the chamber," looks more like a modern form of speech, than a primitive way of denoting an eclipse of the sun. It occurs nowhere else; and although no other eclipse is mentioned in the Shoo, in the other classical writings eclipses of the sun are of common occurrence, and are uniformly denoted by 日有食之 "the sun was eaten." This seems more likely to be the older phrase. And again, with regard to the character 房 *fang,* it is evidently not taken in the Tso-ch'uen for the constellation that now goes by that name, but as equivalent to Shay (舍), any division or mansion of the Zodiac. This interpretation seems also to be favoured by several later writers. The ancient name of the constellation was *Ho* or *Ta-ho, i. e.* Scorpio, and it is only called *fang* in the Book of Rites.

But granting that an eclipse within that part of Scorpio which now goes by the name of *Fang* is intended, no such event could have been witnessed during the reign of Chung-k'ang, if we adopt the current chronology. The eclipse of the astronomers of T'ang, although it happens to agree with that of Gaubil, in being on the fifth year of Chung-k'ang, was reckoned according to some other chronology than that which is current now, and was in fact the eclipse of 2127, which has recently come into favour, after Gaubil's has been set aside as invisible (*See Comm. in loc.*) The astronomers of T'ang distinctly state that it was in the year *kwei-tsze*, the 30th of the cycle of years; and on the day *kang-seŭh*, the 47th of the cycle of days. I have found them right even in the day; which implies a high degree of accuracy in their figures, considering that they were calculating an eclipse at the distance of nearly 3000 years. Is it possible that those Chinese astronomers were superior to Gaubil? or was their success in this instance accidental? It was perhaps too late in the day for the scholars of T'ang to fix the uncertain chronology by astronomical calculation, though those of Han practised this method freely with far inferior knowledge.

Those, however, who like the year 2127 as the date of the eclipse may adopt it now without fear of its being hereafter proved invisible. But it is well to keep in mind that eclipses satisfying the conditions are by no means rare. Eclipses of the sun, visible in the northern hemisphere in the sign Scorpio, might be looked for in any of the following years:—

B. C.			
2154	2024	1894	1764
2135	2005	1875	1745
2127	1997	1867	1737
2108	1978	1848	1718

ECLIPSES RECORDED BY THE ANCIENT CHINESE.

	RECORDED IN THE BOOK OF POETRY.				No.	CALCULATION.				
Emperor's Name.	Year of Reign.	Year of Cycle.	Moon.	Day of Cycle.		Year B.C.	Month & day. New style.	Chinese Moon.	Day of Cycle.	
幽王	6	2	X	28	I	775	August 29	X	28	Early in the morning, *scarcely visible.*
RECORDED IN THE CH'UN TS'EW.										
平王	51	58	II	6	I	719	February 14	III	6	Visible at sunrise.
桓王	11	9	VII	29 total.	II	708	July 8	VIII	29	Total about 3h. P.M.
莊王	2	23	X		III	694	October 3	XI	7	Visible—Afternoon.
惠王	1	42	III		IV	675	April 6	V	49	Sunset.
	8	49	VI	8	V	668	May 18	VI	8	Morning.
	9	50	XII	60	VI	667	November 3	XII	60	Morning.
	13	54	IX	7	VII	663	August 21	IX	7	Afternoon.
	22	3	IX	45	VIII	654	August 11	IX	45	Afternoon.
襄王	4	10	III	7	IX	647	March 29	V	7	Afternoon.
	7	13	V		X	644	January 28	III	21	*Not visible.*
	26	32	II	60	XI	625	January 26	III	60	Visible at Noon.
匡王	1	46	VI	38	XII	611	April 20	V	38	Sunrise.
定王	6	57	VII	1 total.	XIII	600	September 12	X	1	Total about 3h. 30m, P.M.
	8	59	IV	53	XIV	598	February 26	IV	53	Visible at Sunrise.
	15	6	VI	40	XV	591	October 5	XI	8	*Not visible.*
簡王	11	23	VI	3	XVI	574	May 1	VI	3	Visible at Noon.
	12	24	XII	54	XVII	573	October 17	XI	54	Morning.

ECLIPSES RECORDED BY THE ANCIENT CHINESE.—*Continued.*

					No.	B.C.					Remarks
靈王	13	39	II	32	XVIII	558	January	8	II	32	Noon.
	14	40	VIII	54	XIX	557	May	23	VI*	54	*Scarcely visible at Sunrise*
	19	45	X	53	XX	552	August	25	X	53	Noon.
	20	46	IX	47	XXI	551	August	13	IX	47	Noon.
	20	46	X	17	XXII	551	September		X		*No Eclipse.*
	22	48	II	10	XXIII	550	December	30	II	10	Visible at Sunrise.
	23	49	VII	1 total.	XXIV	548	June	12	VII	1	Total about 1h. 15m. P.M.
	23	49	VIII	30	XXV	548	July		VIII		*No Eclipse.*
	26	52	XII	12	XXVI	545	October	7	XI	12	Visible in the Morning.
景王	10	3	IV	41	XXVII	534	March	11	IV	41	Forenoon.
	18	11	VI	54	XXVIII	526	April	10	V	54	Forenoon.
	20	13	VI	11	XXIX	524	August	14	IX	10	Afternoon.
	24	17	VII	19	XXX	520	June	3	VII	19	Forenoon.
	25	18	XII	10	XXXI	519	November	18	XII	10	Afternoon.
敬王	2	20	V	32	XXXII	517	April	1	V	32	Sunrise.
	9	27	XII	48	XXXIII	510	November	7	XII	48	Forenoon.
	15	33	III	48	XXXIV	504	February	10	III	48	Noon.
	22	40	XI	3	XXXV	497	September	15	X	3	Forenoon.
	25	43	VIII	17	XXXVI	494	July	15	VIII	17	Forenoon.

* Intercalary

CHAPTER IV.

THE ANNALS OF THE BAMBOO BOOKS.

THE BAMBOO BOOKS IN GENERAL;—THEIR DISCOVERY
AND SUBSEQUENT HISTORY.
THE ANNALS.
HOW FAR THE ANNALS ARE TO BE RELIED ON;—CONCLUSION FROM THEM AS
TO THE GENERAL CHARACTER OF THE EARLY RECORDS OF THE SHOO.

1.　Having made such frequent reference in the last chapter to the Bamboo Books, I have thought it would be well to devote a chapter specially to them, embodying the text, with a translation, of that portion of them which is most important, and from which the shorter scheme of Chinese chronology is derived.　Some Sinologues, like Father De Mailla, have written about them without sufficient discrimination, and have not done them justice; while other students ₁ chronology, like Freret and Bunsen, unable to examine them for themselves, have attached a greater value to them than can be fairly claimed.　The student will be glad to have the ancient history of China, as indicated in them, in the same volume with the records of the Shoo; and it will be found that they give important corroboration to some of the views which I have advanced on the older portions of the classic.

'The Bamboo Books' is a comprehensive designation.　It is not, indeed, so wide as De Mailla represents, when he says:—'It is the general name given to all ancient Books written on tablets of bamboo, before the manner of making paper was discovered.'　Such books might be spoken and written of as 'Bamboo Books.'　*The* Bamboo Books is the name appropriate to a large collection of ancient documents, discovered in A.D. 279, embracing nearly twenty different Works, which contained altogether between seventy and eighty chapters or Books.

What is meant by 'The Bamboo Books.'

1 See the first of the P. De Mailla's letters to Freret, prefixed to 'L'Histoire generale de la Chine.'

The discovery of those Works is thus related in the history of the emperor Woo, the first of the sovereigns of Tsin, whose supremacy

Manner of their Discovery.   over the empire is acknowledged in chronology :—'In the 5th year of his reign under the title of Hëen-ning [2] [= A.D. 279, the year before the chronological commencement of the Tsin dynasty], some lawless parties in the department of Keih dug open the grave of king Seang of Wei [Died B.C. 295], and found a number of bamboo tablets, written over, in the small seal character, with more than 100,000 words; which were deposited in the imperial library.' But before the tablets were placed in the library, they had sustained various injury and mutilation. The emperor referred them to the principal scholars in the service of the government, to adjust the tablets in order, having first transcribed them in modern characters. The chief among these was one Wei Hăng,[3] famous for his knowledge of the old forms of the characters. He was assisted by Shuh Sih, Ho Këaou, Seun Heuh, and others,—all men of note in their day. In two years their labours were completed, and the tablets were placed in the library in order. De Mailla says that the scholars reported to the emperor unfavourably of the Bamboo Books :—that 'they were filled with reveries, extravagances, and manifest falsities.' I have not found in the Books of Tsin [7] that they gave any such sweeping decision. They made out the names of 15 different Works, the tablets of which, more or less complete, could be arranged together. Some of these Works were, indeed, full of extravagant legends and speculations ;—they soon fell into neglect, if they have not entirely perished. There were two among them, however, of a different character :—a copy of the Yih King, in two Books, agreeing with that generally received ; and a book of Annals, beginning with the reign of Hwang-te, and coming down to the 16th year of the last emperor of the Chow dynasty, B.C. 298. This was in 12 or 13 chapters.

If the scholars of Tsin sent in to the emperor any formal report of their labours, and of their judgment on the different portions of 'the Bamboo Books,' it has not been preserved; but we have the most satisfactory evidence of the points I have just stated, in the appendix or *l'envoi* affixed by Too Yu to his well known edition of the Tso Chuen.[8] He tells us, that on returning, in A.D. 280, from a

---

[2] 咸寧五年. See the Books of Tsin, 帝紀第三, p. 13.   [3] 衞恒

[4] 束皙   [5] 和嶠·   [6] 荀勗·   [7] See in particular the history of

Shuh Sih, 列傳第二十一   [8] 杜預左傳後序·

106]

military expedition to Woo, he completed his great Work, when his attention was called to the Bamboo Books which had been recently discovered; that, by the carelessness of the parties who first found them, they had suffered much damage; and that, when he saw them in the library, the portions most complete and distinct were a copy of the Yih King, and certain Annals, relating, in the latter part of them, more particularly, the affairs of the State of Tsin.

The reader will be conscious of a disposition to reject at once the account of the discovery of the Bamboo Books. He has read so much of the recovery of portions of the Shoo from the walls of houses, that he must be tired of this mode of finding lost treasures; and smiles when he is now called on to believe that an old tomb opened, and yielded its literary stores, long after the human remains that had been laid in it had mingled with the dust. From the death of king Sëang to B.C. 279 were 595 years;—so long had these Books been in the bosom of the earth. The speed, moreover, with which the tablets were transcribed and arranged was surprising. It is hard to credit that so much work was done in so brief time. Against the improbabilities in the case, however, we have to place the evidence which is given in support of it. The testimony of Too Yu, especially, a witness entirely competent and disinterested, and which was probably in A.D. 281 or 282, seems to place it beyond a doubt, that there had been a large discovery of ancient Works in a tomb a few years before, of which a most valuable portion was that which is now current under the name of 'The Annals of the Bamboo Books.' How far some of the other portions have been preserved, I am not able to say; but these Annals have held their place in the literature of China. They are mentioned in the catalogues of the Suy and T'ang dynasties.

How the Annals have kept their place in literature. Shin Yŏ,[9] a scholar and officer of the Lëang dynasty, (A.D. 502—557) published an edition, with a commentary, in the 6th century: Under the Sung dynasty, Choo He made several references to them, not unfavourable. Two scholars of Yuen, Hoo Ying-lin [10] and Yang Shing-gan,[11] laboured upon them; and in the present dynasty five or six different editions and commentaries have been published;—showing that, notwithstanding the generally unfavourable opinion of scholars, the Work has not yet been put out of the court of criticism.

I now subjoin the text and a translation, with a few annotations.

[9] 沈約字休文·   [10] 胡應麟·   [11] 楊升庵·

有鳳凰集不食生蟲不履生草
齋于中宮坐于玄扈洛水之上
時見於攝提名曰景星帝黃服
一星凡三星皆黃色以天清明
相連赤方中有青方中有氣
有景雲之瑞赤方中有兩星青方中有氣
二十年景雲見以雲紀官
元年帝即位居有熊初制冕服○
草指之是以佞人不敢進
之草生於庭佞人入朝則
定聖德光被羣瑞畢臻有屈軼
獸之力以女魃止淫雨天下既
之應龍攻蚩尤戰虎豹熊羆四
言龍顏有聖德劾百神朝而使
十五月而生帝於壽丘弱而能
北斗樞星光照郊野感而孕二
黃帝軒轅氏　母曰附寶見大電繞
竹書紀年卷之一

2. THE ANNALS OF THE BAMBOO BOOKS.

PART. I.

The reigns of Hwang-te; Che; Chuen-heuh; and Kuh.

I. HWANG-TE; DYNASTIC TITLE HËEN-YUEN.[1]

Note. His mother was called Foo-paou. She witnessed a great flash of lightning, which surrounded the star *ch'oo* (α Dubhe) of the Great Bear with a brightness that lightened all the country about her, and thereupon became pregnant. After 25 months, she gave birth to the emperor in Show-k'ew. When born, he could speak. His countenance was dragon-like; his virtue that of a sage. He could oblige the host of spirits to come to his court, and receive his orders. *He employed* Ying-lung to attack Ch'e-yew, the fight with whom was maintained by the help of tigers, panthers, bears, and grisly bears. By means of the *Heavenly* lady Pă, he stopped the extraordinary rains *caused by the enemy.* When the empire was settled, his sage virtue was brightly extended, and all sorts of auspicious indications appeared. The grass K'euh-yih grew in the court-yard of the palace. When a glib-tongued person was entering the court, this grass pointed to him, so that such men did not dare to present themselves.[2]

1   In his 1st year, when he came to the throne, he dwelt in Yew-hëung.[3] He in-
2   vented the cap with pendents, and the robes to match.   In his 20th year, brilliant clouds appeared; and he arranged his officers by names taken from the colours of the clouds.[4]

Note. The auspicious omen of brilliant clouds was in this way:—The vapours of the red quarter [the south] extended so as to join those of the green [the east]. In the red quarter were two stars, and in the green, one;—all of a yellow colour, which appeared, when the heavens were clear and bright, in Shĕ-t'e, and were named the brilliant stars. The emperor in yellow robes fasted in the Middle palace. When he was sitting in *a boat on the* Yuen-hoo, above *its junction with* the Lŏ, there came together phœnixes, male and female. They would not eat any living insect, nor tread on

1   1 Sze-ma Ts'ëen says that Hwang-te's name was Hëen-yuen; and many others take 氏 here as = 名. It seems to me preferable to take it as in the case of Yaou, who was 陶唐氏; and of Shun's 有虞氏 See the Introductory notes to the Canons of Yaou and Shun, Hëen-yuen may have reference to the invention of carriages, which is commonly ascribed to Hwang-te, though these Annals do not mention it; or it may have been the name of a place. There are many methods of accounting for it.

2 This and other notes which follow are supposed by some to be a portion of the text of the Annals. The more likely opinion is, that they are additions to the text by difft. hands;— several of them, but not all, by Shin Yŏ. As they are not many, I have translated them; but they abound so much in extravagant, monstrous, statements, and besides are so full of errors, that I will rarely occupy space with comments on them.

3 Yew-hëung must be the name of a State. It is referred to what was called 'new Ch'ing' (新鄭), in the pres. Ho-nan.   4 The chiefs

或止帝之東園或巢於阿閣或鳴於庭
其雄自歌其雌自舞麒麟在囿神鳥來庭
儀有大螻如羊大蟥如虹帝以土氣勝遂以土德王
五十年秋七月庚申鳳鳥至帝祭于洛水。
牧容成曰於公何如天老曰臣聞之國亂其主好
安其主好文則鳳凰居之國鳳凰翔於東郊而樂
武則鳳凰去之今鳳凰居之國亂其主好
之其鳴音中夷則與天相副以是觀之召史卜之
天有嚴教以賜帝帝勿犯也帝卜之
龜燋史曰臣不能占也其間之聖人帝
曰龜不違聖故占游于洛水
之上見大魚殺五牲以醮之天乃甚雨
七日七夜魚流於海得圖書焉龍圖出
河龜書出洛流赤文篆字以授軒轅接萬
神於明庭今塞門谷口是也
五十九年貫胸氏來賓長股氏來賓○七
十七年昌意降居若水產帝乾荒○一百

living grass. Some of them abode in the emperor's eastern garden; some built their nests about the corniced galleries *of the palace;* and some sang in the courtyard, the females gambolling to the notes of the males. K'e-lins also appeared in the parks; and *other* spirit-like birds came with their measured movements. Four-horned *low* were produced as large as a goat, and the *yin* worms like rainbows. The emperor, considering that the influence of earth was thus predominant, reigned by the virtue of earth.

3   In his 50th year,[5] in the autumn, in the 7th month, on *the day* Kang-shin [57th of cycle], phœnixes, male and female, arrived. The emperor sacrificed at the river Loh.

Note. Beginning with Käng-shin, the heavens were wrapt in mist for three days and three nights. The emperor asked T'ëen-laou, Leih-muh, and Yung-shing, what they thought of it. T'ëen-laou said, 'I have heard this:—When a kingdom is tranquil, and its ruler is fond of peace, then phœnixes come and dwell in it; when a kingdom is disordered, and its ruler is fond of war, then the phœnixes leave it. Now the phœnixes fly about in your eastern borders rejoicing, the notes of their singing all exactly harmonious, in mutual accord with Heaven. Looking at the thing in this way, Heaven is giving your majesty grave instructions, which you must not disobey.' *The emperor then* called the recorder to divine about the thing, when the tortoise-shell was *only* scorched. The recorder said, 'I cannot divine it; you must ask your sage men.' The emperor replied, 'I have asked T'ëen-laou, Leih-muh, and Yung-shing.' The recorder then did obeisance, twice, with his face to the earth, and said, 'The tortoise will not go against their sage wisdom, and therefore its shell is only scorched.'

When the mists were removed, he made an excursion on the Lŏ, and saw a great fish; and sacrificed to it with five victims, whereupon torrents of rain came down for seven days and seven nights, when the fish floated off the sea, and the emperor obtained the map-writings. The dragon-writing came forth from the Ho, and the tortoise-writing from the Lŏ.

In red lines, and the seal character, they were given to Hëen-yuen. He entertained the myriad spirits in Ming-t'ing, the present valley of Han-mun.

4   In his 59th year, the chief of 'The Perforated Breasts'[6] came to make his sub-
5   mission. So also did the chief of 'The Long Legs.'[6]   In his 77th year, Ch'ang-e[7] left the court, and dwelt by the Jŏ-water; he begat the emperor K'ëen-
6   hwang.   In his 100th year, the earth was rent. The emperor went on high.[9]

of the difft. departments were called—'He of the green cloud; he of the white cloud (白雲 氏), &c.   5 Some editions read here—'the 57th year,' instead of the 50th.

6 'The Perforated Breasts' and 'The Long Legs' are of course fabulous. We read of them, and other equally monstrous barbarian tribes, in the 'Classic of Mountains and Seas' (山 海經).   7 Ch'ang-e was a son (1st or 2d is debated) of Hwang-te, and, not being able for the empire, was sent away to a State near the Jŏ-water, in the pres. Sze-ch'uen. Others have it that he went away himself, in virtuous humility;—all is fabulous.   8 When this son of

年地裂帝陟。

帝王之崩皆曰陟書稱新陟王謂新崩也帝以土德王應地裂而陟葬羣臣有左徹者感思帝德取衣冠几杖而朝饗之諸侯大夫歲時為朝焉

帝摯少昊氏
母曰女節見星如虹下流感生少昊登帝位有鳳凰之瑞或曰名清不居帝位以鳥紀官方

帝顓頊高陽氏
母曰女樞見瑤光之星貫月如虹感已於幽房之宮生顓頊於若水首戴干戈有聖德生十年而佐少昊

氏二十而登帝位

元年帝即位居濮○十三年初作歷象○二十一年作承雲之樂○三十年帝產伯鯀居天穆之陽○七十八

Note. The death of emperors and kings is thus spoken of as a going on high. In the Shoo we have 'the recently ascended king,' for the recently deceased [Pt. V. BK. XXIII. 3]. Hwang-te reigned by the virtue of earth;—it was right that his death should be preceded by the rending of the earth. After he was buried, one of his ministers, named Tso-ch'ĕ, affected by the thought of the emperor's virtue, took his clothes, cap, bench, and stick, and offered sacrifice to them in a temple. The princes and great officers every year paid their court before them.

II. THE EMPEROR CHE; DYNASTIC TITLE SHAOU-HAOU.[1]

Note. His mother was called Neu-tsëĕ. She witnessed a star like a rainbow come floating down the stream to the islet of Hwá. Thereafter she dreamed she had received it, and was moved in her mind, and bore Shaou-haou. When he ascended the throne, there was the auspicious omen of phœnixes. Some say that his name was Ts'ing, and that he did not occupy the throne. He led an army of birds, and dwelt in the west, where he arranged his officers by *names taken from birds.*

III. THE EMPEROR CHUEN-HEUH; DYNASTIC TITLE KAOU-YANG.[1]

Note. His mother was called Neu-ch'oo. She witnessed the Yaou-kwang star (η Benetnasch) go through the moon like a rainbow, when it moved itself in the palace of Yew-fang, after which she brought forth Chuen-heuh near the Jŏ-water. On his head he bore a shield and spear; and he had the virtue of a sage. When 10 years old, he assisted Shaou-haou; and when 20, he ascended the imperial throne.

1 In his 1st year, when he came to the throne, he dwelt in Puh. In his 13th
2 year, he invented calendaric calculations and delineations *of the heavenly bodies.*
3 In his 21st year, he made the *piece of* music called 'The Answer to the Clouds.'
4 In his 30th year, he begat Pih-k'wăn, who dwelt in the south of T'ëen-muh.
5 In his 78th year, he died. Shuh-k'e made disorder, and was made an end of by the prince of Sin.

Ch'ang-e was emperor, we do not know; some identify him with Chuen-heuh; others make that emperor his son. 8 陟. See the last par. of the Canon of Shun.—Many accounts say that Hwang-te did not die, but went up to Heaven on a dragon. Hăng Ch'in-fung gives the following passage, quoted by some writers as from the Bamboo Books:—

黃帝既仙去其臣左徹削木為黃帝之像帥諸侯朝奉之

'Hwang-te having gone away as one of the Immortals, Tso-ch'ĕ, one of his ministers, cut an image of him in wood, and led the princes to pay court and reverence to it.' Here

was idolatry at a very early time.—This statement was no doubt in one of the Bamboo Books, but not in the Annals. The same may be said of another,—that this 'Tso-ch'ĕ raised Chuen-heuh to the throne, 7 years after Hwang-te's death.'

II. 1 Some editions of the Annals give this notice as an addition of Shin Yŏ's. Others separate the name and title from the note, and put them in the text.—Sze-ma Ts'een does not give this emperor Che at all. There are many discussions about him, whether he was a son of Hwang-te, or a grandson; or whether he was not rather descended from Fuh-he. His title of Shaou-haou would seem to be in relation with Fuh-he's of T'ae-haou.

III. 1 Chuen-heuh was a son, or a grandson of Ch'ang-e mentioned above. The title of Kaou-

陟
九帝
年子
而摯
廢立

陟
命
十帥
五師
年滅
帝有
錫鄶
唐○
侯六
命十
三
年
帝

十帝
六即
年位
帝居
使亳
重○
四

元
年
帝
○

鼗鼓
皇鐘
擊磬
而舞
鳳

侯天
代下
高使
陽羣
氏人
拊

氏帝
聖嚳
生德高
而初辛
駢封
齒辛
有

年帝
辛陟
侯術
滅器
之作
亂

IV. THE EMPEROR KUH; DYNASTIC TITLE KAOU-SIN.

Note. He was born with double rows of teeth; and had the virtue of a sage. He was at first made prince of Sin, and afterwards succeeded to Kaou-yang as monarch of the empire. He made blibd men beat drums, and strike bells and sounding stones, at which phœnixes flapped their wings, and gambolled.

1 In his 1st year, when he came to the throne, he dwelt in Poh.   In his 16th year,
2 he made Ch'ung lead an army, and extinguish the State of Yew-kwae.   In his
3 45th year, he conferred on the prince of T'ang the appointment to be his successor.
4 In his 63d year, he died.

Note. The emperor's son Che was deposed, after having been appointed nine years.

yang must be derived from some place where he ruled; but two places of this name are assigned to him at different periods of his life:— the 1st in the pres. dis. of Ke, dep. of K'ae-fung, Ho-nan; the 2d in the dep. of Paou-ting, Chih-le.

2 This Puh was probably in the pres. dep. of Tung-ch'ang, Shan-tung.   3 Comp. 歷 象, in Can. of Yaou, p. 2. Some editions read 12th instead of 13th.   4 Hăng Ch'in-fung would remove this notice to the 20th year of Hwang-te.   5 This Pih K'wăn, or baron K'wăn, is commonly supposed to be the father of Yu the Great; but in that case K'wăn would be well on to 200 years old, when Yaou calls him to regulate the waters. T'ëen-muh was a mountain, '20,000 feet high,' acc. to the Classic of Mountains and Seas; and on the north of the Jŏ-water, acc. to one of the sporadic passages of the Bamboo Books, found elsewhere (是惟 若陽). 術器云云, generally appears as a note, but it belongs to the text. Shuh-k'e is said to have been a descendant of Shin-nung, and son of the emp. Kuh.

IV. 1 Kuh was the grandson of Yuen-heaou (元囂), one of Hwang-te's sons. Where the principality of Sin, from which he has his dynastic name, was, seems not to be known. See the dict. *in voc.* 2 This was probably what was afterwards the southern Pŏ. See introd. note to 'The Speech of T'ang.' 3 Yew-kwae was in the pres. dis. of Yung-yang, dep. of K'ae-fung. On who Ch'ung was, see the notes of Hăng Ch'in-fung. 4 The prince of T'ang is Yaou. See on the title of 'The Book of T'ang.' I must translate 錫唐侯命 as I have done. Comp. 錫虞舜命, under the 70th year of Yaou below. The difficulty in the way of the construction is the concluding note about the emperor's son Che; but this may be got over, by transferring it, as an appendix to this par. His appointment was to the succession, and his unworthiness being proved, his father himself deposed him from his place as heir, and gave the succession to his younger brother Yaou. Ch'in-fung argues for this construction, and re-arrangement of the text. I had adopted the construction, however, before reading his remarks.

洛○五十八年帝使后稷放帝子朱
山乘素車玄駒○五十三年帝祭于
年景星見于翼○五十年帝游于首
年春僬僥氏來朝貢沒羽○四十二
賓○
年十九年命共工治河○二十九
十二年初治兵○十六年渠搜氏來
○五年初巡狩四岳○七年有麟○
元年丙子帝即位居冀命羲和歷象
攀天而上高辛氏衰天下歸之夢
及長身長十尺有聖德封於唐
十四月而生堯於丹陵其狀如圖
翼宿既而陰風四合赤龍感之孕
餘長七尺二寸面銳上豐下足履
文要曰赤受天祐眉八彩鬢髮
常有龍隨之一旦龍負圖而至其
常有黃雲覆其上及長觀于三河
帝堯陶唐氏 母曰慶都生於斗維之野
竹書紀年卷之二

PART. II.

The reigns of Yaou and Shun.

I. EMPEROR YAOU; DYNASTIC TITLE, T'AOU AND T'ANG.

Note. His mother was called K'ing-too. She was born in the wild of Tow-wei, and was always overshadowed by a yellow cloud. After she was grown up, whenever she looked into any of the three Ho, there was a dragon following her. One morning the dragon came with a picture and writing. The substance of the writing was:—'The red one has received the favour of Heaven.' The eyebrows *of the figure* were like the character 八, and of varcigated colours. The whiskers were more then a cubit long; and the height was 7 cub. 2 in. The face was sharp above, and broad below. The feet trode on the constellation Yih. After this came darkness and winds on every side; and the red dragon made K'ing-too pregnant. Her time lasted 14 months, when she brought forth Yaou in Tan-ling. His appearance was like that in the picture. When he was grown up, his height was ten cubits. He had the virtue of a sage, and was invested with the principality of T'ang. He dreamed that he clinbed up to heaven. When Kaou-shin was decaying, the empire turned to him.

In his 1st year, which was *ping-tsze*[2] (13th of cycle;=B.C. 2,145), when he came to the throne, he dwelt in K'e;[3] and commanded He and Ho to make calendaric calculations and delineations *of the heavenly bodies*.[4]   In his 5th year, he made the first tour of inspection to the four mountains.   In his 7th year, there was a *k'e-lin*.   In his 12th year, he formed the first standing army.   In his 15th year, the chief of K'eu-sow came to make his submission.   In his 19th year, he ordered the minister of Works[8] to undertake the regulation of the Ho.   In his 29th year, the chief of the Pigmies[9] came to court in token of homage, and offered as tribute their feathers which sank in water.   In his 42d year, a brilliant star appeared in Yih [? Crater].   In his 59th year, he travelled for pleasure about mount Show,[10] in a plain carriage drawn by dark-coloured horses. In his 53d year, he sacrificed near the Loh.   In his 58th year, he caused

I. 1 See on 'The Songs of the Five Sons,' p. 7. 2 This is the 1st determination of a year by cycle names in the Annals. We fix the year to be B.C. 2,145, by calenlating back on the cycle from the 6th year of king Yew of Chow, which (as we have seen) is certainly known. I shall call attention below to the fact that all these cycle names of the years in the Annals were introduced into them after their recovery or discovery. 3 K'e is of course K'e-chow.

於丹水○六十一年、命崇伯鯀治河○六十

九年黜崇伯鯀○七十年春正月帝使四岳

錫虞舜命。

帝在位七十年景星出翼鳳凰在庭朱草

生嘉禾秀甘露潤醴泉出日月如合璧五

星如聯珠廚中自生肉其薄如箑搖動則

風生食物寒而不臭名曰箑脯又有草夾

階而生生月朔始生一莢及晦而盡月小

十六日以後日落一莢焉則五莢

一莢焦而不落名曰蓂莢一曰歷莢洪水

既平歸功於舜將以天下禪之乃潔齊修

壇場於河洛擇良日率舜等升首山遵河

渚有五老游焉蓋五星之精也相謂曰河

圖將來告帝以期知我者重瞳黃姚五老

因飛爲流星上入昴二月辛丑昧明禮備

風搖乃有龍馬銜甲赤文綠色緣壇而上

至於日昃榮光出河休氣四塞白雲起而

吐甲圖而去甲似龜背廣九尺其圓以白

玉爲檢赤玉爲柙泥以黃金約以青繩檢

文曰闓色授帝舜言虞夏當授天命率羣乃

寫其言藏於東序後二年二月仲辛率羣乃

12 his son Choo to be sent in banishment by prince Tseih to Tan-shwuy.   In his
13 61st year, he ordered the baron K'wan of Ts'ung to regulate the Ho.   In his 69th
14 year, he degraded K'wan.   In his 70th year, in the spring, in the 1st month, he
caused the *chief* of the four mountains to convey to Shun of Yu his charge *to succeed
to the throne.*

Note. When the emperor had been on the throne 70 years, a brilliant star issued from the constellation Yih, and phœnixes appeared in the courtyards of the palace; the pearl grass grew, and the admirable grain flourished; sweet dews moistened the ground, and crystal springs issued from the hills; the sun and moon appeared like a pair of gems, and the five planets looked like threaded pearls. In the *imperial* kitchen there appeared of itself a piece of flesh, as thin as a fan, which, when shaken, raised such a wind that all eatables were kept cool and did not spoil. It was called the fan flitch. A kind of grass, moreover, grew on each side of the palace stairs. On the 1st day of the month, it produced one pod, and so on, every day a pod, to the 15th; while on the 16th one pod fell off, and so on, every day a pod, to the last day of the month; and if the month was a short one (of 29 days), one pod shrivelled up, without falling. It was called the felicitous bean, and the calendar bean. When the flooded waters were assuaged, the emperor, attributing the merit of that to Shun, wished to resign in his favour. He thereon purified himself and fasted, built altars near the Ho and the Lŏ, chose a good day, and conducted Shun and others up mount Show. Among the islets of the Ho, there were five old men, walking about, who were the spirits of the five planets. They said to one another, 'The river scheme will come and tell the emperor of the time. He who knows us is the double-pupilled yellow Yaou.' The five old men on this flew away like flowing stars, and ascended into the constellation Maou. On the 2d month, on the sin-ch'ow day, between the dark and light, the ceremonies were all prepared; and when the day began to decline, a glorious light came forth from the Ho, and beautiful vapours filled all the horizon; white clouds rose up, and returning winds blew all about. Then a dragon-horse appeared, bearing in his mouth a scaly cuirass, with red lines on a green ground, ascended the altar, laid down the scheme, and went away. The cuirass was like a tortoise shell, nine cubits broad. The scheme contained a tally of white gem, in a casket of red gem, covered with yellow gold, and bound with a green string. On the tally were the words, 'With pleased countenance given to the emperor Shun'. It said also that Yu and Hëa should receive the appointment of Heaven. The emperor wrote these words, and deposited them in the Eastern college. Two years afterwards, in the 2d month, he led out all his ministers, and dropped a *peih* in the Lŏ. The ceremony over, he retired, and waited for the decline of the day. Then

It is a wide word.   4 See on Can. of Yaou, p. 2.   5 The 'four mountains' are those mentioned in the Can. of Shun, p. 8.   6 兵 is to be taken here in the sense of soldiers, and not merely as weapons of war.   7 See on 'The Tribute of Yu,' Pt. i., p. 83.

8 I should take 共工 as a proper name, but for the Can. of Shun, p. 21.   9 The nation of Pigmies, like the 'Perforated Breasts' and 'Long Legs,' is mentioned in the classic of the Hills and Seas. The 括地志 places it

帝舜有虞氏

意感而生舜於姚
母曰握登見大虹

帝子丹朱避舜于房陵舜讓不克朱遂
封于房爲虞賓三年舜即天子之位

十有二州○一百年、帝陟于陶。
九十年、帝游居于陶○九十七年、司空巡
建十有二州○八十九年、作游宮于陶○
六年、司空入觀贄用元圭○八十七年、初
七十六年、司空伐曹魏之戎克之○八十
初巡狩四岳○七十五年、司空禹治河○
春正月舜受終于文祖○七十四年虞舜
七十一年帝命二女嬪于舜○七十三年、
壇其書言當禪舜遂讓舜
臣沈璧于洛禮畢退俟至于下昃赤光起元龜貝書而出背甲赤文成字止于

虛目重瞳子故名重華龍顏大口黑色
身長六尺一寸舜父母憎舜使其塗廩
自下焚之舜服鳥工衣服飛去又使浚
井自上填之以石舜服龍工衣自旁而

a red light appeared; a tortoise rose from the waters, with a writing in red lines on its back, and rested on the altar. The writing said that he should resign the throne to Shun, which accordingly the emperor did.

15　In his 71st year, he commanded his two daughters to become wives to Shun.
16　In his 73d year, in the spring, in the 1st month, Shun received the resignation of the
17　emperor in *the temple of* the accomplished ancestor.　　In his 74th year, Shun of
18　Yu made his first tour of inspection to the four mountains.　　In his 75th year, Yu,
19　the superintendent of Works, regulated the Ho.　　In his 76th year, the super-
20　intendent of Works smote the hordes of Ts'aou and Wei,[12] and subdued them.　　In
his 86th year, the superintendent of Works had an audience, using for his article of
21　introduction a dark-coloured mace.　　In his 87th year, he instituted the division
22　*of the* empire into 12 provinces.　　In his 89th year, he made a pleasure palace in
23　T'aou.　　In his 90th year, he took up his residence for relaxation in T'aou.
24　In his 97th year, the superintendent of Works made a tour of survey through the 12
25　provinces.　　In his 100th year, he died in T'aou.

Note. The emperor's son Choo of Tan kept away from Shun in Fang-ling. Shun tried to yield the throne to him, but in vain. Choo was then invested with T'ang, and became the guest of Yu. After three years, Shun ascended the throne of the son of Heaven.

II.　THE EMPEROR SHUN; DYNASTIC TITLE YEW-YU.[1]

Note. His mother was named Uh-täng. She saw a large rainbow, and her thoughts were so affected by it, that she bore Shun in Yaou-heu. His eyes had double pupils, whence he was named 'Double Brightness.' He had a dragon countenance, a large mouth, and a black body, 6 cubits, 1 inch long. Shun's parents hated him. They made him plaster a granary, and set fire to it beneath:—he had on birds'-work clothes, and flew away. They also made him deepen a well, and filled it with stones from above:—he had on dragons'-work clothes, and got out by the side. He ploughed in Leih. He dreamed that his eyebrows were as long as his hair. Accordingly, he was raised and employed.

on the north of the Roman empire (在大秦國北). 10 Mount Show is the Luy-show of 'The Tribute of Yu,' Pt. ii. 1. 11 Tan-shwuy is referred to the pres. dis. of Nan-yang, dep. Nan-yang, Ho-nan. There was there, no doubt, a stream called Tan.

12 Ts'aou and Wei are two well known States in the time of the Chow;—the former lay in the pres. Shan-tung, the latter in Shen-se. I am not sure that those in the text were the same. They would seem too far apart.
II. 1 See note on the name of Part II. of the Shoo. 2 西王母,—lit., 'the mother

出耕於歷夢眉長於髮遂登庸

已未帝即位居冀作大韶之樂。
元年

三年命皐陶作刑○九年西王母來朝。

帝即位蓂莢生於階鳳凰巢於庭擊石拊石以
歌九韶百獸率舞景星出于房地出乘黃之馬

西王母之來朝
獻白環玉玦。

十四年卿雲見命禹代虞事。

在位十有四年奏鐘石笙管未罷而天大雷雨
疾風發屋拔木桴鼓播地鐘磬亂行舞人頓伏
一人之天下也亦乃見于鐘石笙筦乎乃薦禹
于天使行天子事也于時和氣普應慶雲典百工鳥
樂正狂走舜乃擁璿持衡而笑曰明哉天下非

若烟非烟若雲郁郁紛紛蕭索輪囷
相和而歌慶雲帝乃倡之曰慶雲爛兮糺縵縵
分日月光華旦復旦兮羣臣咸進稽首曰明明
上天爛然星陳日月有常星辰有行四時從經萬姓允誠
日日月月有行
之軒乎舞之精華以竭寨裳去之於是八風循鼓
子論樂配天之靈遷于聖賢莫不咸聽饗乎

1   In his 1st year, which was *ke-wei* (56th of cycle, = B.C. 2,042), when he came to the throne, he dwelt in K'e; and made the music called Ta-shaou.

Note. On his accession, the felicitous bean grew about the stairs, and phœnixes nested in the courts. When they beat and tapped the musical stones, to accompany the nine performances of the Shaou, all the beasts came after one another gambolling. A brilliant star came out in Fang. The earth produced the horse Shing-hwang.

2   In his 3d year, he commanded Kaou-yaou to make *the code of* punishments.

3 In his 9th year, *messengers* from the western Wang-moo 2 came to do homage.

Note. The coming to court from the western Wang-moo was to present white stone rings and archers' thimbles of gem.

4   In his 14th year, auspicious clouds appeared; and he ordered Yu to consult about affairs for him.

Note. In the 14th year of Shun's reign, at a grand performance with bells, musical stones, organs, and flutes, before the service was concluded, there came a great storm of thunder and rain. A violent wind overthrew houses, and tore up trees. The drumsticks and drums were scattered on the ground, and the bells and stones dashed about confusedly. The dancers fell prostrate, and the director of the music ran madly away; but Shun, keeping hold of the frames from which the bells and stones were suspended, laughed and said, 'How clear it is that the empire is not one man's empire! It is signified by these bells, stones, organs, and flutes.' On this he presented Yu to Heaven, and made him perform actions proper to the emperor; whereupon harmonious vapours responded on all sides, and felicitous clouds were seen. They were like smoke, and yet not smoke; like clouds, and yet not clouds; brilliantly confused; twisting and whirling. The officers in mutual harmony sang of those felicitous clouds, the emperor thus leading them on:—'How bright are ye, felicitous clouds! In what order are ye gathered together! The brightness of the sun and moon Is repeated from morn to morn. All the ministers then advanced, and bowing low, said:—'Brilliant are the heavens above, Where the shining stars are arranged. The brightness of the sun and moon Enlarge our one man.' The emperor sang again, 'The sun and moon are constant; The stars and other heavenly bodies have their motions. The four seasons observe their rule. The people are sincere in all their services. When I think of music, The intelligences that respond to Heaven Seem to be transferred to the sages and the worthies. All things listen to it. How do its rolling sounds thrill! How does it inspire the dance!' When the essential brightness was exhausted, the clouds shrivelled up and disappeared. Thereupon

of the king of the west,' or 'the queen-mother of the west.' But the characters are merely the name of a State or kingdom in the distant west. See Hăng's Comm. *in loc.*

3 The prince of Hea is Yu. See the introd. note on the name of the third Part of the Shoo.

通慶雲叢聚蟠龍
魚踊躍於其淵龜
奮迅於其藏蛟
鼇咸出其穴遷

虞而事夏舜乃設壇於河依堯故事至于下昃榮光休至黃龍負圖
長三十二尺廣九尺出于壇
畔赤文綠錯其文言當禪禹
十五年帝命夏后有事于太室○十
七年春二月入學初用萬○二十五
年息慎氏來朝貢弓矢○二十九年
帝命子義鈞封于商○三十年葬后
育于渭○三十二年帝命夏后總師
遂陟方岳○三十三年春正月夏后
受命于神宗遂復九州○三十五年
帝命夏后征有苗有苗氏來朝○四
十二年玄都氏來朝貢寶玉○四十
七年冬隕霜不殺草木○四十九年
帝居于鳴條○五十年帝陟。
義鈞封于商是謂商均后育娥皇
也鳴條有蒼梧之山帝崩遂葬焉
今海州

the eight winds all blew genially, and *other* felicitous clouds collected in masses. The crouching dragons came hurriedly out of their dens; iguanadons and fishes leaped up from their deeps; tortoises and turtles came out from their holes,—removing from Yu to serve Hea. Shun then raised an altar at the Ho, as Yaou had done before. When the day declined, there came a fine and glorious light; and a yellow dragon issued and came to the altar, bearing a scheme on his back, 32 cubits long and 9 cubits hroad, in lines of red and green intermingled, the words of which were that he should resign in favour of Yu.

5 In his 15th year, he commanded the prince of Hea to conduct the *sacrificial*
6 duties in the Grand apartment.   In his 17th year, in the spring, in the 2d month, when he entered the college, he used for the first time the myriad *dance*. 5
7 In his 25th year, the prince of Seih-shin came to do homage, and paid tribute of
8 bows and arrows.   In his 29th year, the emperor invested his son E-keun with
9 *the principality of* Shang.   In his 30th year, he buried queen Yuh near the Wei.

Note. Queen Yuh was Ngo-hwang.

10 In his 32d year, he commanded the prince of Hea to take the superintendence
11 of the people, who thereupon visited the mountains of the four quarters.7   In his 33d year, in the spring, in the first month, the prince of Hea received the appointment *to be successor*, in *the temple of* the spiritual ancestor; and restored the division
12 *of the empire* into nine provinces.   In his 35th year, he commanded the prince of Hea to lead a punitive expedition against the Yew-mëaou. The prince of Yew-
13 mëaou came to court and did homage.   In his 42d year, the chief of Heuen-too
14 came to court, and paid as tribute precious articles and gems.   In his 47th year,
15 the hoar-frosts of winter did not kill the grass or trees.   In his 49th year, he
16 dwelt in Ming-t'ëaou.8   In his 50th year, he died.

Note. E-keun had been invested with Shang, and is called Keun of Shang. Queen Yuh was Ngo-hwang. In Ming-t'ëaou was the hill of Ts'ang-woo. There Shun died and was buried. It is now Hae-chow.

4 The classic of Hills and Seas makes 太室 the name of a mountain. The meaning in the transl. is much preferable;—the principal apartment in the ancestral temple.
5 萬 is here the name of a dance (萬，舞名也).   6 Seih-shin;—elsewhere Suh-shin.   7 Comp. 'The Counsels of Yu,' p. 9. 夏后陟 is to be understood as the subject of lit. 'to ascend,' but here='to visit.'

8 See on the last par. of the Can. of Shun.—Some strange passages are gathered from other portions of the Bamboo Books, and supposed to have belonged to 'The Annals,' which give quite a different account of the relations between Yaou and Shun. They make Shun dethrone Yaou, and keep him a prisoner, raise Choo for a time to the throne, and then displace him; and thereafter allow no intercourse between father and son. See Hăng Ch'in-fung's Supplement to the Annals, in the last chapter of his Work.

竹書紀年卷之三

帝禹夏后氏　母曰修己出
行見流星貫
昂夢接意感既而吞神珠修己背
剖而生禹於石紐虎鼻大口兩耳
參鏤首戴鈎鈐胸有玉斗足文履
己故名文命長有聖德長九尺九
寸夢自洗於河取水飲之又有白
狐九尾之瑞當堯之世舜舉之禹
觀於河有長人白面魚身出曰吾
河精也呼禹曰文命治水言訖授
禹河圖言治水之事乃退入于淵
禹治水既畢天錫玄珪以告成功
夏道將興草木暢茂青龍止于郊
祝融之神降于崇山乃受舜禪即
天子之位洛出龜書是為
洪範三年喪畢都于陽城
元年壬子帝即位居冀〇
國〇二年咎陶薨〇五年巡狩會諸
侯于塗山。

PART. III.

The dynasty of Hea.

I. THE EMPEROR YU; DYNASTIC TITLE, HEA-HOW.

Note. His mother was called Sew-ke. She saw a falling star, which went through the constellation *Maou*, and in a dream her thoughts were moved till she became pregnant, after which she swallowed a spirits' pearl. Her back opened *in due time*, and she gave birth to Yu in Shih-new. He had a tiger nose and a large mouth. His ears had three orifices. His head bore *the resemblance of the stars* Kow and K'een. On his breast seemed a *figure* in gem of the Great Bear, and in the lines of his feet he seemed to tread on the character 己 ;—hence he was called Wǎn-ming. When he grew up, he had the virtue of a sage, and was 9 cub. 6 in. long. He dreamt that he was bathing in the Ho, and drank up the water. He had also the happy omen of a white fox with 9 tails. In the time of Yaou, Shun brought him forward. As he was looking at the Ho, a tall man, with a white face and fish's body, came out and said, 'I am the spirit of the Ho.' He then called Yu, and said, 'Wǎn-ming shall regulate the waters.' Having so spoken, he gave Yu a chart of the Ho, containing all about the regulating of the waters; and returned into the deep. When Yu had done regulating the waters, Heaven gave him a dark coloured mace, with which to announce his completed work. When the fortunes of Hea were about to rise, all vegetation was luxuriant, green dragons lay in the borders, and the spirit of Chuh-yung descended on mount Ts'ung:—Shun resigned, and Yu ascended the throne. The Lŏ produced the tortoise Book, called 'The great Plan.' When the three years of mourning were over, he made his capital in Yang-shing.

1　In his 1st year, which was *jin-tsze* (49th of cycle,=B.C. 1,989), when he came to the throne, he dwelt in K'e. He published the seasons of Hea throughout the

3　regions and States.　　In his 2d year, Kaou-yaou died.　　In his 5th year, he made a tour of inspection, and assembled the princes at mount T'oo.[1]

I. 1 Mount T'oo,—see on the 'Yih and Tseih', par. 8. 2 The name of Hwuy-k'e remains in the dis. so called, dep. of Shaou-hing, Chě-keang. Many wonderful stories are related of the chief of Fang-fung; but all agree that Yu killed him bẻcause he came late to the meeting.—Among other notices of Yu, which are not in the Annals, but are elsewhere found, quoted as from them, is this,—that ·from Hwang-te to Yu were 30 generations,' or reigns (黃帝至禹為世三十世). If this were ever really in the Annals, much of them must be lost.

117]

師征西河武觀來歸○十六年陟。
野○十一年放王季子武觀于西河
訟○十年帝巡狩舞九韶于天穆之
益薨祠之○八年帝使孟涂如巴涖
王帥師伐有扈大戰于甘○六年伯
侯于璿臺○二年費侯伯益出就國諸
于鈞臺諸侯從帝歸于冀都大饗諸
元年癸亥帝即位于夏邑大饗諸侯

帝啟

禹立四十五年禹薦益於天七
年禹崩三年喪畢天下歸啟

稽。
八年春會諸侯于會稽殺防風氏夏
六月雨金于夏邑秋八月帝陟于會

南巡狩濟江中流有二黃龍負舟
舟人皆懼禹笑曰吾受命于天屈
力以養人生性也死命也奚
憂龍哉龍于是曳尾而逝

Note. On his way to the south, when crossing the Këang, in the middle of the stream, two yellow dragons took the boat on their backs. The people were all afraid; but Yu laughed and said, 'I received my appointment from Heaven, and labour with all my strength to nourish men. To be born is the course of nature; to die is by *Heaven's* decree. Why be troubled by the dragons?' On this the dragons went away, dragging their tails.

4   In his 8th year, he assembled the princes at Hwuy-k'e,2 when he put the chief of Fang-fung to death. In the summer, in the 6th month, it rained gold in the *capital* city of Hea. In the autumn, in the 8th month, he died at Hwuy-k'e.

Note. Yu reigned (as associate, or as sovereign) 45 years. He presented Yih to Heaven, and died seven years after. When the three years of mourning were ended, the empire turned to K'e (his son).

II. THE EMPEROR K'E.

1   In his 1st year, which was *kwei-hae*1 (60th of cycle,=B.C. 1,978), when he came to the throne in the *capital* city of Hea,2 he made a great feast to the princes in the tower of Keun,3 after which they followed him back to the capital in K'e, when he
2   made a *second* great feast to them in the tower of Seuen.   In his 2d year, Pih-yih, the prince of Pe, left *the court*, and went to his State. The king led his forces
3   to punish the prince of Hoo, when there was a great battle in Kan.4   In his 6th
4   year, Pih-yih died, and *the emperor* appointed a sacrifice to him.5   In his 8th
5   year, he sent Mang T'oo to Pa, to preside over litigations.   In his 10th year, he
6   made a tour of inspection, and celebrated a complete service of Shun's music in the wilderness of T'een-muh.   In his 11th year, he banished his youngest son,
7   Woo-kwan, beyond the western Ho.   In his 15th year, Woo-kwan with the people about the western Ho rebelled. The baron Show of P'ang led a force to
8   punish them, when Woo-kwan returned to his allegiance.   In his 14th year, the king died.

II. 1 From 壬子, the 1st year of Yu, to this 癸亥, both inclusive, are twelve years; Yu must have died in 已未, leaving 3 complete years, before K'e's accession. This is the rule in these Annals all through the Hea dyn. The years of mourning are left between the deceased emperor and his successor; but this interregnum varies from 2 to 4 years.
2 This is the city in par. 4 of the last reign. Yu had moved his capital, or made a second one. A dis. of Kwei-tih dep. is still so called.

Near or in this was the tower of Keun. 諸侯從 may be construed by itself:—'the princes agreed to follow him;' as if the feast had been a political gathering to secure the throne to K'e. 4 See 'The Speech at Kan.' 5 This account does not agree with the account of the death of Yih, which is often attributed to the Annals, and which was no doubt in some of the Bamboo Books; viz. that 'Yih was aiming at the throne, and K'e put him to death' (益干啟立啟殺之).

118]

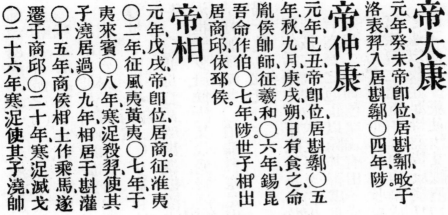

III. THE EMPEROR T'AE-K'ANG.

1   In his 1st year, which was *kwei-wei* (20th of cycle,=B.C. 1,957), when he came
to the throne, he dwelt at Chin-sin. He went hunting beyond the Loh, when E
2 entered and occupied Chin-sin.   In his 4th year, he died.

IV. THE EMPEROR CHUNG-K'ANG.

1   In his 1st year, which was *ke-ch'ow* (26th of cycle,=B.C. 1,951), when the em-
2 peror came to the throne, he dwelt in Chin-sin.   In his 5th year, in the autumn,
in the 9th month, on the day kăng-seuh (47th of cycle), which was the first day of
the month, there was an eclipse of the sun, when he ordered the prince of Yin to
3 lead the imperial forces to punish He and Ho.[1]   In his 6th year, he conferred
4 on *the prince of* Keun-woo the appointment of leader among the princes.[2]   In his
7th year, he died. His son Sëang went away, and dwelt in Shang-k'ew,[3] where he
was supported by the prince of P'ei.[4]

V. THE EMPEROR SEANG.

1   In his 1st year, which was *mow-seuh* (35th of cycle,=B.C. 1,942), when he came to
the throne, he dwelt in Shang;[1] and led a punitive expedition against the hordes of
2 the Hwae.   In his 3d year, he proceeded against the hordes of Fung and Hwang.
4   In his 7th year, the hordes of Yu came to make their submission.   In his
8th year, Han-tsuh put E to death, and made his own son Këaou dwell in Ko.[2]
6   In his 9th year, Seang dwelt in Chin-kwan.[3]   In his 15th year, Seang-
t'oo, the prince of Shang, prepared carriages and horses, and removed to Shang-
8 k'ew.   In his 20th year, Han-tsuh extinguished *the House of* Ko.[4]   In his
26th year, Han-tsuh made his son Këaou lead an army, and extinguish *the House of*

III. 1 The site of Chin-sin is not well ascertained. The dict. places it in the dis. of
Wei (濰縣) dep. of Lae-chow, Shan-tung.
Others—more correctly, I think,—refer it to the
dis. of Kung, dep. of Ho-nan. 2 See on 'The
Songs of the Five Sons.'
    IV. 1 See on the 'Punitive Expedition of
Yin.' 2 There is repeated mention below of
昆吾氏, and therefore I take the two
characters here as in the transl. The country
of Keun-woo was the 衞 of subsequent times.

伯 here=霸, chief or leader among the princes.
When the five *pa* are not all referred to the
dyn. of Chow, this chief of Keun-woo heads
the list. 3 Shang-k'ew is still the name of a
dis. in the dep. Kwei-tih. For 依邘侯
some copies read 依同姓諸侯斟
灌斟鄩.
    V. 1 *I. e.* in Shang-k'ew, the chief city of the
Shang family, which now begins to come into
prominence. 2 This Ko is ref. to the dis. of

而不為備少康使汝艾謀澆初浞娶純
之燼以伐浞浞恃澆娛日忘其惡
官職夏之遺臣伯靡自有鬲氏收二斟
旅能布其德而兆其謀以收夏衆撫其
之以二姚而邑諸綸有田一成有衆一
有虞為之庖正以除其害虞思於是妻
能戒之澆使椒求之將至仍少康逃奔
明年后緡生少康既長為仍牧正浞澆
歸于夏邑乙巳年
年子杼帥師滅戈〇伯靡殺寒浞少康自綸
浞世子少康使汝艾伐過殺澆甲辰〇伯
乙酉〇伯靡自鬲帥斟鄩斟灌之師以伐
夏世子少康生年丙寅〇少康自有仍奔虞
斟灌之墟是為帝邱后緡方娠逃出自竇歸于有仍伯靡奔有鬲氏
澆弑帝后緡歸于有仍伯靡出奔鬲
濰覆其舟滅之〇二十八年寒浞使其子
師滅斟灌〇二十七年澆伐斟鄩大戰于

9   Chin-kwan.   In his 27th year, Këaou attacked Chin-sin. There was a great battle in Wei, when the boat *of the prince of Chin-sin* was overturned, and he was

10 put to death.5   In his 28th year, Han-tsuh made his son Këaou murder the emperor. The empress Min fled to Yew-jing; 6 and Pih-mei made his escape, and fled to Kih.7

Note. The site of Chin-kwan was what was Te-k'ew. The empress Min, who was pregnant, made her escape by a hole, and returned to *her father, the prince of Jing.* Pih-mei fled to the chief of Kih.

11   The heir of the line of Hea, Shaou-k'ang, was born in the year *ping-yin* (=B.C.

12 1,914).   He fled from Yew-jing to Yu,9 in the year *yih-yew* (=B.C. 1,895).

13   Pih-mei led the forces of Chin-sin and Chin-kwan from Kih to attack Tsuh; and the heir-son Shaou-k'ang sent Joo-e to attack Ko; and put Këaou to death, in the year *këă-shin* (=B.C. 1,876). His eldest son, Ch'oo, led a force against Ko, and extin-

14 guished it.   Pih-mei put Han-tsuh to death, and Shaou-k'ang returned from Lun to the capital of Hea, in the year *yih-ke* (=B.C. 1,875).

Note. In the year after *her flight*, the empress Min gave birth to Shaou-k'ang, who became, when he was grown up, chief herdsman in Jing, and was on the watch against the evil designs of Keaou. Këaou having sent Tsëaou to look for him, Shaou-k'ang fled, before his arrival, to Yu, where he became chief cook. Sze, *the prince* of Yu, gave him his two daughters in marriage, and the city of Lun. There his fields were a *le* square; and his followers amounted to 500. He displayed his virtue, and formed his plans to collect the multitudes of Hea, and raise the hopes of the old officers. An old servant of Hea, called Pih-mei, issuing from Kih, collected all the people that were left of the two Chin, to attack Tsuh. Tsuh trusted in Këaou, and felt quite at ease, giving no thought to his wickedness, and making no preparations. *At the same time,* Shaou-k'ang sent Joo-e to spy out Keaou's condition. Now Tsuh had married a daughter of Shun-woo, by whom he had a son who died early, leaving a widow called Neu-k'e. Këaou obliged *one* Yu to go to her house, and pretend that he had something to ask of her. On this Neu-k'e mended his lower clothes, and they passed the night in the same house. Joo-e sent a party, took them by surprise, and cut off the head of Neu-k'e. Keaou, being very strong and swift, *made his escape;* E then

Yih (㧍縣) in Lae-chow. Këaou and a brother are said to have been the sons of Han-tsuh by the wife of E; but they must have been born before E's death. See concluding note in Pt. III. of the Shoo. 3 Chin-kwan is ref.—but not certainly—to the dis. of Show-kwang, dep. Ts'ing-chow, Shan-tung. 4 This Ko lay between the States of Sung and Ch'ing. 5 This Chin-sin would agree with the dis. of Wei. Were there two places of the same name? 6 Yew-jing was in the pres. sub. dep. of Tung-p'ing, dep. of T'ae-ngan, Shan-tung. 7 Kih was in the pres. dis. of P'ing-yuen, dep. Tse-nan.

120]

侯或作帝寧一曰伯杼杼能
帥禹者也故夏后氏報焉

杼或作帝寧一曰伯杼杼能

元年己巳帝即位居原○五年自原遷于老邱○
八年征于東海及三壽得一狐九尾○十三年商
侯冥死于河○十七年陟。

帝杼

后稷之後不窋失官至是而復
十一年使商侯冥治河○十八年遷于原○二十
一年陟。

元年丙午帝即位諸侯來朝賓虞公○二年方夷
來賓○三年復田稷。

帝少康

狐氏有子旱死其婦曰女岐寡居澆強圉往至
其戸陽有所求女岐為之縫裳共舍而宿汝艾
夜使人襲斷其首乃女岐也澆既多力又善走
艾乃田獵放犬逐獸因嗾澆顛隕乃斬澆以歸
于少康於是夏眾滅浞奉少康歸于夏邑諸
侯始聞之立為天子祀夏配天不失舊物

hunted him, and let loose a dog, which seized him, so that he fell, when they cut off his head, with which E returned to Shaou-k'ang. After this the multitudes of Hea put Tsuh to death, and carried Shaou-k'ang back to the capital. As soon as the princes heard of it, they raised him to the throne, to sacrifice to his ancestors along with the sacrifices to Heaven; and thus the old possession was not lost.

VI. THE EMPEROR SHAOU-K'ANG.

1 In his 1st year, which was *ping-woo* (43d of cycle, =B.C. 1,874), when he came to the throne, the princes came to court to do homage. He entertained the duke of Yu
2 as his guest.   In his 2d year, the hordes of Fang came to make their submission.
3 In his 3d year, he restored *the descendant of prince* Tseih, the minister of Agriculture.

Note. Puh-f'uh, a descendant of prince Tseih, had lost the office, which was now restored.

5 In his 11th year, he caused Ming, the prince of Shang, to regulate the Ho.   In
6 his 18th year, he removed to Yuen.[2]   In his 21st year, he died.

VII. THE EMPEROR CH'OO.

1 In his 1st year, which was *ke-sze* (6th of cycle, = B.C. 1,851), when he came to
2 the throne, he dwelt in Yuen.   In his 5th year, he removed from Yuen to Laou-
3 k'ew.   In his 8th year, he went on a punitive expedition towards the eastern
4 sea, as far as San-show, and got a fox with 9 tails.   In his 13th year, Ming, the
5 prince of Shang, died, *pursuing his labours* on the Ho.   In his 17th year, he died.

Note. The name Ch'oo is written with a difft. character (宁). The emperor is also called Pih-ch'oo. *There was a younger brother*, a worthy descendant of Yu, who was therefore rewarded by the emperor.

Who Mei was is all uncertain. He had been, say many, an adherent of E. This is very unlikely. He appears here a strong partizan of the House of Hea.   9 Yu was in the pres. dis. of Yu-shing, dep. Kwei-tih.
VI. 1 The descendant of Tseih here intended,

as restored to the ministry of Agriculture, was probably the famous Kung-lew.   2 Yuen is ref. to the pres. dis. of Tse-yuen, dep. Hwae-k'ing, Ho-nan.
VII. 1 Laou-k'ew is referred to the dis. of Ch'in-lew, dep. of K'ae-fung.

121]

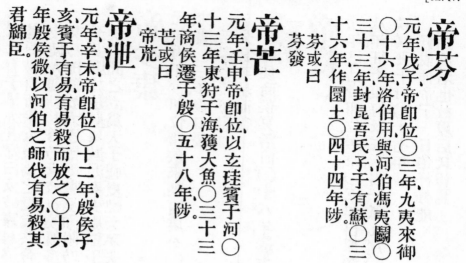

君綿臣。
年殷侯微以河伯之師伐有易殺其
亥賓于有易有易殺而放之○十六
元年辛未帝卽位○十二年殷侯子
帝泄
帝荒
芒或曰
芒荒
年商侯遷于殷○五十八年陟。
十三年東狩于海獲大魚○三十三
元年壬申帝卽位以玄珪賓于河○
帝芒
芬或曰
芬發
十六年作圜土○四十四年陟。
三十三年封昆吾氏子于有蘇○三
○十六年洛伯用與河伯馮夷鬪○
元年戊子帝卽位○三年九夷來御
帝芬

VIII. THE EMPEROR FUN.

1 　　His 1st year was *mow-tsze* (25th of cycle, = B.C. 1,832), when he came to the
2 throne. 　　In his 2d year, the 9 wild tribes of the east came to perform service.
3 　　In his 16th year, Yung, the baron of Loh, fought with Fung-e, the baron of Ho.2
5 　　In his 33d year, he appointed the son of the chief of Keun-woo to Soo.3　　In
6 his 36th year, he made a circular enclosure *for a prison*.4　　In his 44th year, he
died.

Note. Fun is by some called Fun-fă.

IX. THE EMPEROR MANG.

1 　　In his 1st year, which was *jin-shin* (9th of cycle, = B.C. 1,788), when he came to
2 the throne, he *went* with the dark-coloured mace to receive the *baron of* Ho.1　　In
his 13th year, on a tour of inspection to the east as far as the sea, he got a large fish.
4 　　In his 33d year, the prince of Shang removed to Yin.2　　In his 58th year, he
died.

Note. Mang is in some editions called the emperor Hwang.

X. THE EMPEROR SËEH.

1 　　His 1st year was *sin-wei* (8th of cycle, = B.C. 1,729), when he came to the throne.
2 　　In his 12th year, Tsze-hae, prince of Yin, went as guest to Yew-yih, the chief of
3 which put him to death, and sent away *his followers*.　　In his 16th year, Wei,
prince of Yin, with the forces of the baron of Ho, attacked Yew-yih,1 and killed its
ruler Mëen-chin.

VIII. 1 夷 is to be taken here in its proper meaning of 'wild tribes of the east.' 御＝侍 御, 'to wait upon and serve,'—perhaps as warders, guards, &c. 2 Fung-e appears in many writers as a monster or spiritual being. He is evidently in the text merely the chief of the State Ho, or charged with the care of the Ho. 3 Soo was in Tse·yuen, above. 4 All prisons, it is said, in the three dynasties, were circular.

IX. 1 I have translated acc. to the view of Hăng Ch'in-fung:—以元珪往聘河 伯耳; but perhaps some service to the Ho is meant. The mace is that of Yu the Great. 2 This Yin is ref. to the dis. of Shang-shwuy, dep. Ch'in-chow.

X. 1 There is a small dep. in Chih-le, called Yih-chow, which may correspond to the ancient Yew-yih.

殷侯子亥賓于有易而淫焉有易之君
綿臣殺而放之故殷侯上甲微假師于
河伯以伐有易滅之遂殺其君綿臣
中葉衰而上甲微復興故殷人報焉
二十一年命畎夷白夷玄夷風夷赤夷黃
夷〇二十五年陟

帝不降
元年己亥帝即位〇六年伐九苑〇三十
五年殷滅皮氏〇五十九年遜位于弟扃

帝扃
元年戊戌帝即位〇十年帝不降陟。
三代之世內禪惟
不降實有聖德

帝廑
一名胤甲
十八年陟。
元年己未帝即位居西河〇四年作西音。

Note. The prince of of Yin, Tsze-hae, visited Yew-yih, and was guilty of licentious conduct, so that the ruler of Yew-yih, Mëen-chin, slew him, and drove *his followers* away. In consequence of this, Shang-këä-wei of Yin obtained the services of the army of the baron of Ho, attacked and extinguished the State of Yew-yih, putting Mëen-chin to death. For a time Yin had decayed, but when Shang-këä-wei revived its power, the people avenged the wrong that had been done.

4 In his 21st year, he conferred regular dignities on the chiefs of the hordes of
5 K‘euen, of the white hordes, the dark hordes, the hordes of Fung, the red hordes, and the yellow hordes.   In his 25th year, he died.

XI. THE EMPEROR PUH-KËANG.

1 His 1st year, was *ke-hae* (36th of cycle, = B.C. 1,701), when he came to the
2 throne.   In his 6th year, he attacked *the country of* Kew-yuen.[1]   In his
4 35th year, Yin made an end of the House of P‘e.[2]   In his 59th year, he resigned the throne to his younger brother Këung.

XII. THE EMPEROR KËUNG.

1 His 1st year, was *mow-seuh* (35th of cycle, = B.C. 1,642), when he came to the
2 throne.   In his 10th year, the emperor Puh-këang died.

Note. In the period of the three dynasties there was only one resignation of the throne,—that by Puh-këang. He must have had the virtue of a sage.

3 In his 18th year, he died.

XIII. THE EMPEROR KIN.

Note. Also called Yin-këä.

1 In his 1st year, which was *ke-wei* (56th of cycle, = B.C. 1,621), ·when he came
2 to the throne, he dwelt on the west of the Ho.[1]   In his 4th year, he made the music of the West.   The chief of Keun-woo removed to Heu.[2]

XI. 1 Kew-yuen=the 'nine pasturages,' probably a tract of flat country in the pres. Chih-le.
2 The territory of P‘e was in the pres. dis. of Ho-tsin, dep. Keang Chow, Shan-se. It is observed that the extinction of this State was the 1st step of the kind, taken by Shang, to the imperial sway.
XIII. 1 That is, he lived in Shen-se. 'The western Ho' denotes the country west of K‘e-chow.   2 Heu corresponded, probably, to the pres. Heu Chow, Ho-nan.

昆吾氏遷于許。巳姓名樊封于衞夏衰爲伯遷于舊許。

八年天有祅孽十日並出、其年陟。

帝孔甲

元年乙巳帝卽位居西河廢豕韋氏使劉累豢龍○三年王畋于萯山○五年作東音○七年劉累遷于魯陽

王好事鬼神肆行淫亂諸侯化之夏政始衰田于東陽萯山天大風晦盲孔甲迷惑入于民室主人方乳或曰后來見貢日也之子必有殃孔甲聞之曰以爲余一人子夫誰殃之乃取其子以歸大吉或又曰不勝也之子必有殃孔甲聞之必曰以爲余一人子夫誰殃之乃取其子以歸旣長爲斧所妷乃作破斧之歌是爲東音旣而使求之懼而遷于魯陽其後爲范氏累所畜龍一雌死潛醢以食夏后夏后饗之

九年陟。殷侯復歸于商邱。

帝昊
昊一作皋

Note. The surname *of the founder of Keun-woo* was Ke, and his name Tan. He had been invested with Wei, and when Hea was decaying, *the chief of the House* was Head of the princes, and removed to old Heu.

5   In his 8th year, there was an inauspicious portent in the sky;—ten suns appeared together. In that year the emperor died.

XIV. THE EMPEROR K'UNG-KEA.

1   In his 1st year, which was *yih-sze* (mistake for *ke-sze*, 6th of cycle,=B.C. 1,611), when he came to the throne, he dwelt on the west of the Ho. He displaced the
2   chief of Ch'e-wei, and appointed Lew-luy to feed the dragons.[1]   In his 3d year,
3   the king hunted on mount Foo.[2]   In his 5th year, he made the music of the East.
4   In his 7th year, Lew Luy removed to Loo-yang.[3]

Note. The king was superstitious, and acted in a disorderly and licentious way. The princes became like him, and the govt. of Hea began to go to decay. He was hunting on mount Foo of Tung-yang, when in a great wind the sky was all overcast. The emperor lost his way, and went into the family of a peasant, whose wife had just been confined. Some said, 'The emperor has come to see you;—it is a good day. This child will have great good fortune.' Some said, 'Not so. This child will be unfortunate.'—When K'ung-kёа heard this, he said, 'Let it be the child of me, the emperor; then who can harm it?' Accordingly he took the child with him; but when it was grown up, it was killed by a hatchet, on which he made the song of 'Break the Hatchet;'—what is called 'The music of the East.'

A female dragon of those which Lew Luy had the keeping of died, when he privately made pickle of it, and set it before the emperor, who enjoyed it; and ordered Luy to look for the missing dragon. Luy was afraid, and removed to Loo-yang, where his descendants became the Fan family.

5   In his 9th year, he died. The prince of Yin returned to Shang-k'ew.

XV. THE EMPEROR HAOU.

Note. Also called Kaou.

XIV. 1 The State of Ch'e-wei is ref. to a place in the dep. of Ta-ming, Chih-le. It is hard to say what is meant by feeding the dragons, though there are many legends about it.   2 It is strange how the title of 'king' is here employed for 'emperor.'   3 Or 'to the south of mount Loo;'—in the pres. dis. of Loo-san, dep. Joo-chow, Ho-nan.

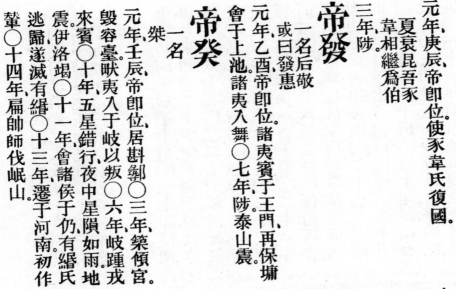

元年庚辰帝即位使豕韋氏復國。
夏衰昆吾豕韋相繼爲伯
三年陟。

帝發
一名后敬或曰發惠
元年乙酉帝即位諸夷賓于王門。再保
會于上池諸夷入舞〇七年陟泰山震。

帝癸
一名桀
元年壬辰帝即位居斟鄩〇三年築傾宮。
毀容臺畎夷入于岐以叛〇六年岐踵戎
來賓〇十年五星錯行夜中星隕如雨地
震伊洛竭〇十一年會諸侯于仍有緡氏
逃歸遂滅有緡〇十三年遷于河南初作
輦〇十四年扁帥師伐岷山

1   His 1st year was *kang-shin* (17th of cycle,=B.C. 1,600), when he came to the throne.   He restored the representative of the House of Ch'e-wei to his State.

Note. In the decay of the Hëa, chiefs of Keun-woo and Ch'e-wei succeeded one another as Head of the princes.

2   In his 3d year he died.

XVI. THE EMPEROR FAH.

Note. Also called the emperor King; and Fă-hwuy.

1   In his 1st year, which was *yih-yew* (22d of cycle,=B.C. 1,595), when he came to the throne, various wild tribes came and made their submission at the king's gate.[1] He again repaired the walls.   There was a meeting on the upper pool, when the wild
2   people came in, and performed their dances.   In his 7th year, he died.   Mount T'ae shook.

XVII. THE EMPEROR KWEI.

Note. Called also Këĕ.

1   In his 1st year, which was *jin-shin* (29th of cycle,=B.C. 1,588), when he came to
2   the throne, he dwelt in Chin-sin.   In his 3d year, he built the K'ing palace, and pulled down the Yung tower.[2]   The K'euen hordes penetrated as far as K'e, with
3   the standard of revolt.[3]   In his 6th year, the hordes of K'e-chung[4] came to
4   make their submission.   In his 10th year, the five planets went out of their courses. In the night, stars fell like rain. The earth shook. The E and Loh became
5   dry.   In his 11th year, he assembled the princes in Jing, when the chief of Yew-min
6   fled home, on which the emperor extinguished Yew-min.[5]   In his 13th year, he removed to the south of the Ho.[6] He made for the first time men-drawn carriages.[7]
7   In his 14th year, Pëen led the imperial forces, and smote Min-san.[8]

xv. 1 王門 should probably be 玉門, 'the gate of gems,'—one of the gates of the palace, so called.

xvi. 1 The meaning of 再保至池 is very much debated. See Hăng Ch'in-fung, *in loc.*

xvii. 1 This, no doubt, was in the dis. of Kung, dep. Ho-nan.   2 For conjectures on the meaning of the names here , see Hăng, *in loc.*

3 Hăng thinks this par. belongs to the reign of king Muh or king E of Chow.   4 The country of K'e-chung, (岐=跂) or 'the people who walked on their toes,' without the heel touching the ground, is placed beyond the Moving sands.   5 See on the time of Shaou-k'ang.   The Min *family* occupied the State of Jing.   6. Some city is intended; but commentators are not agreed which.   7 These

癸命扁伐山民山民進女于桀二人
曰琬曰琰后愛二人女無子焉斲其
名于苕華之玉苕是琬華是琰而棄
其元妃于洛曰妹喜於傾宮飾瑤臺
之居

十五年商侯履遷于亳〇十七年商使
伊尹來朝〇二十年伊尹歸于商及汝
鳩汝方會于北門〇二十一年商師征
有洛克之遂征荊荊降〇二十二年商
侯履來朝命囚履于夏臺〇二十三年
釋商侯履諸侯遂賓于商〇二十六年
商滅溫〇二十八年昆吾氏伐商商會
諸侯于景亳遂征韋商師取韋遂征顧
太史令終古出奔商〇二十九年商師
取顧三日竝出費伯昌出奔商冬十月
鑿山穿陵以通于河〇三十年瞿山崩
殺其大夫關龍逢商師征昆吾冬聆隧
災〇三十一年商自陑征夏邑克昆吾

Note. Some copies read San-min, or hill-people. Kwei ordered Pëen to attack San-min, whose prince presented Kĕĕ with two ladies, called Yuen and Yen. The emperor loved them, tho' they had no children; and had their names cut on the gems Teaou and Hwa. That on the T‘eaou was Yuen; on the Hwa, Yen. He also sent away his first wife Me-he to Lŏ, placing her in the Yaou tower of the K‘ing palace.

In his 15th year, Le, prince of Shang, removed to Poh.9

Note. This was the 1st year of T‘ang the Successful.

In his 15th year, Shang made E Yin come to court.　　In his 20th year, E Yin, returning to Shang, met with Joo Kew and Joo Fang at the north gate.　　In his 21st year, the forces of Shang went on a punitive expedition against the prince of Lŏ, and subdued him. They then went against King,10 which made submission.　　In his 22d year, Le, prince of Shang, came to court, when the emperor ordered him to be imprisoned in the tower of Hea.11　　In his 23d year, he set Le at liberty, when the princes went and offered their submission to Shang.　　In his 26th year, Shang extinguished Wun.12　　In his 28th year, the chief of Keun-woo attacked Shang. Shang assembled the princes in King-poh13 and proceeded against Wei, which its forces took. They then proceeded against Koo. The Grand recorder Chung Koo left the court and fled to Shang.　　In his 29th year, the forces of Shang took Koo.15 Three suns appeared together. The prince of Pe, Ch‘ang, left the court and fled to Shang.　　In the winter, in the 10th month, they chisselled through mountains, and tunnelled hills, to open a communication with the Ho.16　　In his 30th year, there was a fall of mount K‘eu.17 *The emperor* put to death his great officer Kwan Lung-fung. The forces of Shang marched to punish Keun-woo. In the winter, there was a fire in Ling-suy.18

In his 31st year, Shang proceeded by way of Urh against the capital of Hea; and overcame Keun-woo. Amid great thunder and rain a battle was fought in Ming-

carriages are said to have been made for Me-he, Kĕĕ's wife.　　8 The comm. identify this Min-san with a Mung-san (蒙山);—perhaps corresp. to Mung-san, dep. Ya-chow, in Sze-ch‘uen.　　9 This was the 'southern Pŏ.' 10 King;— known afterwards as Ts‘oo.

11 This was a State prison;—near Chin-sin. 12 The pres. dis. of Wun, dep. Hwae-k‘ing. 13 This is said to have been the 'northern Pŏ.'　　14 Probably=Ch‘e-wei.　　15 Supposed to have been in pres. dis. of Wun-ching, dep. Ts‘aou-chow, Shan-tung.　　16 This should not have been done in the winter.

大雷雨、戰于
鳴條、夏師敗
績、桀出奔三
腆、商師征三
腆、戰于郕、獲
桀、戰于焦門、放
之于南巢。

自禹至桀
十七世有桀
王與無王
用歲四百
七十
一年

t‘eaou, when the army of Hea was defeated. Këeh fled away to San-tsung,[19] against which the army of Shang proceeded. A battle was fought at Ching,[20] and Këeh was taken in Tsëaou-mun. He was then banished away to Nan-ch‘aou.

Note. From Yu to Këĕ were 17 reigns. Calculating reigns and interregnums, the dynasty lasted 471 years.

17 K‘eu is better known as mount Chin 岑 山). 18 See the comment of Sun Che-luh, cited by Hăng. For 聆 some read 聆.

19 San-tsung is ref. to the dis. of Ting-t‘aou, dep. Ts‘aou-chow. 20 In the sub. dep. of Tung-p‘ing, T‘ae-ngan.

于之壇沈湯在亳能修其德伊摯將應湯命夢乘船過日月之旁湯乃東至于洛觀帝堯壇化爲黑玉又有黑龜並赤文成字

日生湯號天乙豐下銳上晳而有顣句身而揚聲長九尺臂有四肘是爲成湯

功於民受封於商後十三世生主癸之妃曰扶都見白氣貫月意感以乙吞之遂孕胸剖而生契長爲堯司徒成

甚好二人競取覆以玉筐簡狄先得而

分玄鳥至之日從帝祀郊禖與其妹浴于玄邱之水有玄鳥銜卵而墜之五色

至乃同尊天乙履爲天子三讓遂卽天子之位初高辛氏之世妃曰簡狄以春

侯八譯而來者千八百國奇肱氏以車

湯有七名而九征放桀于南巢而還諸

履名

殷商成湯

竹書紀年卷之四

PART. IV.

The Dynasty of Shang.

1. T'ANG THE SUCCESSFUL, OF SHANG OR YIN.

Note. His name was Le. T'ang, *indeed*, had 7 names, and conducted 9 punitive expeditions. When he returned from confining Këë in Nan-ch'aou, the princes, having 8 interpreters, came to him, to the number of 1,800. The chief of the 'Wonderful Arms' also came in his chariot. They all wished him, Teen-yih Le, to assume the imperial dignity, to which, after declining thrice, he acceded.

In ancient times, the empress of Kaou-sin, called Këen-teih, at the vernal equinox, when the dark swallow made its appearance, had followed her husband to the suburbs to pray for a son, and was bathing with her sister in the Water of Heuen-k'ew, when a dark swallow dropt from her mouth a beautifully variegated egg. The two sisters strove to cover it with baskets which they had; but Këen-teih succeeded in getting it. She swallowed it, became pregnant, and by-and-tion by her chest opened, and she gave birth to Sëĕ. When he grew up, he was minister of Instruction to Yaou, who conferred on him the principality of Shang because of his services to the people.

After 13 generations, Sëĕ's descendant, Choo-kwei, was born, whose wife was called Foo-too. She saw a white vapour go through the moon; was moved to pregnancy; and on the day Yih bore T'ang, who was therefore styled T'ëen-yih. The lower part of his face was broad, and it tapered above;—it was white and whiskered. His body was one-sided, and his voice was loud. He was 9 cubits high, and his arms had four joints. He became T'ang the Successful.

T'ang lived in Pŏ, and cultivated his virtue. When E Chi was about to comply with T'ang's invitation, he dreamed that he passed by the sun and moon in a boat.

T'ang came east to Lŏ, to see the altar of Yaou. He dropped a gem in the water, and stood at some distance. Lo! yellow fishes leaped up in pairs; a black bird followed him, and stood on the altar, where it changed into a black gem. There was also a black tortoise, with red lines forming characters, which said that Këë of Hea was unprincipled, and that T'ang should supersede him. At the same time, the spirit of T'aou-wuh was seen on mount P'ei. Another spirit, dragging a white wolf, with a hook in his mouth, entered the court of Shang. The virtue of metal waxed powerful:

二年陟。

元年乙亥王即位居亳命卿士伊尹○

名勝

外丙

十九年陟。

獻令○二十七年遷九鼎于商邑○二

林雨○二十五年作大濩樂初巡狩定

三年大旱○二十四年大旱王禱于桑

大旱鑄金幣○二十二年大旱○二十

夏桀卒于亭山禁弦歌舞○二十一年

十九年大旱氏羌來賓○二十年大旱。

十八年癸亥王即位居亳始屋夏社

改天下之號曰殷

桀夢及天而舓之遂有天下商人後

金德將盛銀自山溢湯將奉天命放

于邳山有神牽白狼銜鉤而入商朝

言夏桀無道湯當代之禱杭之神見

silver overflowed from the hills. When T'ang was about to put Kёё away, in reverence of the command of Heaven, he dreamed that he went to the sky, and licked it. After this he became possessor of the empire. The people of Shang afterwards changed the title of the dynasty into Yin.

1 In his 18th year, which was *kwei-hae* (60th of cycle,=B.C. 1,557), when he came to the throne, he dwelt in Poh.2 He roofed over, for the first time, the altar to the 2 spirits of the land dedicated by the House of Hea.3   In his 19th year, there was a great drought. The people of Te-kёang came and made their submission.4

3 In his 20th year, there was a great drought. Kёeh of Hea died at mount T'ing, when 4 it was forbidden to play on stringed instruments, to sing and to dance.   In his 6 21st year, there was the great drought. He cast metal money5   In his 22d and 7 23d years, the drought continued.   In his 24th year, the drought still continuing, 8 the king prayed in the mulberry forest, and it rained.6   In his 25th year, he made the music of Ta-hoo.7 He went for the first time on a tour of inspection, and 9 fixed the rules for offerings.   In his 27th year, he removed the nine vases to the 10 capital of Shang.   In his 29th year, he died.

II. WAE-PING.

Note. Named Shing.

1   In his 1st year, which was *yih-hae* (12th of cycle, = B.C. 1,545), when the king 1 came to the throne, he dwelt in Poh; and confirmed the appointment of E Yin as 2 prime minister.2   In his 2d year, he died.

I. 1 The years of T'ang are counted from his accession to the principality of Shang, B.C. 1,574.   2 This was, probably, the western Pŏ,—in the pres. dis. Yen-sze, dep. Ho-nan. 3 T'ang had wished to remove the altars of Hea. Diverted from that purpose, he 'housed' them, or roofed them over,—to remain a monument of the justice of Heaven.   4 See in the She, the 5th of the Praise-songs of Shang.

5 This is understood to have been done for the poor, that they might redeem their children whom they had sold in the famine.   6 See the prayer of. T'ang, from Mih-tsze, in the proleg. to Mencius, pp. 116,117. It is singular

the Shoo says nothing of this drought. Sze-ma Ts'een says it lasted 7 years; the Ch'un-Ts'ew of Leu, 5 years; these Annals, 6 years. Ts'een makes Shwang-lin the name of a wilderness; others say—'the wood of mt. Shwang.'   7

大濩＝大護, 'great salvation;'—celebrating T'ang's exploits and prayers.

II. 1 王, 'king,' here replaces 帝, applied in these Annals to the sovereigns of Hea.   2 We must take 命 here in this way. See Hăng, *in loc.*

絢名 沃丁　十年大饗于太廟初祀方明○十二年陟。　不類蓋後世所益　約按此文與前後　于伊陟、伊奮命復其父之田宅而中分之。　七年王潛出自桐殺伊尹、天大霧三日乃立其　誤以攝政爲眞爾　約按伊尹自立蓋　甲于桐乃自立。　元年辛巳王卽位居亳命卿士伊尹、伊尹放太　至名　太甲　元年丁丑王卽位居亳命卿士伊尹○四年陟。　庸名　仲壬

III. Chung-jin.

Note. Named Yung.

1 In his 1st year, which was *ting-ch'ow* (14th of cycle, = B.C. 1,543), when he came
2 to the throne, he dwelt in Poh, and confirmed the appointment of E Yin.   In his
4th year, he died.

IV. T'ae-kĕah.

Note. Named Che.

1 In his 1st year, which was *sin-sze* (18th of cycle, = B.C. 1,539), when he came to
the throne, he dwelt in Poh, and confirmed the appointment of E Yin. E Yin sent
T'ae-kĕah away, and confined him in T'ung, seizing the throne himself.[1]

Note by Yŏ. It is a mistake to say this. The truth is that he only acted as regent.

2 In his 7th year, the king privately escaped from T'ung, and put E Yin to death.
The sky was overspread with mists for three days, when he raised to office Yin's sons,
E Chih and E Fun, ordered their father's fields and houses to be restored, and equally
divided between them.

Note by Yŏ. This par. does not accord with the text before and after it. It is, probably, the
addition of an after time.

3 In his 10th year, he celebrated a great service to all his ancestors in the Grand
ancestral temple. For the first time he sacrificed to the Intelligences of the *four*
4 quarters.[2]   In his 12th year, he died.

V. Yuh-ting.

Note. Named Heuen.

IV. 1 This and the next notice are so difft.
from the current and classical accounts of E
Yin and T'ae-kĕä, that the friends of these
Annals are in great perplexity about them.
Hăng Ch'in-fung would refer them to the
'Fragmentary Words' of the Bamboo Books.
Seu Wăn-tsing contents himself with saying,
after the original commentator, that they are
the additions of a later hand.

2 方明＝四方之神明. This
is the easiest interpretation. Some suppose the
六宗 of Can. of Shun, p. 5, to be meant.

小庚

元年、癸巳王即位、居亳命卿士咎單○八年、
祠保衡○十九年陟。

辨名

小甲

元年、壬子王即位、居亳○五年陟。

高名

雍巳

元年、丁巳王即位、居亳○十七年陟。

佃名

太戊

元年、甲戌王即位、居亳○十二年陟。

密名

元年、丙戌王即位、居亳命卿士伊陟臣扈○

1　In his 1st year, which was *kwei-sze* (30th of cycle, = B.C. 1,527), when he came to the throne, he dwelt in Poh; and confirmed the appointment of Kaou Shen as prime
3　minister.　　In his 8th year, he appointed sacrifices to Paou-hang.[1]　　In his 19th year, he died.

VI. SĔAOU-KANG.

Note. Named Pĕen.

1　In his 1st year, which was *jin-tsze* (49th of cycle, = B.C. 1,508), when he came to
2　the throne, he dwelt in Poh.　　In his 5th year, he died.

VII. SĔAOU-KĔAH.

Note. Named Kaou.

1　In his 1st year, which was *ting-sze* (54th of cycle, = B.C. 1,503), when he came to
2　the throne, he dwelt in Poh.　　In his 17th year, he died.

VIII. YUNG-KE.

Note. Named Tĕen.

1　In his 1st year, which was *kĕah-seuh* (11th of cycle, = B.C. 1,486), when he came to
2　the throne, he dwelt in Poh.　　In his 12th year, he died.

IX. T'AE-MOW.

Note. Named Meih.

1　In his 1st year, which was *ping-seuh* (23d of cycle, = B.C. 1,474), when he came to the throne, he dwelt in Poh, and confirmed the appointments[1] of E Chih and Chin

v. 1 This was E Yin. See on the T'ae-kĕă, Pt. i. p. 1.

ix. 1 From the 15th notice in the preface to the Shoo, Chin-hoo would seem to have been alive in T'ang's time, so that in T'ae-mow's time, acc. to the current chron., he must have been nearly 200 years old. Even acc. to these Annals, he must have been over 100.

元年庚戌王即位居囂邳人姺人叛〇十年陟。

外壬
名發

元年辛丑、王即位、自亳遷于囂于河上〇六年、征藍夷〇九年陟。

仲丁
名莊

宗

太戊遇祥桑側身修行三年之後遠方慕明德重譯而至者七十六國商道復興廟爲太

七年、有桑穀生于朝〇十一年、命巫咸禱于山川〇二十六年、西戎來賓王使王孟聘西戎〇三十一年、命費侯中衍爲車正〇三十五年、作寅車〇四十六年、大有年〇五十八年、城蒲姑〇六十一年、東九夷來賓〇七十五年陟。

1 Hoo, as his principal ministers.   In his 7th year, a mulberry tree and a stalk
2 of grain grew up together in the court.   In his 11th year, he commanded Woo
3 Hëen to pray to the hills and rivers.   In his 26th year, the hordes of the West
came to make their submission. He sent Wang Măng, as his envoy, with presents
4 to those hordes.   In his 31st year, he appointed Chung-yen, prince of Pe, to be
6 master of his carriages.   In his 35th year, he made *yin* carriages.2   In his
7 46th year, there was a very abundant harvest.   In his 58th year, he walled
8 P'oo-koo.3   In his 61st year, the nine hordes of the East came to make their
9 submission.   In his 75th year, he died.

Note. After T'ae-mow met with the warning mulberry tree, he inclined himself to the cultivation of his conduct; and after 3 years, there were 76 States from distant regions, which sent messengers, with interpreters, to his court, in admiration of his wise virtue. The fortunes of Shang again revived. His sacrificial title was T'ae-tsung.

Note. Named Chwang.

x. CHUNG-TING.

1   In his 1st year, which was *sin-ch'ow* (38th of cycle, = B.C. 1,399), when he came
2 to the throne, he removed from Poh to Gaou 1 on the Ho.   In his 6th year, he
3 went on an expedition against the hordes of Lan.2   In his 9th year, he died.

Note. Named Fă.

xi. WAE-JIN.

1   In his 1st year, which was *kang-seuh* (47th of cycle, = B.C. 1,390), when he came
to the throne, he dwelt in Gaou. The people of P'ei 1 and of Sëen 2 revolted.
2   In his 10th year, he died.

2 Hăng Ch'in-fung says these carriages were of roots of the mulberry tree;—perhaps, referring to their colour.

3 Probably in the pres. dis. of Pŏ-hing, dep. Ts'ing-chow, Shan-tung.

x. 1 Gaou was on a mount Gaou (敖 山),

in the pres. dis. of Ho-yin, dep. K'ae-fung. Up to this time, the capital had been the western Pŏ.   2 Perhaps in the dis. of Yang-k·euh, dep. T'ae-yuen, Shan-se.

xi. 1 P'ei—the pres. sub. dep. of P'ei Chow, dep. of Seu-chow, Këang-soo.   2 The dis. of Ch'in-lew, dep. K'ae-fung.

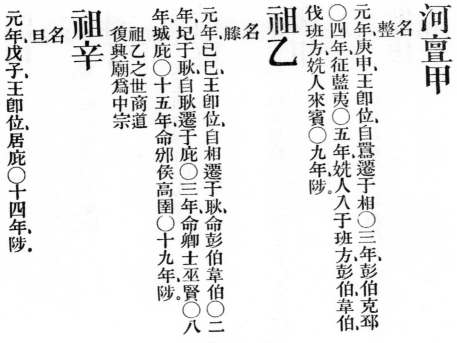

河亶甲

整名

元年庚申、王卽位、自囂遷于相○三年、彭伯克邳○四年、征藍夷○五年、姺人入于班方、彭伯韋伯伐班方、姺人來賓○九年陟。

祖乙

滕名

元年己巳、王卽位、自相遷于耿、命彭伯韋伯○二年、圯于耿、自耿遷于庇○三年、命卿士巫賢○八年、城庇○十五年、命邲侯高圉○十九年陟。

祖乙之世商道復興廟爲中宗

祖辛

旦名

元年戊子、王卽位、居庇○十四年、陟。

XII. HO-TAN-KËAH.

Note. Named Ching.

1   In his 1st year, which was *kang-shin* (57th of cycle, = B.C. 1,380), when he came
2 to the throne, he removed from Gaou to Sëang.[1]   In his 3d year, the baron of P'ang
3 subdued P'ei.   In his 4th year, he made an expedition against the hordes of Lan.
4   In his 5th year, the people of Sëen entered the region of Pan, when the barons of
P'ang and Wei attacked it, and the people of Sëen came to make their submission.
5   In his 9th year, he died.

XIII. TSOO-YIH.

Note. Named T'ăng.

1   In his 1st year, which was *ke-sze* (6th of cycle,=B.C. 1,371), when he came to the
throne, he removed from Sëang to Kăng.[1]   He gave appointments to the barons of
2 P'ang and Wei[2]   In his 2d year, Kăng was inundated, when he removed to
3 Pe.[3]   In his 3d year, he confirmed the appointment of Woo Heen as prime
5 minister   In his 8th year, he walled Pe.[3]   In his 15th year, he gave an
6 appointment to Kaou-yu, prince of Pin.[4]   In his 19th year, he died.

Note. The fortunes of Shang flourished again under Tsoo-yih. His sacrificial title was Chung-tsung.

XIV. TSOO-SIN

Note. Named Tan.

   In his 1st year, which was *mow-tsze* (25th of cycle, = B.C. 1,352), when he came
to the throne, he dwelt in Pe.   In his 14th year, he died.

XII. 1 In the pres. dis. of Ngan-yang, dep. Chang-tih, Ho-nan.
XIII. 1 In the pres. dis. of Ho-tsin, Këang Chow, Shan-se. 2 What appointments is not said. Many comm. say—'The appoint. of Pa, or chiefs of the princes;' but the text will not bear that construction. 3 Some would go away to the dis. of P'ing-hëang, dep. Shun-tih, Chih-le, for this Pe;—which is very unlikely. 4 In Pin Chow, Shen-se. Kaou-yu was a descendant of Kung-lew. Here was the seat of the Chow family.

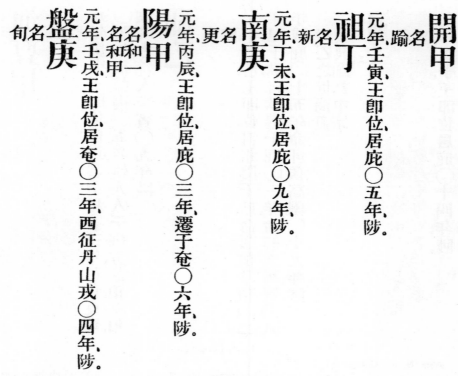

開甲

祖丁　名新
名歈　元年、王壬寅即位居庇○五年陟。

南庚　名更
元年丁未王即位居庇○九年陟。

陽甲　名和甲一名和甲
元年丙辰王即位居庇○三年遷于奄○六年陟。

盤庚　名旬
元年壬戌王即位居奄○三年西征丹山戎○四年陟。

XV. K'AE-KĔAH.

Note. Named Yu.

1　In his 1st year, which was *jin-yin* (39th of cycle,＝B.C. 1,338), when he came to
2　the throne, he dwelt in Pe.　　In his 5th year, he died.

XVI. TSOO-TING.

Note. Named Sin.

1　In his 1st year, which was *ting-we* (44th of cycle,＝B.C. 1,333), when he came to
2　the throne, he dwelt in Pe.　　In his 9th year, he died.

XVII. NAN-KANG.

Note. Named Kăng.

1　In his 1st year, which was *ping-shin* (53d of cycle, ＝ B.C. 1,324), when he came
3　to the throne, he dwelt in Pe.　　In his 3d year, he removed to Yen.1　　In his
6th year, he died.

XVIII. YANG-KĔAH.

Note. Named Ho.　Some style him Ho-kĕa.

1　In his 1st year, which was *jin-seuh* (59th of cycle, B.C. 1,318), when he came to
2　the throne, he dwelt in Yen.　　In his 3d year, he made an expedition to the west
3　against the hordes of mount Tan.　　In his 4th year, he died.

XIX. PWAN-KANG.

Note. Named Seun.

XVII. 1 Yen is no better known than Pe. Some make it out to have been in Shan-tung, in Loo.

XIX. 1 Probably in the dis. of Loo-san, dep. of Joo, Ho-nan.　2 The 'northern Mung '＝ northern Pŏ, what is called 'King Pŏ,' under

小辛

元年丙寅、王即位居奄○七年、應侯來朝○十
四年、自奄遷于北蒙曰殷○十五年、營殷邑○
十九年、命邠侯亞圉○二十八年陟。

頌名

元年、甲午、王即位居殷○三年陟。

小乙

斂名

元年丁酉、王即位居殷○六年、命世子武丁、居
于河學于甘盤○十年陟。

武丁

昭名

元年丁未王即位居殷命卿士甘盤○三年夢
求傅說得之○六年命卿士傅說視學養老○
十二年報祀上甲微○二十五年王子孝已卒

1　In his 1st year, which was *ping-yin* (3d of cycle, = B.C. 1,314), when he came to
2　the throne, he dwelt in Yen.　　In his 7th year, the prince of Ying[1] came to do
3　homage.　　In his 14th year, he removed from Yen, to the northern Mung,[2] which
5　was called Yin.　　In his 15th year, he built the city of Yin.　　In his 19th year,
6　he confirmed the appointment of A-yu, prince of Pin.　　In his 28th year, he died.

xx. Seaou-sin.

Note. Named Sung.

1　In his 1st year, which was *keah-woo* (31st of cycle, = B.C. 1,286), when he came
2　to the throne, he dwelt in Yin.　　In his 3d year, he died.

xxi. Seaou-yih.

Note. Named Lëen.

1　In his 1st year, which was *ting-yew* (34th of cycle, = B.C. 1,283), when he came
2　to the throne, he dwelt in Yin.　　In his 6th year, he ordered his heir-son, Woo-ting,
3　to dwell by the Ho, and study under Kan Pwan.　　In his 11th year, he died.

xxii. Woo-ting.

Note. Named Ch'aou.

1　In his 1st year, which was *ting-we* (44th of cycle,=B.C. 1,273), when he dwelt in
2　Yin, he confirmed the appointment of Kan Pwan as prime minister.[1]　　In his 3d
3　year, in consequence of a dream, he sought for Foo-yuĕ, and found him.　　In his
　　6th year, he confirmed Foo-yuĕ in the dignity of prime minister; and inspected the
4　schools where they nourished the aged.[2]　　In his 12th year, he offered a sacrifice
5　of thanksgiving to Shang-keah Wei.[3]　　In his 25th year, his son Heaou-e died in

the 28th year of Kĕĕ's reign; and Yin under
the reign of the emperor Mang.
　　xxii. 1 See on the Charge to Yuĕ, Pt. iii.,
par. 1.　　2 These schools were asylums. They
were called schools, because the aged who were

supported in them would enforce the duties of
filial duty and submission.　　3 See the note
above, on the 16th year of the emp. Mang.
4 To which he had been banished, many say,

于野○二十九年肜祭太廟有雉來○三十二年

伐鬼方次于荊○三十四年王師克鬼方氐羌來

賓○四十三年王師滅大彭○五十年征豕韋克

之○五十九年陟○

王殷之大仁也力行王道不敢荒寧嘉靖殷邦
至于小大無時或怨是時與地東不過江黃西
不過氐羌南不過荊蠻北不過朔方
而頌聲作禮廢而復起廟號高宗

祖庚 曜名

元年丙午王卽位居殷作高宗之訓○十一年陟。

祖甲 載名

元年丁巳王卽位居殷○十二年征西戎冬王返
自西戎○十三年西戎來賓命邠侯組紺○二十
四年重作湯刑○二十七年命王子囂王子良○
三十三年陟。

1 a wilderness.4   In his 29th year, at the supplementary sacrifice in the Grand
2 ancestral temple, a pheasant made its appearance.5   In his 32d year, he smote the
3 country of the demons,6 and camped in King.   In his 34th year, the king's forces
subdued the Demon-region, when the tribes of Te-keang came and made their sub
4 mission.   In his 43d year, his forces extinguished the State of Ta-p'ang.
6 In his 50th year, he led an expedition against Ch'e-wei, and subdued it.   In his
9th year, he died.

Note. Woo-ting was the great benevolent sovereign of Yin. Vigorously did he carry out the
royal principles, not allowing himself in idleness. Admirably did he still the States of Yin, so
that, great or small, they never murmured against him. In his time, the empire, on the East, did
not extend beyond the Kёang and Hwang; on the West, it did not extend beyond Te-kёang; on
the South, it did not extend beyond King and Man; on the North, it did not extend beyond Sŏ-
fang. But Praise-songs were heard again, and ceremonies revived from their decay. He received
the sacrificial title of Kaou-tsung.

XXIII. TSOO-KANG.

Note. Named Yaou.

1 In his 1st year, which was *ping-woo* (43d of cycle,=B.C. 1,214), when he came to
2 the throne, he dwelt in Yin; and made 'The Instructions of Kaou-tsung.'   In his
11th year, he died.

XXIV. TSOO-KĔAH.

Note. Named Tsae.

1 In his 1st year, which was *ting-sze* (54th of cycle, = B.C. 1,203), when he came to
2 the throne, he dwelt in Yin.   In his 12th year, he led a punitive expedition
3 against the hordes of the West; from which he returned in the winter.   In his
13th year, the hordes of the West came to make their submission. He confirmed
4 the appointment of Tsoo-kan, prince of Pin.   In his 24th year, he established
5 anew the penal statutes of T'ang.   In his 27th year, he gave appointments to his
6 sons, Gaou and Lёang.   In his 33d year, he died.

by his father. But this may be an invention of | of Shang.   6 See the concluding note to the
future times.   5 See the ixth of the Books | said Book.

王舊在野及卽位知小人之依能保惠庶民不侮鰥寡迫其末也繁刑以攜遠殷道復衰

馮辛
名先史記
作廩辛

元年庚寅王卽位居殷〇四年陟。

庚丁
名囂

元年甲午王卽位居殷〇八年陟。

武乙
名瞿

元年壬寅王卽位居殷邠遷于岐周〇三年自殷遷于河北命周公亶父賜以岐邑〇十五年自河北遷于沬〇二十一年周公亶父薨〇二十四年周師伐程戰于畢克之〇三十年周師伐義渠乃獲其君以歸〇三十四年周公季歷

Note. This king had lived, when young, away from the court, so that, when he came to the throne, he knew the necessities of the inferior people, protected them with kindness, and allowed no contumely to the wifeless and widows. Towards the end of his reign, however, by multiplying punishments, he alienated the people of distant regions; and the fortunes of Yin again decayed.

XXV. FUNG-SIN.

Note. Styled Lin-sin in the Historical Records. His name was Sëen.

1 In his 1st year, which was *kang-yin* (27th of cycle,＝B.C. 1,170), when he came
2 to the throne, he dwelt in Yin.　In his 4th year, he died.

XXVI. KANG-TING.

Note. Named Gaou.

1 In his 1st year, which was *këah-woo* (31st of cycle,＝B.C. 1,166), when he came to
2 the throne, he dwelt in Yin.　In his 8th year, he died.

XXVII. WOO-YIH.

Note. Named K'eu.

1 In his 1st year, which was *jin-yin* (39th of cycle,＝B.C. 1,158), he dwelt in Yin.
2 *The prince of* Pin removed to Chow near mount K'e.[1]　In his 3d year, the king removed from Yin to the north of the Ho.[2]　He confirmed the dignity of T'an-foo as
3 duke of Chow, and conferred on him the city of K'e.　In his 15th year, he
4 removed from *the place he then occupied on* the north of the Ho to Mei.[3]　In
5 his 21st year, T'an-foo, duke of Chow, died.　In his 24th year, the forces of Chow
6 smote Ch'ing.　A battle was fought at Peih, which was subdued.[4]　In his 30th year, the forces of Chow attacked E-k'eu,[5] and returned with its ruler as a captive.
7 In his 34th year, Ke-leih, duke of Chow, came and did homage at court, when the king conferred on him 30 *le* of ground, ten pairs of gems, and ten horses.

XXVII. 1 The prince of Pin, who made this removal, was T'an-foo, or king T'ae, celebrated in the She, and by Mencius. K'e-san is still the name of a dis. in Fung-ts'ëang dep., Shen-se. By this move the House of Chow brought its principal seat nearly 100 miles farther east.

2 I agree with Ch'in-fung that it is better not to try to identify this 'North of the Ho' with any particular site. 3 See on the 'Announcement about Drunkenness,' par. 1. 4 Ch'ing and Peih were in the dis. of Heen-ning, dep. Se-gan. 5 In the pres. dep. of

來朝、王賜地三十里、玉十瑴、馬十匹〇三十
五年、周公季歷伐西落鬼戎、王畋于河渭、大
雷震死。

文丁

吏記作太
丁非名托

元年丁丑王卽位居殷〇二年、周公季歷伐
燕京之戎敗績〇三年、洹水一日三絶〇四
年、周公季歷伐余無之戎、克之、命爲牧師〇
五年、周作程邑〇七年、周公季歷伐始呼之
戎、克之〇十一年、周公季歷伐翳徒之戎、獲
其三大夫來獻捷、王殺季歷。

王嘉季歷之功、錫之圭瓚秬鬯九命、爲伯
旣而執諸塞庫、季歷困而死、因謂文丁殺
歷季

十二年、有鳳集於歧山〇十三年、陟。

8　　In his 35th year, Ke-leih, duke of Chow, smote the demon hordes of the Western tribes.6　The king was hunting between the Ho and the Wei, when he was frightened to death by a great thunderstorm.

XXVIII. WĂN-TING.

Note. Wrongly styled T'ae-ting in the Historical Records.　His name was T'ŏ.

1　In his 1st year, which was *ting-ch'ow* (14th of cycle, = B.C. 1,123), when he came
2　to the throne, he dwelt in Yin.1　　In his 2d year, Ke-leih, duke of Chow, attacked
3　the hordes of Yen-king,2 and was defeated.　　In his 3d year, the Yuen-water
4　thrice ceased to flow in one day.　　In his 4th year, Ke-leih attacked the hordes of Yu-woo, and subdued them, after which he received the dignity of Pastor and
6　Teacher.　　In his 5th year, Chow built the city of Ch'ing.　　In his 7th year,
7　Ke-leih attacked the hordes of Ch'e-hoo, and subdued them.　　In his 11th year, Ke-leih smote the hordes of E-t'oo, and, having taken their three great chiefs, came with them to court to report his victory.　The king put Ke-leih to death.

Note. The king *at first* appreciated the services of Ke-leih, gave him a libation mace, with flavoured spirits of the black millet, and the nine ensigns of distinction as chief of the princes; and after all that, he confined him in the house of restraint, so that Ke-leih died from the trouble, and gave occasion to the saying that Wǎn-ting killed him.

In his 12th year, phœnixes collected on mount K'e.

Note. This was the 1st year of king Wǎn of Chow.

In his 15th year, the king died.

K'ing-yang, Kan-suh.　　6 These 'demon hordes' are difft. from the people of the 'demon region,' subdued by Woo-ting. 落＝部落, a tribe.
　　XXVIII. 1 There is a note here that 'he returned from Mei to Yin.' But Ch'in-fung denies this, and argues that, while his father had moved from the old capital, T'ŏ had continued always in it.　　2 The hill of Yen-king was in the pres. dis. of Tsing-lŏ, dep. of Yin, Shan-se.　　8 There is nothing improbable in this. The sovereign of the decaying dynasty might, in a sudden fit of jealousy, thus make away with the Head of the rising House. As the fact, however, is not elsewhere mentioned, the friends of the Annals labour to explain away the passage, or to show that it is corrupted.

138]

羨名　　帝乙

元年庚寅、王卽位、居殷○三年、王命南
仲、西拒昆夷、城朔方、夏六月、周地震○
九年陟。

帝辛
名受卽紂、
也曰受辛。

元年己亥、王卽位、居殷、命九侯周
侯、西周伯爲○三年、有雀生鸇○四年、大
○周侯昌

蒐于黎作炮烙之刑○五年、夏築南單
之臺、雨土于亳○六年、西伯初禴于畢
○九年、王師伐有蘇、獲妲己以歸、作瓊
室、立玉門○十年、夏六月、王畋于西郊
○十七年、西伯伐翟、冬、王遊於淇○二
十一年春正月、諸侯朝周、伯夷叔齊自
孤竹歸于周○二十二年冬、大蒐于渭

XXIX. TE-YIH.

Note. Named Sëen.

1　In his 1st year, which was *kang-yin* (27th of cycle, = B.C. 1,110), when he came
2　to the throne, he dwelt in Yin.　　In his 3d year, he ordered Nan Chung to oppose
the hordes of Keun on the west, and to wall *the city of* Soh-fang.　In the summer, in
3　the 6th month, there was an earthquake in Chow.　　In his 9th year, he died.

XXX. TE-SIN.

Note. Named Show. This was Chow. He is also called Show-sin.

1　In his 1st year, which was *ke-hae* (36th of cycle, = B.C. 1,101), when he came to
the throne, he dwelt in Yin.　He gave appointments to the princes of K'ew, Chow,
and Yu.

Note. The prince of Chow was Ch'ang, chief of the West.

3　In his 3d year, a sparrow produced a hawk.　　In his 4th year, he had a great
4　hunting in Le.[1]　He invented the punishment of Roasting.[2]　　In his 5th year, in
the summer, he built the tower of Nan-tan.[3]　There was a shower of earth in Poh.
5　In his 6th year, the chief of the west offered sacrifice for the first time to his an-
6　cestors in Peih.[4]　　In his 9th year, the royal forces attacked the State of Soo,
and brought away Tan-ke as a captive.　*The king* made an apartment for her, with
7　walls of carnation stone, and the doors all-adorned with gems.　　In his 10th year,
8　in the summer, in the 6th month, he hunted in the western borders.　　In his 17th
year, the chief of the west smote the Teih.[5]　In the winter, the king made a pleasure
9　excursion in K'e.[6]　　In his 21st year, in the spring, in the 1st month, the princes
went to Chow to do homage.　Pih-e and Shuh-ts'e[7] betook themselves to Chow
10　from Koo-chuh.　　In his 22d year, in the winter, he had a great hunting along

xxx. 1 九 here is read as 仇. It was the
name of a State, which was also called 鬼,—
probably in the pres. dep. of Chang-tih, Ho-nan.
The three princes here seem to have been the
three *kung*.　2 See on the ixth of the Books
of Shang.　3 What is called in the Shoo
'the Stag tower.'　4 Ke-leih had been buried
in Peih. Ch'in-fung supposes this was a sacrifice at his tomb.　5 These were different
tribes, occupying the northern regions, west of
the Ho.　6 The pres. dis. of K'e, dep. Wei-
hwuy.　7 See the Ana., V., xxii., *et al.*

11 the Wei.   In his 23d year, he imprisoned the chief of the west in Yew-le.8
12   In his 29th year, he liberated the chief of the west, who was met by *many of* the
13 princes, and escorted back to Ch'ing.   In his 30th year, in the spring, in the 3d
    month, the chief of the west led the princes to the court with their tributes.   In
14 his 31st year, the chief of the west began to form a regular army in Peih, with Leu
15 Shang as its commander.   In his 32d year, there was a conjunction of the five
    planets in Fang. A red crow lighted on the altar to the spirits of the land in Chow.
    The people of Meih invaded Yuen, when the chief of the west led a force against
16 Meih.9   In his 33d year, the people of Meih surrendered to the army of Chow,
    and were removed to Ch'ing. The king granted power to the chief of the west to
    punish and attack *offending* States on his own discretion.

    Note by Yŏ. King Wăn thus for 9 years received the appointment *of Heaven;* and the empire
    was not yet all secured by him *at his death.* His plenipotent authority to punish and attack, in
    which the will of Heaven might be seen, commenced in this year.

17   In his 34th year, the forces of Chow took K'e and Yu; and then attacked Ts'ung,
    which surrendered. In the winter, in the 12th month, the hordes of Keun overran
18 Chow.   In the 35th year, there was a great famine in Chow; when the chief of
19 the west removed from Ch'ing to Fung.   In his 36th year, in the spring, in the
    1st month, the princes went to court at Chow, and then they smote the hordes of
20 Keun. The chief of the west made his heir-son Fă build Haou.   In his 37th
21 year, *the duke of* Chow built an imperial college.9   In his 39th year, the great
22 officer Sin-këah fled to Chow.   In his 40th year, *the duke of* Chow made the
23 spirit-tower. The king sent Kaou-kih to seek for gems in Chow.10   In his 41st
    year, in the spring, in the 3d month, Ch'ang, the chief of the west, died.

    Note. King Wăn of Chow was buried in Peih;—30 *le* west from Fung.

24   In his 42d year,—(the 1st year of king Woo of Chow)—Fah chief of the west, received
    the vermilion book from Leu shang.11 A girl changed into a man.   In his

8 In the dis. of T'ang-yin, dep. Chang-tih.
9 Both Meih and Yuen were in the pres. dep.
of P'ing-lëang, Kan-suh.   9 The building
of a P'eih-yung in Chow was the exercising an

imperial prerogative. See on the She, Pt. II,
Bk. III., Ode. ii.
10 There is a story of a tablet of gem belonging to the princes of Chow, which Show coveted,

年十六　十九王用歲四百九　湯滅夏以至于受二　殷。名邢邱曰懷　緊伐殷至邢邱更　師有事于上帝、庸蜀羌　微彭盧濮從周伐　于鮮原。冬十有二月、周　寅、周始伐殷。秋、周師次　子出奔。○五十二年、庚　囚箕子殺王子比干、微　子、周師渡盟津而還。　五十一年、冬十一月、戊　年夷羊見。二日並出。戊　向摯出奔周。○四十八　伐黎。○四十七年、內史　崩。○四十四年、西伯發　四十三年、春、大閱。嶰山

25 43d year, in the spring, he had a grand review. *Part of* mount K'aou fell down.
26 In his 44th year, Fah smote Le. In his 47th year, the recorder of the Interior,
27 Hëang Che, fled to Chow. In his 48th year, the E goat[12] was seen. Two suns
28 appeared together. In his 51st year, in the winter, in the 11th month, on the day *mow-tsze* (25th of cycle), the army of Chow crossed the ford of Mang; but returned. The king imprisoned the viscount of K'e; and put his relative, Pe-kan, to
29 death; while the viscount of Wei fled away. In his 52d year, which was *kang-yin* (27th of cycle), Chow made its first attack on Yin. In the autumn, the army of Chow camped in the plain of Sëen. In the winter, in the 12th month, it sacrificed to God. The tribes of Yung, Shuh, Këang, Maou, Wei, Loo, P'ang, and Puh, followed Chow to the attack of Yin.[14]

Note. They marched to Hing-k'ew, the name of which was changed to Hwae.
From the extinction of Hea by T'ang to Show were 29 kings, and 496 years.

and wished thus to get for himself. 11 This was a book of Counsels, containing the principles of Hwang-te, and Chuen-heuh. 12 This was a prodigious thing, 'a spirit-like animal,'— variously described. 13 This was in K'e Chow. 14 See on 'Speech at Muh.'

141]

竹書紀年卷之五
周武王

名發初高辛氏之世妃曰姜嫄助祭郊禖
見大人迹履之當時歆如有人道感已遂
有身而生男以爲不祥棄之隘巷牛羊避
而不踐又送之山林之中會伐林者又取
而置寒冰上大鳥以一翼藉覆之姜嫄以
爲異乃收養焉名之曰棄枝頤有異相長
爲堯稷官有功於民后稷之孫曰公劉有
德諸侯皆以天子之禮待之初黃帝之世
讖言曰西北爲王期在甲子昌制命發行
誅旦行道及公劉之後十三世而生季歷
季歷之十年飛龍盈於殷之牧野此蓋聖
人在下位將起之符也季歷之妃曰大任
夢長人感已溲于豕牢而生昌昌是爲周文
王龍顏虎肩身長十尺胸有四乳大王曰
吾世當有興者其在昌乎季歷之兄曰太
伯知天命在昌適越終身不反弟仲雍從
之故季歷爲嗣以及昌昌爲西伯作邑於
豐文王之妃曰太姒夢商庭生棘太子發

PART V.

The dynasty of Chow.

1. KING WOO.

Note. Named Fă. Of old time, Këang Yuen, the wife of the emperor Kaou-sin, was assisting him at a sacrifice in the borders in order to obtain a son, when she saw the footstep of a large man, and trod upon it. At the instant she felt after a certain manner, and, becoming pregnant, by and by gave birth to a son. Thinking the whole thing unlucky, she threw the child away in a narrow lane, but the goats and cattle avoided it, and did not trample on it. She then placed it in a wood, where it was found by a woodcutter. She took it then, and laid it upon the ice, and there a large bird came and covered it with one of his wings. Këang Yuen, surprised by all this, received the child at last, and nursed him, giving him the name of 'Cast-away.'

The lower part of the child's face was largely developed, and his appearance altogether extraordinary. When he was grown up, he became minister of Agriculture to Yaou, and rendered great services to the people. He is known as prince Tseih. His grandson Kung-lew was eminently virtuous, so that the princes behaved to him with the same ceremonies as they did to the emperor.

In the time of Hwang-te, there had been a prophecy, to the effect that 'the chief of the west should become king, in a certain *keă-tsze* year; that Ch'ang should lay the foundations of the dignity, Fă exercise the judgments necessary to it, and Tan develope its principles.' In the 13th generation, accordingly, from Kung-lew, Ke-leih was born; and in his 10th year, a multitude of flying dragons filled the pasture lands of Yin;—an emblem of a sage in an inferior position, who should in course of time rise to his proper distinction.

The wife of Ke-leih was called T'ae-jin, who became pregnant after dreaming that she had been with a tall man. Afterwards, when relieving nature, she gave birth to Ch'ang. This Ch'ang became king Wăn of Chow. He had a dragon's countenance, with a tiger's shoulders; was 10 cubits high; and had 4 nipples on his chest. *His grandfather*, king T'ae, said, 'It will be Ch'ang, in whom our family shall rise to distinction.' Ke-leih's eldest brother was T'ae-pih who, knowing

142]

穀焉穀者紀后稷之德火者燔魚以告天
以告天有火自天止於王屋流爲赤烏烏銜
文成字言紂可伐以世字魚文消燔魚赤
白魚躍入王舟王俯取魚長三尺目下有赤
比干箕子微子去之乃伐紂渡孟津中流
不期而會咸曰紂可伐矣武王不從及紂殺
武王駢齒望羊將伐紂至于孟津八百諸侯王
昭理四海文王既沒太子發代立是爲武
移不得復入靈祇遠離百神吹去五星聚房
王之都書文曰殷無道虐亂天下皇命已
山孟春六日五緯聚房後有鳳凰鳴於文岐
昌者子文王夢日月著其身又鸞鳳銜書游於
齊尚出游見赤人自洛出授尚書命曰呂佐
璜其文要曰姬受命昌來提撰爾洛鈐報呂佐在
乃今見光景于斯尚立變名答曰望七玉
溪之水呂尚釣於渭王下趨拜曰望釣得玉年
曰將大獲非熊非羆大遺汝師以佐昌臣卜在
祖史疇爲禹卜畋得皐陶其兆類此至于磻太
曰姬昌蒼帝子亡殷者紂王將畋史編卜之
爵銜書及豐置于昌戶昌拜稽首受其文要
王幣率羣臣與發竝拜吉夢季秋之甲子赤
植梓樹於闕間化爲松栢械柞以告文王文

that Heaven's purpose was to be realized in Ch'ang, went away to Yuĕ, and never returned. His next brother, Chung-yung, followed this example; so that Ke-leih remained to be his father's heir, and the succession descended to Ch'ang, who became chief of the West, and made his capital city in Fung.

The wife of king Wăn was called T'ae-sze. She dreamed that in the courtyard of the imperial palace there were thorns growing, while her eldest son Fă planted some *tsze* trees about their own gate, which changed into a fir, a cypress, a *yih*, and a *tsŏ*. This dream she told to king Wăn, who prepared gifts, and led his ministers along with Fă to give thanks for it.

On the keă-tsze day, in the last month of autumn, a red bird came to Fung with a writing in its beak, which it put down at the door of Ch'ang. Ch'ang received it with a reverential obeisance, and found the writing to this effect:—'Ke Ch'ang is the son of the God of the empyrean. The destroyer of Yin is Chow.' The king was about to go to hunt, when the recorder Pĕen divined the meaning of this writing, and said:—'You will get great spoil; but not a bear nor a grisly bear. Heaven is sending a Grand-tutor to aid you. My ancestor, the recorder Ch'ow, divined once for Yu about hunting; and then he met with Kaou-yaou,—from an omen like that which has now occurred.' The hunting party went on, and at the water of P'wan-k'e, there was Leu Shang, fishing on the bank. The king descended, hastened to him, and said with a bow, 'I have been hoping to meet with you for seven years, and now I find you here.' Shang instantly changed his name at these words, and answered, 'I, Hope (the looked for), fished up a semicircular gem with this inscription:—"Ke has received the appointment of Heaven; Ch'ang will come and take it up. You have fished this up in the Lŏ, and will have your reward in Ts'e."'

Shang went out *one day* rambling, when he saw a red man come out from the Lŏ, who gave him a writing, with the words:—'As a backbone, you must assist Ch'ang.'

King Wăn dreamt that he was clothed with the sun and moon. A phœnix duck sang on mount K'e. In the first month of spring, on the 6th day, the five planets had a conjunction in Fang. Afterwards a male and female phœnix went about Wăn's capital with a writing in their beaks, which said:—'The emperor of Yin has no principle, but oppresses and disorders the empire. The great decree is removed; Yin cannot enjoy it longer. The powerful spirits of the earth have left it; all the spirits are whistled away. The conjunction of the five planets in Fang brightens all within the four seas.'

When king Wan was dead, his eldest son Fă ruled in his stead. His teeth were one piece of bone, and he had a shepherd's eyes. When he was about to attack Chow, and had reached the ford of Măng, 800 princes came together, without any previous understanding, all saying, 'Show may be smitten.' King Woo, however, did not listen to them; but when Show had killed Pe-kan, imprisoned the viscount of K'e, and was abandoned by the viscount of Wei, then he assailed him. When he was crossing the river at the ford of Măng, in the middle of the stream, a white fish leaped into the king's boat. The king stooped down and took it up. It was 3 cubits long, and under its eyes were red lines which formed the characters—'Chow may be smitten.' The king wrote over them the character for 'dynasty,' and the words disappeared. After this he burned the fish in sacrifice, and announced the event to Heaven. Lo! fire came down from heaven, and rested over Wang uh, gradually floating away into a red bird, with a stalk of grain in its beak. The

火流下應以吉也遂東伐紂勝
於牧野兵不血刃而天下歸之
乃封呂尚於齊周德旣隆草木
茂盛蒿堪爲宮室因名蒿室旣
有天下遂
都于鎬
十二年辛卯王率西夷諸侯伐殷
敗之于坶野王親禽受于南單之
臺遂分天之明立受于祿父是爲
武庚夏四月王歸于豐饗于太廟
命監殷遂狩於管作大武樂〇十
三年巢伯來賓獻殷俘馘于太廟遂
封諸侯秋大有年〇十四年王有
疾周文公禱于壇墠作金縢〇十
五年肅慎氏來賓初狩方岳誥于
沫邑冬遷九鼎于洛〇十六年箕
子來朝秋王師滅蒲姑〇十七年
命王世子誦于東宮冬十有二月
王陟年五十四。

grain was in commemoration of the virtue of prince Tseih; the fire was an auspicious response from heaven to the burnt-offering of the fish.

Woo then went eastward and attacked Show, whom he vanquished in the wilderness of Muh. His soldiers did not need to stain their swords with blood, *so easily* did the empire turn to him. He invested Leu Shang with the principality of Ts'e. Through the abundance of the virtue of Chow, all vegetation was most luxuriant; even the southernwood could supply materials for building a palace, and hence we have the name—'southernwood house.' When he was possessed of the empire, Woo fixed his capital in Haou.

1   In his 12th year, which was *sin-maou* (28th of cycle, = B.C. 1,049), the king led the tribes of the west and the princes to attack Yin, and defeated *Show* in the wilderness of Muh. He took with his own hand Show prisoner in the tower of Nan-tan;[2] and entered into the participation of the bright appointment of Heaven,[3] setting up, *to continue the sacrifices to his ancestors*, Luh-foo, the son of Show, known as Woo-kang.[4] In the summer, in the 4th month, he returned to Fung, and sacrificed in the ancestral temple. He appointed Inspectors of Yin, and went himself on a tour of
2   inspection to Kwan.[5] He made the music Ta-woo.   In his 13th year, the baron of Ch'aou came to make his submission. He presented *the captives of Yin* in the Grand ancestral temple;[6] and afterwards granted great investitures to the princes.
3   In the autumn there was a very abundant harvest.   In his 14th year, the king was unwell, when the duke Wan of Chow prayed *for him* on an altar-area, and
4   made 'The Metal-bound Coffer.'[7]   In his 15th year, the prince of Suhshin came to make his submission. He made his first tour of inspection to the mountains of the four quarters, and made an announcement to the cities of Me.[8] In the winter, he
5   removed the nine tripods to Loh.   In his 16th year, the viscount of Ke came to
6   do homage. In the autumn, the royal forces extinguished P'oo-koo.   In his 17th year, he appointed his heir-son Sung in the eastern palace to be his successor. In the winter, in the 12th month, he died, being 94 years old.

I. 1 Reckoning from the 42d year of Show, when Woo succeeded his father, as duke of Chow.   2 禽=擒 See the acct. of Show's death in the note on par. 1 of 'The Successful Completion of the War.'   3 It is diffi. to translate 分天之明. I take 明=明命. Some take 分 as by mistake for 受; but I have brought out the same meaning which that would give. The text will not allow the meaning of—'before day-break' (天尙未明), which Wän-tsing gives.   4 The 立 or 'setting' up of Show's son is to be understood only as I have indicated. There was no participation of the empire with him, as the 分 preceding seems to make Biot suppose.   5 See the note on par. 12 of 'The Metal-bound Coffer.'

6 That is, he presented the left ears which had been cut off. See the She, Pt III., Bk. I. Ode vii., 8.   7 See the Shoo Pt. V., Bk. VI.. 8 This was 'The Announcement about Drunkenness;' but, see, in the notes on that Bk. of the Shoo, the controversies about the date and the author. 沫邑=沫邦.

成王

名誦

元年丁酉春正月王即位命冢宰周文
公總百官庚午周公誥諸侯于皇門夏
六月葬武王于畢秋王加元服武庚以
殷叛周文公出居于東〇二年奄人徐
人及淮夷入于邶以叛秋大雷電以風
王逆周文公于郊遂伐殷〇三年王師
滅殷殺武庚祿父遷殷民于衞遂伐奄
滅蒲姑〇四年春正月
初朝于廟夏四月初嘗麥王師伐淮夷
遂入奄〇五年春正月王在奄遷其君
于蒲姑夏五月王至自奄遷殷民于洛
邑遂營成周〇六年大蒐于岐陽〇七
年周公復政于王春二月王如豐三月
召康公如洛度邑甲子周文公誥多士
于成周遂城東都王如東都諸侯來朝

滅蒲姑故周文公伐之
減殷殺武庚祿父遷殷民于衞遂伐奄
王逆周文公于郊遂伐殷〇三年王師
人及淮夷入于邶以叛秋大雷電以風

11. KING CHING.

Note. Named Sung.

1   In his 1st year, which was *ting-yew* (34th of cycle, = B.C. 1,043), in the spring, in the 1st month, when he came to the throne, he ordered the prime minister, duke Wăn of Chow, to take the leadership of all the officers.   On the day *kang-woo* (7th of cycle), the duke of Chow made an announcement to the princes at the great gate.[1] In the summer, in the 6th month, they buried king Woo in Peih.   In the autumn, the king assumed the covering for the head.[2] Woo-kăng with the people of Yin

2   rebelled.   Duke Wăn of Chow left the court to reside in the east.[3]   In his 2d year, the people of Yen and of Seu, with the hordes of the Hwae, entered Pei[4] with the standard of rebellion.   In the autumn, there was a great storm of thunder and lightning, with wind, when the king met the duke of Chow in the borders; and

3   immediately after, they smote Yin.   In the 3d year, the king's armies extinguished Yin; Woo-kăng Luh-foo was put to death; the people of Yin were removed to Wei;[5] Yen was forthwith invaded; and P'oo-koo was extinguished.[6]

Note. Koo was aiding in the rebellion of the four kingdoms; and therefore the duke of Chow extinguished it.

4   In his 4th year, in the spring, in the 1st month, he first gave audience *to the princes* in *his father's* temple.   In the summer, in the 4th month, he first tasted *the first fruits of* the wheat.[7] The army smote the hordes of the Hwae, and then entered

5   Yen.   In his 5th year, in the spring, in the 1st month, the king was in Yen, and removed its ruler to P'oo-koo.   In the summer, in the 5th month, he came from Yen, and removed the people of Yin to the city of Loh; and thereon proceeded to build

6   Ching-chow.   In his 6th year, he made a grand hunting expedition on the south

7   of mount K'e.   In his 7th year, the duke of Chow restored the government to the

11. 2 The 'great gate' was on the left of the 5th or last of the principal gates of the palace. The duke would harangue the nobles in the usual place of 'Audience of govt.' 2 元= 首, 'the head.' 'The dress for the head'=the cap. King Ching was now, it is generally said, 14 years old. His capping=the acknowledgement of him as king.   3 See on 'The Metalbound Coffer,' pp. 12, 13.   4 The portion of Yin, ruled by the king's uncle, Ch'oo.   5 See on the 9th of the Books of Chow. 6 This was said to be done in the last reign.   7 See

鼎鳳凰見遂有事于河。
成○十八年春正月王如洛邑定
四年齊師圍曲城克之冬洛邑告
戎夏六月魯大禘于周公廟○十
命○十三年王師會齊侯魯侯伐
十二年王師燕師城韓王錫韓侯
約按周平公卽君陳之弟
治東都。
唐叔歸禾于周文公。
春正月王如豐唐叔獻嘉禾王命周平公
來朝周文公出居于豐○十一年。
○十年王命唐叔虞爲侯越裳氏
慎氏來朝王使榮伯錫蕭慎氏命
年春正月王有事于太廟初用勺。蕭
十月王師滅唐遷其民于杜○九
父齊侯伋遷庶殷于魯作象舞○冬
春正月王初蒞阼親政命魯侯禽○八年
冬王歸自東都立高圉廟。○八年。

king. In the spring, in the 2d month, the king went to Fung. In the 3d month, duke K'ang of Shaou went to Loh, to measure *the ground for* the city. On the day *këah-tsze* (1st of cycle), the duke Wăn of Chow made an announcement to the numerous officers in Ching-chow; and thereon they walled the eastern capital. The king then went to it, and the princes came to do him homage. In the winter, he

8 returned from it, and appointed *anew* a shrine to Kaou-yu.8   In his 8th year, in the spring, in the 1st month, he first took his position as imperial host, and administered the government for himself. He gave orders to K'in-foo, prince of Loo, and K'eih, prince of Ts'e, to remove the multitudes of Yin to Loo. He made the pantomimic dance, called Sëang. In the winter, in the 10th month, his forces extinguished

9 the State of T'ang,9 and removed its people to Too.10   In his 9th year, in the spring, in the 1st month, he had a great sacrificial service in the grand ancestral temple, when he first used the *choh*.11   The chief of Suh-shin came to do homage,

10 when the king employed the baron of Yung to convey his Charge to him.12   In his 10th year, he appointed his brother Yu of T'ang to be *head of all the* princes.13 The chief of Yueh-chang 14 appeared to do homage. The duke of Chow left the court,

11 and resided in Fung.   In his 11th year, in the spring, in the 1st month, the king went to Fung. His brother of T'ang presented a stalk of fine grain, and was ordered to convey it to the duke Wăn of Chow.   The king appointed duke P'ing of Chow to govern the eastern capital.15

Note by Yŏ. This duke P'ing of Chow is Keun-ch'in, the son of the duke of Chow, and younger brother of Pih-k'in.

12   In his 12th year, the king's forces and those of Yen walled Han; 16 and the king
13 gave a Charge to the prince of Han.   In his 13th year, the king's forces assembled with *those of* the princes of Ts'e and Loo, and smote the hordes of the Jung. In the summer, in the 6th month, *the prince of* Loo offered the grand imperial sacrifice in

14 the temple of the duke of Chow.   In his 14th year, the forces of Ts'e invested the city of K'euh,17 and subdued it. In the winter, the announcement was made of

15 the completion of Loh.   In his 18th year, in the spring, in the 1st month, the king went to Loh, and settled *the place of* the tripods there. Phœnixes made their appearance, and a sacrifice was offered near the Ho.

on the Le Ke, Bk. IV., Pt. iii., p. 17.   8 See on the 15th year of Tsoo-yih.   9 Occupied by descendants of Yaou;—in the pres. dis. of Yih-shing, dep. P'ing-yang.   10 In the dis. of Ch'ang-gan, dep. Se-gan.   11 The *chŏ* was a song, with music, made by the duke of Chow, and used at a certain part of the service. 勺＝汋＝酌.   12 See the Pref. to the Shoo, 56th Notice.   13 There is no end of difficulty in fixing the meaning of this sentence.

14 See the Introductory note to the xxist of the Books of Chow.   15 That is—'appointed him who was subsequently duke P'ing of Chow.' *The* duke of Chow was not yet dead. 16 Prob. in the pres. dis of Koo-ngan, dep. of Shun-t'ëen. Not far from Yen.   17 A place of an eastern tribe, in the pres. dep. of Tung-lae.   18 See on the xxth of the Books of Chow.

武王沒成王少周公旦攝政七年制禮

作樂神鳥鳳凰見蓂莢生乃與成王觀

于河洛沈璧禮畢王退俟至于日昃榮

光出幕河青雲浮至青龍臨壇銜玄

甲之圖坐之而去禮于洛亦如之玄龜

青龍止于壇背甲刻書赤文成字周公

援筆以世文寫之書成文消龜隨甲而

去其言自周公訖于秦漢盛衰之符麟

鳳遊苑鳳凰翔庭成王援琴而歌曰鳳

凰翔兮于紫庭余何德兮以感靈賴先

王兮恩澤

胥樂兮分民以寧

十九年王巡狩侯甸方岳召康公從歸于

宗周遂正百官黜豐侯○二十一年除治

象。周文公薨于豐○二十二年葬周文公

于畢○二十四年於越來賓○二十五年、

王大會諸侯于東都四夷來賓冬十月、歸

自東都大事于太廟○三十年離戎來賓。

約按離戎驪山之戎也

爲林氏所伐告于成王

Note. When king Woo died, king Ching was still young; and Tan, duke of Chow, acted as regent for 7 years. He made the institutions and music of the dynasty. Spirit-like birds and phœnixes appeared; and the mysterious bean grew up. After this he went with king Ching to view the Ho and the Lǒ. Having dropt a gem into the water, and finished all the ceremonies, the king retired and waited till the day declined. Then rays of glory came out, and shrouded all the Ho; and green clouds came floating in the sky. A green dragon came to the altar, carrying in his mouth a dark-coloured shell, with a figure on it, which he placed on the altar, and went away. They did in the same way at the Lǒ, and the same things happened. On the shell in red lines were characters, which the duke of Chow copied in the current forms of the age. When his writing was finished, the tortoise dropped the shell, and went away. The writing was all about the rise and fall in the fortunes of the empire down to the dynasties of Ts'in and Han. K'e-lins wandered in the parks; phœnixes flew about in the courtyards; king Ching took a lute, and sang:—

> 'The phœnixes fly
> All around my hall.
> What virtue have I
> So spirits to call?

> 'From the former kings
> This influence comes;
> Theirs the joy that rings
> In the people's homes.'

16 In his 19th year, the king made a tour of inspection to the *how* and *teen* domains, and to the four mountains, the duke K'ang of Shaou being in attendance on him. When he returned to Tsung-chow, he settled the various orders of officers,[18] and
17 degraded the prince of Fung.[19]   In his 21st year, he removed the representations
18 of the penal laws.[20] The duke Wan of Chow died in Fung.   In his 22d year,
19 he buried duke Wan in Peih.   In his 24th year, *the chief of* Yu-yueh came to
20 make his submission.[21]   In his 25th year, the king held a great assembly of the princes in the eastern capital, when the wild tribes of the four quarters came to make their submission. In the winter, in the 10th month, he returned from the eastern
21 capital, and performed a great service in the grand ancestral temple.   In his 30th year, the hordes of Le came to make their submission.

Note by Yǒ. The hordes of Le belonged to mount Le. They had been smitten by the chief of Lin, who announced the event to king Ching.

19 It is said that when king Woo occupied Haou as his capital, he granted Fung as the appanage of one of his younger brothers, whom Ching degraded for drunkenness.   20 Such representations were hung up before one of the palace gates, and perhaps the gates of public offices generally. Ching thought the people were now so accustomed to the rule of Chow, and acquainted with the laws, that they did not need the lessons of such figures and descriptions.   21 The rulers of Yuĕ, called Yu-yuĕ

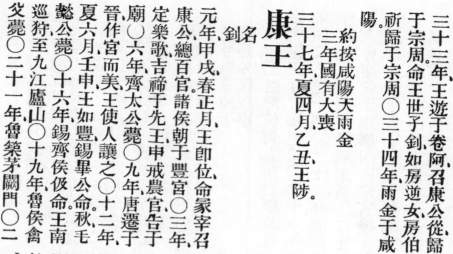

三十三年、王遊于卷阿、召康公從、歸
于宗周。命王世子釗如房逆女、房伯
祈歸于宗周○三十四年、雨金于咸
陽

約按咸陽天雨金
三年國有大喪

三十七年、夏四月乙丑、王陟。

康王

釗名

元年甲戌春正月、王即位、命冢宰召
康公總百官、諸侯朝于豐宮○三年、
定樂歌、吉禘于先王、申戒農官告于
廟○六年、齊太公薨○九年、唐遷于
晉作宮而美、王使人讓之○十二年、
夏六月壬申王如豐、錫畢公命、秋毛
懿公薨○十六年、錫齊侯伋命、王南
巡狩至九江廬山○十九年、魯侯禽
父薨○二十一年、魯築茅闕門○二

22   In his 33d year, the king rambled in Keuen-o,22 with duke K'ang of Shaou in attendance, and then returned to Tsung-chow. He ordered his heir-son Ch'aou to go to Fang 23 to bring home his bride. K'e, the baron of Fang, escorted her to Tsung-
23 chow.   In his 34th year, it rained gold in Hëen-yang.24

Note by Yð. It rained gold in Hëen-yang; and in 3 years, the empire sustained a great loss.

24   In his 37th year, in the summer, in the 4th month, on the day *yih-ch'ow* (2d of cycle), the king died.

Note. Named Ch'aou.

III. KING K'ANG.

1   In his 1st year, which was *keah-seuh* (11th of cycle,=B.C. 1,006), in the spring, in the 1st month, when he came to the throne, he ordered the prime minister, duke K'ang of Shaou, to take the leadership of all the officers. The princes did homage
2 in the palace of Fung.   In his 3d year, he fixed the songs for the different musical performances. The period of mourning being over, he offered the imperial sacrifice to his predecessor.2 He renewed the admonitions to the officers of agriculture,3 and
3 announced them in the ancestral temple.   In his 6th year, duke T'ae of Ts'e
4 died.4   In his 9th year, *the prince* of T'ang removed to Tsin,5 and made a palace
5 in a beautiful style. The king sent and reproved him.   In his 12th year, in the summer, in the 6th month, on the *jin-shin* day (9th of cycle), the king went to Fung, and gave his Charge to the duke of Peih.6 In the autumn, duke E of Maou died.
6   In his 16th year, he give a Charge to K'eih, the duke of Ts'e. He went south
7 on a tour of inspection, as far as mount Loo of Kew-keang.   In his 19th year,
8 K'in-foo, prince of Loo, died.   In his 21st year, the prince of Loo made *a palace*, with the sentry lofts above the gates covered with rushes.   In his

(于, or 於, 越), were descendants of Yu the Great. The capital was on the north of Hwuy-k'e.   22 See on the She, Pt. III., Bk. II., Ode. viii.   23 The pres. dis. of Fang, dep. Yun-yang, Hoo-pih. Here, it is said, Shun placed Choo, the son of Yaou.   24 A dis. of dep. Se-ngan. Here Ke-leih had at one time his capital.

III. 1 The duke of Chow had made the music;

king K'ang now fixed the songs for different pieces.   2 That is, he made all the necessary changes connected with the introduction of his father's shrine into the temple, and sacrificed to him.   3 Supposed to be in 3d of the 2d Bk. of the Praise-songs of Chow.   4 It would appear from 'The Testamentary Charge,' par. 10, that he was dead before this.   5 This change of site was not great.   6 See the xxivth of the Books of Chow.   7 Here the battle about the

昭王　名瑕

穆王　名滿

十四年召康公薨○二十六年秋九月己未王陟。

元年庚子春正月王即位復設象魏○六年王錫郇伯命冬十二月桃李華○十四年夏四月恒星不見秋七月魯人弑其君宰○十六年伐楚涉漢遇大兕○十九年春有星孛于紫微祭公辛伯從王伐楚天大曀雉兔皆震喪六師于漢王陟。

元年己未春正月王即位作昭宮命辛伯餘靡冬十月築祇宮于南鄭。

自武王至穆王享國百年穆王以下都于西鄭

9　44th year, duke K'ang of Shaou died.　　In his 26th year, in the autumn, in the 9th month, on the day ke-wei (56th of cycle), the king died.

IV. KING CH'AOU.

Note. Named Hëa.

1　In his 1st year, which was *kang-tsze* (37th of cycle,=B.C. 980), in the spring, in the 1st month, when the king came to the throne, he restored the practice of suspend-
2　ing the representations of the penal laws.　　In his 6th year, he gave a Charge to the baron of Seun.　In the winter, in the 12th month, peach trees and plum trees
3　were in flower.　　In his 14th year, in the summer, in the 4th month, the regular stars were invisible.　In the autumn, in the 7th month, the people of Loo killed
4　their ruler Tsae.　　In his 16th year, *the king* attacked Ts'oo; and, in crossing
5　the Han, met with a large rhinoceros.　　In his 19th year, in the spring, a comet appeared in the space Tsze-mei.[2]　The duke of Tse[3] and the baron of Sin[4] followed the king against Ts'oo.　The heavens were dark and tempestuous.　Pheasants and hares were terrified.　The king's six armies perished in the Han.　The king died.

V. KING MUH.

Note. Named Mwan.

1　In his 1st year, which was *ke-wei* (56th of cycle, = B.C. 961), in the spring, in the 1st month, after he came to the throne, he built the palace of Ch'aou, and gave a Charge to Yu-mei, the baron of Sin.　In the winter, in the 10th month, he built the palace of Che in Nan-ch'ing.[2]

Note. From king Woo to Muh, the empire was possessed 100 years.　From Muh downwards the capital was in Se-ch'ing.

'Nine Keang' is fought over again.　See on 'The Tribute of Yu.'
　IV.　1 In dis. of E-she, dep. P'oo-chow, Shan-se.　　2 Including the stars about the north pole.　　3 In Ch'ing Chow, dep. K'ae-fung. Its chiefs were of the family of the duke of Chow.　　4 In the dis. Ch'ang-tsze, dep. Loo-ngan, Shan-se.

v.　1 This palace is supposed to have been somehow in commemoration of his father, king Ch'aou.　The baron of Sin is represented in some accounts as having rescued him from the Han, though he died in consequence of the fright and injuries received.　　2 In Hwa Chow, dep. T'ung-chow, Shen-se.　　3 In the

王西征至昆侖邱見西王母其年
舊蠆王命造父封于趙〇十六年霍侯
澤觀鹽池非是一作王幸安邑
昆氏來賓作重璧臺冬王觀于鹽
萍澤作虎牢〇十五年春正月留
作范宮秋九月翟人侵畢冬十
戎克之夏四月王畋于軍邱五月
于宗周〇十四年王帥楚子伐徐
賓徐戎侵洛冬十月造父御王入
王西征次于陽紆秋七月西戎來
征犬戎〇十三年春祭公帥師從
從王伐犬戎冬十月王北巡狩遂
二年毛公班共公利逢公固帥師
十一年王命卿士祭公謀父〇十
騄耳〇九年築春宮王所居有〇
八年春北唐來賓獻一驪馬是生
六年春徐子誕來朝錫命爲伯〇

2 　In the 6th year, Tan, the viscount of Seu,3 came to do homage, when the title of
3 baron was conferred on him. 　　　In his 8th year, *the chief* of the northern T'ang
came to do homage, and presented a very swift mare, which produced *the famous*
4 Luh-urh.4 　　　In his 9th year, he built the Spring palace.

Note. The king resided in the spring palace, and that of Ch'ing.

5 　In his 11th year, he gave additional distinction and a Charge to Mow-foo, duke of
6 Tse, the prime minister. 　　　In his 12th year, Pan, duke of Maou, Le, duke of
Kung,5 and Koo, duke of Fung, led their forces, in attendance on the king, against
the hordes of the K'euen. In the winter, in the 10th month, the king being on a tour
7 of inspection in the north, punished those hordes. 　　　In his 13th year, the duke of
Tse attended the king with his forces on an expedition to the west, when they encamped in Yang.6 In the autumn, in the 7th month, the hordes of the west came to
make their submission. The hordes of Seu invaded Loh. In the winter, Ts'aou-foo
8 drove the king *in triumph* into Tsung-chow. 　　　In his 14th year, he led the viscount
of Ts'oo against the hordes of Seu, and subdued them. In the summer, in the 4th
month, he hunted in Keun-k'ew. In the 5th month, he made the palace of Fan. In
autumn, in the 9th month, the people of Teih invaded Peih. In the winter, there
9 was a grand hunting in the marsh of P'ing.8 He built Foo-laou.9 　　　In his 15th
year, in the spring, in the 1st month, the chief of Lew-keun came to make his submission. The king made the tower of Chung-peih. In the winter, he surveyed the Salt
marsh.11

Note. One copy has here:—'The king went to Ngan-yih, and viewed the Salt pond.' This is
wrong.

10 　In his 16th year, Kew, prince of Hoh, died. The king gave a Charge to Ts'aou-
11 foo, and invested him with Chaou.12 　　　In his 17th year, he went on a punitive
expedition to mount Keun-lun; and saw the western Wang-moo. That year the chief

pres. dep. of Seu-chow, Keang-soo. 　4 King
Muh was famous for his horses; he had several,
—'Spurn the earth,' 'Mount the clouds,' &c.
5 Should probably be Tsing (井). 　6
Undetermined. Some say it was in K'e-chow;
others, in Ts'in; others far beyond, 3,000 *le* from
Tsung-chow. 　　7 An ancestor of the House
of Ts'in, famous for his skilful and rapid driving. 　　8 Probably in dis. of Hea-yih, dep.
Kwei-tih. It was near the capital of the early
kings of Hea. 　　9 That is 'Tigers' Hold,'
in dis. of Ke-shwuy, dep. K'ae-fung. Muh kept
tigers here. 　　10 That is of 'storied *peih*
gems.' 　　11 Supposed to be in the very distant west. Biot says:—'The great lake of the
country of Cashgar.' 　12 Dis. of Chaou-

命〇十二年王陟。

元年甲寅春正月、王即位〇四年王師滅密
〇九年春正月丁亥王使內史良錫毛伯遷

名繄扈

共王

〇五十五年王陟于祇宮。

魯侯賁薨〇五十一年作呂刑命甫侯于豐

〇三十九年王會諸侯于塗山〇四十五年

江架黿鼉以爲梁遂伐越至于紆荊人來貢

荊人于泲〇三十七年大起九師東至于九

作記〇三十五年、荊人入徐毛伯遷帥師敗

一年祭文公薨〇二十四年王命左史戎夫

十八年春正月、王居祇宮、諸侯來朝〇二十

有九萬里

還履天下億

其五王以東西征于青鳥所解山

王北征行流沙千里積羽千里征犬戎取三危西征

西王母來朝、賓于昭宮。秋八月、遷戎于太原。

of Wang-moo came to court, and was lodged in the palace of Ch'aou. In the autumn, in the 8th month, *certain* hordes were removed to T'ae-yuen.

Note. The king, in his expeditions to the north, travelled over the country of the Moving Sands, for 1,000 *le*, and that of 'Heaps of Feathers,' for 1,000 *le*. Then he subdued the hordes of the K'euen, and returned to the east, with their five kings as captives. Westwards, he pushed his expeditions to where the green birds cast their feathers (the hill of San-wei). On these expeditions he travelled over 190,000 *le*.

12　In his 18th year, in the spring, in the 1st month, he dwelt in the palace of Che,
13　where the princes came and did homage.　　　In his 21st year, duke Wăn of Tse
14　died.　　　In his 24th year, he ordered Jung-foo, the recorder of the Left, to make a
15　Record.13　　　In his 35th year, the people of King entered Seu, when Ts'ëen, baron
16　of Maou, led his forces, and defeated them near the Tse.14　　　In his 37th year, the
king raised a great force of nine hosts, and proceeded eastward to Këw-keang, where
he crossed the water on a bridge of tortoises and iguanadons piled up.15　After this,
he smote the people of Yuĕ as far as Yu.　The people of King came with tribute.
18　In his 39th year, he assembled the princes at mount T'oo.　　　In his 45th year,
19　Pe, prince of Loo, died.　　　In his 51st year, he made the code of Leu on Punish-
20　ments, and gave a Charge to the prince of P'oo in Fung.16　　　In his 59th year, he
died in the palace of Che.

VI. KING KUNG.

Note. Named E.

1　His 1st year was *këah-yin* (51st of cycle, = B.C. 906), when he came to the
3　throne.　　　In his 4th year, the royal forces extinguished Meih.　　　In his 9th
year, in the spring, in the 1st month, on the day *ting-hae* (24th of cycle), the king made Lëang, the recorder of the Interior, convey a Charge to Ts'ëen, baron of Maou.
4　In his 12th year, the king died.

shing, dep. P'ing-yang.　13 It is understood that this Record was a history of the rise and fall of dynasties and States, down to the commencement of the Chow dyn. King Muh had come to himself, and was ashamed of his wars, wanderings, and extravagance.　14 泲=濟 See the Tribute of Yu, Pt. ii. p. 10.　15 Häng makes this out to be only a bridge of boats　16. See the 27th of the Books of Chow.

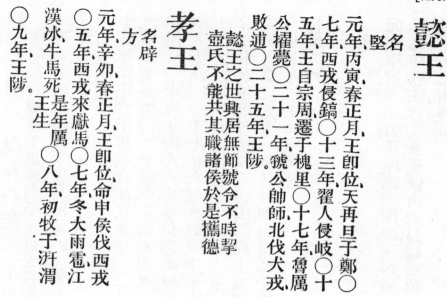

○九年王陟。
漢冰牛馬死是年厲王生
○八年初牧于汧渭
○五年西戎來獻馬○七年冬大雨雹江
元年辛卯春正月王即位命申侯伐西戎

方
名辟

孝王

懿王之世與居無節號令不時挈
壺氏不能共其職諸侯於是攜德

敗逋○二十五年王陟。
公擢薨○二十一年虢公帥師北伐犬戎
五年王自宗周遷于槐里○十七年魯厲
七年西戎侵鎬○十三年翟人侵岐○十
元年丙寅春正月王即位天再旦于鄭○

懿王
堅名

VII. KING E.

Note. Named Kёen.

1   In his 1st year, which was *ping-yin* (3d of cycle, = B.C. 894), when he came to
2 the throne, there were two sunrisings in Ch'ing.   In his 7th year, the hordes
3 of the west invaded Haou.   In his 13th year, the people of Teih invaded K'e.
4   In his 16th year, the king removed from Tsung-chow to Hwae-le.[1]   In his
6 17th year, Chih, the duke Le of Loo, died.   In his 21st year, the duke of K'woh
led his forces north, against the hordes of the K'euen, by whom he was defeated and
7 put to flight.   In his 25th year, the king died.

Note. The movements of king E were without proper regulation; the orders of his government
were ill-timed; the holder of the *time*-jar did not attend to his duty :—and the consequence was
that the princes began to lose their virtue.

VIII. KING HEAOU.

Note. Named Peih-fang.

1   In his 1st year, which was *sin-maou* (28th of cycle, = B.C. 869), in the spring, in
the 1st month, when he came to the throne, he ordered the prince of Shin[1] to smite the
2 hordes of the west.   In his 3d year, the hordes of the west came, and presented
3 horses.   In his 7th year, there were great rain and lightnings about the Kёang
and the Han; and oxen and horses died.

Note. In this year king Le was born.

4   In his 8th year, they made pasture grounds for the first time of the country about
5 the Keen and the Wei.[2]   In his 9th year, the king died.

VII. 1 Given as in the dis. of Hing-p'ing, dep. Se-ngan (Biot). Hăng Ch'in-fung contends this was a different place, and that the site is not known. He strongly repudiates the idea that in the movement of king E, or the previous one of Muh to Ch'ing, we are to understand anything like a transference of the capital.

VIII. 1 In dis. of Nan-yang, dep. Nan-yang, Ho-nan.   2 Fei-tsze, of the House of Ts'in, was employed to look after the king's horses here.

夷王
變名

元年庚子春正月、王即位○二年、蜀人呂
人來獻瓊玉、賓于河用介珪○三年、王致
諸侯、烹齊哀公于鼎○六年、王獵于社林、
獲犀牛一以歸○七年、虢公帥師伐太原
之戎、至于俞泉、獲馬千匹○冬、雨雹、大如礪。
楚子熊渠伐庸、至于鄂○八年、王有疾、諸
侯祈于山川、王陟。

厲王

名
○居戲有汾水焉
胡○故又曰汾王
元年戊申春正月、王即位、作夷宮、命卿士
榮夷公落楚人來獻龜貝○三年、淮夷侵
洛、王命虢公長父伐之、不克○齊獻公山薨
○六年、楚子延卒○八年、初監謗、芮伯良
夫戒百官于朝○十一年、西戎入于犬邱

IX. KING E.

Note. Named Sëĕ.

1 His 1st year was *kang-tsze* (37th of cycle, = B.C. 860), when he came to the
2 throne. In his 2d year, the people of Shuh[1] and the people of Leu[2] came to present carnation and other gems. *The king* performed a service of homage to the Ho,
3 using the large mace.[3] In his 3d year, he assembled the princes, and boiled duke
4 Gae of Ts'e in a tripod.[4] In his 6th year, when hunting in the forest of Shay,[5] he
5 captured a rhinoceros, and carried it home. In his 7th year, the duke of Kwoh led his forces, and smote the hordes of T'ae-yuen as far as Yu-ts'euen, capturing 1,000 horses. In the winter, there was a storm of hail as large as whetstones. Hëung-k'eu,
6 the viscount of Ts'oo, smote the country of Yung[6] as far as Goh.[7] In his 8th year, the king was ill, when the princes prayed to the hills and streams. The king died.

X. KING LE.

Note. Named Hoo. He dwelt at Che, where there is the Fun-water, and hence he is styled also king Fun.

1 In his 1st year, which was *mow-shin* (45th of cycle, = B.C. 852), when he came to the throne, he built the palace of E,[1] and gave a Charge to the prime minister Loh, the duke E of Yung.[2] The people of Ts'oo presented tortoise and other shells. In
2 his 3d year, the hordes of Hwae invaded Loh, when the king ordered Ch'ang-foo, duke of Kwoh, to act against them, which he did without effect. Shan, the duke Hëen
4 of Ts'e, died. In his 6th year, Yen, viscount of Ts'oo, died. In his 8th year, he began the watch for any who reviled him.[3] Lëang-foo, the baron of Juy,[4]
5 cautioned all the officers in the court. In his 11th year, the hordes of the west

IX. 1 Dep. of Ching-too, Sze-ch'uen. 2 In the pres. dis. of Sin-ts'ae, dep. Joo-ning, Ho-nan. 3 See under the 1st year of the emp. Mang of the Hea dynasty. I know not whether this service was connected with the reception of the people of Leu and Shuh, or not. 4 See the history of the House of Ts'e (齊世家), in the Historical Records.

5 Hăng would change 社 into 杜. dis. Chuh-san, dep. Yun-yang, Hoo-pih. 6 In dis. of Woo-ch'ang. 7 In

x. 1 As king Muh built a palace after the name of his father, king Ch'aou. 2 Yung must be the name of a principality. The dict., however, says nothing of this on the character. 3 Acc. to the Chow Joo, the king employed

宣王

名靖

元年甲戌、春正月、王即位、周定公召穆公

廢之不怒、逍遙得志于共山之首

靖、共和遂歸國、和有至德、尊之不喜、

陽、兆曰厲王為祟、周公召公乃立太子

大旱既久、廬舍俱焚、會汾王崩、卜于太

靖為王、共伯和歸其國、遂大雨。

年、大旱、王陟于彘、周定公召穆公立太子

麂○二十五年、大旱、楚子嚴卒○二十六

大旱、宋僖公麂○二十四年、大旱、杞武公

○二十二年、大旱陳幽公麂○二十三年、

蔡武侯麂楚子勇卒○十九年曹夷伯麂○

鄙召穆公帥師追蠻至于洛○十六年、

行天子事、號曰共和○十四年、玁狁侵宗周西

公之子殺之○十三年、王在彘共伯和攝

○十二年、王亡奔彘、國人圍王宮、執召穆

6   penetrated to K'euen-k'ew.   In his 12th year, the king became a fugitive, and fled to Che.5 The people surrounded the palace; and having seized the son of duke

7   Muh of Shaou, they put him to death.6   In his 13th year, the king was in Che; and Ho, baron of Kung, administered the imperial duties.7

Note. This is styled the period of Kung-ho.

8   In his 14th year, *the hordes of* the Yen-yun8 overran the western border of Tsung-chow. Duke Muh of Shaou led his forces in pursuit of the southern hordes of King

9 as far as the Loh.9   In his 16th year, prince Woo of Ts'ae died; and also Yung,

11 the viscount of Ts'oo.   In his 19th year, the baron E of Ts'aou died.   In

12 his 22d year, there was a great drought; and duke Yew of Ch'in died.   In his 23d

13 year, the drought continued; and duke He of Sung died.   In his 24th year, the

14 drought continued; and duke Woo of K'e died.   In his 25th year, still the

15 drought. Yen, viscount of Ts'oo, died.   In his 26th year, there was still the drought, when the king died in Che. The dukes, Ting of Chow and Muh of Shaou, then raised his eldest son Tsing to the throne; Ho, baron of Kung, returned to his State; and there was a great rain.

Note. The great drought had continued so long, that all huts were burned up. When king Fun died, they consulted by the tortoise-shell the *spirit of the* sun, and were answered that Le had been done to death by some monstrous thing. When the dukes of Chow and Shaou had raised his oldest son Tsing to the throne, Ho of Kung returned to his State. He was a man of the greatest virtue. Honours did not make him *overmuch* glad, nor did neglect move him to anger. He afterwards sought his own ease and pleasure in retirement on the top of mount Kung.

XI. KING SEUEN.

Note. Named Tsing.

1   In his 1st year, which was *keah-seuh* (11th of cycle, = B.C. 826), in the spring, in the first month, he came to the throne, when the dukes, Ting of Chow and Muh of

a diviner or magician in this work.   4 In dis. of Chaou-yih, dep. Se-ngan.   5 In dis. of Fun-se, dep. P'ing-yang.   6 The king's son was hidden in the duke of Shaou's house, who gave up his own son instead of him. 7 This is a sure epoch, acknowledged by all Chinese chronologists. Instead of there being only one regent, however, as these Annals say, the more common accounts make out two, Kung and Ho, the dukes of Chow and Shaou.   8 These were afterwards known as the Hëung-noo.   9 If this be the Lŏ river, or the State so called near it, we must suppose that the hordes of Ts'oo had come far north on an invading raid.

年、蔡夷侯甍○二十一年、魯公子伯
文公命○十六年、晉遷于絳○十八
公子赤○十五年、衛釐侯甍王錫號
魯武公甍齊人弒其君厲公無忌立
會諸侯于東都遂狩于甫○十二年、
武公來朝錫魯世子戲命○九年、王
樊侯仲山甫城齊○八年、初考室。魯
楚子霜卒○七年、王錫申伯命。王命
歸自伐徐錫召穆公命西戎殺秦仲。
戎、皇父休父從王伐徐戎次于淮、王
年、召穆公帥師伐淮夷王帥師伐徐
太原秋八月、方叔帥師伐荊蠻○六
四年、王命蹶父如韓韓侯來朝○五
王命大夫仲伐西戎齊武公壽甍○
甍。曹公子蘇弒其君幽伯疆○三年、
年、錫太師皇父司馬休父命魯慎公
輔政。復田賦。作戎車燕惠侯甍○二

Shaou, assisted in the government. He restored the field levies.1 He made chariots
2 of war. Prince Hwuy of Yen died. In his 2d year, he gave a Charge to Hwang-
foo, the Grand-tutor; and one to Hew-foo, the Master of the Horse. Duke Shin of Loo
died. Soo, a younger son of the House of Ts'aou, murdered his prince, Këang, the
3 baron Yew. In his 3d year, the king ordered the great officer Chung to attack
4 the hordes of the west. Show, the duke Woo of Ts'e, died. In his 4th year,
the king ordered Kwei-foo to go to Han, after which the prince of Han came to court.
5 In his 5th year, in the summer, in the 6th month, Yin Keih-foo led his forces, and
smote the Yen-yun, as far as T'ae-yuen.3 In the autumn, in the 8th month, Fang
6 Shuh led his forces, and smote the southern hordes of King.4 In his 6th year,
the duke Muh of Shaou led his forces against the hordes of the Hwae. The king
led his forces against the hordes of Seu, having Hwang-foo and Hew-foo in attendance on him, when he camped on the Hwae. When he returned from the expedition,
he gave a Charge to duke Muh of Shaou. The hordes of the west killed Chung of
7 Ts'in. Seang, viscount of Ts'oo, died. In his 7th year, the king gave a Charge
to the baron of Shin. The king ordered Chung Shan-foo, prince of Fan, to wall
8 Ts'e.5 In his 8th year, the king first completed the apartments *of one his palaces.*
Duke Woo of Loo came to court, when the king appointed his heir-son He to succeed
9 to the principality. In his 9th year, the king assembled the princes in the eastern
10 capital, after which they hunted in Foo.7 In his 12th year, duke Woo of Loo
died. The people of Ts'e murdered their ruler, Woo-ke, known as duke Le, and
11 appointed his son Ch'ih in his room. In his 15th year, prince Le of Wei died.
12 The king gave a Charge to duke Wăn of Kwoh. In his 16th year, Tsin removed
14 its capital to Keang.8 In his 18th year, prince E of Tse died. In his 21st
year, Pih-yu, of the ducal House of Loo, murdered his prince He, known as duke E.

XI. 1 These were charges for military ser-
vices, regulated by the quality of the lands.
They had been neglected during the exile of the
last king. 2 This coming of the prince of
Han to court is celebrated in the She, Pt. III.,
Bk. III., Ode vii. Mention is made of Kwei-foo.
3 This expedition is celebrated in the She,
Pt. II., Bk. III., Ode iii. 4 See the She, Pt. II.,
Bk. III., Ode iv. 5 See the She, Pt. III., Bk.
III., Ode vi. Fan was in the dis. of Tse-yuen,
dep. Hwae-k'ing. We are to understand the
metropolis of Tse. 6 考=成 'to finish.'
What apartments are intended, it is impossible
to say. They may have been, as many suppose,
those of a palace in honour of his father. 7
See the She, Pt. II., Bk. III., Ode v. 8 On
the north of the dis. of T'ae-p'ing, dep. P'ing-

御弒其君懿公戲○二十二年、王錫王
子多父命居洛○二十四年、齊文公赤
薨○二十五年、大旱王禱于郊廟遂雨
○二十七年宋惠公覵薨○二十八年、
楚子狗卒○二十九年初不藉千畞
三十年、有兎舞於鎬京○三十二年王
師伐魯殺伯御命孝公稱于夷宮陳僖
公薨薨有馬化爲人○三十三年齊成
公薨王師伐太原之戎不克○三十七
年有馬化爲狐燕僖侯卒楚子鄂卒○
三十八年王師及晉穆侯伐條戎奔戎
王師敗逋○三十九年王師伐姜戎戰
于千畞王師敗逋○四十年料民于太
原。于戎人滅姜邑晉人敗北戎于汾隰
四十一年王師敗于申○四十三年王
殺大夫杜伯其子隰叔出奔晉晉穆侯
費生薨弟殤叔自立世子仇出奔○四
十四年、年丁巳元○四十六年王陟。

15　In his 22d year, the king gave his Charge to To-foo, a scion of the royal House,
16　to reside at Loh.9　　　In his 24th year, Ch'ih, the duke Wan of Ts'e, died.　　In
17　his 25th year, there was a great drought, when the king prayed at the border altars
18　and in the ancestral temple; and there was rain.　　In his 27th year, Këen, the
19　duke Hwuy of Sung, died.　　In his 28th year, Seun, viscount of Ts'oo, died.
20　In his 29th year, the king for the first time neglected the setting an example of
21　husbandry in his thousand acres field.　　In his 30th year, hares appeared gam-
22　bolling in the capital Haou.　　In his 32d year, the royal forces attacked Loo,
　　and put Pih-yu to death; and the king invested Ch'ing, known as duke Heaou, with
　　the principality, in the palace of E.　Heaou, the duke He of Ch'in, died.　A horse
23　changed into a man.　　In his 33d year, the duke Ching of Ts'e died.　The royal
24　forces attacked the hordes of T'ae-yuen without success.　　In his 37th year, a
　　horse changed into a fox.　The prince He of Yen died.　Goh, the viscount of Ts'oo,
25　died.　　In his 38th year, the royal forces aud prince Muh of Tsin proceeded
　　against the hordes of the T'eaou and the Pun, when they were defeated and put to
26　flight.　　In his 39th year, the royal forces attacked the Këang hordes, and
27　were defeated, and put to flight in a battle in Ts'ëen-mow.12　　In his 40th year,
　　he numbered the people in T'ae-yuen.13　The western hordes destroyed the city of
28　Këang.14　The people of Tsin defeated some northern hordes in Fun-sih.15　　In
29　his 41st year, his forces were defeated in Shin.　　In his 43d year, he put to death
　　the great officer Too Pih, whose son Sih-shuh then fled to Tsin.　Fei-sang, the prince
　　Muh of Tsin, died, when his brother Seang-shuh usurped the principality, and the
30　heir-son K'ew fled.　　His 44th year was ting-sze, the 1st year of Shang-shuh of Tsin.
　　In his 46th year, the king died.

yang, between it and the small dep. of Këang.
The old capital Yih was also in dep. of P'ing-
yang.　　9 To-foo was a younger son of king
Le, and a brother of king Seuen.　　10 In a
field of 1,000 acres, the emperor turned up a
furrow in the spring, to set the people an example of husbandry; the princes did the same
in one of 100 acres.　From a passage in the
Chow Joo, we are led to suppose that Seuen had
neglected this practice from the beginning of
his reign.　The Annals here give us a different
impression.　The phrase 藉田 is variously
explained.　　11 Hăng Ch'in-fung thinks that
T'ëaou and Pun were the surnames of the wild
tribes spoken of.　Those who make them the
names of places entirely fail in identifying Pun.
　12 This seems to have been in the dis. of Gŏ-
yang, dep. P'ing-yang.　The Këang hordes, said
to be descended from Yaou's principal minister,
'the Four Mountains,' were numerous and powerful.　　13 This T'ae-yuen was in dis. King-
yang, dep. Se-ngan.　　14 In the dis. Paou-ke,
dep. Fung-ts'ëang.　　15 In dis. of K'euh-yuh,
dep. P'ing-yang.

幽王 涅名

元年庚申、春正月、王即位。晋世子仇歸
于晋、殺殤叔、晋人立仇、是爲文侯。王錫
太師尹氏皇父命。○二年、侯元年晋文
渭洛竭岐山崩、初增賦晋文侯同王子
多父伐鄶克之、乃居鄭父之邱、是爲鄭
桓公○三年、王嬖襃姒、冬、大雷電○四
年、秦人伐西戎、夏六月、隕霜、陳夷公薨○
○五年、王世子宜臼出奔申皇父作都
于向○六年、王命伯士帥師伐六濟之
戎、王師敗逋西戎滅蓋冬十月、辛卯、朔、
日有食之○七年、虢人滅焦○八年、王
錫司徒鄭伯多父命王立襃姒之子曰
伯服、爲太子○九年、申侯聘西戎及鄶
○十年、春、王及諸侯盟于太室、秋、九月、
桃杏實、王師伐申○十一年、春正月、日

XII. KING YEW.

Note. Named Nëĕ.

1 His 1st year was *kang-shin* (57th of cycle,=B.C. 780), when he came to the throne. K'ew, the heir son of Tsin, returned thither, and slew Shang-shuh. The people then raised him to the government;—he is known as prince Wan. The king gave a

2 Charge to Yin Hwang-foo, the Grand-tutor. In his 2d year,—*sin-yew,* the 1st year of prince Wăn of Tsin,—the King, Wei, and Loh, all became dry. *A part* of mount K'e fell down. *The king* began to increase the taxes, Prince Wan of Tsin, with To-foo, of the royal House, attacked, Tsang, and subdued it. After this *To-foo* took

3 up his residence on the hill of Ch'ing-foo. He was duke Hwan of Ch'ing.[1] In his 3d year, the king became enamoured with *his concubine* Paou-sze. In the winter,

4 there was great thunder and lightning. In his 4th year, the people of Ts'in smote the western hordes. In the summer, in the 6th month, there fell hoar-frost.

5 The duke E of Ch'in died. In his 5th year, his heir-son, E-k'ew, fled from the

6 court to Shin. Hwang-foo prepared *another* capital in Heang.[2] In his 6th year, the king ordered Pih-sze with the royal forces to attack the hordes of Luh-tse,[3] but they were defeated and put to flight. The western hordes destroyed K'ae. In the winter, in the 10th month, on the day *sin-maou,* there was an eclipse of the sun.

8 In his 7th year, the people of Kwoh extinguished Ts'ëaou.[4] In his 8th year, the king gave an additional dignity to To-foo, baron of Ch'ing, his minister of In-

9 struction. He made Pih-fuh, the son of Paou-sze, his heir apparent. In his 9th year, the prince of Shin sent an embassy to the western hordes, and to Tsang, and

10 entered *into an engagement with them.* In his 10th year, in the spring, he made a solemn agreement with the princes in the grand apartment of the ances-

11 tral temple.[5] In the autumn, in the 9th month, the peach trees and almond trees were in fruit. The king led his army against Shin. In the 11th year, in the

XII. 1 To-foo, mentioned here, was a younger brother of king Seuen, by whom he had been invested with the principality of Ch'ing. He wished to appropriate the State of Tsăng, which was afterwards done by one of his successors. That State was at this time only subdued.

Where Ch'ing-foo was, is not exactly known.

2 As if anticipating the capture, which took place ere long, of the existing capital; but where this Heang was is much debated. 3 These belonged to the Keang tribes. 4 ? In Shen

五年秦襄公帥師伐戎卒于師宋戴公
鄭伯命○四年燕頃侯薨鄭人滅虢○
邾岐之田○三年齊人滅祝王錫司徒
會衞侯鄭伯秦伯以師從王入于成周
元年辛未王東徙洛邑錫文侯命晉侯
事王即位皆不書
名宜臼○自東遷以後始紀晉
平王
年共二百八十一年自武王元年
己卯至幽王庚午二百九十二年
武王滅殷歲在庚寅二十四年歲在
甲寅定鼎洛邑至幽王二百五十七
立王子余臣于攜是爲攜王
二王並立
侯魯侯許男鄭子立宜臼于申虢公翰
桓公犬戎殺王子伯服執褒姒以歸申
暈申人鄫人及犬戎入宗周弒王及鄭

spring, in the 1st month, the sun and moon had haloes. The people of Shin, of Tsăng, and the hordes of the K'euen, entered Tsung-chow, and murdered the king and duke Hwan of Ch'ing. The *chief of the* K'euen killed the king's son, Pih-fuh, and took Paou-sze as his captive. The princes of Shin and Loo, with the *nan* of Heu and the young lord of Ch'ing, raised E-k'ew, who was in Shin, to the throne; but Han, duke of Kwoh, declared another son of Yew, named Yu-chin, who was in Hwuy, to be king.

Note. This last is known as king Hwuy. There were thus two kings at the same time.—When king Woo made an end of Yin, the year was in *kang-yin.* Twenty-four years after, in the year *kĕä-yin,* the vases were finally placed in the city of Lŏ. From that time to king Yew, were 257 years;—giving us in all 281 years. From *sin-maou,* the 1st year of Woo, to *kăng-woo,* the last of Yew, were 292 years.

XIII. KING P'ING.

Note. Named E-k'ew. From the removal of the capital to the east, the chronicler relates the affairs of Tsin; and the king's coming to the throne is not mentioned.

1   In his 1st year, which was *sin-wei* (8th of cycle,=B.C. 769), the king removed the capital to the east, to the city of Loh. He conferred the dignity *of chief among the princes* on prince Wan.[1] The prince of Tsin united with the prince of Wei, the barons of Ch'ing and Ts'in, and with their troops escorted the king to Ching-chow.[2]

2   In his 2d year, Ts'in made the western altar.[3] Hëaou of Loo died. The king
3 conferred on Ts'in and Tsin the fields of Pin and K'e. In his 3d year, the people of Ts'e extinguished Chuh.[4] The king conferred an additional dignity on the
4 baron of Ch'ing, his minister of Instruction.[5] In his 4th year, the prince king
5 of Yen died. The people of Ch'ing extinguished Kwoh. In his 5th year, the duke Sëang of Ts'in led his forces against the *western* hordes, and died on the ex-

Chow, Ho-nan.   5 太室 is to be taken here as on the occasion of its previous occurrence. This is plain from the She, Pt. II., Book V., Ode iv., which, probably, refers to this meeting of king Yew and the princes.

XIII. 1 See the xxxth of the Books of Chow.
2 Ching-chow is Lŏ. The transference of the capital is the subject of the She, Pt. II., Bk. V.,

Ode ix.   3 時=神靈之所依止, 'the place where the spirit rests.' Seang, the prince of Ts'in, elated with his new acquisitions in the west, made this altar, where he sacrificed to God. The presumption was somewhat disguised by making the sacrifice be to 'the white god' (白帝).   4 A small State on the north of Ts'e.   5 ? The dignity of duke. The

麋○六年燕哀侯麋。鄭遷於溙洧○七
年楚子儀卒○八年鄭殺其大夫關其
思○十年秦還于汧渭○十三年魏武
公麋○十四年晉人滅韓○十八年秦
文公大敗戎師于岐來歸岐東之田○
二十一年晉文侯殺王子余臣于攜○
二十三年宋武公麋○二十四年秦初
陳寶祠○二十五年晉文侯麋秦初用
族刑○二十六年侯元年丙申晉昭封其弟
成師于曲沃○三十二年晉潘父弒其
君昭侯納成師不克立昭侯之子孝侯、
晉人殺潘父○三十三年癸卯晉孝侯
人侵申○三十六年衞莊公麋王人戌
申○四十年齊莊公麋晉曲沃桓叔成
師卒子鱓立是爲莊伯、自是晉侯在
四十一年辛亥莊伯元年春大雨雪○四十二

6 pedition. The duke Tae of Sung died. In his 6th year, the prince Gae of Yen
7 died. Ch'ing removed its capital to near the Ts'in and the Hwuy.6 In his 7th
8 year, E, viscount of Ts'oo, died. In his 8th year, *the baron of* Ch'ing put his
9 great officer, Kwan K'e-sze, to death. In his 10th year, Ts'in removed its capital
10 to near the Këen and the Wei. In his 13th year, the duke Woo of Wei died.
12 In his 14th year, the people of Tsin extinguished Han.8 In his 18th year,
the duke Wăn of Ts'in inflicted a great defeat on the western hordes in K'e, and
13 came to restore the fields on the east of K'e. In his 21st year, the prince Wăn
14 of Tsin put the king's brother, Yu-chin, to death in Hwuy. In his 23d year,
15 the duke Woo of Sung died. In his 24th year, Ts'in instituted the sacrifices to
16 the Precious ones of Ch'in.9 In his 25th year, prince Wăn of Tsin died. Ts'in
17 for the first time, used the punishment of destroying criminals' relatives. In his
26th year,—ping-shin, the 1st year of prince Ch'aou of Tsin,—the prince of Tsin invested
18 his younger brother Ching-sze with the city of K'euh-yuh.10 In his 32d year,
Fan-foo of Tsin murdered his ruler, prince Ch'aou, and called Ching-sze to the
throne;—without success. The people of Tsin then called the son of Ch'aou, who
19 was the prince Heaou, to the sovereignty, and put Fan-foo to death. In his
33d year,—kwei-maou, the 1st year of prince Heaou of Tsin—the people of Ts'oo overran
20 Shin. In his 43d year, the duke Chwang of Wei died. The king's subjects
22 took guard of Shin. In his 40th year, duke Chwang of Ts'e died. Ching-sze,
Hwan-shuh of K'euh-yuh, died; and was succeeded by his son Shen, who is known
as Chwang-pih.

Note. From this time the prince of Tsin dwelt in Yih, and is known as the prince of Yih.

23 In his 41st year,—sin-hae, the 1st year of Chwang-pih,—in the spring, there was a great

10th ode of the She, Bk. V., Pt. II., is referred to this time. 6 The dis. of Hwuy-ch'uen, dep. K'ae-fung. The Ts'in flowed into the Hwuy. See the 13th of the Songs of Ch'ing, in the She, Part I. 7 The Keen is a tributary of the Wei. It gives name to the dis. of Këen-yang, dep. Fung-ts'ëang. 8 A Han, we saw, was walled by Yen in the 12th year of king Ching. That was in dis. of Koo-ngan, dep of Shun-t'ëen. A branch of that House had settled itself in the dis. of Han-shing, dep. T'ung-chow, Shen-se, which was the Han here spoken of. 9 The story is, that two boys, who changed into pheasants, had made their appearance, and it was known, in a wonderful way, that he who got the female would become chief

使虢公伐晉之曲沃晉鄂侯卒曲沃莊
公請成于翼至相而還作桐○二年王
焚曲沃之禾而還翼侯伐曲沃大捷武
子萬救翼荀叔軫追之至于家谷翼侯
元年壬戌十月莊伯以曲沃叛伐翼公

名林

桓王

春二月己巳日有食之三月庚戌王陟。
隱公及邾莊公盟于姑蔑○五十一年。
惠公薨○四十九年。己未魯隱公元年魯
侯○四十八年。戊午晉鄂侯無雲而雷魯
弒孝侯晉人逐之立孝侯子郤是為鄂
諭止之○四十七年晉曲沃莊伯入翼。
公使宰讓請郊廟之禮王使史角如魯
年狄人伐翼至于晉郊。宋襄公薨。魯惠

24 storm of rain and snow. In his 42d year, the wild tribes of the north attacked Yih,[11] and penetrated to the borders of Tsin. The duke Sëang of Sung died. The duke Hwuy of Loo sent Tsae Jang, to request liberty to use the ceremonies of the imperial border sacrifices and of the ancestral temple. The king sent the recorder 25 Këoh to go to Loo to stop the assumption. In his 47th year, Chwang-pih of K'euh-yuh of Tsin entered Yih, and murdered the prince Heaou. The people of Tsin drove him out, and raised to the sovereignty Keih the son of Heaou, known as 26 prince Goh. In his 48th year,—mow-woo, the 1st year of the prince Goh of Tsin,— 27 there was thunder without any clouds. The duke Hwuy of Loo died. In his 49th year,—ke-wei, the 1st year of duke Yin of Loo. In this year, the Ch'un-Ts'ew begins,— the duke Yin of Loo and the duke Chwang of Choo [12] formed an alliance at Koo- 28 mëë. In his 51st year, in the spring, in the 2d month, on the day yih-sze (42d of cycle), there was an eclipse of the sun. In the 3d month, on the day kang-seuh, the king died.

XIV. KING HWAN.

Note. Named Lin.

1 His 1st year was *jin-seuh* (59th of cycle,=B.C. 718). In the 10th month, Chwang-pih rebelled in K'euh-yuh, and attacked Yih. Wan, of the ruling House, came to the rescue of Yih, and Chin, the chief of Seun,[1] pursued Chwang-pih as far as the valley of Kea. The prince of Yih then burned the standing grain of K'euh-yuh, and returned. *Afterwards* he attacked the place, and gained a great victory. *Chwang-pih's son, afterwards* duke Woo, solicited peace, came as far as Sëang (or T'ung), 2 and returned. In his 2d year, the king made the duke of Kwoh attack K'euh-yuh of Tsin. The prince Goh of Tsin died, when Chwang-pih attacked Tsin. *The*

among the princes, while the possessor of the male would become king. They were called 'The precious ones of Ch'in,' from the place where they appeared. Duke Wăn of Ts'in caught the female, which changed into a stone; and he appointed a sacrifice to them in the pres. dis. of Paou-ke, dep. Fung-ts'ëang. 10 In the dis. so called of dep. P'ing-yang. 11

Mentioned in the note above as the capital of Tsin from the time of prince Heaou. It was in the dis. of Yih-shing, dep. of P'ing-yang. 12 In the dis. of Tsow, dep. Yen-chow. 13 In the dis. of Sze-shwuy, dep. Yen-chow.

XIV. 1 To the west of the river Fun (汾水). 2 That is, could only bring into the

伯復攻晉立鄂侯子光是爲哀侯〇三年、
甲子、晉哀侯〇四年曲沃莊伯卒子稱立是
爲武公尚一軍〇五年、曲沃武公元年
人董伯皆叛曲沃〇十一年、晉小子侯元年
晉哀侯晉人立哀侯子爲小子侯芮伯萬出
奔魏逐萬之母〇十二年王師秦師圍魏取芮
伯萬而東之〇十三年冬曲沃伯誘晉小子
侯殺之晉曲沃滅荀以其地賜大夫原氏黯。
是爲荀叔人逆芮伯萬于郊〇十四年王
命虢仲伐曲沃立晉哀侯弟緡于翼爲晉侯
〇十五年、晉侯緡元年〇十六年春滅翼〇十九
年鄭莊公薨〇二十三年三月乙未王陟。

莊王　名佗
元年乙酉曲沃尚一軍異于晉〇六年五月、
葬桓王〇十五年王陟。

4 *people of* Tsin raised Kwang, the son of prince Goh, to the sovereignty. He is known
as prince Gae.　　His 3d year was *keah-tsze*, the 1st year of prince Gae of Tsin.　　In

5 his 4th year, Chwang-pih of K'euh-yuh died, and was succeeded by his son Ch'ing,
the duke Woo. *The State* had still only one army.[2]　　In his 5th year,—the 1st

6 year of duke Woo of K'euh-yuh,—the people of Juy, Shing-king,[3] the people of Seun,
and the baron of Tung,[4] all rebelled against K'euh-yuh.　　In his 11th year,—1st
year of the prince Seaou-tsze of Tsin,—*the chief of* K'euh-yuh took prince Gae of Tsin
prisoner, when the people of Tsin put Gae's son, known as prince Sëaou-tsze, in his
place.　Wan, the baron of Juy, fled to Wei.[5]

Note. Wan was driven out by his mother.

7 In his 12th year, the royal forces and those of Ts'in besieged Wei, took Wan, the

8 baron of Juy, and carried him to the east.　　In his 13th year, in the winter, the
baron of K'euh-yuh enticed prince Sëaou-tsze of Tsin *to an interview,* and killed
him.　He then extinguished *the House of* Seun, and gave its territory to his great
officer Yuen Gan, who became the chief of Seun.　Some people of one of the western

9 hordes met Wan, the baron of Juy, in Keaou.[6]　　In his 14th year, the king ordered
Chung of Kwoh to smite K'euh-yuh, and to raise Min, a younger brother of prince

10 Gae, to be prince of Tsin in Yih.　His 15th year was the 1st year of prince Min of Tsin.

11 In his 16th year, in the spring, *K'euh-yuh* extinguished Yih *as the capital of*

12 *Tsin.*　　In his 19th year, the duke Chwang of Ch'ing died.　　In his 23d
year, in the 3d month, on the day *yih-wei,* the king died.

XV. KING CHWANG.

Note. Named T'o.

1 In his 1st year, which was *yih-yew* (22d of cycle, = B.C. 695), K'euh-yuh still

2 maintained only one army, different from Tsin.　　In his 6th year, in the 5th

3 month, he buried king Hwan.　　In his 15th year, he died.

field 12,500 men.　3 There seems to be some- | Shan-se.　6 This 郊 must be the name of
thing wanting here.　4 In dis. Yung-ho, dep. | a place. There is the reading of 郏.
T'ung-chow.　5 In the small dep. of Kёae,

趙鳳滅魏以賜大夫畢萬韓魏萌於此○

絳○十六年晉獻公作二軍滅耿以賜大夫趙○

入王府多取玉玉化爲蜮射人○九年晉城

兔舞于市○二年王子頹亂王居于鄭鄭人

元年乙巳晉獻公元年

閬名

惠王

晉武公卒子詭諸立爲獻公王陟。

晉猶不與齊桓公之盟緝是年滅

王命武公以一軍爲晉侯○四年十八年

亂○三年曲沃武公滅晉侯緡以寶玉獻王

元年庚子春齊桓公會諸侯于北杏以平宋

齊名胡

釐王

王如成周。周有白

左傳註晉侯○五年

晉武公三

XVI. KING LE.

Note. Named Hoo-ts'e.

1   In his 1st year, which was *kang-tsze* (37th of cycle, = B.C. 680), duke Hwan of Ts'e assembled the princes at Pih-hing,[1] to bring to order the troubles of Sung.

2   In his 3d year, duke Woo of K'euh-yuh made an end of prince Min of Tsin, and presented *many of* the precious relics of the State to the king, who appointed him to 3 be prince of Tsin, maintaining only one army.   In his 4th year,—the 38th year of duke Woo of Tsin,—Tsin still declined to be present at one of the meetings called by the duke Hwan of Ts'e.

Note. A note in the Tso Chuen says it was in this year prince Min of Tsin was made an end of.

4   In his 5th year, duke Woo of Tsin died, and was succeeded by his son Kwei-choo, known as duke Hëen.   The king died.

XVII. KING HWUY.

Note. Named Lëang.

1   In his 1st year, which was *yih-sze* (42d of cycle, = B.C. 675), the 1st year of duke Hëen of Tsin, the duke Hëen of Tsin went to court.   The king went to Ching-chow.

2   There a white hare appeared, dancing in the market place.   In his 2d year, his son T'uy raised a rebellion, and the king *went and* dwelt in Ch'ing, where the people entered his treasury, and took *many* gems, which changed into *yih* that shot 4 *their venom at* men.[1]   In his 9th year, Tsin walled Këang.[2]   In his 16th year, the duke Hëen of Tsin formed two armies, and extinguished the State of Kăng,[3] which he gave to his great officer Chaou Suh.   He also extinguished Wei, and gave it to his great officer Peih Wan.

Note. This was the germ of the extinction of Tsin by its great officers of Chaou, Han, and Wei.

XVI.   1 In the dis. of Tung-o, dep. T'ae-ngan.
XVII.   1 蜮,—see the She, Pt. II., Bk. V., Ode v., st. 8.   It is described as 'a short fox,' which lived in the water, where it filled its mouth with sand, which it shot at the shadows of persons on the bank, who thereon became sick.   3 In the small dep. of Këang, Shan-se. This had been one of the capitals of Shang.

十七年、衞懿公及赤狄戰于洞澤、作洞當○

十九年、晉獻公會虞師伐虢滅下陽虢公

醜奔衞虢公命瑕父呂甥邑于虢都○二十

五年春正月狄人伐晉王陟。

襄王　名鄭

元年、庚午、晉獻公卒、立奚齊里克殺之、及

卓子立夷吾○二年、辛未晉惠公殺里克

○三年、雨金于晉○七年秦伯涉河伐晉

○十五年晉惠公卒子懷公立秦穆公

帥師送公子重耳圍令狐桑泉白衰皆降

于秦師狐毛與先軫禦秦至于廬柳乃謂

秦穆公使公子縶來與師言次于郇盟于

軍公子重耳涉自河曲○十六年文公元

年、晉殺子圉○十七年晉城荀○二十

周襄王會諸侯于河陽○二十二年齊師

5　In his 17th year, duke E of Wei fought with the red hordes of the north at the
6　marsh of Tung (or K'eung).　　In his 19th year, duke Hëen of Tsin united his
forces with those of Yu, and, attacking Kwoh, destroyed Hea-yang.[4]　Ch'ow, duke
of Kwoh, fled to Wei, and *Hëen* ordered Hea-foo Leu-sang[5] to occupy his capital.

7　In his 25th year, in the spring, in the 1st month, some of the northern hordes
attacked Tsin.　The king died.

XVIII. KING SËANG.

Note. Named Ch'ing.

1　In his 1st year, which was *kang-woo* (7th of cycle,=B.C. 650), duke Hëen of Tsin died,
and He-ts'e was raised to the sovereignty.　Le K'ih, *however,* put him to death, and
2　Ch'oh-tsze *also,* whereon E-woo was chosen.　　In his 2d year,—*sin-we,* the 1st year
3　of duke Hwuy of Tsin,—*the duke* of Tsin put Le K'ih to death.　　In his 3d year,
4　it rained gold in Tsin.　　In his 7th year, the chief of Ts'in crossed the Ho and
5　attacked T'sin.　　In his 15th year, duke Hwuy of Tsin died, and was succeeded
by his son Yu, known as duke Hwae.　Duke Muh of Ts'in, with a force, escorted
duke Hëen's son, Ch'ung-urh, to the State, and invested Ling-koo,[1] Shwang-ts'euen,[2]
and K'ew-shwae,[3] which all surrendered.　Koo Wei and Sëen-chin went to Loo-lew [4]
to oppose Ts'in, when duke Muh sent his son Chih to speak with them, after which
they camped in Seun,[5] and entered into an engagement with Ch'ung-urh in the
6　midst of the army, he having crossed the Ho at Ho-k'euh.[6]　　In his 16th year,—
7　*yih-yew,* the 1st year of duke Wăn of Tsin,—Tsin put Tsze-yu to death.[7]　　In his 17th
8　year, Tsin walled Seun.[8]　　In his 20th year, king Sëang of Chow assembled the
9　princes in Ho-yang.[9]　　In his 22d year, the army of Ts'e drove out Ch'e, the

---

4 A city of Kwoh.　　5 This name is difficult to explain. Hea, perhaps, was the name of the officer's city, from which he was called Hea-foo. Then Leu would be his name, and Sang would denote his relationship to duke Hëen.

XVIII.　1 In dis. of E-she, dep. P'oo-chow. 2 In Lin-tsin dis., same dep.　　3 In Këae

Chow.　　4 Also in Këae Chow.　　5 In north-west of Këae Chow.　　6 Or 'the Bend of the Ho,' in dep. of P'oo-chow, where the river bends to the east.　　7 Tsze-yu=duke Hwae. 8 Mentioned under the 13th year of king Hwan.　　9 Probably in the dis. Măng, dep. Hwae-k'ing. The style of this par. is sufficient-

秦諜殺之絳市六日而蘇○七年晉成公卒于

元年乙卯晉成公元年○六年晉成公與狄伐秦獲

瑜名

定王

穿迎公子黑臀于周立之王陟。

元年己酉○六年晉靈公為趙穿所殺趙盾使

班名

匡王

元年癸卯○六年彗星入北斗王陟。

臣名
壬

頃王

年○三十三年王陟。

卒○二十五年公驪元年○三十年洛絕于洞

○三十一年晉襄公卒○三十二年公夷皇元

逐鄭太子崗奔城張南鄭○二十四年晉文公

甲午晉襄○三十年洛絕于洞晉靈

10　heir-prince of Ch'ing, who fled to Shing-chang Nan-ch'ing.10　　　　In his 24th
11　year, duke Wan of Tsin died.　　　　His 25th year was *kĕă-woo*, the 1st year of Hwan,
12　the duke Sëang of Tsin.　　　In his 30th year, the Loh was dried up at Hëang.11
13　　In his 31st year, duke Sëang of Tsin died.　　　His 32d year was *sin-ch'ow*, the 1st
14　year of E-kaou, the duke Ling of Tsin.　　　In his 33d year, the king died.

XIX. KING K'ING.

Note.　Named Jin-chin.

2　　His 1st year was *kwei-maou* (40th of cycle, = B.C. 617).　　　In his 6th year, a
comet entered the Great Bear (Northern Bushel); and the king died.

XX. KING K'WANG.

Note.　Named Pan.

2　　His 1st year was *ke-yew* (46th of cycle, = B.C. 611).　　　In his 6th year, duke
Ling of Tsin was killed by Chaou Ch'uen, who was then sent by Chaou Tun to
Chow, to fetch the prince Hih-t'un, and raise him to the dukedom.　The king died.

XXI. KING TING.

Note.　Named Yu.

1　　His 1st year was *yih-maou* (52d of cycle, = B.C. 605), the 1st year of duke Ching of
2　Tsin.　　　In his 6th year, duke Ching of Tsin, with some of the northern hordes,
attacked Ts'in, and captured a spy, whom they put to death in the market place of
3　Këang, and who came to life again six days after.　　　In his 7th year, duke Ching

ly remarkable.　The king appears on a level
with the princes.　　10 The text of this par.
is evidently corrupt and defective.　　11 This
name is not elsewhere found.　Ch'in-fung gues-

ses that it should be 洞 or 向.

XXI.　1 In dis. Yung-yang, dep. K'ae-fung.
2 See the account of the affair in the Ch'un

扈○八年、壬戌晉景○十八年齊國佐來獻玉磬

紀公之齋○二十一年王陟。
公元年

簡王
名夷

元年丙子○五年晉景公卒○六年、辛巳晉厲
十三年晉厲公卒楚共王會宋平公于湖陽○十
四年公元年
已丑晉悼王陟。

靈王
名泄

元年庚寅○十四年晉悼公卒○十五年、甲辰晉
年○二十七年王陟。
平公元

景王
名貴

元年丁巳○十三年春有星出婺女十月晉平公
卒○十四年公元年
庚午晉昭河水赤于龍門三里○十

4　of Tsin died in Hoo.[1]　　　　His 8th year was *jin-seuh*, the 1st year of duke King of Tsin.

5　　In his 18th year, the Aid of the State of Ts'e came to present some musical stones

6　of gem, and the boiler *which Ts'e had taken* from the duke of Ke.[2]　　　In his 21st
year, the king died.

XXII. KING KEEN.

Note. Named E.

2　　His 1st year was *ping-tsze* (13th of cycle,=B.C. 584).　　　In his 5th year, the

3　duke King of Tsin died.　　　His 6th year was *sin-sze*, the 1st year of duke Le of Tsin.

4　　In his 13th year, the duke Le of Tsin died. The king Kung of Ts'oo had a

5　meeting with the duke P'ing of Sung in Hoo-yang.[1]　　　In his 14th year, *ke-ch'ou*,
the 1st year of duke Taou of Tsin, the king died.

XXIII. KING LING.

Note. Named Sëe.

2　　His 1st year was *kang-yin* (27th of cycle,=B.C. 570).　　　In his 14th year, the

3　duke Taou of Tsin died.　　　His 15th year was *kёǎ-shin*, the 1st year of the duke P'ing

4　of Tsin.　　　In his 27th year, he died.

XXIV. KING KING.

Note. Named Kwei.

2　　His 1st year was *ting-sze* (54th of cycle,=B.C. 543).　　　In his 13th year, in the
spring, a star issued from the constellation Woo-neu.[1] In the 10th month, duke P'ing

3　of Tsin died.　　　In his 14th year,—*kang-woo*, the 1st year of duke Ch'aou of Tsin,—the

Ts'ew and Tso Chuen, under the 2d year of duke
Ching.
XXII. 1 Probably in dep. of Keih-gan, Këang-se.

XXIV. 1 'The widow;'—four stars, about the
middle of Capricorn.

165]

九年晉昭公卒冬十二月桃杏花〇二十年〇

丙子晉頃〇二十五年晉頃公平王室亂立

公元年

敬王。

敬王

名丐

元年壬午〇八年晉頃公卒〇九年庚寅晉

〇十四年漢不見于天〇二十六年晉青

虹見〇二十八年洛絕于周〇三十六年淇

絕于舊衞〇三十九年晉城頓邱〇四十三

年宋殺其大夫皇瑗于丹水之上丹水壅不

流〇四十四年王陟。

元王

名仁

元年丙寅晉定公卒〇二年丁卯晉出〇四

於越滅吳〇六年晉㵁絕于梁丹水三日、

年

4　waters of the Ho at Lung-mun were red for 3 *le*.　In his 19th year, duke Ch'aou
　of Tsin died.　In the winter, in the 12th month, peach trees and almond trees were
5　in flower.　His 20th year was the 1st year of the duke K'ing of Tsin.　In his
6　25th year, duke K'ing of Tsin pacified the disorders of the royal House, and placed
　king King on the throne.

XXV. KING KING.

Note. Named K'ae.

2　His 1st year was *jin-woo* (19th of cycle,=B.C. 518).　In his 8th year, duke
3　K'ing of Tsin died.　His 9th year was *kăng-yin*, the 1st year of duke Ting of Tsin.
5　In his 14th year, the milky way was not visible in the sky.　In his 26th year,
6　an azure rainbow was seen in Tsin.　In his 28th year, the Loh was dry in Chow.
8　In his 36th year, the K'e was dry in Old Wei.[1]　In his 39th year, Tsin walled
9　Tun-k'ew.[2]　In his 43d year, *the duke of* Sung killed his great officer Hwang
　Yuen near the Tan-water, the course of which was stopt, so that it did not flow.[3]
10　In his 44th year, the king died.

XXVI. KING YUEN.

Note. Named Jin.

1　In his 1st year, which was *ping-yin* (3d of cycle,=B.C. 474), the duke Ting of
3　Tsin died.　His 2d year was *ting-maou*, the 1st year of duke Ch'uh of Tsin.　In his 4th
4　year, *the State of* Yu-yueh extinguished *that of* Woo.[1]　In his 6th year, the course
　of the Kwei[2] of Tsin ceased at Lëang.　The course of the Tan[3] water was interrupted,

xxv. 1 'Old Wei;'—*i. e.* Chaou-ko, formerly
the capital of Wei, but now belonging to Tsin.
2 In dis. Ts'ing-fung, dep. Ta-ming, Chih-le.
3 There were no fewer than 7 Tan-waters.
The one here was also called the P'ëen (汳);
on which see the dictionary.

xxvi. 1 These two States lay along the sea-
board, embracing a considerable portion of
Keang-soo and Chĕ-keang.　Woo was the more
northern of the two.　2 The Kwei took its
rise from a mountain in the east of dis. of Kĕang,
in the dep. of the same name, in Shan-se.　3
This took its rise in the dis. Kaou-p'ing, dep.
Tsih-chow.

貞定王 名介

絶不流○七年齊人鄭人伐衞王陟。

元年癸酉、於越徙都瑯琊○四年十一月、於
越子句踐卒、是爲菼執次鹿郢立○六年、晉
河絶于扈○七年晉荀瑤城南梁公二十年出
一本晉出
○十年、於越子鹿郢卒、不壽立○十一年、晉
出公出奔齊○十二年、河水赤三日晉荀瑤
伐中山、取窮魚之邱○十三年晉韓龐取盧
氏城○十六年、晉十二年
薨乃立昭公之孫是爲敬公○十七年晉出公
公元○十八年庚寅敬
次朱句立○二十二年楚滅蔡○二十四年、
年○二十年、於越子不壽見殺是爲盲姑、
楚滅杞○二十八年、公十一年王陟。

5 and stopped for 3 days.　　　　In his 7th year, the people of Ts'e and of Ch'ing
attacked Wei. The king died.

XXVII. KING CHING-TING.

Note. Named Këae.

1 In his 1st year, which was *kwei-yew* (10th of cycle,＝B.C. 467), Yu-yueh removed its
2 capital to Lang-ya.1　　In his 4th year, in the 11th moath, Kow-ts'een, the viscount
of Yu-yueh, known as Tan-chih,2 died, and was succeeded by *his son*, Luh-ch'ing.
4 In his 6th year, the Ho of Tsin stopt its course at Hoo.　　In his 7th year,
Seun Yaou of Tsin walled Nan-lëang.3

Note. One copy adds:—'In the 20th year of duke Ch'uh of Tsin.'

5 In his 10th year, Luh-ch'ing, the viscount of Yu-yueh died, and was succeeded by
7 Puh-show.　　In his 11th year, the duke Ch'uh of Tsin fled to Ts'e.　　In his
12th year, the waters of the Ho were red for three days. Seun Yaou smote Chung-
8 san,4 and took the hill of K'ëung-yu.5　　In his 13th year, Han P'ang of Tsin
9 took the city of Loo She.6　　His 16th year was the 22d year of the duke Ch'uh of Tsin.
10 In his 17th year, the duke Ch'uh of Tsin died, when a grandson of duke Ch'aou,
11 known as duke King, was raised to the dukedom.　　His 18th year was the 1st year
12 of duke King of Tsin.　　In his 20th year, Puh-show, the viscount of Yu-yueh,
13 known as Mang-koo, was put to death, and was succeeded by Choo-kow.　　In
14 his 22d year, Ts'oo extinguished Ts'ae.　　In his 24th year, Ts'oo extinguished
15 K'e.　　In his 28th year, the 11th year of duke King of Tsin, the king died.

XXVII. 1 There was more than one Lang-ya. That here was in the dis. of Choo-shing, dep. Ts'ing-chow, Shan-tung. 2 Kin Le-ts'eang observes that Tan-chih are to be read together as one word, 'after the syllabic way of the west,' being the viscount's name in the speech of Yuĕ. 3 In the dep. of Joo, Ho-nan. 4 In dis. of T'ang, dep. Paou-ting. 5 Supposed to be a place on the river Lae (溇). 6 In the dis. of Loo-she, Shen Chow, Ho-nan.

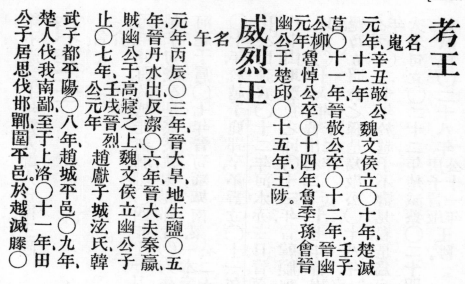

XXVIII. KING K‘AOU.

Note. Named Wei.

1 In his 1st year, which was *sin-ch‘ow* (38th of cycle,=B.C. 439), the 12th year of the duke
2 King, the prince Wan of Wei came to his inheritance.   In his 10th year, Ts‘oo
4 extinguished Keu.1   In his 11th year, duke King of Tsin died.   In his 12th
year,—*jin-tsze*, the 1st year of Lew, the duke Yew of Tsin,—the duke Taou of Loo died.
5   In his 14th year, Ke-sun of Loo had a meeting with the duke Yew of Tsin in
6 Ts‘oo-k‘ew.2   In his 15th year, the king died.

XXIX. KING WEI-LĔEH.

Note. Named Woo.

2   His 1st year was *ping-shin* (53d of cycle,=B.C. 424).   In his 3d year, there
3 was a great drought in Tsin, and the ground produced salt.   In his 5th year,
the waters of the Tan of Tsin 1 left *their natural course*, and battled in an opposite
4 direction.2   In his 6th year, Ts‘in Ying, a great officer of Tsin, murdered duke
Yew in the Lofty chamber, when prince Wan of Wei raised Che, the son of duke
5 Yew, to the dukedom.   In his 7th year, which was *jin-seuh*, the 1st year of duke Lĕĕ
of Tsin, Hĕen-tsze3 of Chaou walled Heuen-she,4 and Woo-tsze of Han,5 made his
6 capital in P‘ing-yang.   In his 8th year, Chaou walled the city of P‘ing.6   In
7 his 9th year, the people of Ts‘oo attacked our south border as far as Shang-loh.7
8   In his 11th year, Keu-sze,8 a son of the ducal Head *of the House* of T‘ĕen,9 attacked Han-tan,10 and besieged the city of P‘ing.   Yu-yueh extinguished T‘ang.11

XXVIII. 1 In the dis. of Ngan-k‘ew, dep. Ts‘ing-chow, Shan-tung.   2 Probably in dis. of Keu-yay, dep. Ts‘aou-chow.
XXIX. 1 In dep. of Tsih-chow, Shan-se.   2 潔 here is taken as=擊.   3 The incidents referred to here are not clearly related else-where. I am strongly inclined to believe, with some critics, that for 大夫 we should read 夫人; so the meaning is that duke Yew was murdered by his wife, a lady of the House of Ts‘in, in his chamber,—his own private and peculiar apartment.   4 The 子 here=officer or chief.   5 In dis. of Ling-ch‘uen, dep. Tsih-chow.   6 In dis. of Ch‘ang-loh, dep. Ts‘ing-chow.   7 In Shang Chow, Shen-se. ——By 'our' southern border is meant the south-ern border of Wei. Whereas the Annals have, from the accession of king P‘ing, been those more particularly of Tsin, from the 1st year of king K‘aou, the 1st also of prince Wan of Wei, they relate to that State.   8 This Keu-sze

陜．氏趙氏韓氏爲諸侯○二十四年王
齊入長垣○二十三年王命晉卿魏
八年王命韓景子趙烈子及我師伐
邱及田布戰于龍澤田師敗逋○十
田布圍廩邱翟角趙孔屑韓師救廩
大夫公孫孫公孫會以廩邱叛于趙
還築汾陰郃陽田悼子卒田布殺其
邑新城○十七年魏文侯伐秦至鄭
平邑邯鄲之師敗逋遂獲韓舉取平
○十六年齊田聆及邯鄲韓舉戰於
歸○十四年於越子朱勾卒子翳立
十二年於越子朱勾伐郯以郯子鴣

安王　名驕
元年庚辰○九年晉烈公卒子桓公
立○十年已丑傾元年○十五年魏

9 　In his 12th year, Choo-kow, the viscount of Yu-yueh, attacked T'an,[12] and carried
10 off captive its viscount Koo. 　　In his 14th year, Choo-kow, viscount of Yu-yueh,
11 died, and was succeeded by his son E. 　　In his 16th year, T'een P'an of Ts'e fought
near P'ing with Han Keu of Han-tan, when the forces of Han-tan were defeated and
put to flight, and *T'ëen P'an* took Han Keu prisoner, and captured the city of P'ing
12 and Sin-shing.[13] 　　In his 17th year, the prince Wan of Wei invaded Ts'in as far
as Ch'ing, and on his return built Fun-yin and Hoh-yang.[14] 　T'ëen Taou-tsze died;
and T'ëen Poo put to death his great officer Kung-sun Sun. 　Kung-sun Hwuy took possession of Lin-k'ëw,[15] and rebelled against Chaou. 　T'ëen Poo laid siege to Lin-k'ëw,
to the rescue of which came Teih Këoh,[16] K'ung Sëë of Chaou, and the army of Han,
who fought with Poo near the marsh of Lung, defeated him, and put him to flight.
13 　In his 18th year, the king ordered the chiefs King of Han and Lëeh of Chaou, and
our forces, to attack Ts'e; when we penetrated within the Long wall.[17] 　In his 23d
year, the king conferred on the nobles of Tsin, each of the Heads of the Houses of
14 Wei, Chaou, and Han, the title of prince.[18] 　　In his 24th year, the king died.

XXX. KING NGAN.

Note. Named Këaou.

1 　His 1st year was *kang-shin* (17th of cycle, = B.C. 400). 　　In his 9th year, duke
2 Lëeh of Tsin died, and was succeeded by his son, duke Hwan.[1] 　　His 10th
3 year was *ke-ch'ow*, the 1st year of K'ing, the duke Hwan of Tsin. 　In his 15th year,

is not read of elsewhere. 　9 At this time
the family of T'ëen had engrossed the power of
Ts'e, over which it asserted ere long sole authority. Still a prince of the House of Leu was
nominally ruling, and we can only translate
田公 as I have done. 　10 In dis. of Han-
tan, dep. Kwang-p'ing, Chih-le. This was the
chief city of the House—shortly, the State—of
Chaou, one of the dismemberments of Tsin, and
we shall find it often used for Chaou. 　11
The dis. T'äng, dep. Yen-chow. 　12 Dis. of
T'an-shing, dep. E-chow, Shan-tung. 　13 Not
clearly ascertained. 　14 Both these places
were in dep. of T'ung-chow, where there is still
the dis. of Hö-yang. 汾 seems to be a mistake

for 洛. 　15 In the dis. of Yun-shing, dep.
Ts'aou-chow. In most editions of the Annals,
Lin-k'ew is said to have been held by Kung-sun
Sun, which is evidently wrong. Häng Ch'in-
fung reads 會 instead of 孫. The events
indicated in the par. cannot be clearly gathered
from other sources. 　16 Teih Keoh was of
Wei. 　17 This appears to have been a wall
built by the chiefs of T'een, running from Mt.
T'ae to Lang-ya. 　18 Here was the imperial
sanction to the extinction of the ancient State
of Tsin, and the usurpations of the three Houses
mentioned. See the note on Mencius, I., Pt. I.,
i. 1.

韓共侯趙成侯遷晉桓于屯留、更無
山堅賊其君哀侯○六年、成王元年、辛亥、以後
諸侯于范臺晉桓公邑哀侯于鄭韓
伐韓、韓將韓襄敗胡蘇于酸水、魏觸
無余是爲恭安○二年秦胡蘇帥師
地名
邯鄲趙、於越大夫寺區定越亂立初
元年丙午、魏公子緩、如邯鄲以作難。
喜名
○二十一年、韓滅鄭、哀侯入于鄭○
二十三年、於越遷于吳○二十六年
王陟、魏城洛陽、及安邑王垣、七月、於
越太子諸咎弒其君翳十月越人殺
諸咎越滑吳人立孚錯枝爲君

烈王

文侯卒。在位五大風晝昏。晉太子喜
出奔○十六年、侯擊元年乙未魏武封公子緩

the prince Wan of Wei died, having enjoyed his dignity 50 years. There was great wind, and it was dusk at noon. He, the oldest son of the duke of Tsin, fled away. In

4 his 16th year, which was yih-wei, the 1st year of Keih, the prince Woo of Wei, one of the sons of Woo, called Hwan, was appointed to a government *away from the capital.*2 In

5 his 21st year, Han extinguished *the State of* Ch'ing, and the prince Gae *of Han*
6 took possession of its capital. In his 23d year, Yu-yueh removed its capital to
7 Woo. In his 26th year, the king died. Wei walled Loh-yang,3 Ngan-yih,4
8 and Wang-heuen.5 In the 7th month, the oldest son of the viscount of Yu-yueh, named Choo-kew, murdered his ruler E.6 In the 10th month, the people of Yueh put Choo-kew, *also called* Yueh-hwah, to death, and put Foo-ts'oh-che in his place.7

Note. Named He.

XXXI. KING LEEH.

1 In his 1st year, which was *ping-woo* (43d of cycle,=B.C. 374), Hwan of the ruling House of Wei went to Han-tan, to produce troubles. Han-tan is the name of a place in Chaou. Sze-k'eu, a great officer of Yu-yueh, settled the disorders of the State, and

2 placed Ts'oo-woo-yu, known as Mang-ngan, at its head. In his 2d year, Hoo Soo of Ts'in led a force against Han, and was defeated by Han Seang, the general of Han, near the Swan-water.1 Wei feasted the princes in the tower of Fan.2 Duke Hwan of Tsin sanctioned the occupation of Ch'ing by prince Gae *of Han* as his

3 capital. Shan Keen of Han slew his ruler, the prince Gae. In his 6th year,— *sin-hae,* the 1st year of king Hwuy-ching of Leang,—the princes Kung of Han and Ching of Chaou removed the duke Hwan of Tsin to T'wan-lew;3 —after this, we have nothing more about the affairs of Tsin. Yen, the prince Ching of Chaou, and Joh, the prince E

XXX. 1 These were merely nominal dukes. 2 It is necessary to supplement the text here. The ruler of Wei sent away his son Hwan to avoid future troubles;—which, however, occurred in course of time. 3 Should, probably, be 汾陽, still the name of a dis., dep. Fun-chow. 4 In Këae Chow. 5 In Këang Chow. 6 His ruler was also his father. The thing is related confusedly, here and elsewhere.

7 I have translated here according to the suggestions or conjectures of Hăng Ch'in-fung, who thinks the text is corrupt or mutilated. The capital being now in Woo, 吳人＝越人.

XXXI. 1 In the south of the dis. of Yen-tsin, dep. Wei-hwuy. 2 Hăng argues that this passage should come in under the 12th year of king Hëen. 3 In dis. of Ch'ang-tsze, dep. Loo-

顯王

扁名

晉
趙成侯偃韓懿侯若伐我葵郊〇七
年王陟。我師伐趙圍濁陽齊田壽帥師
事

伐我圍觀觀降魏大夫王錯出奔韓。

元年癸丑鄭城邢邱。
命爲藍君〇二年河
〇三年公子景賈帥師伐鄭韓明戰于
韓我師敗逋〇四年夏四月甲寅徙都于
于大梁。王發逢忌之藪以賜民於越寺
區弟思弑其君莽安次無顯立〇五年，
雨碧于郢地忽長十丈有餘高尺半〇
六年我師伐邯鄲取列人我師伐邯鄲。
取肥。雨黍于齊〇七年我與邯鄲榆
次陽邑王會鄭釐侯于巫沙〇八年入
河水于圃田又爲大溝，而引圃水瑕陽

水赤于龍門三日
稱曰鄭改秦子向

自此韓改秦子向

4 of Han, attacked our city of K'wei.4　　In his 7th year, the king died.　Our forces attacked Chaou, and invested Ch'uh-yang.5　T'ëen Show of Ts'e came with a force against us, and besieged Kwan,6 which surrendered.　Wang Ts'oh, a great officer of Wei, fled to Han.

XXXII. KING HËEN.

Note. Named Peen.

1　In his 1st year, which was *kwei-ch'ow* (50th of cycle,=B.C. 367), Ch'ing walled Hing-k'ew.1

　　Note. From this, the name of Han is exchanged for Ch'ing.

2　Tsze-hëang of Ts'in was appointed ruler of Lan.2　　In his 2d year, the waters
3　of the Ho were red for three days at Lung-mun.　　In his 3d year, King Këa of our ruling House led a force against Ch'ing, when Han Ming fought with us in
4　Han,3 and our forces were defeated and put to flight.　　In his 4th year, in the summer, in the 4th month, on the day *këah-yin*, we removed our capital to Ta-lëang.4　Our king threw open his preserves in *the marsh of* Fung-ke for the benefit of the people.5　Sze, a younger brother of Sze-k'eu of Yu-yueh, murdered him,—Mang-
5　ngan,—his ruler, who was succeeded by Woo-chuen.　　In his 5th year, it rained *peih* stones in Ch'ing.6　Some ground there suddenly became longer by 100 cubits and more,
6　and higher by a cubit and a half.　　In his 6th year, our forces attacked Han-tan, and took Lëeh-jin.　They attacked it again, and took Fei.8　It rained millet in Ts'e.
7　　In his 7th year, we gave to Han-tan Yu-tsze 9 and Yang-yih.9　Our king had
8　a meeting with the prince Le of Ch'ing at Woo-sha.10　　In his 8th year, we led the waters of the Ho into *the marsh of* P'oo-t'een,11 and also made great ditches to

ngan.　　4 In dis. of Ho-nuy, dep. of Hwae-k'ing.　　5 In dis. of Ch'ang-kŏ, dep. of Heu. It formerly belonged to Han, but had now, perhaps, passed into the possession of Chaou.　6 In dis. of Kwan-shing, dep. Tung-ch'ang.
　　XXXII. 1 In dis. of Ho-nuy, dep. Hwae-k'ing.
　2 In dis. of Lan-t'ëen, dep. Se-ngan.　　3
This battle was at a place called Puh-yang (濮
陽), on the Puh-water, which had formerly belonged to Wei, but was now held by Han or Ch'ing.　4 Dis. city of Ts'ëang-foo, dep.

K'ae-fung;—what is called K'ae-fung.　　5 This marsh was not far from the capital.　This was one of the measures for which king Hwuy took credit with Mencius.　See Mencius, I. Bk. I., iii., 1.　　6 In dis. of Këang-ling, dep. King-chow, Hoo-pih.　　7 Probably in dis. of Kwang-p'ing, dep. Kwang-p'ing, Chih-le.
　　8 In dis. Fei-hëang, same dept.　　9 Both in dep. T'ae-yuen, where we have still the dis. of Yu-tsze.　10 A place upon the river Tse.　11 In dis. of Chung-mow, dep. K'ae-fung.　　12 The construction of this passage is not easy.

171]

我師敗逋東周與鄭高都鄭釐
年齊田期伐我東鄙戰于桂陽
及燕戰于泃水齊師遁〇十五
邯鄲伐衛取漆富邱城之齊師
公孫壯伐鄭圍鄭上枳安陵山氏
秦公孫壯帥師圍焦城不克秦民
侯會燕成侯于安邑〇十四年
卯次無疆立〇十三年邯鄲成
來朝於越子無顓卒是爲菼蠋
魯恭侯宋桓侯衛成侯鄭釐侯
宅陽之圍歸釐于鄭〇十二年
鹿王及鄭釐侯盟于巫沙以釋
諸邑及鄭馳道我取枳道與鄭
使許息來致地平邱戶牖首垣
取屯留尚子〇十一年鄭釐侯
外龍賈帥師築長城于西邊。鄭
十年楚師出河水以水長垣之
九年秦師伐鄭次于懷城殷〇
人自秦導岷山青衣水來歸〇

lead off the waters of the marsh. The people of Hea-yang led the waters of the

9 Ts'ing-e of mount Min all the way from Ts'in to our State.12　　In his 9th year,

10 the forces of Ts'in attacked Ch'ing, camped in Hwae, and walled Yin.13　　In his 10th year, an army from Ts'oo led out the waters of the Ho to overflow the country outside the Long wall.14　Lung Këa led a body of troops to build the great wall on

11 our western border.15　Ch'ing took T'wan-lew and Shang-tsze.16　　In his 11th year, the prince Le of Ch'ing sent Heu Shih to surrender to us the cities of P'ing-k'ew, Hoo-yew, and Show-yuen, with the country as far as the highway of Ch'ing; while we *ourselves* took Che-taou and Ch'ing-luh.17　The king had an interview with the prince Le at Woo-sha, where he agreed to raise the siege of Tsih-yang, and

12 to restore *the city of* Le to Ch'ing.17　　In his 12th year, the princes Kung of Loo, Hwan of Sung, Ching of Wei, and Le of Ch'ing, all came to our court, *in acknowledgment of submission*.　Woo-chuen, the viscount of Yu-yueh, known as

13 T'an-ch'uh-maou, died, and was succeeded by Woo-këang.　　In his 13th year, the prince Ching of Han-tan had an interview with the prince Ching of Yen in

14 Ngan-yih.　　In his 14th year, Kung sun Chwang of Ts'in attacked Ch'ing, and besieged the city of Tsëaou, without being able to take it. He then led his army, and walled Shang-che,18 Ngan-ling,19 and San-min. Han-tan attacked Wei, took the hill of Ts'ih-foo,20 and walled it. The army of Ts'e fought with Yen near the Kow-

15 water,21 and was put to flight.　　In his 15th year, T'ëen K'e of Ts'e attacked our eastern border, when a battle was fought at Kwei-yang,22 in which our forces were

---

The Ts'ing-e flows from the dis. of Loo-san, dep. Ya-chow, Sze-ch'uen, and ultimately joins the Këang. Seu Tsing-san thinks the meaning is that the people of Hea-yang had performed the service described for Ts'in, and in this year came back to Wei. The meaning in the translation is more natural, and is preferred by Hăng Ch'in-fung.　13 In dis. Ho-nuy, dep. Hwae-k'ing. But the reading is not sure.　14 楚 is here evidently corrupt. Granting that there was in its dominions an erection called 'The Long Wall,' it was too remote from the Ho to allow of our supposing any such attempt on its part as is described. Hăng Ch'in-fung would substitute 韓 for 楚.　15 It is observed that this was the commencement of

the Great Wall.　16 Shang-tsze is another name for Ch'ang-tsze, pres. name of the district to which T'wan-lew is referred. See above.　17 Wei was at this time pressing Han hard, and the surrenders here mentioned were made to obtain peace. 'The highway of Ch'ing' had formerly been called 'The general Road' (達路). All the places spoken of are to be looked for in dep. of K'ae-fung.　18 In dis. of Tse-yuen, dep. Hwae-k'ing.　19 In dis. Yen-ling, dep. K'ae-fung.　20 In dis. of Ch'ang-yuen, dep. Ta-ming, Chih-le.　21 Flows thro' the dis. of P'ing-kuh, dep. Shun-t'ëen.　22 Kwei-yang,—prob.=the north of the Kwei river. I have not found any deter-

地堮西絶于汾○二十四年魏
陽秦孝公會諸侯于逢澤絳中
及鄭師伐楚取上蔡孫何取讙
伐徐州○二十三年魏章帥師
年壬寅孫何侵楚入三戶郟楚
燕還取夏屋城曲逆○二十二
二十一年魏殷臣趙公孫裒伐
衞命公子南爲侯○二十年○
築防以爲長城○十九年王如
立武隄澤舜漁處○雷澤卽
代人救濁鹿敗燕師于勺晉取
七年燕伐趙圍濁鹿趙靈王及
使趙口破之不知是何年○十
我于桂陵秦伐韓閼與惠成王
使楚師舍來求成邯鄲之師敗
以韓師敗諸侯師于襄陵齊侯
會齊師圍我襄陵○十六年王
侯來朝中陽。宋景鼓衞公孫倉。

defeated and put to flight. The eastern Chow,23 gave Kaou-too,24 to Ch'ing. The prince Le of Ch'ing came to acknowledge submission *to our king* in Chung-yang. King Koo of Sung and Kung-sun Ts'ang of Wei united their forces with those of

16 Wei, to besiege our Sëang-ling.25 　　In his 16th year, our king, with the army of Han, defeated the forces of *those* princes at Sëang-ling, when the prince of Ts'e sent King Shay of Ts'oo to come and ask for peace. The forces of Han-tan defeated us at Kwei-ling.26 Ts'in attacked *the city* Oh-yu 27 of Han, when our king Hwuy-ching sent Chaou—and defeated Ts'in.

Note. It is not known under what year this last notice should be ranged.

17 　In his 17th year, Yen attacked Chaou, and laid siege to Chuh-luh, which was saved by king Ling of Chaou, and the people of T'ae, who defeated Yen at Choh.28 Tsin took Yuen-woo and Hwoh-tsih.29

Note. Hwŏ-tsih is the same as Luy-tsih, the marsh of Luy, where Shun fished.

19 　In his 18th year, Ts'e built a dyke as a part of its great wall.30 　　In his 19th year, our king went to Wei, and commanded that Nan the son of its duke should

21 *only* be prince. 　　His 20th year. 　　In his 21st year, Yin Chin of Wei and Kung-sun Fow of Chaou attacked Yen; and on their return, took Hea-uh,31 and

22 walled K'euh-yih.31 　　In his 22d year, which was *jin-yin*,32 Sun Ho invaded Ts'oo, and penetrated to the suburbs of San-hoo.33 Ts'oo attacked Seu-chow.

23 　In his 23d year, Chang of Wei, supported by the forces of Ch'ing, led an army against Ts'oo, and took Shang-ts'ae.34 Sun Ho took Yin-yang.35 The duke Heaou of Ts'in had an interview with several *of the* princes in Fung-tsih.36 In Keang

24 there was a rent of the earth, extending west to the *river* Fun. 　　In his 24th year,

mination of the place. 　23 This was the emperor, now merely 'the shadow of a great name.' 　24 In dis. Lŏ-yang, dept. Ho-nan. 　25 In sub. dep. of Shuy, dep. Kwei-tih. 　26 In dis. O-tsih, dep. Ts'aou-chow. 　27 Dis. of Yu-shay, dep. Lëaou, Shan-se. 　28 In dis. Wang-too, dep. Paou-ting. 　29 Hwŏ-tsih,—the marsh of Hwŏ, but here the name of a city in the dis. of Yang-shing, dep. Tsih-chow. Yuen-woo must also be the name of a city. But this notice is evidently out of place.—What have we to do at this date with Tsin?

30 This wall of Ts'e has been mentioned before, under the 18th year of king Wei-lëĕ. It was intended as a protection against Ts'oo. 防, 'a dyke' or embankment against a stream, is used here for a wall, a defence against an enemy. 　31 Both in the pres. Ting Chow, Chih-le. 　32 Here is evidently a corruption of the text. *Jin-yin* was not the 22d year of king Hëen. Seu Wăn-tsing supposes we should read 王命. 　33 Prob. in dis. of Nuy-hëang, dep. Nan-yang. 　34 Still the name of a dis., dep. Joo-ning. 　35 Belonging to Ts'oo, dis. of Lin-ying, Hëen Chow. 　36 The marsh of Fung;—has occurred before.

敗韓馬陵○二十五年○二十六年穰疵帥
師及鄭孔夜戰于梁赫鄭師敗逋與齊田盼
戰于馬陵○二十七年五月齊田盼及宋人
伐我東鄙圍平陽○九月秦衞鞅伐我西鄙○十
月邯鄲伐我北鄙○王攻衞鞅我師敗逋○二
十八年城濟陽秦封衞鞅于鄔改名曰商○
二十九年邳遷于薛三月爲大溝于北郹以
行圃田之水○三十年○三十一年秦蘇胡
帥師伐鄭韓襄敗秦蘇胡于酸水年不知何
三十二年○三十三年鄭威侯與邯鄲圍襄
陵○三十四年魏惠成王三十六年改元稱
一年王與諸侯會于徐州於越子無彊伐楚
○三十五年楚吾得帥師及秦伐鄭圍綸氏
不知何○三十六年楚圍齊於徐州遂伐於
年附此○三十七年龍賈及
越殺無彊○三十八年龍賈于巫
秦師戰於雕陰我師敗逋王會鄭威侯于巫
沙○三十九年秦取我汾陰皮氏○四十年○
○四十一年秦歸我焦曲沃○四十二年九

26　Wei defeated Han at Ma-ling.[37]　　　His 25th year.　　　In his 26th year, *our*
　　Jang Ts'ze led a force, and fought with K'ung Yay of Ch'ing in Lëang-hih,[38] when
　　the army of Ch'ing was defeated and put to flight. *Afterwards*, we fought with T'een
27　P'an at Ma-ling.　　　In his 27th year, in the 5th month, T'een P'an of Ts'e, with
　　the people of Sung, invaded our eastern border, and besieged P'ing-yang. In the 9th
　　month, Yang of Wei, on the part of Ts'in, attacked our western border. In the 10th
　　month, Han-tan attacked our northern border.　　Our king attacked Yang of Wei, when
28　our troops were defeated and put to flight.　　In his 28th year, we walled Tse-yang.[39]
29　Ts'in invested Yang of Wei with Woo, the name of which was changed into Shang.[40]
　　　In his 29th year, P'ei removed its capital to Sëeh.[41] In the 3rd month, we made
30　a great ditch in our northern suburbs, to carry off the waters of P'oo-t'ëen.　　His
31　30th year.　　　In his 31st year, Soo Hoo of Ts'in led a force against Ch'ing, and
　　was defeated by Sëang of Han near Swan-water.

　　Note. It is not known in what year this took place; but it is given here.

33　　His 32d year.　　　In his 33d year, the prince Wei of Ch'ing, with Han-tan,
34　besieged Sëang-ling.　　　In his 34th year, Hwuy Ch'ing of Wei, this being his
　　36th year, changed the style of his reign, and called it his 1st year. The king had
　　a meeting with *several* of the princes in Seu-chow. Woo-këang, the viscount of Yu-
35　yueh, attacked Ts'oo.　　　In his 35th year, Woo-tih of Ts'oo led a force, and in
　　conjunction with Tsin, attacked Ch'ing, and besieged Lun-she.[42]

　　Note. It is not known in what year this took place; but it is given here.

36　　In his 36th year, Ts'oo besieged Ts'e in Seu-chow, and then attacked Yu-yueh, and
38　slew Woo-këang.　　　His 37th year.　　　In his 38th year, *our* Lung Këa fought
　　with an army of Ts'in at Tëaou-yin,[43] when our forces were defeated, and put to flight.
39　Our king had a meeting with the prince Wei of Ch'ing at Woo-sha.　　　In his 39th
41　year, Ts'in took from us Fung-yin[44] and P'e-she.[45]　　　His 40th year.　　　In
　　his 41st year, Ts'in restored to us Tsëaou and K'euh-yuh.　　　In his 42d year, the

37 *I.e.* 'the hill of Ma,' in dep. Ta-ming.
38 Near K'ae-fung. Perhaps we should translate—'fought at night with K'ung of Ch'ing.'
39 Dis. Tse-yang, dep. Tse-nan.　40 Shang

Chow of Shen-se.　　41 In dep. of T'ǎng, dep.
Yen-chow.　　42 In dis. Tǎng-fung, dep. Ho-
nan.　　43 In dis. of Kan-ts'euen, dep. Yen-
ngǎn, Shen-se.　　44 In dis. Yung-ho, dep.

坂關四月越王使公師隅來獻舟三百箭
○三年韓明帥師伐襄邱秦王來見于蒲
齊地景長丈餘高一尺魏以張儀爲相
公子平不克齊師殺子之醢其身○二年、
元年丁未十月鄭宣王來朝梁燕子之殺
蓋赧聲相近
史記作赧王名延

隱王

月城陽向更名陽爲河雍向爲高平。
五年○六年鄭侯使韓辰歸晉陽及向二
成王薨○三年癸卯今王元年○四年○
元年辛丑秦取我曲沃平周○二年魏惠

定名

慎靚王

四十七年○四十八年王陟。
○四十五年楚敗我襄陵○四十六年○
鼎淪泗沒于淵○四十三年○四十四年

43 nine vases were sunk in the Sze, and lost in the deep.   His 43d year.   His
45 44th year.   In his 45th year, Ts'oo defeated us at Seang-ling.   His 46th
48 year.   His 47th year.   In his 48th year, the king died.

XXXIII. KING SHIN-TSING.

Note. Named Ting.

1 In his 1st year, which was *sin-ch'ow* (38th of cycle, = B.C. 319), Ts'in took from
2 us K'euh-yuh and P'ing-chow.[1]   In his 2d year, king Hwuy-ching of Wei died.
4 His 3d year, *kwei-maou*, was the 1st year of our present king.   His 4th year.
6 His 5th year.   In his 6th year, the prince of Ch'ing sent Han Shin to restore to
us Tsin-yang and Hëang. In the 2d month, we walled Yang and Hëang, changing
the name of the former into Ho-yung,[2] and of the other into Kaou-p'ing.[3]

XXXIV. KING YIN.

Note. The Historical Records call this sovereign king Nan, named Yen. This must be owing
to the similarity of sound in Nan and Yin.

1 In his 1st year, which was *ting-we* (44th of cycle, =B.C. 313), in the 10th month,
king Seuen of Ch'ing came to acknowledge submission in our court of Lëang. Tsze-che
of Yen attempted to kill his ruler's *eldest* so P'ing, but without success. The army
2 of Ts'e killed Tsze-che, and made pickle of his body.   In his 2d year, in the
country of Ts'e, *the ground where they measured* the length of the sun's shadow
lengthened more than ten cubits, and was elevated a cubit.[1] Wei made Chang E its
3 prime minister.   In his 3d year, Han Ming led a force against Sëang-k'ew. The
king of Ts'in came, and had an interview with our king at the pass of P'oo-fan.[2] In
the 4th month, the king of Yueh sent Kung-sze Yu to present 300 boats, 5,000,000
arrows, with rhinoceros horns, and elephants' teeth.[3] In the 5th month, Chang E

P'oo-chow.   45 In dis. Ho-tsin, Këang Chow.
46 This statement is much debated. What
could have taken the vases to the Sze?
XXXIII. 1 In dis Këae-hëw, dep. Fun-chow,
Shan-se.   2 In dis. Ho-nuy, dep. Hwae-

k'ing.   3 In dis. Tse-yuen, dep. Hwae-k'ing.
XXXIV. 1 I suppose the meaning is what I
have given. We had the account of a similar
phenomenon before, tho' 景長 here occasions

今王終二十年。○十六年王與齊王會于韓。王于釜邱楚入雍氏楚人敗十四年。○十五年薛侯來會軍大夫適子代史皆貂服○鄲命吏大夫奴遷于九原將蒲坂晉陽封谷○十三年邯○十一年、○十二年秦拔我邯西風○九年城皮氏○十年皮氏翟章帥師救皮氏圍○八年秦公孫爰帥師伐我疾年翟章救鄭次于南屈此的年七帥師來會我次于襄邱○章雨疾風河水溢酸棗。楚庶山水大出○六年十月大霖、趙將韓舉○五年洛入成周,敗儀卒○四年翟章伐衞敗張五百萬、及犀角象齒。五月、

4 died. In his 4th year, Teih Chang attacked Wei. Wei defeated Han Keu, the
5 general of Chaou. In his 5th year, the Loh entered Ching-chow. Waters issued
6 from the hills abundantly. In the 6th year, there were great rains and violent
winds. The waters of the Ho overflowed Swan-tsaou.4 Shoo-chang of Ts'oo came
with a force to have a meeting with us, and encamped at Sëang-k'ew. In his
7 7th year, Teih Chang came to the rescue of Ch'ing, and encamped at Nan-këuh.5
8 In his 8th year, Kung-sun Yuen of Ts'in led a force against our *city of* P'e-she,
the siege of which was raised by the succour of Teih Chang. There was a violent
10 west wind. In his 9th year, we walled P'e-she. His 10th year. His
12 11th year. In his 12th year, Ts'in destroyed our P'oo-fan, Tsin-yang, and Fung-
13 kuh. In his 13th year, Han-tan ordered the Le, the great officers, and their
servants, to remove to Këw-yuen.6 The generals, great officers, sons of the 1st wife,
14 and recorders of Tae, all wore dresses of martens' skins. His 14th year. In
15 his 15th year, the prince of Sëeh came, and had a meeting with our king at Foo-k'ew.
16 The people of Ts'oo penetrated to Yung-she,7 and were defeated. In his 16th
year, our king had a meeting with the king of Ts'e in Han.
This chronicle was finished in the 20th year of our present king.

difficulty. 2 In dis. of Yung-tse, dep. P'oo-
chow. 3 This notice must be out of place.
Why should Yuĕ have sent these things to Wei,
and how could it have sent the boats? 4
Yen-tsin, dep. Wei-hwuy. 5 In Sih Chow, Shan-se. 6 Very remote, north-west of the pres. Yu-lin, Shem-se, more than 700 *le*. The par. is obscure, and the event is not elsewhere clearly related. 7 In sub. dep. of Yu, dep. K'ae-fung.

3. The Reader has now had the opportunity of making himself acquainted with the Annals of the Bamboo Books. As a specimen

General remarks on the Annals.

of the manner in which Chinese scholars deliver their opinion against them, I may quote the language of Wang Ming-shing. He says:—'It may be assumed as certain that they are a compilation which was imposed on the world by Shuh Sih. The forced versions of events in them, with their additions and combinations, are not only not worthy to be believed, but they are not worthy to be discussed. In every age there have been men capable of such mischief and falsehood. What we have to depend on, is that, while the man of knowledge will altogether reject such books, he who may have doubts about so dealing with them will put them on one side. That is the proper way to pursue in studying them.'[1] I cannot by any means agree in so unfavourable a judgment. The sketch of the discovery of *all* the Bamboo books, given in the first paragraph of this chapter, is sufficient to prove that they were not fabricated by Shuh Sih, or by any other, at the beginning of the Tsin dynasty. They had, no doubt, been lying for nearly six centuries in the tomb in which they had been first deposited, when they were then brought anew to light.

At the same time, the usage to which the tablets were subjected on their discovery, led to the loss of some, the mutilation of others, Corruptions must be admitted in the Text. The causes of them. and a general confusion of their order, which leave abundant room for the exercise of critical ingenuity on the Annals as we now have them. The haste, too, with which the ancient writing was deciphered and transcribed in the current characters of the age, gives occasion to doubt whether that important work could have been executed with the care which its difficulty required. I have called attention in the notes to some of the many transpositions of paragraphs of the present text, which are proposed by Hăng Ch'in-fung, the latest editor of the Annals, and an able and voluminous commentator on them. And there are other paragraphs, which he would cast out altogether, as having been incorporated with them from other portions of the mass of documents found in the tomb of king Sëang. What was called 'Fragmentary Sayings,'[2] or Narratives, of which there were eleven Books, appears to have supplied most of such additions. From the nature of the paragraphs supposed to be derived from this source, and of other fragments collected from various books where they appear as quotations from 'The Bamboo Books' (of which the account of the relations between Yaou and Shun, in note 8, p. 116, may be taken as an example), it appears that, besides the ore of the Annals, the tomb contained a large amount of dross, consisting of the wildest and most ridiculous legends and fables. From this material mainly were composed the long notes which we find interspersed through the Work, the more numerous and the more extravagant and absurd the more distant the times to which they

1 必是束皙僞譔‥‥‥‥其穿鑿附會, 不旦不足信, 亦不足辯也, 大約妄人何代蔑有, 全賴有識者屏黜之, 有疑則闕, 方爲善讀書. See the 十七史商榷, on the 竹書紀年.

2 璅語十一篇.

relate. In what must be acknowledged as really belonging to the Annals, there are, moreover, absurdities enow:—entries of prodigious phenomena, showers of gold, monstrous animals, transformations of sex, &c. The reader is often reminded of the marvels in Livy's History. Even if we were sure that we had the chronicle as it was placed in the tomb of king Sëang, we should have to be wary in our treatment of its contents; and much more must we be so, considering that we have it—here with mutilations, and there with additions.

With the reign of king P'ing, B.C. 769, there is a change in the character of the chronicle. From Hwang-te to that time, the Annals are those of the empire. The sovereigns

Different characters of different parts of the Annals. Probable date of the compilation of the earliest part.

of the different dynasties are the principal figures, in subordination to whose history the events of the various States are detailed. But from the date mentioned, the princes of Tsin become the principal figures; and they continue to be so, down to B.C. 439, when those of Wei, one of the three States, into which Tsin was dismembered, come into the foreground.[3] From B.C. 769, therefore, the Annals are those of the State of Tsin, composed by its Recorders, and digested subsequently into a more compendious form by one of the officers, bearing that title, of the State of Wei. The earlier chronicle, which is more important and of more general interest, was compiled, probably, about the time that the second portion was commenced, by one of the Recorders of Tsin, and kept in the archives of that State, as an appropriate introduction to its particular affairs.

This view conducts us to an important conclusion respecting the Shoo. While denying, in the second chapter of these *prolegomena*,

Conclusion from the Annals against the earlier portions of the Shoo.

that in the older portions of the Shoo we have contemporaneous records of the events which they relate, I have given my opinion, on p. 66, that 'the Tribute of Yu' was, notwithstanding, among the written monuments of the dynasty of Shang, and passed over from its historiographers to those of the dynasty of Chow. I am not going now to retract or modify that opinion; but the fact that these Bamboo Annals contain so little of what the Shoo contains about Shun and Yu, appears to me to have a great significance. The accounts in the Shoo could not have been generally known, or, if known, not generally accepted, when the Annals were made. The character of the two Works is, indeed, different. The Annals give but the skeleton of the history of ancient China; the Shoo gives the flesh and drapery of the body at particular times. The one tells of events simply, in the fewest possible words; the other describes the scenes and all the attendant circumstances of those events. The numerous appointments, however, of officers by Shun, and the grand labours of Yu, all related in the Shoo, ought, according to the plan of the Work, to have their brief commemoration in the Annals. That they are not so corroborated, proves that they were not accepted as matter of veritable history by the author of our chronicle. I shall dwell somewhat more minutely on this point in the next paragraph. It may suffice here to point it out distinctly. In one respect, the compiler of the documents of the Shoo has shown more discrimination than the compiler of the Annals. He did well in not attempting to go back into the shadowy age before Yaou; but I submit it to my readers, whether the want of corroboration, in the Annals, of the Shoo's accounts of the government of Shun and the labours of Yu, does not bear out my view, that the latter are merely the devices of philosophical romance, intended to present the first beginnings of Chinese history on a grand scale, and under heroes of sagely wisdom and gigantic achievement, who should be a model to sovereigns in all future ages.

4. There are two points in which the Annals of the Bamboo Books differ seriously from the generally received views of Chinese history. The one is in the mat-

Differences between the Annals and the common views of Chinese History.

ter of chronology, the years assigned in the Annals to the period between king P'ing of the Chow dynasty and the beginning of Yaou's reign being fewer by 211 than those commonly allowed. The other is that insisted on immediately above,—the contrast between them and the Shoo, in regard to the government of Shun and the labours of Yu.

On the former of these points, something was said in the last chapter. The history of China is certainly shortened in these Annals by the amount just mentioned. The number of sovereigns which they assign is the same as that in the common chronology, excepting in the case of the Shang dynasty, where we have two additional reigns, which, however, would lengthen the period by only 6 years, if the schemes otherwise agreed. The names or titles of the sovereigns, moreover, are for the most part the same, as will be seen in the table subjoined to this chapter. Where the length of the reigns differs, the years assigned in the Annals will generally, though not always, be found to be fewer than in the common tables. We know nothing of the authority on which the duration of the greater num-

179]

ber of the reigns is determined in the one scheme or in the other.

Neither the chronology of the Annals, nor that more commonly acknowledged, is supported by sufficient evidence; but it is right that I should point out here the grounds there are for believing that the numbers given in the text of the Annals have been corrupted. This corruption is two-fold.

The chronology of the Annals has been corrupted.

First, from the commencement of Yaou's reign downwards, the 1st year of the reigns is almost always indicated by the ordinary cycle characters. These, I maintain, were added after the discovery of the tablets;— not immediately, indeed, but by a gradual process, which was not completed until the Sung dynasty. In support of this view, I allege the following considerations :—

The cycle denominations of the reigns are spurious.

[i.] It has been shown, on pp. 82, 83, that, before the second Han dynasty, the cycle characters were employed to chronicle days, and not years. In coming to that conclusion, Chinese scholars have not taken these Annals into account. They reach it from a study of all the ancient books known previous to the Han dynasty. The Bamboo Books turn up in the last quarter of our 3d century; and if we are to receive the cycle dates as contemporaneous with the rest of this chronicle, then all the arguments for the conclusion go for nothing. Here was a practice, exceedingly elegant and convenient for marking dates, prevalent when the Annals were composed; and yet no other instance of its use can be adduced from any of the acknowledged early Writings, while Sze-ma Ts'ëen and the other scholars, who first erected chronology in China into a science, knew nothing of it. Only an extreme credulity will admit this.

[ii.] The reader will have observed that a good many dates do not form part of the text of the Annals, but are introduced as notes. Let me refer him particularly to those on p. 120. The inference from this is, that the addition of the cycle dates was not made complete at once, and that subsequent insertions to perfect the system, after the work had become the possession of the public, were thus made in notes;—it was not possible then to enter them in the text.

[iii.] The early citations, under the Tsin dynasty and even later, of passages from the Annals, do not contain these cycle dates. This fact is decisive on the point. Upon the 1st date, that of *ping-tsze*, marking the 1st year of Yaou's reign, Hung E-heuen, a scholar and officer of the present dynasty, in the reigns Këa-k'ing and Taou-kwang, observes :—'The various books which quote the Bamboo

Annals, do so without the cycle dates. It is not till we come to the chapter on chronology in the Books of Suy that we find the 1st year of Yaou quoted as *king-tsze*. Subsequently [in the Sung dynasty], a comment to the "After Chronicle of the Loo Sze" quotes the year as *ping-tsze*,—as we find it in the present copies of the Annals.'[1]

[iv.] If the Annals on their discovery had contained the cycle dates, we could not have had the errors which are found in the concluding notes to the dynasties of Hea and Shang on the length of those periods. This consideration is equally decisive on the matter in hand. Those notes were of early origin. Now, the Hea dynasty began with the year *jin-tsze* and ended with *jin-seuh;* it lasted, therefore, 6 cycles and 11 years,=431, whereas the annotator says its duration was 471 years. The Shang dynasty began with the year *kwei-hae* and ended with *kăng-yin*, comprising 8 cycles and 28 years,=508, whereas the annotator assigns to it 496 years. The error in the one case amounts to 40 years, and in the other only to 12;—if the reigns had been marked at the date of those annotations, as they are now, there could not have been any error at all. We must conclude, on all these grounds, that the cycle names, used to denominate the first years of the reigns throughout the Annals, are an addition made subsequent to the period of their discovery.

Second, there is ground for thinking that the number of years

The lengths of the reigns have also been altered. assigned to the several reigns has also been altered in some cases. There are two considerations which make this probable.

[i.] Apart from the question of the cycle dates, the annotator had only to add together the years assigned to the different sovereigns, to obtain the length of the Shang dynasty. It is difficult to suppose that he should not have executed so simple an operation correctly.

[ii.] With the Hea dynasty the case is different. The addition of all the reigns, taking in the 40 years between Sëang and Shaou-k'ang, gives us only 403 years. About 40 years are dropt, being those of mourning, between the death of one sovereign and the 1st year of his successor. But now in the history of Shuh Sih, referred to on p. 106, it is stated that in the Bamboo Annals 'the years of the Hea dynasty were more than those of Shang.'[2] Attention is

---

[1] 洪頤烜曰,諸書引竹書紀年,皆無甲子紀年,惟隋書, 律歷志,引竹書紀年,堯元年景子,路史後紀註引帝堯 元年丙子,與今本同. Quoted by Hăng Ch'in-fung on the 1st year of Yaou.

[2] 夏年多殷.

called to the fact, as one of the peculiarities of the Annals, distinguishing them from the commonly accepted histories of those ancient times. Hăng Ch'in-fung observes upon it:—'When the history of Shuh Sih says that the dynasty of Hea was longer than Shang, whereas in our present copies Shang lasted longer than Hea, I do not know on what ground the statement rested.'[3] He might well say so. But the memoir of Shuh Sih affords us one of the most satisfactory testimonies to the discovery of the Bamboo Books, and the fullest account of the various documents comprehended under the name. The express statement to which I have called attention cannot be got rid of. And it obliges us to conclude, that not only were the cycle characters for years introduced into the Annals after their emergence from the tomb, but that the lengths of the reigns also were altered, so that the value of the chronicle, as a guide in chronology, is altogether taken away.

The second point of difference, mentioned at the beginning of this paragraph, between these Annals and other histories of China, The Annals are more credible than the Shoo on the period of Yaou, Shun, and Yu. is to my mind of much greater importance. My own researches and reflections having led me to consider most of what we read in the Shoo about the well-ordered government of Shun and the labours of Yu, as the invention of later times, intended to exalt the characters and achievements of those worthies, and place them at the head of Chinese history on a pinnacle of more than human wisdom and greatness, I am pleased with the confirmation which my views receive from the accounts in the Annals. Let the reader compare them carefully with the documents in the Shoo, and I do not think he can fail to be struck with them as I have been. There are points of agreement between the two, as could not but be the case, the authors of them both, whatever they might add of their own, drawing on the same general stock of traditions. But the details of the Annals present the men and their doings in reasonable proportions. We see in them the chiefs of a growing tribe, and not the emperors of a vast and fully organized dominion.

[i.] The labours of Yu are confined in the Annals to the regulation of the Ho. Yaou assigns to him no greater task than Sëaou-k'ang, one of his own successors, has to assign, about 100 years later, to one of the princes of Shang. The same task has often been assigned to officers in subsequent times; might very well be assigned to one in

[3] 夏年多殷 今本仍殷多夏 不知此傳何所據而云也。

the present reign. Nothing is said of a far-extending, devastating deluge; nothing of Yu's operations on the mountains, or on the general face of the country, or on any river south of the Ho. Had it been in the accepted history of China, when these Annals were compiled, that Yu performed the more than Herculean tasks which the Shoo ascribes to him, it is unaccountable that they should not have mentioned them.

[ii.] The Shoo presents us with a picture of the government of Shun, which makes it appear to have been wonderfully complete. Not only has he Yu as his prime minister, and Kaou-yaou as minister of Crime; but he has his ministers of Instruction, Agriculture, Works, and Religion; his commissioner of Woods and Forests; his director of Music; his minister of Communication. According to the plan of the Annals, the appointment of all those ministers should have been mentioned; but the only names which they contain are those of Yu and Kaou-yaou. It is clear, that of the two-and-twenty great ministers by whom the Shun of the Shoo is surrounded, the greater number were the invention of speculators and dreamers of a later day, who, regardless of the laws of human progress, wished to place at the earliest period of their history a golden age and a magnificent empire, that should be the cynosure of men's eyes in all time.

If the space which I have given in these prolegomena to the Bamboo Annals appear excessive, the use to which I have turned them, to support the conclusions which I had been led on other grounds to form, must be my excuse. Even if it could be substantiated (which it cannot be), that the Annals were fabricated in the Tsin dynasty, the fact would remain, that their fabricator had taken a more reasonable view of the history of his country than any other of its writers has done, and indicated views, which, I venture to think, will be generally adopted by inquirers in the West. Those who come after me will probably assail the hitherto unchallenged accounts of ancient times with a bolder hand and on a more extensive scale than I have done in the present essay.

TABLE OF ANCIENT CHINESE CHRONOLOGY,

According to THE COMMON SCHEME, and to THE BAMBOO ANNALS.

Common Scheme.   *Bamboo Annals.*

Emperor's Name.	Emperor's Name.	Years of Reign.	1st Year on Reign.	1st Year of Reign.	1st Year of Reign.	1st Year of Reign.	Years of Reign.	Emperor's Name.	Emperor's Name.
堯	Yaou,	100	B.C. 2,356	甲辰	丙子	B.C. 2,145	100	Yaou,	堯
舜	Shun,	50	„ 2,254	丙戌	己未	„ 2,042	50	Shun,	舜

HEA DYNASTY, WITH TITLE OF 王 or 后, SOVEREIGN.   HEA DYNASTY, WITH TITLE OF 帝, EMPEROR.

Emperor's Name.	Emperor's Name.	Years of Reign.	1st Year on Reign.	1st Year of Reign.	1st Year of Reign.	1st Year of Reign.	Years of Reign.	Emperor's Name.	Emperor's Name.
禹	Yu,	8	B.C. 2,204	丙子	壬子	B.C. 1,989	8	Yu,	禹
啟	K'e,	9	„ 2,196	甲申	癸亥	„ 1,978	16	K'e,	啟
太康	T'ae-k'ang,	29	„ 2,187	癸巳	癸未	„ 1,957	4	T'ae-k'ang,	太康
仲康	Chung-k'ang,	13	„ 2,158	壬戌	己丑	„ 1,951	7	Chung-k'ang,	仲康
相	Sëang,	27	„ 2,145	乙亥	戊寅	„ 1,942	28	Sëang,	相
	Usurpation,	40	„ 2,118	壬寅	丙午	„ 1,914	40	Usurpation,	
少康	Sh'aou-k'ang,	22	„ 2,078	壬午	己巳	„ 1,874	21	Sh'aou-k'ang,	少康
杼	Ch'oo,	17	„ 2,056	甲辰	戊子	„ 1,851	17	Ch'oo,	杼
槐	Hwae,	26	„ 2,039	辛酉	壬申	„ 1,832	44	Fun,	芬
芒	Mang,	18	„ 2,013	丁亥	辛未	„ 1,788	58	Mang,	芒
泄	Sëĕ,	16	„ 1,995	乙巳	己亥	„ 1,729	25	Sëĕ,	泄
不降	Puh-keang,	59	„ 1,979	辛酉	乙亥	„ 1,701	59	Puh-këang,	不降
扃	Pëen,	21	„ 1,920	庚申	戊戌	„ 1,642	18	Pëen,	扃
廑	Kin,	21	„ 1,899	辛巳	己未	„ 1,621	8	Kin,	廑

184]

TABLE OF ANCIENT CHINESE CHRONOLOGY.—Continued.

名	Name	Reign	B.C.	Cycle
孔甲	K'ung-kĕă	31	1,878	壬寅
臯	Kaou	11	1,847	癸酉
發	Fă	19	1,836	甲申
癸	Kwei	52	1,817	癸卯

DYNASTY OF SHANG, WITH TITLE OF 王, OR KING.

名	Name	Reign	B.C.	Cycle
湯	T'ang	13	1,765	乙未
太甲	T'ae-kĕă	33	1,752	戊申
沃丁	Yuh-ting	29	1,719	辛巳
太康	T'ae-kang	25	1,690	庚戌
小甲	Sëaou-kĕă	17	1,665	乙亥
雍己	Yung-ke	12	1,648	壬辰
太戊	T'ae-mow	75	1,636	甲辰
仲丁	Chung-ting	13	1,561	己未
外壬	Wae-jin	15	1,548	壬申
河亶甲	Ho-t'an-kĕă	9	1,533	丁亥
祖乙	Tsoo-yih	19	1,524	丙申
祖辛	Tsoo-sin	16	1,505	乙卯
沃甲	Yuh-kĕă	25	1,489	辛未
祖丁	Tsoo-ting	32	1,464	丙申
南庚	Nan-kang	25	1,432	戊辰

名	Name	Reign	B.C.	Cycle
孔甲	K'ung-kĕă	9	1,611	乙巳
臯	Haou	3	1,600	庚辰
發	Fă	7	1,595	乙酉
癸	Kwei	31	1,588	壬辰

DYNASTY OF SHANG, WITH TITLE OF 王, OR KING.

名	Name	Reign	B.C.	Cycle
湯	T'ang	12	1,557	癸亥
外丙	Wae-ping.*	2	1,545	乙亥
仲壬	Chung-jin	4	1,543	丁丑
太甲	T'ae-kĕă	12	1,539	辛巳
沃丁	Yuh-ting	19	1,527	癸巳
小庚	Sëaou-kang	5	1,508	壬子
小甲	Sëaou-kĕă	17	1,503	丁巳
雍己	Yung-ke	12	1,486	甲戌
太戊	T'ae-mow	75	1,474	丙戌
仲丁	Chung-ting	9	1,399	辛丑
外壬	Wae-jin	10	1,390	庚戌
河亶甲	Ho-t'an-kĕă	9	1,380	庚申
祖乙	Tsoo-yih	19	1,371	己巳
祖辛	Tsoo-sin	14	1,352	戊子
開甲	K'ae-kĕă	5	1,338	壬寅
祖丁	Tsoo-ting	9	1,333	丁未
南庚	Nan-kang	6	1,324	丙辰

TABLE OF ANCIENT CHINESE CHRONOLOGY.—*Continued.*

Name	Reign (years)	B.C.
陽甲 Yang-këä	7	B.C. 1,407
盤庚 Pwan-käng	28	" 1,400
小辛 Sëaou-sin	21	" 1,372
小乙 Sëaou-yih	28	" 1,351
武丁 Woo-ting	59	" 1,323
祖庚 Tsoo-käng	7	" 1,264
祖甲 Tsoo-këä	33	" 1,257
廩辛 Lin-sin	6	" 1,224
庚丁 Käng-ting	21	" 1,218
武乙 Woo-yih	4	" 1,197
太丁 Tae-ting	3	" 1,193
帝乙 Te-yih	37	" 1,190
紂 Chow-sin	32	" 1,153

Name	Reign (years)	B.C.
陽甲 Yang-këä	4	B.C. 1,318
盤庚 Pwan-käng	28	" 1,314
小辛 Sëaou-sin	3	" 1,286
小乙 Sëaou-yih	10	" 1,283
武丁 Woo-ting	59	" 1,273
祖庚 Tsoo-käng	11	" 1,214
祖甲 Tsoo-këä	33	" 1,203
馮辛 Fung-sin	4	" 1,170
庚丁 Käng-ting	8	" 1,166
武乙 Woo-yih	35	" 1,158
文丁 Wän-ting	13	" 1,123
帝乙 Te-yih	9	" 1,110
帝辛 Te-sin	52	" 1,101

DYNASTY OF CHOW, WITH TITLE OF 王, OR KING.

Name	Reign (years)	B.C.
武 Woo	7	B.C. 1,121
成 Ching	37	" 1,114
康 K'ang	26	" 1,077
昭 Ch'aou	51	" 1,051
穆 Muh	55	" 1,000
共 Kung	12	" 945
懿 E	25	" 933
孝 Hëaou	15	" 908

DYNASTY OF CHOW, WITH TITLE OF 王, OR KING.

Name	Reign (years)	B.C.
武 Woo	6	B.C. 1,049
成 Ching	37	" 1,043
康 K'ang	26	" 1,006
昭 Ch'aou	19	" 980
穆 Muh	55	" 961
共 Kung	12	" 906
懿 E	25	" 894
孝 Hëaou	9	" 869

TABLE OF ANCIENT CHINESE CHRONOLOGY.—*Continued.*

	Ruler	Reign	Cyclic	B.C.		B.C.	Cyclic	Reign	Ruler	
夷	E.	16	丁卯	893		860	庚子	8	E.	夷
厲	Le.	51	癸未	877		,, 852	戊申	26	Le.	厲
宣	Seuen	46	甲戌	826		,, 861	甲戌	46	Seuen	宣
幽	Yew	11	庚申	780		,, 780	庚申	11	Yew	幽
平	P'ing	51	辛未	769		,, 769	辛未	51	P'ing	平
桓	Hwan	23	壬戌	718		,, 718	壬戌	23	Hwan	桓
莊	Chwang	15	乙酉	695		,, 695	乙酉	15	Chwang	莊
僖	He.	5	庚子	680		,, 680	庚子	5	Le.	釐
惠	Hwuy	25	乙巳	675		,, 675	乙巳	25	Hwuy	惠
襄	Seäng	33	庚午	650		,, 650	庚午	33	Seäng	襄
頃	K'ing	6	癸卯	617		,, 617	癸卯	6	K'ing	頃
匡	K'wang	6	己酉	611		,, 611	己酉	6	K'wang	匡
定	Ting	21	乙卯	605		,, 605	乙卯	21	Ting	定
簡	Këen	14	丙子	584		,, 584	丙子	14	Këen	簡
靈	Ling	27	庚寅	570		,, 570	庚寅	27	Ling	靈
景	King	25	丁巳	543		,, 543	丁巳	25	King	景
敬	King	44	壬午	518		,, 518	壬午	44	King	敬
元	Yuen	7	丙寅	474		,, 474	丙寅	7	Yuen	元
貞定	Ching-ting	28	癸酉	467		,, 467	癸酉	28	Ching-ting	貞定
考	K'aou	15	辛丑	439		,, 439	辛丑	15	K'aou	考
威烈	Wei-lëĕ	24	丙辰	424		,, 424	丙辰	24	Wei-lëĕ	威烈
安	Ngan	26	庚辰	400		,, 400	庚辰	26	Ngan	安

TABLE OF ANCIENT CHINESE CHRONOLOGY.—Continued.

列	Lëĕ,	7	B.C. 374	丙午
顯	Hëen,	48	" 367	癸丑
愼靚	Shin-tsing.	6	" 319	辛丑
赧	Nan,	29	" 313	丁未

列	Lëĕ,	7	B.C. 374	丙午
顯	Hëen,	48	" 367	癸丑
愼靚	Shin-tsing.	6	" 319	辛丑
隱	Yin,		" 313	丁未

CHAPTER V.

THE ANCIENT EMPIRE OF CHINA.

ENTRANCE OF THE CHINESE INTO CHINA.　OTHER EARLY SETTLERS.
GROWTH OF THE TRIBE INTO A NATION.　RELIGION AND SUPERSTITIONS.
FORM AND ISSUES OF THE GOVERNMENT.

1.　About two thousand years before our Christian era, the Chinese tribe first appeared in the country, where it has since increased

First arrival of the Chinese tribe in its future home.

so greatly. It then occupied a small extent of territory, on the east and north of the Ho,—the more southern portion of the present province of Shan-se. As its course continued to be directed to the east and south (though after it crossed the Ho, it proceeded to extend itself westwards as well), we may conclude that it had come into China from the north-west. Believing that we have in the 10th chapter of the Book of Genesis some hints, not to be called in question, of the way in which the whole earth was overspread by the families of the sons of Noah, I suppose that the family, or collection of families,—the tribe,—which has since grown into the most numerous of the nations, began to move eastwards, from the regions between the Black and Caspian seas, not long after the confusion of tongues. Going on, between the Altaic range of mountains on the north and the Tauric range, with its continuations, on the south, but keeping to the sunny and more attractive south as much as it could, the tribe found itself, at the time I have mentioned, between 40° and 45°, N. L., moving parallel with the Yellow River in the most northern portion of its course. It determined to follow the stream, turned south with it, and moved along its eastern bank, making settlements where the country promised most advantages, till it was stopped by the river ceasing its southward flow, and turning again towards the east. Thus the present Shan-se was the cradle of the Chinese empire. The tribe dwelt there for a brief space, consolidating its strength under the rule of chieftains, who held their position by their personal qualities more than by any privileges of hereditary descent; and then gradually forced its way, east, west, and south, conflicting with the physical difficulties of the country, and prevailing over the opposition of ruder and less numerous neighbours.

2. Neighbours? Yes. The arrival of the Chinese tribe had been anticipated by others. These may have left the original seat of Other early immigrant tribes. our infant race in the West earlier than it; or they may have left it at the same time. If they did so, the wave of emigration had broken in its progress. Some portions had separated from the main body, and found their way into the present province of Shen-se; and others, pursuing the same direction with it, but moving with more celerity, had the:. been pushed forward, by its advance, towards the sea, and subsequently along the sea-board, trying to make good a position for themselves among the mountains and along the streams of the country. We are not to suppose that the land was peopled by these tribes. They were not then living under any settled government, nor were they afterwards able to form a union of their forces, which could cope with the growing power of the larger people. They were scattered here and there over the region north of the Ho, gradually extending southward toward the Këang. Hostilities were constantly breaking out between them and the Chinese, over whom they might gain, once and again, temporary advantages. They increased in their degree, as well as those, and were far from being entirely subdued at the end of the Chow dynasty. Remnants of them still exist in a state of semi-independence in the southwestern parts of the empire. Amid the struggles for the supreme power, which arose when one dynasty gave place to another, and the constant contentions, which prevailed among the States into which the empire was divided, the princes readily formed alliances with the chiefs of these wilder tribes. They were of great assistance to king Woo in his conflict with the last sovereign of the dynasty of Shang. In the speech which he delivered to his forces before the decisive battle in the wild of Muh, he addressed the 'men of Yung, Shuh, Këang, Maou, Wei, Loo, P'ang, and Poh,'[1] in addition to his own captains, and the rulers of friendly States. We are told that the wild tribes of the south and north, as well as the people of the great and flowery region, followed and were consenting with him.[2]

---

[1] The Shoo, Pt. V., Bk. III., parr. 2–4.   [2] Pt. V., Bk. IV., p. 6.

Edward Biot calls attention to the designation of the early Chinese tribe or colony as 'the black-haired people,' saying that they were

Epithet of black-haired, applied to the early Chinese.

doubtless so named in opposition to the different or mixed colour of the hair of the indigenous race.[3] But I cannot admit any 'indigenous race,'—any race that did not come from the same original centre of our world's population as the Chinese themselves. The wild tribes of which we read in the Shoo and Chinese history, were, no doubt, black-haired, as all the remnants of them are at the present day. If we must seek an explanation for the name of 'black-haired people,' as given to the early Chinese, I should say that its origin was anterior to their entrance into China, and that it was employed to distinguish them from other descendants of Noah, from whom they separated, and who, while they journeyed to the east, moved in an opposite and westward direction.

3. It was to their greater civilization, and the various elements of strength flowing from it, that the Chinese owed their superiority

Characteristics of the early Chinese which made them masters of the country.

over other early settlers in the country. They were able, in virtue of this, to subdue the land and replenish it, while the ruder tribes were gradually pushed into corners, and finally were nearly all absorbed and lost in the prevailing race. The black-haired people brought with them habits of settled labour. Their wealth did not consist, like that of nomads, in their herds and flocks. Shun's governors of provinces in the Shoo are called Pastors or Herdsmen, and Mencius speaks of princes generally as 'Pastors of men;'[1] but pastoral allusions are very few in the literature of China. The people could never have been a tribe of shepherds. They displayed, immediately on their settlement, an acquaintance with the arts of agriculture and weaving. The cultivation of grain to obtain the staff of life, and of flax to supply clothing, at once received their attention. They knew also the value of the silk-worm, and planted the mulberry tree. The exchange of commodities—the practice of commerce on a small scale—was, moreover, early developed among them. It was long, indeed, before they had anything worthy of the name of a city; but fairs were established at convenient places, to which the people resorted from the farms and hamlets about, to barter their various wares.

In addition to the above endowments, the early Chinese possessed

3 See his Introduction to his translation of the Chow Le. p. 5.
1 Mencius, I., Pt. I., vi. 6.

the elements of intellectual culture. They had some acquaintance with astronomy, knew approximately the length of the year, and recognized the necessity of the practice of intercalation, to prevent the seasons, on a regard to which their processes of agriculture depended, from getting into disorder. They possessed also the elements of their present written characters. The stories current, and which are endorsed by statements in the later semi-classical books, about the invention of the characters by Ts'ang-këĕ, in the time of Hwang-te, are of no value; and it was not till the Chow dynasty, and the reign particularly of king Seuen (B. C. 825—779), that anything like a dictionary of them was attempted to be compiled;[2] but the original immigrants, I believe, brought with them the art of ideographic writing or engraving. It was rude and imperfect, but it was sufficient for the recording of simple observations of the stars in their courses, and the surface of the earth, and for the orders to be issued by the government of the time. As early as the beginning of the Shang dynasty, we find E Yin presenting a written memorial to his sovereign.[3]

The habits of the other settlers were probably more warlike than those of the Chinese; but their fury would exhaust itself in predatory raids. They were incapable of any united or persistent course of action. We cannot wonder that they were in the long run supplanted and absorbed by a race with the characteristics and advantages which I have pointed out.

4. The reader will understand that what I say in this paragraph on the religion and superstitions of the early Chinese will be based

Religion and superstition of the early Chinese.

almost entirely on the documents of the Shoo; and that Book has to do with the sayings and doings of the emperors. By and by, we shall have before us all the testimony of all the classical writings, and be prepared to consider these important subjects, as they entered into and affected the life of the people at large. I would willingly have deferred any discussion of them at present; but it was necessary to my design in the present chapter to touch cursorily upon them.

The chiefs and rulers of the ancient Chinese were not without some considerable knowledge of God; but they were accustomed, on their first appearance in the country, if the earliest portions of the Shoo can be relied on at all, to worship other spiritual Beings as well.

2 See the Introduction to Morrison's Dictionary, and an Essay by Father De Mailla,—, Recherches sur les Characteres Chinois,'—the 7th of the essays, appended to Gaubil's Shoo-king.

3 The Shoo, Pt. IV, Bk. V., Pt. i., par. 1.

There was no sacerdotal or priestly class among them; there were no revelations from Heaven to be studied and expounded. The chieftain was the priest for the tribe; the emperor, for the empire; the prince of a State, for his people; the father, for his family.

Shun had no sooner been designated by Yaou to the active duties of the government as co-emperor with him, than 'he offered a special sacrifice, but with the ordinary forms, to God; sacrificed purely to the six Honoured ones; offered their appropriate sacrifices to the rivers and hills; and extended his worship to the host of spirits.'[1] Subsequently, in the progresses which he is reported to have made to the different mountains where he met the princes of the several quarters of the empire, he always commenced his proceedings with them by 'presenting a burnt-offering to Heaven, and sacrificing in order to the hills and rivers.'[1] I do not refer to these passages as veritable records of what Shun actually did; but they are valuable, as being the ideas of the compilers of the Shoo of what he should have done in his supposed circumstances.

The name by which God was designated was *the Ruler*, and *the Supreme Ruler*, denoting emphatically His personality, supremacy, and unity. We find it constantly interchanged with the term *Heaven*, by which the ideas of supremacy and unity are equally conveyed, while that of personality is only indicated vaguely, and by an association of the mind. By God kings were supposed to reign, and princes were required to decree Justice. All were under law to Him, and bound to obey His will. Even on the inferior people He has conferred a moral sense, compliance with which would show their nature invariably right.[2] All powers that be are from Him. He raises one to the throne and puts down another. Obedience is sure to receive His blessing; disobedience, to be visited with His curse.[3] The business of kings is to rule in righteousness and benevolence, so that the people may be happy and good. They are to be an example to all in authority, and to the multitudes under them. Their highest achievement is to cause the people tranquilly to pursue the course which their moral nature would indicate and approve.[4] When they are doing wrong, God admonishes them by judgments,—storms, famine, and other calamities; if they persist in evil, sentence goes forth against them. The dominion is taken from them, and given to others more worthy of it.

Their idea of God.

---

1 The Canon of Shun, parr. 6, 8.   2 Pt. IV., Bk. III., par. 2.   3 Pt. IV., Bk. IV., p. 2; *et passim*.   4 Pt. IV., Bk. III., p. 2.

The duke of Chow, in his address on 'The Establishment of Government,'[5] gives a striking summary of the history of the empire down to his own time. Yu the Great, the founder of the Hea dynasty, 'sought for able men, to honour God.' But the way of Kĕĕ, the last of his line, was different. He employed cruel men;—and he had no successors. The empire was given to T'ang the Successful, who 'greatly administered the bright ordinances of God.' By and by, T'ang's throne came to Show, who was all violence, so that 'God sovereignly punished him.' The empire was transferred to the House of Chow, whose chiefs showed their fitness for the charge by 'finding out men, who would reverently serve God, and appointing them as presidents and chiefs of the people.'

It was the duty of all men to reverence and honour God, by obeying His law written in their hearts, and seeking His blessing in all their ways; but there was a solemn and national worship of Him, as ruling in nature and providence, which could only be performed by the emperor. It consisted of sacrifices, or offerings rather, and prayers. No image was formed of Him, as indeed the Chinese have never thought of fashioning a likeness of the Supreme.

Who the 'six Honoured ones,' whom Shun sacrificed to next to God, were, is not known. In going on to worship the hills and

Their worship of other spiritual Beings.

rivers, and the host of spirits, he must have supposed that there were certain tutelary beings, who presided over the more conspicuous objects of nature, and its various processes. They were under God, and could do nothing, excepting as they were permitted and empowered by Him; but the worship of them was inconsistent with the truth that God demands to be recognized as 'He who worketh all in all,' and will allow no religious homage to be given to any but Himself. It must have always been the parent of many superstitions; and it paved the way for the pantheism which enters largely into the belief of the Chinese at the present day, and of which we find one of the earliest steps in the practice, which commenced with the Chow dynasty, of not only using the term *Heaven* as a synonym for God, but the combination *Heaven and Earth*.[6]

There was also among the early Chinese the religious worship of their departed friends, which still continues to be observed by all

Worship of Ancestors.

classes from the emperor downward, and seems of all religious services to have the greatest hold

---

5 Pt V., Bk., XIX.   6 Pt. V., Bk. I., Pt. i., p. 3.

upon the people. The title given in the Shoo to Shun's minister of Religion is that of 'Arranger of the Ancestral temple.'[7] The rule of Confucius, that 'parents, when dead, should be sacrificed to according to propriety,'[8] was, doubtless, in accordance with a practice which had come down from the earliest times of the nation.

The spirits of the departed were supposed to have a knowledge of the circumstances of their descendants, and to be able to affect

Ancestors supposed to know the affairs of their descendants, and to be able to affect them.

them. Events of importance in a family were communicated to them before their shrines; many affairs of government were transacted in the ancestral temple. When Yaou demitted to Shun the business of the government, the ceremony took place in the temple of 'the accomplished ancestor,'[9] the individual to whom Yaou traced his possession of the supreme dignity; and while Yaou lived, Shun, on every return to the capital from his administrative progresses, offered a bullock before the shrine of the same personage.[10] In the same way, when Shun found the toils of government too heavy for him, and called Yu to share them, the ceremony took place in the temple of 'the spiritual ancestor,' the chief in the line of Shun's progenitors. In the remarkable narrative, which we have in the 6th of the Books of Chow, of the duke of Chow's praying for the recovery of his brother, king Woo, from a dangerous illness, and offering to die in his stead, he raises three altars,—to their father, grandfather, and great-grandfather; and prays to them, as having in heaven the charge of watching over their great descendant. When he has ascertained by divination that the king would recover, he declares that he had got Woo's tenure of the throne renewed by the three kings, who had thus consulted for a long futurity of their House.

This case shows us that the spirits of good kings were believed to be in heaven. A more general conclusion is derived from what we read in the 7th of the Books of Shang. The emperor Pwan-kăng, irritated by the opposition of the wealthy and powerful Houses to his measures, and their stirring up the people also to murmur against them, threatens them all with calamities to be sent down by his High ancestor, T'ang the Successful. He tells his ministers, that their ancestors and fathers, who had loyally served his predecessors, were now urgently entreating T'ang, in his spirit-state in heaven, to execute great punishments on their descendants. Not only, therefore,

7 Canon of Shun, p. 23.   8 Ana., II., v.   9 Canon of Shun, p. 4.   10 Ib., p. 8.

did good sovereigns continue to have a happy existence in heaven; but their good ministers shared the happiness with them, and were somehow round about them, as they had been on earth, and took an interest in the progress of the concerns which had occupied them during their lifetime. Modern scholars, following in the wake of Confucius, to whom the future state of the departed was all wrapt in shadows, clouds, and darkness, say that the people of the Shang dynasty were very superstitious.—My object is to bring out the fact, and the nature of their superstition.

There is no hint in the Shoo nor elsewhere, so far as I am aware, of what became of bad emperors and bad ministers after death, nor,

No hint of the fate of the bad after death; and no inculcation of future rewards and punishments.

indeed, of the future fate of men generally. There is a heaven in the classical books of the Chinese; but there is no hell; and no purgatory. Their oracles are silent as to any doctrine of future rewards and punishments. Their exhortations to well-doing, and their warnings against evil, are all based on a reference to the will of God, and the certainty that in this life virtue will be rewarded and vice punished. 'Of the five happinesses, the first is long life; the second is riches; the third is soundness of body and serenity of mind; the fourth is the love of virtue; and the fifth is doing or receiving to the end the will of Heaven.'[11] There is no promise of rest or comfort beyond the grave. The virtuous man may live and die in suffering and disgrace;—let him be cheered. His posterity will reap the reward of his merits. Some one, sprung from his loins, will become wealthy, or attain to distinction. But if he should have no posterity:—it never occurred to any of the ancient sages to consider such a case.

I will pass on from this paragraph with a reference to the subject of divination. Although the ancient Chinese can hardly be said to

Divination.

have had the knowledge of a future state, and were not curious to inquire about it, they were anxious to know about the wisdom and issues of their plans for the present life. For this purpose they had recourse to divination. The duke of Chow certainly practised it; and we have a regular staff of diviners among the officers of the Chow dynasty. Pwan-kǎng practised it in the dynasty of Shang. And Shun did so also, if we can put faith in 'The Counsels of Yu.' The instruments of divination were the shell of the tortoise and the stalks of a certain grass or reed. By various caustic

11 Pt. V., Bk. IV., par. 39.

operations on the former, and by manipulations with the latter, it was supposed possible to ascertain the will of Heaven. I must refer the reader to what I have said about the practice on the seventh section of 'The Great Plan.' It is difficult to understand how the really great men of ancient China could have believed in it. One observation ascribed to Shun is worthy of remark. He tells Yu that 'divination, when fortunate, must not be repeated.'[12] I once saw a father and son divining after one of the fashions of the present day. They tossed the bamboo roots, which came down in the unlucky positions for a dozen times in succession. At last a lucky cast was made. They looked into each other's faces, laughed heartily, and rose up, delighted, from their knees. The divination was now successful, and they dared not repeat it!

5. When the dignity of chief advanced to that of sovereign, and the Chinese tribe grew into a nation, the form which it assumed was that of a feudal empire. It was probably not until the Chow dynasty, that its constitution was fully developed and consolidated; as it is only then that we find in the last part of the Shoo, in the Ch'un Ts'ew, the Rites of Chow, and other Works of the period, materials to give a description of it. King Woo, we are told, after he had overthrown the last sovereign of the line of T'ang, arranged the orders of nobility into five, from duke downwards, and assigned the territories to them on a scale proportioned to their different ranks.[1] But at the beginning of the Hea dynasty, Yu conferred on the chiefs among his followers lands and surnames.[2] The feudal system grew in a great measure out of the necessities of the infant empire. As the ruder tribes were pushed backwards from its growing limits, they would the more fiercely endeavour to resist further encroachment. The measure was sometimes taken of removing them to other distant sites, according to the policy on which the kings of Assyria and Babylon dealt with Israel and Judah. So Shun is reported to have carried away the San-mëaou. But the Chinese empire was too young and insufficiently established itself to pursue this plan generally; and each State therefore was formed with a military constitution of its own, to defend the marches against the irruptions of the barbarians.

Constitution and Issues of the ancient Chinese empire.

12 Pt. II., Bk. II., p. 18.

1 Pt. V., Bk. III., p. 10.   2 See the Tribute of Yu, Pt. ii., p. 16. I seem to see clearly now, that this paragraph and the six that follow should be interpreted of Yu the emperor, and not of him as a minister of Yaou.

What was designed to be the central State of the empire was the appanage of the sovereign himself, and was of the same dimensions as one of the largest of the feudatory States.[3] Over this he ruled like one of the other princes in their several dominions; and he received, likewise, a certain amount of revenue from all the rest of the country, while the nobles were bound to do him military service, whenever called upon. He maintained also a court of great ministers, who superintended the government of the whole empire. The princes were little kings within their own States, and had the power of life and death over the people. They practised the system of sub-infeudation; but their assignments of lands were required to have the imperial sanction.

It was the rule, under the Chow dynasty, that the princes should repair to the court every five years, to give an account of their administration of their governments; and that the emperor should make a general tour through the country every twelve years, to see for himself how they performed their duties. We read in the Canon of Shun, that he made a tour of inspection once in five years, and that the princes appeared at court during the intermediate four.[4] As the empire enlarged, the imperial progresses would naturally become less frequent. By this arrangement, it was endeavoured to maintain a uniformity of administration and customs throughout the States. The various ceremonies to be observed in marriages, funerals and mourning, hospitalities, religious worship, and the conduct of hostilities; the measures of capacity, length, weight, &c.; and the written characters of the language:—these were all determined by imperial prerogative. To innovate in them was a capital offence.[5]

The above is an imperfect outline of the feudal constitution of the ancient empire of China, which was far from enjoying peace and prosperity under it. According to the received accounts, the three dynasties of Hea, Shang, and Chow were established, one after another, by princes of great virtue and force of character, aided in each case by a minister of consummate ability and loyal devotion. Their successors invariably became feeble and worthless. After a few reigns, the imperial rule slackened. Throughout the States there came assumptions and oppressions, each prince doing what was right in his own eyes, without fear of his suzzerain. The wild tribes round

---

3 Here is the true account of the origin of the names Chung Kwoh (中 國), 'Middle State,' and Chung Pang (中 邦), 'Middle Region.'   4 Can. of Shun, par. 9.   5 See the Canon of Shun, par. 8; and the Doctrine of the Mean, Ch. XXVIII.

THE ANCIENT EMPIRE OF CHINA.

PROLEGOMENA.

about waxed bold, and kept up a constant excitement and terror by their incursions. Then would come an exceptional reign of more than usual vigour, and a partial order would be established; but the brief prosperity was only like a blink of sunshine in a day of gloom. In the Shoo, the termination of the dynasties of Hea and Shang is attributed to the wickedness of their last emperors. After a long array of feeble princes, there suddenly appear on the throne men of gigantic physical strength, the most daring insolence, and the wildest debaucheries, having neither piety nor ruth; and in contrast with them are princes, whose fathers have for several generations been attracting general notice by their righteousness and benevolence. When Heaven and men can no longer bear the iniquity of the tyrants, the standard of revolt is raised, and the empire speedily comes under a new rule. These accounts are, no doubt, much exaggerated and embellished. Kĕĕ and Show were not such monsters of vice, nor were T'ang and Woo such prodigies of virtue. More likely is it that the earlier dynasties died out like that of Chow, from sheer exhaustion, and that their last sovereigns were weaklings like king Nan, rather than tyrants.

The practice of polygamy, which was as old as Yaou, was a constant source of disorder. A favourite concubine plays a conspicuous part in the downfall of the dynasties of Shang and Hea, and another signalizes a calamitous epoch in that of Chow. In the various States, this system was ever giving rise to jealousies, factions, usurpations, and abominations which cannot be told. No nation where polygamy exists can long be prosperous or powerful; in a feudal empire its operation must be peculiarly disastrous.

The teachings of Confucius in the Chow dynasty could not arrest the progress of degeneracy and dissolution in a single State. His inculcation of the relations of society and the duties belonging to them had no power. His eulogies of the ancient sages were only the lighting up in the political firmament of so many suns which communicated no heat. Things waxed worse and worse. The pictures which Mencius draws of the misery of his times are frightful. What he auspiced from the doctrines and labours of his master never came to pass. The ancient feudal empire was extinguished, amid universal anarchy, in seas of blood.

The character and achievements of the founder of the Ts'in dynasty have not yet received from historians the attention which they deserve. He destroyed the feudal system of China, and introduced, in its room, the modern despotic empire, which has now lasted rather more than 2,000 years.

6. The ancient empire of China passed away, having been weighed in the balances and found wanting.   Under the system of rule, which superseded it, the boundaries of the empire have been greatly extended, and the people have grandly increased.   Now, however, it would seem to be likewise approaching its end.   It would not have endured so long, but for the position of the country at the extremity of the Asiatic continent.   Its neighbours were not more powerful than itself, and they were less civilized.   Once and again the country has been overrun and subjugated by the descendants of the tribes which disputed the possession of the soil with its earliest colonists; but it has subdued them in its turn by its greater cultivation, and they have become more Chinese than the Chinese themselves.   The changes of dynasty since the end of the old empire or classical period have not been revolutions, but only substitutions of one set of rulers for another.   In the present century new relations have arisen between China and the rest of the world.   Christian nations of the West have come into rude contact with it.   In vain did it fall back on the tradition of the 'Middle State,' and proclaim its right to their homage.   The prestige of its greatness has vanished before a few ships of war, and the presence of a few thousand soldiers. The despotic empire will shortly pass away as the feudal one did, but with less 'hideous ruin and combustion.'   It is needless to speculate on the probabilities of the future.   God will be His own interpreter. China, separated from the rest of the world, and without the light of revelation, has played its part, and brought forth its lessons, which will not, I trust, be long without their fitting exposition. Whether it is to be a dependent or independent nation in the future, to be broken up or remain united, the first condition to happiness and prosperity is *humility* on the part of its scholars and rulers.   Till they are brought to look at their own history and their sages, falsely so called, according to a true estimate, and to cease from their blind admiration of them, there is no hope for the country.

The Future.

CHAPTER VI.

LIST OF THE PRINCIPAL WORKS WHICH HAVE BEEN CONSULTED IN THE PREPARATION OF THIS VOLUME.

SECTION I.

CHINESE WORKS.

1   In the 十三經註疏 (see proleg. to vol. I., p. 129):—

[i.] 尙書註疏, containing the commentary of K'ung Gan-kwŏ, and the expositions made and collected by K'ung Ying-tă and other scholars of the T'ang dynasty (see above, p. 31).

[ii.] 爾雅註疏. This is a sort of dictionary to the classics. The comments are by Kwoh P'oh (郭璞), of the Tsin dynasty, and the exposition, glosses and disquisitions, by Hing Ping (邢昺), of the Sung. 爾雅 may be translated—'The Ready Rectifier.'

3   欽定書經傳說彙纂, 'Compilation and Digest of Comments and Remarks on the Shoo King. By imperial authority.'   In 24 Books.   I have generally in my notes called this Work—'Yung-ching's Shoo.'   It was commanded in 1721, the 60th year of the period K'ang-he, the last year but one of the emperor Benevolent; and appeared with a preface by his son and successor, the emperor Pattern, in 1730, the 8th year of the period Yung-ching.   Many great scholars were employed in its preparation and publication. They drew on the writings of 380 scholars,—from the Ts'in dynasty downwards.   First, they give the commentary of Ts'ae Ch'in, the disciple of Choo He (see above, pp. 35, 36), interspersed with illustrative glosses.   Then follows a collection of passages, confirmatory of Ts'ae's views, taken from their authorities (集說).   This is often followed by an appendix of different views of the text, which are conceived to be worthy of examination (附錄).   Occasionally, the editors give their own decisions, where they think they have more light than their predecessors had (案).   There are maps and illustrations at the beginning, and a critical introduction; while the preface

201]

ascribed to Confucius is given and commented on at the end. This Work may serve the student in lieu of many others. It is a monument of industry and research ;—beyond all praise.

4   I have made frequent reference to the other imperial editions of the Classics, mentioned in proleg. to vol. I., p. 131 ; especially, to the 春秋傳說彙纂, which embodies the *Chuen* of Tso-k'ew, Kung-yang, and Kuh-lëang.

5   欽定周官義疏, 'Discussion of the Meaning of "The Officers of Chow." By imperial authority.' In 48 Books. This Work, with two others on the 'Rites,' was ordered in 1748, the 13th year of the reign K'ëen-lung, by the emperor Pure, to complete the labours of his father, the Benevolent, on the Classics. Edward Biot thus characterises it :—'It is worthy to be compared with the best Works executed in Europe on the different parts of the Bible. I should even say that it is superior to them, if I did not fear being accused of partiality' (Introduction to the Translation of 'The Rites of Chow,' p. xxxv.) The eulogy is deserved, so far as the exhaustive research is concerned. In range of thought and speculation, commentaries on the Chinese Classics and the Bible cannot be compared.

6   御製日講書經解義, 'Daily Lectures, Explaining the Meaning of the Shoo King. By imperial authority.' In 13 Books. It was ordered by the emperor Benevolent in 1,680. I have often quoted it under the name of 'The Daily Explanation.' It has all the qualities which I ascribed to the sister work on the Four Books, 'being full, perspicuous, and elegant.'

7   三山拙齋林先生尚書全解, 'A Complete Explanation of the Shang Shoo, by Lin Chueh-chae of San-shan.' In 40 Books. The author is commonly called Lin Che-k'e ; and so I have generally referred to him. His commentary is very voluminous. It is older than Ts'ae Ch'in's, and, in my opinion, superior to it.

8   臨川吳澄今文尚書纂言, 'Digest of Remarks on the Modern Text of the Shang Shoo, by Woo Ching of Lin-ch'uen.' In 4 Books. See above, p. 36. This is *the* commentary of the Yuen dynasty ;—terse and original.

9   陳氏師凱書蔡傳旁通, 'The Commentary of Ts'ae on the Shoo Illustrated by Ch'in Sze-k'ae.' Published in 6 Books, in 1,520. It is a commentary on Ts'ae Ch'in's commentary. The author draws his illustrations from 88 different Works.

10   王耕野先生讀書管見, 'Imperfect Views (views through a tube), by Wang Kăng-yay, of passages in the Shoo.' In 2 Books.

This also is a Work of the Yuen dynasty. The views are sometimes very ingenious.

11 王魯齋書疑 'Wang Loo-chae's Doubts about the Shoo. In 8 chapters. The author was of the Sung dynasty. He is also called Wang Pih (王柏).

12 The 皇淸經解, (See proleg. to vol. I., p. 133) contains many Works on the Shoo, or on portions of it. Those which I have made most use of are:—

[i.] 尙書集註音疏 'Comments of himself and others on the Meaning of the Shang Shoo, and on the Pronunciation of the Characters.' The author was a Këang Shing (江聲), of the district of Woo, dep. Soo-chow. It occupies Books 390–403 of the collection;—a Work of vast learning, but dogmatical.

[ii.] 尙書後案, 'Latest Decisions on the Shang Shoo.' By Wang Ming-shing (王鳴盛), an acquaintance of Këang Shing, and of the same district. His main object is to bring out the views of Ch'ing K'ang-shing, as the true exposition of the Classic. The Work occupies Books 404–434, and took the author 34 years to complete it. His research is vast; but his object is one-sided.

[iii] 尙書今古文註疏, 'The Shang Shoo in the Modern and Ancient Text Commented on and Discussed.' Books 735–773. The Work appeared in 1,815. The author was Sun Sing-yen (孫星衍), an officer of high employments. His 'ancient text' is not that current under this designation, but the variations from Fuh-săng's text, which are found in Ch'ing K'ang-shing and other Han writers.

[iv.] 古文尙書撰異, 'The various Readings of the Ancient Text of the Shang Shoo Collected.' Compiled in the reign of K'ëen-lung, by Twan Yuh-tsae, (段玉裁). The writer uses the designation 'Ancient Text' in the same way as Sun Sing-yen, Këang Shing, and Wang Ming-shing. Books 567–599.

[v.] 禹貢錐指, 'The Needle-touch applied to the Tribute of Yu.' Published in the reign K'ang-he, by Hoo Wei (胡渭). The author had previously been employed, with many other officers, in preparing a statistical account of the present empire. The Work cannot be too highly spoken of. Books 27–47.

17 古文尙書疏證, 'A Discussion of the Evidence for the Ancient Text of the Shang Shoo.' By Yen Jŏ-keu (閻若璩); published in

1,704. The Work is a vehement onset against the genuineness of the commonly received 'Ancient Text,' and was intended to establish, beyond contradiction, the views of Këang Shing, mentioned above. The plan of it extends to 128 Chapters or Arguments; but not a few of them are left blank. It is, no doubt, very able; but, as is said of it in the catalogue of the Imperial Libraries. it is too discursive, and full of repetitions.

18 Of the writings of Maou K'e-ling (proleg. to vol. I., p. 132), bearing on the Shoo, there are :—

[i.] 古文尙書冤詞, 'The Wrongs of the Ancient Text of the Shang Shoo.' In 8 Books. This was intended as an answer to the Work of Yen Jŏ-keu; and it seems to me that Maou has the best of the argument.

[ii.] 尙書廣聽錄, 'New Essays for Readers of the Shang Shoo.' In 5 Books. Throws light on several passages; but the author is too devoted to the commentary of Gan-kwŏ.

[iii.] 舜典補亡, 'The Lost Portions of the Canon of Shun Supplied.' In 1 Book.

21 洪範正論, 'A Correct Discussion of "The Great Plan."' In 5 Books. By Hoo Wei, whose Work on the Tribute of Yu has been noticed above. This is a fit companion to the other.

22 經義考, 'An Examination of the Explanations of the Classics.' In 300 Books. By Choo E-tsun (朱彝尊). It contains a list of all the Works on the Thirteen Classics, lost or preserved, of which the author's industry could ascertain the names, from the earliest time down to the present. Much information is given about many of them; and critical questions connected with them are discussed. The Work was ordered by the emperor Pure (K'ëen-lung), and appears with an Introduction from his pencil.

23 御纂朱子全書, 'A Grand Collection of the Views of Choo He. By imperial authority.' Compiled in 66 Books, in the 52d year of the period K'ang-ke. Books 33 and 34 are on the Shoo.

24 陔餘叢考, 'A Collection of Essays, written at intervals of Filial Duty.' In 43 Books. By Chaou Yih (趙翼). Published in 1,811.

25 Ma Twan-lin's General Examination of Records and Scholars; and its Continuation. See proleg. to vol. I., p. 134.

27 A Cyclopædia of Surnames, or Biographical Dictionary, &c. See proleg. to vol. I., p. 133.

28 The Complete Works of the Ten *Tsze*. See proleg. to vol. I., p. 133.

29　　The Philosopher Mih.　See proleg. to vol. II., p. 126.

30　　The Collected Writings of Han Ch'ang-le.　See proleg. to vol. II., p. 126.

31　　說文解字, 'Definitions and Explanations of Characters.'　This is the dictionary of Heu Shin.　See note on p. 1, above.　It was not finished A.D. 100, as there stated, but in 121.

32　　釋名, 'Explanation of Terms.'　In 4 Books.　By Lew He (劉熙), a scion of the imperial House of Han.

33　　經典釋文, 'An Explanation of the Terms and Phrases in the Classics.'　In 30 Books.　By Luh Tih-ming (陸德明), of the T'ang dynasty.　This is more a dissection of the Classics, excluding Mencius, and including Laou-tsze and Chwang-tsze, giving the sounds of characters, and the meaning of them single and in combination, than a dictionary.　It is valuable as a repertory of ancient views.

34　　御定康熙字典, 'The Dictionary of K'ang-he.　By imperial authority.'　In 42 Books.

35　　經韻集字析解 ⎫
36　　四書羣經字詁 ⎬ See below, pp. 731, 735.
37　　經籍纂詁 ⎭

38　　國語, 'Narratives of the States.'　In 21 Books.　Belongs to the period of the 'Divided States' (列國); and is commonly ascribed to Tso-k'ew Ming.　It is always published with comments by Wei Ch'aou of Woo (吳韋昭), one of the 'Three States.'

39　　戰國策注, 'Plans of the Warring States, with Comments.'　In 33 Books.　Belongs to the closing period of the Chow dynasty.　It was compiled in the first instance by a Kaou Yew (高誘), of the Han dynasty; but was subsequently largely supplemented.

40　　呂氏春秋, 'The Ch'un Ts'ew of Leu.'　In 26 Books.　Ascribed to Leu Puh-wei, the prime minister of the founder of the Ts'in dynasty.　It is tiresome to read, but is useful in studying the Classics.

41　　吳越春秋, 'The Ch'un Ts'ew of Woo and Yuĕ.'　See above, pp. 67, 68.

42　　昭明文選,李善註, 'Selection of Compositions, by Ch'aoum'ing, with the Comments of Le Shen.'　In 30 Books. Ch'aou-ming is the posthumous title of the compiler, who was heir to the throne during the Lëang dynasty (A.D. 503–557), but died early.　The compositions are of various kinds,—poems, letters, epitaphs, &c.; from Tsze-hëa downwards to the first Sung dynasty.　The commentator was of the Sung dynasty.

43   二十四史, 'The Historians.'   See proleg. to vol. I., p. 134.

44   御批通鑑輯覽一百十六卷附明唐桂二王本末三卷, 'Grand Collection of the General Mirror of History, in 116 Books; with a Supplement, containing the History of the two kings, T'ang and K'wei, in the Ming dynasty, in 3 Books. With the imperial views.' A noble work, commanded in the 33d year of K'een-lung.

45   資治通鑑綱目, 'General Mirror of History, in Heads and Particulars, for the Assistance of Government.' My copy is an edition of 1,807, in 101 Books, to the end of the Yuen dynasty.

46   綱鑑易知, 'The Mirror of History, made Easy.' In 29 Books. By Woo Sing-k'euen (吳乘權). Published in the 50th year of K'ang-he.

47   竹書紀年, 'The Annals of the Bamboo Books.' In 2 Books. By a Woo Kwan (吳琯), of the Ming dynasty. Contains only the Text, and comments of Shin Yŏ, of the Lëang dynasty.

48   竹書紀年統箋, 'The Bamboo Annals, with a Complete Annotation.' In 12 Books. By Seu Măn-tsing (徐文靖), of the present dynasty. There is also a preliminary Book, carrying the History up to Fuh-he; and one on the Evidences of the Annals. The Geographical notes are most valuable.

49   竹書紀年集證, 'The Bamboo Annals, with Collection of Evidences.' In 50 Books. Published in 1,813, by Ch'in Fung-hăng (陳逢衡). The Work is very carefully executed; by a most able scholar; and seems to exhaust the subject of the Annals.

50   十七史商榷, 'The Seventeen Histories Examined and Displayed.' In 100 Books. By Wang Ming-shing, whose 'Latest Decisions' on the Shoo King have been noticed above. Like that other Work, this also displays amazing research.

51   大清一統志, 'Statistical Account of the Empire under the Great Pure dynasty.' Commanded in the 29th year of the Emperor Pure, A. D. 1,762. In 424 Books.

52   歷代統紀表; and 歷代疆域表. See proleg. to vol. I., pp. 134, 135.

54   日知錄, 'Essays, the Fruit of Daily Acquisitions.' In 32 Books. By Koo Yen-woo (顧炎武) The essays are on a Multitude of subjects, likely to engage the attention of a Chinese Scholar. Published in 1695.

55   太平御覽. A monstrous miscellany, in 1,692 Books, prepared by order of the second emperor of the Sung dynasty, in 977. The

style of his reign at the time was 太平興國; hence the name of the Work.

56　格致鏡原. A miscellany of the present dynasty, inquiring into the origin of the things discussed. In 100 Books. By Ch'in Yuen-lung (陳元龍).

57　事物紀原, 'Record of the Origin of Affairs and Things.' A miscellany of the Sung dynasty. Contains 1,765 articles.

58　丹鉛總錄, 'Miscellaneous Pencillings.' In 27 Books. Originally published under the Ming dynasty in 1,524.

SECTION II.

TRANSLATIONS AND OTHER FOREIGN WORKS.

SEVERAL of the Works, mentioned in the prolegomena to vol. I, pp. 135, 136, have been frequently consulted by me. In addition to them, I have used:—

LE CHOU-KING, un des Livres Sacrés DES CHINOIS, qui renferm les Fondements de leur ancienne Histoire, les Principes des leur Gouvernement et de leur Morale, Traduit et enrichi des notes, par FEU LE P. GAUBIL, Missionaire a la Chine. Revu et corrige, &c., par M. DE GUIGNES, &c. A Paris, 1,770.

THE SHOO KING, or THE HISTORICAL CLASSIC, being the most ancient authentic Record of the Annals of the Chinese Empire, illustrated by LATER COMMENTATORS. Translated by W. H. MEDHURST, Sen. Shanghae, 1,846.

DESCRIPTION Geographique, Historique, Chronologique, Politique, et Physique, DE L'EMPIRE DE LA CHINE, et DE LA TARTARIE CHINOISE, &c., par le P. J. B. DU HALDE, de la Compagnie de JESUS. Tomes quatre; fol. A Paris, 1,735.

JOURNAL ASTATIQUE. Particularly the Numbers for April, May, and July, 1,836; for December, 1841; for May, and August and September, 1842.

LE TCHEOU-LI, ou RITES DES TCHEOU, Traduit pour la premiere fois du Chinois, par FEU EDOUARD BIOT. Tomes deux; 8vo. Paris, 1851.

A SKETCH OF CHINESE HISTORY, Ancient and Modern, &c. By the REV. CHARLES GUTZLAFF. Two volumes; 8vo. London, 1834.

MELANGES ASIATIQUES, &c.; par M. ABEL-REMUSAT. Tomes deux; 8vo. Paris, 1826.

EGYPT'S PLACE IN UNIVERSAL HISTORY. An Historical Investigation in five Books. By C. C. J. BARON BUNSEN, &c. Translated from the German by CHARLES H. COTTRELL, Esq., M.A. London, 1859.

ETUDES SUR L'ASTRONOMIE INDIENNE ET CHINOISE, par J. B. Biot. Paris, 1,862.

THE NUMERICAL RELATIONS OF THE POPULATION OF CHINA, DURING THE 4000 YEARS OF ITS HISTORICAL EXISTENCE, &c. By T. SACHAR-OFF, Member of the Imperial Russian Embassy in Peking. Translated into English, by the REV. W. LOBSCHEID. Hongkong, 1864.

堯　虞　位　將　宅　文　堯　昔　一節　書
典。舜、讓　遜　天　思　聰　在　　序
○　作　于　于　下、光　明　帝

1　I. Anciently there was the emperor Yaou, all-informed, intelligent, accomplished, and thoughtful. His glory filled the empire. He wished to retire from the throne, and resign it to Shun of Yu. *Descriptive of all this*, there was made THE CANON OF YAOU.

PREFACE TO THE SHOO KING. This is often called 'The small Preface' (小序), to distinguish it from the larger one (大序 and 尙書序), prefixed by K'ung Gan-kwŏ to his commentary on the Classic. It was among the other monuments recovered from the wall of Confucius' house, which were given to Gan-kwŏ to be deciphered and edited. He incorporated it with the Work itself, breaking it up into its several parts, and prefixing to each Book the portion belonging to it. Other scholars of the Han dynasty edited it in its complete form at the end of the classic. It seems to me better, and to afford more facility of reference to it hereafter, to prefix it here as a whole.

If it were indeed the work of Confucius himself, its value would be inestimable; but its many peculiarities of style, as well as many inanities, forbid us to believe that it is the composition of the Sage. Ch'ing K'ang-shing (鄭康成), Ma Yung (馬融), and Wang Suh (王蕭), those great scholars of the Han dynasty, all attribute it to him; and to justify them for doing so, Keang Shing (江聲) appeals to the words of Sze-ma Ts'een (in the 史記孔子世家):—' He prefaced the Records of the Shoo, from the times of T'ang and Yu, down to Muh of Ts'in, arranging their subjects in order (see 江徵君尙書集注音疏 on the 序). This, however, would only be evidence at the most that Confucius had made a preface to the Shoo King; but Ts'een's statement, in which he has been followed by many subsequent chroniclers, was grounded merely on the existence of this document itself, many parts of which he has introduced into his histories (本記), though not all in the order in which they are given by Gan-kwŏ. It is enough to admit with Choo He, that this preface was the production of some writer in the end of the Chow or the beginning of the Ts'in dynasty.—I shall discuss here but sparingly its various statements. That will be done, where necessary, in the introductions to the several Books.

九共九篇、　類作汨作、　方別生分　土方設居　○帝釐下〔三節〕　難作舜典。〔三節〕　位歷試諸　明將使嗣　堯聞之聰　虞舜側微、〔二節〕

2   II. Shun of Yu was in a low and undistinguished position, when Yaou heard of his comprehensive intelligence, and wishing to make him successor to his throne, made proof of him in many situations of difficulty. *With reference to this*, there was made THE CANON OF SHUN.

3   The emperor regulated the territories, appointing *nobles* to every quarter to reside in them, giving them surnames of distinction, and defining the constituents of each. *Descriptive of this*, there were made the KWUH TSŎ, the KEW KUNG, in nine Books, and the KAOU YU.

I. This paragraph contains, according to the arrangement of the Books which I have adopted, and for which I have elsewhere given the reasons, the notice of only one Book, the first part of the Classic. 'The Canon of Yaou' is edited as the first of 'The Books of Yu,' by those who divide the Work into four parts; and as the first of the Books of Yu-Hea, by those who make only three divisions. 遂 is best explained, with Gan-kwŏ, by 遁, 'to withdraw,' though the 于 following would more readily be translated by 'to' than by 'from.'

   Both Gan-kwŏ and Ch'ing K'ang-shing understand the 讓 as denoting not the resignation of the throne, but simply of the management of affairs. Yaou was still emperor till his death, and Shun was only his vice. 作 堯典,—the 作 is at first referred to 堯 as its subject. The character must be so connected with the principal word in many sentences of the preface. The nominative here, however, is not 堯. In this and many other sentences the 作 is quite vague. We might take it intransitively.—'These subjects *form* the matter of the Canon of Yaou.' The 集傳 says—作者追言作書之意如此, '作 says retrospectively that to relate these matters was the object of the maker of the Book.'

   II. This paragraph contains the prefatory notices to the Books of Yu, forming the second part of the classic, though it may be questioned whether another arrangement of some of them would not be more correct. This question has been touched on in the prolegomena. I have thought it sufficient to indicate my own view there, not wishing to make in this volume any further change in the ordinary arrangement of the Books, beyond what I have done in separating the 'Canon of Yaou' from the Books of Yu. Those amounted in Confucius' time, it will be seen, to 15, of which only 4 are now existing, allowing the genuineness of 'The Counsels of the great Yu,' and the right of the 'Canon of Shun' to stand by itself separate from the 'Canon of Yaou,' and of the 'Yih and Tseih' to be separate from the 'Counsels of Kaou Yaou.'

   Not. 2. This is a very imperfect account of the Canon of Shun. 'The Book must contain the governmental affairs, first and last, of Shun's reign, and the preface would make it appear that the proof of him in various difficult situations was all the matter treated of!' (See the 集傳.)   3. I have translated after Gan-kwŏ. Keang Shing points differently, and gives quite another view of the meaning. K'ung Ying-tă (孔穎達), Gan-kwŏ's glossarist of the T'ang dynasty (flour. in greater part of the 7th cent.), says—'In such cases, where the text of the classic is lost, we shoot at the meaning in the dark. Gan-kwŏ interpreted according to the words, whether correctly or not cannot be known.' For this reason I have for the most part given the Chinese names of the lost Books, without attempting to translate them. 汨作 may mean 'The Achievements of Government.' 九共 has been translated 'The nine Laws' (共=法); and 'The nine Contributions' (共=給); also 'The nine Hills' (共=邱). All is uncertain. And so also is the meaning of 稾飫.   4. 帝

作胤征。○自契至于成　淫廢時亂日、胤往征之、[九節]　作五子之歌。○羲和湎　邦昆弟五人須于洛汭、[八節]　之野、作甘誓。○太康失[七節]　九州隨山濬川任土作貢。○啟與有扈戰于甘[六節]　禹皋陶謨益稷。○禹別[五節]　成厥功、帝舜申之、作大　稟飫。○皋陶矢厥謨禹[四節]

4   Kaou Yaou unfolded his counsels; Yu completed his work; the emperor Shun made him go on to further statements. *With reference to these things*, there were made THE COUNSELS OF THE GREAT YU, and OF KAOU YAOU, and the YIH AND TSEIH.

5   III.   Yu marked out the nine provinces; followed the course of the hills, and deepened the rivers; defined the imposts on the land, and the articles of tribute.

6   K'e fought with the prince of Hoo in the wilderness of Kan, when he made THE SPEECH AT KAN.

7   T'ae-k'ang lost his kingdom; and his five brothers waited for him on the north of the Lŏ, and made THE SONGS OF THE FIVE SONS.

8   He and Ho, sunk in wine and excess, neglected the ordering of the seasons, and allowed the days to get into confusion. *The prince of* Yin went to punish them. *Descriptive of this*, there was made THE PUNITIVE EXPEDITION OF YIN.

9   IV.   From Sëĕ to T'ang the Successful, there were eight changes

---

舜申之,—申之, 'repeated it,' has reference probably to the commencing words of the 'Yih and Tseih'—'The emperor said, Come Yu, you *likewise* must have admirable words.'

III. The four Books in this paragraph constitute the third part of the Shoo. The genuineness of two is questioned; but it is remarkable that Confucius found among the relics of the Hea dynasty, B.C. 2204—1766, only these four documents worthy to be transmitted to posterity. And, indeed, the first of them should belong more properly to the Books of Yu.

Not. 5. 任土作貢,—all the commentators make the 任土 auxiliary to the other characters,='he assigned the tribute according to the nature and productions of the land.' It seems much simpler to take them as I have done; comp. Mencius, IV. Pt. I. xiv. 3. It will be seen the notice is defective, and wants 作禹貢 at the end. Ch'ing has called attention to this. 6. The style of this notice is considered sufficient evidence that the preface is not the work of Confucius, who would never have represented the emperor and his vassal as if they were fighting on equal terms—與...戰. (See the 集傳.) 7. 須=待. In the text of the Book we have 係. 8. 胤= 胤侯. IV. This paragraph, containing 23 prefatory notices, enumerates 31 different documents, in

4   PREFACE TO THE SHOO KING.

遷其社不可作夏社疑至、

野、作湯誓。○湯既勝夏、欲
十三節

自陑遂與桀戰于鳴條之

汝方。○伊尹相湯伐桀升
十二節

門、乃遇汝鳩汝方作汝鳩

醜有夏復歸于亳入自北

湯征。○伊尹去亳適夏、既
十一節

侯、葛伯不祀湯始征之作

居作帝告釐沃。○湯征諸
十節

湯、八遷湯始居亳從先王

of the capital. T'ang at first dwelt in Pŏ, choosing the residence of the first sovereign of his House. *Then* were made the TE KUH, and the LE YUH.

10   When T'ang chastised the various princes, the chief of Kŏ was not offering the *appointed* sacrifices. T'ang began his work by chastising him, and *then* was made the T'ANG CHING.

11   E Yin went from Pŏ to Hea. Indignant with the sovereign of Hea, he returned to Pŏ; and as he entered by the north gate, met with Joo Kew and Joo Fang. *With reference to this* were made the JOO KEW, and the JOO FANG.

12   E Yin acted as minister to T'ang, and *advised* him to attack Këĕ. They went up from E, and fought with him in the wilderness of Ming-t'eaou. *Then* was made THE SPEECH OF T'ANG.

13   When T'ang had vanquished Hea, he wished to change its sacrifices to the Spirit of the land, but concluded not to do so. *With*

40 Books or chapters (篇), all belonging to the dynasty of Shang, B.C. 1765—1122. More than half of them are lost,—the first five, classed by some among the Books of the Hea dyn.; the 7th, 8th, 9th, and 10th; the 13th, 15th, and 16th; the 19th to the 25th; and the 29th. Of the remaining 11 documents, there are only 5 whose genuineness is unchallenged. The order in which they stand, moreover, differs somewhat in the preface as edited by Gan-kwŏ, and as approved by Ch'ing and other Han scholars.

Not. 9. Sëĕ, from whom the sovereigns of the Shang dyn. traced their descent, was a son of the emp. 嚳, B.C. 2432; whose capital was Pŏ. Kuh must therefore be the 先王, and

probably the 帝 in 帝告, 'The Announcement to the Emperor.' 釐沃 may mean 'The Rule of Enrichment.'

10. 湯征, 'The Punitive Expedition of T'ang.' See Men. III. Pt. II. v., and the Announcement of Chung Hwuy. Those who object to the Shoo King of Gan-kwŏ say that the passages of Hwuy's Announcement referred to are a remnant of this Book; see the 尙書後案 of 王鳴盛, *in loc.* 11. Joo Kew and Joo Fang, we may suppose, were two ministers, with whom E Yin discussed the affairs of Hea. 13. 欲遷其社—

復歸于亳思庸、伊尹作太
立不明、伊尹放諸桐三年、
伊訓肆命祖后。○太甲既
湯既沒太甲元年、伊尹作
湯誥。○咎單作明居。
湯既黜夏命復歸于亳作
夏至于大坰仲虺作誥。○
伯仲伯作典寶。○湯歸自
之遂伐三朡俘厥寶玉誼
臣扈。○夏師敗績湯遂從

reference to this there were made the HEA SHAY, the E-CHE, and the CHIN-HOO.

14　The army of Hea being entirely defeated, T'ang followed it and smote Săn-tsung, where he captured the precious relics and gems. *Then* E-pih and Chung-pih made the TEEN PAOU.

15　When T'ang was returning from *the conquest of* Hea, he came to Ta-këung, where Chung Hwuy made his ANNOUNCEMENT.

16　T'ang having made an end of the sovereignty of Hea, returned to Pŏ, and made THE ANNOUNCEMENT OF T'ANG.

17　Kaou Shen made the MING KEU.

18　After the death of T'ang, in the first year of T'ae-kĕă, E Yin made THE INSTRUCTIONS OF E, the SZE MING, and the TSOO HOW.

19　When T'ae-kĕă was declared emperor, he proved unintelligent, and E Yin placed him in T'ung. After three years he returned with him to Pŏ, when he had applied his thoughts to the course of duty. *Then* E Yin made the T'AE-KEA in three Books.

see Mencius, VII. Pt. II. xiv.; he says that the spirits of the land and grain might be changed on proof of their powerlessness, and much more might this be done on a change of dynasty as here. But whom was T'ang to place as the 土神句龍, or human assessor of such, in room of, to whom the Hea dyn. had sacrificed? None was found so worthy. E-che and Chin-hoo were probably two ministers consulted on the subject. 14. The precious relics and gems were those of the Hea emperors. 17. This notice contains no prefatory explanation. There are three others of the same kind. Kaou Shen (so the name is to be read), according to Ma Yung, was minister of Works. 明居 may mean—'Illustration of the way to settle the people.' 18. 肆命 = 'A declaration of the way of Heaven,' acc. to Gan-kwŏ; 'of the principles of government,' acc. to Ch'ing. 祖后, 'the past (= deceased) sovereign;' referring to T'ang. 19. 思庸,—王天與 (of the Yuen dyn.) says, 'Gan-kwŏ explains this phrase by *he thought of the constant course of duty;* Soo by *he thought of using the words of* E *Yin;* Ch'in says, The meaning is expressed by Mencius (V. Pt. I. vi. 5.),—*He repented of his errors, was*

甲三篇。○伊尹作咸有一德。○_{廿一節}沃丁既葬伊尹于亳、咎單遂訓伊尹事作沃丁。○伊陟相太戊、_{廿二節}亳有祥桑穀共生于朝、伊陟贊于巫_{廿三節}咸作咸乂四篇。○太戊贊_{廿四節}于伊陟、作伊陟、原命。○河_{廿五節}亶丁遷于囂、作仲丁。○河亶_{廿六節}甲居相作河亶甲。○祖乙_{廿七節}圯于耿作祖乙。○盤庚五

20　E Yin made the BOTH POSSESSED PURE VIRTUE.

21　When Yuh-ting had buried E Yin in Pǒ, Kaou Shen then set forth as lessons the doings of E Yin, and there was made the YUH-TING.

22　E Chih was prime minister to T'ae-mow, when ominous appearances showed themselves in Pǒ. A mulberry tree and a stalk of grain grew up in the court. E Chih told Woo Heen, who made the HEEN E in four Books.

23　T'ae-mow spoke on the subject with E Chih, and there were made the E CHIH and the YUEN MING.

24　Chung-ting removed to Heaou, and there was made the CHUNG-TING.

25　Ho-tan-kĕ̆ lived in Sëang, and there was made the HO-TAN-KEA.

26　Tsoo-yih met with calamity in Kăng, and there was made the TSOO-YIH.

contrite, and reformed himself, &c.' See the 集說, *in loc.*

22. Gan-kwǒ and others refer to 桑穀 as two trees growing together. But how can a stalk of grain be represented as a *tree?* The 說文 dict. explains the char. 楮 by 穀 (? radical 木 and not 禾), a kind of mulberry tree from the bark of which both cloth and paper can be made. We should probably read 穀桑, one tree. Gan-Kwǒ says it attained its size in seven days; Sze-ma Ts'een says one evening! 巫咸,—see the 君奭, par. 7.

Ch'ing interprets 'Heen. the Wizard,'—perhaps correctly. Ts'een says that Hëen made the Hëen E, and the T'ae-mow. 23. These last Books are supposed to have been on the subject of the ominous appearances. 原 is the name of a minister. 原命, 'The charge to Yuen.'

25. Ho-tan-kĕ̆,—this is always given as the name of the 10th emp. of the Shang dyn. We may suppose that Tan-kĕ̆ was his name, and that 河 was added, because of some peculiar troubles in his time with that river. See the 通鑑綱目. 26. 圯,—'was overthrown;' *i.e.*, the capital was injured by an

○惟十有一錯天命微子作誥父師少師。告于受作西伯戡黎。○殷既始咎周周人乘黎祖伊恐奔作高宗肜日高宗之訓。○殷雉升鼎耳而雊祖己訓諸王命三篇。○高宗祭成湯有飛工營求諸野得諸傅巖作說庚三篇。○高宗夢得說使百遷將治亳殷民咨胥怨作盤

年武王伐殷一

27　Pwan-kang made the fifth change *of capital,* and was about to repair Pŏ, *as the cradle of the* Yin. The people murmured, and expressed themselves resentfully to one another. *With reference to this* there was made the PWAN-KANG, in three Books.

28　Kaou-tsung dreamed that he got Yuĕ, and made all his officers institute a search for him in the wilds. He was found in Foo-yen; and THE CHARGE TO YUE was made in three Books.

29　Kaou-tsung was sacrificing to T'ang the Successful, when a pheasant flew up, and lighted on the ear of a tripod, aud *there* crowed. Tsoo Ke lessoned the king *on the subject,* and made THE DAY OF THE SUPPLEMENTARY SACRIFICE OF KAOU TSUNG, and THE INSTRUCTIONS TO KAOU-TSUNG.

30　Yin's first hatred of Chow was occasioned by its conquest of Le. Tsoo E, full of dread, hurried off to inform Show. *With reference to this* there was made THE CHIEF OF THE WEST'S CONQUEST OF LE.

31　Yin having cast away the sovereignty conferred on it by Heaven, the count of Wei made his announcement to the Grand Tutor and to the Junior Tutor.

32　V. In the eleventh year king Woo smote *the power of* Yin. On the mow-woo day of the first month, his army crossed *the Ho at* Măng-

overflow of the Ho.　　31. 錯＝廢, as in Ana. II. xix.

V. This paragraph contains notices—such as they are—of 38 different documents in 40 Books, extending from the commencement of the Chow dynasty, B.C. 1121, to 626, within little more than half a century of the birth of Confucius. Eight of the pieces have been lost,—the 5th, 7th, 11th, 12th, 22d, 23d, 27th, and 28th; there are two documents, very different in themselves, each of which claims to be ' The Great Speech;'

殷邦諸侯、班宗彝作

作洪範。○武王旣勝 卅六節

受立武庚以箕子歸、 卅五節

武成。○武王勝殷殺

伐歸獸識其政事作

牧誓。○武王伐殷往 卅四節

人、與受戰于牧野作

車三百兩虎賁三百

泰誓三篇。○武王戎 卅三節

月戊午、師渡孟津、作

tsin. *Descriptive of this* there was made THE GREAT SPEECH, in three Books.

33   King Woo, with three hundred chariots of war and three hundred tiger-like officers, fought with Show in the wilderness of Muh. *Then* was made THE SPEECH AT MUH.

34   King Woo smote Yin; and the narrative of his proceeding to the attack, and of his return and sending his animals back to their pastures, with his governmental measures, form THE COMPLETION OF THE WAR.

35   When king Woo conquered Yin, he slew Show, and appointed Woo-kăng *over the original principality of his House.* He got the count of Ke to return to him, and THE GREAT PLAN was made.

36   When king Woo had conquered Yin, he appointed the princes of

of the remaining Books 20 are of unchallenged genuineness, and the claim of the others—the 3d, 6th, 10th, 21st, 26th, 29th, 32d, 33d, and 34th—has been discussed and mainly admitted in the prolegg. These 29 Books form now the fifth and last part of the classic.

Not. 33. 戎車三百兩, 虎賁 三百人,—see Men. VII. Pt. II. iv. 4, where this sentence appears to be quoted; but with 革 for 戎, and 三千人 for 三百 人. Sze-ma Ts'een also has 三千人. Mih Teih, again, says that Woo had 100 chariots, and of 虎賁之卒四百人 (明鬼 篇下). Another enumeration of 800 is also found. See the 尙書今古文注疏 of 孫星衍, *in loc.* The 虎賁 are said to have been 勇士, 'brave officers,'— centurions, according to Gan-kwŏ (百夫 長). 35. 殺受—Show, like another

Sardanapalus, burned himself, after being defeated by king Woo.   Woo-kăng was Show's son, called also 祿父 (or 甫), was appointed by Woo over the original seat of his House to continue the sacrifices to his forefathers.

箕子—the 大傳, or Introduction to the Shoo, ascribed to 伏生, says, that 'the count of Ke on being delivered from the prison, where he had been put by Show, unwilling to become a servant to the new dynasty, fled to Corea, of which Woo appointed him ruler. This obliged him to come to Woo's court to acknowledge the king's grace, and then it was that the Great Plan was obtained from him.' Others say that his appointment to Corea was a subsequent affair. If so, another explanation of 以箕 子歸 has to be sought.   36. 分器, may be translated—'The apportioned vessels.' 邦=封. It was one of the ceremonies of investiture, to give part of the furniture of the ancestral temple of the emperor to the deputed noble. See the 集說 The principles

命唐叔歸周公于東、作歸

禾異畝同穎獻諸天子、王

後作微子之命。○唐叔得

命殺武庚命微子啟代殷〔四十二〕

殷作大誥。○成王既黜殷〔四十一〕

淮夷叛周公相成王、將黜

作金縢。○武王崩、三監及〔四十節〕

旅巢命。○武王有疾、周公〔卅九節〕

旅獒。○巢伯來朝、芮伯作〔卅八節〕

分器。○西旅獻獒、太保作〔卅七節〕

the various States, and distributed among them the vessels of the ancestral temple. *With reference to this* there was made the FUN K‘E.

37 The western people of Le made an offering of some of their hounds; and the Grand Guardian made THE HOUNDS OF LE.

38 The chief of Ch‘aou having come to court, the chief of Juy made and impressed on him the CH‘AOU MING.

39 King Woo was sick, which gave occasion to the Book about the duke of Chow's making THE METAL-BOUND CASKET.

40 When king Woo had deceased, the three overseers and the wild tribes of the Hwae rebelled. The duke of Chow acted as prime minister to king Ching; and having purposed to make an end of *the House of* Yin, he made THE GREAT ANNOUNCEMENT.

41 King Ching having made an end of the appointment *in favour of the House* of Yin, and put Woo-kăng to death, he appointed K‘e, the count of Wei, to take the place of the descendants of Yin. *Descriptive of this*, there was made THE CHARGE TO THE COUNT OF WEI.

42 The *king's* uncle, the prince of T‘ang, found a head of grain, *two stalks* in different plats of ground growing into one ear, and presented it to the king. The king ordered him to send it to the duke of Chow in the east. *Upon this* was made the KWEI HO.

on which the distribution to different ranks was made were probably described in this last Book.

38. There is a difficulty in translating 旅 In not. 43 it = 陳, by which it is explained here; the diff. arises from its following 作. It is said in the 集說 —‘The chief of Juy, being in the court and making the royal charge, must have been a minister of the king. 旅= 陳. He set forth the majesty and virtue of the king to charge Ch‘aou.' 42. The prince of T‘ang was a younger brother of king Ching's mother; see the 左傳、昭十五年

遷　卜　周　作　宅　誥　王　天　禾
殷　作　公　召　洛　梓　既　子　○
頑　洛　往　誥　邑　材　伐　之　周
民　誥　營　○　使　○　管　命　公
周　○　成　召　召　成　叔　作　既
公　成　周　公　公　王　蔡　嘉　得
以　周　使　既　先　在　叔　禾　命
王　既　來　相　相　豐　以　○　禾
命　成　告　宅　宅　欲　殷　成　旅

四十三

四十四

四十五

四十六

四十七

43　The duke of Chow having got the *king's* charge and the head of grain, set forth the charge of the sovereign, and made the KEA HO.

44　The king Ching having smitten his uncles, the prince of Kwan and the prince of Ts'ae, invested his uncle K'ang with the rule of the remnant of Yin. *With reference to this*, there were made THE ANNOUNCEMENT TO K'ANG, THE ANNOUNCEMENT ABOUT WINE, and THE GOOD MATERIALS.

45　King Ching being in Fung, and wishing to fix his residence at Lŏ, sent the duke of Shaou in the first place to survey the localities. *Then* was made THE ANNOUNCEMENT OF SHAOU.

46　The duke of Shaou having surveyed the localities, the duke of Chow went to build *this capital, called* Ching Chow, and sent a messenger to announce the divinations. With reference to this THE ANNOUNCEMENT ABOUT LO was made.

47　When Ching Chow was completed, the obstinate people of Yin were removed to it. The duke of Chow announced to them the royal will, and THE NUMEROUS OFFICERS was made.

Gan-kwŏ takes 畝＝壟, 'a hillock,' 'a mound;' so Choo He elsewhere explains the character. Ch'ing makes it ＝苗, 'a stalk of growing grain,' which gives a good meaning, but made for the occasion. 孫星衍 would explain it by 母＝拇, 'toes or fingers,' a figurative expression for the grain dividing from the stalk. 歸禾 may be translated 'The Presented Grain.' 43. 得命和, —Ch'ing says, 受王歸已禾之命 與其禾, *i.e.*, we must understand an *and* between 命 and 和. Both Keang Shing and Sun Sing-k'een quote here, from 韓詩 外傳, what appears to be another legendary account of this head of grain, formed by *three* stalks growing through a mulberry tree into one ear of marvellous size. I have only got the copy of the 外傳, given in the 三代兩 漢遺書, which does not contain the legend; and, indeed, Keang Shing quotes from the 外傳五. A similar account is found in 劉向's 說苑, 辨物篇. 嘉禾 ＝ 'The Excellent Grain.' 44. It is disput-

告作多士。○周公作無逸。○召
公爲保周公爲師相成王爲左
右召公不悅周公作君奭。○蔡
叔既沒王命蔡仲踐諸侯位作
蔡仲之命。○成王東伐淮夷遂
踐奄作成王政。○成王既踐奄
將遷其君於蒲姑周公告召公
作將蒲姑。○成王歸自奄在宗
周誥庶邦作多方。○周公作立
政。○成王既黜殷命滅淮夷還

48　The duke of Chow made the Book AGAINST LUXURIOUS EASE.

49　The duke of Shaou acted as guardian and the duke of Chow as tutor, the chief ministers of king Ching, his left and right-hand men. The duke of Shaou was not pleased, and the duke of Chow made the PRINCE SHIH.

50　After the death of the king's uncle, the prince of Ts'ae, the king appointed his son Chung to take his place as a prince *of the empire.* Then was made the CHARGE TO CHANG OF TS'AE.

51　King Ching having smitten the wild tribes of the Hwae on the east, at the same time extinguished the State of Yen. Then was made the CHING WANG CHING.

52　King Ching having extinguished Yen, and wishing to remove its ruler to P'oo-koo, the duke of Chow announced the thing to the duke of Shaou. *Then* there was made the TSEANG P'OO-KOO.

53　King Ching returned from Yen, and in the honoured city of Chow made an announcement to all the States. *Then* was made THE NUMEROUS REGIONS.

54　The duke of Chow made THE ESTABLISHMENT OF GOVERNMENT.

ed whether 康叔 should be translated—'his uncle, K'ang,' or 'his uncle, the prince of K'ang.' See on the 康誥.　51. 踐 is taken by Ch'ing as = 翦, and explained by

滅. Gan-kwŏ agrees with him. 成王政 probably meant 'The Completion of the Royal Government.' See the 集說. 52. 蒲姑 is 薄姑 in the 史記. I don't know

康王既尸天子、遂誥諸侯作　公率諸侯相康王作顧命。○　君陳。○成王將崩、命召公畢　泆命君陳分正東郊成周作　畢告周公作亳姑。○周公既　泆欲葬成周、公薨成王葬于　賄肅慎之命。○周公在豐將　東夷、肅慎來賀王、俾榮伯作　歸在豐作周官。○成王既伐

六十節　　　　　　五十九　　　　　　五十八　　五十七　　　　　　五十六

55   When king Ching had made an end of the House of Yin, and extinguished the wild tribes of the Hwae, he returned to Fung; and there was made THE OFFICERS OF CHOW.

56   When king Ching had smitten the wild tribes of the east, Suh-shin came to congratulate him. The king made the chief of Yung make the CHARGE TO SUH-SHIN, and gave him presents also.

57   The duke of Chow was in Fung and about to die. He wished to be buried in Ching chow; but on his decease king Ching buried him in Peih, making an announcement at his bier. Then was made the PO-KOO.

58   After the death of the duke of Chow, Keun-ch'in was commissioned with the separate charge of regulating Ching Chow in the eastern border, and there was made the KEUN-CH'IN.

59   When king Ching was about to die, he ordered the duke of Shaou and the duke of Peih to take the lead of all the princes to support

what to make of the 將.   56. 蕭 (al. 息) 慎 was the chief of some wild tribe; but in what quarter is disputed. See the 左傳, 昭 九年; and the 國語, 五卷, 魯語, 下.
    The 集傳 explains 賄 by 賂, and adds that the writer does not understand the meaning of the word as used here. In the passage of the 國語 just referred to, it is said that king Woo made the wild tribes bring the

productions and articles of their countries as tribute (以其方賄來貢). Suh-shin, I suppose, had brought such, and the emperor ordered him gifts in return.   57. Sze-ma Ts'een says that Chow-kung on his death-bed said, 'Bury me in Ching-chow, to show that I dare not leave king Ching.' The king, however, buried him in Peih, beside king Wăn, to show that he did not dare to look on Chow-kung as a servant (see the 魯周公世家).

告周公作亳姑. This is very ob-

康王之誥。○康王命作 六十一

册畢分居里成周郊作

畢命。○穆王命君牙爲 六十二

周大司徒作君牙。○穆 六十三

王命伯冏爲周大僕正、

作冏命。○呂命穆王訓 六十四

夏贖刑作呂刑。○平王 六十五

錫晉文侯秬鬯圭瓚作

文侯之命。○魯侯伯禽 六十六

宅曲阜徐夷並興東郊

king K'ang. *With reference to this*, there was made THE TESTAMEN-
TARY DECREE.

60   When king K'ang occupied the sovereign place, he made an
announcement to all the princes, and there was made THE AN-
NOUNCEMENT OF KING K'ANG.

61   King K'ang ordered that a document of appointment should be
made for the duke of Peih, severally defining the localities in the
borders of Ching chow.   There was then made the CHARGE TO THE
DUKE OF PEIH.

62   King Muh appointed Keun-ya to be the minister of instruction
of Chow; and there was made the KEUN-YA.

63   King Muh appointed Pih-keung to be the master of his household; and there was made the CHARGE TO KEUNG.

64   *The prince of* LEU was charged by king Muh to set forth the lessons of Hea on the redemption of punishments; and there was made
LEU ON PUNISHMENTS.

65   King P'ing gave to prince Wăn of Tsin spirits of the black
millet mixed with odoriferous herbs.   *With reference to this*, there
was made the CHARGE TO PRINCE WAN.

66   When Pih-k'in, prince of Loo, first dwelt in K'euh-fow, the Seu
and other wild tribes rose together in insurrection.   The gates on

scure. The announcement must have been to
the duke on his bier, or by means of a sacrifice.
Some suppose that 亳姑 should be 蒲姑,
not 52, and that the subject announced had
something to do with the removal of the ruler
of Yen, a measure which had originated with
Chow-kung. 60. 旣尸天子,—the

use of 尸 here is strange. It leads us to 太
康尸位 in 'The Songs of the five Sons,'
and to 羲和尸厥官 in 'The Punitive
Expedition of Yin.' The writer of the preface
would seem to have had those passages in view;
but the 尸 here simply ＝ 主, and intimates
nothing condemnatory of king K'ang.

作　崤　師　襄　伐　秦　費　不
秦　還　敗　公　鄭　穆　誓。開
誓。歸。諸　帥　晉　公　○　作

六十七

the eastern frontier were kept shut, and there was made THE SPEECH
AT PE.

67   When duke Muh of Ts'in was invading Ch'ing, the duke Seäng
of Tsin led an army, and defeated his forces in Heaou.   When they
returned, he made THE SPEECH OF THE DUKE OF TS'IN

SUMMARY. From this preface it appears that the Shoo-king, as compiled by Confucius, contained 81 Documents in 100 Books. The preface has no division of those into Parts. According to the arrangement made in this volume, Part I., or the Book of T'ang, contained 1 document still existing: Part, II., or the Book of Yu, contained 7 documents in 15 Books, of which 3 in 11 Books are lost; 4 remain, but not all equally allowed: Part III., or the Book of Hea, contained 4 documents in 4 Books, all of which remain, though the genuineness of two of them is questioned: Part IV., or the Book of Shang, contained 31 documents in 40 Books; 20 documents in 23 Books are lost; 11 documents remain, only 5 of which, however, are unquestioned: Part V., or the Book of Chow, contained 38 documents in 40 Books; 8 documents in 8 Books are lost; of 1 there are two very different versions; 20 documents are fully admitted.

THE SHOO KING.

PART I. THE BOOK OF T'ANG.

THE CANON OF YAOU.

于　被　恭　思　勳　帝　曰一
上　四　克　安　欽　堯　若節
下　表　讓　安　明　曰　稽　尚　尚
。　。　光　允　文　放　古　堯　唐　書
○　格　　　　　　　典　書

1   I. Examining into antiquity, *we find that* the emperor Yaou was
called Fang-heun. He was reverential, intelligent, accomplished, and
thoughtful,—naturally and without effort. He was sincerely courteous, and capable of *all* complaisance. The display *of these qualities* reached to the four extremities *of the empire*, and extended from

TITLE OF THE WHOLE WORK. 尚書.—
Anciently, the Work was simply called the Shoo.
So Confucius, in the Analects, and Mencius
refer to it. See Ana. II. xxi., &c.; Men. I. Pt.
II. iii. 7, &c. The addition of 尚,—上,
'High,' is by Ch'ing K'ang-shing attributed to
Conf. He says, 'Conf., honouring it, gave it
the denomination of 尚書. Honouring and
emphasizing it as if it were a Book of Heaven,
he therefore called it "The Highest Book,"'
(尊而重之若天書然,故曰
尚書). Gan-kwŏ in his preface ascribes the
name to Fuh-shang, who called it, he says, the
尚書 'as being the book of the highest
antiquity' (以其上古之書). The
use of the name by Mih Teih in his 明

鬼篇, however, shows its existence before
Fuh's time. With whom and how it originated,
we cannot positively say. 書, given by
the 說文 as being formed from 聿 and 者
(＝著),＝what is described or related with a
pencil, 'a writing.'

TITLE OF THE PART. 唐書.—In so deno-
minating this portion of the work, I follow the
authority of Hea Shin (許慎, of the 2d
cent.), who in his dict. (the 說文) quotes
part of par. 8 as from the 唐書. Keang
Shing and Maou K'e-ling, likewise, both say that
this was the arrangement of Fuh-shang himself;
see the 集注音疏 of the former *in loc.*,
and the 古文尚書冤詞, 卷一,

p. 9, of the latter. Besides, Yaou constituted a dynasty by himself. He and Shun were as distinct from each other as were Shun and Yu. 唐者堯有天下之號 'T'ang is the dynastic designation of Yaou.' Before he succeeded to the empire, he was prince of T'ang (唐侯). The name is still retained in the district so called of 保定 dep., in Chih-le.

TITLE OF THE BOOK. 堯典, 'The Canon of Yaou.' Yaou is to all readers substantially the name of the emperor. Whether it was so or not, see on par. 1. 典 is found in K'ang-he's dict., under 八, but the 說文 gives it under 丌, 'that which is high and level.' '冊 being placed over it, there is thus indicated the exalted nature of the document. The character indicates what is classical, invariable, what may serve as a law, and rule.' The sayings and doings of Yaou and Shun form a pattern for all ages.—With regard to the relative position of the three titles, they are placed here according to modern usage. Under the Han dynasty, the relative position was just the reverse. The title of the Book was put highest, and that of the Work lowest.

CONTENTS OF THE BOOK. Yaou is the subject of the Book; first in his personal character, and the general results of his government; next in his special care for the regulation of the calendar, and the labours of agriculture; and lastly, in his anxiety to find a man to whom in his declining years he could intrust the administration of affairs, and who might succeed him on the throne. He appears before the reader—the sage; the administrator; the patriotic sovereign. There are in all, according to the ordinary, though not unexceptionable arrangement only 12 paragraphs (節), which may be divided into 3 chapters (叚 or 大叚). Ch. I. contains the parr. 1 and 2; ch. II. contains parr. 3—8; ch. III. contains parr. 9—12.

CH. I. THE SAGELY VIRTUES OF YAOU, AND THE BENEFICENT CHARACTER AND SUCCESSFUL RESULTS OF HIS GOVERNMENT. Par. 1. Choo He gave his decided opinion that the six characters 曰若稽古帝堯 were to be construed together without stop, and were 'the introductory words of the chronicler' (see 朱子全書, 卷三十三, 堯典)=— 'When we make a study of the ancient emperor Yaou.' Anciently, however, a comma was put at 古; 曰 (read also 粤) 若 were taken as a formula of introduction; and 稽古帝堯 were a sentence, of which 帝堯 was the subject, and 稽古 the predicate. K'ang-shing makes 稽=同 and 古=天, and explains, 'Yaou was able to accord with Heaven, and his actions were of equal merit with its' (see any of the comm. of the present dyn.). Support is thought to be given to this view by

Conf. words, Ana. VIII. xix. But it is plainly inadmissible. Ma Yung and Gan-kwŏ, taking only 曰 as introductory, make 若=順, and 稽=考. The latter explains, 'He who could accord with and examine ancient principles, and practise them, was the emperor Yaou.' There is not so much violence here to the meaning of terms, as in Ch'ing's interpretation; but Maou K'e-ling points out another and much simpler construction, taking 曰若稽古 as an ancient formula prefixed by chroniclers to their narratives. (Instances may be seen in 孫星衍, in loc.) The four characters, then, = 'When we examine into antiquity,' and 堯帝 are the subject of the 曰 which follows; see Maou's 尙書廣聽錄, 卷一. 帝堯曰放勳 (al. 勛),— The uniform testimony of antiquity is that 放勳 was Yaou's name; 重華 that of Shun; and 文命 that of Yu. So expressly, Sze-ma Ts'een Ch'ing, Ma, and Chaou K'e. Mencius also seems to countenance this, V. Pt. I. iv. 1; though I there, in deference to the Sung scholars, translated the words by 'The Highly Meritorious.' Gan-kwŏ was the first to treat the characters as a descriptive phrase, taking 放 (up. 2d tone) = 'to learn,' 'to imitate;'—'it may be said of him that he imitated the merit of the highest ages?' Choo He's disciple 蔡沈, improved on this, making 放=至, and the phrase = 'The Highly Meritorious.' But it is better to revert to the ancient view. For the difficulty in its way, arising from Pt II. iii. 1, see in loc. But if Fang-heun, &c., were the names of Yaou and the other sages, what account is to be given of the terms 堯, 舜, &c., themselves? This question cannot be settled beyond dispute. They were not 謚, honorary, posthumous titles, as Ma Yung says; for, not to insist on the point that the giving of such titles originated with the Chow dyn., we find both Shun and Yu spoken of and spoken to by those styles;—see, par. 8: Pt. II. i. 3; iv. 1. I must regard them as a kind of 號 or 字, designations. Yaou's reign commenced B.C. 2356. He is the fourth of the "five Te," with whom Sze-ma Ts'een commences his history. After Shun, the sovereigns of China were called by the humbler title of 'Wang' or King, down to the Ts'in dynasty, B.C. 220. 帝 is a synonym of Heaven, and properly denotes 'God.' The 說文 defines it by 諦, 'to judge; and K'ung Ying-tă, expounding the application of it, says that Heaven exercises an impartial rule, judging righteous judgment, and that the name is given to the earthly sovereign, the vicegerent of Heaven, as expected to do the same; see Ying-tă's paraphrase on the first par. of the preface. 欽明文思 (up. 3d tone, exp. by

變　黎　和　昭　姓　平　族　九　德　克二部
時　民　萬　明　百　章　既　族　以　明　俊
雍。於　邦　協　姓　百　睦　九　親　俊

2 earth to heaven. He was able to make the able and virtuous
distinguished, and thence proceeded to the love of the nine classes
of his kindred, who all became harmonious. He *also* regulated and
polished the people *of his domain*, who all became brightly intelligent. *Finally*, he united and harmonized the myriad States *of
the empire;* and lo! the black-haired people were transformed. The
result was *universal* concord.

Ch'ing—慮深通敏, 'in cogitation profound, in penetration active.') 安安,—欽
'reverential,'=cherishing a constant feeling of
responsibility. This, it is said, is the 'one word'
in the Book, indicating the one virtue out of
which all Yaou's other qualities grew. Gan-kwŏ
takes 安 as a verb—'by these four virtues he
gave repose to those to whom repose was due.'
Much better to take the phrase as in the translation, with Choo He. Ch'ing read 宴宴.
光被 (3d tone,＝及) 四表,—Gan-kwŏ
expl. 光 by 充—'those virtues filled up and
reached to,' &c. Fuh-shang's text seems to have
read 橫 (see the 後案); but in the prefatory
notice we read 光. 表＝外, 'that
which is outside.' Acc. to Ch'ing, 四表＝
四海之外, 'the remotest limits of the
four seas.' 上下＝天地, heaven
above and earth beneath.

　2. 克明俊德,— see the Great Learning, Comm. i. 4, where for 俊 we have 峻.
There the 'great virtue' is that of Yaou himself;
but the preceding has spoken sufficiently of that.
Ch'ing and Gan-kwŏ both take the meaning as
in the transl., which moreover agrees with Conf.
teaching, Doct. of the Mean, xx. 12, 13, where
親親 follows 尊賢. The commentator
in the Great Learning *accommodates* the text of
the Classic. 九族＝all of the same
surname, all the relatives of consanguinity, from
the great-great-grandfather to the great-great-
grandson. Gow-yang (歐陽), and other interpreters of Fuh-shang's Books, understood the
nine classes to be 4 on the father's side, 3 on
the mother's, and 2 on the wife's (see Ying-tă *in
loc.*). Ch'ing and Gan-kwŏ rightly prefer the
former view; but we may say with Ts'ae Ch'in
that the relatives by affinity should here be
understood as included with the others. 平

章百姓,—I have given 百姓, after
Ts'ae Ch'in, as meaning 'the people of the
imperial domain.' That the phrase must be
restricted in signification is plain from the
萬邦 and 黎民 that follow. Gan-kwŏ,
however, says that 百姓＝百官, 'the
various officers.' Ch'ing substantially agrees
with him;—百姓＝羣臣之父子
兄弟. That 'the hundred surnames' was a
designation of the great families of the State
under the Chow dyn. is shown clearly by Ying-
tă, *in loc.* But in the Shoo-king, where the
phrase occurs some 14 times, much the more
natural interpretation of it is as＝民, 'the
people.' Part V. x. 10; xvi. 9 are exceptions to
this, but the ordinary usage is as I have said.
For 平 the 'Historical Records' give 便, and
Ch'ing interpreted by 辨, 'to distinguish, to
separate.' Hence it has been contended that the
original reading was 采, the old form of which
was liable to be mistaken for that cf 平. [I
cannot in these notes enter much into the question
of various readings, and discuss the correctness of
the text. The subject has been treated generally
in the prolegg.] 萬邦＝萬國 (so
it is in the 史記), 'the myriad States,' *i.e.*,
the States of all the princes beyond the imperial
domain. 黎＝'black,' *i.e.*, black-haired.
Some simply expl. it by 衆, 'all' 於, an
excl., read *woo.* 時＝是. Gan-kwŏ
brings out the concluding clauses thus:—天下
衆民,皆變化從上,是以風俗
大和, 'All the people under heaven were
transformed, and followed the example of the
sovereign, so that their manners became greatly
harmonious.'

義○乃_{三節}
和、欽命
若昊天、
曆象日
月星辰、
敬○授人
時。
命羲義仲
宅嵎夷、
日暘谷、
分_{四節}

3   II. Thereupon *Yaou* commanded He and Ho, in reverent accordance with *their observation* of the wide heavens, to calculate and delineate *the movements and appearances of* the sun, the moon, the
stars, and the zodiacal spaces; and so to deliver respectfully the seasons to the people.

4   He separately commanded the second brother He to reside at
Yu-e, in what was called the Bright Valley, and there respectfully to

CH. II. THE MEASURES OF YAOU TO SECURE
A CORRECT CALENDAR IN ORDER TO PROMOTE
THE BUSINESS OF AGRICULTURE.   Par. 3. 乃
being a conjunction, we naturally connect this
par. with the preced., as following it in time.
Such is not the case, however. Parr. 1 and 2
should be taken as the words of the chronicler
whoever he was, and whensoever he wrote,
giving his general impressions of Yaou's character and government. Here he begins to make
use of documents, yet condensing them in his
own language, till we arrive at par. 8. 乃 is
equivalent to our 'now.'   About the Hes
and Hos we need not seek to be wise above what
is written here and in Pt. III. iv. It is attempted to connect them with a Ch'ung and Le
(重黎) descended from the emp. Shaou-haou,
B.C. 2594 (see on Pt. V. xxvii. 6), as hereditary occupants of their offices. They come
before us receiving their appointment from Yaou
to form a Board of astronomy, and specially
to regulate the calendar,—a work so necessary
for the purposes of agriculture. Gaubil
says they were charged likewise 'to correct the
abuses and disorders which had been introduced
into manners and religion' (Le Chou-king, p.
6., n. 2); but there is nothing in the text to justify
this. It is queried whether those mentioned in
par. 3 were elder brothers of the others, heads
of their respective families, or merely those
brothers, so that we should translate 羲和—
'the Hes and the Hos.' Were there three of
each surname or only two? The point cannot
be settled. I receive the impression that there
were three.   欽若(=順)昊天,—
'reverently to accord with the vast heaven.'
昊天 is the name specially appropriated to
the firmament of summer, when an air of vigour
and vastness seems to fill all space. We are
not to think of anything beyond the visible ex-
panse and the bodies in it.   The 集傳 defines
曆 as 'the writings in which calculations were
recorded,' and 象 as 'the instruments with
which the heavens were surveyed.' This cannot

be. The characters are verbs. 曆 is 'to
calendar,' implying calculations and writings;
象, 'a figure,' 'a resemblance,' and, as a verb,
'to imitate,' must here = 'to delineate,' 'to represent.' 星, 'the stars,' generally; both the
fixed stars and the planets. 辰, 'the zodiacal
spaces.' These, it is said in the 集傳, by
the conjunctions of the sun and moon, divide
the circumference of heaven into twelve mansions (十二次). For 人時 we should
probably read 民時; see 段玉裁's 古
文尙書撰異, *in loc.*

Parr. 4–7. It is supposed the work enjoined in the prec. par. has been done. That there
may be no mistake in a matter of such importance,—to test the accuracy of the calendar,
two members of each of the families He and Ho
are appointed to the work of verification at different points.   P. 4. The second brother
He has his appointment at 嵎夷 (see Pt.
III. i. 上. 22), not, as often stated, the present
Tăng-chow in Shan-tung, but a place farther to
the east in Corea. There was a spot convenient
to observe the sun coming up, as from a valley,
to enlighten the earth, from which it got its
name. The 宅 would seem to denote that He's
proper residence was at Yu-e, but perhaps it
only indicates a sojourn there to make the
necessary observations. So in the other parr.
This is Choo He's opinion. He was to receive
the rising sun, acc. to the 集傳, by carefully
noting the length of the shadow cast from a
gnomon; but this is not said in the text.
The special object of his observation was to
ascertain that mid-spring, the vernal equinox,
was correctly fixed; and the final end was that
the 東作 'labours of the east' might be
adjusted. Those labours of the east are the
labours of spring; and in the other parr. the
south stands for summer, the west for autumn,
and the north for winter. On this see the

寅賓出日、平秩東作。日中星鳥、以殷仲春。厥民析、鳥獸孳尾。○〔五節〕申命羲叔、宅南交、平秩南訛、敬致日永星

receive as a guest the rising sun, and to adjust and arrange the labours of the spring. "The day," *he said*, "is of the medium length, and the star is in *Neaou*; you may thus exactly determine midspring. The people begin to disperse; and birds and beasts breed and copulate."

5　He further commanded the third brother He to reside at Nankeaou, and arrange the transformations of the summer, and respectfully to observe the extreme limit *of the shadow*. "The day," said

易經, 說卦傳, ch. v. The idea underlying the representation seems to be that of an analogy between a day and the year,—the morning, with the sun in the east, corresponding to spring; noon, with the sun in the south, to summer, &c.　To guide He in his observations, he is told, 1st, that he would find 日中, 'the day of the average length,' *i.e.*, a mean between its lengths at the solstices, or more probably of the same length as the night, determined by a clepsydra (so, Ma Yung); and 2d, that 'the star was *Neaou*.' But *Neaou* (鳥) is not the name of a star, but of a constellation, or space of the heavens, extending over 112° (see Keang Shing), and embracing 'the seven constellations of the Southern quarter.' called 井, 鬼, 柳, 星, 張, 翼, and 軫. Gankwŏ thinks the meaning is that all those seven constellations would be visible on the evening of the vernal equinox. This view cannot be correct, however, because in the next three paragraphs the 星 is the star or 宿, which culminated on each occasion. We have then to adopt as the star indicated here, the central one of the space *Neaou*, which was the view of Ma Yung and K'ang-shing; and it is stated by Ts'ae Ch'in that 張一行, a very learned Buddhist priest of the T'ang dynasty (in the reign of 元宗, A.D. 713–756) calculated this to be the star 鶉火, corresponding to Cor Hydra of the west.

Here Dr. Medhurst in his translation of the Shoo King has made the following note:—'If Cor Hydra culminated at sun-set on the day of the vernal equinox in the time of Yaou, the constellation on the meridian at noon of that day must have been Pleiades in Taurus. Now as by the retrocession of the equinoxes the stars of the zodiac go back a whole sign in 2000 years, it would take 4000 years for the sun to be in Pleiades at the time of the vernal equinox, which is about the time when Yaou is said to have flourished, and affords a strong confirmation of the truth of Chinese chronology. For Pleiades is 56 degrees and one third from the point where the ecliptic crossed the equinoctial A.D. 1800, and as the equinox travels backwards 50 seconds and one tenth per annum, it would take about 4000 years for Pleiades to be in the zenith at noon of the vernal equinox. Referring to Chinese records, we find that Yaou's reign closed 2254 years before Christ, which added to 1800 makes 4054; and a retrocession of 50 seconds and one tenth per annum would give 4050.' See a note to the same effect by the editors of the 書經傳說, *in loc.*

By the equal length of day and night, and the culminating star, He-chung would be able exactly to determine (殷一正, Gan-kwŏ) midspring. Two popular characteristics of the season are added. The people would be dispersed, scattered, that is, from their homes and villages where they had been congregated during the winter, and engaged in field work; and animals would be beginning to breed. For 鳥獸孳尾, Sze-ma Ts'een has 鳥獸字微; but the meaning is substantially the same.

5. Another He is sent to Nan-keaou, the border of 安南, Annam, or Cochin-china, called also 交阯. Sze-ma Ts'een says that the sway of the emperor 顓頊 extended 'from 幽陵 on the north to 交阯 on the south.' Ch'ing, supposes that the characters 曰明都, (= 'in what was called the Bright Capital)' have dropt out of the text after 交.　南訛 (*al.*, 譌 and 為),—訛=化 'to transform;' with reference to the changes of things

夷、鳥獸毛毬。 殷仲秋、厥民 宵中星虛以 日平秩西成、 昧谷、寅餞納 和仲宅西、曰 希革。○分[六節]命 厥民因、鳥獸 火、以正仲夏、

he, "is at its longest, and the star is *Ho*; you may thus exactly determine mid-summer. The people are more dispersed; and birds and beasts have their feathers and hair thin, and change their coats."

6   He separately commanded the second brother Ho to reside at the west, in what was called the Dark Valley, and *there* respectfully to convoy the setting sun, and to adjust and arrange the completing labours of the autumn. "The night," *he said,* "is of the medium length, and the star is *Heu*; you may thus exactly determine mid-autumn. The people begin to feel at ease; and birds and beasts have their coats in good condition."

in the productive operations of summer (化 育之事, acc. to Gan-kwŏ).   敬致, —I have translated acc. to what is generally supposed to be the meaning, and which can claim the authority of Ch'ing;—see Keang Shing and Sun Sing-yen. A similar measurement was to be practised, it is said, at the other seasons; only Shing will have it, that at the equinoxes it was the shadow cast by the moon which was to be ascertained. Gan-kwŏ, however, may be right when he interprets more simply—敬行其教以致其功, 'reverently carrying out your instructions to give to those productive operations their largest results.'   The culminating star at dusk of the summer solstice would be 火 or 'Fire,' the central star of 'the Azure Dragon' (蒼龍), which embraced the seven constellations of the eastern quarter, 角, 亢, 氐, 房, 心, 尾, and 箕, and corresponding to the Heart of Scorpio. The editors of the 書經傳說 say here:—'At the summer solstice in Yaou's time the sun was in 星 (α Hydræ Alphard; Reeves), whereas now it is in 嘴 (λ Orion).' This work was ordered in the 8th year of Yung-ching, A.D. 1730.   厥民因,—因 = 'to be going on from,' *i.e.,* 析而又析, 'the people were still more scattered and in the fields than in the spring.'

6. To two younger members of the house of Ho the examination of the times of the autumnal equinox and winter solstice was assigned. The particular place in the west to which Ho-chung had to repair cannot be specified. 餞, 'to convoy;'—by measuring the shadow of the gnomon, acc. to the 集傳; but see on par. 4.   No particular reason but the writer's or the emperor's thought at the time need be sought for the use of 宵 here rather than 夜. The culminating star was *Heu,* the centre one of 'The Dark Warrior' (玄武), which embraced the seven constellations of the northern quarter, 斗, 牛, 女, 虛, 危, 室, and 壁, and corresponding to β Aquarius. It is observed here in Yung Ching's Shoo King, 'At the autumnal equinox in Yaou's time the sun was in 房 (β δ π ρ Scorpio); while now it is in 翼 (α Crateris [Alkes]).'   厥民夷,—夷 = 平. Gan-kwŏ, Ts'ae Ch'in, and Keang, all agree in thus defining 夷, but the meaning they attach to 平 is different. K'ung says that 'the people are still at their labours in the fields, *the same as* in the summer.' Këang says that the people now come down, because of the bleak winds, from the summer heights which they had preferred, and live in the low *level* grounds? The only reasonable interpretation is that of Ts'ae —'The great heats are over, and the people

暨 曰、氄 民 正 短 在 曰 叔、○
和 咨 毛 隩 仲 星 朔 幽 宅 申 七節
暴 汝 ○ 鳥 冬、昴 易 都 朔 命
三 羲 帝 八節 獸 厥 以 日 平 方、和

7 He further commanded the third brother Ho to reside in the northern region, in what was called the Sombre Capital, and there to adjust and examine the changes of the winter. "The day," *said he*, "is at its shortest, and the star is *Maou*; thus you may exactly determine mid-winter. The people keep their *cosy* corners; and the coats of birds and beasts are downy and thick."

8 The emperor said, "Ah! you, He and Ho, a round year consists of three hundred, sixty, and six days. By means of an intercalary

feel at ease.' 7. The 史記 for 朔方 reads 北方. 朔, doubtless, means 'the north.' It is used also for the 'first day of the new month.' Both these are applications of the term, which is explained by 穌, 'to come alive again,' the winter being to the year what its last quarter is to the moon, a season of disappearance and decay, to be succeeded by revival. 平在 (=察) 朔易.—朔易, 'the changes of the winter:'—the former things pass away; all things become new. The labours of the season are therefore called 'changes.' For 朔易 Ts'een has 伏物, 'the hidden things,' with reference to the energies of nature now working in concealment. 昴, the culminating star, is the centre of the 'White Tiger' (百虎), comprehending the seven constellations of the western quarter, 奎, 婁, 胃, 昴, 畢, 觜, and 參. It is our Pleiades. 'In the time of Yaou, at the winter solstice, the sun was in *heu* (虛, β Aquarius), while now at the same season it is in Ke (箕, γ Sagittarii)'; see the 書經傳說. 厥民隩—隩 (read *yuh*) is with Ch'ing = 內, 'inside,' and with K'ung = 室, 'house,' 'apartment.' In winter the people keep mostly within, in the warmest places.

Par. 8. The verifications in the four prec. parr. are supposed to have been made; and now the emperor addresses either the two chiefs of the He and Ho families, or all their members whose services had been employed, on the important subject of making the calendar complete by an intercalary month. 咨=嗟, an interjection, 'ah!' 暨=及, 'and.' 暴三

百有六旬 is quoted by Heu Shin, under 棋, which is defined 復其時, 'a revolution of the time.' Gan-kwŏ defines it—匝 四時日暮, 'The circuit of the four seasons is called 暮.' Yaou does not speak scientifically, but says that the round year consists of 366 days. On this Gaubil observes (Le Chou-king, p. 7, n. 4), 'We see that Yaou knew the Julian year of 365¼ days; the fourth year consists of 366 days. We see also that they then intercalated some months to divide the year into four seasons.' But there is nothing in the text to indicate that every fourth year was reckoned 366 days. If it had been so, Yaou's calendar would have been the same as the Julian, and there would have been no necessity for the intercalation of a month at certain regular periods which is indicated. We may well be surprised to find this ancient emperor of China speaking as he does here, in the 24th century before Christ, with so close an approximation to the correct length of the year. On this as gradually ascertained in China with an increasing exactness, I shall quote the following note by the editors of Yung-ching's Shoo:—

'When it is said that the year consists of 366 days, we are to understand that Yaou was speaking in round numbers. The period in question is now called the value of the year. It has been differently estimated by the astronomers of successive dynasties.

'In the Books of the Han dynasty' [ended A.D. 263], 'the circuit of the heavens is divided into 365¼°; and a degree of the heavens is made to correspond to a day of the calendar. At that time it was taken for granted that a circuit of the heavens' [a sidereal year] 'was the same as a circuit of the year' [a tropical year].

'Under the eastern Tsin dynasty' [A.D. 318 —420], 'Yu He' [died about the middle of the 4th century. Ts'ae Ch'in says that he was the *first* to distinguish the sidereal year from the tropical, and to bring forward the doctrine of

百　有　日、閏　定　時　歲、鼇　工、

有　六　以　月　四　成　允　百　庶

month do you fix the four seasons, and complete the *determination of the year. Thereafter*, in exact accordance with this, regulating the various officers, all the works *of the year* will be fully performed."

the precession of the equinoxes, which he estimated at one degree in 50 years] 'reckoned the circuit of the heavens' [= the sidereal year] 'at 365°.26, rather more than 365¼, and the circuit of the year' [= the tropical year] 'at 365.24 days; rather less than 365¼.

'Under the Sung dynasty' [*i.e.,* the northern Sung, which succeeded the Tsin], 'Ho Ching-t'een' [about the middle of the 5th century] 'made another alteration in these reckonings, and estimated the circuit of the heavens at 365°.255, and the tropical year at 365.245 days.

'Under the Yuen dynasty, Kwoh Show-king' [died A.D. 1316, at the age of 86], 'on a comparison of ancient and modern observations, fixed the circuit of the heavens at 365°.2575, and the tropical year at 365.2425 days. The accumulation of decimal figures, however, in both of these quantities' [while the degree was made to correspond to a day] 'made all calculations founded upon them difficult.

'But the philosopher Shaou' [邵堯夫; died A.D. 1017; his tablet has a place in the temples of Confucius], 'in his 元會運世 adopted the number 360 as an arbitrary standard, the circumference of the heavens being the basis of his calculations. That being once fixed' [at 360°], 'it became comparatively an easy matter to deal with the other fractional quantities.' [It must be observed that the phrase 天周, circuit or circumference of the heavens, here changes its meaning; and the value assigned to it, in its former sense, of 365.2575, now to be reckoned in days, is as necessary to astronomical calculations as ever.] 'Accordingly, the calendar now published by authority determines the circumference of heaven to be 360° (a degree containing 60 minutes, a minute 60 seconds and all the parts below continuing to be reckoned by 60); and the tropical year consists of 365 days, 5 hours, 48 minutes, 45 seconds (365.2421875).

'Through successive ages, though the fractional parts have been now a little more and now a little less, the determinations have all been based on the round number in this Canon of Yaou, and have served to illustrate it. As to the conjunctions of the sun and moon, determining the changes and first days of months, and the conjunctions of the sun and' (various fixed stars in) 'the heavens, determining the equinoxes and solstices,—whereas the solar period and the lunations do not correspond, so that there arise what are called the surplus of the former and the deficiency of the latter, there is required the use of intercalation to make the four seasons come each in its proper place. This is the practice indicated in this Canon of

Yaou, which constitutes it the model for all ages.'

Yaou certainly commanded his officers to use intercalations;—how they did so we cannot tell. Previous to the Han dynasty, Chinese history does not furnish us with details on the subject of intercalation. In the time of that dyn., however, we find what is called the Metonic cycle well known. It is not mentioned as any discovery of that age. See the 'History of the Former Han' by Pan Koo (班固), finished about A.D. 80, in the 律歷志, 第一, 下, where the whole process is fully described. No doubt it came down to the Han from the Chow, and was probably known in China long before Meton reformed the Athenian calendar according to its principles, B.C. 432. I abstract the following account from Woo Ch'ing (吳澄) of the Yuen dynasty's Work on the Shoo:—A common year of 12 months of 30 days each, or 360 days, is assumed. Not that there ever was such a year in China, as Medhurst says by mistake (Shoo King, p. 8, note); but it is convenient to lay down that as the length of the year in order to exhibit the process of intercalation. Now, the sun makes his circuit of the heavens in 365 days and ¼, or 365 days and 235–940ths (a day being divided into 940 parts). The year as determined by the sun, therefore, is 5 days and 235–940ths over 360, which excess is denominated 氣盈. A synodic revolution of the moon, again, takes place in 29 days and 499–940ths, so that 12 months = 354 days and 348–940ths, short of 360 by 5 days and 592–940ths, which deficiency is denominated 朔虛. Adding the excess and the deficiency, we have 10 days and 827–940ths, the difference of the two from 360 in one year.

In the third year this amounts to 32 days and 601–940ths, when the first intercalation of one synodic period is supposed to be made, leaving 3 days and 102–940ths unabsorbed.

In the sixth year there have accumulated 35 days and 703–940ths, which a second intercalation reduces to 6 days and 204–940ths. A third intercalation in the ninth year would leave 9 days and 306–940ths, which by the eleventh year would amount to 31 days and 80–940ths, reduced by intercalation to 1 day and 521–940ths.

A fifth intercalation in the fourteenth year would leave 4 days and 623–940ths.

A sixth in the seventeenth year would leave 7 days and 725–940ths, which in the nineteenth year would amount to 29 days and 499–940ths, which the last intercalation would exactly absorb.

績咸熙。^{九節}帝曰、疇咨。若時登庸。放齊曰。子朱啟明。帝曰、吁嚚訟。可乎。○^{十節}帝曰、疇咨。若予采。驩兜曰、都。共工塊曰、都。共

9　III. The emperor said, " Who will search out for me a man according to the times, whom I may raise and employ? " Fang-ts'e said, " There is your heir-son Choo, who is highly intelligent." The emperor said, " Alas! he is insincere and quarrelsome:—can he do."

10　The emperor said, " Who will search out for me a man equal to the exigency of my affairs? " Hwan-tow said, " Oh! there is the minister of Works, whose merits have just been displayed in various

It is to be observed that the above division of a day into 940 parts was different from that of the Han dynasty, and indeed only began to obtain in the time of the great Sung dyn. Practically, moreover, a month must be estimated by a whole number of days; and hence the Chinese have so many short months in the year of 29 days, while the rest are of 30 days. 允釐百工, 庶績咸熙 is very well given by Sze-ma Ts'een—信飭百官, 衆功皆典. 百工＝百官, 'the hundred' (*i.e.* all, the various) 'officers,' each office having its special department of *work*. It is not said that He and Ho had any further charge of the officers beyond supplying them with a correct calendar.

Ch. III. The anxiety of Yaou to find the right men for the exigencies of the times, and especially the best man, on whom to devolve the throne:—all illustrating his freedom from every selfish consideration. The events described in the prec. 6 parr. are referred by the compilers of Chinese history to the 1st and 2d years of Yaou's reign; but we really cannot say when they took place. Par. 12 belongs to the 70th year of his reign; par. 11 is referred with some probability to the 61st; the 10th must be of about the same date.

P. 9. *Yaou inquires—prob. in open court—for an officer whom he may employ in high affairs.* What the affairs were we cannot know. Ma Yung thinks that by this time the four Hes and Hos were dead, and that one was wanted to enter on their duties as ministers of the four seasons. A meaning is thus found for 時 as ＝四時; but the view is to be rejected at once. Gan-kwŏ takes 時 as＝是, 'these,' and connects the par. with the 8th, making the inquiry to be for a premier to direct all the officers, and all the works of the year, (so also Ts'een); but the only connection between the parr. is of fragments brought together into the present canon. The matter must be left indefinite.

疇＝誰, 'who.' 咨 is here not a particle of exclamation, as hitherto, but a verb,＝訪問, 'to inquire for.' 若 as in p. 3, 'to accord with.' It is observed that in those times of wise antiquity, forceful control was not the way of sovereigns and ministers, but a cautious accordance with nature and circumstances. 庸＝用, 'to use.' Fang-ts'e (Ying-tă makes 放 in the 2d tone) only appears here. He must have been a minister. Sze-ma Ts'een for 胤子 has 嗣子. 胤＝'to continue, to succeed;' and I have translated accordingly. Gan-kwŏ takes 胤 for the State so called, (see Pt. III. iv.), and 子 for the title of its ruler,＝'count;' and Ying-tă says it seems to him unnatural for the emperor's son to be recommended and spoken of as here. But that only serves to exalt the character of Yaou, who was free from the partialities of common men, that 'do not know the wickedness of their own sons' (Great Learning, Comm. viii. 2). The difficulty would disappear, if we could suppose that Yaou is here proposing to resign his throne. 吁 is a particle of exclamation, intimating the speaker's decided dissent.

P. 10. *Yaou again makes inquiry for a minister who might be equal to the management of his affairs.* Such seems to be the meaning of 采, which is given by Gan-kwŏ as＝事. Ma Yung explains it by 官, 'officers,' as if it were a prime minister to be over all the other ministers, who was wanted. Hwan-tow and the K'ung-kung appear in the next Book, p. 12, as two of the four great criminals whom Shun dealt with. 共工 is the name of the one's office. In the next Book, p. 21, Shun calls Ching to the same. It is about＝Minister of Works. Ch'ing sup-

工方鳩僝功。帝曰吁靜言庸違象恭滔天。○帝曰咨四岳湯湯洪水方割蕩蕩懷山襄陵浩浩滔天下民其咨有能俾乂。僉曰於鯀

ways." The emperor said, "Alas! when unemployed, he can talk; but when employed, his actions turn out differently. He is respectful *only* in appearance. See! the floods assail the heavens."

The emperor said, "Oh! *chief of* the four mountains, destructive in their overflow are the waters of the inundation. In their vast extent they embrace the mountains and overtop the hills, threatening the heavens with their floods, so that the inferior people groan and murmur. Is there a capable man, to whom I can assign the correction *of this calamity?* All *in the court* said, "Oh! there is

poses that the Kung-kung here was the 水官, 'officer of the Waters.' He had no doubt, as we shall see, been employed to relieve the distress occasioned by the prevailing floods.   都 is an exclamation, the opposite of 吁, indicating approval and commendation.   Choo He says that 方鳩僝功 cannot be understood, but that the old view—as in the transl.—may be allowed to stand. Sze-ma Ts'een gives Hwan-tow's reply:—共工旁聚布功可用.   靜, 'to be still,'—unoccupied. Gan-kwŏ explains it by 謀, 'to plan;' but that meaning only arises from the context here.

滔天 is joined by Gan-kwŏ to the prec. characters:—'He appears to be respectful, but his heart is full of pride as if it would inundate the heavens.' Dissatisfied with this, Ts'ae Ch'in declares the two characters to be unintelligible, and that they dropt into the text here somehow from the next par. In the transl. I have followed an art. on the passage in the 盧學士, 龍城札記, which forms the 388th Book of the 皇清經解. The writer starts from an intimation in the 'Annals of the Bamboo Writings' (竹書紀年), that Yaou in his 19th year appointed the Kung-kung to the management of the Ho. That management had been on the whole unsuccessful. The result was the existing state of inundation, to which Yaou in the text points as evidence of the officer's incompetency.

P. 11. *The appointment of K'wăn to remedy the distress occasioned by an overflowing flood.* This overflow of waters has been called by some western writers 'the deluge of Yaou;' and it has been endeavoured to identify it with the deluge of Noah. The descriptions in the classic, however, will not permit this; see on Pt. III. i.

The emperor addresses himself to the 四岳 (or 嶽), literally 'The four Mountains:'—those mentioned in the next Book, par. 8, Tae-tsung or Mount T'ae on the east (in the present Shantung); Mount Hwăng in the south (in Hoonan); Mount Hwa in the west (in Shan-se); and Mount Hăng, in the north. Those were central points in the empire, to which different quarters of it were referred. In the text does Yaou address one great officer styled the chief of the four Mountains, or does he address the body of great officers in charge of the different quarters? Gan-kwŏ held that the four Yŏ were four individuals, the successors of the Hes and Hos, parr. 4–7. K'ang-shing thought that at the time of Yaou's reign to which this par. belongs, the places formerly held by those Hes and Hos were filled by eight chiefs (八伯), who are addressed. Choo He determined that only one man was intended, the president of all the nobles of the empire, regulator of the relations between the court and its feudal retainers. To this opinion I must give in my adhesion. It has its difficulties; but when Yaou proposes to the 四岳, in the next par., to take his place upon the throne, it is impossible to suppose that more than one individual is denoted.   湯 (read *Sëang*) 湯洪水方割=湯湯=水盛貌, 'the appearance of water in

巽　載、朕　帝　績　往　可　岳　哉　哉。
朕　汝　在　曰　用　欽　乃　曰、　方　帝
位。　能　位　咨　弗　哉、　已、　异　命　曰、
岳　庸　七　四　成。　九　帝　哉、　圯　吁、
曰、　命、　十　岳　○　載　曰、　試　族。　咈

K'wăn." The emperor said, "Alas! no, by no means! He is disobedient to orders, and tries to injure his peers." His Eminence said, "Well but——. Try him, and then you can have done with him." The emperor said to K'wăn, "Go; and be reverent!" For nine years he laboured, but the work was unaccomplished.

12　The emperor said, "Oh! you *chief of the* four mountains, I have been on the throne for seventy years. You can carry out my appointments;—I will resign my throne to you." His Eminence said, "I have not the virtue; I should *only* disgrace the imperial seat."

abundance,' a sheet of water; 方, as in prec. par.,＝旁, 'on all sides;' 割 'to cut with a knife,' hence generally 'to injure.' 滔 is expl. by 漫, 'great water,' 'water flooding, and destroying things.' 下民其咨 —下民 is exp. by Woo Ch'ing, 居處卑下之民, 'the people who live in the low places'; but the phrase, of not unfrequent occurrence in the mouths of great men in the Shoo, denotes simply the people, in distinction from themselves. Observe the use of 其, completing the rhythm of the clause, and giving the force of a double nominative to the verb. 僉＝皆, 'all;' *i.e.*, all in the court, not the 四岳 only, but the other nobles with him. Of course it may be said that as the inquiry was addressed only to the Yŏ, and the answer is prefaced by 僉, this character shows that Yŏ was a designation not of one but of many. But tho' there were 4 or 8 Yŏ, I should understand 僉 of others beside them;—so does Yingtă, yet believing that the Yŏ were four.

K'wăn was a minister of Yaou, the father of the great Yu (禹), and chief of the state of Ts'ung (崇伯), corresponding to the present Hoo-heen (鄠縣) in the dep. of Se-ngan in Shen-se. 方命,—方＝放, 'to disregard, neglect.' Ch'ing and Ma Yung both take the character so, and Ch'ing would also read it as

放, 3d tone. It is merely a conceit, which is given in the 集傳, that 'what is round moves, and what is square (方) stops,' so that 方 comes to mean 'to disregard,' or 'to disobey!' 异 哉,—the 說文 defines 异 by 舉, a meaning which I don't see how to understand here. Ts'ae Ch'in says he does not understand the character. The rest of the Yo's reply is given more fully by Sze-ma Ts'een,—不 試 可 用 而 已. Ch'ing's view is not so good —'Try him. He is fit for this, though not for other duties, in which you need not to employ him.' 載, 'a year.' For this, acc. to Yingtă, in the Hea dyn. they subsequently used 歲, in the Shang, 祀; and in the Chow, 年. 績用不成,—we may suppose that the force of 用 merges in that of 績.＝功.

P. 12. *Yaou, having been 70 years on the throne, wishes to resign the administration of affairs to the worthiest, and Shun appears on the stage.* 朕, the imperial We, was anciently simply ＝I, used both by superiors and inferiors. It was one of the characteristic actions of the founder of the Ts'in dyn. to appropriate it to the sovereign. 庸（＝用）命,—'use, carry out my orders.' 巽＝遜, 'to yield, to resign.' Ch'ing takes it＝入, 'to enter into.' He interprets Yaou's inquiry thus,—'Among all you princes is there

否德忝帝位。

明明揚側陋師

錫帝曰、有鰥在

俞予聞如何岳

下曰虞舜帝曰、

曰瞽子父頑母

嚚象傲克諧以

孝烝烝乂不格

姦帝曰、我其試

哉女于時觀厥

The *emperor* said, "Point out some one among the illustrious, or set forth one from among the poor and mean." All *in the court* said to the emperor, "There is an unmarried man among the lower people, called Shun of Yu." The emperor said, "Yes, I have heard of him. What is his character?" His Eminence said, "He is the son of a blind man. His father was obstinately unprincipled; his *step*-mother was insincere; his *half brother* Seang was arrogant. He has been able, however, by his filial piety to live in harmony with them, and to lead them gradually to self-government, so that they no longer proceed to great wickedness." The emperor said, "I will try him!

one, who, acting in harmony with things and obeying the orders of Heaven, can enter in and occupy my throne, discharging the duties that devolve on the emperor?' This is very far-fetched. It is found in a note in the 史記, whose own version of the passage is decisively in favour of what is now the common view:— 汝能庸命踐朕位. 否德, —Ts'een has 鄙德, with substantially the same meaning. 明 (a verb)=舉, 'to recommend;' 明 (an adj.)=高明者, 'those already high and distinguished.' 側陋= 微賤之人, 'men small and mean.' Yaou wants to find the worthiest, in whatever social position. 師=僉 in the former par., 'all,' and not as Ch'ing thinks, 'the chiefs of the princes.' 錫 is expl. by 與;—'All said to the emperor.' Ts'een has it 眾皆言於 堯曰. 虞舜,—see on the title of next Part. 瞽子—'the son of a blind man.' Gan-kwŏ says that Shun's father was not physically blind, but mentally and morally, so that people spoke of him as if he were really blind, and he received the designation of Koo-sow (瞽瞍). It may have been so, but the general belief of antiquity, and the language of the text

are not to be received in other than their natural significancy on mere surmise. 母,— 'mother;' not Shun's real mother, but his step-mother. Sze-ma Ts'een says so in express terms. 諧=和, 'harmony.' It is not easy to say whether we should take it actively —'to bring them to harmony,' or intransitively— 'to live in harmony with them.' The usage of the term in the next Book is in favour of the former view. 烝, properly,='steam.' But steam ascends and moves forward; hence here 烝烝乂='to move by gradual progress to self-government.' The account here given of the influence which Shun had produced on his parents and brother is not borne out by the statements in Mencius, Book V. Pt. I., i. and ii.

我其試哉.—'I will test him,' or 'Let me test him.' The 其 has a peculiar force, which neither Premare in his Grammar, nor Morrison, Medhurst, or Williams, in their Dictionaries, has pointed out. The usage is specified in K'ang-he's dictionary, but with no further explanation than that 其 is then 'a particle, helping the sense.' It gives to the whole sentence a half hortatory, half imperative force.

Yaou would test Shun, and a very strange trial it was to which he put him. It impresses my mind with grave doubts as to the trustworthiness of the whole history. As it stands, it shows us one thing,—that polygamy had at this early time obtained among the Chinese.

欽　帝　于　汭，于　二　釐　二　刑
哉。曰，虞。嬪　嬀　女　降　女。于

I will wive him, and then see his behaviour with my two daughters."
On this he gave orders, and sent down his two daughters to the
north of the Kwei, to be wives in the family of Yu. The emperor
said *to them*, "Be reverent!"

From 帝曰 to the end, I have translated according to Choo He's view of the passage:—that down to 刑于二女 we have Yaou's words; from 釐降 to 于虞, what he did; and that the 欽哉 at the end were addressed to his daughters. The construction is not easy; but the interpetation of Gan-kwŏ, and that of Keang Shing in the pres. dyn., make confusion worse confounded. 女 (3d tone),—'to give a daughter to a man to wife.' 刑＝法, 'example,' 'behaviour.' The names of Yaou's two daughters are said to have been *Wo-wang* (娥皇) and *Neu-ying* (女英). 'The former,' says Woo Ch'ing, 'became Shun's wife, and the other his concubine.' But this is said, applying the ways of subsequent times to Yaou's age. We cannot acknowledge any inferiority of the one to the other. 嬪 (＝婦, 'to be wife to)' applies equally to both. The 嬀 is a small stream in Shan-se, rising where the two depp. of P'ing-yang (平陽) and P'oo-chow (蒲州) border on each other, and flowing southwards to the Ho. 汭 is defined 'the north of a stream;' or it may be, there was a smaller stream so called, which flowed into the Kwei, not far from its junction with the Ho. A note on the 集說 in Yung-ching's Shoo says that there is such a stream so called, but that people may have been led by the text of the Classic to give it that name. Here was the dwelling-place of Shun.

"I will wive him, and then see his behaviour with my two daughters."
On this he gave orders, and sent down his two daughters to the
north of the Kwei, to be wives to the family of Yu. The emperor
said to them, "Be reverent."

THE SHOO KING.

PART II. THE BOOKS OF YU.

BOOK I. THE CANON OF SHUN.

乃　玄　溫　濬　華　帝　曰　　　尚
命　德　恭　哲　協　舜　若　虞　書
以　升　允　文　于　曰　稽　書
位。　聞、　塞、　明、　帝、　重　古、　舜
　　　　　　　　　　　　　　　典

1 I. Examining into antiquity, we find that the emperor Shun was called Ch'ung-hwa. He corresponded to the *former* emperor; was profound, wise, accomplished, and intelligent. He was mild and respectful, and entirely sincere. The report of his mysterious virtue was heard on high, and he was appointed to occupy the *imperial* Seat.

TITLE OF THE PART. 虞書.—Yu is the dynastic designation of Shun, as T'ang was that of Yaou. It does not appear so clearly, however, how it came to be so. Ts'ae Ch'in, after K'ang-shing, says that 虞 was the 氏 or family name of Shun. Wang Suh said that it was the name of a place or country (地名), held to have been the pres. district of 安邑 in the dep. of 解州 in Shan-se. Some think that Yaou, after marrying his daughters to Shun, appointed him chief of this State (see the 通志 quoted in the 通鑑綱目, on the 70th year of Yaou's reign); but this is inconsistent with the first mention of Shun to Yaou, in the prec. Book. It is commonly held that Shun's ancestors had been lords of the principality of Yu to the time of his father, who somehow lost his patrimony and was reduced to the rank of a private man. It may have been so, and the old title would continue to be cherished, though without the accessories that made it valuable. As to the history of the family of Yu, there is much difficulty in tracing it. Mencius, Book IV. Pt. II. i., tells us that Shun was of the wild tribes of the east, born in Choo-fung. Sze-ma Ts'een makes him descended from Hwang-te through the emp. Chuen-heŭh. But as Yaou was also descended from Hwang-te through the emp. K'ŭh, Yaou and Shun must have had the same surname, and the idea of the one marrying his daughters to the other is so abhorrent to Chinese notions of propriety, that Choo He denounces Ts'een's genealogy as highly injurious to the fame of the sages. As Shun and the ladies would be cousins about ten times removed, a foreigner cannot sympathize with the horror expressed at the thought of their union. From the 國語, 晉語九, and the 左傳, 昭公八年, it appears that there was, or at least that in the time of the Chow dyn. it was believed there was, high up among Shun's ancestors, one of the name of Mǒh (幕), who has no place in Ts'een's genealogy; and some, discrediting entirely the account in the "Historical Records," would fix on this Mǒh as being the progenitor of Shun, chief of the principality of Yu, and not of the lineage of Hwang-te.—I have given these details to illustrate the many uncertainties that attend questions relating to Chinese antiquity.

TITLE OF, AND DISPUTES ABOUT, THE BOOK.

一舜典, 'The Canon of Shun.' For the characters themselves, see on the title of the Canon of Yaou, and on par. 1 of that Book. This Canon is all found, with the exception of the first par., both in the texts of Fuh-shang, and of Gan-kwǒ. Fuh-shang, however, taught it as a part of the preceding Canon, and those who now deny the authenticity of the Books additional to his have no Canon of Shun in their editions.

On this question it may be observed :—First, the ancient preface to the Classic shows that there were originally two Canons—that of Yaou, and that of Shun—distinct from each other.

Secondly, about one half of the Book, as we have it, might very well belong to the Canon of Yaou, the parr. 2–12 being all occupied with the trial of Shun and his doings as acting emperor, while Yaou was yet alive. Par. 2, moreover, follows naturally the last par. of the prec. Book.

Thirdly, from par. 14th to the end we have the doings of Shun as emperor, which can with no propriety form a part of the Canon of Yaou.

The natural conclusion from these points is, that in the Canon of Shun we have the whole or a part of what was anciently and properly so called, and another portion which has been improperly separated from the Canon of Yaou. The Shoo has still its two Tëen, but the point of division between them has been incorrectly marked.

It accords with this conclusion, that Mencius, Bk. V. Pt. I. iv, quotes par. 13, as from the Canon of Yaou. Other similar quotations of portions of the first part of the Book are adduced. No quotation of any par. of the second part, as belonging to the Canon of Yaou, can be found.

In the 'Historical Records' (五帝本紀), immediately after the account of Yaou's death, as in par. 13, there follow various accounts of Shun,—legendary, indeed, in their character, but having the sanction of Mencius, Bk. V. Pt. I. i., et al.—which are not now found in the Canon of the Classic. No doubt, the original and less *gossiping* version of those accounts formed, before the dyn. of Ts'in, part of the Shoo; and so much of the Canon of Shun I believe to be lost. See an attempt by Maou K'e-ling to reconstruct the whole, appended to his 尚書廣聽錄.

It is more difficult to come to a conclusion on another question, with which that about the

Division of the Canons has been unnecessarily complicated,—the question of the

GENUINENESS OF THE FIRST PARAGRAPH. These twenty-eight characters have a history of their own. Fuh-shang knew nothing of them, nor is it clear that Gan-kwǒ did. Had he found them among the other portions of the Shoo which were recovered from the wall of Confucius' house, the two Canons must have been from the first accurately divided by them.

When the work of Gan-kwǒ was first presented to the Government, as containing the Shoo in larger measure than Fuh-shang's Books, by Mei Tsih (梅賾), sometime in the beginning of the eastern Tsin [unfortunately, the Histories of the Tsin dynasty are some of them lost. The 'Book of Tsin' from which K'ung Ying-tǎ quotes his account of Tsih does not now exist; and it does not seem possible to ascertain the year when Gan-kwǒ's work was authoritatively recognized], this paragraph was wanting.

During the dyn. of the Southern Ts'e (南齊), in A.D. 497, one Yaou Fang-hing (姚方興), found 'in a large ship' (於大航頭得; so, Ying-tǎ; in the 'Books of the Suy dynasty [A.D. 589–617], however, it is said that Fang-hing 於大桁市, 'bought it in a large 桁. That character is given in the dict. as used synonymously with 航) a copy of Gan-kwǒ's Canon of Shun with the par. complete. He memorialized the Government on his discovery, and acc. to Maou K'e-ling, divided the Canons as we now have them. Not even yet, however, was the par. publicly recognized. Soon after the presentation of his memorial, Fang-hing was put to death; and the matter continued undecided till the early part of the reign of the first Suy emperor, when another copy was found containing the sentences in question.

This late recognition of the introductory portion of Shun's Canon justifies a suspicion of its genuineness. On the other hand, Ying-tǎ says that, while Mei Tsih's copy wanted this par., they supplied it from Wang Suh and Fan Ning, the former of whom had written on all the classic, and the latter specially on this Canon. (See the list of Books on the Shoo, in the time of the Suy dyn.) Now Wang Suh died A.D. 259, himself an adherent of the House of Wei (魏), yet before the final extinction of the Han. The industry of critics has also discovered portions of the par. in the remains of writers prior to Suh. Maou K'e-ling quotes especially from Wang Ts'an (王粲), who died A.D. 216, and from Wang Yen-show (王廷壽), more than half a century earlier; and contends that the par. must have been with the rest of the Canon deciphered by Gan-kwǒ. Against this conclusion has to be put the fact of the improper division of the Canons, which I have pointed out. My own opinion is that some such par. did originally belong to the Canon of Shun. The fact of the Canon of Yaou, and the Counsels of Kaou Yaou (to say nothing of the Counsels

徽　典　典　從　于　揆　揆　敘　于
○慎　五　五　克　納　百　百　時　賓　四
二
節

2　II. *Shun* carefully set forth the beauty of the five cardinal duties;
and they came to be universally observed.　Being appointed to be
General Regulator, the affairs of each department were arranged in
their proper seasons.　Having to receive *the princes from* the four

of Yu), being so prefaced, renders it all but
certain that this Book had a similar introduction.　Portions of this floated about among
scholars from one source and another, and
gradually coalesced into the par. which we now
have.　Maou K'e-ling is the best defender of
its genuineness, in the second chapter of his
古文尚書寃詞.　Against it, see the
60th art. in the 尚書古文疏證 of
Yen Jŏ-keu (閻若璩).

CONTENTS OF THE BOOK.　The meagre and
misleading account of the Book given in the prefatory notice of it has been pointed out.　Looking
at the Canon as it is now edited, we may conveniently divide it into six chapters;—the first,
cont. par. 1, describing Shun's virtues and
advancement; the second, cont. parr. 2–4, describing Yaou's trial of Shun, and resignation
to him of the administration of affairs; the
third, cont. parr. 5–11, describing the acts of
Shun as Yaou's vicegerent; the fourth, parr. 13
and 14, describing the demise of Yaou, and accession of Shun to the throne; the fifth, parr.
15–27, describing Shun's choice of ministers,
and other arrangements; and the sixth, par. 28,
recording his death.　As Yaou was the subject
of the last Book, so is Shun of this.

CH. I.　THE SAGELY VIRTUES OF SHUN, AND
HIS CONSEQUENT ADVANCEMENT TO DIGNITY.　On
the constr. of 曰若稽古, and on 舜
曰重華, see on the last Book, p. 1.　When
重華 is taken as descriptive of Shun, and
not as his name, the interpretation is—'there
was anew a display of virtue in him equal to that
of Yaou.'　協于帝,—the 帝 of course
is Yaou.　允塞,—塞 'to stop up;' then,
'fill up,' and hence, 'what is solid,' 'solidity.'
It is observed by Chin Tih-show (眞德秀,
of the Sung dyn.), that in the times of T'ang
and Yu they had not yet the character 誠
sincerity, and that that is the meaning conveyed
here by 允塞　玄德,—玄=幽
潛, 'dark and hidden.'　An obj. is taken to the
genuineness of the whole par. from the phrase,
which belongs to the school of Taouism.　No
doubt it is a common phrase with Taouists, but
I do not see why other writers might not use it
also to express the idea of 'mysterious virtue.'
升聞, 'ascended and was heard of,'

i.e., came to the ears of Yaou.　乃命
以位,—acc. to Ts'ae Ch'in, 位 is simply
職位, 'office,' or 'offices,' with reference to
the various posts in which Shun was tested.
Such an interpr. supposes the par. to be in its
proper place; but it has been shown that it
should stand after par. 13, and 位 = the throne,
the imperial Seat.

CH. II.　SHUN FULLY SATISFYING YAOU'S
HOPES IN VARIOUS OFFICES, THE EMPEROR AFTER
THREE YEARS COMMITS TO HIM THE ENTIRE
ADMINISTRATION OF AFFAIRS.　P. 2.　It is
supposed that Shun, after receiving the emperor's two daughters in marriage, ruled his house
well, and Yaou proceeded to try him, first as minister of Instruction.　徽=美, 'to beau-
tify.'　Some expl. it by 和, 'to harmonize.'
五典, 'the five Canons,'—what are
elsewhere called 五教, 'the five lessons,' and
五常, 'the five constant duties,' the virtues
belonging to the five social relations of husband
and wife, father and son, sovereign and subject,
elder and younger brother, and friends.

Thereafter Shun 納于百揆, 'was introduced into the office of General Regulator.'
揆, 'to consider,' 'to calculate,' = 度.　百
揆=揆度百官之事, '百揆
expresses the regulation of the business of all
the officers.'　The office of General Regulator
is not heard of in subseqent dynasties.　That
of 冢宰 or premier corresponded to it under
the Chow.　It is said in the 'Historical
Records' that in discharging the duties of
minister of Instruction, Shun employed the
services of 'the eight good men' (八元),
descended from Kaou-sin (高辛氏) or the
emp. K'uh, whom Yaou had not been able to
employ; and in the office of prime minister,
that he availed himself of the help of the 'eight
triumphant ones' (八愷), descended from
Kaou-yang (高陽氏), or the emp. Chuen-
heŭh.　The same thing is found in the 左傳.
Why may we not suppose that such legends,
existing in the ancient documents, were purposely rejected by Confucius himself?

門、　納　風　○　舜、　乃　三　位。　弗　上
四　于　雷　帝　詢　言　載　舜　嗣。　曰、
門、　大　雨　曰、　事　底　汝　讓　○　受
穆、　麓、　弗　格、　考　可　陟　于　正　終
穆。　烈　迷。　汝、　言、　績、　帝　德　月　于

quarters of the empire, they all were docilely submissive. Being sent to the great plains at the foot of the mountains, amid violent wind, thunder, and rain, he did not go astray.

3　　The emperor said, "Come, you Shun. I have consulted you on *all* affairs, and examined your words, and found that your words can be carried into practice;—*now* for three years. Do you ascend the imperial throne." Shun wished to decline in favour of some

4 one more virtuous, and not to consent to be successor. On the first day, of the first month, *however*, he received Yaou's retirement *from the imperial duties* in the *temple of the* Accomplished ancestor.

Shun was finally tried as the president of the nobles, in the office of the Sze Yŏ (四岳). 賓于四門,—賓, 'a guest,' and also 'to receive a guest,' 'to act the host.' This is its sense here. Ch'ing read it in the 3d tone, as if it had been 儐. 四門,—'to act the host at the four gates,' *i.e.*, to receive the nobles coming from the different quarters. So, Ma Yung. Keang Shing says ingeniously that the four gates were those of the 明堂, or Hall of Audience. The 'Historical Records' have a legend of Shun's banishing away 'the four bad ones' (四凶), in connection with the duties of this office. It is difficult to know what to think of the last part of the par. 麓 is expl. by Ch'ing as 山足, 'the foot of a mountain.' The 'Historical Records' take the account literally as in the transl. Looking at the phrase 納于大麓, following so close upon 納于百揆, it is natural to interpret it in the same way, as indicating Shun's appointment to some office. This Gankwŏ has done, and after him Wang Suh. They say—麓, 錄也, 堯納舜于尊顯之官, 使大錄天下萬機之政, 'Luh means to record. Yaou appointed Shun to an honourable and distinguished office, that he might record the govt. of the empire with its myriad springs.' This might be admitted as a good enough explanation of the phrase, but the sequel about the wind and rain cannot be made to harmonize with it. See in the

集說 various attempts to explain the passage, all unsatisfactory.

P. 3. 詢=容謀, 'to consult about.' 乃 is in the sense of 汝, 'you.' 底=致, 'to come to, result in.' The paraphrase of the 'Daily Lessons' puts 詢 and 考 in the past complete tense:—'Formerly, when I called you to employment, I consulted you on what you would do, and examined the plans you laid before me.' But why should we suppose that the two had not been in frequent intercourse all along? Ch'ing strangely takes the 'three years' to be three years subsequent to Shun's receiving the nobles of all quarters. The last clause might also be translated—'Shun declined on the ground of his virtue's not being equal to the succession.'

P. 4. This demission of the actual conduct of affairs is referred to the 73d year of Yaou's reign. 正月上日,—see on p. 14. Here 正 (in this sense often, but not necessarily, read in the 1st tone) 月='the first month;' 上日='the first day.' This has been disputed but without reason; see the remarks of Lin Che-k'e (林之奇) in the 集說. Certainly, if this natural interpr. of 上 be rejected, we are altogether at sea as to its meaning. 受終 intimates that 'now Yaou *ended* his imperial administration, and Shun undertook it' (so, Ts'ae Ch'in). 于文祖 must be understood 'in the temple of,' or

禮上類○七以玉璿○文
于帝于_{六節}肆政。齊衡璣在_{五節}祖。

5 III. He examined the gem-adorned turning sphere, and the gem transverse *tube*, that he might regulate the seven Directors.

6 Thereafter, he sacrificed specially, but with the ordinary forms, to

'before the shrine of, the accomplished ancestor.' By this ancestor must be intended the individual to whom Yaou traced his possession of the throne,—perhaps Hwang-te. Ma Yung understood by 文祖 Heaven, saying that 'Heaven is the Father (祖) who beautifies all things, and therefore is called 文祖.' This would give a good meaning; but had it been intended, the text would have been different. K'ang-shing thought that Yaou had a Hall of audience and worship, called 五府, corresponding to the 明堂 of the Chow dynasty, the several parts of which were dedicated to 'the five Tes,' the Gods or divine powers presiding over nature; and that 文祖 was the name of the hall of the Red Te (赤帝), but is used here, a part for the whole, intending the whole structure. This view comes to be substantially the same with that of Ma Yung. The belief of five Tes was long posterior to the times of Yaou and Shun.

Ch. III. LABOURS AND ADMINISTRATION OF SHUN OCCUPYING THE THRONE AS VICEGERENT OF YAOU. P. 5. *Astronomical labours.* 在 = 察, 'to examine,' as in the Canon of Yaou, p. 7. 璿 is the name of some kind of gem; the particular kind can hardly be ascertained. 璣 is given in the dict. as being 器名, 'the name of an instrument,' with a reference to this passage. Ts'ae Ch'in takes the char. as = 機, 'a spring,' 'a contrivance.'

We can easily understand that the 玉 was an addition of subsequent times to both characters. Fuh-shang seems to have read 旋機, 'the turning contrivance' (see his 'Preface to the Shoo,' and Keang Shing, *in loc.*). There is no difference about the reading of the next two characters, which mean 'the gem transverse,' and the 玉 there will justify the same in the two previous characters. According to Ts'ae Ch'in, following the ancient interpreters, Gan-kwŏ, Ch'ing, and Ma Yung, the four characters describe a kind of armillary sphere, the 璿璣 representing the revolution of the heavens, and the 'transverse' being a tube made of a precious stone, and placed athwart the sphere, for the purpose of celestial observation. Earlier than Gan-kwŏ, a different view seems to have obtained.

Fuh-shang says:—'What was the 旋機? 旋 means to revolve; and 機 means a spring, what is minute. That whose own motion is very small, while the movements which it produces are great, is what is called here 旋機. The words denote the north pole' (尚書大傳). Keang-shing says he approves of this view, but taking the four characters to be a description of the 'Great Bear,' called in Chinese the 'Northern Peck' (北斗). The 'handle' is the 'transverse' of the classic. 天璇 is the name still given to α Dubhe of Ursa Major; 天機 to β Dubhe; and 玉衡 to ε Alioth. This explanation is marked by simplicity, but the text of the classic will not admit of it. The writer must have had some constructed instrument in his mind's eye. De Guignes observes that the details are very singular for the time to which they refer, and asks whether astronomy had then made so much progress (Le Chou King, p. 13, note). But the existence of instruments of the character indicated is in accordance with the astronomical knowledge which we have seen that Yaou possessed. With regard to the form of Shun's sphere, it was no doubt very simple. The figure in Yung Ching's Shoo, said to represent it, is all of modern device.

The object of Shun's labours on the sphere and tube was 'to regulate (齊, "make uniform") the seven Governments.' By these 七政 Ma Yung understood the seven stars of the Great Bear. K'ang-shing said they meant 'spring, autumn, winter, and summer, astronomy, geography, and anthropology' (see Keang Shing, *in loc*). These opinions may be set aside at once. The consent of later times is all but universal to the view of Gan-kwŏ, that the seven governments were the sun, the moon, and the five planets, Mercury, Venus, Mars, Jupiter, and Saturn, each of which had its own rules of government.

According to this, we ought to translate 七政, 'the seven regularly governed Bodies.' But we have seen that the study of astronomy in those early times was all for practical purposes. The motions of the heavenly bodies were ascertained, to be a help to the movements of the government on earth. I prefer therefore to render the terms by 'the seven Directors.'

P. 6. *Acts of religious worship.* 肆 = 遂, 'upon this,' 'thereafter.' Gan-kwŏ (especially

觀 乃 旣 五 ○ 群 徧 山 望 六
四 日 月、瑞、輯 七節 神。于 川、于 宗、

God; sacrificed purely to the six Honoured *ones*; offered their appropriate sacrifices to the hills and rivers; and extended his worship to the host of spirits.

7　He called in all the five tokens of gem; and when the month was over, he gave daily audience to the *chief of the* four Mountains, and all the Pastors, *finally* returning the tokens to the several nobles.

as expounded by Ying-tă) makes the char. follow in logical sequence from the prec. par., as if Shun had discovered by his examination of the heavenly bodies, that Yaou's urging him to occupy the throne was from Heaven, and immediately he proceeded to announce his compliance to all superior spiritual powers.

類 禋, and 望 are the names of different sacrifices. 類 denotes a sacrifice offered to the Highest, on an extraordinary occasion, which characteristic is faintly indicated in the name, 類 being = 'of a sort,' 'a class.' Hence K'ang-shing says that Shun now sacrificed to Shang Te at the round mound, *i.e.*, at the place and with the ceremonies appropriate to the imperial worship of Heaven at the winter solstice. By 上帝 we are to understand God, the supreme Ruler. It is not till we come down to the times of the Chow dyn. that anything can be discovered to lead us to think of Shang Te as other than one and supreme. During the Chow there grew up the doctrine of five Tes, sometimes represented as distinct from Shang Te, and sometimes as different manifestations of Him. It has not, however, maintained itself. K'ang-shing's view of the name here has been indicated above. Ma Yung held that Shang Te was 'The supreme One' (太一); see the Record of Rites, 禮運, Pt. iv. 4. The whole of his comment is:— 上帝太一、神在 紫微宮、天之最顯者, 'Shang Te is the great One; his spirit occupies the palace of Tsze-wei' [a celestial space about the pole], 'the most distinguished of the heavenly Powers.' The blending of astrological fancies with the classical truth appears in it. Wang Suh made Shang Te here simply to be synonymous with Heaven; and Gan-kwŏ himself had defined the name as = 'Heaven and the five Tes' (天及五帝). I cannot doubt but Shang Te is here the name of the true God; but the truth concerning Him and His worship had been perverted even in this early time, as appears from the other clauses of the paragraph.

禋 is supposed by Ch'ing K'ang-shing to be connected with 煙, 'smoke,' and have reference to the burnt sacrifices which were

presented; but this view cannot be sustained. The word applies to a sacrifice offered 'with purity and reverence.' Who the 'six Honoured ones' were, it is not possible to ascertain. Fuh-shang and his earlier followers held that, though six were mentioned, only one Being or Power was intended,—a sort of plastic influence, working between heaven and earth and the four cardinal points (see Sun Sing-yen, *in loc.*) Subsequently every interpreter had his own view, as may be seen in Ying-tă. Acc. to Gan-kwŏ, followed by Wang Suh, the six Honoured ones are 'the seasons, cold and heat, the sun, the moon, the stars, and drought.' Of course we must understand that the emp. sacrificed to certain spirits, ruling over these phenomena and things, and residing probably in different stars.

望 is the name of sacrifices offered to the hills and streams. The sacrificer would probably *look towards* the quarter where each mountain or stream was situated. We are to understand that 'the hills and rivers' were all throughout the empire, not the more famous of them only, but all, with their presiding spirits.

Finally, Shun did homage to 'the herd of spirits,'—all spirits of heaven, earth, and men, not included in the above three clauses;—'to mounds, dykes, plains, forests, and the sages and worthies of ancient times.' So says Ying-tă, who points out also how, in thus sacrificing to 'all spirits' (百神), Shun was exercising an imperial prerogative. Such was the solemn worship of Shun, a sage, a perfect man, according to the Chinese ideal. It was offered in the year B.C. 2283, so soon had men departed from the truth of God, and added to His worship of their own inventions.

P. 7. *Shun gives audience to the nobles of the empire, and confirms them in their fiefs.* 五 瑞,—'the five gem-signets.'—It is difficult to get a word exactly corresponding to 瑞. Medhurst transl. it by 'sceptre.' The fiefs of the empire were divided into five classes, the chiefs of which were known respectively by the titles of Kung, How, Pih, Tsze, and Nan (see Mencius, Bk. V. Pt. II. ii.); so it was in the Chow dyn., and there was an arrangement, the same or similar, in the earliest times. Each ruler, on obtaining his appointment from the emperor, received a token, differing in size and form according to the rank. This he kept, and brought with him whenever he appeared at

度　正　后、　川、　望　于　東　○　瑞　岳
量　日、　協　肆　秩　岱　巡　歲　于　群
衡、　同　時　觀　于　宗　守　二　群　牧、
修　律　月、　東　山　柴、　至　月、　后。　班

八師

8　　In the second month of the year, he made a tour of inspection eastwards, as far as Tae-tsung, where he presented a burnt-offering to Heaven, and sacrificed in order to the hills and rivers. Thereafter he gave audience to the nobles of the East, putting in accord their

court. The separate tokens were so constructed that they fitted into a sort of frame kept in the imperial treasury, by which their genuineness was tested, so that an impostor might in this way be detected. The token held by the *Kung*, or nobles of the highest rank, was called 桓圭; that of the *How*, 信圭; of the *Pih*, 躬圭; of the *Tsze*, 穀璧; and of the *Nan*, 蒲璧 (see the 周禮, 春官, 大宗伯, 二). On Shun's accession to the administration of the empire, it was necessary that all the nobles should have their appointments confirmed by him.

There is a difficulty with the interpretation of 既月. 既 is taken as ＝ 盡, so that the phrase ＝ 'when a month was completed.' That month is understood to be the first month of the year after his accession. The summons had been sent to the nobles, and at the expiry of a month they began to arrive. . The 羣牧 were the chiefs of the nobles in the different provinces, the lord-lieutenants, whose official chief again was the 四岳. To them Shun gave daily audience on the subject of the diff't. nobles, whom they would introduce, and who were then sent back with their tokens to their various fiefs, to maintain the authority of the vicegerent.

P. 8. *Tours of Inspection.* 巡守 appears in Mencius, I. Pt. II. iv. 5, *et al.*, as 巡狩, ＝ 'perambulated the Charges *of the nobles.*' To what year this first tour is to be referred cannot be determined. Ma Yung held that it was the 5th year after Shun undertook the govt. Gan-kwŏ again makes it the same as that in which he confirmed the nobles. The arranged chronol. places it in the year after, the 74th of Yaou's reign. Perhaps it was so. In making the circuit, Shun first travelled east, as far as 岱宗, called elsewhere and now 泰山, 5 *lc* to the north of the district city of T'ae-gan (泰安) in the dep. of the same name

in Shan-tung [Lat. 36°30′, N., Lon. 1°, E., Med.] This mount. was deemed the first of all the hills of China, and therefore it has the epithet of 宗 or 'Honourable.' When his work was done here, Shun went to the South.

卒乃復,—Gan-kwŏ and Ma Yung take 復 actively:—' he returned the five instruments of gem.' I have followed them. K'ang-shing takes it intrans., and supposes that Shun returned to the capital and sacrificed a single victim at the end of each tour. Choo He, foll. of course by Ts'ae Ch'in and others, also takes it intrans., but without suppos. a return to the cap. Shun simply turns back from his eastward course, and goes in another direction. They also suppose that the text has got transposed, and read 五玉、三帛、二生、一死、贄, immediately after 東后. There is no necessity for such a violent measure, if we take 復 actively, as I have done. From mount T'ae, Shun proceeded to the Southern mountain, generally supposed to have been mount Hwǎng (衡), 30 *le* to the north of the dis. city of Hwǎng-san (衡山), in Hwǎng-chow dep. (衡州), Hoo-nan [Lat. 37°30′, N., Lon. 4°15′, W., Med.] This has been thought too remote, and other hills not so far south have been fixed on. From mount Hwǎng, Shun trav. west to the Western mountain, or mount Hwa (華山), called T'ae-hwa (太華) in the 'Tribute of Yu.' It is 10 *le* south of the dis. city of Hwa-yin (華陰), in Shen-se, dep. of Se-ngan. [Lat. 34°30′, N., Lon. 6°30′, W., Med.]. From the west, he proc. north, to the Northern mountain. or mount Hǎng (恒山), considered, in the sacrificial statutes of the pres. dyn., to be 20 *le* to the south of Hwǎn-chow dis. (渾州), dep. of Ta-t'ung (大同), in Shan-se [Lat. 37°30′, N., Lon. 2°30′, W., Med.] From the north he ret. to the cap., which was at no great distance, in the pres. dep. of P'ing-yang (平陽) in Shan-se; and there he sacrificed **a**

西岳如初。　巡守、至于　禮。八月、　南岳、如岱　巡守、至于　復。五月、　五器、卒、乃　一死、贄、如　三帛、二生、　五禮、五玉、

seasons and months, and rectifying the days; he made uniform the standard tubes, the measures of length and of capacity, and the steel-yards; he regulated the five *classes of* ceremonies. As to the several articles of introduction,—the five instruments of gem, the three kinds of silk, the two living animals, and the one dead one, when all was over, he returned the five instruments. In the fifth month, he made a similar tour to the south, as far as the southern mountain, observing the same ceremonies as at Tae. In the same way, in

bull (特＝一牛), in the temple of the Cultivated ancestor, announcing the completion of his circuit. 藝祖 is probably the same as 文祖, p. 4. So, Gan-kwŏ and K'ang-shing.

On arriving at each of his halting places, Shun first pres. a burnt-offering to Heaven. 柴, lit., = 'firewood.' On the altar a pile of wood was reared, on which the victim and other offerings were placed. The practice is the same at the pres. day. The old interp. placed no comma after 宗, but placed one after 柴. Choo He pointed at 宗, and then read on to 川. I put a comma both at 宗 and 柴. 秩, 'in order,' = 如其秩次, 'acc. to their order.' Difft. ranks were assigned to the hills and rivers, and the ceremonies paid to them varied accordingly.

Shun's business at the various points, after giv. audience to the nobles was:—1st, to see that they had the calendar correct—協時 (＝四時) 月 (謂月之大小, i.e., which months were long and which short. So, Gan-kwŏ; and this would imply a process of inter-calation like the present) 日 (謂日之甲乙, i.e., the names of the days, their designation by the cycle-characters); 2d, to see that the weights, measures, &c., of the difft. States were uniform. 同律,—'he made uniform the regulation-tubes.' 律 is defined by 分, 'that which divides.' The name was given to twelve tubes, originally made of bamboo, then of some gem, and in the time of the Han dyn. of brass or copper. They were a little more than three tenths of an inch in diameter.

and the circumference of the bore was exactly nine tenths. The longest was called 'the yellow cup' (黃鐘), 9 in. long, and the shortest 'the responsive cup' (應鐘), only 4.66 in. The name of 律 more especially belonged to six of them, which gave the sharped notes in music. The others, giving the flat notes, were called 呂. The twelve together about formed, I believe, a chromatic scale. But besides their applica-tion to music (see on p. 24), the *hwang chung* was the standard measure of length. The 90th part of it was 1 *fun* (分); 10 *fun* were 1 inch (寸); 10 inches were 1 foot (尺); 10 feet were 1 *chang* (丈); and 10 *chang* were 1 *yin* (引). [It is said that the breadth of a grain of millet (一黍之廣) made a *fun*, and that 90 of them determined the length of the 1st tube. See the 'Commentary of Ts'ae Illustrated' (蔡傳旁通), by Ch'in Sze-k'ae (陳師凱) of the Yuen dyn. (pub. A.D. 1321)]. The same tube was the standard for measures of capacity. 13⅓ millet grains filled a *fun* of it, and 1200 grains filled the whole. So much made a *yoh* (龠); 2 *yoh* made a *kŏh* (合); 10 *kŏh*, 1 *shing* (升); 10 *shing*, 1 *tow* (斗); 10 *tow*, 1 *hoh* (斛). The tube, again, supplied the stan-dard for weights. 100 grains of millet weighed a *choo* (銖); 24 *choo*; 1 *lëang* (兩) or tael; 16 taels, 1 *kin* (斤), or catty; 30 catties, 1 *keun* (鈞); and 4 *keun*, 1 *shih* (石), or stone. From all these applications of 'the yellow cup' we find it spoken of as 'the root of all human affairs' (黃鐘爲萬事根本).

試 奏 后 一 特。于 西 于 朔 十
以 以 四 巡 ○ 藝 禮。北 巡 有
功 言 朝 守 九二 祖 歸 岳 守 一
車 明 敷 群 載 用 格 如 至 月

節

the eighth month, he travelled westwards, as far as the western mountain; and in the eleventh month he travelled northwards, as far as the northern mountain. When he returned *to the capital, he* went to the *temple of the* Cultivated ancestor, and offered a single bullock.

9   In five years there was one tour of inspection, and four appearances of the nobles at court. They set forth a report of their government in words. This was clearly tested by their works. They received chariots and robes according to their services.

Shun would carry with him from the capital standard tubes, measures, steelyards and beams, and weights.   There was a 3d subject to occupy him. He had also 'to regulate the five ceremonies.' By these Ch'ing understood the ceremonies to be observed in appearing at court and in their intercourse with one another by the five classes of nobles indicated in the last par. Gan-kwŏ and Ma Yung take the ceremonies to be the same with those recognized under the Chow dyn.,—the various ceremonies of worship (吉禮); the ceremonies appropriate to calamity and mourning (凶禮), the ceremonies appropriate to guests of State (賓禮); the ceremonies appropriate to war (軍禮); and festive ceremonies (嘉禮) appropriate to marriages and other occasions of joy. This latter interpretation is to be preferred.

The nobles in waiting upon Shun brought with them their tokens of investiture,—the 五端 of last par., called here 五玉 and 五器; and also various articles which prepared the way for their audience, and are here called 贄. 'A man's gift maketh room for him, and bringeth him before great men.' This obtains in the east more than elsewhere, and obtained from the earliest times. The statutes enacted even in Shun's days recognized it, and endeavoured to regulate it and prevent its abuse.   三帛,—'three fabrics of silk.'

Ch'ing says they were red silk (赤繒), on which the descendants of Kaou-sin presented their signets; black silk, on which those of Kaou-yang presented theirs; and white silk, used by the other nobles. Gan-kwŏ and Wang Suh, again, say that they were silks of a deep red, brought by the eldest sons of princes; dark

azure silks, brought by 三公之孤; and yellow silks, brought by the chiefs of small attached territories.   二生, 'two living animals,'—lambs or kids, brought by the highest officers in the various States (卿); and geese, brought by inferior officers (大夫).

一死, 'one dead animal,'—pheasants brought by the smaller officers, and scholars expecting employment (士).   如五器, 'as to the five instruments,' *i.e.,* the signets. Those who would transpose this clause (see above) are obliged to expl. 如 by 同, 'to make uniform.'

This year of inspection must have been a busy one to Shun. Many commentators have doubted the possibility of his accomplishing all the work. Some things indicated have been pushed up, I must suppose, from the practices of a subsequent age.

P. 9. *Regular periods of tours of inspection and appearances of the nobles at court, with the results of such appearances.*   After the circuit detailed in last par., it was probably enacted by Shun that such a tour should be made every five years. During the intermediate four years, the nobles and princes of the difft. divisions of the empire presented themselves at court. Ma and K'ung suppose that the 'four appearances' were those at the four points of meeting during the year of the imperial circuit. The other view—more in accord with the phrase 四朝—is given by Ch'ing. He says 'the nobles came separately,' intending, we may suppose with Ts'ae Ch'in, that the first year those of the east came, those of the south on the second, &c.

敷奏以言,—敷＝陳, 'to lay out, set forth;' 奏＝進 'to present,' ＝to represent. In want of any expressed nominative

服以庸。○肇[十節]十有二州、封十有二山、濬[十一節]川。○象[十二節]以典刑、流宥五刑、鞭作官刑、扑作五刑、

10　*Shun* instituted the division of the empire into twelve provinces, raising altars upon twelve hills in them. He *likewise* deepened the rivers.

11　He gave delineations of the statutory punishments, enacting banishment as a mitigation of the five *great* inflictions; with the whip to be employed in the magistrates' courts, the stick to be employed in schools, and money to be received for redeemable crimes.

to these verbs, we may take them indefinitely. —'There was setting forth and representation by means of words.' So with the other clauses.

功, 'meritorious service,' is specially applied to 'service to the State' (國); while 庸 is 民功, 'service rendered to the people' like the teaching them agriculture (see the 周禮,夏官,司馬,第四之三).

車服以庸,—see the She King Pt. II., Bk. VII., viii. 以 is here somewhat difft. from its use in the prec. clauses, and = 'according to.'

P. 10 *Division of the empire into twelve provinces, and attendant circumstances.* This division must have taken place several years after Shun's accession to the administration. While Yu was labouring on the flooded provinces, their number was only nine, and the rearrangement of them as twelve must have been subsequent to the conclusion of his work. It is referred by the Annalists to the 81st year of Yaou. Fuh-shang in his Preface assigns it to the first year of Shun's independent reign, which would seem to be more likely. For the provinces, see next Part, Bk. I. Shun divided K'e into the three provinces of Ping (幷), K'e (冀) and Yew (幽); and Ts'ing into Ts'ing (青) and Ying (營). See Ying-tă *in loc.* This division into twelve provinces did not last beyond Shun's reign. 封十有二山, —封, 'to raise a mound,' here = 封土爲壇, 'to raise up earth for an altar' (Keang Shing). In every province Shun selected a mountain,—the largest probably,—and made it the 'guardian' of the territory (鎭山). See the 周禮,夏官,司馬,第四之六. 濬, in p. 1, 'profound,' 'deep;' here a verb, = 'to deepen.' The mention of this leads us to refer the whole of this par. to Shun's own

reign, some years after the completion of Yu's work.

P. 11. *Punishments.* Comp. p. 20; and Pt. V., Bk. XXVII. 象以典刑 — 象, 'to delineate;' as in the Canon of Yaou, p. 3. There is much dispute about the meaning of the char. here. Gan-kwŏ takes it as = 法, 'laws,' and expl.—'according to the laws, he used the regular punishments, not going beyond the laws.' This view may at once be set aside. Ts'ae Ch'in says we are to understand it as in the phrase—'Heaven hangs out its appearances to show to men' (天垂象以示人); which gives us the idea of pictorial representation. 典刑,—'regular punishments,' said to be five in the next clause. Those were branding (on the forehead) (墨); cutting off the nose (劓); cutting off the feet (刖); castration (宮); and death [which might be by various modes of execution] (大辟).

It is maintained by some Chinese scholars that Yaou and Shun did not use those severe punishments. They did not need to do so, it is said. Ma Yung says on the text:—'Kaou Yaou instituted these five punishments, but none made themselves obnoxious to them. There were the representations (其象), but not the criminals' (其人). Fuh-shang speaks of persons liable to these punishments being dressed so as to attract attention, which made a greater impression than the infliction of the penalties would have done. These objections were made at a very early time, and answered by Seun K'ing, in the 3d cent. before Christ. Others allowing that Yaou and Shun had the punishment of death, say that the other four penalties in the flesh (肉刑) originated with the Hea dyn.; but neither is this correct. See Maou K'e-ling's 廣

工　○　之　哉　欽　終　肆　刑　金　作
于　流　恤　惟　哉　賊　赦　眚　作　教
幽　共　哉　刑　欽　刑　怙　災　贖　刑

Inadvertent offences and those which might be caused by misfortune were to be pardoned, but those who offended presumptuously or repeatedly were to be punished with death. "Let me be reverent; let me be reverent," *he said to himself.* "Let compassion rule in punishment."

12   He banished the minister of Works to Yew island; confined Hwan-tow on mount Tsung; drove the *chief of* San-meaou *and his people*

聽錄, 一, *in loc.* Branding and the cutting off of the nose and feet were abolished by the emp. Wǎn (文帝) of the Han dynasty (B.C. 178-156). Castration, however, remained on the statute book till the first emperor of the Suy dyn. (A.D. 579-600). From that time to the present the five punishments have been—beating with the bamboo (答); with the cudgel (杖); the shorter banishment (徒); the longer (流); and (死) death [which may be by decapitation, strangulation, cutting or slicing to pieces, &c.] K'e-ling observes that in this respect the ways of modern times are more humane than the ways of the ancient sages were.

流宥五刑 = 'banishment to mitigate the five severe penalties.' 鞭,—'a whip,' 'a piece of leather tied to a stick.' 扑 (p'uh),—'to beat;'—the Dict. says 'with a stick' (杖); Gan-kwŏ, 'with bramble-twigs, or with branches of the 榎.' The crimes punishable with the whip and stick are supposed to be slighter offences, not only below the penalty of the five inflictions, but also below banishment. The whip was employed against officers in the courts; and the stick against officers in the schools. Medhurst, indeed, translates—'the birch for the flagellation of scholars.' But if the next clause be correctly taken as applying to offences under these two heads, which is the common view of it, a commutation of the birch for a fine in schools becomes absurd,—to say nothing of Shun's condescending to such matters. 金,—'metal,' here = 'copper.' See Sun Sing-yen, *in loc.* 無心之過 誤謂之眚, 'offences without intention are called 眚.' 不幸而獲過謂之災, 'offences by mishap are called 災:'—see the 日講. The old interpreters joined the two together—'injuries done without pur-

pose.' 肆=縱, 'to let go.' 怙終賊刑,—Ch'ing expands:—怙其姦而終身以爲殘賊則用刑之, 'those who persist in their villainy, and all their lives are criminals, are to be punished.' It is better, with Gan-kwŏ, to take 賊=殺, and 怙 as in the translation; 怙=有恃, and 終=再犯. 欽哉云云,—it is best to take these two sentences as addressed by Shun to himself.

P. 12. *How Shun dealt with the four great criminals of the empire.* We do not know when the transactions here mentioned took place. Sze-ma Ts'een, I mentioned above, has a legend of 'four villains' (四凶), banished by Shun while Yaou was testing him; but he has also incorporated the present par. with his Work, so that he must have considered the 四罪 and the 四凶 to be different individuals.

The minister of Works, Hwan-tow, and K'wǎn have all occurred in the Canon of Yaou. 三苗 was the name of a country. This appears clearly from a passage in the 左傳, 昭元年, and especially from the 戰國策, 卷十四, where Woo K'e (吳起) tells one of the princes of Wei (魏) that 'San-meaou had on its left the waves of the P'ang-le (彭蠡), and on its right the waters of the Tung-t'ing (洞庭), Mount Wan (汶山) on the South, and Mount Hwǎng (衡) on the north.' This agrees with other accounts of its situation. It possessed the territory now occupied by the depp. of Woo-ch'ang (武昌) in Hoo-pih, Yŏ-chow (岳州) in Hoo-nan, and Kew-keang (九江) in Keang-se. Why it was

姓 乃 有 服。 而 羽 危 三 于 洲、
如 殂 八 ○ 天 山。 殛 苗 崇 放
喪 落、 載、 二 下 四 鯀 于 山、 驩
考 百 帝 十 咸 罪 于 三 竄 兜

十三節

into San-wei, and kept them there; held K'wăn till death a prisoner on mount Yu. These four criminals being thus dealt with, universal submission prevailed throughout the empire.

13   IV. After twenty-eight years the emperor demised, when the people mourned for him as for a parent for three years. All within the

called the 'three Meaou,' it is only attempted to account for by foolish legends.

From the 國語,楚語,下, we see it was thought in the Chow dyn. that Yaou had been in hostilities with the people of Meaou, and we shall see in the next Book that Yu had likewise to proceed against them. Shun's measure seems to have been to remove their Chief and probably a portion of his people to another part of the country. We must suppose that their chief is specially intended, to make one in the quaternion of four great criminals. 流 = 'to banish.' 放 = 'to put in a place and confine there.' 竄 = 'to drive to, and keep as in prison.' 殛 would seem to mean 'to put to death,' and Ch'ing and Ma Yung expl. it by 誅, 'to take out of the way;' but Gan-kwŏ says that every one of the four criminals was dealt with in the way of 誅. A lighter meaning therefore is given to the term; and indeed, it is not easy to suppose that while Yu was his right hand, and rendering the greatest services to the empire, Shun would put his father to death. Woo Ch'ing says, 殛謂待死于此,以終其身. 幽洲 must originally have been 幽州, the 水 being a subsequent addition. This place was somewhere in the north;—it is said outside Chih-le province, to the north east of Meih-yun (密雲) dis., dep. of Shun-t'een. I am not sure, however, whether it is right to translate 洲, by 'island.' 崇山 was in the south, in the pres. Hoo-nan, in the dis. of Yung-ting (永定) in Le-chow (澧洲) 三危 was a district in the west, deriving its name from a hill of the same name. 'It rises,' says the Statistical Account of the empire under the pres. dyn., 'in the south-east of the dep. of Gan-se (安西) in Kan-suh, with three precipitous summits, which seem threatening to

fall' (如危欲墜). 羽山 was in the east, in the pres. Shan-tung, 70 le to the northeast of the dis. city of T'an-shing (郯城), in E-chow (沂州).

四罪,—the char. 罪 originally was 皇, for which the founder of the Ts'in dyn. ordered 罪 to be used, disliking its similarity to the char. 皇. After 四罪 we must understand some characters equal to—'being thus discriminatingly dealt with.'

Ch. IV. The death of Yaou and accession of Shun to the throne. P. 13. 二十有八載,—it seems to me that every unprejudiced reader of the classic must understand this as meaning 28 years, reckoning from Shun's accession to the administration of affairs, mentioned p. 4, so that Yaou's death would occur in the 100th year of his reign, B.C. 2257. The matter is complicated, however by what is related in the ·Historical Records,' that Yaou, getting Shun in the 70th year of his reign, employed him for 20 years, and only then resigned to him the administration, dying himself 8 years after. This account would make Yaou's reign extend over 98 years. The conclusion we draw from the classic is all against this view.

殂落 together = 'to decease.' Ts'een has 崩. Choo He says that at death the animus goes to heaven, and the anima to the earth. In this case, 殂 ought to denote 'to ascend,' but it simply = 往, 'to go away.' 百姓, —as in last Bk., p. 2, the 四海 corresponding to the 萬國 and 黎民 there. Keang Shing remarks that the mourning for three years proves that 百姓 must be confined to officers; but this assumes that 喪 is to be understood in the sense of 'wearing mourning,' and not in that of 'lamenting' generally. Besides, the people of the imperial domain had to

明　闢　于　祖。格　元　○　密　四　姒．
四　四　四　○　于　日、月　八　海　三
目、門、岳、詢　文　舜　正　音。過　載．
　　　　十五節　十四節　　　　　

four seas, the eight instruments of music were stopped and hushed.

14 On the first day of the first month, Shun went to the *temple of the* Accomplished Ancestor.

15   V. He deliberated with the *chief of the* four Mountains, how to throw open all the doors *of communication between the court and the empire*, and sought to see with the eyes and hear with the ears of all.

wear mourning for three months (集傳, *in loc.*); and here they extended of themselves the rule to three years.   考 = a father, deceased; 姒, a mother, deceased.   四海, —'the four seas.' Anciently, the territories occupied by the nine *E* (夷), the eight *Teih* (狄), the seven *Jung* (戎), and the six *Man* (蠻), were called 'the four seas.' All within the four seas was divided into the 'nine provinces.' Within the nine provinces there were arranged the 'five domains,' divided into three, —the imperial, the nobles', the peaceful,—called the 'Middle Kingdom,' and two,—the domain of restraint, and the wild domain,—called the country of the 'four wild tribes;'—see Hoo Ming-king's (胡明經) Introduction to his Work on 'The Tribute of Yu.' According to this view, which is that of the ancient Dictionary, the 爾雅, 'the four seas' is a designation having nothing to do with the seas. The scholars and thinkers of the Sung dyn. did not understand how it could have arisen, and rejected this account of it. The phrase must have had its origin in some idea of the habitable territory as bounded on every side by water (see Con. Ana., XII. v., note). Yen Jŏ-keu, in his 'Topography of the Four Books.' art. 四海, says that the phrase has two meanings; generally it is to be taken in accordance with the ancient view, but sometimes it has a vast and vague signification, and = 天下, 'all under heaven.' Practically, this account is correct, but it says nothing of the origin of the phrase.—In the text, we must take the phrase vaguely, comprehending the empire. Even allowing the account of the 爾雅, 四海 must = 四海 之內, or 九州. The writer could not have the barbarous territory beyond the empire in his mind.

八音,—' the eight sounds,' *i.e.*, all musical instruments, made of metal, of stone, of silk, of bamboo, of a gourd, of earth, of leather, or of wood.

P. 14. *Shun's accession to the throne.* This did not take place the year that Yaou died, nor the year after, but when the three years' mourning was expired. Nor did Shun then immediately occupy the throne. He allowed time for the expression of opinion from the nobles and people, and was willing that Yaou's son Choo should succeed to his father. Neither nobles nor people, however, would have any other but Shun to reign over them. See Mencius, Bk. V. Pt. I. v. 7. The date of the accession was B. C. 2254.   月正元日,—comp.

p. 4., 正月上日. Gan-kwŏ and Wang Suh supposed the two passages identical, and that 月正 and 元 in the one and 正月 and 上 in the other are only variations of style, which a writer may indulge in without any great reason. Ch'ing on the other hand contends that the changes teach an important fact,—that Shun on his accession to the throne changed the first month of the year, from the month after the winter solstice, to the month beginning with it. It is slender ground on which to build such a conclusion. Suh says that it was only the Yin and Chow dynasties which changed the beginning of the year, and that the Hea dyn. and all previous times made it commence with the third month after the winter solstice; see on Con. Ana. XV. x. An expression in Pt. III. Book. II. p. 3. may be pressed in support of Ching's view. I do not know that there is any other evidence of it, and must here leave the point undetermined.   格

于文祖,—文祖, see on p. 4. Shun went now to the temple to announce his accession to the throne; but henceforth he would go to the temple of his own ancestors.

Ch. V. Acts of Shun as Emperor. With this par., or the prec., commences what is properly the Canon of Shun, or rather a fragment of that Canon. It wants the beginning, and we may say it wants the end also;—hardly carrying us beyond the events of one year.

P. 15. *Measure of Shun to call forth the good and able to public service, and make himself acquainted with the state of the empire* 詢 is here more than 'to inquire;' it conveys the idea of plans

有能奮庸　曰咨四岳　率服。○舜〔十七節〕　任人蠻夷　允元而難　能邇惇德　惟時柔遠　牧曰食哉　咨十有二〔十六節〕　達四聰。○

16   He consulted with the twelve Pastors, and said, "The food!—it depends on *observing* the seasons. Be kind to the distant, and cultivate the ability of the near. Give honour to the virtuous, and your confidence to the good, while you discountenance the artful:—so shall the barbarous tribes lead on one another to make their submission."

17   Shun said, "Ah! *chief of* the four Mountains, is there any one who can vigorously display his merits, and give wide development

and measures (see the 書經備旨).

闢四門,— 'to open the four gates,' *i.e.*, to open the gates of the four quarters, remove every hindrance obstructing the access of worth and ability, wherever situated, to the notice of the sovereign and his service. K'ang-shing supposes an allusion to the audience given by the emperor to his officers 'in the gate.' Keang Shing brings in his favourite idea of 'the four gates of the Hall of Audience.' It is not necessary to be so minute. All agree in the general meaning, that Shun's object was—廣賢路, 'to widen the way of the worthy.' There is more difficulty in apprehending precisely the remaining two phrases—明四目,達四聰. Gan-kwŏ's expl. of them will suffice:—廣視聽於四方, 使天下無雍塞, 'to enlarge his seeing and hearing throughout the four quarters, that nothing in the empire might be shut up or hid from him.' Good officers, in sympathy with him, would be eyes and ears to him.

P. 16. *Counsels to the twelve pastors of provinces.* 牧, 'pastor,' 'shepherd,' was a name given in the times of Yaou and Shun to the chief or superintendent of all the princes and nobles in a province; indicating that the nourishment of the people should be his chief concern. This is the reason why 'food' is here mentioned first. 食哉惟時,—'Food!—Only the seasons.' This is the second time we find the part. 惟 (see p. 11), which is of very frequent occurrence in the Shoo, and of varied *usus.* As to the sentiment, see Mencius, I. Pt. I. iii. 能邇,—能 is taken by K'ang-shing as = 恣, 'to be indulgent to.' So also the modern comm. Gan-kwŏ and Wang Suh, unwilling to

adopt such a meaning, interpreted :—'give repose to the remote, and then you *can* do so to the near.' It does not appear to me that we need to depart from the usual meaning, only giving the term a *hiphil* force. 元=仁厚之人, 'men of benevolence and generosity.' 任人=佞人, 'artful people,' especially in speech. The standard interpretation of 任 is 包藏凶惡之人, 'men who treasure wickedness in their bosoms.' Instead of 任, we have 壬 in Bk. III. 2. [The Dict. gives the 任 of the text in the 3d tone, which must be a mistake.] 蠻夷,—'the wild tribes of the south and the east,' used for such tribes generally. 率=相率, 'lead on one another.'

P. 17. *Appointment of Yu to be General Regulator to Shun, as Shun had formerly been to Yaou.* 舜曰,—the use of 舜 here would seem to be purposely to mark that Shun was now the emperor. Hereafter the phrase is 帝曰. 奮=起, 'to put forward.' It gives the idea of vigour. Ma Yung explains it by 明, 'to illustrate,'—wrongly. 庸=功, 'services,' 'merits.' 熙,—as in the Canon of Yaou, p. 8. 帝之載,—the emp. of course is Yaou; 載, as in Doctr. of the Mean, xxxiii. 6. 百揆,—see par. 2. 亮 柔,—亮=相, 'to assist,' 'to act as minister to' (see note by Lin Che-k'e in the 集傳); 柔=事, as in the Can. of Yaou, p. 10. 惠疇—惠=順, 'to accord with; 疇=

熙帝之載使宅
百揆亮采惠疇。
僉曰伯禹作司
空帝曰俞咨禹、
汝平水土惟時、
懋哉禹拜稽首、
讓于稷契暨皋
陶。帝曰俞汝往
哉。○帝曰棄黎
十八節

to the undertakings of the emperor, whom I may make General Regulator, to aid me in all affairs, and manage each department according to its nature?" All *in the court* said, "There is baron Yu, the superintendent of Works." The emperor said, "Yes. Ah! Yu, you have regulated the water and the land. In this *new office* exert yourself." Yu did obeisance with his head to the ground, and wished to decline in favour of the minister of Agriculture, or Sëĕ, or Kaou-yaou." The emperor said, "Yes; but do you go, *and undertake the duties.*"

18   The emperor said, "K'e, the black-haired people are *still* suffering

類, 'a class.' The meaning of the phrase, so far as it can be ascertained, is given in the transl. Lin Che-k'e says;—謂天下之事, 各以其類, 無不順也, 'The meaning is, that all the affairs of the empire should be managed naturally, each according to its nature and class.' 僉曰,—as in the Can. of Yaou, p. 11. 伯禹,—Baron Yu. Yu must by this time have superseded, or succeeded to, his father, as chief of Tsung; see on Can. of Yaou, p. 11. 司空,—see Pt. V. Bk. XX. 12. The 司空 was one of the great officers of the Chow dyn.; but only here do we find the name in connection with earlier times. In Yaou's time the minister of Works was styled 共工 (Can. of Yaou, p. 10), and we find the same designation continued in this Bk., p. 21. K'angshing supposed that 司空 was a special designation given for the time to Yu. It certainly had to do with his labours on the mountains and streams of the flooded empire. 惟時 (=是) 懋哉,—'now in this exert yourself!' Ma Yung takes 懋=美, 'to beautify;' but the meaning in the transl. is to be preferred. 禹拜稽首,—稽首 is exegetical of the 拜, which signifies 'to do obeisance,' 'to pay one's respects.' In

the Chow Le, 春官 宗伯 第三之九, there are specified nine 拜, of which the first is 稽首, 'laying the head to the ground.' 稷 is the name of an office, that of the minister of Agriculture. The individual here mentioned had rendered, it is supposed, such services to the State in his office, that he came to be distinguished by it, and not by his own name which was K'e (棄). He was a son of the emp. K'uh (高辛氏); and to him the emperors of the Chow dyn. referred as their progenitor. See the wonders of his birth and infancy, and the achievements of his life, in the She King, Pt. II. Bk. II. i., *et al.* During Shun's administration of the empire, K'e had been apointed ruler of the state of T'ae (邰), to which his mother had belonged. 契 (Sëĕ), was a half-brother of K'e, and had been appointed ruler of Shang (商). From him the emperors of the Shang dyn. were descended. See the accounts of his birth, &c., in the last portion of the She King, the 'Praise-songs of Shang.' 皋陶,—see on Bk. III.

P. 18. *Confirmation of K'e as minister of Agriculture.* This is the confirmation of K'e, not his appointment. As Yu had mentioned him with Sëĕ and Kaou-yaou, the emperor turns to them, and praises them for their services, which they were to continue. All the old interpreters put the verbs in the past tense:—

汝作士五刑　夏寇賊姦宄　皐陶蠻夷猾　在寬。○帝曰　徒敬敷五教　不遜汝作司　姓不親五品　○帝曰契百　稷播時百穀。　民阻飢。汝后

十九節　　二十節

the distress of hunger. It is yours, O prince, the minister of Agriculture, to sow *for them* these various kinds of grain."

19　　The emperor said, "Sëĕ, the people continue unfriendly with one another, and do not observe docilely the five orders *of relationship*. It is yours, as the minister of Instruction, reverently to set forth the lessons of duty belonging to those five orders. Do so with gentleness."

20　　The emperor said, "Kaou-yaou, the barbarous tribes disturb our bright great land. There are *also* robbers, murderers, insurgents, and traitors. It is yours, as the minister of Crime, to employ the five

'The people were suffering,' &c. Perhaps we should so translate; but it seems more natural to render as I have done,—after Woo Ch'ing, and the 'Daily Explanation.' 阻=厄, 'to be straitened.' For 阻 Sze-ma Ts'een has 始, from which some suppose the original reading was 祖, which, indeed, Ma Yung gives. Rather we may suppose that originally there was simply 且. 后稷,—K'e was 后, 'prince,' as being chief of T'ae; as minister of Agriculture he was called 稷, 'millet,' that being considered the best of the five principal grains (Woo Ch'ing.) 時=是,—'these.' Ch'ing would have it read as 蒔, 'to transplant.' 百穀,—the hundred grains,' *i.e.*, all the various kinds of grain. Fan Sze-lin (潘士遴, Ming dyn.), indeed, makes out 100 in this way:—under the name of *leang* (粱), including millet, wheat, &c., 20 kinds; of *taou* (稻), including rice, and all grains that grow in water, 20 kinds; of 菽, *i.e.*, beans, peas, &c., 20 kinds; of vegetables (蔬), 20 kinds; and of fruits (果), 20 kinds.

P. 19. *Confirmation of Sëĕ as minister of Instruction.* 百姓 is here plainly the people. The commen. who have hitherto insisted on the phrase denoting 'the officers,' say nothing about it here. 不親,—I have said 'continue unfriendly,' to indicate the reference to the past services of Sëĕ, which is properly supposed. 五品,—品 = 'a class,' 'a rank;' 五品, 'the five ranks,' under which human society may be arranged;—parent and child, sovereign and subject, husband and wife, brothers, and friends. 五教, 'the five lessons of duty, belonging to those orders. See Mencius, III. Pt. I. iv. 8, who puts his seal to the meaning of 五品 and 五教. There need be no hesitation, therefore, in rejecting K'ang-shing's view, that the 'five 品' are 'father, mother, elder brother, younger brother, and son,' and the five 教 the duties belonging to those. 在寬,—lit., 'it is in gentleness,' *i.e.*, the people must be drawn, they can't be forced, to those duties.

P. 20. *Confirmation of Kaou-yaou as minister of Crime.* 猾夏,—猾 = 亂, 'to throw into confusion.' Ch'ing expl. it by 侵亂, 'to invade and throw into confusion.' 夏 is a name for 'the middle country,' conveying the ideas of 'brightness and greatness.' The character 華 is generally found with it.

姦宄,—在外曰姦, 在內曰宄, 'external troublers are called 姦; internal, 宄.' The latter are *traitors*, members of one's household or State; the former are insurgents.

工　咨　哉。工　曰、克　三　有　三　有
垂　垂、帝　僉　疇　允。居、宅　就　服、
拜　汝　曰、曰、若　○　惟　五　五　五
稽　共　俞、垂　予　帝(廿一節)明　宅　流　服

punishments for the treatment of offences, for the infliction of which there are the three appointed places; and the five banishments, with their several places of detention, for which three localities are assigned. Perform your duties with intelligence, and you will secure a sincere submission."

21　The emperor said, "Who is equal to the duty of superintending my workmen?" All *in the court* said, "There is Suy." The emperor said, "Yes. Ah! Suy, you must be minister of Works." Suy did obeisance, with his head to the ground, and wished to decline in

or invaders. 作士,—Ch'ing exp. 士 as 'one who presides over the examination of civil and criminal causes'; Ma says he was 'the chief of such judges.' During the Chow dyn. there was the 士師, or chief criminal judge, but he was only a subordinate to the minister of Crime. Kaou-yaou's office was that of the 大司寇 of the Chow dyn. On the interpr. of 五刑有服,五服三就,五流有宅,五宅三居, opinions are much divided. The five punishments, we may assume, are the branding, castration, &c., mentioned on p. 11. 服, says Woo Ch'ing, 猶衣服之服,謂加其身,'服 indicates the application of the punishment to the body, as a garment is put on'. I do not think we can translate in English more closely than if we say—'There are the five punishments which are to be undergone, and for the undergoing of them there are three places to be resorted to.' What those three places were, cannot be determined.—Ch'ing says—'the open country (原野); the market-place and court (市朝); and the place where the 甸師氏 executed his functions' [more privately, on members of the imperial House]. Ma Yung takes the same view. Gan-kwŏ had determined the three places to be the open country, the market place, and the court,—from misunderstanding a passage in the 國語,魯語,上,大刑用甲兵,云云. Dissatisfied with these explanations, Ts'ae suggested that it may have been that capital sentences were carried into effect in the market place, castration, in some place corresponding to the 'mulberry apartment' (蠶室) of the Han dyn., and the other

three punishments, in some other place, screened from the wind.—We must leave the subject undetermined.

The five severe inflictions might be commuted for banishments,—to a greater or less distance. Each banishment was undergone in a certain place (宅); but those five localities were comprehended within three larger divisions of territory. This is the extent of the conclusion to which we can come on this part of the passage. Gan-kwŏ says the lesser banishment was to a distance of a thousand *le*: the second was beyond the limits of the nine provinces; and the third was to the remotest region of barbarism. Ch'ing has a strange view. He would read 宅 as 侂 (*ch'a*), and thinks it means handcuffs, fetters, &c., with which the criminals were secured. 惟明克允,—does this mean, 'Be intelligent and you will secure the acquiescence of the people,' or 'Be intelligent and your sentences will be in accordance with the truth of the cases?' The characters will admit of either meaning. Ts'ae Ch'in joins them together, but a translation can only admit one of them.

P. 21. *Appointment of Suy to be minister of Works.* This office was vacant in consequence of Yu's appointment to be General Regulator. The minister of Works, it would appear, had to look after all the workers, or guilds of workers, in earth, stone, metal, leather, &c.

若予工,—see on 若, in Can. of Yaou, p. 9. 垂 (read *Suy*, like 瑞; see the Dict.),—mention is made of 'the bamboo arrows of Suy,' preserved as precious relics in the times of the Chow dyn.; see Pt. V. Bk. XXII. 19. The Taouist philosopher Chwang also speaks of 'the finger of Suy' (倕); see the 南華外篇,第三). Suy would appear from this to have

首讓于殳斨
暨伯與。帝曰、
俞往哉汝諧。
○帝曰、疇若 廿二節
予上下草木
鳥獸僉曰益
哉。帝曰、俞咨
益汝作朕虞。
益拜稽首讓
于朱虎熊羆。

favour of Shoo, Ts'eang, or Pih-yu. The emperor said, "Yes; but do you go and undertake the duties. Effect a harmony *in all the departments.*"

22   The emperor said, "Who is equal to the duty of superintending the grass and trees, with the birds and beasts, on my mountains and in my marshes." All *in the court* said, "There is Yih." The emperor said, "Yes. Ah! Yih, do you be my Forester." Yih did obeisance, with his head to the ground, and wished to decline in favour of Choo, Hoo, Heung, or Pe. The emperor said, "Yes; but do you go, and undertake the duties. You must manage them harmoniously."

been himself a skilful worker. 殳斨, 暨伯與 are three men in the 集傳, the two first being supposed to have got their names from their skill in making the weapons which the characters denote. The old interpr. made them two men—殳斨 and 伯與, which Keang Shing would identify with 朱斨 and 伯譽, in the 古今人表 of the Former Han. No doubt it was the object of Pan Koo there to mention the names in this par. 汝諧, is perhaps simply = 'make things go on harmoniously.' Yang Shaou-fang (楊肇芳, Ming dyn.) says:—'Under Suy and Yih there were many departments, which were to be carried on harmoniously.' Some take 諧=偕, 'together with,' and make it refer to Choo, Ts'eang, and Pih-yu, who were to be Suy's assistants, and in concert with whom he was to manage his duties;—so, Woo Ch'ing.

P. 22. *Appointment of Yih to be forester.*

上下,—in the Can. of Yaou, p. 6, these characters were equiv. to 'heaven and earth;' here they = 山林, 'hills and forests,' on high ground, and 澤藪, 'marshes and fens,' in low.

益—Yih had assisted Yu in his labours upon the flooded provinces. We are told that 'Shun then committed to him the direction of the fire to be employed, when he set fire to the forests and vegetation of the mountains and marshes, so that the birds and beasts fled away to hide themselves (Men. III. Bk. I., iv. 7).

Some make him a son of Kaou Yaou, but this is not likely (see the 集說, *in loc.*). According to Sze-ma Ts'een he was descended from Chuen-heuh, and, receiving from Shun the surname of Ying (嬴), became the progenitor of the rulers of Ts'in (秦). Ts'een gives his name 伯翳 and not 伯益 (see 秦本紀 第五). As Yih had been associated with Yu, this may be the reason why Ch'ing, Ma, and Wang Suh all read 禹曰益哉 instead of 僉曰益哉. This is considered a flagrant proof of the falsehood of the common text. The 'Historical Records,' however, for 僉曰 read 皆曰. The text from which Sze-ma copied must have had 僉曰. 虞=山澤之官, 'the officer of the hills and marshes.' In the time of the Chow dyn. each department had its superintendent, and the office was of smaller importance. 虞 means 'to consider,' 'to calculate' and the warden of the forests' was so styled, it is said, because he had so much to think about! Some would also make the name of the office to be 朕虞. 朱、虎、熊、羆,—lit., 'the fir,' 'the tiger,' 'the bear,' 'the grisly bear.' These were four officers, brothers, it is said, the sons of Kaou-sin. *Their* names, and those in the last par., might make us compare Shun's court to a council of Red Indians. The Historical Records add that these four men became Yih's assistants. This agrees with the meaning

帝曰、俞往哉汝

諧。○帝曰、咨四

岳、有能典朕三

禮。僉曰、伯夷。帝

曰、俞咨伯夷、汝作

秩宗夙夜惟寅、

直哉惟清。伯拜

稽首讓于夔龍。

帝曰、俞往欽哉。

○帝曰、夔命汝

廿四節

廿三節

23　The emperor said, "Ah! *chief of* the four Mountains, is there any one who can direct my three *religious* ceremonies?" All *in the court* said, "There is the baron E." The emperor said, "Yes. Ah! baron, you must be the Arranger of the ancestral temple. Morning and night you must be respectful. Be upright, be pure." The baron did obeisance with his head to the ground, and wished to decline in favour of K'wei or Lung. The emperor said, "Yes; but do you go, and undertake the duties. Be reverential."

24　The emperor said, "K'wei, I appoint you to be Director of music, and to teach our sons, so that the straightforward may yet be mild,

which I said on last par. some give to the diff. word 諧

P. 23. *Appointment of Pih-e to be minister of Religion.* The 四岳 is specially consulted with reference to the appointment of Yu, p. 17, and the app. here;—showing, it is supposed, the superior importance of the two offices of General Regulator and minister of Religion. 典 —here a verb,= 主, 'to preside over,' 'to direct.' 三禮,—'the three ceremonies.' There is no difference of opinion as to the understanding of these. They are all the observances in the worship of the spirits of heaven (天神), the spirits of earth (地祇), and the spirits of men (人鬼). The ceremonies of the first went by the name of 祀; of the second by that of 祭; of the third by that of 享. The minister of religion under the Chow dyn. was called 大宗伯, and the duties of his office will be found described at length under that name in the 'Rites of Chow' (夏官).

伯夷,—'the baron E, 伯 being his title (爵, Woo Ch'ing). How it is that the emperor addresses him simply by the title, and that the historian describes him simply by it is a difficulty, which has not been solved (see

段玉裁's Work, *in loc.*). The 'Historical Records' do not use 伯 alone, but always say 伯夷. 秩宗,—秩=敍次, 'to arrange,' 'to dispose in order'; 宗=祖廟, 'the ancestral temple' (this is the proper meaning of the character). That this—Arranger of the ancestral temple—should be the name given to the minister of Religion, shows strikingly the chief place occupied by the worship of their ancestors in the religion of China, from the earliest times. 夙夜惟寅, 直哉惟清.—Choo He says:—'From reverence there will come uprightness, and from uprightness purity' (惟寅故直, 惟直故清). I suppose it is so, but it is very difficult to discover in the text the grammatical nexus of the different clauses.

P. 24. *Appointment of K'wei to be minister of Music.* It is singular how great an importance is here attributed to training in music, and that this should have been a special department regulated by imperial statutes from the earliest times. Under the Chow dyn., the minister of Music was styled 大司樂; see the chapter on his duties in the 'Rites of Chow,' 春官, 宗伯 第二之六　夔 is the name of a monstrous animal, 'a dragon with one leg.' I can find no other information about the officer thus designated, besides the notice here

於　人　無　聲　聲　言　簡　栗　直　典
予　以　相　八　依　志　而　剛　而　樂
擊　和　奪　音　永　歌　無　而　溫　教
石　蘷　倫　克　律　永　傲、　無　寬　冑
拊　曰。　神　諧、　和　言、　詩　虐、　而　子、

the gentle may yet be dignified, the strong not tyrannical, and the impetuous not arrogant. Poetry is the expression of earnest thought; singing is the prolonged utterance of that expression. The notes accompany that utterance, and they are harmonized themselves by the pitch pipes. *In this way* the eight different kinds of instruments can all be adjusted so that one shall not take from or interfere with another, and spirits and men will thereby be brought into harmony."

and in Bk. IV., p. 9. 冑 is expl. by Gan-kwŏ by 長, 'eldest,' and he adds—'meaning the eldest son *of the emperor*, and the younger branches of the families of the nobles and officers.' He had before him a passage in the Le Ke,—the 王制, Pt. iv. p. 4, where we are told the minister of Music (樂正) taught 'the poems, ceremonies, and music of the former kings,' and was resorted to by the eldest and other sons of the king, the eldest sons of all the feudal princes, the eldest sons (by their proper wives) of the nobles and officers, and by the promising youth of the kingdom.' 冑, however, denotes descendants generally; and there was at an early time another reading of 育 for 冑, leaving the 子 quite unqualified. In 無虐,無傲·無＝毋. 詩言志,歌永言,—志 is defined by 心之所之, 'that to which the mind moves,' and hence it is translated by 'will,' 'aim,' 'purpose.' It denotes thought, but thought earnest and ardent, which seeks display and development. Shun's definition of poetry is not much amiss. 永 is, lit., 'water flowing on long and unbroken.' Ch'ing explains it here by 長, 'to prolong.' Singing is the poetic language 'in linked sweetness long drawn out.' 聲依永,律和聲,—依 is 'to rely on,' 'to be according to,' 'to keep close to.' Its force is well brought out in the 'Daily Explanation:'—'This singing gives rise to the distinction of notes into high and low, treble and bass,—the five notes of music, indeed, which all come out in connection with the prolonged

utterance' (皆依永而出). These five notes (聲) constitute the imperfect scale, common perhaps to all nations in their early attempts to form a musical system, into which no interval of less than a tone is admitted. Their names are *kung* (宮), *shang* (商), *këŏ* (角), *che* (徵, gen. read *ching*, but not in this sense), and ?*u* (羽). The tubes (律) which produce and subsequently harmonize (和) these notes, are said to measure, in ninths of an inch, 81, 72, 64, 54, and 48 respectively. The next number in this series, corresponding to the octave to *kung*, should of course be $\frac{1}{2}$ of 80 $=40\frac{1}{2}$; and we have thus according to our notation G, A, B, D, E, g. The series is constructed, starting from 81 as a basis, by making perfect fifths ascending (3:2), and perfect fourths descending (3:4). Thus from 81 is obtained 54; 54 gives, by the second proportion, 72; 72 again gives 48; and 48 gives 64. Carrying on this process, increasing or decreasing each time, as the case requires, the following set of twelve is obtained:—81, $75\frac{2}{3}$, 72, $67\frac{1}{3}$, 64, $59\frac{2}{3}$, $56\frac{2}{3}$, 54, $50\frac{2}{3}$, 48, $44\frac{2}{3}$, $42\frac{2}{3}$. (The fractions are not very accurate.) Twelve tubes of these several lengths constituted what I have called 'the standard tubes,' whose various application has been pointed out above. As regards the theory of music, could we be sure that the details which have been given, had really been wrought out in Shun's time, we could not refuse them our meed of admiration. The progress of the Chinese in music has not corresponded to such beginnings. A theoretical difficulty and a practical one have hindered them. They have found it impossible in theory for A to hold the same proportion to D as D to g; and in practice they have found that while their calculatons might be applied to stringed instruments, the

石、百獸率舞。○帝曰、龍、朕堲讒說殄行、震驚朕師、命汝作納言、夙夜出納朕命、惟允。

廿五節

[K'wei said, "Oh! I smite the stone; I smite the stone. The various animals lead on one another to dance."].

25　The emperor said, "Lung, I abominate slanderous speakers, and destroyers of *right* ways, who agitate and alarm my people. I appoint you to be the minister of Communication. Early and late give forth my orders and report to me, seeing that every thing is true."

tube g must be made considerably less than half the length of the tube G in order to sound the octave to it. Their division of the tubes into 6 律 and 6 呂, moreover, has complicated the subject, and thrown around it the perplexity of their reasonings about the *yin* and *yang* principles. 八音克諧—see p. 13. 神人以和,—on this the 'Daily Explanation' says:—'The instruments thus in harmony being played at the sacrifices to Heaven and in the ancestral temple, the spirits are all harmonious; being played in the court, men are all harmonious:—what then must be the power of music in teaching our youth!' 夔曰, 云云,—see Bk. IV. 9. There can be no doubt the reply of K'wei is out of place here,—appears here in fact from some displacement of the ancient tablets.

P. 25. *Appointment of Lung to be minister of Communication.* We are in ignorance of Lung just as we are of K'wei. 堲＝疾, 'to detest.' In the 'Historical Records' we have instead of it 畏忌, 'to fear and suspect.' 讒說—'slanderous speeches.' The Taouist Chwang defines 讒 as 'the liking to speak of the evil of others' (漁父篇). 殄＝絕, 'to subvert.' 'to make an end of;' 殄行 (3d tone)＝'to subvert the conduct.' The question arises,—Is the conduct subverted that of the individuals themselves? or that of others, so that this clause is an appendix to the former, a description of the object of the slander? Gan-kwŏ and Ma Yung take the latter view, and are followed by the modern interpreters (the 'Daily Explanation' expands—傷絕善人君子所行之事, 'they injure and keep out of view the actions of good and superior men'). Ch'ing takes the former view and explains the two phrases 讒說 and 殄行 by a reference to the words of Ana. XII. xx. 6.—'assuming the appearance of virtue, while opposing it in conduct.' This appears to me

the more natural interpretation,—to take the clauses as coordinate. 師＝眾, as in Can. of Yaou, p. 12, but does it mean 'all the people,' or 'all those in office'? Ch'ing restricts it to 'ministers' (眾臣); we may take it more generally. 納言 is the name of the office, which may be translated—'Communicator of words.' It is perhaps easier to describe the office, than to translate the terms, or those of the sentence below—出納朕命. Gan-kwŏ says:—'納言 was the officer of the throat and tongue. Hearing the words of those below, he brought them before the sovereign; receiving the words of the sovereign, he proclaimed them to those below:—in either case there was required fidelity' (納言喉舌之官, 聽下言, 納于上, 受上言, 宣于下, 必以信). Here at the end of Shun's appointment of ministers, Woo Ch'ing has the following note:—'Shun gave nine commissions, of which four were new appointments,—those of Yu, Suy, Yih, and the baron E. On occasion of *their* wish to decline the appointments, he confirmed five ministers in their old offices:—Tseih, Sëĕ, Kaou-yaou, K'wei, and Lung. Some have thought, from the words "I appoint" standing before the designation of these two last, that they likewise were new men. But this is wrong. When the emperor asks advice and then appoints, and the designate makes obeisance and wishes to decline, the appointment is new. When he appoints without asking advice, and the designate does not make obeisance nor wish to decline, there is only a confirmation. Can we suppose that K'wei and Lung would not have made obeisance, on first receiving their appointments? The commentator Wang Yen (王炎) has observed:—"The General Regulator was the head of all the ministers, and therefore Yu first received his appointment. The nourishment of the people is the beginning of royal government, and therefore the minister of agriculture was next appointed. When people are well off, instruction may be given them; hence there followed the appointment of Sëĕ. Punishment

惟允。○帝 廿六節
曰咨汝二
十有二人、
欽哉惟時
亮天功。○ 廿七節
三載考績
三考、黜陟
幽明、庶績
咸熙。分北 廿八節
三苗。○舜

26 The emperor said, "Ah! you, twenty and two men, be reverent, and so shall you aid *me* in performing the service of Heaven."

27 Every three years there was an examination of merits, and after three examinations the undeserving were degraded, and the deserving promoted. By this arrangement the duties of all the departments were fully discharged. The people of San-meaou were discriminated and separated.

is intended to help instruction; hence followed the appointment of Kaou-yaou. Workers make implements and utensils for the benefit of the people:—this is the conclusion of government; hence Suy was appointed, and so far as men are concerned, the organization of the government was pretty well complete. Shun then proceeded to care for the grass and trees, for birds and beasts, appointing Suy. This done, the time came for the cultivation and development of ceremonial observances and music. These two things are the grand consummation of government, by which service is done to Heaven, to earth, and to spirits, and all things are brought to harmony and order; hence there were the appointments of E and K'wei:—of E first and then of K'wei, because music must be a sequel to the ceremonial observances. With music the work of government might be supposed to be ended, but notwithstanding the abundance of able ministers, let slanderous dividers once go abroad, and the men of worth and ability would be made restless, and what had been done would come to nought. On this account the appointment of Lung was made last of all. The design of this was the same with that of Shun's concluding charge to the pastors of the twelve provinces, that they should *make it hard for the artful;* and with Confucius' concluding lesson on the administration of a country—*to keep far from specious talkers.*" (Ana. XV. xx. 6).

P. 26. *General address to all his principal ministers.* 汝二十有二人,—Who were these 22 men? There ought to be but one answer to the question,—that which we find in Ts'ae Ch'in. They were the chief of the four Mountains, the twelve presidents of the provinces, and the nine ministers, whose appointments or confirmations have been related. The old interpreters, thinking that the 四岳 were four individuals, mistook the meaning.

Ch'ing is obliged to leave them out altogether, and says the 22 were the 12 presidents of provinces, with Yu, Suy, Yih, Pih-e, K'wei, Lung, Shoo-ts'eang, Pih-yu, Choo-hoo, and Heung-pe; and Wang Ming-shing argues, in his 後案, that this view should not be changed! Gan-kwŏ and Ma Yung leave out Tseih, Sëě, and Kaou-yaou, and say the 22 men were Yu, Suy, Yih, Pih-e, K'wei, Lung, the 12 presidents of provinces, and the four ministers called 四岳. This view is followed by Keang Shing. 惟時亮天功,—時=是; 亮 as in p 17. Sze-ma Ts'een has 敬哉惟是 相事天.

P. 27. *Institution of examinations; and further discipline of the Meaouites.* 黜陟幽明, *i.e.*, 黜幽陟明; 幽 'the dark,'—the idle and undeserving; 明 is the opposite of this. 庶績咸熙,—see Can. of Yaou, p. 8. 分北三苗,—北 (read p'ei, 3d tone), 'to separate.' Keang Shing would read it pëě, contending, that the original character was two 八, one over the other, the old form of 別. In what year the Meaou were thus dealt with we cannot tell. Wang Suh thinks that after the discipline of them mentioned p. 12, those who were left in their original seat again proved insubordinate, and another separation and banishment of them had to be made.

CH. VI. SUMMARY OF SHUN'S LIFE; AND DEATH. There is no dispute about the first clause; all allow that Shun, when he was thirty, was called to employment by Yaou, and the testing of him began. The reading of 三十

○ 乃 陟 十 位、十 庸、十 生
死。方 載、五 在 三 徵 三

28   VI. In the thirtieth year of his life Shun was called to employment.   Thirty years he was on the throne *with Yaou*.   Fifty years
after, he went on high and died.

在 位 is much disputed. Ch'ing read 二
十, making Shun's life to have amounted altogether to 100 years. And there *was* a reading
of 二十 for 三十. Wang Ming-shing
and Twan Yuh-tsae adduce many proofs of it.
But on p. 13 we saw that the 28 years there
could only be understood of the years during
which Shun acted as Yaou's vicegerent. Adding
to them the three years of his testing, p. 3, we
should have 31 years; but one of those three
may naturally be considered the year in which
he was called from his obscurity. We shall
thus have the 三十 of the text. As to the
50 years on the throne, these must include
the two years (three, including the year in
which Yaou died) of mourning for Yaou, when
opportunity was given for the accession of
Yaou's son. Altogether then, Shun was on the
throne, with universal recognition, 48 years,
his life extended over 110 years; and he died
ʙ.ᴄ. 2202. Gan-kwŏ, not deducting the two
years after Yaou's death, makes Shun's age 112.

陟 方 乃 死,—I have translated this
clause after Ts'ae Ch'in, who relies chiefly on
the usage of the 'Bamboo Annals,' where 陟
is used of the death of the emperors, and =
崩. The 方 after it is a difficulty, and so is

the 乃 死, for the going on high should be
mentioned after the death, and not before it.
Gan-kwŏ, to avoid these difficulties, takes 方 in
the sense of region, and says 昇 道 南 方
巡 狩 死, 'he went up the way towards the
southern region, on a tour of inspection, and
died.' Maou K'e-ling argues for this view; but
it is inadmissible as an explanation of the text
of this paragraph. He builds principally on
the account of Shun's life and death in the
'Historical Records.' It is there said :—'When
Shun was 20, he was heard of for his filial piety ;
at 30, he was promoted by Yaou ; at 50 he
undertook the administration of affairs for
Yaou, and when he was 58, Yaou died. At 61,
he took his place, and occupied the imperial
throne 39 years, after which, being on a tour
of inspection in the south, he died in the wilderness of Ts'ang-woo (蒼 梧), and was buried
at Kew-e (九 疑) of Keang-nan, in Ling-ling.'
Ling-ling is the name of a district in the pres.
dep. of Yung-chow (永 州) in Ho-nan, where
they still show, or pretend to show, the grave
of Shun. Mencius (IV. Pt. II. i.) gives another
name to the place of his death.

THE BOOKS OF YU.

BOOK II. THE COUNSELS OF THE GREAT YU.

于　海、　敷　曰　古、　曰　一節　　大禹
帝。　祗　于　文　大　若　　　　　謨
〇　承　四　命、　禹　稽

1　I. On examining into antiquity, we find that the great Yu was called Wăn-ming. Having arranged and divided *the empire*, all to the four seas, in reverent response to the *inquiries of the former* emperor,

TITLE OF THE BOOK.—大 禹 謨, 'The Counsels of the great Yu.' The Books of the Shoo have been arranged in six classes, according to the nature of their subject-matter. Of those classes the 'Counsels' form the second, containing the wise remarks and suggestions of high officers on the subject of government. In one of the Writings ascribed to K'ung Foo (孔 鮒), Confucius is made to say—'In the Counsels of the great Yu, I see the loyalty and diligence, the service and merits of Yu' (孔 叢 子, 卷 一, 論 書 篇) 謨＝謀, 'plans;' but it is implied that the plans are the result of deliberation. Heu Shin defines it 'plans of deliberation;' and his expounder adds:—'The thoughtful consideration of a subject, and the description of a plan in consequence, is what is indicated by 謨.' Yu, it has been seen in the prev. Book, was the son of K'wăn, the chief of Tsung. According to Sze-ma Ts'een, K'wăn was a son of the emp. Chuen-heuh, so that Yu was the great-great-grandson of Hwang-te. He is here called 'the Great,' 'because of the greatness of his merit' (Gan-kwŏ),—the services he rendered on occasion of the great inundations which devastated the empire.

Into the question which is agitated about the GENUINENESS of the Book I do not here enter; the reader is referred to what has been said on the subject in the *proleg.*, and to the remarks that will be found on particular passages in the annotations. The 'Counsels of Yu' were a portion of the Shoo edited by Confucius. The preface, and many references to it in other books, sufficiently prove this. It was not among the portions recovered and taught by Fuh-shang, but it was among those recovered by K'ung Gan-kwŏ. In the words of Ts'ae Chin:—'The modern text wants it; the ancient text has it' (今 文 無, 古 文 有).

CONTENTS. The Book may be divided into three chapters:—the first, embracing 8 parr., and containing various counsels of Yu and Yih on principles and methods of good govt.; the second, parr. 9–19, occupied with Shun's resigning the administration of the govt. to Yu, and cont. many sage observations and maxims; the third, parr. 20, 21, describing Yu's measures against the people of Meaou. The *style* differs from that of the Canons. It is sententious as befits the subject: and we observe in it a tendency to fall into rhythm.

CH. I. YU; HIS COUNSELS AND THOSE OF YIH ON GOVERNMENT; COMPLIMENTS BETWEEN THE EMPEROR AND THOSE MINISTERS. P. 1. *The achievement of Yu, and occasion of delivering his*

告不廢困窮惟　己從人不虐無　咸寧稽于眾舍　野無遺賢萬邦　茲嘉言罔攸伏、　○帝曰俞允若　乃乂黎民敏德。　臣克艱厥臣、政　曰后克艱厥后、

2 he said, "If the sovereign can realize the difficulty of his sovereignship, and the minister can realize the difficulty of his ministry, government will be well ordered, and the people will sedulously
3 seek to be virtuous." The emperor said, "Yes; let this really be the case, and good words will nowhere lie hidden; no men of virtue and talents will be neglected away from court; and the myriad States will all enjoy repose. *But* to ascertain the views of all; to give up one's own opinion and follow that of others; to refrain from oppressing the helpless; and not to neglect the straitened and poor:—it

counsels. 曰若稽古, 大禹曰 文命. Gan-kwŏ, followed by Ts'ae Ch'in, takes 文命 as two nouns, the subject of the verb 敷,—'his accomplished virtue and the lessons of his teaching were spread abroad to the four seas,' according to what is said in the last par. of the 'Tribute of Yu.' The commen. Soo Shih (蘇軾), or Soo Tung-po, moreover, asks to what 敷于四海 can be referred, if 文命 be taken as the name of Yu. The first words of the 'Tribute of Yu' enable us to answer the question,—禹 敷 土, 'Yu divided the land.' To the same effect, in the She-king, Pt. IV., in the 4th of the Praise-songs of Shang, we have 禹敷下土方, where 敷 is explained by 治, 'to regulate.' The meaning therefore may very well be as I have given it in the translation. 四海,—see Bk. I. p. 13. 祇(＝敬)承于帝,—'he reverently received—took it up—from the emperor.' Wang K'ang-t'ang (王肯堂, Ming dyn.) says:—'The emp. with his love of questioning and delight in excellence addressed his inquiries to his minister, who reverently responded to his sovereign, laying on him what was difficult and setting forth what was excellent.'

P. 2. *Good govt. depends on sovereign and minister not shrinking from the difficulties of their* position. Comp. Con. Ana., XII. xv. 后＝ 君, 'the sovereign,' 'ruler.' 敏, 'active,' 'alert,' here as a verb,＝'to follow earnestly.' It is better to take the char. thus, than to interpret,—'will quickly be virtuous,' though earnest endeavours will speedily attain their object.

P. 3. *Shun's response to Yu's sentiment, and disclaimer of such merit in himself.* 允＝信, 'truly.' 攸＝所; 罔攸, 'nowhere.' 'Good words will nowhere lie hidden,' *i.e.*, all capable of giving lessons of good will find their way to notice. 野, 'the wilds,' 'the fields,' ＝ away from court. 'The myriad States will enjoy repose,' being ruled and directed by the wise and good. 舍己從人,—see Men., II. Pt. I. viii. 3. 不虐無告, 不 廢困窮,—comp. in 莊子, 天道篇, —堯曰, 吾不敖無告, 不廢窮 民. It is argued that the text is forged from these passages. I cannot but draw the opposite conclusion. In the chapter of Mencius, especially, he is evidently quoting from various books, in no case specifying their names or sections; the 2d par.,—禹聞善言則拜, —is taken from the Counsels of Kaou-yaou, p. 1;—shall we say that Book of the Shoo is also forged? 惟帝時克,—the emperor is Yaou; 時＝是; Ying-tă paraphrases :—

帝時克。○益 四節

曰都乃帝德廣

運乃聖乃神

乃武乃文乃皇

天眷命奄有

四海為天下

君。○禹曰惠 五節

迪吉從逆凶

惟影響。○ 六節

曰吁戒哉微

4　was only the emperor *Yaou* who could attain to this." Yih said, "Oh! your virtue, O emperor, is vast and incessant. It is sagely, spiritual, awe-inspiring, and adorned with all accomplishments. Great Heaven regarded you with its favouring decree, and suddenly you obtained all within the four seas, and became sovereign of the empire."

5　Yu said, "Accordance with the right is good fortune; the following of evil is bad:—the shadow and the echo." Yih said,

6　"Alas! be cautious! Admonish yourself to caution, when there

惟帝堯於是能爲此行, 'it was only Yaou in these matters who could act thus.'

P. 4. *Yih repudiates Shun's disclaimer, and celebrates his virtue.* I can by no means agree with Gan-kwŏ and Ch'in, that the 帝 in 帝德 refers to Yaou. Ch'in observes, indeed, that to take 帝 as some do, as referring to Shun himself, would make the whole plain, and is in harmony with the style of 'The Counsels,' 帝 in the mouth of Shun being Yaou, but 帝 in the mouth of Shun's ministers being Shun. He decides against it, however, because in the simple honesty of those early times Yih would not have praised Shun so to his face! But this is no more than what Kaou-yaou does in this same Book, p. 12. 都,—see on Can. of Yaou, p. 3. Choo He here says that 都 meaning the capital, the place where superior men assemble, when used as an exclamation, it conveys the idea of admiration (see the 集說).

運, 'to revolve,' here = 行之不息, 'to move without ceasing.' 乃聖 乃神,—see Men. VII. Pt. II. xxv. 7, 8.

乃武乃文.—as the civil (文) always takes precedence in China of the military (武), it is thought necessary to note here that the terms are inverted from the necessity of the rhythm (note in the 集傳). 眷, 'to look round to,'—with the idea of kindly regard.

奄 is taken by Gan-kwŏ as = 同, of

which I can't make sense. Ch'in explains it by 盡, 'entirely,' 'the whole of.' The meaning which I have foll. seems more natural; and the rise of Shun might very well be thus described.

In the 呂氏春秋 十三卷 (near the end), we find a portion of this par. quoted from 'the Books of Hea.'—夏書曰, 天子之德廣運, 乃神乃武乃文. Wang Ming-shing argues that the par. of the text was made from this, the maker inserting 乃聖 before 乃神, to complete the rhythm and flow of the whole passage. But is it not more natural to suppose that Leu quotes the Classic incorrectly?

P. 5. *The certain connection between the right and happiness, between the wrong and misery.*

惠＝順, 'to follow,' 'to accord with,' as in Bk. II. p. 17. 迪, 'to advance,' 'to go forward,' and here opposed to 逆, 'going backwards,' 'rebelliousness,'＝'the right way.'

惟影響 and not 如影響 is an emphatic way of representing the truth of the two prec. statements; so, to say 'is good fortune,' rather than 'leads to good fortune' is not only a literal rendering, but is necessary to give exactly Yu's sentiment. 'We are not to look,' says Ch'in King (陳經, Sung dyn.) 'for good fortune or bad, beyond the complacency or displacency of the mind.' Yu's object by this remark was to deepen the impression of his previous observation.

P. 6. *Exhortation founded on Yu's proposition.*

吁,—see Can. of Yaou, p. 10. 儆

戒無虞罔失法度、
罔遊于逸罔淫于
樂任賢勿貳去邪
勿疑疑謀勿成百
志惟熙罔違道以
干百姓之譽罔咈
百姓以從己之欲、
無怠無荒四夷來
王。○禹曰、於帝念
哉德惟善政政在

七節

seems to be no reason for anxiety. Do not fail in due attention to the laws and ordinances. Do not find your enjoyment in indulgent ease. Do not go to excess in pleasure. In your employment of men of worth, let none come between you and them. Put away evil without hesitation. Do not try to carry out doubtful plans. Study that all your purposes may be with the light of reason. Do not go against what is right to get the praise of the people. Do not oppose the people to follow your own desires. *Attend to these things* without idleness or omission, and from the four quarters the barbarous tribes will come and acknowledge your sovereignty."

7   Yu said, "Oh! think *of these things*, O emperor. Virtue is seen in the goodness of the government, and the government is tested

(Choo He says the original read. was 敬) 戒 無 虞,—'be reverently cautious where there is no calculating,' no forecasting, *i.e.*, no occasion for anxiety. 法 度,—not only 'the laws of State and ordinances of govt.,' but all the rules for the regulation of conduct, be it even in eating and drinking (see a note in the 集 傳). 淫, 'to go beyond,'—'like water overflowing and not returning.' 貳, —'in employing men of worth, to let mean men come between you and them is called 貳' (集 傳). 百 志 惟 熙,—'your hundred movements of mind,—let them be bright.' It is observed by She Lan (時 瀾, Sung dyn.): —'The movements of the sages are accordant with reason. Whithersoever their spirits and mental exercises carry them, these are brightly intelligent and great; hence it is said 百 志 惟 熙' (集 說). 來 王,—the wild tribes outside the provinces did not come regularly to court, but every chieftain of a tribe came once, on his taking the rule, to acknowledge the

imperial supremacy; this was called 來 王. So it was in the Chow dyn. See a note by Ch'in Sze-k'ae in the 集 傳.

In a pass. in the 國 策, the clauses 任 賢 勿 貳 去 邪 勿 疑 are quoted from the Shoo in an inverted order;—a proof, it is said, that the pres. 'Counsels' is a forged compilation. But such arguments have no force. Irregular quotations from the acknowledged Books are not uncommon. The clause 無 怠 無 荒 is found in the Books of the After Han, 卷 五 十 二, near the end of the sketch of 崔 駰, only we have 殆 for 怠. But there are other passages of the classics in the same sketch, without any specific acknowled. See Maou K'e-ling and Wang Ming-shing, *in loc.*

P. 7. *Further exhortations and details by Yu on the subject of government.* Choo He observes that parr. 2—6 were all one conversation, but whether what follows was spoken at the same time cannot be known. P. 7 is gen. connected with the prec. in the manner indicated in the transl., but the 念 哉 may = 'think of

以　用　用　惟　惟　惟　利　惟　金　養
九　威　休　歌　敘　和　用　修　木　民
歌　勸　董　戒　九　九　厚　正　土　水
俾　之　之　之　敘　功　生　德　穀　火

by its nourishing of the people. There are water, fire, metal, wood, earth, and grain,—these must be duly regulated; there are the rectification of *the people*'s virtue, the conveniences of life, and the securing abundant means of sustentation,—these must be harmoniously attended to. When the nine services *thus indicated* have been orderly accomplished, let that accomplishment be celebrated by songs. Caution the people with gentle words; correct them with the majesty of *law;* stimulate them with the songs on those nine subjects,—in order that your success may never suffer diminution."

what I am now going to say.' 於 (*woo*),—as in Can. of Yaou, p. 2 德惟善政,—惟 connects the two parts of the clause; but I have spoken before of the difficulty in determining exactly the force of the particle. 'Virtue—just *is* good government;'—this is expanded in the Daily Explanations:—'Virtue does not exist ineffectively in one's own mind merely. It should be seen in the conduct of affairs, making the govt. entirely good, and then 'it is real virtue.'　Now follows a description of good govt. as consisting in the nourishment of the people,—not the bare support of their bodies, but the sustenance and development of their whole being. We must wish, however, that the description were given in plainer terms.

First, to get food for the people, water, fire, metal, wood, earth [see V. Bk. IV. 5, which purports to be part of Yu's teaching], and grain must be regulated. The grain is the principal thing here, and the result of the whole process of regulation. Fire acting on metal melts it, and metal implements may be fashioned. These act on wood, and wooden implements are made. We have now the plough, &c., to act upon the earth, and by-and-by there will be the grain. But what use of water has been made in this process? Here is a difficulty. Ch'in Sze-k'ae says, 'Water acts on fire—subdues it, makes it subservient—for cookery'!

Second, food being provided, govt. goes on to 正德,—not, as Gan-kwo would make it, the rectification by the ruler of his virtue as an example to the people, but the getting the people to be virtuous—fathers kind, sons filial, &c. To this succeeds 利用, 'the facilitating of things used,' attained by the promotion of arts and commerce; and also 厚生, 'the enrichment of living,' abundant comforts and luxuries.

These three great objects, it is said, 惟和, are to be harmonious,' to be attained by the measures appropriate to each, without any collision between them.

Third, the aid of song is to be called in, 九功,—'the nine services,' referring to the management of water, of fire, &c., and the other things just detailed. 叙 = the 修 and 和 above. 董 = 督責, 'to urge and reprove.'

In the 左傳, 文七年, we find—夏書曰,戒之用休,董之用威,勸之以九歌,俾勿壞,九功之德皆可歌也,謂之九歌,六府三事,謂之九功,水火金木土穀,謂之六府,正德利用厚生,謂之三事,義而行之,謂之德禮,云云. Here, it is said, are four clauses quoted from the Shoo, and then the author of the Chronicle gives his own explanations of their meaning, which the compiler of the present Book has taken and fashioned into part of the classic. I come to a different conclusion. There is so much quotation, and so much explanation;—and the writer of the 左傳 is fond of such a style. But the explanation would be absurd, if it were not founded on other passages of the Classic. To my mind the 左傳 testifies to the whole of this paragraph and the next.

種德德乃降黎民
克民不依皋陶邁
師。○禹曰、朕德罔
勤、汝惟不怠、總朕
有三載耄期倦于
禹朕宅帝位三十
乃功。○帝曰、格汝
允治萬世永賴時
平天成六府三事
勿壞。○帝曰、俞、地

8　The emperor said, "Yes. The earth is *now* reduced to order, and *the influences of* heaven operate with effect; those six magazines and three businesses are all truly regulated, so that a myriad generations may perpetually depend on them:—this is your merit."

9　II. The emperor said, "Come, you, Yu. I have occupied the imperial throne for thirty and three years. I am between ninety and a hundred years old, and the laborious duties weary me. Do

10　you, eschewing all indolence, take the leadership of my people." Yu said, "My virtue is not equal *to the position;* the people will not repose in me. *But there is* Kaou-yaou, with vigorous activity sowing

P. 8. *Complimentary response of Shun.* Yu has urged Shun to a certain style of govt., and Shun responds that the possibility of its realization was all owing to him. 地平,— this refers to Yu's labours on the inundated provinces. 天成,—'Heaven completes.' The meaning is that there could now be seed-time and harvest. Gan-kwŏ foolishly says'— 五行序曰成, 'the five elements acting in order is what is called 成'; and Ying-tă more foolishly expands the 'five elements' into the spirits of the five elements' (五行之神). We find this sentence quoted as from the 'Books of Hea' in the 左傳, 僖二十四年. 六府,—'six treasuries' (see Con. Ana. XI. xiii). Those are the water, fire, &c., of the prec. par., the six treasuries' or magazines of nature. 三事,—three businesses,' *i.e.,* the rectification of the people's virtue, &c. 時=是, 'this.' 乃=汝 'you.' This par. prepares the way for the proposal in the next. CH. II. YU IS CALLED TO ACT AS SHUN'S VICEGERENT, AND IS OBLIGED UNWILLINGLY TO ACCEPT THE DIGNITY. P. 9. *Shun on the ground of his age requests Yu to relieve him of the*

toils of government. Ninety years of age is called 耄; a century, 期. Shun describing himself by both the terms, we are to understand that he was between 90 and 100, which, indeed, must have been the case after he had been on the throne 33 years. 倦于勤,—Leu Tsoo-hëem (呂祖謙, Sung dyn.) says, 止倦於勤而已, 非倦於道. This is exactly our distinction ;—'weary *in* the service, not weary *of* it.' 總朕師,—'gather together' (=take the lead of) 'my multitudes' (including both ministers and people). The language differs from that of Yaou to Shun —汝陟帝位, Bk. I. p. 3, because Yaou wished then to resign the throne altogether.

P. 10. *Yu wishes to decline the proposal in favour of Kaou-yaou.* 邁種德—邁 = 勤, giving 'the idea of bold movement and strong action;' 種德 is 'to sow virtue,' to exhibit it so as to awaken responsive feeling in others. 念茲在茲,—in transl. these difficult sentences I have followed the view given of them in the 集傳. A difft. view was taken by Gan-kwŏ:—'If you would think of this (= any) man (*i.e.,* to employ him), it must be on the ground of this (= some)

予治刑期于無　以弼五教期于　作士明于五刑、　罔或干予正、汝　皐陶惟兹臣庶、　帝念功。○帝曰、（十一節）　允出兹在兹惟　兹名言兹在兹、　兹在兹、釋兹在　懷之、帝念哉念

abroad his virtue, which has descended on the black-haired people, till they cherish him in their hearts. O emperor, think of him! When I think of him, my mind rests on him, *as the man for this office;* when I would put him out of my thoughts, they still rest on him; when I name and speak of him, my mind rests on him *for this;* the sincere outgoing of my thoughts about him is that he is the man. O emperor, think of his merits!"

11　　The emperor said, "Kaou-yaou, that of these my ministers and people, hardly one is found to offend against the regulations of my government, is owing to your being the minister of Crime, and intelligent in the use of the five punishments to assist the *inculcation of the* five duties, with a view to the perfection of my government, and

merit; if you would not employ him, it must be on the ground of some fault.' As to his expl. of the next clauses, I can really not get hold of it with sufficient definiteness to attempt to describe it. The whole passage from 念兹 to the end is found quoted in the 左傳, 襄 二十一年, and an explanation of it different both from Gan-kwŏ's and from Ch'in's, but so vague that I cannot adopt it.

The words of the par., 皐陶邁種 德, 德乃降, are also found in the 左 傳, 莊 八年, and it is argued that this portion of the pres. 'Counsels of Yu' was evidently plagiarized from that place. We have Too Yu's (杜預, Tsin dyn.) commentary on the 左傳, acc. to which the words of the Shoo King are only 皐陶邁種德, and the 德乃降 are an observation of duke Chwang. Here, it is said, the ignorance of the forger has betrayed him. He found a quotation from the Shoo, and he incorporated it with his compilation, but he incorporated with it what was not a portion of the Shoo. But it may be that it was Too Yu who was in error here. He had not seen the 'old text' of Gan-kwŏ; he had not seen our present Book; and from his own reading of the 左傳 he supposed the quotation from the Shoo terminated at 德, and not at 降. From a study of the 傳, I am persuaded he was in error. Looking at the whole passage where the quotation occurs, I conclude that 德乃降 is a portion of the 'Books of Hea,' whether 降 be read *hèarg,* or *këang,* about which there is some unnecessary dispute.

Parr. 11—13. *Shun, not listening to Yu's recommendation of Kaou-yaou to be his vicegerent, yet praises the latter for his merits as minister of Crime. Kaou-yaou disclaims the merit, and attributes it to the emperor.*　11. 罔或干予正, —罔或, 'none, perhaps,' = our 'hardly any'; 干=犯, 'to offend against,' diff. from its use in p. 6; 正 is by Ying-tǎ expounded 正道, 'right ways,' but it is better with Ch'in to make it = 政, 'government,' 'regulations of govt.'　期, in both instances, has the force of 'aiming at.' The 集傳 defines well:—期先事取必之謂, 'anticipating the issue beforehand.' Gan-kwŏ

刑.民協于中時乃功、
懋哉。○皐陶曰、帝德 十二節
罔愆臨下以簡御眾
以寬罰弗及嗣賞延
于世宥過無大刑故
無小罪疑惟輕功疑
惟重與其殺不辜寧
失不經好生之德洽
于民心兹用不犯于 十三節
有司。○帝曰俾予從

that through punishment there may come to be no punishments, but the people accord with the *path of the* Mean.　*Continue to* be strenu-

12 ous."　Kaou-yaou said, "Your virtue, O emperor, is faultless.　You condescend to your ministers with a liberal ease; you preside over the multitude with a generous forbearance.　Punishments do not extend to the criminal's heirs; while rewards reach to after generations.　You pardon inadvertent faults, however great; and punish purposed crimes, however small.　In cases of doubtful crimes, you deal with them lightly; in cases of doubtful merit, you prefer the high estimation.　Rather than put to death an innocent person, you will run the risk of irregularity and error.　This life-loving virtue has penetrated the minds of the people, and this is why they do not render themselves liable to be punished by your

13 officers."　The emperor said, "To enable me to follow after and

badly takes it in the first case as = 當 期 于 予 治,'—'aiming at my govt.'　The 治 is in the 3d tone, with an intensive meaning, as in the transl.　民協于中,—Wang Ming-shing quotes from the 韓詩外傳:—聽獄執中者,皐陶也,故曰民協于中.　時乃功,—as in p. 8.　12. 臨 and 御 are both terms of imperial application.　'When a superior visits an inferior, 臨 designates the act'; 'wherever the son of Heaven stops is called 御' (see the Dict.).　The diff. between them is indicated by the employment of them in the text. 臨 describ. Shun in his relation to his ministers (下), and 御 in his relation to the peo-

ple.　嗣 and 世 are here synonyms, = 子孫, 'descendants.'　過 is equal to 眚, Bk. p. 11; 故 is crimes done 'on purpose.'　失不經,—'to fail by being not regular,' not according to the standard.　兹用 = 所以, 'therefore,' 'it is hereby that.' 有司,—'the officers,' 'an official;' see Ana. XX. ii 3, *et al.*　I cannot but think that Kaou Yaou intended himself by the phrase, and feel inclined to translate:—'this is why they do not render themselves liable to be punished by *me, who am but an officer.*'　In the 左傳, 襄二十六年, we find quoted from the 'Books of Hea'—與其殺不辜,寧失不經.　13. Shun reiterates his sense of Kaou-yaou's merits. 惟

功予懋乃德嘉乃　伐天下莫與汝爭　與汝爭能汝惟不　汝惟不矜天下莫　不自滿假惟汝賢　勤于邦克儉于家　允成功惟汝賢克　來禹洚水儆予成　惟乃之休。○帝曰，十四節　欲以治四方風動

obtain what I desire in my government, the people everywhere responding as if moved by the wind;—this is your excellence."

14   The emperor said, "Come, Yu. The inundating waters filled me with dread, when you realized all that you represented, and accomplished your task,—thus showing your superiority to other men. Full of toilsome earnestness in the service of the State, and sparing in your expenditure on your family; and this without being full of yourself or elated; you *again* show your superiority to other men. Without any prideful presumption, there is no one in the empire to contest with you the palm of ability; without any boasting, there is no one in the empire to contest with you the claim of me-

乃之休,—乃=汝; 休=美, 'excellence.' In the Works of the philosopher Seun, 大畧篇, we find the first part of this par. with a slight change. He says—舜曰，維子從欲而治.

Parr. 14–19. *Shun returns to insist on Yu's becoming his vicegerent; delivers various admonitions to him; disallows his repeated attempt to decline the dignity; and finally Yu undertakes the government.* 14. 來禹, 洚水儆予,—see in Men. III. Pt. II. ix. 3, 書曰洚水警余. Ts'ae Ch'in says the old text read 降; and according to that char., Gankwŏ explains—'the waters flowing down.' No doubt the text of Mencius has prevailed to change 降 into 洚. 成允成功 is literally—'you accomplished sincerity, you accomplished merit.' I have translated according to the expansion of the meaning in the 集傳. There can be no doubt that by the 'merit' which Yu accomplished is intended his management of the inundating waters. The passage is quoted in the 左傳 襄六年

and explained in harmony with the case which it is adduced to illustrate :—'when one's good faith is established, he can accomplish his services.' 汝賢=汝賢於人, 'you are superior to, you surpass others;' see this meaning of 賢 in Ana. XI. xv., et al. 克勤于邦, 克儉于家,—comp. Ana. VIII. xxi. 假,—in the sense of 大, 'great.' 自假,—'making one's-self great,' being elated. 矜 is defined 自賢, 'making one's-self superior,' and 伐 自功, 'arrogating to one's-self merit.' There is something like the four clauses beginning 汝惟不矜 in Seun's 君子篇, and also in Laou-tsze's 道德經; but we need not assume that the pres. text was compiled from those passages. 懋 is properly 'to urge,' it may be to urge another, or to exert one's-self, and Ying-tă makes the meaning here—'I urge your virtue.' But this is quite unsuitable, and hence Choo He says that 懋 and 楙 were anciently interchanged, and so understands it in

丕
績
天

之
曆
數

在
汝
躬、

汝
終
陟

元
后。
○

人
心
惟

危
道
心

惟
微、
惟

精
惟
一、

允
執
厥

（十五節）

rit. I see how great is your virtue, how admirable your vast achievements.　The determinate appointment of Heaven rests on your person; you must eventually ascend *the throne of* the great sovereign.

15 The mind of man is restless,—prone *to err*; its affinity for the *right*
way is small.　Be discriminating, be undivided, that you may sin-

the sense of 'great,' 'to consider great.'　天
之 曆 數 在 汝 躬,—see Con. Ana.,
XX. i. 1, where this and other parts of the pres.
parr. are given as having been spoken by Yaou
to Shun, though it is added that Shun used the
same language in giving charge to Yu.　　15.
Warning on the proneness of man to err.
Medhurst translates the first two clauses:—
'The carnal mind is treacherous, while the
virtuous feeling exists only in a small degree.'
Gaubil says:—'The heart of man is full of
shoals (*ecueils*); the heart of Taou is simple and
thin (*delie*)'; and adds in a note:—'The heart of
man is here opposed to that of Taou.　The
discourse is of two hearts,—one disengaged (?)
from passions, the other simple and very pure.
Taou expresses the right reason.　It is very
natural to think that the idea of a God, pure,
simple, and Lord of men, is the source of these
words.'　Neither translation is good, and the
note is altogether fanciful.　The first clause
does, indeed, suggest to a Christian reader of the
classic what is said in the New Testament of
the 'carnal mind;' but that phrase is not the
correspondency of 人 心. 危, moreover, is
not 'treacherous,' but 'insecure,' 'tottering,'
'threatening to fall.'　When the statement in
this clause is taken in connection with that in
the next, we have the idea of 'the carnal mind.'
道 心 is, indeed, a difft. expression; and we
seem to want in 道 some entity or being corresponding to 人.　But that cannot be.　The
道 心 is still the 人 心, the mind of man
in its relation to the path of duty.　The two
clauses together tell us very truly that the mind
of man, uncertain, unstable in what is good, is
ever more likely, without a careful self-government, to fall into the way of evil.

Ying-tǎ, in paraphrasing Gan-kwǒ, seems to
take 人 as == 民, as if Shun were cautioning
Yu only about the proclivities of the *people*.
But the term is of universal application.　Choo
He and other philosophers of the Sung dyn.
have written much on this text.　One of the
scholars Ch'ing says:—'The heart of man which
is restless denotes the desires of man; the reason
to which it has little affinity is heavenly prin-

ciple' (集 說).　Choo He says:—'The mouth,
the nose, the ears, the eyes, and four limbs all
belong to one's own body; they are the things
which are of one's self, and are not like the conviction of right and duty (道), which belongs to
one with all others.　Thus we have at once the
root of selfishness, and there is a proneness to
it moreover; yet this is not in itself bad;—it is
only the root of what is bad.'　'Take what is
here called the 人 心, and regulate and
control (收 之) it, and you have the 道 心;
take the 道 心, and leave it uncared for (放
之), and you have the 人 心.'　Putting the
question, whether it could be said of the mind
of the sages, that it was also restless and prone
to err, he replies that the affinity for the right
in them completely predominated so as to rule
the other.　(See the 集 說).　　惟 精
惟 一,—these denote the exercise of mind and
force of will by which the 人 心 can be kept
from disturbing the 道 心, and there will
result in practice the strict adherence to the
Mean,—the course which neither exceeds nor
comes short of what is right.

允 執 厥 中 is found in the Con. Ana.,
XX. i. 1.　The rest of the par., it is said, was
made up in the time of the Tsin dyn. by Mei
Tsih from Seun K'ing's 解 蔽 篇.　We
certainly find there, and quoted as from 道 經,
the passages 人 心 之 危 道 心 之
微.　There is also much in the context about
being 精 於 道, and 一 於 道.　Seun
K'ing has written nothing which he was not
likely to do, if he had the Shoo with this passage
in his mind.　And, on the other hand, it must
be allowed that a forger might have compiled
the first three clauses of the par. from him.　His
quoting from the 道 經 can hardly be said
to be decisive in the question, for as we refer
to the Bible often as 'The word of Truth,'
'The book of Truth,' the phrase in question

可願四海困　有位敬修其　邦欽哉慎乃　非衆罔與守　元后何戴后非　畏非民衆非　可愛非君可　之謀勿庸。○　言勿聽弗詢。　中。○無稽之

十七節　　　十六節

16 cerely hold fast the Mean.　Do not listen to unsubstantiated words;
17 do not follow undeliberated plans.　Of all who are to be loved, is
not the sovereign the chief?　Of all who are to be feared, are not the
people the chief?　If the multitude were *without* the sovereign, whom
should they sustain aloft?　If the sovereign had not the multitude,
there would be none to guard the country for him.　Be reverent.
Carefully demean yourself on the throne which you will occupy,
respectfully cultivating *the virtues* which are to be desired in you.
If within the four seas there be distress and poverty, your Heaven-

may denote the Shoo under a similar designation. One thing is certain,—the sentences were put together before the time of Mei Tsih, for **Ma Yung** in his 忠經 quoted—惟精惟一, 允執厥中 (see the 尚書冤詞, *in loc.*). He who has found reason to accept these 'Counsels' as genuine on other grounds will not have his faith disturbed by the difficulties connected with this passage.

It has been impugned not only on the critical grounds which I have indicated, but as containing heretical doctrine. Wang Ch'ung-yun (王充耘) of the Yuen dyn., and Mei Tsuh (梅鷟) of the Ming, especially, have contended that the idea of human nature which it gives is quite contrary to the orthodox truth; but even Ming-shing condemns them for being carried so far by their detestation of Mei Tsih.

16. *An admonition to prudence and caution in counsel and action.* 稽=考證, 'to examine and attest.' 'Unsubstantiated words' are counsels for which no precedents can be adduced. 'Undeliberated plans' are plans that have not been submitted for general consideration. 庸=用.

The 正名篇 of Seun K'ing concludes with a sentence which would seem to have been suggested by this paragraph:—無稽之言, 不見之行, 不聞之謀, 君子慎之.

17. *Shun intimates his determined purpose that Yu should undertake the duties of the govt., and impresses on him various important considerations.*

The first clause, 可愛非君, and the next are to be taken interrogatively. The 日講 gives them;—民所可愛, 豈非君乎, 君所可畏, 豈非民乎. Comp. a somewhat similar construction in Mencius, II. Pt. I. ii. 22, *et al.* 元后, —as in p. 14.; 元=大, 'great.' We find the clauses—衆非元后, 何戴, 后非衆, 無與守邦, quoted from the 'Books of Hea,' in the 國語, 周語, 上. 戴,—' to carry on the head ;' and thence, 'to respect,' 'to honour.' 慎乃有位. I take as =慎汝將有之位, and the next clause also as addressed to Yu in his own person. 可願 is very much the same as 可欲 in Men., VII. Pt. II., xxv. 3. 四海困窮, 天祿永終,—see Ana. XX, i. 1. I have adhered to the translation of this sentence which I gave in the Analects. Gan-kwŏ takes quite a different view of it. 'By 困窮,' he says, 'are intended the sufferers of distress through the empire, who have none to appeal to. Let the emperor cultivate the virtues appropriate to him, and care for these, and the possession of the throne will abide for ever in his person' (天之祿籍, 長終汝身). Maou K'e-ling shews that previous to the time of the 'Eastern Tsin' this was the

首　卜　神　先　昆　禹　臣　再　出　窮
固　不　其　定　命　官　惟　○　好　天
辭　習　依　詢　于　占　吉　禹　興　祿
帝　吉　龜　謀　元　惟　之　曰　戎　永
曰　禹　筮　僉　龜　先　從　枚　朕　終
毋　拜　協　同　朕　蔽　帝　卜　言　惟
惟　稽　從　鬼　志　志　曰　功　不　口

conferred revenues will come to a perpetual end. It is the mouth
which sends forth what is good, and gives rise to war. My words
I will not repeat."

18   Yu said, "Submit the meritorious ministers one by one to the
trial of divination, and let the fortunate indication be followed."
The emperor said, "Yu, the officer of divination, when the mind
has been made up on a subject, then refers it to the great tortoise.
Now, in this matter, my mind was determined in the first place. I
consulted and deliberated with all *my ministers and people*, and they
were of one accord with me. The spirits signified their assent, the
tortoise and grass having both concurred. Divination, when fortunate, may not be repeated." Yu did obeisance, with his head to
the ground, and firmly declined the throne. The emperor said, "Do

received interpretation of the language while
that which I have followed (and which is much
more likely and natural) prevailed from that
time; and he argues that if the commentary of
Gan-kwŏ were indeed a forgery of Mei Tsih he
would not have given the explanation which
had by his time gone into disuse. 惟口
出好興戎,—see 墨子, 尚同, 中.
Mih quotes the words as from 'The Books of
the former Kings,' a usual formula with him
when quoting from the Shoo King. It is not
easy to trace what connection the truth declared
in them has with the other remark of Shun.
    18, 19. *Yu, still wishing to decline, and to have
his appointment submitted to the trial of divination,
is overruled by Shun, and finally enters on the duties
of the administration.* 枚卜功臣,—
枚, 'the stalk of a plant;' used also for a tally
in reckoning things. From this comes its
use in the text—枚卜, 'one by one divine
about.' 卜,—'to divine;' properly, by
means of the tortoise. Here it would seem, to
sig. 'to divine generally,' including both the 龜

and 筮 below. 官占,一占, composed
of 卜 and 口, indicates the answer supposed
to be returned to the divination. 官占 was
the officer who determined this. 蔽—in
the sense of 斷, 'to determine.' 昆—in
the sense of 後, 'afterwards.' Wang Shih-
p'ǎng (王十朋, Sung dyn.) observes, 'The
ancients understood 昆 as the elder brother;
he is after the father:—hence the character is
explained by 後.' 命于元龜, Ts'ae
Ch'in and others explain 命 by 令. He says
令之于龜, 'charges it to the tortoise.'
This I do not well understand. Whatever we
make of the 命, the general meaning is evidently that given in the transl. We find the whole
sentence, with the alteration of one character,
quoted from the Books of Hea, in the 左傳,
哀十八年,—夏書曰, 官占惟
能蔽志; 昆命于元龜 朕

道敗德君子在野、
不恭侮慢自賢反
命蠢茲有苗昏迷
濟濟有眾咸聽朕
會群后誓于師曰、
弗率汝祖征。禹乃
曰咨禹惟時有苗
官若帝之初。○帝（廿節）
受命于神宗、率百
汝諧。○正月朔旦、（十九節）

19 not do so. It is you who can suitably *occupy my place.*" On the
first morning of the first month, *Yu* received the appointment in the
temple of the spiritual Ancestor, and took the leading of all the
officers, as had been done at the commencement of the emperor's
government.

20   III. The emperor said, "Alas! O Yu, there is only the prince of
the Meaou, who refuses obedience;—do you go and correct him."
Yu on this assembled all the princes, and made a speech to the host,
saying, "Ye multitudes, listen all to my orders. Stupid is this
prince of Meaou, ignorant, erring, and disrespectful. Despite-
ful and insolent to others, he thinks that all ability and virtue are
with himself. A rebel to the right, he destroys *all the obligations*

志先定, 詢謀僉同, 鬼神其
依, 龜筮協從, 卜不習志,—see
on Pt. V. Bk. IV., pp. 20–31. It is observed by
Chin Tih-sew (眞德秀), that we have
here the first occurrence in the classics of the
phrase 鬼神.   19. 神宗 is explained
by Ts'ae Ch'in, as being 'the ancestral temple
of Yaou.' But this would be contrary to all
analogy. Shun received this appointment in
the temple of Yaou's ancestors, and Yu would
receive his in the temple of Shun's ancestors.
That Shun had established such a temple appears
from Confucius' words, Doct. of the Mean, xvii.
1. Ch'in was led into the error by misunderstanding a passage in the 禮記, 祭法,
where Shun is spoken of as having 宗 ed
Yaou;—see Maou's 尙書廣聽錄, *in loc.*
    This accession of Yu to the administration
took place B.C. 2222.
    CH. III. YU UNDERTAKES AN EXPEDITION A-
GAINST THE MEAOUITES; ITS CONDUCT AND RE-
SULTS.   P. 20. *Yu, being charged to act.*
against the prince of Meaou, assembles his host, and
makes a speech to it. 惟旹 (= 是) 有苗

弗率.—有苗 = 有苗之君; such is
generally the force of 有 before the name of a
country throughout the Shoo. We might render
the charr. literally—'the possessor of Meaou.'
率 is here = 遵 or 循, 'to honour' 'to be
obedient.'   It has been said that as Shun
had twice dealt with the Meaouites (see Bk. I.,
pp. 12 and 27), there was nothing left for Yu
to do with them. But there is no one chapter,
perhaps, in the Shoo King which is so abundantly corroborated by citations from it and
references to it in books of the Chow and Han
dynn. as the present;—see the 後案, *in loc.*
The prince of Meaou against whom he proceeded
would not be the one whom Shun banished to
San-wei, but some chieftain of the whole or a
portion of the tribe who had been left in their
native Seat. That Yaou, Shun, and Yu were
all obliged to take active measures against them
only shows the restlessness of the people, and
the difficulty which those sage emperors had in
establishing their sway over the country.
誓于師,—'made a speech to the host.'
This is the proper meaning of 誓, throughout
the Shoo. Formed from 折 and 言, 'to

小人在位民棄不

保天降之咎肆予

以爾眾士奉辭伐

罪爾尚一乃心力

其克有勳。○三句。

苗民逆命益贊于

禹曰惟德動天無

遠弗屆滿招損謙

受益時乃天道帝

廿一節

of virtue. Superior men are kept by him in obscurity, and mean men fill all the offices. The people reject and will not protect him. Heaven is sending calamities down upon him. On this account I have assembled you, my multitude of gallant men, and bear the instructions *of the emperor* to punish his crimes. Do you proceed with united heart and strength, so shall our enterprize be crowned with success."

21   At the end of three decades, the people of Meaou continued rebellious against *the emperor's* commands, when Yih came to the help of Yu, saying, "It is virtue which moves Heaven; there is no distance to which it does not reach. Pride brings loss, and humility receives increase:—this is the way of Heaven. In the early time of the

decide' by 'words,' it often = 'an oath;' but in the classic its application is to the solemn charge laid upon his soldiers by a general, a speech delivered to a host. It is said in the 禮記, 檀弓下, p. 11, that 誓 were first made in the time of the Yin or Shang dyn.; but incorrectly, as the present instance is sufficient to show. The speech of Yu is given by Mih Teih, with some omissions and alterations, in the last part of his chapter on 'Universal Love.' 濟 濟 is given in the Dict. as meaning 'the appearance of multitudes' (眾盛之貌), to which Ts'ae Ch'in would add, 'and of marshalled order.' 有眾 simply = 爾眾. This use of 有, in sententious, half rhythmical passages, is not uncommon. 蠢, from 'summer' and 'insects,' signifies 'insects moving about,' brought to all their activity by the summer heat. 'To be insubordinate,' and 'to be stupid,' are secondary significations. It is here a term of contempt, applied to the chief of Meaou, buzzing, heedless, as an insect. 咎 = 災, 'calamities';—this is the meaning given

to the character in the 說文. 奉辭 = 奉帝之辭 'bear the words—instructions—of the emperor.' 爾尚一乃 (= 汝)心力,—尚 is defined in the Dict., and by Ts'ae, as = 庶幾. It has the force of exhortation and entreaty. Hing Ping (邢昺) says, 'it indicates the hope of the mind' (謂心所希望). 其克有勳,—其, 'this,' *i.e.,* such union and energy being realized.   21. 苗民逆命,—Ts'ae explains, 苗頑猶不聽服, 'the *prince of* Meaou obstinately still refused to submit.' The most natural conclusion is that Yu's expedition was unsuccessful, and that the people of Meaou were too strong for him. 益贊, —Yih assisted Yu when labouring to regulate the waters. Here we find him also in Meaou. Afterwards he was his chief minister. There seems to have been a peculiar intimacy between the two. 贊 = 佐 or 助, 'to assist.' 時乃天道,—時 = 是, 'this.'

七德振拜感慄載父日初
旬舞旅昌神瞽母號于
有干帝言矧亦瞽負泣歷
苗于乃曰茲允瞍罪于山
格羽誕俞有若夔引旻往
○于敷班苗至夔慝天于
兩文師禹誠齊祗于田
階振神齊載

emperor, when he was living by mount Leih, he went into the fields,
and daily cried with tears to compassionate Heaven, and to his parents, taking to himself and bearing all guilt and evil. *At the same
time*, with respectful service, he appeared before Koo-sow, looking
grave and awe-struck, till Koo also became truly transformed by his
example. Entire sincerity moves spiritual beings;—how much more
will it move this prince of Meaou!" Yu did homage to the excellent words and said, "Yes." *Thereupon* he led back his army, having drawn off the troops. The emperor *also* set about diffusing his
accomplishments and virtue more widely. They danced with shields
and feathers between the two staircases *of the court*. In seventy days
the prince of Meaou came to make his submission.

帝初于歷山,—the 初 here is
always referred to Shun's early life, before he
was taken notice of by Yaou. The 日講
here expands it—帝微賤之初,曾
耕于歷山, 'early in the emperor's life,
when he was in a low and private station, he
ploughed upon mount Leih.' In opposition to
this, however, Mencius says the weeping and
crying to heaven and his parents took place
when Shun was 50 years old. See Men. V. Pt.
I. i. 5. There is no way of reconciling these representations. Mount Leih is referred to a
hill, 30 le south of P'oo-chow (蒲州), dep. of
P'ing-yang (平陽), in Shan-se.   號
泣于旻天,于父母,—see Men., *loc
cit.*, p. 1.   祗載見… 允若,—see Men.
V. Pt. I. iv. 4. The 日講 expl. 祗載 by
敬修爲子之事, 'he reverently per-
formed the service of a son.' In Men. I translated 允若 by 'believed him and conformed to virtue,' but parag. 3 may satisfy us that
允 is to be taken adverbially.   禹拜

昌言,—see Men. II. Pt. I. viii. 2.   班
師振旅,—Ts'ae and others take 振 in the
sense of 整, 'to adjust,' 'to trim,' and make
the whole equal to 'he withdrew his army in
good order.' Ts'ae gives also another view,
without disapproving of it, according to which
班師 intimates the quitting Meaou, and 振
旅 describes what was done on their re-entering
the capital. We find the phrase 振旅, however, in the She King, Pt. II., Bk. III., iv., st.
3, where it means 'to draw off the troops.' With
reference to that passage, the Dict. explains it
by 止, and so I have translated it here.
文德 is explained by Ts'ae Ch'in by 文
命德教. I have a persuasion myself that
the best translation would be—'the virtues
of peace,' 文 being used in opposition to 武.
War had been tried, and found ineffectual; they
would now see what effect would be produced
by an exemplification of the blessings of *peace*.
舞干羽于兩階,—see on Ana.
III. i. The 舞 was more a posture-making

than what we call *dancing*. 于兩階＝ 于兩階之間, 'between the two staircases,' that appropriated to the sovereign as host, and that employed by his guests. The expression ＝ the 於庭 of the Analects. The shield was a weapon of war appropriate to a war-dance. On this occasion Shun wanted by this exhibition in the court to show how he disliked war. And the consequences, we are told, justified Yih's advice. The prince of Meaou came and made his submission.————From the whole of this 3d. chapter, I conclude that Yu's expedition against Meaou was unsuccessful. He had to retreat. The advice of Yih, with the subsequent measures, and their result, serve merely to gloss over the real fact.

THE BOOKS OF YU.

BOOK III. THE COUNSELS OF KAOU-YAOU.

如　禹　明　厥　曰、　古　曰一節　皋
何。　曰、　弼　德　允　皋　若　陶
皋　俞、　諧。　謨　迪　陶　稽　謨

1　I. On examining into antiquity, we find that Kaou-yaou said,
"If *a sovereign* sincerely pursue the course of his virtue, the counsels *offered to him* will be intelligent, and the aids *of admonition* will
be harmonious." Yu said, "Yes; but explain yourself." Kaou-yaou

TITLE OF THE BOOK.—皋陶 (Yaou) 謨,
'The Counsels of Kaou-yaou.' 'Counsels,'—see
on the title of the last Book.　　Kaou-yaou
was minister of Crime to Shun (Bk. I., p. 20).
Tsze-hea has recorded his merit, saying, 'Shun,
being in possession of the empire, selected from
among all *the officers* and employed Kaou-yaou,
on which all who were devoid of virtue disappeared' (Ana. XII. xxii. 6). There are few or
no reliable details of his history. In the 左
傳 he appears with the style of T'ing-këen
(字庭堅), one of the 'eight able sons'
(才子八人) of the emp. Chuen-heuh;
and Wang P'oo-meih (皇甫謐), of the Tsin
dyn., says, in his 帝王世紀, that Kaou-
yaou was born in K'euh-fow (曲阜, still the
name of a district in Yen-chow dep. [兗州],
Shan-tung), in the country of Yen (偃), whence
he was surnamed Yen. Sze-ma Ts'een in his
Record of the sovereigns of Hea (夏本記
二), says that Yu, on his accession to the throne,
made Kaou-yaou his chief minister, with the
view of his ultimately succeeding him, but the
design was frustrated by Kaou-yaou's death,
and that then his son was appointed to the principality of Ying-luh (英六, in the prov.
of Gan-hwuy. We have still the dis. of 英
山, in the dep. of 六安), which was extinguished under the Chow dyn., by the power of
Ts'oo (楚), and an end was made of the representatives of Kaou-yaou. See a note on
Kaou-yaou in the 四書經註集證,
Ana. XII. xxii.　　There is still a clan of the
surname Kaou which traces its origin to Kaou-
yaou (see the 氏姓譜, 皋氏); but Kaou
and yaou are to be taken together as the minister's name.

CONTENTS. The Book is found in the texts
both of Fuh-shang and K'ung Gan-kwŏ, so that
there is no question of its genuineness. I have
divided it into four chapters. The first, pp. 1,
2, enunciates the principle that in govt. the
great thing is for the prince to pursue the
course of his virtue, which will be seen in his
knowledge of men, and giving repose to the
people. The second chap., pp. 3—5, is designed

陶曰、都　慎厥身、　修思永、　惇敍九　族庶明、　勵翼邇　可遠在　兹。禹拜　昌言禹　俞。○皇二節　曰、

said, "Oh! let him be careful about his personal cultivation, with thoughts that are far-reaching, and then he will effect a generous kindness and nice observance of distinctions among the nine classes of his kindred; all the intelligent *also* will exert themselves in his service; and from what is near he may reach in this way to what is distant." Yu did reverence to the admirable words, and said,

to illustrate the former of these things,—the knowledge of men; and the third, pp. 6, 7, treats of the repose of the people. In the fourth chap., p. 8, Kaou asserts the reasonableness of his words, and humbly expresses his own desire to be helpful.

CH. I. THE DUTY OF A SOVEREIGN TO BE TRULY VIRTUOUS; ITS HAPPY EFFECTS; ITS NATURE; ITS GRAND EVIDENCES; AND ITS DIFFICULTY.   1. *Kaou-yaou and Yu on the nature and consequences of a sovereign's course of virtue.* 日若稽古,—see on the 1st par. of the previous Books. Those who would accept K'ang-shing's expl. of 稽古, as applied to Yaou, allow that it is not admissible as applied to the minister; and they say that we must not obstinately think that the same words have always the same meaning in the classics (不可泥于一說, Keang Shing)! When we go on to the next clause—皇陶曰允 德云云, however, we cannot explain according to the analogy of the corresponding passages. Tung-po asks—'Will those who take Fang-heun, Ch'ung-hwa, and Wăn-ming, as the names of Yaou, Shun, and Yu, say that Yun-teih (允迪) was the name of Kaou-yaou'? This certainly cannot be said, but we are in no better case if we take Fang-heun and the other expressions as descriptive epithets. *Yun-teih* is neither the name of Kaou-yaou, nor any honourable description of his doings or character. In whatever way we interpret the passages in the other Books, 皇陶 (or, as Keang Shing and others edit, 咎繇) 曰 must be translated, 'Kaou-yaou said.'   允迪厥德謨 明弼諧,—it is not easy to understand this passage. In the 'Historical Records' it appears as—信其道德, 謀明輔和, 'Believing his path *of duty* and virtue, his plans will be intelligent and his aids harmonious,' 允 being taken as an active verb, = 信, and 迪 = 道, as in the last Book, p. 5. Keang Shing and Sun Yen adopt the same view. But

if this were the correct view, we should have read—允厥迪德. All suppose, it will be seen, that Kaou-yaou is speaking of *the sovereign*.   Gan-kwŏ takes 迪 as = 蹈, 'to tread on,' 'to walk,' so that 迪德 = 'to pursue the course of virtue.' He takes a peculiar view, however, of 厥, which is with him not = 'his,' but 'their,' and 厥德 is 'the virtue of the ancients;' and he expounds the whole:—'A sovereign ought sincerely to tread the path of the virtue of the ancients, planning how to enlarge his intelligence in order to assist and harmonize his govt.'   Woo Ch'ing has a view of his own, and takes 允迪厥德 as descriptive of a minister's duty to his sovereign. He defines 迪 by 導, 'to lead forward,' and 明 by 明哲之人, 'intelligent men.' His expos. is:—'The duty of ministers to their sovereign is truly and really to stimulate and promote his virtue. In taking their counsels, he must strive that he have the intelligent to assist him, and must harmonize them.'   None of these interpretations is satisfactory, and unable to suggest one more so, I have followed in the transl. the view of Ts'ae Ch'in, who expounds:—' If the sovereign really pursue the course of his virtue, what his ministers counsel will be intelligent, and wherein they would aid him, they will be harmonious.'

This agrees better with what is said in the sequel, though it has its difficulties. An ingenious note by Wang Kăng-t'ang (王肯 堂; Ming dyn.) is given in the 集傳; —謨 indicates the setting forth of counsels and 弼, the exercise of correction. 謨 and 弼 belong to the ministers; 明 and 諧, to the sovereign. When they offer counsels on occasion of occurring affairs, he can understand their mind, without any doubts; when they differ from him and offer admonitions, he can harmonize with their words, and not put himself against them.' This is ingenious, but too refined. While approving of Kaou's words, Yu

陶曰、都、在知人、在
安民。禹曰、吁、咸若
時、惟帝其難之、知
人則哲能官人、安
民則惠黎民懷之
能哲而惠何憂乎
驩兜何遷乎有苗、
何畏乎巧言令色
孔壬。○皇陶曰、都
亦行有九德亦言

2　"Yes." Kaou-yaou said, "Oh! it lies in knowing men, and in giving repose to the people." Yu said, "Alas! *to attain to* both these things was a difficulty even to the emperor *Yaou.* When *a sovereign* knows men, he is wise, and can put men into their proper offices. When he gives repose to the people, he is kind, and the black-haired people cherish him in their hearts. When *a sovereign* can be *thus* wise and kind, what occasion will he have for anxiety about a Hwan-tow? what to be removing a prince of Meaou? what to fear any one of fair words, insinuating appearance, and great artfulness?"

3　II. Kaou-yaou said, "Oh! there are in all nine virtues to be discovered in conduct; and when we say that a man possesses *any* virtue, that

might well ask—如何, 'what do you mean?' 慎厥身修思永 are to be understood as a sort of explanation of what is intended by 迪厥德. The remaining clauses describe the effects of such a course of virtue. First, there will be 惇敍九族, 'the making generous, and nicely observant of discriminations, the nine classes of his kindred,' equivalent to the regulation of the family or clan, in the Great Learning; second, there will be 庶明勵翼, 'all the intelligent exerting themselves as wings,' equiv. to the govt. of the State: thirdly, there will be the good order of the whole empire, 邇, 'the near,' being the Family and the State, and 遠, 'the distant,' being the empire.—In this way it is attempted to interpret the text,—not very satisfactorily.

2. *Kaou-yaou explains by what processes such effects are realized, and Yu enlarges on their difficulty.* The concluding 'Yes' of the last par. was pronounced, we may suppose, in a tone equiv. to another 如何. 咸若時 (=是),—'all as this,' *i.e.,* to attain to both these things. 惟帝其難之,—Gankw̆o, followed by Ts'ae Ch'in, supposes the emp.

intended to be Yaou,—correctly, I think. Woo Ch'ing and Keang Shing suppose Shun is referred to. The former gives a hortatory turn to the clause:—'the emperor should feel the difficulty of this.' The latter supposes the force of the 其 is to *insinuate* an advice:—'the emperor—yes, perhaps,—he feels the difficulty of this.' The clause is to me declarative simply. 能官人,—'can *office* men,' *i.e.,* put men into the offices for which they are fit. By 巧言令色孔壬 (壬, comp. 任人, Bk. I., p. 16) it is supposed the 共工 of the Can. of Yaou, p. 10, is intended. This would give three of 'the four criminals' of Yaou's reign, whom Shun punished, leaving only K'wăn, Yu's father, unmentioned, 'Yu,' says K'ang-shing,' purposely concealing *his* name.'

CH. II. ON KNOWING MEN:—THE VIRTUES BY WHICH THEY MAY BE KNOWN; RIGHT MEN IN THE RIGHT PLACES; AND THE IMPORTANCE OF THE EMPEROR'S PERSONAL EXAMPLE. 3. 行有九德,—'Actions (行, 3d tone) have nine virtues.' There is a difficulty with the 亦 before 行. Ts'ae defines it by 總, 'altogether,' 'in all;' and expounds:—'Speaking comprehensively of the virtues which appear in conduct, they are in all nine.' I don't see

其人有德乃言

曰載采采禹曰、

何。皐陶曰寬而

栗柔而立愿而

恭亂而敬擾而

毅直而溫簡而

廉剛而塞彊而

義彰厥有常吉

哉。○曰宣三德　四節

夙夜浚明有家、

is as much as to say—he does such and such things." Yu said, "What *are the nine virtues?*" Kaou-yaou said, "Affability combined with dignity; mildness combined with firmness; bluntness combined with respectfulness; aptness for government combined with reverence; docility combined with boldness; straightforwardness combined with gentleness; easiness combined with discrimination; vigour combined with sincerity; and valour combined with righteousness. *When these qualities are* displayed, and that permanently, have we not the good *officer?*

4   When there is a daily display of three *of these* virtues, their possessor could early and late regulate and enlighten the Family, *of*

what else the char. can mean here, but this signification of it is not in the Dict., nor have I seen any other example of it. Keang Shing arguing from the definition of 亦 in the 説文, says that 亦 and 掖 were anciently, interchanged. They were so in the sense of the 'armpit.' 掖 has a secondary mean.—'to uphold,' 'to sustain,' and attributing that also to 亦, he interprets—'supporting the actions of men, there are nine virtues.' I cannot accede to this view. The 亦 which follows has its common meaning of 'and,' 'and moreover.' 載采采,—'He does such and such things.' The Historical Records read, instead of these characters, 始事事; and Woo Ch'ing and Keang Shing both interpret 載 here by 始. It is certainly easier to take it with Gan-kwŏ as =行. Ying-tă says:—'載 has the signification of transport and movement (運行之義), hence we define it by 行.' 采=事, as in Can. of Yaou, p. 10. 載事事=其人行某事某事. 寬而栗,—as in Bk. I. p. 24. So also 直而溫. 愿而恭.—on 愿 (*al.*

原), see Ana. VIII., xvi; XVII. xiii; and esp., Men. VII. Pt. II. xxxvii. 8, 9. I translate it here by 'bluntness,' acc. to the account of it by Ying-tă—愿者遅鈍外失於儀. 亂=治, 'to govern,' here 治才, an aptness for government, often associated with a spirit of lightness and self-confidence.

簡而廉,—in Bk. I. p. 24, we have 簡而無傲, where I have translated 簡 by 'impetuous.' The impetuous will overlook many things, and in their hot haste not discriminate. The same want of discrimination may result from an easy indifference, which is the force of 簡 here.

The pairs of different qualities specified are understood to constitute the unity of the virtue; it is not that the one compensates for the other. 吉=善, 'good.'

4. This par. is specially illustrative of 哲, 能官人 in p. 2. It sets forth the knowledge of men turned to the right account by employing them according to their capacity and aptitude. Perhaps as close a translation of the first portion of the par. as can be given (to be intelligible) would be:—'The daily displayer of three virtues *would be* early and late a regulating and brightening holder of a Family.' The 'Daily Explanation' expands it thus:—九德之中有其三者、能日宣而

教逸欲有邦 績其凝。○<small>五節</small>無 撫于五辰庶 師百工惟時 在官百僚師 德咸事俊乂 翕受敷施九 德亮采有邦 日嚴祗敬六

which he was made chief. Where there is a daily severe and reverent cultivation of six virtues, their possessor could brilliantly conduct the affairs of the State, *to which he was constituted ruler.* When such men are all received and employed, the possessors of these nine virtues will all have their services. Then men of a thousand and men of a hundred will fill the offices *of the State;* the various ministers will emulate one another; all the officers will accomplish their duties at the proper times, observant of the five *elements-regulated* seasons:—and thus their various duties will be fully accomplished."

"Let not *the emperor* set to the rulers of States an example of

克德夫以明 廣之而治治 之有常者有其家 使之常者必有其家 益之也使夜能家之事 以著之夜事 此為匪無不 三大懈不

'When a man has three of these virtues, and can daily display and enlarge them, making them still more conspicuous, he is a man of whom those three virtues are a permanent characteristic. Let him be made a great officer, the head of a Family, and he will be found early and late ruling that Family with all diligence, and its affairs will all be brilliantly regulated.' 浚 is here taken, after Ts'ae, as = 治. The second portion might be similarly translated and expanded. 亮 is here best defined by 明. 翕受敷施,—this is spoken of the supreme authority,—of the emperor. 翕=合. 敷施=布而 用之. 俊乂在官,—Ma, Wang, and Ch'ing, all describe 俊 as being men in ability and virtue beyond a thousand, and 乂 as men exceeding in the same way a hundred. 百僚師師,—同官曰僚, 'those who are in office together are called 僚;' hence the term is often = 'companions,' 'colleagues.' 師師,—'the one will make the other his model.' 百工惟時,—the 百工

are the same as the 百僚, called 工 with reference to their duties, the work they had to do. 惟時,—comp. the same phrase in Bk. II. p. 16. 撫于五辰—撫=順, 'obedient to,' 'accordant with;' 辰 is defined in the Dict. with ref. to this passage, by 時, and Ch'in says 五辰,四時也, 'the five 辰 are the four seasons.' Of the five elements, wood predominates in the spring; fire in the summer; metal in the autumn; and water in the winter; while earth is to be recognized equally in all the seasons. We read in the Le Ke 禮運, Pt. iii. 2, 播五行於四時, 'the five elements are distributed over the four seasons;' and in the context of that passage much is said on the doctrine of the *Yin* and *Yang*, the five elements, five virtues, five tones, &c., much of which is mystical, and much absurd. In the Historical Records, after 俊 乂在官 we have only 百吏肅謹. The rest of the paragraph is wanting;—possibly because Ts'een and his father did not well understand this phrase. 庶績其凝 (=成),—comp. in Can. of Yaou, p. 8, 庶績 咸熙, which follows after the settlement of the seasons, and the regulation of the officers in accordance with them, which is perhaps all that is meant here by 百官惟時,撫于五 辰.

5. *How the emperor must himself set the*

協恭和衷哉　有庸哉同寅　禮自我五禮　惇哉天秩有　勅我五典　○天敘有典。　工人其代之。　無曠庶官。天　日二日萬幾、　兢兢業業一

六節

indolence or dissoluteness. Let him be wary and fearful, *remembering* that in one day or two days there may occur ten thousand springs of things. Let him not have the various officers cumberers of their places. The work is Heaven's;—it is men's to act for it."

6   III. "From Heaven are the *social* arrangements with their several duties; to us it is given to enforce those five duties, and then we have the five courses of generous conduct! From Heaven are the *social* distinctions with their several ceremonies; from us proceed the observances of those five ceremonies, and then do they appear in regular practice! When *sovereign and ministers* show a common

example of careful attention to his duties, and so get all his officers and nobles to give the same.

無教逸欲有邦—'do not teach idleness and desires to the holders of States.'

無＝毋. Gan-kwŏ explains:—不爲逸豫貪欲之教,是有國者之常, 'Do not practise the lessons of idle pleasure and inordinate desires, which is the constant way of the holders of States.' He does not suppose the counsel given to the emperor for his personal benefit, but to concern generally princes and officers; but his interpretation altogether is inadmissible. 教 is the teaching of example; —非必教令,謂上行而下效也 (Ts'ae Ch'in). 幾, 'that which is small and minute,'＝機, 'the spring' or motive force, which, indeed, is Keang Shing's text. Gan-kwŏ explains 曠 by 空, 'empty.' The phrase in the transl. gives its force. 天工,人其代之,—Keang Shing says that 人 is the sovereign. So it is, but embracing the officers employed by him;—'the king as supreme, and governors that are sent by him.'

Cʜ. III. Oɴ ɢɪᴠɪɴɢ ʀᴇᴘᴏsᴇ ᴛᴏ ᴛʜᴇ ᴘᴇᴏᴘʟᴇ:—ᴛʜᴇ ᴀᴄᴄᴏᴍᴘʟɪsʜᴍᴇɴᴛ ʙʏ ᴍᴇᴀɴs ᴏғ ɢᴏᴠᴇʀɴ-ᴍᴇɴᴛ ᴏғ Hᴇᴀᴠᴇɴ's ᴘᴜʀᴘᴏsᴇs ғᴏʀ ᴛʜᴇᴍ. 6.

天敘有典,—Keang Shing reads 五典 after Ma Yung; but as we have below—天秩 有禮, &c., 有典 is here probably the correct text. And, acc. to the same analogy,

有典 must＝a concrete noun, under the govt. of 敘, like 有罪, 有德, under the govt. of 討 and 命. We might render therefore: —'Heaven arranges in their orders those who have the cardinal duties.' The orders are of course the constituent relations of society,—sovereign and minister, father and son, brothers, husband and wife, and friends. 勅我 五典,—'charges on us the five duties.' 正 is accepted by all the commentators as the explanation of 勅 here. A much better meaning comes from the ordinary signif. of the char. By 我 is intended the sovereign and his ministers and officers,—the sovereign specially, as the head of govt. 五典,—as in Bk. I. p. 2, *et al.* 五惇哉,—perhaps we should give this clause as nearly literally as our language will permit, if we said;—'and to the five there is a large obedience!' 天秩有禮—'Heaven arranges in their ranks those who have the ceremonies.' The 典 belong to the essential constituents of society; the 禮 have their foundation also in the mind, which seeks for an outward recognition of the different ranks that actually obtain in society. 自我五禮—'from us'—that is, the sovereign and his ministers—'are the definition and ordering of the five ceremonies.' But what are 'the five ceremonies?' Keang Shing supposes the

天命有德五
服五章哉天
討有罪五刑
五用哉政事
懋哉懋哉。○
天聰明自我
民聰明天明
畏自我民明
威達于上下、
敬哉有士。○

七節

reverence and respect for these, do they not harmonize the moral nature *of the people?* Heaven graciously distinguishes the virtuous;—are there not the five habiliments, five decorations of them? Heaven punishes the guilty;—are there not the five punishments to be severally used for that purpose? The business of government! —ought we not to be earnest in it? ought we not to be earnest in it?

7 "Heaven hears and sees as our people hear and see; Heaven brightly approves and displays its terrors, as our people brightly approve and would awe:—such connection there is between the upper and lower worlds. How reverent ought the masters of the earth to be!"

ranks spoken of to be the different orders of nobility, and that the 禮 are the ceremonial distinctions appropriate to each. But this can hardly be correct, though K'ang-shing and Wang Suh both give a partial sanction to it. Down to 衷哉, Kaou-yaou seems to have before him the influence of govt. on the mass of the people. I take myself 五禮 as = 五者之禮, all the ceremonies belonging to the distinctions of rank in connection with the five constituent relations of society. This is the most natural view in the connection. I have hesitated between it and an interpretation in accordance with the use of the phrase in Bk. II. p. 8, which indeed may be harmonized with it. 有 庸哉,—here Ma Yung read 五庸哉, which should probably be adopted, on the same ground that 有典 should be sustained,—the analogy, namely, of the other clauses. 同 寅協恭 和衷哉,—I have followed Choo He and Ts'ae in translating this clause. Keang Shing, in acc. with his view of the prec. one to which I have referred, explains:—'all who advance together to position in the court will be respectful both in body and mind.' He takes 寅 as = 進; 協恭, reverence of the body; and 和衷, reverence of the mind. The view is quite inadmissible. 天命有 德,—命 = 眷命, 'to regard and appoint,'

i.e., to distinguish graciously. 五服五章哉,—see on next Book, p. 4. 五刑 五用哉,—see on Bk. I. 11. The commentator She Lan (時瀾) observes:—'In connection with the distinguishing of the virtuous, and punishment of the guilty, there is no reference to anything to be done by us (不云我), to show that reward and punishment are to be simply in harmony with the mind of Heaven. The social arrangements and ceremonial distinctions have indeed their foundation in the mind of Heaven, but man is necessary, with his help and regulations, to complete them. But in the matter of rewards and punishments, man may not introduce one jot or tittle of his own.' This is a good instance of the way in which Chinese critics refine upon the letter of the classical texts.

7. *The sympathy between Heaven and the people.*—A warning to rulers, that they strive to give repose to the people. 天聰明自 我民聰明,天明畏自我民 明威 (Ma Yung read 威 in both places),— comp. Pt. V. Bk. I. i. p. 11; ii. 7. 達于 上下,—'this reaches to above and below.' Here 上 refers to heaven, and 下 to the people. 敬哉有土,—on 有土 Ying-tā quotes from K'ang-shing:—'The em-

贊　思　未　陶　可　乃　禹　可　朕　皐　_{八節}
襄　曰　有　曰　績　言　曰　厎　言　陶
哉　贊　知　予　皐　厎　俞　行　惠　曰

8　IV. Kaou-yaou said, "My words are reasonable, and may be put in practice." Yu said, "Yes; your words may be put in practice, and crowned with success." Kaou-yaou said, "*As to that* I do not know, but I wish daily to be helpful. May *the government* be perfected!"

peror, the princes, high nobles, and great officers, —all who have their domains—are styled 君; and from the great officer upwards all may be comprehended in the 有土 here, though its chief reference is to the emperor.'

Ch. IV. Kaou-yaou's confidence in his principles; and his humility. 惠＝順 於理, 'accordant with reason;' comp. the use of 惠 in Bk. I. p. 17; II. p. 5. 厎行; 乃言厎可績,—comp. Bk. I. p. 3. 思曰贊贊襄哉,—the 'Historical Records' have here simply 思贊道哉 Gan-kwŏ and Ying-tă join the 思 to the upper

clause:—'*As to that* I do not know nor think about it.' On the 曰 they make no remark. Keang Shing supposes there may be a transposition of 思曰 for 曰思. and then he would take 曰 as ＝妥. It is certainly an easier solution of the difficulty to say with Ts'ae Ch'in that 曰 is here a mistake for 曰　贊,— as in the last Book., p. 21. It is repeated, to show that Kaou-yaou would be helpful in any way (所助非一事). At the second 贊 I put a comma, and read 襄哉 by itself, taking 襄 as ＝成. For other interpretations, see Keang Shing and Wang Ming-shing.

THE BOOKS OF YU.

BOOK IV. YIH AND TSEIH.

皋 曰 言 帝 拜 昌 禹 帝 一節
陶 孜 予 予 曰 言 汝 曰 益
曰 孜 思 何 都 禹 亦 來 稷

1 I. The emperor said, "Come Yu, you also *must* have admirable words *to bring before me.*" Yu did obeisance, and said, "Oh! what can I say *after Kaou-yaou,* O emperor? I can only think of maintaining a daily assiduity." Kaou-yaou said, "Alas! Will you

TITLE OF THE BOOK.—益稷, 'Yih and Tseih.' The names Yih and Tseih occur in the first paragraph, and occasion is thence taken so to entitle the whole Book. But without good reason;—for those worthies do not appear at all as interlocutors in it. Yu is the principal speaker; the Book belongs to the class of 'Counsels.'

Ying-tă says that Ma, Ch'ing, and Wang edited this Book as a portion of the 'Counsels of Kaou-yaou,' and that, in the preface to the Shoo which they made use of, this Book, or, rather, what they considered to be another Book, was called 棄稷, and not 益稷. Keang Shǐng, acting on this note of Ying-tă's, gives the 4th par. of the preface—咎繇矢厥謨, 禹成厥功, 帝舜申之, 作大禹, 咎繇謨棄稷. On first reading there the combination 棄稷, I concluded there was a misprint, on the ground that it was most unnatural to join together the name and the office of the same man in such a way. This is the very point urged by Ying-tă against Ch'ing and the others. He says:—'棄 and 稷 are one man. It is improper to give his name, and then besides to give his office.

Those scholars were mistaken' (棄稷一人, 不宜言名, 又言官, 是彼誤耳). As to incorporating the Book with the preceding one, that had been done by Fuh-shang; and the 'modern text' (今文) is always published with this Book as the conclusion of the 'Counsels of Kaou-yaou.'

CONTENTS. These have been divided into three chapters. The first, embracing parr. 1—9, relates a conversation between Yu and the emperor, in the presence of Kaou-yaou. Yu relates his own diligence and achievements as a model to the emp., and administers various advices; and Shun on the other hand insists on what his ministers should be. The second chapter, parr. 9, 10, has no apparent connection with the former. K'wei appears in it as minister of Music. In the third chapter, p. 11, Kaou-yaou and Shun sing to each other on the mutual relations of the sovereign and his ministers.

CH. I.   P. 1. *Yu, urged by the emperor to counsel him, describes his own diligence and labours to remedy the calamity of the inundating waters.*

來禹, 汝亦昌言,—the 亦, 'also,' connects this Book closely with the prec.; —so closely, indeed, that many contend it is only a portion of it, and should not stand by itself as a division of the Shoo. But the expres-

暨　濬　九　庶　刊　乘　下　浩　洪　吁、
稷　畎　川　鮮　木、　四　民　懷　水　如
播　澮　距　食、　暨　載、　昏　山　滔　何。
奏　距　四　予　益　隨　墊　襄　天、　禹
庶　川。　海、　決　奏　山　予　陵、　浩　曰、

describe it?" Yu said, "The inundating waters seemed to assail the heavens, and in their vast extent embraced the mountains and overtopped the hills, so that people were bewildered and overwhelmed. I mounted my four conveyances, and all along the hills hewed down the woods, at the same time along with Yih showing the multitudes how to get flesh to eat. I *also* opened passages for the streams throughout the nine provinces, and conducted them to the sea. I deepened *moreover* the channels and canals, and conducted them to the streams, at the same time along with Tseih

sion in the prefatory notice, 帝舜申之, which is all there is of introduction to the 'Yih and Tseih,' quite agrees with this close connection between it and the other 'Counsels.' 予何言,—'what can I say?' All commen. understand here something equivalent to the '*after Kaou-yaou*' of the translation. 予思曰孜孜,—comp. the closing words of last Book. 孜—the 說文 defines 孜 by 汲汲, 'unceasingly assiduous.' The Historical Records give 孳孳. 皐陶曰, 吁,如何,—the Historical Records read— 皐陶難禹,曰,云云, 'Kaou-yaou troubled Yu with the question,' &c. 洪水滔天,浩浩懷山襄陵,—comp. Can. of Yaou, p. 11, from which Yu would almost seem to be quoting. 下民昏墊 —K'ang-shing defines 昏 by 沒, 'to sink in the water,' so that it and the next character have the same meaning. I have followed the better expl. of Gan-kwǒ, who defines 昏 by 瞀. 予乘四載,—the Historical Records give this sentence at much greater length, and Yu is made to say:—'To travel along the dry land, I used a carriage (乘車); to travel along the water, I used a boat (乘舟); to travel through miry places, I used a sledge (泥行乘橇 [k'eaou]. To designate this sledge several other

characters are used. It is described as being like a sieve, and slid easily over the surface of the soft and marshy ground); to travel on the hills, I used spikes' (乘橇 [keuh]. This contrivance is also expressed by various characters. It was only a shoe with a spike, 'like an awl,' under it, to prevent the feet from slipping). 隨山刊木,—隨 is defined by 行. It is better to take it as = 'along,' 刊, written also 栞 and 栞, acc. to older forms, = 'to hew down,' 'to remove.' 暨益奏庶鮮食,—暨 = 與, 'along with;' 奏 = 進, 'to introduce;' 庶 = 衆 or 民, 'the people;' Ma Yung defines 鮮 by 生, meaning, as applied to meat, 'raw,' 'fresh.' 鮮食 is flesh meat, the flesh of birds, beasts, fishes, turtles, &c. But it is not to be supposed that this was eaten raw. Mencius tells us that Shun, in connection with Yu's labours, entrusted to Yih the direction of the fire to be employed, and Yih consumed the trees and tangled vegetation of the forests and marshes, so that the birds and beasts were driven away. In this way the people, unable yet to cultivate their inundated fields, had in the capture of animals a resource against starvation. 奏庶鮮食 = 進衆民于鮮食. Some prefer to expand it— 進衆鳥獸魚鼈之肉於民. 決九川距四海,—決, 'to open a passage for a stream;' comp. Men. VI. Pt. I. ii. 九川 is best taken, after Wang Suh,

惟康其弼直、　安汝止惟幾　帝曰俞禹曰、　帝慎乃在位。　言。○禹曰都　曰俞師汝昌　邦作乂皇陶　烝民乃粒萬　遷有無化居　艱食鮮食懋

二節

sowing *grain*, and showing the multitudes how to procure the food of toil *in addition to* flesh meat. I urged them *further* to exchange what they had for what they had not, and to dispose of their accumulated stores. In this way all the people got grain to eat, and all the States began to come under good rule." Kaou-yaou said, "Yes; *we ought to* model *ourselves* after your excellent words."

2　Yu said, "Oh! be careful, O emperor, of the manner in which you occupy the throne." The emperor said, "Yes." Yu said, "Find your rest in your resting-point. Attend to the springs of things, study stability; and let your assistants be upright:—then

as 九州之川, 'the streams of the nine provinces.' Some have enumerated '*nine* rivers,' as intended by the phrase; but in fact, the rivers on which Yu laboured, as will be seen in the next Book, were many more than nine. 距＝至, 'to,' 'to reach to.' 距四海,— 'to the four seas.' But what were those 'four seas?' This passage shows to my mind that this phrase, in the mouth of Yu and others, with reference to his labours, has more sound than sense. 濬 (as in Bk. I. p. 10) 畎澮 距川,—畎 and 澮 were artificial channels cut in the fields for the purposes of agriculture. The 畎 was the smallest of such channels, a foot deep and a foot wide; the 澮 was the largest, 16 feet wide, and as many deep. Between them there were 遂, 溝, and 洫. So it was at least in the Chow dynasty;—see the Rites of Chow, 考工記之四. 'To the streams' is definite enough, and we ought to have as substantial a meaning in the 'four seas.'

暨稷播—播, must be taken as ＝ 布種五穀, 'to sow the various kinds of grain.' K'ang-shing, indeed, will have the sowing and cultivating here to be only of vegetables, such as could be grown in marshy ground. 艱食,—'the food of toil,' a good name for the produce of agriculture. Ma Yung read 根食, 'root-grown food.' 懋遷有無化居,—Keang Shing reads 貿 principally

on the authority of a passage in Fuh-shang's Introduction to the Shoo, which is now lost. It would give a good enough meaning. 遷,— to remove,' 'as,' says Lin Che-k'e, 'to convey fish and salt to the hilly country, and bring the lumber of the woods to the low grounds.' 居 is defined in the Dict., with reference to this pass., by 積也, 蓄也, 'stores,' 'accumulated materials.' 粒,—米食曰粒 'rice food is called 粒.' The rice is eaten whole, and not ground. But we should not confine the meaning of 粒 to rice.

P. 2. *Yu admonishes the emperor on the way to secure the blessing and favour of Heaven.* 都 帝慎乃在位,—comp. 慎乃有位, in Bk. II. p. 17, noting the diff. of 在 and 有. 安汝止,—comp. the Great Learning, T. 2, *et al.* But after this reference, it is difficult to say exactly what Yu means. 惟幾惟康,—惟＝思, 'to think of.' Immediately below, however, in 惟動, it is the particle, whose various application is so difficult to determine. 惟動丕應徯志 is expanded in the Daily Explanation thus:— 一有動作，布之政令，則天下翕然丕應，若先待我志之發矣 'on the occasion of any move-

右　耳　臣　曰　鄰　吁　用　帝　志　惟
有　目　作　俞　哉　臣　休　天　以　動
民　予　朕　○　臣　哉　○　其　昭　丕
汝　欲　股　帝　哉　鄰　帝　申　受　應
翼　左　肱　曰　禹　哉　曰　命　上　徯

（四節）（三節）

will your every movement be greatly responded to, *as if the people only* waited for your will, and you will brightly receive *gifts from God.* Will not Heaven renew its favouring appointment, and give you blessing?"

3 The emperor said, "Alas! ministers! associates! Associates! ministers!" Yu said, "Yes."

4 The emperor said, "*My* ministers constitute my legs and arms, my ears and eyes. I wish to help and support my people;—you give effect to my wishes. I wish to spread the influence *of my go-*

ment, when you send forth yonr orders about it throughout the empire, they will with one accord greatly respond to them, as if they had first been waiting for the intimating of your will.' 昭 受 上 帝,—'you will brightly receive God.' We must understand 上 帝 之 命, or some similar phrase. 申 命 用 休,—the force of the 其 = 'will it not be that'—? Woo Ch'ing well expanded the clause:—天 亦 申 重 其 已 然 之 命 而 嘉 美 之. 'Heaven likewise will renew its existing regard, and indicate its favour and esteem.' He interprets the prev. clause, however:—'you will brightly respond to the favour which you have received from God.'

P. 3. *The emperor enlarges on his dependence on his ministers, and the services which they render.*

3 吁,—'alas'! Shun speaks, it is said, under excitement, unable to receive all that Yu had just said, and with special reference to 其 弼 直. Ts'ae says:—'臣 indicates the men; 鄰 indicates the office.' Woo Ch'ing makes them two classes, 臣 being the ministers in the administration of business, and 鄰, those in personal attendance on, and intercourse with, the emp. The 臣 and the 隣 must be the same persons, the former term express. their official station, and the latter the personal intimacy of the emp. with them;—see a note by Chang Wang (張 綱, Sung dyn.) in the 集

說. 4. 臣 作 朕 股 肱 耳 目,—the emp. himself is the head,—元 首; see below, p. 11. 左 右 有 民,—左 右 = 助, 'to assist.' Ma Yung says:—左 右 助, 'to assist on the left hand and the right.' 有 民 = 我 所 有 之 民, 'the people which I have,' = my people. 翼,—'wings;' to serve as wings to; then, metaphorically, 'to assist,' 'to give effect to' (成). The literal meaning is lost in the text. 宣 力,—'to proclaim my strength.' Gan-kwǒ defines by 治 功, 'the services of govt.' 古 人 之 象,—'the ancients.' Gaubil observes:— 'It is remarkable that Shun, who is so ancient, speaks of the figures on the dresses of the ancients' (Le Chou-king, p. 36, note). In the first supplement to the Yih King (繫 辭 下 傳, Ch. II. p. 5) we read that Hwang-te, Yaou, and Shun let fall their robes, and the empire was governed (黃 帝 堯 舜 垂 衣 裳 而 天 下 治). By 'the ancients,' therefore, we may be conducted to Hwang-te, 'the Yellow emperor,' the inventor of the cycle, ʙ.ᴄ. 2637, but not beyond him. There were twelve figures, six painted on the upper garment or robe (衣), and six embroidered on the lower garment (裳). They were called altogether 'the twelve ornaments' (十 二 章). Those

予欲宣力
四方、汝爲
予欲觀古
人之象日、
月星辰山、
龍華蟲作
會宗彝藻
火粉米黼
黻絺繡以
五采彰施

vernment through the four quarters;—you are my agents. I wish to see the emblematic figures of the ancients,—the sun, the moon, the stars, the mountain, the dragon, and the flowery fowl, which are depicted *on the upper garment;* the temple-cup, the aquatic grass, the flames, the grains of rice, the hatchet, and the symbol of distinction, which are embroidered *on the lower garment:*—*I wish to see all these displayed with the five colours, so as to form the official*

on the robe were the sun, the moon, stars (Gan-kwŏ would place a comma in the text after 星, and make the 辰 refer to the three prec. nouns, and be in apposition with them. Ch‘in Ts‘eang -taou [陳祥道] says the 星 were the five planets, and 辰, the twelve zodiacal spaces. But 星辰 go together, and simply = stars), a mountain, a dragon, and a pheasant (華蟲, ‘the variegated animal.’ 蟲 is often used not for insects only, but for living creatures generally. These figures—prob. two of each—were painted (作會. 會 is used for 繪). The figures on the lower garment were a cup, used in the services of the ancestral temple (of the temple cups, one had the figure of a tiger on it [虎彝], and another of a kind of monkey [蜼彝]. One or both of these was on the 裳), some kind of water plant, flames, grains of rice, an axe-head (黼. This character denotes a texture of black and white stripes, ornamental. The Dict. says that an axe or hatchet is so called from its white head and black handle. I should rather suppose that 黼 was used for 斧, from their agreement in sound), and what I have called the symbol of distinction (黻. This is defined as a texture of black and azure stripes. As applied to the embroidered ornament, that was made in the form 亞, or two 已 placed back to back). These figures were embroidered (絺繡. Ch‘ing takes 絺 to be for 黹, ‘to embroider,’ syn. with 繡. Gan-kwŏ would take it in its ordinary sense of ‘fine cloth made of the fibres of the 葛.’ I do not see how it is then to be construed).

以五采

彰施于五色,—Ch‘ing says that 采 and 色 refer to the same thing, only 采 is the substance of the various colours, unused, and 色 those colours employed in painting and embroidery. The sacrificial robes of the emperor had all these 12 figures painted or embroidered upon them, emblematic of various attributes, which I will not attempt to specify. The 公 or highest nobles were restricted from the use of the sun, moon, and stars; the 侯 and 伯 were further restricted from the mountain and dragon; and, by a constantly decreasing restriction, five sets of official robes were made, indicating the rank of the wearers. See last Book, p. 6,—天命有德, 五服五章哉. [The practice of the earlier times in the use of these ornaments was a good deal altered during the Chow dynasty. The subject is often perplexed, from not bearing this in mind.]

六律, 五聲, 八音,—see Bk. I. p. 24. As to what follows—在治忽以出納五言, I am far from clearly understanding it. 在 is supposed to = 察, ‘to examine,’ as in Bk. I. p. 5. 忽 is taken as ‘the opposite of 治,—misrule. 五言 is made = 五聲. The ‘Daily Explanation’ paraphrases the passage thus:—

事惡由政事
廷納政之因
之之以朝忌
驗聲間納之
風民于所由
之德君播政

音和由政事
之修治事惡
忽其之以廷
所出察朝納
歌謠言所之
樂章者播驗

有　無　違　汝　出　在　五　欲　服、于
後　面　汝　聽。　納　治　聲　聞　汝　五
言、　從、　弼、　○　五　忽　六　明、　色、
欽　退　汝　子 五節　言、　以、　音、　律　予　作

robes; it is yours to adjust them clearly.　I wish to hear the six
pitch-tubes, the five notes *determined by them*, and the eight kinds
of musical instruments, *regulated again by these*, examining thereby
the virtues and defects of my government, according as the *odes*
that go from *the court*, and the *ballads* that come in *from the people*
5 are ordered by those five notes:—it is you who hear for me.　When
I am doing wrong, it is yours to correct me;—do not follow me to
my face, and when you have retired, have other remarks to make.
Be reverent, ye who stand before and behind and on each side

而我不盡自聽也, 'The harmony of all musical instruments is owing to the happy order of the govt., and their dissonance to its being ill attended to. The method of examining into the matter is to look upon the elegant compositions which proceed from the court, and the songs and ballads which are brought in from the people,—all pieces, in fact, which are put together in harmony with the five notes, and set to music, as evidence of the sovereign's virtue and the people's manners; and I am not able to hear them all for myself.'　Gan-kwŏ gives substantially the same view of 在 治 忽 as the above, but he takes the clause 出 納 五 言 differently, and explains:— 'Moreover, the use of music, thus regulated, is to communicate instructions about the five virtues of benevolence, righteousness, propriety, knowledge, and faith, giving them forth to the people to accomplish their transformation.'
The reading—在 治 忽 is by no means certain. The 'Historical Records' give, instead of it, 來 治 滑, which is unintelligible. Ch'ing read 在 治 曶, and took 曶 as = 笏, a writing-tablet of gem, ivory, or other material, according to the rank of the bearer. The nobles and officers carried this with them into the court. 'The sovereign also,' says Ch'ing, 'was provided with one, to communicate to the principal officers (五 官) the lessons of govt.' But what have those tablets to do with music? Ch'ing's reading does not make the passage any plainer. The reading—采 政 忽 has had its advocates, but its meaning would not differ from that of the *textus receptus*.
In the Books of the 'Former Han' dyn., however, 律 曆 志 上, we have the passage—

書曰, 予欲聞六律, 五聲, 八音, 七始, 詠, 以出納五言, 女聽.　No doubt this was a current reading in the early times of the Han. It makes the whole clause refer somehow to the subject of music, without introducing the matter of examining about the govt., and so far it is to be preferred. But what are we to understand by the 七 始, or 'seven beginnings?'　Pan Koo, the historiographer of Han, says they are 'heaven, earth, man, and the four seasons.' So far as I can understand Woo Ch'ing, he understands by them the complete musical scale, containing the five notes (五 聲) and two semitones. They are no doubt terms with some musical significance.　A sinologue, understanding the theory of music, and having some practical acquaintance with the art, might succeed in elucidating the subject.　Pan Koo takes 出 納 五 言 in the same way as Gan-kwŏ. 五 言 = 五 常 之 言.—We go on to the next par., wishing that the second part of this were more apprehensible, or that we understood it better.　5. *The duty of ministers freely and openly to correct the sovereign's faults.* 予 違,—'I am opposing;' *i.e.*, going contrary to the right (有 違 戾 於 道).　汝 弼, —with reference to 其 弼 直 in p. 2.　弼 has the idea of *correction*.　後 言 = after and other words.　欽 四 鄰,—I have translated 四 鄰 after Gan-kwŏ, in illustration of whose interpr. Ying-tǎ refers to 惟 予 一 人 無 良, 實 賴 左 右 前 後

則　而　以　並　用　以　以　不　頑　四
承　颺　納　生　識　記　明　在　讒　鄰。
之　之　言　哉　哉　之　之　時　說　○
庸　格　時　工　欲　書　撻　侯　若　庶　六節

6 of me.　As to all the obstinately stupid and calumniating talkers, who are not to be found doing what is right, there is the target to exhibit their true character; the scourge to make them remember; and the book of remembrance!　Do we not wish them to live along with us?　There are also the masters of music to receive the compositions which they make, and continually to set them forth *in*

有 位 之 士 匡 其 不 及. in Pt. V., Bk. XXVI., p. 3. Fuh-shang and K'ang-shing after him supposed that there were four ministers attendant on the person of the emp., specially called 鄰,—'a helper on the left, a corrector on the right, a solver of doubts before, and a stimulator of purpose behind.'　There is no evidence that there were such officers. 鄰 is here equivalent to 臣, as in p. 3.　6. *That ministers are not only to be strictly faithful to their sovereign, but are to use stringent measures to correct others, and provide a supply of good men for the use of the State.* 庶 頑 讒 說,— these are the 讒 說 殄 行 of Bk. I. p. 25. We are to understand these words not of the people generally, but 'of the sons of officers, and youths of greatest promise of ability, who may be expected to discharge hereafter the functions of the State' (see Woo Ch'ing, *in loc*). 若 不 在 時,—the 時＝是. Gan-kwŏ takes it as the 是 emphatic, == 'what is right.'　Woo Ch'ing, with ref. to his observation on the prec. clause, says 不 在 是 選 者, 'who are not in this selection,' *i.e.*, selection to office. 侯 以 明 之,—'there is the target to show them clearly.'　Archery was made much of anciently in China; see the 儀 禮, 卷 八 至 十 四. Wang Ming-shing, quoting from the 射 義, says, 'The archers must advance, retreat, and move round, according to the proper rules.　Where the aim of the mind is right, the adjustment of the body will be correct; and thus archery supplies an evidence of character.　Unworthy men will not be found hitting frequently.　There were three ceremonial trials of archery, belonging to the emperor, the princes, the high ministers and the great officers.　First, there was the Great archery, used to select those who should assist at the sacrificial services.　Second, there was the

Guests' archery, used on occasion of the princes appearing at court, and their visiting among themselves.　Third, there was the Festive archery, used at entertainments generally.　From the first kind expectant scholars were excluded; but they could take their part in the other trials.'　He then goes on to describe the various targets used at those trials.　What we call the 'bull's-eye,' was the figure of a small bird (鵠　See Doctr. of the Mean, xiv. 5).　Confucius more than once spoke of archery as a discipline of virtue (see Ana. III. xvi., *et al.*).　Certain vices will of course unfit men for the successful practice of archery, but to lay down success in archery as a test of moral character is tearing a subject to tatters.　The most famous archers of Chinese antiquity were very bad men: see Men. IV., Pt. II., xxiv. 撻 以 記 之,—'there is the scourge to make them remember.'　The archery field was, according to this, truly a place of discipline.　This illustrates the 扑 作 教 刑 of Bk. I. p. 11. 書 用 (＝ 以) 識 (read *che*) 哉,—'there is the *book*,' not, it must be borne in mind, a book of paper and printing, but a record made on cloth or on a tablet.　It does not appear that the record should be confined to the result of the trials in archery;—see the 周 禮, 地 官, 司 徒, 第 二 之 四, where the Heads of districts are all supposed to keep a register of the characters of the people, in reference to the laws generally. 欲 並 生 哉,—the object of the trial, the punishment, and the record, is to effect a reformation.　The characters may be translated—'Oh! we wish them to live together *with us*.'　Keang Shing defines 生 by 進, 'to advance;' and explains it by 'to advance to goodness.'　This is far-fetched. 工 以 納 言, 時 而 颺 之,— 工 is, no doubt, ＝ 樂 官, 'an officer of mu

誰　功、以　帝　共　生　至　帝　○　之、
敢　車　言、時　惟　萬　于　光　禹　否
不　服　明　舉、帝　邦　海　天　曰　則
讓　以　庶　敷　臣、黎　隅　之　俞　威
敢　庸、以　納　惟　獻　蒼　下、哉、之。

song. If they become reformed, they are to be received and employed; if they do not, let the terrors *of punishment* overtake them."

7　Yu said, "Yes, but let your light, O emperor, shine all through the empire, even to the grassy shores of the seas, and in the myriad States the most worthy of the people will all wish to be your ministers. Then, O emperor, you may advance them to office. They will set forth, and you will receive, their reports; you will make proof of them severally by their merits; you will confer chariots and robes according to their services. Who will then dare

sic.' All commentators agree in this. As to the interpretation of the whole clause, I have followed Ts'ae Ch'in, as in the concluding part of p. 4, without feeling sure of being right. To quote here again from the 'Daily Explanation,' we have there this paraphrase:—然必觀其改過與否, 又當命樂官取彼所進納之言, 播于樂章, 時時而宣颺之, 其言和平, 是能改過, 'But it must be seen whether they really reform or not. The officers of music must also be charged to take the words which they present and send in, and set them to music, continually rehearsing them. If their words are harmonious and mild, it is an evidence of their reformation.' On the other hand, Gan-kwŏ, foll. by Woo Ch'ing and others, thinks the use of the musical officers in the matter was to bring their songs and sentiments to bear on those who had undergone the discipline described, in order to complete their reformation. This is, perhaps, the preferable view. 格則承之,—格, as in Ana. II. iii.　7. *Yu suggests to the emperor that his chief dependence must be on himself, and not on any assistance or correction of his ministers.* 俞哉,—'Yes!' Tung-po says that while this phrase expresses the assent of the mouth, it indicates that the mind does not quite consent. But this is hypercriticism, suggested by the design apparent in the sequel of the paragraph. 海隅蒼生—隅=角, 'a corner;' 蒼生 is given in the 'Daily Explanation' as equivalent to 黎民, 'all the people;' and

this is a meaning now often attached to the phrase. But it is contended that it was not so understood before the Tsin dynasty. 蒼 properly denotes the green colour of grass, and Gan-kwŏ connects the phrase with 海隅 as in the translation (至于海隅蒼蒼然生草木). 黎獻—獻=賢, 'the worthy,' 'the wise,' as in Ana. III. ix, 黎 may be taken as = 'all;' or in the sense we have hitherto attached to it :—'the wise of the black-haired race.' 時舉—時=是. The whole clause = 'and your Majesty will simply have to employ them.' 敷納以言, 明庶以功, 車服以庸,—comp. Bk. I. p. 9. Ying-tă explains the slight difference between the two passages, saying that the first is descriptive of Shun's dealings with the princes, whose standing was recognized, and this speaks of the first selection and employment of officers. Hence we have here 納 and 庶, 納 denoting the receiving and choice of them, and 庶, the distinction of them from their fellows (納謂受取之, 庶謂在羣眾). This is ingenious, though the 庶 has to me a suspicious appearance. Choo He would read 試. Keang Shing reads the whole according to a quotation from the 'Books of Hea' (which, however, may possibly be of the passage in the Can. of Shun) in the 左傳,

創　用　舟　頟　是　遊　丹　罔　時　不
若　殄　朋　頟　作　是　朱　功　敷　敬
時　厥　淫　罔　罔　好　傲　。○　同　應
娶　世　于　水　晝　傲　惟　無　日　帝
于　予　家　行　夜　虐　慢　若　奏　不

not to cultivate a humble virtue? Who will dare not to respond to you with reverence? If you, O emperor, do not act thus, all *your ministers* together will daily proceed to a meritless character.

8 "Do not be like the haughty Choo of Tan, who found his pleasure only in indolence and dissipation, and pursued a proud oppression. Day and night, without ceasing, he was thus. He would make boats go where there was no water. He introduced licentious associates into his family. The consequence was that he brought the honours of his House to an end. I took warning from his course. When I

傷,二十七年,–賦納以言,明試以功,車服以庸. 帝不時,敷同日奏罔功.–時=是 不時=不若是, 'not thus.' 敷同 is taken as =普同, 'all together,' i.e., even the ministers of good character whom you at present employ, to say nothing of the calumniating parties whom you talk about our reforming. We read in the 'Historical Records'—帝即 不時,布同善惡,則無功. The compiler of these would seem to have understood 敷同 in the sense of—'if you employ together the good and the bad.' 8. *Yu proceeds to warn Shun by the example of himself. Shun in reply compliments both Yu and Kaou-yaou.* In the 'Historical Records' this par. appears introduced by a 帝曰, while after the equivalent there for 予創若是, we have the addition of 禹曰. Keang Shing follows Ts'een, and edits his text accordingly. He adduces other evidences of the reading, as in the 楚元王傳, in the Books of the Former Han, where we find (in the acct. of 向子政) –帝舜戒伯禹, 毋若丹朱敖 帝曰 There must have been the readings of 帝曰 and 禹曰 in some copies of the Shoo during the Han dyn. But, if we are to judge in the matter by the canon that the more difficult reading is to be preferred, we shall adhere to the *textus receptus*. It is startling to find Yu

lecturing Shun, and warning him not to be like Choo of Tan.—Dared a minister to speak so to the sage emperor? This diffi. is somewhat got over by introducing the characters 帝曰, which again necessitate the 禹曰 below. 丹朱,—it is stated, in the 漢書律曆志, that 'Yaou placed his son Choo in 丹淵,' from which it is concluded that Tan was the name of a State to which Yaou appointed his son. 頟頟 is defined 不休息貌 'the appearance of unceasingness.' Ch'ing connects the phrase with the clause below, and says:— 'Choo having seen people moving about in boats during the inundation, after the waters were reduced, would still live in a boat, and made men unceasingly push it along.' Wang Ming-shing argues for a metaphorical explanation of 罔水行舟, making it = Mencius 從流忘反 (I. Pt. II. iv. 7),—absurdly, it appears to me. 朋淫家內,—this is illustrated from the orgies of Këë, the last emp. of the Hea dyn., who dug a pool, and made a night palace, where men and women lived promiscuously together, and where he once remained himself for a whole month.' 用殄 厥世,—殄=絕, 'to extinguish.' Ts'ae Ch'in says 世者世堯之天下也, '世 means making hereditary—handing down to future generations—the empire of Yaou.' 予創若時 (=是),—創 (1st tone), 'a wound inflicted by a knife;' here=as in the transl. Gan-kwŏ defines it by 懲, 'to repress,'

咸　外　十　于　成　度　弗　癸　塗
建　薄　有　五　五　土　子、　甲、　山、
五　四　二　千、　服　功、　惟　啟　辛
長、　海、　師、　州　至　弼　荒　呱　壬

married in T'oo-shan, *I remained with my wife only* the days *sin, jin, kwei, and keă*. When *my son* K'e was wailing and weeping, I did not regard him, but kept planning with all my might my labour on the land. *Thus* I assisted in completing the five tenures, extending over 5,000 *le; in appointing* in the provinces twelve Tutors; and in establishing, in the regions beyond, extending to the four seas, five Presidents. These all pursue the right path and are merito-

'to reprove' and Ying-tă says:—'創 and 懲 have both the meaning of seeing wickedness, and stopping one's-self from a similar course.' Ts'een gives, for this clause, 予不能順 是, which is quite inane. The clause is natural in the mouth of Yu, unnatural from Shun. I do not see how with this clause we can adopt the reading 帝曰 at the begin. of the par.

娶于塗山,—塗山 was the name of a principality, the daughter of the ruler of which was married by Yu. A hill called 塗, gave its name to the territory, and is identified with one in the pres. prov. of Gan-hwuy, 8 *le* to the south-east of the dis. city of Hwae-yuen (懷遠), dep. of Fung-yang (鳳陽). Ch'ing says that Yu was married on the day 辛, and got the emperor's command to undertake the remedy of the inundation on the day 甲, so that he spent only three nights in his house. But I suppose he was already engaged in his great work, and could only spare four days from it for the business of his marriage. 啟呱

呱,—啟 was Yu's son who afterwards succeeded to the throne. The two other characters express the sound of an infant's crying.

弗子, 'did not *son* him,' *i.e.*, did not regard him. Mencius tells us (III. Pt. I. iv. 7) that Yu, when engaged upon the waters, was eight years away from his family, and though he thrice passed the door of his house, did not enter it. 荒=大, 'great,' 'greatly.' 土功 'the service of the land,' *i.e.*, all the work which he had to perform in regulating the waters.

弼成五服,—see on the next Book, Part ii., parr. 18—22. Yu speaks of himself here, it is said, as only 'assisting,' (弼), because he would attribute the great merit to the emp.

Woo Ch'ing, however, considering 弼 to mean, primarily, the effort employed in forming the figure of a bow, explains the text of the figure and formation of the difft. tenures:—a very likely explanation. 州十有二師,— Medhurst has translated this clause:—'In every district I appointed twelve officers,' and then he has a note to the effect that over every province there was established only *one* nobleman, as officer. Gaubil translates the text in the same way as Medhurst:—'Chaque Tcheou eut douze chefs.' It is a vexed question whether in each province there was only one 師, or whether there were eleven. The old interpreters, not without differences among themselves, yet all maintain the larger number. It will be sufficient here to give an abridgment of the views of Ch'ing.—'Inside the tenure of Restriction (要 服) were the nine provinces (九州), containing altogether a space of 49,000,000 square *le*. Deducting from these the imperial domain, there remain 48,000,000; or 6,000,000 square *le* to each province. Now, when Yu assembled the princes of the empire at Hwuy-k'e (會稽), they amounted to 10,000. Such was the number of the States of the nine provinces. Over every province was a Pastor (牧), and the worthiest of the princes were selected to be tutors or counsellors (師) to him. For every hundred States there was one 師, and 12 師 would suppose 1200 States. Each province contained of States 100 *le* square, 200; 70 *le* square, 400; 50 *le* square, 800:—altogether 1400. Deduct 200 of these, as an allowance for waste lands, and there remain 1,200 States. Multiply these by 8; we have 9,600, and allowing 400 for States within the imperial domain, we have the 10,000 States forming the empire.' The value of these statements and figures will have to be considered in connection with the next Book. In the meantime, according to these views there were in all

刑　敘　陶　功　朕　哉。工、苗　各
惟　方　方　惟　德　帝　帝　頑　迪
明。施　祗　敘　時　曰、其　弗　有
○　象　厥　皋　乃　迪　念　即　功、

rious; but there are *still* the *people of* Meaou, who refuse to acknowledge their duty. Think of this, O emperor." The emperor said,
"That my virtue is followed, this is the result of your meritorious
services, so orderly displayed. And now Kaou-yaou is respectfully
carrying out your arrangements, and employing the represented
punishments with entire intelligence."

96 Tutors or Counsellors in the empire. The ancient commentators agree in this view, and many of the moderns follow them,—Ts'ae Ch'in for instance, and the authors of the 'Daily Explanation.' On the other hand, many scholars maintain that, the 12 師 are the same as the 12 牧 of Bk. I., p. 16; and that the appointment of them here is not to be referred to the time when Yu reduced the waters of the inundation, and the provinces were nine in number, but to the subsequent period, when Shun had altered that division, and made twelve provinces (Bk. I. p. 10.) This was the prevailing opinion in the Yuen dyn. Woo Ch'ing advocates it, and so does Wang Kang-yay (王耕野). I may quote the language of the latter:—'Twelve Tutors in provinces were the same officers as those elsewhere denominated pastors. It was their duty to nourish the people, and therefore they were called pastors; it was their duty also to be the instructors of the people, and therefore they were called tutors. Don't let it be supposed that, besides the 12 pastors, there were other 12 princes appointed in every province to be their tutors' (see the 讀書管見, 卷上, *in loc.*) This was the view which occurred to myself on the study of the classic, without reference to commentaries, and I am inclined still to prefer it. I have made the translation so literal that it will admit of either view.

外薄四海, 咸建五長,—it is difficult to know the exact meaning here, as much is in the prec. clause. 外 must be 九州之外, 'beyond the nine provinces.' 薄 (p'ŏh) = 被, 'reaching to.' 薄四海 is a vague expression, indicating all the territory beyond the nine provinces, which partially acknowledged the imperial sway. Medhurst translates the clause:—'Beyond these districts, even to the four seas, everywhere I established the five elders,' and in a note, translated from Ts'ae, he says:—'Beyond the nine regions, bordering on the four seas, in every part he separately established five elders as superiors, to take

the general charge of the country.' The translation of Gaubil is entirely incorrect:—Joining the foll. 各迪有功 closely with the clause immediately preceding, he translates the whole: —'Au dehors je renfermai dans leurs bornes les quatre mers, cinq autres choses furent etablies, et je reussis dans mon entreprise.' This is evidently not the meaning; what the meaning is, it is not so easy to determine. According to my interpretation, it is that there were five chiefs to whom was given the superintendence of all this outlying territory. I do not find this view, however, supported by Chinese authorities. Ch'ing said:—' Outside the nine provinces over five States was appointed a chief, to cause' each of them—*i.e.*, the rulers of each—to observe their duties' (外則五國立長, 使各守其職). This view is supposed to be confirmed by a passage in the Le Ke, 王制, ii. 2, where it is said that 'five States formed a connection, and every connection had a chief' (五國以爲屬, 屬有長). Such an arrangement, however, belonged to the Chow dynasty, and it prevailed all beyond the imperial domain. Woo Ch'ing makes the 五長 = 五等諸侯, 'the five kinds of princes,' the kung, how, pih, &c. He adds that the 師 were leaders of all princes in a province, the 長 presided each over one State.—Neither of these interpretations appears to me so likely as the one which I suggest. 各迪有功,— I take 迪 as in the last Book p. 1, only that 迪 is here intransitive, unless we take 有功 together, as a noun governed by it. The meaning adopted in the former passage of 迪 = 導 by Woo Ch'ing would answer here. He of course adheres to it, and Keang Shing here adopts it, making 各迪有功 = 率道諸侯就功 弗即工,—即 =

戛^{九節}　擊　搏　瑟　祖　格　在　后　下　鼓、

曰、　鳴　拊　以　考　位　德　管　合

戛　球、　琴、　詠、　來　賓　讓、　鼗　止

9　　II. K'wei said, "When the sounding-stone is tapped or strongly
struck; when the lutes are swept or gently touched; to accompany
the singing:—the *imperial* progenitors come to the service, the guest
of Yu is in his place, and all the nobles show their virtue in giving
place to one another.　Below there are the flutes and drums and
hand-drums, which join in at the sound of the rattle, and cease at
the sound of the stopper; with the calabash organs and bells:—all

就 工 功、　　　帝曰、迪朕德

云云、—in the Historical Records we read for
this—道 五 德 乃 女 功 序 之 也，
皋 陶 於 是 敬 禹 之 德，令 民
皆 則 禹，不 如 言，刑 從 之，舜
德 大 明. The meaning is substantially the
same as that which I have given, with the
exception of the view which is taken of the
concluding 惟明. It will be seen also that
the compiler of the Records supposed Shun's
words to terminate with 惟 敍, and that what
followed was historical. The first 方 is certainly more natural, considered as narrative; as to
the second, one would gladly follow Keang
Shing, and take it as = 薄.

Ch. II. *K'wei celebrates the power of the music which he superintended.* Ts'ae Ch'in observes
that this chapter is to be considered by itself,
and has no connection with the previous or
subsequent portions of the Book.　Shun, he
observes, reigned more than 50 years, and must
have had many conversations in which Kaou-
yaou, K'wei, and Yih took part.　The historian
has preserved the most remarkable of their
remarks, but not in the sequence of their conversations.　Ts'ae blames, therefore, the efforts
of scholars to force a connection between this
and the context.　It is as well to admit this
view, though the mind naturally likes to think
that we have in the various 'Counsels' so many
integrals.　憂 擊 鳴 球—球 is
defined as 'the sonorous gem-stone (玉 磬),
and also as 'a fine gem' (美 玉). It is, no
doubt, used here in the former application.　I
have seen a *king*, brought in 1861 from the
'Summer palace,' that had been made for the
emp. K'een-lung of jade stone fully an inch
thick, and like a ship-builder's' *knee*, the form
in which the instrument is commonly represented.　When suspended and struck with a
piece of metal, it emitted a rich ringing sound.

輕 敲 曰 憂. 重 敲 曰 擊, 'To strike
lightly is called 憂 ; heavily, 擊.'　The striking in both ways was applied to the stone, and
not, Gan-kwŏ supposes, also to the 柷 and 敔
mentioned below, which he thinks regulated
the music in the raised part of the hall, as
well as that in the lower.　搏 拊 琴 瑟,
—I call the 琴 瑟 *lutes*, whithout having for
myself definite ideas of the instruments.　[I
hope to be able to describe them fully and
correctly in the next volume, upon the She
King].　They were stringed.　Ch'ing K'ang-
shing says the *k'in* had five strings, and the *shih*
twenty-five.　There were different sizes and
forms of them.　A note in the 爾 雅 says:—
'The *k'in* was 5.66 feet long, with five strings
to which other two, called the civil and martial, were subsequently added.　The Great *shih*
was 8.1 feet long, and 1.8 ft. broad, with 27
strings; the Elegant *shih* of the same size, had
23 strings, and one in common use only 19;
the Praise *shih* of the same breadth, but nearly a foot shorter, had 23 strings.　Some ascribe
the invention of the *k'in* to Fuh-he; some,
to Shin-nung: and some to Shun.　搏 is
a forcible striking of the strings; and 拊, a
slighter.　以 詠 is expanded in the 'Daily
Explanation' to 以 合 于 人 聲 之
歌, 'to accord with the singing of the human voice.'　祖 考,—'grandfather and
father,' = ancestors.　祖 考 來 格 = 祖
考 之 神 來 至, 'the spirits of ancestors
come.'　The whole of the service is supposed to
take place in the ancestral temple of Shun.

'The guest of Yu' is Choo of Tan, the son of
Yaou; comp. are 作 賓 于 王 家, Pt. V.
Bk. VIII. 1.　　下 = 堂 之 下, 'in the
lower part of the hall.'　We understand from
this that the sounding-stone and lutes were in

來　鳳　九　簫　蹌　鳥　以　笙　柷
儀。　凰　成　韶　蹌、　獸　閒、　鏞　敔、

filling up the intervals; *when* birds and beasts fall moving. When the nine parts of the service according to the emperor's arrangements have all been performed, the male and female phœnix come with their measured gambollings *into the court.*"

the higher or raised portion of the hall.

管　鼗　鼓,—the 管 was a kind of flute, originally made of bamboo. Accounts differ as to its exact form. It is generally figured as double, two tubes, each with a mouth-hole and five other holes. It is difficult to see how the two could be blown together. Other flute instruments were the 籥 and the 篪. 鼗　鼓.—鼓 is the general name for drums. The 鼗 was a small drum, held by a handle, with two strings fixed to the sides and terminating in knobs. When twirled by the hand, those knobs struck on the ends, and produced the sound. Pedlars now carry a small instrument of this kind about with them, and by the noise it makes attract the public attention. Ts'ae supposes that the two characters of the text belong to the one instrument, the *t'aou*. Woo Ch'ing, with whom I rather agree, takes them to signify the small hand-drum and the large drum. 合　止　柷

敔.—the 柷, it is said, was a lackered box, a foot deep and 2.4 ft. square (other dimensions are assigned), with a handle going down to the bottom, and moveable so as to strike against the sides when turned round. At the sound of this the other instruments struck up. The 敔 is represented as a couchant tiger of wood, with 27 teeth along the ridge of his back, which when rasped against by a handle gave the signal for the music to stop. This is the common account of these instruments and their use, which however does not go higher than the Han dynasty. Woo Ch'ing calls it in question, and with him agrees Sun Ke-yew (孫繼有; Ming dyn. See the 集說). According to them, the 敔 was made of earth, an instrument similar to the 塤. In this way all the 八音, or eight kinds of musical instruments are mentioned by K'wei. This explanation is not unlikely; but I cannot make out fully what Woo Ch'ing says about 合止（合止為 二音合作, 止則敔止, 柷木音 敔當是土音, 塤之類 而舊虎 說相傳以為斷木成 伏聲 狀背有鉏鋙而生鉏 蓋因敔名 樂之義

必不然也). 笙　鏞,—the 笙 was made of reeds or tubes (19 in large instruments, and 13 in smaller), placed upright in an emptied calabash, with a cross piece of metal at the mouth of each tube. G. T. Lay, Esq., in his 'The Chinese as they are,' p. 88, has called the *shang* Jubal's organ, and says:—'This seems to be the embryo of our multiform and magnificent organ, and consists of several tubes varying in length, so as to utter sounds at harmonic intervals from each other. These tubes are inserted into a bowl' (were originally placed in a calabash), 'which must be taken as the humble representative of the wind chest, while the office of bellows is of course discharged by the human breath.' The invention of this primitive organ has been ascribed to a fabulous female sovereign (女媧氏), who followed Fuh-he. 鏞＝ 大鐘, 'a large bell.' The invention of the bell is carried up to Koo-yen (鼓延), a grandson of Fuh-he. 以間 is expanded in the 'Daily Explanation' to 以與堂上衆 樂, 更迭間作, 'to strike up at the intervals, in their turns with the instruments in the higher part of the hall.' Ts'ae says:— 與詠歌迭奏, 'striking up in their turn with' (after) 'the singing.' The meaning is the same. 蹌蹌 is defined 行動 之貌, 'the appearance of moving.' Ts'ae says:—'The music not only moved spirits and men; but even birds and beasts—ignorant creatures—led on one another to gambol to it.' 簫韶九成.—簫韶 are to be taken together as the name of the music of Shun, said to have been made by him in the 5th year of his reign (see the 資治通鑑綱目前 編卷之二). For 簫 we should read 箾, meaning a sort of castanets, held by the dancers as they kept time to the music; but the two characters lose their individual meanings, and represent the music of Shun. 成 is defined by Ying-tă as 樂曲終, 'the completion of the music and song.' He adds that when one song was concluded, another was sung to a different tune; and this was repeated in Shun's music 9 times, with reference to what is said in Bk. II. p. 7,—'when the nine services

念哉率作興事、手稽首颺言曰、工熙哉。皋陶拜哉、元首起哉、百乃歌曰、股肱喜之命惟時惟幾、庸作歌曰、勑天庶尹允諧。○帝拊石、百獸率舞、夔曰、於予擊石

十一節

十節

10　　K'wei said, "Oh! when I strike the stone or tap the stone, all kinds of animals lead on one another to gambol, and all the chiefs of the officers become truly harmonious."

11　　III. The emperor on this made a song, saying, "Being charged with the favouring appointment of Heaven, we must be careful at every moment, and in the smallest particular." He then sang, saying,

　　"When the members work joyfully,
　　The head rises flourishingly;
　　And the duties of all the officers are fully discharged!"

Kaou-yaou did obeisance, with his head to the ground, and with a loud and rapid voice said, "Oh! think. It is yours to lead on,

have been orderly accomplished, let that accomplishment be celebrated in songs.' 鳳凰來儀,—see Ana., IX. viii. In K'ang-he's dict., char. 鳳, several descriptions of the bird will be found. 來儀＝來舞有容儀, as in the transl. Ch'ing's expl. is different, and to me hardly intelligible. He says, 儀, 匹也, 來止巢而乘匹. I suppose he means that they came and bred in the court.———K'ung Ying-tǎ observes that though the descent of the spirits of ancestors is mentioned in connection with the music high up in the hall, and the movements of animals in connection with that below, and the appearance of the phœnix in connection with the whole service, we are not to suppose that the particular effect was owing to the whole or particular part of the service as specified. Ts'ae notices also the opinion of some who explain the statements away, and ask how we can suppose that birds and beasts and phœnixes really came gambolling in the court. He replies that such suspicions merely show ignorance of the power of music, and then he adduces instances duly recorded (見於傳者), quite as marvellous as those in the text. It was the music of Shun, as preserved in Ts'e, which so affected Confucius that for three months he did not know the taste of flesh (Ana. VII. xiii.).　　　P. 10.

See Book I. p. 24. I said the passage was out of place there. It would almost seem to be the same here, though the concluding clause,—庶尹允諧, adds a particular point to the effects of music, not mentioned in the prec. par. 尹 is defined, both by Gan-kwŏ and Ch'ing, by 正, which again ＝官長, 'the heads of the officers,' i.e., the directors of the various official departments. The 'stone' is here mentioned by K'wei (for particular reasons, which exercise the ingenuity of commentators), by synecdoche,—one of the kinds of musical instruments for all the eight kinds.
Cʜ. III. Sᴏɴɢꜱ ᴏꜰ ᴛʜᴇ ᴇᴍᴘᴇʀᴏʀ ᴀɴᴅ Kᴀᴏᴜ-ʏᴀᴏᴜ, ᴏɴ ᴛʜᴇ ᴅᴜᴛɪᴇꜱ ᴏꜰ ᴛʜᴇ ᴇᴍᴘᴇʀᴏʀ ᴀɴᴅ ʜɪꜱ ᴍɪɴɪꜱᴛᴇʀꜱ. This par., if the two prec. did not intervene, might well be taken as a sequel to parr. 4—6 on the part of Shun, and parr. 7, 8, where Yu tells him that his dependence must be on himself, and not on his ministers 庸＝用; but we cannot tell with what reference it is used. It indicates that the reflection and song of Shun were consequent on something previously mentioned, being ＝ 'on this.' There is nothing in the parr. immediately prec. to which the this can be referred. 勑天之命,—勑, as in p. 6. of the last Book :—'being charged with the favouring appointment of

往欽哉。○
墮哉帝拜曰俞、
股肱惰哉萬事
曰元首叢脞哉、
庶事康哉。又歌
明哉股肱良哉、
賡載歌曰、元首
省乃成欽哉。乃
慎乃憲欽哉、屢

and to originate things, with a careful attention to your laws. Be reverent! Oh! often examine what you have accomplished. Be reverent!" With this he continued the song, saying,

"When the head is intelligent,
The members are good;
And all business will be happily performed!"

He again continued the song, saying,

"When the head is vexatious,
The members are idle;
And all affairs will go to ruin!"

The emperor said, "Yes; go ye, and be reverently *attentive to your duties!*"

Heaven.' 惟 時,—comp. 食哉惟 時, Bk. I. p. 16. 股肱—see p. 4. 元首,—the sovereign is evidently intended by this phrase. In Ying-tă's paraphrase (foll. by K'ang-he's dict., char. 元), 元 is taken as = 首; but it is rather an adj., with some eulogistic meaning, = 'the great,' 'the superior.' 百工熙哉,—comp. in Can. of Yaou, p. 8, 允釐百工, 庶績咸熙. 颺言曰 念哉—Gan-kwŏ defines 颺 by 大言而疾, 'with great words and rapid.' 念哉 is evidently addressed to the emp. Ch'ing says that they are a summons to all the ministers to give heed to the warning just uttered by the emperor; and Ming-shing and Keang Shing, in their prejudice, endorse the view. 憲 = 法, 'the laws.' A careful attention to these on the part of the emp.

would be a good example to the officers to attend to their duties. 'Examine what you have accomplished;'—*i.e.*, that you may carry on your undertakings and govt. with the same success. 賡載歌曰,—賡 = 續, 'to continue.' 載 is taken by Ch'ing as = 始, making the meaning,—'he continued and sung his *first* song,' with ref. to 又歌 below. Gan-kwŏ takes it as = 成, 'to complete.' making the meaning—'he continued and completed the meaning of the emperor.' 叢脞哉,—Ch'ing explains 叢脞 by 總聚小小 之事, 'a general collection of small affairs.' To the same effect, substantially, are the views of Gan-kwŏ and Ma Yung. 'Vexations,' as in the transl., seems to give the idea, though it is not easy to collect it from the several characters. 墮 (read *to*) = 壞, 'to fall in ruins.' 往欽哉,—see Can. of Yaou, p. 11, *et al.*

THE SHOO KING.

PART III.

THE BOOKS OF HEA.

THE SHOO KING.

PART III. THE BOOKS OF HEA.

BOOK I. THE TRIBUTE OF YU. PART i.

夏書

禹貢上

大
川。高
山木
奠山
刊隨
土
敷
禹_一
節
上

1 I. Yu divided the land. Following the course of the hills, he hewed down the woods. He determined the high hills and great rivers.

NAME OF THE PART.—夏書, 'The Books of Hea.' 夏 is the dynastic designation under which Yu and his descendants possessed the empire, B.C. 2,204—1,766, a period of 439 years. Hea was a small territory, which still retains the name of Yu (Yu-chow [禹州], dep. of K'ae-fung in Ho-nan), to which he was appointed after the conclusion of his labours on the inundated empire. Hwang-poo Mih (皇甫謐), in his 'Chronicle of Emperors and Kings,' says:—'Yu was constituted Chief of Hea, south of Yu-chow, the present Yang-chih (陽翟) of Ho-nan' (Mih wrote dur. the Tsin dyn.); 'and afterwards, when he succeeded to the throne which Shun resigned in his favour, he took the dynastic designation of Hea.' I have not, indeed, found the appointment of Yu to Hea in the 'Historical Records;' but the tradition of it was current during the Chow dynasty. In the 國語, 周語 下, under the year B C. 549, after

a long rambling account of Yu's labours, it is said that 'Great Heaven was pleased with him, and gave him the empire, while there was conferred on him' (we must understand by Yaou) 'the surname of Sze (賜姓曰姒), and the clan-name of Holder of Hea (氏曰有夏).' This part of the Shoo King never consisted of more than the four Books, which compose it at present—a fact difficult to be accounted for; and the first of them, much more extensive than all the others together, is descriptive of what took place during the vice-gerency of Shun, before the death of Yaou. Ying-tă says that originally it was among the Books of Yu, but that the historiographers of Hea placed it among those of their dynasty, or perhaps Confucius was the first to assign to it its present place. Whensoever it was first placed among the Books of Hea, there can be no doubt that Ts'ae Ch'in gives the true reason for that arrangement, when he says that the merit here described was the ground of Yu's advancement to the imperial seat.

NAME OF THE BOOK.—禹貢, 'The Tribute of Yu.' Tribute, however, is not here to be understood in the sense of a contribution *paid by one nation to another* in acknowledgment of subjection and testimony of fealty, but as the contribution paid by subjects to their proper rulers. The barbarous tribes round about the 'Middle Kingdom' bring here, indeed, their 貢, and the attempt by the rulers of the present Manchow dynasty to give the same name to the presents sent to them from Great Britain and other countries was an assumption which needed to be repressed and rebuked; but such offerings occupy a very inferior place, as compared with the 賦 or contribution of revenue, levied from each province. We might rather expect that the Book should be called 禹賦. 貢, however, has the general signification of 'an offering made by inferiors' (下之所供謂之貢), and may embrace the 賦, while that term is more restricted and could not be employed to comprehend the 貢 properly so called. This is the account given by Ying-tǎ of the name of the Book, and I think correctly. Ts'ae Ch'in endorses a view somewhat different:—'In the Book we have both 貢 and 賦, and yet it is called only by the former. Mencius observes that the sovereign of the Hea dynasty enacted the 50 *mow* allotment, and the payment of a proportion of the produce (夏后氏五十而貢, Bk. III. Pt I. iii. 6). This proportion was determined by taking the average of several years, so that, accord. to this acct., 貢 was the general name for the revenue levied under the Hea dynasty from the land.'

CONTENTS. The name,—'The Tribute of Yu,' gives a very insufficient account of the contents. The determination of the revenue, and of the various articles of tribute was, indeed, very important, but the Book describes generally the labours of Yu in remedying the disasters occasioned by the overflowing waters. Having accomplished that, he went on to define more accurately the boundaries of the different provinces, and to divide the empire into five tenures. It may be regarded as a domesday book of China in the 23d century before Christ: but when we consider that it is contained in the compass of a few pages, we cannot expect very much information from it. Choo He says in several places, that much of what is said about the geography of the country—the mountains and rivers—cannot be understood, in consequence of the changes of names, and the actual changes in nature which have taken place. This is doubtless the case; but when we shall have an accurate and scientific survey of China, and it is known to us in the length and breadth of its provinces as any of the countries of Europe is, this ancient document will be invested with a new interest, and have a light thrown upon it, for want of which we can at present in many places only grope our way. The division of the Book into two parts, which is found in Yung Ching's Shoo, and I have here followed, is convenient, but of modern device. It is still unobserved in many editions, of which I need only mention the 'Daily Explanation.' The first part is conveniently arranged in ten chapters, the first containing only one paragraph; and each of the others containing the account of one province in a good many paragraphs.

On the title of 'The Counsels of the Great Yu' it was observed that the Books of the Shoo have obtained a sixfold classification accord. to their subject-matter. This Book has been referred with reason to the class of the Canons. Chang Kew-ching (張九成, Sung dyn.) has the following observations on the authorship of it:—'Are we to suppose that it was composed by the historiographers? But they could not have known all the minutiæ which we find in it about the regulation of the waters. I venture to give my opinion in this way:—There are the first and last paragraphs, about Yu's dividing the land, &c., and returning his mace;—these are from the historiographers. But all between, from 冀州 down to 訖于四海, is the narrative by Yu himself of his various labours, —his narrative as presented to the emperor, and kept in the bureau of history, whence it was edited by the proper officers with some modifications of the style.'

CH. I. A SUMMARY OF YU'S SCHEME OF OPERATIONS UPON THE INUNDATED EMPIRE. It is the general opinion that this par. lays down the plan on which Yu proceeded to his task; and though there is nothing in the language to determine absolutely in fav. of this interpret., I think it is the most likely. First, he divided the land into nine provinces, and arranged in what order they should be taken in hand. Next, he travelled along the hills, and possessed himself with a general idea of what was to be done to afford a vent for the waters, and conduct them by their natural channels, Lastly, the waters being carried off, he defined the boundaries of the provinces more accurately than had been done before, by reference to the principal mountains and streams. 禹敷土,—敷土, comp. 'Counsels of Yu,' p. 1. Ch'ing defines 敷 by 布, 'to spread out,' 'to arrange,' adding 布治九州之水土, 'he arranged and reduced to order the water and land of the nine provinces.' Ma Yung says that 敷＝分; and in Gan-kwŏ we find all these terms together: 洪水汎溢禹分布治九州之土, 'amid the overflowing of the inundating waters, Yu divided, arranged, and reduced to order the land of the nine provinces.' It may be questioned whether the division of China into nine provinces originated with Yu. The first territorial arrangement of the country is referred to Hwang-te, who, it is said, 'mapped out the country, and divided it into provinces, making in all 10,000 States of 100 *le* each (畫野分州, 得百里之國萬區; see the 歷代疆域表, under Hwang-te).

于　底　○　于　太　○　梁　口　既 三節　冀 二節
衡　績 六節　覃　岳　原 五節　既　及　○　載　州
漳。　至　懷　陽。　至　修　岐。　治 四節　壺　○。

2　II. With respect to K'E-CHOW,—he did his work at Hoo-k'ow and
5　took effective measures at Lëang and K'e. Having repaired *the works* on T'ae-yuen, he proceeded on to the south of *mount* Yŏ. He
6　was successful with his labours on Tan-hwae, and went on to the cross-flowing stream of Chang.

In the accounts of Chuen-heuh, the grandson of Hwang-te, we read that he 'established nine provinces,' the names of which are the same as those of Yu. The 'Historical Records' give 傳 instead of 敷, and introduces this par. thus:—'Yu, along with Yih and Tseih, received the emperor's commands, and ordered the princes and people to call forth labourers to divide and arrange the land.' I introduce this passage because it helps us to understand how Yu accomplished his great work. We are too apt to think of him alone in connection with it. He had the merit of suggesting, directing, and superintending; but all the talent and strength of the empire were helping. Yih and Tseih are mentioned by himself as his coadjutors. Passages from the Shoo itself, the 'Historical Records,' &c., indicate that he was also in correspondence with Kaou-yaou, the Sze-yŏ, Pih-e, and the pastors of the provinces, and so had all the resources of the empire at his disposal. This has suggested to Hoo Wei (胡渭) another ingenious view of the meaning of 禹敷土. Taking 敷=傅=賦, 'to give,' 'to assign,' he says:—'What is expressed by 敷 took place before Yu went over his door. K'e-chow was to be assigned to so and so; Yen-chow to so and so; and so on. This was simply the choice and employment of men for the several portions of the work.' 隨山刊木,—see 'Counsels of Yu,' p. 1. Sze-ma Ts'een gives 行山表木, and Keang Shing inclines to interpret 刊 by 表; but we cannot admit this. The woods were hewn down to open up paths for men, and channels for the waters. Mencius tells us that Yih employed fire to destroy the forests and rank vegetation. We may suppose that fire was had recourse to, when peculiar difficulties opposed the use of the axe. 奠高山大川,—奠=定, 'to fix.' He fixed the great rivers and mountains;—but for what purpose? Ts'ae Ch'in answers:—'To distinguish accurately the boundaries of the different provinces.' Yĕh Mung-tih (葉夢得; early in the Sung dyn.) answers:—'As guiding marks to determine the application of the forces necessary to accomplish the work in hand' Gankwŏ and Ma Yung answered:—'To determine their order and degree, with reference to the sacrifices that should be offered to them.' This last view has found a vigorous advocate in Maou K'e-ling, who argues that 奠 denotes the preliminary sacrifices at the commencement of the work, and 旅, those offered at the conclusion of it, so that the 奠高山 here is in correlation with the 九山刊旅 in Part ii., p. 14. But with what is the 奠大川 in correlation? If it be said—with the 九川 滌源, there is no notion of sacrifice there. We might accept either the view of Ch'in or that of Mung-tih, but not that advocated by Maou.

CH. II. THE ACCOUNT OF K'E-CHOW. *Pp.* 2—6. *Engineering labours on the rivers and country.*

P. 2. 冀州. The old interpreters all read on 冀州既載, and placed a comma at 載, making the meaning to be=='A description of the work to be done in K'e-chow was first prepared.' No doubt it seemed to them that 既, being generally equivalent to our sign of the perfect tense, presupposed a subject already mentioned. But in p. 5, 既修大原, it introduces a clause in an absolute manner. It is much more in consonance with the analogy of the commencing parr. of the other chapters on the other provinces to put a stop at 州. The only difference is that those others are all defined by certain boundaries, whereas no boundaries are assigned to this. The reason may be, as Ts'ae says, that all the others being defined, the boundaries of this might thence be known; or, as it said by others, it is left undefined, a mark of distinction, as containing the imperial seat, the capital of the empire. Hwang-te is said to have had his capital in Choh-luh (涿鹿); Chuen-heuh, his in Te-k'ew (帝邱); Kaou-sin, his in Poh (亳);

Yaou, his in P'ing-yang; and Shun, his in P'oo-fan (蒲坂);—all of which places were within K'e-chow.   As to the actual boundaries of the province, it had the Ho—what is called the Yellow River—on three sides of it, the west south, and east. On the west, between it and Yung-chow, was all that portion of the Ho, which forms the present dividing line of Shen-se and Shan-se, in a course of about 500 miles, according to Williams (The Middle Kingdom, vol. I., p. 15). At the south-western corner of Shan-se, the Ho turns to the east, and first dividing that province from Ho-nan, flows through Ho-nan on to the south-west point of Shan-tung, and afterwards traverses Keang-soo, with a southerly incline, finally disembogueing itself in about lat. 34°. At any rate, one would have so described its course a few years ago; it is said now to pursue a north-easterly course from somewhere in the border between Shan-tung and Ho-nan. It did this in the time of Yu. It turned north at about the place where Chih-le, Shan-tung, and Ho-nan all touch, and its waters flowed north and east into the present gulph of Pih-chih-le. The southern boundary of K'e-chow, therefore was the Ho in its south-eastern flow, which divided it from Yu-chow; and its eastern boundary was the Ho in its north-eastern flow, which divided it from Yen-chow. [This north-eastern portion is often called the Ho of Yu;—the first change in its direction to a more southerly course took place in the 5th year of the emp. Ting (王定) of the Chow dyn. B.C. 601.] The northern boundary of K'e-chow must be left altogether indefinite.

From this account of the province, it will be seen that Medhurst is in error when he speaks of it as corresponding to the present Shan-se.(Shoo King, p. 83). It was of much larger extent. As stated in 'The Boundaries of the empire in Successive Dynasties,' K'e-chow embraced the present provinces of Chih-le and Shan-se, with the three departments of Chang-tih (彰德), Wei-hwuy (衞輝), and Hwae-k'ing (懷慶) in Ho-nan, and the western portion of Shing-king or Leaou-tung.

Pp. 3, 4. 既載壼口, 治梁及岐,
—If 既載 be joined, as by the old scholars, with 冀州, it is not possible to construe 壼口. They have said nothing, however, which would indicate that they saw the difficulty.

載 is best taken as = 事, 'to perform service.' Ts'ae and others would combine the meanings of 始 'first,' and 事. He says:—經始治之謂載; but this is not necessary.

壼口 is the name of a hill which we might translate 'Pot's-mouth.' It is 70 le to the south-east of the small dep., city of Keih (吉), in Shan-se. Medhurst gives its position as in lat. 36°15', N., long. 6°5', W. of Peking. The Ho passes it in its southward flow, 'seething like a boiling pot' (see a note in the 集傳), and I suppose that in the time of Yu

some spur of the mountain encroached upon the stream. South of Hoo-k'ow was the Lung-mun (龍門) or 'Dragon Gate,' an important point of the Ho, so called from a hill of that name; and north of it was the 孟門, or Great Gate,' also an important point. Before Yu's labours, the waters of the Ho not finding free course from Măng-mun downwards, there overflowed, and inundated both K'e-chow and Yung-chow. By what he did on Hoo-k'ow, and his immediately subsequent operations on mount Leang, he achieved one of the most notable of his 'labours,' and 'opened the Dragon-gate.' Leang and K'e are the names of two hills,—belonging, say the scholars of the Sung dyn. to K'e-chow; belonging, said the older interpreters, to Yung-chow. Acc. to Ts'ae, Leang was the Leu-leang (呂梁) hill, corresponding to the present 'Spine hill' ('骨脊山), in the north-east of the small dep. of Yung-ning (永寧), belong. to the larger one of Fun-chow (汾州); and K'e was the Hoo-k'e, or 'Fox-peaks,' hill in the same dep. of Fan-chow, in the west of Heaou-e district (孝義縣). Ts'ae says that the waters of the Ho passed at the base of both these hills. But it is objected by Hoo Wei that 'Spine hill' is fully 150 le from the Ho, and 'Fox-peaks' more than 330. I must conclude that while it was natural for the Sung scholars to look for Leang and K'e in K'e-chow, they have not been successful in finding them there. Turning to the old interpreters, who refer the hills to Yung-chow, Leang is the pres. mountain of that name, 90 le to the north-west of the dis. city of Han-shing (韓城), dep. Se-ngan, in Shen-se; and K'e, called also 'Heaven's pillar' (天柱) is 90 le north-east from K'e-san (岐山) dis. city, dep. of Fung-Ts'eang (鳳翔). The former was not far from the western bank of the Ho, and near to Lung-mun. We can easily see how some operations on it should have been necessary to complete the accomplishment of the object contemplated in beginning at Hoo-k'ow. But why should he have gone westward to mount K'e? Hoo Wei answers:—'By dealing with mount Lëang, a free passage was made for the Ho, and the calamity of inundation was removed from the country on the right and left of this western portion of it. But that country still remained unfit for the purposes of agriculture, covered with pools, undrained, and it was for Yu, acc. to his own words, 'to deepen the channels and canals, and conduct them to the rivers, that Tseih might proceed to his business. But why should he defer proceeding at once to his work on T'ae-yuen and Yŏ-yang, which were near the imperial seat? If he had now gone at once eastward, not a few years must have elapsed before he could come back to this point; and we may conclude also that it was of great importance to the capital itself that this part of the country should be regulated without delay.' These observations seem to give a sufficient explanation of Yu's turning aside a little from K'e-chow to the adjoining prov. on the west. There remains still another point to be touched on, before we proceed to the next par.—We get the impression that Yu's labours commenced at Hoo-k'ow and mount Lëang. But Choo He has questioned this. Referring again to Hoo Wei, he observes :—'Choo in his 語錄 says that he cannot fully credit the common view as to the commencement of Yu's labours, for that if he had opened the passage of the 'Dragon Gate' without previously clearing the channels below, the out-rush of the Ho would only have been more disastrous than before. It was Yu's plan to commence at the lowest point, and therefore in K'e-chow he must have begun at Këĕ-shih, and the nine Ho. These views have been followed, especially by Foo T'ung-shuh (傅同叔); and it is generally concluded that Yu began to deal with the waters in Yen-chow. But let us attend to the aspect of the inundation, as it presented itself to Yaou. He said :—"Destructive is the overflow of the waters. In their vast extent, they embrace the mountains and overtop the hills, threatening the heavens." Mencius' account is :—"In the time of Yaou, the waters flowing out of their channels, inundated the Middle kingdom. Snakes and dragons abounded, and the people had no place where they could settle themselves. In the low grounds they made nests for themselves, and in the high grounds they made caves." This was the aspect of the inundation as it appeared to Yaou, and frightened him ; it is described by him accordingly. It was occasioned chiefly by the outburst of the Ho above Măng-mun, and no other place so urgently required that measures should be taken with it. If Yu could manage the Ho at Lung-mun and mount Leang, he would find no insurmountable difficulties elsewhere ; if he could not do this, the capital must have become the home of fishes. But without reference to the capital, here was the spot where it was necessary to take the first measures to remedy the terrible evil.' K'ung Ying-tă reasons in a similar way, and insists that the waters of K'e-chow did not flow through Yen-chow.

P. 5. 既修太原,至于岳陽,— 既修, 'having repaired.' This is understood to have reference to the labours of K'wăn, Yu's father, which had not been altogether ineffectual. Choo Hoh-ling (朱鶴齡; of the pres. dyn.) has said :—'On the north of the Ho there are many of K'wăn's dykes. The capital being within the space here indicated, K'wăn had wrought with peculiar energy to defend it from the waters. Yu entered into his labours, availed himself of them and completed them. But there was this difference between the father and the son. Yu went first to the source of the evil, and made a free course for the Ho ; whereas K'wăn had confined himself to a branch of it, to the course of the Fun in those parts.' 太原,—lit., 'the great plain ;' but the name still exists as that of the principal prefecture of Shan-se, and also of a district of the same.

The city of T'ae-yuen is in lat. 37°45', N., lon. 3°55', W. of Peking. 岳陽,—'the south of Yŏ.' Yŏ, called also T'ae-yŏ, was the principal mountain in K'e-chow. It is now the Hoh-t'ae (霍太) hill, 30 le to the east of Hoh-chow city, belong. to the dep. of P'ing-yang. It is said to be 200 le in circumference, and its southern skirts touch on the two districts of Yoh-yang (岳陽), and Chaou-shing (趙城). Hereabouts Yaou, it is said, had his principal city when marquis of T'ang ; but this is doubtful. The 修......至, indicate continuousness of operation, and indeed this paragraph is descriptive of Yu's regulation of the river Fun (汾), which rose in T'ae-yuen, pursued a devious course to Yoh-yang, and afterwards joined the Ho.

P. 6. 覃懷底績.至于衡漳,—Yu is now operating on the borders of the Ho in its eastward course from the south-western corner of the pres. Shan-se. The name of Tan-hwae still partly remains in that of the dep. of Hwae-k'ing (懷慶), in Ho-nan, whose prin. city is in lat. 35°6', N., 3°28', W. of Peking. The territory was low and level, easily inundated therefore, and requiring more toil to be spent on it. The toil and the eventual success are indicated in the phrase 底績 ;—comp. Can. of Shun, p. 3, and Coun. of Kaou-yaou, p. 8. Having done all that was necessary for the present on the southern portion of the Ho, Yu went on to the junction of the Chang with the Ho ; or, as Lin Che-ke says, we may suppose that he crossed over the country, across the mountain ranges of 太行, to the sources of the Chang, and regulated its course, and the country which it drained, all the way to the Ho. 衡 is taken as = 橫, and 衡漳 is 'the cross-flowing Chang,' so called with reference to its course from east to west, or the contrary ; a course from north to south or from south to north being described as natural (從) ;—see the 集說. Ma Yung and Wang Suh were of opinion that 衡 was the name of one river, and 漳 that of another, but there is no evidence to support their view. It appears, however, that the 衡漳 was formed by the union of a 'clear' (清漳) and a 'muddy' (濁漳) Chang.' The foll. account of them is taken from the 地理今釋, or 'Modern Geography:'—'The Clear Chang rises 30 le to the south-west of the district city of Lŏ-p'ing, (lat. 37°35', N ; lon. 2°40', W.), dep. T'ae-yuen. Flowing south-east to the dis. of Shê-heen (涉縣), dep. Chang-tih (彰德), Ho-nan, it is there joined by the muddy Chang, at " the Meeting of the Chang." Thence it flows north-east to Chih-le, and in the dis. of Kwang

中。惟 厥 上、惟 厥_{八節}壤。惟 厥_{七節}
〇 中 田 錯、上 賦 〇 白 土

8　The soil of this province was whitish and mellow.　Its contribution of revenue was the first of the highest class, with some proportion of the second.　Its fields were the average of the middle class.

p'ing (廣平), in the dep. of the same name, it throws off a branch which joins the Wei, (衞河), while the main stream, skirting the borders of Shan-tung, in the dis. of K'ew-heen (邱縣; dep. Ts'ing-chow) again divides, and sends off a branch northwards to the marsh of Ta-luh (大陸澤), passing on itself through the dep. of Ho-këen (河間) in Chih-le, into dep. of T'een-tsin, where, in the dis. of Ts'ing-hëen (青縣), it unites with the Wei.　Thence flowing northwards as far as Se-koo of T'een-tsin, it receives various streams, and holds an eastward course to the sea.　At this quarter it is called the Old Chang, to distinguish it from the branch of itself which went off to Ta-luh, and rejoins it at Se-koo, under the name of the New Chang.' (Se-koo, 'the western Koo' [西沽], to distinguish it from Ta-koo (大沽), a name become sufficiently familiar of late years).　'The muddy Chang has its rise in the dis. of Ch'ang-tsze (長子), dep. of Loo-ngan (路安), Shan-se, and also follows a south-eastern course to the "Meeting of the Chang."'　Of course, in Yu's time, the Chang, being absorbed in the Ho, had no subsequent course of its own to the sea.　Its junction with the Ho took place in the pres. dep. of Ho-këen, dis. of Fow-shing (阜城; lat. 37°55'. N., lon. about 15', W.).

Pp. 7, 8.　*Soil and Revenue.*　7.　土 here denotes the soil or ground, with general reference to the whole province; and it is described by regard both to its colour and nature.　Its colour was 'white,' = whitish, and its nature was 壤.　This term may be interchanged with 土 in the general sense of soil or ground;—see the 'Rites of Chow,' 地官, 司徒, 第二之二, esp. pp. 23, 24.　Here, however, where it denotes a particular kind of soil, the word *mellow*, signifying, in this application, 'soft, easily pulverized,' very well represents its meaning.　Gan-kwŏ defines it by 無塊, 'without lumps,' and the 說文 by 軟土, 'soft

earth.'　In the portion of the 'Rites of Chow' just referred to, we have much said about the practical uses to which a knowledge of the different soils should be turned, but the simple statement of the text does not require that I should enter on that subject.　8. Both the revenue and the fields—that is, the cultivable ground—were arranged in three classes (see Part ii., p. 15), and under each class were three divisions.　Thus the value of the ground ranged from the 1st to the 9th degree; and the amount of revenue did the same, the general rule, I apprehend, in regard to it being that it should be a tenth of the produce.　The amount of revenue would be very much regulated by the character of the ground, but not entirely so.　A poor tract of country well cultivated would produce more than a rich one, left to go to waste.　The actual produce depended on many other circumstances in addition to the character of the soil, such as the density or sparseness of the population, the system of irrigation, manuring, &c.　Here in K'e-chow, the revenue was the highest of the highest class, (厥賦惟上上), with an admixture of the second degree of the same. Such is said to be the force of 錯.　Gan-kwŏ and K'ang-shing both define that term in this connection by 雜.　Gan-kwŏ says:—雜出第二之賦, 'it mixedly produced the revenue of the second degree.'　Ma Yung took a different view (地有上下錯通率第一); but allowing their meaning, we are still unable to say when and where the reduction from the highest amount of revenue was admitted.　In the account of the other provinces, the description of the fields always precedes that of the revenue, as is proper, the revenue chiefly depending on the ground; but here the order is reversed.　The revenue is mentioned first, and the quality of the fields follows.　The most likely explanation, perhaps, of this is that suggested by Lin Che-k'e, that K'e-chow being the imperial domain, its income would be derived not only from the fields, but from a groundrent, and imposts on gardens, orchards, &c., as well.　In the other provinces, again, mention is made of 貢, 'articles of tribute,' in addition to the 'revenue.'　Those were expressions of their fealty presented by the princes.　There was no occasion for them in the imperial domain.

恆九節 既 大 既 島十節 夾十一節 碻 入 河。
衞 從、 陸 作。 夷。皮服。 右。石 于 ○

9　The *waters of the* Hăng and Wei were brought to their proper channels; and Ta-luh was made capable of cultivation.

10　The wild people of the islands brought dresses of skins.　Keeping
11　close on the right to the rocks of Kĕĕ, they entered the Ho.

P. 9.　*Other engineering labours.*　It is difficult to say why this par. does not immediately follow the 6th.　We may reasonably suppose that the country was all rescued from the inundation before measures were taken to fix the revenue.　從=從其故道, 'to follow their old channels.'　從 has a *hophal* signification. The Hăng river takes its rise from a valley of the hill of the same name, in the pres. dis. of Keuh-yang (曲陽; lat. 38°39′, N.; long. 1°40′, W.), dep. Chin-ting (眞定, called also 定州).　Near its source it is called the 'Long Streamlet' (長溪); it pursues an eastern course, to the borders of K'e Chow (祁州), dep. Paou-ting (保定), receiving difft. names in its progress.　At this point it unites with the Tsze (滋河), and by-and-by flows into the T'ang water (唐水), called also the Kow (滱).　The Wei, under the name of Luy-kow (雷溝), rises in the district of Ling-show (靈壽; lat. 38°18′, N., long. 1°57′, W.), and flowing to the south, enters the Hoo-t'o (滹沱).　Hoo Wei contends that by the Hăng of the text we are to understand the Kow, and by the Wei the Hoo-t'o.　The Kow and the Hoo-t'o now unite their streams, and travelling eastwards pass the city of T'een-tsin, and on to the sea.　The Hăng and the Wei in Yu's time poured their united waters into the Ho.

大陸既作.—K'ang-shing says that 大陸 is 'the name of a marsh or lake, on the north of Keu-luh' (鉅鹿; lat., 37°17′, N., lon., 1°17′, W.).　Modern writers incline to consider it the name of a large tract of flat ground, 'embracing,' says the Daily Explanation, 'the district of Hing-t'ae (邢臺), and the smaller depp. of Chaou (趙州), and Shin (深).'　I apprehend the modern view is correct, 陸 having the signification, given in the 爾雅, of 'what is high and level.'　As to the lake of Ta-luh, called also Kwang-o (廣阿), it is still very considerable.　It touches the dis. of Shuh-

luh (束鹿), dep. of Paou-ting (保定); that of Keu-luh, dep. of Shun-tih (順德); those of Lung-p'ing (隆平), and Ning-tsin (寧晉) in Chaou-chow; and Shin-chow :— see a note in the 集傳, and the description of the lake in the 'Statistical Account of the Empire of Ta-ts'ing,' under Shun-tih foo.)　The Hăng and the Wei were to the north of Ta-luh, and I suppose that their waters overflowing and running south into the lake made the country difficult of cultivation.　Still the repetition of the 旣=旣從, 旣作—implies that a good deal of independent labour had to be expended on Ta-luh,—the country, I suppose, all round the lake, before it was possible to cultivate it, which is the meaning of 作.

Pp. 10, 11.　*Tribute brought by barbarous tribes, and their route to the capital.*　10 島夷皮服,—The 'Historical Records' read 鳥夷; as did Ch'ing, Ma, Wang, and others of the Han dynasty.　Gan-kwŏ determined that 島 was the proper reading, which was subsequently introduced into the text.　He defines the character by 海曲, 'bends of the sea,' *i.e.*, bays, with islands in them that could be inhabited.　But the proper definition of 島 is 'an island' (海中可居者曰島).　If 鳥 be the proper reading, then 鳥夷, or 'Bird barbarians,' would be the name of a tribe of wild people, for whom we are to look in the islands or mainland, north and east from K'e-chow.　Assuming that Gan-kwŏ was right in thinking we should read 島, we are restricted from the mainland.　Hoo Wei thinks that only the Japanese and the people of San-han (三韓 (see a long, but extravagant description of this tribe or tribes in the Books of the 'After Han,' 卷七十五) can be intended.　But I cannot suppose that, if Japan was then occupied, its people had any intercourse with China, far less acknowledged its sovereignty.　The 'skin dresses,' no doubt = furs, rather lead our thoughts to the mainland, to the regions northeast from K'e-chow.　11 夾右碻

12 III. *Between* the Tse and the Ho was YEN-CHOW.

13 The nine branches of the Ho were conducted by their proper
15 channels.   Luy-hea was formed into a marsh; *in which the waters of*
16 the Yung and the Tseu were united.   The mulberry grounds were
made fit for silkworms, and then *the people* came down from the
heights, and occupied the ground *below.*

17 The soil of this province was blackish and rich; the grass in it
18 became luxuriant, and the trees grew high.   Its fields were the
lowest of the middle class.   Its revenues just reached what could
be deemed the correct amount; but they were not required from it
as from the other provinces, till after it had been cultivated for
19 thirteen years.   Its articles of tribute were varnish and silk; the
baskets from it were filled with woven ornamental *fabrics.*

20 They floated along the Tse and T‘ă, and so reached the Ho.

石,—we might translate almost literally—'they *hugged* on the right the rocks of Kĕĕ.' Evidently these were somewhere on the northern shore of the gulph of Pih-chih-le;—though some have supposed that 碣石 might be the name of a hill, some distance inland, which served as a land-mark to boats—for we can hardly use another term for the craft of those times—entering the Ho. But this view affords no explanation of the expressive phrase 夾右.

In the time of the founder of the Ts‘in dynasty, the rock or rocks of Kĕĕ were well known. He visited them, and had an inscription engraved—we may suppose on the most conspicuous. Subsequently, the emp. Woo (武) visited the place in the year B.C. 109. It is generally referred now to the coast of the dis. of Foo-ning (撫寧; lat. 39°56′, lon. 2°52′, E.) in the dep. of Yung-p‘ing (永平). No traces of such a rock or rocks are now to be found

there; but this may be accounted for by encroachments of the sea. See again on Part ii. p. 1.   The Ho in Yu's time must have entered the sea in not much less than 40° N. lat.

入于河,—this is evidently descriptive of the route of the wild people with their tribute of furs. The Ho is mentioned as the grand channel by which communication was held with the capital in connection with the tribute of every province. There can be no other meaning here; and when Gan-kwŏ says that it was Yu who returned by the Ho to the capital, to report his labours, and Ch‘ing K‘ang-shing also interprets the words of Yu, though somewhat differently, we feel that the old interpreters may be very unsafe guides to the understanding of the text.

CH. III. THE ACCOUNT OF YEN-CHOW.
P. 1. *The boundaries.* Those were the river Tse on the south and east, and the Ho on the north and west. The former separated it from Yu-chow and Ts‘ing-chow; the latter, from K‘e-chow. The 濟, anciently called also the 泲 had its origin, under the name of the 沇

in 'King's-house' hill (王屋山), in the pres. Tse-heen (濟縣), dep of Hwae-k'ing, Ho-nan;—see Part ii. p. 10. This would give its rise in about lat. 35°5', N., lon. 4°46', W. Flowing eastwards it now enters the sea, as the 小清, at about lat. 37°15' N., lon., 1°55', E. Its name appears in its course in that of Tse-nan (濟南), the principal dep. of Shan-tung. Yen-chow did not commence at or near its source. We must place the boundary point between Yen and Yu in the pres. Ts'aou-chow (曹州);—see Hoo Wei, *in loc.* The same critic says on the Ho as the boundary-line of Yen on the west and north:—'At the pres. dis. of Tsoo-shing (lat. 35°20', N.; lon. 2°6', W.), dep. Wei-hwuy of Ho-nan, the Ho proceeded north-east towards the dep. of Ta-ming in Chih-le, and at the hill of Ta-p'ei (大伾), in the dis. of Seun-heen (濬縣; lat. 35°45', N.; lon. 1°38', W.), it made a bend to the west, and flowed northwards past the dep. of Chang-tih in Ho-nan. Then turning eastwards again, it flowed through various depp. of Chih-le-Kwang-p'ing, Shun-tih, Chin-ting, and Ho-kien, on to the sea. This was the old course of the Ho of Yu, the same as the course of the Chang described in the Han dynasty.' According to this account, the Ho of Yu must have disembogued where the Pe-ho (北河, 'the northern Ho') now does. With these boundaries, Yen-chow (兗 is sometimes called 沇) may be said to have contained—of the pres. Shan-tung, the dep. of Tung-ch'ang (東昌), the northern portion of Tse-nan, and western of Yen-chow; and of Chih-le, the dep, of Ta-ming, with portions of those of Ho-keen and T'een-tsin:—see the 歷代疆域表. It was not a large province.

Pp. 13—16. *Engineering labours.* 13. 九河既道,-既道 seems properly explained by Ts'ae—既順其道, 'were made to follow their courses.' The whole sentence gives the idea that the nine streams or branches were already existing, and that Yu's work was to clear and direct them. K'ang-shing seems rather to have thought that the nine channels were opened by Yu, to diminish the force of the mighty stream (河水自上至此,流盛而地平無岸,故能分爲九,以衰其勢); but such a view cannot be thought of. The truth seems to be that the Ho discharged itself into the sea by many branches, in addition to the main stream described in the last note. These all occupied the northern part of Yen-chow, which formed the delta of the Ho, and Yu, selecting eight or nine of the streams, cleared their course, and by means of them drained the country. It has always been, and still is, a curious inquiry among Chinese scholars, to determine, if pos-

sible, the nine Ho. The 爾雅, as if they had all been existing in the Chow dyn., gives their names as T'oo-hae (徒駭); T'ae-she (太史); Ma-kёё (馬頰); Fuh-foo (覆鬴); Hoo-soo (胡蘇) Kёen-kёё (簡潔); Kow-p'wan (鈎盤); Kih-tsin (鬲津). These are only eight names; and some therefore divide the sixth name into two, making the Kёen one stream, and the Kёё another, while others, more probably, make out the nine by adding to those eight the 'Ho of Yu,' or the main stream, already described. As early as the Han dynasty, it was the opinion of many that it was of no use trying to identify these various streams, the face of the country being so much altered from the time of Yu. Some, indeed, were of opinion even then, that the whole of the delta of the Ho of those early days had been swept away into the sea. Others, however, thought that the Kёen-kёё, the Kow-p'wan, and the Kih-tsin were then determinable; and the researches of the scholars of the T'ang dynasty are said to have determined other three;—but these matters are very doubtful. It is sufficient for us to know that the northern part of Yen-chow, the delta of the Ho, was rescued from the inundating waters by Yu. 14. In the south-east of the small dep. of Puh (濮), sub. to Ts'aou-chow (曹州), is the marsh of Luy, still retaining part of the ancient name. It was in the waters of Luy-hea that Shun fished, according to the 'Historical Records,' and hereabouts also Yaou is said to have rambled (堯作游成陽; 成陽 has been the name of Puh-chow under various dynasties). 'Luy-hea was marshed;'—we are not to suppose that Yu now for the first time formed a marsh at this point, but that by draining and embanking he reduced and confined the waters to their proper limits.

Ts'ae quotes a story from the 山海經 about a spirit of thunder with a dragon's body and a man's head, which dwells in the lake and makes a noise like thunder by thumping on its belly. 'Thus,' concludes Ts'ae, 'the lake, originally called the Hea, got its name of Luy-hea, the Thunder-hea.' One Le Che-tsaou (李之藻), of the Ming dyn, ridiculing this story, says that at certain seasons the waters seem to be sucked through some passage at the bottom with a loud noise. 15. I do not think that the Yung and the Tseu have been distinctly identified. They were streams in the neighbourhood of the Luy-hea, and it seems proper to join this par. with the prec., and to read that the two streams were united in the marsh. Yet it may not have been so. Both Gan-kwŏ and K'ang-shing thought so. The latter, indeed, as if he were describing what he had seen, says that the streams first met each other from opposite directions, and then entered the lake in one stream (雍 [so he reads for 灉] 水沮水相觸,而合入此澤中). On the other hand, we read in the 'Daily

Explanation:'—'The Yung issuing from the Ho, and the Tseu issuing from the Tse, when the Tse was regulated, the Yung flowed into the Tseu, and they were conducted in one stream to the Ho.'

16 桑土既蠶,—'when the mulberry country was *silkworm-ed*;'—Medhurst translates —'supplied with silkworms;' but the meaning must be rather as I have given. The silkworm dislikes moisture;—as the country was drained, and the waters confined to their proper places, the people could attend to it with success, What particular tract of the country was intended by 桑土 we do not know. The whole of Yen-chow was distinguished for its mulberry trees and silkworms, but especially the region about Puh. K'ang-shing quotes, in illustration, from the 樂記 Bk. I. 6, 桑閒濮上之音. 是(=於是)降(*i.e.*, 民降)丘宅土,—丘 or 邱 is defined by 小陵, 'a small mound' (see the 廣雅); by 土性自然, 'the natural formation of the ground' (孫炎). In Yen-chow the hills were few, but the mounds or rising grounds were many. While the inundation prevailed, the people were driven to these, but now they could descend from the heights, and dwell on the level ground. 宅土=宅平土.

Pp. 17—19. *Soil, revenue, and tribute.* 17. The colour of the soil was the opposite of that of K'e-chow, being 'black,' or blackish. I find it difficult to determine exactly the meaning of 墳 (2d tone). Ma Yung defines it by 膏肥, 'rich and fat;' Gan-kwŏ, by 墳起, as if it meant rising up in mounds or ridges. It is better to abide by Ma's meaning. 厥草惟繇,—繇=茂, 'luxuriant.' The 說文 quotes the passage under 蘨, with the expl. of 草盛皃. 條=長, 'tall.'

Lin Che-k'e observes that the provinces on the north and west were very hilly, and naturally rich in grass and forests, so that there was no occasion to speak of these things in connection with them. The provinces in the south and east, however, were low and wet; they suffered especially from the inundation; all vegetation in them was stunted or unnaturally rank; and therefore the grass and trees of Yen, Seu, and Yang are all made mention of.

Hoo Wei observes that this account of the grass and trees of Yen-chow, growing luxuriantly and tall after Yu's labours, would seem to be inconsistent with Mencius' observation that the inundation made all vegetation more luxuriant (Bk. III., Pt. I., iv. 7); and replies that Mencius' idea is that the overflowing waters caused everywhere a rank jungly growth, whereas here the description is of the country under the hand of man, drained of the excessive floods, and responding readily to the toil put forth on it.

18. The fields of this province were ranked in the 6th degree,—the lowest of the middle class. Its revenue was 貞. This char. is defined, both by the ancient and modern interpreters as 正, 'correct,' 'exact,' and further they all agree in saying that the revenue of this province was the lowest of all. Ts'ae brings this meaning out of 正 thus:—'The revenue of Yen was the lightest of all; and the sovereigns of the empire consider that the lightest revenue is the correct thing' (以薄賦爲正). The rest of the par.,—作十有三載乃同, he considers an additional circumstance. Not only was the revenue fixed at the lowest degree, but even that amount was not levied till after 13 years of cultivation, so much more had Yen suffered from the overflow of the waters than the other provinces. This interpretation is upon the whole the best that has been proposed. To take 作 as descriptive of the cultivation of the land is in harmony with its meaning everywhere else in this Book. The old interpreters,—Gan-kwŏ, Ch'ing, and Ma Yung,—all took 作十有三載 as descriptive of the length of time that it took to deliver Yen from the inundating waters, so that it was the very last of the provinces on which the work could be reported as completed. Gan-kwŏ gets a meaning for 貞 = 正 out of this circumstance:—'Yen was the ninth rescued from the flood, and so its revenue was fixed the ninth or last in degree.' Ch'ing read on 貞=正 with the next characters, with an adverbial meaning, = 'just,' This may be done, but then there is nothing in the sentence to indicate that the revenue was fixed at the lowest rate.   18, 厥貢,—Choo

He says:—'貢 denotes the offerings presented by the princes to the emperor; therefore in all the eight provinces, beyond the imperial domain, we have mention of them.' Under the Chow dyn., those offerings were of nine kinds:—'Offerings available for sacrifice' (祀貢), victims, &c.; 'offerings for the ladies of the harem' (嬪貢), as silk and hemp; 'offerings available for vessels,' (器貢), metal, sounding stones, varnish, &c.; 'offerings available for presents (幣貢), gems, silks, horses, &c.; 'building materials' (材貢); 'offerings of commodities' (貨貢): 'dresses, and materials for dresses' (服貢); 'feathers and hair' (旉貢); 'sundries' (物貢), as fish, fruits, &c.; (see the 'Rites of Chow,' 天官冢宰第一之二.) The articles from Yen-chow consisted of varnish, the province producing largely the trees which yield it, and silk.

達于濟。○
筐厭絲。○
怪石、萊夷
錯岱畎絲枲鉛松
厥貢鹽絺海物惟
上下厥賦中上。○
濱廣斥。○厥田惟
道。○厥土白墳海
夷既畧。○濰淄其
海岱惟青州。○　嵎

廿一節　廿二節　廿三節　廿四節　廿五節　廿六節　廿七節
浮于汶、厥牧厥

21　IV. The sea and the Tae *mountain* were *the boundaries of* Ts'ING-
CHOW.

23　*The territory of* Yu-e was defined; and the Wei and Tsze were
conducted by their proper channels.

24
25　The soil of this province was whitish and rich; near the sea were
wide tracts of salt land. Its fields were the lowest of the first class,
and its contribution of revenue the highest of the second.

26　Its articles of tribute were salt, fine grass-cloth, and the productions of the sea, of various kinds; with silk, hemp, lead, pine-
trees, and strange stones, from the valleys of the Tae. The wild
tribes of Lae were taught tillage and pasturage, and brought in
their baskets the silk from the mountain mulberry.

27　They floated along the Wăn, and reached the Tse.

厥筐織文,—the 筐 were round bamboo
baskets, in which manufactured fabrics were
sent to the capital. The 織文 would be
various kinds of silks, flowered or ornamented;
—but not, some say, woven with various colours.
　P. 20. *Course to the Ho, en route for the capital.*
To pass from one river into another, without
having to take the land and cross the country,
is what is denoted by 達. Some think they
passed from the Tse into the T'ă, and then into
the Ho. It might be so in some cases, but not
always. The T'a (in the 說文 we find 濕,
and not 漯) had its rise in the pres. dis. of
Chaou-shing (朝城; lat. 36° 8′, N., lon. 43′,
W.), dep. Ts'aou-chow, and entered the sea
near the pres. dis. city of Lŏ-ngan (樂安;
lat. 37° 5′, N., lon. 2°10′, E.) dep of Ts'ing-chow.
Yu is said to have made a junction between
one of the branches of the Ho, which he led
away from Ta-p'ei, and the T'ă. By this the
tribute bearers could reach the Ho; and thence
their course to the capital was well defined.
　CH. IV. THE ACCOUNT OF Ts'ING-CHOW.
P. 21. *Its boundaries.* These are given very

indefinitely,—the sea and Tae. Tae is the same
as Tae-tsung, Can. of Shun, p. 8, the well known
T'ae-shan (泰山). In the note on that pass.,
the district of T'ae-ngaл, where the mountain
is, is said to belong to the dep. of Tse-nan. So it
formerly did; but T'ae-ngan is now constituted
itself an independent department. The position
of T'ae-ngan city is given from Medhurst in
the same place as 36°30′, N. lat., 1° E. Lon.
According to Biot, the lat. is 36°14′, N., and the
lon. 45′, E.　Tae must be understood in the
text as defining the boundary of Ts'ing on the
west and south. A line drawn in the same lat.
would soon reach the Ts'e on the west, and the
sea on the east, dividing Ts'ing from Seu-chow.
In the time of the Chow dynasty, we find references to a wall (長城) built by princes of
Ts'e, to mark this division, and protect themselves from encroachment on the south. See the
禹貢錐指, *in loc.* The sea, again, formed
the boundary on the north and east; it would
do so on the north so far, to the point where it
received the Tse, which would then become the
dividing line between Ts'ing and Yen-chow. As
to the boundary on the east, the text would
never give the idea that it passed beyond the
sea which washes the north and east of the

pres. Shan-tung, so that the territory of Ts'ing-chow extended indefinitely into Leaou-tung, and Chaou-seen or Corea. So it would appear, however, to have done. When Shun extended Yu's nine provinces to twelve (Can. of Shun, p, 10), he divided Ts'ing-chow into Ts'ing and Ying (營);—he cut off, that is, from Ts'ing all the indefinitely extended portion lying north and east across the sea, from the present Shan-tung; and constituted it into a new province. In confirmation of this, the 爾雅 may be referred to, where, in the enumeration of the nine provinces, we do not have the name of Ts'ing-chow, but read instead—齊曰營州, 'Ts'e was called Ying-chow.' Now Ts'e embraced nearly all of Ts'ing-chow west of the sea. The calling it 營 proves how Ts'ing and Ying were connected, and is a sufficient answer to the view of some who contend that the Ying-chow of Shun was a section of K'e-chow, and not of Ts'ing-chow. The 'Boundaries of the Empire in successive Dynasties' says :—'Ts'ing-chow embraced the three departments of Ts'ing, Tăng, and Lae, with the western portion of Tse-nan, extending also to all the parts of Leaou-tung and Ting-leaou.'

Pp. 22, 23. *Engineering labours.* 22. 嵎 夷既略,—Gan-kwŏ defines 略 by 用 功小, 'to expend a little labour upon;' but the term—used only here in the description of Yu's operations—has probably a more definite signification. In the first meaning given to 略 in the dict., it is coupled with 經,—經 略, meaning 'to define'—or, perhaps to survey —'the boundaries.' Ts'ae adopts this meaning, and adds 為之封畛, 'to raise dykes and boundaries about it.' Yu-e is the same as the Yu-e, to which Yaou sent the second brother He, to observe the rising sun (Can. of Yaou, p. 4). The name 嵎夷 is writen also 堣夷, 昌 銕; 嵎鐵 (evid. a mistake for 銕), and perhaps in other ways. Those who confine Ts'ing-chow within the pres. Shan-tung refer this place to the small dep. of Ning-hae (寧 海州,; lat. 39°35', N., lon. 4°18', E.) in Tăng-chow. But as Yaou would send He to the remotest point eastwards, which was within the limits of the empire, and we have seen that Ts'ing-chow extended to the pres. Corea, it is more natural to conclude that Yu-e was some tract in that region. 23. 濰淄其道, —*lit.*, 'the Wei and the Tsze, their channels,' *i.e.,* were conducted by their proper channels. 其 道=既道, p. 8. Ts'ae says, indeed, that 其道 indicates that Yu led the rivers here to their proper channels, while 既道 shows that they were new channels which he made to divide the force of the Ho; but we saw reason to question this view of that portion of Yu's labours. The river Wei rises in the north-

east of Keu-chow (lat., 35°35', N.; lon. 2°52', W.), dep. of E-chow (沂州), and flowing east passes by Choo-shing (諸城) in Ts'ing-chow. Thence proceeding north, it enters the sea, 50 *le* to the north-east of Ch'ang-yih (昌邑縣; lat., 36°52', N.; lon., 2°15', E.). The Tsze (淄 is not found in the 說文. Keang-shing edits 甾, with which 蓄 was interchanged) rises in the northern slope of Yuen hill (原 山), 25 *le* to the West of Poh-san dis. city (博 山); thence it flows north-eastwards past the districts of Yih-too (益都), Lin-tsze (臨 淄), Loh-ngan (樂安), and Show-kwang (壽光),—all in Ts'ing-chow. Not far from this last city (lat. 36°55', N.; lon., 2°32', E.), it enters the sea by the embouchure of the Ts'ing water (清水泊). With the Wei and Tsze, Yu's labours in Ts'ing-chow terminated; —he had less to do here than in other provinces.

Pp. 24—26. *Soil, revenue, and tribute.* 24. 厥土白墳,—see pp. 7 and 17. 海 濱廣斥,—斥謂地鹹鹵 '斥 is descriptive of a country which is salt.' Accord. to the 說文, 斥 and 鹵 are synonyms, salt tracts in the east being described as 斥, and similar tracts in the west as 鹵. The country intended in the text was doubtless the coast of the two departments of Tăng and Lae, where there is an active preparation of salt at the present day. The ancient kingdom of Ts'e was noted for its advantages of salt and fish. 25. The fields of this province were only second in the empire to those of Yung and Seu. 26. 絺,—this char. denotes a fine fabric made of the fibres of the 葛, or *dolichos tuberosus.* A coarser fabric of the same kind was called 綌. Hoo Wei observes that in subsequent ages these fabrics were required only from the southern regions, with the single exception of 15 pieces of 絺葛, which continued to be required from Lin-tsze (臨淄),—a relic of Yu's arrangements. 海物惟錯,—海物, 'things of the sea,' *i.e.*, fishes, crabs, oysters, &c. Gan-kwŏ here defines 錯, as in p. 8, by 雜非一種, 'mixed, not of one kind only.' In opp. to this, Lin Che-k'e says that 海 物 sufficiently declares the variety of the articles, without the addition of 惟錯 to convey the same idea. Comparing the sentence with 齒革羽毛惟木, p. 44, he argues that 錯 must be something different

○ 州。徐 惟 淮 及 岱 海 ^{廿八節}

28   V. The sea, the Tae *mountain*, and the Hwae were the *boundaries* of Ts'EU-CHOW.

from 海物, and = 'grinding stones.' Woo Ch'ing, adopts the same view, and argues that 惟 in the middle of a clause is a conjunctive particle, meaning 'and.' The interpretation itself is not unlikely, but the meaning given to 惟 cannot be sustained;—as, *e.g.*, in p. 21.

岱畎 絲 枲 鉛 松 怪 石,—畎 here = 谷, 'valleys,' difft. from its use in the 'Yih and Tseih,' p. 1. The 'strange stones' are very perplexing to commentators. Ts'ae gets over the difficulty by supposing they were articles indispensable in the making of certain vessels, and not curiosities, merely to be looked at.   萊 夷 作 牧,—the note of Gan-kwŏ on this is:—萊 夷 地 名, 可 以 放 牧, 'Lae-e is the name of a country, adapted for the pasturing of flocks.' This must be a mistake. 萊 夷 can only be 'the wild people of Lae.' Yen Sze-koo (顏 師 古) said they were 'the wild people of mount Lae;' and this mountain is referred to the dis. of Hwang-heen (黃 縣) in Tăng-chow. No doubt their name remains in that of the dep. of Lae-chow. We may suppose they were spread over the country embraced now in the two depp. of Tăng-chow and Lae-chow. They continued, notwithstanding Yu's discipline and teaching of them, wild and intractable down into the Chow dyn. They figured at the famous interview between the princes of Loo and Ts'e at Keă-kuh, where Confucius distinguished himself (vol. I. proleg. pp. 73, 74). Gan-kwŏ, and Ts'ae after him, make 作 牧 one thing, and so did Sze-ma Ts'een who reads 萊 夷 爲 牧. The view in the transl. is more in acc. with the usage of 作 in this Book. Woo Ch'ing and Hoo Wei both approve it.   厥 is the name of a mountain mulberry tree. Silkworms fed on its leaves produced a very tough silk, which made good strings for lutes. We can hardly read the text otherwise than that the baskets of this silk were brought by the wild people of Lae. I make this note because some would extend the 厥 to the whole province, like the 厥 貢 at the beginning of the par.

P. 27. *Route of conveyance to the capital.* Arriving at the Tse, the tribute-bearers would go on to the Ho; and thence to the capital. This we readily infer from the former notices of the routes of conveyance. The subject of the Wăn river is a good deal perplexed. There were five streams so called, finally, it would appear, all uniting their waters. The course of the main stream may be thus described. It took its rise in the dis. of Lae-woo (萊 燕; lat., 36°16', N., lon., 1°25', E.), dep. of T'ae-ngan. Flowing past the districts of T'ae-ngan, Fei-shing (肥 城), and Ning-yang (寧 陽), on to the subordinate dep., of Tung-p'ing (東 平; lat., 36°07', N., lon., 03, E.), it entered the Tse. This ancient course of the Wăn cannot now be traced. It was diverted, during the Yuen and Ming dynasties, to feed the Grand Canal.

Ch. V. THE ACCOUNT OF SEU-CHOW. P. 28. *Boundaries.* Three boundaries of this province are mentioned, while of the other provinces only two are specified. There was the sea on the east; the Tae mountain on the north; and the river Hwae on the south. For the Hwae see on Part ii., p. 11. It is sufficient here to state that it takes its rise in the dis. of T'ung-pih (桐 柏, lat. 32°20', N., lon. 3°10', W.), dep. Nan-yang, of Ho-nan. Flowing east, the main stream of it joins the Yellow river in the dis. of Ts'ing-ho (清 河; lat. 33°35', N., lon. 2°34', E.), dep. Hwae-ngan (淮 安), in Keang-soo. In Yu's time it held its own way to the sea, and was the dividing line between Seu-chow and Yang-chow.   The Tae mountain is as indefinite a boundary for the north of Seu, as we saw it was for the south of Ts'ing-chow. The north-east dividing-line of the two was where the two depp. of E-chow and Ts'ing-chow now touch.   No western boundary is mentioned. In the time of Chow, according to the 爾 雅, 'westward from the Tse to the sea was Seu-chow' (濟 東 日 徐 州). We may conclude, therefore, that the Tse was, to some distance at least, the boundary between Seu-chow and Yu-chow. According to the 'Boundaries of Successive Dynasties,' Seu-chow embraced the territory of the pres. dep. of Yen-chow in Shan-tung and all the country south to Seu-chow in Keang-soo; and from the small dep. of Suh-chow (宿 州) in Fung-yang, and Sze-chow 泗 州, (both in Ngan-hwuy), eastward through Keang-soo, by Seu-chow and the north of Hwae-ngan dep., on to the dep. of Hae-chow (海 州).   A more detailed account given in a note in the 集 傳, from the 'Geography Modernized,' (地 理 今 釋), is to the effect that the present Seu-chow (in Keang-soo); the four districts of Hwae-yuen (懷 遠), Woo-ho (五 河), Hung-heen (虹

五色羽畎夏 ○ 厥賦惟中土 卅五節 厥貢惟土 厥田惟上中、卅四節 草木漸包。○ 厥土赤埴墳、卅三節 東原底平。○ 卅二節 大野既豬。○ 卅一節 蒙羽其藝。○ 卅節 淮沂其乂。廿九節

30 The Hwae and the E *rivers* were regulated. The *hills of* Mung
31 and Yu were brought under cultivation. The *lake of* Ta-yay was
32 confined within its proper limits. The *country of* Tung-yuen was
successfully brought under management.

33   The soil of this province was red, clayey, and rich. The trees and
34 grass became more and more bushy. Its fields were the second of
the highest class; its contribution of revenue was the average of
the second.

35   Its articles of tribute were earth of five different colours; with
the variegated feathers of pheasants from the valleys of the Yu;

縣), and Ling-peih (靈璧), in the dep. of Fung-yang, with the small depp. of Sze and Suh (all in Ngan-hwuy); the six districts of T‘aou-yuen (桃源), Ts‘ing-ho (清河), Ngan-tung (安東), Suh-ts‘ëen (宿遷), Suy-ning (睢寧), and Kan-yu (贛榆), in the dep. of Hwae-ngan, with the small depp. of P‘ei-chow (邳州) and Hae-chow (all in Keang-soo); and the whole of Yen-chow, the south of P‘ing-yin (平陰) district, and Tung P‘ing (東平州), in T‘ae-ngan, the dep. of E-chow, and portions of Tse-nam and Ts‘ing-chow (all in Shan-tung):—all these were comprehended in the Seu-chow of Yu.

    Pp. 29—32. *Engineering labours.*   29. 其 乂,—comp. 其道, p. 23. 乂＝治, ‘to bring to order,’ ‘to regulate.’ On the Hwae, see the prec. note and below, Part ii., p. 11. Ts‘ae quotes from Tsăng Yen-ho (曾彦和; like Ts‘ae, of the Sung dyn., but earlier) a remark that the Hwae came out of Yu-chow, and when it reached the borders of Seu and Yang, its stream was large, and the injury it did was specially great in Seu, so that the regulation of it is only mentioned in conn. with that prov. It is observed on this, in the 禹貢錐指, that the country of Yang was lower than Seu; the overflow of the Hwae could not be less injurious in the more southern province; and that Yu, no doubt, employed a portion of his assistants at the same time upon the Yang side, and delivered both provinces at once from the evil. Compare what was said on 治梁及岐, p. 4.   The E rises in the dis. of E-shwuy (沂水, lat. 35°46′, N., lon. 2°32′, E.; difft. hills 艾山 沂山, &c., are assigned as its source. Probably difft. streamlets from the same mountain range coalesced in one) of E-chow, and passing through that of T‘an-shing (郯城), it enters Këang-soo. There in the sub. dep. of P‘ei (邳) in Seu-chow, it unites with the Sze (泗), and proceed. south-east to the dis. of Ts‘ing-ho, it enters the Hwae. [There were other rivers called E in Seu-chow. That mentioned Ana., XI. xxv. 7 (浴乎沂) was one of them.]   30. The hill of Mung is 40 *le* to the south of the district city of Mung-yin (蒙陰; lat. 35°50′, N., lon. 1°42′, E.), extending to the borders of the dis. of Pe (費). It is the same with that called by Confucius the eastern Mung (Ana. XVI. i. 4). It is mentioned in the Statistical Account of the present dynasty, that K‘ëen-lung, who several times passed the mountain in his visits to Këang-soo and Chĕ-këang, wrote some pieces of poetry on the sight of its snow-covered summits.   Mount Yu is 0 *le* to the north of the dis. city of T‘an-shing, lat. 34°45′, N., lon. 2°17′, E. This is said to have been the hill where Shun kept K‘wăn a prisone. (Can. of Shun, p. 12). The ‘Statistical Account’ says there can be no doubt on the point, for on the top of the hill there are two springs which unite and form a deep pool (羽潭), and we are told in the 左傳, that the spirit of K'wăn was changed into a yellow bear, which sprang into the gulf of Yu (羽淵)! Hoo Wei, however, and not without apparent reason, would refer the place of K'wăn's banishment to a mount Yu, farther to the east, in the dis. of Fung-lae (蓬萊) in Tăng-chow. 其藝, 'were planted.' Hoo Wei observes: 方耕曰作; 旣種曰藝, 'Just ploughed is called 作; already planted is called 藝.' When the E was regulated, the country on the west of it to Mung, and on the east of it to Yu, would be so far drained that Yu could proceed to whatever other labours were necessary upon it.   31. 大野旣豬,—Sze-ma Ts'een reads:—大野旣都. He avoids, as is common with him, the unusual and difficult character. Gan-kwŏ defines:—水所停曰豬, 'where water rests is called 豬.' To the same effect is Wang Suh's definition:—水所停止深者曰豬. The waters overflowed the borders of the lake; by reducing them and by embankments, Yu succeeded in confining them within their proper limits.   We can only speak, it will be seen, of the Ta-yay lake or marsh in the past tense. It was in what is now the district of Keu-yay, lat. 35°27', N., lon. 12', W., of the dep. of Ts'aou-chow. In subsequent times it was often called the lake of Keu-yay, 大 and 鉅 having the same signification of 'great.' It had a connection on the south with the Choo (洙) and the Sze, and on the north with the Ts'ing and the Tse, so that it must have been liable to risings of its waters. The country all about it has been liable to inundations of the Ho. A great one happened A.D. 131, which it took more than 20 years to remedy. Repeated inundations from the time of the Han dyn. obliterated all traces of the labours of Yu. In A.D. 1344. the Ho spread over all the districts of Keu-yay, Kea-ts'ëang (嘉祥), Wăn-shang (汶上), and Jin-shing (任城); and when it retired south again, this lake was left quite dry, a tract of level ground;—see the 禹貢錐指, in loc. [These notices are interesting They show that the state of the country which called forth Yu's services was not peculiar to his time.]   32. Tung-yuen, 'the eastern plain,' is now the sub. dep. of Tung-p'ing, and some adjacent territory, in the dep. of T'ae-ngan. It was in the north of Seu-chow, but is spoken

of as eastern, with reference to its position east of the Tse. 底平,—the 底, as has been observed before, implies the putting forth of effort. The two characters = 'could be levelled;' but we must understand 平 as Gan-kwŏ did. He says:—言可耕, 'the meaning is that it could be cultivated.' Wang Yen (王炎) observes:—'The confining the waters of Ta-yay, and then bringing Tung-yuen under management, were things of which the one was the sequel of the other' (集說).

Pp. 33—35. *Soil, revenue, and tribute.*   33. 土黏曰壚, 'earth adhesive is called clay.' There can be no doubt of the meaning. Ch'ing instead of 壚 read 戠.   草木漸包 —the 說文 quotes this sentence as 草木蔪苞. 包 or 苞 has the signification, as applied to trees or shrubs, of 'bushy.' Wang Suh explains:—包相包裹也, '包 means embracing one another,'—showing that he read 包, and an intelligible description of a bushy shrub.   漸 = 'gradually,' 'advancing by degrees.'   34. The cultivable ground of Seu ranked in the second grade, and its revenue was only in the fifth.   35. 土五色,—the soil of Seu-chow was red. Such was its general character, but in different parts earth of different colours must have been found; especially was the country about the pres. districts of Choo-shing (諸城), and T'ung-shan (銅山) in Seu-chow, famed for its coloured earths. The meaning of this tribute is thus expanded by Ying-tă from Gan-kwŏ:—'The emperors raised a mound of earth of the five colours, as an altar to the spirits of the land. On the investiture of any prince, a quantity of earth, of the colour characteristic of the region where his principality lay, was cut away and given to him, which he took home to build an altar with. All the altars thus built, however, were covered with yellow earth. The earth was given to each prince, in bundles covered with white rushes, emblematic of purity.' Ying-tă quotes also from Han Ying's preface to the She King, to the effect that the emperor's altar was five cubits square, green on the east, red on the south, white on the west, black on the north, and all covered with yellow earth. [Comp. Naaman's request to Elisha, 2 Kings, v. 17.]   羽畎夏翟,—羽畎 comp. 岱畎, p. 26. The dict., with reference to this passage, defines 夏 by 五色, 'having the

翟、嶧陽孤桐、泗濱浮磬。淮夷蠙珠暨魚、厥筐玄纖縞。○浮于淮、泗、達于河、○　卅六節

the solitary dryandra from the south of *mount* Yih; and the sounding stones that *seemed to* float near the banks of the Sze. The wild tribes about the Hwae brought oyster-pearls and fish; and their baskets full of deep azure silks, and other silken fabrics, chequered and pure white.

36　They floated along the Hwae and Sze, and so reached the Ho.

five colours,' variegated, and we may accept this meaning, though some would make 夏翟 together the name of a pheasant found about the Yu. 翟 (*teih*) alone means a long-tailed pheasant. The ancient Chinese made great use of feathers on their flags and banners, and for ornament generally. 嶧陽孤桐,—嶧陽, 'the south of Yih.' There were two mountains of this name, one north in the pres. dis. of Tsow (鄒縣) in Yen-chow, and the other south, called 葛嶧, in the sub. dis. of P'ei (邳) in Seu-chow. It is the latter which is intended in the text. The wood of the dryandra is always considered good for making lutes. The older and loftier the tree, the better for the purpose. One that stood solitary on the hill-side or top, having outlived all its compeers, would possess a special value. This is, I suppose, the force of the 孤, or 'solitary.' 泗濱浮磬,—the Sze, which rises in the dis. of Sze-shwuy (泗水; lat. 35°48′, N., lon. 1°2′, E. The dis. takes its name from the stream, and that again, named from the fact that it is formed by *four* streamlets, each with its separate spring, in Yen-chow, is now one of the feeders of the Grand canal. In Yu's time it flowed into the Hwae in the country of the present Seu-chow. It was after its entrance into the pres. Keang-soo, in the pres. district of T'ung-shan (銅山), that the sounding stones of the text were found. The reason why they are spoken of as 'floating' seems to be that suggested in the translation by the addition of 'seemed to.' At any rate, that is the explanation of the older interpreters. Other views may be seen in the 禹貢錐指, *in loc.* 淮夷蠙珠暨魚,—淮夷 can only mean 'the wild people about the Hwae.' They continued rebellious and in-

tractable long after Yu's time;—see Confucius' Preface, parr. 40, 55. Gan-kwŏ blunders here, as we saw he did upon 萊夷, p. 26. He says that 淮 and 夷 are the names of two rivers. Wang-Suh and Ma Yung agreed with him; but Ch'ing explained as in the translation. 蠙 is another name for 蚌, the common term for the pearl oyster. 厥筐玄纖縞,— here these baskets of silks would seem to have been brought also by the wild tribes of the Hwae, and so the Daily Explanation expressly says (三者亦淮夷所出,命其盛諸筐而貢焉);—comp. on p. 26. Still, 厥筐 may refer to the whole province, like 厥貢 above. 玄、纖, and 縞, are descriptive of three kinds of silken fabrics :— the first expressing the colour as being 赤黑, 'red and black,' a deep azure; the second indicating a chequered silk, with a black warp and white woof (黑經白緯); and the third, a fabric white and unornamented. Other accounts of these characters may be found in Hoo Wei.

P. 36. *Route of conveyance to the Ho.* 達于河,—Keang Shing edits 達于菏, after the 說文; but the analogy of the corresponding par. in the account of the other provinces is sufficient to justify the reading of the text. We have 河, moreover, in the 'Historical Records.' As to the route itself, it will suffice to give the paraphrase of the 'Daily Explanation:'—'The tribute was conveyed northwards from Seu. First, they floated in boats along the Hwae, and from the Hwae entered the Sze. Proceeding then still north, they went on to the Ho from the Sze, either by the Yung (灉) or by the Tse.'

旣 三^{四十節} 居。 烏 ○ 旣 彭^{卅八節} 州。 惟 淮^{卅七節}
入。 江 ○ 攸 陽^{卅九節} 豬。 蠡 ○ 揚 海

37　VI. The Hwae and the sea formed *the boundaries of* YANG-CHOW.

38　*The lake of* P'ang-le was confined to its proper limits; and the sun

40　birds had places to settle on. The three Këang were led to enter the sea; and it became possible to still the marsh of Chin.

CH. VI. THE ACCOUNT OF YANG-CHOW.

P. 37. *Boundaries.* The Hwae was the boundary on the north, and it is natural to suppose that the other boundary mentioned, the sea, should be referred to the south of the province. This was the view of Gan-kwo (北據淮南距海). If it were really so, Yang-chow must have extended along the coast as far as Cochin-china, and not a few Chinese scholars are ready at the present day to argue that it did so. Others restrict it to more likely dimensions. Hoo Wei contends that the sea which has been specified as a boundary of the provinces of Ts'ing and Seu was that along their east coast, and similarly ought we to think of the sea as a boundary of Yang. K'ang-shing had said, rather indefinitely, that 'the boundaries of Yang-chow were from the Hwae southwards to the sea along the east (揚州界自淮而南至海以東). If I have caught the exact meaning of his words,— 至海以東—I think the amount of his interpretation is all that we can conclude from the text. Yang-chow extended from the Hwae southwards along the coast, but how far is not said. No other province was beyond it in the south, but that it did not extend to the southern shores of the pres. Kwang-tung we may be sure;—where it really did terminate we cannot tell. The articles of tribute and revenue in Yu's time, and the hills and waters mentioned in the account of the empire under the Chow dynasty, lead us to conclude that the imperial dominions did not then extend beyond what is called the 'southern mountain-range,' and the 'five mountains' (南嶺 and 五嶺). Williams in his 'Middle Kingdom,' p. 127, says of this:—'The Nan Ling runs along the north of Kwang-tung, between it and Keang-se and Hoo-nan. The chain takes forty or fifty names in its course from Kwang-se to Fuh-këen, but no part of it is so well-known as the road, twenty four miles in length, which crosses the Mei ling, between Nan-ngan and Nan-heung' [The names of the 'Five ling,' in Hoo Wei's charts, are 越城 on the west, 萌渚, 騎思 大庾, and 揭陽 on the east.] Of course the territory of China proper gradually extended south and west; but it was the ambition of the founder of the Ts'in dynasty, which first formally incorporated the southern regions with it. Among the forty tracts (郡) into which he divided his empire, we have those of Nan-hae (南海), Kwei-lin (桂林), and Sëang (象), embracing Kwang-tung and Kwang-se on to An-nam or Cochin-china. Hoo Wei, tracing the eastern border of Yang-chow along the coast of Keang-soo, Chĕ-keang, and Fuh-keen, extends it to Ch'aou-yang (潮陽; lat. 23°22', N., lon, 13', E.) dis., of Ch'aou-chow dep., in Can. province. This is certainly bringing it far enough south.

The western boundary of Yang-chow is left quite undefined. Along the greater part of its course it was conterminous with King-chow, and in the north-west with Yu-chow.

The 'Boundaries of Successive Dynasties' speaks within bounds, when it assigns to Yang-chow the present Chĕ-keang, Keang-se, and Fuh-këen (今南直浙江江西福建皆是). To those three provinces the 'Daily Explanation' adds Kwang-tung, of which only a small portion, if any, can be assigned to it. And neither of these accounts carries the province so far west as it went, nor do they give the more northern portion of it. A note in the 集傳, from 'Geography Modernized,' gives the area more in detail. Modernizing its statements a second time, we may say that Yang-chow contained—of Keang-soo, the departments Keang-ning (江寧), Soo-chow (蘇州), Sung-keang (松江), Chang-chow (常州), Chin-keang (鎮江), and Yang-chow (陽州), with the districts of Shan-yang (山陽), and Yen-shing (鹽城), in the dep. of Hwae-ngan (淮安); of Ngan-hwuy, the departments Ngan-k'ing (安慶), Hwuy-chow (徽州), Ning-kwŏ (寧國)-Ch'e-chow (池州), T'ae-p'ing (太平), Leu-chow (廬州), with the smaller depp. of Ho Chow (和). Seu Chow (滁), and Kwang-tih (廣德), together with the small dep. of Show Chow (壽), and the districts of Fung-yang (鳳陽), Ting-yuen (定遠),

and Ling-peih (靈璧), in Fung-yang dep., the districts of Hoh-k'ew (霍邱) and T'ac-ho (太和), in dep. of Ying-chow (潁州), and those of Yu-ch'e (盱眙), and T'een-ch'ang (天長), in Sze Chow (泗州); of Ho-nan, the districts of Kwang-shan (光山), and Koo-ch'e (固始) in the small dep. of Kwang (光州); and of Hoo-pih, the small dep. of Ke (蘄州) and the districts of Lo-t'een (羅田), Ke-shwuy (蘄水), Kwang-tse (廣濟), and Hwang-mei (黃梅), in the dep. of Hwang-chow (黃州). The above may be considered the northern portion of the province. Southwards, according to the same detail, were Chĕ-këang, Keang-se, Fuh-këen, and the dep. of Ch'aou-chow in Kwang-tung.

Pp. 38—41. *Engineering labours.* 38. 既豬,—see p. 31.   The P'ang-le is the famous lake well known as the Po-yang, so called from the name of an island in it (都陽山). It is in the northern part of Këang-se, and is stated to be 450 *le* in circumference, its waters lapping the coast of 4 difft. depp.,—Nan-ch'ang (南昌; lat. 28°37′, N. lon. 38′, W.), whose chief city is dis. from it to the south-west 150 *le*; Jaou-chow on the east (饒州; lat. 28°59′, N., lon. 14′, E.) distant from it 40 *le*; Nan-k'ang in the north-west (南康; lat. 29° 31′, N., lon. 27′, W.) distant 5 *le*; and Kew-këang, also on the northwest (九江; lat. 29°54′, N., lon. 24′, W.), dis. 90 *le*. The P'ang-le marsh or lake received many streams. (Lew Hin, of the Han. dyn., enumerated nine). The services of Yu were required to regulate its banks, and keep the waters within their proper limits.   39. 陽鳥攸居,—one scholar, Lin Che-k'e, supposes that 陽鳥 may be the name of a place. This view might come substantially to the same as the common traditional interpretation, which there is the less reason, therefore, to call in question.   陽＝日, 'the sun,' as the great source of energy and brightness. 陽鳥, 'sun birds,' are wild geese, who follow the course of the sun. 'In the winter months they live upon the islets of this lake, in flocks which may be counted by hundreds and thousands. The sun in summer travels south, and in winter north. The geese come south in the 9th month, and in the first month go north again. Thus they avoid the cold and repair to the regions of heat, and are therefore called sun birds' (Woo Ch'ing). The overflowing and disarrangement generally of the lake had driven these birds from their former haunts, to which they could now return after Yu's operations.   It does seem a trivial circumstance to mention in such a condensed account

of Yu's labours; and it was not unnatural for Lin Che-k'e to cast about for another explanation.

Pp. 40, 41. 三江既入,—the disputes about the three Keang are endless; and I do not think it is possible to settle them so as to place the meaning of the text beyond dispute. It seems proper to join the par. with the next,— 震澤底定; and there is an agreement in the opinion that the 'Shaking Marsh' was what is now called the 'Great Lake,' (太湖), in the south-west of the dep. of Soo-chow, and in the borders between Keang-soo and Chĕ-këang. It would seem that it was owing to the operations on the three Kĕang that it became possible (底) 'to settle' the disturbed waters of the lake. This would take us away from the great Kĕang, the Yang-tsze, which flows through Kĕang-soo to the sea considerably north of Soo-chow. Accordingly, Ts'ae Ch'in follows the authority of Yu Chung-ch'oo (庾仲初; Tsin dynasty. Died about the middle of the 4th century), who made the three Keang to be the Sung-keang (松江), with the two branches into which it separates 70 *le* after issuing from the lake, the L'ow Keang (婁 [in this sense read *low*] 江), flowing north-east into the sea, and the Tung Keang (東江), flowing south-east. The place where the Sung divided, was called the 'Mouth of the three Keang,' (三江口); and we have still the same name, in the north of the dis. of Woo-keang (吳江). This view would seem to satisfy the requirements of the text, but it is objected to it that the existence of the Tung Keang has never been proved;—see Maou K'e-ling, *in loc.* The Sung and the Low might be accepted as one of the three Keang, but cannot be the whole three. When we turn, moreover, to the 國語, we find in the 越語 mention made more than once of the 'three Keang.' It is said paticularly in one place that 'the three Keang surrounded' (= traversed in various directions) 'the States of Woo and Yuĕ' (三江環之,民無所移). The three Keang of Chung-ch'oo by no means answer to this description.

The oldest view of the passage—and it is that followed by Soo Tung-po, which Ts'ae mentions, but only to argue against it—considered the 'three Keang' to be only another name for the 'Great Keang,'—the Yang-tsze. It was founded on the expressions 南入于江, 東爲北江, p. 8, Part. ii., and 東爲中江, p. 9. Ch'ing K'ang-shing said :—'On the left uniting with the Han, it became the northern Keang, and after meeting with the P'ang-le it became the southern Keang; between these was the Min Keang, which was the middle Keang;—so at least it was called after issuing

震　四十一
澤
底
定。

○篠　四十二
蕩
既
敷
厥
草
惟

夭
厥
木
惟

喬
厥
土
惟
塗　四十三
泥
○
厥

田
惟
下
下、

厥
賦
下
上、　四十四

上、
○
厥

土
錯。
○厥

貢
惟
金
三

42   The bamboos, small and large, then spread about; the grass grew long and thin, and the trees rose high; the soil was all miry.

43   The fields of this province were the lowest of the lowest class; its contribution of revenue was the highest of the lowest class, with a proportion of the class above.

44   Its articles of tribute were gold, silver, and copper; yaou and

from the P'ang-le. The three Keang separating at the P'ang-le into three openings (or orifices) entered eastwards into the sea';—see the 後案. This account is not very intelligible. One part of it would seem to make the one stream of the Yang-tsze, called by three names in three parts of its course, to be the 'three Keang,' and again this stream would seem to have separated into three at the P'ang-le. As, however, the one or the three entered into the sea, without approaching the 'Shaking Lake.' we do not see how the settlement of that should be connected with the 'three Keang.' Gan-kwŏ thought 'that the three Keang' were the 'Great Keang,' and said, with Ch'ing, that it divided into three after leaving the P'ang-le, but those three branches he conducted all to the 'Shaking Lake,' from which again they proceeded by three courses to the sea. This cannot be the true view. It would oblige us to suppose an alteration from the ancient channel of the grand stream to that which it now pursues of which we have no evidence. As I said, at the beginning of the note, we do not know what rivers the three Keang were. Ch'in Sze-k'ae, in his notes upon Ts'ae's commentary, says at this place:—'If we would interpret the text without reference to views which have been urged, and would look over Yang-chow for the rivers of most advantage or capable of being most injurious to it, we shall find none equal to the Great river,—the Yang-tsze, the Sung Këang, and the Chĕ Keang. Maou K'e-ling, again, makes them out to be the Sung Keang, the Chĕ Keang, and the P'oo-yang (浦陽). The Yang-tsze is too far removed from the others, and too vast in itself. to allow us to couple it with them. The Chĕ Keang, from which Che-keang province takes its name, and the Sung Keang were perhaps two of the three Keang; but I cannot hazard a conjecture about the third.

Pp. 42—44. *Vegetation; soil, revenue, and tribute.* 42. Acc. to the analogy of parr. 17 and 33, we should expect the account of the vegetation to follow, and not to precede, the description of the soil. I have not found a satisfactory explanation of the different order observed here. 篠蕩既敷—篠 is the name of a small-stemmed bamboo. Gan-kwŏ explains it by 竹箭; but we are not to interpret 箭 by 'arrow.' It is merely here a synonym of the term in the text. 蕩 is the name of a large species of bamboo, 'the joints of whose stem are a fathom apart';—so said Le Seun (李巡; Han dynasty). 敷=布. Gan-kwŏ expands:—水去已布生, 'when the water was removed, they spread about and grew.' 夭,—comp. the quotation from the She in the Great Learning, comm. ix. 6,—桃之夭夭. Gan-kwŏ explains it here by 少長, the meaning of which I have endeavoured to give in the translation. 喬=高, 'tall.' 厥土惟塗泥,—the 說文者 defines 泥 by 黑土在水中, 'black earth in the midst of water.' We can hardly accept this as a description of the soil of a province so large as we have seen Yang-chow described to be. It shows, however, how greatly the country, where Yu had been, had suffered from the overflow of the rivers.

43. The fields were of the lowest or ninth grade; the revenue was of the seventh, with a proportion of the sixth. 土錯,—see on par. 8. This 上 is in the second tone, meaning 'going up' into the class above. 44. 金三品,—'the three grades of metal.' Those were gold, silver, and copper. In the 'Historical Records,' 卷三十, 平準書, we read: 古者金有三等, 黃金為上, 白金為中, 赤金為下. 'Among

貝、篚 服、夷 木、毛 革 蕩、琨 品.
厥 織 厥 卉 島 惟 羽 齒 篠 瑤

keun stones; bamboos small and large; elephants' teeth, hides, feathers, hair, and timber.　The wild people of the islands brought
garments of grass.　The baskets were filled with woven ornamented

the ancients there were three degrees of metal:
—the yellow metal, the highest in value; the
white metal, the next; and the red metal, the
lowest.' I don't know how or where K'ang-shing
got his idea that the text meant 'the three
colours' (= qualities) 'of copper' (銅三
色). Hoo Wei has collected a mass of evidence to show that gold was found in Jaou-chow
dep.; that silver also was found there, and in the
dep. of Lin-keang (臨江), and that there
were copper mines in various parts of Keang-
soo. [It is to the western provinces of Yun-nan
and Sze-ch'uen that we are now commonly
referred for the precious metals.]　瑤琨
are said by Gan-kwŏ to be 'beautiful gems'
(美玉). Wang Suh, however, describes them
as 'fine stones inferior to gems.' He is supported
by the 說文 expressly in his account of the
second, and probably also in that of the first;—
see the 後案. The 篠 were used for arrow-
shafts. One statement says they were solid,
which I do not know that any bamboo can be.
The 蕩 were used,—the larger of them for
small packing and other cases, the smaller for
flutes and similar instruments.　齒 革 羽
毛 惟 木,—惟 is here a connective particle,
= 曁, 'and.' See note on par. 26, upon 惟
錯. Lin Che-k'e says that 'by teeth, hides,
feathers and hair we are to understand whatever
about animals was available for articles of use or
for ornament.' More specially, Gan-kwŏ understood by 'teeth' the teeth of elephants, and by
'hides' (革 supposes the hair to be taken
off) the hides of the rhinoceros. This view is
generally acquiesced in. Are we to suppose
then that the rhinoceros and elephant were
found in Yang-chow in Yu's time? They
may very well have been so.　Hoo Wei
observes that from the mention or supposed
mention of these animals some argue for the
extension of the limits of the province beyond
the southern mountain-range to Kwang-tung,
Kwang-se, and An-nam, and replies that the
princes might be required to send articles of
value and use purchased from their neighbours,
as well as what they could procure in their own
territories.　島 夷 卉 服,—Keang
Shing here reads 鳥 夷, as in p. 10. The
Historical Records read as in the text. The

occurrence of the name again confirms the
ordinary reading. One tribe of wild people,
north or south, might have been called the
'Bird barbarians;' but when the name is applied
equally to the two extremities of the empire
along the sea-board, we must take the phrase
as having nothing special in its signification.
Hoo Wei would carry us chiefly to Japan for
the people here intended; but that is too remote.
Possibly the name may include the inhabitants
of Formosa, and the Chusan archipelago, as well
as of the islands generally along the east coast.
卉 草 之 總 名, 卉 is a general
name for grasses.' Ts'ae would extend it to
'cotton,' the production of a plant, so that 卉
服 should include dresses of cotton; but the
cultivation of cotton was first introduced into
China during the Sung dynasty. The 卉 服
were garments, I apprehend, made of grass or
straw, manipulated indeed, but not having
undergone any operations of machinery, however
rude.　織 貝,—Gan-kwŏ takes these for
two things,—'fine woven fabrics,' and 'fine
shells.' Those shells, it has been supposed, were
to serve as pieces of money, for purposes of
exchange. But such a use of shells cannot
be proved to have existed in the time of Yu.
織 貝 would rather seem to be the name of
some kind of silken manufacture. So this phrase
is generally taken. Ch'ing, on the authority of
a passage in the She King, defines 貝 by 錦
名, 'the name of variegated silks.' Woo Ch'ing
says:—'When the silk was dyed of various colours, and then woven into patterns, the fabric was
called 織 貝; where the patterns were made
with silk not so dyed of various colours, the
fabric was called 織 文.'　The 橘 is a
small orange, the citrus mandarinus. It grows
farther north than the common orange. The
柚 or pummelo seems to grow best in Fuh-këen.
錫 命,—Gan-kwŏ says:—錫 命 乃 貢,
言 不 常 也, 'when the order was given,
they were sent; this was not a regular tribute.'
Wang Suh gives the same explanation, and
adds that these fruits were only required from
Yang-chow as a supplement to those of King-
chow. K'ang-shing took a difft. view, but what
he understood exactly by 錫 can hardly be
known. He says:—'When there was 錫, it

陽 及 ○ 淮 達 江 沿 〔四十五〕貢 ○ 柚 包
惟 衡 荆〔四十六〕泗 于 海 于 錫 橘

silks.　The bundles contained small oranges and pummeloes:— rendered when specially required.

45　They followed the course of the Këang and the sea, and so reached the Hwae and the Sze.

46　VII. The King *mountain* and the South of *the mountain* Hwang were *the boundaries of* KING-CHOW.

was sent; when there was none, it was not sent as tribute. It is with 錫 that we soften metal' (有錫則貢之，或時乏則不貢，錫所以柔金也)。 錫 certainly has the meaning of tin; but any mineral article of tribute would not be mentioned here in connection with the fruits. We must adhere to the view of K'ung and Wang.

P. 45.　*Route of conveyance to the capital.*

沿 seems to have the meaning of going with the current and keeping along the shore. The tribute-bearers so passed down the Këang to the sea, and then turning north proceeded along the coast to the mouth of the Hwae, which stream they ascended to the place where it received the Sze. By the Sze they would go on to the Ho.　This par. would seem to show that there is an error in Mencius' account of Yu's labours, Book III., Part I., iv. 7. He there says that 'Yu opened a vent for the Joo and Han, and regulated the course of the Hwae and Sze, so that they all flowed into the Keang' (決汝漢，排淮泗，而注之江)。 Now, we know it was not till the Chow dynasty, that a channel or canal was cut across the country to connect the Hwae and the Keang;—see the 左傳哀九年. Mencius does appear to have made a mistake.

CH. VII.　THE ACCOUNT OF KING-CHOW.
This province was bounded on the north by the mountain King,—the southern King as it is termed (南條之荆山), to distinguish it from the mount King of Yung-chow (p. 76). It is mentioned again, Part ii., par. 3. It is in Hoo-pih, 80 *le* east and north from the dis. city of Nan-chang (南漳; lat. 31°47′, N., lon. 4°46′, W.), dep. of Sëang-yang (襄陽). East and west from it were other hills, and barrier-passes (關) among them, which separated King from Yu-chow. On the south the prov. was bounded by the south of mount Hăng, which is a very indefinite expression. Hăng (or Hwăng)-shan itself is 30 *le* to the west of the dis. city of Hăng-shan (so called from the mount.; lat. 27°14′, N., lon. 3°51′, W., Biot), dep. Hăng-chow, Hoo-nan. It is the southern mountain of the Canon of Shun, par. 8. But what is

meant by 'the south of Hăng?' Ying-tă replies:—'South of Hăng there was no other famous mountain or large river which could be named as bounding the province. The specification of "the south" shows us that the province extended beyond, southwards from the mountain.' I think it likely that King-chow extended towards the southern range, mentioned in speaking of the boundaries of last province. On the east King-chow and Yang-chow were conterminous, and on the west there was Lëang-chow.

The 'Boundaries of Successive Dynasties' says:—'The present Hoo-kwang' (*i.e.*, Hoo-pih and Hoo-nan); the dep. of Tsun-e (遵義; now belongs to Kwei-chow) in Sze-ch'uen, with the south of Chung-k'ing (重慶) dep; the depp. of Sze-nan (思南), T'ung-jin (銅仁, Yin-chow (恩州) and Shih-ts'ëen (石阡), in Kwei-chow; the whole of Kwang-se; and Leen-chow 連州) dep. in Canton:—all these territories were comprehended in King-chow.'　As this authority gave the extent of Yang-chow too limitedly, it thus extends King-chow too much. The 地理今釋 gives the following detail:—'King-chow embraced—of the pres. Hoo-kwang the eleven depp. of Woo-ch'ang (武昌), Han-yang (漢陽), Ngan-luh (安陸), King-chow (荆州), Yŏ-chow (岳州), Ch'ang-sha (長沙), Hăng-chow (衡州), Chang-tih (常德), Shin-chow (辰州), Paou-k'ing (寶慶), and Yung-chow (永州), also the two small depp. of Ch'in (郴) and Tsing (靖), and the wards of Sze-chow (施州衛), together with the dis. of Nan-chang, dep. Sëang-yang, the five districts of Ngan-luh (安陸), Yun-mung (雲夢), Heaou-kan (孝感), Ying-shing (應城), and Ying-shan (應山), and the south of the sub. dep. of Suy (隨),—all in dep. of Tih-ngan (德安), the four districts of Hwang-kang

道○ 潛○ ○ 孔 九^{四八}海。宗 漢○ 荊
○ 旣 沱^{四九}殷。江 ○ 于 朝 江^{四七}州。

47   The Këang and the Han pursued their common course to the sea,
48 as if they were hastening to court.   The nine Këang were brought
49 to complete order.   The T'o and Ts'een were conducted by their

(黄岡), Ma-shing (蔴城), Hwang-pe (黄
陂), and Hwang-ngan (黄安) of the dep. of
Hwang-chow; of Sze-ch'uen, the dis. of Këen-
ch'e (建始) in K'wei-chow (夔州) dep.;
and of Kwang-se, dep. Kwei-lin, the dis. of that
name, and the north of Hing-ngan (興安)
district.'

Pp. 47-50. *Engineering labours.*   47. The
Këang, and the Han,—see on Part ii., parr. 8
and 9. The Këang entered King-chow in the
pres. dis. of Pa-tung (巴東; lat. 31°2', N.,
lon. 6°11', W.), dep. of E-ch'ang (宜昌), and
pursuing an eastern course to the dep. city of
Han-yang, receives the waters of the Han (lat.
30°34', N., lon. 2°18', W.). The Han flows from
Shen-se into Hoo-pih in the dep. of Yun-yang
(鄖陽; dep. city, lat. 32°49', N., lon., 5°37',
W.), and then holds a south-eastern course to
its junction with the Këang.   We may
suppose that Yu expended no small amount of
labour on the two rivers, from their entrance
into King-chow on to the point of their junction.
Particularly is he said to have operated on a
narrow pass in the dis. of Pa-tung (called
巴東峽 and 三峽); but all such
achievement is passed over in the text.   Wang
Ts'ëaou (王樵; Ming dyn.) says:—'The six
characters of the par. bring the mighty stream
of the united rivers rushing to the sea before
our eyes. I have looked at it from Woo-ch'ang,
and the vast flood dashing on brought to my
mind the idea of a man hurrying with all his
speed on some special mission without a thought
of anything else.' 朝 宗 于 海,—, acc.
to Gan-kwŏ and K'ang-shing, 'with the reverence for the sea that is seen in court for the
sovereign.' Ts'ae gives the view of them which
is seen in the translation. The appearance of
the princes at court in the spring, he says, was
called 朝; their appearance in summer was
called 宗.   There is little to choose between
the interpretations. The phrase itself, with a
similar application, is found in the She King,
Part II., Book III., Ode ix.   48. 九江
孔殷,—whatever opinion be come to about
the 'nine Keang,' I do not see that 孔殷 can
with any propriety have a difft. meaning assigned to them from that in the translation, which
is after Ts'ae Ch'in, who says that 孔=甚,

and 殷=正, adding:—九 江 水 道,
甚 得 其 正, 'The channels of the nine
Keang were made to be greatly correct.' K'ang-
shing took 殷=多 and thought that the
par.,—'the nine Këang were very many,' showed
simply the difficulty which Yu had in regulating
them. Gan-kwŏ, again, took 殷=中, and
understood the par. to say that 'the nine Keang
occupied all the middle of the land.' On the
subject of the nine Keang, a hundred pages
would not contain the discussions on one side
and another. I will confine myself here to
the summary given of them by Maou K'e-ling
(尚 書 廣 聽 錄 二):—
'There are two accounts of the nine Keang.
The first is that the Great Keang, on arriving at
King-chow, separated into nine streams;—and
this is the nine Keang of the "Tribute of Yu,"'
(that is, this is the view which Maou himself
prefers.) 'The second is that the nine Keang is
another name for the P'ang-le lake;—and this
is the nine Keang of the Han and Tsin dynasties. As to the view of the Sung scholars,
that the lake of T'ung-t'ing is the nine Keang,
it is a mere speculation.
'On the first view it may be remarked that
the par.—九 江 孔 殷, standing where it
does, proves clearly that the nine Keang were
within the boundaries of King-chow. Now the
comment of Gan-kwŏ is:—" In this province the
Great Keang separated into nine channels,"
which Ying-tă expanded into—"The Great
Keang divided and became nine, just as the
Great Ho separated itself into the nine Ho."
In accordance with this is the statement of
Shwang Yin in his work on "The Waters" (桑
欽 水 經;—Shwang Yin belonged to the
closing times of the Han dynasty. He is a great
authority in geographical matters. His work
is always published with the commentary of Le
Taou-yuen [酈 道 元], of the 'After Wei'
[後 魏] dyn.), that the nine Keang were in
the north-west of Hea-sun in Ch'ang-sha"
(在 長 沙 下 雋 西 北). Their position
must thus have been somewhere to the west of
the present King-chow (荊 州 之 西) and
the north of Yŏ-chow (岳 州 之 北). To the
same effect is the account of Chang Ching (張
滇), that they began in Yŏ-ling (鄂 陵), and

ended at Keang-k'ow (江 口), meeting in Shwang-loh (桑落). All these names would not take us far from the pres. dep. of King-chow. And yet, since the time of Yu, these nine branches of the Great Keang have disappeared, leaving only their names. They cannot be traced any more than "the nine Ho." All the earlier scholars agree in this account. The names of the streams, moreover, are given, and though no two enumerations agree in all the nine, about seven will be found the same in all of them.

'As to the second view, that the nine Keang is another name for the P'ang-le lake, it took its origin from an expression of Sze-ma Ts'een in his Historical Records—" I ascended the hill of Leu, and saw where Yu separated the nine Keang" (余登廬山, 觀禹疏九江). After him Lew Hin said that the nine streams entered into the P'ang-le; and at last, in Pan Koo's Geography of the Han dynasty, under the district of Sin-yang (尋陽) in Leu-keang dep. (廬江郡), we have the note:—"The nine Keang of the Tribute of Yu were in the south of this. They all united eastwards of this, and became the Great Keang." But this view is easily disposed of. According to the classic, the nine Keang were in King-chow, and the P'ang-le was in Yang-chow;—the two had nothing to do with each other. Moreover, the classic says that the Keang, after passing the nine Keang, went on to Tung-ling, and then flowing gently eastwards united in the north with the P'ang-le (Part. ii., p. 9), so that not only were the nine Keang and the P'ang-le not identical, but Tung-ling and a tract of country lay between them. It is quite clear that Sze-ma Ts'een and all who followed him were in error.

'The divisions of the country got their names very much from those of the waters in them, and mistakes, like that which has been pointed out, came to be stereotyped on the face of the land, giving rise to endless discussions about the original site of places. The tract of Kew-keang (九江郡), as originally established by the Ts'in dynasty, was in King-chow between Se-ling and Ke-chun (在荆州西陵蘄春之間). At the commencement of the Han dynasty, it was taken away and afterwards reappointed, but was placed near to Show-ch'un (壽春), made to approach, that is, to Yang-chow. During the usurpation of Wang-mang (王恭), the Kew-keang of Show-ch'un was changed into the tract of Yen-p'ing (延平郡), and the tract of Yu-chang (豫章) in Keang-nan was changed into Kew-keang; and thus it was that the Kew-keang of King-chow passed into the P'ang-le of Yang-chow.'

Maou goes on to relate other changes in the geographical position assigned to Kew-keang, but that last narrated finally asserted itself; and we have still the dep. of Kew-keang in Keang-se, near the Po-yang lake, the old P'ang-

le, as was noticed in the note on par. 38. The demonstration is complete that in the time of Yu the nine Keang and the P'ang-le had no relation together, but were in different provinces, a long way removed from one another.

On the opinion now generally followed, that we are to think of the T'ung-t'ing lake when we read here of the nine Këang, Maou observes that it commenced with Hoo-tan (胡旦, early in the Sung dynasty) He was followed by Chaou Shwǒ-che, (晁說之), Tsǎng Yen-ho, and others, especially Choo He, whose advocacy of the view has secured for it its present general acceptance. There are differences of opinion, in the details of it, as to the nine streams having their common receptacle in the T'ung-t'ing. It is difficult also to reconcile it with Part ii. par. 9. I have less difficulty, however, in supposing that the lake is what now corresponds to the nine Keang of Yu than in believing the view of Gan-kwǒ which Maou endorses. If the Great Keang had ever separated its main stream, and become nine streams, history would not be silent as it is as to their disappearance, and traces of their former existence would still be discoverable on a geological survey of the country. Such a survey may yet throw some new light on the meaning of the text.

49. 沱潛既道,—the same words occur again, p. 64, in connection with Leang-chow. There must have been streams with these names in both the provinces. The 爾雅 says:— 'Streams issuing from the Keang are called 沱; those issuing from the Han are called 潛.' Gan-kwǒ, says that 'T'o is another name for the Këang.' The likeliest view seems to be that at an island in the middle of the great stream, in the present dis. of Che-këang (枝江, 'the branching of the Këang;' lat. 30°24'. N., lon. 5°6', W.), dep. of King-chow, its waters separated, and flowed for a time in two channels, one north and one south, meeting again near the T'ung-t'ing lake. The northern of these channels was called the T'o. Hoo Wei insists also on another stream called the 'E, water' (夷水), which took its rise in the present dis. of Woo-San (巫山, of K'wei-chow dep. in Sze-ch'uen, and after entering King-chow, joined the Keang in the pres. dis. of E-too (宜都), as also to be accounted one of the 沱, which engaged the labours of Yu. For the Ts'een we are referred to the dep. of Ngan-luh in Hoo-pih, where the name is preserved in that of the dis. of Ts'een-keang (潛江; lat. 30°28', N., lon. 3°40', W.) As the character 潛 also signifies 'to abscond,' 'to lie hidden,' Hoo Wei supposes that the Ts'een of the Han flowed from it under ground in the first place, and then coming to the surface found their way back to the parent stream. Among the branches of the Han now there is one called Leu-fuh (蘆洑), in which name we have a reference to an under-

雲土夢作乂。〇厥土惟塗〇泥厥田惟下中厥賦上下。〇厥貢羽毛齒革、惟金三品、杶幹栝柏、礪砥砮丹、箘簵楛三邦、底貢厥名包

50 proper channels. The land in *the marsh of* Yun *became visible*, and that of Mung was brought under cultivation.

51 The soil of this province was miry; its fields were the average of the lowest class; its contribution of revenue was the lowest of the highest class.

52 Its articles of tribute were feathers, hair, ivory, and hides; gold, silver, and copper; the ch'un tree, wood for bows, cedars and cypresses; grindstones, whetstones, arrow-head stones, and cinnabar. *There were also* the k'wăn and loo bamboos, and the wood of the hoo tree, of which the three regions were able to contribute the best specimens. The three-ribbed rush was put in cases, which *again* were wrapped up.

ground current (宜取伏流之意). This, he supposes, may be the Ts'een of the text. The 'Statistical Account' of the present dyn. confirms this view. 50. The reading of this par. is not certain. In the Han dyn. the prevailing reading was 雲夢土作乂. The founder of the T'ang dynasty issued a proclamation settling the reading to be that now published. The reading depends to my mind on the question of whether there were two marshes, the Yun and the Mung, or only one,— the Yun-mung. Each side of this is very plausibly maintained. On the whole I am inclined to agree with the authors of the 'Daily Explanation,' that the marshes were two, 'the Yun on the north of the Keang, spreading over the country of the present depp. of Ngan-luh and Tih-ngan, and all about the sub. dep. of Meen-yang (沔陽); and the Mung, on the south of the Keang, spreading over the districts of Keang-hea (江夏) and Hwa-yung (華容). We can understand how these might be spoken of sometimes as one lake without reference to the Keang between them, and how it might be called sometimes the Yun, and sometimes the Mung. If, indeed, it was only one, then I can make no meaning of the text. The necessity of the case would make us read 雲夢土. If the two portions were spoken of separately, —about which there is to me no doubt,—then we may interpret as in the translation. The large tract of country covered by the marshes was very much drained by the other labours which have been detailed; north of the Keang the water sank till the ground appeared in places; and south of the Keang, portions of the country were left dry, and could be cultivated.

Pp. 51, 52. *Soil, revenue, and tribute.* 51. The soil of this province was of the same character as that of the last,—'all miry'; which we can well believe of the portion of it, not far removed from the courses of the Keang and Han. Its fields were one degree higher in quality than those of Yang-chow; and its revenue was much higher, owing, we may suppose, to its being more thickly peopled. 52. 羽毛齒革、惟金三品,—comp. p. 44. It is supposed that the articles from the two provinces are mentioned in the order of the quality which distinguished them. Thus, Yang-chow was most noted for its precious metals, and they are therefore mentioned first in p. 44.

杶幹栝柏—in Yang-chow we have only 惟木. Here various kinds of wood are enumerated. There are four trees, as Gan-kwŏ and Ch'ing unite in saying, and not three only, as we find in the 集傳. Ts'ae joins the two first characters together, and says—'The wood of the Ch'un tree was fit for making bows.' But I have no evidence that it had such a quality. The wood preferred for bows was that of the 柘, by which Gan-kwŏ here defines 幹. Was it the yew tree? I cannot say exactly what tree the *Ch'un* was. It has got the various names of 杶 櫄 櫄 and 椿, and was good for making musical instruments, and the thills of carriages, and

甌菁茅、厥篚玄纁璣組、九江納錫大龜。○ 五十三 浮于江沱潛于漢、逾于洛、至于南河。○

The baskets were filled with deep azure and purple silken fabrics, and with strings of pearls that were not quite round. From the *country of* the nine Këang the great tortoise was presented.

53 They floated along the Keang, the T'o, the Ts'een, and the Han; crossed over to the Lǒ, and proceeded to the most southern part of the Ho.

for pillars. Was it the dammar? 柏 is probably the cypress; but I do not know that I am right in calling the 栝 the cedar. It is described as having the leaf of the 柏, and the stem of the 松, or common pine, growing very large, enduring cold, and good for making coffins and boats. 礪砥砮丹，—the *le* and *che* were both stones abounding in the hills of King, adapted for purposes of grinding. The former were of a coarser substance; the latter closer and finer. The *noo* were stones, by their natural shape and quality fitted for being made into arrow-heads. The best are said to be found far north, on the banks of the Hih-lung, where they are called 'water flowers, hard and sharp, approaching to the character of iron (名水花石，堅利，入鐵). 丹＝丹砂, 'cinnabar.' 惟箘簬楛，—these were all good for making arrows. The *kwǎn* and *loo* grew about the marsh of Yun-mung (Gan-kwǒ). The *hoo* was a tree. We know that it was famed for the arrows made from it, because Confucius, on one occasion, being asked about a bird which lighted on the palace of the prince of Ch'in and died, pierced with a *hoo* arrow, declared that it was transfixed with one of the famous arrows of Suh-sin;—see the references in the note to par. 56 of the Preface. 三邦底貢厥名，—I think it is most natural to connect this clause with the one immediately preceding, and to suppose that it has reference only to the three articles just specified. Many, however, extend it to all the articles of tribute enumerated. What the three countries were, we cannot tell. Tung-po would make the phrase out to mean all the States of King,—'large, small and middling.' Gan-kwǒ, understanding the par. to extend only to the *kwǎn*, *loo*, and *hoo*, which he thinks grew about the Yun-mung, naturally takes the three countries to have been three States in the neighbourhood of that marsh. 厥名猶言尤美, '厥名—'the best of them';

—so, Chang Kew-shing (張九成). K'ang-shing very strangely puts a point at 貢, and reads 厥名 as part of the next clause. 包匭菁茅，—the rush here spoken of, described as having 三脊, *i.e.*, three-ribbed, was used for straining the wine at the imperial sacrifices. It was packed in small cases, which again were covered over,—showing the value of the article by the care which was taken of it. This seems to be the meaning of the characters. Gan-kwǒ and Wang Suh put a stop at 包, and understand by it 'bundles' of fruit, as in the case of Yang-chow. The former also takes 菁 and 茅 as being two different articles. K'ang-shang defines 匭 by 纏結, 'to tie or wrap round.' These explanations are all erroneous. I prefer also the meaning which I have given to 包匭 to another which is common, and which ＝ 'bundles in cases.' 厥篚玄纁璣組．—纁 is another name for 絳. The silk has received three dippings in the dye-fluid. 璣組 are to be taken together. The former character denotes 'pearls that were not round' (珠不圓者, acc. to the 說文); these were strung, and put into the baskets, as I read the text. Some say they were carried by themselves, and not in the baskets. 九江納錫大龜，—'the great tortoise' attained the size, acc. to the 'Historical Records,' (龜策傳) of two cubits and a half. Such a creature would be esteemed very valuable, where divination was much relied on. Gan-kwǒ explains the 錫 as having the same force with the 錫貢 in par. 44. He says;—龜不常用，錫命而納之, 'the tortoise was not a regular article of tribute, but was presented when required by express command.' But the phraseo-

荊河惟豫州。〔五十四〕

伊洛瀍澗既〔五十五〕

入于河。○○榮〔五十六〕

波既豬。○○導〔五十七〕

菏澤被孟豬。

下土墳壚。○〔五十八〕

厥土惟壤。○

厥田惟中上。〔五十九〕

厥賦錯上中。

54   VIII. The King *mountain* and the Ho were *the boundaries of* YU-CHOW.

55   The E. the Lŏ, the Ch'ëen, and the Këen, were conducted to the
56   Ho. The *marsh of* Yung-po was confined to its proper limits. *The*
57   *waters of the marsh of* Ko were led to that of Măng-choo.

58   The soil of this province was mellow; in the lower parts it was
59   *in some places* rich, *in others* dark and thin. Its fields were the
highest of the middle class; its contribution was the average of the
highest class, with a proportion of the very highest.

logy is different, and the nature of the case was different also. The tortoise might not be found, even when specially called for. It is better to take 錫 as a synonym of 納, —a meaning which it often has. The people presented the tor. whenever they met with it. It was always a welcome contribution.

P. 53.   *Route of conveyance to the capital.* They floated along the Keang, the T'o, and the Ts'een,—not necessarily from the one of these to the other, but rather, I suppose, according to the place where the various articles were being brought from. It was necessary, however, to reach the Han, which took them to the borders of Yu-chow, where they had to leave their boats, and cross over the country to the Lŏ, by which they might proceed to the southern portion of the Ho, the boundary between Yu-chow and K'e-chow.

CH. VIII. THE ACCOUNT OF YU-CHOW.
P. 54.   *Boundaries.* On the south was mount King, which has been spoken of as the northern boundary of King-chow. On the north was the Ho, that is, the southern portion of it which flowed with nearly a direct course from west to east. On the north-west, this prov. touched on the northern slopes of mount Hwa, which is sometimes described as belonging to it. On the east it was conterminous with the provinces of Yen, Seu, and Yang. Yu-chow, indeed, was the central one of Yu's nine divisions of the empire, and was conterminous, for a greater or less distance, with all of them except Ts'ing-chow, which lay off in the east by itself.

The 'Boundaries of Successive Dynasties' says:—'Yu-chow comprehended the present Ho-nan with the department of Yun-yang in Hoo-pih.' The more detailed and exact account of the 'Geography Modernized' is:—'Yu-chow embraced—of the present Ho-nan, the five de-partments of Ho-nan, K'ae-fung (開封), Kwei-tih (歸德), Nan-yang (南陽), and Joo-ning (汝寧), with the small dep. of Joo (汝州); of Chih-le, the two districts of Tung-ming (東明) and Ch'ang-hwan (長桓), dep. of Ta-ming (大名); of Shan-tung, the four districts of Ting-t'aou (定陶), Shing-woo (城武), Ts'aou (曹), and Tan (單), dep. of Ts'aou-chow (曹州); of Ngan-hwuy, the four districts of Fow-yang (阜陽), Ying-shang (潁上), T'ae-ho (太和), and Mung-shing (蒙城), with the sub. dep. of Pŏ (亳), in the dep. of Ying-chow (潁州); and of Hoo-pih, the five districts of Seang-yang (襄陽), Kwang-hwa (光化), E-shing (宜城), Tsaou-yang (棗陽), and Kuh-shing (穀城); with the sub. dep. of Keun (均州), in the dep. of Seang-yang, the district of Yun (鄖) in the dep. of Yun-yang, and the northern part of the sub. dep. of Suy (隨) in the dep. of Tih-ngan (德安).

Pp. 55—57.   *Engineering labours.*   55.
Comp. Part ii., par. 13, from which it appears that the four streams or rivers here mentioned, did not separately enter the Ho. The Lŏ received the waters first of the Këen and the

Ch'ëen, and last those of the E, and then proceeded, with them all to the Yellow river. In the text we are told, I suppose, the order in which Yu operated upon them. First, he took in hand the E, and having cleared its course to the Lŏ, continued his labours on that stream on to the Ho, after which he turned to do what was necessary for the Ch'ëen and Këen.

The E-water (伊水) has its source in Bear's-ear hill (熊耳山), in the dis of Loo-she (盧氏) lat. 34°01', N. lon. 5°32', W.), in the small dep. of Shen-chow (陝州), Ho-nan. Passing into the dep. of Ho-nan, it flows east, close by the dis. city of Ts'ung (嵩). Bending towards the north, it passes through the districts of E-yang (伊陽) and Lŏ-yang (洛陽), into that of Yen-sze (偃師; lat. 34°45', N., lon. 3°45', W.), 5 le to the south-west of whose dis. city it enters the Lŏ. The Lŏ rises in the Ts'in range (秦嶺), 50 le to the north of the dis. city of Lŏ-nan (洛 or 雒南; lat. 34°06', N., lon. 6°22', W.), in the small but independent dep. of Shang (商州), in Shen-se. It enters Ho-nan in the dis. of Loo-she, and flows north and east through Shen-chow, on to Ho-nan dep. Proceeding northeast, through the south of the dis. of Yung-ning (永寧), and the north of E-yang (宜陽), it traverses the dis. of Lŏ-yang, where it receives the Ch'ëen and Këen. Going on eastwards through Yen-sze, where it receives the E, its course is through the north-west of Kung (鞏縣), into the dis. of Fan-shwuy (氾水), dep K'ae-fung, where it enters the Ho.

The Ch'ëen and the Këen are both on the north of the Lŏ. The former rises in the west of the dis. of Măng-tsin (孟津; lat. 34°52', N., lon. 3°50'. W.). and flowing south to that of Lŏ-yang, it runs south-east into the Lŏ.

The Këen rises in White-stone hill (白石山), in the north of Min-ch'e district (澠池; lat. 34°46', N., lon. 4°47', W., and flows east, south of Sin-ngan (新安) district city, to the west of Lo-yang dis., where it joins the Ho.

Another Yu has often been wanted since Yu's time to remedy the devastations done by these four streams. In B.C. 184, the E and Lŏ overflowed and carried away nearly 2000 families. In A.D. 223, the same streams occasioned immense loss of life and property. In A.D. 722, a rising of the E destroyed a portion of the city of Tung-too (東都); and another in 800 was equally calamitous. Injuries quite as great are recorded from risings of the Ch'ëen and Këen; —see the 禹貢錐指, in loc.

56. Ts'ae Ch'in says that the Yung and the Po were 'two waters,' the former connected with the Tse and the latter with the Lŏ. This view is followed in the 'Daily Explanation;' but it has been satisfactorily refuted by Hoo Wei and others. An older view now commands general acceptance, for it was Yen Sze-koo of the T'ang dynasty, who first advocated the opinion adopted by Ts'ae. Gan-kwŏ, K'ang-shing, and Ma Yung all hold that the two characters should go together (滎波 or 滎播), as the name of a marsh, that formed by the waters of the Tse, rising up remarkably out of the ground, as described Part ii, par. 10. The name partly remains in those of the districts Yung-tsih (滎澤) and Yung-yang (滎陽) in the dep. of K'ae-fung. The marsh itself in the days of K'ang-shing was dried up, and become so much level ground (今塞爲平地). 57. Following the course of the Tse, Yu proceeded on to the marsh of Ko, taking its name from the hill of Ko, near the pres. dep. city of Ts'aou-chow in Shan-tung, lat. 35°20', N., lon. 52', W. It was also formed by the waters of the Tse, and unable to bring it entirely under management by itself, Yu led off the excess of its waters to the marsh of Măng-choo. This name is variously written,—孟豬, 望諸 in the 'Rites of Chow,' 明都 by Sze-ma Ts'een. A memorial of it remains in the tower of Măng-choo (孟諸臺), 10 le to the north-east of the dis. city of Yu-ching (虞城; lat. 34°38', N., lon. 19', W.) dep. of Kwei-tih in Ho-nan. The marsh itself cannot now be traced, and Hoo Wei observes that repeated overflowings of the Ho, which commenced A.D. 1266, and laid the country about Kwei-tih under water, have obliterated all traces of Yu's labours in that quarter. Whether there was a connection between the marsh of Ko and that of Măng-choo which he only cleared, before Yu's time, or whether he opened such a connection in order to carry off the excessive waters of the former, we cannot tell. 被=及, as in Can. of Yaou, par. 1. As the Ho might be considered one of the rivers of Yu-chow and beyond comparison the greatest of them, we may be surprised that nothing is said of any labours performed upon it. We must suppose that when Yu was operating on the northern bank of it, about mount Yoh, and Tan-hwae (pp. 5,6), he had sent detachments over to Yu-chow, and finished at once all that was necessary to be done for the great stream. This left him free to direct his attention first to the Lŏ and its tributary streams in the west of the province, and then to the Tse and the evils it gave rise to in the east.

Pp. 58—60. *Soil, revenue, and tribute.*

58. 壤,—see per. 7. K'e-chow and Yuchow agreed in the general character of their soil, but no colour is assigned to that of Yu-chow, because, we are to suppose, no uniformity characterized it in this respect. 墳壚,—墳, see par. 17, where I adopted Ma Yung's meaning of the term as = 'rich.' This places it in direct opposition to Ts'ae's definition of 壚 as =疏, 'thin,' 'poor.;' such also was K'ang-shing's ac-

潛　旣　州。黑　河。　于　磬　纖　厥六十
旣　藝。　○　水　○　洛　錯。　纊　絺　貢節
道。　○　岷六十　惟　華六十　達　○　錫　厥　漆
○　沱六十三嶓　梁　陽二　于　浮六十錫　篚　枲
　　四　　　　　　　一

60   Its articles of tribute were varnish, hemp, a finer hempen cloth,
and coarser hempen cloth.   The baskets were filled with fine silken
fabrics, and fine floss-silk.   Stones for polishing sounding-stones
were rendered, when required.

61   They floated along the Lŏ, and reached the Ho.

62   IX. The south of *mount* Hwa and the Black-water were *the boundaries* of LEANG-CHOW.

64   The *hills* Min and Po were brought under cultivation.   The T‘o

count of it. The 說文 defines the char. by
黑剛士, 'black, hard, earth.' I have done
the best I could with the two terms.   59. If
we look only at the revenue of the province, we
should expect its fields to rank much higher than
they do; the reason of the disproportion, according to Foo T‘ung-shuh (傅同叔), was that
the black hard tracts in the lower parts of it were
unfit for the cultivation of grain. The student
will observe how the place of the 錯 is different
from what it occupies in parr. 8 and 43.

60. 漆, 枲, 絺, 絟,—漆, see par. 19;
枲 and 絺, see par. 26; 絟 is a coarse kind
of hemp,—a perennial plant, acc. to Luk Ke
(陸璣—絟亦麻也, 宿根在
地, 至春自生). A kind of cloth was
made from it which was called by the same name.
Ts‘ae says he cannot tell whether we should
understand here the raw material, or the manufactured article. We must suppose, I think,
that, as the character follows 絺, we are to
understand the cloth. 厥篚纖纊—
纖, see par. 35; 纊=綿, 絮之細者,
as in the translation. 錫貢,—see par. 44.
There the phrase *follows* the articles so contributed, they being sufficiently marked off from
the other articles by the 厥包 which precede.
Here it *precedes* the articles, because, if it followed them, its force might be extended to the
others previously mentioned. The 錯 were
stones used for polishing other stones and gems,
differing from the grinding-stones and whetstones of King-chow, the use of which was to
polish articles of metal.

   P. 61. *Route of conveyance to the capital.* From
the eastern parts of Yu-chow they could at once

reach the Ho. From the western, they reached
it by means of the Lŏ.

CH. IX.   THE ACCOUNT OF LEANG-CHOW.
   P. 62. *Boundaries.* There is no dispute
about the former of the boundaries mentioned.
Mount Hwa is 'the western mountain' (西
岳) of the Canon of Shun, par. 8, standing 8
le on the south of the dis. city of Hwa-yin
(華陰; lat. 34°35′, N., lon. 6°31′, W., Biot),
in the dep. of T‘ung-chow (同州), acc. to
the latest arrangement of Shen-se province.
In the small adjacent dep. of Shang (商) is the
dep. of Shan-yang (山陽), which is said to be
identical with the Hwa-yang of the text. Mount
Hwa served as boundary mark to three of Yu's
provinces—Leang, Yu, and Yung.   On the
other boundary,—the Black-water,—there is not
the same unanimity of opinion. Gan-kwŏ said:
—'On the east this province reached to the
south of mount Hwa, and on the west to the
Blackwater.' If, indeed, the Blackwater was
the boundary of Lëang-chow on the west, we
are led to identify it with the river of the same
name, also the western boundary of Yung-chow,
and described in Part ii., p. 6, as ·flowing into
the southern sea.' This view leads to great
difficulties, quite as great as those attending
the extension of Yang-chow round the sea-coast
to Cochin-China. The first distinctly to con-
trovert it appears to have been Sëe Sze-lung
(薛士龍; Sung dyn.), who took the boundaries mentioned in the text as the northern
and southern, and not those on the east and west:
—'The northern boundary of Leang-chow was
the south of mount Hwa, and on the south it
stretched along the Blackwater, the present
Loo-water (南距黑水, 黑水今瀘
水也).' The name of the Loo had taken
the place of the Blackwater in the Han dynasty,
and subsequently to the T‘ang, the stream has

been called the 'river of the Golden Sands' (金沙江); but it is sufficiently proved that this stream, or at least that portion of it from its junction with the Shing-shwuy (繩水) and the Jŏ-shwuy (若水) to their merging in the Min Këang, was called the Black-water.

Combining the statements of the 'Geography Modernized,' and the ' Statistical Account of the present dynasty,' we have the following description of the southern boundary of Lëang-chow:—'The present Golden Sands of Yun-nan is the Black water of Leang-chow. Its sources are very remote, farther off than those of the Yellow river, in 27°50', west lon.' (this must surely be an error, as it would take us to about the long. of Calcutta), and between 35° and 36° north lat. Flowing south-east, it enters Yun-nan, near the pass of Tä-shing (塔城), in the border dep. of Le-keang (lat. 26°51', N., lon. 16°01', W.). Flowing through the northern part of this province, it enters Sze-ch'uen in the dep. of Ning-yuen (寧遠), and, bending more northwards, enters the Keang in the south of the dep. of Seu-chow' (叙州: lat. 28°38', N., lon. 11°63')'.

After the junction of the Loo and the Keang, the latter great stream would continue the southern boundary of Lëang on to King-chow. On the east it was conterminous with Yu-chow and King-chow. Its western boundary cannot, I think, be laid down with any certainty.

It is worthy of remark that neither of the two great dynasties which followed Yu,—neither the Yin nor the Chow, included the province of Leang. Portions of it were embraced in their provinces of Yu and Yung, but the greater part was considered as wild, savage territory, beyond the limits of the Middle Kingdom. We can hardly suppose that the territory of China ever diminished so greatly. It is more reasonable to think that Yu pushed his labours in this direction, not so much because the country was really included in Yaou's empire, as because it was necessary for him to operate upon it for the benefit of the more eastern parts.

The 'Daily Explanation' says:—'Leang-chow embraced the present provinces of Sze-ch'uen, Kwei-chow, and Yun-nan, with the dep. of Han-chung (漢中) in Shen-se, and the small dep. of Këae (階州) in Kan-suh.' This representation is beyond the truth; and that in the 'Boundaries of Successive Dynasties,'—that 'Leang-chow extended over the present Sze-ch'uen, and the dep. of Han-chung in Shen-se,' seems to be too narrow.

The following is the detail in the 'Geography Modernized':—'Leang-chow embraced—of Shen-se, the dep. of Han-chung, and the small depp. of Hing-ngan (興安) and Shang (商州); of Kan-suh, the small dep. of Keae, and the two districts of Hwuy (徽) and Leang-tang (兩當), in dep. of Ts'in (秦州); of Hoo-pih, the three districts of Fang (房), Chuh-

san (竹山) and Chuh-k'e (竹谿), and the west of Yun-se dis. (鄖西), dep. of Yun-yang (鄖陽); and the prov. of Sze-ch'uen.'

Pp. 63—66. *Engineering labours.* 既藝,—see on par. 30. 岷嶓,—see Part ii, parr. 3, 4, 8 and 9. In these mountains were the springs of branches of the great streams of the Keang and Han. Mount Min (the 'Historical Records' read 汶 instead of 岷) is in the most north-western part of Sze-ch'uen, called the T'ing of Sung-p'wan (松潘廳), given by Biot as in lat. 32°38', N., lon. 12°52', W. The 'Geography of the Shoo Modernized' says that 'from the small dep. of Min (岷州) in Kung-ch'ang (鞏昌) of Shen-se [now of Kan-suh], a range of lofty mountains with deep valleys stretches westwards to the western borders of the department of Ching-too (成都). The snowy ridges of Mow-chow (茂州) and other famous elevations are to be reckoned to this range. Where Yu began his operations was at the mountain of Lang-kea (浪架) on the very borders on the north-west of Sung-p'wan.

Mount Po, called Po-ch'ung in Part ii, p. 3, was not so far west. There were two mountains of the name:—one 90 *le* to the north of the present sub. dep. of Ning-keang (寧羌州; lat. 32°42', N., lon. 10°, W.), in Han-chung dep. of Shen-se, whence the waters of the eastern Han issued. This was the Po-ch'ung of Part ii. The other was in the pres. small dep. of Ts'in (秦州; lat. 34°36', N., lon. 10°42', W.) of Kan-suh; and from it the waters of the western Han issued. The two were distant from each other, north and south, between three and four hundred *le;* but they are to be considered as belonging to the same range. Yu's work on these two mountains is described as 'the clearing the springs of the Keang and the Han' (江漢滌源之事). The text tells us that the country about the foot of the mountains themselves was brought under cultivation. 64. See on par. 46. Gan-kwŏ thought that the T'o and the Ts'een here were the same as those of King-chow, the upper portion of their courses being here referred to. But this view cannot be adopted. Woo Ch'ing says:—'These were the separately flowing branches of the Keang and Han that were in Leang-chow. In the east of the pres. district of Pe, (郫縣) lat. 30°47', N. lon. 12°32', W.) dep. of Ching-too was a T'o, which flowed westwards into the Keang. In the south-west of the dis. of Taou-keang (導江) in P'ang-chow' (彭州) [these are names of former territorial divisions; we have now the dis. of P'ang in Ching-too dep., and the dis. of Kwan (灌縣) in the same corresponds to Taou-keang] 'there was another T'o which flowed east into the Keang.

蔡蒙旅平。○和夷厎績。○厥土青黎。○厥田惟下上。厥賦下中三錯。○厥貢璆鐵銀鏤砮磬熊羆狐狸織皮。

65 and the Ts‘een were conducted by their proper channels. Sacrifices were offered to the hills Ts‘ae and Mung, on the regulation of the country about them.

66 *The country of* the wild tribes about the Ho could *now* be successfully operated on.

67 The soil of this province was greenish and light.

68 Its fields were the highest of the lowest class; its contribution of revenue was the average of the lowest class, with proportions of the rates immediately above and below.

69 Its articles of tribute were musical gem-stones, iron, silver, steel, stones for arrowheads, and sounding-stones; with the skins of bears, great bears, foxes, and jackals, and articles woven with their hair.

Again, in the dis. of Chin-foo (眞符) in Yang Chow (洋州) [we have now the dis. of Yang in the dep. of Han-chung, in Shen-se], there was the water of Ts‘een-kuh (灙谷), which was a Ts‘een. But the branches flowing from the Keang and Han, whether large or small, long or short, all went by the names in the text, and are to be looked for in various places. When the mountains Min and Po were brought under cultivation, the upper parts of the two streams were regulated; and now their courses through all the province were cleared by the measures taken with the various T‘o and Ts‘een.'   65. The hills of Ts‘ae and Mung are both referred to the present dep. of of Ya-chow (雅州; lat. 30°3', N., lon. 13°25', W). Mount Mung seems to be sufficiently well ascertained. The ‘Statistical Account’ of the pres. dynasty says that it stands on the borders of the three districts of Ya-ngan(雅安), Ming-san (名山), and Loo-san (蘆山), of the above department, and that the best tea of all Sze-ch‘uen is grown upon it. Mount Ts‘ae is not so well determined. The ‘Geography of the Shoo Modernized’ identifies it with the hill of Chow-kung (周公山), 5 le to the east of Ya-chow city, and the Statistical Account of the Ming dyn., adopting that view, adds that 5 le further off there is a place called Leu-p‘ing (有地名旅平), where it is probable that Yu offered his sacrifices. But this Leu-p‘ing was not heard of till modern times, and, indeed, Yeh Mung-tih (葉夢得), of the Sung dyn., was the first to say that the hill of Chow-kung was the Ts‘ae of the Shoo. The Geography of the Han dyn. does not mention the Ts‘ae at all. Hoo Wei inclines to the opinion that we are to look for it in one of the famous Ngo-mei hills (峨眉山) in the dis. of the same name (lat. 29°32', N., lon. 12°50', W.), dep of Kea-ting (嘉定).   旅平, 一旅 is applied to designate sacrifices offered to mountains;—see Ana. III. vi. The ‘Daily Explanation’ expands the whole paragraph thus:—‘The Mei-water had flowed between the hills of Ts‘ae and Mung with a rapid and destructive course, but now all this was remedied, and Yu sacrificed to the mountains, and announced the completion of his work’ (蔡蒙二山之間，沫水所經，其勢漂疾，于是旅爲害，今水土既平，而告成功焉，祭其山)

66. Ts‘ae gives two views of the meaning of this paragraph, neither of which he accepts as quite satisfactory, though he rather inclines himself to the former of them. It is that propounded by Gan-kwŏ, that the two characters were the name of a tract of country. The other is that Ho and E were the names of two streams.   A more natural interpretation is that of K‘ang-shing, that 和夷＝和上之夷, ‘The wild people upon the Ho,’ though, taking the two characters in connection with the rest of the par., we must understand them of the territory occupied by those people.

The 和水 is another name for the 洣水, which came through the pres. Mow Chow (茂州), and, after a long course of about 3,000 *le*, flowed into the Këang in the dep. of Kea-ting. But we can hardly think that the tribes mentioned dwelt along all the stream, even in that portion of it which was in Sze-ch'uen.

Pp. 67—69. *Soil, revenue, and tribute.*

67. In interpreting this par., Ts'ae follows Gan-kwŏ, who gives 黎 as = 黑, 'black,' a meaning which it often has, but which does not seem appropriate here. We should thus be told only the colour of the soil, and nothing about its nature. Gan-kwŏ adds, indeed, to 黑 the charr. 而沃壤 'and rich and mellow;' but this cannot be all indicated by 黎, and the next par. is inconsistent with such a view of the soil of Lëang. The 'Historical Records' read 驪 for 黎, which variation does not assist us at all in determining the meaning. In these circumstances we must look about for another meaning of 黎, and Ma Yung, followed by Wang Suh, has suggested that which I have adopted in the translation. He defined the character by 小疏, 'small and thin.' This suits the passage well enough. The difficulty with it is that we do not find such a meaning of the term elsewhere, and hence it is not given in the Dictionary.

68. Its fields were ranked in the second grade, and the revenue in the 8th, though this sometimes, or perhaps in some places, rose to the 7th, and again fell to the 9th. The 'Daily Explanation' says:— 其賦爲下中,三錯,本第八等,或一年而進第七等,又或一年而降第九等,共三等. The revenue of this province was thus only not so low as that of Yen-chow. On this Tsăng Yen-ho has observed that Leang-chow was very mountainous, while the provv. of Yen and Yang had suffered and were still suffering more than others from the overflow of water, and in consequence of these circumstances their revenue was so small. These circumstances would have their influences on the revenue, but still more powerful would be the denseness or sparseness of the population.

In the course of time, the States of Woo (吳) Yuĕ (越), Min (閩), and Shuh (蜀),—all belong. to Yang-chow and Lëang-chow, became the most famous for their fertility of all in the empire. 69. 璆鐵銀鏤砮磬.— Ts'ae adopts the meaning of 璆 as 玉磬, 'musical stones of gem,' taking the char. as a synonym of 球. Gan-kwŏ simply defines it by 玉名, 'the name of a gem.' Either of these meanings suits the passage well enough; but K'ang-shing read 鏐, which he defines—

黃金之美者, 'the finest gold,' and this, could it be fully established, would suit the passage still better. The regions of Lëang-chow have always been famous for their gold, while the situations and excellence of their gems are unchronicled. By 鐵 we are to understand 'soft iron,' and by 鏤, 'hard iron,' or 'steel.' The latter character is often used for 'to cut and engrave,' with reference to the hardness of the tools necessary for such a purpose. In the time of the Han dynasty, 'Iron-masters' (鐵官) were appointed in several districts of the old Leang-chow to superintend the iron works. Ts'ae refers to two individuals mentioned in the 'Historical Records,' one of the surname Ch'ŏ (卓氏), and the other of the surname Ch'ing (程), both of this part of the empire, who became so wealthy by their smelting that they were deemed equal to princes. 銀 is the 'white metal,' or silver. 砮磬,—see on previous paragraphs. 熊羆狐貍,織皮,—熊 is 'the bear;' the 羆 is described as 'like the bear, of a yellowish white' (爾雅); 'like the bear, with a long neck, and long legs, very fierce and strong, able to pull up trees' (郭璞); 'there are yellow *pe*, and red (赤) *pe*,—it is larger than the 熊, and the grease is coarser.' I do not think we can at present determine exactly the species of the *pe*. The 狐 is 'like a dog, but with a long tail;' the 貍 are 'a small sort of 狐.' Ts'ae, after Soo Tung-po, takes 織皮 as two different things, the former denoting a sort of felt (罽), made from the hair of the animals; the latter denoting furs (以罽者曰織,以裘者曰皮). Other commentators make the two characters to denote only one thing—a fabric woven from the skins tanned, and cut into very small and thin strings (Woo Ch'ing). The view adopted by Ts'ae is to be followed. Quite unnatural is the view of K'ang-shing, who puts a stop at 貍, as if they were the living animals which were sent as tribute, and then takes 織皮 as the name of a barbarous territory:—(西戎之國). There is more reason in the opinion of Woo Ch'ing, Hoo Wei, and others, who instead of stopping at 皮, carry the paragraph on to 來. The furs and hair-cloth are thus the tribute from the wild tribes lying west and north of the province, and the description of the route of conveyance commences in the same way as in the previous provinces.

西七十節　是　潛　于　水　雍　水　屬　沮
傾　　　　來、逾　河。西　州。既　渭　既
因　　　　浮　于　○　河　○　西　汭　從
桓　　　　于　沔、黑七十一惟　弱七十三涇七十三漆七十四灃七十五
　　　　　渭、亂

70　From Se-k'ing they came by the course of the Hwan; floated along the Ts'een; crossed the country to the Mëen; *then* entered the Wei; and ferried over the Ho.

71　X. The Blackwater and the Western Ho were the boundaries of YUNG-CHOW

73　The Weak-water was conducted westwards.　The King was led to

74　mingle its waters with those of the Wei.　The Tseih and the Ts'eu

P. 70.　*Route of conveyance to the capital.* 西傾因桓是來,—see the conclusion of last note. 西傾 is the name of a mountain, which belonged to Yung-chow; its southern slopes, however, passed into Lëang. It is often identified with the mountain of the same name in the district of Chang (漳縣; lat. 34°40′, N., lon. 11°50′, W.), dep. of Kung-ch'ang in Kan-suh;—see below, Part ii., p. 2. The river Hwan took its rise on the south of the mountain. It is also called the White-water (白水), and flowing into Sze-ch'uen, in the dis. of Ch'aou-hwa (昭化; lat. 32°16′, N., lon. 10° 38′, W.), dep. Paou-ning, it proceeds to join the western Han. This western Han was the Ts'een, and going up it they should have been able to pass into the Mëen, another branch of the Han, for it flows out of the pres. dis. of Lëö-yang (略陽), dep. of Han-chung, and running south-east into the dis. of Mëen, called after it, it there joins the great stream. Perhaps there were shallows in the course of the Ts'een, which rendered it necessary to leave their boats, or it may have been a saving of time and labour to leave the water at some point, and go across the country to the Mëen (see a note in the 集說, by Foo Yin [傅寅]).　From the Mëen it was necessary to get to the north, into the Wei, which was in Yung-chow. From the text,—入于渭,—we should conclude that this was accomplished without taking the land again. But this was impossible, their being no water-communication between the Han and the Wei. In the dep. of Fung-ts'eang (鳳翔), however, of Shen-se, and dis. of Mei (郿縣; lat. 34°13′, N., lon. 8°38′, W.) is the mountain of Ya (衙嶺), from which the stream of Paou (襃水) flows south into the Mëen,

while another stream on the north side, the Seäy (斜川), flows into the Wei. Probably, the tribute-bearers ascended the Paou as far as they could, and then went overland to the Seäy. For the Wei, see Part ii., p. 12. It enters the Ho, and of course brought the travellers to that stream, which they ferried across at some suitable point. 絕河而渡曰亂.

Ch. X. The Account of Yung-chow.

P. 71.　*Boundaries.* The western boundary is here assigned and the eastern. The former—the Black-water—is difft. from the river of the same name, which formed the southern boundary of Lëang-chow;—see on par. 62. It is no doubt the same with the Black-water of Part ii., p. 6, which see. It will be sufficient here to quote from the 禹貢錐指:—' According to Shwang Yin's work on the Waters, with the comment. of Taou-yuen. "The Black-water issued from Fowl-hill in Chang-yih (出自張掖雞山; Chang-yih is now the principal dis. in the dep. of Kan-chow (甘州, lat. 39°, N., lon. 15°32′, W.), and flowing south to T'un-hwang (燉煌), the prin. dis., dep. of Ngan-se (安西), passed by the hill of San-wei (三危山), and flowed on to the southern sea." Acc. to the Compilation of Geography (括地志; a work of the T'ang dynasty), "The Black-water rose 120 *le* to the north of E-woo district in E-chow (伊州伊吾縣), and flowing south was lost about the hill of San-wei, in Sha-chow (沙州), 46 *le* to the south-east of the district city of T'un-hwang." We cannot tell which of these accounts is correct. The T'ung-teen (通典; by 杜佑, of the Tsin dynasty) says:—" Accomplished scholars like K'ung and Ch'ing did not know where the Black-water was, because, perhaps, in the lapse of time, it had become dried up.'' About the eastern boundary,—the western Ho,—there is no uncertainty. This was the Ho, where it runs from north to south, between the present Shan-se and Shen-se;—called the 'western,' as being the western boundary of K'e-chow, the imperial province. The length of its course from the point in Yu-lin dep. (榆林), where it enters Shen-se, to the district of Hwa-yin, amounts, it is said, to 1,700 *le*.

On the south, Yung-chow was conterminous with Lëang-chow, from mount Hwa westwards, on to Se-k'ing, and again westwards on to Tseih-shih, from which Yu traced the course of the Ho (Part ii., par. 7), and thence again to the Black-water. The northern boundary of the province is not at all intimated in the Shoo, but it must have extended from the position of the pres. city of Yu-lin, lat. 38°18', N., lon., 7°7'. W., westwards along the north of Shen-se and Kan-suh as far as the south boundary did. Hoo Wei says that of Yu's nine provinces this was the largest, and that next to it were K'e and Lëang. 'The extent of Yung, from east to west, was about 3,700 *le*, and from north to south, about 2,500 *le*, while in all this great space there was not much of unoccupied territory.'

Pp. 72—78. *Engineering labours.* 72. The Weak-water,—see Part ii., p. 5. In the 'Statistical Account of the present dynasty,' under the dep. of Kan-chow in Kan-suh, we find the following account of the Jŏ, or Weak-water :—'It rises in the south-west of San-tan district (山丹), and flows north, west of the city, into the district of Ch'ang-yih. Passing that district city on the north, it enters, going on still to the north-west, the borders of Kaou-t'ae (高臺) in Suh-chow (肅州; lat. 39° 45', N., lon. 17°21', W.) This is the Weak-water of the Tribute of Yu.' Some accounts say that it can be crossed in coracles of skin, while yet a piece of straw thrown upon its surface would sink to the bottom. To this feeble sluggishness of its stream its name is ascribed. 旣西,—'was conducted westwards.' This was its natural course, and in this it is unique among the rivers mentioned in this Book, all the rest flowing east, with the exception of the Black-water of this province, whose course was south. In the general disorder, which had prevailed, however, we may suppose that it had taken a direction to the south-east, and mingled its waters with those of the Ho. 73. 涇 屬渭汭.—屬 is read *chuh*, up. 4th tone,—相連, 'to be connected together.' Gankwŏ defined it by 逮=及; and Ma Yung by 入. These meanings are all connected, and it is strange that the dictionary should give Gankwo's explanation under the second sound of the character,—*shuh*, low. 4th tone. 渭汭 are to be taken together like 嬀汭 in the Can. of Yaou, par. 12. Ts'ae makes 汭 to be the

name of a stream which entered the King, before it joined its waters with those of the Wei. If this had been intended, we may be sure that the text would have been different. 汭 is defined—水北, 'the north of a stream; 水之隈曲, 'the bending bank of a river;' 水中州, 'an island in a river;' and by the 說文 水相入, 'the meeting of two rivers.' The second and last of these meanings may easily be harmonized. As regards the first meaning, there is no difficulty in the text where the King flows from the north to the Wei. The King, according to the 'Statistical Account of the present dynasty,' makes its appearance in Shen-se in the west of Shun-hwa dis. 淳化; lat. 34°55', N., lon. 7°58', W.), in the small dep. of Pin (邠州); thence it flows past the small dep. of K'een (乾), enters the dep. of Se-ngan, and takes its way, through the districts of Le-ts'euen (醴泉), and King-yang (涇陽), on to that of Kaou-ling (高陵; lat. 34°30', N., lon. 7°24', W., in the south-west of which it joins the Wei. It is said to have its rise in Ke-t'ow hill (笄頭山), 'in the south-west of Ping-lëang dis. 平涼; lat. 35°34', N., lon. 9°48', W.,), dep. of the same name in Kan-suh. The Wei,—see below, Part ii. ,p. 12. The stream of the King was muddy and that of the Wei clear; and the muddiness of the former became more evident after their junction. There are many poetic allusions to these circumstances ;—see the She-king, Part I. Book III., Ode x. 74. 漆沮旣從.—we have 恆衞旣從 in par. 9, but the 旣從 cannot here be taken in the same way. There the phrase indicated that the Hăng and Wei were made to follow their natural channels; here it signifies that the Tseih and Ts'eu were made to join the Wei. Tung-po says :—'The following here is like that with which a youth follows his elder. The Wei was great and the Tseih and the Ts'eu were small ; hence it is said that they were made to follow' (note in the 集說). Acc. to the 'Geography of the Shoo Modernized,' the Tseih takes its rise in the pres. dep. of Se-ngan, in the north of the dis. of T'ung-kwan (同官; lat. 35°6', N., lon. 7°25', W.), and flowing past that city on the east, is there joined by the T'ung-kwan river. Proceeding thence south-west to the sub. dep. of Yaou (耀州; lat. 34°56', N., lon. 7°35', W.), it unites with the Ts'eu. The Ts'eu rises in the dis. of Chung-poo (中部; lat. 35°38', N., lon. 7°16', W.), in the small dep. of Luh (鄜州), and after flowing through the dis. of E-keun (宜君), passes into the dep. of Se-ngan, traverses the dis. of T'ung-kwan, on to the south of Yaou Chow, where it unites with the Tseih. Their united waters proceed

厥賦中下。○
厥田惟上上、
土惟黃壤。○ 八十節
苗丕敍。○ 厥 七十九
三危既宅、三 七十八
至于豬野。○
鼠原隰底績。 七十七
惇物。至于
岐既旅、終南
水攸同。○ 荆 七十六

75 were led in a similar way *to the Wei;* and the waters of the Fung found the same receptacle.

76 The mountains King and K'e were sacrificed to, and those of Chung-nan and Shun-wŭh *were also regulated,* and all the way on to

77 that of Neaou-shoo. Successful measures could now be taken with

78 the plains and swamps, even to the marsh of Choo-yay. The *country about* San-wei was made habitable, and the *affairs of the people of* San-meaou were greatly arranged.

79 The soil of the province was yellow and mellow.

80 Its fields were the highest of the highest class; its contribution of revenue was the lowest of the second.

into the district of Foo-p'ing (富平), where they receive the name of Shih-ch'uen (石川河), and holding on in the same direction enter the Wei in the district of Lin-t'ung (臨潼; lat. 34°20′, N., lon. 7°28′, W.)

75. 灃水攸同,-攸=所. Gan-kwŏ says 灃水所同, 同之于渭 'The waters of the Fung found the same place, *i.e.,* they were conducted in the same way to the Wei.' The Fung has its rise in the hill of Chung-nan, in the south east of the dis. of Hoo (鄠縣, 東南終南山; the city of Hoo is in lat. 34°8′, N., lon. 7°50′, W.), of Se-ngan dep., and enters the Wei in the south-east of the district Heen-yang (咸陽). It was on the south of the Wei. Lin Che-k'e observes:—'The territory of Yung-chow bordered on the western Ho, so that before the regulation of that stream, it suffered as well as K'e-chow from the overflow of its waters. After the operations of Yu, however, on Hoo-k'ow, and on the mountains K'e and Lëang, the great stream pursued its way to the east; and when he arrived at Yung-chow he had only to deal with the Weak-water, conducting it to the west, and to lead the waters of the King, the Tseih and the Ts'eu, and the Fung, to the Wei, in which they all went on to the Ho.'

76. 既旅,—see on par. 65. The King mountain here is not that of King-chow. We are referred for it to a mountain 10 *le* to the

south-west of Foo p'ing (富平; district city, lat. 34°42′, N., lon. 7°41′. W.) Mount K'e is the same which I supposed to be meant in par. 4 Chung-nan is 50 *le* to the south of the dis. city of Ch'ang-ngan, the dep. city in fact of Se-ngan; lat. 34°16′, N., lon. 7°31′, W.) On the east it extends to the dis. of Lan-t'een (藍田; lat 34°5′, N., lon. 7°8′, W.) and on the west to the district of Mei (郿縣; lăt. 34°13′, N., lon. 8°38′, W.), stretching along altogether an extent of 800 *le*. Shun-wŭh is supposed to be the same with what is now called T'ae-pih hill (太白山) in the south of the district of Mei, called also T'ae-yih (太一 and 太乙). Neaou-shoo, or Bird and Rat mountain, is farther west, and conducts us to the district of Wei-yuen (渭源; 35°8′, N., lon. 12°12′, W.), dep. of Lan-chow (蘭州) in Kan-suh.

Hoo Wei here makes the following note:— 'Ch'in Ta-yew (陳大猷, Sung dyn.) says, "The ancients felt it right to sacrifice on occasion of any great undertaking, and it was specially right to do so in connection with such an undertaking as Yu's. But we have mention of his offering sacrifice only in the provinces of Yung and Leang, because these were the two last provinces where he operated, and his sacrificing in them shows that he had done so in the other provinces as well. Further, Yu's sacrificing is mentioned only in connection with the hills of Ts'ae and Mung in Leang, and those of

King and K'e in Yung, because Ts'ae and Mung were the last hills of Leang, and King and K'e were the first of Yung, so that we may understand he sacrificed to all the others; and thence it is said below that *the hills in all the nine provinces were cleared of their wood and sacrificed to.*" These observations are good, but do not give the proper reason for the use of the term 旅. At Hoo-k'ow the object was the clearing of the Ho: at Lëang and K'e it was the clearing of the Ho and of the country as well;—and hence we have the terms 載 and 治. At Mung, Yu, Min, and Po, the object was the cultivation of the country, and therefore we have the term 藝. At Ts'ae, Mung, King, K'e, Chungnan, Shun-wǔh, and Neaou-shoo, the object was to clear the streams in the valleys, and had nothing to do with the fields or country, and hence we could not have 藝, but only 旅. At San-wei the object was both to clear the Blackwater, and the valley-streams, so that the country might be inhabited, and hence we have the term 宅. The words used in every case have a peculiar appropriateness to the circumstances. They have all a reference to Yu's labours upon the disordered country. We are not to lay stress upon the idea of sacrificing in 旅.

This is ingenious; but Wei has not told us the peculiar and appropriate meaning in the use of 旅.

77. 'Ground wide and level is called 原; low and wet is called 隰. What we read in the She,—"He measured the plains and marshes," has the same local application as the phrase in the text.' So, Ts'ae Ch'in, following Ch'ing K'angshing. The ode referred to is the 6th in the 2nd Book of the 大雅, celebrating the praises of duke Lew, who founded the fortunes of the House of Chow in the territory of Pin (豳). If we thus interpret the text, the region of these operations of Yu was the present Pin-chow (邠州) in Shen-se. Possibly, however, the phrase may have a more extensive reference. Even at present, in a multitude of the districts of Shense and Kan-suh there are one or more not able 原, many of which in Yu's time would be in a marshy condition. For the marsh of Choo-yay we have to go to Kan-suh, 80 *le* east of the district of Chin-fan (鎮番; lat. 38°35′, N., lon. 13°20′, W.), dep. of Leang-chow (涼州). In the geography of the Han dynasty it is called the marsh of Hew-ch'oo (休屠). To reach this Yu must have crossed the Ho. 78. 三危.—see Can. of Shun, par. 12. The hill identified with this San-wei is in the south-east of the district of T'un-hwang. Thither Shun had removed the most unprincipled and insubordinate of the people of San-mëaou. The

banishment had not been without its effect in softening and subduing them, and now when Yu came to ameliorate the condition of their settlement, the moral effect of his kindness is said to have completed the work of their transformation. The Black-water, it was seen on par. 71, passed by the mountain of San-wei. We must suppose that it was by operating on its troubled stream, that Yu effected the change which is intimated in the character of the country around. 三苗丕敍.—Gan-kwǒ explains this:—三苗之族大有次敍, 'the tribe of the San-meaouites had great order and arrangement;' adding—'This is said to set forth the merit of Yu.' I cannot see my way clear to adopt the common modern view that the phrase 丕敍 celebrates the merit of the Meaouites. Ch'ing Heaou, for instance (鄭曉; Ming dyn.), says on 敍:—是遷善改過革其凶頑, 'it expresses how they became good, reforming their faults and putting away their malignant stolidity.'

I find two interesting notes on this par. The first is by Leu Tsoo-heen (呂祖謙; of the Sung dynasty), who says:—'The people of San-meaou were driven to San-wei for their evil conduct, and according to the views of after ages they might have been left as banished criminals to themselves, to destroy themselves or to keep themselves alive, without being cared for or pitied. But such was not the mind of those early sages. When they were criminals, it was necessary to banish them; but after that punishment was inflicted, it was thought right to show kindness to them, and to extend to them the influence of good government. Thus it was that Yu having regulated the waters as far as to San-wei, there laid out for the Meaouites the plan of their settlements.'

The other note is by Tsae Ts'in:—'When Shun drove out the people of San-meaou, it was only the worst among them whom he removed to San-wei, while he left the rest in their settlements. But here we find the banished portion displaying great merit, while the others still continued bad and insubordinate. The old settlements of the San-meaouites were amid the strengths of hills and streams, the influence of which fostered such a spirit. Even now-a-days we find the people about the T'ung-t'ing lake ever and anon breaking out and displaying such a spirit; and when they are captured and questioned, most of them are found to have the surname of Meaou.— Are they the descendants of the ancient tribe?'

Ps 79—81. *Soil, revenue, and tribute.*

79. Yellow is considered the proper colour of soil. The soil of Yung-chow was thus the best of all the provinces. 80. The disproportion here between the character of the fields, which were in the first grade, and the amount of the revenue which was only of the sixth grade is very great. It is generally explained by saying that the population was very thin; and I do not see how it can otherwise be accounted for. Hoo Wei having argued for the wide extent of the province, and said

厥貢惟球^{八十一}
琳琅玕。○
浮于積石、^{八十二}
至于龍門于
西河.會于
渭汭。○織^{八十三}
皮崑崙、析
支渠搜西
戎即敍。○

81   Its articles of tribute were the k'ew and lin *gem-stones*, and the lang-kan *precious stones*.

82   From as far as Tseih-shih they floated on to Lung-mun on the western Ho; they then met, on the north of the Wei, *with the tribute-bearers from other quarters*.

83   Hair-cloth and skins *were brought from* Kwǎn-lun, Seih-che, and K'eu-sow;—the wild tribes of the West all coming to submit to *Yu's* arrangements.

there were few empty, uninhabited districts in it, feels the pinch of the difficulty, and tries to get over it by arguing that Yu only levied revenue from the fertile country on either side of the Wei, in which moreover there were many high hills and long valleys. But his reasoning is not satisfactory;—it is tantamount, in fact, to the giving up many of his former statements.   81. Ch'ing defines 球 by 美玉, 'an admirable gem.' The 說文 calls it 玉磬, 'a sounding-stone of gem,' which would agree with the use of the term in Part II., Bk. IV., p. 9. We may conclude that the 球 was a jade suitable for the manufacture of such instruments.   The 琳 is called by Ch'ing 美石, 'a beautiful stone.' But in this he stands alone. The 說文 and other authorities agree in referring it also to the class of 玉, or gems.   The two characters 琅 and 玕 go together. Gan-kwǒ describes the substance denoted by them as 'a stone, but like a pearl.' Some speak of it as a kind of coral, but we cannot look for coral in the hilly and inland districts of Yung-chow. Possibly it was lazulite, or the *lapis lazuli*.

82.   *Route of conveyance to the capital.* Two routes are here indicated. The one—and we may suppose it the principal one—was by the Wei, which would be available for the more southern portion of the province. The other was by the Ho, which was available from the mountain of Tseih-shih (see Part ii., p. 7: it is in the sub. dis. of Ho (河州), lat. 35°44', N., lon. 13°28', W.). Parties living more to the east could of course take the Ho at the most convenient part of its course towards its highest northern latitude when it turned south, and then descend with it as far as the mountain of Lung-mun, on its western bank; in the north-

east of Han-shing dis. (韓城; lat. 35°32', N., lon. 5°3', W.). Not far from this, a little south of it, they met with the boats which had come to the Wei, and tracked up from the junction of that stream with the Ho. Here I suppose they all took the shore, and travelled through K'e-chow to the capital.

83.   *Other articles of tribute. The par. should form part of par. 81.* In this view of the concluding portion of the Part, I agree with Soo Tung-po, to whom Ts'ae Ts'in also inclines. The analogy of 織皮 in par. 69 seems to necessitate it. As the account of all the other provinces, moreover, concludes with the route of conveyance to the capital, we cannot understand why this should not do the same. On par. 69, K'ang-shing took 織皮 as the name of a country; here, with strange inconsistency, he takes them as descriptive of the tribes from K'wǎn-lun, Seih-che and K'eu-sow, all 'skin-wearing.'   K'wǎn-lun, Seih-che, and K'en-sow are understood to be the names of mountains, giving name to the regions and tribes about them. We have only to conceive of them as representing three tribes of what were called the western barbarians, and those three the greatest of them all, so it is added that all the tribes came and submitted to Yu's arrangements. So says Hoo Wei:—三國皆西三國皆來入日戎而西戎不止於三國、服、故國乃西戎大者皆賓就貢則其餘無不即=就 'to come to.' 西戎即敍。 Gan-kwǒ explains 即敍 by 皆就次敍, which is equivalent to the 丕敍 in par. 78.

THE BOOKS OF HEA.

BOOK II. THE TRIBUTE OF YU. PART ii.

禹貢下

導𡸂及岐、
至于荆山、
逾于河、
口、雷首至
于太岳底
柱析城至
于太
于王屋至太
行、恆山至

I. *Yu* surveyed and described the hills, beginning with K'ëen and K'e, and proceeding to mount King; then, crossing the Ho, Hoo-k'ow and Luy-show, going on to T'ae-yŏ. After these came Te-ch'oo and Seih-ching, from which he went to Wang-uh; then there were Ta-hang, and mount Hăng, from which he proceeded to Kĕĕ-shih, where he reached the sea.

CONTENTS. It has been stated, on page 93, that the division of the Book into two parts is a modern arrangement, and by no means universally followed. It is convenient, however. The first part gives a view of Yu's labours in each particular province. This gives a general view of the mountain ranges of the empire, and of the principal streams, and relates some other labours of Yu, not alluded to before,—his conferring lands and surnames, and dividing the whole territory into five domains. The contents may be divided into five chapters:—the first, parr. 1—4, describing the mountains; the second, parr. 5—13, describing the rivers; the third, parr. 14, 15, containing a summary of all the labours of Yu, hitherto mentioned; the fourth, parr. 16—22, relating his other labours, how he gave lands and surnames, and divided the empire into five domains; and the fifth, par. 23, celebrating Yu's fame, and the completion of his work.

CH. I. THE RANGES OF MOUNTAINS ALONG WHICH YU OPERATED. It is difficult to know how we ought to translate 導 here. We can see how the term, signifying 'to lead,' 'to guide,' may be applied to streams; but there could be no *leading* of the great mountains. Ying-tă says:—' What was done on the hills was for the sake of the waters, and therefore it got the name of 導山.' In the dictionary, 導 is defined by 治, 'to regulate,' with reference to this passage, and on the ground, probably, assigned by Ying-tă. We should understand then, on this view, that Yu went along the mountains indicated, clearing the channels of innumerable small streams, which he conducted to the larger rivers whose names are given. But the question arises—when did he do this? Was it immediately after he divided the land, as mentioned Part i., p. 1? or was it while he was carrying out his operations in each province? It was not while he was operating in each province, for he then proceeded from east to west, and not, as here described, from west to east; and we have no reason to believe that any practical steps were taken till the work was begun at Hoo-k‘ow, Part i., p. 3. Following the account of the regulation of the nine provinces, the paragraph here should describe what was done by Yu subsequent to that regulation; and in the first two chapters we seem to have a view of the position of the principal mountains, and the courses of the principal streams, as if Yu had paused to look back upon his work, and take a bird's-eye view of the country. We cannot suppose that he travelled again along the hills or the rivers, for in that case his toil would have been endless, and he must have gone again and again over the same ground. He surveyed mentally the mountains and rivers, and made delineations of them,—their ranges and courses. This is the meaning which I venture to attach to 導,—'to survey and describe.'

Sze-ma Ts‘een between 導 and 汧 inserts 九山,—'He surveyed the mountains of the nine provinces.' So we must interpret 九山. Twenty-seven mountains are immediately specified; it is impossible that the mention of them should be preceded by a statement that Yu only dealt with 'nine mountains.' With regard to the order in which the mountains are enumerated, it has given occasion to divide them into different ranges. Ma Yung and Wang Suh considered that there were three;—the northern range (北條), embracing from mount K‘ëen to Këě-shih; the middle range (中條), embracing from Se-k‘ing to Pei-wei; and the southern range (南條), embracing the rest. Ch‘ing K‘ang-shing made four ranges of them (四列);—the northern (陰列), from K‘ëen to Këě-shih; the next-northern (次陰), from Se-k‘ing to Pei-wei; the next-southern (次陽), from Po-ch‘ung to Ta-pëě; and the southern (正陽), from mount Min to Foo-tseën. His object, we can see, was to make these ranges correspond to the courses of the principal streams,—the Ho, the Hwae, the Han, and the Keang. Since the publication of Ts‘ae's commentary, it is customary to speak only of two ranges, a northern and southern. This is only a simplification of K‘ang-shing's arrangement.

P. 1. The mountains K‘ëen, K‘e, and King were all in Yung-chow,—all in the pres. Shen-se. The 'Statistical Account of the present dynasty' gives mount K‘een (Keang Shing edits 汧 and not 岍) as in the west of the sub. dep. of Lung (隴州; lat. 34°48′, N. 9°31′, W.), dep. Fung-ts‘eang. Others have identified it with a mount Woo (吳山), in the south of the same Lung Chow. The authors of the Statistical Account say the two hills were anciently considered as one. K‘e and King,—see Part i., p. 76. The former, like K‘ëen, belongs to the dep. of Fung-

ts‘eang. The latter, we saw, was in that of T‘ung-chow. Hoo Wei observes that there were anciently three mountains called King:—that in the text, where Yu is said to have cast his nine famous vases (大禹鑄鼎處); that on the borders of the provv. Yu and King, where Pëen Ho found his famous gems. (卞和得玉處; see in the Biographical Dictionary [氏姓譜], surname 卞); the third, not mentioned in the Shoo, in the prov. of Yu, at a place referred to the pres. dep. of Shen (陝州), in Ho-nan, where Hwang-te is said to have cast some vases. 逾于河,—the point at which the Ho was crossed, or supposed to be crossed, is said to have been 35 *le* to the east of the district city of Chaou-yih (朝邑; lat. 34°48′, N., lon. 6°26′, W.), dep. of T‘ung-chow. The phrase certainly reads as if an actual progress of Yu were described; but I must understand it as meaning simply that, had such a progress been made, the Ho must have been crossed here. 壺口、雷首，至于太岳,—壺口, see Part i., p. 4. 雷首 is in the south of the district of Yung-tse (永濟; lat. 34°54′, N., lon. 6°13′, W.), dep. of P‘oo-chow (蒲州). The mountain received in course of time many names. Among them were those of mount Show (首), and Show-yang (首陽), at the foot of which Pih-e and Shuh-ts‘e died of hunger (Ana. XVI. xii). 太岳,—see on 岳陽, Part i., p. 5. Yu had come south from Hoo-k‘ow to Luy-show, and now again he turns north, in consequence of the urgency with which relief was called for from the capital. The T‘ae-yoh is 30 *le* to the east of Höh-chow (霍州; lat. 36°34′, N., lon. 4°45′, W.). 底柱析城，至于王屋,—底 (Sze-ma Ts‘een has 砥) 柱; Gan-kwŏ says on this, at par. 7, below, that it was the name of a mountain, where the waters of the Ho separated, and passed by, embracing the hill, so that it appeared in the waters like a pillar (山名，河水分流，包山而過，山見水中，若柱然). The place is now referred to the small dep. of Shen in Ho-nan, 40 *le* northeast from the dep. city, lat. 34°45′, N., lon. 5°23′, W., and is also called by the name of the 'Hill of the three Gates,' or Passages (三門山). The 'Book of the Waters' (水經注) says:—'When Yu was regulating the evils of the inundation, when he found a stream impeded by a mountain, he chiselled through it. So he cut through this hill of Te-ch‘oo, perforating it in three places called the "Three Passages."' Chaou

于敷淺原。○　衡山、過九江、至　岷山之陽、至于　四節　方、至于大別。○　冢、至于荆山、內　于陪尾。○三節　導嶓　耳、外方、桐柏、至　鼠、至于太華、熊　西傾、朱圉、鳥　○三節　于碣石、八于海。

2　*South from the Ho, he surveyed* Se-k'ing, Choo-yu, and Neaou-shoo, going on to T'ae-hwa; then Heung-urh, Wae-fang. T'ung-pih, from which he proceeded to Pei-wei.

3　He surveyed and described Po-ch'ung, going on to *the other* mount King; and Nuy-fang, from which he went to Ta-pëĕ.

4　He *did the same with* the south of mount Min, and then went on to mount Hăng. From this he crossed *the lake of* Kew-këang, and went on to the plain of Foo-tsëen.

Tung-he (趙冬曦), a writer of the T'ang dynasty, describes the hill of Te-ch'oo as consisting of six peaks, all rising up in the midst of the stream. On the most northern of them were two pillars, over against each other, standing up near the bank, and forming the passage of the 'Three Gates.' We cannot say what labours Yu performed at this point, nor what was the appearance presented in his time by the hill. Notwithstanding what he did, the Ho has here occasioned incalculable evil to the people, and incalculable trouble to the government. Hoo Wei has made a precis of attempts to overcome the natural difficulties of the passage, from the Han to the Sung dynasty, the result of which appears to have been to aggravate the evil rather than remove it. The hill of Seih-shing is found in the dep. of Tsih-chow (澤州), in the south-west of the district of Yang-shing (陽城; lat. 35°26', N., lon. 3°52', W.). Wang-uh is in the dep. of Hwae-k'ing, in Ho-nan, 80 *le* to the west of the dis. city of Tse-yuen (濟源; lat. 35°7', N., lon. 3°49', W.). It extends to the borders of Yang-shing district, just mentioned, and presents an appearance as if it consisted of three storeys, like a house. 太行、恆山、至于碣石、入于海。—T'ae-hang is in the south of Fung-t'ae dis. (鳳臺) in Tsih-chow (lat. 35°30', N., 3°39', W.). South of it lies the district of Ho-nuy (河內), dep. of Hwae-k'ing, while, stretching along to the north-east, it touches in its range on the district of Ling-ch'uen (陵川), on the districts of

Hoo-kwan (壺關), Loo-shing (潞城), and Le-shing (黎城), dep. of Loo-ngan (潞安), on the dis. of Woo-heang (武鄉) in Pe Chow (沁州), on the dis. of Ho-shun (和順) in Leaou Chow (遼州), and on that of Lŏ-p'ing (樂平) in P'ing-ting dep. It is called by a hundred different names in different parts of its range, but it is really the same mountain of T'ae-hang. 恆山,—see on Can. of Shun, par. 8. It is the northern mountain, the limit of Shun's excursions to the north, and according to the determination of the pres. dyn., is in about lat. 39°41', N., lon. 2°43', W. I don't know where Dr. Medhurst got the latitude which I have assigned to it from him on page 35. According to the geography of the Han dyn., we should look for mount Hăng in Keuh-yang dis. (曲陽; lat. 38°39', N., lon. 1°40', W.), dep. of Chin-ting, in Pih-chih-le. This opinion prevailed through many dynasties. In the Sung dynasty a more northern position began to be claimed for the northern hill, and the Ming dyn. decreed that the proper Hăng was in Shan-se. It did not, however, remove the sacrifices from Keuh-yang. This was done in the 17th year of Shun-che of the present dynasty. We must conclude that the decision of the Ming and the present dynasties is incorrect. The Hăng hill of Shan-se would take us away from the Ho, along which this range of hills is evidently laid down from K'ëen to Këe-shih.. 碣石,—see on Part i., p. 11. I must believe that Këe-shih was something like Te-ch'oo, only not far from the mouth of the river.

Some would claim for the name the dignity of a mountain like T'ae-hang or Hăng, but this is no more necessary than that Te-ch'oo should have been equal to Seih-shing or Wang-uh. The rocks of Kĕĕ-shih were existing, it was seen, at the beginning of our era, but they have long disappeared before the encroachments of the sea. It is vain to attempt to lay down their place with nice precision. 入于海, —Ying-tă makes this phrase refer to the range of mountains, which here terminated in the sea. Hoo Wei contends on the other hand that we must understand it of Yu,—that it takes up 逾河, and tells us that Yu here took a boat, and went out some distance to take a survey of the rocks of Kĕĕ. The view which I have taken of 導 renders it unnecessary to suppose any personal action of Yu; but on the application of the phrase, I choose to agree with Ying-tă rather than with the modern scholar.

P. 2. 西傾,朱圉,鳥鼠至于太華,—this par. contains the 'second row' of northern hills, according to K'ang-shing's phraseology. Tsăng Yen-ho observes that as no 導 precedes 西傾, we must bring the verb on from the commencement of the prec. par. We must do so, but we can hardly read the two paragraphs together. We have travelled from west to east; and now we return to the west again. 西傾,—see on Part i., p. 70. I have said there that it is often identified with mount Se-k'ing in the dis. of Chang, dep. of Kung-ch'ang. So it is in the Statistical Account of the Ming dyn., but that of the pres. dynasty says this is a mistake. The compilers of that find it rather beyond the extreme west of that dep., within the boundaries of Koko-nor, about 350 *le* to the south-east of the T'ing of T'aou-chow (洮州廳; lat. 34°35′, N., lon. 12°57′, W.). With them agree Hoo Wei and other scholars. This view is probably the correct one. The mountain has also the names of K'eang-t'ae (强臺), and Se-keang (西彊). 朱圉,—this mountain is 30 *le* to the south-west of the district of Fuh-keang (伏羌; lat 34°38′, N., lon. 11°4′, W.), in the depart. of Kung-ch'ang. Yen Jŏ-keu says that he visited the mountain, and found it of no very great size, having a reddish appearance; on a rock were the four words engraved—'Choo-yu fixed by Yu' (禹奠朱圉).

鳥鼠,—see on Part i., p. 76, and below, p. 12. The Wei had here its source. Hoo Wei observes at this point:—'Yu in his survey of the hills did not always go forward in a straight course, but went sometimes round about or retraced his steps. Thus instead of going east from Luy-show he went north to T'ae-yŏ, the urgent need of the capital requiring him to do so. As Neaou-shoo was on the east of the T'aou-water (洮水), Yu's most direct and convenient route would have been from Se-k'ing along that stream to Neaou-shoo, instead of which he

first went to Choo-yu, and then retraced his way westwards to the other mountain. This is strange, and may lead us to suppose that the names of Choo-yu and Neaou-shoo have somehow changed places in the text.' 太華 is the 'western mountain' of the Canon of Shun, and the mount Hwa of Part i., p. 62. Between Neaou-shoo and T'ae-hwa were the hills of Shun-wuh and Chung-nan (Part i., p. 76), which are not mentioned here. 熊耳,外方,桐柏,至于陪尾,—熊耳 hill is in the south of Loo-she district (盧氏; lat. 34°1′, N., lon. 5°32′, W.), of Shen-chow, in Ho-nan. There are two peaks, it is said, which rise up covered with verdure, and look like a bear's ears, from which it takes its name. Yu commenced his work on the Lŏ here;—see p. 13. 外方,—this mountain is identified with mount Ts'ung (嵩 or 崇山) in the district of Tăng-fung (登封; lat. 34°30′, N., lon. 3°27′, W.), dep. Ho-nan in Ho-nan prov. It has received also the names of Ts'ung-kaou (崇高) and T'ae-shih (太室). It came in subsequent times to be considered as the 'Central Mountain' (中嶽), and emperors still make progresses to it. 桐柏,—this mountain has given its name to the district of T'ung-pih (lat. 32°20′, N., lon. 3°10′, W.) in the dep. of Nan-yang (南陽) of Ho-nan. The Hwae has its source near to it;—see par. 11. Hoo Wei considers that two other hills,—Ta-fuh (大復) 30 *le* east of the dis. city, and T'ae-tsan (胎簪), 30 *le* to the north-west of it, are branches of T'ung-pih, and to be included in the name in the text. 陪尾,—Gan-kwŏ, referring Wae-fang, T'ung-pih, and Pei-wei, all to Yu-chow, sought for the last of them in the hill of Hwang-wei (橫尾), 30 *le* to the north of the dis. city of Ngan-luh (安陸), dep. of Tih-ngan (德安), Hoo-pih, which he says the river Hwae passed by. But this was a mistake. Pei-wei is in Shan-tung, dep. of Yen-chow, and the district of Sze-shwuy (lat. 35°48′, N., lon. 1°2′, E.). The Sze-water (泗水) had here its sources. The 至于 before 陪尾 indicates that there was a considerable distance between it and the last named mountain of T'ung-pih.

P. 3. We return now to the west again, and have to do with the mountains of the southern range. 導嶓冢至于荊山,—嶓冢 see Part i., p. 63, and below, p. 8. Ts'ae says that the appearance of the mountain was like a 冢 'the tumulus of a grave,' and hence it was called Po-ch'ung. Gan-kwŏ on 岷嶓

河　海。入　于　黑　沙。八　黎　至　導 ^{五節}
積　〇　于　三　水、〇　于　餘　于　弱
石、導 ^{七節} 南　危　至　導 ^{六節} 流　波　合　水、

5　　II. He surveyed the Weak-water as far as Hŏ-le, from which its superfluous waters went away among the Moving sands.

6　　He surveyed the Black-water as far as San-wei, from which it went away to enter the southern sea.

既藝 does not define the situation of mount Po, and Ying-tă, quoting from the Geography of Han, refers it to the tract of Lung-se (隴西郡). This was a mistake, and has occasioned much perplexity in subsequent works on the subject of this mountain, which is in the dep. of Han-chung, in Shen-se. —see Part i, p 46. 荆山,

內方至于大別,—Nuy-fang is identified with mount Chang (章山), in the south-west of the district of Chung-ts'eang,(鍾祥; lat. 31°12', N., lon. 3°57', W.), dep. of Ngan-luh in Hoo-pih. It was in King-chow. The Han passes near it. It is generally laid down in modern maps by the name of Ma-lang hill (馬良山).

大別 was also in King-chow. It is close by the dep. city of Han-yang (漢陽; lat. 30°34', N., lon. 2°18', W.), by the junction of the Han and the Kêang;—see par. 8. There was also a 小別, 'the small Pĕĕ,' in the district of Han-ch'uen (漢川).

Par. 4. We turn back again, and farther east. 岷 (in the Books of Han, 嶓) 山之陽至于衡山,—岷山,—see on Part i., p. 63. Hoo Wei observes that there are four different mountains which are said now to represent the mount Min of the Shoo. The first is in the ward of Sung-p'wan—that described in the note just referred to; the second is in Mow Chow, called often 汶山, which name appears in that of Min-ch'uen district (汶川); the third is in the dis. of Kwan (灌縣), dep of Shing-too; and the fourth is in Min Chow(岷州), dep., of Kung-ch'ang in Kan-suh. Woo Ch'ing's observation is correct, that all the mountains near the sources of the Keang went by the common name of Min. We must bear in mind, however, that what he and others call the sources of the Keang are only sources of branches of it within the limits of China, and flowing from the north to meet the Këang of the 'Golden Sands,' which must be traced westwards to find the true springs of the great river. 衡山, —see on Part i., p. 46. In going on to this, Yu left the Këang five or six hundeed le to the north. Gan-kwŏ very strangely says that the Këang passed by mount Hăng. 過九江至于敷淺原,—we saw, on Part i., p. 48, how it is all but impossible to come to a definite conclusion about what the Shoo calls the 'Nine Keang.' Whether what is now the T'ung-t'ing lake was intended by the phrase or not, however, the region indicated by it was not far from the site of that. Passing by this region, Yu went on to the plain of Foo-tseen, the place of which is about as difficult of determination. Gan-kwŏ says that this was also called the hill of Foo-yang (傅陽山), and this name conducts us to the district of Po-yang in Jaou-chow, Keang-se. How there should be mention of a plain, while the discourse is of hills, it is not easy to see. I suppose that, in travelling north-east from mount Hăng, whatever hills there were up to the termination of the progress at Foo-tseen, were of so little note that it was not thought worth while to mention their names. From the P'angle eastwards the hills were so few or small, that here the survey of them was concluded.

Ch. II. The account of the rivers. We must continue here the same meaning which we have attached to 導 in the preceding paragraphs. It is not so absurd in itself, indeed, to speak of leading the waters of the streams as it is to speak of leading the hills; and 導 is used in this sense, as in 導菏澤被孟豬, Part i., p. 57. But we cannot admit that meaning here. In clearing the channels and conducting on the rivers, it was necessary for Yu to begin at the lowest part of their course, and gradually proceed towards their sources; and this he did, as we have seen in the details of his operations in the several provinces. Here, however, he goes from the source to the mouth,—evidently surveying the work that had been accomplished. Hoo Wei says:—'By his personal agency, or by the deputed services of his assistants, Yu had finished his work in the nine provinces, and now he took a boat, and went from the sources of the streams to see whether the work was properly done.' It is not necessary to suppose even this travelling, according to the view which I have taken. We have in the paragraphs simply a description of what would have been seen on such a survey.

P. 5. Sze-ma Ts'een, after 導 (with him, 道) has 九川, as we found the addition of 九山 in par. 1; and it so happens that only *nine rivers* are specified. Still the phrase 導九川 must be taken in analogy with 導九山, as speaking not of 'the nine rivers,' but of 'the rivers of the nine provinces.'

The Weak-water,—see on Part i., par. 73.

Hŏ-le is the name of a hill rising in the north-west of the dis. of Chang-yih, and stretching along in a north-west direction from the dep. of Kan-chow into the adjoining one of Suh. The 'Statistical Account' gives it in both of the departments. The 'Geography Modernized' says:—'The Moving Sands lie beyond the pass of Kea-kuh' (嘉峪關) in Shen-se [this pass is in the north of Suh Chow, prov. of Kan-suh, at the termination of the great wall], from Soh-ko-ngoh-moo (索科鄂模) northwards, on the east as far as mount Ho-lan (賀 蘭山), and on the west as far as the borders of the discontinued Sha-chow (西至廢沙 州界; Sha-chow has again been replaced as the Ward of Sha-chow [沙州衞] by the pres. dynasty, in the extreme west of Ngan-se dep.). They extend from north to south more than 1,000 *le*, and from east to west several hundred *le*. The sand rises up and moves or flows along before the wind. Everywhere in the tract indicated this is to be seen.' In the rough map of China and its territories in the 'Universal Geography' (瀛環志略), published by Seu (徐繼畬), the governor of Fuh-këen in 1849, these moving sands are laid down very distinctly. On the east and north they are called Han-hae (瀚海), and on the west the deserts of Gobi (戈壁). The description of the Weak-water in the 'Statistical Account' does not enable us to understand the text, which Hoo Wei has conceived and described in the following way, from a study of all the references to it in older books:—Finding its waters near its source in a troubled condition and flowing eastwards, Yu conducted them from the hill of K'eung-shih (窮石), where they had their origin, north and west to the hill of Hŏ-le. There the main stream took a turn to the north-east, and proceeded to the marsh of Keu-yen (居延澤), which was among the moving sands,—what is called, in the preceding extract from the 'Geography Modernized' Soh-ko-ngoh-moo. But there were times when its waters were so swollen, that instead of all flowing east from the passage in the Hŏ-le hills, a portion overflowed and went westwards. These were the 'superfluous waters' of the text, and they were led away to the west, and lost in the sands of what is now the desert of Gobi. All this is ingeniously conceived and supported; but any distinct traces of this labour of Yu can hardly be expected to be discernible after the lapse of so long a time.

P. 6. The subject of the Blackwater is quite as difficult as that of the Weakwater;—see on Part i., p. 71. There it is given as the western boundary of Yung-chow, corresponding to the western Ho. But on the west of Kan-suh we find no stream answering at all to this description. Black-waters there are, besides that which is given as the boundary of Yung-chow, about ten in number, but not one of them satisfies the requisitions of the text. The last particular stated,—that the Black-water flowed to the southern sea, proves, indeed, that there could have been no such stream in the quarter assigned to the hill of Sau-wei. In his comments on the 'Book of the Waters,' Le Taou-ynen says:— 'The Black-water took its rise in Fowl-hill of Chang-yih, and flowing south to T'un-hwang passed by San-wei, from which it went away still south to the southern sea; but Chang-yih and T'un-hwang were both on the north of the Ho. The way in which the Black-water was able to cross the Ho, and proceed to the southern sea, was that westward from Tseih-shih the course of the Ho is often under ground, so that another stream might flow over it towards the south.' This view is absurd enough. There are no recent observations to support it. After taking the Black-water in this way across the Ho, it would still be necessary to carry it over the main stream of the Këang.

Hoo Wei, seeing that this account could not be adopted, supposes that the stream turned west after passing the hill of San-wei, and after getting beyond the sources of the Ho and the Këang, flowed south again, and entered the southern sea. Of course in thus writing, he knows not what he writes about. Of the rivers flowing south into the sea to the west of China there are the May-këang, or River of Cambodia, the Mei-nam of Siam, the Salween, and the Irawaddy. Many have tried to identify the Black-water with the first of these, which rises in Tibet, and flows through Yun-nan as the Lan-ts'ang (瀾滄江). Here is a river certainly which flows into the southern sea, but the northern part of it can in no ways be made into a boundary of Yung-chow.

Yu's geographical knowledge certainly was at fault in the case of the Black-water. Referring back to Part i., p. 62, where we saw reason to believe that the river of this name there mentioned was the southern boundary of Lëang-chow, and correctly identified with the 'Golden Sands,' or a portion of it, the main stream of the Keang. Now the 'Golden Sands' was known as the Black-water only after it had received the Shing, the Jŏ and the Loo. The Loo, moreover, has itself the name of the Black-water. We can conceive that this was supposed to extend indefinitely to the north, and run along both Lëang-chow and Yung-chow. This would enable us to believe that Yu, or whoever compiled this Book from his memoranda and reports, had the idea, however erroneous, of only one stream in his mind, when speaking of the boundaries of the two provinces. But after this simplification there remains the point of the

至于龍門、南至于華陰、又東至于厎柱、又東至于孟津、東過洛汭、至于大伾、北過澤水、至于大陸、又北播為九河、同為逆河、入于海。○

7 He surveyed the Ho from Tseih-shih as far as Lung-mun; and thence, southwards, to the north of mount Hwa; eastward then to Te-ch'oo; eastward again to the ford of Măng; eastwards still he passed the junction of the Lŏ, and went on to Ta-pei. From this the course was northwards, past the Keang-water, on to Ta-luh; north from which the stream was distributed and became the nine Ho, which united again and formed the meeting Ho, when they entered into the sea.

river's flowing to the southern sea. That cannot be got over. There is here a very serious error in the details of the Shoo.

P. 7. *The course of the Ho.* 導河積石 至于龍門,—on Tseih-shih, see Part i., p. 82, where its position is given as on the north-west of Ho Chow in the dep. of Lan-chow (蘭州). The compilers of the Statistical Account of the present dynasty, however, place it much farther off, and give it within the boundaries of the territory of Ts'ing-hae (青海) or Koko-nor. The mountain of Ho Chow was indeed, they say, called Tseih-shih as well as the other, but was distinguished from it by the prefix of 'little' (小積石), while the more western one was called the 'great.' Hoo Wei agrees in this view; and if it be correct, then Yu must have proceeded, or at least penetrated by his assistants, a long way west beyond the boundaries of the present China proper.

But if he got as far as the 'Snowy Mountain' (雪山),—which I find it difficult to believe, he was still distant from the sources of the Ho. Those are in the extreme west of the Koko-nor. The stream at first and, indeed, through most of its progress in the Koko-nor, is called the river of O-urh-tan (阿爾但河). It is not till it has pursued a tortuous course of more than 2,300 *le* to the fortified post of Kwei-tih (貴德堡), that it receives the name of the 'Yellow River' (黃河). A further progress of between 400 and 500 *le* brings it to the pass of Tseih-shih, flowing past which it enters the boundaries of Ho Chow.

[The Chinese Government cannot be said to have been indifferent to the discovery of the sources of the Ho. The Han, the T'ang, and the Yuen dynasties sent out special officers to trace the stream to its fountain-head. The emperor K'ang-he of the present did the same. We should read the reports of their expeditions with more interest, if it were not for the uncouth form which the names of the mountains and rivers of the Koko-nor assume when represented by Chinese characters. After all that the Chinese themselves have done, much distinction yet awaits the explorer from the west who shall visit the springs of this most fast-rushing and unmanageable of the great rivers of our globe.]

Lung-mun,—see on Part i., p. 82. The Ho, after entering Kan-suh in Ho Chow, flows east and north through the dep. of Lan-chow, and passes into that of Ning-hea (寧夏). This it traverses, now outside, now inside the great wall, going more north than east, and, at length, east of the district of P'ing-lo (平羅; lat. 38°52', N., lon. 4°22', W.), it goes again beyond the great wall into the country of the Ortous Mongols (鄂爾多斯界), which it quite embraces, only entering China proper again in Yu-lin (榆林), the north-eastern department of Shen-se. After this it flows south, sometimes inclining to the west, to the hill of Lung-mun, dep. of T'ung-chow. Hoo-k'ow, we saw, was somewhat to the north of Lung-mun, on the eastern or Shan-se side of the river; and hereabouts Yu commenced his labours. From Tseih-shih to Lung-mun, along the course of the Ho, is a distance of more than 3,000 *le*.

南至于華陰,—華陰 must be translated 'the north of mount Hwa;' see on Part i., p. 62. There is now the district city of Hwa-yin, but there could be no such place in

Yu's time. The north of mount Hwa is specified, as marking the point at which the Ho turned from its southern course to proceed east. Here also we must suppose that Yu had to put forth his skill and resources in its regulation. 東至于底柱,—see on par. 1. 又東至于孟津,—'the ford of Măng' still gives its name to the district of Măng (孟縣; lat. 34°55′, N., lon. 3°38′, W.), dep. of Hwae-k'ing in Ho-nan. The whole name, indeed, remains in a district of Ho-nan dep., which borders with the dis. of Măng on the north and east, the Ho being between them. The ford is about 20 *le* to the south of the dis. city of Măng. Lin Che-k'e supposes that it was not till he reached this point that Yu found it possible to ford the Ho; but there were during the Chow dynasty other fords between this and Te-ch'oo. Măng was most conveniently situated with reference to the capital. This is the reason why it is specified. 東過洛汭,—see on Part i., p. 55. Here, with reference to the stream of the Ho, we may very well read 洛汭 as in the translation. Elsewhere, as in Book III. par. 3, we must render differently. At the place of junction of the two streams, Yu must have performed some labour. 至于大伾,—the character 伾 is disputed. 岯, 坯, 阫, and 郱, all have their advocates. Connected with the form of the character are the opinions as to whether we should regard 大伾 as the name of a district or place, or of a hill. We may acquiesce in the conclusion of the Statistical Account of the present dynasty that we are to find it in the present Le hill (黎山), 20 *le* to the south-east of the dis. city of Seun (濬縣; lat. 35° 45′, N., lon. 1°38′, W.), in the dep. of Wei-hwuy of Ho-nan. [This is a recent arrangement; this dis. used to be reckoned in the dep. of Ta-ming, Chih-le.] From the ford of Măng to this point, the Ho had been gradually bending northwards. 北過洚水,至于大陸,—the Keang-water [洚 should probably be 降; in the Statistical Account we have 絳] rises in the south-west of the dis. of Chun-lew (屯留), dep. of Loo-ngan in Shan-se, and flowing into the dis. of Loo-shing (潞城), joins the 'Muddy Chang,' (濁漳), which, according to the Geography Modernized, is in consequence also called the Keang-water (降水). This river flowing east entered the Ho of Yu between Ta-pei and Ta-luh. The particular point was probably in the district of Fei-heang (肥鄉), dep. of Kwang-p'ing. Ta-luh,—see on Part i.. par. 9. There, however, we have to take 大陸 as the name of a district; here we have to think of some definite place, to be found

probably in the district of Ping-heang (平鄉; lat. 37°2′, N., lon. 1°23′, W.), 11 *le* to the north of which we have the site of the old city of Ken-luh. 又北播爲九河,—see on Yen-chow, Part i., par. 13. The successive changes in the course of the main stream of the Ho, and encroachments of the sea since the time of Yu, make it impossible for us now to ascertain those nine streams. The same things also render the rest of the paragraph difficult of elucidation. 同爲逆河,入于海,—it would seem from this that the nine Ho again united their waters, and formed one great river which seemed to contend with the advancing waves of the sea. The union of so many streams in one before entering the sea is difficult to suppose in the circumstances. Can we suppose that by the 逆河 is meant the coast water all along the space included between the Ho and its extreme southern branch, kept in a constant state of agitation by so many channels emptying themselves into it at no great distance from one another? This appears to be what in subsequent times was called the Pŏ-hae (渤海).

[It is clear from the above details that we cannot look for the Ho of Yu on the present face of the country. As it received the Chang river, however, before reaching Ta-luh, which still pursues its course to the sea, and enters it in the dep. of T'een-tsin, we may suppose that the north-eastern part of the Ho's course was not much difft. from the present course of the Chang. By the time of the famous duke Hwan of Ts'e in the Chow dyn., B.C. 684–642, of the nine Ho all but one had disappeared, and not long after, B.C. 601, in the 5th year of the emp. Ting (定王), 1675 years, acc. to the 'Annals of the various dynn.,' after Yu's labours, the first great change in the course of the stream took place. This, however, did not affect its northern portion. The main stream broke off, not far from Ta-pei, and after running for some time in the T'ä (漯川), broke off from it again, and proceeding east and north, rejoined the Chang, and went on as before to the sea. A second change, more extensive, took place more than 600 years later. In the third year of the usurper Mang (王莽), A.D. 11, the channel from the T'ä northwards disappeared, and the Ho, now in the channel of the T'ä and now north of it, flowed east to the sea, which it entered in the pres. district of Le-tsin (利津; lat. 37°32′, N., lon. 1°52′, E.), dep. of Woo-ting (武定), Shan-tung. For more than 1000 years a struggle was maintained to prevent the stream from going further south, but in A.D. 1194, the main stream broke off in the dep. of Wei-hwuy in Ho-nan, about the district of Sin-heang (新鄉; lat. 35°22′, N.. lon. 2°22′, W.), and flowing east and north as far mount Lëang (梁山),

八于海。東爲北江。澤爲彭蠡、于江東匯、大別南入、三澨至于、浪之水、過。又東爲滄、東流爲漢、嶓冢導漾、八節

8　　From Po-ch'ung he surveyed the Yang, which, flowing eastwards, became the Han. Farther east, it became the water of Ts'ang-lang; and after passing the three great dykes, went on to Ta-pëe, southwards from which it entered the Keang. Eastward still, and whirling on, it formed the marsh of P'ang-le; and from that its eastern flow was the northern Këang, as which it entered the sea.

in the dis. of Show-chang (壽張), dep. of Yen-chow, it there divided into two branches, one flowing north and east, and entering the sea in the dis. of Le-tsin, the other going east and south till it joined the Hwae, and went on in its channel to the sea. After this, the northern branch gradually became less and less. During the Yuen and Ming dynasties, The Ho finally broke off in the district of Yung-tsih (滎澤), dep. of K'ae-fung, and proceeded east with a very gradual inclination to the south till it joined the Hwae. I have not met with an account of the changes which it has undergone since. Until within a few years it discharged itself into the sea by the old channel of the Hwae.]

P. 8. *The course of the Han.* 嶓冢導漾 (in Sze-ma Ts'een and others, 瀁), 東流爲漢,—see on Part i., p. 63. It is there stated that there were two mountains called Po-ch'ung, one in Kan-suh, in the small dep. of Ts'in (秦州), 60 *le* to the south-east of the dep. city, in which what is called the Western Han (西漢水) takes its rise. Flowing through Ts'in Chow and Keae Chow (階州) into Sze-ch'uen, it is lost in the Kealing, which proceeding south through the departments of Paou-ning (保寧), and Shun-k'ing (川慶), enters the Keang, near the dep. city of Chung-k'ing (重慶; lat. 29°42′, N., lon. 9°48′, W.). The Geography of the Han supposed that this western Han was the Yang of the text, and that we were to look for the Po-ch'ung mountain in the pres. Kan-suh. But there is no connection between the two Hans;—there is none now, nor is it likely that there ever was. The mistake made in the Han dynasty has led to much perplexity and debate on the sentence under notice. The Po-ch'ung of Yu was, no doubt, the mountain in the north of Ning-kёang Chow (寧羌州), dep. of Han-chung.

Here the Han rises, and for some time after issuing from its springs it was called the Yang. Flowing east along the south of the district of Mёen (沔縣), it passes the dep. city in the dis. of Nan-ch'ing (南鄭), whereabouts the name of Yang ceased, and was superseded by that of Han. From the dep. of Han-chung, the Han passes into that of Hing-ngan, out of which it proceeds from Shen-se into Hoo-pih in the dep. of Yun-yang (鄖陽) Entering from this that of Seang-yang in the sub. dep. of Keun (均州), it took the name of the Water of Ts'ang-lang:—又東爲滄浪之水. There was an island here according to Le Taou-yuen in the middle of the stream, called Ts'ang-lang (漢水中有洲、日滄浪洲), which gave occasion to the name which was retained to the junction of its waters with the Keang. It is perhaps a more likely account of the name, that it was given to the stream here from the bluish tinge of its waters. 過三澨至于大別、南入于江,—this describes the course of the stream from Keun Chow till it mingles its waters with the Heang. On Ta-pëe, see on par. 3. The only difficulty is with 三澨, which Ts'ae says was the name of a stream, or streams. Such also was the view of the older commentators,—Gan-kwǒ, Ch'ing Heuen, Ma Yung, and Wang Suh. The 說文, however, defines 澨 as 'a large dyke on a river's bank where people could dwell' (埤增水邊、土人所止). This meaning is the better established of the two. Hoo Wei fixes on three points, all in the pres. district of Seang-yang, where he supposes three dykes to have been raised to sustain the impetus of the waters entering the Han, and considers them to be the positions indicated in the text.

東匯澤爲彭蠡、東爲北江、入于海,—these clauses present

岷山導江、東別為沱、又東至于灃、過九江、至于東陵、東迤北會于匯、東為中江、入于海。○導沇水、東流為

9　　From mount Min he surveyed the Këang, which branching off to the east formed the T'o; eastward again it reached the Le; after this it passed the nine Këang; and flowing eastward and winding to the north, it joined *the Han* in its eddying movements; from that its eastern flow was the middle Këang, as which it entered the sea.

10　　He surveyed the Yen water, which flowing eastward became the Tse, and entered the Ho. *Thereafter* it flowed out, and became the

no small difficulties. First, the waters of the Han have now mingled with the Këang;—why should it still be spoken of as if it were a distinct stream? Second, the P'ang-le lake has its own sources and feeders, independent of the Këang, and is moreover a very considerable distance from the river;—it cannot with propriety be represented as being formed by the Han and Këang. Laborious efforts have been made to clear up these points,—with some, but by no means complete, satisfactoriness. I apprehend that the face of the country changed very considerably during the 2,000 years and more that elapsed between Yu and the Han dynasty; whether the changes can still be traced remains to be seen:—see what was said on the nine Këang, pp. 113, 114. The way in which Chinese scholars have dealt with the difficulties of the text will be seen from the two following quotations. First, on the second perplexity which I have indicated, Choo-foo-tsze says:—'The marshing of P'ang-le took place, indeed, to the south of the great Keang. But it did so in consequence of the nature of the ground, which high in the north and low in the south impeded the discharge of the waters from the P'ang-le. Unable to find a sufficient vent, they gathered themselves up, and spread abroad in the form of the lake which we have, several hundred *le* in extent.' Again, on the whole passage Woo Ch'ing has said:—'The Han flowing south enters into the Keang, and then along the northern bank of the Keang, flows eastward, the northern portion of the Keang, and so enters the sea (東行為江之北，而入于海). But the Han having once entered the Keang, the two became one stream, and yet it is here said—"it flowed eastward as the northern Keang," as if there were still a separate stream;—how is this to be accounted for? Let us bear in mind that the sources of the Han were remote, and its stream great, barely second to the Keang, and all but its peer. Another way of speaking was necessary here than the style usual on the junction of a small stream with a large one; and hence in Part i., p. 47, the Keang and the Han are both mentioned as pursuing their common course to the sea. The Keang is not permitted to absorb both the waters and the name of the Han, but the Han shares in the name of the Këang, becomes in fact "the northern Keang." There are again "the four principal rivers" whose discharge from their basins into the sea is commemorated (記其入海者，著其為瀆也). Three of them are just one stream, but the fourth is twice commemorated,—as the Keang, and also as the Han. Not that the Ho, for instance, did not carry with it to the sea the waters of many other rivers, but they are all small as compared with it, and might be supposed to be swallowed up in it; but not so with the Han and the Keang. The former must still retain an individuality to the last.'

P. 9. *The course of the Keang.* 岷山 導江、東別為沱,—see on Part i., pp. 49, 63, and 64; and on par. 3 of this Part. At whatever point in the range of hills going by the name of Min, this branch of the Keang takes its rise, it appears in the north-west of Sze-ch'uen, and flows south through the Ward of Sung-p'wan into the small dep. of Mow (茂州). Thence flowing more easterly, it enters the dept. of Ching-too, and in passing through the district of Kwan (灌縣; lat. 30°59', N., lon. 12°46', W.), it throws off the first T'o, often called the river of Pe (郫江), because it immediately passes on the east through the dis. of that name. It goes on south of the small dep. of Mei (眉州); thence through the dep. of Kea-ting (嘉定), to that of Seu-chow (敍州), not far from which (lat. 28°38', N., lon. 11°43', W.) it receives, we are told, the river of Ma-hoo (馬湖). It would be more correct to say that here it joins *the* Keang, the river of the 'Golden Sands' which received the waters of the Ma-hoo not long before. From this point the course of the stream is eastwards, and generally with a gradual inclination to the north. First it traverses the small dep. of Loo (瀘州), on the south-east of the dep. city of which (lat. 28°56′, N., lon. 10°55′, W.) it again receives the T'o, which has collected various streams in its course. From this it proceeds east and north through the depp. of Chung-k'ing (重慶) and K'wei-chow (夔州), and in the Fung-tsëë (奉¹節) dis. of the latter, it threw off at one time a second T'o. This was the E-water (夷水), which left the Këang at this point, and flowing to the south-east was joined by a stream from the dep. of She-nan (施南) in Hoo-pih, with which it went away east-ward, and rejoined the Këang, which has passed from Sze-ch'uen into Hoo-pih,—rejoined it, after passing the districts of Pa-tung (巴東) and Ch'ang-yang (長陽), dep. of E-ch'ang (宜昌), close by the district city of E-too (宜都), dep. of King-chow. At this point the river from She-nan still flows into the Këang, but the branch which flowed off from the great stream in Fung-tsëë district has long been dried up. I have abridged the above details from the 禹貢錐指. They bring the present course of the Min-keang sufficiently well before us. From the text, however, one gets the impression that, if the main stream was not called by the name of the T'o, it was the branch or branches so styled which engaged the chief attention of Yu.

又東至于澧, 過九江, 至于東陵,—the former clause left as near the district city of E-too, lat. 30°28′, N., lon. 5°9′, W. This brings us to Pa-ling the chief city and district of the dep. of Yŏ-chow (岳州府巴陵縣), lat. 29°24′, N., lon. 3°33′, W. In Yu's time, 東陵, 'the eastern hill,' would simply be the name of the hill which now occupies the south-western part of the dep. city, called Pa-ling, Pa-k'ew (巴邱), and T'een-yŏ (天岳). Among the old interpreters there is a difference of view, whether 澧 (Sze-ma Ts'een and the Books of Han read 醴) is the name of a hill or of a stream; and Ch'ing lays down a canon, which must be considered arbitrary, to settle the point. He says that in this Book after 過 and 會 we have the names of rivers, but after 至 the names of hills or marshes. Whichever we understand by the term, the name remains in the small dep. of Le, the chief city of which is in lat. 29°37′, N., lon. 4°45′, W. We have also the Le-water, which rising in the dis. of Yung-ting (永定), in the extreme west of the dep., flows eastwards through the whole of it, and passes into Hwa-yung (華容) dis., dep. of Yŏ-chow, where it flows

into the T'ung-t'ing lake. Of the 'nine Këang' enough has been already said. This passage certainly assigns the place of them near where the T'ung-t'ing lake is. The great difficulty in my way against acceding to the view of the Sung scholars is that neither here nor elsewhere in the Tribute of Yu are the 'nine Keang' spoken of as a marsh or lake.

東迤北會于匯,—this clause is attended with no little difficulty. Gan-kwŏ took 迤 in the sense of 溢 'to overflow,' and says that 'the stream, overflowing as it went east, divided into separate channels, which all went north and united to form the P'ang-le' (東溢分流, 都共北會爲彭蠡). Woo Ch'ing, ingeniously but too violently, removed the clause 東匯澤爲彭蠡, and read it after the text—東迤北會于匯, 東匯澤爲彭蠡. 匯 is then a name, in the first place, for the meeting of the Han and Keang, and in the next for the stream of their united waters. These attempts at explanation only show the difficulty of the text. We must suppose that in this par. the Shoo takes no notice of the junction of the Han and the Këang, but the 匯 in it and the prec. par. have the same reference,—are to be understood of the turbulence of the united streams, which caused the formation of the P'ang-le. This turbulence, however, is primarily predicated of the Han, and here the Keang is supposed by an eastward course, winding (迤) to the north, to merge its waters at that point in those of the Han. 東爲中江, 入于海,—Gan-kwŏ says:—' We had the northern Kèang; here we have the middle one; that there was a southern one is plain' (有北, 有中, 南可知). The Han was called the northern Keang in the last par., after its junction with the great stream. Here the great stream after leaving the P'ang-le, or the point at which the waters which formed it tried to discharge themselves, is called the middle Keang. Possibly, the portion of those waters which did enter may be regarded as the southern Këang, or southern part of the river. Still as the Shoo makes no mention of a southern Këang, we need not trouble ourselves with it. We get the idea certainly of one stream flowing to the sea from this point, and I conclude that the three Keang of Yang-chow (Part i., p. 40) have nothing to do with the Yang-tsze.

P. 10. *The course of the Tse.* What is most remarkable in the account of this river is that it is described as first on the north of the Ho, then crossing that powerful stream, and reappearing on the south of it. The former part of it is called by Woo Ch'ing 'the northern Tse,' the latter, 'the southern.' The name of the Tse still remains north of the Ho. On the south it has long been lost, but the ancient course of the stream must have been much the same as that of the present Scaou Ts'ing (小清河)

東　自　又　穴、　東　導　比　陶　濟
會　熊　東　東　八　淮　會　丘　入
于　耳、　過　會　于　自　于　北、　于
伊、　東　漆　于　海。　桐　汶、　又　河、
又　比　沮、　灃、　○十二節　柏、　又　東　溢
東　會　入　又　導　東　比　至　爲
比　于　于　東　渭　會　東　于　滎、
八　澗　河、　會　自　于　八　菏、　東
于　瀍、　○十三節　于　鳥　泗　于　又　出
河。　又　導　涇、　鼠　沂、　海。　東　于
　　　　洛　　同　十一節

Yung *marsh*. Eastward, it issued forth on the north of Taou-k'ew, and flowed further east to the *marsh of* Ko. North-east from this it united with the Wăn, and after flowing north went eastwards on to the sea.

11　He surveyed the Hwae from *the hill of* T'ung-pih. Flowing east, it united with the Sze and the E; and with an eastward course *still* entered the sea.

12　He surveyed the Wei from Neaou-urh-tung-heuĕ. Flowing eastwards it met with the Fung, and eastwards again with the King. Farther east still, it passed the Tseih and the Tseu; and entered the Ho.

13　He surveyed the Lŏ from Heung-urh. Flowing to the north-east, it united with the Kĕen and the Ch'ĕen; eastwards still, it united with the E; and then on the north-east entered the Ho.

導沇水、東流爲濟入于河,—the Statistical Account says of the Tse-water, under the dep. of Hwae-k'ing in Honan:—'It has another name, that of the Yen-water. It rises in the hill of Wang-uh, in the west of the dis. of Tse-yuen, and flowing east along the north of the district, it passes with a south-east course through the north of the district of Măng, and on to the Ho.' There is another stream,—'the Wide Tse' (廣濟),—in the same department, having a longer course very much parallel to this, and more to the east, which some would rather identify with the river of the text. It is not worth the time and space to enter into the discussions of the critics on the subject. For some time after leaving its source the stream was called the Yen, but ere long it was known as the Tse, and soon lost in the Ho. 溢爲滎,—here Gan-kwŏ says:—'The Tse having entered the Ho flows along with it ten *le* and more, and then shooting across to its south bank, flows along with it again for several *le*, and issues out, as the marsh of Yung, on the south-east of Gaou-ts'ang' (在敖倉東南). All this, about a small stream like the Tse entering a mass of fast-rushing water like the Ho, and yet preserving itself distinct, &c., is absurd. Yung is the same as the marsh of Yung-po, Part i., p. 56;—see the note on that par. 溢 must be understood as flowing out, not from the river but from the ground. The water of the marsh was most likely derived from the Ho, finding its way by some underground communication to the place, but we cannot suppose for a moment that the water of the marsh was that of the Tse, flowing into the Ho from the north and passing through it. 東出于陶丘北，又東至于菏，—陶丘 = 'the small hill of T'aou.' A hill that seems to be composed of two parts, rising like storeys one above the other, is called 陶丘 (再成為陶丘，再成，其形再重也). The name remains in the district of Ting-t'aou (定陶; lat. 35°11', N., lon. 44', W.), dep. of Yen-chow, the hill being 7 *le* to the south-west of the district city. The hill of T'aou was about 500 *le* from the Yung marsh, and here again there bubbled up a spring from the ground, which was strangely supposed to be the waters of the Tse reappearing after so long a subterranean travel. Woo Ch'ing says that the 出 should lead us to think of a well-spring, sending up its waters to the surface from its own bosom. These waters flowed away to the marsh of Ko which they served to augment;—see Part i., p. 57. 又東北會于汶，—the waters of what we may now call the Southern Tse flowed through the marsh of Ko, and on the north-east of it were met by those of the Wǎn-water, which is now one of the feeders of the Grand Canal;—see on Part i., p. 27. 又北，東入于海，—the Tse, augmented now by the Wǎn, flowed north as far as about the pres. district city of Yang-kuh (陽穀; lat. 36°9', N., lon. 29', W.), and then pursued its way to the sea, very much in the course of the present Seaou-ts'ing (小清), the name of 清, 'clear,' having taken its rise from the purity for which the waters of the Tse had always been famous.

P. 11. *The course of the Hwae.* The Hwae rises in the hill of T'ung-pih (see on par. 2), Honan prov., dep. of Nan-yang, dis. of T'ung-pih (lat. 32°20', N., lon. 3°10', W.). It met with the united streams of the E and the Sze (see on Part i., par. 30) in Keang-soo, dep. of Hwaengan, dis. of Ts'ing-ho (lat. 33°35', N., lon. 2°34', E.), and from that point went on east to the sea. The eastern portion of the Hwae's course is now very much changed. From the dis. of T'ung-pih, dep. Nan-yang, it flows east and north through the small dep. of Kwang, where it receives the Joo (汝水), and from the dis. of Koo-ch'e (固始; lat. 32°18', N., lon. 51', W.). it passes into Ngan-hwuy. Entering this prov. in the dep. of Ying-chow (潁州) it traverses it, flowing nearly due east, and collecting many waters, to the small dep.

of Sze (泗州; lat. 35°8', lon. 1°52', E.) when it passes through the lake of the 'Great marsh' (洪澤湖), which may be said to be formed by it, into Keang-soo, and from which lake on the north-east it discharges itself again into the Yellow River, in the dis. of Ts'ing-ho dept. Hwae-ngan. Thenceforth its course is lost in that of the Ho. At the same point the Grand Canal also issues from the Ho, so that we may say there is a connection between the Hwae and the Yang-tsze, which we saw, Part i., p. 45, began to be established in the Chow dynasty. On the northern side of the Ho, the canal now receives the waters of the E and the Sze, which used to flow into the Hwae. In the mention of both the E and the Sze, after their waters had been blended together, Woo Ch'ing finds a case analogous to that of the Han's retaining its individuality after joining the Keang, as in p. 8. The streams, he says, were of about equal size, and therefore the name of each must be preserved. The whole course of the Hwae from T'ung-pih to the sea is about 1,800 *le*.

P. 12. *The course of the Wei.* See on Part i., pp. 73–75. The river rises in the hill of Neaou-shoo-t'ung-heuĕ, in the west of the district of Wei-yuen (渭源), dep. of Lan-chow, Kan-suh. In par. 2, and Part i., p. 76, the mountain is called Neaou-shoo, but here we have its full name, meaning 'Bird and Rat in the Same Hole.' Gan-kwŏ, with his fondness for the marvellous, says that 'a bird and a rat lived in the same holes on this mountain, and paired together as male and female.' The Urh-ya had said that 'a bird called T'oo (鵌), and a rat, called Tuh (鼵), lived here together in the same hole.' This is conceivable; the addition of their pairing is of course absurd. From Lan-chow dep. the river flows into that of Kung-ch'ang, and thence to the small dep. of Ts'in (秦州), from which it passes into Shen-se, the whole of which it traverses till it meets the Ho at the termination of its southward flow. The whole length of its course is now under 1,500 *le*, whereas in the Han dynasty it was given as nearly 1,900. It may have altered its course in some parts.

P. 13. *The course of the Lŏ.* See on Part i., p. 55. 熊耳,—see on par. 2. The Heung-urh hill there mentioned is, no doubt, that of the text, from which Yu began his survey of the Lŏ; but the sources of the stream are more distant, in the small dep. of Shang, in Shen-se, as stated on Part i., p. 55. There is also a Heung-urh hill there, distinguished from this by the prefix of 'Western.' According to the Geography of the Han dynasty, the course of the Lŏ was altogether 1,970 *le*.

十四節
九州攸同、四
隩既宅九山
刊旅九川滌
源九澤既陂、
四海會同六
十五節
府孔修庶土
交正厎慎財
賦咸則三壤、
成賦中邦。○

14　　III. *Thus*, throughout the nine provinces a similar order was effected:—the grounds along the waters were everywhere made habitable; the hills were cleared of their superfluous wood and sacrificed to; the sources of the streams were cleared; the marshes were well banked; access to the capital was secured for all within the four seas.

15　　A great order was effected in the six magazines *of material wealth;* the different parts of the country were subjected to an exact comparison, so that contribution of revenue could be carefully adjusted according to their resources. The fields were all classified with reference to the three characters of the soil; and the revenues for the Middle region were established.

Ch. III. Pp. 14, 15. A SUMMARY OF THE LABOURS OF YU THUS FAR DESCRIBED. 14. 九州攸同,—this clause is a summary of the whole par.; the other clauses give the particulars of the general order which was established. The phrase 攸同 occurred before, where after Gan-kwŏ, I explained 攸 by 所, its frequent synonym;—see Part i., p. 75. K'ung seems to take the character in the same way here, his comment on the clause being—所同事在下, 'the particulars in which they were made to agree are given below.' This is forced, however. The dict. gives 攸 as sometimes merely 'a helping word' (語助詞), an expletive, and quotes from the She King. Part III., Bk. I., Ode x., stt. 4,5, 四方攸同, which is much akin to the text. We may consider the 攸 therefore as simply supplying the place of the copula. The nine Chow are of course the nine provinces described in Part i. 洲 and 州 were originally interchangeable; and the Urh-ya defines 洲 as 'inhabitable gronnd in the midst of water,' (水中可居者). Now all the habitable ground the ancient Chinese knew was conceived of as surrounded by water, and hence it was called a 州 or continent, and the subdivision was again made of the nine Chow, embracing the empire proper;—see Hoo Wei *in loc.* 四隩既宅,—隩, see Can. of Yaou, p. 7. But we must seek for a different meaning here. That which I have adopted is after Le Seun (李巡), who says:—涯內近水爲隩. Under Yen-chow we are told, Part i., p. 16, that the people could come down from the heights and dwell on the low ground, and under Yung-chow (p. 78), that the country about San-wei was made habitable; the text says that throughout the nine provinces all the low ground near the streams that had formerly been inhabited was recovered from the waters 四隩=四方之隩. This is better than to take it, with Ts'ae and the Daily Explanation, as =四海之隩. 九山刊旅,—九山 =九州之山;—see the Introduction to Ch. I. Wang Ts'ëaou (王樵) says:—'刊 and 旅, describing the beginning and end of the work on the hills, embrace all the operations on them. The cutting down the wood was the first step in the regulation of the waters; the sacrificing was the announcement of the completed work.' On 旅, see on Part i., pp. 65,76. 九川滌源,—九川=九州之川; see on par. 5. 滌源, 'had their

錫十
土六
姓。節

○
祗十
台七
○節

德
先
不
行。

距
五十
百八
節

○
朕
行。

里
甸
服。
百

百
里
里
賦

納
總、
納
二

百
里
里
納

銍、
三
百

16　IV. He conferred lands and surnames. *He said*, "Let me go
17　before the empire with reverent attention to my virtue, that none
may act contrary to my conduct."

18　　Five hundred *le* constituted THE IMPERIAL DOMAIN.　From the first

sources cleared,' is a somewhat difficult expression. Ying-tă says it means that from the source of the rivers to their mouth, Yu cleared all their channel, so that they had no obstruction in their course. This is, no doubt, intended, but the question is as to how it is said by the characters employed. Hoo Wei approves a remark by one of the critics Kin (金氏), that when it is said here that the sources of the rivers were cleared, and not their courses, we must understand by the text the work described by Yu himself—'I deepened the channels, and canals, and conveyed them to the streams.' In this way there were no pools of water about the country to lead to the obstruction of rivers. The remark is well enough, but it leaves the difficulty of the language untouched. We may conclude that if the sources were cleared, the courses would also be attended to;—this is probably the ground of Ying-tă's observation. 九澤既陂,—九澤 must be taken in analogy with 九山 and 九川, as =九州之澤. It does happen, indeed, that we can make out nine marshes mentioned in the first Part,—Luy-hea in Yen-chow; Ta-yay in Ts'eu-chow; P'ang-le and the Shaking marsh in Yang-chow; Yun-mung in King-chow (supposing only *one* marsh intended in p. 50); Yung-po, the marsh of Ko, and Măng-choo in Yu-chow; and Choo-yay in Yung-chow. Notwithstanding this coincidence, we must deal with 九澤 as with 九川. 陂==障, 'a bank or dyke,' used here as a verb. It is synonymous with 隄 in the general signification, but the terms are differently applied, 隄 denoting the high banks on both sides of a river to confine the waters to their channel; 陂, the embankment surrounding a marsh, with sluices to admit water, and others to let it out. 四海會同,—two interpretations have been proposed of this clause. There is that given in the 集傳:—四海之水, 無不會同, 各有所歸, 'the waters within the four seas all met in a similar way,—each had its place to which it came.' The other, which I

have followed in the translation, is that proposed by Gan-kwŏ. Lin Che-k'e explains it by a reference to the conclusion of each chapter on the provinces, which sets forth an account of the route of conveyance to the capital. A commentator Chang (張) observes:—'When the calamity of the inundation was removed, not only could the people of the nine provinces without obstruction, but the barbarous tribes, east, west, north, and south, could likewise all assemble in the capital. We are sent back to the discussions about the meaning of the phrase, 'the four Seas;'—see on the Canon of Shun, p. 13. In this place we must take, I think, the general indefinite signification of the phrase. 會同,—see on Ana. XI., xxv., 6.

P. 15. This is a sort of summary of the portions of Part i., on the soil, fields, revenue, and tribute of the different provinces. 六府孔修,—see on 'The Counsels of Yu,' pp. 7,8. 庶土变正,底慎財賦,—it seems most natural to take 土 here in the sense belonging to it in the first Part,—as meaning the soil, and 庶土, the soil everywhere, with the different characters attaching to it. It will also cover 'the fields,' the account of which always follows it;—to this we are led by the 咸慎 which follows in the next clause. 底慎 indicates the care and diligence with which Yu proceeded, according to the force that we have seen attaches throughout this Book to 底. The 財 preceding 賦 occasions some perplexity. I have endeavoured to give what I consider is the meaning. 咸則三壤,成賦中邦,—則 is a verb,—法, signifying 'according to,' 'taking as a law;' 三壤, 'the three soils,' *i.e.*, the three grades of quality as 'highest, middle, and lowest,' every grade having also, as we have seen, a threefold subdivision. 中邦 'the middle region,' is held by Hoo Wei to denote the territory in the three first of the domains spoken of in the next chapter.

Ch. IV. Pp. 16—22. Another territorial and political division of the country. The division of the empire into nine provinces was mainly regulated by the natural features of the country,—a reference to the hills and streams. The division here described was of another character and mainly political. Not a few difficult questions arise out of it, which I shall briefly touch on, after discussing exegetically the meaning of the several paragraphs.

P. 16. 錫土姓, 'He conferred lands and surnames,'—this must be understood in close connection with the paragraphs below. The evils occasioned by the overflow of the waters had been in a great measure removed; the lands had everywhere been surveyed; the revenues which they ought to yield had been fixed;—it was necessary that provision should now be made for the government of the multitudes, and the maintenance of the order which had been established. Yu therefore now assigned throughout the province, according to the plan which is subsequently detailed, different portions of territory to those whose birth, or services, or virtue, most entitled them to the distinction. He was himself, indeed, only a minister, a servant, and what he did in this way must have been subject to the approval of Yaou, by whom it was necessary that his acts should be confirmed;—we may well suppose that they were never disallowed. And we may suppose also, that in his conferring lands his first regards were given to the officers who had rendered him the most effectual assistance in his arduous labours.

This assignment of lands was like the action of a conqueror who dispossesses the original possessors of the kingdom which he has subdued, and portions it out among his followers. And there was probably an element of this nature in the action of Yu. The tribes of San-meaou, for instance, were doubtless put under some minister of Yaou. But the strifes of the founders of the Chinese empire with the earlier occupants of the country are barely intimated. Yu's subjugation of it was mainly a reclaiming of it from the wildness of nature, and the disasters brought about by the overflowing of its rivers.

When it is said that Yu conferred surnames as well as names, we cannot but think of his era as that of the real origin of the Chinese empire. Gan-kwŏ's exposition of the par.—it must be borne in mind that he understood Yaou and not Yu as the nominative to 錫—is :—'The emperor, establishing the virtuous, gave them surnames after their places of birth, meaning that such and such a virtuous man was born in such a place, and therefore the name of that place was given to him as a surname to distinguish him, (天子建德因生以賜姓 [this is a quotation from the 左傳, 隱八年], 謂有德之人生此地, 以此 地名賜之姓, 以顯之). The surname, however, was given not only from the birth-place, but after the name of the fief conferred, from the office held by the receiver or one of his ancestors, from any remarkable incident in his life, and from a variety of other

circumstances;—the history of surnames among the Chinese is just like the same history in other nations. Subsequent to Yu's time, and especially on the changes of the early dynasties, we have instances of the conferring of lands and surnames; but not at all on the large scale which the text suggests to us as practised by him.

As closely connected with this paragraph and the whole of the chapter, we should keep in mind Yu's own statement in the 'Yih and Tseih,' p. 8 :—'I assisted in completing the five tenures, extending over 5,000 *le*; in appointing in the provinces twelve Tutors; and establishing, in the regions beyond, extending to the four seas, five presidents.'

P. 17. I have introduced '*He said*' before this paragraph, understanding it to be a remark made by Yu, related here, amid the account of his achievements, to show how he himself set the chief store by his personal virtue. It seems out of place, indeed, but we cannot help that. Gan-kwŏ rather supposes it to be describing the thought of the emperor, and in an indirect form, from the narrator, and not from the sovereign. 祇=敬 · 台=我 · 台 and 朕 have the same reference. We have seen how 朕, before the founder of the Ts'in dynasty, was used indifferently by the emperor and by his ministers.   Hoo Wei observes :— 'From 冀州 (Part. i., p. 2) downwards discribes the business of good government and the nourishment of the people; from 錫土姓 describes the business of good instruction and the transformation of the people. 成賦中 邦 (par. 25) is what I call good government; —it gets the wealth of the people. 聲教 訖于四海 (par. 23) shows what I call the good instruction;—it gets the hearts of the people.'

Pp. 18—22. *The five domains.* 18. 五百 里甸服,—I do not see how to translate 服 in this and the other paragraphs otherwise than by 'domain, if, indeed, that word can be called a translation of the Chinese character. The dictionary gives the 五服, and the cognate phrases of 六服, 九服, as a distinct signification of the term, without attempting to deduce it from others that are more common. It is often represented as meaning 'service,' 服事, such and such service being rendered to the emperor here, and such and service being rendered there. So Gan-kwŏ explains 甸服 as denoting 爲天子服治田, 'for the emperor doing service in the cultivation of the fields.' In whatever way this application of it arose, the character is in effect here simply a designation of territory. 甸 is defined by Ts'ae as =田, 'fields;' and he says :—'Because all the business of this territory was to supply the

里、納
秸、服、
四百粟、
里
里五百米。
○ 十九節
百里
侯服、
百里

hundred *le* they brought, as revenue, the whole plant of the grain; from the second, they brought the ears; from the third, they brought *only* the straw, but had to perform other services; from the fourth, *they gave* the grain in the husk; and from the fifth, the grain cleaned.

19   Five hundred *le beyond* constituted THE DOMAIN OF THE NOBLES. The first hundred *le* was occupied by the cities and lands of the

revenue, from the fields, therefore it is called 甸服. Here again the dictionary is very cautious, and defines the term (from the 說文) 'the emperor's 500 *le* of land.' There is, I think a connection between 甸 and 田; but without attempting to indicate what it is, I translate 甸服, 'the imperial domain.' The 500 *le* are understood to extend every way, north, south, east, and west, from the capital, so as to form a square of 1,000 *le*, which may be represented thus :—

The whole would contain an area of 1,000,000 square *le*.

百里賦納總—總, meaning 'to collect and bind up,' then = 'all,' 'the whole.' Here applied to the produce of the land it means 'the whole plant.' Ts'ae's definition is very good:—禾本全曰總. 賦 = 'as revenue;'—not that they brought all the produce to the imperial granaries, but the proportion of it—probably one tenth—as assessed. This was the rule for the first hundred *le* round about the capital. We have no mention of the payment of revenue in the other domains. It was, no doubt, on some arrangement analogous to that made for this *fuh*. The princes occupying the several territories received it, and then paid a tithe of their incomes to the emperor not in kind but in value, in other articles produced in their principalities;—such at least is the account given by Hoo Wei. 二百里納銍—銍 primarily means 'a short sickle for reaping grain;' it is then used for the grain reaped with it. Ts'ae says:—刈禾曰銍. He adds, however, 半藁 'half the stalk.' We are to understand the ear, with a small portion of the stalk, by which the ears could conveniently be bundled together. 三百里納 秸、服、—秸 denotes 'the straw,' the plant

without the ears or grain. Ts'ae defines it 半 藁去皮, which I do not understand. The contribution of revenue from this portion of the domain was thus the least valuable of all, and therefore the inhabitants were called upon to perform other service, which is denoted by 服. Ts'ae would extend this to the first and second hundred *le* as well, and some would extend it to all the other four. But this is quite arbitrary. The service must be confined to the third hundred *le*. What it was we cannot well say, but Kin Keih-p'oo (金吉甫) ingeniously conjectures that it was specially the conveyance of their revenue for the inhabitants of the 4th and 5th hundred *le* beyond. He finds in this an explanation for the omission of 納 in the account of their revenues; he sees also the imperial grace in the arrangement :—those at a moderate distance from the capital paid a small contribution of revenue, and made up for it by their personal service, while those farther off, paying a larger contribution, were spared the labour of conveying it. We can see generally that the contributions from the different hundreds were arranged with reference to their distance from the capital and trouble of conveyance. 四百里粟、五百里米、 —粟 and 米 are sometimes used indifferently, with the general signification of 穀 or 'grain.' When a distinction is made between them as here, their meaning is as in the translation :— 有殼曰粟、無曰米. [Hoo Wei takes the opportunity to touch here on the burdensome system of transporting the revenue in kind (漕運之法), which has prevailed in China since the time of the Han dynasty. It was a consequence of the change from the feudal system to a centralized government,—an evil in itself, but less than other evils. In times of weakness and confusion like the present it must be found very burdensome.]

P. 19. 五百里侯服、—侯服 = 侯國之服, 'the domain containing the principalities of the nobles.' By 侯 we must understand all the nobles of the five ranks, (see Mencius, Bk. V. Pt. II., ii.); nor are we to

武衞。○奮　百里。里　文教、二　百里揆　綏服、三　五百里　廿節　諸侯。○　三百里　里、男邦、　柔、二百

high ministers and great officers; the second, by the principalities of the Nan; the other three hundred were occupied by the various princes.

20　　Five hundred *le still beyond* formed the PEACE-SECURING DOMAIN. In the first three hundred *le* they cultivated the lessons of learning and moral duties; in the other three hundred they showed the energies of war and defence.

suppose that they occupied only this domain;—the next was occupied by them as well. Outside the imperial domain, this extended 500 *le* in every direction (Ts'ae). The following figure may be taken as a representation of it:—

The domain was thus altogether three times the size of the imperial domain, and would contain 3,000,000 square *le*. 百里柔、—Ts'ae says:—柔、卿大夫邑地, '柔 was the cities and lands allotted to the chief ministers and officers.' Those were the nobles and officers in the emperor's immediate service, having their offices within the imperial domain. Outside of it the first hundred *le* was assigned them for their families and support. They took rank in various degrees with the feudal princes. Under the Chow dyn., acc. to Mencius, a chief minister received as much territory as a How, a great officer as much as a Pih, and a scholar of the first class as much as a Tsze or a Nan. Perhaps the arrangement made by Yu was much the same. 二百里爲男邦、—二百里 = 'the second hundred *le*.' The 男 was the lowest of the five ranks of nobility, but the territory assigned to it in the Chow dyn. was the same as that of the Tsze (子). It may have been different under Yaou. The ministers and officers of the emperor took rank, it has been said, with the feudal princes, but from the territories of the Nan being called here 邦, we may conclude that the 柔邑

地 were not recognized as principalities. 三百里諸侯、—三百里 is not the third hundred *le* but 'the *remaining* three hundred *le*.' 諸侯 embraces the Kung, How, Pih, and Tsze,—the princes of all the ranks above the Nan. It is conjectured that the smaller principalities were placed next to the imperial domain at once to receive and to afford shelter from the encroachments not unlikely to be attempted by the more powerful lords.

P. 20. 五百里綏服、—this domain was likewise occupied by the princes. 'Being more distant from the imperial seat,' says one of the commentators Chang (張氏), 'the name was changed to 綏, that its occupants might know that the reason why principalities were established was to secure the repose of the royal House.' According to this comment, I have translated 綏 by 'peace-securing.' The domain extended 500 *le* in every direction from that of the nobles in the following way:—

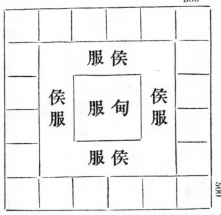

It was thus five times the size of the imperial domain, and contained 5,000,000 square *le*. 三百里揆文教、—'through the first

蔡。百 夷 百 服 里 五　廿
○ 里 二 里 三 要 百　一節

21 Five hundred *le, remoter still,* constituted THE DOMAIN OF RESTRAINT. *The first* three hundred *le* were occupied by the tribes of the E; *the next* two hundred by criminals undergoing the lesser banishment.

'three hundred *le* of this domain they cultivated lessons of learning and moral duties.' 揆二 度, 'to measure,' 'to calculate;'—see on Canon of Shun, p. 2. By its use here we are to understand, it seems to me, that some selection was made in the lessons and instruction which were here given. In all stages of society, especially in the earlier, learning and polite manners must be expected to flourish most in the capital and near it. There will be the higher seminaries and institutions; in distant provinces, schools of no great pretensions, teaching the substance of human duty and the more important acquirements, will be sufficient. 二百里奮 武衞,—the principalities in this part of the empire approached the nature of military colonies on the frontiers. They bordered on the wild tribes; it was necessary they should always be prepared to resist aggression. We need not suppose that here they paid no attention to literary and moral training, or that in the inner portion of the domain they altogether neglected the art of war;—the characteristics of the two parts simply were as in the text.

P. 21. 五百里要服,—the dict. deals with 要服 as we saw it did with 服, defining the phrase simply as the name of a territory, without trying to account for its being

denominated *Yaou.* In his dictionary, Dr. Medhurst explains 要服, 'the Important Tenure,' in which case we must read 要 in the third tone. This view has the support of Soo Tungpo; but it cannot be admitted. In his translation of the Shoo, Dr. Medhurst renders the phrase—'the Restricted Tenure.' This is more in accordance with the prevailing view. Gankwŏ says the domain 要束以文教, *i.e.,* 'was bound and restrained by the instructions of learning.' The idea of restraint seems to be correct; 'the instructions of learning,' as the instrument of that restraint, are foreign to the subject. Many critics assign to 要 the idea of 要約, 'summary,' 'perfunctory.' Thus Leu Tsoo-hëen in the 集說:—'This domain was all occupied by wild tribes, but it was still near the Middle Kingdom, and an easy, summary, jurisdiction was exercised over it;— it was not governed with attention to every particular.' I prefer the view given in the translation, with which indeed this other is not inconsistent. The territory was assigned to the nobles; but with reference to its indigenous inhabitants, they governed them in a 'rough and ready' way, just sufficient to keep them in subjection. It extended in every direction from the Peace-securing domain 500 *le*—thus:—

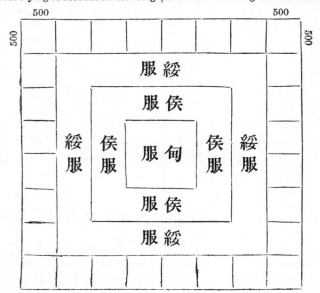

流。百 蠻 百 服 里 五廿二
○里 二 里 三 荒 百 節

22   Five hundred *le*, *the most remote*, constituted THE WILD DOMAIN.
Threé hundred *le* were occupied by the tribes of the Man; two
hundred, by criminals undergoing the greater banishment.

It was thus 7 times the size of the imperial
domain, and contained 7,000,000 square *le*.
三百里夷, 二里百蔡,—there
is nearly a consent on the meaning of 蔡. It
is taken as = 放, in Can. of Shun, p. 12, meaning 'to banish and confine.' In the 左傳,
定四年, we read—王於是乎殺
管叔而蔡蔡叔. There the opposi-
tion of 蔡 and 殺 fixes the meaning of the
term. A note, however, says that the, first 蔡
is to be read *shă*, and we find the explanation of
this in the character's being given in the 說
文 as 𣿬, with the meaning of 'to scatter.'
This must have been afterwards mistaken for
蔡. [Here perhaps we have also the explanation of how the 竄三苗, of the Can. of
Shun, *loc. cit.*, appears in Mencius, Bk. V. Pt.

I., iii. 2, as 殺三苗.] By 蔡, then in
the text we must understand banished criminals;
and in contrast with the 流 of the next par.,
that their banishment was of a lighter character,
and not to the greatest distance.
   The first three hundred *le* were occupied by
wild tribes which had not yet been merged in
the conquering race, nor driven by it from their
original seats. The attempts to explain 夷 as an
adjective = 易 or = 平, may be seen in 禹
貢錐指. Hoo Wei very pertinently compares with the text the language of Mencius,
Bk. IV., Pt. II., i.
   P. 22. 五百里荒服,—we have
come to the last of the domains. It was called
the 荒服 with reference, we may suppose, to
the rude character of the inhabitants, and the
wildness of the country. It extended 500 *le* in
every direction beyond the fourth domain—
thus :—

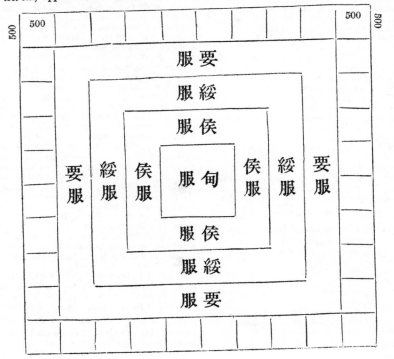

It was thus nine times the size of the imperial domain, and contained 9,000,000 square *le*.

三百里蠻, 二百里流,—蠻 corresponds to the 夷 of the prec. par. The *Man* were considered still more rude and barbarous than the *E*. Properly speaking, 蠻 was the name of the wild tribes on the south; 夷, that of those on the east; 戎, that of those on the west; and 狄, that of those on the north. 蠻夷, however, is used as a designation for *all* the wild tribes, and also 戎狄. Similarly we find the single terms 蠻 and 夷 employed.

流 is used as in Can. of Shun, p 12. It must denote a more distant banishment than 蔡 in the last par. It is not meant that criminals occupied the whole territory, but they had their position assigned to them here among the *Man*.

[The five *Fuh* constituted what we may call the China Proper of Yu's time. Beyond them there was still an outlying territory, over which the ancient emperors claimed authority, and where Yu went on to make political arrangements. 'I assisted,' he says in the Yih and Tseih, p. 8, 'in completing the five domains, extending over 5,000 *le;* in appointing in the provinces twelve Tutors; and in establishing in the regions beyond, extending to the four seas, five presidents.' The nine Chow and the five Fuh covered the same territory, the former being its natural divisions, the latter its artificial and political ones. A subdivision of the five Fuh is insisted on by many, by which the three inner domains constituted the Middle Kingdom,' and the two outer the territory of the 'Four *E*.' On this it is not necessary to dwell. With regard to the five Fuh, certain questions present themselves to the mind. .

First, the five domains of Yu formed a square of 5,000 *le*. If the *le* were of the same length as that of the present day, Yu's China must have extended rather more than 1,700 miles from north to south, and from east to west, and contained an area of nearly 3,000,000 square miles. The largest area which can possibly be assigned to the 'Eighteen Provinces' of the present day does not come up to 2,000,000 sq. m.;—see Williams' 'Middle Kingdom,' Vol. I., p. 7. It is not possible that the *le* of Yu could have been equal to the *le* now; but scholars have not been able to determine its measurement. Koo Yen-woo (顧炎 武), in the beginning of the present dynasty, contended that the ancient *le* was only 31–50ths of the modern one, but his views do not seem to have obtained general acceptance. If they could be established, Yu's five Fuh would have been rather more than 1,100 miles in each way, which we might admit, so far as the question of extent is concerned.

But second, the five Fuh of Yu surround the imperial domain, which is represented as a square of 1,000 *le* exactly in the centre of them (see in 'Le Chou King,' p. 333, a strange parallel attempted to be drawn by De Guignes between this arrangement and the division of the Holy Land described in the last chapters of Ezekiel). Now the imperial seat of Yaou was in K'e-chow, the most northern of the provinces. His capital was in P'ing-yang, the name of which remains in the dep. P'ing-yang, in Shan-se, lat. 36°6', N., lon. 4°55', W. It could not, therefore, have been in the centre of the domains. This difficulty is clearly seen by Chinese critics. Ts'ae Ch'in observes:— 'Though we extend the northern territory of K'e-chow to Yun-chung (雲中; we are to look in the 'Six T'ing of the city of Kwei-hwa' in the extreme north of Shan-se for this. The city of Yun-chung is now the city of T'oh-kih-t'oh [托克托]), to Chŏ (涿; ? dis. of 涿 州, dep. of Shun-t'een), and to Yih (易; ? the small dep. of Yih Chow), I am afraid we shall not have 2,500 *le*. Even if we have them, they will consist of a sandy desert without vegetation. On the other hand, in the east and south, whence the greatest revenue now comes, we must put down the domain of Restraint, and the Wild domain. The account of the domains does not seem to harmonize with the nature of the country. Looked at with reference to this, it is unintelligble. I may observe, however, that territories have been very different in ancient and modern times, in regard to their prosperity and the reverse. The country on the north of K'e-chow may not have been the wild and desert tract which we find there in subsequent times; while the regions of Fuh-këen and Chĕ-keang, which were then jungly fens, occupied by barbarous tribes, have now become rich and populous, territory of the highest character. The character of a region cannot be pronounced from its appearance at one era.' This effort of Ts'ae to remove the difficulty cannot be regarded as successful. Barrenness or fertility is one element in it. Even on that point we could not admit Ts'ae's views, unsupported, as regards the north of K'e-chow, by historical evidence; but the main point is that of geographical position. Ch'in Sze-k'ae shows how, on the arrangement described, we must carry the wild domain on the east, into the sea; on the west, beyond Tseih-shih; on the north, 1,200 *le* beyond Yun-chung; while on the south it would not have reached mount Hăng. There is no laying down the five domains on the surface of China. I cannot regard them as anything but an ideal mapping out of the country. This much we may admit,—that Yu placed the smaller principalities next to the imperial, and the larger ones farther off, the indigenous tribes being more strong and numerous according as the distance from the capital increased. In name, the divisions probably existed, and nobles and wild chiefs might be said to belong to one Fuh and another, but there could only be a rough and general approximation to the scheme which Yu had in his mind.

Third, a division of the empire into nine, or more properly ten Fuh, was made under the Chow dynasty. It is twice given in the Chow Le, first in Bk. XXIX., where the domains are called Ke (畿), and again in Bk. XXXIII., where all but the king's Ke are called Fuh. This arrangement may be represented thus:—

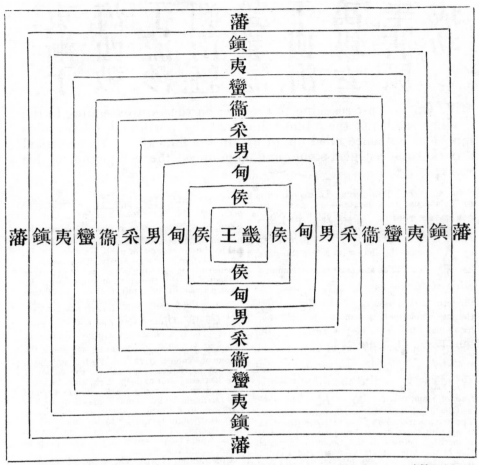

It will be seen that not only are the number of the domains double what Yu made them, but that, where the same names are retained, the order in which they are placed is different. That is a matter, however, to be explained when we come to the 'Chow Le.' The point to be remarked here is that the domains of Han are said to be distant from each other 500 *le*, like those of Yu, and we have the country represented as a square of 10,000 *le*. [The spaces between them in the diagram are smaller than in the prec. diagrams, in order to get the figure upon the page.] How to reconcile the Shoo and the Rites of Chow is a question of much perplexity.

The method adopted by Ch'ing K'ang-shing is the most remarkable. He supposes that the first clause in each of the paragraphs 18—22 gives the Fuh as it had been in the previous part of Yaou's reign, and that the other clauses, always describing 500 *le* in difft. portions, give an addition made by Yu. For instance, the 200 *le* of the Nans' principalities and the 300 of the other princes' were added by him to the second domain, making it altogether 1,000 *le* in each direction from the first. This addition is in-tended, he contends, by the term 弼 in the Yih and Tseih, p. 8. Making the nine provinces terminate with the Man Fuh of the Chow dynasty, 7,000 *le* from the capital, he gets the 49,000,000 square *le* which I have mentioned in the note on that passage, as the area of the empire proper. The mingled violence and ingenuity of this treatment of the Shoo cannot be contemplated without moving us to smile.

Other methods of reconciling the two accounts have been proposed. Yu's measurements, it is said, were as the bird flies, the Chow dynasty's were as men travel, up and down and winding about. Again, it is urged, the *le* of Yu was double that of Chow, and moreover, the domains of Chow include all the territory beyond Yu's Fuh, which he describes as extending to the four seas. As Ts'ae says, 'To sum the matter up, nothing certain has been said about it' (要之, 皆非的論). The more we extend Yu's domains, the greater difficulty we have to reconcile the classic with the actual face of the ground,—the everlasting hills, the bounding deserts, and the sea embracing the empire on the east and south.]

東 海 于 朔 聲 于 禹 圭 成
漸 西 流 南 教 四 錫 告 功
于 被 沙 暨 訖 海 玄 厥 ○

廿三節

23   V. On the east reaching to the sea; on the west extending to the moving sands; to the utmost limits of the north and south:—his fame and influence filled up all within the four seas.   Yu presented a dark coloured gem-stone, and announced the completion of his work.

CH. V. P. 23. THE UNIVERSAL RECOGNITION OF YU'S FAME, AND HIS ANNOUNCEMENT OF HIS COMPLETED WORK. 東漸于海,— 漸 (the first tone) is explained by Gan-kwŏ by 入; so also the dict., with ref. to this pass., has 流入. Ts'ae and most recent commentators explain the term by 漬, 'to soak.' As the term is here used along with 被 and 暨, the less emphatic it is made the better. Gan-kwŏ's definition is to be preferred.   西 被于流沙,—被, as in Can. of Yaou, p. 1, *et al.*   流沙,—see par. 5.   朔 南暨,—朔 = 北, the north';—see on Can. of Yaou, par. 7.   暨 = 及. The whole = 'the south and the north being come to.' The extension of Yu's fame in these directions is left thus indefinite, and no place of boundary is specified, because in the Book the termination of the nine provinces north and south is left undefined.   聲教訖于四海, —it does not seem appropriate to bring in 教, 'instructions,' here. Yu has appeared in the whole of the Book as a worker and not as a teacher. The 教 was that given by his doings and character, and not by his works. I have ventured therefore to use 'influence' in the translation, instead of 'instructions.' This is according to the definitions of the term which are the oldest;—see those quoted in the dict. from the 說文 and 釋名. Hoo Wei says that 'the four seas' denote the E on the east, the Jung on the west, the Man on the south, and the Teih on the north. I cannot think so. 訖于四海 is to me a vague phrase, by which the writer would express in the widest admissible terms the extent of Yu's fame. Compare the eulogium of the perfect sage in the Doctrine of the Mean, ch. xxxi.   禹錫玄圭, 告厥成功,—錫 as in Can. of Yaou, p. 12. and more particularly, Part i., p. 52—九江納錫大龜,

= 'to present.' 圭 = 瑞玉, 'an auspicious gem.' Of the 'five tokens of gem,' Can. of Shun, p. 7, three were called 圭;—see the note on that passage. The gem-token was conferred by the emperor on the noble,—a delegation to him of his dignity and authority. There seems an incongruity in speaking of one, as in the text, as presented by the minister to the emperor. So strongly has this been felt, that Sze-ma Ts'een produces the passage as—帝錫禹玄圭, 以告成功, and Gan-kwŏ takes the same view. The text, however, will not admit of it. The 圭 is called 玄, because, say some, the colour of water is dark, and Yu has regulated the waters; because, say others, the colour of the heavens is of a deep dark, and Yu was engaged on a heavenly work. These sayings are far-fetched; Yu found somewhere such a dark-coloured precious stone, so remarkable that he thought it worthy to be presented to the emperor. The emperor was Yaou, but the stone would be presented in the first place to Shun, as his vice-gerent.

CONCLUDING NOTE. The standard chronology fixes the year in which Yu thus announced the completion of his work as that B. C, 2276, the 80th year of Yaou's reign, and the seventh of Shun's association with him in the government.

According to Mencius (Book III., Pt. I., iv. 7), Yu was eight years employed on the regulation of the waters. There is a different statement in the Historical Records, Bk. XXVII., 河渠書, where it is said, as if from the Books of Hea, that Yu was engaged on the inundating waters for thirteen years (夏書曰, 禹抑鴻水, 十三年). This estimate of 13 years arose probably from mistaking the meaning of Part i., p. 18.

There was another tradition, that Yu's work extended only over three years. Ma Yung says: —'Yu dealt with the waters for three years, and eight of the provinces were brought to order, on which Yaou considered the work as good as done, and resigned the administration to Shun. All this took place in twelve years after the regulation of the waters had been taken in hand' (*i.e.,* by K'wăn). 'In the year after, the 13th year, Yen-chow was also brought to order, and

Shun publicly accepted the administration.' Ying-tă writes to the same effect. They both include in the thirteen years the nine in which K'wăn laboured in vain.

We may be sure that the work ascribed in this Book to Yu was not done in three or four years. Mencius' assignment of eight years is short enough. Hoo Wei supposes that so much time was occupied with the labour upon the nine provinces, and that the conferring of lands, and arrangement of the five *fuh* occupied so much time more. As to the exact year in which Yu began his labours; when they terminated; and how many years the deluge of Yaou lasted:—these are questions which we cannot determine categorically.

BOOK II. THE SPEECH AT KAN.

六　曰、　○　六　乃　于　大᷉᷉　甘
事　嗟、　王᷉᷉　卿。　召᷉᷉　戰　誓

1 There was a great battle in Kan. *Previous to it*, the emperor call-
2 ed together the six leaders of his hosts; and said, "Ah! all ye

INTRODUCTORY AND CONNECTING NOTE. It was observed in the first note on the last Book, that though 'The Tribute of Yu' appeared as the first of the Books of Hea, it is descriptive really of what took place during the reign of Yaou. It terminates, accord. to the received chronology, B.C. 2276, 22 years before the accession of Shun to the throne upon Yaou's death. 'The Counsels of the Great Yu' bring us farther down. We have there the accession of Yu to the administration of the empire under Shun, B.C. 2222, and his reduction of the Meaouites, referred to B.C. 2220. The Shoo tells us nothing of Yu's accession to the throne, nor the events of his reign. Shun died B.C. 2207. Yu carried on the government during the years of mourning for his death, and then withdrew, to allow his son, Shang-k'eun (尚均), an opportunity of ascending the throne. The people, however, would not have him to be their king;—they preferred Yu (Mencius, Book V., Part I., vi.), whose reign accordingly dates from B.C. 2204.

Yaou had given him the surname of Sze (姒). Old and worn out with the fatigues he had undergone, he died after a reign of eight years, short as compared with the reigns of Yaou and Shun. Kaou-yaou whom he had associated with him in the administration died the year after. He then made Yih his prime minister, with the view of his succeding him. He died on a

progress to the south, B.C. 2197, in Hwuy-k'e (會稽), in the pres. dep. of Shaou-hing (紹興), in Chĕ-këang. He was succeeded by his son K'e (啟), whose reign dates from B.C. 2196, and to whom is attributed the speech recorded in this Book which is assigned to B.C. 2194, the third year of his reign.

[The Chinese chronologists are pleased to lay it down so, and it is hardly worth while quarrelling with the arrangement. Still it is not quite accurate. According to Mencius, Yih administered the govt. during the period of mourning for Yu, and it was not till that was expired, that the people called K'e to occupy his father's place in preference to Yih. His reign therefore should date only from B.C. 2194; should be reckoned only six years instead of nine; and the expedition against the prince of of Hoo be referred to his first year instead of his third.]

That the speech at Kan was made by K'e rests on the authority of the Preface to the Shoo, par. 6, which is followed by Sze-ma Ts'een. The Taouist Chwang-tsze, indeed, and Lew Heang, in his 說苑, Bk. VII., 政理篇, say that Yu fought with the prince of Yu; and others speak of the emperor Seang (夏

于　○　行　今　勑　三　五　扈　告　之　　
左、　左　天　予　絕　正、　行、　民　汝。　人、　　
汝　不　之　惟　其　天　怠　威　○　予　　
不　攻　罰。　恭　命、　用　棄　侮　有　誓　　

who are engaged in my six armies, I have a solemn announcement
to make to you.

3　　"The prince of Hoo wildly wastes and despises the five elements,
and has idly abandoned the three acknowledged commencements
of the year. On this account Heaven is about to destroy him, and
bring to an end the favour it has shown to him; and I am reverently executing the punishment appointed by Heaven.

4　　"If you, left-side men, do not do your work on the left, it will be
a disregard of my orders. If you, right-side men, do not do your

后相), three reigns later than K'e, as his
antagonist. The statements of Chwang-tsze
and Lëw Heang might possibly be reconciled
with the Preface, but Mih-tse, (明鬼篇,
三), quotes (with variations) most of the Book,
attributing it to Yu. There were evidently
two traditions during the Chow dynasty, after
the time of Confucius, as to when and by whom
the speech at Kan was made.

TITLE OF THE BOOK.—甘誓, 'The Speech
at Kan.' 誓,—see on 'The Counsels of the
Great Yu', p. 28. The 誓 or 'martial speeches'
are given by Ying-tă as the 5th of the component elements of the Shoo. This at Kan is
the first of them that forms a distinct Book.
We had a speech of Yu to his troops in the
passage just referred to. 甘 was the name of
the place where the speech was made.

CONTENTS. The emperor, about to engage
in battle with a rebellious vassal, assembles
his generals and troops, and addresses them.
First he declares obscurely the grounds of the
expedition which he had undertaken, and concludes by stimulating the soldiers to the display
of courage and observance of order by promises of reward and threats of punishment. It
is so short that it is not worth while to divide
it into chapters.

P. 1. Occasion of the speech. 大戰
于甘,—the battle is called 'great,' we might
suppose, because of the numbers engaged in it,
and the obstinacy with which it was contested.
Another reason is assigned, however, for the
denomination,—that the wickedness of the
prince of Hoo, in compelling the emperor to
take the field against him, might be more
strongly set forth. On the principle of Mencius, VII., Pt. II., ii., the emperor did not fight

戰), but only 'punished;' nor did he take the
field till after the means which the constitution
of the govt. provided had proved ineffectual.
Such came to be the rule, when the feudal
system had become fully developed;—we can
hardly seek to apply it regularly to the case
of K'e at so early a period. 甘 is given
by some as the name of a place in the southern
border of the principality of Hoo; by others, as
the name of a river; by others again, as the
name of a marsh; and by others, as the name
of a wilderness. There is an agreement, however, as to the locality, and all the representations might be reconciled. We have still the
'Shed of Kan' (甘亭), with the water from
the 'valley of Kan' flowing past it, in the dis.
of Hoo (鄠縣); lat. 34°8′, N., lon. 7°50, W.)
dep. of Se-ngan, Shen-se. The Shed or Portico
marks, it is said, the place of the battle.

乃召六卿,—we must bring 王 from
the next par. as the nominative to 召. The
whole Book is only a fragment. This par.
must have been the proper sequence originally
of a preceding narrative. I introduce 'previous
to it' in the translation, after Sze-ma Ts'een,
who has—啟伐之, 大戰 於甘, 將
戰 作甘誓, 乃召六卿申之.
六卿,—'the six high nobles,' here evidently
the leaders of the 'six armies' (六軍, and
六師), which composed the military force of
the emperor. This is the view of all the commentators.—Ch'ing says:—六卿者六
軍之將. We need not trouble ourselves
to inquire further what offices these k'ing

sustained in time of peace. In the Chow dynasty, a 軍 or army consisted of 12,500 men.

Pp. 2, 3. *The grounds of the expedition against Hoo.* The king commences his speech with a sigh,—an Ah! (嗟),—because of the gravity of the matter;—so, Ts'ae. 六事之人,—Ch'ing observes that the change of style from 六卿 to 六事 indicates that the king was addressing not the generals only, but the inferior officers and common soldiers as well. Of course he could not be heard by such a multitude, but his speech would be circulated throughout the host. Gan-kwǒ says:—各有軍事, 故曰六事. I have translated accordingly.   3. 有扈氏 = the holder of, *i.e.*, the prince invested with, Hoo. This Hoo was the present territory of the district of Hoo in Shen-se. The name in the text was changed in the Ts'in dynasty to the present 鄠. The prince of Hoo, according to Sze-ma Ts'een and the older interpreters, was of the surname Sze, the same as the emperor. I have read of him somewhere as K'e's 庶兄, his elder brother by a secondary wife. Ts'ae does not seem willing to admit so much. The surname is not a point of importance.   威侮五行, 怠棄三正,—these two clauses state the crime of Hoo, but in obscure and mystical terms. Ch'ing defines 五行 by 四時, 'the four seasons,' making the phrase analogous with 五辰 in the 'Yih and Tseih,' p. 4;—see the note there. He calls 三正 = 天地人之正道, 'the correct way of heaven, earth, and man,' meaning probably the same with Ma Yung, that the phrase denotes the commencement of the year in 子 the 11th month, or midwinter, which was called the 天正, the commencement in 丑, the 地正, and the commencement in 寅, the first month of spring, the 人正. This last was the beginning of the year with the Hea dyn.; the Shang began it with the 地正; and the Chow with the 天正. The text would imply, on this view of it, that these difft. commencements had been employed before;—see note on the Canon of Shun, p. 14. If it were so, perhaps the prince of Hoo wanted to begin the year with some other month, as the founder of the Ts'in dyn. afterward adopted the month 亥, the 10th, the first month of winter.   Maou K'e-ling's view of the subject is not unreasonable. He considers these two clauses as an obscure intimation from K'e that Hoo refused to acknowledge him as the right successor of Yu. This is an old view. Yaou had been succeeded by Shun, as the worthiest man in the empire, and

Shun had been succeeded by Yu. Why should Yu's throne descend to his son? This afforded the pretext for rebellion. Maou further tries to show that by the language used K'e makes the rebellion a crime against Heaven, and not merely an attempt against himself. See the 尙書廣聽錄, *in loc.* We can hardly doubt that the object of the expedition was to put down a dangerous rival.   天用勦絕其命,—勦 is given in the 說文 as 剿 and defined by 絕; 命 is not to be taken as = 'life,' but the position of the prince of Hoo, as invested with that principality, though, in being deprived of that, we may presume, he would pay the forfeit of his life as well; 用 = 'on this account,' as in the 'Yih and Tseih,' p. 8, *et al.*

P. 4. *Rules to be observed by the troops.* 左不攻于左, 云云,—左 = 車左, 'the left of the chariot;' 右 = 車右, 'the right of the chariot.' It appears that in the warfare of those early times, chariots were much used in China, as in other nations in a similar or less advanced stage of civilization, —among the ancient Gauls and Britons, for instance. The ordinary war-chariot for the troops contained only three men,—an archer on the left, a soldier armed with javelins and pike or spear on the right, and the charioteer in the centre. This continued down to the Chow dynasty;—see the 集傳 and 後案, *in loc.* 攻 = 治; 治其事, 'do your work,' *i.e.*, observe the rules laid down for your guidance. So, also, 非其馬之正; comp. Mencius, Bk. III., Pt. II., i. 4. [The pictures of those chariots are not unlike those given of similar war *materiel* on Egyptian and Assyrian monuments.]

P. 5. *The martial law of K'e;—rewards and punishments.* 用命, 賞于祖, 不用命, 戮于社,—祖 = 遷廟之祖主, 'the spirit-tablets of his ancestors which had been removed from the regular hall of ancestral worship to the special shrine appointed for them;'—see on The Doctrine of the Mean, Ch. xix. So 社 = 社主, 'the tablets of the spirits of the land.' It would appear from this, that it was the practice of the emperors, when they went on a warlike expedition, to carry with them these two classes of tablets, that they might have with the host, hovering about them, the spirits of their ancestors and the tutelary spirits of the country or dynasty. A variety of passages are adduced to prove the existence of the practice in the Chow dynasty;—it had come from the earlier time. Those tablets were to K'e and his army like the ark of God in the camp of the Israelites. Martial law also was executed before them. And strict law it was.   予則孥戮汝,—孥 is defined by Gan-kwǒ and others by 子, 'children.' But it may

恭命右不
攻于右汝
不恭命、御
非其馬之
正汝不恭
命。〇用命、
賞于祖不
用命、
戮于
社、子則孥
戮汝。〇

（五節）

work on the right, it will be a disregard of my orders. If you, charioteers, do not observe the rules for the management of your
5 horses, it will be a disregard of my orders. You who obey my orders shall be rewarded before my ancestors; and you who disobey my orders shall be put to death before the spirits of the land; and I will also put your children to death."

include wives as well. The threat=‘I will also exterminate your families.’ Attempts are made to weaken the force of both the terms 戮 and 孥, but without success. A different meaning of 戮 cannot be admitted here from what it has in the preceding clause. Kaou-yaou praised Shun, because with him ‘punishments did not extend to the criminal's heirs;’—see ‘The Counsels of Yu,’ p. 12. The practice of K‘e was very different. It may be said that the text is speaking only of military law; and it must be replied that it was the military law of a very cruel and barbarous state of society.

CONCLUDING NOTE. The Pere de Mailla, in his ‘Histoire Generale de la Chine,’ has wonderfully amplified (? and improved) the account of the battle of Kan. He says (Vol. I., p. 125):—‘On the approach of the imperial army, the prince of Hoo drew up his in order of battle. The emperor arranged his troops in this way:—On the two wings he placed his chariots of war which carried 25 men, armed with arrows, pikes, and sabres, and his cavalry in the centre; after which he addressed them as follows:—

“Remember that you are fighting for Heaven. You who are on the wings, be attentive to the orders which will be given you; let it be seen that you are well skilled with your arrows and your pikes. These are my orders; respect them. And you cavaliers, at the first signal which shall be made to you, enter with courage into the ranks, which the arrows will have opened,” &c., &c.

The Shoo does not mention the issue of the battle. According to Sze-ma Ts‘een, it was the defeat and death of the prince of Hoo (遂滅有扈氏). We find, however, in the ‘History made Easy’ (綱鑑易知錄) this account:—‘Not succeeding, his generals begged to renew the engagement. K‘e said, “My present failure is owing to the slenderness of my virtue, and because my instructions are not good.” On this he returned with his army to the capital; silenced all his music; sat on a single mat, and confined himself at meals to a single dish. At the same time he was affectionate to his relations, and respectful to his elders; he gave honour to the worthy, and office to the able;—brooding silently over his affairs (隱神; this is an unusual combination, and not found in the Thesaurus. Without other examples, we can only guess at its meaning). After a month, the prince of Hoo submitted and was put to death.’

All this is plainly an imitation of the account of Yu's expedition against the tribe of San-meaou, Pt. II., Bk. II., pp. 19, 20. It is a clumsy imitation of it. Why should the prince of Hoo, thus submitting himself to the emperor's virtue, have been put to death?

We may suppose that K‘e was successful at Kan, and put down the rising rebellion. We know nothing of the subsequent events of his reign. He died B.C. 2188, and was succeeded by his son, T‘ae-k‘ang.

THE BOOKS OF HEA.

BOOK III. THE SONGS OF THE FIVE SONS.

五子之歌

一節
太康尸位以
逸豫滅厥德
黎民咸貳乃
盤遊無度畋
于有洛之表
十旬弗反。○

1 I. T'ae-k'ang occupied the throne like a personator of the dead. By idleness and dissipation he extinguished his virtue, till the black-haired people all began to waver in their allegiance. He, however, pursued his pleasure and wanderings without any restraint. He went out to hunt beyond the Lŏ, and a hundred days elapsed with-

TITLE OF THE BOOK.—五子之歌. 'The Songs of the five Sons.' It would have been more correct to name it 'The Songs of the five Brothers.' The singers were the brothers of T'ae-k'ang, bewailing in these strains his evil course and evil fate. The word 'Sons' is probably used with reference to the fact that they were with their mother at the time,—left to her, while he who should have been her chief support had got himself outcast both from her and his kingdom; still there is not a word in the songs having special reference to her. The Book ranks in that division of the Books of the Shoo, which goes by the name of 'Instructions' (訓). Though the form be poetical, the subject-matter is derived from the lessons left by Yu for the guidance of his posterity.

CONTENTS. After three introductory paragraphs, relating the occasion of the Songs, we have the Songs themselves,—one from each brother. The first deplores how the emperor had lost the affections of the people; the second speaks of his dissipation and extravagance; the third mourns his loss of the imperial seat; the fourth deplores his departure from the principles of Yu, and its disastrous consequences; and the fifth is a wail over their miserable condition. I have divided the whole into two chapters,—the Introduction, and the Songs.

The GENUINENESS of the Book is disputed. It is sufficient to say here that a Book substantially the same as this did form part of Confucius' compilation of the documents of the Shoo.

CH. I. Pp. 1—3. HOW T'AE-K'ANG LOST HIS KINGDOM, AND IN WHAT CIRCUMSTANCES HIS BROTHERS COMPOSED THEIR SONGS.

I

作歌。○　禹之戒以　咸怨述大　之汭五子　從徯于洛　御其母以　厥弟五人、｜三節　距于河。○｜三節　因民弗忍、　有窮后羿．｜二節

2 out any sign of his return. *On this*, E, the prince of K'ëung, taking advantage of the discontent *of the people*, resisted *his return* upon

3 the *north of the* Ho. The emperor's five brothers had attended their mother in following him, and were waiting for him on the north of the Lŏ; and, *when they heard of E's movement*, all full of dissatisfaction, they related the cautions of the great Yu in the form of songs.

太康尸位,—T'ae-k'ang was the eldest son of K'e, and succeeded to the empire on his death. His reign dates from B. C. 2187. 尸 is defined by Gan-kwŏ by 主, = 'to preside over.' The character has that meaning ;—see the dict. Its proper signification, however, is 'a corpse,' and it is often used for the personator of the dead in the funeral ceremonies of antiquity ;—see the dict., which defines it in this application by 神象, 'the image of the spirit.' Ts'ae has improved on Gan-kwŏ by interpreting the text on this use of the char.—T'ae-k'ang was but a personator on the throne, little better than a sham sovereign.

逸豫—逸 is 'idleness,' and 豫 is 'pleasure,' 'dissipation.' The meaning of the terms is akin. 貳,—comp Pt. II., p. 5—任賢勿貳. But the usage in the two passages is not identical. Here 咸貳＝皆有二心, 'all had two hearts.' 盤遊—盤＝樂, 'pleasure.' We find 般 in Mencius, in the same sense,—e. g., Bk. II., Pt. I., iv. 4, 般樂怠敖. 有洛之表,—for the Lŏ, see the Tribute of Yu, Part i., p. 55, *et al.*; 表＝外, 'beyond,' 'the country beyond,'; the 有 is not at all needed for the sense, and I cannot account for its introduction. 2. 有窮后羿,—窮 was the name of a principality, referred to the present sub. dep. of Tih (德州), dep. of Tse-nan in Shan-tung. Its holder in the time of T'ae-k'ang was named E. There was a tradition in the Chow dynasty, which made him

a descendant of the master of the archers, centuries before, in the time of the emp. Kuh 嚳), whose office was indicated by the character, the name of the office having become hereditary as a personal name in the family. The history of the individual in the text is very obscure, and will be found, so far as it can be ascertained, in the concluding notes to this Book and the next. In the text he appears simply withstanding the return of T'ae-k'ang to his capital. Medhurst translates 距于河 by 'drove him beyond the Yellow river,' but 'drove' is much too strong. T'ae-k'ang had gone beyond the Ho, we know not how far; and E opposed his return. His doing so cannot be defended, but we do not know his motives. He was enabled to do what he did, 因民弗忍, 'because the people could not bear,' *i.e.*, could not bear the indifference and extravagance of T'ae-k'ang. 3. 御其母以從,—御＝侍, 'to be in attendance on.' The movement of the mother and brothers had perhaps been previous to the movement of E. The composition of the songs, however, could only have taken place after they had heard of that ;—they look on K'e-chow, the peculiar patrimony of their family, as being as good as lost. It is most natural to suppose that while they were waiting for the long delayed return of T'ae-k'ang, they heard of E's action against him. 五子咸怨,—the dissatisfaction is to be supposed to be directed against T'ae-k'ang. See Mencius' defence of such dissatisfaction with a relative, Book VI., Pt. II., iii.

其一曰皇祖有
訓民可近不可
下民惟邦本本
固邦寧。○予視
天下愚夫愚婦
一能勝予一人
三失怨豈在明
不見是圖予臨
兆民懍乎若朽
索之馭六馬為

四節

五節

4　II. The first said,
"It was the lesson of our great ancestor:—
The people should be cherished;
They should not be down-trodden:
The people are the root of a country;
The root firm, the country is tranquil.

5　When I look throughout the empire,
Of the simple men and simple women,
Any one may surpass me.
If I, the one man, err repeatedly;—
Should dissatisfaction be waited for till it appears?
Before it is seen, it should be guarded against.
In my relation to the millions of the people,
I should feel as much anxiety as if I were driving six horses
　　with rotten reins.

Ch. II. Pp. 4—9. The Songs of the brothers.
Pp. 4, 5. *The first brother's song.—How T'ae-
k'ang had carelessly lost the affections of the
people.* 4 其 一 = 'the first of them;'
—*i.e*, the first in order who spoke, probably the
oldest. 皇祖,—Gan-kwŏ takes 皇 = 君;
Ts'ae makes it = 大. On whichever view,
the two characters refer to Yu. 民可近,
不可下,—literally, 'the people should be
neared, they should not be *put down*.' In the
國語, 周語, 中, we have this passage
quoted as 民可近,不可上. Hence
it is said that the compiler of this present Book
plagiarized the passage from the 國語,
changing 上 into 下. I should rather suppose that the speaker in the 國語 changed
下 into 上 from the frequency of that word
in his mouth at the time. On this and the
next clause, comp. the words of Shun to Yu, Pt.
II., Bk. II ,17. 予視天下,—the 予,

according to Ts'ae, is the speaker's designation
of himself and his brothers. I am not sure of
this. Possibly he is still reciting the words of
Yu; or he may be speaking in the person of
his brother the emperor. This last view is
that which I prefer.—It is only in the last two
lines, 為人上者,奈何不敬, that
we have the speaker's own reflection. 一
人 三 失, 怨 豈 在 明, 不 見
是 圖,—we find this quoted in the 國 語,
晉 語, 三, and also the two last clauses of
it in the 左 傳, 成 十 六 年. If we
connect the first clause closely with the other
two, the lesson which is taught is of a doubtful
character. I have therefore tried to indicate
in the translation that the clause which should
properly complete the first one is wanting.
予 臨 兆 民, 懍 乎 若 朽 索 之 馭
六 馬,—this passage shows plainly that
these words are spoken in the person of the
emperor. 兆 民—'the millions of the people,' in opposition to 'the one man.' 以 尊

亂其紀綱、乃底　冀方、今失厥道、　惟彼陶唐、有此　不亡。○其三曰、　有一于此、未或　嗜音、峻宇彫牆、　外作禽荒、甘酒、　有之、內作色荒、　敬。○其二曰、訓　人上者、奈何不

The ruler of men—
How can he be but reverent *of his duty?*"

6　The second said,
　　"It is in the lessons:—
　　When the palace is a wild of lust,
　　And the country a wild for hunting:
　　When wine is sweet, and music the delight;
　　When there are lofty roofs and carved walls,—
　　The existence of any one of these things,
　　Has never been but the prelude to ruin."

7　The third said,
　　"There was the prince of T'aou and T'ang,
　　Who possessed this country of K'e.
　　Now we have fallen from his ways,
　　And thrown into confusion his rules and laws;
　　The consequence is extinction and ruin."

適卑曰臨, 'when the high go to the low, the action is called *lin*.' Ming-shing quotes from Hwae-nan's 說林訓, 君子居民上, 若腐索御奔馬, and from Confucius in the 家語, 致思篇, 懍懍焉若持腐索扞馬,—passages very like this, but as likely to have been suggested by it as to have suggested it. He also contends that it was not till the Ts'in dynasty that the emperor used *six* horses in his carriage. The point is by no means certain. On the rhymes in this song, see Maou K'e-ling, on 'The Wrongs of the Old Text of the Shoo,' Bk. III.

P. 6. *The song of the second brother.—On the dissipation and extravagance of T'ae-k'ang.* Gan-kwŏ defines 荒 here by 迷亂, 'led astray and disordered.' Such a meaning of the term, however, is not justified by examples. Its proper signification of 'a wild' answers sufficiently. 內外, 'within' and 'without,'=='the palace' and 'the country.' 禽荒==禽

includes 獸. In the 國語, 越語下, we read—王其且馳騁弋獵、無至禽荒、宮中之樂、無至酒荒、音==八音, 'the eight kinds of musical instruments; here == 'music' generally.

Mencius might seem to have had this passage in view, when he spoke as in VII. Bk. II., xxxiv.

P. 7. *The song of the third brother.—How the imperial patrimony was lost.* 惟彼陶唐, —'there was that T'aou and T'ang.' No doubt it is Yaou who is here intended. He ascended the throne from being prince of T'ang, the name of which remains in the dis. of T'ang, dep. of Paou-ting, Chih-le. [Others, however, will have it that the principality of T'ang was in the pres. district of T'ae-yuen, dep. T'ae-yuen, in Shan-se.] Before he ruled in T'ang, he had been princelet, it is said, in T'aou, referred to the dis. of Ting-t'aou, dep. Ts'aou-chow, Shan-tung. [Others will have it that Yaou lived first in T'ang, and then in T'aou.—So uncertain are such early matters.] Ts'ae says that when raised to the empire, he made T'aou his capital. [In this case T'aou

絕祀。○其（九節） 厥緒、覆宗 則有、荒墜 和鈞、王府 子孫、關石 有則、貽厥 之君、有典 我祖、萬邦 四曰、明明 滅亡。○其（八節）

8 The fourth said,
"Brightly intelligent was our ancestor,
Sovereign of the myriad States!
He had canons, he had rules,
Which he transmitted to his posterity.
The standard Stone and the equalizing Quarter
Were in the imperial treasuries.
Wildly have we dropt the clue he gave us,
Overturning our family and extinguishing our sacrifices."

ought to be the same as P'ing-yang.] Setting little store by all these statements, we have the fact that Yaou is often referred to as 陶唐氏. 有此冀方,—Yaou of course possessed the whole empire; but it was in K'e-chow that he had his capital, and it was from it that T'ae-k'ang was now kept. We therefore find it specified in this way.

紀綱,—'rules and laws;' = the lesser regulations and the greater. 紀 properly signifies 'to separate and arrange sorts of silk,' a fine delicate manipulation; 綱 is the large rope of a net, to which the whole is attached.

We find the whole of this song with two slight variations, and the addition of one line, in the 左傳. Under the 8th year of duke Gae, Confucius appears quoting from the Books of Hea—惟彼陶唐, 帥彼天常, 有此冀方, 今失其行, 亂其紀綱, 乃滅而亡.

P. 8. *The fourth brother's song.*—How unworthy a successor of Yu T'ae-k'ang had been. 有典有則,—Gan-kwŏ defines 典 by 經籍, 'standard writings,' or 'books,' and 則 by 法. Ts'ae, much more happily, illustrates the phrases by referring to the second Book of the Rites of Chow, where the six 典, the eight 法, and the eight 則, are all described as in the special charge of the first minister of the crown (冢宰). The *teen* were the general regulations about government, and its several departments of instruction, ceremonies, offices, punishment, and employments. The *tsih* were the special rules about sacrifices, emoluments, the collection of revenue, &c. Yu's canons and rules were more compendious probably than those of a later period; but they would be of the same general nature. 關石和鈞, 王府則有,—關 is here explained by 通, and Medhurst translates—'He rendered uniform the weights and harmonized the measures.' But this is wrong. 關 and 和 are two adjectives, qualifying 石 and 鈞, which latter term moreover is not a measure, but the quarter of the 石. Choo He gave it as his opinion that the two phrases were simply the denominations of the weights. We may translate 關 by 'current,' or 'standard,' and 和 by 'equalizing.' By the use of these weights there was an end of petty strifes among the people,—they were made 'harmonious.' The royal treasury contained the standard measures of capacity and length as well; that we must understand:—so widely and carefully had Yu provided for the working of the government. We find this passage quoted in the 國語, 周語, 下, where the glossarist, Wei Ch'aou (韋昭; of Woo, one of the 'Three Kingdoms'), would make 關 = 'the customs,' a meaning which might be adopted but for the following 和. 覆宗 'overturning our ancestral temple,' = causing our family to be cast out from the empire.

雖　弗　厚　乎　疇　仇　之　曷　五
悔　慎　有　予　依　予　悲　歸　曰
可　厥　忸　心　鬱　予　萬　予　嗚
追。　德。　怩。　顏　陶　將　姓　懷　呼

9　The fifth said,
　　"Oh! whither shall we turn?
　　The thoughts of our breasts make us sad.
　　All the people are hostile to us;
　　On whom can we rely?
　　Anxieties stand thick in our hearts;
　　Thick as are our faces, they are covered with blushes.
　　We have not been careful of our virtue;
　　And though we repent, we cannot overtake the past."

P. 9. *The song of the fifth brother.—A wail over the sad condition to which they were reduced.* 子懷之悲,—'I dwell on this and am sad;' or, as in the 'Daily Explanation,' 此子懷之所以悲, 'this is why the thoughts of my bosom are sad.' The 子, in this and other places, I have translated in the plural, the brothers in this way taking to themselves the blame attaching to T'ae-k'ang. 鬱陶乎予心,顏厚有忸怩. —comp. Mencius, V., Bk. I., ii 3—鬱陶思君爾, 忸怩. Ming-shing contends that the text is plagiarized from that passage. But Mencius must there be quoting from histories of Shun current in his days;—most probably he is quoting from the first part of the Canon of Shun, which is now lost. If this be denied, we may say that Mencius appropriated the language of the text, with quite as much reason as that it was modelled from him. As to the meaning of 鬱陶, it is very much disputed. K'ung explains it by 哀思, 'anxiously, mournfully, thinking.' Others again, as Yen Jŏ-keu, assuming 陶 to mean 'joy,' 'to be joyful,' make the phrase = 'the first emotion of joy not yet finding vent.' This meaning would be quite inappropriate in the text, and they say that this being the proper meaning of the phrase, its use here arose from misunderstanding it in Mencius, and shows the hand of the plagiarist. But the other meaning suits the passage in Mencius much better than this, and is not to be so readily sent out of court. 鬱 properly denotes 'trees growing bushy;' then, 'tangled.' 陶 is 'a potter's furnace;' it is also used for potters' work. The phrase in the text will then signify the 'tangled workings of the mind,' appropriate to its anxious thoughts, rather than its joyful emotions. 顏厚,—'our faces are thick';—this is said to show the strong working of their shame.

CONCLUDING NOTE. Neither from the Shoo nor from the 'Historical Records' do we learn anything about T'ae-k'ang but what is contained in the first three paragraphs of this Book; and from them we cannot say in what year of his reign he undertook his hunting expedition beyond the Lŏ, or what was the result of the movement of E against him. The chronologists, however,—on what authority it is not necessary here to discuss,—refer the expedition to the 19th year of his reign, B.C. 2169: and they say he was never able to recross the Ho. He lived on for ten years in Yang-hea (陽夏), corresponding to the pres. dis. of T'ae-k'ang, dep. of Ch'in-chow, in Ho-nan. His name is there perpetuated. Some writers say that E built a city for him there, and allowed him to occupy it as his capital, and to continue nominally to be emperor. Whatever hand E had in it, chronology recognizes T'ae-k'ang as emperor till his death, B.C. 2159; and the reign of his brother Chung-k'ang, with whom we have to do in the next Book, dates from the year following, B.C. 2158.

THE BOOKS OF HEA.

BOOK IV. THE PUNITIVE EXPEDITION OF YIN.

祖征。○告^{三節} 后承王命 于厥厥邑胤 厥職酒荒 師義和廢 侯命掌六 位四海胤 惟^{一節}仲康肇 胤征

1　I. When Chung-k'ang commenced his reign over all within the four seas, the prince of Yin was commissioned to take charge of the imperial armies. *At this time* He and Ho had neglected the duties of their office, and were sunk in wine in their *private* cities, and the prince of Yin received the imperial charge to go and punish them.

NAME OF THE BOOK.—胤征. 'The Punitive Expedition of Yin.' 胤 is the name of a State; —where it was situated I have not been able to ascertain. The 胤侯 in par. 1 makes it clear that we must take the first character as the name of a principality. K'ang-shing makes it, in his comment on the 8th par. of the Preface, the name of a minister, which would seem to be a gross blunder. It can be accounted for, however. The Book is one of those whose genuineness is controverted. K'ang-shing had not seen it. To guide him in determining the meaning of 胤, he had only the expression in the Preface, and its occurrence in Pt. V., Bk. XXVI., p. 14. His error is quite excusable. 征, 'punitive expedition,'—the meaning is laid down by Mencius, VII. Pt., II., ii., 2. The Book is rightly assigned to the division of the Shoo, which consists of 誓, 'martial speeches.'

CONTENTS. He and Ho, ministers of the Board of Astronomy, had grossly neglected their duties, and given themselves over to licentious indulgence. The emperor considers them worthy of death, and commissions the prince of Yin to destroy them. The prince on his part assembles his forces, and addresses them on the object of the expedition, setting forth the justice of the punishment to be inflicted, and summoning them to second him with all their energies. This is all that appears on the surface of the Book;—whether we are to understand other ends as contemplated in the expedition will be considered in the notes. I have divided it into two chapters:—the first containing only the first paragraph, and stating generally the grounds of the expedition; the second occupying all the other paragraphs, which contain the speech of the prince of Yin.

Ch. I. P. 1. THE OCCASION OF THE EXPEDITION. 惟仲康肇位四海,胤侯命掌六師,—we can give no meaning to the 惟, standing, as it does here, at the commencement of the Book. In modern style,

謹 王 保 徵 訓 有 眾 予 曰 于
天 克 先 定 明 謨 聖 有 嗟 眾

2　II. He made an announcement to his hosts saying, "Ah! ye, all my troops, there are the well-counselled instructions of the sage *founder of our dynasty*, clearly verified in their power to give stability and security *to the State*:—'The former kings were carefully

for 肇 位 四 海 we should say 始 卽 位, 臨 御 四 海. 命 must be taken passively,—'was charged,' 'was appointed.' 掌 六 師,—'to handle the six armies.' The prince of Yin was raised to the office of 大 司 馬, made, in our phraseology, commander-in-chief of the imperial forces. 六 師＝六 軍, 'the six armies,' indicated in Book II., as forming the military force of the emperor;—see on Ana., VII. x. 2.　This was the first step of Chung-k'ang on his accession to the throne,—to put his armies in the charge of the prince of Yin.　The editors of Yung-ching's Shoo give their opinion that Chung-k'ang succeeded his brother in Yang-hea, and that he was not in possession of Yu's capital called Gan-yih (安 邑), and the name of which still remains in the dis. of Gan-yih, in the small dep. of K'eae (解 州), separated by the pres. dynasty from P'ing-yang.　They suppose that E kept him as well as T'ae-kang from all the country north of the Ho.　This is against the view of Gan-kwŏ and Ying-tă, that E called Chung-k'ang to the throne in the room of his brother.　Looking at the text, I cannot suppose that Chung-k'ang reigned only over part of the empire.　The phrases 四 海 and 六 師 would seem designed as a protest against such a view.　Then he is represented as exercising an authority quite independent in the appointment of the prince of Yin, and sending him subsequently against He and Ho.　How it was that Chung-k'ang could possess such an authority, situated as he was between his brother, whom E kept from the best part of the empire, and his son whom E cast out of the whole of it,—this is a historical difficulty which we have not facts enow to enable us to solve.　There is much speculation about it among the critics. The wiser course in such a case is to rest contented in our ignorance. 羲 和 廢 厥 職, 酒 荒 于 厥 邑,—this He and Ho would be descendants—sons or grandsons—of the ministers of Yaou; and Ts'ae says that the different offices sustained by them in Yaou's time had now been united in one.　We need not think so.　He and Ho here may very well be the chiefs of the two families, as they rather seem to be in the Can. of Yaou, p. 3.　On Ts'ae's view,

厥 邑 will be singular, and Gaubil has accordingly translated 'leur ville.' As they were 卿 or high nobles in the employment of the emperor, their cities would be in the territory next to the imperial domain, the first hundred *le* of the *How fuh*, and probably not far from each other.　The phrase 廢 厥 職, in conn. with the next clause, implies that they had both neglected their duty and abandoned their posts. 酒 荒,—comp. 色 荒 in the last Book, p. 6.　脩 后,—not 脩 侯, as above.　Ts'ae observes that when the princes of the empire took up their residence at court as high ministers, their style was changed from 侯 to 后.

Some time may have elapsed between the prince of Yin's being appointed commander of the imperial armies and his receiving this commission to punish He and Ho; but we naturally conclude that he led all his powers against them.　And was it necessary to do this?　They were not living in their own fiefs, surrounded by other nobles yielding a reluctant submission to their suzerain.　This circumstance harmonizes with the view that He and Ho were in league with E, and that the main object intended by such a display of force was to overawe that dangerous chief, and to weaken his power by cutting off his confederates.

Ch. II. Pp. 2—7. THE SPEECH OF THE PRINCE OF YIN.　Pp. 2, 3.　*Principles of the State for the guidance of officers and others;—preparatory to the introduction and condemnation of He and Ho.*

2. 嗟,—the speech begins like that at Kan, Bk. II., p. 2.　聖 有 謨 訓, 明 徵 定 保,—the 聖 here must refer to Yu. The 'Daily Explanation' paraphrases the passage thus:—我 夏 聖 祖 大 禹, 著 有 謨 訓, 其 言 皆 明 切 徵 驗 可 以 定 國 保 邦.　It is quoted in the 左 傳, 襄 二 十 一 年, with 動 for 訓,—聖 有 謨 動, 明 徵 定 保.　A meaning is there also put upon it not so natural as that which I give to it here.　What follows are the counsels of Yu.　The 'Daily Explanation' goes on to paraphrase them with a—謨 訓 有 曰.　Lin Che-k'e observes that 謨 means the counsels offered by a minister to his sove-

戒　有　官　后　○　春　木　路　規　事
臣　常　修　惟　三節　遒　鐸　官　工　以
人　憲　輔　明　　每　人　徇　師　執　諫
克　百　厥　明。　歲　以　相　藝　其
　　　　　　　孟　　于

attentive to the warnings of Heaven, and their ministers observed the regular laws *of their offices.* All the officers, *moreover,* watchfully did their duty to assist *the government,* and the sovereign became

3　entirely intelligent.' Every year in the first *month* of spring, the herald with his wooden-tongued bell goes along the roads, *proclaiming,* 'Ye officers able to direct, be prepared with your admonitions. Ye workmen engaged in mechanical affairs, remonstrate on the

reign, as in the 'Counsels of the great Yu,' 'Counsels of Kaou-yaou,' &c.; but that the rules laid down by a sovereign for the guidance of his descendants are also called by the same name, as in the 'Instructions of E.,' p. 8. The usage of 訓 is similar. 先王克謹 天戒,—'the former kings,' as spoken of by Yu, must refer to Shun and Yaou, and what others he had heard of before them. Compare the language of Shun in the 'Yih and Tscih,' p. 4,—古人之象. 克謹, 'were able to attend sedulously to;'—克, joined to a verb, often serves to emphasize its meaning. 天戒, —'warnings of Heaven,' such as were supposed to be conveyed by eclipses, and other unusual heavenly phenomena. 臣人,—this is understood to mean the great ministers,—輔 弼大臣, while the officers generally, large and small, are spoken of in the phrase 百官 below. The 人 after 臣, however, is peculiar; but it must merge in the 臣. 臣人 corresponds to the 先王 before; we cannot render it 'ministers and people.' 明明 is the redoubled adjective, expressing the meaning intensely.　3. Not only was this general principle laid down in the counsels of Yu, that the ministers and officers should all be earnestly assisting to the sovereign, but there was also a special institution to call forth the experience of all classes for the same object. 遒人 is defined by Gan-kwŏ and in the dictionary by 宣令之官, 'the officer who proclaims the orders.' Ying-tă tries to deduce the meaning from one of the significations of 遒, in which it = 聚, 'to collect.' This officer collected

the people, and gave them their orders, and hence was derived his name.' We may translate the phrase by 'herald.' 木鐸, —see Ana. III. xxiv. The wooden-tongued bell was used for civil, peaceful objects; in war a metal-tongued bell was used. 徇=徧; 徇于路 = 'all along the roads.' What follows—官師, 云云,—is to be understood as the language of the herald's proclamation. So it is taken in the 'Daily Explanation.' This view is established likewise by the account of a similar practice in the Chow dynasty;—see the Chow Le, Bk. III. (天官, 小宰), par. 52,—正歲帥治官之屬, 而觀 治象之法, 徇以木鐸, 曰, 不 用法者, 國有常刑. 官師相 規,—官 and 師 are not two classes, but one. They are called 官 as having office, and 師 as supposed to be men of principle and knowledge, fitted to instruct. So, Ts‘ae;—官以 職言, 師以道言. 規,—'a compass,' then used as = 正, 'to correct,' the use of a compass being necessary to make correct circles. There is a difficulty with 相. We naturally interpret 相規, 'to correct one another;' but this would give no pertinent meaning. How would the officers' not correcting one another bear on the guilt of He and Ho in not admonishing their sovereign? The object of the 規 must be defects in the emperor's conduct or government. The paraphrase in the 'Daily Explanation' brings out this very clearly:—凡職官有道者, 或遒 朝廷之德政闕失, 卽直言

或不恭邦有
常刑。○惟時　四節
義和顛覆厥
德沈亂于酒、
畔官離次、俶
擾天紀遐棄
厥司乃季秋
月朔、辰弗集
于房、瞽奏鼓、
嗇夫馳庶人

subject of your business! If any of you disrespectfully *neglect this requirement*, the country has regular punishments for you.'

4　"Now here are He and Ho.   They have entirely subverted their virtue, and are sunk and lost in wine.   They have violated the duties of their office, and left their posts.   They have been the first to allow the regulations of heaven to get into disorder, putting far from them their proper business.   On the first day of the last month of autumn, the sun and moon did not meet harmoniously in Fang. The blind *musicians* beat their drums; the inferior officers and common people bustled and ran about.   He and Ho, however, as if they

以相規正, 'all ye officers, being men of principle, if you see that there are defects in the virtue or government of the court, speak out directly that you may correct them.'   This meaning of 相 does not first occur to the reader, but it is admissible;—the emperor is the other party opposite to whom the officers are to suppose themselves placed.   工執藝事以諫,—here we go below the official class; even mechanics might see extravagance in the expenditure of the court on articles of their departments, which they were bound to find some way of remonstrating about,—so earnest was Yu, and such precautions had he taken, that the errors of the sovereign should be brought to his notice.

[Both Gaubil and Medhurst err egregiously in translating these last two clauses.   De Mailla hits the meaning of the former, but loses entirely that of the second. Grosier, in a note to De Mailla's version, seems to approve that of Gaubil.]

We find from 遒人 to 以諫 quoted as from the 'Books of Hea' in the 左傳 襄十四年.   其或不恭—on this use of 恭, see Mencius, IV., Pt., I., i., 13.

P. 4.   *The crimes of He and Ho; and the punishment due to them.*   惟時(=是)義和, 顛覆厥德 沈亂于酒,—comp. the She-king, Pt. III., Bk. III., Ode. ii. 3. 畔官離次,—the dict. explains 畔 with

ref. to this passage, by 離, 'to leave.'   It is better, however, to take it in the sense of 'to disobey,' 'to violate.'   官 = 'the duties of office'; 次 = 'the place,' 'the post'   俶擾 天紀—俶 = 始, 'the first;' 擾 = 亂, 'to throw into confusion;' 天紀, 'the heavenly regulators.'   See Part V., Bk. IV., p. 8, where those regulators are said to be five,—the seasons of the year, the sun, the moon, the stars, and the calculations of the calendar. The phrase in the text is to be taken generally: —He and Ho had neglected the contemplation of the Heavens, and attention to the calendar, so putting far from them 'their proper business' (厥司 = 其所司之事).   乃季秋月朔, 辰弗集于房,—here is a specific and flagrant instance of the neglect of duty by those astronomers.   On the first day of the last month of autumn it had happened that 辰弗集于房.   The year when this took place is not mentioned, but we cannot do other than suppose that it was the same year in which the speech was made, or the one immediately before it.   The prince of Yin could not have spoken as he did, if a second autumn had intervened between the phenomenon and the date of his speech.

房—see on the Can. of Yaou, par. 5, where we saw that this was the central constellation of the larger group of constellations in the eastern quarter, called the 'Azure Dragon.' It begins with the star π of Scorpio and ends with σ, and extends over a space of less than 5½° (see Gaubil's Shoo-king, pp. 68, 69, and

走義和尸
厥官罔聞
知昏迷于干
天象以
先王之誅
政典曰先
時者殺無
赦不及時
者殺無赦。
○今予以
五節

were mere personators of the dead in their offices, heard nothing
and knew nothing;—so stupidly went they astray *from their duty* in
the matter of the heavenly appearances, and rendering themselves
liable to the death appointed by the former kings. The statutes of
government say, 'When they anticipate the time, let them be put to
death without mercy; when they are behind the time, let them be
put to death without mercy.'

J. B. Biot's 'Etudes sur l' Astronomie Indienne
et Chinoise,' p. 375). The clause 辰弗集
于房 has always been understood as describing the fact of an eclipse of the sun, on
the day and month indicated, in that portion
of the heavens; and there can be no doubt the
interpretation is correct. Down to the present
day ceremonies substantially the same as those
which the prince of Yin goes on to describe
are observed on the occurrence of such a phenomenon. The passage is quoted moreover in
the 左傳, 昭十七年, corresponding
to B.C. 524, and this explanation given of it.—
There can be no doubt therefore as to the
meaning. As to the characters themselves,
Medhurst translates them.—'There was a conjunction of the sun and moon without being
fully combined, in the constellation of Fang;'
and Gaubil has :—'Le soleil et la lune en conjunction n'ont pas été d'accord dans Fang.'
Gaubil's version is a literal translation from
the interpretation of Ts'ae Ts'in, who bases it
on the fact that in the Books of Han instead
of 集 we have 輯, and says that the two
characters may be interchanged, adding:—日
月會次, 不相和輯. I doubt the
interchangeableness of 集 and 輯; but the
former has the established significations of 合,
齊,
[this is Gan-kwŏ's explanation *in loc.*], and
which give the ideas of 'harmonious, regular
union.' 辰 must be the conjunction of the
sun and moon for the month in question;—see
the Canon of Yaou, par. 3. 瞽奏鼓,
嗇夫馳 庶人走,—these were
customs observed on occasion of an eclipse;
similar practices were observed under the
Chow dynasty; and with some modifications
they are prescribed by the Chinese government
at the present time. See Biot's Studies above

referred to, pp. 357—360. 瞽奏鼓,—by
'the blind' we must understand the musicians
who were employed in antiquity because of
their blindness, their loss of the sense of sight
being supposed to sharpen that of hearing. 奏
=伐, 'to strike.' 嗇夫 is explained
by Ts'ae—小臣, 'small officers;' according
to K'ang-shing, they were *employés* under the
Minister of Works. By 庶人 are in-
tended what Mencius, V., Pt. II., ii., 6, calls 庶
民在官者, 'such of the common people
as were employed about the government offices';
—see the note on that passage. Of what
these people ran, and the smaller officers
galloped about for, we get an idea from the
passage of the 左傳 where this text is
quoted. We are there told that when an eclipse
happened, the emperor fasted, and had the
drums beat before the altar of the spirits of
the land, while the princes of States presented
offerings before that altar and had the drums
beat in their court. [It would appear from
the same passage, that in the Chow dynasty
these things were observed only when eclipses
happened on the first day of the first month
of the year. In this point the custom of Hea,
with which the present usage agrees, differed
from that of Chow.] Again, in the Chow Le,
Bk. XXXVII. (near the end), we read of the
bow and arrows used to deliver the sun, and
those used to deliver the moon. On an eclipse
of the sun, they shot their arrows into the sky
to frighten away the injurious moon, and *vice
versa.* See the long note of K'ung Ying-tă
on the passage, where immense lore is brought
to bear on its illustration. While the
phenomenon was occasioning so much excitement, He and Ho were entirely indifferent to
it. 尸厥官,—comp. Bk. III., p. 1. 昏
迷于天象,—'darkly going astray in

regard to the heavenly appearances.' 迷,—comp. Canon of Shun, p. 2.

政典,—see on the last Book, p. 8, 有典有則.　先時者, 云云,—there is considerable diversity of view in interpreting this sentence. First, the 'Daily Explanation' paraphrases it thus:—曆官職掌, 凡躔度節候, 俱要推算合時, 或失于先時, 或失于後時, 罪當殺無赦, 'They who are intrusted with the office of regulating the calendar must calculate exactly to the time the degrees of motion of the heavenly bodies, with the terms of the year. If they err by being too early or too late, their crime requires that they be put to death without mercy.' This view is approved by Gaubil, who translates:—'Celui qui devance on qui recule les tems doit être, sans remission, puni de mort;' and he adds in a note, 'Une loi si severe contre les calculateurs d'éclypses, dans des tems si reculés, denote une ancienne methode pour les éclypses.' Possibly astronomers of this high antiquity in China may have been able to calculate eclipses after a fashion, by means of the cycle of 19 years,—if indeed they were acquainted with that, which is quite uncertain; but I find it difficult to believe they had attained so far. Nor is this interpretation of the text sufficiently evident or attested by tradition to bring us to Gaubil's conclusion.

Second, Gan-kwŏ gives a more general and plausible interpretation. By 時 he understands 'the four seasons, and the four and twenty terms into which they were divided, with the times of new and full moon and the two quarters' (四時節氣, 弦望晦朔). On this view the statute was to the effect that the astronomers neglecting their work, and allowing the months and seasons to get into confusion, were to be punished with death. It does not bear directly on the special crime of He and Ho's absence from their posts on the occurrence of the eclipse; but we can conceive of the prince of Yin's thinking it sufficiently to the purpose to appeal to it in addressing his troops.

Third, Lin Che-k'e separated the passage from the par. to which in all editions it is here united, and joined it to the part of the speech which follows. The prince of Yin has done with He and Ho when he has once said that they were liable to the death appointed by the former kings, and then turns to his troops to urge them to do their duty, prefacing his remarks with this reference to the canons of Government on military law, by which neglect of orders, whether in anticipating movements or in delaying them, was punishable with death. This view has been ingeniously supported by Ch'in Leih (陳櫟);—see the 附錄. Choo He condemned Che-k'e's interpretation, on the ground that it was forced, the passage being connected more naturally with the preceding part of the speech than with what follows. The editors of Yung-ching's Shoo, however, profess themselves unable to decide positively between this view

and the first. The ordinance is too severe, they say, against the astronomers, who might easily make a mistake in their figures, while it may be acknowledged if it form part of the stern code of martial law. For myself I have hesitated between the second and third views, abiding for the present by the second. The passage, with the slight variation of 逮 for 及, is found in Seun-tsze, 君道篇, but not in a connection which enables us to judge of the meaning he put upon it.

[The eclipse of the sun related in this paragraph has always been a subject of great interest to students of history in China and elsewhere. Could it be satisfactorily verified, a date would be established in Chinese history, which would for ever settle all doubts as to its antiquity and general certainty.

The accession of Chung-k'ang dates, it has been seen, B.C. 2158 (Gaubil says 2159. But there is no real difference between him and me, as I do not reckon the year of our Lord's birth, the dates in my scheme of Chinese chronology running thus:—A.D. 1; A.D.; B. C. 1. Gaubil reckoning—A.D. 1; B.C. 1, my B.C. 2158 is with him B.C. 2159). The Shoo does not say expressly that the eclipse took place in that year, though the ordinary, and perhaps the readiest, inference has been that it did do so. But such an inference may not be correct. The appointment of the prince of Yin may have been one of the first acts of Chung-k'ang, and the expedition against He and Ho may not have been undertaken till some years after. If the eclipse could be verified any time during the reign, i.e., between B.C. 2158 and 2146, there would be a sufficient harmony between the chronology and the astronomy. More than this, in the scantiness of dates and the uncertainties attaching to the particular reigns of the Hea emperors from Yu to Këĕ, one of which uncertainties I pointed out in the concluding note to the last Book, I should almost be prepared to regard with satisfaction a verification of the eclipse in any year of the first half of the 22d century before our era, or even, I will venture to say, between B.C. 2050 and 2158. To be sure, the genuineness of 'The Punitive Expedition of Yin' is called in question; but in regard to this eclipse, we know, on the authority of the 左傳, which I have adduced, that the record of it was in one of the Books of Hea. Whether the Books of the Shoo additional to those derived from Fuh-shang were a compilation of the times of the Tsin dynasty or not, one of them—the real 'Expedition of Yin'—did contain the same passage that we have in the present text.

Now, the year B.C. 2158 must be given up as the date of the eclipse. No such phenomenon could have then occurred. Ts'ae tells us, however, that the astronomers of the T'ang dynasty (by which time they began to have such a knowledge of the precession of the equinoxes as enabled them to attempt these investigations) determined that the eclipse took place in the fifth year of Chung-k'ang. Several of the early Jesuit missionaries applied themselves to solve the point,—none with such devotion to the inquiry

爾有眾奉將

天罰爾眾尚士

同力王室

弼予欽承天

予威命。○火 六節

炎崑岡玉石

俱焚天吏逸

德烈于猛火

殲厥渠魁脅

從罔治舊染

5   "Now I, with you all, am entrusted with the execution of the punishment appointed by Heaven. Unite your strength, all of you warriors, for the imperial House. Lend me your help, I pray you, reverently to carry out the dread charge of the son of Heaven."

6   "When the fire blazes over the ridge of Kwǎn, gems and stones are burned together; *but* when a minister of Heaven exceeds in doing his duty, the consequences are fiercer than raging fire. I will so

as Father Gaubil, who brought out the result, in harmony with the conclusions of the T'ang scholars, that the eclipse occurred on the 11th October (old style) of the year B.C. 2155 (2154 in my scheme), the 5th year of Chung-k'ang, and that it was visible at Gan-yih at 6h. 49m. in the morning. Here was an important result; the only circumstance to render one dissatisfied with it was that the eclipse must have been very small, extending only over a sixth part of the sun's diameter, so that it was little likely to arrest attention.

Since Gaubil's time the tables used in those calculations have been rendered more accurate, and the conclusions arrived at possess a greater certainty. My friend, the Rev. Mr. Chalmers of Canton, took in hand in the present year to verify the eclipse, and confirmed Gaubil's conclusion so far as regarded the year, the month, and the day, but found that it must have occurred during the night, before the rising of the sun at Gan-yih, and not after it. I have since found that the same result was obtained in France in 1840 by Largeteau, an able astronomer (see Biot's 'Etudes,' p. 377). It would seem then that we must give up the year 2154 as well as 2158. And yet the matter may be considered as still *sub judice*. It is only in the present century that the secular variation of the moon's mean motion, which seriously affects the calculation of eclipses so remote as this of Chung-k'ang, has been determined with an approach to nice exactness. It may yet come out, as the lunar tables are perfected, that the eclipse of 2154 was visible at Gan-yih, and in that case we shall not hesitate to accept it as the one referred to in this Book.

Mr. Chalmers has determined that there were eclipses of the sun, in or near the constellation Fang, in the years B.C. 2135 (or 2136), 2127 (or 2128), and 2108 (or 2109). Of these that B.C. 2127 was visible in China, and very high Chinese authority has contended that it was to it that the prince of Yin referred. For the reasons which I have assigned I could accept either of the dates 2154 or 2127. I can hardly doubt that on one or other of them there was the phenomenon, by their disregard of which He and Ho afforded the ground which is alleged for their punishment. The text on which I have dwelt so long is to be regarded as a strong confirmation of the substantial truth of Chinese history.]

P. 5. *The troops are exhorted to be brave and energetic.* Compare Yu's speech to his army, Pt. II., Bk. II., 20. The 'Daily Explanation' paraphrases 以爾有眾 by 率爾六軍眾士, which is, plainly enough, the meaning, though we cannot give 率 as a synonym of 以. We may say here that 以＝用. 將＝行, 'to execute.' 同力王室＝同心盡力于王室. A preposition like 于, or a verb signifying 'to maintain,' has to be supplied. 承...命,—承 is 'to receive,' but must be taken here with the pregnant meaning of 'executing' as well.

P. 6. *How the imperial charge was to be executed with discrimination, and justice tempered with forbearance.* 火炎崑山,—Ts'ae says that 崑 is 'the name of a mountain, which produces gems.' Gan-kwǒ's account is substantially the same. It is best taken so. The dict. would lead us to say that 崑崙 is meant, which is now referred to the 枯爾坤山, in the west of the Koko-nor, where the Yellow river has its sources. But the text leads us to conceive of the Kwǎn as a volcanic mountain, which I have not read that the Kwǎn-lun is 天吏,—see Mencius, II., Pt. I., v. 6, *et al.* 逸德,—逸＝過, 'to go be-

汗俗、咸與惟新。○嗚呼、威克厥愛、允濟、愛克厥威、允罔功。其爾眾士、懋戒哉。〔七節〕

destroy *only* the chief criminals, and not punish their forced followers, while those who have long been stained by their filthy manners will be allowed to renovate themselves."

7 "Oh! when sternness overcomes compassion, then things are surely conducted to a successful issue. When compassion overcomes sternness, no merit can be achieved. All ye, my warriors, exert yourselves, and be cautious."

yond.' 逸德 is virtue—conduct in the performance of what may be considered duty—carried to its utmost, going beyond. 渠魁,—'the great chiefs.' He and Ho are intended. 脅從—脅=迫脅, 'pressed.' Those parties had been forced into combination with He and Ho. The expressions here certainly give support to the view that those astronomers were associated with some rebellious movement against the imperial authority.

咸與惟新,—the 'Daily Explanation' has here—皆與赦除,使之改過自新。與 is to be taken as=許, 'to allow,' 'to grant to.'

P. 7. *The severity of martial law.* We are to understand that the prince of Yin here warns his troops, that if they do not do their duty, they must not expect him to deal with them on any principle of indulgence. As to their duty in the circumstances, the 'Daily Explanation' finds it in the concluding words 懋戒哉, the 懋 referring to p. 4, where they were urged to unite their strength for the imperial House, and the 戒 to p. 6, where it is laid down how their justice was to be tempered. It paraphrases:—懋勉于同力,警戒于逸德,以共濟弼承王命之功哉. This is finding a great deal of meaning in the terms. Yen Jŏ-keu argues strongly that this paragraph is adapted from the 左傳,昭二十三年, where a general of Woo (吳), says:—吾聞之,作事,威克其愛,雖小必濟. It is more likely, however, that the general of Woo was adapting the words from the copies of the Shoo current in his time. His applica-

tion of them is not happy;—it is enigmatical indeed, but Jŏ-keu's argument is here, as in many other places, too eagerly pursued.

CONCLUDING AND CONNECTING NOTE. With this Book terminate Confucius' selections from the monuments of the Hea dynasty subsisting in his time. Seventeen reigns altogether are assigned to it. Chung-k'ang's was the fourth. Of the twelve that follow, the Shoo gives us no intimation; but the name of the last emperor and his wickedness are often mentioned and dwelt upon in the Parts of the classic that follow this.

Sze-ma Ts'een gives us little more than a catalogue of the emperors' reigns, how they came to the throne and how they died. He has not a word on the length of their reigns; and only on K'ung-këă, the 13th from Yu, and Këĕ, the last, does he give a few brief notices of their characters. His whole account is comprised in less than a page. The fragments of the history of those times that have been gathered from other sources, more or less trustworthy, and are found in Choo He's 'General Mirror of History' (通鑑綱目), and in what may be called the 'Standard Annals' (歷代統紀表), may be related in brief space.

Chung-k'ang's reign of 13 years terminated B.C. 2146. We should like to know the relations that existed between him and E, but all we are informed of is that this chief put to death Pih-fung, or the baron Fung (伯封), one of his ministers, a son of K'wei, Shun's minister of Music. We are left in uncertainty as to whether the act was one of justice, the punishment of a criminal, or one of hostility, the cutting off a faithful adherent.

Chung-k'ang was succeeded, B.C. 2145, by his son Seang (后相), who reigned for 27 years. In the first year of his reign he had to withdraw across the Ho to Shang-k'ew (商邱), still the name of the principal district in the dep. of Kwei-tih, Ho-nan. He was driven to this step, we may well believe, by E, who now exercised the supreme authority in K'e-chow. In 2138 E was killed by a minister of his own, or at least on his instigation. The minister's name was Han-tsuh, or perhaps we should rather say Tsuh of the State Han (see the 左傳, 襄四年; and comp. Mencius IV. Pt. II. xxiv). He took to himself E's wife, and by her had two sons, Këaou (澆) and He (豷), the former of whom by his father's orders put the emperor to death in Shang-k'ew, B.C. 2118, he himself being only 20 years of age. Various 'punishments' of barbarous tribes are ascribed to Seang in the early years of his reign, which it is difficult to believe he was capable of in his circumstances. We may infer from the accounts, however, that the wild tribes, in and about the empire, took advantge of the weakness and confusion of the government to try and regain their independence or to make plundering incursions.

On the death of Seang, Tsuh claimed the empire, and maintained himself on the throne for 39 years. When the emperor was killed, however, one of his wives, who was pregnant, made her escape to her native State of Jing (仍), of which her father was chief. There she gave birth to a son, known as Shaou-k'ang (少康), who lead a perilous life for nearly 40 years. His existence was known to the usurper, who made various attempts to get him in his power. At one time he was chief herdsman to the chief of Jing; at another he was chief cook to the prince of Yu. The latter chief recognized his worthiness, and gave him his two daughters in marriage, and an establishment in the pres. dis. of Yungho, dep. of P'ing-yang. There his capacity and character still more developed themselves. The old adherents of his House took heart. The people remembered Yu. An end was made of the usurping family, and Shaou-k'ang was raised to the throne of his father in B.C. 2078.

Shaou-k'ang's recovery of the throne [we might say K'ang the third; Chung-k'ang was K'ang the second, and T'ae-k'ang K'ang the first] was followed by the reverent acknowledgment of the chiefs of the empire, and the submission of the wild tribes. The only event of his reign which is recorded, however, is his appointment of one of his sons by a secondary wife to be the chief of Yuĕ (越), there to maintain the sacrifices at the tomb of Yu, who died, we saw, at Hwuyk'e, in the pres. Chĕ-keang. The emperor's son was styled Woo-yu (無餘). He was the first

feudal chief established in the regions of Woo and Yuĕ, so slowly did the conquering Chinese firmly establish their rule over the country.

Shaou-k'ang was succeeded, B.C. 2057, by his son Ch'oo, (后杼); and he was followed, after a reign of 17 years, in B.C. 2039, by his son Hwae (后槐).

After Hwae came his son Măng (后芒), B.C. 2013; then Măng's son, Sĕĕ (后泄), B.C. 1995; then, Sĕĕ's son, Puh-këang (后不降), B.C. 1979; then, Puh-këang's brother, Keung (后扃), B.C. 1920; then, Keung's son, Kin 后厪, B.C. 1899; then, a son of Puh-keang, called K'ung-këä (后孔甲), B.C. 1878.

Sze-ma Ts'een pauses in his list of all but nameless sovereigns to dwell on the character of K'ung-këä, whom he pronounces to have been superstitious and dissipated, so as to alienate from him the hearts of all the 'princes. In the 27th year of his reign, B.C. 1851, there occurred an event, most important to the fortunes of the Hea dynasty,—the birth of Le (履), son of the chief of Shang, who became in due time T'ang the Successful, the founder of a new line of emperors.

K'ung-këä was succeeded by his son Kaou (后皋), B.C. 1847; and he again by his son Fă (后發), B.C. 1836. Fă died B.C. 1816, leaving the throne to his son Kwei, (癸), with whom the sovereignty of the line of Yu came to an end.

Kwei is better known by his name of Kĕĕ, 'the Injurer of men and Destroyer of many' (賊人多殺日桀). The first three and thirty years of his long reign are a blank. Possessing extraordinary strength, able to twist bars of iron about like ropes, he gloried in his vigour, and wearied out the people with expeditions of war. In B.C. 1785, he proceeded to attack the chief of She (有施氏), in the neighbourhood of mount Mung in the present Shantung. The chief propitiated his anger by presenting him with his daughter Me-he (妹喜), of surpassing beauty, but more depraved, if possible, than the emperor himself. All thoughts of prudence were lost amid the enjoyment of her charms. He gratified all her caprices. He made her a chamber of carnation-stone, with side apartments of ivory, a splendid tower, and a bed glittering with gems. Around this he heaped up, in their wild dissoluteness, mounds of flesh, hung dried meats on all the trees, filled a pond with wine till they could row a boat on it, while three thousand people would make their appearance at beat of drum and drink up the liquor like so many oxen. All government was neglected. In the mean time the avenger was growing up. T'ang succeeded to his father's principality, B.C. 1783, and soon drew the regards of all thoughtful men to himself. The great officers who felt ashamed of Kĕĕ's vices, and mourned the condition of the empire, betook themselves to Shang; the people who groaned beneath the oppression of their lords, too many of whom followed Kĕĕ's example, sighed for the gentle rule of T'ang. The emperor was roused to fits of jealousy, and at one time got T'ang in his power, and imprisoned him. He let him go, however; and at last, B.C. 1765, after many misgivings, T'ang took the field against his sovereign. There could be no doubt as to the result. Heaven and earth combined with men to show their detestation of the tyrant. Two suns fought in the sky. The earth shook. Mountains were moved from their strong foundations. Rivers were dried up. Kĕĕ was routed, and fled south to Ts'aou, which is still the name of a district in the dep. of Loo-chow (盧州), in Ngan-hwuy, and there he was kept a prisoner till his death three years after. His son and some of his adherents made their way to the wilds of the north, and mingled among the barbarous tribes.

Thus miserably ended the dynasty of Hea, having extended, including the usurpations of E and Tsuh, over 439 years.

THE SHOO KING.

PART IV. THE BOOKS OF SHANG.

BOOK I. THE SPEECH OF T'ANG.

商書

湯誓

一節
王曰、格爾
衆庶悉聽
朕言非台
小子、敢行
稱亂、有夏
多罪、天命
殛之。○今
二節

1   I. The king said, "Come, ye multitudes of the people, listen all to my words. It is not I, the little child, who dare to undertake *what may seem to be* a rebellious enterprize; but for the many crimes of the sovereign of Hea Heaven has given the charge to destroy him.

NAME OF THE PART.—商書, 'The Books of Shang.' 商 (the reader will distinguish the character from 尙, which is the title given to the whole of the Shoo. A Chinese scholar can discriminate them by their different tones) is the dynastic designation by which T'ang and his descendants possessed the empire, B.C. 1765—1122, a period of 644 years. The family traced their origin up to Hwang-te, through Sëĕ, (势), a son of the emperor Kuh, and minister of Instruction to Yaou and Shun. For his services at that time he was invested with the principality of Shang, a part or the whole of the territory now forming the small department of Shang in Shen-se, and received the surname of Tsze (子). From Sëĕ to T'ang were fourteen generations; and we find the latter at a considerable distance from the ancestral fief, and having his capital in the first place, before he dethroned Këĕ, at the southern Pŏ, which seems correctly referred to the dis. of Shang-k'ew (商邱), dep. of Kwei-tih, in Ho-nan. The title of the dynasty, however, was derived from the original Shang to which Sëĕ was appointed.

We saw, on the 9th paragraph of the Preface, that more than one half the documents originally composing this Part of the Shoo were lost, while of the 11 Books which still claim to be received in it there are only 5 whose genuineness is not contested.

NAME OF THE BOOK.—湯誓, 'The Speech of T'ang.' We must regard 湯, not as the honorary posthumous title, but as the designation of the emperor during his lifetime;—see in the note on the Canon of Yaou, par. 1. His name, as we have it from himself, was Le (履). Sze-ma Ts'een says it was 天乙, of which I have not met with a satisfactory explanation.

誓,—see on 'The Speech at Kan.'

正。帝　罪、言、惟　割　我　恤　曰、爾
○不　子　夏　聞　正　稽　我　我　有
今敢　畏　氏　汝　夏。事、衆、后　衆、
汝不　上　有　衆　予　而　舍　不　汝

2　"Now, ye multitudes, you are saying, 'Our prince does not compassionate us, but is calling us away from our husbandry to attack and punish *the ruler of* Hea.' I have indeed heard *these* words of you all: *but* the sovereign of Hea is an offender, and, *as* I fear God, I dare not but punish him.

'The Speech of T'ang' is found in both 'the old and modern texts.' It is now the first of the Books of Shang, though it was in the time of Confucius only the sixth. The five that preceded it have been lost;—see on the 'Preface of Confucius.'

CONTENTS. T'ang having summoned his people to take the field with him against Këĕ, and finding them backward in the enterprise, he addresses them, and sets forth his own reasons for attacking the tyrant, in order to remove their hesitation, and silence their murmurs, while in the end he uses both promises and threats to move them to obey his orders. The whole Book is very short; but I have divided it into two chapters,—the first containing three parr., and giving T'ang's reasons for his course; and the second, in only one par., laying down his martial law. The speech must have been made at Pŏ, and in the year B.C. 1765.

Ch. I. Pp. 1—3. T'ANG'S REASONS FOR ATTACKING KEE, AND THE UNREASONABLENESS OF HIS SUBJECTS' MURMURS. 1. 王曰,— we have no introductory paragraphs as in the 'speech at Kan,' telling us the occasion of the speech. We can, however, supply the want from the preface, p. 12. The use of 王 to denominate T'ang, when he was not yet on the throne, has occasioned a good deal of criticism. Ts'ae says that it is a case of prolepsis by the recorder of the speech. Yet as T'ang was the 天吏, or 'minister of Heaven,' the moment that he took the field, he was the rightful sovereign of the empire, and Këĕ was only an ordinary man. 非台小子,敢行 稱亂,一台 (read *e*) =我, the first personal pronoun. 小子, 'the little child,' is a frequent designation, humbly applied to themselves by the emperors. Ts'ae Peen (蔡卞) says:—'In an announcement to the myriad regions, and in distinction from their multitudes, the emperor calls himself "the one man." Realizing his relation to God, and feeling as in His presence, he calls himself "the little child" (以天子告萬方,故稱予一

人, 對上帝而言, 故稱台 小子). 稱=舉, 'to raise up,' 'to undertake.' Keang Shing edits the character with 人 at the side, on the authority of the 說 文. T'ang states very distinctly the reason of his movement. Këĕ, 'the holder of Hea,' was a criminal condemned by Heaven which had given charge to cut him off. But how had Heaven done this? and how was the charge given to T'ang? The answer to both questions is the same :—'By the voice of the people.' 2. Acc. to the view of Gan-kwŏ (and here he is followed by Keang Shing), T'ang addresses in this par. not his own people, but the subjects generally of Këĕ. 我后, 'our sovereign,' is Këĕ, and 舍我稽事而割正— 'he disregards our husbandry, and exercises a cruel government.' 割 is explained by 剝, with reference to cruel dismemberments inflicted by Këĕ; and 正 is taken as =政, 'government.' Gan-kwŏ takes no notice of the 夏 after 正. and Keang Shing argues that the character is spurious. With the same critics, moreover, the clause 夏氏有罪 is the language of the people, the words which T'ang had heard from them.

This view has many difficulties,—is inadmissible, indeed. 夏 is here in the text, and we cannot throw it out. Nor can we take 正 in 割正 differently from its mean. in 不敢 不正. No similar difficulties attach to the interpretation given by Ts'ae, which I have followed in the translation. 正=治罪, 'to punish,' a well established meaning of the character. 夏氏,—this usage is much akin to our own of calling men by their estates and

其曰、夏罪其如台。夏
王率過眾力、率割夏、
邑有眾率怠弗協、曰、
時日曷喪、予及汝皆
亡。夏德若茲、今朕必
往。○爾尚輔予一人、 〔四節〕
致天之罰、予其大賚
汝、爾無不信、朕不食
言、爾不從誓言、予則
孥戮汝、罔有攸赦。

3 "Now you are saying, 'What are the crimes of Hea to us?' The king of Hea does nothing but exhaust the strength of his people, and exercise oppression in the cities of Hea. His people have all become idle *in his service*, and will not assist him. They are saying, 'When will this sun expire? We will all perish with thee.' Such is the course of *the sovereign of* Hea, and now I must go *and punish him.*

4 II. "Assist, I pray you, me, the one man, to carry out the punishment appointed by Heaven. I will greatly reward you. On no account disbelieve me;—I will not eat my words. If you do not obey the words which I have spoken to you, I will put your children with you to death;—you will find no forgiveness."

possessions. 3. 夏罪其如台.—Gan-kwŏ takes 如台 as = 如我所聞之言, 'according to the words which we have heard.' Here Keang Shing rightly declines to follow him, and follows Sze-ma Ts'een, who reads—有罪其奈何, which he interprets as an exclamation of despair. More accordant with the tone of the whole speech, and better warranted by usage is the meaning given in the translation. The two 其 intensify the language;—see on Can. of Yaou, p. 11. 率過, 率割, 率怠.—in all these cases 率 is to be taken as = 一切, 'in every thing,' 'universally.' Gan-kwŏ is unable to think of any meaning for it but 'to lead,' and labours hard, but unsuccessfully, to explain the passages accordingly. 割夏邑,—here 割 must be explained by 剝. 時 (= 是) 日曷喪, 予及汝皆亡,—see on Mencius, I. Pt. II., iv. 4. Ch'ing

would seem to make this passage the words of Këĕ himself. He says:—'Këĕ seeing that the people wished to rebel, compared himself to the sun, saying, "Has ever that sun perished? If that sun perish, then I and you will also all perish." He made use of the sun's security from danger, to make the people dread himself;'—see the 後案, *in loc.* Mencius is a safer guide as to the meaning of the text than K'angshing. We may well believe, however, that Këĕ had compared himself to the sun. Different traditions say it was in reply to the remonstrances of E Yin that he did so. 夏德若此,—this is a very evident instance of the use of 德 for evil conduct.

Ch. II. P. 4. T'ANG'S DETERMINATION TO HAVE HIS ORDERS OBEYED.—PROMISES OT REWARD, AND THREATS OF PUNISHMENT. Comp. Yu's speech in the 'Counsels of Yu,' p 20, and 'The speech at Kan.' 予其大賚爾.—賚 = 賜, 'to give to,' 'to confer gifts,' = 'to reward.' Sze-ma Ts'een has 理, which it is difficult to account for. The 其 here is strongly intensive. The usage approaches to that pointed out on Can. of Yaou, p. 12.

汝不從誓言, 我則孥戮汝,—the want of such a clause as 汝不從誓言 is felt in 'The speech of Kan,' p. 5. 我則孥戮汝 is there so unconnected that Woo Ch'ing supposes it slipped in by mistake from the present passage.

CONCLUDING NOTE. Though T'ang professed to have it in charge from Heaven to destroy Kёё, and the charge of Heaven was ascertained from the voice of the people, it is plain from this speech that it cost him some trouble to get the co-operation even of his own subjects. The will of Heaven is not always clearly intimated in providence. Even when it is so, it must be wrought out by those who perceive it amidst and against many conflicting interests and prejudices.

This speech was followed by the battle of Ming-t'eaou (Preface, p. 12), not far from the capital of Hea, and by the defeat and downfall of the tyrant.

BOOK II. THE ANNOUNCEMENT OF CHUNG-HWUY.

嗚　乃　實。　以　予　有　于　成^一　仲
呼、惟　作　○　台　恐　慙　南　湯^節　虺
惟　誥　仲　爲　來　德、巢、放　之
天　曰、虺　口　世　曰、惟　桀　誥

1　I. When T'ang, the Successful, was keeping Kĕĕ in banishment in Nan-ch'aou, he had a feeling of shame on account of his conduct, and said, "I am afraid that in future ages men will fill their mouths with me."

NAME OF THE BOOK.—仲虺之誥, 'The Announcement of Chung-hwuy.' Chung-hwuy was one of the principal ministers of T'ang, descended from a He-chung (奚仲), Master of the carriages (車正), under the Hea dynasty, and who at first occupied the territory of Sëĕ (薛), which was in the pres. dis. of T'ang, (滕), dep. of Yen-chow, Shan-tung. He-chung removed to the pres. sub. department of P'ei (邳) in Këang-soo, but Chung-hwuy appears still in Sëĕ;—see the 左傳定元年 (near the beginning). The family traced their line up to Hwang-te; their surname was 任;—see the 歷代疆域表. Chaou K'e and many other scholars have made Chung-hwuy the same as Lae-choo (萊朱), a minister of T'ang, mentioned by Mencius, VII., Pt. II., xxxviii. 2; but it is only by inferential reasoning that the point can be made out. 誥=告, 'to tell,' 'to an-nounce to.' 'Announcements' form one of the divisions of the Shoo, and this is the first of them. They are distinguished from the 誓, which are speeches made to an army, as being made in a general assembly for the information of all (誓,用之于軍旅,誥,用之于會同,以喩衆). From this account of them, we must understand that the 'Announcement of Chung-hwuy' was not ad-dressed to T'ang only, but was spoken or publish-ed for the general information.

On a reference to the Preface, it will be seen that there were originally four other Books, which are now lost, between the 'Speech of T'ang' and this. The time that elapsed between the Speech and the Announcement, however, could not have been long; and, indeed, the one follows the other in the arrangement of the Books, which we derive from Ch'ing Heuen and other scholars, who were not acquainted with Gan-kwo's discoveries. According to the Preface, the Announcement was made at a place called Ta-keung, for which in the 'His-torical Records' we find T'ae-keuen-t'aou (泰

典　舊　正　錫　墜　有　生　主　生
奉　服　萬　王　塗　夏　聰　乃　民
若　茲　邦　勇　炭　昏　明　亂　有
天　率　繼　智　天　德　時　惟　欲
命。厥　禹　表　乃　民　乂、天　無

2　　II. On this Chung-hwuy made the following announcement:—
"Oh! Heaven gives birth to the people with *such* desires, that
without a ruler they must fall into all disorders; and Heaven *again*
gives birth to the man of intelligence whose business it is to regulate
them.　The sovereign of Hea had his virtue all-obscured, and the
people were *as if they were* fallen amid mire and charcoal.　Heaven
hereupon gifted *our* king with valour and wisdom, to serve as a
mark and director to the myriad States, and to continue the old
ways of Yu.　You are now only following the standard course,

卷陶; the 陶 is probably spurious).　Ts'een
also says that in the interval T'ang, by the
advice of E Yin, had proclaimed himself
emperor.　We are still, therefore, in the year
B.C. 1765.

CONTENTS.　T'ang is suffering from a feeling
of remorse at having dethroned Kĕĕ, and is
afraid that his fame will suffer from his act.
Ch'ung-hwuy sets himself to vindicate the
course of his chief, and shows first that he was
called to the throne by the will of Heaven;
next, that he was called to it by the wishes of
the people; and finally, he urges on him various
wise counsels.　The whole naturally falls into
4 chapters:—the first, in one par., giving the
occasion of the Announcement; the second, in
two parr., showing that T'ang had only obeyed
the guidance of Heaven; the third, in three
parr., containing how men consented with
Heaven in the matter; and the fourth, in three
parr., containing Chung-hwuy's own counsels.

CH. I. P. 1. T'ANG'S DOUBT AS TO THE
RIGHTEOUSNESS OF HIS COURSE.　成湯,
—Gan-kwŏ says:—武功成, 故曰成
湯, 'His military operations were brought to
a successful issue, and therefore he was styled
成湯.'　Gaubil and De Mailla don't translate
成 at all, but transfer it; Medhurst has 'the
accomplished T'ang',—which is not good.

放桀于南巢,—Kĕĕ had fled to Nan-
ch'aou, and T'ang simply took measures that
he should remain there.　We must not lay
much emphasis on the 放.　The southern
Ch'aou is identified with the pres. dis. of the
same name, dep. of Loo-chow in Gan-hwuy.

有戡德.—'He thought,' says the 'Daily
Explanation,' 'how Yaou had resigned the
throne to Shun, and Shun had resigned it to
Yu, and Yu had wished to resign it to Yih, and
now he had got it by attacking Kĕĕ and banishing him, and he was ashamed that his
virtue was not equal to that of those ancients'
(戡愧其德不如古).　It is simpler
to take the phrase as in the translation; we may
understand 於 after 戡.　Comp. Mencius II.,
Pt. II., ix., 1.　以台爲口實,—lit., 'take
me to be a mouth-full.'　T'ang's fear evidently
was lest future ages should misunderstand his
motives, and suppose him to have been actuated
by a selfish ambition.　The critics refine on the
point, and suppose that his anxiety was lest
ambitious men should justify their rebellious
attempts from his example.

Ch. II.　CHUNG-HWUY'S ANNOUNCEMENT.
Pp. 2, 3.　THAT T'ANG WAS CALLED BY HEAVEN
TO DO AS HE HAD DONE.　有欲,—the 'desires'
are the senses and the passions, the lusts of men's
own hearts.　時乂,—時=是.　Gan-
kwŏ says:—是治民亂, 'his it is to rule
the disorders of the people.'　There is a force in
the conciseness of the language, which tells us
that not only is it the business of the Heaven-
appointed to regulate disorders, but that he
does do so.　塗炭,—comp. Mencius, II.,
Pt. I., ix., and V., Pt. II., i.　There, sitting in
mire and charcoal is used to give the idea of
being defiled; and Ming-shing says that as here
the phrase gives the idea of misery, it is not
rightly employed.　The compiler, he argues,
borrowed it from Mencius, and misunderstood
its meaning.　This is very small criticism.　To

若　若　我　實　○　命　不　命　誣　夏三
粟　苗　邦　繁　簡四　用　臧　于　上　王節
之　之　于　有　賢節　爽　式　下　天　有
有　有　有　附　厥　商　帝　以　罪
秕　莠　夏　徒　勢　師　受　用　布　矯

3 honouring and obeying the appointment of Heaven. The king of Hea was an offender, falsely pretending to the sanction of supreme Heaven, to spread abroad his commands among the people. On this account God viewed him with disapprobation, caused *our* Shang to receive His appointment, and employed you to enlighten the multitudes of the people.

4 III. "Contemners of the worthy and parasites of the powerful,—many such followers he had indeed, *but* from the first our country was to the sovereign of Hea like weeds among the springing corn,

sit in dust and ashes very strongly conveys the idea of misery. 表正萬國，-表= 'to serve as a signal to,' *i.e.*, by example and all personal ways; 正= 'to correct,' *i.e.*, by laws and institutions. 纘禹舊服=繼 禹舊所服行, 'to continue what Yu of old time practised and did.' 兹率厥 典，奉若 (a verb, as in Can. of Yaou, p. 3) 天命,—Gaubil translates—'en suivant ses loix, c'est suivre celles de ciel,' making 厥 refer to Yu, and 厥典='his laws.' Medhurst does the same. They are both wrong. If we are to find an antecedent to 厥, it must be 天 and not 禹. Wang Ts'eaou says well:— 上言天意如此，故此言王 于此，惟循其常道以順天, 'Above it has been said that such is the mind of Heaven, and hence it is here said, that the king in this course is only pursuing its regular way to be obedient to Heaven. 3. 矯誣 上天,—矯 and 誣 are often found together. They both denote, 'falsification,' but the latter has the idea of 'slandering' as well. 帝用不臧-用, as in the 'Speech at Kan,' p. 3, *et al.*,= 'on this account;' 臧 善, here taken actively, 'to approve.' 帝, the personal name, the Judge and Ruler, very evidently, takes the place here of the vague

phrase—'high Heaven.' 式=用, 'to use,' 'to employ.' The 'Daily Explanation' uses 使, 'to cause,' for it. 用爽厥師,-爽 =明, 'to enlighten,' used probably with reference to the 有夏昏德 of last par.

Jŏ-keu calls attention to the manner in which this paragraph appears in Mih-tsze, who has quoted it in every one of his chapters, called 'Against prevailing views of the Decrees or Appointments of Heaven' (非命篇). First we have—於仲虺之告曰，我聞 于夏人，矯天命布命于下， 帝伐之惡，襲喪厥師. Next it is—我聞有夏人，矯天命布 命于下，帝式是惡，用闕師. The third time we have—我聞有夏人， 矯天命于下，帝式是增，用 爽厥師. It seems absurd to argue from these passages against the genuineness of the present text.

Ch. III. Pp. 4—6. The Announcement continued.—That T'ang was called by men to do as he had done. P. 4. *It was necessary for T'ang to dethrone Kĕĕ in order to his own preservation.* 簡賢附勢，實繁 有徒,—Medhurst translates :—'*The sovereign of Hea* contemned the wise and attached himself to the mighty, which substantially increased his followers.' Gaubil has the same view. But they are both wrong. The 'Daily Explanation'

東征西夷怨南征、
伯仇餉初征自葛、
彰信兆民。○乃葛
過不吝克寬克仁
懋賞用人惟己改
利德懋懋官功懋
不邇聲色不殖貨
言足聽聞。○惟王
于非辜矧予之德
小大戰戰罔不懼

五節　六節

and blasted grains among the good. *Our people*, great and small, were in constant apprehension, fearful though they were guilty of no crime. How much more was this the case, when our *prince's* virtues made them a theme *eagerly* listened to! *Our king* did
5 not approach to *dissolute* music and women; he did not seek to accumulate property and money. To great virtue he gave great offices; to great merit he gave great rewards. He employed others as *if their abilities were* his own; he was not slow to change his errors. Rightly indulgent and rightly benevolent, from the display *of such virtue* confidence was reposed in him by the millions of the people.
6 "When the chief of Kŏ showed his enmity to the provision-carriers, the work of punishment began with Kŏ. When it went on

paraphrases:—夏王既用者,已皆同不簡慢惡而道其所任,阿附權勢寶多,又之人肇我邪于我邪,哲濟徒泉有夏云云.—I put a comma after 肇, and take it adverbially,—'from the first.' 我邪 is then in the nominative, the subject of the sentence; and 于有夏 = 'in relation to—or simply to—'the ruler of Hea.' The 'Daily Explanation' makes 于有夏=于有夏之間, 'in the country of Hea.' But 有夏 is 'the holder,' and not the country, 'of Hea.' The whole meaning, moreover, comes out much better on the view I have taken. It sounds strange to have Shang likened to weeds and blasted grains; but it was only Kĕĕ who was thus affected by the presence of Shang. The point of comparison is the detestation such things awaken in the mind of the husbandman.
秕 is not 'chaff,' as Medhurst has it, but 穀之不成者, 'the grain that has not ripened.' It is to be distinguished from the 稗 which

Mencius mentions, VI., Pt. I., xix. 矧子之德,言足聽聞,—Gan-kwŏ read this passage without a stop.—'How much more when our virtues and words became sufficient to attract attention!' Choo He approved of putting a comma at 德, and making 言足聽聞 a clause by itself. I have followed this view in the translation. 5. *A description of T'ang's virtues.* Medhurst puts all this paragraph in the imperative mood,—'Only let your Majesty not become too familiar with music and women,' &c., &c.;—this is wrong in grammatical construction, and not pertinent to the context. Gaubil translates in the indicative mood, which is correct, but in the present tense, which is wrong. Chung-hwuy is describing the virtues of T'ang, which had attracted universal regard to him, and made the people long that he would dethrone Kĕĕ. Wang K'ang-t'ang (王肯堂) says:—此言湯德足人聽聞之寶,乃指為諸侯時言之, 'This speaks of the virtues of T'ang when he was one of the princes of the empire.'
6. *A reference to T'ang's former exploits, to show how the people desired him.* See Mencius, I., Pt. I., xi. 2; III., Pt. II., iii., 2—5; and VII., Pt. II. iv. 3. Read also the notes on those

北狄怨曰奚
獨後予攸徂
之民室家相
慶曰徯予后
后來其蘇民
之戴商厥惟
舊哉。○^{七節}佑賢
輔德顯忠遂
良兼弱攻昧
取亂侮亡推

in the east, the wild tribes of the west murmured; when it went on in the south, those of the north murmured:—they said, 'Why does he make us alone the last?' To whatever people he went, they congratulated one another in their chambers, saying, 'We have waited for our prince;—our prince is come, and we revive.' The people's honouring *our* Shang is a thing of long existence.

7　　IV. "Show favour to the able and right-principled *among the princes*, and aid the virtuous; distinguish the loyal, and let the good have free course.　Absorb the weak, and punish the wilfully blind; take their States from the disorderly, and deal summarily with those going to ruin.　Thus overthrowing the perishing and strengthening what is being preserved, how will the States all flourish!

passages.　　The Tsin compiler, it is said, made up this passage from Mencius, and Mencius moreover, is quoting from one of the lost Books, the T'ang Ching or 'Punitive Expeditions of T'ang.'　Mencius, however, does not particularize any Book, but only quotes generally from the Shoo.　I can well believe that he does quote from the T'ang Ching, and also that Chung-hwuy does the same,—if, indeed, we need to suppose any quotation in Chunghwuy's case.　He adduces facts and speeches which were flying about through the mouths of the people at the time.

Ch. IV. THE SPEECH CONCLUDED.—COUNSELS TO T'ANG TO HELP HIM TO PRESERVE THE POPULARITY AND THE THRONE WHICH HE HAD GAINED.　　Ch'in Leih (陳櫟) says:— 'The shame of T'ang was the natural feeling of his mind, when he thought of the position which he occupied, as a minister who had effected a revolution and taken the place of his sovereign.　Ch'ung-hwuy, in dissipating that feeling, was at first led to praise T'ang, but then he became anxious lest the feeling of shame should give place to one of exultation and pride, and concluded by admonishing him;—such is the way in which a great minister should lead on his sovereign in the right path' (see the 集說 on the first par).　　7. 佑賢輔德,—有才德兼備,是謂賢者, 'those who are largely endowed both with talents and virtue are the *heen*; 有積善 行仁,是謂有德者, 'those who have

accumulated good deeds and shown benevolence are the *tih*.'　'Aid the virtuous,' *i.e.*, reward them, honour them, encourage them to virtue in every way. 遂良,—奉公守 法,是謂良者, 'those who seek the common weal and keep the laws, are the *lëang*;' 遂 'to accord with,' 'to make to feel comfortable;' here it denotes every arrangement which could encourage the good in their course.

兼弱,—'the weak' are princes incapable of managing their affairs.　They are to be put under a powerful neighbour, or have a 'resident' located with them (after our Indian fashion) from the court. 攻昧,—the 'Daily Explanation' says:—'Punish them, and strip them of a portion of their territory.' 侮亡,—see Mencius, I., Pt. II., iv. 6, 樂酒無厭謂 之亡. The 亡 are those who are utterly lost to all virtue, and in the way to certain ruin. 侮 is 'to contemn.'　Such princes are to be dealt with summarily and at once.

推亡,—the 亡 here has a slighter meaning than in the clause above, and embraces the 弱, 昧, 亂, and 亡; while the 推 applies to 兼, 攻, 取, and 侮.　Similarly 固存 extends to the first four clauses.

莫　得　昆　禮　民　昭　九　昌　亡
已　師　子　制　以　大　族　○八節　固
若　者　聞　心　義　德　乃　德　存
者　王　曰　垂　制　建　離　日　邦
亡　謂　能　裕　事　中　王　新　乃
好　人　自　後　以　于　懋　萬　其

8   "When *a sovereign's* virtue is daily being renewed, he is cherished
throughout the myriad States; when he is full of his own will, he is
abandoned by the nine classes of his kindred.   Exert yourself, O
king, to make your great virtue illustrious, and set up the *pattern
of the* Mean before the people.   Order your affairs by righteousness;
order your heart by propriety:—so shall you transmit a grand
example to posterity.   I have heard the saying:—'He who finds
instructors for himself, comes to the supreme dominion; he who says
that others are not equal to himself, comes to ruin.   He who likes
to ask becomes enlarged; he who uses *only* himself becomes small.'

This par. is partially and imperfectly quoted
in the 左傳 three times.   The first is under
the 12th year of duke 宣; the second, under
the 14th year of 襄; and the third, under the
30th year also of Sëang.   See the arguments
that have been raised on the first quotation
against the genuineness of this Book, in Ming-
shing's 後案, and the reply of Maou K'e-
ling, in the 'Wrongs of the old Text of the Shoo,'
Book. V, upon the 'Announcement of Chung-
hwuy.'   The quotations certainly prove that we
are not to look for verbal accuracy in passages
adduced from the classics in the 左傳, and
I will add other ancient Books.   8. The above
paragraph contained counsels of administration; in this the minister becomes more personal,
and tells T'ang what he must do in the government of himself.   德日新......乃離.
—these are general propositions, the personal
application of which commences with the next
clause—王懋昭大德.   Ts'ae ingenious-
ly suggests that the inscription about daily
renovation on T'ang's bathing-tub, 'Great Learning,' C., ii. 1, may have been in consequence
of Chung-hwuy's remark here—德日新
建中于民,—comp. 允執厥
中, in the Counsels of Yu, p. 15.   以義
制事, 以禮制心,—'righteousness' is
what the judgment of the mind determines to

be 'right' in reference to what is beyond ourselves; 'propriety' is the regulation of our own
feelings and behaviour, in accordance with all
the Heaven-established relations of society.
垂裕後昆,—in the Counsels of Yu, p.
18, we had 昆 in the sense of 'afterwards.' Here,
joined with 後, the phrase 後昆 = 'future
futurity,' 'future ages.'   The 'Daily Explanation' paraphrases the clause:—且非特
可建中于民也,即垂諸後
世,凡子孫之欲制事制心而有
者,其家法自足相承云云
餘裕矣,予聞云云,—all this
is intended to inculcate humility on T'ang.
王,—low. 3d tone, 'to exercise, or come to exercise, the imperial authority;'—it often occurs
in Mencius.   莫已若者,= 莫若
已者,—an instance of the negative adverb
attracting the pronoun to itself.

In Seun-tsze, 堯問篇, we find 其在
仲虺 (must be for 虺) 之言也曰, 得
諸侯者王,得師者存,得友而
者自爲得疑者亡,自爲謀
者霸得者存
莫已若者亡 And in Leu Puh-wei,
Lew Hëang, and other later writers, we have

問　自　小。呼、終、始　禮、暴、天　保
則　用。○　慎　惟　殖　覆、欽、道、天
裕、則　鳴　厥　其　有　昏　崇　永　命。

9　"Oh! he who would take care for his end must be attentive to
his beginning. There is establishment for the observers of propriety,
and overthrow for the blinded and wantonly indifferent. To revere
and honour the way of Heaven is the way ever to preserve the
favouring regard of Heaven."

Chung-hwuy's words, much to the same effect.
Of course the impugners of the 'Old Text,' seize
on the discrepancy between this and what we
read in the Shoo to discredit it. Maou K'e-
ling contends that 得友者霸, &c.,
are Seun-tsze's own addition; and we may
suppose have been quoted from him by subsequent writers. But in the text Chung is
quoting from a saying common in his time.
We need not suppose that he quotes the whole
of it, but only so much as suited his purpose.
It was easy to enlarge his couplet, and the whole
might be ascribed to him. 9. Chung-hwuy
concludes with words of warning. T·ang must
at once attend to his counsels, and never intermit in the observance of them. 殖有禮,

覆昏暴,—we may take 昏 as＝the 自
棄者, and 暴 as＝the 自暴者, of
Mencius, IV., Pt. I., x. The 'Daily Explanation' paraphrases the two clauses thus:—
福善禍淫, 上天不易之道,
有禮者, 天必篤厚而培植
之, 昏暴者, 天必厭棄而傾
覆之, In par. 5 it is said—王不殖
貨利, with ref. to which the dict. defines
the term by 與生財利; with ref. to its
use in this par., it defines it, after Gan-kwŏ, by
封殖, 'to promote.'

THE BOOKS OF SHANG.

BOOK III. THE ANNOUNCEMENT OF T‘ANG.

明 方 嗟、○ 告 于 克 王一節 湯
聽 有 爾 王二節 萬 亳 夏 歸 誥
予 眾、萬 曰、方。誕 至 自

1   I. The king returned from vanquishing Hea, and came to Pŏ.
There he made a grand announcement to the myriad regions.

2   II. The king said, "Ah! ye multitudes of the myriad regions,
listen clearly to the announcement of me, the one man. The great

THE NAME OF THE BOOK.—湯 誥, 'The
Announcement of T‘ang.' The characters have
been already sufficiently explained. There is
no difficulty in the use of 誥 here. The Announcement was addressed to the whole empire
and delivered, no doubt, in the first place in
an assembly of the princes and nobles. The
Book is one of those whose genuineness in its
present form is controverted.

CONTENTS. The notice in the Preface says
that T‘ang 'had put an end to the sovereignty
of Hea, when he made this Announcement.'
We may consider it a coronation speech on the
inauguration of the new dynasty. The emperor
first shows how he had assumed the dignity
in reverent submission to the will of Heaven,
and goes on to show the sense he had of the
duties devolving on him, and the spirit in which
he would discharge them, calling at the same
time on the princes and people to co-operate
with him. I have divided the whole into three
chapters:—the first, in one par., stating the
occasion of the Announcement; the second, in
4 parr., referring to the downfall of Hea, and his
own elevation to the will of Heaven; and the
third, also in 4 parr., announcing the sort of
sovereign he meant to be, and asking for
sympathy and co-operation.

CH. I. P. 1. THE TIME AND PLACE OF THE
ANNOUNCEMENT. We are led to conceive that
T‘ang was encouraged by the address of Chung-
hwuy, and continuing his march from Ta-
keung, he arrived at Pŏ his capital. We are
still to think here of 'the southern Pŏ,;'—see
on the Name of Book I.

CH. II. Pp. 2—5. THE ANNOUNCEMENT.—
THAT THE OVERTHROW OF HEA AND HIS OWN
ELEVATION WERE BOTH THE WORK OF HEAVEN.
1. HOW THE GREAT GOD HAS MORALLY EN-
DOWED MEN, AND WHAT IS THE DUTY OF THE
SOVEREIGN. 嗟—as at the commencement
of the speech at Kan. 爾 萬 方 有 眾,
明 聽 予 一 人 誥—On 予 一 人,
see on the 'Speech of T‘ang,' p. 1. T‘ang
summons all the people in all the empire to hear
his announcement. They might be considered
as all present with him by their representatives;
and I suppose measures were taken to have
his declaration of views made generally known.
惟 皇 上 帝 降 衷 於 下 民,—
we have had the phrase 皇 天, 'great Heaven,' in the 'Counsels of Yu,' p. 4, and it often
occurs throughout the Shoo; here, and only

一　誥　皇　帝　衷　下　若　恆　克　厥
人　惟　上　降　于　民　有　性　綏　猷

God has conferred *even* on the inferior people a moral sense, compliance with which would show their nature invariably right. *But* to cause them tranquilly to pursue the course which it would indicate, is the work of the sovereign.

here, I think, we have 皇上帝, though once, Part V., Bk. XII., p. 9, we find 皇天上帝. Medhurst translates here—'the great Supreme'; and Gaubil—'L'auguste Chang-ti,' giving the meaning of the characters Chang and Ti in a note as 'Souverain Maître.' The predicate here, and the interchange of the name with 'Heaven,' sufficiently tell us who 'the august sovereign Master,' the 'great supreme Ruler' is. I always translate 上帝 and also 帝, when used with the same application, by 'God,' believing the radical idea in our word to be the same as that in the Chinese,—the idea of supreme rule. Medhurst translates 衷 by 'the due medium,' after Ts'ae, who himself follows his master Choo He. He's language is that '衷 just is 中' (衷只是中). But what is conferred by God is not the due medium as something without man, but the mind that can appreciate such a standard and rule of duty ;—see the remarks on the title of The 'Doctrine of the Mean.' vol I., pp. 246, 247. Gaubil translates the term by ' la raison.' 'A moral sense' appears to come nearer to the signification than any other term in English I can think of.

Gan-kwŏ defined it simply by 善, 'good,' which Choo He rightly says gives no appropriate meaning. The word occurs not unfrequently in the 國語 in this sense of 'good'=happiness; and twice we have the phrase 降衷, but only =' sending down happiness ;'—see the 晉語, 二, and the 吳語.　若有恆性, —' according with —obeying—*this*, they have a constant nature.' By the 'constant nature' we are to understand what Mencius calls ' the constant heart ;'—see his Works, I., Pt. I., vii., 20, and III., Pt. I., iii. 8. The meaning is as given in the translation. Mencius also enables us to understand why T'ang should specify ' the inferior people,' for he says that 'they are only men of education who, without a certain livelihood, are able to maintain a fixed heart.' T'ang has in his mind's eye the millions of the people, all in contradistinction from ' the one man,' and he says that every one of them has a God-given nature, which, if he obeyed it, would lead him in the path of virtue.　克

綏厥猷惟后,—猷=道, 'the path' or 'course'; 厥猷, 'its course,' is that which the nature points to. Chin Tih-sew says, 'When we intend the nature in itself, we speak of 性; when we intend it in action, we speak of 道' (以體言曰性, 以用言曰道). 綏=安, to give tranquillity—security—to.' This is the business of the sovereign.

In explaining this paragraph Gan-kwŏ is more than ordinarily unhappy. His view of 衷 has been adverted to. At 人 he makes a full stop, and then 若有恆性, 克綏厥猷 is all the predicate of 惟后,—describes what is the business of the sovereign,—to accord, namely, with the constant nature which men have, when he can tranquilly set up the lessons for their course' (順人有常之性, 能安立其道教, 則惟爲君之道).

[The editors of Yung-ching's Shoo pause here to enlarge on the wisdom of T'ang, and his services in completing the doctrine of human nature. Yaou had simply told Shun to hold fast the Mean (Con. Ana. XX. i. 1), and Shun, in transferring the lesson to Yu, had said, 'The mind of man is restless, prone to err ; its affinity for the *right* way is small. Be discriminating, be undivided, that you may sincerely hold fast the Mean.' The whole doctrine about the endowments of the nature, and those endowments as from Heaven, was contained, it is said, in those sentences, but darkly and enigmatically. It was for T'ang to declare the doctrine clearly, showing a profound thoughtfulness, and an intelligence peculiar to himself, beyond what was to be gained from Yaou and Shun.

I think that T'ang is deserving of this eulogium ; the student should not pass lightly from this paragraph to the next. We cannot but admire the distinct recognition of the great God, the Father of man's spirit, the Former of all men for a life of virtue. There is then recognized the proneness of men to go astray, and the sovereign is called on, by the position in which God has placed him, to correct their errors, and keep them right. The whole doctrine of human nature is not here, but there is much of important truth, from which we must start in guiding the Chinese to a knowledge of that doctrine. A hard task is assigned to the sove-

惟后。○夏王
滅德作威以
敷虐于爾萬
方百姓爾萬
方百姓罹其
凶害弗忍荼
毒並告無辜
于上下神祇
天道福善禍
淫降災于夏

3　"The king of Hea extinguished his virtue and played the tyrant, extending his oppression over you, the people of the myriad regions. Suffering from his cruel injuries, and unable to endure the wormwood and poison, you protested with one accord your innocence to the spirits of heaven and earth.　The way of Heaven is to bless the good and to punish the bad.　It sent down calamities on *the House of* Hea, to make manifest its crimes.

reign, and no account is taken of the fact that he is as prone to go astray himself as any of the inferior people; but it was not an ordinary mind which could thus conceive of what a sovereign should propose to himself. The lessons of T'ang here are the same which Mencius expounds at length, and vindicates in the first Part of his sixth Book. They have the same excellences and the same deficiencies.]

P. 3.　*How the last ruler of Hea had failed to fulfil his duty, and brought on himself the wrath of Heaven.* 滅德,—comp. 敗德, 'Counsels of Yu,' p. 20, and 顛覆厥德. 'Pun. Expedition of Yin,' p. 4; but the phrase in the text is stronger then either of those passages. Këë had cast from him that 'benevolence,' which is the greatest of the virtues, and acc. to Mencius, the grand characteristic of humanity. 萬方百姓,—see on the 'Can. of Yaou,' p. 2, where a distinction is made between 萬方 and 百姓, the former having a more extensive signification than the latter. In the text the phrases are co-extensive. 百姓 must = our 'the people.' We are not to lay stress on the 'hundred.' It is used indefinitely. When a people are surnamed, considerable progress has been made in civilization. 弗忍荼毒,—荼 is the name of a bitter herb; 毒 is used for 'poison.' An old form of 毒 shows it formed from 虫 instead of 毋, so that its original meaning was probably 'venom.' The two terms together denote 'smarting pain,' 'suffering.' 告無辜于上下神祇＝上下＝天地. Comp. 'Can. of Yaou,' p. 1, and 'Coun-

sels of Kaou-yaou,' p. 7. 上下神祇＝天神地祇;—see the note on 'Can. of Shun,' p. 23. 神 and 祇 may be considered in themselves synonyms. The dict. defines 祇 by 地神; but in usage they denote the spirits of heaven and of earth respectively. In the text, the people appear before us crying out in distress to all superior powers. T'ang himself immediately represents 'Heaven' as responding to their cry. They called on they knew not whom or what　Ts'ae refers in illustration to a passage in the 'History of Keuh Yuen' (屈原傳; the 集傳 simply says 屈原曰, which is a mistake. See the 84th Bk. of the 'Historical Records'), which is worth giving at greater length than he does;—天者人之始也,父母者人之本也,人窮則反本,故勞苦倦極未嘗不呼天也,疾痛慘怛未嘗不呼父母也. 'From Heaven man derives his beginning; from his parents he grows as his root. When a man is brought to extremity, he turns back to his root, and thus it is that when men are toiled, embittered, and worn out, we hear them always calling upon Heaven, and when they are sick, pained, afflicted, and grieved, we hear them always calling on their parents.' 淫, as opposed here to 善, has the general sense of 'bad,' 'evil;'—see 'Counsels of Yu,' p. 6. 降災,—these 'calamities' are to be understood of the convulsions of nature and various strange phenomena which preceded the fall of Këë.

以彰厥罪。○

肆台小子，將

四節
天命明威不
敢赦，敢用玄
牡，敢昭告于
上天神后，請
罪有夏、聿求
元聖、與之戮
力，以與爾有
眾請命。○ 上
五節

4　"Therefore, I, the little child, charged with the decree of Heaven and its bright terrors, did not dare to forgive *the criminal*. I presumed to use a dark coloured victim, and making clear announcement to the spiritual Sovereign of the high heavens, requested leave to deal with the ruler of Hea as a criminal. Then I sought for the great sage, with whom I might unite my strength, to request

P. 4. *How T'ang felt himself called on, and prepared himself, to punish the crimes of Kee.*
肆＝故, 'therefore.' 將＝奉 or 承, 'to bear,' 'to have received.' 奉 and 將 are used together in the 'Punitive Expedition of Yin,' p. 5. 天命明威,—the 'Daily Explanation' paraphrases this by 天命之顯然可畏者, 'the conspicuous terrors of the charge of Heaven.' 玄牡,—under the Hea dynasty they preferred in their victims of sacrifice a dark colour. Under the Shang, it was the reverse ; their victims were white. At this time T'ang continued to follow the practice of Hea. K'ang-shing assigns another reason, not so good, for the use of the dark victim, —see the 後案, *in loc.* 上天神后,—Ts'ae by 神后 understands 后土, 'Sovereign Earth.' Lin Che-ke does the same. He says :—神后者后土,皇地祇也, '"The spiritual Sovereign" is the Sovereign Earth, the great spirit of the earth.' In this way the text is equivalent to the 上下神祇 of the last par. I translate upon a different view, having reference to the form in which this passage appears in the Confucian Analects, XX. i. 3, where for 上天神后 we have 皇皇后帝. In Mih-tsze, moreover, who also quotes T'ang's language, we have only 上天后. 聿求元聖 —聿＝遂, 'then;' 元聖, 'the great sage,' is to be referred to T'ang's principal adviser and minister, E Yin ;—see on the next Book. 戮力＝同力. 戮 is here used in

the sense of 勠. The two characters are found interchanged. 以與爾有眾請命,—this is paraphrased in the 'Daily Explanation:'—以與爾萬方百姓,請更生之命于天. A good portion of this paragraph is found in the Con. Ana., as already referred to, but with some considerable variations ; and with the addition of p. 8, also with variations. The same portion with the same and other additions is found in the works of Mih-tsze ;—see the Prolegomena to Mencius, pp. 116, 117. The rest of the par. is also found with a variation in another part of Mih-tsze. In the second of his chapters 'On Honouring men of Talents and Virtue' (尚賢中), we find 湯誓曰,聿求元聖與之戮力,同心以治天下. These words, moreover, are given as from 'The Speech of T'ang,' and not from the 'Announcement,' while the rest of the paragraph is quoted by him as 'Words of T'ang,' (湯說), without reference either to 'Speech' or 'Announcement.' To add to the perplexity of the subject, Ho An, quoting K'ung Gan-kwŏ's comment on the passage in the Analects, makes him say that Mih-tsze quotes the 'Speech of T'ang' in the same way as it appears in the text there. I do not see my way clear to an explanation of all these difficulties. The passages of the Shoo quoted in the 20th Bk. of the Analects are brought together in a very loose and irregular manner. As to the comment given by Ho An there from Gan-kwŏ, which speaks of Mih's quoting from the 'Speech of T'ang,' Mih does not say that the passages in the text of the Analects are from that 'Speech,' but only 'Words of T'ang.' Moreover, the additions in Mih would make us refer the language of T'ang not to the time of the 'Speech,' nor to the

天孚佑下民、
罪人黜伏、天
命弗僭、賁若
草木、兆民允
殖。○俾予一
人、輯寧爾邦
家、茲朕未知
獲戾于上下、
慄慄危懼、若
將隕于深淵。

5 the favour *of Heaven* on behalf of you, my multitudes. High Heaven truly showed its favour to the inferior people, and the criminal has been degraded and subjected. Heaven's appointment is without error;—brilliantly *now* like the blossoming of flowers and trees, the millions of the people show a true reviving.

6　III. "It is given to me, the one man, to give harmony and tranquillity to your States and Families; and now I know not whether I may not offend *the powers* above and below. I am fearful and trembling, as if I should fall into a deep abyss.

time of the 'Announcement' but to a time subsequent to both, towards the close of the seven years of drought which followed his assumption of the empire. If all the discrepancies tell against the genuineness of the 'Announcement,' they tell as much against the 'Speech,' as it is found both in Fuh-shang's text, and in that attributed to Gan-kwŏ. Keang Shing, aware of this, edits the 'Speech of T'ang' with the addition of the par. from the Analects, and of the sentence 聿求元聖、云云, from Mih-tsze. But if he take one part from Mih, why should he not take the whole?

We need not wonder that we should meet with such difficulties. Our course seems to be to state them, and where no satisfactory solution of them presents itself, to leave them, without reasoning from them against the modern text or the ancient.

P. 5. *The righteousness of T'ang's dethronement of Kёĕ proved by the issue, and consequent prosperity.* 孚＝信, 'truly.' So 允 in the last clause. Hwang Too (黃度) puts the first clause very plainly:—天佑下民、信矣. 罪人, 'the criminal;' this of course is Kёĕ. 天命弗僭,—僭＝差, 'in error.' 'The appointment of Heaven' is the withdrawal of its favour from Hea, and the conferring of it on Shang,—the calling T'ang to the throne in the room of Kёĕ. 賁若草木、兆民允殖,—this is a passage which has wonderfully exercised the ingenuity of the interpreters. 賁 (read *pe*)＝飾, 'to adorn,' 'to be ornamented.' What is it that the adorning is here predicated of? The

two K'ungs, Gan-kwŏ and Ying-tă, say—'the empire.' The language of the former is :—'The evil-doer being cut off from the empire, all is brilliantly adorned, and beautiful as flowers and trees, while the people truly enjoy their life.' Choo He takes the clauses as epexegetical of the preceding 天命弗僭, and the whole ＝'What Heaven appoints is entirely right ;— the world of things and the world of men are made beautiful and happy by it.' The editors of Yung-ching's Shoo give a great variety of views, several preferable, they say, to that of Gan-kwŏ, but none so good as that of Choo He. I prefer to abide by the oldest view.

Ch. III. Pp. 6—9. T'ANG'S FEELINGS AND PURPOSES IN THE POSSESSION OF THE THRONE, AND WISH FOR THE CO-OPERATION OF HIS PRINCES AND PEOPLE. 6. 俾予一人,—this clause and the next would seem to flow on from something preceding, and in some editions it is given as belonging to p. 5, in which case 上天 would be the nominative to 俾. Whether we do so join it, or take the 俾 as I have done in the translation, the 'gift' must be understood as from Heaven. 茲朕未知獲戾于上下,—茲, 'now,' might very well be taken as beginning a new par. 戾＝罪. 上下,—as in par. 3. Gan-kwŏ makes the whole to be a humble expression of doubt in T'ang's mind whether he had really been right in dethroning Kёĕ,—'I do not know whether I may not have offended,' &c. But we must suppose T'ang to have now done with Kёĕ. The prec. chapter shows him sufficiently assured on the subject of his dealings with him. Mih-tsze, in the passage referred to on p. 4, has

一人有罪、無以
罪、在予一人、
心、其爾萬方有
惟簡在上帝有之、
朕躬、弗敢自赦、
朕弗敢蔽、罪當
天休。○爾有善、
各守爾典、以承
匪彝、無卽慆淫、
凡我造邦、無從

七節

八節

7　"Throughout all the States that enter on a new life under me, do not, *ye princes*, follow lawless ways; make no approach to insolent dissoluteness: let every one observe to keep his statutes:—that so 8 we may receive the favour of Heaven.　The good in you, I will not dare to conceal; and for the evil in me, I will not dare to forgive myself;—I will examine these things in harmony with the mind of God.　When guilt is found anywhere in you who occupy the myriad regions, it must rest on me.　When guilt is found in me, the one man, it will not attach to you who occupy the myriad regions.

未知得罪于上下.　7. We are to understand that here T'ang addresses the princes of the different States. This is clear enough from 凡我造邦......各守爾典.　造邦,—the 'Daily Explanation' says that this phrase ═新造之邦, 'newly established kingdoms,' adding:— 侯邦惟舊, 商命惟新, 悉與更始, 故曰造邦, 'The princes and their States were old, but the rule of Shang was new, and they were all with it making a new beginning,—hence the phrase 造邦.'　卽═就 'to approach to.'

In the 國語, 周語, 二, we have the following passage:—先王之令有之曰, 天道賞善而罰淫, 故凡我造國, 無從非彝, 無卽慆淫, 各守爾典, 以承天休.

8. This par. is closely connected with p. 2. There T'ang gives his very high estimate of the duties of the sovereign; here he says how he would try to come up to it. There he lays it down that the sovereign has to lead the people in the right path, and hence he says here that for all that is wrong among them he must be accountable.　'I will not dare to conceal it,'—the meaning is that virtue and talents will not go with him unrewarded.

惟簡在上帝之心,—Medhurst translates this:—'I shall only submit to the inspection of the supreme mind.' In his 'Dissertation on the Theology of the Chinese,' however, he renders—'The inspection of these things rests with the mind of the Supreme Ruler.' Gaubil construes in the same way:—'Tout est marqué distinctement dans la cœur du Chang-ti.' In the Analects I have translated:—'The examination of them is by Thy mind, O God,' which is not sufficiently definite. But the meaning is not exactly as thus represented; the present translation is more accurate. 惟簡 connects the clause closely with what has preceded, so that we must understand the 簡, or 'examination,' as predicated of T'ang himself, and 在上帝之心 as laying down the rule by which he will be guided in it. Choo He says well:—'Heaven knows all our good and all our crimes. It is as if Heaven noted them down and numbered them up. Your good deeds are all before God, and my evil deeds will also be all before Him.' T'ang declares that he will judge himself and others righteously,—in harmony with the judgment of God. 無以爾萬方═于爾萬方何與焉. On the manner in which this par. appears in quotations, see on par. 4.

爾　方.　鳴九　尙　時　乃　有
萬　○　呼.　克　忱、　亦　終。

9　"Oh! let us attain to be sincere in these things, and so we shall likewise have a happy consummation."

P. 9. 尙克時忱.—時＝是, referring to what has been said in the three prec. paragraphs on the obligations of the sovereign and the princes; 忱＝信 or 誠, 'sincere.'

乃亦有終.—有終, 'have an end,' *i.e.*, our dynasty will have a long and happy course.

[In the 'Historical Records,' Sze-ma Ts'een, after giving the 16th paragraph of the Preface, gives a fragment which we should suppose, from his usual practice, was a part of the 'Announcement of T'ang.' Keang Shing, indeed, edits it as being the only portion of the real Announcement that remains. Though not concurring in that view, I have thought it well to append the fragment here:—

至　毋　后　羣　告　諸　侯　於　東　郊
不　乃　予　事　力　勤　於　民、　有　功
大　梟　古　日　其　毋　予　怨、　於　汝、
陶　乃　禹　平　其　有　功　其　勞　于　外,
乃　爲　民、　濟、　爲　江、　東　南　爲　淮、
民　西　萬　播　修　四　瀆　已　后　有
百　殖　農　于　功　尤　降　咸　公
后　故　民、　民、　當　帝　昔　立
大　其　與　乃　不　百　（？土）、
有　予　弗　可　姓　言　作
不　曰,　勉　不　之　亂　先
怨　我　女　國　在　王　毋
。　This

may be translated:—'In the third month, the king came himself to the eastern suburb, and announced to all the princes and the nobles,—' see that you all achieve merit, and vigorously discharge your duties. *If you do not*, I will severely punish you, and put you to death; do not murmur against me.' He said, 'Anciently, Yu and Kaou-yaou laboured long without, and performed meritorious service for the people, who were enabled to dwell in tranquillity. On the east there was the Këang; on the north the Tse; on the west, the Ho; on the south,' the Hwae. These four great streams were brought to order, and the people were able to dwell. *Then* my lord Tseih instructed them how to cultivate the various kinds of grain. These three Kung all achieved merit on behalf of the people and were enfeoffed. Formerly Ch'e-yew and his officers stirred up rebellion among the people, and *Hwang-te* disallowed him, and held him as guilty. The words of the former kings

should act as goads to us.' He said, 'Have no unprincipled ways in your kingdoms. *If you have, and I punish you,* do not murmur against me.'

Sze-ma Ts'een adds—'Thus he gave charge to the princes.' It would be a waste of space to make any remarks on such a farrago]

CONCLUDING NOTE. We here take leave of T'ang, the one, perhaps, of all the ancient princes of China who gets the strongest hold of our sympathies and esteem. Dr. Gutzlaff has said well:—' From his frequent invocations of Shang-te, we might be led to believe that he was a pious prince, who knew something of the true God.' (China Opened, Vol. I., p. 306). His mild but able government of his paternal State drew to him the attention of all the people suffering from the tyranny of Këĕ. The universal voice called him to do the work of the avenger, and to assume the sovereignty of the empire. He dethroned the oppressor, but not without some misgivings, the natural workings of compassion in a high-toned generous mind. His conception of the imperial duties was high, and he bent himself with hearty earnestness to discharge them. Here the Shoo stops, and none of the lost Books contained anything of his history after his assumption of the throne.

According to the 'Standard Annals,' his reign terminated B.C. 1753, so that his sway over the empire lasted only 13 years. The first 7 of them were a season of trial and calamity. No rain fell. Famine was the consequence of the drought. The sufferings of the people were intense. The issues of the mint were freely distributed among them, but money was of little use when grain was scanty. It was suggested at last, we are told, that some human being should be offered in sacrifice to Heaven, and prayer for rain presented at the same time. 'It is for the people,' said T'ang, 'that rain needs to be sought. If a man must be the victim for such an object, I will be he.' He then fasted, cut off his hair and his nails, and in a plain carriage drawn by white horses, clad in white rushes, in the guise of a sacrificial victim, he proceeded to a grove of mulberry trees, and there prayed, asking whether the calamity was owing to any failure in his government, or misemployment of officers, or extravagance in palaces, or excessive devotion to beauty, or the practice of bribery, or allowance of calumniators. He had not done speaking when a copious rain fell over several thousand *le*.

This account is doubtless much embellished, but through the cloud of exaggeration we can see the generous sovereign sympathizing with the general distress, fasting, and praying for the removal of the calamity.

According to the current chronology, T'ang was succeeded by his grandson, T'ae-kĕă;—see on the next Book par. 1.

THE BOOKS OF SHANG.

BOOK IV. THE INSTRUCTIONS OF E.

祖之成德以訓 伊尹乃明言烈 總已以聽冢宰、 群后咸在百官 祗見厥祖、侯甸 于先王奉嗣王 月乙丑、伊尹祠 惟元祀十有二 一節 伊訓

1   I. In the 12th month of the first year, on *the day* Yŭe-ch'ow, E Yin sacrificed to the former king, and presented the heir to the throne reverently before his ancestor. All the princes from the domain of the nobles, and the imperial domain, were present; the various officers *also* were in attendance with their several duties to receive orders from the prime minister. E Yin then clearly described the accomplished virtue of the meritorious ancestor for the instruction of the *new* king.

NAME OF THE BOOK.—伊訓, 'The Instructions of E.'   E was the chief minister of T'ang, and was to him almost what Shun had been to Yaou, and Yu to Shun, and Yih to Yu. Mencius gives him his place among sage ministers and counsellors as 'the one most inclined to take office' (V., Pt. II., i). And this was from no facility of temper, or desire for the gains of office. He reasoned:—'Heaven's plan with mankind is that they who are first informed should instruct those who are later in being informed, and they who first apprehend principles should instruct those who are slower in doing so.' 'He thought,' says Mencius, 'that if there were any of the common men and women who did not enjoy such benefits as Yaou and Shun

conferred, it was as if he himself pushed them into a ditch.'

Having this character of being so fond of employment, the romancers of the Chow dynasty embellished his history accordingly. He was a native of Sin (莘), the present Shen Chow of Ho-nan, and in Mencius' time the story went that when T'ang was marrying a daughter of the House of Sin, E Yin managed to go to Shang in her train, and got himself taken notice of by T'ang through his skill in cookery. Mencius denies the account, and says that E was a farmer on the lands of Sin, delighting in the principles of Yaou and Shun, and ready to spurn an offer of the empire, if it were made to induce him to do anything contrary to those principles. T'ang heard of his wisdom and ability, and sent messengers with costly presents, inviting him to his court. Twice their visit to him was fruitless, but when they came a third time, being satisfied of T'ang's sincerity, he said, 'Had I not better make this prince a prince like Yaou or Shun, and this people like the people of Yaou or Shun;'—see Men. V., Pt. I., vii. T'ang received him with great deference, and reposed in him entire trust. He sent him to the court of Këě, hoping that his counsels might move the emperor to change his evil course. It was in vain. Five times E went backwards and forwards between Këě and T'ang, till, convinced that the former was incorrigible, he moved T'ang to raise the flag of rebellion, and take the empire for himself. After T'ang's death he continued the watchful guardian of his throne. Of the way in which he dealt with T'ae-këă we shall have to speak in treating of the next Book. The surname of 伊 was derived from the river E, near which he and his parents lived. Leu Puh-wei tells a story of a princess of Sin finding an infant, when she was picking mulberries, in a hollow mulberry tree. This was E. Her father gave him to his cook to bring him up, and on inquiry it was found that his mother had lived on the banks of the E. One might she dreamt, during her pregnancy, that a spirit told her that the sun would discharge a flood of water, and that she must run off to the east. When she rose in the morning, she looked to the sun, and lo! it was as in her dream. Giving the alarm to her neighbours, she fled, and after running ten *le*, she paused to look back, when she saw the town overflowed with water, and was herself changed to a hollow mulberry tree,—the same in which the infant was found! E's name is generally understood to have been Che (摯). Sze-ma Ts'een says it was O-hăng (阿衡);—see next Book, p. 1. Yin (尹) was his 字 or designation. 訓, 'instructions;' this we saw, on the name of Pt. III., Bk. III., was the name of one of the divisions of the Shoo. The 'instructions,' acc. to Lin Che-k'e are of three kinds:—lessons of antiquity transmitted for the guidance of future ages; lessons of ancestors intended specially for the guidance of their posterity; and lessons of faithful ministers like E Yin, addressed to their sovereigns.

According to the Preface, p. 18, in the year that T'ang died, E Yin made three Books, of which these 'Instructions' were one. Of the other two only the names remain; and the genuineness of this is disputed.

CONTENTS. T'ae-këă comes to the throne of his grandfather, young and of unstable character. T'ang's counsellor and friend uses the privilege of his years and station to advise the young monarch,—warns him by the fate of Këě, and stimulates him with the example of T'ang. I have divided the Book into four chapters: the first, in one par., giving the occasion when E Yin delivered his 'lesson;' the second, parr. 2—4, showing how the throne had come down from the great Yu, and was now possessed by T'ae-këă, the scion of another line; the third, parr. 5—7, celebrating the example of T'ang; and the fourth, par. 7., warning T'ae-këă of the fate he would incur if he neglected the advice given to him.

CH. I. P. 1. THE OCCASION OF E's INSTRUCTIONS. 惟元祀十有二月乙丑,—Hea had used 歲 for 'year;' in the Shang dynasty they preferred the char. 祀. 元祀 must mean the first year of T'ae-këă. The Hea dynasty had begun the year with the month 寅, the first of spring. The Shang removed the commencement of the year a month back, beginning it with 丑. In this way the 12th month of the text is understood to be the 12th month of the Hea year, and the first month of the Shang, so that these instructions of E were delivered in the first month of the year after the death of T'ang. This is the view of Ts'ae and the scholars generally of the Sung dynasty; and Ts'ae goes largely into the proof of what seems a strange thing,—that while the Shang and Chow dynasties differed from Hea as to the commencement of the year, they yet often numbered the months as Hea had done. Maou K'e-ling denies the argument of Ts'ae, and maintains that the 12th month of the text is the 12th month of the Shang year,—the 12th month also of the year in which T'ang died. At the same time, 元祀 is with him the first year of T'ae-këä. According to him, under the Chow dynasty, the new sovereign succeeded of course to the throne immediately on the death of his predecessor, but his first year was reckoned only from the first month of the year which followed. The practice of the Shang sovereigns was different. A month after the death of an emperor, the style of the year was changed, and what remained of it was reckoned to the first year of his successor. This was the view of Gan-kwŏ and Ying-tă. According to it T'ang must have died in the 11th month of the year, and the Instructions of E were delivered in the month after.—I will not undertake at present to decide between these views;—see on the next Book, Pt. ii., 1.   What day of the month 乙丑 was we cannot tell. Had it been the first, we should have read 朔, instead of these two characters.

伊尹祠于先王,奉嗣王祇見厥祖.—祠=祭, 'to sacrifice.' The term is used specially for the sacrifices offered in spring in the ancestral temple, but we cannot think of any such ceremony in the text. The 'heir-king' of course is T'ae-këě, and 先王 and 厥祖, are in the singular,—'the former king,' and 'his ancestor,' referring to T'ang.

[This seems to be the place to notice the historical difficulty which there is respecting the succession to T'ang. The Shoo gives no hint of any individual's having interposed between him and T'ae-këă. Indeed the language of the Preface,—'After the death of T'ang, in the first year of T'ae-këă, E Yin made the Instructions of E.' &c., seems to forbid the supposition that T'ae-këă did not immediately follow his grandfather on the throne. The current chronology

災︒有德懋后夏古嗚○于
山天罔厥先方先呼︑曰二節王︒

2　II. He said, "Oh! of old, the earlier sovereigns of Hea cultivated
earnestly their virtue, and then there were no calamities from Heaven.
The spirits of the hills and rivers likewise were all in tranquillity;

has been arranged accordingly. T'ang's death
is entered ʙ.ᴄ. 1753, and the reign of T'ae-kĕă
commences the following year, ʙ.ᴄ. 1752.

When we refer to the 'Historical Records,'
however, it is said after the mention of the death
of T'ang:—'His eldest son, T'ae-ting, died
before he could come to the throne, and a
younger son, Wae-ping, succeeded. He was
the emperor Wae-ping (是爲帝外丙).
Wae-ping died after reigning three years, and
was succeeded by a younger brother,—a third
son of T'ang's,—called Chung-jin. He was the
emperor Chung-jin (是爲帝中壬).
Chung-jin reigned four years, and on his death
E Yin raised to the throne T'ae-kĕă, son of
T'ae-ting, and the eldest grandson of T'ang.
He was the emperor T'ae-kĕă, (是爲帝
太甲). Whatever other authority Ts'een
may have had for this account, there can be
no doubt he took it chiefly from Mencius, V.,
Pt. I., vi. 5; and the interpretation which he
gives of Mencius' words is the most natural,
though the passage is not unsusceptible of
another interpretation;—see the Works of Mencius, pp. 236, 237. Those who follow the natural
reading of Mencius in preference to the natural
reading of the Preface to the Shoo, hold, of
course, that the mourning of T'ae-kĕă, which
the text supposes, was for Chung-jin and not
for T'ang. There is a difficulty;—that must be
admitted. For myself, I should follow the
Preface, and the standard chronology, holding
that T'ae-kĕă immediately followed T'ang upon
the throne.]

What sacrifice E Yin performed to T'ang
can hardly be determined. In the Books of the
'Former Han' (律歷志,下), we find
the first part of the paragraph, with the
addition of 朔 after 丑, and the clause 誕
資有牧方明 after 先王. Possibly
this clause may be an addition of Pan Koo, the
Han chronicler, but the whole passage shows
that he understood the sacrifice to be the
solemn one to God, offered at the winter solstice.
Be this as it may, and I do not think it unlikely,
the conducting T'ae-kĕă to appear before his
ancestor was a different ceremony. The appearance was, I suppose, before the coffin of T'ang.
侯甸羣后咸在,—侯甸＝侯
服甸服;—see 'The Tribute of Yu,' Pt.
ii., pp. 18, 19. Perhaps these two domains are
mentioned by synecdoche for all the five; or
there may not have been time for the nobles

who were more remote to reach the court.
The mention of the presence of these princes
shows us that the occasion was the solemn
inauguration of T'ae-kĕă as successor to T'ang.
百官總已以聽冢宰,—
see the Analects, XIV., xiii., 2. I there said
that 總已 was a difficult expression, and I
do not find it easier now. Gaubil does not try
to translate it. Medhurst mistakes the meaning, and has:—'The various officers gave a
general account of their affairs, in order to wait
for orders from the prime minister.' The 'Daily
Explanation' paraphrases:—百官各總攝
已職,以聽命于冢宰. Is the phrase
simply = 'all and each'? 烈祖,—烈
= 'ardent,' as in Pt. III., Bk. IV., p. 6; here it
is defined by 'meritorious' (功), and Ying-tă
says, 'T'ang had achieved the lasting service
of settling the empire, and was the founder of
the dynasty of Shang;—hence he is styled 烈
祖.'

[De Mailla's view of this paragraph is seen
in the expansion which he gives of it, Vol. I., p.
176.—'Having resolved that T'ae-kĕă should
succeed to T'ang, E Yin, as prime minister
and as president of the tribunal of rites,
assembled all the princes who were at court,
and made them recognize T'ae-kĕă. It was
then the 12th month, and the funeral ceremonies for T'ang were not yet performed. E
Yin ordered them with great magnificence,
and then brought T'ae-kĕă, whom he placed on
a throne which he had prepared for that purpose in the hall of the ancestors of the Shang
dynasty, saluted him emperor, and made him
receive in this character the homage of the grandees, the vassal princes, the mandarins and the
people. Thereafter, addressing himself to the
young emperor, he exhorted him to imitate the
virtue of the great prince whom he succeeded,
and gave him these advices.'——]

Ch. II. Pp. 2—4. Tʜᴇ Iɴsᴛʀᴜᴄᴛɪᴏɴs ᴏғ E.—
Lᴇssᴏɴs ғʀᴏᴍ ᴛʜᴇ Hᴇᴀ ᴅʏɴᴀsᴛʏ; ғʀᴏᴍ ᴛʜᴇ
ʀɪsᴇ ᴏғ T'ᴀɴɢ; ғʀᴏᴍ T'ᴀᴇ-ᴋᴇᴀ's ᴏᴡɴ ᴘᴏsɪᴛɪᴏɴ
ᴀᴛ ᴛʜᴇ ᴄᴏᴍᴍᴇɴᴄᴇᴍᴇɴᴛ ᴏғ ʜɪs ʀᴇɪɢɴ.　2.
有夏先后,—'the former emperors possessing Hea.' Lin Che-k'e says that we are to
understand all the Hea sovereigns before Kĕĕ.
That cannot be. K'ung-kĕă has been singled
out for his wickedness; only Yu himself would
fully answer to E's description. It suits his
purpose to speak of a line of good princes; and
many of them would be considered so in com-

昭聖武代虐 | 惟我商王布 | 三節 朕哉自亳。○ | 造攻自鳴條、 | 手于我有命、 | 皇天降災、假 | 其子孫弗率、 | 魚鼈咸若、鳥獸 | 川鬼神、亦莫 不寧、暨鳥獸

and the birds and beasts, the fishes and tortoises, all realized the happiness of their nature. But their descendant did not follow *their example*, and great Heaven sent down calamities, employing the agency of our *ruler*, who had *received* its favouring appointment. The attack *on Hea* may be traced to Ming-t'eaou, and our *attack on it*

3 began in Pŏ. Our king of Shang had brilliantly displayed his sacred prowess. When for oppression he substituted his generous gentle-

parison with Kĕĕ. 方 is an adverb, and stress is to be laid on it. The dict. defines it by 今, 'now.' It = 'then,' 'so long as.' 咸若=皆順適其性 而得遂其生, 'all quietly followed their nature, and had the enjoyment of their life.' From 山川 down to this describes fancifully, but not without a truth to which the mind responds, the happy condition of the well-governed empire. Ch'in Ta-yew (陳大猷) directs attention to the last par. of the 1st chap. of the 'Doctrine of the Mean,'—致中和, 天地位焉, 萬物育焉. 于其子孫,—by 子孫 Kĕĕ is pre-eminently intended. Perhaps E had other earlier and unworthy sovereigns in his mind as well, but Kĕĕ was the impersonation of all the wickedness of Hea. 于='in the case of.' 皇天降災,—Lin Che-k'e illustrates this by saying that 'the spirits of the hills and rivers could no longer be in tranquillity. Hills fell; rivers were dried up; strange sounds were emitted. Birds and beasts, fishes and tortoises, no longer followed their nature, and many of them were changed into monstrous and prodigious things.' I quote this, as showing how the Chinese share in the feeling of a sympathy between the course of nature and the character and doings of men, so that 'the whole creation groans' and writhes to be delivered from the curse of human wickedness. 假手于我有命,—'borrowed a hand from our having the appointment.' Lin Che-k'e expands the clause well:—假手于我商有天

命之成湯 使之伐夏救民, 以爲天吏.

[Up to this point the paragraph is found, but in a very different form, in the only remaining part of Mih-tsze's Book on 鬼 (明鬼篇, 下). He gives it as from the 'Books of Shang:' 一嗚呼, 古者有夏, 方未有禍 之時, 百獸貞蟲, 允及飛鳥 莫不比方, 矧在人面, 胡敢 異心 山川鬼神 亦莫敢不 寧, 若能共允任 天下之合 下土之葆. Mih's text is evidently corrupt; yet he could hardly have the 'Instructions of E,' as we now read them.]

造攻, 云云,—compare Mencius, V., Pt. I., vii. 9. There we have 'the palace of Muh' (牧宮) instead of Ming-t'eaou. But from the Preface, par. 12, we know that Ming-t'eaou was not far from the cap. of Kĕĕ. It was there probably that he had the palace of Muh, where his orgies alienated the people from him, and awoke the vengeance of Heaven. [There was another Ming-t'eaou towards the east, where Shun died, according to Mencius, IV., Pt. II., i, 1.] 'Our attack commenced (哉=始) in Pŏ,'—the meaning is that the virtues of T'ang, pleasing to both Heaven and men, first displayed in Pŏ, marked him out as the punisher of Kĕĕ, and the successor to the empire.

P. 3. 聖武,—'his sacred prowess.' 'It is not simply said,' observe the commentators, 'showed his *prowess*, but his *sacred* prowess. The expression intimates that his prowess came from the valour of virtue and righteousness, by

以寬，兆民允懷。○今王嗣厥德[四節]，罔不在初，立愛惟親，立敬惟長，始于家邦，終于四海。○嗚呼[五節]！先王肇修人紀，從諫弗咈，先民時若，居上克明，為下克忠，與人不

4 ness, the millions of the people gave him their hearts. Now your Majesty is entering on the inheritance of his virtue;—every thing depends on *how* you commence *your reign*. To set up love, it is for you to love your elders; to set up respect, it is for you to respect your relatives. The commencement is in the family and State; the consummation is in the empire.

5 III. "Oh! the former king began with careful attention to the bonds that hold men together:—he listened to expostulation, and did not seek to resist it; he conformed to *the wisdom of* former people; occupying the highest position, he displayed intelligence; occupying an inferior position, he displayed his loyalty; he allowed *the good qualities* of others, and did not seek that they should have every talent;

which he was able to destroy oppression, deliver the people, and give repose to the empire.'

P. 4. 今王嗣厥德,—T'ae-keă was inheriting the throne. But it was a throne that had been acquired by virtue, and E Yin therefore puts his succession before him in this way. 初=即位之初, 'the beginning of his reign.' The other observations of the paragraph are the same as the lessons set forth at so much length in the concluding chapters of 'The Great Learning.'

Ch. III. Pp. 5—7. THE INSTRUCTIONS CONTINUED.—THE CHARACTER AND REGULATIONS OF T'ANG. 6. 肇修人紀,—Ts'ae says that the 人紀 are 三綱五常, 'the three relations' [prince and minister, husband and wife, father and son] 'and five constant virtues' [benevolence, righteousness, propriety, &c.]. Somewhat differently, Chang Kew-shing tells us:—'Sovereign and minister, father and son, elder and younger brother, husband and wife, elders and juniors, with friends:—all these relationships are held together by propriety and righteousness which are called the "bonds of men"' (有禮義以相維謂之人紀). We are to understand by 人紀 the fundamental relationships of society, and the moral virtues by which they are securely and happily maintained. Kĕĕ had disregarded these virtues and disorganized society; the first

work of T'ang was—unconsciously to himself—to exhibit the virtues and reform society. All the rest of the paragraph is an expansion of this clause. 先民時若=先民是順, 'with the former people he was accordant.' By the 'former people' are intended sage men of ancient times, the lessons of whose wisdom had been transmitted. Ying-tă says that 民 is used to indicate that the wisdom was from 'the people.' But the character need not have that force;—compare Pt. V., Bk. XII., p. 11,—相古先民有夏. The sentiment is that T'ang did not consider that all wisdom was with himself, but was ever ready to learn. 爲下克忠,—T'ang's dethroning Kĕĕ, and taking the empire to himself, would seem to be contrary to this affirmatiom of his loyalty, but it was not of his own will merely, nor till he had used every method of remonstrance and advice, that he took the field against his sovereign. 與人不求備—求備,—see Con. Ana., XIII., xxv.; 與人=與人之善, 'he allowed to men their good qualities.' 與=許; the 檢身 in the parallel clause shows that we are to take 與 as a verb. 以至于萬方—, this language well indicates how T'ang was

淫色巫宮位○人惟以求
風恆風酣曰制俾艱至備
敢于敢歌敢官輔哉于檢
有遊有于有刑于。有身
侮畋殉室恆儆爾敷萬若
聖時于時舞于後求邦不
言謂謂于有嗣哲茲及

in the government of himself, he seemed to think he could never sufficiently attain.—It was thus he arrived at the possession of the myriad regions. How painstaking was he in these things!

6 He extensively sought out wise men, who should be helpful to you

7 his descendants and heirs. He laid down the punishments for officers, and warned them who were in authority, saying, 'If you dare to have constant dancing in your palaces, and drunken singing in your chambers,—that is called sorcerers' fashion; if you dare to set your hearts on wealth and women, and abandon yourselves to wandering about or to hunting,—that is called the fashion of dissipation; if you dare to contemn the words of sages, to resist the loyal and

carried on, as by the force of circumstances, and not by any ambition of his own, to the supreme dominion. 茲惟艱哉— the 艱 suggests the idea that the clause does not celebrate T'ang's surmounting all difficulties that opposed his possession of the empire, but his being able to display the virtues which insured his possession of it. Seun-tsze, in his Book on the 'Ways of a Minister' (臣道篇), quotes a passage from the Shoo, which must be another form of the first part of this paragraph. He has:—書曰,從命 而不拂,微諫而不倦,爲上 則明,爲下則遜. 6. 敷= 廣, 'widely.' Ch'in King (陳經) says:— 'T'ang attained the empire with the greatest difficulty, and therefore his anxious thoughts about it went very far forward; it was right he should seek for men of talents and virtue to hand it down to his posterity.' 7. Lin Che-k'e says;—'Although T'ang had sought out wise men to be a help to his descendants, he was still afraid lest the men whom they employed should only think of securing themselves in their offices, and not attend to their duty to remonstrate with and guide their sove-

reign. He therefore instituted these punishments for officers to admonish them.' E Yin, in calling the young emperor's attention to such ordinances, had regard, no doubt, to the vices and errors into which he saw that T'ae-kĕä was prone to fall.

巫風,—Ying-tă observes that the wizard is called 覡 and the witch 巫, but that 巫 is applicable both to men and women. These persons had intercourse with spiritual beings, and hence the service of spirits is called 巫 (事鬼神曰巫). We have only to think of the frenzied excitement of the ancient sibyls to see how strong and contemptuous is the language of T'ang in reference to the officers of this fashion. 風 is here = 'ways,' 'fashion.' Properly it denotes 'the wind;' thence it is applied to what is exciting and influences others.

殉 is here in the sense of 求, 'to desire,' 'to seek for.' 淫風,—淫=過, 'excess.' 遠耆德,比頑童,—遠 (3d tone) = 疎遠, 'to be distant to and keep at a distance;' 比=狎比, 'to be familiar

逆忠直、遠耆
德比頑童時
謂亂風惟茲
三風十愆
士有一于身、卿
家必喪邦必君
一于身、國必
亡臣下不匡、
其刑墨、其訓　八節
于蒙士。○嗚

upright, to put far from you the aged and virtuous, and to be familiar with procacious youths,—that is called the fashion of disorder. Now if a high noble or officer be addicted to one of these fashions with their ten evil ways, his Family will surely come to ruin; if the prince of a country be so addicted, his State will surely come to ruin. The minister who does not *try to* correct *those vices in the sovereign* shall be punished with branding.' These rules were minutely enjoined *also* upon cadets in their lessons.

and keep company with.' 頑 is paraphrased by 頑鈍無恥, 'obstinate, stupid, and shameless.' The case of Rehoboam with the counsellors of Solomon and his own young companions will occur to most readers. 三風十愆,—the 'three fashions' are those just mentioned, and the 'ten vices' are the evil ways enumerated in connection with them:—two under the sorcerers' fashion; and four under each of the other two fashions. 必喪,—家 is here very evidently used for the whole establishment of the noble or officer. 臣下不能匡,其刑墨,—the 'Daily Explanation' paraphrases:—若天子而犯此風愆,則在位有匡扶之責者也,皆當盡言直諫而忠言,君以墨刑加之,其是則必食祿, to the effect that any officer suffering the emperor to proceed in any of those evil ways without remonstrating with him should be punished with branding. With this the words of T'ang terminate. We are to understand the concluding clause as from E Yin himself. 其訓于蒙士,—the dict., with ref. to this passage, explains 蒙 by 蒙稚卑小之稱, 'the designation of the young and little.' 蒙士 are the sons

of officers and nobles being trained in schools to fit them for the duties of mature life. 'They were minutely instructed,' says Ts'ae, 'in these duties, that when they entered on office they might know to administer reproof.'

[Mih-tsze has a passage in his only remaining chapter 'Against Music' (非樂篇上), where he quotes part of this par. and the next, but evidently his text is very corrupt. He says:—先王之書,湯之官刑有曰,其恆舞于宮,是謂巫風,其刑君子出絲二衛小曰上不喪其家必壞,黃徑二乃言孔亡,上帝弗常,其邢似二伯倖九有以亡,其家必壞,舞常有百殃,人降之百殃,嗚呼弗降,上帝必順。

From this corrupt and mutilated passage we perceive there was a book in Mih's time known as 'The Penal Laws of T'ang.' Of course if such a book was really made by T'ang, we can suppose that E Yin should be quoting from it here. Yen Jŏ-keu contends that such a book was made towards the close of the Shang dynasty, and not by T'ang, and concludes, therefore, that our present 'Instructions of E' bear upon them in this place the manifest stamp of forgery. But he has no direct evidence to show that we should refer 'The Penal Laws of T'ang' to a period several hundred years later than that emperor. All his reasoning on the point is singularly weak.]

呼．嗣王祗厥身、

念哉聖謨洋洋、

嘉言孔彰惟上

帝不常作善降

之百祥作不善

降之百殃爾惟

德罔小萬邦惟

慶爾惟不德罔

大墜厥宗。

8　IV. "Oh! do you, who *now* succeed to the throne, revere *these instructions* in your person. Think of them!—Sacred counsels of vast importance, admirable words forcibly displayed. *The ways of God are not invariable;*—on the good-doer He sends down all blessings, and on the evil-doer He sends down all miseries. Do you be but virtuous, without consideration of the smallness *of your actions*, and the myriad regions will have cause for congratulation. If you be not virtuous, without consideration of the greatness *of your actions, they* will bring the ruin of your ancestral temple."

CH. IV. P. 8. THE INSTRUCTIONS CONCLUD-ED.—A SOLEMN ADMONITION TO T'AE-KEA TO FOLLOW THE EXAMPLE OF T'ANG, AND TAKE HEED TO HIS WAYS. 祗厥身,—we might translate this—'be reverent of his person,' but the commentators generally prefer to make the lessons of the last par. the object of 祗, and expand the passage by 敬之于身, 'respect them in his person.' 洋洋,—'vast;' comp. 'Doctrine of the Mean,' xvi., 3. 孔=大, 'great,' or 'greatly.' 爾惟德云云,—Lin Che-k'e has said on this passage:—K'ung of Han says, "Cultivate your virtue, and not on a small scale; then the whole empire will have cause for congratulation. Do what is not virtuous, and that not on a great scale, and you will overthrow your ancestral temple. These are the instructions of E, showing his true royalty." The meaning of K'ung was that the emperor's virtue must be extremely great, and then he would make the myriad regions happy, while for the overthrow of his ancestral temple it was not necessary that his want of virtue should be great; and this advice showed the true devotion of E Yin. K'ung of T'ang lost this meaning of Gan-kwŏ, and explains it thus:—爲善無小, i.e., all states will rejoice in your little virtue, and how much more will they do so if it be great! 爲惡無大, i.e., a little wickedness will overthrow your ancestral temple, and how much more will great wickedness do so! These two expressions—罔小罔大 are antithetic, but their meaning is the same. Lin then endeavours to show that Gan-kwŏ's interpreta-tion is the only one admissible. The antithetic phrases are certainly somewhat perplexing. I consider that the one of them supposes also the other. 罔小 is equivalent to—'be it small or large,'; and 罔大 to—'be it large or small.' The *tendency* of virtue and vice, without reference to their amount or degree, is as several-ly represented.

THE BOOKS OF SHANG.

BOOK V. T‘AE KEA. PART i.

太甲上

一節　惟嗣王不惠于阿衡。

二節　○伊尹作書曰先王顧諟天之明命以承上下神祇社稷宗廟罔不祗肅天監厥德用集大命撫綏萬方惟尹躬克左右厥辟宅師肆嗣王丕承基

1 　I. The king, on succeeding to the throne, did not follow *the*
2 *advice of* A-hăng. *He, that is,* E Yin, then made the following
writing:—'The former king kept his eye continually on the bright
requirements of Heaven, and served and obeyed the spirits of
heaven and earth, of the land and the grain, and of the ancestral
temple;—all with a reverent veneration. Heaven took notice of
his virtue, and caused its great appointment to light on him, that
he should soothe and tranquillize the myriad regions. I, Yin, then
gave my assistance to my sovereign in the settlement of the people.
And thus it is that your Majesty, inheriting the crown, have become
charged with the line of the great succession.

NAME OF THE BOOK.—太甲, 'T‘ae-kĕa.'
This was the name, we saw on the 1st par. of
the last Book, of T‘ang's grandson and successor.
The names of all the Shang emperors after
T‘ang are made up of the first series of the
cyclical characters, called the 'Heavenly Stems'
(天幹), with another distinguishing character added. This was the fashion of the
dynasty. The Book is divided into three

Parts, each of which is called a *p‘ëen* (篇). The
first Part might stand very well by itself; the
second and third have nothing in their contents
specially to require a separation of them from
each other. Lin Che-k‘e observes that the
division of several of the Books of the Shoo into
Parts arose from their length. Being written
or engraved originally on tablets of wood or
bamboo, very many of these could not be kept
together so as to be read with comfort. A book

was therefore tied up in two bundles, marked 上, 下, or in three, marked 上, 中, and 下, as the case might be. The division was made for convenience' sake, rather than from regard to any difference in the matter. This is only partially correct. There are some Books that are not divided, which yet are longer than others that are.   Sze-ma Ts'een gives the name as 太甲訓 'The Instructions delivered to T'ae-kĕä.' It may have been current during the Han dynasty under that title. It does belong to the division of the Shoo which embraces 'Instructions.'   The genuineness of the Book is called in question.

CONTENTS. E Yin finds the young sovereign disobedient to his counsels, and insensible to repeated remonstrances. On this the minister takes a high-handed measure, removes the emperor from his palace and companions, and keeps him in a sort of easy confinement, near the grave of his grandfather, all the period of mourning. T'ae-kĕä becomes penitent and truly reformed. This is the subject of the first Part. Delighted with the change, E Yin brings T'ae-kĕä back in state to the capital. He congratulates him on his reformation, and the emperor makes a suitable reply; after which E again proceeds to his favourite work of counselling and advising. This first Part is divided into ten parr., which are again arranged in three chapters. The first, containing 3 parr., tells of T'ae-kĕä's waywardness, and how E Yin called him in a letter to follow the example of his grandfather. The second, in 4 parr., tells of T'ae-kĕä's continued misconduct, and how E Yin by word of mouth expostulated with him. The third, in 3 parr., shows us the minister's patience worn out, with the bold measure which he took, and its happy effects.

CB. I. Pp. 1—3. T'AE-KEA'S WAYWARDNESS. E YIN REMONSTRATES WITH HIM IN WRITING.

1. 不惠于阿衡,—惠=順, 'to accord,' 'to be obedient.' Compare its use in Pt. II., Bk. I., 17; Bk. II., 5; Bk. III., 8. 阿衡,—this is said by Sze-ma Ts'een to have been the name of E; and it saves the translator considerable trouble to follow this view. The more common opinion, however, and that followed by Ts'ae, is that the characters were the title of an officer—the prime minister in fact—under the Shang dynasty. 阿 is taken as＝倚, and the name is then＝'support and steelyard,' 'buttress and director.' Others make 阿＝保, which gives the same result. The name, it is said, was given to E Yin, because of his services to T'ang and to the empire. 2. E Yin presses in writing the example of T'ang's religious reverence upon T'ae-kĕä. 伊尹作書,— this is the first time that we read in the Shoo of any communication addressed otherwise than by word of mouth. Ch'in Leih suggests that perhaps the presenting written or engraved memorials commenced at this time. We are not to think of E Yin as using pencils, ink, and paper. His memorial was on one or more slips of wood or bamboo, lightly engraved, or described perhaps with some colouring matter on the plain surface. Lin Che-k'e observes that down to the Han

dynasty the memorials were all upon such slips, and were presented tied up in black bags. 先王顧諟天之明命,—see 'The Great Learning,' C., i., 2. The meaning of 諟 is not well ascertained. It evidently serves to give emphasis to 顧. Choo He and the Sung school generally take 明命, as referring to 'man's nature,' the bright gift conferred on and entrusted to him by Heaven, and the statement is that 'T'ang assiduously cultivated his virtue.' This is twisting the Shoo to support the dogmas of a school. T'ang had regard to the will of Heaven in reference to the whole course of his life and duty. That led him to cultivate his personal virtue, but it took him out of himself also, to do what his circumstances called him to; more especially did he feel it was required of him by Heaven that he should be reverent and devout,—religious, according to his lights. We may believe that T'ae-kĕä was glaringly neglectful of all religious worship. 承＝奉, 'to serve.' 以承, 'so as to serve;' i.e., his regard to the requirements of Heaven did actually make him a regular and reverent worshipper. 天監厥德,用集大命,—commentators call attention to the manner in which the first of these clauses responds to 顧天之命. T'ang looked up to Heaven, and Heaven looked down on him. 用＝'and so;'—we have had several instances of this usage. 集, 'to collect;' here ＝'to make to light upon.' Compare the She-king, Pt. III., i., Ode II., 4,—天監在下,有命既集. 惟尹躬克左右厥辟宅師,—尹躬='Yin's-self,' 'Yin himself.' According to Leu Puh-wei and others, E's name was Che (摯), but he here speaks of himself as Yin. We must suppose that he was styled 尹, because of his services, and better known among the people as 'the Regulator,' 'the Corrector,' than by his name. Here he accepts the designation. 辟 (peih),—'a sovereign.' It was applied to the emperor and to princes of States. 師＝眾, 'the multitude,' 'the people.' Wang Ts'ëaou says:—'The phrase 宅師 follows from the preceding 撫綏. What is meant by settling—locating—the people, is that after their oppressions were taken away and a gentle rule exercised, they were arranged so that every man was in his proper place' (處之各得其所). 丕承基緒,—緒, comp. III., Bk. III., p 8; 基 is 'a foundation,' that on which any thing rests. Joined with 業, it denotes 'an inheritance,' 'a transmitted property.' The phrase in the text has the same meaning. Ts'ëaou says on the

尹　庸　忝　爾　終　克　終　周　見　緒。
乃　罔　厥　厥　嗣　有　其　有　于　○惟
言　念　祖。　辟　王　終、　後　終、　西　尹三節
曰、　聞。　○　辟　戒　相　嗣　相　邑　躬
先　○四節　不　哉　亦　王　亦　夏、　先
王　伊五節　辟、　祗　罔　罔　惟　自

3 "I have seen it myself in Hea with its western capital,—that when its sovereigns went through a prosperous course to the end, their ministers also did the same; but afterwards when their successors could not attain to such a consummation, neither did their ministers. Take warning, O heir-king. Reverently use your sovereignty. The sovereign, if you do not play the sovereign, you will disgrace your ancestor.'

4 II. The king would not think *of these words*, nor listen to them.

5 On this E Yin said, "The former king, before it was light, sought to have large and clear views, and then sat waiting for the morn-

clause that it means that T'ae-kĕä had come 'to the myriad regions, all established, and to the multitudes of the people, all settled.'

3. *That the minister is more dependent on his sovereign for prosperity than the sovereign on his minister.* T'ae-kĕä had probably, half in insolence and half in flattery, been saying that he might follow his heart's lusts, while the government was safe in the hands of such a minister as E. 西邑夏,—'Hea of the western city.' The reference must be to Gan-yih, the capital of Hëa, which was farther west then Pŏ, the cap. of Shang. 自周 有終,—the 周 here has occasioned much perplexity. On the authority of an expression in the 國語, Gan-kwŏ and others since him have explained it by 忠信, 'loyal and true.' Choo He remarked that to say—以忠信 自周, 'by loyalty and faith to perfect one's-self,' would be well enough, but that to define 周 as meaning 'loyal and true' was not allowable; and that the characters 自周 in the text were unintelligible. Wang Pih (王柏), foll. by Kin Le-ts'ëang (金履祥), thought that for 周 we should read 君, the ancient form of which was 㑆, that might easily be mistaken for 周 The editors of Yung-ching's Shoo

express their approval of this emendation, and I have translated accordingly. 有終,—comp. Bk. II., 9. 祗爾云云,—爾 厥辟—'your that being sovereign.' Compare 君君、臣臣, &c., in Con. Ana., XII. xi. In the Book of Rites, 坊記, p. 22, we find the two last clauses,—厥辟不辟、忝 厥祖, quoted from the Shoo, with an interpretation and application, different from their meaning in E's writing.

Ch. II. Pp. 4—7. T'AE-KEA CONTINUES CARELESS, AND E YIN EXPOSTULATES WITH HIM, AND TRIES TO WIN HIM ON TO WHAT WAS RIGHT.

4. Many put a comma at 庸, and explain it by 常.—'T'ae-kĕä treated E Yin's words as if they were only ordinary and unimportant.' This is Ts'ae's interpretation. Gan-kwŏ, pointing in the same way, explained, —'T'ae-kĕä kept his ordinary way, and did not change.' Choo He proposed to read the paragraph without a stop at 庸, and to take that character in the sense of 用, so that it simply emphasizes the verbs below;—comp. Bk. VIII., Pt. i., p. 2, —王庸作書以誥 I have translated on this view. 5. 昧爽丕顯,—昧 爽, 'the dark and light;'—as we say, 'between the dark and the light,' = 'the grey dawn;'

昧爽丕顯坐以
待旦、旁求俊彥、
啟迪後人、無越
厥命以自覆。○
六節 慎乃儉德、惟懷
永圖。○七節 若虞機
張、往省括于度、
則釋、欽厥止、率
乃祖攸行、惟朕
以懌、萬世有辭。

ing. He *also* sought on every side for men of ability and virtue to instruct and guide his posterity. Do not frustrate his charge *to me*,

6 and bring on yourself your own overthrow. Be careful to strive

7 after the virtue of self-restraint, and cherish far-reaching plans. Be like the forester, who, when he has adjusted the spring, goes to examine the end of the arrow, whether it be placed according to rule, and then lets go;—reverently determine your end, and follow the ways of your ancestor. Thus I shall be delighted, and be able to all ages to show that I have discharged my trust.

丕顯, 'was greatly clear.' Kin Le-ts'eang says well, that the whole clause shows how T'ang kept his eye continually on the requirements of Heaven (此即先王顧諟之功). 俊,—see on 'Counsels of Kaouyaou,' p. 4. 彥＝美士, 'admirable officers.' The 說文 defines it—美士有文人所言也. 旁求……後人,—this shows how T'ang's anxieties were not merely for himself and for the time being. 無越厥命,—無＝毋; 越 is here not＝踰, 'to transgress,' but 墜, 'to let fall,'＝'to bring to nought;' 厥命 is the charge of T'ae-këă which E supposes to have been specially committed to himself by T'ang. 6. T'ae-këă was losing all self-restraint, plunging into extravagance, and thinking only of the day before him;—hence the two admonitions in this par. 乃＝汝. 儉德,—comp. in last Bk., p. 5,—檢身若不及. 7. Gan-kwŏ takes 虞 in the sense of 度, 'to consider,' 'to calculate,' and 若虞機張＝'as when you calculate the adjusting the spring *of your crossbow*.' This is admissible; but Choo He prefers, and I think rightly, to take 虞 in the sense of 虞人, or 'forester.' 機, is defined by 弩牙, the tooth of the cross-bow.' We are

to understand the spring by touching which the instrument was discharged. 括＝矢末, 'the end of the arrow,' which was placed against the string, and on the correct placing of which—its being 合於法度—depended the success of the archery. 欽厥止,—compare 'The Great Learning,' C., iii., 3. 萬世有辭,—Ts'ae explains 辭 by 譽, 'praise,' and makes the clause refer to T'aekëă, ＝'all ages will celebrate you.' Lin Che-k'e makes it refer to E Yin, and ＝'through all ages be able to say *that I have discharged my trust*,' *i.e.*, be able to give an account of myself. The editors of Yung-ching's Shoo rather approve of this view of Lin's. I have followed it, because it retains the proper signification of 辭. I do not know that the meaning which Ts'ae puts on it can be supported by other examples;—comp. 汝永有辭, Pt. V., Bk. XIII., p. 10.

[In the 'Record of Rites,' and the Book called 緇衣 p. 16, we have quite an array of quotations from the 太甲, more or less agreeing with the received text.—太甲曰、無越厥命、以自覆也、若虞機張、往省括于厥度、則釋。 Here par. 6 is omitted. 尹吉曰、惟尹躬天見于西邑夏、自周有終 相亦惟終 Here 吉 is perhaps an error

允德。｜宮居憂克終｜迷。○十節王徂桐｜其訓無俾世｜宮密邇先王｜弗順營于桐｜成子弗狎于桐｜不義習與性｜九節伊尹曰、兹乃｜八節王未克變。○

8, 9　　III. The king was not yet able to change *his course*. E Yin said *to himself*, "This is *real* unrighteousness, and is becoming by practice *a second* nature. I cannot bear to be near *such* a disobedient *fellow*. I will build *a place* in the palace at T'ung, where he can be quietly near *the remains of* the former king. This will be a les-

10 son which will keep him from going astray all his life." The king went accordingly to the palace in T'ung, and dwelt during the period of mourning. In the end he became sincerely virtuous.

for 告, or, more probably, 尹吉 should be 伊尹, and 天 may be for 先.]

Ch. III. Pp. 8—10. T·AE-KEA CONTINUING VICIOUS, E SENDS HIM FROM THE PALACE, AND KEEPS HIM IN CONFINEMENT,—WHICH ENDS IN HIS REFORMATION. 8. 伊尹曰,—曰 is the reflection in E's mind. It is better to take it thus than to expand it with Ying-tă,— 'E Yin announced to all the ministers in the court, saying,'—. 兹乃不義習與 性成—Gan-kwŏ explains this:—習行 不義將成其性, 'the practice of unrighteousness will become his nature.' This is no doubt the meaning, but it gives us no ex-planation to account for the use of the 與. Ts·ae avoids the same difficulty by expanding: —伊尹指太甲所爲乃不義 之事, 習惡而性成者也. If we had 而 in the text instead of 與, the whole would be easy. The 'Daily Explanation' tries to bring out the force of the 與 thus:—習 爲不善, 若天生性成者然, 'he is practising what is not good as if his nature from his birth were so constituted.' Lin Che-k·e treats it substantially in the same way; and I do not see that anything better can be done. 子弗狎于弗順,— 'I will not be near the disobedient.' Such is the natural rendering of the words, and such was the view of them taken by Choo Ho. Ying-tă, however, and Ts·ae, subsequently, thinking this language would be too harsh in E's mouth, softened it down to—'I will not *allow him to be*

near the disobedient.' There is no reason why we should strain the text to avoid the very decided expression of his opinion which E gave, and to maintain in him the Chinese ideal of a hero-sage. He spoke evidently under strong provocation. 營于桐宮,—'T·ung' was the place where T·ang's tomb was. It was, probably, in the pres. dis of Yung-ho (榮河), dep. of P·oo-chow (蒲州), in Shan-se. The site or supposed site of the grave there was washed away by the Fun (汾河), under the Yuen dynasty, when a stone coffin was removed to another position, near which, under the Ming dynasty, an imperial tomb was built. [The sub. dep. of Pŏ (亳), in Gan-hwuy, likewise prefers a claim to include the place of T·ang's grave.] From Mencius, V., Pt. I., vi, 5, we are led to infer that T·ung was the name of a city or district;—nothing is said of it as the place where T·ang had been buried. Ts·ae manipulates the text to 營宮于桐, 'built a palace in T·ung;' and Ying-tă had done the same 營於 桐墓立宮. But why should we use such violence with the language, when we are not compelled to do so in order to make any meaning out of it? The text leads us to suppose that there was already a palace in T·ung. E Yin determined to build or fit up some apartment in it, where T·ae-kĕa might reside,—be confined in fact,—till he gave proof of reformation. 密邇先王其訓,—all the commen-tators take 密邇 as＝親近. We get a better meaning, it seems to me, by taking 密 as＝'secretly,' 'silently.' We do not know what to do with the 其訓. Lin Che-k·e represents E.'s idea thus :—'I will make him dwell there, to be near the former king, and think of his instructions.' Ts'ae has :—'I will make him be near the grave of T'ang, where thinking mournfully morning and night, he may rouse up the good that is in him :—thus I will instruct him.' My translation is more after Ts'ae's view.

10. 居憂,—Gan-kwŏ has 居憂位, 'dwelt in the place of sorrow.' There T'ae-kĕä could not help himself, and had to observe all the established customs of mourning.

CONCLUDING NOTE. [i.] The action of E Yin in dealing with his sovereign has been much canvassed. Mencius was bound on his principles to defend it, and he did not scruple to do so. When Kung-sun Ch'ow asked him whether worthies, being ministers, might indeed banish their vicious sovereigns in this way, he answered, 'If they have the same purpose as E Yin, they may ; if they have not the same purpose, it would be usurpation' (VII., Pt. I., xxxi.). This doctrine is startling, but sound. A man in the position of E Yin must be a law to himself, wherever his actions will not clash with the moral laws of God.

[ii.] According to the Shoo, the confinement of T'ae-kĕä in T'ung took place during the period of mourning, and lasted only to the end of it,—we may say, in round numbers, for three years, as Mencius does. Sze-ma Ts'een gives a different account. We read in the 'Historical Records :'—'When T'ae-kĕä had been on the throne three years, he proved unintelligent and oppressive, paying no regard to the laws of T'ang, and being guilty of all sorts of disorderly conduct. On this E Yin confined him in the T'ung palace for three years, while he himself administered the government of the empire, and gave audience to the princes. When T'ae-kĕä had been in T'ung for three years, he became penitent, reproved himself and returned to good, on which E Yin brought him back to the capital, and resigned the government into his hands. The emperor then cultivated his virtue ; the princes all signified their allegiance ; the people enjoyed tranquillity ; and E Yin, in admiration, made the "Instructions to T'ae-kĕä," in three Parts, in his praise.' We cannot say positively from Mencius that Ts'een's account is incorrect, but we must set it aside, if on no other ground, yet certainly on the authority of the Preface to the Shoo.

THE BOOKS OF SHANG.

BOOK V. T'AE KEA. PART ii.

太甲中

惟二節

十有三祀。

月朔。

尹以冕

服。

王○歸二節作于

書亳。曰。民

1   I On the first day of the 12th month of the 3d year, E Yin took the imperial cap and robes, and escorted the young king back to

CONTENTS OF THE SECOND PART. The confinement of T'ae-këä in T'ung having produced the desired effect, E Yin brings him back with honour to Po, to undertake the duties of the government, and presents him with a congratulatory address on his reformation. T'ae-këä responds with a proper acknowledgment, and asks the continued assistance and guidance of the minister, who on his part is happy to resume his favourite work of delivering instructions.

The first two parr. form a chapter, describing the emperor's return, and giving the address on his reformation. T'ae Këä's penitent reply, in par. 3, forms a second chapter. The remaining 3 paragraphs, in which E resumes his lessons and counsels, on the example of T'ang, and the duties of T'ae-këä, conclude the part with a third chapter.

Ch. I. THE YOUNG KING IS BROUGHT BACK WITH HONOUR TO PO. E YIN CONGRATULATES HIM AND THE EMPIRE ON HIS REFORMATION.

惟三祀十有二月朔,— this note of time follows from that in the 'Instructions of E,' par. 1. Two years have elapsed from that time. The same question arises.— Is the 12th month the 12th month of the Hea year or of the Shang? I am more inclined to believe that in both passages we have nothing to do with the Hea year. T'ang having died in the eleventh month, T'ae-këä had immediately commenced the formalities of mourning for him,—with no sincerity indeed, but yet

nominally. It was now the 26th month since T'ang's death. T'ae-këä was entered into the third year of mourning. At the end of the 24th month it was competent for him to lay aside his sad apparel, array himself in his ordinary robes, and go about all the duties devolving on him. The period of mourning for parents and grandparents is indeed said to be three years; but as the Chinese say that they are three years old, not when they have completed three years of 12 months each, but when they have lived in three years, so T'ae-këä might now, in the 12th month of the 3d year in which he had been on the throne, be considered to have fulfilled the duties of mourning for his grandfather, and take the administration of affairs into his own hands.

Jŏ-keu argues that two years are not enough for all the events that are supposed to have taken place,—the repeated remonstrances with T'ae-këä, his proving himself insensible to advice, his banishment to T'ung, his reformation, and his proving its sincerity. We have not sufficient information to enable us to solve all the difficulties that may be raised; the view of the time which I have followed seems to me more likely then any other;—see the 後案 of Wang Ming-shing, on the one side, and the 尙書廣聽錄, on the other.

冕服,—the distinctive name of the ceremonial bonnet or crown under the Yin or Shang

子不明于德 稽首曰予小 休○王拜手 萬世無疆之 克終厥德實 有商俾嗣王 方皇天眷佑 民罔以辟四 匡以生后非 非后罔克胥

2 Pŏ. At the same time, he made the following writing:—"Without the sovereign, the people cannot have that guidance which is necessary to *the comfort of their* lives; without the people, the sovereign could have no sway over the four quarters *of the empire.* Great Heaven has graciously favoured the House of Shang, and granted to you, O young king, at last to become virtuous. This is indeed a blessing that will extend without limit to ten thousand generations."

3 II. The king did obeisance with his face to his hands, and his head to the ground, saying, "I, the little child, was without under-

dynasty was 冔 (see the Record of Rites, 王制, Pt. V., p, 11). Here, however, the general term 冕 is used. Under the Chow dynasty, the emperor had six diff't. crowns, with robes appropriate to each. In sacrificing to Heaven, he used one kind of crown and robes, in sacrificing to his ancestors, a different kind; &c., (see the Rites of Chow, 卷二十一, 春官, 司服). Whether the practices under the Shang dyn. were the same, we have no means of knowing. The crown was always in the form of a student's cap, with tassels on which pearls were strung hanging down before and behind, except on the occasion of sacrificing to Heaven, when it is said there were no tassels; on the other occasions the number of pendents and pearls and gems varied, and perhaps the colour. As the text does not say for what particular ceremony T'ae-kĕă was now arrayed, though I should judge it was either to perform the great solstitial sacrifice to Heaven, or to announce his entering personally on the duties of the government in the ancestral temple, more need not be said on the crown and robes.

2. 民非后...四方, these clauses show how the people and the sovereign are necessary to one another. The only difficulty is with 胥匡以生. Medhurst translates:—'The people have nothing wherewith they may correct each other so as to preserve their lives'; and Gaubil:—'The people cannot live either in peace or in order.' Medhurst's version appears to be the more literal; but we must deal with 胥 here in the same way as with

相 in the clause 官司相規, 'Pun. Expedition of Yin,' par. 3. [In the Record of Rites, 表記, par. 11, we have the passage quoted—太甲曰, 民非后, 無能胥以寧, 后非民無以辟四方.]

皇天......厥德,—the commentators call attention to the way in which it is here taught that T'ae-kĕă's becoming virtuous was to be ascribed to the influence of Heaven exerted on him. Ts'ae says that 'Heaven secretly drew on his better nature' (陰誘其衷). Shin She-hing (申時行) says:—'In the matter of his thoughts, it was as if Heaven awakened him; in the matter of his actions, it was as if Heaven helped him' (其思也, 若或啟之, 其行也, 若或翼之).

Ch. II. P. 3. T'AE-KEA'S PENITENT REPLY. HE CONFESSES HIS FAULTS IN THE PAST, AND ASKS E YIN TO CONTINUE HIS GUIDANCE TO HIM. 自底不類—不類=不肖; —see 'Doctrine of the Mean,' iv., 1. The 'Daily Explanation' has:—以自入于不肖, 'and thereby entering among the unworthy.' 欲敗度, 縱敗禮,—these words are quoted in the 左傳昭十年. 欲=多欲, 'many desires,' or 'lusts;,

自厎不類欲敗度縱
敗禮以速戾于厥躬
天作孽猶可違自作
孽不可逭既往背于厥師
保之訓弗克于厥初
尚賴匡救之德圖惟
厥終。○〔四節〕伊尹拜手稽
首曰修厥身允德協
于下惟明后。○〔五節〕先王
子惠困窮民服厥命

standing of what was virtuous, and was making myself one of the
unworthy. By my desires I was setting at nought all rules *of
conduct*, and by my self-indulgence I was violating all rules of propriety:—the result must have been speedy ruin to my person.
Calamities sent by Heaven may be avoided, but from calamities
brought on by one's-self there is no escape. Heretofore I turned
my back on the instructions of you, my Tutor and Guardian;—my
beginning has been marked by incompetency. May I still rely on
your correcting and preserving virtue, keeping this in view that
my end may be good!"

4　　III. E Yin did obeisance with his face to his hands, and his head
to the ground, and said, "To cultivate his person, and by being
sincerely virtuous, bring *all* below to harmonious concord with
5　him;—this is the work of the intelligent sovereign. The former
king was kind to the distressed and suffering, as if they were his

縱=縱肆, 'unrestrained indulgence.' Ts'ae
says that 度 has reference to the conduct, the
ends pursued, and 禮 to the behaviour, the
demeanour to others. 天作孽......可
逭,—this is twice quoted by Mencius, with
活 instead of 逭;—see Vol. II., p. 15, and p.
175. In the Record of Rites, however, the Bk.
緇衣, par. 16, we find it exactly as in the
text. 既往=已往. It is an adver-
bial phrase = 'in the past.' 圖惟厥
終,—comp. 有終, 罔終, Part i., p. 3.
　　Ch. III. Pp. 4—6. E Yin resumes his
instructions. 4. *Description of an intelligent sovereign.* 伊尹拜手稽首,—see
on 'Canon of Shun,' p. 17. This humble obeisance was due from the minister to the sovereign.

For the sovereign to pay it to the minister as in
the last paragraph, and as we shall see it hereafter often rendered to the duke of Chow, was
an act of extreme reverence and condescension.
　　On 修厥身 She-hing has well said
that it implies two things:—'the ordering one's
affairs by righteousness' (Bk. II., p. 8), in which
there will be no 'setting at nought, through
lusts, the rules of conduct;' and 'the ordering
one's heart by propriety,' in which case there
will be no 'violating the rules of demeanour.'
允德協于下, 'and to have sincere
virtue harmonizing in *the sphere* beneath.' The
'Daily Explanation,' paraphrases this:—出乎
身而加乎民, 將誠實之德,
孚契于人, 自然人心協和
無不愛戴。　　5. *How T'ang by his kind-
ness and sympathy with the distressed drew the hearts
of all the people to himself.* 子惠困窮,

無聰遠孝豫視罰有罔
斁朕惟接怠乃○有邦不
承明下○烈王邦厥悅
王聽思奉祖懋鄰並
之德恭先無乃徯乃其
休惟視思時德我曰

<small>六節</small>

<small>七節</small>

后
后
來
無

children, and the people submitted to his commands, all with
sincere delight.   Even in the States of the neighbouring princes the
people said, 'We are waiting for our sovereign; when our sovereign
comes, we shall not suffer the punishments *which we now do?*'

6　"O King, zealously cultivate your virtue.   Regard *the example of*
your meritorious ancestor.   At no time allow yourself in pleasure
7　and idleness.   When honouring your ancestors, think how you can
prove your filial piety; in receiving your ministers, think how you
can show yourself respectful; in looking at what is distant, try to
get clear views; have your ears ever open to listen to virtue:—then
shall I respond to the excellence of your Majesty with an untiring
devotion to your service!"

一子 = 'son-ned,' *i.e.*, treated as his children.
並其有邦厥鄰乃曰, Gan-
kwŏ explains this:—湯俱與鄰並有
國, 鄰國人乃曰, 'T'ang and his
neighbours were equally possessors of kingdoms,
but the people of the neighbouring kingdoms
said.' Choo He's representation of the construction is the same:—湯與彼皆有土
諸侯, 而鄰國之人乃曰, 'T'ang
and those were all princes possessing States,
and yet the people of the neighbouring States
said.' They have both caught the meaning.
We read 並其有邦厥鄰 without a
stop.—'Compeers *with him were* those possessed
of States, his neighbours.'　Then 乃曰

= 'but it was said,' *i.e.*, it was said in their
States by their people.　徯我后云
云,—see the quotation of this by Mencius, III.,
Pt. II., v., 4.　　6, 7.　*E Yin exhorts T'ae-këă
to cultivate his virtue after the example of T'ang;
calls his attention to several important points in
which he might make his profiting appear; and
promises his own untiring aid.*　朕承王
之休無斁,—I will receive the excellence
of the king without satiety. The paraphrase
in the 'Daily Explanation' is:—尹承王
之休美益思左右匡救而
不遺其力矣, 其何敢厭斁
哉.'

THE BOOKS OF SHANG.

BOOK V. T'AE-KEA. PART iii.

惟親親.民　惟天無　曰.嗚呼.　誥于王　伊尹申　一節　太甲下
罔常懷.　克敬　　親.克敬　　　申　　下
懷于有　　民　　　　　　　　　　　申

1　I. E Yin again made an announcement to the king, saying, "Oh! Heaven has no affections;—only to those who are reverent does it show affection. The people are not constant to those whom they cherish;—they cherish only him who is benevolent. The spirits

CONTENTS OF THE THIRD PART. In the first three paragraphs E Yin dwells on the high and difficult charge to which the emperor is called; points out how good government is to be secured; and concludes by once more exhibiting T'ang as a model. The next five paragraphs contain various counsels and cautions addressed to T'ae-këä. In the last par. a lesson is given at once to sovereigns and ministers.

This portion of the T'ae-këä was perhaps delivered at a later period than the previous one. There is no allusion in it to the emperor's early follies and vices; there is supposed to be an allusion in the close to E's desire to withdraw from public life. In this way we find a reason for its separation from the previous Part. The compiler arranged his documents according to the knowledge which he had of the date of their contents. To the same effect with these remarks are the observations of Ch'in Ta-yew, which we find in the 集說;—'The "Instructions of E" were made before the faults of T'ae-këä had shown themselves, and the minister, wishing to guard against his tendency to self-indulgence, used language stern and severe. The first Part of the "T'ae-këä" was made when the emperor's faults were showing themselves, and E, not wishing to provoke him, slightly changed his plan, and made his language gentle and insinuating. The second Part was made when T'ae-këä had begun to repent, and E, full of joy and consolation, made his language bland and encouraging. The third

Part was made after T'ae-këä had reformed, and then E, anxious lest perhaps the change should not hold out to the last, fashioned his language so as to convey profound and stimulating exhortation. The consummate words of the great minister, now shallow and now deep, are all to be accounted for in this way.'

Ch. I. Pp. 1—3. THE DIFFICULTY OF RIGHTLY OCCUPYING THE IMPERIAL SEAT; THE RULES OF GOOD GOVERNMENT; THE EXAMPLE OF T'ANG.

1. 惟天無親＝天無所親. 'Heaven has none whom it loves.' We may supply 常 before 親, after the analogy of the clauses below, 一常懷常享; and then the meaning will be that 'Heaven is not invariable in its likings;' and we find this idea expressed very many times in the Shoo and other classical books. There must be a reason, however, why we do not have 常 before 親 in the text, and I conceive it is this.—Heaven stands out to the mind of E as the head of all government, the supreme Power and Authority in the world. To rule, as rule, reverence is due from the ruled; from the ruler we look for justice, not love. He has to do with men not simply as men, but as good men or as bad men, to reward the former and to punish the latter. Hence in the text we have it barely and broadly affirmed that 'Heaven has no affections.' This is not the whole truth, which was held by the ancient

配　時　明　始　同　道　否　艱　享　仁、
上　懋　后。　慎　事　罔　德　哉。　于　鬼
帝、　敬　○　厥　罔　不　亂　○　克　神
今　厥　先　與　不　興　與　德　誠　無
王　德　王　惟　亡、　與　治　惟　天　常
嗣　克　惟　明　終　亂　同　治　位　享.

do not always accept the sacrifices which are offered to them;—
they accept only the sacrifices of the sincere. A place of difficulty
2 is the Heaven-*conferred* seat! Where there are *those* virtues, good
government is realized; where they are not, disorder comes. To
maintain the same principles as those who secured good government
will surely lead to prosperity; to pursue the course of disorder
will surely lead to ruin. He who at last, as at first, is careful as
3 to whom and what he follows is a truly intelligent sovereign.—The
former king was always zealous in the reverent cultivation of his

Chinese, about Heaven, as it is not the whole
truth which is held by us about God; yet as it is
proper for us to speak of God as 'the Lord of
hosts that judgeth righteously,' so the affirmation in the text is properly put forth without
any qualification. 鬼神無常享,
—享 is 'to enjoy,' *i.e.*, to accept the sacrifices
and oblations of the worshipper. We can hardly
make a distinction between 鬼 and 神. Medhurst calls them here—'the demons and spirits.'
Gaubil simply has—'les esprits.' The spirits
of dead ancestors, which might be styled 鬼,
and all other spirits from the highest to the
lowest, which might be called 神, are embraced
in the phrase. E's lesson is that the emperor
as the subject of Heaven has to be reverent; as
the sovereign of the people, he has to be benevolent; as the head of all religious worship, he
has to be sincere. If he be not reverent, Heaven
will punish him; if he be not benevolent, men
will reject him; if he be not sincere, no spirits
will regard him. Well might he add—天位
艱哉. Compare on 兹惟艱哉, Bk.
III., p. 5.

[Chin Tih-sew observes that here for the first
time we have the virtues of reverence, benevolence, and sincerity, announced distinctly and
in their connection and references,—a step in
the development of the doctrine of Yaou and
Shun, Yu and T'ang. The observation is correct. In later times, Confucius, Mencius, and
others, made much of E's lessons.]

2. 德惟治,—the 德 is to be taken in
close connection with the reverence, benevolence,
and sincerity of the prec. par. 治 (3d tone) is
good government realized. In 與治 and 與
亂 the 與 has a verbal force. This appears
from the 慎厥與 which follows. Ts'ae
observes that the 道 or principled course of
good government is spoken of, because though
there may be differences of administrations and
ordinances, required by difft. times, a common
principle will be found underlying all variations.
On the other hand we have only the 事 or
courses of disorder, princes who are going to
ruin doing so as they are hurried on and away
by their several hearts' lusts. 慎厥與,
—'be careful of his concurring.' She Lan says
ingeniously, but with an over refinement :—
'what is intended by 與 is something very
subtle ;—it is the concurring tendency of the
mind.' 惟明明后,—here again is the
redoubled adjective, = a superlative. 3. 先
王,—this of course is T'ang. 懋敬厥
德,—Ts'ae makes this = 'strove to make his
virtue reverent,'—with special reference to the
reverence towards Heaven mentioned in the first
par., and the one of the virtues there specified
being adduced here as inclusive of the other
two. This seems to be straining the language
too much. 克配上帝,—this phrase

人　慮　求　道　言　危　事　逷　若　四節
元　胡　諸　有　逆　○　惟　必　升　有
良　獲　非　言　于　愼　難　自　高　令
萬　弗　道　遜　汝　終　無　邇　必　緒
邦　爲　○　于　心　于　安　○　自　尚
以　胡　嗚　汝　必　始　厥　無　下　監
貞　成　呼　志　求　○　位　輕　若　茲
○　一　八節　弗　必　有　惟　民　陟　哉
　　　　　　　諸　七節　　　五節　　○
　　　　　　　　　　六節

virtue, so that he was the fellow of God.　Now, O king, you have
entered on the inheritance of his excellent line;—fix your inspection
on him!

4　II. "*Your course must be* as when in ascending high you begin
　　from where 'tis low, and when in travelling far you begin from where
5　'tis near.　Do not slight the occupations of the people;—think of
　　their difficulties; do not yield to a feeling of repose on your throne;—
6, 7　think of its perils.　Be careful for the end at the beginning.　When
　　you hear words against which your mind sets itself, you must
　　inquire whether they be not right; when you hear words which
　　accord with your own mind, you must inquire whether they be
8　not contrary to what is right.　Oh! what attainment can be made
　　without anxious thought? what achievement can be made without
　　earnest effort?　Let the one man be greatly good, and the myriad
　　regions will be rectified by him.

has two meanings.　It is spoken of the *virtue* of
a sovereign, so admirable in the present or the
past that he can be described as the mate of God,
—as a sovereign upon earth, the one correlate
of the Supreme Sovereign above.　It is spoken
also of the *honours* of a departed sovereign, exalted to association with God in the great sacrificial
services rendered to him by the reigning emperor.
We are to take the phrase here in the first
meaning.　配上帝 occurs again and again
in the She King; in the Shoo we have it only
in the text, though below we shall meet with
配天,配皇天, in several places.
令緒,—'the excellent line or clue.'　Compare
基緒, Part i. p. 2.
　Ch. II.　Pp. 4—8.　Vᴀʀɪous counsels.
4.　*How T'ae-kĕă's progress in virtue should be
persistent and progressive.*　Comp. in the 'Doctrine of the Mean,' xv. 1, 君子之道辟

如行遠必自邇, 云云.
has commonly the signification of 升, 'to
ascend.'　We must take it here in the general
sense of 'to advance.'　5.　*The emperor
should sympathize with the people's toils, and think
of the perils of his own position.*　無=毋.
民事,—'the affairs of the people,' *i e.*, their
toilsome occupations of husbandry, &c.　惟
難,—Ts'ae expands this by 而思其難,
'but think of their toilsomeness.'　On this
use of 惟, compare 惟幾, 惟康, in the
'Yih and Tseih,' p. 2.　6.　*To end right the
best plan is to begin right.*　7.　*T'ae-kĕă should
judge what he hears not by his own likings or dislikings.　Palatable advice is probably bad; unpa-
latable, good.*　Wang Ts'ëaou observes well
that this is an expansion of 聽德惟聰, in
Part ii., p. 7.　Compare Con. Ana., IX., xxiii.,

陟

休。永功利罔舊辯君
孚邦居以政言罔
于其成寵臣亂以

9 III. "When the sovereign will not with disputatious words throw the old rules of government into confusion, and the minister will not for favour and gain continue in an office whose work is done;—then the country will lastingly and surely enjoy happiness."

and Mencius, II., Pt. I., ii., 17.　　*8. An appeal to T'ae-kĕă from the importance of his influence to be anxiously thoughtful, and earnest in his doings.*

Ch. III. P. 9. E YIN EXPRESSES HIS HOPE THAT THE EMPEROR WILL HOLD ON IN THE IMITATION OF T'ANG, AND INTIMATES HIS OWN INTENTION TO WITHDRAW FROM PUBLIC LIFE. 居成功,—'dwell in accomplished service.' The meaning is as in the translation. Ying-tă says:—'That E Yin addressing his sovereign should turn to speak of the duty of a minister, though his words are general, and announce a great principle, shews that he had himself formed the purpose of retiring.' - Soo Tung-po says:—'The disorders of the empire arise from division between the sovereign and his ministers. When the sovereign proceeds disputatiously to change the old rules of government, the minister becomes afraid; and when the minister, for the sake of favour and gain, presumes on the service he has done, the sovereign comes to doubt him. It is thus that disorder begins.'　　See the 集說.

THE BOOKS OF SHANG.

BOOK VI. BOTH POSSESSED PURE VIRTUE.

保　常、　難　曰、二節　戒　告　政　伊一節　咸
厥　常　諶　嗚　于　歸、　厥　尹　有
位、　厥　命　呼、　德。　乃　辟　既　一
厥　德　靡　天　○　陳　將　復　德

1　I. E Yin, having returned the government into the hands of his sovereign, and being about to announce his retirement, set forth admonitions on the subject of virtue.

2　II. He said, "Oh! it is difficult to rely on Heaven;—its appointments are not constant. *But if the sovereign see to it that* his virtue

NAME OF THE BOOK.—咸有一德, 'Both possessed pure virtue.' This is part of a sentence in the Book itself; and as the object of the whole is to inculcate the cherishing and maintaining of virtue pure and unchanging, the words are taken to form the name or title.

The author of the Book was E Yin, excepting of course the first paragraph, which is merely a note by the historical compiler. There is a controversy, as will be seen from the next note but one, as to whom E Yin was addressing, but the style is of a piece with that of the last two Books. The Book comes under the head of 'Instructions.'

CONTENTS. E Yin having returned the government into the hands of T'ae-këä, and wishing to withdraw from public life, addresses some cautions to the emperor on the subject of virtue. This is told us in the first par., forming the first chapter. In four parr. E shows how the possession or loss of the empire depends on the virtue of the sovereign or his want of it, and illustrates his theme by reference to the downfal of Këë and the rise of T'ang. This forms a second chapter. In the next four parr, forming the third chapter, E dwells on the nature and results of pure virtue, and urges the

cultivation of it on T'ae-këä. The two last parr., which form the concluding chapter, tell how this virtue will surely be acknowledged, and how the sovereign may find help to it even among the people.

TO WHOM THE INSTRUCTIONS OF THIS BOOK WERE ADDRESSED. There can be no doubt on this point, if we receive the Book, as we now have it, as genuine. The 'Instructions' in it were delivered to T'ae-këä. And this is confirmed by the position of the note on this Book in the Preface to the Shoo, as printed at the beginning of this volume. It follows immediately the note about the 'T'ae-këä.' In the 'Historical Records,' however, the same note appears in a different place. Ts'een places it immediately after the note of 'The Announcements of T'ang,' and before the death of that emperor. This order is followed by all who impugn the genuineness of the present 'old text.' The 'Both possessed pure virtue' must, they say, have been addressed to T'ang:—that the present copies all make it addressed to T'ae-këä is a clear evidence of their being forged.

The note itself is one of those in the Preface which give no account of the occasion on which the Book or Books that they refer to were

神　一　有　萬　弧　庸　夏　有　德
主　德　命　方　保　德　王三　以　靡
惟　俾　眷　啟　監　慢　弗節　亡。　常
尹　作　求　迪　于　神　克　○　九

be constant, he will preserve his throne; if his virtue be not con-
3 stant, the nine provinces will be lost by him. The king of Hea
could not maintain the virtue *of his ancestors* unchanged, but
contemned the spirits and oppressed the people. Great Heaven
no *longer* extended its protection to him. It looked out among
the myriad regions to give its guidance to one who might receive
its favour, fondly seeking *a possessor of* pure virtue, whom it might

composed. It says nothing but 'E Yin made the BOTH POSSESSED PURE VIRTUE.' It so happens that there is only one sentence in the present text whose genuineness is beyond dispute. All the rest of the Book may be forged, but this one sentence was in the original 'old text.' It is the part of the 3d par.— 惟尹躬暨湯咸有一德, which is quoted in the 'Record of Rites,' the Bk. 緇衣, par. 10, in the form—尹吉 (see on the last Book, Pt. ii., p. 2) 曰惟尹躬及湯咸有壹德 If it were proved that 湯 were the honorary, post-humous title of the founder of the Shang dynasty, this quotation would prove that the lessons of the Book were *not* addressed to him. I have said, however, on the name of 'The Speech of T'ang,' that T'ang ought not to be regarded as an honorary title, but as the designation of the emperor in his life. Still, for the minister thus to introduce his sovereign's designation in an address delivered to that sovereign himself would be an instance of unexampled freedom. It does not appear to be straining the point, to conclude from this passage that the 'Both possessed pure virtue' was not addressed to T'ang. That established, we may believe, without much misgiving, that it was addressed to T'ae-kĕă.

CH. I. P. 1. OCCASION WHEN THE 'BOTH POSSESSED PURE VIRTUE' WAS SPOKEN. These instructions were delivered when E Yin was about to announce his retirement from public life;—in what year, we cannot tell. The returning of the govt. into the hands of T'ae-kĕă took place B.C. 1750, and E may very soon after have announced his intention to retire from all toils of administration. So far as the language of this par. is concerned, how-ever, years may have elapsed between the two events. Par. 8 below would rather connect the two things closely together, but in opposi-tion to this is a statement in the 左傳襄,

二十一年, that E Yin, though he had kept T'ae-kĕă in confinement, yet afterwards acted as prime minister to him (尹伊放太甲而相之). Ying-tă supposes that, though E may have declared his wish to withdraw from the court shortly after the reformation of the emperor, T'ae-kĕă would not receive his resignation, and prevailed on him to continue at the head of affairs. This is not improbable, and it affords a satisfactory solution of the difficulty. 于德= 'on the subject of virtue.' The 'Daily Explanation' says:—以德之當勉陳戒于君.

CH. II. Pp. 2—5. THE FAVOUR OF HEAVEN IS NOT TO BE RELIED ON;—IT DEPENDS ON THE VIRTUE OF THE SOVEREIGN. THIS TRUTH IL-LUSTRATED BY REFERENCE TO THE OVERTHROW OF THE HEA DYNASTY, AND THE RISE OF THE SHANG. 2. Comp. last Book., Pt. iii., pp. 1, 2. 天難諶—諶=信, 'to be believ-ed,' 'to be trusted.' We have the same phrase in Pt. V., Bk. XVI., p. 4, where the same assertion is made in p. 6, in the words— 天不可信 靡=無 九有 以亡—九有, 'the nine possessions,'= 九州, 'the nine provinces.' This clause is held to prove that the Shang dynasty continued to retain Yu's division of the empire into nine provinces. 3. *The fall of Kĕĕ and rise of T'ang,—proving the doctrine just affirmed.* 夏王,—this of course is Kĕĕ. 弗克庸德,—Gan-kwŏ explains this by 不能常其德, 'could not make his virtue constant.' Lin Che-k'e adopts his language, and the 'Daily Explanation' says more explicitly—弗能有此純常之德, 'could not have

正。爰有以天天德咸躬
○革之有明心克有暨
非夏師、九命、受享一湯、
　四節

make lord of *all* the spirits. *Then* there were I, Yin, and T'ang, both possessed of pure virtue, and able to satisfy the mind of Heaven. He received *in consequence* the bright favour of Heaven, and became master of the multitudes of the nine provinces, and

this pure and constant virtue.' The translation shows that I take a different view of the phrase here. There was no virtue at all about Këĕ; it seems absurd to make E speak of him as if there could have been expected from him virtue of the highest style. 慢神虐民,—comp. last Book, Pt. iii., p. 1. 神 here is equivalent to 鬼神 there. 啟迪有命,—Gan-kwŏ says for this—有天命者開導之,'to guide on the possessor of the decree of Heaven.' Lin Che-k'e, more correctly and as in the translation, expands—擇其將有天命而開導之. 眷求一德,——德 is not 'one virtue,' but 'virtue all-one.' Ts'ae says that it means—純一之德,不雜不息之義,即上所謂常德也, 'virtue pure and one, unmixed, unceasing, what is called above "constant virtue."' It is the 誠, 'the singleness or sincerity,' of the 'Doctrine of the Mean,' by which the three virtues of knowledge, magnanimity, and energy are carried into effect. 神主,='lord of the spirits.' Ts'ae says:—神主,百神之主, 'By 神主, is meant lord of the hundred (= all the) spirits.' It is a name for the emperor as chief of the religion of the empire,—in our phrase, 'Head of the Church' of China. Cheang Kew-shing observes:—'The sovereign is lord of all the spirits. Thus we read in the She King (Pt. III., Bk. II., Ode viii., st. 3), "May you be the lord of all the spirits!" Being lord of the spirits, it follows that he is lord of the people. On the other hand we read in the "Many Regions," (Pt. V., Bk. XVIII., p. 6)—"Heaven on this sought a lord of the people." Being lord of the people, it follows that he is lord of the spirits.' This is to the effect that the 'Head of the Church' is the 'Head of the State' as well, and that either of the designations must be understood as inclusive of the other. The term 主, however, cannot be taken with the same force exactly in both the phrases. The 'lord of the people,' is high above them, their ruler; the 'lord of the spirits' is only the president and director in their worship.

[A passage in the Record of Rites, Bk. 祭法, par. 3, makes this modified meaning of the term 'lord,' as applied to the emperor in his relation to 'spirits,' very plain. It is there said —有天下者祭百神,諸侯在其地則拜之, 'The possessor of the empire sacrifices to all the spirits; the princes only sacrifice to those that are within their territories.' As sacrificing to the spirits, the emperor is their host (主人). In this passage of the 'Laws of Sacrifice,' I know that the hundred 神 are the *shin* of the hills, rivers, forests, valleys, &c., and do not embrace the spirits of heaven or those of men. It was probably this prerogative of the emperor to sacrifice to all of these which first originated the designation of him as 百神之主. But the phrase has now a wider application. Gan-kwŏ says that the 神主 in the text—天地神祇之主, 'lord of the spirits of heaven and the spirits of the earth.']

克享天心,—享 is taken here as = 當, 'to be suitable to,' 'to correspond to.' Ying-tă says:—'When one's virtue corresponds to the mind of the spirits, then they accept his offerings (德當神意,神乃享之); hence 享 is to be taken as = 當.' This is beating about for a meaning. 受天明命,—there can be no doubt as to the meaning of 明命 here. Compare last Book, Pt. i., p. 2. 爰革夏正,—爰= 於是, 'and thereupon.' The dict. calls the char. 引詞, 'a connective conjunction.' T'ang made the year commence in 丑, the last month of winter, instead of the beginning of spring, after the practice of the Hea dyn. Lin Che-k'e says that from the language here we may infer that the alteration of the commencement of the year began with T'ang, and was unknown before the Shang dyn. Whether this practice began with T'ang or not is a

天私我有商、惟天佑
于一德非商求于下
民惟民歸于一德。○
_{五節}德惟一、動罔不吉德
二三、動罔不凶惟吉
凶不僭在人、惟天降
災祥在德。○_{六節}今嗣王
新服厥命、惟新厥德、
終始惟一、時乃日新。
○_{七節}任官惟賢材、左右

4 proceeded to change Hea's commencement of the year. It was not that Heaven had any partiality for the ruler of Shang;—Heaven simply gave its favour to pure virtue. It was not that Shang sought *the allegiance of* the lower people;—the people simply turned

5 to pure virtue. Where the *sovereign's* virtue is pure, his movements are all fortunate; where his virtue is wavering and uncertain, his movements are all unfortunate. Good and evil do not wrongly befall men, because Heaven sends down misery or happiness according to their conduct.

6 III. Now, O young king, you are newly entering on your *great* appointment;—you should be making new your virtue. At last

7 as at first have this as your one object, so shall you make a daily renovation. Let the officers whom you employ be men of virtue and ability, and let the ministers about you be the right men.

disputed point; but Lin infers more than the text will sustain him in doing.

4, 5. *The rise of T'ang was altogether to be ascribed to his pure consistent virtue; and such virtue is ever the sure way to prosperity.* 德二三,—'virtue two and three.' It is said of a man who is unstable, that 朝二, 夕三, 'in the morning he is for two, and in the evening for three.' He is 'a double-minded man, unstable in all his ways.' 不僭 在人, 云 云,—compare 天 命 弗 僭, Bk. III., p. 5.

Ch. III. Pp. 6—9. COUNSELS TO T'AE-KEA ON THE DUTY AND THE MEANS OF REALIZING IN HIMSELF THIS PURE AND CONSTANT VIRTUE.

6. *For the maintenance of virtue a daily progress in it is necessary.* 新 服 厥 命,—'newly *invested* with your appointment.' 惟新 厥 德,—comp. Bk. II., p. 8. 終 始 惟

一, 時 (=是 or 於是) 乃 日 新,—Choo He explains this by:—'This principle (= way of proceeding) must be connectedly kept up without stopping, and there will be a daily renovation. If there be any intermission, this cannot take place.' Chin Tih-sew says:—'Former scholars have observed, that, if men be not daily going forward in their learning, they will be daily going back. So virtue must be daily renewed.' See the 集 說. 7. *Right officers and ministers; and how to make them helpful to the sovereign's virtue.* 賢 材,—賢 often embraces 材. The 材 or 'ability' being here expressed, we must confine 賢 to the idea of 'virtue.' 左 右=輔 弼 大 臣;—see on the 'Yih and Tseih.' p. 2, 其 弼 直, and p. 5, 欽 四 鄰. 其 人,—'*the men*,' = 'the right men.' 為 上……為 民,

惟其人臣
為上為德
為下為民
惟其人臣

其難其慎
惟和惟一。

○惟和惟一。

師德善無常
師善主善無為常

主協于克
一○俾萬克

The minister, in relation to *his sovereign* above him, has to promote
his virtue; and, in relation to the *people* beneath him, has to seek
their good. How hard must it be *to find the proper man*! what
careful attention must be required! *Thereafter* there must be
harmony *cultivated with him*, and a one-ness of confidence placed in
him!

8　　"Virtue has no invariable model;—a supreme regard to what is
good gives the model of it. What is good has no invariable
characteristic to be supremely regarded;—it is found where there

—all the 為 here are in the low. 3d tone, and
have a verbal force, = 'to be for.' Ts'ae says
that we have 為德 instead of 為君, to
show that to be virtuous is the course for the
sovereign, and, I may add, that to promote his
virtue is the great business of the minister with
him. 其難其慎惟和惟一,
—it is not easy to satisfy the mind as to the
connection and meaning of these brief, emphatic
expressions. Gan-kwŏ made them all refer to
the duty of ministers whose business has just
been described. Ying-tă thus expounds his
view:—'This passage expands the business of
ministers. Since what they have to do is so
difficult, let them not deem it easy; and since it
demands so much care, let them not make light
of it. Ministers are thus warned not to slight
their duties or consider them easy. Since their
duties are not to be deemed light, they ought
harmoniously to serve their sovereign;—the
whole body of ministers should have one heart
in serving him, and so his government will be
good. The 一心一德, so that ministers
also are required to have this pure and constant
virtue.' In the 語類, Choo He makes
其難其慎 an instruction to the sovereign, while 惟和惟一 are addressed to
the ministers. He says:—'The meaning of 其
難其慎 is that, since his officers should be
thus virtuous and able, and his ministers just the
proper men, the sovereign should feel the difficulty in getting them, and the necessity of his
being cautiously attentive. The meaning of 惟
和惟一 is that, since ministers are charged
with such duties, to promote the virtue of their
sovereign above them, and the welfare of the
people below them, they must be harmonious

and united in discharging them.' A third view
is that which I have followed in the translation.
According to it, each expression contains a
counsel to the sovereign in his relation to his
officers and ministers. To suppose, with Gan-
kwŏ and Ying-tă, that E is speaking here of
ministers and for them very much breaks the
continuity of his discourse. To suppose, with
Choo He, that part is spoken to the sovereign,
and part to his ministers, is liable to the same
objection, and is like guessing out the meaning
rather than reasoning it out. The 'Daily Explanation' thus paraphrases at length the view
which I have followed:—人臣之繫于
人其輕詳其灼猜相雜君
國也不綦重哉故其知不必伺之以得恐
君不用之難用未能灼而而得也待可不惟恐
賢才則官實及其賢以一初不乘于審人之以此譽不惟恐
授核間知恩滿方才以其也其才可以一終無其才也
8. *How
to secure a uniformly virtuous course.* 德無
常師,—師 is taken in the sense of 法,
'law,' or 'model.' It might be taken as =
'teacher,' as when it is said that 'Confucius had
no regular teacher' (何常師之有, Ana.
XIX., xxii.). It is better, however, to understand it here as in the translation. 德 or
'virtue' is employed as the general designation

萬　可　七　生　厎　王　心　曰　哉　姓
夫　以　世　○　烝　之　克　一　王　咸
之　觀　之　鳴　民　祿　綏　哉　言　曰
長　德　廟　呼　之　永　先　王　又　大
　　　　　十　之　　　王

9 is conformity to the uniform decision *of the mind.* *Such virtue* will make *the people* with their myriad surnames all say, 'How great are the words of the king!' and also, 'How single and pure is the king's heart!' It will avail to maintain in tranquillity the *great* possession of the former king, and to secure for ever the *happy* life of the multitudes of the people.

10　　IV. "Oh! *to retain a place* in the seven-shrined temple of ancestors is a sufficient witness of virtue. To be acknowledged as chief by the myriad heads of families is a sufficient witness of one's government.

of all good actions. By what model shall a man order his conduct that it shall always be virtuous? No invariable model can be supplied to him. But let him have a chief regard to this point,—that his actions be good, and he will not go far wrong. 主,—as in Ana. I., viii., 2. But what is to be the decisive characteristic of what is good? The answer to this question is in the last clause,—協于克一,—'harmony in attaining to the one.' It is not easy to say precisely what is meant. Ts'ae says the idea is not far different from that of Confucius in his famous saying,—吾道一以貫之 (Ana. IV., xv.) The 一 has reference to the 一德, which is in the title of the Book. Man has a monitor in regard to what is good and what is evil in his own breast. Let him only give a uniform obedience to the voice of this monitor, and his whole conduct will be ordered virtuously. 9. *The happy and great results of such a virtuous course.* 俾＝使, 'will cause.' A nominative is to be brought on from the last paragraph. 大哉王言,—the 'words of the king' are those published in his ordinances of State. 克綏先王之祿,—the same nominative is to be supplied to 克 as to 俾. 祿 is the 天祿, 'Heaven-conferred revenues,' of the 'Counsels of Yu,' par. 17.

Ch. IV. Pp. 10, 11. THE CHARACTER OF ONE'S GOVERNMENT AND VIRTUE WILL COMMAND ACKNOWLEDGMENT IN THE PRESENT AND THE FUTURE. THE SOVEREIGN SHOULD BE PREPARED TO ACCEPT HELPS TO HIS VIRTUE EVEN FROM THE LOWEST OF THE PEOPLE. 七世之廟 —'the ancestral temple of seven generations.'

The emperors had in their ancestral temple the shrines with the spirit-tablets of seven of their ancestors;—see on the 'Doctrine of the Mean,' xix. 4. But in the case of an emperor's possessing great merit, having displayed great virtue and rendered great services to his dynasty, his shrine might remain in addition to the seven regular shrines of the temple. This seems to be the motive presented to T'ae-këa,—that by being greatly virtuous, he might insure to all time a niche—a shrine—in the ancestral temple, and be looked up to by his descendants to the latest period of his dynasty. 萬夫之長,—Lin Che-k'e observes that 萬夫＝萬姓 or 萬民, 'the myriad surnames,' or 'the myriads of the people,' and that the whole phrase is equivalent to 天子, or 'emperor.' No doubt this explanation is correct, and I suppose that 夫 is to be taken in the sense of 'husband,' or head of a family. The idea is that when all the people readily submit to the emperor, the excellence of his government may be predicated.

[No little controversy has been raised on this paragraph, and especially on the clause 七世之廟. That the imperial temple of ancestors in the Chow dynasty was fitted up with seven shrines as the rule is acknowledged on all hands; and there is no intimation in the classical books, or in any writings of a high antiquity,—with perhaps one exception, which will be pointed out,—that the practice was different under the dynasties of Shang and Hea. About the middle of the second century of our era, Wei Yuen-shing (韋元成), a great scholar and minister, put forth the view that under the Shang dynasty, the shrines in the imperial temple

與　盡　婦　人　自　罔　○　可
成　民　不　匹　廣　罔　十節　以
厥　主　獲　夫　以　事　后　觀
功。　罔　自　匹　狹　無　非　政。
　　　　　　　　　　非　民

11　"The sovereign without the people has none whom he can employ; and the people without the sovereign have none whom they can serve. Do not consider yourself so enlarged as to deem others small in comparison. If ordinary men and women do not find the opportunity to give full development to their *virtue*, the people's lord will be without the proper aids to complete his merit."

were only five. Lew Hin and others opposed this opinion; but subsequently it was adopted with some modification by Ch'ing Heuen and Ma Yung; as an opponent to whom Wang Suh put himself forward. The question will not be admitted to be settled yet. The impugners of the present 'old text' hold to the decision of Ch'ing, while Maou K'e-ling has written at great length on the other side in his 廟制折衷.

I have said that there is perhaps one exception to the universal silence in books before our era on there having been any difference in the number of shrines in the early dynasties. That exception is in the 呂氏春秋, in the 13th Bk. of which, and the chapter 諭大, we have the passage—商書曰，五世之廟可以觀怪，萬夫之長可以生謀. But I cannot persuade myself that our present text was made by altering this strange quotation.]

11. 后非民……罔事,—comp. last Book, Pt. ii., p. 2. 匹夫匹婦—comp. Con. Ana., XIV., xviii., 3. 不獲自盡—'do not obtain to develope themselves to the utmost.' Ts'ae says:—匹夫匹婦，有一不得自盡於上，則善不備,—'Let but one common man and woman not be able to display their virtue completely to the sovereign, then there is one instance of what is good not provided,' *i.e.*, not provided to be an example to him. E Yin's idea was that the emperor could and ought to learn good from all, however far they might be beneath him. It must be allowed that there is a falling off in these two concluding paragraphs. They are but an impotent conclusion to the Book.

CONCLUDING NOTE. [i.] *About E Yin*. E Yin had certainly played a most important part in the overthrow of the Hea dynasty, and the establishment of the Shang. Whether he spent his last years in retirement as he wished to do, or was persuaded to continue to be prime minister to his death, we do not know; but he survived T'ae-këă, and died, according to the preface to the Shoo, and to Sze-ma Ts'een, B.C. 1712, more than 100 years old, in the 8th year of Yuh-ting, T'ae-këă's son and successor. He was buried with imperial honours, and a narrative of the transactions of his life was drawn up by another minister called Kaou Shen, which formed one of the documents of the Shoo, but is unfortunately lost.

No credit can be given to the statements in the 'Bamboo Books,' that E was keeping T'ae-këă in confinement, while he reigned in his stead, and that T'ae-këă, having escaped in the 7th year of his imprisonment, put him to death, when Heaven put the emperor in such terror by a dense mist of three days' duration that he invested E's son with his honours and possessions.

[ii.] *About T'ae-këă*. History is silent on the events of T'ae-këă's reign after his reformation. He must have held on, however, in the course of virtue, for he earned for himself the shrine in the ancestral temple, and occupied it with the title of 太宗. His reign ended B.C. 1720.

THE BOOKS OF SHANG.

BOOK VII. PWAN-KANG. PART i.

盤　盤一節　于　不　居　眾　矢
庚　庚　殷　適　率　感　言。
上　遷　民　有　籲　出

1　I. Pwan-kăng wished to remove to Yin, but the people would not go to dwell there.　He therefore appealed to all the discontented, and made the following protestations.

INTRODUCTORY HISTORICAL NOTE.　T'ae-kĕä's reign ended B.C. 1720, and Pwan-kăng's commenced B.C. 1400.　More than three centuries of the Shang dynasty is thus a blank in history, so far as the documents of the Shoo are concerned.　They were filled up by the reigns of 14 emperors, of whom we know from all other sources little more than the names.

Originally there were 7 other Books between the 'Both possessed pure virtue,' and the 'Pwan-kăng;' but hardly a shred of any of them can now be collected.

The names of the intervening emperors, with all the information that can be brought together about them, are as follow :—

[i.] Yuh-ting (沃丁).　He was a son of T'ae-kĕä; succeeded to his father, B.C. 1719; died, B.C. 1691.　We have seen that E Yin died in his reign, and was buried by him magnificently in Pŏ.　Soon after this there was made the lost Book, called 'Yuh-ting.'

[ii.] T'ae-kăng (太庚).　He was a brother of Yuh-ting.　He died, B.C. 1666.

[iii.] Sëaou-kĕä (小甲).　He was a son of T'ae-kăng.　He died, B.C. 1649.

[iv.] Yung-ke (雍已).　He was a brother of Sëaou-kĕä.　He died, B.C. 1637.　During his reign, the government became very weak, and many of the princes did not think it worth their while to appear at court.

[v.] T'ae-mow (太戊).　He was a brother of Yung-ke.　His prime minister was E Chih, the son of E Yin.　In his time there occurred at Pŏ an ominous appearance of a mulberry tree and a stalk of grain growing together.　According to Ts'een, T'ae-mow in great alarm consulted his minister about it, when Chih replied, 'I have heard that portents do not overcome virtue.　May there not be defects about your government?　Let your Majesty cultivate your virtue.'　This advice was taken.　The emperor became greatly virtuous.　The strange growth withered away, and the affair was commemorated in a Book, which is now lost, by a worthy minister called Woo Heen.　T'ae-mow reposed great confidence in Chih; the dynasty revived; the princes acknowledged their allegiance; and when the emperor died in B.C. 1562, after reigning 75 years, he received, in the ancestral temple, the title of 中宗　[We might be inclined to doubt the length of this reign.　Chow-kung mentions it particularly, in Pt. V., Bk. XV., par. 5.]

[vi.] Chung-ting (仲丁).　He was the son of T'ae-mow.　He transferred the capital from Pŏ to Gaou (囂; Sze-ma Ts'een writes the name 隞), in the pres. dis. of Ho-yin (河陰), dep. of K'ae-fung, Ho-nan.—There was a Book in the Shoo, giving an account of this removal; but it is lost. His reign was marked by insurrections and incursions of wild tribes, and by 'internal disorders.' It ended B.C. 1549.

[vii.] Wae-jin (外壬). He was a brother of Chung-ting. His reign ended B.C. 1534, amidst a renewal of 'internal disorders.'

[viii.] Ho-tan-këä (河亶甲). He was a brother of Chung-ting and Wae-jin. An overflow of the Ho made him remove the capital in his first year from Gaou to Sëang, a place in the pres. dep. of Chang-tih (彰德), Ho-nan. His reign was a feeble one, and the fortunes of Shang began again to wane. A Book, which is now lost, commemorated the transference of the seat of govt. The addition of Ho (河) to the emperor's name must have been somehow connected with this. He died B.C. 1525.

[ix.] Tsoo-yih (祖乙). He was a son of Tan-këä. He was obliged to remove the capital from Sëang to Kăng (耿), in the pres. dis. of Ho-tsin (河津), in Këang Chow (绛州), Shan-se. The Book of the Shoo commemorating this is lost. Subsequently he made another charge from Kăng to 邢, in the pres. dis. of Hing-t'ae (邢臺), dep. Shun-tih, Chih-le. [It may be doubted, however, whether 邢 and 耿 were not identical. See Sze-ma Ts'een.] He had for his chief minister Heen (賢), a son of Woo Heen of T'ae-mow's reign, and his govt. displayed a vigour which anew commanded the submission of the princes. He died B.C. 1506.

[x.] Tsoo-sin (祖辛). He was a son of Tsoo-yih. He died B.C. 1490.

[xi.] Yuh-këä (沃甲). He was a brother of Tsoo-sin. He died, B.C. 1465, amid confusion and disorder.

[xii.] Tsoo-ting (祖丁). He was a son of Yuh-këä. He also died in the midst of troubles, B.C. 1433.

[xiii.] Nan-kăng (南庚). He was another son of Yuh-këä. It is the same story;—he died amid troubles, B.C. 1408.

[xiv.] Yang-këä (陽甲). He was a son of Tsoo-ting. The fortunes of the House of Shang seemed to be at a low ebb in his time. He died in B.C. 1401, and was succeeded by his brother Pwan-kăng.

NAME OF THE BOOK.—盤庚, 'Pwan-kăng.' This was the name of the 17th emperor of the Shang dynasty. It is sometimes written 殷庚. He is by some reckoned the 19th emp., two reigns—of Wae-ping and Chung-jin—being interposed between T'ang and T'ae-këä. The 左傳 refers to the Book as the 'Announcement of Pwan-kăng;' and it is properly placed in the division of the Shoo which embraces 'Announcements.' The Book is found both in the old text and the modern. There are many passages in it difficult of interpretation. As edited by Confucius, it was in three Parts, which arrangement is retained in the old text, while Fuh-shang had either forgotten, or did not mark it.

CONTENTS. The whole Book centres round the removal of the capital from the north of the Ho to Yin on the south of it. The emperor saw that the removal was necessary, but he was met by the unwillingness of the people and the opposition of the great families. The first Part relates how he endeavoured to justify the measure. It contains two addresses, to the people and to those in high places respectively, designed to secure their cordial co-operation. The second Part brings before us the removal in progress. They have crossed the river, but there continues to be dissatisfaction, which the emperor endeavours to remove by a long and earnest vindication of his policy.

The third Part opens with the removal accomplished. The new city has been founded, and the plan of it laid out. The emperor makes a third appeal to the people and chiefs to forget all their heart-burnings, and co-operate with him in building up in the new capital a great destiny for the dynasty.

The first Part has been divided into 17 paragraphs, which may be be divided again into 2 chapters. The former, parr. 1—4, contains, after an introductory reference to the occasion of its delivery, an address, by Pwan-kang, chiefly to the people, vindicating his measure on the authority of precedents, and the advantages it would secure. The other, parr. 5—17, is an address, to those in high places chiefly, complaining of the manner in which they misrepresented him to the people, and consulted only their own selfishness, and threatening them with his high displeasure, if they did not change their ways.

Ch. I. Pp. 1—4. OCCASION OF THE ADDRESSES IN THIS PART. NECESSITY AND DUTY OF REMOVING THE CAPITAL; THE MEASURE VINDICATED BY PRECEDENTS; ADVANTAGES TO BE GAINED BY IT. 1. 盤庚遷于殷,—'Pwan-kăng was removing (the past incomplete tense, = wished to remove) to Yin.' The removal must have been from Kăng, or from 邢, if Tsoo-yih made a second change of his capital; and it was probably necessitated by an overflow of the Ho. The site chosen for the new capital was 殷, called 殷亳 in the prefatory note on the Book, which I have there translated—'Pŏ, the cradle of the Yin.' Gan-kwŏ says here that '殷 is another name of 亳.' Others say that Pŏ was the name of the territory, and Yin that of a particular place in it. The site of Pwan-kăng's new capital was what is called 'the western Pŏ,' in the pres. dis. of Yen-sze (偃師), dep. of Ho-nan, Ho-nan. This was not the Pŏ where T'ang had his capital, when he commenced his work of punishment among the princes with the chief of Kŏ (Bk. II., p. 6). He had, however, probably dwelt previously in this Yin-pŏ, as intimated in the 9th notice of the preface.

曰我王來、既爰宅于兹重我民無盡劉不能胥匡以生、卜稽曰 二節

其如台。○先王有服、恪謹天命、兹猶不常 三節

2　He said, "Our king came, and fixed on this settlement. He did so from a deep concern for our people, and not because he would have them all die, where they cannot *now* help each other to preserve their lives. I have examined the matter by divination, and obtained

3　the reply—'This is no place for us.' When the former kings had any business, they reverently obeyed the commands of Heaven. In

[After this removal of Pwan-kăng to Yin, the name of the dynasty appears to have been changed from Shang to Yin. Pwan-kăng and his successors all appear in the 'Kang-muh' as kings of Yin, in contradistinction from his predecessors, who are entered as kings of Shang. It is there stated also that he changed the title of the dynasty.]

適有居,—適=往 or 之, 'to go to.' The 'Daily Explanation' has for the whole—往 適安居之地, 'go to the place of tranquil dwelling.'　率籲眾慼—率=總; 籲 (the dict. says should be without the 竹)=呼; 慼=憂. Gan-kwŏ took 率 as =領, and 籲 as =和. Ying-tă expands his view:—率領和諧眾憂之人, 'He conducted and *tried to* harmonize all the grieving.' The view given in the translation is much to be preferred.　The 說文 quotes the passage with 戚 for 慼, which has unnecessarily made Këang Shing and others insist on 眾戚 as meaning—'all his relatives,'= 'all the high officers.'　出矢言,—矢 =誓. Comp. Con. Ana., VI., xxvi.

2. *The necessity and the sanction of a change of capital.*　我王來,—the 王 or king here must be Tsoo-yih.　既爰宅于兹 —既爰= 'and thereupon.' 爰, however, between 既 and 宅 is perplexing.　于 兹=於此, 'here,' referring to Kăng. 重我民、無盡劉—劉=殺, 'to kill,' or 'to be killed.' Keang Shing gives as the meaning of the passage:—'He governed well, and made the people prosperous. Altho' there were the evils of occurring inunda-

tions, they did not hurt the people, and they did not all die.' The view of Gan-kwŏ is better than this:—'Tsoo Yih removed here, because he valued the people, and would not have them all die,' *i.e.*, would not have them all die in Sëang (see the preface, not. 25). The meaning given in the translation is that of Ts'ae, as expanded in the 'Daily Explanation.' It is certainly more germane to the argument of the whole Book.　不能胥匡以生,—comp. Bk. V., Pt. ii., p. 2; but there is not the same difficulty with the 胥 here. [But that that passage of the 'T'ae-këă' is guaranteed by its being expressly quoted in the Le Ke, we should certainly have had Jŏ-keu, and all the impugners of the received 'old text,' referring to this paragraph as the original of it, and insisting that 'here the plagiarist of Tsin stole from the Pwan-kăng.']　卜稽之=稽之 於卜.　曰其如台,—this is the answer returned to the divination, but expressed in Pwan-kăng's words.　其如台,— comp. Bk. I., p. 3,—夏罪其如台. Ts'ae explains by:—亦曰, 此地無 若我何, 言耿不可居, 決當 遷.

3. *Precedents of removal in the histories of former reigns.*　服 is to be taken in the sense of 事, 'business,' 'affair.' The 'Daily Explanation' says:—'The former kings, in great governmental emergencies of the empire,' &c.　兹猶不常寧,—兹, 'this,' = in such a matter as this transference of the capital. 猶 is well expressed by 'especially.' The force of it is to connect the clause closely with the preceding.—'If in all matters they obeyed the will of Heaven, how much more did they do so in a matter like this!'　于今五邦,—'by

由乃在位以常舊
方。○盤庚斅于民、<small>五節</small>
王之大業、厎綏四
于兹新邑、紹復先
由蘗、天其永我命
烈。○若顛木之有<small>四節</small>
曰其克從先王之
罔知天之斷命、矧
五邦今不承于古、
寧、不常厥邑于今

a case like this especially they did not indulge a constant repose, —they did not abide ever in the same city. Up to this time *the capital has been in* five regions. If we do not now follow the practice of the ancients, we shall be refusing to acknowledge that Heaven is making an end of our dynasty here;—how little can it be said of us that we are following the meritorious course of the former

4　kings! As from the stump of a felled tree there are sprouts and shoots, Heaven will perpetuate its decree in our favour in this new city; —the great possession of the former kings will be continued and renewed; tranquillity will be secured to the four quarters *of the empire.*"

5　　II. Pwan-kang, in making the people, aware of his views, began with those who were in *high* places, and took the constantly recur-

now there have been five regions.' We must understand as in the translation. There is some difficulty in making out the five capitals. They are commonly enumerated as—T'ang's capitals in Shang K'ew and Pŏ, Chung-ting's in Gaou, Ho-tan-këă's in Sëang, Tsoo-yih's in K'ăng. But Shang-k'ew and the Pŏ of T'ang —the Pŏ where he first appears in the Shoo— were identical. If he had previously moved from the 'western Pŏ,' that was anterior to the commencement of the dynasty;—only our capital can be counted to him in the enumeration. Reckoning from T'ang's eastern Pŏ, and including the present change to Yin, or the western Pŏ,—which is the way of many,—we have five capitals; but to include the change which was only in contemplation seems forbidden by the clause which follows—今不承 于古. The number of five may be made out by allowing two movements to Tsoo-yih. The point is really of little importance; and to suppose that Pwan-kăng is speaking of five changes which be had made himself, 'though it is the view of Sze-ma Ts'ëen, is inadmissible. 罔知天之斷命,—the meaning of 斷命 is very much determined by the 永命 in the next par., which is in contrast

with it. 矧 corresponds to 猶 above. 猶 = 'how much more'; 矧 = 'how much less.' The commentators all explain 烈 by 業. We get a much better meaning by taking it as = 功,—as in Bk. IV., p. 1.

4. *How a reviving and prosperity would come with a change of capital.* 若顛木之 有由蘗,—蘗 (see the dict. on the form of the character) = 斫木餘, 'the remains of a tree that has been cut down.' This justifies —requires, indeed—the translation which I have given of 顛木, which is simply 'a fallen tree.' 由 is defined by 木生條, 'the sprouts and shoots of a tree;'—see the dict. on this use of the character.

Ch. II. Pp. 5—17. PWAN-KANG'S ADDRESS TO THOSE IN HIGH PLACES. HE EXPOSTULATES WITH THEM, AND THREATENS THEM, BECAUSE OF THEIR OPPOSITION TO THE PROPOSED REMOVAL OF THE CAPITAL. 5. Lin Che-k'e and Ts'ae preface this chapter in the following way :—The site of Kăng, being low and liable to inundations, was peculiarly unhappy for the poorer people, who were driven from their homes and

服正　法度，曰，或　伏　人　攸　王　衆　至
正度，無　敢　小　之　箴，命　悉　于

ring circumstances of former times to lay down the right law for the *present emergency*, saying, "Let none of you dare to suppress the remonstrances of the poorer people." The king ordered all in common to come to his hall.

scattered about. It had advantages, however, for the large and wealthy families, who were therefore unwilling to leave it, and contrived by unsubstantial statements to bring many of the lower orders to resist the proposed movement along with themselves. They could not blind the minds of all, but they came between those who wished to represent the grievances of their situation and the emperor, preventing the interchange of their views. These were the circumstances, which occasioned Pwan-kăng his difficulties, and to deal with which is his object in this chapter. These observations seem to be correct, and by keeping them in mind, we can better understand the whole of the chapter.

敎于民—敎＝教, 'to teach,' or, better, ＝覺悟, 'to awaken, make aware.'

由乃在位, 以常舊服正法度,—this is a difficult passage, as appears from the difft. views that have been taken of it. Gan-kwŏ, taking 由＝用, and 乃＝汝, supposed the words to be spoken to the people. Ying-tă thus paraphrases his interpretation:—'Pwan-kăng instructing the people, said, "You ought to follow the orders of your superiors, and use the constant practice of former times to rectify the law." He wished to charge the people to remove in obedience to the orders of the ministers.' It is added—" He also cautioned the ministers, saying," &c. This is hardly intelligible, and we cannot admit the interposition of a 曰 after the first clause. Keang Shing, Sun Yen, and other interpreters of the present dynasty, take 由 and 乃 in the same way as Lin and Ts'ae, but view the whole differently. Their interpretation is:—'Pwan-kăng, wishing to make the people aware of his views, would do so by means of those in places of authority, and would use the constant practice of former times to lay down the correct way of proceeding. He therefore said to the officers,' &c. On this construction, the constant practice of former times (常舊服,—服 ＝事, as in par. 3) is not the practice of removing the capital, but that of calling a general assembly of the people to deliberate on such an important measure. 正法度, also, does not mean, as in the translation, to lay down the law of proceeding in what was already determined on, but to consider whether such a proceeding should be taken or not. An insuperable objection to this view is the address

which follows, in which no proposition is laid before the assembly, but the ministers and officers simply are sharply spoken to. I append the paraphrase of the 'Daily Explanation':—

其(＝盤庚)敎于民也, 自在位動遷度,乎者, 意者始之都見先王亦若曰云云. 然亦惟以威事之已. 非以繩之以先王之舊日者,取度法職之. 以正天臣之上命. 舊法守其大. 常法度. 則恪遵乎命其職之上.

無或敢伏小人之攸箴—無＝毋; 伏＝藏匿, 'to conceal;' 攸 ＝所; 箴＝諫, 'to remonstrate.' 箴 prinasily denotes 'a sewing needle,' made of course of bamboo; then a pointed stone used for puncturing the flesh in disease. From this second use of the term comes that in the text. 箴言 are 'pungent words,' that probe the conscience. 王命衆悉至于庭,—王, 'the king.' This of course is Pwan-kang; and it might be well to separate this sentence from the rest of the paragraph, and let it stand by itself, as Lin Che-k'e does. I have said that 'the king of course is Pwan-kăng but Keang Shing and others will have it that we are to understand, after K'ang-shing, that the King was Yang-kĕa Pwan-kăng's brother and predecessor.' They will have it that, at the time to which this first Part refers, Pwan-kăng was acting as prime minister to him, and was carrying out his wishes in advocating the removal of the capital. They admit at the same time that in the second and third parts Pwan-kăng himself is 'King,' so that we must suppose the transference to have been contemplated and agitated for a considerable time. This theory is altogether gratuitous, and I can find no substantial ground for it in the language of any part of the Book. Sun Yen to support it makes 王命,云云, to be the words of Pwan-kăng;—'Do not venture to conceal from the people that the King commands all,' &c. But the 攸箴 forbid such a construction. In the 衆悉 we must understand both the people and the officers and ministers. They were

變今汝聒聒起　有逸言民用丕　指王用丕欽罔　告之修不匿厥　舊人共政王播　先王亦惟圖任　傲從康○古我　汝猷黜乃心無　汝眾予告汝訓　庭○王若曰格

六節　七節

6　The king spoke to this effect:—"Come, all of you; I will announce to you my instructions. Take counsel how to put away your *selfish* thoughts. Do not with haughty *disregard of me* follow after your own ease.

7　"Of old, our former kings had it as a principal object in their plans to employ the men of old families to share in the government. When they wished to proclaim and announce what was to be attended to, those did not conceal the imperial views, and on this account the kings greatly respected them. They did not exceed the truth *in their communications with the people*, and on this account the

gathered to 'the hall,' congregated, I suppose, all about the royal residence. The meeting, however, was not for deliberation. We may suppose that the people would enjoy the *schooling* of the officers.

[If we will not be satisfied without a reason for the change of style from 'Pwan-kăng' to 'the king,' and think that the inartistical manner in which the compiler did his work does not sufficiently account for it, I see no course but to resort to the theory of different documents, which certain critics make so much use of in accounting for the change from one name of the Supreme Being to another in the Book of Genesis!]

6. *Reproof of the insolence and selfishness of the officers.* 王若曰,—若曰 intimates that what follows is not all in the exact words of the king, but the substance of what he said. Others will have it that the 若 is appropriate in the mouth of a minister speaking in the name of the sovereign, as we shall find it several times in the next Part; but even there the 若 = 'substantially thus.' 格爾眾, —the 眾 must be co-extensive with the same term in the last par., embracing officers and people, but the address is at once directed to the officers only. 猷黜乃心,—猷 = 謀; 黜 = 去; 乃 = 汝. 無傲 從康,—無 = 毋; 傲, 'haughty,' 'insolent,' as in the 'Yih and Tseih,' p. 8. The

whole is paraphrased:—毋得傲上之 命,從已之安.

7. *Degeneracy of Pwan-kăng's ministers and officers as compared with those of former times.* 古我先王,—these 'former Kings' are to be taken generally, as intending all the sovereigns of the dyn. from T'ang downwards. 亦惟圖任舊人共政,—亦, 'also,' *i.e.,* in the same way as Pwan-kăng himself; 惟圖, is not 'only planned,' but 惟 may be taken as the copula, or as amalgamating with the meaning of 圖; 舊人 = 世臣 舊家之人, 'hereditary ministers and men of old families.' Gan-kwŏ takes 舊人 as = 老成之人, old and experienced men;' but the meaning is clearly indicated in par. 14, and other places. 共政 = 共治 其政. 王播告之修,不匿 厥指,—Gan-kwŏ explains this:—王 布告 人以所修之政,不匿其 指, 'when the kings were publishing (= wished to publish) to the people the government which was to be cultivated, they did not conceal their views.' This must be the meaning of the 修, which, standing alone in the text, is enigmatic. The 'Daily Explanation,' finds a

信險膚予弗
知乃所訟。○
非予自荒茲 八節
德惟汝含德
不惕予一人
予若觀火予
亦拙謀作乃
逸。○若網在 九節
綱有條而不
蓁若農服田

people became greatly changed. Now, *however*, you keep clamouring, and get the confidence *of the people* by alarming and shallow
8 speeches. I do not know what you keep wrangling about. In
this movement I am not myself abandoning my proper virtue,
but you conceal the goodness of my intentions, not standing in
awe of me, the one man. I see you as clearly as one sees fire;
but still by my undecided plans I have produced your error.

9   "When the net has its line, there is order and not confusion;
and when the husbandman labours upon the fields, and spends his

great deal of meaning in the clause—不匿
厥指, saying it = 'they proclaimed the
favour of the sovereign to the people, and reported the remonstrances of the people to the
sovereign.' I cannot see more in it than I have
expressed in the translation.   罔有逸
言,—逸＝過; 逸言 are 'words going
beyond' the truth.   今汝聒聒,—the
說文 quotes this passage not under 聒, but
under 䛟, which seems also to have been the
reading of Ch'ing K'ang-shing. The meaning
of the phrase is given variously. We have—
多言之意, 'clamorous' (the 日講 and
集傳); 無知之貌, 'the appearance
of stupidity' (Gan-kwǒ); 拒善自用之
意, 'self-opinionated, resisting what is good'
(Ma Yung and the 說文); 難告之貌,
'the appearance of being difficult to be spoken
to' (Ch'ing).   起信險膚,—the connec-
tion shows that by 險膚 the speeches of the
officers are characterized. 險, 'precipitous,'
'hazardous,' = 'alarming.' 膚, 'the skin,'
here = 'shallow,' words not more than skin
deep.   The translation of 起信 is after
Lin Che-k'e and Ts'ae. Këang Shing has a
different view, and takes 起＝造, and 信
(1st tone) = 申, the two together = 'you raise
and put forth.'   8 *While rev roving the*

perverse opposition of his ministers, Pwan-kăng
acknowledges his own weakness. The meaning of
this par. given in the translation is again after
the 集傳. 荒＝廢; comp. its use in Pt.
III., Bk. III., p. 8.   茲德,—'this virtue,' *i.e.*,
the virtue proper to the sovereign, *to love the
people.*   含德,—'conceal the virtue,' *i.e.*,
the virtue of the emperor proposing the removal
of the capital with a view to the benefit of the
people.   予若觀火＝我視汝情,
明若觀火, 'I see your feelings and ways
as clearly as if I were looking at fire.'
拙謀,—'stupid plans.' 'Stupid' = undecided, not using force of will and appliances to
compel obedience.   作乃逸＝成汝
過失.   Gan-kwǒ takes a different view of
惟汝含德 and makes it = 'but you
cherish evil thoughts.' Keang Shing agrees
with this; but his explanations of 茲德 and
予觀若火 are peculiar. See his comm.
in loc.

9, 10. *The officers are exhorted to put away
their selfishness, and to do real good to the people.
The good effects of their doing so are illustrated.*

9. 若網在綱,—'if the net be on the
rope.' The rope, going round the mouth or
edge of the net, keeps it in order, and affords
the means of handling it easily.   有條,
—'there are the separate divisions or parts,' =
there is order. What the rope is to the net,
that the sovereign is to the ministers; and they
must allow to him a control over them and

力穡、乃亦有秋。

○十節 汝克黜乃心、

施實德于民、至

于婚友、丕乃敢

大言汝有積德。

○乃十一節 不畏戎毒

于遠邇、惰農自

安不昏作勞、不

服田畝越其罔

有黍稷。○汝十二節 不

10 strength in reaping, there is then the *abundant* autumn. If you can put away your *selfish* thoughts, you will bestow real good upon the people, reaching to your relatives and friends, and may boldly venture to make your words great, and say that you have accumulated

11 virtue. You do not fear the great evils which are far and near. *You are like* the husbandman who yields himself to ease, and is not strong to toil and to labour on his acres, and who in such a case

12 cannot have either rice or millet. You do not use friendly and good

guidance of them. This portion of the par. is understood to have reference to the haughty disregard of him shown by Pwan-kăng's ministers,—their 傲 (par. 6). 若農 云云, —服田=服勞于田畝; 力穡 =盡力于稼穡。 The 'reaping' is to be taken as inclusive of the 'sowing.' This portion is understood to be directed against the officers' seeking their ease,—the 從康 of par 6.

10. 實德,—'real, substantial, virtue.' The meaning is that if they would put away their selfishness (see par. 6), and cordially co-operate with the emperor in promoting the removal to Yin, they would be really benefiting the people.

It is not easy to show how the diff. parts of the paragraph depend on one another. No commentator that I have examined has succeeded in doing so. They all, from Gan-kwŏ downwards, have lost the clue to a fair and consistent interpretation, by making the two clauses—汝克黜乃心, 施實德于民 run on as if they were connected by an *and*, whereas we should take 施實德 云云, as the results that would flow from their putting away their selfishness. The two first clauses must be joined by a 則, and not by 而, or the 及 of a looser style. 至于婚友,—'reaching—which will reach—to relatives and friends.' 婚 properly denotes 'the kindred of the wife'; here it = 'relatives' generally. The great families were opposed to

the contemplated movement, as Kăng was sufficiently advantageous to them. Pwan-kăng here tells them that they likewise, as well as the people generally, would be benefited by it. 丕乃敢大言,—'great(=bold) may be your venturing to magnify yourselves and say,' ——.. The straits to which the commentators are put by the language here may be seen in Gan-kwŏ and Keang Shing. The placing of a 則 between the two first clauses makes the interpretation much more easy.

11, 12. *Further reproof of those in high places for their self-seeking and disregard of the emperor's wishes.* 11. 乃不畏戎毒于遠邇,—戎=大, 'great;' 毒=害, 'injuries,' 'evils.' Pwan-kăng has reference to the desolation wrought by the overflowing waters, of which the wealthy families hardly seemed to be conscious. Keang Shing says he can get no meaning from the sentence thus construed, and places a stop at 毒, and explains 于遠邇 by 徒計校于遠近, 'you vainly calculate, and compare the distant and the near.' This does not make the meaning more intelligible or the construction more easy. 不昏作勞,—昏=暋, Pt. V. Bk. IX., p. 15, 'to be strong,' 'energetic.' 越 is defined by Ying-tă by 於; but then 於 must be taken as an adverb, =於是, 'thereupon.' Keang Shing gives 卒 for it, = 'the result is.' 12. 汝

告　短　有　胥　何　乃　身　姦　汝　和
朕　長　逸　顧　及　奉　乃　宄　自　吉
而　之　口　于　相　其　既　以　生　言
胥　命　矧　箴　時　恫　先　自　毒　于
動　汝　予　言　憸　汝　惡　災　乃　百
以　曷　制　其　民　悔　于　于　敗　姓
浮　弗　乃　發　猶　身　民　厥　禍　惟

words to the people, and are only producing suffering for yourselves.
As destroyers and calamities, villains and traitors, the punishment
shall come on your persons. You set the example of evil, and must
feel its smart,—what will it avail you then to repent? Look at
the poor people;—they can still consult together about remonstrances *which they wish to address to me*, but when they begin
to speak, you are ready with your extravagant talk:—how much
more ought you to have me before your eyes, with whom it is to
make your lives long or short! Why do you not report their

不……生 毒,—吉—善, 'good.' 和
吉言, are 'soothing and good words,' by
which the officers might have allayed the excitement of the people, and led them to fall in
with the emperor's wish to remove to Yin.
惟汝自生毒 must be = the 自
災于厥身 below. Pwan-kăng begins
to take a higher tone with the officers, and
threatens them. Gan-kwŏ supposes the 百
姓 here to be the 百官, 'the various officers,' and the lesson to be administered to the
公卿, or 'high nobles' above them. It is a
strange and inadmissible interpretation. 乃
敗禍……厥身,—the 'Daily Explanation'
has for this:—敗禍姦宄之刑亦
且災于汝之身矣. The 乃 may
be taken either as =汝, or as a conjunction.
敗禍 are co-ordinate with 姦宄, and are
designations applied to the officers, opposing
the emperor as they did. Among all the commentators only Sun Yen has attempted to grap-
ple with the difficulty of these terms, and he
only partially and unsuccessfully. 乃
既……何及,—乃=汝; 先惡=惡

之先, 'the precedents of wickedness;'—so,
Ts'ae. 恫=痛. 悔身無及,—
the 身 occasions a difficulty here. It is to be
joined to 何及. Gan-kwŏ says:—悔之
而于身無所及, 'you may repent,
but that will not avail your persons.'
時憸民……之命,—相=視. 'to
look at;' 時=是, 'these;' 憸民=小
民, 'the lower people.' 憸 (the original form
of the char. is disputed) properly means 'sharp-
mouthed,'='litigious,' 'flattering.' This meaning is retained in the phrase, in Pt. Y., Bk. XIX.,
p. 20. It would be inappropriate here, and
therefore the signif. of 小民 is accepted in
its stead. 猶胥顧云云,—I have trans-
lated after the paraphrase of the 'Daily Explanation.' Ts'ae seems to interpret after Lin
Che-k'e, who says:—'Look at those poor people;
—they can still regard one another in their
remonstrances, fearing lest, in the words which
they utter, they should transgress with their
mouths, and bring misery on themselves. So
are the poor people in awe, with reference to
the remonstrances which they would speak,
and yet you, with regard to me who have
the power of life and death over you in
my hands, do not stand in awe of me, but
haughtily disregard me, and follow your own

舊　求　有　有　作　則　其　原、若　言、
惟　舊　言　咎。弗　惟　猶　不　火　恐
新。器、曰、○　靖　爾　可　可　之　沈
○　非　人　遲　非　衆　撲　嚮　燎　于
古十四節　求　惟　任十三節　予　自　滅、邇、于　衆、

words to me, but go about to excite one another by empty speeches, frightening and involving the multitudes in misery? When a fire is blazing in the plains, so that it cannot be approached, can it still be beaten out? Thus for you to cause dispeace in this way: —it is not I who am to blame.

13　"Ch'e Jin has said, 'In men, we seek individuals of old families;

ease.' You are not equal to the poor people.' Gan-kwŏ took the same view of the passage as Lin. The modern view is more in harmony with the tenor of the whole Book.

汝曷弗告......于衆,-恐=恐動之以禍患, 'frightening and exciting them about the calamity.' 沈=沈陷之於罪惡, 'plunging and sinking them in wickedness.' 若火......撲滅,—in interpreting this sentence, I am obliged to differ from Lin Che-k'e and the 'Daily Explanation.' They understand Pwan-kang as saying that a blazing fire which could not be approached, might still be beaten out, and he would cause the officers to know that when he arrayed himself in his terrors, they would be consumed before him, and have an end made of all their speeches. But is it true in nature that a fire not approachable can yet be beaten out? There could not be such a thing without appliances of which Pwan-kăng could have no idea. The passage is twice quoted in the 左傳 (隱. 六年, and 莊 十四年,) with 惡之易, before 若火之燎, and the meaning is that prolonged wickedness becomes irremediable. It can't be remedied, and must produce its natural result of ruin. So Pwan-kăng threatens his officers, it would be with them. 則惟爾衆自作弗靖非予有咎,—the king's anger does not allow him to bring his meaning out fully. He means to say—'In the same way, when you all of yourselves make this dispeace, and will have to take the consequences, you will have only yourselves to blame. You cannot ascribe your suffering to

me.' The 'Daily Explanation' says:—此皆汝等不能安靜以奉上命,自速其禍耳,豈予樂用威刑以加汝也.

[Lin Che-k'e observes at the close of this paragraph, that the style of the Pwan-kăng is very full of repetitions, the same thought being brought out again and again, and the same illustrations. He compares 予若觀火,云云, of par. 8, with 若火之燎云云, here, and 若農服田,云云 of par. 9, with 惰農,云云, of par. 11, adding that however the style may be in *disjecta membra*, there is yet a unity of thought, and though the language be involved and irritating, difficult to understand, yet a man may by repeated exercises of his mind upon it make out the meaning. I think he is correct in saying that the general meaning may be made out; but the style is very rugged. We have to make our way through it, as.　　　[or rare.] 'O'er bog or steep, through straight, rough, dense.

13, 14. *Pwan-kăng seeks to stimulate his officers by reminding them of their fathers, for whose sakes he would deal justly and even kindly with them.*

13. Who Ch'e Jin was is not known. Ch'ing says he was an ancient historiographer. A Chow Jin (周任) is quoted in the same way in the Analects, XVI., i. 人惟求舊,—舊人 must be taken here as in par. 7. Perhaps Ch'e Jin may have intended 'old, experienced men,'—the wiser for the length of their experience,—but Pwan-kăng applies the

我先王、暨乃
祖乃父胥及
逸勤、予敢動
用非罰、世選
爾善茲予不掩
享于先王、爾
祖其從作
之作福災、
予亦不敢動

14 in vessels, we do not seek old ones, but new.' Formerly, the kings, my predecessors, and your forefathers and fathers, shared together the ease and labours *of the State ;*—how should I dare to lay undeserved inflictions on you? For generations the toils of your *families* have been approved, and I will not conceal your goodness. Now when I offer the great sacrifices to my predecessors, your forefathers are present to share in them. *They observe* the happiness I confer and the sufferings I inflict, and I cannot dare to reward virtue that does not exist.

phrase in that other sense.　14. 胥及 逸勤,—相與同其勞逸. The 'Daily Explanation' has it—君臣一德 無事則同享其逸, 有事則 共任其勤, 'sovereigns and ministers possessed a common virtue. In times of quiet, they enjoyed the ease in common; in times of trouble, they shared the burden of the toil together.' 予敢, 云云,—we may take this interrogatively, or supply a 不 before 敢, after the analogy of 予亦不敢 in the last clause. 世選爾勞,—'generations have selected your toils.' The meaning is as in the translation. 茲予……享之, —under the Chow dynasty, as we learn from the 'Rites of Chow,' Bk. XXX. (夏官司 馬, 第四之三), there was a 'Recorder of merits' (司勳), who entered the names of meritorious ministers and officers among the imperial kindred when alive, and regulated the arrangement of their spirit-tablets at the sacrifices in the ancestral temple, when they were dead. The text shows that the practice of giving a place to worthy ministers at imperial sacrifices had descended from the Shang dynasty. The 從 intimates that the spirits of the ministers were supposed not to be present as principals, but as assessors.　作福作 災, 云云,—the 亦 is to be explained from the relation of the sentence to the preced-

ing. Ts'ae has expressed it:—作福作災, 皆簡在先王與祖之心,—'in my rewards and punishments, I seek to be in harmony with the judgment of my predecessors and of your forefathers.' Their judgment is just, and Pwan-kăng wishes that his may *like-wise* be so.　動用,—'to move and use ;' *i.e.*, he would not of his own motion do anything contrary to what was just.

[Choo He has a note on this passage which is worth referring to. He observes that Pwan-kăng speaks of his predecessors and the forefathers of his ministers, as if they were real existences above them (若有眞物在 其上), observing his proceedings from day to day. The meaning, he says, is that Pwan-kăng in his proceedings felt himself, as it were, in the presence of spiritual beings, and no doubts about their justice arose in his mind (質諸鬼神而無疑; see the 'Doct. of the Mean,' xxix. 3). But the common belief of the Yin dynasty venerated spirits (殷俗 尙鬼), and therefore he wanted to guide his ministers by what they profoundly believed in. Were there then those beings as real existences after their death? 'The sages,' answers the critical philosopher, 'felt a difficulty in speaking about the spirits of the dead (鬼神之理, 聖人蓋難言之). To say that they were really existing, would be wrong, and to say that they were *not* really existing, would also be wrong. The subject, being beyond our *sensible* understanding, may be put on one side.' See the 朱子全書, Bk. xxxiv. Was there

爾身弗可悔。

恭爾事齊乃位度乃口罰及

其惟致告自今至于後日各

惟予一人有佚罰。○凡爾衆

善邦之臧惟汝衆邦之不臧

遠邇用罪伐厥死用德彰厥

力聽予一人之作猷。○無有

孤有幼各長于厥居勉出乃

之有志汝無侮老成人無弱

用非德。○予告汝于難若射

十五節　十六節　十七節

15　"I have announced to you the difficulties *of the present enterprise.* My will is that of an archer. Do not you despise the old and experienced, and do not make little of the helpless and young. Seek every one long continuance in your *new* abode; exert yourselves to

16 listen to the plans of me, the one man. There is *with me* no distinction of distant and near. The criminal shall die the death; and the good-doer shall have his virtue displayed. The prosperity of the country must come from you all. If it fail in prosperity, that must arise from me, the one man, erring in the application of punish-

17 ment. All of you be sure to make known this announcement. From this time forward attend respectfully to your business; have *the duties of* your offices regularly adjusted; bring your mouths under the rule of law:—lest punishment come upon you, when repentance will be of no avail."

ever a thinker who more reversed the rule of 'walking by faith and not by sight?']

15. *Pwan-kăng intimates his settled purpose to remove the capital, and summons the officers to co-operate with him.* 予告汝于難—于難, 'about the difficulties;' *i.e.* the difficulties of the contemplated movement. 若射之有志,—the archer thinks only of hitting his mark. Everything else is forgotten. So was Pwan-kăng bent to carry out his purpose. 汝無(＝毋)侮老成人, 無(＝毋)

弱孤有幼,—Keang Shing would read the first clause 汝無老侮成人. Such was the reading of K'ang-shing, who says both 老 and 弱 have the meaning of 'despising.' This we might allow, but there is then no proper contrast between 侮 and 孤. 孤 有幼＝孤與幼, 有 being in the 3d tone, ＝又 (so, at least Tung-po). There were old people who wished to signify their approbation of the removal, but the officers would not hear them, nor represent their views to the emperor. The young were the greatest

sufferers by remaining at Kăng, but the officers made no account of them. 各長
于厥居,—'let every one be long in this
abode.' He would have them look forward to
a permanent abode in Yin, and labour with
him to secure it.   16. *How Pwan-kăng
would exercise a strict justice. The great responsibility which he felt to be devolving on himself*
遠邇,—'distant and near'; here spoken
with reference to kindred and others, and to the
various ties by which officers might think they
had a claim on the emperor's regard.
用 罪=爲 惡, 'the doer of evil'; 用
德=爲 善, 'the doer of good.'   The
meaning of 伐 厥 死 is plain enough, but
the terms do not severally correspond with the
corresponding clause—彰 厥 善. 善 and
死 don't match each other.   邦 之 臧,

云 云,—伏=失, 'to mistake,' 'to err.'
Compare the whole sentiment with T'ang's in
Bk. III., p. 8. It is by no means so noble, and
yet the first part of it might call forth the
sympathy of the higher classes.   17. *Concluding counsels to the officers to co-operate with
himself, and avoid the consequences of continuing
to oppose him.*   凡 爾 衆; 其 惟
致 告,—the 其 has here its strongly hortative force, 致 告 'carry out the announcement.' Leu Tsoo-heen observes :—'Only those
who were in the hall could hear what he said.
He charges them therefore to transmit his
words, and make them generally known.' If
they 'attended respectfully to their business,'
there would be no more 'haughty disregard' of
their sovereign ; if they 'regularly adjusted the
duties of their offices,' they would no longer
'follow their own ease' ; if they 'brought their
mouths under the control of law,' they would
no more give utterance to their 'unsubstantial
and exaggerated speeches.'

BOOK VII. PWAN-KANG. PART ii.

庭　勿　有　告　之　遷　涉　盤一節　盤
盤　藝　眾　用　乃　河　庚　庚
庚　在　咸　亶　率　話　以　作　中
乃　王　造　其　誕　民　民　惟

1　I. Pwan-kăng arose, and crossed the river with the people, moving them to *the new capital*. By and by he addressed himself to those of them who were still dissatisfied, and made a full announcement to their multitudes, to induce a sincere *acquiescence in the measure*. They all attended, and *being charged* to take no liberties in the royal

CONTENTS OF THE SECOND PART. Pwan-kăng has commenced the carrying out of his resolution. They have just crossed, or are about to cross, the river on their way to Yin. But dissatisfaction still exists among a portion of the people, and he calls a great assembly to his hall or tent, and argues at length the wisdom of the movement in which they were engaged. First, he insists on his only acting after the example of former kings, and strives to bring the people to see the measure in its proper light as intended for their good, so that they should entirely sympathize with him in it. This brings us to the 10th par., and may form a chapter by itself. Next, he threatens them with the anger of their forefathers, who would punish them for their disobedience to him, as the founder of his House would punish him, if he did not move from a site now all-unfit to be occupied by the people. This subject forms a second chapter, and brings us to par. 14. In the remaining three parr., he calls them to obedience and sympathy, threatening them with severe punishment, if they continued to murmur at the removal or to resist it.

CH. I. OCCASION OF THE ADDRESS. THE REMOVAL OF THE CAPITAL WAS NOT A NEW THING; IT WAS ALTOGETHER INTENDED FOR THE GOOD OF THE STATE; THE DISSATISFACTION OF THE PEOPLE WAS SHORT-SIGHTED AND BLAME-WORTHY. 1. 盤庚作，惟 涉河，以民遷.—Gan-kwŏ and Ch'ing read the first six characters here without a stop, and made the meaning—'Pwan-kăng prepared the vessels, or arranged the measures, for crossing the Ho.' The 惟 ought on this view to have a substantive meaning, which Wang Suh has endeavoured to express,— 盤庚爲此思南渡河之事, 'Pwan Kăng did this thing,—the thinking on the south to cross the Ho.' All this is very harsh. It is much better to put a stop at 作, and take that character as='to arise,' 'to put one's-self in motion,' which is a common use of it. 惟涉河 will then have the meaning in the translation, 惟 having the slightest possible independent signification. The clause taken in this way describes a fact,—the

登進厥民。○曰明聽二節朕言、無荒失朕命。○嗚呼、古我三節前后、罔不惟民之承、保后胥慼、鮮以不浮于天時。○

2 hall, he called them before him, and said, "Listen clearly to my words, and do not disregard my commands.

3 "Oh! of old time my royal predecessors cherished every one and above every thing a respectful care of the people, who again upheld their sovereign with a mutual sympathy. Seldom was it that they were not superior to any *calamitous* time sent by Heaven.

crossing of the river. 乃話民之 弗率,—the 說文 defines 話 by 會合善言, 'good words in conference.' Keang Shing accordingly thinks he is justified in taking it in the sense simply of 會合, 'to assemble!' It seems to have been used originally with reference to the speaking of 'good words,' but that force is now lost. We need not even seek to find it in the text. 民之弗 率=民之猶弗聽命者. 誕=大, 'great'; 亶=誠 'sincere.' The 'Daily Explanation' puts a stop at 亶, so that 誕告用誠='he made a full announcement with sincerity.' Gan-kwŏ read on to 其有 衆, before putting a stop, —'he made a great ann., using sincerity with his multitudes.' Keang Shing points in the same way, but takes 誠 actively, —'to make sincere;' and I have pointed and translated according to this view.

Ma Yung would carry the sentence on to 造, before putting a stop. That character he defines by 爲, 'to make,' so that the meaning is,—'he addressed them that he might bring them all with sincerity to make—get ready—boats to cross the Ho.' This again is too harsh. We must stop at 衆, and then 造 (ts'aou, 3d tone)=至. 勿藝在王庭,—this passage has wonderfully exercised the ingenuity of the critics. Keang Shing takes 勿 in the sense of 'flags,' and would change 藝 into 達, making the meaning 'flags were set up to collect the people in the royal hall.' But this is too violent. Sun Yen makes 勿=未, and 藝=近, and, running the sentence on to what follows, makes out—'Pwan-kăng made the people who were not near to the royal hall come forward that he might consult them.' But the meaning he would give to 藝 cannot be sustained. Letting the text stand as it is, we must supply something equivalent to the 'being charged' of the translation before 勿. Leu Tsoo-heen observes that as they had left the old capital, and had not arrived at the new, we can only understand the king's tent by the 'royal hall' (王庭蓋道路行宫). 登進厥民,—登 and 進 combine their meaning together. Ying tă has well:—延之、使前而告之. Tsoo-heen says that at such a meeting as is indicated, the ministers were in front, and the people behind them, but that here the king called the people—it could only be the chief among them—to the front. I have dropt 厥民 in the translation. 2. 無荒失朕命,—無=毋; 荒失, comp. 荒墜, Pt. III., Bk. III., p. 8.

3. *The kindly sympathy between former emperors and their people, and its happy effects.* 罔不惟民之承=' were always and every one the reverent *protectors* of the people.' 承=敬, 'to respect,' 'to have a reverent care of.' The use of the term here is well illustrated by the words of Confucius (Ana. XII., ii.)— 使民如承大祭. 保后胥慼,—we must understand this as spoken of the people. The 'Daily Explanation' has:—百姓亦莫不保愛其君. Keang Shing and others would join the 保 to 承, which would not be objectionable in itself; but then to take 后胥慼 as a clause by itself makes the style too jagged. Shing, however, tries to meet this, as we shall see, by adopting the reading 高 instead of 慼. 鮮以

四節 殷降大虐先
王不懷厥攸
作視民利用
遷汝曷弗念
我古后之聞、
承汝俾汝惟
喜康共非汝
有咎比于罰。
五節 ○予若籲懷
兹新邑亦惟

4 When great calamities were coming down on our empire of Yin, the former kings did not fondly remain in their place. What they did was with a view to the people's benefit, and therefore they moved *their capital*. Why do you not reflect that I, according to what I have heard of the ancient kings, in my care for you and actings toward you, am only wishing to rejoice with you in a common repose? It is not that any guilt attaches to you, so that this

5 movement should be like a punishment. When I call you to cherish this new city, it is simply on your account, and as an act of great

不浮于天時,—鮮＝罕, 'seldom.' Gan-kwŏ takes 浮 in the sense of 行, 'to go,' 'to do.' 'A boat's floating along,' says Ying-tă, 'is its movement on the water, and hence 浮 may be used for "to go."' In this way 浮于天時 is made out to mean—'They acted according to the times of Heaven,' *i.e.*, as we should say, 'the requirements of Providence.' Ts'ae, after Soo Tung-po, takes 浮 as ＝勝, 'to overcome,' 'get the better of.' It often means 'to overflow,' 'to go beyond,' and hence this signification is evolved. But why need we feel so much difficulty with the term? If we say that 浮于天時 ＝ 'they floated over—tided over—the times of Heaven,' we are brought to an interpretation substantially the same.

I have said above that Keang Shing reads 高 for 感; he also takes 鮮 in the sense of 'great hills in distinction from little ones' (see the dict.), and makes the whole to mean—'The sovereigns ascertained where the high hills were, and removed to them.' The interpretation is so far-fetched, that we can only laugh at it.

4 *The people could not but approve of the measures of the former kings;—why should they disapprove of the present measure, which was conceived in the same spirit as those?* 殷降大虐,—we think at first that 殷 must be the nominative to 降, but that would give no meaning. 殷 stands absolutely, ＝ 'in our dynasty of Yin.' Then 天 must be understood

as the nominative to 降, or that character may be taken passively. The 'Daily Explanation' says:—昔我殷邦,河水爲災,天降大害,云云. 懷＝安居, 'to dwell at ease.' 汝曷弗念我古后之聞……康共,—the interrogation reaches on to 康共, and 古后之聞 is parenthetical. It might be as well perhaps to end the interrogation at 聞.—'Why do you not think of what you have heard about the former kings, my predecessors?'

Then, however, we must understand a 我 as the nominative to 承 and 俾. 承汝,—承 as in last par.; 俾汝,—'give to you,' ＝ 'do to you, 'call you to do.' 非汝有過,比于罰,—there is some difficulty here with the 比, which is read with the 3d tone, and ＝ 'to be near to,' 'equivalent to.' The 于 following makes it necessary to tone and interpret it thus. The whole ＝ 'It is not that you have any fault, so that I should be, as it were, punishing you, and banishing you by this removal.' 5. *The movement might be considered as in accordance with the people's wishes.* 予若……汝故,—懷 is here defined by 來, 'to come.' We get a better meaning by taking it in its more common signification of 'to cherish.' Gan-kwŏ, taking 若＝順, 籲

臭若爾以不之以志汝
厥乘惟忱宣邦○故
載舟自動汝今以
爾汝鞠子不憂予丕
忱弗自一宣朕將從
不濟苦人乃心試厥
　　　欽　咸　安
　　　念　大　定六節
　　　　　攸　厥
　　　　　困　心

6 accordance with your wishes. My present undertaking to remove with you, is to give repose and stability to the State. You *however*, have no sympathy with the anxieties of my mind; but you all keep a great reserve in declaring your minds, *when you might* respectfully think by your sincerity to move me, the one man. You only exhaust and distress yourselves. The case is like that of sailing in a boat;—if you do not cross the stream *at the proper time*, you will destroy all its cargo. Your sincerity does not respond to

一和, and 懷=歸, makes the meaning—'I turn to this new city, in accordance with right principles, and to harmonize you all.' He would then put a stop at 汝, and join the 故 to the last clause,—'I wish to benefit you, and therefore I boldly follow the first impulses of my will, and remove to it.' No one will be found now to advocate such a construction of the text. It is not more objectionable, however, than that proposed by Keang Shing, who would put a stop at 以, reading 亦惟汝故以, as if 以 were =已, (comp. Mencius, I., Pt. I., vii. 2). He then takes 不 as =丕, and the meaning is —'I, in accordance with reason, call you to come to this new city, simply and solely for your good. I cannot follow your *wayward* wishes.' The construction of Lin Che-k‘e, Ts‘ae and others, which I have followed, is much more easy, and the meaning which it gives is in harmony with the whole address. If it be asked how the removal contrary to their wishes could be represented as an act of great accordance with the peo., it may be answered with Yuen Hwang (袁黃), 'To follow the people's temporary wishes would have been a small act of accordance with them; to gratify their desire for the benefit of permanent establishment was an act of great accordance' (從民之欲者,其從小;從民一時之利者,其從大. 故曰丕從).

6. *The people are reproved for their want of sympathy, and the folly and fruitlessness of their*

opposition to the movement pointed out. 今予將試,='my present experiment,' 'my present undertaking.' 汝不憂朕心之攸困=不憂我憂, 'you do not sorrow with my sorrow,' *i.e.*, you do not enter at all into my trouble of mind about the calamities which threaten us in the old capital. 咸大不宣乃(=汝)心,— 'you all greatly do not declare your minds.' 欽念以忱動予一人,—these two clauses are to be read closely together. 念=敬想, 'reverently thinking' 自鞠,—鞠=窮. 汝弗濟,—we must supply 以時 before 濟. 臭厥載, —臭=敗壞, 'to ruin;' comp. Con. Ana., X., viii. 2. The removal from Kǎng to Yin was like crossing a stream in a boat. If they delayed, the calamity of inundation would be upon them. 汝忱不屬,—屬 is read *chuh*, 'to be connected with.' It seems most natural to understand the meaning to be as in the translation. From this to the end, the 'Daily Explanation' paraphrases:—汝從焉沈爾違,從亦于此從,則及如決,不屬惟相害昭察以早,斷間濟乎利,誠有而曾不稽察,上之能溺民

迁　臭　一　上　罔　勸　以　瘳　其　屬
乃　恐　無　○　後　憂　思　○　或　惟
心　人　起　今　汝　今　乃　汝　稽　胥
○　倚　穢　予　何　其　災　不　自　以
予　乃　以　命　生　有　汝　謀　怒　沈
迓　身　自　汝　在　今　誕　長　曷　不

mine, and we are in danger of going together to destruction. You notwithstanding will not examine the matter:—though you anger yourselves, what cure will that bring?

7 "You do not consult for a distant day, nor think of the calamity that must befal you. You greatly encourage one another in what must prove to your sorrow. Now you have the present, but you may not have the future. What deliverance can you look for from

8 above? Now I charge you to have but one mind. Do not let wicked thoughts arise to ruin yourselves. I am afraid that men bend your persons, and pervert your minds."

但自生怨疾忿怒亦曷救
于沈溺之苦哉子不能爲
汝解已 Gan-kwŏ's interpretation was
rather different. He says:—汝忠誠不
屬逮古苟不欲徒相與沈
溺何瘳差乎.
　Keang Shing reads 迪 (＝道) for 稽,
and 怨 for 怒, and interprets:—爾柬誠既
不連屬于我同謀共濟其
臭厥載惟相與沈水不
有生道矣 (＝'you have no way of life'),
雖自怨恚何瘉乎.
　7, 8. *Pwan-kăng reproves the short-sightedness
of the people, and warns them against being
misled.* 7. 汝不謀長以
思乃災＝汝不爲長遠之
謀, 以思不遷之禍, 'you do not
adopt any far-reaching counsels to think about
the calamity that must result from your not
removing.' 勸憂＝以憂自勸,
'you advise one another about what will prove
to your sorrow.' Ts'ae, after Lin Che-k'e,
refers to the case adduced by Mencius (IV., Pt.

I., viii.) of those princes who 安其危而
利其災, 樂其所以亡, as an in-
stance of 勸憂. 今其有今罔
後,—this does not mean, as Gan-kwŏ supposed, 'you have no plans for the future,' but
死亡無日, 'your death will soon happen'
(see Keang Shing, *in loc.*). 汝何生
在上,—for 在上, Gan-kwŏ said 在人
上, 'among men.'; Lin Che-k'e, in the same
way, 在生民上; Keang Shing says 在
地上, 'upon the earth.' Ts'ae alone, and
I think correctly, makes 上, 'above,'＝天
'heaven,' referring to 子迓續乃命于
天, which passage and the text, he says, explain
each other (相首尾之辭). 8. 命
汝一＝命汝專一乃心, 從我遷
徒, 'I charge you to have but one heart to follow
me in the proposed movement.' 無 (＝毋)
起穢以自臭,—穢 is explained in the
dict., with ref. to this passage, simply by 惡,
'wickedness.' It stands related to 臭, which
denotes the fetid odour of articles in a state of
decomposition. Pwan-kăng chooses such terms

崇　兹　失　用　予　后　予　奉　予　續
降　高　于　懷　丕　丕　念　畜　豈　乃
罪　后　政　爾　之　克　我　汝　汝　命
疾　丕　陳　然。　勞　羞　先　眾。　威　于
曰　乃　于　○　爾　爾　神　○　用　天、
　　　　　　　先　　后
十一節　　　十節　　　　　　　十節

9　"My measures are forecast to prolong your lease of life from Heaven. Do I force you by my majesty? My object is to support
10　and nourish you all. I think of the toils of my predecessors, *who are now* the spiritual sovereigns, for your ancestors; I would in the same way greatly nourish you, and cherish you.
11　II. "Were I to err in my government, and remain long here, my High sovereign, *the founder of our House*, would send down great punishment for my crime, and say, 'Why do you oppress my peo-

to show his contempt for the injurious speeches by which the people were led astray. 倚 =偏. 迂=曲.

9, 10. *Pwan-kăng, like his predecessors, had but one object in his measures,—the good of the people.* 9. 迂=迎, 'to meet.' 予迂續乃命于天,—'I am going forward to a continuance (prolongation) of your lives from heaven'; *i.e.*, by removing them from Kăng to Yin, he would prolong their lives and prosperity. 用奉畜汝眾,—畜=養, 'to nourish.' 奉畜, 'to bear up and nourish,'= to nourish with all kindly and respectful care. 用 is used with reference to the removal which Pwan-kăng had in his mind, and = 'I am using this—my object in it is—to,' &c. 10. 我先神后,—'my predecessors, the spirit sovereigns.' I think the meaning is as I have given it in the translation. From the last Part, p. 14, and the parr. which follow here, we see how Pwan-kăng thought of his ancestors as still sovereigns, and their ministers as still ministers, in the world of spirits. 我先后之勞爾先—the 'Daily Explan.' takes 勞 act. = 'to make to toil' (我思我先后之勞爾先人,而先人不以爲勞). Lin Che-k'e takes 先 as = 'toiled with your ancestors' (我先后與爾先祖相與勤勞). I venture to let the view of the meaning, which first occurred to me, stand as in the translation.

羞=養, or the 畜 of the last par. Keang Shing reads 不克 instead of 丕克, and makes the 然 at the close stand by itself, connecting the whole with the next par.—'I think how my predecessors removed their capital, and escaped from the evils threatening them. And I cannot get you to go to this land of enjoyment, where I could give you repose. If indeed it prove so, I shall be failing in my government,' &c.

Ch. II. Pp. 11—14. SPIRITUAL SANCTIONS. HOW FORMER EMPERORS AND THE PEOPLE'S FOREFATHERS WOULD PUNISH FROM HEAVEN BOTH EMPEROR AND PEOPLE, IF THEY DID NOT REMOVE TO YIN. 11. 陳于兹,—陳=久, 'long.' 陳 and 塵, it is said, were anciently interchanged, and as 'dust' accumulated on any thing shows it must have been for some time undisturbed in its place, there grew up the meaning of 'long,' 'long continuance.' However the meaning arose, we must acknowledge it in this passage. 高后,—Lin Che-k'e insists that this phrase here should be taken in the plural, and with the same general reference as 先后 before and after. His reasoning on the subject is not without weight, but I prefer, on the whole, with Ts'ae to understand the 'high sovereign' as being T'ang. 崇=大, 'great,' 'greatly.' 罪疾,—'the pain of—suffering for—crime.' 虐朕民,—not that Pwan-kăng oppressed the people; but his sin of *omission* in not removing them from Kăng would be reckoned to him

我畜民汝有戕則
乃祖乃父汝共作
○十三節古我先后既勞
其罰汝汝罔能迪。
比故有爽德自上
曷不暨朕幼孫有
不降與汝罪疾曰
一人獻同心先后
民乃不生生暨予
曷虐朕民。○汝萬　十二節

12 ple?'　If you, the myriads of the people, do not attend to the perpe-
tuation of your lives, and cherish one mind with me, the one man,
in my plans, my predecessors will send down on you great punishment for your crime, and say, 'Why do you not agree with our
young grandson, but so go on to forfeit your virtue?'　When they
13 punish you from above, you will have no way of escape.　Of old,
my royal predecessors toiled for your ancestors and fathers.　You
are equally the people whom I nourish; but your conduct is in-

as a sin of *commission*.　12. 不生生,
—Wang Suh and Gan-kwŏ both explained 生
生 by 進進, = 'an earnest joyful alacrity,'
i.e., in adopting the proposal to transfer the
capital.　Che-k'e adopted the explanation of Soo
Shih as being preferable, in which he was foll.
by Ts'ae:—we have in the 集傳;—樂生
與事, 其生也厚, 是謂生生,
'a joyous life, with vigorous enterprises,—a life
strong and rich; this is what is meant by 生
生.'　Much better than either of those views
is that in the 'Daily Explanation,' which I have
followed;—生生者, 生養不窮之
意.　暨予一人獻,—hitherto we
have had 暨=及, 'and,' a conjunction simply;
here and below, it =與.　Keang Shing reads
縣 for 獻, and takes it in the sense of 從,
but I cannot construe the sentence so.
降與爾罪疾,—here the use of 與,
where we should expect 于, is strange. 朕
幼孫,—'our young grandson.' This of course
is Pwan-kang.　有比,—比,=合 or
同　Keang Shing takes it in the sense of 下

順, which also gives a good meaning.　故
有爽德,—this clause is joined with the
preceding, in the 'Daily Explanation,' which
also takes 爽 in the sense of 失.　Gan-kwŏ
joined the clause with what follows, and took
爽 as = 明.—'Therefore he who has the brilliant virtue (*i.e.,* T'ang) from above will punish,'
&c.　This is inadmissible.　Keang Shing, following 賈逵 in an explanation of the same phrase
in the 國語, gives it by 貳德, which
comes to much the same with 失德.　汝
罔能迪,—迪=道.　Ts'ae says:—汝
無道以自免也, 'you will have no
way to make your escape.'　13. 故我
先后……畜民,—see on parr. 10 and 9.
汝有戕, 則在乃心,—I hardly
know what to make of this passage. The 'Daily
Explanation' paraphrases it:—汝不法
汝祖父而從我以遷, 是即
戕害生民矣. 若有戕害在
汝之心, 我先王云云, 'you do
not imitate your ancestors by falling into my
view of removing.　In this you prove yourselves
hurtful to the life of the people, and since you
have such an injurious object in your hearts, my

乃　于　我　乃　政　乃　父　乃　在
崇　朕　高　祖　同　死　乃　祖　乃
降　孫　后　乃　位　。　斷　乃　心
弗　迪　曰　父　其　○　棄　父　我
祥　高　作　丕　乃　兹　汝　乃　先
。　后　丕　乃　貝　予　不　祖　后
○　丕　刑　告　玉　有　救　乃　綏
嗚　　　　　　　　亂

十四節

jurious,—it is cherished in your hearts. Whereas my royal predecessors made happy your ancestors and fathers, your ancestors and fathers will cut you off and abandon you, and not save you from death. Here are those ministers of my government, who share with me the offices *of the State;*—and yet only think of hoarding up cowries and gems! Your ancestors and fathers urgently represent to my High sovereign, saying, 'Execute great punishments on our descendants.' So they intimate to my High sovereign that he should send down great calamities.

predecessors,' &c. Keang Shing would take 在＝察, as in the Canon. of Shun, par. 5,—'What sort of mind does your resistance to my commands betoken? But if you occasion injury to any, my predecessors will examine your hearts. I am afraid they will punish you.'

As much difficulty is found with what follows,—我先后綏乃祖乃父, 云云, The 'Daily Explanation' continues the paraphrase which I have just quoted:—'My predecessors, thinking of the great and real toils of your forefathers, will soothe them till there is awakened the thought of punishing you' (必安慰汝祖父, 致其用罰之意). Keang Shing takes 綏＝妥＝止, 'to stop,' and says:—'My predecessors will stop your forefathers, and require them not to save you.' The view which I take will be seen in the translation. Gan-kwŏ interpreted 綏 differently, but his view of the argument, so to speak, was similar. He says:—'My predecessors reposed in the loyalty of your forefathers; and now that you are disloyal, your forefathers will cast away your lives, and not save you from death.' 14. Ts'ae observes on this par. that 'former scholars had taken it as addressed in reproof to Pwan-kăng's ministers,

but that, on looking closely at the style, we see that it is a reproof of the ministers indeed, but spoken not directly to them, but of them to the people.' Ts'ae is right in saying that the first portion—兹予有亂政同位, 具乃貝玉, is to be understood as spoken about the ministers, but I do not see my way to interpret 乃祖乃父, 'their ancestors and their fathers,' as he does. Here is the difficulty;—why should the ancestors of the people ask their descendants to be punished for the evil conduct of the ministers? A reason can be given, and we may suppose that it was indicated by the tone of voice, though it was not expressed in words. It was that the people by listening to the speeches of such men, and in obedience to them disobeying their sovereign, greatly aggravated their guilt. 亂＝治. 同位＝共天位. 具＝多取而兼有, 'amassing.' 貝玉,—貝＝海介蟲, 'a shelled insect of the sea.' Ying-tă says that 'anciently they used the shell as money.' The text is a proof that such a medium of exchange was known in the Shang dynasty. 'Amassing cowries and gems' is a description of the selfish covetousness of the ministers.

永建乃家。

生今予將試以汝遷、

于茲新邑。○十七節往哉生

之、無遺育無俾易種

遇姦宄我乃劓殄滅

吉不迪顛越不恭暫

中于乃心。○十六節乃有不

分猷念以相從、各設

敬大恤無胥絶遠汝

呼十五今予告汝不易、永

15   III. "Ah! I have now announced to you my unchangeable purpose: —do you perpetually respect *my* great anxiety; let us not get alienated and removed from one another; share in my plans and thoughts, and be prepared to obey me; let every one of you set up the true

16   rule of conduct in his heart. If there be bad and unprincipled men, precipitously or carelessly disrespectful *to my orders*, and taking advantage of this brief season to play the part of villains or traitors, I will cut off their noses, or utterly exterminate them. I will leave none of their children. I will not let them perpetuate their seed in this new city.

17   "Go! preserve and continue your lives. I will now transfer you to the new capital, and there for ever establish your families."

Ch. III. Pp. 15—17. Pwan-kang announces his settled purpose to proceed to Yin, and summons all to sympathizing co-operation with him, while recusants are threatened with punishment and death.

15. 告汝不易,—Wang Suh and Gan-kwŏ read 易 in the 3d tone, and interpreted—'I have announced to you what is not easy,' so that the meaning is the same as that of the first clause, p. 16, Pt. i. Ts'ae adopts this view: but that in the transl., which was originally proposed by K'ang-shing, is followed by Lin Che-k'e and Keang Shing. 大恤 =大憂, 'the great sorrow.' Pwan-kăng thus characterizes the movement which had occasioned him so much anxiety. 汝分猷念,—Kĕang Shing reads 比 for 分; but the meaning is the same. 設中于乃心,—'set up the middle in your hearts.' 中=大中至正之則, 'the great exact, and perfectly correct rule.' 16. 乃

有不吉不迪,—吉=善; 迪=道; 不吉不迪, are 'men without goodness or principle.' 顛越不恭,=Ts'ae explains these terms by—'overthrowing, transgressing, or not respecting *my commands*;' but we may as well take 越 here as in 無越厥命, V., Pt. i., 5. 暫遇姦宄,—Lin Che-k'e says that the two words 暫遇 are not in harmony with the rest of the sentence, and unintelligible to him; and he will therefore say nothing about them. Ying-tă, giving Gan-kwŏ's view of them, says—'they mean that such persons plundered men whenever they met them; that they did so without intermission' (謂逢人卽刦, 爲之無已). I have done the best with them I could. [Keang Shing puts them out of the text, as an addition by the compiler of the present 'old text.' He reduces the whole par., indeed, to small dimensions,—其有顛越不共, 則劓殄 云云. His reason for doing so is that so much is found quoted in the 左傳, 哀十一年. But because only so much is quoted, it is absurd to conclude that there never was any more.] 我乃劓, 云云,—we may compare this with the conclusion of 'The Speech at Kan,' and of 'The Speech of T'ang.' 'Cutting off the nose' was one of the ancient regular punishments;—see on the 'Canon of Shun,' p. 11. 易種,—易＝移. 17. 往哉,—comp. 'Can. of Shun,' p. 17, *et al.* 生生,—see p. 12. 今予, 云云,—see p. 6.

盤　盤一節　遷　攸　正　緩　衆。　無　戀
庚　庚　奠　居　厥　爰　○　戲　建
下　旣　厥　乃　位　有　曰二節　怠。　大。

1　1. Pwan-kang having completed the removal, and settled the places
of residence, proceeded to adjust their several positions, and then
2　he soothed and comforted the multitudes, saying to them, " Do not
play or be idle, but exert yourselves to build here a great destiny
for us.

CONTENTS OF THE THIRD PART. The removal
has been accomplished. Emperor, officers, and
people are all at Yin, when he once more addresses them. First, in 7 parr., he goes over much
the same ground with the people as he had done
before, justifying the measure which he had
taken; and then, in the remaining 6 parr. he
charges all the chiefs and officers to labour with
him in a common sympathy for the good of the
people.

Ch. I. Pp. 1—7. OCCASION OF THE ADDRESS.
THERE SHOULD BE ENTIRE CONFIDENCE BE-
TWEEN SOVEREIGN AND PEOPLE. THE REMOVAL
OF THE CAPITAL WAS IN ACCORDANCE WITH
FORMER PRECEDENTS; REQUIRED FOR THE GOOD
OF THE PEOPLE; APPROVED BY GOD. 1.
Occasion of the address. 奠 厥 攸 居,
乃 正 厥 位,—Ch'ing supposed that the
former of these clauses described the settlement
of *the people,* and the latter the laying out the
official residences and public buildings,—such
as the ancestral temple, the court, &c. Gan-
kwŏ takes the second clause in the same way,
and naturally extends the former to the settlement of the officers as well as of the people. Lin
Che-k'e argues against this view of the second
clause, and says that Pwan-kăng would have
had the city laid out, before moving from Kăng,
as Chow-kung did afterwards when he wished

to make Lŏ the capital of the Chow rule. To
my mind the style corroborates this reasoning.
The parties interested in 'the dwellings' (攸
居) are the same as those concerned in the
'positions' (厥 位); but the 乃 intimates an
interest of a diff't. kind. I am prepared therefore to agree farther with Lin Che-k'e in taking
正 厥 位 of the arrangements made for the
positions of the various classes at a public assembly, where Pwan-kăng gave the address that
follows. Woo Ch'ing follows this view. Ts'ae,
dissatisfied with that of Gan-kwŏ and Ch'ing,
makes the positions to be those of 'sovereign,
ministers, high, and low;' but the relations of
all these were determined before. 緩 爰
有 衆,—both Gan-kwŏ and Ch'ing again agree
in def. 爰 by 于, and explain the clause by
安 於 有 衆, and 安 隱 于 其 衆.
The construction would be easier, but the sym-
metry not so good, without the 爰. 2.
*The great object to be kept in view by them all at
their present crisis.* 無 戲 怠. The comment of Woo Ch'ing on this par. is very good :—

命。○ 今予其
敷心腹腎腸、
歷告爾百姓
于朕志罔罪
爾衆爾無共
怒協比讒言
予一人。○古
我先王將多
于前功適于
山用降我凶

3　"Now I have disclosed my heart and belly, my reins and bowels, and have fully declared to you, my people, all my mind. I will not treat any of you as criminals; and do not you *any more* help one another to be angry, and form parties to defame me, the one man.

4　"Of old, my royal predecessor, that his merit might exceed that of those who had gone before him, proceeded to the hill-site. Thereby he removed our evils, and accomplished admirable good for our country.

'When Pwan-kăng tells them "not to play," he requires that they should *reverently* attend to their duties (欲其敬事); when he tells them "not to be idle," he requires them to attend *diligently* to them. By "a great destiny" he intends the destiny of themselves and of the kingdom; and he speaks of "building" this, just as Mencius speaks of "establishing it" (猶孟子言立命; see Men. VII., Pt. I., i., 3). Our destiny depends, indeed, on Heaven, but the establishing it is our own work, by which the people may be made to have the enjoyment of their life, and the fortunes of the kingdom be prolonged. At that time a disregard of the emperor and a seeking of their ease, with an addiction to sport and idleness, were characteristics of the Yin people. Before the removal of the capital, they were afraid of the trouble; after the removal, they thought they had done enough, saying now their lives would be perpetuated, and they need not exert themselves any more. It was to meet all this that the emperor cautioned them as in the text.'

3. *The openness of Pwan-kăng with the people and his kindness should make them respond to him with entire confidence.* 今予其敷,—the 其 is strongly intensive. 敷=布, or 布露 歷告=盡告 I think the verbs here should be translated in the present complete tense, with reference to all that the emp. had said to them. 白姓,—'the people;' including also the 'various officers,' says Ts'ae, 'and their clans,'

[The reading of the first part of this par. adopted by Këang Shing is peculiar, and he is put to great straits to make any sense of it. What he does make is not in harmony with the tenor of the Book. He has:—今我其敷

優臥、揚歷告爾、云云〕　罔 罪爾衆,—Medhurst translates—'not that I would blame you all;' which is very different from the meaning. Pwan-kăng promises to forget all the past, and goes on to hope that they will not do as they had done.

協比=合同附和.

4. *What advantages T'ang had secured by fixing his capital in a high situation.* 古我 先王,—'the former king' must be T'ang. The characterizing him as 古, 'ancient' is in favour of this view, and from his time the emperors had been obliged to leave one capital after another, in consequence of their low situation exposing them to inundations. We might have expected that it would have been more clearly indicated that the hill-site of T'ang was that to which they were now returned;—but we must take the Book as it is. Those early settlements could not have been built of very permanent materials and structure.

將多于前功,—將=欲, 'to wish.' 將, as the sign of the future, indicates also the purpose out of which that future grows. One of the definitions of it in the dict. is—將有 其意也. 用降我凶德,—用 ='thereby;' 降=下 Hwang Too, more intelligibly, defines it here by 減少, 'to diminish.' 我凶德 == 'our suffering condition,' referring to the evils of a low situation, exposed to inundation. Lin Che-k'e would make the meaning—'removed our evil habits,' arguing from the Mencian doctrine that want and calamities are the parents of wickedness (see

非廢厥謀弔由靈、　新邑。○肆予冲人、　承民命用永地于　我家朕及篤敬恭　我高祖之德亂越　遷。○肆上帝將復　朕曷震動萬民以　居罔有定極爾謂　今我民用蕩析離　德嘉績于朕邦。○

5 Now you, my people, were by your position dissipated and separated, and obliged to leave your dwellings, so that you had no abiding place. And yet you asked why I was troubling your myriads by
6 removing you here. But God being about to restore the virtue of my High ancestor, and secure the *good* government of our empire, I with the sincere and respectful *of my ministers* felt a reverent care for the lives of the people, and have made a lasting settlement in this new city.

7   "I, a youth, did not slight your plans;—I *only* used what were

Men. Bk. VI., Pt. I., vii.), where as T'ang removing the people to a location which required industry, and rewarded it, greatly improved their moral tone. 嘉績,—another reading is 綏績.

It will be seen that Pwan-kăng throws himself and his people a long way back, to identify themselves with their fathers in the time of T'ang, nearly 400 years before.

5. *How Pwan-kăng had emulated T'ang's proceeding, against the general sentiment, but having the approval of some, and, as he thought, the sanction of God.* 用=以; 以其居處, 'in consequence of their position.' 極=止.

罔有定極 'had no fixed place of rest.' 爾謂云云,—we must understand, as preliminary to this, something equivalent to —'a removal was urgently called for.' The 'Daily Explanation' has—乃陷于凶 德,而宜急圖嘉績之時. [Keang Shing reads 今 before 爾, and 惠 for 謂, making the interpretation still more difficult.] 6. 肆上帝 云云—肆, as 'an introductory particle indicating a change in the thought' (更端辭), is defined in the dict. by 故, 'therefore,' and 今, 'now.' Neither

of these terms, however, expresses exactly what seems to be its force here. 'But' comes nearer to it, and Ts'ae indeed explains it by 乃. Pwan-kăng evidently ascribes the movement to an influence exerted by God on the mind of himself and some of his ministers. 亂越 我家,—亂=治; 越=及; 家=國 家. The meaning of the clause is as in the transl. The only critic who takes a difft. view is Lin Che-k'e, who would retain the common meaning of 亂, 'to confound.' He says:— 'God, being about to restore the virtue of T'ang, and make the empire flourish anew under his descendant, brought about the disorder and calamities in Kăng, to lead Pwan-kăng to move to Yin;' and then he goes on to speak of the uses of adversity. This is too ingenious.

朕及篤敬,—we can only understand that the emperor is speaking here of some of his ministers who were of the same mind with himself. Ts'ae says:—我與一二篤 敬之臣. Keang Shing would make 及=汲汲, so that the discourse is only of Pwan-kăng, himself.—'I roused to earnest reverence,' &c. 7. *Forgetting their past differences, the emperor is willing to suppose there had been a substantial agreement between the people and himself. The paragraph is hardly intelligible.* Ch'in Leih has said:—'Choo He doubted the

念　懋　哉　人、百　邦　賣。卜　各
敬　簡　○　尚　執　伯　○　用　非
我　相　予　皆　事　師　嗚　宏　敢
眾。爾、其　隱　之　長、呼　茲　違

the best of them. And you did not presumptuously oppose the decision of the tortoise:—so we are *here* to enlarge our great inheritance.

8　II. "Ah! ye chiefs of regions, ye heads of departments, all ye, the hundreds of officers, would that ye were animated by a true
9　sympathy! I will exert myself in the selection and guiding of you;

genuineness of this Part from 多于前功 (in par. 4), and there are passages like 弔由靈宏茲賣 here, which are truly difficult to understand. Our best plan is to be content with what the early scholars said about them.' Such a course might be our best plan; but no one whose judgment is worth anything will be content to take it. 予沖人,—幼少在位曰沖. 'a youth on the throne is called 沖.' In the 5th Part of the Shoo we shall find the phrase 沖人 employed several times by the emperors as a humble designation of themselves. This is the first instance of its occurrence. Pwan-kăng was not 'a youth' at this time, but he is pleased to speak as if he were. 弔 (also 逆) = 至; 由 = 用; 靈 = 善. Ying-tă says:—'On occasion of any great matter, the rule was to consult with all about it. Pwan-kăng did so, and therefore he says, "I did not neglect consulting with you." But in such a case there could not but be different views, and he therefore followed what he considered the best' (故至極用其善者. One hardly knows the exact force of 至極. Perhaps it = 'in the extremity'). It would appear that the emperor submitted the conclusion to which he came to the decision of the tortoise, and when the divination approved of the transference of the capital, the people ceased their opposition. 用宏茲賣,—宏 and 賣 (read *fun*) have both the meaning of 大 'great;' but the former is a verb, = 'to enlarge,' and the latter = a concrete noun,—'great inheritance.' Such is the view of the par. given by the early scholars. Tung-po took another view of the last term, which he read *pe;*—see the 附錄, and a note by the editors of Yung-ching's Shoo. Keang Shing, as usual, strikes out a path here for himself, and with more than his usual ingenuity.

I am not sure but it would be well to interpret the par. after him—'I did not slight your plans; but as the best rule felt it right to follow the intelligent tortoise. And you, did not venture to resist the divination,' &c.

Ch. II. Pp. 8—13. CHARGE TO THE NOBLES AND OFFICERS TO SYMPATHIZE WITH HIMSELF, AND SEEK THE GOOD OF THE PEOPLE. 8. By 邦伯 Lin Che-k'e and Ts'ae understand 邦之諸侯, 'the princes of regions:' by 師長, 眾官之長, 'the heads of all the officers,' the six high nobles (六卿 and 公卿); and by 百執事之人, 'all the officers,' subordinate to these last. Gan-kwŏ and Ying-tă differed only in their view of 邦伯, by which they understood all the princes of the nine provinces, and two superior princes who exercised a control over them. But the institution of those two princes belonged to the next, or Chow dynasty. And we can hardly suppose that the princes of all the provinces were collected on this occasion. The 邦伯 must be restricted to those within the imperial domain,—the 甸服. Much more must we restrict the 師長, which we should otherwise be inclined to understand according to Yu's use of the terms in the 'Yih and Tseih,' p. 8. 隱 = 痛, 'to feel pained,' = to look with sympathy upon the condition of the people. [Keang Shing for 隱 read 乘, which he explains by 治職.] 9. 簡 = 擇, 'to select'; 相 = 導, 'to lead.' Others take 簡 = 閱, 'to examine,' and 相 = 視, 'to see;' giving the meaning,—'I will assiduously examine, and see whether you think reverently of my people.' This meaning is as

朕不肩好貨敢
恭生生、鞠人謀
人之保居敘欽。
○今我既羞告
爾于朕志若否、
罔有弗欽。○無
總于貨寶、生生
自庸、○式敷民
德永肩一心。

10 —do ye think reverently of my multitudes. I will not employ those who are fond of wealth; but those who are rigorously yet reverently labouring for the lives and increase of the people, nourishing them and planning for their enduring settlement, I will use and respect.

11 "I have now brought forward and announced to you my mind, whom I approve and whom I disallow;—let none of you but reve-

12 rence *my will.* Do not seek to accumulate wealth and precious things; *but* in fostering the life of the people seek to find your merit.

13 Reverently display your virtue in behalf of the people. For ever maintain *this* one heart."

good as that in the translation. 10. 肩, 'to bear on the shoulder,' is here taken as = 任, 'to employ.' The whole par. is very difficult. Ts'ae acknowledges that he does not understand 鞠人, 謀人, adding that some take 鞠 in the sense of 養, 'to nourish.' Such was the view of K'ang-hing. I have translated after the 'Daily Explanation.' Other views may be seen in Woo Ch'ing and Keang Shing. 叙 = 次叙, 'to arrange,' = to give employment and emolument to according to their qualities. 欽, 'to respect,' = to treat with reverent politeness. 11. 羞 = 進, 'to bring forward.' 若否,—若 = 若者, 'those whom I approve,'—those characterized in the prec. par., as 'labouring for the lives and comfort of the people.' 否 = 否者,—those whom I disallow,'—'those who were fond of wealth.' Keang Shing takes the two characters differently.—'I have shown you my thoughts. Whether you approve of them or disapprove, reverence my will.' 12. 無 總于貨寶,—無 = 毋; 總 = 聚; 貨寶 = the 貝玉, of last Part, p. 14. 庸 denotes 民功, 'service done to the people.' Woo Ch'ing, says:—以民之生生爲已責. 13. 式 = 敬, 'to reverence,' 'reverently,' 民德爲民之德 肩, 'to, bear on the shoulder,' = 'to bear about with one, 'to maintain.'

CONCLUDING NOTE. History tells us nothing special of Pwan-kăng after his transference of his capital to Yin. It is only said that he revived the government of T'ang, and the dynasty of Shang prospered again. He reigned 28 years, and died B.C. 1373.

THE BOOKS OF SHANG.

BOOK VIII. THE CHARGE TO YUE. PART i.

說命上

言式惟明嗚群既王一
臣王君哲呼臣免王節
下言萬實知咸憂宅
罔惟邦作之諫亮
攸作百則曰于陰
稟命官天明王三
令不承子哲曰祀

1   I. The king passed the season of sorrow in the mourning shed for three years, and when he had ceased mourning, he still did not speak. The ministers all remonstrated with him, saying, "The man of *quick* knowledge is said to be intelligent; and the intelligent man forms a model. The emperor rules over the myriad regions, and all the officers depend on and reverence him. When the king speaks, *his words* form the commands *for them*; if he do not speak,

INTRODUCTORY HISTORICAL NOTE.   Pwan-kăng's reign ended B.C. 1373. Between him and Woo-ting, some events of whose time are commemorated in this and the following Book, there intervened a space of 50 years, occupied by the reigns of Seaou-sin (小辛) and Seaou-yih (小乙), both brothers of Pwan-kăng and Yang-kĕä, so that we have the remarkable fact of four brothers occupying the throne in succession. Seaou-sin and Seaou-yih are all but nameless sovereigns. Sze-ma Ts'een tells us that the fortunes of the house of T'ang began again to wane under the former, who died B.C. 1352. Of Seaou-yih nothing at all is chronicled, but we are told that in his 26th year Tan-foo (亶父) removed from (豳) to K'e (岐), and gave his settlement the name of Chow. The dynasty which was to supplant that of Shang (or Yin) is already looming in the distance. Seaou-yih died B.C. 1324, and the next year was the first of Woo-ting (武丁), who earned a place for himself in the 'seven-shrined temple,' under the title of 'The High and Venerable' (高宗), and arrested for a time the downfal of his House.

Nᴀᴍᴇ ᴏꜰ ᴛʜᴇ Bᴏᴏᴋ.—說命, 'The Charge to Yuĕ.' This is the first of the 'Charges' which form one of the divisions of the Shoo. They relate the designation by the emperor of some officer to a particular charge or fief, with the address delivered to him on the occasion. Here the charge is to Yuĕ on his appointment to be prime minister. The name, however, is not happily chosen. It does very well for the first Part of the Book, but in the other two Parts Yuĕ is the principal speaker, and not the king. They would be classified properly among the 'Counsels.'　　Yuĕ was a recluse, living in obscurity,—on account, we may suppose, of the disorder of the times. Woo-ting's attention was drawn to him in the manner related in the Book, and he was discovered in Foo Yen, or the crags of Foo, from which he was afterwards known as Foo Yuĕ, as if Foo had been his surname. The Book is only found in the 'old text.' It has been alleged against its genuineness that Sze-ma Ts'een does not say anything about its composition. But this can only be an omission. Ts'een gives several particulars about Yuĕ; the Preface to the Shoo, and many references in other books, leave no doubt as to the fact of there having originally been a 'Charge to Yuë.'

Cᴏɴᴛᴇɴᴛꜱ. The first Part tells us how the emperor was led to meet with Yuĕ, and appointed him his prime minister, with the charge, which he then delivered to him, and Yue's response to it. In the second Part, Yuĕ appears counselling the emperor on a variety of points, and the king responds admiringly. In the third Part, the king presents himself first as a pupil at the feet of Yuĕ, and is lectured on the subject of study, or enlarging his knowledge. Finally, the emperor says he looks to Yuĕ to be another E Yin, to make him another T'ang.

Cᴏɴᴛᴇɴᴛꜱ ᴏꜰ ᴛʜᴇ ꜰɪʀꜱᴛ Pᴀʀᴛ. The whole is edited in 11 paragraphs. The first three form a chapter, relating the peculiar circumstances in which Woo-ting found Yuĕ. The next 7 parr. relate the elevation of Yuĕ to the premiership, and the charge which was then given him. The last par. contains Yue's dutiful reply, and expresses his confidence in the emperor's wisdom.

Ch. I. Pp. 1—3. Oᴄᴄᴀꜱɪᴏɴ ᴏꜰ ᴛʜᴇ ᴄʜᴀʀɢᴇ. Wᴏᴏ-ᴛɪɴɢ ᴇxᴄɪᴛᴇꜱ ᴛʜᴇ ꜱᴜʀᴘʀɪꜱᴇ ᴏꜰ ʜɪꜱ ᴍɪɴɪꜱᴛᴇʀꜱ ʙʏ ʜɪꜱ ᴘʀᴏᴛʀᴀᴄᴛᴇᴅ ꜱɪʟᴇɴᴄᴇ, ᴡʜɪᴄʜ ʟᴇᴀᴅꜱ ᴛʜᴇᴍ ᴛᴏ ʀᴇᴍᴏɴꜱᴛʀᴀᴛᴇ ᴡɪᴛʜ ʜɪᴍ. Hᴇ ᴇxᴘʟᴀɪɴꜱ ᴛʜᴇ ʀᴇᴀꜱᴏɴ, ᴛᴇʟʟɪɴɢ ᴛʜᴇᴍ ᴏꜰ ᴀ ᴅʀᴇᴀᴍ ɪɴ ᴡʜɪᴄʜ ᴀ ꜱᴀɢᴇ ᴍɪɴɪꜱᴛᴇʀ ᴡᴀꜱ ᴘʀᴇꜱᴇɴᴛᴇᴅ ᴛᴏ ʜɪᴍ, ᴡʜᴏ ɪꜱ ꜰᴏᴜɴᴅ ᴀɴᴅ ᴘʀᴏᴠᴇꜱ ᴛᴏ ʙᴇ Yᴜᴇ. 1. 王宅憂亮陰三祀.—宅憂＝居喪, 'to occupy—to abide—during mourning.' 亮陰,—this is a phrase which has occasioned much speculation as to its meaning. The characters are variously written. In Pt. V., Bk. XV., p. 5, they are the same as here. In the Analects, XIV., xiii., we have 諒陰; and in other places we have 諒闇. However we write them, the first should be pronounced in the low. 1st tone, and the second is read an or gan, up. 1st tone. As to the mean., Choo He, on the Analects, says he does not know it. Gan-kwŏ

made it out to be 信默,—'trusting the premier, and silent himself.' In this sense we should have to read 陰 in the usual way; but the explanation is most unlikely. We are indebted to Ch'ing for the view that we are to understand by the phrase the 凶廬, or what is called in the 儀禮,喪服, Pt. I., 倚廬, the mourning shed which the emperor was supposed to occupy during the period of mourning. Here Woo-ting spent the prescribed period of 'three years,' or 25 months, 'without speaking' (see the pass. in the next Part, Bk, XV.). Not that we are to suppose he preserved an absolute silence; but he abstained from speaking of governmental matters, and left them in the hands of his prime minister.

At the end of this time, he *still* kept silence. We must understand 其惟不言 in this way. The 'Daily Explanation' has:—及大祥後,喪服已除,猶未發號施令,裁決庶務. 知之＝有先知之德, 'he who has the ability of earlier apprehension.' There was probably a reference in the minds of the speakers to the language of E Yin about the duty of 'those who are first informed, and first apprehend principles,' to instruct and enlighten others. They compliment the emperor with being such a man, 'knowing,' says Kin Le-ts'ëang, 'his extraordinary natural gifts' (天資之不凡). 明哲,—Shin She-hing (申時行) explains 'the man of brightness (明者) as one whose large comprehension embraces all principles (方寸虛靈,無一理之不具), and the man of wisdom, (哲者) as one who has examined the minute and knows the displayed, as if a light were thrown on every principle' (察微知著,無一理之不燭). 百官承式,—Ts'ae seems to take 式 as a noun ＝ 'rules,' gov. by 承 'to receive.' It is better to take 承 absolutely. The officers represent themselves as receiving every thing from the emperor. Then 式＝敬, 'to respect,' 'to reverence.' The 'Daily Explanation' says:—百官之所仰承而欽式者. 稟 (pin; 2d tone)＝受命, 'to receive commands.' [The question of Tsze-chang in the Analects, in which he quotes the Shoo as saying that 'Kaou-tsung, while mourning in the usual imperial fashion, was for three years without speaking,' was founded probably, not on the text, but on Pt. V., Bk. XV., p. 5.]

求　象、言。良　道　弗　于　誥　王二節
于　俾　○　弼　夢　言　四　曰、庸
天　以　乃三節　其　帝　弗　方、以　作
下、形　審　代　賚　恭　台　台　書
　　旁　厥　予　予　默　故　恐　正　以

2 the ministers have no way to receive their orders." The king on
this made a writing, and informed them, saying, "As it is mine to
secure what is right in the four quarters *of the empire*, I have
been afraid that my virtue is not equal *to that of my predecessors*,
and therefore have not spoken. *But* while I was respectfully
and silently thinking of the *right* way, I dreamt that God gave me
3 a good assistant, who should speak for me." He then minutely
described the appearance of the person, and caused search to be

2. 王庸作書以誥,—庸=
用. It emphasizes the 作;—see on Bk. V., Pt.
i., p. 4. 正于四方,—comp. 表正
萬邦, Bk. II., p. 2. 德弗類.—Gan-
kwŏ makes 類=善, 'good.' It is better to
take it as in the translation. Ts'ae says:—恐
德不類于前人. 思道,—
'thinking of the way.' By 道 we are to understand 'the principles and course of good
govt.' (治道). 賚=與, 'to give.'
弼,—see the 'Yih and Tseih,' parr. 2 and 4.
審厥象,—審, 'to discriminate.' Woo-
ting brought back the dream to his mind, till
he could distinguish and make out the linea-
ments and form of the man whom he had seen.
The 'Daily Explanation' says:—乃追夢
中之所見而諦審其象,繪
畫成形. 旁求=遍求, 'to search
everywhere,' on all 'sides.' 誥 (read Yuĕ)
築, 云云,—Ts'ae takes 築 as=居, 'to
dwell,' and is foll. by the 'Daily Explanation;'
—I know not upon what authority. We ought
not to depart from its common signification,
sanctioned as that is by Mencius, who tells us
that 'Yuĕ was called to office from the midst
of his building frames' (傅說舉於版
築之間; Men., VI., Pt. II., xv.). 傅巖
之野,—Mih-tsze (尚賢,下篇) speaks
of 'the city (? wall) of Foo-yen' (傅巖之

城). Gan-kwŏ calls the place—'the crag of
the Foo family' (傅氏之巖), and says
that the public road went by it, and was injured
by a mountain stream. It devolved on a convict
in the place to repair it, when Yuĕ, who was
living a recluse life in that quarter, and was
in great poverty, undertook to do the work, 'in
order to get food' (以供食). Sze-ma
Ts'een for 傅巖 has 傅險, Whether
we call the place Foo-yen, or 'the crag of Foo,'
it is agreed that it was 25 *le* north-east from the
pres. dis. city of P'ing-luh (平陸; lat, 34°
47', N., lon. 5°25', W.), in Kĕae Chow (解州),
Shan-se. Mih-tsze tells us that Yuĕ wore
coarse clothes of hair cloth, with a rope for a
girdle; and Seun-tsze says that 'his person was
like a fish standing up' (傅說之狀,身
如植鰭, *lit.*, 'like a perpendicular dorsal
fin,' but see the gloss *in loc.* 荀子,非相
篇). These are merely the stories floating
about in the Chow dynasty.

[As we might expect, this dream of Woo-ting
has given rise to no little speculation among
Chinese crities. Some have said that the emperor in his wanderings through the empire, to
which he alludes at the commencement of Part
iii., had become acquainted with the worth and
ability of Yuĕ, and knew very well where to
find him, so that his telling the courtiers about
a dream, and sending through the country to
look for Yuĕ, was only an expedient to make
them readily acquiesce in his elevation of him
to the highest dignity. This view, however,
is rejected, as it would subject Woo-ting to a
charge of hypocrisa ynd falsehood.

○　左　諸　王　作　爰⁴⁸⁴⁸ 肖。野、巖　築
命⁵ 右。其　置　相。立　○　惟　之　傅

made for him by means of a figure throughout the empire.　Yuĕ, a builder in the country of Foo-yen, was found like.

4   II. On this the king raised and made him his prime minister, keeping him also at his side.

[Choo He observes that, according to the account in the Shoo, God did really appear to Woo-ting in his dream, and say to him—'I give you a good assistant.' But now people, when they speak of God, intend only the idea of Rule and Government, and say that He has no form, which, it is to be feared, is not a correct mode of expression. If we should say, on the other hand, that the common representations of God as like the 'Great God, Yuh-hwang' are right, this also would be improper. What are we to say in the matter? He leaves this question unanswered. See 朱子全書, Bk. XXXIV.]

[It may be as well here to refer to a passage in the 國語, 楚語, 上, where we find a great deal of what we have in the 'Charge to Yuĕ.' A minister of king Ling of Ts'oo (靈王, ʙ.ᴄ. 539-528), remonstrating with him, says:—昔殷武丁能聳其德，至於神明，以入于河，自河徂毫。於是乎三年默以思道。既得道，乃不敢專制，使以夢象旁求四方之賢。得傳說以來。升以爲公，而朝夕規諫。曰：「若金，用女作礪；若津水，用女作舟；若歲大旱，用女作霖雨。啟乃心，沃朕心。若藥不瞑眩，厥疾不瘳；若跣不視地，厥足用傷。」……使朝夕規諫曰：「必交修余，無余棄也。」……云云。

The above passage contains most of the 1st Part, and some sentences of the third. It is not quoted as from the Shoo, but there can be no doubt it really was taken from the classic,

known both to king Ling and his minister. The historical portions are condensed, and brought together to serve the purpose of the speaker. The whole appears, as it would naturally do, if drawn—not quoted—from our present text. To contend that the text was plagiarized and 'made up' from the 國語 is a strange turning of the tables. Even if it were so, we still have in it so much of the original 'Charge to Yuĕ.']

Ch. II. Pp. 4—10. Tʜᴇ ᴇʟᴇᴠᴀᴛɪᴏɴ ᴏꜰ Yᴜᴇ, ᴀɴᴅ ᴛʜᴇ ᴇᴍᴘᴇʀᴏʀ's ᴄʜᴀʀɢᴇ ᴛᴏ ʜɪᴍ.　4. I have translated 相 by 'prime minister,' though I am not sure that the term had, in the Yin dynasty, more than the general meaning of 'assistant.' The proper name for prime minister was then 冢宰;—see Ana., XIV., xliii. It was to this office that Yuĕ was raised—總百官, as it is expressed in Pt. ii., p. 1. Yuĕ became to Woo-ting what E Yin had been to T'ang.　王置諸（＝於）左右,—'in these words,' says Ts'ae, 'is intimated Yue's appointment to be "tutor and guardian" as well as prime minister' (以冢宰兼師保也). I do not know, however, that we should find any appointment to offices in the language,—anything more than the emperor's wish that Yuĕ should always act as his most intimate counsellor.　We find in Ma Twan-lin (Bk. XXIX., 職官, 宰相) that T'ang appointed two 相;—E Yin and Chung Hwuy, the Seang of the right and left respectfully, and that Yuĕ was called to discharge both of their offices. But we cannot pronounce positively, it seems to me, on the offices of so early a time.

爰, at the beginning of the par., ＝於是, 'on this,' 'hereupon.'　Sze-ma Ts'een says that Woo-ting conferred with Yuĕ, and made proof of him, finding that he was really a sage, before he raised him to these dignities; and Ts'ae says that not to have done so would have been unreasonable. We can well suppose that the emperor entered at once into conference with the strange man, but the Shoo leads us to think only of the dream as the cause of Yue's

乃　乃　地　厥　朕　作　舟　礪　台　之
辟　僚　厥　疾　心　霖　楫　若　德　曰
俾　罔　足　弗　○　雨　若　濟　○　朝
率　不　用　瘳　若　○　歲　巨　若　夕
先　同　傷　若　藥　啟　大　川　金　納
王　心　○　跣　弗　乃　旱　用　用　誨
迪　以　惟　弗　瞑　心　用　汝　汝　以
我　匡　　視　眩　沃　汝　作　作　輔

（六節・七節・八節・九節）

5　　He charged him, saying, "Morning and evening present your
6　instructions to aid my virtue.　Suppose me a weapon of steel;—I
will use you for a whetstone.　Suppose me crossing a great stream;
—I will use you for a boat with its oars.　Suppose me in a year
7　of great drought;—I will use you as a copious rain.　Open your
8　mind, and enrich my mind.　*Be you* like medicine, which, if it do
not distress the patient, will not cure his sickness.　*Think of me* as
one walking *barefoot*, whose feet are sure to be wounded, if he do
not see the ground.

6　　"Do you and your companions cherish all the same mind to
assist your Sovereign, that I may follow my royal predecessors, and
tread in the steps of my High ancestor, to give repose to the

elevation.　　5.　納誨—納＝進, 'to present,' 'to bring forward;' 誨, 'instructions.'—including both teachings and remonstrances. 'The emperor,' says Wang Yen, 'speaks here of instructions and not of remonstrances, in his humility, showing his anxiety to be taught.'

6.　*Various illustrations of the advantages of Yuĕ's teaching.*　若金, and the other commencements of the clauses, are descriptive of the emperor himself.　霖雨,—'a copious rain.' 霖 is defined as 'rain continuous for at least three days,' 'rain unceasing.' The three clauses rise, it is said, in intensity of meaning, one above the other. The first shows how Yuĕ would help the king to accomplish himself (成器); the second has reference to the overcoming of difficulties; the third to the dispensing benefits to the people.　　7.　沃朕心, —'to enrich my mind.' The figure of a copious rain is here continued. The 說文 defines 沃 by 灌溉, 'to moisten,' 'to irrigate.'

8.　*Illustrations of the advantages of Yuĕ's remon-* strances.　若藥 and 若跣 are here also descriptive of the emperor;—in the first place as under medical treatment, and in the second place, as walking in a thoughtless and unguarded manner, needing to be warned of his danger. 若藥……瘳,—see Men., III., Pt. I., i.,

5. 瞑 (read *mĕen*, 3d tone.' Keang Shing edits 眄眩) are understood to be descriptive of the violent operation of medicine. So decided, and regardless of their immediate effect on himself, would Woo-ting have Yuĕ's words to be.　跣 is defined in the 說文—足親地, 'the foot close to the ground,' *i.e.*, 'barefoot.' This illustration requires Yuĕ to point out boldly whatever dangers the emp. might be heedlessly going into.　　9.　*Yuĕ must get all under him to have the same mind with himself.*　惟暨 乃僚,—we must understand 汝 before 暨, and then the clause = 'you and your associates.' Whether we take 暨 as＝及 or＝與, it stands awkwardly at the beginning of the

之休命。
疇敢不祇若王
聖臣不命其承、
從諫則聖后克
木從繩則正后
說復于王曰惟
命其惟有終。○
○嗚呼欽予時
高后以康兆民。

十一節

10　millions of the people. Oh! respect this charge of mine;—so shall you bring your work to *a good* end."

11　　III. Yuĕ replied to the king, saying, "Wood by the use of the line is made straight; and the sovereign who follows reproof becomes sage. When the sovereign can *thus* make himself sage, his ministers, without being charged, anticipate his orders;—who would dare not to act in respectful compliance with this excellent charge of your Majesty?"

clause. 以匡乃辟,—匡 may be taken as in the translation, or as＝救 or 正, 'to save,' or 'to correct,' 'to keep right.' The 先王 are all former wise kings of the Shang dyn.; 高后 is specially T'ang. 率 is 循 其道, 'to follow their path;' 迪 is 蹈 其迹, 'to tread in his footsteps.' 10. 時命＝是命. 其惟有終,— 有終, see Bk. II., p. 9; Bk. V., Pt. i., p. 3; *et al.* Ts'ae takes 惟 in the sense of 思, 'to think.'—'Respect this charge, thinking from the first upon the issue.'

Ch. III. THE DUTIFUL REPLY OF YUE TO THE ABOVE CHARGE. 說復于王,—

復, see on Men., I., Pt. I., vii., 10. 后 克聖,—Medhurst translates this—'When the sovereign is a sage;' but we must lay stress on the 克, and connect the clause with the preceding. When ministers see that the sovereign yields himself to be moulded by them,— is like wood in the hands of the carpenter,— they are encouraged to all assiduity in doing their duty. 臣不命其承,—the 'Daily Explanation' expands this:—凡為臣者, 爭欲仰承德意, 進獻讜言, 雖不命之言, 猶且先意承 之, 若王之休命,—若＝'such an'; 'an excellent charge like yours.'

THE BOOKS OF SHANG.

BOOK VIII. THE CHARGE TO YUE. PART ii.

說命中

一節
惟
說。
命
總

百官。
○乃
二節

進于
王曰，

嗚呼，
明王、

奉若
天道，

建邦
設都，

樹后
王君

公承
以大

1   I. Yuĕ having received charge to take the presidency of all the
2   officers, he presented himself before the king, and said, "Oh!
intelligent kings act in reverent accordance with the ways of Heaven.
The founding of States, and setting up of capitals; the appointing
of sovereign kings, of princes and dukes, with their great officers

CONTENTS OF THE SECOND PART. It has
already been observed that this Part should be
called 'The Counsels of Yuĕ.' In answer to
the charge which he had received, Yuĕ presents
his advice on various points, all connected with
the duty of the sovereign, and the successful
conducting of government. In the two last
parr., the emperor and the minister give expression to their confidence and complacency in
each other.

Ch. I. Pp. 1—11. THE COUNSELS OF YUE.
1, 2. *Occasion of the counsels. All government
is not for the gratification and glory of the governing,
but for the good of the people.* 1. 總百官，
—總＝將領, 'to take the lead of.' Lin
Che-k'e understands the phrase as denoting
that Yuĕ continued to act as the representative
of the emperor, doing everything for him, as the
prime minister did during the period of mourning. Perhaps it was so, Woo-ting had said
that his 'good assistant' should speak for him.

2. 進于王，—進 may be taken
as in the translation, or we may we under-
tand 誨 as the object of the verb. With regard
to what follows—嗚呼, 明王, 云云,
there is considerable difficulty. 明王 would
seem to be the subject of all the verbs that
follow,—奉若, 建, 設, and 樹. 后王,
'sovereign king,' is understood to be a designation of the emperor (天子), and 君公 to
stand for 諸侯 all the feudal princes under
him. In this way, 明王 must be taken as
singular, and to have reference to the first
sovereign, the founder of the Chinese empire.
This was the view of Gaubil. He translates:—
'Le roi intelligent, qui autrefois se conforma
avec respect a la loi du ciel, fonda l'empire et
etablit une cour. Il assigna des lieux on devoient
resider le roi, les grands vassaux, et les grands
officiers. Ce prince intelligent ne s'occupa pas
des plaisirs; il n'eut que le gouvernement du
peuple en vue.' To this translation he appends
the following note:—'Here Yuĕ speaks of the
first king of China, but what follows does not
give us any light on the time when he reigned.
One might still translate, it appears to me, in
the plural, and say—the intelligent kings, the

夫　不　豫　亂　惟　明、　時　臣　惟　乂。
師　惟　惟　民。　天　惟　憲、　欽　民　○
長、　惟　以　○　聰　聖　惟　若、　從　惟

and heads of departments :—were not designed to minister to the idleness and the pleasures *of one*, but for the good government of the people.

3　"It is Heaven which is all-intelligent and observing. Let the sage *king* take it as his pattern :—then his ministers will reverently accord with him; and the people will consequently be well governed.

founders of the empire. Yuĕ spoke of the first king as of a known personage. In the commentaries on the Yih-king, Confucius speaks of Fo-he as the first king; and on this subject the authority of Confucius is preferable to that of others.'

I have not attempted to turn Gaubil's French version of the text into English, that the reader may see it as from his own hand. An intelligent comparison of it with the original will show that it gives the meaning of hardly a single phrase correctly. Several of the renderings are made in order to harmonize the whole with his view that 明王 is in the singular, and denotes the founder of the Chinese empire; but independently of this, the translation is inadmissible. Medhurst takes 明王 indefinitely, and renders it by 'an intelligent king.' His version is better than Gaubil's in the several phrases; but upon the whole it is not satisfactory.

For myself, I must construe the paragraph differently from any critic, native or foreign, that I have read. 明王 cannot be, as Gaubil supposes, 'the intelligent king,'—*the founder of the Chinese State ;*—it must be translated—'intelligent kings,' or 'an intelligent king.' 后王 is to be understood, with Ts'ae and other scholars, as denoting 'the emperor,' or 'emperors.' To speak of intelligent kings as appointing emperors (明王樹后王) is absurd, and therefore 明王 cannot be the nominative to 建 and the other verbs. I put a stop at 道; and take 建邦, &c., as clauses in the nominative, the verb of which they are the subject being found in 不惟逸豫. By whom States were founded. and capitals set up, emperors, princes, and dukes, appointed, with all sustaining office under them is indicated in the phrase 天道, and the term 天, with which the next par. commences. It was by Heaven or God, constituting such a social order with a view to the benefit of the people. This construction

may appear rather harsh, but it gives a consistent meaning to the whole paragraph, which we fail to get from any other interpretation. It is confirmed in so far by a passage in Mih-tsze (尚同中), where he seems to be partly quoting, and partly commenting on, the text.

He says :—先王之書，相年之道，王大使帝長貴萬民，乃作后（for 卿）維辯者上正祿爲萬曰，夫建國設都也，設泰用，否否用此語國都厚將以云云。君公師天治鬼神也，均之高錯之均則建其爵之其害云云。夫治鬼神也，佚與利除害，

3. *The imitation of Heaven by the supreme earthly power is the first step, and surely leads, to good government.* 惟天聰明,—see the 'Counsels of Kaou-yaou.' p. 8. 時憲,— 時＝是; 憲法, 'to imitate.' 欽若,— see 'Can. of Yaou,' p. 3. The four clauses of this par. are like pearls, lying side by side. We must take them, and string them together in the manner indicated in the translation. But how is 'the sage king' to imitate Heaven, all-intelligent and observing? The commentators labour to answer this question. The 'Daily Explanation,' for instance, says :—'Heaven aloft on high, without prepossession, entirely just, most spiritual and intelligent, needs not to hearken, and yet hears every thing; needs not to look, and yet sees every thing. The excellences and defects of govt., the happiness and suffering of the people, do not escape its observation. And not only this.—Of all that is done in darkness and in privacy, where there are neither ears nor eyes, nothing escapes its notice. Such is the intelligence and observation of Heaven ;—it is for the wise sovereign to take this for his pattern. When his likings and dislikings are free from the becloudings of

及惡德惟其賢。 昵惟其能爵罔 庶官官不及私 休。〇惟治亂在 五節 兹克明乃罔不 躬王惟戒兹允 笥惟干戈省厥 起戎惟衣裳在 口起羞惟甲胄

4 "It is the mouth which gives occasion for shame; they are the coat of mail and helmet which give occasion to war. The upper robes and lower garments *for reward should not be lightly taken from* their chests; before shield and spear are used, one should examine himself. If your Majesty will be cautious in these things, and, believing this about them, attain to their intelligent *use, your government* will in every thing be excellent.

5 "Good government and bad depend upon the various officers. Offices may not be given to men because they are favourites, but only to men of ability. Dignities may not be conferred on men of evil practices, but only on men of worth.

partiality, and his rewards and punishments are all in accordance with right,—like the all-seeing and all-hearing of Heaven; then he can give the law to the empire,' &c. All this is not without truth and force; but Yuĕ's lesson is too vaguely expressed to be of much practical use. Gaubil, however, observes justly that those who have affirmed that the ancient Chinese only understood by Heaven the material heavens have not paid sufficient attention to such passages as the present.

4. *Instances of things in which the endeavour to imitate Heaven will be seen; and the happy effect of doing so.* From the commencement of this par. to 厥躬, is found in the Le Ke, Bk. 緇 衣, p. 16, quoted as from the 兌 (evidently for 說) 命. Choo He says that the clauses beginning with 惟 are independent of one another. Lin Che-k'e, on the other hand, finds in the third clause the complement of the first, and in the 4th that of the second. It is not worth our while to enter on this question. The tongue is man's glory, but very easily abused; and then it turns out to his shame. The coat of mail and helmet are weapons of defence, but the confidence of strength often leads to insolence and quarrels. The robes in the imperial stores are intended to reward the good and meritorious; but, if distributed carelessly, they are productive of evil effects. Shield and spear are the weapons with which one goes to punish offenders;—but woe to him who undertakes this duty, while his heart condemns himself! The four things are of great importance and easily offended in; and Yuĕ therefore calls the attention of Woo-ting to them. 起戎,—戎= 兵, 'an offensive weapon.' 衣裳,—see the 'Yih and Tseih,' p. 4. 笥 is defined as 'an article of furniture for holding food or clothes' (飯及衣之器). Its figure was square, We may translate it by 'chest.' 戒兹, 允兹,—the former of these 兹 seems to = 'these,' the things, namely which had been spoken of; the latter = 'this,' and indicates what had been said or implied about the mouth, &c.

5. *How the imitation of Heaven should be seen in conferring offices and dignities.* Ying-tă says: 'The performance of duties is called 官; the receiving of rank is called 爵' (治其事 謂之官, 受其位謂之爵). We are not to think, however, here of the different dignities among the feudal princes, but of the ranks among the officers in the imperial domain. 私昵,—昵= 近, or 親近, 'near to,' 'familiar with.' 私昵, are the emperor's 'private intimates,' his favourites. 惡德= 包藏凶惡之 人, 'men who cherish all evil in their bosoms.'

慮善以動、動惟厥時。○有其善、喪厥善、矜其能、喪厥功。○惟事事、乃其有備、有備無患。○無啟寵納侮。○惟厥作非。○惟厥攸居政事、惟醇。○于祭祀、時謂弗

(六節 / 七節 / 八節 / 九節 / 十節 / 十一節)

6   "Anxious thought about what will be good should precede your movements.   Your movements also should have respect to the time for them.

7   "The indulged consciousness of goodness is the way to lose that goodness.   Boasting of ability is the way to lose the merit it might produce.

8   "For all affairs let there be adequate preparation.   With preparation there will be no calamities.

9   "Do not open the door for favourites, from whom you will receive contempt.   Do not be ashamed of mistakes, and thus make them crimes.

10   "Let your mind rest in its proper objects, and the affairs of your government will be pure.

11   " "Officiousness in sacrifices is called irreverence; ceremonies when

The clause—爵罔及惡德 is found, like most of the last par., in the Le Ke, Bk. 緇衣, quoted in the same way from the 兌命.

6. *How the same should be seen in thoughtful and timely action.*   善 is here defined by 當乎理, 'that which is agreeable to right reason or principle.'   7. *And in repressing all prideful thoughts.* 有其善＝自有其善, 'having his goodness to one's-self,' thinking of it, resting in it.

8. *And in preparation for all undertakings, and against emergencies.*   On 事事 Gan-kwŏ says 非一事, 'not in one affair merely,' ＝'in all affairs.' Ts'ae seems to take the first char. as a verb—惟事其事, 乃其有備, 'in doing his affairs there should be preparation.'   This par. would seem to have been at one time somewhat different. In the 左傳, 襄, 十一年, we find—書曰, 居安思危, 思則有備, 有備則無患. This quotation, however, may be from some other Book of the Shoo, among those that are lost.

9. *And in avoiding favouritism and persistence in mistakes.* 無(一毋)啟寵,—'do not open favouritism.' The 'contempt,' it is understood, will be from the favourites themselves, bred to it by the familiarity to which they are admitted. 無心失理謂之過, 有心背理謂之非, 'an unintentional failure to do what is right is called a mistake; an intentional violation of what is right is called a crime.'   In the 左傳 定元年, we read—啟寵納侮, 其此之謂矣.   10. *And in the keeping of the heart.* 惟厥攸(一所)居,—居＝止. The clause is quite elliptical, and ＝惟居其所止. Comp. 'The Great Learning,' Comm. ch. 3. 醇＝粹清, 'pure and clear,'＝unmixed. There will be no evil thoughts and bad objects to disturb the govt.   11. *On the service of spirits.* 黷

說不言有厥答。 于先王成德惟協 王忱不艱允協 之艱行之惟艱、 拜稽首曰、非知 予罔聞于行。十三節 服乃不良于言惟 旨哉、說乃言惟 神則難。○王曰、十二節 欽禮煩則亂事

burdensome lead to disorder. To serve the spirits *in this way* is difficult."

12 11. The king said, "Excellent! Your words, O Yuĕ, should indeed be carried out in the conduct. If you were not so good in counsel,

13 I should not have heard these things for my practice." Yuĕ did obeisance with his head to the ground, and said, "It is not the knowing that is difficult, but the doing. If your Majesty know this, however, there will not be the difficulty, and you will become really equal in complete virtue to the former king. Wherein I, Yuĕ, do not express myself, the blame rests with me."

于祭祀—黷, means 'to soil,' 'dirty.' The phrase 䙝黷 is used, with reference to spiritual beings, in the sense of 'to defile,' 'to profane.' Wherein the profanity which Yuĕ wanted to guard the emperor against consisted, we cannot say precisely. One meaning of 黷, given in the dict., is 數, 'frequently,' 'forwardly.' Now from the next Bk. we shall see that Woo-ting was prone to be officious in the worship of the spirits of the departed, and we have seen how later times charge the Shang dynasty with being superstitious. Officiousness —sacrificing unnecessarily to certain spirits, and at unnecessary times,—and the attempt to please them by the multitude of observances, would seem therefore to be the things here condemned by Yuĕ. 時=是. The last clause— 事神則難 would seem to be co-ordinate with the preceding. All the critics, however, understand it as in the translation. [This par., with some alterations and additions, appears in the Le-ke, Bk. 緇衣, p. 25, referred to already under p. 5. We have :—兌命曰,

爵無及惡德、民立而正事 純而祭祀是爲不敬、事煩 則亂,事神則難,]

Ch. II. Pp. 12, 13. THE COMPLACENCY OF WOO-TING AND YUE IN EACH OTHER, 12. 旨哉,—旨=美, 'admirable.' Ts'ae says that the ancients, in eating and drinking, when any thing particularly pleased their palate, pronounced it 旨; and Woo-ting thus characterizes Yuĕ's words as if they had a flavour. 乃(=汝)言惟服,—服=行, 'to practise.' 13. 王忱不艱=王 忱信之, 亦不爲難, 'if your Majesty sincerely believes this,—the difficulty of action, —it likewise will not prove to be a difficulty.' In the conclusion of the first Part, Yuĕ says that the sovereign's giving heed to his advisers would encourage them to do their duty. His concluding words here show how the ready ear the emperor yielded to his lessons was spurring him on.

THE BOOKS OF SHANG.

BOOK VIII. THE CHARGE TO YUE. PART iii.

厥　河　宅　于　盤　舊　說　王一節
終　祖　于　荒　既　學　台　曰　　說
岡　亳　河　野　乃　于　小　來　　命
顯。　暨　自　乃　遯　甘　子　汝　　下

1 I. The king said, "Come, O Yuĕ. I, the little one, first learned with Kan Pwan. Afterwards, I lived concealed in the rude country, and then I went to *the inside of* the Ho, and lived there. From the Ho I went to Pŏ;—and the result has been that I am

CONTENTS OF THE THIRD PART. The emperor tells Yuĕ of his early disadvantages, and begs him now to instruct him, enlightening his ignorance, and supplying his deficiencies. To this Yuĕ replies by enlarging on the subjects most important to be learned, and the spirit of the learner. From the 8th paragraph to the end, the emperor praises Yuĕ for what he had already done for him, and expresses his hope that the minister would prove a second E Yin, and frame of him a second T'ang; to which Yuĕ suitably responds.

Ch. I. Pp. 1—7. WOO-TING DEPLORES THE DISADVANTAGES OF HIS EARLY YEARS, AND BEGS YUE TO INSTRUCT HIM. YUE SPEAKS OF THE SUBJECTS OF LEARNING, AND THE SPIRIT REQUIRED IN THE LEARNER. 1. *The early life of Woo-ting.* 台小子舊學于甘 盤,—we saw before that 小子, 'the little child,' was appropriately used by the emperor as a humble designation of himself in relation to God. It came, however, to be employed, as in the text, where we can hardly suppose any reference in the mind to that relation. 舊,—'of old;'—we may render it by 'first.' From this clause we should suppose that Kan Pwan had been a learned master, who imparted to Woo-

ting the rudiments of learning. From Part V., Bk. XVI., p. 7, however, we learn that he was a great minister. He is there mentioned, indeed, as *the* minister of Woo-ting's time, while nothing is said of Foo Yuĕ. We may suppose that he acted as prime minister on the death of Seaou-yih, and died himself before the period of mourning was expired. What Woo-ting learned with him would be lessons of govt., and such subjects as are treated in 'The Great Learning.'

既乃遯于荒野, 云云,—既 stands absolutely, = 'afterwards.' 遯 = 'to withdraw from public life, and live in obscurity.' Chow-kung says, Pt. V., Bk. XV., p. 5, that 'Kaou-tsung toiled, away from the court, among the inferior people.' What was the reason of his doing so, we do not know. Gan-kwŏ says his father sent him for a time to this mode of life, that he might know the hardships of the common people. It is more likely that he was compelled to it by some dire necessity, arising from convulsions of the State with which we are unacquainted. From the fields of the people Woo-ting 'entered the Ho and dwelt,'—resided, acc. to Gan-kwŏ, 'on some island in the Ho.' It is more probable that we should take 入

匪說攸聞。○惟學
不師古、以克永世、
于古訓乃有獲、事
多聞、時惟建事、學
訓。○說曰、王人求
予棄予惟克邁乃
鹽梅爾交修予、罔
蘗若作和羹爾惟
若作酒醴爾惟麴
○爾惟訓于朕志、

2 unenlightened. Do you teach me what should be my aims. Be to me as the yeast and the malt in making sweet spirits; as the salt and the prunes in making agreeable soup. Give your help to cultivate me; do not cast me away:—I shall attain to practise your instructions."

3 Yuĕ said, "O king, men seek to hear much, having in view to establish their affairs. But to learn the lessons of the ancients is the way to attain this. That the affairs of one, not making the ancients his masters, can be perpetuated for generations, is what I have not heard.

宅于河 as—入居于河內, understanding 河內, 'the inside of the Ho' as a designation of K'e-chow generally. From the north of the Ho he removed again to Pŏ,—the capital as re-established by Pwan-kăng;—and the end was (暨厥終) that he was, or thought himself, little versed in the subjects necessary for him to know as emperor. 2. *He asks Yuĕ to instruct him* 爾惟訓 予朕志,—'do you instruct me about my aims.' 若作酒醴爾惟麴蘗, —酒 is commonly translated 'wine,' but incorrectly. The term denotes 'spirits, distilled from rice.' 醴 is the product in its earlier stage, before the process of distillation is commenced, after the mashing and fermentation, when 'the juice and the refuse are mixed together,' what is called 'sweet spirits' (醴成 而汁滓相將, 如今甜酒) —酒母, 'yeast.' 麴 蘗=牙米, 'the sprouting rice,' 'malt.' 爾交修 予,—this clause and the next are found in the long quotation which I made in the first Part from the 國語. In Pt. V., Bk. XXVI.. p.

4, we have 交修不逮, where the 交 refers to the united services of many ministers. Here the char. is used with single reference to Yuĕ in his relation to Woo-ting. 邁= 行, 'to practise,' indicating the efforts which he would put forth. 3. *Yuĕ replies—first, that the lessons of the ancients are the most important thing to be learned.* 王人求多 聞,—Gan-kwŏ joins 王人 together as = 王者, 'royal men,' 'kings.' It is better to take 王 in the vocative. Yuĕ addresses Woo-ting—'O king,' as Yu, in the 'Yih and Tseih,' p. 7, addresses Shun, 'O Emperor.' 時惟 建事,—時=是, 'thus.' The 'Daily Explanation' says:—是其意惟欲建 立修身治天下之事業耳 古訓,—'ancient lessons,' such as are contained in the Canons of Yaou and Shun, and the Counsels of Yu and Kaou-yaou. Ming-shing calls attention to a passage in Ts'een's history of the founder of the Ts'in dynasty— 事不師古而能長久者、非 所聞也, from which he thinks the last part of the par. was taken. Much more likely

嗚呼、說、四海之內、

列于庶位。○王曰、

克欽承、旁招俊乂、

永無愆。○惟說式

監于先王成憲其

學厥德修罔覺。○

學半、念終始典于

積于厥躬。○惟斅

乃來、允懷于茲道

遜志、務時敏、厥修

4　"In learning there should be a humble will, and a striving to maintain a constant earnestness. In such a case *the learner's* cultivation will surely come. He who sincerely cherishes these

5　things will find all truth accumulating in his person. To teach is one half of learning. When a man's thoughts from first to last are constantly fixed on *such* learning, his virtuous cultivation comes unperceived.

6　"Survey the perfect pattern of the former king;—so may you

7　for ever be preserved from error. Then shall I be able reverently to meet your views, and on every side to look out for men of eminence to place in the various offices."

8　II. The king said, "Oh! Yuĕ, within the four seas, all look up

is it to have been adopted by the speaker in the passage referred to from the text. 4. *Second, that success in learning depends on docility and persevering earnestness.* 允懷于茲 —'he who sincerely cherishes these things,'— the humility, namely, and persevering earnestness. 道積于厥躬—道 denotes all the principles of self-cultivation and of govt. taught and practised by the ancients. In the Le Ke, Bk. 學記, par. 9, we read 兌命曰、敬孫、務時敏、厥修乃來. 5. *Third, that learning is perfected by communicating what has been acquired.* 斅學半,—'teaching is the half of learning.' The words are quoted in the 學記, par. 3, and explained.—'When one learns,' it is said, 'he knows his deficiencies. When he teaches, he knows the difficulties *of learning.* A knowledge of his deficiencies leads him to self-inspection; a knowledge of the difficulties leads him to exert himself' (學然後知不足、教然後知困、知不足、然後能自反也、知困、然後能自

强也). 念終始典于學—典=常, 'constant,' 'constantly.' 學 here must be understood to include both the learning and teaching. The clause is found twice in the Le Ke,—once in the 學記, p. 2, and once in the 文王世子, Pt. ii., p. 23. 6, 7. *Finally, that the emperor should adopt T'ang as his model, and Yuĕ would surround the throne with ministers like himself.* 先王成憲,—先王 here is to be taken as referring to T'ang. 憲=法, 'law,' 'pattern.' 惟說式克,—式=用, 'to use;' —taken adverbially as 用 itself often is, == 'hereby.' The emperor's goodness would be to Yuĕ the greatest impulse to do all that devolved on him. 俊乂,—see 'Counsels of Kaouyaou,' p. 4. CH. II. Pp. 8—11. THE EMPEROR PRAISES YUE, AND LOOKS FOR STILL GREATER ADVANTAGES FROM HIM. YUE UNDERTAKES TO RESPOND TO THE EMPEROR'S WISHES. 8. *What Yuĕ had done for the emperor.* Comp. Shun's language to Yu, II., Bk. II., p. 8, ending 時乃功.

爾　賢　阿　于　曰　恥　克　保　惟　咸
克　不　衡　皇　時　若　俾　衡　人　仰
紹　乂　專　天　予　撻　厥　作　良　朕
乃　惟　美　爾　之　于　后　我　臣　德
辟　賢　有　尚　辜　市　惟　先　惟　時
于　非　商　明　佑　一　堯　王　聖　乃
先　后　○　保　我　夫　舜　乃　○　風
王　不　惟　予　烈　不　其　曰　昔　○
永　食　后　罔　祖　獲　心　予　先　股
綏　其　非　俾　格　則　愧　弗　正　肱

9 to my virtue:—all through your influence. As his legs and arms
form the man, so does a good minister form the sage *king*.

10　"Formerly there was the premier of our dynasty, Paou-hăng,
who made my royal predecessor. He said, 'If I cannot make my
sovereign like Yaou or Shun, I shall feel ashamed in my heart, as
if I were beaten in the market place.' If any one common man did
not find *all he should desire*, he said, 'It is my fault.' Thus he
assisted my meritorious ancestor, so that he became equal to Great
Heaven. Do you give your preserving aid to me, and not let
O-hăng engross all the good service to the House of Shang.

11 The sovereign should share his government with none but worthy
ministers. The worthy minister should accept his support only
from the proper sovereign. May you now succeed in making
your prince a successor of my royal ancestor, and in securing the

風 here = 'influence.'　　9. *The same sub-*
ject.　　10. *The emperor wishes Yŭe to be to him*
what E Yin had been to T'ang. 先正保
衡,—正 is here explained by 長, 'chief,'
'president.' As applied to E Yin, it denotes
his presidency of all the other ministers,—his
being premier. On 保衡, see the note on the
'T'ae-kĕă,' Pt. i., p. 1.　　作我先王,—
作 exactly corresponds here to our 'made.'
Ch'in King (陳經) says:—學于伊
尹,湯之爲聖乃尹與起而
作成之　子弗克,云云,一

comp. Men., V., Pt. I., vii.; Pt. II., i., and other
places where he speaks of E Yin.　　格于
皇天,—'he reached to great Heaven.' This
is a wild and blasphemous exaggeration, like
many of the assertions about the perfectly
sincere man and Confucius in the 'Doctrine of
the Mean.' The 'Daily Explanation' paraphrases it :—烈祖德業之成,直與
天地同流而無間焉.　　11.
Woo-ting and Yŭe both rest complacently in their
adaptation to each other, and auspice great things.
不乂=不與共治, 'does not
share the government with.' 不食=不
食其祿, 'does not eat his revenue.' 其

休 子 揚 敢 首 拜 民。
命。之 天 對 曰、稽 說

lasting happiness of the people!"　　Yuĕ did obeisance with his head
to the ground, and said, " I will venture to respond to, and display
abroad, your Majesty's excellent charge."

爾,—we might invert the order of these characters; 其 has its hortatory force.　對＝
答, ' to answer,' ' to respond to.'

[Choo He observes :—' The lessons of E Yin
to T'ae-kĕä are different from those of Foo Yuĕ

to Kaou-tsung.　The words of E Yin are repeated again and again, as the small natural
comprehension of T'ae-kĕä required.　This was
not necessary with Kaou-tsung.　His natural
ability was good, and he was not chargeable
with many faults.']

THE BOOKS OF SHANG.

BOOK IX. THE DAY OF THE SUPPLEMENTARY SACRIFICE OF KAOU-TSUNG.

夭永典曰事惟雊高高
民有厥惟○先雉宗宗
民不義天乃格○肜肜
中永降監訓王祖日日
絕非年下于正己越
命。天有民、王厥曰、有

1   I. On the day of the supplementary sacrifice of Kaou-tsung, there
2 appeared a crowing pheasant. Tsoo Ke said, "To rectify this
affair, the king must first be corrected."
3 Accordingly he lessoned the king, saying, "In its inspection of
men below, Heaven's first consideration is of their righteousness;
and it bestows on them *accordingly* length of years or the contrary.
Heaven does not cut short men's lives;—they bring them to an end

NAME OF THE BOOK.—高宗肜日, 'The day of the Supplementary Sacrifice of Kaou-tsung.' Kaou-tsung, I have already observed, was the title given to Woo-ting in the ancestral temple. Sze-ma Ts'een says that it was conferred on him by his son and successor Tsoo-kăng, with reference to the circumstances commemorated in this Book,—his being taught to be virtuous by the appearance of a pheasant in the manner described. He says also that it was on occasion of this canonization, so to term it, that this Book, and another which is lost,—the 'Instructions to Kaou-tsung' (高宗之訓)—were composed. That the Book was not composed in the reign of Woo-ting is sufficiently proved by the use of the sacrificial title which was given to him; that that title was conferred on him with reference to the occurrence here related is extremely improbable.

肜日,—肜 (Keang Shing has 融. See the note in the 後案 on the history and form of the character) was the name of a supplementary sacrifice, offered on the day following the regular and more solemn service (祭明日又祭). I have not been able to find any precise account of the reason and manner of such an observance. K'ang-shing says it was common to all sacrifices,—'those to Heaven and Earth, to the spirits of the land and the grain, of the hills and rivers, and of ancestors.' It was continued under the Chow dynasty, and was called 繹. Subsequently, it seems to have fallen into disuse.

The words—高宗肜日 may be translated 'The day of the supplementary sacrifice to

Kaou-tsung, and this rendering of them has its advocates, who are foll. by De Mailla in his 'Histoire Generale de la Chine.' This view seems to have prevailed in the Yuen dynasty. The editors of Yung-ching's Shoo say that Kin Le-ts'ëang and Tsow Kwei-yew (鄒季友) both thought that the reproof of Tsoo Ke must have been addressed to a young emperor,—to Tsoo-kăng, and that it is not conceivable as addressed to Woo-ting. They say themselves that the words of the 4th par.—乃曰其如台 are not to be thought of as addressed to Woo-ting after his character had developed under the counsels of Foo-yuĕ. They therefore suppose the appearance of the pheasant to have taken place in the first year of Woo-ting, and advert to the 11th par. of the second Part of 'The Charge to Yuĕ,' as showing that there was a superstitious element in his character, which might have then given occasion to the remarks of Tsoo Ke. The Preface to the Shoo must be held as conclusive that the sacrificer was Woo-ting, and not Tsoo-kăng. We there read, note 29, 'Kaou-tsung was sacrificing to T'ang the Successful, when a pheasant flew up, and lighted on the ear of a tripod, and there crowed. Tsoo Ke lessoned the king,' &c.   The Book is found both in the 'old text and in the modern.' It is classed among the 'Instructions.' Fuh-shang appended it to the 'Pwan-kăng,' so that it was not a separate Book in the 'modern text.'

CONTENTS. A pheasant suddenly makes its appearance and crows, while Kaou-tsung is engaged in the supplementary sacrifice to T'ang. This is understood to be indicative of something wrong in the service, and Tsoo Ke, a worthy minister, proceeds to lecture the emperor on the subject, whose particular fault is intimated in the last par.

Par. 1. *The appearance of a pheasant.* 高宗肜日,—see the note on the name of the Book.   越有雊雉—we cannot translate 越. The 'Daily Explanation' calls it 發語辭, 'an introductory, or initial particle.' Ying-tă defines it by 於是, 'on this.'   The 說文 says that '雊 is the cry of the male pheasant.' The preface to the Shoo and Sze-ma ts'een, after it, say that the pheasant lighted on the ear—one of the handles—of a tripod. Such an event would of course be understood to be ominous, and the older writers wearied themselves in endeavours to explain the meaning of it, some supposing it a good omen, and some a bad one. Maou K'e-ling ridicules their varying conjectures;—see the 尚書廣聽錄, *in loc.* The only explanation of it I will mention here is that of Fuh-shang (尚書大傳), which is peculiar to himself, and the more strange because it is inconsistent with the tenor of the Book. He says: —'Woo-ting was sacrificing to T'ang, when a pheasant flew up on the handle of a tripod, and crowed. Woo-ting asked Tsoo-ke what it meant, who replied, "The pheasant is a wild bird, and

ought not to mount the tripod. Its doing so now shows that it wants to be employed (今升鼎者, 欲爲用也).   Shall we not have people from distant regions coming to the court?"   On this Woo-ting examined himself, and reflected on the ways of the former kings; and in three years envoys, with twisted hair, who needed an interpreter, came to court from six kingdoms (三年編髮重譯來朝者六國).   Confucius said, "I have observed how speedily virtue is rewarded in what is related of Woo-ting and the day of his supplementary sacrifice."'

2. *Remark of Tsoo Ke on the subject.* Tsoo Ke was evidently a worthy minister of Woo-ting; but we know nothing of him more than is here related. I suppose 祖 to be the surname. 惟先格王,—王 is here ＝正, 'to correct,'—see Men., IV., Pt. I., xx., 惟大人爲能格君心之非.   Gan-kwŏ takes it as an adj.,＝至, and says—'a sovereign of the highest style of principle, when he meets with extraordinary events, corrects his affairs, and the prodigies of themselves pass away.'   The 先 before 格 is sufficiently decisive against this view.   正厥事,—'to rectify this affair.' I understand the reference to be to the affair or circumstance, which, in Tsoo Ke's opinion, had occasioned the ominous appearance of the pheasant.   This remark was not made to the emperor, but to Tsoo Ke's companions, or perhaps we should understand it simply as the thought in his mind.

3, 4. *Tsoo Ke's attempt to rectify the emperor's mind.   3. Men's prosperity does not depend on the arbitrary will of Heaven, but on their own conduct.*   下民,—comp. the 'Announcement of T'ang,' p. 2. There, however, I have translated the phrase—'the inferior people,' the people being spoken of in contradistinction from the sovereign. In the text, people and sovereign are all comprehended, and 'men below' seems to give the meaning. 典＝主, 'to put first,' 'to make the principal consideration.' 永＝長, 'long.'   天 means 'to die prematurely' (不盡天年謂之天. 殀 is more common). It is used here actively,＝'to cause to die prematurely.' Ts'ae observes that it would appear from this language that Woo-ting had been praying in connection with his sacrifice for length of years. The conclusion is not unnatural;—it is more natural than the view of K'ang-shing that shortness of life is here as a specimen of the calamities which men dread, being the one most readily apprehensible by even stupid persons. All calamities are the consequence of men's unrighteousness, and Tsoo Ke would have Woo-ting understand this, by bringing home to his thoughts the one calamity of premature death. Ying-tă follows Ch'ing in this exposition, which

于　典　罔　王　台　乃　命　罪　若　○
昵　祀　非　司　。　日　正　天　德　民　四節
。　無　天　敬　○　其　厥　既　不　有
豐　胤　民　嗚　如　德　孚　聽　不
　　　　呼　五節

4 in the midst themselves. Some men may not have complied with virtue, and will not acknowledge their crimes, but when Heaven has evidently charged them to correct their conduct, and they still say, 'What is this to us?'—

5 "Oh! Your Majesty's business is to care reverently for the people. And *all* your *ancestors* were the heirs of *the empire favoured by* Heaven;—attend to the sacrifices to *them*, and be not *so* excessive in those to your father."

seems to me very far-fetched. 4. *When men are deaf to the special warnings of Heaven, their case is desperate.* According to the translation, this paragraph is not complete. It was not easy for Tsoo Ke to speak out plainly and fully what was his meaning. He fancied that the emp. was thinking but little of the omen of the pheasant, and wished to warn him against heedlessly pursuing his own course, regardless of the admonitions of Heaven. The transl. is in acc. with the paraphrase of the 'Daily Explanation,' which I subjoin. It will be seen how the meaning is completed in it.—

然　天　未　嘗　遽　絶　之　也　斯　民
之　中　有　不　不　乎　理　而　肆　意
妄　爲　不　服　順　其　而　飾　非　拒
諫　者　天　未　其　罪　以　妖　孽　爲
信　驗　以　嘗　罪　未　夫　天　罪　諼
告　欲　其　戒　出　嘗　聽　罪　無　乃
謂　妖　順　德　上　違　偶　然　仁　我
何　孽　特　不　遑　不　天　愛　心
矣　則　重　聽　誅　之　絶　之　不
聽　天　豈　罪　哉

—'will not hear of their offences,'= 'will not acknowledge them, and put them away.' 孚, 'sincerely,' = with evidenced sincerity. There is a reference to the appearance of the pheasant as an evident intimation that there was something wrong, needing to be reproved and corrected. Sze-ma Ts'een gives 附 instead of 孚, and Keang Shing reads 付, which he says was anciently interchanged with 附, in the sense of 與, 'to give.' The meaning which he puts on the par. seems to be this:—'Some men do not comply with virtue, and will not acknowledge their crimes. Heaven then gives them charge to correct their conduct, and they say, "What shall we do?"' This

interpretation is not by any means so apt to the occasion as that which I have followed. Gan-kwŏ gives still another view of the clause—乃日其如台;—see the 註疏, *in loc.*

5. *How Tsoo Ke tried to correct the special error of Woo-ting.* 司 is taken in the sense of 主, having the same meaning as 典, in par. 3. Ts'ae says:—'Your Majesty's office is to reverence the people; to be looking, on a peradventure, for happiness from spirits is not your business' (王之職主於敬民而已, 徼福於神, 非王之事也). 胤=嗣; 'to inherit,' 'heirs.' 罔非 supposes a subject in the thoughts, which is most naturally expressed by 祖宗, 'your ancestors.' 典=主; 典祀, 'attend to the sacrifices,' *i.e.*, the sacrifices prescribed to all your ancestors. The 'Daily Explanation' has:—吾王承其後, 而主其祭, 只當一體孝敬, 'your Majesty, succeeding to them, and presiding over the sacrifices to them, should cherish an equal filial reverence for them all.' 昵 (read *ne*, low 2d tone)=禰,—'the shrine appropriated to a father's spirit-tablet in the ancestral temple.' It would appear from this that Woo-ting's fault was the paying some excessive and superstitious reverence to the spirit of his father. This is the one important meaning of the par., and it will be found that the critics, differing in the view they take of the first clauses—王司敬民, 罔非天胤, yet agree in this.

CONCLUDING NOTE. Woo-ting had a very long reign of 59 years, and died B.C. 1265. It is mentioned of him, in the 63rd diagram of the Yih King, that he 'attacked the demon-land, and subdued it in three years' (高宗伐鬼方,三年克之.) This 'demon-region' seems to have been the country of the wild tribes in the north, who never ceased to press upon the more civilized Chinese, till they made themselves masters of the empire, about 2,500 years after Woo-ting's time. A note in the 綱鑑易知 says that in the Hea dynasty they were called 獯鬻; in the Yin, 鬼方; in the Choo 玁狁; under Ts'in and Han, 匈奴; under the T'ang, 突厥; and under the Sung, 契丹.

The last of the Praise-songs of Shang, in the She King, is understood to celebrate the martial prowess of Woo-ting against the wild tribes of King-tsoo, and Choo He supposes that *they* were the people of the 'demon-regions.' In this case we should have to look for those regions on the south of Pŏ, which is not at all likely. If there was a strong effort by the northern hordes against the Chinese supremacy, we may suppose that the half-subdued tribes within the boundaries of the empire took advantage of the opportunity to rise against the government. The movement, however, whether from within or without, was effectually quelled. Woo-ting subdued rebellion, and made peace within all his borders. He arrested the decline of the Shang dynasty, but he could not turn it back. There is duly chronicled in the 41st year of his reign, B.C. 1282, the birth of Leih (季歷), the father of king Wăn, the founder of the dynasty of Chow.

THE BOOKS OF SHANG.

BOOK X. THE CHIEF OF THE WEST'S CONQUEST OF LE.

西伯戡黎

一節　西伯既戡黎、祖伊恐奔告于王。○二節曰天子、天既訖我殷命格人元龜罔敢知吉、非先王不相我後人惟王

1
2

The chief of the West having subdued Le, Tsoo E was afraid,
and hastened to report it to the king. He said, "Son of Heaven,
Heaven is bringing to an end the destiny of our dynasty of Yin;
the wisest of men and the great tortoise equally do not venture to
know any thing fortunate for it. It is not that the former kings
do not aid us, the men of this after time; but by your dissoluteness

INTRODUCTORY HISTORICAL NOTE. Woo-ting's
reign terminated in B.C. 1265, and 'the Conquest of Le by the Chief of the West' took place
B.C. 1123. Here, therefore, there is again a gap
in the history of the Shang dynasty, so far as
it might be collected from the documents of the
Shoo. Nor is the gap owing to the insensate
measure of the founder of the Ts'in dynasty in
burning the ancient Books. In the Shoo as it
came from the hand of Confucius, the 'Conquest
of Le' immediately followed the 'Instructions
to Kaou-tsung.'

The conquest of Le took place in the 31st
year of Chow-sin, the last emperor of the House
of Shang, who succeeded to the throne B.C.
1153. The time between him and Woo-ting
was filled up by the reigns of seven sovereigns.
[i.] Woo-ting was succeeded by his son
Tsoo-kăng (祖庚). Nothing is related of
him. He appears to have been a weak ruler,
and died, after a reign of seven years, B.C. 1258.

[ii.] Tsoo-këä (祖甲) followed his brother Tsoo-kăng. One account says that Woo-
ting, knowing Tsoo-këä to be worthier and abler
than his brother, had wished to leave the empire
to him, but that he himself, not to be charged
with supplanting Tsoo-kăng, withdrew and kept
himself concealed for some time. In B.C. 1257
the people called him to the throne, which he
occupied for 33 years.

The standard chronology chronicles no events
of his time in which he bore a part. It is noted
that in his 28th year, B.C. 1229, Ke-leih the
youngest son of Tan-foo, 'the old duke' of
Chow, had a son, Ch'ang (昌), by his wife T'ae-
jin (太任), whom Choo He delights to celebrate for her many virtues. Ch'ang is known
in history as 'king Wăn,' and his father as
'king Ke.' It would appear that Tan-foo died
in the same year, but not till he had seen something remarkable about the infant Ch'ang,

which made him say that he would greatly advance the fortunes of their House. In consequence of this, his two eldest sons, T'ae-pih (太伯; see Con. Ana., VIII., i.,) and Chung-yung, (仲雍; *alias*, 虞仲) both declined the dukedom of Chow in favour of Ke-leih, the first year of whose rule, as duke of Chow, dates in B.C. 1228.

Sze-ma Ts'een says that Tsoo-këä was lewd and disorderly (淫亂), and reigned only 16 years.

[iii.] Lin-sin (廩辛) succeeded to his father Tsoo-këä, B.C. 1224, and died after a short reign of six years. That is all history records of him.

[iv.] Lin-sin was followed by his brother Kǎng-ting (庚丁), who occupied the throne 21 years.

[v.] Woo-yih (武乙), the son of Kǎng-ting, commenced his brief reign of 4 years in B.C. 1197. On this 1st year, or in the year after, he removed the capital from Pŏ once more to the north of the Ho, somewhere in the dep. of Wei-hwuy, Ho-nan. He may have done this to be nearer the eastern part of the empire, which was disturbed in his time by risings of the wild tribes between the Hwae and mount T'ae.

Woo-yih occupies an unenviable place in the annals of China, many attributing to him the first making of idols in China ;—see Morrison's 'View of China for Philological purposes,' and De Mailla's History, Vol. I., p. 217. The action on which the charge is based, however, was more that of a madman than of a devotee, a freak of licentious folly, and not the birth of any religious feeling, however perverted. Sze-ma Ts'een simply tells us :— 武乙無道, 爲偶人, 謂之天神, 與之博, 令人爲行, 天神不勝, 乃僇辱之, 爲革囊盛血, 仰而射之, 命曰射天. 'Woo-yih was without any right principle. He made the image of a man, and called it "the Spirit of Heaven." Then he gamed with it' (博 = 'played dice, or at chess),' causing some one to play for the image. "The spirit of Heaven" was unsuccessful, on which he disgraced it, and made a leather bag which he filled with blood, and then placed aloft and shot at' (the image probably was in the bag as well), 'calling this "shooting at Heaven."' This is all the account we have in the 'Historical Records.' De Mailla, I imagine, *is making for himself* the narrative which he gives, that the emperor 'required all the people to adore the image, and address their vows to it.'

In the 4th year of his reign, while hunting between the Ho and the Wei, Woo-yih suddenly died. Ts'een says that he was struck dead by lightning; and people recognize in that event the just and appropriate vengeance of Heaven which he had insulted.

[vi.] Woo-yih was succeeded by his son T'ae-ting, whose brief reign of three years ended B.C. 1191.

[vii.] Te-yih (帝乙), the son of T'ae-ting, succeeded to his father, and reigned for 37 years, dying in B.C. 1154. During his time the House of Chow greatly increased in power and grew in favour with the people throughout the empire. In the previous reign duke Ke had signalized himself by repelling the incursions of certain wild hordes in the north. Having performed several similar exploits in the first year of Te-yih, the emperor gave him the title, first of 'Master of the Pastors' (命爲牧師), and subsequently invested him with the dignity of 'Chief of all the princes' (侯伯).

In B.C. 1184, duke Ke-leih died, and was succeeded by his son Ch'ang, who thenceforth appears in history under the style of the 'Chief of the West' (西伯). The benevolence which he displayed in the govt. of his own principality made the people everywhere long to be under his rule, and the men of greatest virtue and ability began to collect around him. In B.C. 1168, according to the generally acknowledged chronology, his son Fǎ (發), afterwards King Woo, the first emperor of the Chow dynasty, was born.

Chow-sin (紂辛) succeeded to the empire, B.C. 1153. He had two brothers older than himself,—K'e, known as the viscount of Wei (微子啟), and Chung-yen (仲衍); but when they were born, their mother had only a secondary place in the harem. Before the birth of Chow-sin, however, she was raised to the dignity of empress, and she and Te-yih were persuaded, against their better judgment, to name him on that account successor to the throne, in preference to K'e. He appears in history with all the attributes of a tyrant. His natural abilities were more than ordinary; his sight and hearing were astonishingly acute; his strength made him a match for the strongest animals; he could make the worse appear to be the better reason, when his ministers attempted to remonstrate with him; he was intemperate, extravagant, and would sacrifice everything to the gratification of his passions. He was the first, we are told, to use ivory chopsticks, which made the viscount of Ke (箕子) sorrowfully remonstrate with him. 'Ivory chopsticks,' said he, 'will be followed by cups of gem; and then you will be wanting to eat bears' paws and leopards' wombs, and proceed to other extravagancies. Your indulgence of your desires may cost you the empire.' Such admonitions were of no use.

In B.C. 1146 in an expedition against the prince of Soo (有蘇氏), he received from him a lady of extraordinary beauty, called Tǎ-ke (妲己), of whom he became the thrall. It is the story of Këe and Me-he over again. Tǎ-ke was shamelessly lustful and cruel. The most licentious songs were composed for her amusement, and the vilest dances exhibited. The court was at a place in the pres. dis. of K'e (淇縣), dep. of Wei-hwuy, and there a palace was erected for her, with a famous terrace or tower, two *le* wide, and the park around stocked with the rarest animals. This expenditure necessitated heavy exactions, which moved the resentment of the people. At Sha-k'ew (沙丘), in the pres. dis. of P'ing-heang (平鄉), in Chih-le, there was still greater extravagance and dissipation. There was a pond of wine; the trees were hung with flesh; men and women chased each other about, quite naked. In the palace there were nine market-stances, where they drank all night. The princes began to rebel, when Tă-ke said that the majesty of the throne was not sufficiently maintained;—that punishments were too light, and executions too rare. She therefore devised two new instruments of torture. One of them was called 'The Heater,' and consisted of a piece of metal, made hot in a fire, which people were obliged to take up in their hands. The other was a copper pillar, greased all over, and laid above a pit of live charcoal. The culprit had to walk across the pillar, and when his feet slipped, and he fell down into the fire, Tă-ke was greatly delighted. This was called the punishment of 'Roasting' (炮烙之刑). These enormities made the whole empire groan and fume with indignation.

Chow appointed the Chief of the West, the prince of K'ew (九侯), and the prince of Gŏ (鄂侯), his three principal ministers (三公). The two last met a sad fate. The prince of K'ew added his own daughter to the harem, and when she would not enter into its debaucheries, Chow put her to death, and made minced meat of her father. The prince of Gŏ ventured to remonstrate, and was sliced to pieces for his pains. Ch'ang fell at the same time under suspicion and was put in prison (囚于羑里), in a place called Yew-le.

These events are referred to B.C. 1143. Ch'ang, it is said, occupied himself, in prison, with the study of Fuh-he's diagrams, and composed a considerable portion of the present Yih King. In 1141, his sons and subjects propitiated the tyrant with immense gifts; the exigencies of the empire were likewise very pressing, in consequence of risings and incursions of the wild tribes; Ch'ang was released, and invested with greater authority than before. If he had raised the flag of rebellion, he could easily have dethroned the emperor, but he preserved his allegiance, obtained the abolition of the punishment of Roasting, and drew the hearts and thoughts of princes and people more and more to himself and his House. History tells us of his exploits, virtually regent of the empire, till his death in B.C. 1134, when he was succeeded by his son Fă, who inherited his authority and his virtues. Ten years pass on, of the events of which nothing important is related, and we come to B.C. 1123, to which the conquest of Le is referred.

NAME OF THE BOOK,—西伯戡黎, 'The Chief of the West's conquest of Le.' In the details of the preceding note I have followed the account of the closing years of the Shang

dynasty, which is now generally received, and acc. to which the chronology in the 歷代統紀表 is arranged; and the Chief of the West who subdued Le is said to have been Fă, the subsequent king Woo. Ts'ae, on the contrary, ascribes the conquest to Ch'ang or king Wăn, agreeing with Fuh-shang, Sze-ma Ts'een, Ch'ing, and all the older critics. The question is discussed at length in the 通鑑綱目, under the 31st year of Chow-sin. It hardly appears to me capable of a clear determination. Choo He was appealed to about it by one of his disciples who said, 'Most of the old interpreters thought that the Chief of the West here was king Wăn; but Ch'in Shaou-nan (陳少南), Leu Pih-kung (呂伯恭), and Sëë Ke-lung (薛季隆), have given their opinion that it was king Woo. Woo Ts'ae-laou (吳才老), also says that the conquest of Le must have closely preceded the attack on Chow himself.' The questioner then proceeded to indicate his own conclusion in favour of the more recent opinion, and asked for the master's decision. Choo He wisely replied, 'We may as well put on one side such questions where the evidence is so scanty' (此等無證據可且闕之).

By the 'West' in the designation 'Chief of the West,' we are to understand the province of Yung on the north, with those of Leang and King on the south,—the western part of the empire in fact.

Sze-ma Ts'een has Ke (飢), for Le, and Fuh-shang had K'e (耆). It is agreed, however, that the country designated extended over what are now the two districts of Le-shing (黎城) and P'ing-shun (平順), dep. of Loo-ngan (潞安) in Shan-se. This was only about 100 miles from Chow's capital, and within the boundaries of the imperial domain. The Chief of the West was no longer confining himself to the west. It was this approach of the army of Chow to the neighbourhood of the emperor which filled with alarm all who continued to cherish any attachment to the House of Shang. What provocation the duke of Chow may have had to attack Le, or by what motives he was actuated, we cannot tell; but it now became plain to all, that however loyally inclined he might be, there was a tide of affairs carrying Chow on to the supremacy of the empire. This is the meaning of the expression in the Preface, that 'Yin's first hatred of Chow was occasioned by the conquest of Le.' The Book is found in both the texts.

It is referred, not very satisfactorily, to the class of 'Announcements.'

CONTENTS. The Chief of the West having overthrown the prince of Le, Tsoo E filled with alarm hurries away to inform the emperor. He sternly sets the truth before him,—that the rule of Yin is hastening to a close through his own evil conduct. The tyrant gives no heed to his

○王曰嗚呼　今王其如台。　威大命不摯　曰天曷不降　民罔弗欲喪　率典。○今我　虞天性不迪　不有康食不　○故天棄我　淫戲用自絶。
五節　　　　　　　　　　　　　　　　　　　　四節　　　　　　　　三節

3 and sport, O king, you are bringing on the end yourself. On this account Heaven has cast us off, so that there is distress for want of food; there is no consideration of our heavenly nature; there is no

4 obedience to the statutes *of the empire*. *Yea*, our people now all wish *the dynasty* to perish, saying, 'Why does not Heaven send down its indignation? why does not *some one with* its great decree make *his* appearance? what has the present king to do with us?'"

5 The king said, "Oh! is not my life secured by the decree of

remonstrances, but returns an absurd reply; on which Tsoo E withdraws, and sighs over the ruin which he sees cannot now be averted.

P. 1, *Introductory paragraph. The occasion of Tsoo E's address.* 西伯戡黎— see on the Name of the Book. The 爾雅 defines 戡 by 殺, 'to till;' but the meaning of 勝 or 克, 'to overcome,' 'to subdue,' is to be accepted here. Tsoo E was probably a descendant of Tsoo Ke, the worthy minister of Woo-ting. He hurried away, *i.e.*, from his own city, probably between Le and the capital, to give information to Chow.

Pp. 2—5. *Tsoo E's address.* 2. *That the dynasty of Yin was about to be extinguished,— entirely through the wickedness of Chow.* 天 既訖我殷命,—訖=絶, 'to extinguish,' 'to bring to an end.' 我殷命=殷 之王命, 'Yin's appointment to the sovereignty' (Gan-kwǒ). 格人元龜— 格=至, 'perfect,' 'of the highest class;' 元 =大, 'great.' The tortoise employed for divination at the imperial court was so called by way of eminence, and supposed to measure, length-ways and across, a cubit and two inches. Sze-ma Ts'een has 假人 for 格人, and Keang Shing edits 假爾, reading 假 in the up. 2d tone, = 'to avail of.' He compares the text with the language of the Le Ke, 曲禮, Bk. I., Pt. v., p. 24, 假爾泰龜; but the interpretation is intolerably forced and harsh. 惟王淫戲自絶,—Sze-ma

Ts'een has 虐, 'oppression,' instead of 戲 'sport.' The meanings are both appropriate. The paraphrasts supply 于天 after 絶,— 'you cut yourself off from Heaven.' This does not seem to be necessary. 3. *Evidences of Heaven's abandonment in the miserable and demo- ralized condition of the people.* 不有康 食,—'we have no eating in comfort.' Famine was stalking abroad. 不虞天性,—虞 =度, 'to consider,' 'to act upon consideration of.' Demoralization followed upon want. 不 迪率典,—典=國家之常典, 'the regular statutes of the empire.'—'We do not tread in and follow the statutes.' Social disorder followed hard on demoralization. Such is the interpretation of this paragraph, and it is the most likely which I have seen. See others in the 註疏, in Keang Shing, and in the 後案. 4. *How the people were openly declaring their longing for the end of the dynasty.* 罔弗欲喪=無不欲 王之喪, or 殷之喪, 'the ruin of your Majesty,' or 'the ruin of the dynasty.' 大命不摯=摯=至, 'to come.' The 'great decree' is the appointment of Heaven to the sovereignty of the empire. Sze-ma Ts'een has 大命胡不至.

P. 5. *The defiant reply of Chow.* 我 生,—Chow intends, not only his 'life,' but his 'position' also. The 'Daily Explanation' para- phrases:—爾雖云民心背畔,

戮于爾邦。　乃功不無　之即喪指　于天。○殷　乃能責命七節　多參在上　嗚呼乃罪　祖伊反曰六節　命在天。○　我生不有

6 Heaven?" Tsoo E returned, and said, "Ah! your crimes which are many are set above;—and can you speak of your fate as if you
7 give it in charge to Heaven? Yin will very shortly perish. As to all your deeds, can they but bring ruin on your country?"

將實有我　然我尊爲天子,
欲天生何　我主萬民,獨不
亡在命矣　生天乎小民亦無如
我　　　　　　　　6,7. *Tsoo E's withdrawal and soliloquy on Chow's reply.*　6. 反＝還, 'to return.' He left the court, and returned to the place whence he had hurried to bring the news of the conquest of Le. Gan-kwŏ, however, makes the meaning to be—'returned for answer.' 乃(＝汝)罪多參在 上,—參 is a rank or cluster of 'three, orderly arranged;' hence it has here the meaning of 列, 'arranged in order.' 能責命 于天,—'can you charge your fate to Heaven? *i.e.*, can you speak as if you were safe through the decree of Heaven in favour of your House? Only the good-doer can look to Heaven with hope.

7. I have translated here after the 'Daily Explanation' supposing 殷 之即喪 to be a sentence complete,＝殷 之喪亡,直在旦夕,不能久 延矣. The interpretations of the paragraph, however, are very various. I will only give that of Keang Shing, which ＝ 'When Yin soon comes to ruin, shall not the destroyer declare your deeds, and put you to death in your kingdom?'

[It is remarkable that Tsoo E does not say a word about the growing power of the House of Chow,—makes not a single reference to the Chief of the West. Ts'ae supposes that he knew the loyal feeling of Ch'ing and Fǎ,—that neither of them was prompted by an ambition to gain the empire, and that even now, if the emperor could only be got to reform, the regent would sustain the dynasty of Shang. We can only note the singularity of the fact;—our hypotheses to account for it may be right or wrong.]

THE BOOKS OF SHANG.

BOOK XI   THE VISCOUNT OF WEÏ.

微子

微[一節]子若曰父
師少師殷其
弗或亂正四
方我祖厎遂
陳于上我用
沈酗于酒用
亂敗厥德于
下。○[二節]殷罔不

1　I. The viscount of Weï spoke to the following effect :—" Grand Tutor and Junior Tutor, *the House of* Yin, we may conclude, can no longer exercise rule over the four quarters of the empire.　The great deeds of our founder were displayed in former ages, but by our being lost and maddened with wine, we have destroyed *the effects*

HISTORICAL NOTE. The conversation recorded in this Book is referred in the chronology to B.C. 1122, the year immediately following the conquest of Le, and that in which the dynasty of Shang perished.　The chron. does not make mention, indeed, of this document ; but it places in the above year the events mentioned in the 18th Bk. of the Con. Ana., Ch. i,—how the viscount of Weï withdrew from Chow-sin's court, and the viscount of Ke became a slave, while Pe-kan was put to death ; and those events are supposed to have followed almost immediately after the conference between the worthies which is here related.　Difficulties might be raised against this view ; but it is not worth while arguing a point of little importance, and where absolute certainty cannot be attained.　The conversation between the viscount of Weï and his friends must have taken place near the time assigned to it,—in one of the closing years of the Shang dynasty.

NAME OF THE BOOK.—微子, 'The Viscount of Weï.'　This name seems to have been given after the fashion of the Books of the Confucian Analects.　The characters begin the Book and are therefore adopted as its name.　The Preface speaks of the viscount of Weï making his *announcement* to the Tutors, and the Book is accordingly placed in the division of 'Announcements.'　Like that of the last Book, this arrangement is convenient rather than satisfactory.

Weï (微) was the name of a principality of the 4th order (Men. V., Pt., ii. 3), the holder of which had the title of 子, which some have translated by 'viscount,' others by 'count,' and others again by 'marquis.'　It was within the limits of the imperial domain, in the pres. dis. of Loo-shing (潞城), dep. of Loo-gan (潞

安), Shan-se. It has been stated in the introductory note to the last Book, that the viscount of Wei was named K'e (啟), and that he was an elder brother of the emperor, by the same mother, who was, however, only a concubine when K'e was born, and subsequently raised to be empress before the birth of Sin. Such is the account of Sze-ma Ts'een, and other old writers. The authority of Mencius is pleaded in favour of the view that K'e was an uncle of the emperor;—see Men. VI., Pt. I., vi., 3. But Mencius does not allege this himself;—it only appears as an opinion current in his time. As K'e is in this Book addressed as 王子, 'son of the king,' and still more is called 殷王元子, 'the eldest son of the king of Yin,' in the 8th Book of the next Part, par. 1, the account in the 'Historical Records' ought not to be called in question. The Book is found in both the texts.

CONTENTS. Saddened with the thought of the impending ruin of their dynasty, the viscount of Wei seeks the counsel of two other high nobles, and after pourtraying in lively colours the mad dissoluteness of the emperor, and the demoralization of the people, asks them to tell him what was to be done. One of them, —the Grand Tutor—replies to him, describes in still stronger language the sad condition of the empire, and the unavoidable overthrow of the dynasty, and concludes by advising the viscount to make his escape, declaring that he himself would remain at his post and share in the unavoidable ruin. We may make a separate chapter of the language of each of them.

CH. I. Pp. 1—3. THE ADDRESS OF THE VISCOUNT OF WEI TO THE GREAT TUTOR AND THE JUNIOR TUTOR. 1. *How Yin, through the drunkenness of Chow, could no longer sway the empire.* 微子若曰,—compare what is said on 若曰 in the Pwan-käng, Pt. i., p. 6. 父師, 少師,—父 is here == 太, 'great,' 'grand.' Under the Chow dyn., we find from the next Part, Bk. XXV., there were the 'three *Kung*' (三公) one of whom was styled 太師, and the 'three *Koo*' (三孤), one of whom was the 少師 the highest officers of the empire, and who seem to have formed a sort of privy council to the sovereign. There were inferior officers of the same titles, mentioned by Fuh-shang (大傳),—retired magistrates and scholars who afterwards exercised something like the duties of schoolmasters in the villages, and were called 父師 and 少師. There

were also the grand and the assistant music-masters, who were styled 太師 and 少師;—see the Ana., XVIII., ix. The terms in the text must be understood as having the first of these three applications,—as designations of the highest officers about Chow's government. We do not know that there were, in the Shang dyn., the three *Kung* and three *Koo*, as subsequently in the Chow, but the 'grand Tutor' and 'junior Tutor' were of the class of those dignitaries. The individuals thus designated are said to have been 'the viscount of Ke' and 'Pe-kan,' who are both classed with the viscount of Wei in the Analects, XXIII., 1.; all the other commentators say so; and though Sze-ma Ts'een has some expressions both in the 殷本記, and in the 宋微子世家, which seem inconsistent with it, it is hardly worth while to discuss the subject. 殷其弗或亂正四方,—亂 = 治, 'to rule.;' 亂正四方, —comp. 治正于四方, 'Charge to Yue,' Pt. i., p. 2. Woo Ch'ing says that '其 and 或 are both expressions expressive of uncertainty' (皆非必然之辭). This is true of 或, but not true of 其, though it belongs to the peculiar usage of it, which has been more than once pointed out, to *insinuate* the meaning of the speaker. 我祖底遂陳于上,—T'ang is intended by 'our ancestor.' Ts'een gives 敗湯德 instead of 敗厥德 immediately below. We must take 遂 in the sense of 成, 'to accomplish,' and then 底遂 is equivalent to what we call a verbal noun,—'his carrying to the utmost his achieving,' == 'his great deeds.' 陳 = 列, 'to arrange.' 上, and 下 in the end of the par., are used with reference to time. 我用沈酗于酒,—Sze-ma Ts'een has 紂 instead of 我. Chow is no doubt intended, but K'e delicately takes the blame of his vices to all the descendants of T'ang;—compare the use of the pronoun in the 'Songs of the five Sons.' Ts'een also omits the 用, which adds emphasis to the verbs 沈 and 酗. The dict. defines 酗 by 醉怒, 'the anger or fury of drunkenness.' Luk Tih-ming (陸德明) explained the char. by 以酒爲凶, 'the practice of malignant wickedness under the

越　津　涉　殷　相　獲　辜　師　姦　小
至　涯　大　其　為　小　罪　非　宄　大
于　殷　水　淪　敵　民　乃　度　卿　好
今　遂　其　喪　讐　方　罔　凡　士　草
○ c 喪　無　若　今　興　恆　有　師　竊

2 *of* his virtue in these after times. The people of Yin, small and great, are given to highway robberies, villainies and treachery. The nobles and officers imitate one another in violating the laws; and for criminals there is no certainty that they will be apprehended. The lesser people *consequently* rise up, and make violent outrages on one another. The dynasty of Yin is now sinking in ruin;—its condition is like that of one crossing a large stream, who can find neither ford nor bank. That Yin should be hurrying to ruin at the present pace!"—

influence of spirits.' 　　2. *How the people, high and low, were demoralized and lawless, so that there was no hope for the dynasty.* 草竊 —Gan-kwŏ explains this by 草野盜竊 'steal and rob in the grassy wilds,' making one think of the notoriety in former days of Hounslow heath in England as a place for robberies. Keang Shing takes 草 in the sense of 莠 'hurtful weeds,' so that it is used adverbially and metaphorically. I prefer the old explanation. 師師非度,—師師＝互相傚效, 'imitate one another.' 凡有辜罪,乃罔恆獲,—辜＝罪. The two characters here form a complex term ＝ 'crime,' or 'criminals.' 　Woo Ch'ing supposes that this clause follows from the prec. He says:—'The nobles and officers are the model of the people, but instead of using the regular laws to apprehend criminals, they forbear with and allow them (卿士為民師表,凡有辜罪之人,反容縱之,無常法捕獲者). This is the most natural exegesis, and I have followed it. The old interpreters took the passage difftly. Gan-kwŏ interprets:—'They are all' (taking 凡＝皆, and referring it to 卿士) 'criminals, and there is not one who can regularly hold fast the due Mean' (皆有辜罪, 無秉常得中者). Still more absurd is the view given by K'ang-shing:—'All the

ministers are thus criminals, and as to their dignities and emoluments, they do not always get them. The meaning is that the ministers attacked and plundered one another' (羣臣皆有是罪,其爵祿又無常得之者,言屢相攻奪). 相為敵讐＝相敵相讐, 'fight with one another, revenge themselves on one another.' 今殷其淪喪,—Sze-ma Ts'een has 典喪 instead of 淪喪, so that the meaning is —'The statutes of Yin, every bond of order and govt., are now gone to ruin, and the dyn. is in a condition like that,' &c. This would give a good enough meaning, but we cannot, because we find 典 in Ts'een, conclude that the 淪 in the text is erroneous. One crossing a great stream where there was neither ford nor bank could only sink in the waters. 殷遂喪, 越至于今,—越, like the same char. in Bk. IX., p. 1, can hardly be translated. Ma Yung and Gan-kwŏ both try to bring out its meaning as＝於是;—but unsuccessfully. See the 後案, and the 註疏. I consider the clause to be incomplete. The 'Daily Explanation' paraphrases it:—豈意我殷之盛,一旦喪亡相及,至于如此之甚乎, 'How could it have been supposed that on our Yin, once so flourishing, ruin would have suddenly come upon ruin, to such a degree as at the present time?'

（三節）曰、父師少師、我其發出狂、吾家耄遜于荒、今爾無指、告予顛隮、若之何其。○（四節）父師若曰、王子、天毒降災荒殷邦、方興沈酗于酒。○（五節）乃罔畏畏、咈其耉長舊有位

3 He added, "Grand Tutor and Junior Tutor, we are manifesting insanity. The venerable of our families have withdrawn to the wilds; and now you indicate nothing, but tell me of the impending ruin; —what is to be done?"

4 II. The Grand Tutor made about the following reply:—"King's son, Heaven in anger is sending down calamities, and wasting the country of Yin. Thence has come about that lost and maddened
5 condition through wine. He has no reverence for things which he ought to reverence, but does despite to the aged elders, the old

P. 3. *K'e represents their sad condition still more vividly, and begs his friends to give him counsel.* 我其發出狂,—Chow is intended here by 我, as in par. 1 耄,—'a person 90 years old is called 耄;—see Pt., Bk. II., p. 9. 顛隮,—Ying-tă defines and distinguishes these terms, saying that 顛 means 'to fall from a height,' and 隮, 'to fall into a ditch.' Nothing can be made of the 其 at the end. we must be content to take it as a mere expletive.' These notes and the translation are all after Ts'ae Ch'in, Gan-kwŏ interprets differently; —thus:—'When I think of this ruin of Yin, I feel as if unwell and become maddened. In my family, my heart is wearied and confused, and I wish to withdraw to the wilds. Now you do not inform me of your views, but tell me of the downfal of the country, and ask what is to be done.' Sza-ma Ts'een's text is a good deal dift.—曰, 太師少師, 我其發出往, 吾家保于喪, 今女無故告, 予顛躋如之何其, 'I will arise and go forth away. My family will be preserved in the ruin. Now you tell me nothing (?). I may fall *into a wrong course*;—what should I do?' Keang Shing's text nearly agrees with Ts'een's, but not quite. I believe the received text is the most correct, and that Ts'ae's interpretation is to be preferred to all the others.

CH. II. Pp. 4—9. REPLY OF THE GRAND TUTOR. 4. *He enlarges on what K'e had said about Chow's drunkenness.* 王子,—see the note on the Name of the Book. 毒降,—'is poisonously sending down.' It is difficult to know how to interpret 方興, and connect it with what precedes. We want a nominative expressed to 興, as in par. 2;—to suppose one in 邦, as Gan-kwŏ does is too violent. The meaning given by him, as expanded by Ying-tă, is:—Heaven, sending down cruel and poisonous calamities, gave birth to this insensate and oppressive sovereign, to waste and confound the kingdom of Yin. Chow having proved a drunkard, the people throughout the four quarters are all acted on by him, and addicted to the same vice, so that nothing can be done.' It would appear that the Grand Tutor attributes the ruin of the dynasty to Heaven, and that not in permission or retribution merely. 'He puts it upon Heaven,' says Ts'ae, 'his loyalty and reverence for the emperor not permitting him to put it on him!' If the crimes through which the dynasty was going to ruin were produced by Heaven, that ruin certainly could not be arrested. Ts'een omits altogether the second part of the par., and gives the first—太師曰, 王子, 天篤下災, 亡殷國. 5. *He illustrates what K'e had said on the madness of Chow, and the withdrawal of the old and experienced.* 罔畏畏—不畏其所當畏, as in the

今其有災我
瘠罔詔。○商　八節
罪合于一、多
召敵讐不怠
民用乂讐斂
災。○降監殷　七節
以容將食無
之犧牷牲用
乃攘竊神祇
人。○今殷民　六節

6 official fathers.　Now the people of Yin will even steal away the pure and perfect victims devoted to the spirits of heaven and earth; and their conduct is connived at, and though they proceed to eat 7 the victims, they suffer no punishment.　*On the other hand*, when I look down and survey the people of Yin, the methods of government to them are hateful exactions, which call forth outrages and hatred; —and this without ceasing.　Such crime equally belongs to all *in authority*, and multitudes are starving with none to whom to 8 appeal.　Now is the time of Shang's calamity;—I will arise and share in its ruin.　When ruin overtakes Shang, I will not be the

translation. Comp. Con. Ana., XVI., viii. 耇長=老成之人, 'old, accomplished men.' 耇 denotes 'the appearance of a frosted pear.' Such-like are the faces of old men, and hence the char. is used for 'old.' 6. *He intensifies what had been said of the robberies and villainies of the people of Yin.* The people were guilty not of ordinary robberies only;—they committed sacrilege, and were allowed to do so with impunity. 攘 is 'to steal upon occasion offered,' to appropriate, for instance, a neighbour's sheep trespassing on one's ground; but we cannot here insist on that peculiar meaning of the term. 牲=='victim,'—ox, sheep, or pig. 犧 is the victim 'uniform in colour.' 牷 is the same, 'complete,' without blemish. 用以容.—Ts'ae supposes that this clause speaks of 'the officers.'—有司用 相容隱. Keang Shing makes Chow himself to be the subject of it. Gan-kwŏ ingeniously joins the 用 to the clause above, and explains it as meaning 'the offerings of fruit and grain.' Maou K'e-ling says that in his earlier years he could not away with this interpretation, but was inclined to adopt it on maturer thought;—see the 尚書廣聽 錄, Bk. II,, *in loc.* 7. *He describes the outrages and misery of the people in consequence of the oppressions of those in authority.* 降= 下, 'down,' 'descending.' 用乂讐斂

=凡上所用以治之者, 無非 讐斂之事, 'all the methods used by their superiors to govern them are only exactions of enemies.' Ma Yung read 稠 for 讐; but the meaning is substantially the same. 召敵讐,—'which call forth outrages and hatred.' This is understood to have reference to 相爲敵讐 in paragraph 2. It would seem to be so; and we may understand the outrages there spoken of as further described here as done in defiant despite to the government. 罪合于一,—'the crimes' are those of the emperor and of the officers generally. 罔詔,—詔=告, 'to tell,' 'to appeal to;'—comp. the use of 告 in the phrase 無告者, Mencius, I., Pt. II., v., 3. 8. *The Grand Tutor declares his own intention to abide all risks at his post, but he advises K'e to withdraw and save himself.* 商今......臣 僕,—the reader who has Lin Che-k'e's commentary will be amused by reading his view of this passage. I do not introduce it here, because, though ingenious, it does not show Lin's usual soundness of judgment. 詔王子 出迪,—the 'Daily Explanation' paraphrases this:—我告王子, 惟出而遠去 乃合于道, 'I tell you, O king's son, that to quit and go far away is the right course for you.' 我舊云刻子=我前

我不顧行遯。　自獻于先王、　隮。○自靖、　弗出我乃顛　云刻子、王子　子出迪、我舊　爲臣僕、詔王　其淪喪、我罔　興受其敗、商
　　　　　　自靖、　　九節
　　　　　　人

servant *of another dynasty.* *But* I tell you, O king's son, to go away as being the course *for you.* Formerly I injured you by what I said, but if you do not go forth now, our *sacrifices* will entirely

9 perish. Let us rest quietly *in our several parts,* and present ourselves to the former kings. I do not think of making my escape.

日所言、適以害子, 'what I formerly said served to injure you.' It has been mentioned that Te-yih and his empress wished to leave the throne to K'e, and not to Chow-sin, but were dissuaded from the purpose. It is supposed that the text refers to the advocacy at that time by the Grand Tutor of K'e's claims to the throne, which had made him all along an object of jealousy and dislike to Chow.

Gan-kwŏ takes 刻 as = 病, 'to be distressed for;'—see the 註疏 *in loc.* Keang Shing, always ready to reject the received text, adopts from Wang Ch'ung (王充) the reading of 孩子; but the meaning which he ingeniously brings out of 舊云孩子 comes in effect to the same thing as that usually followed. 我乃顛隮,—it must be understood that the Grand Tutor speaks here of the sacrifices offered to the founder and all the departed emperors of the House of Shang. He must himself have belonged to the imperial line. If, as is most likely, he was the viscount of Ke, he was an uncle of the emperor;—so the relationship between them is commonly represented. Ts'ae expands the text:—我商家宗祀、始隮墜而無所托矣. 9. *They must, each of them, do what they felt to be right.* 自靖,—靖 = 安, as in Bk. VII., Pt. i., p. 12. Ts'ae says :—各安其義之所當盡, 'let each man rest in the performance of what his circumstances require him to do.' Gan-kwŏ, and here for a wonder Kĕang Shing is at one with him, takes 靖 in this pass., and in the Pwan-kăng, as = 謀, so that 自靖 = 'take counsel with yourself.' It is difficult to say what is the precise idea in 'presenting themselves to the former kings.' I

think it is this,—that if they did what was right, they should have consciences void of offence, as now beheld by their ancestors, or as hereafter to appear before them. 顧 is used as in the T'ae-kĕă, Pt. i., p. 1, 顧諟天之明命.

[FATES OF THE MEN MENTIONED IN THIS BOOK. The viscount of Wei appears to have acted on the advice given him by the Grand Tutor, and to have withdrawn from the court of Yin. The expression in the Ana., XVIII., i.,—微子去之, may be considered as proving this. When and how he withdrew, however, it is not possible to ascertain. According to a description in the 左傳、僖六年, and the account given by Sze-ma Ts'een, after the death of Chow, he went out to meet king Woo at the head of his army, having with him the sacrificial vessel of the House of Shang. He presented himself in miserable plight, almost naked, with his hands bound behind him, and moving forward on his knees, when king Woo received him honourably, and restored him to his former office, whatever that was. This legend has been called in question. In the next Part of the Shoo we shall meet with the viscount again, and see him finally enfeoffed with the principality of Sung, there to continue the representative of the House of Shang.

If the viscount of Ke, whose name was Seu-yu (胥餘), was indeed the Grand Tutor of the text, he did not die with the dynasty, as he seems to have expected. The passage of the Analects referred to says 'he became a slave.' According to Ts'een, he reproved Chow in the first place, and when his friends urged him to make his escape, he refused, and feigned himself to be mad, allowed his hair to hang about uncared for. King Woo found him in prison, and set him free, when he fled away to Corea. We shall meet with him also again in the next Part.

The Junior Tutor is supposed to have been Pe-kan, also a member of the imperial House, though his precise relationship to Chow is uncertain. Mencius calls him 王子, 'king's son' (Book. II., Pt. I., i. 8); Ts'een says no more than that he was 'a relative' (親戚); Ch'ing and others say he was 'an uncle.' He does not appear as a speaker in the text; but the part which he chose was a harder one than the parts of his friends. When he saw how the reproofs of the viscount of Ke were received, he brought the truth before the tyrant with still sterner vehemence. 'I have heard,' said Chow, 'that the heart of a sage has seven apertures;—let us see if it be so.' With this he made Pe-kan be put to death, had his heart cut out, and glutted his eyes with the sight of it.]

[FINAL OVERTHROW OF THE SHANG DYNASTY.

The dynasty closes, in the chronology, in B.C. 1122, the same year to which the conference between the viscount of Wei and his friends is referred. It was in the year after, however, that Chow-sin died, and for the contest between him and the duke of Chow we must look to the commencing Books of the next Part. The duke of Chow after many delays at last took the field against the tyrant. We are surprised to find that Chow-sin, notwithstanding the general detestation with which he was regarded, was able to bring together an immense host, vastly outnumbering that of the other side. The two armies met in the plain of Muh, in the south of the pres. dis. of Ke, dep. of Wei-hwuy, Ho-nan. Chow-sin's troops failed him in the hour of need. He was totally defeated, and fled to the palace which had been the scene of so many debaucheries with Tă-ke. Arrayed in his most gorgeous robes, and covered with gems, he set fire to the 'Stag Tower,' which he had built for her, and perished in the flames;—yet not so but that his body was found by the duke of Chow, now king Woo, who cut off the head, and had it exhibited on a pole. Tă-ke apparelled herself splendidly, and went out to meet the conqueror, thinking he might be conquered by her charms. She was made prisoner, however, by a detachment of his troops, and put to death by his order, without having the opportunity to present herself before him.]

THE

CHINESE CLASSICS:

WITH

A TRANSLATION CRITICAL AND EXEGETICAL NOTES,
PROLEGOMENA, AND COPIOUS INDEXES.

BY

JAMES LEGGE, D.D.,

OF THE LONDON MISSIONARY SOCIETY.

IN SEVEN VOLUMES.

VOL. III.—PART II.

CONTAINING

THE FIFTH PART OF THE SHOO KING,
OR THE BOOKS OF CHOW; AND THE INDEXES.

London:

HENRY FROWDE,

OXFORD UNIVERSITY PRESS WAREHOUSE, AMEN CORNER, E.C.

HONGKONG:

PRINTED AT THE LONDON MISSIONARY SOCIETY'S
PRINTING OFFICE.

THE SHOO KING.

PART V. THE BOOKS OF CHOW.

BOOK I. THE GREAT DECLARATION. PART i.

周
書

泰
誓
上

惟^{一節}
十
有
三

年、
春
大
會

于^{二節}
孟
津。
我
○

王
曰、
嗟
我
友
邦
冢
君、

越
我
御
事

庶
士、
明
聽

1 　In the spring of the thirteenth year, there was a great assembly
2 at Măng-tsin.　The king said, "Ah! ye hereditary rulers of my
friendly States, and all ye my officers, managers of my affairs, listen
clearly to my declaration.

NAME OF THE PART.—周書, 'The Books of Chow.'　Chow is the dynastic designation under which Woo and his descendants possessed the empire from B.C. 1121—255, a period of 867 years.　They traced their lineage up to K'e (棄), the minister of Agriculture (后稷) under Shun.　K'e is said to have been a son of the emperor K'uh (B.C. 2432).　The marvels of his birth and infancy are pleasantly described in the second Part of the She King, and are duly chronicled by Sze-ma Ts'een (周本紀).　He was invested with the principality of T'ae (邰), the pres. dis. of Foo-fung (扶風), dep. of Fung-ts'ëang (鳳翔), in Shen-se.　In the time of Këĕ, B.C. 1796, the fortunes of the family, which had for some time been waning, revived under Kung-lew (公劉), who established himself in Pin (豳), the pres. small department of 邠.　There his descendants remained till B.C. 1326, when Tan-foo, afterwards styled king T'ae in the sacrificial ritual of the dynasty, removed to the foot of mount K'e in the pres. dis. of K'e-san (岐山), dep. of Fung-ts'ëang;—see Men., I., Pt., II., xiv., and xv.　The State which he established there was called Chow.　King T'ae was succeeded by his son Ke-leih, or king Ke, and he again by his son Ch'ang, or king Wăn, who transmitted his hereditary dominions, greatly increased, and his authority to his son Fă or king Woo.　Woo then adopted Chow as the designation of the dynasty which he founded.

The Books of Chow were more numerous, as we might expect, than those of the previous dynasties,—even though they belong only to little more than the first half of its history.　Nor did they suffer so much in consequence of the fires of Ts'in as those of the Shang dynasty.　Out of 38 documents there remain 20 whose genuineness is uncontested; and only 8 have been entirely lost. I have said that we might have expected that the Books of Chow would be more numerous than those of Shang; but we could not have expected that so much larger a proportion of them should escape the various dangers to which all were equally exposed.

THE NAME OF THE BOOK.—泰誓, 'The Great Declaration.' 泰=大, 'great.' King Woo, having at last taken the field against Chow, makes three speeches to his officers and men, expounding the grounds of his enterprise, urging them to play the man with him in the cause of humanity and Heaven. Those are brought together, and constitute one grand whole,—'The *great* Declaration.'

THE DIFFERENT TEXTS OF THE BOOK. This subject has been treated of in the prolegomena; and I will content myself here with giving the summary of the discussions that have been raised upon it, which is quoted in the 通鑑綱目 from Kin Le-ts'ëang's 通鑑前編, merely interjecting a remark or two, where his statements can be fairly called in question. The text preferred by Keang Shing and other modern scholars will also be found, with a translation of it, in an appendix to the Book.

Le-ts'ëang says:—'The Shoo of Fuh-shang did not contain the "Great Declaration."' [But see the first Book of Maou K'e-ling's 'Wrongs of the old Text of the Shoo.' The 'Great Declaration' *was* in the Books of Fuh-shang.] 'It was in the "Old Text," found in the wall of Confucius' house; but as the commentary of K'ung Gan-kwŏ was not entered in the imperial college during the Han dynasty, his edition of it did not then become current. Chang Pa (張霸) then fraudulently made a "Great Declaration," in three Parts, which became current, and contained the passage about "a white fish entering king Woo's ship," &c., which is found in Chung-shoo (仲舒) and Sze-ma Ts'een.' [This passage is found in those writers, and also in Fuh-shang's Introduction to the Shoo. There is no necessity to say that the 'Great Declaration,' current during the Han dynasty, was forged by Chang Pa.] 'But in the time of the Eastern Han, Ma Yung and other scholars became aware that this was not the genuine document; and it fell into general discredit, when the "Old Text" made its appearance at the commencement of the Eastern Tsin dynasty. Recently, however, this same Old Text has come to be suspected by the scholar Woo (吳氏). "Its language," he says, "is vehement and arrogant, not to be compared with that of the Declaration of T'ang. As the document appeared so late, we may suppose that the whole of it is not the original text."

'In my opinion, the conduct and language of T'ang and Woo were equally responsive to Heaven and accordant with men. They differed because the circumstances of the men differed. T'ang was the founder of the fortunes of his House; Woo entered into an inheritance which was already flourishing. T'ang's enterprise commenced when men were beginning to look to Shang; Woo's was undertaken when many of the princes had long been followers of the Chiefs of Chow. The battle of Ming-t'eaou was fought by the people of Pŏ, while at Măng-tsin there was a grand assemblage of the princes with their hosts. With such differences of circumstances, we should expect differences of style and manner. As to what is said of Chow's being worse than Kĕĕ, and the language being more ornate, these things are accounted for by the difference of time. Even allowing that the style was somewhat modified and improved, when the document made its reappearance, we may well believe that it gives us the views of king Woo.'

CONTENTS. These may be stated in the language with which Le-ts'ëang concludes his observations.—'In the first Part, king Woo addresses himself to the princes and others of inferior rank; in the second, to the hosts of the princes; and in the third, to his officers. The ruling idea in the first is the duty of the sovereign,—what he ought to be and do; with this it begins and ends. There is not the same continuity of thought in the second, but the will and purpose of Heaven is the principal thing insisted on. The last Part shows the difference between the good sovereign and the bad, and touches on the consent that there is between Heaven and men. The Book is brilliantly composed, and far transcends the powers of any man of a later age to have made it.'

CONTENTS OF THE FIRST PART. At a great assemblage of the princes, king Woo sets before them the reasons of his proceeding against Chow-sin. Starting from the position that the sovereign is ordained by God for the good of the people, he shows how the king of Shang acted only to the injury of the people. King Wăn would have punished him if he had lived, but now the duty was devolved upon himself, and with their help he would proceed to obey the requirement of Heaven. They need have no fears as to the issue. Favoured by God and men, the expedition could not but be crowned with success. There are eleven paragraphs which are so connected as to form only one chapter.

Par. 1. *The time, place, and occasion of the Declaration.* The time was the spring of the 13th year; but it is hardly possible to place beyond dispute the prior date from which we are to calculate this 13th year. In the first place, the Preface assigns the time to the 11th year (note 32); and there is no way that can be admitted of reconciling the two accounts. The general view is that the 11 in the preface is a mistake for 13, but Lin Che-k'e takes the opposite view, and contends that the 13 in the text should be 11. In the second place, admitting the text to be correct, we find that the standard or common chronology reckons from the 1st year of king Woo's accession to the principality of Chow, which it places in B.C. 1133. This view is ably argued by Ts'ae Ch'in *in loc.* On the other hand, Gan-kwŏ said that the 13th year was to be reckoned from king Wăn's receiving (as indicated by circumstances) the appointment of Heaven to the sovereignty of the empire. He is supposed to have then changed the style of his reign,—to have begun it afresh with a new 'first year.' Nine years then elapsed, and his work was not completed;—the tyrant was still upon the throne, and Wău

民　元　作　亶　物　惟　物　天　誓。
父　后　元　聰　之　人　父　地　○
母。作　后、明　靈、萬　母、萬　惟三節

3　　"Heaven and Earth is the parent of all creatures; and of all creatures man is the most highly endowed.　The sincere, intelligent, and perspicacious *among men* becomes the great sovereign; and

died. Two years more passed by,—the period of mourning for him; and then king Woo took the field, but it was not till the year after, the 4th year of his reign, that the contest between him and Chow-sin was decided. This view is strongly advocated by Maou K'e-ling, against Ts'ae and others, in the third Book of his 尚書廣聽錄.　But the various data on which it is endeavoured to decide the question are by no means certain;—see a note in the 歷代統紀表, on the date of king Woo's birth, under B.C. 1168. I must for the present suspend the expression of any opinion of my own on the point.

A controversy, nearly as perplexing, is waged about the time intended by 'the spring,' where we should hardly think there was room for any difference of view. It has been already observed (on 'The Instructions of E' Pt. i., p. 1) that while the Hea dyn. began the year with the 1st month of spring (the month 寅), the Shang began it with the last month of winter (the month 丑). The Chow dynasty removed the commencement of the year farther back still, and made it begin with the second month of winter (the month 子). Ts'ae and a host of followers say that by 'the spring' is intended the months of the Hea year; and this appears reasonable, for however different dynasties might begin their year in different months, they could not change the order of the seasons. The 'spring' of Chow was the same as that of Hea; and if we suppose, as is most natural, that the historian is speaking in the text with reference to the Chow year, then the month intended by 'the spring' must be the first month of that season. Gan-kwŏ, however, understands the month intended to be the *first* of the Chow year, and Maou K'e-ling supports his view. This question will come up again in the course of this and the two next Books.

The place where the declaration was made was Măng-tsin, or at the 'Ford of Măng:'—see the Tribute of Yu, Pt. ii., p. 7. There was there a great assembly of all the princes who already acknowledged the supremacy of Chow, and were confederate with Woo to make an end of the tyrant. Gan-kwŏ says they were the princes of the two thirds of the empire, who had followed the banner of king Wăn (Ana., VIII., xx., 4), and the chiefs of many of the wild tribes;—along with their various hosts.

P. 2.　*Opening of the address.*　王曰,

—Woo is here styled 'king,' or emperor, by anticipation. Had he been defeated, he would have been 'a rebel;' but as his enterprise was crowned with success, from the moment he began to operate against Chow-sin, he was the sovereign of China, and the other was only 'a solitary fellow' (獨夫; Pt. III., 4).　我友邦冢君,—Ying-tă says—同志爲友, 'they were 友, as having the same mind and aim with him.'　冢君 is literally 'highest rulers,' or 'great rulers.' The 'Daily Explanation' explains the phrase by—各國嗣立之君, which I have followed in the translation.　越我御事庶士,—越＝及, 'and;' 御＝主 or 治, 'to preside over,' 'to manage.' 御事＝治事者, 'managers of affairs.' The 'Daily Explanation' would include the soldiers among the 士 as well as the officers,—衆士卒; but it is better not to extend the meaning of the term so far in this passage. Medhurst strangely and quite erroneously translates 越我御事 by—'it has fallen to me to manage these affairs.' The address begins with 嗟, the exclamation which ordinarily precedes these military speeches.

3.　*The sovereign is ordained by Heaven and Earth, because of his virtues, for the good of the people.*　Compare the 'Announcement of T'ang,' p. 2. What is to be remarked here is the style of speaking which is new, and places 'Heaven and Earth' in the place of 'Heaven' simply, or 'God.' Woo does not always employ this style. In this same Part he employs both the terms which I have mentioned. There can be no doubt that the deification of 'Heaven and Earth,' which appears in the text, took its rise from the Yih King, of which king Wăn may properly be regarded as the author. No one who reads what Wăn says on the first and second diagrams, and the further explanations of his son Tan (the duke of Chow), can be surprised to find king Woo speaking as he does in the text.　惟人萬物之靈,—'it is man who is the most intelligent of all creatures.' By 萬物 in the first clause we understand

池侈服以　室臺榭陂　以世惟宮　以族官人　暴虐罪人　冒色敢行　民。○沈湎（五節）　天、降災下　受、弗敬上　○今（四節）商王

4 the great sovereign is the parent of the people. *But* now, Show, the king of Shang, does not reverence Heaven above, and
5 inflicts calamities on the people below. He has been abandoned to drunkenness, and reckless in lust. He has dared to exercise cruel oppression. Along with criminals he has punished all their relatives. He has put men into office on the hereditary principle. He has made it his pursuit to have palaces, towers, pavilions, embankments, ponds, and all other extravagances, to the most painful injury of you,

'all things,' inanimate as well as animate; in the second clause we must confine the meaning to animate creatures. The various tribes of animals have their several measures of intelligence, but all are very inferior to men.

Then, as men are superior to other creatures, there appear among them those who are superior to their fellows;—the sages, who are raised up by Heaven, and become the rulers, teachers,—parents, in fact—of the mass. Ch'in King says on this:—'Man is one among all creatures. Other creatures, however, get but a portion of the energizing element of nature, while he receives it complete:—it is this which makes the nature of man more intelligent and capable than that of other creatures. But though men are endowed with this capacity and intelligence, there are those who are not able to preserve and maintain it, and there must be the quick-apprehending and understanding ruler to be a parent to them. In this way the people are able all to complete their intelligence. The sage possesses before me that of which I have the seeds in common with himself; and among intelligent beings he is the most intelligent'

（人之所此得民先靈　者偏以靈聰始得之　萬人獨有明得我靈　物得靈不之以各之　之氣於能君各之以　一也此人靈母靈然　物此人靈母靈然物　得人雖此炎母靈而　氣性有必斯人為聖而）

Pp. 4, 5. *How Chow had forfeited all his title to the empire, and king Wăn had been charged to punish him.* 4. 商王受,—I have hitherto called the tyrant of Shang by the name of Chow (紂), after Sze-ma Ts'een and Mencius. Here and elsewhere he appears as

Show, which Ts'ae says was 'the name of Chow.' Chow is his epithet in history, conferred upon him for his cruelty and wickedness;—see the Dict. on the character (殘忍損義曰 紂). Lin Che-k'e says that 紂 was interchanged with 受 from the similarity of the two characters in sound, but he must be wrong, because Show is here used by king Woo before the tyrant's death. 上天下民,—I think these phrases may best be taken as in the translation. 5. 沈湎,—comp. 沈酗 于酒, in 'The Viscount of Wei,' p. 1. 冒 色,—冒 is 'to go forward with the eyes covered,'='to pursue blindly and recklessly.' 色＝女色. 罪人以族,—'he crimed men according to their relationships.' The meaning is as in the translation. The 'Daily Explanation' has:—加罪于人, 不但誅其一身,并其族屬, 而刑戮之. Mencius points it out as one of the glories of king Wăn's administration of K'e, that 'the wives and children of criminals were not involved in their guilt' (罪人不 孥; Bk. I., Pt. II., v. 3.) It was one of the principles of Shun that punishments should not be extended to the offender's children (Counsels of the Great Yu, p. 11.) We have seen Yu's son, (The Speech at Kan, p. 5) and even T'ang, (The Speech of T'ang, p. 4) menacing their troops with the death of their children, if they did not do their duty. That may have been a measure of war; and Chow carried it into all the penal administration of his govt. To what extent the punishment of relations was carried by Chow, we do not learn from the text. Gankwŏ supposes that the parents, brothers,

商、惟受罔有　冢君、觀政于　發、以爾友邦　○肆子小子　威、大勳未集。　文考、肅將天　天震怒命我　剖剔孕婦、皇　姓、焚炙忠良、　殘害于爾萬

六節

the myriad people.　He has burned and roasted the loyal and good.
He has ripped up pregnant women.　Great Heaven was moved
with indignation, and charged my deceased father Wăn reverently
to display its majesty; but *he died* before the work was completed.

6　"On this account I, Fă, who am but a little child, have by
means of you, the hereditary rulers of my friendly States, contemplated the government of Shang; but Show has no repentant

wives and children, (三族) all suffered
with the offender. 官人以世、
—'he officed men according to their generation,
or genealogical connection.' The 'Daily Explanation' makes the meaning to be that Chow
put into office all the friends of his favourites.
一其用人、則不論賢否、但其
心之所喜、即幷其子弟親
屬悉寵任之. But this view of 以
世 is unwarrantable. Mencius, in the passage
above referred to, says that king Wăn salaried
the descendants of meritorious officers. But
tho' such men might be salaried, they were called
to office only when they had the virtue and
ability necessary for its duties. Chow did not
look out for able and good men to fill the offices
of the State. This is the burden of this part of
the indictment against him. 惟宮室
……萬姓—惟='he only cared for.'—其
所務者惟在宮室、云云. The
說文 defines 宮 by 室. The former term
is the building as a whole; 室, the apartments
in it. Le Seun says:—臺 is a high terrace of
earth, made for the purpose of observation;
when a house or houses are built on the top of
it, they are called 榭.' 侈服=凡
侈靡諸事, 'all extravagances;' 服=
事. 焚炙忠良,—this refers to the
punishment of Roasting, described in the historical note on the 'Conquest of Le.' 剖
剔孕婦,—we saw how Chow caused the
heart of Pe-kan to be cut out;—Hwang-poo

Meih, of the Tsin dyn., says that he also caused
Pe-kan's wife to be ripped up. No earlier account to that effect, however, is known. King
Woo is no doubt rehearsing things which were
commonly charged upon the tyrant at the time.
皇天,—see on the 'Announcement of
T'ang,' p. 2. 命我文考,—考 is the
name for a father deceased. King Woo speaks
in this way of his father having been charged
to punish Chow, to vindicate all the better his
own present course. We are not to suppose
that any such commission was ever expressly
given to Wăn; and Confucius speaks of him as
having been faithful to the dyn. of Shang to the
last;—see Ana., VIII., xx., 4. 大勳未
集=大功未成. We must complete
the meaning by adding 而崩, as in the translation.
P. 6. *The task of punishing Chow being now
devolved on him, he sets forth the evidence of his
hopeless wickedness.* 肆=故, 'therefore.'
以爾……于商.—觀政 is ex-
plained by a reference to the same phrase in the
'Both possessed pure Virtue,' p. 10. The princes
of the States were to Woo an index of the govt.
of Chow. Had they remained loyal to him,
that would have shown that his govt. was good.
As they were now in the mass revolted from
him, and following Woo's banner, it was clear
that he was no longer fit to be emperor. Such
is the explanation of this passage by Ts'ae, and
what is now commonly received; and I see no
better course than to acquiesce in it. Gan-kwŏ
and the earlier scholars explained it with reference to an assembly, which they imagined, of
Woo and the princes at the ford of Tsin, two
years before the period of this 'Declaration.'
Then he had thoughts of attacking Chow, but
on contemplating his govt., concluded that the
time was not yet come, and withdrew his troops.

曷敢有越厥志。○
四方、有罪無罪、予
其克相上帝寵綏
作之君、作之師、惟
其侮。○天佑下民、
吾有民有命罔懲
盛既于凶盜乃曰
宗廟弗祀犧牲粢
上帝神祇遺厥先
悛心乃夷居弗事

heart. He abides squatting on his heels, not serving God or the spirits of heaven and earth, neglecting also the temple of his ancestors, and not sacrificing in it. The victims and the vessels of millet all become the prey of wicked robbers; and still he says, 'The people are mine: the decree is mine,' never trying to correct his

7 contemptuous *mind*. *Now* Heaven, to protect the inferior people, made for them rulers, and made for them instructors, that they might be able to be aiding to God, and secure the tranquillity of the four quarters of the empire. In regard to who are criminals and who are not, how dare I give any allowance to my own wishes?

Such a meeting is not properly substantiated; and the view is otherwise liable to many objections. 夷居,—compare 夷俟, Con. Ana., XIV., xlvi. 弗事上帝神祇遺厥先宗廟弗祀,—Ts'ae, after Gan-kwŏ, gives for this—廢上帝百神宗廟之祀, 'he has discontinued the sacrifices,—to God, the hundred spirits, and the spirits of his ancestors.' Ying-tă observes that the meaning is that Chow had no religion, rendered no service to spiritual beings (不事神祇); God, as the highest of all such beings, being mentioned, to show the enormity of his wickedness. In this way a distinction is made between 上帝 and 神祇, the latter phrase being synonymous with 百神. On the other hand, the 'Daily Explanation,' for 弗事上帝神祇 has—忽慢天地神祇不知奉事, 'he slights and contemns the spirits of Heaven and Earth, and renders not service to them.' This would confound God with the spirits of Heaven and Earth, which is by no means inconceivable in Woo, when we consider the language of p. 3. Compare also the language of parr. 3 and 4 in the 'Announcement of T'ang.' Upon the whole, however, the gradation of thought in the passage may determine the scale in favour of the former view. 犧牲粢盛既于凶盜,—犧牲, see the last Book, p. 6; 粢盛, see Men., III., Pt. II., iii., 3; 既＝盡, 'are consumed,' or 'are all taken.' The whole corresponds with the words of the Grand Tutor in the par. of the 'Viscount of Wei' just referred to. 有民, 有命, —comp. the 'Conquest of Le,' p. 5. 罔懲其侮＝無有懲戒其侮慢之意.

P. 7. *He returns to the principles declared in par. 3, and shows that he was constrained by them to attack Chow.* See this par. as it is quoted by Mencius, I., Bk. II., iii., 7. The difference between the text here, and that which he gives is very considerable. We cannot suppose that the present text of the Shoo was forged from Mencius. A plagiarist, attempting such an imposition as is ascribed to 'the false K'ung,' would have taken the language exactly from his copy. We can only believe that Mencius had a copy of the 'Great Declaration' before him, differing not a little from the present, or that he quoted from memory, and allowed himself great license in altering the classic. 寵綏四方,—'to show favour and tranquillize the four quarters *of the empire*.' 予曷敢有越厥志。＝我何敢

爾　上　懼　　弗　貫　千　億　義　同
有　帝　受　○　順　盈　惟　萬　受　力
衆　宜　命　予　天　天　一　心　有　度
底　于　文　小　厥　命　心　子　臣　德
天　家　考　子　罪　誅　○　有　億　同
之　土　類　夙　惟　之　商　臣　萬　德
罰　以　于　夜　鈞　予　罪　三　惟　度
。　　　　祗　。　　　。　　　。

8　" 'Where the strength is the same, measure the virtue of the parties;
where the virtue is the same, measure their righteousness.' Show
has hundreds of thousands and myriads of ministers, but they have
hundreds of thousands and myriads of minds; I have three thousand
9　ministers, but they have one mind. The iniquity of Shang is full.
Heaven gives command to destroy it. If I did not comply with
Heaven, my iniquity would be as great.

10　" I, who am a little child, early and late am filled with appre-
hensions. I have received charge from my deceased father Wăn; I
have offered special sacrifice to God; I have performed the due
services to the great Earth;—and I lead the multitude of you to

有過用其心乎, 'how dare I use
my own mind too much?' Such is the interpretation of Ts'ae;—越厥志, is 'to go
beyond *what is right* with—in accordance with
—my own wishes.' The dict. follows Gan-kwŏ
in defining 越 here by 遠, 'to put away.'—
'My purpose is to destroy the tyrant for the
good of the people. Whether he be guilty or
not guilty, I will smite him. I will not let go
that, my proper purpose.' This is evidently incorrect.

P. 8. *He auspices success from the righteousness of his cause, and the harmony of mind among
his followers, though they were comparatively few.*

The two first clauses are supposed to be
a current saying used against each other by
contending parties;—Lin Che-k'e has adduced
from the 左傳 two examples of similar couplets. The second clause is not so intelligible
as the first. We can understand how when
parties were matched in strength, the struggle
should be expected to terminate in favour of
the more virtuous; but it is difficult to perceive
how 'virtue' and 'righteousness' can be set
against each other. 受有臣億萬,
—Ts'ae says here that 億 denotes 'a hundred
myriads,' or a million. This was probably a
slip of his pencil. 億,= ten myriads, or

100,000. The subject of Show's more numerous host comes up again in the next Part, p.
6. We may admit it as a fact, and it explains the risings and troubles which disturbed
the dynasty of Chow after the death of king
Woo. It is difficult, at the same time, to
reconcile it with the representations of the
general disaffection to the emperor, and of two
thirds of the empire having been for years
devoted to the House of Chow. See the
note on this paragraph in the 後案. It is
instructive, though not conclusive in favour of
the author's views. 9. *It was woe to Woo
himself if he proceeded not to destroy Shang.*
Compare the 'Speech of T'ang,' pp. 1, 2; and
the 'Announcement of T'ang,' p. 4. 商
罪貫盈,—'the crimes of Shang are strung
together and full.' 10. *Woo's caution ana
conscientiousness in proceeding with his enterprise.*
予小子夙夜祗懼,—comp.
the 'Announcement of T'ang,' p. 6. 受
命文考, 類于上帝,宜于
家土.—家=大 'great'; 家土, 'the
great earth,'=大社, 'the altar dedicated
to the great spirit of the Earth.' The sacrifice
at this altar was called 宜　類于上帝,

失。哉 四 人、弼 之 天 之 于 ○
弗 海、永 子 爾 必 所 民、天十
可 時 清 一 尙 從 欲、民 矜一節

11 execute the punishment appointed by Heaven. Heaven compas-
sionates the people. What the people desire, Heaven will be found
to give effect to. Do you aid me, the one man, to cleanse for ever
all within the four seas. Now is the time!—it may not be lost."

—see the 'Canon of Shun,' p. 6.　In the Le
Ke, Bk. 王 制, Pt. ii., 17, we find—天 子
將 出, 類 乎 上 帝, 宜 乎 社, 造
乎 禰, 'When the emperor is about to go forth,
he offers special sacrifice to God, performs the
due services at the altar of the Earth, and goes
to the shrine of his father.' Woo had attended
to all these observances; and it must have been
at the shrine of his father, that he somehow
understood himself 'to receive,' as he says here,
'charge' to attack Chow. 底 天 之 罰,

—comp. 恭 行 天 之 罰, in the 'Speech
at Kan,' p. 3.　11. *The enterprise was a
proof of the compassion of Heaven for the people,
and he summóns all the princes and officers to strenuous cooperation with him.*　Under the 32nd
year of duke Seang, and in another place of the
左 傳, we find the passage—民 之 所
欲, 天 必 從 之, quoted from the 'Great
Declaration.' It is also found in the 國 語.
爾 尙 弼 子 一 人,—see the 'Speech
of T'ang,' p. 4.

THE BOOKS OF CHOW.

BOOK I. THE GREAT DECLARATION. PART ii.

咸　西　○　徇　畢　群　次　惟　　　泰
聽　土　曰　師　會　后　于　戊　　　誓
朕　有　鳴　而　王　以　河　午　　　中
言。眾、呼、誓。乃　師　朔、王

1 On *the day* mow-woo, the king halted on the north of the River. When all the chiefs with their hosts were assembled, the king re-
2 viewed the hosts, and made the following declaration, saying, "Ah! ye multitudes of the West, listen all to my words.

CONTENTS OF THE SECOND PART. Since the delivery of the first address, the army has crossed the Ho, when Woo reviews it, and makes this speech, which is more especially addressed to the troops. He makes Show and Kĕĕ, T'ang and himself, all pass before his men, showing that Show was more wicked than Kĕĕ, and that his punishment of him would be more glorious than T'ang's had been of Kĕĕ. Heaven will surely crown their enterprise with success; and he therefore in conclusion urges them all to go into battle, not despising the tyrant, but with united hand and heart, to accomplish a work that should last for ages. The whole is divided into 9 paragraphs.

Pp. 1, 2. *The time, place, and occasion of the address; and the parties addressed.* The time was the day *mow-woo*, which we are able to determine, from the 1st par. of the 'Completion of the War,' to have been the 28th day of the 1st month. We are there told that Woo began his march to attack Chow on the day *jin-shin*, which was the 2d of the 1st month. Calculating on to the day *mow-woo*, we ascertain that it was the 28th of the same moon. The controversy, described on the 1st par. of the last Part, on the term 'spring,' however, is not

decided by this fixing of the relation between the two dates. Ts'ae will still have the month to be the first of the Hea year,—really the first month of spring; Gan-kwǒ and others will have it to be the first month of the Chow year, the second month of winter. 次于河 北,—次＝止, 'to stop,' 'to be stationed.' In the interval, therefore, between the two addresses, the army had crossed the Ho. 徇 師,—徇 (3d tone)＝循, 'to go about.' Hwang Too explains it from the phrase 拊循, 'to cheer and animate.' 'To review' expresses the meaning accurately enough. Perhaps we are to understand that the king first crossed the river and encamped; and then, when all the princes with their troops, had pitched their tents around him, he went through the host and addressed the soldiers. 2. 西 土有眾,—Woo and his father had both been 'Chiefs of the West,'—viceroys over that part of the empire.

天乃佑命成湯降黜夏
桀弗克若天流毒下國、
天惠民惟辟奉天、有夏
辜籲天、穢德彰聞。〇惟
朋家作仇、脅權相滅、無
人淫酗肆虐、臣下化之、
無度、播棄犂老、昵比罪
日不足、今商王受力行
不足、凶人爲不善、亦惟
〇我聞吉人爲善惟日

3　　"I have heard that the good man, doing good, finds the day insufficient, and that the evil man, doing evil, likewise finds the day insufficient. Now Show, the king of Shang, with strength pursues his lawless way. He has cast away the time-worn sires, and cultivates intimacies with wicked men. Dissolute, intemperate, reckless, oppressive, his ministers have become assimilated to him; and they form parties, and contract animosities, and depend on *the emperor's* power to exterminate one another. The innocent cry to Heaven. The odour of such a state is plainly felt on high.

4　　"Heaven loves the people, and the sovereign should reverence *this mind of* Heaven. Kĕĕ, the sovereign of Hea, could not follow the example of Heaven, but sent forth his poisonous injuries through the States of the empire:—Heaven favoured and charged T'ang, the

P 3. *The dreadful wickedness of Show.*
吉人、凶人,—comp. the use of 吉 and 凶 in the 'Counsels of Yu,' p. 5. Here, however, we are to take the terms in their purely moral signification. This use of them shows the deep conviction that goodness and prosperity, evil and calamity, ought always to be found together. 播棄犂老,—comp. in the 'Viscount of Wei,' p. 3, 毫遜于荒 播 is here explained by 放, very nearly synonymous with 棄 犂 is most simply explained by taking it as for 黧, 'black and yellow,' the colour of old men's faces. Mih-tsze says of Chow that he 播棄黎老, where 黎 is probably intended for the character in the text 昵比罪人.—昵 (*neih*), as in the

'charge to Yuĕ p. 5; 比, as in the 'Instructions of E,' p. 7. 朋家作仇=各立 朋黨, 互爲仇讐. 脅權一 脅, as in the 'Punitive Expedition of Yin,' p. 6, = 進. 'to press,' 'to force.' The phrase here = 'they make forcible use of—press upon with—the power *of the emperor.*' 籲天 =告天 or 呼天, 'appeal to Heaven.' 穢德,—'their filthy, fœtid deeds.' See on the 'Pwan-kăng,' Pt. ii., p. 8. Pp. 4, 5. *Heaven will always overthrow wickedness and tyranny:—illustrated in the case of Kĕĕ and T'ang, and now in that of Show, who was worse than Kĕĕ, and himself.* 4. 惠=愛 'to love.' 有夏桀 is not = 'there was Kĕĕ of Hea,' but 有夏之君, 桀,

襲民王惟謂足賊于命
于朕天不暴行虐桀○
休夢其遠無謂諫剝惟五
祥協以在傷祭輔喪受節
戎朕予彼厥無謂元罪
商卜乂夏鑒益己良浮

有天命謂敬不

5 Successful, to make an end of the decree of Hea. But the crimes of Show exceed those of Këĕ. He has stript and degraded the greatly good man; he has behaved with cruel tyranny to his reprover and helper. He says that his is the decree of Heaven; he says that a reverent care of his conduct is not worth observing; he says that sacrifice is of no use; he says that tyranny is no matter. The case for his inspection was not remote;—in that king of Hea. It would seem that Heaven is going by means of me to rule the people. My dreams coincide with my divinations; the auspicious omen is double. My attack on Shang must succeed.

'Këĕ, the ruler who held Hea.' 流毒 下國,＝流毒于下國, 'flowed out his poison upon the lower States.' Këĕ is conceived of on the throne of the empire, as being raised on high, above his own and all the feudal domains. 降黜夏命,-降黜＝ 'to bring down and put away.' Comp. the expression in the 55th note of the Preface,—成 王既黜殷命. 5. 罪浮于 桀,-浮, comp. on the 'Pwan-kang,' Pt. ii., 3. Here it is evidently ＝勝 or 過, 'to exceed.' 剝喪元良,—剝 'to tear,' 'to peel,' ＝ 'to degrade'; 喪 is 失位, 'to lose one's office,' used, here in a *hiphil* sense. It is supposed that this clause has reference to the viscount of Wei, whose withdrawal from court, it would thus appear, was preceded by violence and oppression on the part of Show. The next clause,—賊 虐 諫 輔, is referred to Pe-kan. 謂 已 有 天 命,—see the 'Conquest of Le,' p. 5. 敬不足行,—'reverence is not worth being practised.' We had better understand the 're-verence' with reference to his own conduct, and to the business of the State. 祭無益,— this was the cry of the wicked Jews in the time of Malachi,—'It is vain to serve God.'

暴無傷,—無傷,—see Men. I., Pt., vii.' 8. 厥鑒 云云,—see the quotation from the She King in Mencius, IV., Pt. I., ii., 5. 天其以予乂民,—observe the force of 其. 朕夢協朕卜、襲 于休祥戎商必克.—We have no other intimation of Woo's being encouraged in a dream to act against Show; his divination may have been before the shrine of his father, referred to in the last Part, p. 10. 襲,＝ 重, 'double,' 'repeated.' 襲于休祥, —'both agree in being auspicious,' 戎, 'a wea-pon,' here ＝ 'to attack with weapons.' Acc. to the interpretation thus indicated, which is after Ts'ae, the omens were only two, which united in being favourable. In the 國語, however, 周語, 下, the passage is quoted, where the speaker is treating of the agreement of *three* omens, and he adds to the passage— 以 三 襲 也. On this view, 襲于休 祥＝ 'agree with the 休祥,' whatever this was. Lin Che-k'e. adopting this construction, refers to the 24th chap. of the 'Doctrine of the Mean,' where it is said that when a nation or a family is about to flourish, there will be 禎祥, seen in the milfoil and tortoise, &c. There, a substantive meaning may be given to those two

姓　自　我　人　周　心　亂　心　億　必
有　我　民　〇　親　同　臣　離　兆　克
過　民　視　天　不　德　十　德　夷　。
在　聽　天　視　如　雖　人　子　人　〇
子　百　聽　自　仁　有　同　有　離　受有

6　"Show has hundreds of thousands and millions of ordinary men, divided in heart and divided in practice;—I have of ministers capable of government ten men, one in heart and one in practice. Although he has his nearest relatives with him, they are not like 7 *my* virtuous men. Heaven sees as my people see; Heaven hears as my people hear. The people are blaming me, the one man, *for my*

characters, as to 休祥 here,—namely the occurrence of certain unusual phenomena;—see Ying-tă on the passage of the 中庸. The editors of Yung-ching's Shoo seem on the whole inclined to favour this view.

P. 6. *The greater number of Show's host and adherents was no cause for doubt as to the issue.* See on the 8th par. of last Part. 夷人,—夷＝平常, 'common, ordinary men.' 子有亂臣十人,—see Con. Ana., VIII., xx. 周親–周＝至, the superlative adverb, 'most.' The phrase 周親, and the whole clause indeed, are difficult. The paraphrase of the 'Daily Explanation' is:—受所信者,雖有同姓至親,我親人，親皆凶人,雖有醜類同惡相濟,是我親人，皆十臣,雖不盡是仁厚有德之人,之戚然皆以經邦濟世, 'Although those in whom Show reposes his most intimate confidence are his nearest relatives of the same surname with himself, yet they are all bad men and detestable, helping him and one another in their common wickedness. My ten ministers, on the other hand, although they are not all my own relatives, are virtuous men, benevolent and generous, fit to rule a country and benefit the age.'

[Confucius said that there was a woman among Woo's ten able ministers;—see the Ana., *loc cit.* She is generally spoken of as 文母, 'mother Wăn,' king Woo's mother, the famous 太姒. Others think Woo's wife, 邑姜, must be intended. It is not easy to believe this.]

P. 7. *The will of Heaven might be seen from the earnest wish of the people that he should destroy Show.* 天視......民聽,—see Men., V., Pt. I., v., 8. It would not be easy to determine the exact meaning of the term 'Heaven' here. The attention of Choo He being called to the applicability of the definition of Heaven as meaning 'Reason,' or 'what is Reasonable' here, replied, 'Heaven certainly means "What is Reasonable"; but it does not mean that only. It means also "the azure vault" (蒼蒼者亦是天); and it means too "the Lord and Ruler who is above" (在上而有主宰者亦是天). The term is to be explained in every place by a consideration of the context. If here you say that it means "what is Reasonable," how can that see and hear? Although the explanations are different, there yet is something common in all the usages. If you know that, you will not be startled by the differences; and if you know them, you will see that they are not inconsistent with the common idea.'—See the passage quoted in the 集說. 百姓有過,在子一人.—Lin Che-k'e takes these words as equivalent to those in the 'Announcement of T'ang,' p. 7, 萬方有罪,在子一人; and most readers will feel inclined at first to agree with him. 過 is to be distinguished, however, from 罪, and the sentiment appropriate to the lips of T'ang, who had vanquished his rival, is not to be expected from Woo, who was only marching to the fight. Gan-kwŏ, as if he had T'ang's words before him, and yet felt the difference between 過 and 罪, interpreted—'It devolves on me, the one man, to teach the people, and correct their

定厥功、惟克永世。
呼乃一德一心立
懍懍若崩厥角嗚
畏寧執非敵百姓
九節 最哉夫子、罔或無
用張于湯有光。○
疆取彼凶殘我伐
我武惟揚侵于之
八節 一人今朕必往。○

8 *delay*;—I must now go forward.　My military prowess is displayed, and I enter his territories, to take the wicked tyrant.　My punishment

9 *of evil* will be shown more glorious than that of T'ang.　Rouse ye, my heroes!　Do not think that he is not to be feared;—better think that he cannot be withstood.　*His* people stand in trembling awe of him, as if the horns were falling from their heads.　Oh! unite your energies, unite your hearts;—so shall you forthwith surely accomplish the work to last for all ages."

errors.' But this idea is foreign to the occasion. Ts'ae's explanation of 過 by 責, 'fault-finding,' 'complaining of,' is very ingenious, and sound.　　See the Con. Ana., xx., i., 5, where also we have the conclusion of the last paragraph.

P. 8.　*The present enterprise was not less but more glorious than that of T'ang.*　Compare the paragraph as quoted by Mencius, Bk. III., Pt. II., v., 6.　It will be seen to be rhythmical, and this may account for the difficulty which we find in construing it.　侵于之疆 ＝侵入受之疆界, 'I invade and enter the boundaries of Show's domain.'　于湯有光,—Ts'ae makes this to ＝ 'and this will reflect light on T'ang,' *i.e.,* will make his mind in attacking Këĕ more clear.　As the editors of Yung-ching's Shoo say, this is too ingenious.　Ts'ae wanted to relieve Woo of a portion of the charge of boastfulness, which is urged against the language of this Book; but foreign students of Chinese history do not feel the pressure of such a charge.　We are content to take king Woo as we find him, and are not concerned to bring his character either up or down to the Chinese idea of a sage.

P. 9.　*He rouses his men to prepare for the fight with stern determination, not undervaluing their enemy, but rather overvaluing him.*　　A good part of this paragraph is also found in Mencius;—see VII., Pt. II., iv. 5.　His variations from the present text are, however, greater, and affect the meaning of the several parts of the par.　How to account for the differences is a difficult question.　To say that our present 'Old Text' is a forgery, is an absurd solution; —the true solution has yet to be found.　夫子,—'my masters,' here ＝ 'my heroes.'　罔或無畏, 寧執非敵 ＝ 無或以紂爲不足畏, 寧執心以爲非我所敵也, as in the translation.　百姓懍懍,—the people are understood to be those of Show's domain, and the parts of the empire in the east.　The next clause represents them as a flock of cattle, whose horns were being broken.　立定厥功,—the 立 is best taken adverbially, ＝ 'forthwith.'

BOOK I. THE GREAT DECLARATION. PART iii.

狷侮五常荒　彰今商王受、　顯道厥類惟　土君子、天有　曰嗚呼、我西　誓眾士。　大巡六師、明　時厥明、王乃　　泰誓下
　　　　　　　　　　　　　　　　　　　　　一節　　二節

1　　The time was on the morrow, when the king went round
his six hosts in state, and made a clear declaration to all his
2 officers.   He said, "Oh! my valiant men of the west, Heaven has
enjoined the illustrious courses *of duty*, of which the *several* characters
are quite plain.   And now Show, the king of Shang treats with contemptuous slight the five constant *virtues*, and abandons himself

CONTENTS OF THE THIRD PART. On the day
after addressing the troops as in the last Part,
Woo had a grand review of all the hosts, and
declared his sentiments more particularly to
the officers.   He sets forth, as before, the crimes
of Show against God and men, as sufficiently
justifying their enterprise, and urges the officers
to support him with all their energies that he
might do his work thoroughly, and utterly
destroy the tyrant.   Having set before them
the prospect of rewards and punishments, he
concludes with a humble but encouraging reference, to his father Wăn.

P. 1.   *The time and occasion of the Declaration,
with the parties addressed.* The day was that
immediately following that on which the last
address was delivered,—the *Ke-wei* day of the
calendar.   It is supposed that the army was
now about to march to meet or seek the enemy.
大巡六師,—大巡, 'went greatly
about.' Lew Ying-ts'ew (劉應秋) says
that 巡 differs from 循, the latter meaning to

go round and cheer, while the former conveys the
ideas of marshalling and warning.   This is very
doubtful. 六師 is used, like 王, throughout the Book, by anticipation.   According to
the subsequent statutes of the Chow dyn., the imperial forces consisted of six armies or brigades,
while those of a great State were only three.   In
reality the hosts now collected on the banks
of the Ho were an imperial force, and so they
are denominated the 'six hosts.' 明誓
眾士,—眾士, 'all the officers;'—Gan-
kwŏ says they were all 'from centurions upwards.'

P. 2.   *That Show, violating the laws of Heaven,
had set both Heaven and men against him.*
西土君子,—'princely men of the western
regions' 君子 is appropriate as addressed
to the officers, though Lin Che-k'e shows that
it might be employed also to designate the common soldiers. 天有顯道、厥類

上帝弗順祝降時　技淫巧以悅婦人　修宗廟不享作奇　囚奴正士郊社不　黜師保屏棄典刑　四海崇信姦回放　心作威殺戮毒痛　涉之脛剖賢人之　結怨于民。○斯朝　怠弗敬自絕于天、三節

to wild idleness and irreverence. He has cut himself off from Heaven, and brought enmity between himself and the people.

3　　　"He cut through the leg-bones of those who were wading in the morning; he cut out the heart of the worthy man. By the use of his power killing and murdering, he has poisoned and sickened all within the four seas. His honour and confidence are given to the villainous and bad. He has driven from him his instructors and guardians. He has thrown to the winds the statutes and penal laws. He has imprisoned and enslaved the upright officer. He neglects the sacrifices to Heaven and Earth. He has discontinued the offerings in the ancestral temple. He makes contrivances of wonderful device and extraordinary cunning, to please his woman. —God will no longer indulge him, but with a curse is sending down

惟彰,—it seems most proper to explain these clauses by what is said below that Show had violated the 'five virtues.' The 'illustrious ways of Heaven,' therefore, are the various relationships, of society, and 'their characters,' are the duties severally belonging to them. This view is advocated by Ying-tǎ, who is followed by Ts'ae. Lin Che-k'e, on the other hand, understood by the 'illustrious ways,' Heaven's love of virtue and hatred of vice, and by 'their characters,' the good and evil which severally attend them;—making reference to the use of the phrase 天道 in the 'Counsels of Yu,' p. 21, and in the 'Announcement of T'ang,' p. 3. This interpretation is ingenious and not without merit; but the other is preferable. 狎侮五常,—狎＝易 or 輕,' 'easily 'lightly;' 狎侮＝ 'slights and contemns.' 五常,—see on 五典, 'Can. of Shun,' p. 2.

P. 3. *An enumeration of Show's wickednesses, and summons to the officers to support the king in punishing him.* 斮朝涉之脛,— Gan-kwǒ tells us that Chow, one winter's day, seeing some people wading through a stream,

thought their legs had a wondrous power of enduring cold, and had them cut off through the shank-bone, that he might see their marrow. 剖賢人之心,—this refers to the case of Pe-kan. 毒痛四海,—痛 ＝病, 'to be sick'; here, 'to make sick.' 姦回,—回＝邪 or 曲, 'the crooked,' ＝ 'the bad.' 囚奴正士,—this was the case of the count of Ke. 郊社,—see on the 'Doctrine of the Mean,' xix. 6 婦人,—this refers to Tǎ-ke. History has not preserved an account of the cunning contrivances referred to. Ts'ae says that since Show contrived 'the punishment of Roasting' to make her laugh, we can well understand that he tasked his ingenuity to the utmost in other things to please her. 祝降時 (＝是) 喪,—Gan-kwǒ defines 祝 by 斷 (up. 2d tone), 'to cut off,' 'to make an end of.' Ts'ae, misunderstanding 斷 for the same char. in the 3d tone, explains the clause by 斷然降

喪、爾其孜孜奉予一人、恭行天罰。○古人有言曰、撫我則后、虐我則讐、獨夫受洪惟作威乃汝世讐、樹德務滋除惡務本肆予小子、誕以爾眾士殄殱乃讐爾眾士其尙迪果毅以登乃辟功多有厚賞不迪有顯戮。○嗚呼惟我文考、若日

on him this ruin. Do ye support with untiring zeal me, the one man, reverently to execute the punishment appointed by Heaven.

4 The ancients have said, 'He who soothes us is our sovereign; he who oppresses us is our enemy.' This solitary fellow Show, having exercised great tyranny, is your perpetual enemy. *It is said again*, 'In planting *a man's* virtue, strive to make it great; in putting away *a man's* wickedness, strive to do it from the root.' Here I, who am a little child, by the powerful help of you, all my officers, will utterly exterminate your enemy. Do you, all my officers, march forwards with determined boldness, to sustain your prince. Where there is much merit, there shall be large reward. Where you advance not so, there shall be conspicuous disgrace.

5 "Oh! *the virtue of* my deceased father Wăn was like the shining

是喪亡, 'is determinedly sending down this ruin.' But 祝, like the Hebrew *barak* is a *vox media*, and may be used for 'to curse' as well as 'to bless.' 孜孜='with unwearied efforts.'

P. 4. *Show had shown himself the enemy of the people, never to be forgiven; and Woo calls his troops to support him in making root and branch work with the tyrant.* 獨夫受,—this was certainly very strong language, applied to Show who was still occupying the throne. See the reference to it by Mencius, I., Pt. II., viii. It is much in his style. Seun-tsze has quoted it as from the 'Great Declaration,' in his 議 兵篇 世讐,—'an hereditary enemy,' one whose memory must be held in detestation in all the future. 樹德...... 務本,—these clauses are probably sayings

of the day like the first two. The former of them appears, slightly varied, as 'an old saying,' in the 左傳, 哀元年. 其尙迪果毅—the union of 其 and 尙. to express earnest exhortation, has occurred more than once. 迪=進, 'to advance.' 果 and 毅 are both defined by 決 and 有決, 'determined.' It is said—致果爲毅 毅 is the intensest determination.' 登乃辟,—登=成, 'to complete.' The 'Daily Explanation' brings the meaning out by saying:—以成爾君弔民伐罪之功, 'to accomplish the work of your ruler in consoling the people and smiting the criminal.'

Pp. 5, 6. *The virtue of King Wăn, and its effects. Success in the present enterprise would be owing to him; failure, if failure there should be,*

月之照臨、于四方、顯于西土、惟我有周、誕受多方。○予克受、非予武、惟朕文考無罪、受克予、非朕文考有罪、惟予小子無良。〔六節〕

and influence of the sun and moon. His brightness extended over the four quarters *of the empire*, and shone signally in the western region. Hence it is that our Chow has received *the allegiance of* 6 many States. If I subdue Show, it will not be my prowess, but the faultless *virtue* of my deceased father Wăn. If Show subdue me, it will not be from any fault of my deceased father Wăn, but because I, who am a little child, am not good."

would all be Woo's own. 5. The greater part of this par. appears in Mih-tsze (兼愛,下篇), thus:—太誓曰，文王若日若月，乍照光于四方于西土。 惟我有周，誕受多方，—I have translated this in the indicative mood, as historical narrative. Such is the view of Gan-kwŏ who explains;—文王德大，故受衆方之國，三分天下，而有其二，'The virtue of king Wăn was so great, that he received the allegiance of the States of many quarters, and had two thirds of the empire.' Ts'ae found in the language an auspice of Woo's success in the enterprise in hand. The 'Daily Explanation,' expanding his construction, says:—文考之德，其所及如此，是以人心戴之，天命歸之，惟我有周，宜其大受多方而有天下，'Thus far-reaching was the virtue of my father Wăn:—the hearts of men cherished him, and the decree of Heaven fell to him. Right it is that our House of Chow should receive the allegiance of the many regions, and possess the empire.' I must prefer to construe with the older scholar.

6. The whole of this par. is found with the verbal variation of 紂 for 受, in the Le Ke, Book 坊記, p. 16. In 無罪，有罪，we must take 罪 lightly, as merely = 過，'fault,' 'error.'

APPENDIX.

I annex here the "Great Declaration," as it appears in Këang Shing's 尚書集註音疏. He has been at great pains to gather up, and put together, the fragments of the Book, as it was when current in the Han dynasty. Wang Ming-shing, or Wang Kwang-luh (王光祿), gives a much briefer edition of it in his 尚書後案, and arranges many of the sentences, moreover, differently. The fragments give us now in many passages but a farrago of absurdities. We may be sure that a Book containing such things never received the *imprimatur* of Confucius :——

維四月、太子發上祭于畢、下至于孟津之上。○

周公曰、都忞哉子聞古先哲王之格言。○太子

發拜手稽首。○乃告司徒司馬司空諸凡齊栗

信哉。○予無知以先祖之有德臣左右小子予

受先公功畢力賞罰以定厥功于先祖之遺○

家典師師尚父左杖黃戉右把白旄以號曰蒼

兒兒總尓衆庶與尓舟楫後至者斬。○太子

發升舟中流白魚入于王舟王跪取出淶以燎

羣公咸曰休哉。○至于五日有火自上復于下

至于王屋流之爲雕其色赤其聲魄五至以穀

俱來。○武王喜諸大夫皆喜周公曰茂哉茂哉

天之見此以勸之也恐恃之○正卟古立功立

事可以永年傳于無窮不天之大律。○使上附

以周公書報誥于王王動色變。○八百諸侯不

召自來。不期同時不謀同詞皆曰受可伐矣王

曰尓未知天命未可伐維丙午王還師前師乃

鼓枻譟師乃搯前歌後舞極于上天下地咸曰

孜孜無怠天將有立父母民之有政有居。○

In the fourth month, Fă, the eldest son and successor, went up and sacrificed at [or, to] Peih, and then proceeded to the neighbourhood of Măng-tsin.

The duke of Chow said, "Oh! exert yourself. I have heard the excellent words of the wise and ancient kings."　　　The prince Fă bowed with his face to his hands, and his head to the ground.

He then addressed the minister of Instruction, the minister of War, and the minister of Works, with all the other appointed officers,—"Be reverent, firm, and sincere.　　　I am without knowledge, but *I look to* the virtuous ministers of my fathers to help me, who am but a little child. I have received the achieved work of the dukes my predecessors, and will exert my strength in rewards and punishments, to accomplish whatever they have left undone."　　　On this he put the host in motion. The *grand* Tutor, Father Shang, carrying in his right hand an axe yellow with gold, and in his left a white flag, to give out his orders, said, "The hoary wild bull! The hoary wild bull! Lead on all your multitudes. There are your boats and oars. The last come shall be beheaded!"

As the prince Fă had got to the middle of the stream in his boat, a white fish entered it. The king knelt down and took it up. He then went on the bank, and burned it, *in sacrifice to Heaven.* All the dukes said, "This is auspicious!"

On the fifth day there was a *ball of* fire which descended from above, till it came to the king's house, and there dissolved into a crow. Its colour was red; its voice was calm and decided; five times it came bringing a stalk of grain.　　　The king was glad, and all his officers also. The duke of Chow said, "Be strenuous! Be strenuous! Heaven has showed this to encourage us. But let us trust in it with dread."　　　"Examining into antiquity, it is by accomplishing merit and accomplishing business, that one can transmit *his work* to perpetual generations, and magnify the laws of Heaven."　　　They sent up this to be joined to the writing of the duke of Chow, and reported to the king, who was moved, and his countenance changed.

Eight hundred princes came of themselves without being called; they came at the same time without previous agreement; without consultation they all spoke to the same effect, saying, "Show may be attacked." The king said, "You do not know the will of Heaven; it is not yet the time to attack him." On the day ping-woo he accordingly withdrew his army. In front the host beat their drums and shouted. Some of the soldiers lowered their spears, and went through their exercise; with songs in front and dancing behind, they made heaven and earth resound, while they cried out, "Let us never be weary. Heaven is about to raise up a parent for us. The people will have good government and dwell quietly."

司馬在前。○今殷王紂乃用其婦人之言、自絕于天、
毀壞其三正。○離逷其王父母弟、乃斷棄其先祖之
樂、乃爲淫聲用變亂正聲以悅婦人、故今台發維襲
行天罰最哉夫子不可再不可三。○附下而罔上者
死附上而罔下者刑。○與聞國政而無益于民者退
上位而不能臨政者逐。○紂夷居不肯事上帝鬼神、
棄厥先神祇不祀、乃曰吾有命毋僇其務天亦縱之、
棄而弗葆。○小人見姦巧乃聞不言也、發皋鈞。○
有億兆夷人亦有離德余有亂十人同心同德。○紂
眠自我民眠、天聽自我民聽。○民之所欲天必從之。
○朕夢協朕卜、襲于休祥戎商必克。○文王若日若
月、照光于四方于西土。○予紂非予武惟朕文考有
無皇紂克子、非朕文考有皇惟子小子無良。○惡乎
君子而有顯德其行甚章爲鑑不遠、在彼殷王謂人
有命謂敬不可行謂祭無益謂暴無傷、上帝不常九
有以亡上帝不順祝降其喪、惟我有周受之大帝。
獨夫紂。○我武惟揚侵于之疆、則取于殘殺伐用張。
于湯有光。○

The minister of War was in front.   "Now, king Chow listens to the words of his woman;—he has cut himself off from Heaven; he has destroyed [and ruined *all his hopes* from heaven or earth or men. He has separated himself from his royal uncles and his maternal relatives. He has cast away the music of his forefathers, and by making dissolute melodies he has changed the correct melodies, to please his woman. On this account I, Fă, reverently proceed to execute the punishment determined by Heaven. Rouse ye, my heroes! Don't let us need a second effort, or a third.   He who deceives those above him, in the interest of those below, dies; he who deceives those below, in the interest of those above, is punished; he who takes counsel on the government of the kingdom, which is of no use to the people, has to retire; he who is in the highest position, and cannot advance the worthy, must be driven out.

"Chow abides squatting on his heels, and will not serve God or spirits. He has cast away, and will not sacrifice to, the spirits of his fathers. He says on the contrary,—'The decree is mine;' and therefore he will not put forth his strength in the duties to them. Heaven allows him to take this course, having thrown him away, and no more preserving him.   A mean man sees villainy and cunning, or hears it, without speaking:—his knowledge makes him as guilty *as the villain.*

Chow has hundreds of thousands and millions of ordinary men, but they are divided in their courses; I have ten able men who are one in heart and in course.   Heaven sees as my people see, and hears as my people hear.   My dreams agree with my divinations; the auspicious omen is double;—my attack on Shang must succeed.   King Wăn was like the sun or the moon. He lightened with his shining the four quarters,—the western regions.   If I vanquish Chow, it will not be my prowess;—it will be the faultlessness of my father Wăn. If Show vanquishes me, it will not be from any fault of my father Wăn, but because I am not good.

"Oh! when the superior man has illustrious virtue, his conduct is grandly displayed. There is a beacon not distant;—it is in that king of Yin. He says to men that the decree is his; that reverence should not be practised; that sacrifice is of no advantage; that oppression does not matter. God is not constant, and the empire is passing from him. God is not allowing him, but sending down his ruin with a curse. Our House of Chow is receiving *the empire* from the great God.   The solitary fellow Chow.   Chow has hundreds and tens of thousands of ministers, who have hundreds and tens of thousands of hearts. King Woo has three thousand ministers with one heart.   My prowess is displayed; I invade his borders, and will take the tyrant. My punishment *of evil* will be exhibited more glorious than that of T'ang."

THE BOOKS OF CHOW.

BOOK II. THE SPEECH AT MUH.

時甲子昧爽，王朝至于商郊牧野，乃誓。王左杖黃鉞，右秉白旄以麾，曰，逖矣西土之　牧誓

1　I. The time was the grey dawn of the day kĕă-tsze.　On that morning the king came to the open country of Muh in the borders of Shang, and addressed his army.　In his left hand he carried a battle-axe, yellow with gold, and in his right he held a white ensign, which he brandished, saying, " Far are ye come, ye

THE NAME OF THE BOOK.—牧誓, 'The Speech at Muh.'　Muh [Keang Shing edits 坶 instead of Muh] was in the south of the pres. district of Ke (淇縣), dep. of Wei-hwuy, Ho-nan.　It was a tract of open country, stretching into the pres. dis. of Keih (汲), and at no great distance from the capital of Show. King Woo had, no doubt, made choice of it as a favourable field for the decisive battle between him and the tyrant.　I return here to the rendering of 誓 by 'Speech,' as in the 'Counsels of the great Yu,' p. 20, and other places.　It would have been well if the term 'Declaration' had not been used instead of it in the last Book. The Speech at Muh is found in both texts. There is more of the martial spirit in it than in any other of the speeches of the Shoo.

CONTENTS.　It is the morning of the day of battle, for which the king had prepared his host in the three speeches of the last Book.　Once more he addresses the confederate princes, his officers, and his men.　He sets forth, much as before, but more briefly, the intolerable wicked-ness of Show, and then instructs and warns the troops on how they should behave them-selves in the fight.　The speech proper begins with the 5th paragraph.　The four parr. that precede may be considered as forming a prelimi-nary chapter.

Ch. I.　Pp. 1—4.　THE TIME AND CIRCUM-STANCES OF THE SPEECH.　1. *The time; and the appearance of the king.*　時甲子昧爽,—the day 甲子 was six days later than mow-woo ('The Great Speech' Pt. ii., p. 1), which was, we saw, the 28th of the 1st month. The speech at Muh, therefore, is held to have been spoken on the 4th day of the second month. 昧＝冥, 'dark;' 爽＝明, 'light;' 昧爽, 'the dark and the light,'＝the grey dawn.

杖＝持, 'to hold in the hand.'　Its tone in this sense was difft. at one time from that which it had in its more common significa-tion of 'a staff.'　It now seems to be used only with the 3d tone.　秉, (from a *hand* grasping *stalks of grain*) is of similar signification to 杖.

The 'axe' is supposed to be called ' yel-low,' from its having been ornamented with gold. The 旄 ensign consisted (according to the figures

矛　戈　彭　庸　長　亞　司　友　人
予　比　濮　蜀　百　旅　徒　邦　〇
其　爾　人　羌　夫　師　司　冢　王二節
誓　干　〇四節　髳　長　氏　馬　君　曰
〇五節　立　稱　微　〇三節　千　司　御　嗟
王　爾　爾　盧　及　夫　空　事　我

2 men of the western regions!" He added, "Ah! ye hereditary
rulers of my friendly States; ye managers of affairs, the ministers of
instruction, of war, and of public works: the many *officers* subordinate
to them: the master of my body-guards: the captains of thousands,
3 and captains of hundreds; and ye, O men of Yung, Shuh, Këang,
4 Maou, Wei, Loo, P'ang, and Pŏ;—lift up your lances, join your
shields, raise your spears:—I have a speech to make."

of it, which agree with the component parts of
the character) of several ox-tails, suspended as
streamers from a staff. By means of this Woo
could intimate his wishes as to the order of their
position, &c., to the troops, and therefore he carried it in his right hand.   Gan-kwŏ says the
axe was in the left hand and the flag in the right,
to show that Woo considered his work was not so
much to kill as to teach.   This is being absurdly
ingenious.   We may be sure that Woo had his
axe in his right hand in the battle.   逖 =
遠, 'far,' 'distant.'   The 'Daily Explanation'
paraphrases the clause thus :—爾 等 皆 西
土 之 人, 我 以 伐 暴 救 民 之
故 率 爾 至 此, 其 行 亦 已 遠
矣.   Ts'ae observes that he spoke thus to
comfort the men under their long travel.
　Pp. 2, 3.   *The different parties addressed.*

2. 我 友 邦 冢 君, 御 事,—see on
the last Book, Pt. i., p. 2. The 'managers of
affairs' were the officers immediately after
specified, belonging to Woo's own govt.,—to
the State of Chow.   The 司 徒, 司 馬,
and 司 空, were three of the 'six ministers'
(六 卿) under the imperial govt. of Chow,
when the dynasty was fully established, and
whose duties are described in Bk. XX., parr.
7—13. A great State, such as Chow was before
the extinction of the Shang dyn., had only *three*
principal ministers, whose names are here given.
But we may inquire what the ministers of instruction and works had to do in the camp.
Ying-tă says that the former superintended all
orders given to the troops, and the latter all

the business of intrenchments. Ts'ae seems
to have thought that they were there as the
generals of the three armies of the State. This
is not likely ;—see Ch'in Sze-k'ae, *in loc.* We
can only form a vague idea on this, as on many
other points in the Shoo.   亞 旅.—亞
= 次, 'secondary,' 'of inferior rank'; 旅 =
眾, 'multitude,' 'many.' I do not find it possible to say whether we are to understand by
these characters the 'multitude of inferior
officers' generally, or two distinct classes of
such. Gan-kwŏ had the former view. He
says :—眾 大 夫, 其 位 次 卿, 'The
phrase denotes all the great officers, whose
posts were inferior to those of the ministers.'
Ts'ae on the other hand supposes that the
亞 were the 大 夫 or 'great officers,' below,
but next in rank to, the ministers, and five of
whom filled up the space between each minister
and his 士, or 'officers,' of whom there were
27, denoted in the text by the term 旅.

師 氏.—'the Instructor.' The functions of
an officer thus designated are given at length
in the 13th Book of the Chow Le (地 官 司
徒 第 二 之 六). He was a ta-foo or great officer of the second grade, and the Tutor of the heir-
apparent, at the same time executing various
duties about the sovereign, and specially having
charge of the guard of foreign—barbarian—mer-
cenaries who kept watch outside the royal gate.
In time of war, or when the sovereign went
abroad for any other cause, he followed in attendance, with the whole or a portion of that
guard. It must have been in this capacity

曰、人　言　牝　無　牝　之　惟　之　○
古　有　曰、雞　晨　鷄　晨　家　索。今
　　　　　　　　　　　　　　　　　六節

5 II. The king said, "The ancients have said, 'The hen does not announce the morning. The crowing of a hen in the morning

that he was present at Muh;—if indeed the 師氏 of the the text was the same officer who is so designated in the Chow Le. Ts'ae follows Gan-kwŏ in saying that the 師氏 were 'the officers who guarded the gates' (以兵守門者). 千夫長, 百夫長.—we can only translate these designations literally as I have done. According to the Chow Le, five men formed a *woo* (伍); five *woo*, or 25 men, formed a *lëang* (兩); four *lëang*, or 100 men, formed a *tsuh* (卒); five *tsuh*, or 500 men, formed a *leu* (旅); five *leu*, or 2,500 men, formed a *sze* (師); and five *sze*, or 12,500 men, formed a *keun* (軍). Gan-kwŏ and Wang Suh both say that the 百夫長, were 'leaders of *tsuh*,' which of course is literally correct; but they say also that the 千夫長 were 'leaders of *sze*,' commanded 2,500 men each. K'ang-shing agrees with them in this, but makes the 百夫長 to have been 'leaders of *leu*' (旅帥),' commanding 500 men each. It seems absurd to insist on such explanations. The arrangements of Woo's army much more probably corresponded with the terms which he employed. 3. The names Yung, Shuh, &c., enumerated here, are said generally to be those of 'eight kingdoms of the rude tribes on the west and south' (西南夷八國名). The first and last are found associated together in the 左傳, 文十六年, in an attack upon the great State of Ts'oo. It is said that 'the people of Yung.... led the hundred *tribes* of the Pŏ to invade Ts'oo;' and from this description of the Pŏ by 'hundreds' it is supposed that they were under no general Head or chieftain, but consisted of many clans, each acknowledging its own chief. The site of the Yung was in the pres. dis. of Chuh-shan (竹山), dep. of Yun-yang (鄖陽), Hoo-pih; that of the Pŏ was in the same prov., dep. of King-chow (荊州), dis. of Shih-show (石首). The country of Shuh was the pres. dep. of Shing-too (成都) in Sze-ch'uen. West and north from this was the country of Këang: while that of Maou and

Wei was to the east, radiating from the pres. dis. of Pa (巴縣), dep. of Chung-k'ing, as a centre. Loo is referred to the present dis. of Nan-chang (南漳), dep. of Sëang-yang (襄陽), in Hoo-pih. The name of P'ang remains in P'ang-shan dis., dep. of Mei (眉), Sze-ch'uen. All these tribes, we may suppose, acknowledged the supremacy of the princes of Chow, and had been summoned to assist king Woo in his enterprise against Show. Some critics, like Wang Loo-chae (王魯齋; see his 'Doubts about the Shoo,' on the Speech at Muh), say that they had come to his banner of their own accord, without being called;—which is very unlikely.

[Gaubil says in a note on this par. (Le Chou-king, p. 157), that Yung, Shuh, &c., were the countries on the south-west,—*e.g.*, in Sze-ch'uen and Yun-nan. To this M. de Guignes appends a very bold and sweeping remark:—' I will add,' he says, 'that all the peoples in the text bear the name of 夷, or *barbarians*. Thus, this conquest of China, made by king Woo, was a conquest effected by the foreigners on the west of China.' The remark is unwarranted. So far as we learn from the Shoo, these tribes were only an inferior and auxiliary force on the occasion.]

4. *Attitude in which the troops were required to listen.* 稱=舉, 'to lift up;' apparently = 'to bear aloft in the right hand.' 立=立於地, 'to erect on the ground,' *i.e.*, to rest the end on the ground, the points being shown above. There were three weapons of the nature of spears or lances, differing in the forms of their points which would be difficult to describe in brief space, but principally distinguished by their lengths,—the 戈, the 戟 and the 矛. Acc. to Wang Ts'ëaou, the handle of the 戈 was 6 ft. 6 in. long; that of the 戟 16 ft.; and of the 矛, 21 feet. Medhurst translates 戈 by 'javelin;' but I have not seen it anywhere stated that the instrument was thrown from the hand. The 干 or 'shield' was long and comparatively narrow, so as to cover most of the body.

Ch. II. THE SPEECH. Pp. 5, 6. *The crimes of Show.* 5. 晨, 'the morning,' here = 晨鳴報曉, 'crows in the morning to an-

商王受惟婦言是
用、昏棄厥肆祀弗
答、昏棄厥遺王父
母弟不迪乃惟四
方之多罪逋逃、是
崇是長、是信是使、
是以為大夫卿士、
俾暴虐于百姓以
姦宄于商邑。○今　七節

6 *indicates* the subversion of the family.' Now Show, the king of Shang, follows only the words of his wife. He has blindly thrown away the sacrifices which he should present, and makes no response *for the favours which he has received;* he has blindly thrown away his paternal and maternal relatives, not treating them properly. They are only the vagabonds of the empire, loaded with crimes, whom he honours and exalts, whom he employs and trusts, making them great officers and nobles, so that they can tyrannize over the people, exercising their villainies in the city of Shang.

nounce the day.' 索 is defined by Gan-kwŏ by 盡; and by Keang Shing, after K'ang-shing, by 散. The two definitions are much akin. Woo's language may seem rather undignified; but it was, no doubt, suited to his audience. And we must bear in mind the character and deeds of Tă-ke against whom it was directed.

6. 昏 (*i.q.* 昏) 棄厥肆祀不答,—comp. the last Book, Pt. i., 6; Pt. ii., 5. 肆=陳, 'to set forth;' 厥肆祀=其所當陳之祭祀, 'the sacrifices which he ought to offer.' K'ang-shing understood by 肆祀 'the name of a sacrifice';—but incorrectly. 答, 'to answer,' 'to make an acknowledgment for favours received,' such being the common meaning of sacrifice with the Chinese; —Tung-po says, 祭所以報也, 故謂之答. Here also K'ang-shing incorrectly defines 答 by 問; and 不答=不問, 'without asking any questions, or thinking about them.' 王父母弟,—Gan-kwŏ takes 王父, as =祖 or 'grandfather,' saying that if he thus treated his grand-uncles, we may be sure he did not treat his uncles any better. Woo Ch'ing says that 王父母弟 =王之諸父, 諸母, 諸弟, 'the royal uncles, royal aunts, royal cousins.' I think we must join 王父 together, and agree with Wang Ts'eaou that 王父母弟=王父弟與母弟. The general meaning is plain enough,—that Show separated himself from all his relatives, both by blood and by affinity, who would naturally have the interests of the imperial House at heart. 不迪,-迪=道, and 不迪=不以道遇之, as in the translation. Keang Shing takes 迪=進 or 登, and 不迪=不用, 'does not employ them.' The meaning is not unsuitable; but it is not so good as that which I have followed. 逋逃=—'refugees.' Woo Ch'ing says:—四方多罪之人逃亡而歸紂, 'the great criminals of all quarters make their escape, and betake themselves to Chow.' 商邑,—'the city of Shang,' probably meaning the capital of Show. We might translate 邑, however, in the plural. Keang Shing takes it as =國, 'kingdom' or 'State.'

爾躬有戮。

夫子。○爾所弗勗其于

迓克奔以役西土勗哉

貔如熊如羆于商郊勗弗

夫子。○尚桓桓如虎如

九節

伐七伐乃止齊焉勗哉

○不愆于四伐五伐六

八節

步乃止齊焉夫子勗哉

日之事不愆于六步七

予發惟恭行天之罰今

7 "Now I, Fă, am simply executing respectfully the punishment
appointed by Heaven. In to-day's business do not advance more
than six or seven steps; and then stop and adjust your ranks:—my
8 brave men, be energetic! Do not exceed four blows, five blows,
six blows, or seven blows; and then stop and adjust your ranks:—
9 my brave men, be energetic! Display a martial bearing. Be like
tigers and panthers, like bears, and grisly bears;—here in the
border of Shang. Do not rush on those who fly *to us in submission,
but receive them* to serve our western land:—my brave men, be
10 energetic! If you are not thus energetic, you will bring destruction
on yourselves."

Pp. 7—10. *Directions about the rules to
be observed in the impending battle.* 7. The
first part of this par. had better be joined to
the one preceding. King Woo speaks in it of
himself in contrast with Show;—of himself as
engaged on behalf of Heaven to punish one who
was an enemy to both Heaven and men. Ts'ae
and others, prefixing it to this and the succeeding parr., make a milder spirit breathe in them
than the reader will easily perceive. The stopping at every seven steps and seven blows was,
they think, that as few of the enemy as possible
might be killed. In this way the tyrant would
be overthrown and Heaven's justice would be
satisfied with the sacrifice of comparatively few
lives! The cautions were evidently given that
the order of battle might be preserved unbroken.
愆=過, 'to exceed.' 步=進
趨, 'to advance hurriedly.', 齊=齊
整, 'to adjust and put in order.' The paraphrase of the 'Daily Explanation' is:—其
進而迎敵 不過于六步, 七

步, 即便止駐, 以整齊部伍,
然後復從而伐之, 'In advancing
to meet the enemy, take no more than six or
seven steps. Then stop and adjust your ranks,
and go forward again to smite them.'
夫子,—see the last Book, Pt. ii., p. 9.
8. 伐=擊刺, 'to strike and thrust.'
They are thus admonished, it is said, lest they
should be hurried on in their rage by a desire
for slaughter. 9. 桓桓=威武貌
'the appearance of martial prowess.' The 說
文 quotes the passage with 狟 instead
of 桓. 貔 is described as 豹屬,
'a kind of panther.' 弗迓克奔—
'do not meet those who are able to—who really
do—run.' The meaning is as in the translation.
Kĕang Shing, however, edits 禦 instead of 迓,
after K'ang-shing. Ma Yung also read 禦

which he explains better than K'ang-shing. Wang Suh read 御, which is susceptible of being taken either for 禦 or 迓. The meaning is substantially the same, whether we adopt 迓 or 禦. 以役西土,—the translation of this is after K'ang-shing. Ma Yung and Wang Suh took the clause as = 'do your best to serve our western land.' Gan-kwǒ understood it differently:—'It is thus you will make them submissively acknowledge the righteousness of our western land.' 10. 爾所不勖,—as 勖哉夫子 has been repeated at the close of the several instructions or admonitions, we must suppose that the warning here belongs to each of them. The 'Daily Explanation' paraphrases the 9th and 10th parr. thus:—

殺拒者西武也，有或而必可
濫抗降我其可而殺令刑矣，
于之來役士戒命貪號常赦，
免者以爾降我走勞將是之或違有攸，
不殘有之哉殺我進是軍有，
則凶于若擊殺于輕降則罔，
勇于之若人奮士勉而殺也身，
過當誅迎之是將不勇紀及爾哉。
惟者勿士勇爾所無失戮不戒

THE BOOKS OF CHOW.

BOOK III. THE SUCCESSFUL COMPLETION OF THE WAR.

商。于 步 己、翼 死 壬 惟_{一節}
○ 征 自 王 日 魄 辰 一 武
厥_{二節} 伐 周、朝 癸 越 旁 月 成

1   I.   In the first month, *the day* jin-shin immediately followed the end of the moon's waning. The next day was kwei-ke, when the king in the morning marched from Chow to attack and punish Shang.

THE NAME OF THE BOOK.—武 成, 'The Successful Completion of the War.' The phrase 一 武 成, meaning, literally, 'military affairs completed,' occurs in the 3d paragraph, and has thence been taken to denominate the Book. It is not objectionable as a designation; though it by no means covers the contents, they all grow up around the accomplishment of Woo's enterprise. The Book is found only in the old Text.

DIFFICULTIES IN THE ARRANGEMENT AND INTERPRETATION. These will fully appear in the course of the exposition; it may be sufficient here to describe them generally, and for that purpose I will use in the first place the words of Ying-tă. He says:—'This Book consists mainly of narrative; the portion composed of the king's words is small. The language of the several parts is without the beginning and the end properly marked, and its composition altogether is different from that of the other Books. From 惟 一 月 (p. 1) down to 受 命 于 周 (p. 4), the historian relates the march to the attack of Yin, and the return from the enterprise, with the assembling of the princes: —as introductory to the words of the king. From 王 若 曰 to 大 統 未 集 (both in p. 5), Woo narrates the rise of their House of Chow; from 子 小 子 (p. 5) to 名 山

大 川 (p. 6), he states how he had inherited the possessions and the duties of king Wăn, and how he declared to the spirits the crimes of Show; from 曰 惟 有 道 (p. 6) to 無 作 神 羞, (p. 8), he repeats his prayer to the spirits. From 既 戊 午 to the end, the historian again resumes his narrative, and tells of the attack on Show, of his death, of Woo's entrance into the capital of Yin, and of his governmental measures.

The prayer, however, which concludes with 無 作 神 羞, is incomplete. According to the analogy of other prayers, recorded in the 左 傳, there ought to be, after those words, some protestation by Woo of his own intentions. And when all the princes and officers were receiving their investitures and commands from the new emperor of the House of Chow, we cannot suppose that he did not address them, in a manner similar to T'ang, in his 'Announcement.' With so many speeches to them before the conflict, we cannot believe that he simply related to them after its close his prayer to the spirits. On these two grounds I must conclude that a portion of the Book, immediately following these words—無 作 神 羞, has been lost.

'Perhaps it was wanting when the tablets were hidden away in the wall; perhaps it was among the confused and broken fragments which Gan-kwŏ says there were in addition to the 58 Books which he recovered. As he found in the tablets of this Book a beginning of it and an end, he did not say anything of the intermediate portion being deficient.'

Ying-tă was thus of opinion that the Book was deficient; but it does not appear that he had any doubts as to the relative order in which the several portions stand. He thought some tablets were lost; but did not suppose that any of those preserved had been displaced. In the Sung dynasty, however, the critics assumed not only that there were portions missing, but that the remaining tablets were all disordered and confused. Ch'ing E-ch'uen (程伊川), Lew Gan-she (劉安世), and others, had their several ways of arranging them so as to produce a consistent narrative; and Ts'ae Ch'in, profiting by the determinations of his master Choo He, produced an edition of the Book, which has superseded the old one in the copies of the Shoo which are now taught in schools. It will be found, with a translation, in an appendix. Scholars of the present dynasty for the most part acquiesce in his views, when they do not discard the old text altogether. There are some, however, who think they can improve on him, and Wang Loo-chae has given a disposition of the paragraphs somewhat different in his edition of 'Doubts about the Shoo.'

Maou K'e-ling will not admit either of disorder or defect in the Book. He has certainly proved by references to the 左傳 and the 國語, that the prayer of Woo to the spirits was a part of his speech or announcement to the princes;—see the 尚書廣聽錄, on the 武成. So far it is established that the disorder in the parts which the Sung critics complained of and tried to remedy,—if indeed we should call it disorder,—existed even during the Chow dynasty. Maou says, 'If the text be not good, we have only to be content with it as it is.' In this he is right. The ingenuity of the critics has not been of service either to history or the classic.

CONTENTS. Those are summarily and correctly stated in the prefatory Notice.—'King Woo smote Yin; and the narrative of his proceeding to the attack, and of his return and sending his animals back to their pastures, with his governmental measures, form 'The Completion of the War.' The whole is divided in Yungching's Shoo into 9 parr., which I have rearranged in 10, including them also in three chapters. The first chapter, containing 4 parr., consists of brief historical notes of the commencement and close of Woo's expedition. The second also contains 4 parr., and gives the address (or a part of it) delivered by Woo to his nobles and officers on occasion, we may suppose, of their solemn recognition of him as emperor, and of his confirming some of them in their old investitures or appointments, and giving new ones to others. The third, in the two concluding parr., is again historical, and relates several incidents of the battle between Woo and Show, going on to subsequent events, and important governmental measures of the new dynasty.

Ch. I. Pp. 1—4. THE MARCH TO THE ATTACK, AND CONQUEST, OF SHANG. THE RETURN, AND MEASURES ON THE CONCLUSION OF THE WAR.

1. 惟一月壬辰旁死魄,
一月, 'the first month'; but whether we are to understand the first month of the Hea year,—the first month of spring; or the first month of the Chow year,—the second month of winter, cannot yet be determined. Ts'ae endeavours here to reinforce his view that the month is the first of the Hea year, by calling attention to the language, 一月, and not 正月; but this circumstance is of little weight. 壬辰 is the calendaric name of the day, and it was 旁 (read p'ang, 3d tone, = 近, 'near to' 'close by') 死魄, 'next to the day of the dead disk.' This expression is generally understood to be descriptive of the first day of the new moon. In p. 4 we find the phrase 生魄, denoting the 15th day or full moon. In p. 2, again, we have 哉生明, 'the beginning of the birth of light,' as denoting the third day, when the moon first becomes visible. It is clear therefore that the term 魄 was applied to the disk of the moon from the the time it began to wane until the new moon reappeared. How it came to be so used, I do not perceive. The 說文 has 霸 instead of 魄, but pronounced in the same way; and in the dict. we find the definition quoted, 一月體黑者謂之霸, 'the body of the moon when dark is called 霸.'

[Fan Sze-lin (潘士遴) observes that after the 1st day of the moon, the light went on to grow, and the darkness of her disk (魄) to disappear; that if the previous month was 'great' (consisted, that is, of 30 days), then on the second day of the month, the 'light' began. He concludes that this was the case here, and that the day denoted by 旁死魄 was not the second but the first day of the month. The editors of Yung-ching's Shoo are inclined to agree with him, saying it is more natural and in rule to find a specification of the first day of the month than of the second. This view does not seem unlikely.]

越翼日癸巳,—越一及; 翼日 =明日, 'the morrow:' 癸巳 follows 壬辰 in the calendar.   王朝步自周, —步=行, 'to travel,' 'to march;' 王步周 is, literally, 'the king paced it.'   王步周 is understood to stand here for Woo's capital,

天　林　放　華　文　乃　商　明　四
下　之　牛　山　歸　偃　至　王　月
弗　野　于　之　馬　武　于　來　哉
服。　示　桃　陽、　于　修　豐、　自　生

2   In the fourth month, at the first appearance of the moon, the king came from Shang to Fung, when he hushed all the movements of war, and attended to the cultivations of peace. He sent back his horses to the south of mount Hwa, and let loose his oxen in the open country of T'aou-lin, showing the empire that he would not use them *again*.

called Haou (鎬), which was 30 *le* south of the pres. dis. city of Ch'ang-gan, dep. of Se-gan, Shen-se. In the next par. it is stated that he returned to Fung, which had been the capital of his father Wan, in the pres. dis. of Hoo (鄠), of the same dep. The two places were only about 8 miles apart; Haou on the east of the river Fung, and Fung on the west of it. The site of Haou was converted into a lake (昆明池) by the emp. Woo (世宗孝武帝, B.C. 139-87) of the Han dyn. 于征伐商,—于=往, 'to go,' 'to proceed.'

[We saw, in the 'Great Speech,' Pt. ii., p. 1, that on the day mow-woo, the 28th day of the 1st month, king Woo halted on the northern bank of the Ho. On that same day he had crossed the river;—see the 9th par. below. The distance from Haou to Măng-tsin is said by Ying-tă to be 1,000 *le*, and I have seen another estimate of it at 900 *le*. Taking the larger number, we have 25 days' marches, of 40 *le* each, or about 14 miles per day, which could be accomplished without difficulty.   Five days after (the day 癸亥), Woo drew up his army in the borders of Shang, and waited for the dawn of the next morning, the 4th day of the 2d month, to decide the contest between himself and Show.

After the battle, Show fled to the 'Stag tower,' and burned himself to death. In the mean time, Woo, having received the congratulations of the princes on his victory, pressed on after the tyrant. On arriving at the capital, the people were waiting outside the walls in anxious expectation,. which the king relieved by sending his officers among them with the words,—'Supreme Heaven is sending down blessing' (上天降休). The multitudes reverently saluted the king, who bowed to them in return, and hurried on to the place where the dead body of Show was. Having discharged three arrows at it from his chariot, he descended, struck the body with a light sword,

and cut the head off with his 'yellow' battle-axe, and made it be suspended from the staff of a large white flag. Much in the same way he dealt with the bodies of two of Show's concu-bines who had killed themselves; and then returned to his army. These accounts are taken from the 'Historical Records,' and are put down by subsequent writers as lying legends, inconsistent with Woo's character.

Next day he entered the capital of Shang in great state, attended by his brothers and the chiefs of his host, and solemnly accepted the charge of the empire. It was said to him, on behalf of all the nobles, 'The last descendant of the House of Yin having destroyed and disowned the bright virtue of his forefathers, having insolently discontinued the sacrifices to the spirits, and having blindly tyrannized over the people of Shang, the report of his deeds ascended to the great God in heaven ' (其章顯聞于天皇上帝). On this, Woo bowed twice, with his head to the ground, and said, 'It is right that I should change the great charge; that I should put away the House of Yin, and receive myself the great appointment of Heaven ' He then again bowed twice, with his head to the ground, and went out.

In this way king Woo took on himself the sovereignty of the empire. One of his first steps was to appoint Show's son, Luh-foo (祿父), prince over the domain of Yin; and he appears to have remained in the capital of Shang between two and three months, employed in the measures described in the last two parr. of this Book, and in others requisite to the establishment of the dynasty of his House.]

Pp. 2, 3. *Measures in the 4th month showing that the war was over.*   2. 旣四月哉 (一始) 生明,—this was the 3d day of the month;—see on the last par. But there had been an intercalary month between This is proved in the following manner.—The day 丁未 of par. 3 evidently belonged to the 4th

成　大　戍　三　豆　奔　侯　廟　祀　○
○　告　柴　日　籩　走　衞　邦　于　丁　三節
既　四節　武　望　庚　越　執　駿　甸　周　未

3   On the day ting-we he sacrificed in the ancestral temple of Chow, when *the chiefs of* the imperial domain and of the teen, how, and wei domains all hurried about, carrying the dishes.   Three days after, he presented a burnt-offering *to Heaven*, and worshipped towards the mountains and rivers, solemnly announcing the successful completion of the war.

month. 甲子, the day of the battle of Muh, was the 4th of the 2d month, which we may suppose had 29 days. This brings us to 庚寅, for the first day of the next month, the 18th of which was a 丁未 day; but it could not be that of the text. We have to count 60 days before we come to the next 丁未 day, which would consequently be in the 5th month, unless there was an intercalary month between the 1st and the 4th. The chronologers are all agreed in supposing that there was a second month intercalary this year; and consequently the ting-we day of the text would be the 18th or 19th of the fourth month. 至于豐 —Fung was the capital of Wăn and here was the ancestral temple of the princes of Chow. That was the reason, as we gather from the next par., why Woo went in the first place to Fung and not to Haou. 偃武修文 —in the rest of the par. we have two instances of the 'hushing of military measures,' (偃 is defined by 臥, 'to sleep,' 'to send to sleep);' what 'the cultivations of peace' were, we are not told. 華山之陽＝華山之南, 'the south of mount Hwa.' For mount Hwa, see on 'The Tribute of Yu,' Pt. i., p. 62.

The 'wild of T'aou-lin' (Peach forest) is referred to the country about 'the hill of Muh-new (牧牛), called also the hill of K'wa-foo (夸父), in the south-east of the pres. dep. of T'ung-chow (同州).   An objection has been taken to the credibility of the account here on the ground that the horses and oxen belonged to the people,—were only contributed by them for the expedition ; and that to appropriate them to himself in this way, instead of returning them to their owners, was an act befitting Show, and not at all to be expected from king Woo. But we may be sure these were Woo's own horses and oxen. If it be granted that the people did supply a portion of the animals used in war, the sovereign himself furnished a larger

number;—see K'e-ling's 古文尙書冤詞, Bk. IV., on the point.

[In the Le Ke, the Bk. 樂記, pp. 29–22, there is an expansion of the text, celebrating King Woo. It may be that the author had before him some copy of the 武成, current in the Han dynasty, fuller than that which we now have. In p. 19, it is said—馬散之華山之陽, 而弗復乘牛散車之桃林之野, 而弗復服甲用, 倒載干戈, 包之以虎皮……然後天下知武王之不復用兵也.]

3. *Various sacrifices, and solemn announcement of the completion of the War.* 丁未祀于周廟,—the fourth month would commence on 已丑 or 庚寅, according as the previous one had 29 or 30 days, and 丁未 must have been the 18th or 19th day. Before setting out on his enterprise, Woo had sacrificed to his father, to God and the earth ('The Great speech,' Pt. i., p. 10) ; here at its close he sacrifices, and, we may suppose, gives thanks at the same altars.   邦, 甸, 侯, 衞,—see the account and figure on pp. 148, 149, of the divisions of the empire under the Chow dynasty. By the 邦 we must understand, I think, the central division,—the imperial domain (王畿) and 甸, 侯, 衞, we have three of the divisions which lay beyond it,—a part for the whole of the five domains which constituted the 'middle kingdom.' We cannot account for the irregularity of the order in which they are given. After 衞 we must understand 諸侯, equivalent to 'the chiefs,' which I have supplied in the translation.

呼、曰、王五節周。命工、暨冢庶生
群嗚若○于受百君邦魄、

4　After the moon began to wane, the hereditary princes of the various States, and all the officers, received their appointments from Chow.

Gan-kwŏ defines 駿 by 大, 'great,' 'in great state;' it is better to take it with Ts'ae after the 爾雅 as ＝速. 豆籩,— see Con. Ana., VIII, iv. 3. It was an honour to the chiefs and princes to assist at the sacrifice. 越三日庚戌,—between ting-we and kăng-seuh there are two days, so the latter was the 21st or 22d day of the month. In Bk. XII., p. 2, we have 丙午越三日戊申, where both ping-woo and mow-shin must be reckoned to make up the three days;—the writers had different methods equally legitimate, of reckoning. 柴,—see on the 'Can. of Shun,' p. 8. 望,—see on the 'Can. of Shun,' p. 6. This sacrifice was offered, I suppose, at the altar of the great earth, mentioned in Bk. I., Pt. i., p. 10. 4. *The princes and officers receive their appointments from Woo, as the first emperor of the dynasty of Chow.* 既生魄, —the moon begins to wane,—the darkness is born—after the full moon. The day indicated in the text is generally supposed to be the 16th; but Ch'in Leih, observes that, if that had been the day, the phrase would have been 哉生魄, corresponding to 哉生明 in p. 2. He would lay stress therefore on the 既, as showing that the darkness was not only 'born,' but had made some growth; and fixes the day as the 17th. But here there is a difficulty.—The historian goes backward instead of forward with his narrative; the 17th would precede the day *ting-we.* Ying-tă calls attention to this circumstance, he himself supposing the day to be the 16th; and in the fact of the chiefs assisting at the sacrifice in the ancestral temple he sees a proof that they had previously received their appointments from king Woo. I should myself extend the force of the 既 much more than Ch'in does. Why may not the phrase 既生魄 indicate any between the 15th and the end of the month, when we should come to the 'death' or end of the darkness? The historian has chosen to indicate thus indefinitely the day when the princes and officers received their appointments from Woo. As to their assisting on the day ting-we at his sacrificial service, that might very well be. Things could not be done in order while the revolution was in progress. From the taking the field against Show down to the new commissioning of rulers under the new supremacy, all was irregular and

only after this would a new *order* of things take its course.

[In the Books of the early Han dynasty, 律歷志, 第一、下, compiled by Lew Hin we find three quotations as from the 武成. The first agrees with the 1st par. of the chapter.—惟一月壬辰旁死霸, 若翼日癸巳, 武王乃朝步自周, 于征伐紂. The second is not found in the received text, nor any trace of it; but it agrees sufficiently with the first par. of the 'Speech at Muh,' and the statement in the 9th par. of this Book.—粵若來二 (some editions have ＝三, incorrectly) 月, 既死霸, 粵五日甲子, 咸劉商王紂. It is then stated that there was a second month intercalary in this year which began with the day 庚寅; that the third month began with 已未, and the fourth month with 已丑. Then comes the third quotation:— 惟四月既旁生霸, 粵六日庚戌, 武王燎于周廟, 翼日辛亥祀于天位, 粵五日乙卯, 乃以庶國祀馘于周廟, 'In the fourth month, on the day kăng-seuh, the 6th after the 16th, king Woo made a fire in the ancestral temple of Chow. Next day,— the day sin-hae,—he sacrificed at the altar of Heaven; and five days after,—on the day yih-maou,—attended by the princes of the various States, he sacrificed and presented the heads *of Show and his two concubines* in the ancestral temple.' Here the intimations of time are different from those which we have in parr. 3 and 4 of the text. Possibly the 燎 here ＝ the 柴 of par. 3;—and they are referred to the same day. We cannot trace any other correspondencies.

The question occurs,—Where did Lew Hin find the copy of the 武成, from which he made these quotations? Yen Sze-koo supposed they were taken from some copy of Fuh-shang's Books; see an art. by Choo He in the 集說 But Fuh-shang did not possess the 武成

后、惟先王建邦
啟土公劉克篤
前烈至于大王、
肇基王迹、王季
其勤王家、我文
考文王克成厥文
勳誕膺天命、以
撫方夏、大邦畏
其力、小邦懷其
德惟九年大統

5   II.   The king spake to the following effect:—"Oh! ye host of princes, the first of our kings founded the State and commenced our territory.   The duke Lew was able to consolidate the merits of his predecessor.   But it was the king T'ae who laid the foundations of the imperial inheritance.   Then king Ke was diligent for the royal House; and my deceased father, king Wăn, completed his merit, and received the great decree of Heaven to soothe the regions of the great bright land.   The great States feared his strength; the small States cherished his virtue.   In nine years, however, the whole

Yen Jŏ-ku, Wang, Ming-shing and others think that he took them from the copy of the 'Old Text,' which Gan-kwŏ had transcribed, and which was preserved in one of the imperial repositories.   We know that Lew Hin had access to this copy, and it is possible that he might quote from the 武成 in it.

There is, however, another way of accounting for the quotations.   There was a copy of the 武成 current in the Han dynasty, as we have seen there was of the 誓泰.   K'ang-shing states that it was lost in the reign of the founder of the eastern Han, A.D. 25-57.   We do not know whence it was derived.   From the last quotation we may suppose that its character was like that of the copy of the 'Great Speech,' which likewise disappeared.   It appears to me more likely that the quotations by Lew Hin were made from it than from the 'Old Text' to which he had access.   The authority of the received text, such as it is, need not be affected by the differences between it and the passages in the 律歷志.

Ch. II. Pp. 5, 7.   ADDRESS OF KING WOO TO THE PRINCES, ON GIVING THEM THEIR INVES-TITURES.   5.   *Sketch of the history of the House of Chow from its founder to king Woo.* See the introductory note to Book I. on the name of this Part of the Shoo.   先王 'the former king,' = 'the first of our kings.' Ying-tă says that we know that K'e, Shun's min. of agriculture, must be intended, because he is mentioned before the duke Lew.   The predi-cates—建邦啟土—sufficiently indicate

the same.   K'e was not a king, but Woo here calls him so.   篤前烈、= 篤厚前人功烈.   K'e is to be understood as Lew's 'predecessor.'   大王、—by king T'ae is intended Tan-foo.   肇基王迹、—'first founded the traces of imperial sway;' see in the She King, the 'Praise-songs of Loo,' iv. 2, where it is said of T'ae that 'he dwelt on the south of mount K'e, and began to shear the dynasty of Shang' (居岐之陽、實始翦商);—not, say the critics, that he had any intention to do it, but the hearts of the people were so drawn to him, that they became devotedly attached to his House.   文考文王、—'my deceased father Wăn, the king Wăn.'   We cannot well repeat the honorary title in the translation.   誕膺、—'greatly received'; 膺 = 受.   以撫方夏 = 以撫安四方諸夏.   On 夏, see the Can. of Shun, p. 20.   大邦畏其力、小邦懷其德—this passage is quoted, as from 'the Books of Chow,' in the 左傳襄三十二年.   大統、—'the great united whole.'   未集 = 未集於其身, 'was not yet collected in his person.'

未集子小子其
承厥志。○厎商
六節
之罪、告于皇天
后土所過名山
大川曰惟有道
曾孫周王發、將
有大正于商、今
商王受無道暴
殄天物害虐烝
民爲天下逋逃

empire was not collected under his rule, and it fell to me, who am but a little child, to carry out his will.

6　Detesting the crimes of Shang, I announced to great Heaven and the sovereign Earth, to the famous hill and the great river, by which I passed, saying, 'I, Fă, the principled, king of Chow, by a long descent, am about to have a great righting with Shang. Show, the king of Shang, is without principle, cruel and destructive to the creatures of Heaven, injurious and tyrannical to the multitudes of the people, chief of the vagabonds of the empire,

[In the 'Doctrine of the Mean,' xviii., 3, it is said that 'the duke of Chow completed the virtuous course of Wăn and Woo,' and that he carried up the title of king to T'ae and Ke, and sacrificed to all the former dukes above them with the imperial ceremonies.' As it was thus the duke of Chow who carried up the title of king to Tan-foo and Ke-leih, completing what Woo had left undone, it has been asked how we find those titles here in the mouth of king Woo. I apprehend that the merit of the duke of Chow was in extending the practice of honouring ancestors, beyond the circle of the imperial family, to 'the princes, the great officers the scholars, and the common people.' King Woo no doubt took counsel on the subject with his brother the duke of Chow. Perhaps it was by his advice that he did it; but there can be no doubt that he had conferred the titles mentioned in the text. The thing is commemorated in the Le Ke, the Bk. 大傳, p. 2. I give the whole paragraph here, because it gives a strong confirmation not only to this par., but also to the two preceding ones.—牧之野、

武王之大
事也、既事而退、柴於上帝、率走、文
於社、設奠於牧室、遂奔走、歷、
祀於下諸侯執豆籩、逋季、尊
天王昌、不王以卑臨尊]

Pp. 6—8. *He relates the prayer which he addressed to the spirits of Heaven and Earth, of mount Hwa and the Ho, in contemplation of the engagement with Show.*

6. 厎商之罪、

—there is much difficulty in giving any appropriate meaning to 厎. It has been defined by 至, 致, and 極數. The last is given in the 'Daily Explanation;' the 'detesting' in the translation is as allowable, and that is all that can be said for it. 皇天后土, —comp. what was said on the phrase 天地 in Bk. I., Pt. i., p. 3. This is the only place in the Shoo where the combination 后土 occurs. Ying-tă understands, I think correctly, by 名山 mount Hwa, and the Ho by 大川. Critics generally take 山 and 川 in the plural. We must understand, of course, that Woo made his announcement to *the spirits of* Heaven, Earth, the mountain, and the river. 有道曾孫,—I take 有道 and 曾孫 as in apposition. Such is the view of Ying-tă, who observes that Woo, in asking the help of the spirits, and speaking of himself in contrast with Show would not affect a false humility. Ts'ae and others say that by 'the principled' Woo refers to his forefathers, and construe the phrase as under the regimen of 曾孫, which means literally 'great-grandson.' 周王發,—Ts'ae supposes that 周王 is an interpolation, —which seems very likely. 大正,— comp. the use of 正 in the 'Speech of T'ang,' p. 2,—不敢不正. 暴殄天物,

征　命　○　罔　華　以　祗　獲　予　主、
綏　肆　恭 七節　不　夏　過　承　仁　小　萃
厥　予　天　率　蠻　亂　上　人、　子　淵
士　東　成　俾。　貊、　畧、　帝、　敢　既　藪、

who collect about him as fish in the deep, and beasts in the prairie.
I, who am but a little child, having obtained *the help of* virtuous
men, presume reverently to comply with *the will of* God, to make
an end of his disorderly ways. The great and flowery region, and
the wild tribes of the south and north, equally follow and consent
7 with me. Reverently obeying the determinate counsel of Heaven,
I pursue my punitive work to the east, to give tranquillity to its

一殄＝絕, 'to destroy utterly' 天物,
'the creatures of Heaven;' 'including men,' says
Lin Che-k'e, 'but they are further specified,'
because of their greater importance.' 為
天下逋逃主, 萃（＝聚）淵藪,
—the paraphrase of this in the 'Daily Explanation' is :—天下有罪在逃之人,
所當誅鋤之, 以安良善者
也, 受反收留之, 與彼為主,
有司莫之敢捕, 如魚之聚
于深淵, 獸之聚于林藪, 'The
criminals and vagabonds of the empire ought
to be taken off and rooted out, to secure the repose of the good, but Show receives and maintains them, and is their chief, so that the officers
do not dare to apprehend them. They are as
fish collected in the deep waters, and as beasts,
gathered together in the forests and thickets.'
予小子既獲仁人,—we have
seen the references made by Woo in the 'Great
Speech,' Pt. ii., 9, *et al.*, to his 'virtuous men.'
We may compare with the sentiment here that
of T'ang in his 'Announcement,' p, 4., where he
says that before taking his measures against
Këĕ, he 'sought for the great sage, with whom
he might unite his strength' (聿求元聖
與之戮力).　承上帝＝承
上帝之意, 'to receive or comply with
the will of God.'　亂畧,—Gan-kwŏ takes
畧 in the sense of 路, 'ways;' Ts'ae takes it
in that of 謀, 'counsels,' 'plans.' Both explanations are allowable.　華夏,—see on
the 'Can. of Shun,' p. 20.　蠻貊,—see
Ana., XV., v. 2.　率俾,—Ts'ae and others

take 俾 here in the sense of 從, 'to follow,'
so that the clause ＝ 'all follow one another to
follow me.' Gan-kwŏ would put a comma at
率, and taking 俾 in its common signification
of 使, join it to the next clause. This has in
its favour, that the 肆 in next par. stands
more naturally at its commencement than as
we read it at present. The rhythm of the style,
however, requires that we join 率 and 俾.

[In the 左傳, 昭七年, we find:—
昔武王數紂之罪, 以告諸
侯, 曰, 紂為天下逋逃主, 萃
淵藪. The quotation is important, not
only as guaranteeing so much of the prayer, but
also as showing that the prayer was a part of
the address which king Woo made to the
princes. It is on this that Maou K'e-ling
mainly relies in protesting against the way in
which Choo He and others propose to break up
and re-arrange the paragraphs of this Book.]

7. See the manner in which this paragraph
is adduced by Mencius, III., Pt. II., v., 5.
There are important alterations in the structure, the philosopher not directly quoting, but
using the passage so as to suit his purpose.
Gan-kwŏ puts all the verbs in the past tense,
saying that the description is of what took
place in the 11th year, when there was the first
assemblage at Măng-tsin, and Woo returned,
without proceeding to the attack of Show. But
there is no sufficient evidence of such a meeting.
The two clauses, moreover,—恭天成命,
肆予東征, fix the whole par. to the time
then being,—the time in which 武 was offering his prayer.　筐厥玄黃,—'bas-
keted their azure and yellow *fabrics*.' See the
many descriptions in the 'Tribute of Yu' of the

俟　癸　戊　無　相　惟　附　王　厥　女
天　亥　午　作　子　爾　我　天　玄　惟
休　陳　師　神　以　有　大　休　黃　其
命　于　逾　羞　濟　神　邑　震　昭　士
甲　商　孟　〇　兆　尚　周　動　我　女
子　郊　津　旣　民　克　〇　用　周　篚

men and women. Its men and women bring their baskets full of
azure and yellow silks, to show forth *the virtue of* us the kings of
Chow. Heaven's favours stir them up, so that they come with
8 their allegiance to our great State of Chow. And now, ye
spirits, grant me your aid, that I may relieve the millions of the
people, and nothing turn out to your shame!"

9 III. On the day mow-woo the army crossed the ford of Măng;
on the day kwei-hae it was drawn up in array in the borders of

offerings brought in baskets. 昭我周
王—'displaying our kings of Chow.' Some
say that azure and yellow are the colours
of heaven and earth respectively, and that the
object of bringing such fabrics was to show
that the kings of Chow were as good and beneficent as Heaven and earth. It is not necessary
to seek for such a recondite meaning. The
bringing of the baskets was an expression of allegiance, and an acknowledgment of the virtues
of the House of Chow. 大邑周,—I
take 邑 here = 國, as we saw that Këang
Shing proposed to do in the last Book, p. 6.

8. 爾有神,—the spirits are those of
Heaven and earth, of the mountain and the river.
The conclusion is sufficiently bold. Woo must
have felt sure that his enterprise was right,
and in accordance with the supreme mind and
will.

Medhurst (Theology of the Chinese, p. 55) has
translated the par.:—'Only may you shins be
enabled to assist me in settling the millions of
the people, and do not bring disgrace on your
shin-ships.' He observes upon it, that 'the
form of expression would intimate that there
was some power above the shins invoked, and
that it was possible they might be unable to
grant the needful assistance.' There is no such
indication in the form of the expression as he
supposes. 尚克相予 is not—'may you
be enabled to assist me,' but 'grant me, I pray
you, your help.' The 克 denotes an efficacy
in the spirits themselves, and gives emphasis,
as we have often seen to be its force, to the
word that follows, so that 克相予 = 'help

me indeed.' It is remarkable how, in the course
of the prayer, reference is expressly made both to
'God' and to 'Heaven,' as supreme. Why was
it not addressed directly to God? There are
both imperfect monotheism and polytheism in
it. God is recognized as supreme, and at the
same time other spirits are recognized, who
would give effect to His will, and might be
prayed to for that purpose. As Woo addressed
his army in the grey dawn of the day at Muh,
we may say that he had but the grey dawn of
religious knowledge in his mind.

I will not add anything here to what I quoted
from Ying-tă in the introductory note on the
abruptness and seeming incompleteness with
which the prayer terminates. It would have
been better if there had been some additional
expression of Woo's own feelings and purposes,
and some inculcation of duties on the princes.
It may be that a portion of the Book has been
lost; or it may be that we do have all which
Woo was pleased to say.

Ch. III. Pp. 9, 10. THE BATTLE OF MUH,
WITH KING WOO'S PROCEEDINGS IMMEDIATELY
AFTER; AND SUBSEQUENT MEASURES. 9.
旣戊午師逾孟津,—comp. the
'Great Speech,' Pt. i., p. 1. On this same day he
delivered the address recorded in that Part.

癸亥陳于商郊,—kwei-hae was
the 3rd of the 2d month, five days after mow-
woo. From Măng-tsin to Show's capital was 400
le, so that Woo must have hurried on his army
with great speed. 俟天休命,—'the
favourable decree' of Heaven was to be seen in
the result of the impending battle, about which
Woo felt quite confident. Gan-kwŏ says that
this clause has reference to the ceasing of the
rains which had fallen all the way from Măng-

昧爽受率其旅
若林會于牧野
罔有敵于我師
前徒倒戈攻于
後以此血流漂
杵一戎衣天下
大定乃反商政
政由舊釋箕子
囚封比干墓式
商容閭散鹿臺

Shang, waiting for the gracious decision of Heaven. On the day kĕă-tsze, at early dawn, Show led forward his hosts like a forest, and assembled them in the wilderness of Muh. But they would offer no opposition to our army. Those in the front inverted their spears, and attacked those behind them, till they fled, and the blood flowed till it floated the pestles about. Thus did *king Woo* once don his arms, and the empire was greatly settled. He overthrew the *existing* government of Shang, and made it resume its old course. He delivered the count of Ke from prison, and raised a tumulus over the grave of Pe-kan. He bowed in his carriage at the gate of

tsin, so that they were able during the night to complete the order of battle. This view is at once far-fetched and shallow. 甲子昧 爽,—see the 'Speech at Muh,' p. 1. 其旅

若林,會于牧野,—see the She King, Pt. III., Bk. I. Ode II., 7, 殷商之旅, 其 會如林, 矢于牧野. Sze-ma Ts'een says that Show's army amounted to 700,000 men, which is doubtless a great exaggeration. 敵于我師,—the historian identifies himself with Woo's army. 以

北,—北=奔, 'to flee.' Ts'een gives a difft. account of the battle. At least he makes no mention of Show's troops falling upon one another, but says that 'Woo sent his general Shang-foo, with a hundred of the most daring warriors, to dash forward at the head of a large body. Show's army had no mind to fight, but really wished king Woo to penetrate their host. They therefore inverted their lances, and made way for his men. They in fact all revolted from Show, who fled at once to the "Stag tower."' This account is not reconcileable, however, with the statement which follows about 'the blood flowing till it floated the pestles of the mortars.'

The remarks of Mencius on the passage— 血 流漂杵 are well known. He attests (VII. Pt. II., iii.) that the 'Completion of the War' contained such a passage, but protests against

believing it.—'When the prince the most benevolent was engaged against him who was the most the opposite, how could such a thing be?' It gives, no doubt, an exaggerated description of the slaughter which took place. 杵 means the wooden pestles of the mortars, which the soldiers carried with them to prepare their rice. We need not suppose, as some do (see a note in the 集傳 by 蔡清), that they were the pestles used for pounding the earth in making the intrenchments. Maou K'e-ling prefers the reading of 鹵, 'shields,' for 杵. Mei Tsuh (梅鷟) would save the credit of Mencius at the expense of the classic. If, he argues, it had appeared, as in the present text, that the slaughter was occasioned by Show's troops turning against one another, there would have been no occasion for the philosopher's remark. The forger of Tsin evidently constructed his text that king Woo might not appear chargeable with the bloodshedding, which Mencius supposed might be attributed to him! It is much more natural to believe that Mencius, in the impulse of his ardent nature, spoke as he did,—unadvisedly. 一戎衣,—'once he put on his martial garb.' See in the 'Doctrine of the Mean,' xviii., 2. Comp. also on 殪戎 殷, Bk. IX., p, 4. 反商政,—'he turned back the govt. of Shang,' *i.e.,* he took away the oppressive laws of Show, and then— 由舊政, 'followed the old govt.' *i.e.,* the

下治。　報功、垂拱而天　惇信明義崇德　五教惟食喪祭　位事惟能重民　惟三、建官惟賢、　列爵惟五、分土　而萬姓悅服。○　粟、大賚于四海、　之財、發鉅橋之

^{十節}

Shang Yung's village. He dispersed the treasures of Luh-t'ae, and distributed the grain of Keu-k'eaou, thus conferring great gifts throughout the empire, and all the people joyfully submitted.

10　He arranged the orders of nobili'y into five, assigning the territories to them on a threefold scale. He gave offices only to the worthy, and employments only to the able. He attached great importance to the people's being taught the duties of the five relations of society, and to take care for food, for funeral ceremonies, and for sacrifices. He showed the reality of his truthfulness, and proved clearly his righteousness. He honoured virtue, and rewarded merit. Then he had only to let his robes fall down, and fold his hands, and the empire was orderly ruled.

govt. of T'ang and the other good sovereigns who succeeded him. 釋箕子囚，封 比干墓,—see the concluding note to the 'Viscount of Wei.' 式商容閭—式, see Con. Ana.. X., xvi., 3. Shang Yung must have been some worthy in disgrace with Show, and living retired in his village. Ying-tă quotes some account of him from Hwang-p'oo Meih's 帝王世記, but it is the production of a later age. 散鹿臺之財，發鉅 橋之粟,—of the 'Stag tower' we have spoken. Keu-k'eaou was in the north east of the pres. dis. of Keuh-chow (曲周), dep. of Kwang-p'ing (廣平). Chih-le, where Show had collected great stores of grain. These two measures were directed to the benefit of the masses of the people, impoverished by the exactions of the tyrant.

P. 10. 列爵惟五, 分土惟三,—this agrees with the account of the arrangement of dignities and emoluments determined by the House of Chow, given by Mencius, Book V., Pt. II., ii. The orders of nobility were the Kung, How, Pih, Tsze and Nan, to the two first of which were assigned a hundred *le* square of territory, each, while the Pih had 70, and the Tsze and the Nan only 50 *le* square each. Yeu

Jŏ-keu absurdly says that this is different from the account of Mencius. It is different, however, from the account which we find in the Chow Le, Bk. IX., (地官, 大司徒). There the orders of nobility are five, as in Mencius, but the divisions of territory are also five. To the Kung, it is said, there were assigned 500 *le* square; to the How, 400; to the Pih, 300; to the Tsze, 200; and to the Nan, 100. I don't see how the two accounts are to be reconciled. If it be said that the five-fold territorial division was made by the duke of Chow at a subsequent period, which is the view of K'ang-shing, why did not Mencius advert to it? If it be said, that the larger dimensions arose from the usurpations of the States among themselves, which is the view of Ying-tă, how is it that they have any place in the Chow Le? 建官惟賢, 位事惟能,—the historian proceeds to Woo's provisions for the officers about his court. His object was to have none in office but men of talents and virtue, and that each man's duties should be those for which he was specially able.

重民五教, 惟食, 喪, 祭,— Gan-kwŏ explained the former of these clauses by inserting an 與 between 民 and 五教, —'he attached importance to the people, and to the inculcation of the five duties.' This is not so good as to take 民 to be under the regimen of 五教. The force of 重 extends to the difft. terms in the second clause, and 惟 is used as a connective particle. Lin Che-k'e compares its use here with the same in the 'Tribute of Yu,' Pt. i., pp. 44 and 51. It is said that Woo gave effect to this solicitude for the instruction of the people by establishing schools,—educational institutions of various kinds; and to make good the provision of food, he enacted 'the hundred mow allotment and the share system' (see Mencius, III., Pt. I., iii.). 惇信明義,=惇=厚, 'to make solid, or real.' The 信 or 'truthfulness' belonged, the critics say, to all his governmental orders, and the fidelity with which they were kept, and the 義 or 'righteousness,' to all his actions. We have in the 'Daily Explanation:'—凡出一令,必守之以信,而始終不渝,凡行一事,必裁之以義而動無過舉. 垂拱=垂衣拱手, 'to let the robes hang down, and fold his hands ceremoniously before his breast.' The meaning is, that by the excellence of his institutions and example, there was superseded the necessity of any further laborious measures or efforts. The good order of the government followed as a matter of course.

CONCLUDING NOTES.　　[i]. *On the investitures granted by king Woo.* The 歷代統紀表, under the year B.C. 1121, gives a list of the principal States into which the empire was divided in the dynasty of Chow ;—viz. Loo (魯), Wei (衞), Ts'ae (蔡), Tsin (晉), Ts'aou (曹), Ch'ing (鄭), Woo (吳), Yen (燕), Ch'in (陳), Sung (宋), Ts'e (齊), Ts'oo (楚), and Ts'in (秦). I will not here enter into particulars on each of those principalities, as I shall have to speak of most of them in connection with one or other of the following Books. I will now only refer to what is in the Bk. 樂記, of the Le Ke, Part iii., par. 19,—that 'king Woo, on the overthrow of the Shang dynasty, before he descended from his chariot, invested the representative of Hwang-te with the territory of Ke (薊; the pres. dis. of Ta-hing, [大興] in the dep. of Shun-t'een); the representative of Yaou with Chuh (祝; the pres. dis. of Ch'ang-ts'ing [長清], in the dep. of Tse-nan); the representative of Shun with Ch'in (陳; the name remains in that of the dep. Ch'in-chow, Ho-nan); and when he had descended from his chariot,—*i.e.*, subsequently,—he invested the representative of Yu with K'e (杞; this name also remains in that of the dis. of K'e, in the dep. of K'ae-fung); and he sent the representative of the House of Yin to the territory of Sung' (宋; the pres. dis. of Shang-k'ëw (商邱), dep. of Kwei-tih, Ho-nan). These appointments were given, not because of services rendered to the new dynasty, as many others were, but from respect to the memories of the great men represented. that the sacrifices to their spirits might not fall into disuse.

[ii]. *On the specifications of time in this and the two preceding Books.* King Woo proceeded from his capital to the attack of Show on the 3rd day of the 1st month of what is called his 13th year, B.C. 1121 (Gaubil, 1122); and in the 28th day of that month 'in the spring' (according to the 'Great Speech,' Pt. i., p. 1), he crossed the Ho at Măng-ts'in. Ts'ae Ch'in supposes that the year intended was that of Hea, which has been that of all the dynasties of China since the Han. Now the first month of the present Chinese year began on the 18th of our February, and the cycle name of the day was mow-shin (戊申). If we multiply 2984 solar years, which have elapsed since the 13th of Woo's reign, by 365.24224, we obtain the number of days from that time up to the end of last Chinese year, = 1,089,882.84416, or 18164 cycles of days and 42 days more. But it will be found, on calculation, that the first day of new moon in February, 2984 years ago, occurred three days earlier that in the present year. Reckoning back therefore 18,164 cycles and 46 days more from mow-shin of the present year, we come to jin-seuh (壬戌), as the first day of the Hea year in the 13th of Woo's reign; and the view of Ts'ae cannot be sustained.

Reckoning back other 30 days from 壬戌, we come to the day jin-shin (壬辰), as the first day of the first month in the year of Shang; and according to the view of Fan Sze-lin, approved of rather by the editors of Yung-ching's Shoo, this is the day intended in the classic as the first day of the first month spoken of. It is only one day after sin-maou. It would thus appear that not only is Ts'ae in error in saying that we are to understand that the months in the text are the months of the year of Hea, but that the other commentators are equally mistaken in referring them to the year of Chow. They are those of the year of Shang, beginning with the last month of winter. This conclusion lightens somewhat the difficulty occasioned by the mention of "the spring," in the "Great Speech," par. 1. This is spoken with reference to the day mow-woo, which certainly was close upon the spring. If it be thought that the whole of the first month is intended to be described as in 'the spring,' we must believe that in consequence of deficient intercalation, an error of one whole lunation had crept into the calendar by the time of the rise of the Chow dynasty. On suggesting that this might be the case to a very intelligent Chinese scholar, he replied, 'How can you think that the sages could have blundered so?' But it will be found, from what will be seen in the prolegomena on the subject of the astronomy and chronology of the ancient Chinese, that this was probably the case.

蔡沈考定武成

惟一月壬辰旁死魄越翼日癸巳王朝
步自周于征伐商。○底商之罪告于皇
天后土所過名山大川曰惟有道曾孫
周王發將有大正于商今商王受無道、
暴殄天物害虐烝民爲天下逋逃主萃
淵藪予小子既獲仁人敢祇承上帝以
遏亂略華夏蠻貊罔不率俾惟爾有神
尚克相予以濟兆民無作神羞。○既戊
午師逾孟津癸亥陳于商郊俟天休命
甲子昧爽受率其旅若林會于牧野罔
有敵于我師前徒倒戈攻于後以北血
流漂杵一戎衣天下大定乃反商政政
由舊釋箕子囚封比干墓式商容閭散
鹿臺之財發鉅橋之粟大賚于四海而
萬姓悅服。○厥四月哉生明王來自商
至于豐乃偃武修文歸馬于華山之陽
放牛于桃林之野示天下弗服。

APPENDIX.

THE COMPLETION OF THE WAR, AS ARRANGED BY TS'AE CH'IN.

In the first month, *the day* jin-shin immediately followed the end of the moon's waning. The next day was kwei-ke, when the king in the morning marched from Chow to attack and punish Shang.

Declaring the crimes of Shang, he announced to great Heaven and the sovereign Earth, to the famous hill and the great river, by which he passed, saying, 'ɪ, Fă, the principled, king of Chow, by a long descent, am about to have a great righting with Shang. Show, the king of Shang, is without principle, cruel and destructive to the creatures of Heaven, injurious and tyrannical to the multitudes of the people, chief of the vagabonds of the empire, who collect about him as fish in the deep, and beasts in the prairie. I, who am but a little child, having obtained *the help of* virtuous men, presume reverently to comply with *the will of* God, to make an end of his disorderly ways. The great and flowery region, and the wild tribes of the south and north, equally follow and consent with me. And now, ye spirits, grant me your aid, that I may relieve the millions of the people, and nothing turn out to your shame!'"

On the day mow-woo the army crossed the ford of Măng; on the day kwei-hae it was drawn up in array in the borders of Shang, waiting for the gracious decision of Heaven. On the day keă-tsze, at early dawn, Show led forward his hosts like a forest, and assembled them in the wilerness of Muh. But they would offer no opposition to our army. Those in the front inverted their spears, and attacked those behind them, till they fled, and the blood flowed till it floated the pestles about. Thus did *king Woo* once don his arms, and the empire was greatly settled. He overthrew the *existing* government of Shang, and made it resume its old course. He delivered the count of Ke from prison, and raised a tumulus over the grave of Pe-kan. He bowed in his carriage at the gate of Shang Yung's village. He dispersed the treasures of Luh-t'ae, and distributed the grain of Keu-keaou, thus conferring great gifts throughout the empire; and all the people joyfully submitted.

In the fourth month, at the first appearance of the moon, the king came from Shang to Fung, when he hushed all the movements of war, and attended to the cultivations of peace. He sent back his horses to the south of mount Hwa, and let loose his oxen in the open country of T'aou-lin, showing the empire that he would not use them *again*.

拱　喪　賢　列　天　其　成　集　小　天　我　王　若　日　甸　命　既
而　祭　位　爵　休　士　命　予　邦　命　文　肇　曰　庚　侯　于　生
天　惇　事　惟　震　女　肆　小　懷　以　考　基　嗚　戌　衞　周　魄、
下　信　惟　五　動　篚　予　子　其　撫　文　王　呼　柴　駿　○　庶
治。　明　能　分　用　厥　東　其　德　方　王　迹、　羣　望　奔　丁　邦
　　義　重　土　附　玄　征、　承　惟　夏　克　王　后　大　走、　未、　冢
　　崇　民　惟　我　黃、　綏　厥　九　大　成　季　惟　告　執　祀　君、
　　德　五　三、　大　昭　厥　志。　年、　邦　厥　其　先　武　豆　于　暨
　　報　教、　建　邑　我　士　○　大　畏　勳、　勤　王　成。　籩。　周　百
　　功、　惟　官　周。　周　女。　恭　統　其　誕　王　建　○　越　廟、　工、
　　垂　食　惟　　　王　惟　天　未　力、　膺　家、　邦　王　三　邦　受

After the moon began to wane, the hereditary princes of the various States, and all the officers, received their appointments from Chow.

On the day ting-we he sacrificed in the ancestral temple of Chow, when *the chiefs of* the imperial domain, and of the teen, how, and wei domains, all hurried about, carrying the dishes. Three days after, he presented a burnt-offering *to Heaven*, and worshipped towards the mountains and rivers, solemnly announcing the successful completion of the war.

The king spake to the following effect :—" Oh ! ye host of princes, the first of our kings founded the State and commenced our territory. The duke Lew was able to consolidate the merits of his predecessor. But it was the king T'ae who laid the foundations of the imperial inheritance. Then king Ke was diligent for the royal House ; and my deceased father, king Wăn, completed his merit, and received the great decree of Heaven to soothe the regions of the great bright land. The great States feared his strength ; the small States cherished his virtue. In nine years, however, the whole empire was not collected under his rule, and it fell to me, who am but a little child, to carry out his will. Reverently obeying the determinate counsel of Heaven, I pursued my punitive work to the east, to give tranquillity to its men and women. Its men and women brought their baskets full of azure and yellow silks, to show forth *the virtue of* us the kings of Chow. Heaven's favours stirred them up, so that they came with their allegiance to our great State of Chow.

He arranged the orders of nobility into five, assigning, the territories to them on a threefold scale. He gave offices only to the worthy and employments only to the able. He attached great importance to the people's being taught the duties of the five relations of society, and took care for food, for funeral ceremonies, and for sacrifices. He showed the reality of his truthfulness, and proved clearly his righteousness. He honoured virtue, and rewarded merit. Then he had only to let his robes fall down, and fold his hands and the empire was orderly ruled.

THE BOOKS OF CHOW.

BOOK IV. THE GREAT PLAN.

居、民、天、呼、乃、箕、祀、惟一節
我相陰箕言子。王十有
不協隲子〇訪三
知厥下惟嗚王二節于

1　　I. In the thirteenth year, the king went to inquire of the vis-
2　count of Ke, and said to him "Oh! viscount of Ke, Heaven, unseen,
has given their constitution to mankind, aiding *also* the harmonious
development of it in their various conditions.　I do not know how
their proper virtues in their various relations should be brought
forth in due order."

THE NAME OF THE BOOK.—洪範, 'The Great Plan.' 洪＝大, 'great.' 範＝法, 'plan.' Other synonyms of 範, given in the dict., are 式 and 模, both conveying the same idea of 'plan,' or 'model.' The name, like that of the last Book, is taken from the Book itself. We read in par. 2, that 'Heaven gave to Yu the Great Plan, with its nine Divisions.' Some would adopt the whole of this,—洪範九疇, as the name; but there would be no advantage gained by departing in such a matter, from the established usage.　The Book is found in both the texts.

HISTORY OF THE BOOK, AND MODE OF INTERPRETATION. The viscount of Ke had said that when ruin overtook the House of Shang, he would not be the servant of another dynasty; —see 'The Viscount of Wei,' p. 8. Accordingly, he refused to acknowledge the sovereignty of king Woo, who had delivered him from the prison where Show had put him, and fled—or perhaps only made it known that he would flee —to Corea.　King Woo respected and admired his attachment to the fallen dynasty, and invested him with that territory.　He now felt constrained to appear at the court of Chow, when the king took the opportunity to consult him on the great principles of government, and the result was that he communicated this 'Great Plan, with its nine Divisions.'　Being first made public under the Chow dynasty, it is ranked among the 'Books of Chow.'　It is often referred to, however, as one of the 'Books of Shang,' as having emanated from the viscount of Ke, who should properly be adjudged to that dynasty.　When we read the Book itself, we see that it originally belonged to the time of Hea, and at least the central portion, or text of it,—par. 4,—should be ascribed to 'the great Yu.'　We have therefore a fragment in it of very ancient learning.　How this had come into the possession of the viscount of Ke we cannot tell.　It does not seem to have occurred to the Chinese critics to make the inquiry.　Whether we should ascribe all the paragraphs from the 5th downwards to the viscount, is also a point on which I cannot undertake to pronounce a positive opinion. Hea Seuen (夏僎; Sung dyn.) says that 'though the words are those of the viscount of Ke, the record of them was made by the historians of Chow.'

That the central portion of the Book, and more or less of the expository part, came down from the times of Hea is not improbable. The use of the number nine, and the naming of the various divisions of the 'Plan,' are in harmony with Yu's style and practice in his 'Counsels,' and in what we may call the 'Domesday Book.'

We are told that 'Heaven—God—gave the plan with its Divisions to Yu.' Upon this Gan-kwŏ says that 'Heaven gave Yu the mysterious tortoise, which made its appearance in the waters of the Lŏ, bearing marks on its back well defined, from 1 to 9; and thereupon Yu determined the meaning of those numbers, and completed the nine divisions of the plan.'

This legend has been fathered on Confucius, as we read in the 'Appendix to the Yih king' (易經. 繫辭), Pt i., p. 38, that 'the Ho gave forth the Scheme, and the Lŏ gave forth the Book (or defined characters), which the sages (or sage) took as their pattern' 河出圖, 洛出書, 聖人則之). If we admit that these words proceeded from Confucius or were edited by him, while it is absurd enough to speak of the two rivers giving forth the Scheme and the Book, he says nothing of the Scheme being on the back of a dragon, which has been the current statement for more than 2,000 years, or of the Book being on the back of a tortoise. Moreover, there is no evidence that he meant to connect the 'Book of Lŏ' with the 'Great Plan' at all. We should rather imagine that he supposed the Scheme and the Book to be equally related to the diagrams of the Yih, and to have been both presented to Fuh-he. I hardly know an interpreter, however, but Lin Che-k'e, who has not adopted the statement of Gan-kwŏ; and the consequence is that the explanations of this Book are overlaid with absurd twaddle about the virtue of numbers as related to Heaven and Earth, to the Yin and the Yang, the cardinal points, &c., &c.. The following figure has been imagined as that which was exhibited to Yu:—

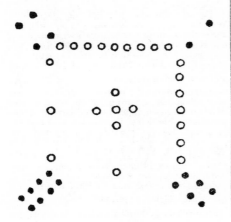

Near the head of the tortoise, it is said, were the nine open marks, and opposite was the one close mark. The two and the four were at the shoulders; the six and the eight were by the feet. Three and seven were on the left and right, and five were in the centre. Out of those numbers, odd and even, heavenly and earthly, now multiplied, now added together, the whole of the Plan and its Divisions is developed, with a glibness of tongue and a leger-de-plume, which only familiarity with the Yih-king, and the applications of it to astrology, geomancy, and other follies can produce. There is of course no 'solid learning' (實 學) in all this. We shall have to endeavour to treat seriously of it, when we come to the Yih-king, but it should be exploded from the study of 'The great Plan.' The Book will be found dark enough in itself, but the viscount of Ke says nothing of occult qualities of numbers, from which the ideas in the different divisions of the Plan could be deduced. It will be my object, therefore, simply to elucidate the meaning of the whole as a scheme of government, intended to guide all rulers in the discharge of their duties.

Gaubil says that 'the Book is a treatise at once of Physics, Astrology, Divination, Morals, Politics, and Religion; and that it has a sufficiently close resemblance to the work of Ocellus the Lucanian.' There is a shadowy resemblance between the *Great Plan* and the curious specimen of Pythagorean doctrine which we have in the treatise *On the Universe*. The dissimilarities are still greater and more numerous. More especially are the different characters of the Greek mind, speculative, and the Chinese mind, practical, apparent in the two Works. Where the Chinese writer loses himself in the sheerest follies of his imagining, he would yet grope about for a rule to be of use in the conduct of human affairs. One of the most interesting curiosities which were obtained in 1861 from the 'Summer palace' near Peking, was a scroll, purporting to be in the handwriting of the emperor K'een-lung, dilating on the meaning of 'The great Plan,' and the lessons to be learned by sovereigns from it. There is a general agreement among the critics in assigning its place to the Book either among the 'Counsels' of the Shoo, or among the 'Instructions.'

CONTENTS. I avail myself here, with a little variation, of the account of these given in the 'Complete Digest' of commentaries on the Shoo (書經備旨).—The whole divides itself into three chapters. The first, parr. 1–3, is introductory, and describes how the 'Great Plan with its Divisions' was first made known to Yu, and came at this time to be communicated to king Woo. The second, in p. 4, contains the Plan and its Divisions. The third, parr. 5–40, contains a particular description of the several Divisions. 'The whole,' says the writer, 'exhibits the great model for the govt. of the empire. The fifth or middle division on Royal Perfection is, indeed, the central one of the whole, that about which the Book revolves. The four divisions that precede it show how this royal Perfection is to be accomplished, and the four that follow show how it is to be maintained.'

Ch. I. Pp. 1—3. KING WOO APPLIES TO THE VISCOUNT OF KE FOR INFORMATION ABOUT

HOW THE GOVERNMENT OF THE EMPIRE SHOULD BE CONDUCTED, AND IS TOLD BY HIM OF THE GREAT PLAN WITH NINE DIVISIONS WHICH YU GOT FROM HEAVEN. 1. 十有三祀．—the commentators observe that 祀, the Shang term for 'year,' is here used instead of the Chow 年, the viscount of Ke using the character to which he had been accustomed. 訪, acc. to Ts'ae,＝就而問之,＝'went to and asked him.' It implies 'consultation.' See the note on the History of the Book. 2. 王乃言曰,—' the king thereupon spoke, saying.' The 乃 protracts the style, and indicates the deliberation with which the king made his inquiry. So in the next paragraph,— 箕子乃言曰. 箕子,—king Woo, it is observed, addressed the noble by his Shang title, not having yet invested him with the territory of Corea. It may be so; but he might also address him thus, the old designation being familiar to him, even if he had already given him his new appointment. 天陰隲下 民, 相協厥居,—陰＝默, 'secretly,' 'by a hidden influence;' 隲＝定, 'to settle.' Sze-ma Ts'een gives the text as 天陰定 下民, which shows at least how he understood the term 隲. The meaning then of the first clause is that 'Heaven, working unseen, has made men with certain hidden springs of character.' As Gan-kwŏ says, 天不 言而默定下民. This interpretation is much to be preferred to that adopted by Këang Shing and others from Ma Yung, who makes 陰＝覆, 'to cover,' 'to overshadow,' and 隲＝升＝舉＝生, 'to produce.' 天陰隲下民 is thus simply ＝'Heaven that overshadows produced the inferior people.' The next clause is continuative, and is to be referred to Heaven as its subject. 相 (3d. tone)＝助, 'to aid.' 協＝合, 'to unite,' 'to harmonize.' 厥居,—'their dwelling or abiding.' This expression is difficult. Both the 'Daily Explanation,' and Këang Shing paraphrase it by 其所當居止之理, 'the principles in which they ought to abide.' Gan-kwŏ's language upon it is enigmatical. He says that 'Heaven thus aids and harmonizes their abiding, so that they shall have a provision for prolonged life,' (是助合其居, 使 有常生之資). Ying-tă in expanding this has some striking things. He says that 'the people have been produced by supreme Heaven (民是上天所生), and both body and soul are Heaven's gift (形神天

之所授). Men have thus the material body and the knowing mind, and Heaven further assists them, helping them to harmonize their lives. The right and the wrong of their language, the correctness and errors of their conduct, their enjoyment of clothing and food, the rightness of their various movements:—all these things are to be harmonized by what they are endowed with by Heaven. Accordance with the right way gives life, and error from it leads to death. Thus Heaven has not only given life to men, and conferred upon them a body and mind, but it further assists them to harmonize their conditions of life, so as to have a provision for its continuance' (天非徒賦 命於人, 授以形體心識, 乃 復佑助諧合其居業, 使有常 生之資). The fact is that the obscure text can only be brought out obscurely. We cannot do better than understand 厥居 as meaning 'the principles in which men should rest in their various conditions,' belonging to the complex constitution which God has given them.

I have said that Heaven is the subject spoken of in 相協厥居. The text certainly supplies no other; but Wang Suh supposed a 王 者, before 相, thinking the meaning to be that 'Heaven having produced men with their peculiar constitution, and taking an interest in them, it devolves on the sovereign to give effect to the wishes of Heaven for men's virtue and happiness.' Keang Shing follows this view. It cannot be said not to be in harmony with the general teaching of the classics. The text is thereby, indeed, brought into strict accordance with that in the 'Announcement of T'ang,' p. 2. But the language in that passage is sufficiently explicit. I can find no subject in the text for 相協 but 天. The next clause, however, must be understood, I think, with reference to the duty of the sovereign, so that the whole paragraph may be considered as very nearly equivalent to that referred to in the 'Announcement of T'ang.'

我不知其彝倫攸敘,—king Woo, say many critics, knew very well all about the subject, but he thus speaks to bring out the learning of the viscount of Ke. We may rather suppose that he speaks with reference to the Great Plan and its Divisions, of which he had merely heard. 彝＝常, 'constant,' 'regular;' meaning here the nature of man, acting according to the regular laws of its constitution appointed by Heaven. Compare in the She King, Pt. III., Bk. III., Ode vi., st. 1, 天生烝民, 有物有則, 民 之秉彝, 好是懿德, 'Heaven, in giving birth to the multitudes of men, to every endowment appointed its appropriate law. The people, holding fast this constant nature, love the virtue which is admirable.' 倫＝人倫, 'the relations of human society,' in which are

其彝倫攸敘。○

三節 箕子乃言曰、我
聞在昔、鯀陻洪
水、汩陳其五行、
帝乃震怒不畀
洪範九疇、彝倫
攸斁、鯀則殛死、
禹乃嗣興、天乃
錫禹洪範九疇、四節
彝倫攸敘。○初

3　The viscount of Ke thereupon replied, "I have heard that of old time K'wăn dammed up the inundating waters, and thereby threw into disorder the arrangement of the five elements. God was thereby roused to anger, and did not give him 'the great Plan with its nine Divisions,' whereby the proper virtues of the various relations were left to go to ruin. K'wăn was then kept a prisoner till his death, and Yu rose up to continue his undertaking. To him Heaven gave 'the great Plan with its nine Divisions,' and thereby the proper virtues of the various relations were brought forth in their order.

seen the virtues of man's nature, intended by 彝 攸＝所; 攸敘＝所以敘, 'how they are arranged.'

I have said that this clause is to be understood with reference to the work and duty of the sovereign. Gan-kwŏ, indeed, supposes that Heaven is still the subject (我不知天所以定民之常道理次敘問何由); but the other view is generally adopted. The explanation of the whole paragraph, given by Ch'in Ya-yen (陳雅言; Ming dyn.) is the best which I have seen:—武王意人君代天理物使以心人以箕子之所必其無者倫敘子是之所以治得相其協秉知此箕爲即意天順天在欲道治洪九疇承之上道我之以告法仰居貴其也之以 . Gaubil's translation is—'Le ciel a des voies secrettes, par lesquelles il rend le peuple tranquille et fixe. Il s'unit à lui pour l'aider à garder son Etat. Je ne connois point

cette regle: quelle est elle?' Medhurst endeavours to keep more close to the text :—'Heaven has secretly settled the lower people, aiding and according with that in which they rest; but I do not know the arrangement of those invariable principles.'

P. 3. 鯀陻洪水,—陻＝塞, 'to dam up.' Instead of finding a vent for the accumulated waters, as his son Yu did, K'wăn attempted to remedy the evils of their inundation by damming them up. 汩陳五行, —for the 'five elements,' see the 5th par. 汩＝亂, 'to confuse,' 'to throw into disorder.' 陳＝列, 'to arrange,' and 陳五行＝上帝所陳列之五行, 'the five elements arranged by God.' How K'wăn's damming the waters—dealing wrongly with one element—should derange all the other elements, is a statement which I can make nothing of. 不畀洪範九疇,—畀＝與, 'to give to;' 疇＝類, 'sorts,' 'classes,' 'divisions.' 彝倫攸斁,—斁 (read too) ＝敗, 'to subvert,' 'to ruin.' How the consequence here stated took place, is likewise a thing which I don't understand. 鯀則殛死,—see the 'Can. of Shun,' p. 12. 天乃錫禹洪範九疇—we have seen, in the second introductory note, how it is fabled that Yu received the great Plan from

一、曰五行、次二、
曰敬用五事、次
三、曰農用八政、次
四、曰協用五
紀、次五、曰建用
皇極、次六、曰
用三德、次七、曰
明用稽疑、次八、
曰念用庶徵、次
九、曰嚮用五福。

4　　II. "*Of those divisions*, the first is called 'The five Elements;' the second is called 'The Reverent Practice of the five Businesses'; the third is called 'Earnest Devotion to the eight objects of Government;' the fourth is called 'The Harmonious Use of the five Arrangements'; the fifth is called 'The Establishment and Use of Royal Perfection'; the sixth is called 'The Cultivation and Use of the three Virtues'; the seventh is called 'The Intelligent Use of the Examination of Doubts'; the eighth is called 'The Thoughtful Use of the various Verifications'; the ninth is called 'The Hortatory Use of the five Happinesses, and the Awing Use of the six Extremities.'

Heaven. Lin Che-k'e held that all which is meant by the text is that Heaven gave Yu the mind and the enlightenment to conceive and describe the Plan. Choo He was asked what he thought of this view, and whether it was not contrary to the Yih King, which says that 'the Lŏ gave forth the Book.' He answered, 'Suppose that Heaven had only now given the Book of Lŏ, if it did not also give the mind to interpret it, no man would understand it! Neither the old account, nor Lin Che-k'e's, is to be set aside' (便使而今天錫洛書、若非天啟其心、亦無人理會得、兩說似不可偏廢也). I have said I don't understand how the virtues and relations were left to go to ruin, in consequence of K'wăn's failure: Ch'in Sze-k'ae has tried to explain the difficulty, but with little success. He says:—陶唐之盛於變斁行迹之必哉雍之際又何斁倫蓋之五鳥憂豈斁時之非言朝倫甚斁以哉斁九功廷也獸蹄謂之斁既道交於未斁堯斁之此綱彝常倫滅中所而後謂之綱

Ch. II. P. 4. THE GREAT PLAN AND ITS NINE DIVISIONS. The reader must not suppose that the great Plan was something different from its nine Divisions. It was merely the combination of them

This paragraph is supposed to be the work of Yu. According to Lew Hin, indeed, the whole 65 characters were upon the back of the tortoise;—see the 前漢書、五行志、上、凡此六十五字、皆洛書本文. Gan-kwŏ says he did not know how many characters were on the back of the tortoise, but that the numbering of the Divisions, 'first,' 'second,' &c., (初一曰、次二日、云云) was done by Yu. In this way there would be 38 characters left. Some take away the half of these again,—those, namely, which have a verbal or hortatory force,' (敬用、農用、云云), leaving the names of the divisions. The prevailing opinion now, however, is that there were only the 45 small circles, open and close, upon the creature; but even thus much cannot be allowed. The whole story of the tortoise and 'the book of Lŏ' is only fit to be told to children. In the paragraph before us, the characters 五行、五事、 &c., had come down from the times of Hea; perhaps the 敬用、農用、 &c., had done the same; 初一曰、次二日、 &c., were spoken by the viscount of Ke in the narrative which he gave to Woo.

While discarding the 'book of Lŏ,' it will be a help to the student's memory, and in his reading of the various lore on the Plan, if I append here an outline of the 'Book' with the

火曰炎 曰潤下 曰土、水 曰金、五 曰木、四 曰火、三 曰水、二 五行、一 極。○ 威用六
五節

5 III. [i.] "First, of the five elements.—The first is named water; the second, fire; the third, wood; the fourth, metal; the fifth, earth. *The nature of* water is to soak and descend; of fire, to blaze and ascend; of wood, to be crooked and to be straight; of metal, to obey and

names of the Divisions added to it. It differs from the common representations of the Plan, by containing the 5th division in the centre, which is ordinarily excluded, from numerical considerations.

For the names of the subjects of the nine Divisions, see on their several paragraphs that follow.   With regard to the 'five 事,' it is said they are to be reverently used. The 事 being personal, belonging to the government of one's self, it is required to be 'reverent' in respect to them. [Keang Shing, after Lew Hin, reads 羞用 for 敬用, but 敬 rests on good authority;—see the 後案, *in loc.*].

The 'eight 政' are to be used 'liberally.' 農 is read as if it were 醲, and defined by 厚. Ma Yung and Wang Suh try to retain the meaning of 農, 'agriculture,'—but ineffectually.   The 'five 紀' are to be used 'harmoniously,'—'to bring the works of men into harmony with the times of heaven.' The 'various 徵' are to be used 'thoughtfully.' 念 = 'with considerate examination.'   The 'five 福' are to usedeb 'encouragingly,'—so

as to attract men 'towards' (嚮) what is desired.   No numbers, it is observed, are used with reference to the fifth Division, the perfection which it indicates not being capable of measurement.

Ch. III. Pp. 5—40. PARTICULAR DESCRIPTION OF THE NINE DIVISIONS.   5. *Of the five elements.* Gaubil does not translate 行, but gives always—'les cinq *hing*.' We have got into the habit of rendering it in English by 'elements.' But it seems hardly possible to determine what the Chinese mean by the term. By 'elements' we mean 'the first principles or ingredients of which all bodies are composed.' The Pythagoreans, by their four elements of earth, water, air, and fire—a classification first made, apparently, by Ocellus—did not intend so much the nature or essence of material substances, as the forms under which matter is actually presented to us. The term 行, meaning 'to move,' 'to be in action,' shows that the original conception of the Chinese is of a different nature; and it is said, in the dict., that 'the five *hing* move and revolve throughout heaven and earth, without ever ceasing, and hence they are so called (五行運于天地間, 未嘗停息, 故名). 'Distributed,' say the editors of Yung-ching's Shoo, 'through the four seasons, they make the "five arrangements;" exhibited in prognostications, they give rise to divination by the tortoise and the reeds; having lodgment in the human body, they produce "the five businesses;" moved by good fortune and bad, they produce "the various verifications;" communicated to organisms, they produce the different natures, hard and soft, good and evil; working out their results in the changes of those organisms, they necessitate here benevolence and there meanness, here longevity and there early death:—all these things are from the operation of the five *hing*. But if we speak of them in their simplest and most important character, they are, as here, what man's life depends upon, what the people cannot do without.'

Leaving all this jargon, and turning to the 'counsels of Yu' parr. 7, 8, we find that 'water, fire, metal, wood, and earth' are, along with 'grain,' the 'six magazines,' from which the people are to be provided with what is necessary for their sustenance and comfort. We may content ourselves, therefore, with under-

恭言曰從視曰　聽五曰思貌曰　言三曰視四曰　事一曰貌二曰　稼作甘。○二五　酸從革作辛稼　上作苦曲直作　稼潤下作鹹炎　曰從革土爰稼　上木曰曲直金

to change; while the virtue of earth is seen in seed-sowing and ingathering. That which soaks and descends becomes salt; that which blazes and ascends becomes bitter; that which is crooked and straight becomes sour; that which obeys and changes becomes acrid; and from seed-sowing and ingathering comes sweetness.

6 [ii.] "Second, of the five businesses.—The first is called demeanour; the second, speech; the third, seeing; the fourth, hearing; and the fifth, thinking. The *virtue of the* demeanour is called respectfulness; of speech, accordance *with reason*; of seeing, clear-

standing 五行 here as 'the five essentials to human life.' From 水曰潤下 downwards is to be taken as the language of the viscount of Ke, or of the chronicler of Chow, to whom we owe the 'great Plan' of the Shoo; but the language is affected by the study of the Yih-king, which had come into vogue.

水曰潤下,—'water may be described as moistening and descending.' 潤下……

從革, it is said, 以性言, 'describe the *nature* of the elements.' But *nature* in such a case is only expressive of some *qualities* belonging to them. 稼穡 again, is said to be descriptive of the *virtue* of earth (以德言); and hence we read 土爰稼穡, and not 土曰稼穡. 'Metal obeys and changes'; *i.e.*, it alters its form when acted on by fire.

From 潤下 to the end we have the 五味 or 'five tastes' of the elements ;—not, however, the tastes that are proper to them, but those which they are found in course of time to assume. This is denoted by 作, which I have translated 'becomes.' Hea Seuen has said, 'The reason why we find 作 used in connection with the five tastes or flavours of the elements is this.—Water as it issues from the spring is not salt;—but when it flows away to the sea, and is there collected and coagulated together for a long time, the salt taste is pro-

duced, and the saltness is made by the soaking and descending. When fire, blazes on without ceasing, charring and scorching for a long time, the bitter taste is produced, and the bitterness is made by the blazing and ascending'; &c., &c. The reader may find a reasonable meaning in all this, if he can. Ts'ae observes that the five elements have their several sounds, colours, and airs, as well as tastes, but the text only speaks of their tastes, those being of greater importance to the people than the others.

P. 6. *Of the five businesses.* To translate 五事 by 'the five businesses' reads awkward and uncouth; but I can do no better with it. Medhurst renders the phrase by 'the five senses,' which is plainly inadmissible. Gaubil gives for it—'les cinq occupations ou affaires.'

From the language of p. 4,—敬用五事, we gather that the 'aspect,' 'the speech,' &c., are not themselves the 事, but what give occasion to them. 貌=容儀, 'carriage,' 'demeanour.' 恭, 從, &c., describe the several virtues or desirable characteristics of the 'businesses' (五事之德). 言曰從, —從=順, 'accordance,' that is, obedience to right and reason. It is strange that the old interpreters, Gan-kwŏ, K'ang-shing, and Ma Yung, all agree in defining 從 by 可從, making the meaning to be—'the virtue of speech is that it move others to follow the speaker.' This is manifestly wrong. 睿=通乎

明聽日聰思日

睿恭作肅從作

父明作哲聰作

謀睿作聖。○

八政一日食二

日貨三日祀四

日司空五日祀四

徒六日司寇七

日賓八日師。○

四五紀一日歲

(八節)

(七節)

ness; of hearing, distinctness; and of thinking, perspicaciousness. The respectfulness becomes manifest in gravity; accordance *with* reason, in orderliness; the clearness, in wisdom; the distinctness, in deliberation; and the perspicaciousness, in sageness.

7　[iii.] "Third, of the eight objects of government:—the first is called food; the second, commodities; the third, sacrifices; the fourth, the minister of works; the fifth, the minister of instruction; the sixth, the minister of crime; the seventh, *the entertainment of* guests; the eighth, the army.

8　[iv.] "Fourth, of the five arrangements.—The first is called the year; the second, the month; the third, the day; the fourth, the

微, 'penetrating to what is minute.' 肅, 乂, &c., describe the consummation of those virtues (五德之用),—what they come to, as is indicated by the 作.

These businesses are represented as being in the human person what the five elements are in nature. Demeanour is the human correspondency of water, speech that of fire. But again leaving all this, can we tell what the writer would be at? Lin Che-k'e refers to what Mencius says, VII., Pt. I., xxxviii.,—'The bodily organs with their functions belong to our Heaven-conferred nature; but a man must be a sage before he can satisfy the design of his bodily organization;' and then adds that this paragraph contains the science of doing this. Certainly if a man have attained to the results here exhibited, he has made much progress in self-government and personal cultivation.

P. 7. *The eight objects of government.* Medhurst translates 八政 by 'the eight Regulators,' and Gaubil by 'les huit regles du Gouvernement.' It means the eight things to be attended to in government, its objects or departments. They seem to be stated in the order of their importance in the view of the speaker. 'Food' belongs to the department of agriculture, and 'commodities' or 'goods' to that of trade and commerce. These two things being secured, the people would have the essentials of life, and would be able to attend to their duties to spiritual beings and to the dead. Then would come in the minister of works, to secure the comfort of their dwellings; and the minister of instruction to teach them all their moral duties; and the minister of crime to deter them from evil. All festive ceremonies, all the intercourses of society, could then be regulated; and finally the efficiency of the army would be maintained, to secure the general well-being of the State.

It will be seen that the three first and two last are the objects to be attended to in their several departments, while the intermediate three are the names of the ministers. No account can be given of this peculiarity of the style. So the author was pleased to write,—very unsatisfactorily.

P. 8. *The five subjects of arrangement.* Medhurst calls the 五紀, the 'five Arrangers,' and Gaubil, 'les cinq Periodes.' He observes in a note that '紀 is used for chronicles and annals; for a revolution of the stars, of cycles, of years; and that it may express a fixed point for chronology and astronomy.' The term properly denotes 'the sorting of threads of silk,' and thence is applied to the digesting of chronicles and arranging of annals. It is hard to say whether it is intended in the text for the objective work of arranging the measures of the things spoken of, or, for those things as measured and arranged.

歲＝天時之一周, 'a complete revolution of the seasons.' 月, 'the moon,' is

極　厥　厥　五　其　五　五　日、二
錫　庶　庶　福　有　皇　曰　四　曰
汝　民　民　用　極　極　曆　曰　月、
保　于　惟　敷　斂　皇　數。　日　三
極。　汝　時　錫　時　建　　　星　曰
　　　　　　　　　　　　　　辰、

<small>九畴</small>

stars and planets, and the zodiacal signs; and the fifth, the calendaric calculations.

9　　[v.] "Fifth, of royal perfection.—The sovereign having established his highest point of excellence, he concentrates in himself the five happinesses, and then diffuses them so as to give them to his people:—then on their part the multitudes of the people, resting

here = 'month,' the period of a lunation,' including the determination of new and full moon, and the intermediate phases. 日, 'the sun,' is here = 'a day.' 星辰,—see Can. of Yaou,' p. 3. 歷數,—comp. the use of this phrase in the Canon of Shun, p. 14. It is here used, in its primary meaning, of the computations by which the measures of the year, the month, the day, &c., are determined, and the calendar fixed.

This division of the Plan is substantially the same as Yaou's instructions to his astronomers. The language is too brief to tell us what improvement had been made in the science of astronomy between the time of Yaou, and that of king Woo

Pp. 9—16.. *Royal perfection*　Medhurst translates 皇極 by 'the princely perfections;' and Gaubil, by 'le terme du Souverain, on le milieu du Souverain.' Gan-kwŏ had defined the terms by 大中, 'the great Mean,' and his explanation seems to have been unquestioned till the time of the Sung dynasty. Then Choo He insisted that 皇 must be taken here in the sense of 君, 'prince,' 'sovereign,' referring to the way in which it is interchanged with 王 in par. 14 (皇之皇君之王）. Choo's criticism is correct.—He is correct also in rejecting the definition of 極 by 中. 極 is 'the utmost point,'—the extreme of excellence, realized in the person of the sovereign, and

serving as an example and attractive influence to all below, both ministers and people. It is supposed to be *in* the centre, the exact middle, but it should not be called the centre or Mean. Take its primary application to 'the beam forming the ridge of a house:'—that is the highest point of the roof, on which the other parts rest, and it is in the centre of it; but it is called 極 and not 中. By 'royal perfection' we are to understand the sovereign, all that he ought to be. Ts'ae dwells upon it in its relation to his personal character, exhibiting all the virtues. Others say it is the accumulation of the personal and governmental excellences described in the previous divisions of the Plan. Our best way is to leave it in its own vagueness.

I have already observed that no place is found for this in the numerical scheme of the 'Great Plan,' arranged according to the principles of the Yih King. There are only 8 diagrams, not 9. This might have shown the critics that this Book was not to be treated on those principles. 9. 斂時（＝是）五福,—'collects these five happinesses,' that is, collects, concentrates them in his own person （斂集是五福于皇躬; see the 日講). Happiness, it is supposed, invariably follows virtue;—compare in the 'Counsels of Yu,' p. 5, 惠迪吉, 從逆凶, 惟影響. The 'five happinesses' must be those of the last Division, and we are surprised to find them mentioned here, with the definitive 時＝是 before them. It is not to be wondered at that Hung Mae (洪邁) should have proposed to remove from this down to 錫之福 in p. 11, to the ninth division. The difficulty is a little lightened by taking 時＝於

而康而色曰、　咎皇則受之、　于極不罹于　則念之不協　有為有守汝　厥庶民有猷　皇作極。○凡^{十一節}　無有比德惟　無有淫朋　○凡^{十節}厥庶民、

(Chinese source has interlinear节 markers 十節 and 十一節)

10 in your perfection, will give to you the preservation of it. That the multitudes of the people have no lawless confederacies, and that men *in office* have no selfish combinations, will be an effect of the sovereign's establishing his highest point of excellence.

11 Among all the multitudes of the people, when any have counsel, and conduct, and keep themselves from evil, do you bear them in mind; those who do not come up to the highest excellence, and *yet* do not involve themselves in crime, let the sovereign receive; and when a placid

是, 'thereon' or 'thereby,' as in the translation. 用敷錫厥庶民,—'uses them, diffusing and giving them to his multitudinous people.' The king, not able to be happy himself only, seeks to make his people happy;—it is not said by what methods. 惟時, 云云,—Ts'ae expands this:—當時之 民守,亦皆於君之極,與之保也, 言皇極君民所以相與者 如此, 'the people, after that, guard and preserve the perfection of the sovereign for him, not daring to lose it or let it drop. This is what is shown by 錫保. The whole tells us what a mutual interest the ruler and the people have in this royal perfection.' It is really difficult to say what the whole tells us. The student will not fail to observe how the viscount of Ke begins here to address himself to king Woo.—汝極. 10. *Royal perfection will banish from the empire all selfish confederacies.* 淫朋=邪黨, 'bad, corrupt parties.' 淫 has here its frequent meaning of 過, 'beyond bounds.' Comp. 朋淫于 家 in the 'Yih and Tseih,' p. 8. 人無有 比德,—the 人 here, in opp. to the 庶 民 above, is understood to mean 有位之 人, 'men having office.' 德 is used in a bad sense. 比德=私相比附, 'selfish combining.' 作極 is about *i. q.* 建極

of the last par. Perhaps 作 indicates the various efforts and steps of progress by which 建, the point of establishment, is attained.

11. *How royal perfection will be seen in dealing with superior men, and with inferior men also, bringing the latter to approve and attain to the highest excellence.* 有猷有為 are men 'mighty in words and deeds.' They are supposed further to be 有守, to have that firm and resolved nature, which will sustain them against temptation. 念之, 'think of them,' 'bear them in mind.' This is = 'give to such your confidence. You may repose trust in them.' 不協于極,—'do not harmonize with—have not yet attained to—the highest excellence.' 不罹于咎 = 不陷於惡. The 不—而不, with the adversative force of 而, 'and yet.' These are a class of mediocre individuals, different from and inferior to the former. 而康而色,—Gan-kwŏ, taking 而=汝, took this as addressed to king Woo:—汝當安汝顏色以謙下人, 'you ought to compose your countenance, and condescend to those inferior men.' But he is then obliged to understand another 人 as the nominative to 曰,—'when men say,' &c,. It is better to take, with Choo He, 而康 而色, as referring to the class of men just described, and = 'when they are pleased, and look so, saying,' &c.. Ts'ae says:—見於

予攸好德汝則錫之福時人斯其惟皇之極。○無虐煢十二節獨而畏高明。○人十三節之有能有為使羞其行而邦其昌凡厥正人既富方穀汝弗能使有好于而家時人斯其辜而其無好德汝雖于其無好德汝雖

satisfaction appears in their countenances, and they say—'Our love is fixed on virtue,' do you then confer favour on them. Those men

12 will in this way advance to the perfection of the sovereign. Do not oppress the friendless and childless; do not fear the high and

13 illustrious. When men have ability and administrative power, cause them still more to cultivate their conduct, and the prosperity of the country will be promoted. All right men, having a competency, will go on to be good: If you cannot make men have what they love in their families, they will only proceed to be guilty of crime;

外而有安和之色,發於中而有好德之言,云云. 錫之福,—福 here = 祿, one of the 'five happinesses.' 時(=是)人其惟皇之極,—the 'Daily Explanation' paraphrases this:—將見惟是庶民感發于錫福而念受之已深鼓舞歸惟皇之極而信能以保極矣斯同

12. Ts'ae says this par. completes the meaning of the one which precedes, and serves to introduce that which follows. To me it interrupts the train of thought, fugitive as that is. Gan-kwŏ says that 煢=單無兄弟, 'solitary, without brothers,' and that 獨 is 無子, 'childless.'

13. Ts'ae says that this paragraph speaks of 'men who are in office' (此言有位者也.) This is in accordance with the distinction made between 庶民 and 人 in par. 10. This is the general view of the critics. I do not think it can be altogether sustained. The 'men' may not be in office, but only aspirants for it. They are inferior to those first

mentioned in par. 11, having the ability, and the practical capacity, but being without the conservative (有守) element. If they can be led on to this—使羞(=進)其行—they may be employed, and their employment will conduce to the prosperity of the country. 凡厥正人,—Gan-kwŏ takes 正人 in a moral sense as = 正直之人, 'correct men.' I think his view is right. Ts'ae understands the phrase in an official sense, and says it = 在官之人, 'men who are in official employment.' The phrase may be so taken; but the other view suits the whole paragraph better. 既富,—'being enriched,' having remunerative office conferred on them. 穀=善, 'good.' 方穀,—'then they will be good.' Ts'ae makes this = 'then you may require them to be good.' The idea is the same with that which Mencius often insists on,—that men, when raised above the pressure of want, are likely, may be expected, to cultivate the moral virtues. Though I have followed Gan-kwŏ in his view of 正人, I cannot accept his explanation of this 方穀; —see the 註疏. 汝弗能……其辜,—the principal difficulty here is with 有好于而家. I take 好 in the 3d tone,

錫之福其作汝用咎。○〔十四節〕無偏無陂遵王之義無有作好遵王之道。無有作惡遵王之路遵王道無黨王道蕩蕩無黨無偏王道平平無

while they do not love virtue, though you confer favour on them, they will involve you in the guilt of employing them *thus* evil.

14   "Without deflection, without unevenness,
        Pursue the Royal righteousness;
        Without any selfish likings,
        Pursue the Royal way;
        Without any selfish dislikings,
        Pursue the Royal path;
        Without deflection, without partiality,
        Broad and long is the Royal path.
        Without partiality, without deflection,
        The Royal path is level and easy;

and 有好 as = 有所好, 'to have what they love,' meaning the means of comfortable living. 而家＝其所有家, 'their families;'—the 而 being taken as merely a pause or rest of the voice. Possibly it may＝ 汝, 'your,' and 家 may be, by synecdoche, for 國家, so that 而家＝'your country.' I prefer the other construction however.

時人斯其辜＝是人則將陷於罪. The whole is in opposition to the preceding clause.—'Let the sovereign employ and remunerate those able and well-meaning men, and they will go on to be really good. If on the contrary they are neglected, and left to suffer penury, they will lose their self-respect, and proceed to become evil.' Hoo Yih-chung (胡一中; Yuen dyn.) explains the passage very much in the same way. He says:—好者，而若自藉其家祿汝不顧于罪有厚善，且所謂當爲彼無陷於罪家，汝能富家也，官方使之有重之足，之其將愛長富祿于人用自正之先重是咎者凡使不愛則無⋯⋯用咎，—such men, falling off into

crime, may afterwards be put in remunerating offices; but the opportunity has been lost by the sovereign. He will only now reap the fruit of his want of wisdom in dealing with them in the past.

P. 14. *An ancient Song, descriptive of the royal perfection, and stimulating men to imitate it.* We may compare with it the songs of Shun and Kaou-yaou in the 'Yih and Tseih.' The lines are composed of four characters, and every two lines rhyme together after a fashion. The general opinion is that the song was not composed by the viscount of Ke, but that it was a well-known piece, which had come down from the Hea times, and which he recites to king Woo. 無偏無陂，遵王之義—Sze-ma Ts'een gives 頗 for 陂, and there can be no doubt this was the reading till the reign of the emperor Heuen-tsung (玄宗) of the T'ang dynasty. A proclamation of his, in the year 744, is still extant, ordering the change from 頗 to 陂, that there might be a rhyme with 義, and referring to the language of the Yih in the diagram 泰,—無平不陂, as suggesting the latter character, which is in meaning much the same as the other. But we might still retain 頗, and read 義 as *go*, to rhyme with it. 儀, which is a derivative from it, is allowed to be sometimes pro-

反無側王
道正直會
其有極歸
其有極。○
曰皇極之
＋五
敷言是彝
是訓于帝
其訓。○
厥庶民極
之敷言是
凡
十六節

Without perversity, without one-sidedness,
The Royal path is right and straight.
Seeing this perfect excellence,
Turn to this perfect excellence."

15   He went on to say, "This amplification of the Royal perfection contains the unchanging *rule*, and is the *great* lesson ;—yea, it is the
16 lesson of God.   All the multitudes, instructed in this amplification of the perfect excellence, and carrying it into practice, will approxi-

nounced so; and, in fact, 我 is the phonetic element in 義 itself.   Këang Shing edits—無偏無頗,遵王之誼. The dict. also says that 誼 was the reading of the old text. I have not found any authority for this.

Ts'ae observes that 偏, 陂, 好 and 惡, in the first three couplets, are descriptive of risings of selfishness in one's own mind, and 偏, 黨, 反, and 側, in the next three, are descriptive of the manifestations of selfishness in one's conduct.   A distinction is made between 道 and 路 in this way :—道 is the ideal character of the Royal course, always right (以其爲事物之當然曰道); 路 is that course, as it is to be actually trodden by all (以其爲天下之共由曰路).   王道平平,—平 is read *p'een*, to rhyme with 偏. The phrase is explained by 平易.   會其有極·歸其有極,—Lin Che-k'e says on this:—建極者如北辰之居所,而會其極,歸其極者,則如衆星之拱北辰也, 'The perfection, set up, is like the north pole-star occupying its place. Meeting with the perfection and turning to it, is like all the other stars moving towards—doing homage to—the pole star.'

Pp. 15, 16. *The viscount of Ke celebrates the description which he has given of the Royal perfection, and the glorious issue to which it leads.*

15. The 曰, at the beginning, must have 箕子 for its subject. Ts'ae calls it 起語辭, 'a term of introduction'; Hea Seuen, 更端辭, 'a term indicating a change in the discourse or argument.'   皇極之敷言,—'the diffuse discourse of Royal perfection.' We must understand all the amplification which the viscount had given of the phrase 皇極. 是彝,—彝＝常;—'it is constant, invariable.' 是訓,—'it is the lesson' for all.   于帝其訓,—'from God is its lesson.'   We must wish that the language of this par. had been more explicit. I will here again make use of the words of Ch'in Ya-yen, while confessing my own want of appreciation of what awakens so much enthusiasm in him, and other Chinese critics :—

聖人在上,下履吟也。爲一大皇不以訓聖而極
既而於天于天踐誦廢理乎之惟而可之人一
復建天歌偏純謂天言豈天聖天
敷言教躬其可常故於也,是乃之之天
言教身以言以示者使不至敷理,故本之之不
蓋身實教者得惟皇謂理降降者其能一
之實得而惟皇謂理降訓者其而
詠而下惟二理極之也,東東視其能二
天下大故皇謂理降訓者天者二
至理是帝於之天者其而
理訓上異君也。人一而者也
訓上異君也。人二而一者也 16.極

高　柔　弗　克　曰　德　天　子　訓
明　克　友　平　剛　一　下　之　是
柔　沈　剛　康　克　曰　王　光　行、
克。　潛　克　正　三　正　〇　曰、　以
〇　剛　爕　直、　曰　直、　十七節　天　近
惟　克。　友　彊　柔　二　六　子　天

mate to the glory of the son of Heaven, and say, 'The son of Heaven is the parent of the people, and so becomes the sovereign of the empire.'

17 [vi.] "Sixth, of the three virtues.—The first is called correctness and straightforwardness; the second, strong government; and the third, mild government. In peace and tranquillity, correctness and straightforwardness *must sway;* in violence and disorder, strong government *must sway;* in harmony and order, mild government *must sway.* For the reserved and retiring there is the strong rule; for the lofty and intelligent there is the mild rule.

之敷言 is of course 皇極之敷言. Medhurst erroneously translates the clause—'carry out these wide-spread instructions.' The people are supposed to repeat and croon over the amplification,—especially the song, teaching themselves and one another, and to be aroused to carry the lessons into practice, till they attain to a perfection in their degree equal to that of the sovereign in this. 曰 天子.云云,—the people are the subject of the 曰 here. Hea Scuen would refer it to 箕子, like the 曰 in the last par., but he must be wrong. 天子,—'the Son of Heaven;'—see Part III., Bk. IV., 5.

Pp. 17—19. *Of the three virtues.* The three virtues are characteristics of the imperial rule;—they are not personal attributes of the sovereign, but the manifestations of the perfection which is supposed to have been described in the last Division. Their names are 正直, 剛克, and 柔克. Ts'ae makes the names 正直, 剛, and 柔,; but the omission of the 克 in the case of the second and third gives them too much the appearance of personal attributes. The second and third are chiefly dwelt on, this division being supplementary to the last,—to show how the Royal perfection will deal with times and cases of an abnormal character.

17. 正直,—see in p. 14, 王道正直. This is the course that the perfect sovereign will naturally and usually take. 剛克,—'strong subduing.' This is the course of the perfect sovereign, when it is necessary for him to put on his terrors. 柔克, 'mild subduing.' This is his course, when it is proper for him to condescend to weaker natures. 彊弗友,—友, 'friendly,' 'disposed to be friendly,' must here be taken as = 順, 'compliant,' 'obedient.' 爕=和, 'harmonious,' 'mild.' 沈潛,—the former of these characters signifies 'to sink beneath the water,' and the second, 'to dive.' 'Disappearance,' 'being hidden,' belongs to both these things, and hence the combination is used in the text to denote individuals who are reserved and retiring, wanting in force of character. In 高明, 'the high and intelligent,' we have the opposite of them, those in whom the forward element predominates. The 'strong rule' must be applied to the former class,—to encourage them, and the 'mild rule' to the latter,—to repress them. The use of the 'virtues' is thus different from what it appears to be in the clauses that precede. Chinese critics do not venture to find fault with this;—to me it makes the text perplexing and enigmatical.

辟作福、惟辟
威、惟辟玉食、臣
無有作福作威
玉食。○臣之有
十九節
作福作威玉食、
其害于而家、凶
于而國、人用側
頗僻、民用僭忒。
二十節
○七稽疑、擇建

18   "It belongs only to the prince to confer favours, to display the
19 terrors of majesty, and to receive the revenues of the empire.   There
should be no such thing as a minister conferring favours, displaying
the terrors *of justice*, or receiving the revenues of the country.   Such
a thing is injurious to the families, and fatal to the States of the
empire;—small officers become one-sided and perverse, and the people
commit assumptions and excesses.

20 [vii.] "Seventh, of the examination of doubts.—Having chosen and

18, 19. *The prerogatives of the ruler must be strictly maintained.*   Some critics would remove these paragraphs to the last Division.   One certainly does not readily perceive what connection they have with the three virtues that have just been spoken of.   We can hardly venture on the step of removing them, however, and putting them in another place;—we must be content with them where they are, acknowledging the vexation which their inconsequence occasions us.   Only the prince 作福, 'rouses up, employs, the various happinesses;' *i.e.*, he is the source of all favours and dignities.   In the same way he only 作威,—is the source of all punishments and degradations.   惟辟玉食,—'only the prince the gemmeous food.' 玉食＝珍食, 'the pearly or precious food,' each grain of rice or other corn being spoken of as a gem or pearl.   There is no 作, it will be seen, between 辟 and 玉食, and we must therefore supply another verb, and one, it seems to me, of a different meaning.   Lin Che-k'e, without repeating the 作, or supplying any other verb, yet understands the clause according to the analogy of the two preceding ones, and takes the 玉食 as meaning all the badges of distinction and favour conferred by the sovereign on his princes and ministers.   There is thus no intelligible difference between the first clause, 惟辟作福, and this. Ts'ae says that the 玉食, 'the precious grain,' is what the people contribute to their rulers (下之所以奉上).   He must be right. 玉食＝'the revenues' of the State; and we must understand the verb, 享, 'to enjoy,' 'to receive,' before the phrase. According to this view, 辟 is to be interpreted not of the emperor only, but of all the princes, large and small, in their several States as well. K'ang-shing, Ma Yung, and Wang Suh all insist on this. Ma Yung's words are—辟, 君也, 玉食, 美食, 不言王者, 關諸侯也. Gan-kwǒ does not speak distinctly on the point; but Ying-tǎ, in his gloss on the other's annotation, refers to Wang Suh's view, observing that, as the princes, in their several States, had the power of rewards and punishments, and, he might have added, the right to the revenue, this interpretation is perhaps correct.   It does seem strange thus to pass from the person and govt. of the emperor; but so it is.

其害于而家, 凶于而國,
—see on 好于而家, in par. 13.   There is the same difficulty in determining the meaning.   The two last clauses show how the injury and ruin will arise.   There will be a general disorganization of social order, each lower rank trying to usurp the privileges of that above it; —comp. Mencius I., Bk. I., i., 4. 人 and 民 are again opposed to each other, as in the 10th and other paragraphs.

Pp. 20—31. *Of the examination of doubts.* The course proposed for the satisfaction of doubts shows us at how early an age the Chinese had come under the power of absurd supersti-

從二人之言。　筮三人占則從。　廿四節立時人作卜　用二衍忒。　凡七卜五占廿三節　曰貞曰悔。廿二節　曰驛曰克。　雨曰霽曰蒙。　命卜筮。○　廿一節立卜筮人乃

21 appointed officers for divining by the tortoise and by the milfoil,
they are to be charged *on occasion* to perform their duties. *In doing
this*, they will find *the appearances* of rain, clearing up, cloudiness,
22 want of connection, and crossing; and *the symbols*, solidity, and re-
23 pentance. In all *the indications* are seven;—five given by the tortoise,
and two by the milfoil, by which the errors *of affairs* may be
24 traced out. These officers having been appointed, when the operations with the tortoise and milfoil are proceeded with, three men are
to obtain and interpret the indications and symbols, and the *consenting* words of two of them are to be followed.

tions. In the 'Counsels of Yu,' p. 18, that sage proposes to Shun to submit the question of who should be his successor on the throne to divination, and the emperor replies that he had already done so. There is no reason to doubt, therefore, the genuineness of the great Plan, as a relic of the Hea times, from the nature of this part of it. As soon as the curtain lifts from China, and we get a glimpse of its greatest men about four thousand years ago, we find them trying to build up a science of the will of Heaven and issues of events, from various indications given by the shell of a tortoise and the stalks of the milfoil! Gaubil observes that according to the text the tortoise and milfoil were consulted only in doubtful cases. But we may be sure that if such was the practice of the sages, superstitious observances entered largely as a depraving and disturbing element into the life of the people. They do so at the present day. The old methods of divination have fallen into disuse, and I cannot say how far other methods are sanctioned by the government, but the diviners and soothsayers, of many kinds, form a considerable and influential class of society.

Pp. 20—24 contain some hints as to the manner in which divination was practised. The same subject is treated in the Chow Le, Bk. XXIV; but it is hardly possible to get the two accounts into one's mind so as to understand and be able distinctly to describe the subject.

20. *Two kinds of divination and the appointment of officers to superintend them.* The two kinds of divination were—first, that by means of the tortoise, or tortoise-shell rather, called 卜; and that by means of the stalks of the 蓍 plant, called 筮. 'The tortoise,' says Choo He, 'after great length of years becomes intelligent;

and the 蓍 plant will yield, when a hundred years old, a hundred stalks from one root, and is also a spiritual and intelligent thing. The two divinations were in reality a questioning of spiritual beings, the plant and the tortoise being employed, because of their mysterious intelligence, to indicate their intimations. The way of divination by the tortoise was by the application of fire to scorch the tortoise-shell till the indications appeared on it; and that by the stalks of the plant was to manipulate in the prescribed ways forty-nine of them, eighteen different times, till the diagrams were formed'

(龜歲久則靈，蓍生百歲者，神兆，爲掛，而成卦，蓍物之神靈，以蓍卦，龜一本百莖，亦物之問鬼神，以其卦，龜爲，分，故假之以柴灼，十有八變，卜筮靈之法，以明火爇九，卜兆楪扐凡十。法以四)

See the Chapter on Divination in the 'Historical Records' (龜策，列傳，第六十八).

Medhurst says the 蓍 was one of the class of plants called *Achillea millefolium.* Williams calls it 'a sort of labiate plant, like verbena,' thereby leading us to think of the 'holy herb' of Dioscorides, the *verbena officinalis.* The correctness, however, of both these accounts may be doubted. There is a figure of the plant in the 本草綱目（草部隰草類上）;

but I have not yet been able to obtain a specimen to have its botanical name and place exactly determined.

We cannot tell how many were the officers of divination in the earlier dynasties, nor what were their several duties. In the Book of the Chow Le, referred to above, we have the 太卜, or 'grand diviner;' the 卜師, or 'master of divination;' the 龜人, or 'keeper of the tortoises;' the 菙氏, or 'preparer of the wood;' and the 占人, or 'the observers and interpreters of the prognostics.' They were all, observe the critics, required to be men far removed from the disturbing influence of passion and prejudice. Only such could be associated with the methods of communication between higher intelligences and men.

Pp. 21—23. *The various indications.* 21. The appearances here described were those made on the shell of the tortoise. The way in which they were obtained seems to have been this.—The outer shell of the tortoise was taken off, leaving the inner portion on which were the marks of the lines of the muscles of the creature, &c. A part of this was selected for operation, and smeared with ink. The fire was then applied beneath, and the ink, when it was examined, according as it had been variously dried by the heat, gave the appearances mentioned. 霽 is defined as 雨止, 'rain stopping,' = 'the weather clearing up.' 蒙 = 蒙昧不明, 'cloudiness, obscurity.' 驛, for which K'ung-shing and others have 圛, is understood to mean certain marks scattered about, without connection or relation;—see the remarks, by the editors of Yung-ch'ing's Shoo, on Gan-kwo's definition of the term by 落驛不屬, and Ts'ae's by 絡驛不屬. 克 = 交錯, meaning lines or cracks in the ink crossing each other. Ts'ae says these appearances belonged severally to the different elements,—that of rain to water, of cloudiness to wood, &c. The whole operation was a piece of absurdity, and we have too little information to say anything certain about it. 22. 貞 and 悔 were the names given to the diagrams formed by the manipulation of the stalks of the *she*. In a complete diagram, composed of two of the eight primary ones, the lower figure is called 'the inner diagram' (內卦), and was styled 貞; the upper figure is called 'the outer diagram' (外卦), and was styled 悔. There were also other conditions according to which these names of 貞 and 悔 were applied to the different figures. How far, however, they obtained in the Hea and Shang dynasties we cannot tell. Our present Yih King is entirely a book of the Chow dynasty;

but the text shows that the manipulation of Fuh-he's lines, and the derivation of meanings from the combination of them were practised, at least in some extent, in the earlier times. The meaning of the names 貞 and 悔 is very much debated; and instead of entering on the discussion here, I will content myself with the words of Heang Gan-she (項安世; Sung dyn.), one of the most voluminous writers on the Yih,—'We only know that the inner diagram was 貞 and the outer 悔; we do not know what was intended by those designations.'

23. We have here a *resumé* of the two last parr. with the addition of the enigmatical phrase 衍忒 at the end. 卜五, 占用二, —we must understand a first 用 between 卜 and 五. The 卜占 here is equivalent to 卜筮 in p. 20, so that 筮 is exchanged for 占. 衍忒,—衍 = 推, 'to infer,' 'to push or carry out;' 忒 may be taken as either = 差, 'error,' or = 變. Ts'ae adopts the former meaning, and interprets—'By this means the errors of human affairs may be traced out,' that is, may be indicated before they occur, and so be avoided. The 'Daily Explanation,' expanding this view, says—所謂推衍者, 推衍于未有過差之先, 非遲廻顧慮于已然之後. Choo He adopted the former meaning, and interpreted—'every changing form of indication and symbol being traced out and determined.' See the quotation from him in the 集說; still, when the operations, thus many times varied, had been concluded, the object would be to obtain the guidance of their results in the conduct of affairs. Woo Ch'ing and many others prefer to say that they do not understand the phrase at all.

24. *Care to be taken in performing the divination.* 立時人作卜筮, 一時 = 是, and the whole = 既立是所擇之人, 以作卜筮之官, 'Having appointed the men thus selected to be the officers of divination.' 三人占,—we are to suppose that they have been charged to perform their duties (乃命卜筮, p. 20), and then three men divine in each way. 占 in the last par. was = 筮; here it is used both for 卜 and 筮, including not only the various manipulations, but also the interpreting the results obtained. It is supposed that each man went through his operation further on a different method.

廿五節
汝則有大疑、謀及乃心、謀及卿士、謀及庶人、謀及卜筮。○汝則從、廿六節卿士從、庶民從、龜從、筮從、是之謂大同、身其康彊、子孫其逢吉。○汝則從、龜從、筮從、卿士廿七節逆、庶民逆、吉。○卿士從、龜廿八節從、筮從、汝則逆、庶民逆、吉。○庶民從、筮從、龜從、汝則廿九節逆、卿士逆、吉。○汝則從、三十節龜

25 "If you have doubts about any great matter, consult with your own heart; consult with your nobles and officers; consult with the
26 masses of the people; consult the tortoise and milfoil. If you, the tortoise, the milfoil, the nobles and officers, and the common people all consent to a course, this is what is called a great concord, and the result will be the welfare of your person, and good fortune to
27 your descendants. If you, the tortoise, and the milfoil all agree, while the nobles and common people oppose, the result will be
28 fortunate. If the nobles and officers, the tortoise, and the milfoil all agree, while you oppose and the common people oppose, the
29 result will be fortunate. If the common people, the tortoise and the milfoil all agree, while you and the nobles and officers oppose,
30 the result will be fortunate. If you and the tortoise agree, while

Pp. 25—31. *Rules for the application of the results of divination, and the varying conclusions of men, to the solution of doubts.* 25. 大疑 is not 'great doubts,' but 'doubts on a great matter.' The 'Daily Explanation' says,—國家大事, 有行止可疑而未決者, 云云. It is not to be supposed that the emperor would on every little matter or private occasion consult both men and spirits in the way proposed. We must keep in mind that 'the Great Plan' is a scheme of government. There are five parties whose opinions were to be weighed:—first, the emperor himself; next, his high nobles and officers generally (卿士); third, the common people; fourth, the tortoise; and fifth, the stalks of the *she*. The student will remember how the emperor in the Pwan-kăng complains that the opinions of the people were kept from him. Compare also, pp. 2 and 3 in 'The punitive Expedition of Yin.' Choo He observes that the opinions of men were first taken into consideration, but as they are liable to be affected by ignorance, and selfish considerations, the views of the spirits, above such disturbing influences, and intimated by the divinations, were to have the greater weight in the final determination. 26. *The case of a great concord, all the five parties agreeing.* 27. *The emperor, the tortoise-shell, and the milfoil, all agreeing, carry it over the nobles and officers, and the people.* 28. *The nobles and officers, with the tortoise and milfoil, carry it over the sovereign and people.* 29. *The people, with the tortoise and milfoil, carry it over the sovereign, and the nobles and officers.* 30. *When the sovereign and the tortoise were opposed to all the other parties.* In this case, not only are the

凶。○八[卅二節]　吉用作、　人用靜、　共違于　○龜筮[卅一節]　作外凶。　作內吉、　庶民逆、　卿士逆、　從筮逆、

the milfoil, the nobles and officers, and the common people oppose, internal operations will be fortunate, and external operations will be unlucky. When the tortoise and milfoil are both opposed to the views of men, there will be good fortune in stillness, and active operations will be unlucky.

31

opinions of men divided, but the spirits also give different intimations. The doubt therefore remained, and the difficulty was settled by a compromise! 'Internal affairs,' acc. to Gankwŏ, were cases of marriages, capping, and sacrifices, within the State; 'external affairs' were military expeditions undertaken beyond it. Choo He says:—'In this case, the tortoise opposing and the milfoil consenting, nothing, it would seem, should be undertaken. But the tortoise-shell was supposed to give surer indications than the plant, and as all the human opinions agreed, it was inferred that internal affairs might be proceeded with and would be fortunate!' It is needless to point out the inconsistency of this. 31. *Where the divinations gave results contrary to all the hnman opinions.* In this case the spirits carried it over men. 用靜、吉,—'using stillness, there will be good fortune.' By 'stillness' is meant refraining from the undertaking doubted of.

[Many Chinese critics of more recent times seem to have an uneasy feeling of dissatisfaction on the subject of the ancient divinations; but hardly one has the courage boldly and fairly to disown them. To do so would be inconsistent with the proper veneration for the sages.

Ts'ae Ch'in said:—義之所當爲 而不爲者,非數之所能 知而爲者,亦不占 之;義之所不當爲也,非 義數之疑 非疑而占,謂之 侮,非義而占,謂之欺.' 'Not to do what in right ought to be done:—no rule for this can be obtained from numbers; and no rule can be obtained from them to do what in right ought not to be done. There should be no divination in reference to what would not be right, and no divination where there are no doubts. To divine where there are no doubts is pronounced "a piece of folly;" to do so in reference to what would not be right is pronounced "a piece of deception."'

Woo Ch'ing observed:—天下之事, 卿士庶民,皆不可而猶有使 吉者,蓋自古未之有也

將龜乘矣,說不／君惟以事其賢／人而得多聞之／世民議此習子／後庶異自箕子／行忽說下尚／之卿從天俗／說士邪入雖／子之而商流／箕棄而蓋不俗／有筮信於

'From the oldest time never has anything turned out fortunate which the nobles and officers, with the common people, all disapproved of. Were the statements of the viscount of Ke to obtain currency and credence, the sovereigns of future ages would be found casting away their high ministers and officers, and slighting their people, attending only to the intimations of the tortoise-shell and the *she*. Perverted talk and strange principles would find their way to influence, and there would be no end to the troubles of the empire. These passages belong to the fondness for superstition which was characteristic of the Shang dynasty; accustomed to hear such things said, people believed them, and even a man of worth, like the viscount of Ke, could not keep himself from going with the current of the prevailing custom.' These observations are unusually free and sound, as coming from a Chinese scholar. The man who expressed himself thus should have gone on to bolder conclusions, affecting the reputation for sageness of Yu and Shun, and even of Confucius himself. I am sorry to find a writer, so sensible in general as Hoo Wei, trying to beat down the remarks of Ch'ing with the authority of the great sage:—草廬說經,往往有賢／智之過,而此說尤爲紕繆／夫子隱,而賛之,易曰,探索吉乎／凶,著成天下之亹亹者,莫大百姓之有會／著龜。能天下又謂人可乎別附／所指疑大而其禹筮／也。子禹筬謂以稽以

蕃　敘　各　者　曰　寒　曰　雨、庶
廡。庶　以　來　時、曰　曰　煥　曰　徵、
○　草　其　備、五　風　曰　暘、曰

32　　[viii]. "Eighth, of the various verifications.—They are rain; sunshine; heat; cold; wind; and seasonableness. When the five come all complete, and each is in its proper order, *even* the various

之邪, 使箕子而溺於流俗, 何以爲箕子, 'Ts'aou-loo' [this is a designation by which Woo Ch'ing is known], 'in his remarks upon the Classics, often speaks about the errors of the worthy and wise; but here he errs and commits himself more than usual. The Master, in his observations on the Yih, has said, "To unravel what is confused, and search out what is mysterious; to hook up what is deep, and reach to what is distant,—thus determining whatever will be fortunate or unlucky, and rousing all men to continuous effort: there is nothing better than the use of the *she* and the tortoise-shell" (see the 繫辭 上傳, p. 37. 'The Master' of course is Confucius]. He also says, "Men are consulted; the spirits are consulted; the common people *also* contribute their ability" (繫辭, 下 傳, p. 69), meaning that thus all things doubted of may be determined. Did the great Yu mean anything else than this by his "Examination of Doubts"? and did the viscount of Ke accommodate to that what he said about divination by the tortoise and the milfoil? Had he been sunk in the current of prevailing custom merely, how could he have been the viscount of Ke?']

Pp. 32—38. *Of the various verifications.* Medhurst translates 庶徵 by 'the general verifications;'—rightly, as regards 徵, but wrong, as regards 庶, which = 非 一 'not one merely,' 'many,' 'various.' Gaubil renders the phrase by 'les apparences,'—unhappily. In a note he says:—'I render the Chinese character 徵 by '*apparences*,' not having found any word which would cover the whole extent of its meaning. In the present case, it signifies *meteors, phenomena, appearances*, but in such a sort that those have relation to some other things with which they are connected;—the meteor or phenomenon indicates some good or some evil. It is a kind of correspondence which is supposed, it appears, to exist between the ordinary events of the life of men, and the constitution of the air, according to the different seasons;—what is here said supposes I know not what physical speculation of those times. It is needless to bring to bear on the text the interpretations of the later Chinese, for they

are full of false ideas on the subject of physics. It may be also that the viscount of Ke wanted to play the physicist on points which he did not know.'

Gaubil describes correctly the way in which the character 徵 is here applied, but the translator should not render it from what it is applied to, but according to its proper signification. In the dict. it is defined by 證, 'to bear witness,' 'to attest,' and by 明, 'to illustrate;' and then there is quoted from par. 4 of this Book, 念用庶徵. 'Verifications' is probably as good a term as can be found in our language. The giving the name to the various phenomena in the. text, and making them indicators of the character of men's conduct, is of a piece with the divinations of the last division. It is another form of superstition. If there underlie the words of the viscount of Ke some feeling of the harmony between the natural and spiritual worlds, which occurs to most men at times, and which strongly affects minds under deep religious thought or on the wings of poetic rapture, his endeavour to give the subject a practical application is so shallow that it only strikes us as grotesque and absurd.

The. Division falls into two parts. In the first parr. 32—34, we have a description of the verifying phenomena, and the interpretation of them.

P. 32. 暘 = 日出, 'the sun coming forth,' or = 明, 'brightness,' 'sunshine.' 煥 = 熱 在中, 'warmth diffused,' or = 煖. 'heat.' The meaning of 暘 and 煥 is sufficiently shown by their opposition to 雨 and 寒, 'rain and cold.' 曰時,—I have translated this by 'seasonablenss,' and would extend its meaning to all the preceding verifications, so that there are only five and not six phenomena. The specification of 'five' immediately after (五者來備), and the way in which the phenomena are mentioned in the next par. with the adjunct of 時, seem to require this interpretation. This was the view also of Gan-kwŏ, and is adopted by Choo He and most other critics. Gaubil however, translates 曰時 by '6. Les saisons.' And this view is contend-

卅三節 一極備凶、一極無凶。○ 卅四節 曰休徵、曰肅、時雨若、曰乂、時暘若、曰哲、時燠若、曰謀、時寒若、曰聖、時風若、曰咎徵、曰狂、恆雨若、曰僭、恆暘若、曰豫、恆燠若、曰急、恆寒若、

33 plants will be abundantly luxuriant. Should any one of them be either excessively abundant, or excessively deficient, there is evil.

34 "There are the favourable verifications:—namely, of gravity, which is emblemed by seasonable rain; of orderliness, emblemed by seasonable sunshine; of wisdom, emblemed by seasonable heat; of deliberation, emblemed by seasonable cold; and of sageness, emblemed by seasonable wind. There are also the unfavourable verifications:—namely, of wildness, emblemed by constant rain; of assumption, emblemed by constant sunshine; of indolence, emblemed

ed for by Lin Che-k'e, who understands 時 of 'the round year, the months, and the days,' of which we have the account in the 35th and foll. paragraphs. He took the view from Ts'ae Yuen-too (蔡元度), a critic also of the Sung dyn., earlier than himself. It supposes a more artificial structure of the text than the study of the whole Book authorizes. 各以其敘,-敘=序, 'order,' 'series.' The order of time and the degree of quantity, are both included, (各得其多寡先後之序). 庶草蕃廡,-廡=豐茂, 'abundant,' 'luxuriant.' This is a very simple truth. It is supposed to be mentioned as one of the least consequences of the seasonableness of the various phenomena, from which all others, however great, may be inferred.

33. Gan-kwŏ's expansion of this is——一者備極過甚,則凶,一者極無不至,亦凶,謂不時失叙.

34. *The favourable or good, and the unfavourable or bad, verifications.* The student will see that this par. and the 6th are closely connected. The successful achievement of each of the 'five businesses' has its verification in the character of the phenomena which have been described, and failure in, or the neglect, of them, has also its corresponding outward manifestation. On the 若, with which each clause terminates, Ying-tă observes:—此休咎,皆曰若者,其所致者,皆順其所行,故言若也, 'In every case, good and bad, the issue is in accordance with the course of the conduct, and therefore we find the character 若.' Opposed to 'gravity,' we have 狂,—妄, 'incoherence,' 'wildness.' Opposed to 'orderliness,' we have 僭=差, 'error,' 'presumptuous error.' Opposed to 'wisdom,' there is 豫, 'idleness,' 'indecision' (Wang Suh read 舒, with the same meaning). Opposed to 'deliberation,' there is 急, 'urgency,' 'haste;' and opposed to 'sageness' there is 蒙, 'stupidity.' The various phenomena, by which these qualities good and bad are responded to in nature and providence, are of course all fanciful. Since the Han dynasty, the critics have nearly all abandoned themselves to vain jangling in speculations on the operation of the five elements, and their distributions through the seasons of the year, *en rapport* with the virtues and failings of men. And yet, as we saw on the last Division, many of them do not endorse the statements of the text without misgivings. Ts'ae observes that 'to say on occasion of such and such a 'business' being successfully achieved, there will be the favourable verification corresponding to it, or that on occasion of such and such a 'business' being failed in, there will be the corresponding unfavourable verification, would betray a pertinacious obtuseness, —would show that the speaker was not a man to be talked with on the mysterious opera-

曰蒙、恆風若。○（卅五）王省惟歲、卿士惟月、師尹惟日。○（卅六節）歲月日時無易、百穀用成、乂用明、俊民用章、家用平康。○（卅七節）日月歲時既易、百穀

by constant heat; of haste, emblemed by constant cold; and of stupidity, emblemed by constant wind."

35　He went on to say, "The sovereign is to examine the character of the whole year; nobles and officers, that of the months; and

36　the inferior officers, that of the day. If throughout the year, the month, the day, there be an unchanging seasonableness, all the kinds of grain are matured; the operations of government are wise; heroic men stand forth eminent; and in the families *of the people* there are peace and prosperity. If throughout the year, the month,

37　the day, the seasonableness is interrupted, the various kinds of grain

tions of nature. It is not easy to describe the reciprocal meeting of Heaven and men. The hidden springs touched by failure and success, and the minute influences that respond to them:—who can know these but the man who has apprehended all truth (必曰某事應、某事失、則通矣、得者則咎徵不人幾、休徵亦造未妙之也、膠化易言微、失道知非、得某而天之孰能識之哉)?' This is in effect admitting that the statements of the text can be of no practical use.

Pp. 35—38. We have here apparently an endeavour to show how the 'various verifications are to be thoughtfully made use of,' according to the language of p. 4. By 師尹 we are to understand all the 有司 or inferior officers. See on 庶尹 in the 'Yih and Tseih' p. 10. We may take 師 here as = 庶 or 眾; with regard to the rank of the 尹 which the text mentions, the whole scope of the passage shows it could only be of a lower grade. The sovereign stands to his nobles and great officers as the year to months, including and leading on them all; and they again stand to their inferior *employés* as the month to the days. Must the sovereign then, by the rule here laid down, wait till the year's end before examining his character and ways? I suppose, as he com-

prehends all dignities in himself, he must be every month doing on himself the examination work of a high officer, and every day that of an inferior. The editors of Yung-ching's Shoo say on this point:—'The sovereign, the high officers, and the inferior officers, it is said here, must examine severally the year, the month, and the day; but this is spoken in a general and vague way, with reference to the different rank of their offices:—we must not stick to a phrase. For instance, a violent wind shall in a day do injury to the grain fields. The wind lasts for a single day only, but its injurious effects extend to the months and the year. Shall we make it relate to the inferior officers? or to the high officers and the sovereign? Whenever any unfavourable verification happens, no one should put the thing off himself. Every one should examine himself, and do so with regard to every matter.' Experience and their own sense have made many in China wiser in many things than their classics, but they will not give up the national idols.

36, 37. 時無易.—'if the times do not change.' But we must take 時 in the same way as in p. 34, meaning 'seasonableness.' The meaning is that if rain and sunshine, heat and cold, and wind all occur seasonably, the various effects enumerated will follow. There is a grain of truth in the assertions, and a bushel of nonsense. Hoo Wei says that 乂 is used with reference to the government of the court (以朝政言之), and 俊民 of individuals who have no office (以無位者言之), while 家 refers to those who are in

用不成乂用
昏不明俊民
用微家用不
宷。庶民惟　卅八節
星星有好風
星有好雨日
月之行則有
冬有夏月之
從星則以風
雨。九五福　卅九節

do not become matured; the operations of government are dark and unwise; heroic men are reduced to obscurity; and in the families *of the people* there is no repose.

38　　　"The common people are like the stars. Some stars love the wind, and some love the rain. The course of the sun and moon give winter and summer. The course of the moon among the stars gives wind and rain.

office. In regard to the last clause, I prefer the view which is given in the translation.

[Gaubil has here the following note:—'There is supposed here a mutual correspondence between the ordinary events of the life of men, especially of kings and grandees, and the constitution of the air; but instead of adopting the false ideas which the viscount of Ke may have had on that subject we may reflect on what has been thought about it in Europe, and on what many people still think and say of a culpable and dangerous character. It appears that the Chinese have admitted a homogeneous matter in all bodies; that they have admitted a soul subsisting after the destruction of the body; that they have admitted spirits, and one spiritual Being, Master of heaven, of earth, and of men. But they have been bad physicists, and have troubled themselves little with metaphysics or with logic. They have not thought too much (?) of examining the grounds of their reasoning on the nature of beings; and they have in no way fathomed the question of the union of the soul with the body, nor that of the operations of the soul.'

There is no danger of our adopting the notions of the viscount of Ke on the correspondence between the weather and the characters of men. A great service would be done by the Sinologue, who should take up 'the Great Plan,' and produce a commentary on it for Chinese readers, clearly and minutely unfolding the errors on the constitution of nature and the course of providence of which it is full. From this ground we might go on to shake the stronghold of their confidence in all the ancient teachings and the wisdom of their so-called sages.]

P. 38. *The people should examine the stars.* 庶民惟星,—Medhurst translates this— 'The common people are like the stars,' and Gaubil, in the same way,—'Les étoiles représentent les peuples.' This also is the view of Ts'ae, who says:—民之麗乎土, 猶星之麗乎天也. But this would make the paragraph of a different character entirely from those immediately preceding. The text is evidently analogous with the clauses of par. 35, and the 省 which we must understand there of the 卿士 and 師尹, we must understand here also after 庶民. 'The people should examine the stars.' But nothing is said of 'verifications' in connection with the stars and the people;—what was to result from the examination of the stars? 'The people,' says Woo Ch'ing, 'would know when it was summer, and when it was winter, when they might expect wind, and when they might expect rain. Knowing these things they could carry on their labours and take their precautionary measures accordingly.' We thus find a meaning in the paragraph, though of a different kind from what the preceding paragraphs would lead us to look for. On the view of the first clause, taken by Ts'ae and the commentators generally, the whole paragraph appears equally out of place, and no reasonable meaning can be given to it. The constellation 箕—the hand of Sagittarius—is said to bring wind, and 畢, or Hyades, to bring rain. Ts'ae goes at great length into the courses of the sun and moon, but all according to the accounts of the astronomers of the Han dynasty. The text specifies no stars from which we might determine the place of the sun in the heavens at the solstices or equinoxes, when the Book was made.

六曰弱。
日貧五曰惡
疾三曰憂四
凶短折二曰
○六極一曰
　四十節
五曰考終命。
四曰攸好德
富三曰康寧
一曰壽二曰

39　[ix]. "Ninth, of the five happinesses.—The first is long life; the second is riches; the third is soundness of body and serenity of mind; the fourth is the love of virtue; the fifth is an end crowning the life.
40　As to the six extremities again, the first is misfortune, shortening the life; the second is sickness; the third is sorrow; the fourth is poverty; the fifth is wickedness; the sixth is weakness."

Pp. 39, 40. *Of the five happinesses and six extremities.* It is said, in p. 4, that 'a hortatory use is to be made of the five happinesses,' and 'an awing use of the six extremities.' It is not easy to see how this division enters into the scheme of the Great Plan. Tsăng Kung (曾鞏) says:—'The nine divisions all describe the course of the sovereign. The happinesses and extremities are conditions by which the sovereign examines his own attainments and defects in reference to the people. That these happinesses should be among the people, is what the sovereign should aim after; and the extremities' being among them is what he should be standing in awe of;'—see the 集說. Hoo Wei, on the other hand, says:—'The five conditions of happiness and six conditions of suffering, are by the doing of Heaven, and not from any arrangements of men. We have it said in the division on Royal Perfection, "He concentrates in himself the five happinesses, and then diffuses them so as to give them to his people;"—we have therefore in this place only the names of the happinesses and their opposites, and nothing about their use' (五福六極設在目, 非人之道具但列其皆天之所爲，也其斂時敷錫之道故此但列其皇極章中，而不言其用).

39. 壽,—'longevity;' without specifying any number of years. Gan-kwŏ says it means 120 years; but this is absurd. A man dying over 50 is spoken of by the Chinese as not having a short life. 60 and upwards is reckoned longevity. Ts'ae says that with long life all the other happinesses can be enjoyed, and therefore it occupies the first place among them. 富,—'riches;' probably meaning a competency according to the rank and station. Lin Che-k'e says, 'a sufficiency for food and clothing is 富.' 康寧 = 'freedom from sickness,' *i.e.*, good health,—according to Gan-kwŏ. Modern critics extend the meaning, as in the translation.—形康而心寧. 攸好德 = 所好者德, 'when virtue is what is loved.' The meaning, says Lin Che-k'e, is a natural disposition tending to the love of virtue rather than of pleasures and other lower things. 考終命,—Ts'ae explains this by the words of Mencius, VII., Pt. I., ii. 1, 順受其正, 'submissively receiving all the will of Heaven.' 考 is generally explained here by 成, 'to accomplish,' and the happiness is that of 'accomplishing to the end the will of Heaven.' This does not differ materially from the view of the translation, which has the advantage of making more evident the proper meaning of 考.

40. 六極,—極 = 窮 = 'exhaustion,' 'being brought to extremity.' It denotes the opposite of 福. 凶短折 is literally 'disastrous short breaking.' The meaning is —the life coming to an untimely and disastrous close. 疾 and 憂 are the opposite of 康寧. 惡—Gan-kwŏ explained this by 醜陋, 'ugliness,' and the last extremity—弱, by 尫劣, 'feebleness;'—perhaps in both cases with some reference to the mind as well as the body. 惡 means probably boldness in what is evil, and 弱, weakness in what is good. The viscount of Ke was not so successful in enumerating the 'extremities,' as with the 'happinesses.'

[Gaubil, in a concluding note, thinks it not unlikely that the viscount of Ke wished to speak of the 'Book of Lŏ,' and under pretence of explaining this enigma, 'has given very excellent instructions on the duties which princes and subjects ought to observe.' I am unable to agree with the learned Jesuit. The Great Plan is little less of an enigma than the Book of Lŏ. It is full of perplexities and absurdities. There are some right principles of morals and government in it, but after hearing it all, king Woo must have been more in the dark than when he went to the viscount at first with the remark that he did not know how the virtues in men's various relations should be brought forth in their proper order.]

I append here a scheme of the whole Plan, modified from that which is given among the cuts in Yung-ching's Shoo :—

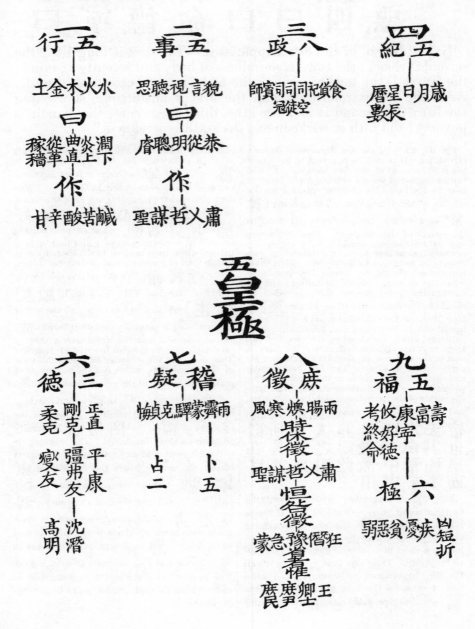

THE BOOKS OF CHOW.

BOOK V. THE HOUNDS OF LEU.

旅 保 厥 旅 八 于 遂 惟　一節
獒 乃 獒 厎 蠻 九 通 克　　旅
用 作 太 貢 西 夷 道 商　　獒

1　　After the conquest of Shang, the way being open to the nine
wild and the eight savage tribes, the people of the western tribe of
Leu sent in as tribute some of their hounds, on which the Great-
guardian made "The Hounds of Leu," by way of instruction to the
king.

THE NAME OF THE BOOK.—旅 獒, 'The
Hounds of Leu.'　The 37th note of the
Preface, on the subject of this Book, says that
the 'western Leu' made an offering of some of
their hounds' (西 旅 獻 獒). Leu, therefore, is to be looked for in the west. It was
the name of one of the rude tribes, lying in
that quarter, beyond the 'nine provinces' of the
empire. 獒 is the name of a kind of hound.
It was, acc. to the 爾 雅, '4 feet—ancient
feet, that is—high.' The 說 文 describes it
as 'knowing the mind of man, and capable of
being employed' (知 人 心 可 使 者).
From an instance of its use, quoted in the
集 傳 from Kung-yang, it was evidently a
blood-hound.　　The critics generally understand the term in the text in the singular;—I
know not why. There is nothing in the Book,
and no ancient references to it, which should
make us do so. We more naturally take it in
the plural, and it seems to me more likely that
several hounds, and not one only, would be
sent to king Woo.
　This is one of the Books found only in Gan-
kwŏ's text. K'ang-shing and Ma Yung had not
seen it, and they have strangely mistaken the
meaning of the prefatory note. '獒,' says

K'ang-shing, 'is read like 豪. The rude tribes
of the west had no princes, but gave the title
of 酋 豪 to the strong among them, who
governed them for the time. The people of the
tribe sent at this time the principal man of
their chiefs, to present himself at the court of
Chow;'—see the 後 案, in loc. But this
view carries its own refutation on the face
of it. The words of the prefatory note are that
'the western Leu presented—as an offering,
expressive of their subjection—their 獒.' To
suppose that their chief was thus made an
article of tribute is absurd. Ch'ing's paraphrase
of 獻 獒 by 遣 來 獻 見 于 周 is
quite inadmissible. The signification of 獒 as
='hound' is not to be disturbed.　　The
Book belongs to the division of 'Instructions.'
　CONTENTS. The Leu people having sent some
of their hounds to king Woo, and he having
received them, or intimated that he would do
so, the Great-guardian remonstrated with him,
showing that to receive such animals would be
contrary to precedent, would be dangerous to
the virtue of the sovereign, and was not the
way to deal with outlying tribes and nations.
　The reader will think that the Book is much
ado about a very small matter, and in truth it
is so. It receives an interest, however, when

用。服　方　邇　無　夷　慎　呼、○　訓
○　食　物　畢　有　咸　德　明　二節曰　于
王三節器　惟　獻　遠　賓。四　王　嗚　王。

2　　He said, "Oh! the intelligent kings have paid careful attention to their virtue, and the wild tribes on every side have willingly acknowledged subjection to them. The nearer and the more remote have all made offerings of the productions of their countries;—

we see in it a specimen of the feeling and procedure by which the rulers of China have all along sought to regulate their intercourse with foreign nations. 'When the sovereign does not look on foreign things as precious, foreigners will come to him:'—this language is a good exponent of the normal Chinese policy. A self-complacent assumption of superiority—superiority both in wisdom and in power—has always been displayed. I have read references to the steam-engine with its various applications, from men versed in all the learning of China, as if it were nothing more than a toy, to be thought of just as the duke of Shaou thought of the hounds of Leu. Statesmen and people are now, in this nineteenth century, having a rude awakening from their dream.

P. 1. *The occasion on which the Book was made.* This par. might have had a place in the Preface, and Ts'ae calls it 'the proper preface of the Hounds of Leu' (此旅獒之本序). 惟克商,—'on the conquest of Shang.' The 'Daily Explanation' expands the clause:—惟我周武王既克商而有天下. The 'General History' refers the tribute of the hounds to the 14th year of king Woo, B.C. 1,120. 遂通道于九夷八蠻,—by the 'nine E and eight Man,' we are to understand the barbarous tribes generally,—expressed in the Can. of Shun, p. 16, by the phrase 蠻夷, and by 蠻貊 in the 'Completion of the War,' p. 6. See also on the 'Tribute of Yu,' Pt. ii., p. 22. The difft. rude tribes round about the nine provinces of the empire are variously enumerated. Here we have the '9 夷 and 8 蠻;' in the Le Ke, Bk. XIV., 明堂位, p. 3, we have the '9 夷, 8 蠻, 6 戎 and 5 狄;' in the Chow Le, Bk. XXXIII., 夏官, 司馬, 第四之六, 職方氏, p. 1, we have the 4 夷, 8 蠻, 7 閩, 9 貉, 5 戎, and 6 狄;' in the 國語魯語 下, we have 'the '9 夷 and 100 蠻.'

The numbers are not to be pressed, and we must be content with finding a statement in the text, that the wild tribes all around came or sent to the court of king Woo;—acknowledging his supremacy. Ts'ae says that we are not to understand from 通道, that king Woo used any efforts to open roads to the barbarous regions beyond the limits of the empire proper;—it was his virtue and fame which drew them, and they came, 'climbing the hills as if they had been ladders, and in boats across the sea.' It certainly would not have been discreditable to king Woo to have good roads made throughout all his dominions; and in the passage of the 國語, referred to above, evidently modelled on this part of the Shoo, the opening of the thoroughfares is described as his work:—仲尼曰, 昔武王克商, 通道於九夷百蠻, 使各以其方賄來貢, 使無忘職業. 底貢,—the same phrase occurs in the Tribute of Yu, Pt. i., p. 52. The force of 底 passes on to the next character, and indicates that what *it* says took effect. 太保,—it is not said anywhere in the Book who the Great-guardian was; but since the commentary of Gan-kwŏ, the prevailing opinion has been that he was Shih,—the duke of Shaou. See on the name of Bk. XII. He was Great-guardian under Woo's successor; and it is supposed—with probability—that he held the office also under Woo.

Pp. 2—10. THE ADDRESS OF THE GREAT-GUARDIAN TO KING WOO AGAINST RECEIVING THE HOUNDS. Pp. 2, 3. *The precedent of former wise kings in receiving articles of tribute, and the use which they made of them.* 2. 明王慎德,—the language here is to be taken historically. Medhurst and Gaubil both miss this point, and render—'When an intelligent prince is careful in the cultivation of his virtue,' &c. The guardian is giving not merely the lesson of duty, but of duty illustrated by example. The 'Daily Explanation' has it:—自古明哲之王, 所以保邦安民者, 要在謹修其德云云. 慎德, 'the careful cultivation of virtue,' is said to be the hinge on which the whole of the address moves. 咸

乃昭德之致于異姓之邦、無替厥服、分寶玉于伯叔之國、時庸展親、人不易物。

3 clothes, food, and vessels for use. The kings have then displayed the things thus produced by their virtue, and *distributed them* to *the princes of* the States of different surnames, *to encourage them* not to neglect their duties. The precious things and gems they have distributed among their uncles in charge of States, thereby increasing their attachment *to the throne*. The recipients have *thus* not despised the things, but have seen in them the power of virtue.

賓,—賓 is not merely =客, 'strangers,' 'guests,' but =賓服;—see in the dict. on the character. 畢獻方物,惟服食器用,—方物=其方所生之物, 'the articles produced by their country,' and we may understand also articles manufactured there. The last clause gives a summary of those articles, and the meaning is that the contributions were restricted to these:—不敢於此外有以奇玩異物進獻者. 3. 異姓之邦,伯叔之國,—the empire being divided into many States or principalities, the emperors of each dynasty apportioned these among their relatives and adherents. 'The States of their uncles' were 同姓之邦, 'regions of the same surname,' *i.e.*, their rulers had the same surname as the emperors. The 'regions of different surnames' were the States ruled by Chiefs, attached to the reigning dynasty, but of a different lineage.

To these the emperors 昭德之致, 'displayed what their virtue *thus* produced,'—the productions of remote territories, the tribute from distant tribes. The transitive meaning of 昭 is very much determined by its correlation with 分 in the next part of the par. The things were sent about as imperial gifts among the States; so they were 'displayed,' and served to warn and encourage the chiefs to loyal service and duty. 無替厥服=無廢其服事之職. 時庸展親—Gan-kwŏ explains this by 是用誠信其親親之道, 'thereby verifying the sincerity with which they held the principle of attachment to their relatives,' taking 展 as =信. Lin Che-k'e supports this interpretation, and quotes with approval the words of Wang Gan-shih,—'Though they loved them, yet if they had not shared their precious things with them, who could have known the sincerity of their love (親之矣而不以所寶分之,則人孰知親親之信也)?' But the clause is evidently related to the preceding 無替厥服, and must describe—not the feeling of the emperors from which the gifts proceeded, but the feeling which they wished to increase in the princes, their relatives. The explanation of 展 by 信 is therefore inadmissible. The meaning in the transl. is given by Ts'ae and in the dictionary:—使之益厚其親.

[In the passage of the 國語 from which I quoted, on the 1st par., the words of Confucius, the sage goes on to say:—於是肅慎氏貢楛矢石砮,其長尺有咫。先王欲昭其令德之致遠也,以示後人,使永監焉,故銘其栝曰:肅慎氏之貢矢,以分太姬,配虞胡公,而封諸陳。古者分同姓以珍玉,展親也;分異姓以遠方之職貢,使無忘服也。]

人不易物,惟德其物,—by 人 is intended the various princes, receiving the imperial gifts; 易=輕 'to slight.' 不易物,—'have not slighted the things,' have not dared to think lightly of them, however little valuable they might be; 德其物,—'they have virtue-ed the things;' *i.e.*, they have looked at the things in the light of the virtue which

惟德其物。○德盛不狎侮狎侮君子罔以盡人心罔侮小人罔以盡其力。○不役耳目百度惟貞○玩人

4   "Complete virtue allows no contemptuous familiarity. When *a prince* treats superior men with such familiarity, he cannot get them to give him all their hearts; when he so treats inferior men, he cannot

5 get them to put forth for him all their strength. If he be not in bondage to his ears and eyes, all his conduct will be ruled by correctness.

6 By trifling with men he ruins his virtue; by finding his amusement in things he ruins his aims.

produced them, and as monitions to the virtue they themselves ought to cultivate. Gaubil's rendering of this part is sententious, but can be of no help to a student:—'Ainsi les choses qui viennent de la vertu retournent à la vertu.'

[This passage appears in the 左傳, 僖五年, along with two other sentences from 'the Books of Chow,' in the following form:—民不易物惟德繄物 The use which is made of it there is to show that virtue is the only sure defence of a State.]

Pp. 4—6. *How the sovereign's careful attention to his virtue will appear in his guarding against improper familiarity with men, and foolish cherishing of useless creatures and things.* This is the meaning that is put upon these paragraphs. The interpretation of them, it will be seen, is perplexing and difficult. 4. 德盛不狎侮.—comp. 狎侮五行, in 'the Great Speech,' Pt. iii., 2. Koo Seih-ch'ow (顧錫疇; Ming dyn.) says upon the terms here:—狎者與之暱也，侮者禮之倨也，一是視爲私人，一是忽爲易與, '狎 is being familiar with them; 侮 is a haughty disregard of the rules of propriety. The former indicates the looking upon them as mere favourites; the latter expresses the treatment of them as easily consorted with.' For the two terms, however, we have the one term 玩, 'to make sport with' in p. 6. The 'Daily Explanation' says, on that par., that the first 玩 is the 玩 of contempt, and the second the 玩 of fondness' (上玩字，玩忽之意，下玩字玩好之意) But we must find a com-

mon idea expressed by the two applications of 狎侮 here, and of 玩 in p. 6. Such an idea is that of contemptuous familiarity. Directed to creatures like the hounds of Leu, it will have more of the character of trifling sport; directed to men, there will be in the ruler who practises it a want both of self-respect, and of the respect which he owes to them. 君子 is descriptive of men in office, who are to be supposed to have a degree of elevated character. They have their minds—their virtues and acquirements—to serve the sovereign with; but when treated with contemptuous familiarity, they will despise him and go away. 小人 are the people, in whom the familiarity of their superiors is sure to breed contempt, so that they will not be careful to labour for them, as they ought to do, with their strength. Ying-tă, aptly enough, quotes, in illustration of 侮狎君子, the words of E Yin, 接下思恭 (太甲, Pt. ii., p. 7); and the words of Confucius, 使民如承大祭 (Ana., XII., ii.), in illustration of 狎侮小人. 5. 不役耳目＝不爲耳目所役, *i.e.*, if he be superior to the external fascinations that assail him through the senses,—what are called 物 in the next paragraph. 百度, 'the hundred measures,'＝百爲之度, 'the measures of all his conduct.' A certain rule—of 'correctness' (貞＝正)—is supposed, by which the ruler, free from the bondage of his senses, will endeavour to regulate all his conduct. 'His words and actions,' it is said in the 'Daily Explanation,' 'will all be conformed to the measure of perfection, and he will not dare to transgress it an inch.' 6. 玩.—see on par. 4. Contemptuous familiarity with men destroys that self-

夜罔或不勤不矜細
則邇人安。○嗚呼夙
則遠人格所寶惟賢
不育于國不寶遠物
土性不畜珍禽奇獸
物民乃足犬馬非其
乃成不貴異物賤用
不作無益害有益功
以道寧言以道接。○
喪德玩物喪志。○志

7　"The aims should repose in what is right; words should be listened to according to their relation to right.

8　"*A prince* should not do what is unprofitable to the injury of what is profitable, and then his merit may be completed. He should not value strange things to the contemning things that are useful, and then his people will be able to supply *all his needs*. *Even* dogs and horses which are not native to his country he will not keep; fine birds and strange animals he will not nourish in his kingdom. When he does not look on foreign things as precious, foreigners will come to him; when it is worth which is precious to him, *his own* people near at hand will enjoy repose.

9　"Oh! early and late never be but earnest. If you do not attend jealously to your small actions, the result will be to affect your virtue

respect and reverence for right which is at the foundation of all virtue. A fondness for, and fondling of, creatures like the hounds of Leu brings the whole mind down to the level of little things.

P. 7. *The rule for a prince's aims, and his intercourse with others.* 道＝所當由之理, 'the principles according to which we ought to proceed.' 言以道接＝人之言以道而接. The first clause is illustrated by Mencius' 持其志 (II., Pt. I., ii. 9), and the second by his 我知言 (*ib.*, p. 11); also by Shun's language in 'The Counsels of Yu,' pp. 14—16. The two sayings are good enough in their way, but the object which they serve in the guardian's address is not very evident;—see the remark of Wang Pih at the conclusion of his 'Doubts' about this Book.

P. 8. *What things a sovereign should abstain from cherishing and pursuing, and what things he should prefer and seek.* In this par. the Guardian comes at last to the subject of the hounds of

Leu, though he does not expressly mention them. 不作至民乃足,—these two clauses are of a general character, and may be applied to an endless variety of subjects. 民乃足,—'the people will be sufficient.' Chin Tih-sew says:—貴異物，則征求多，而民不足, 'If he set a value on strange things, his exactions and requirements will be so many that the people will not be able to meet them.' 犬馬至不畜.—these dogs and horses might be useful, but being foreign, the virtuous sovereign will have nothing to do with them! 珍禽,—珍 is here an adjective, ＝珍美之禽. 不寶至人安,—see the remarks on this in the note on the Contents of the Book.

Pp. 9, 10. *How the sovereign is to cultivate his virtue by an untiring attention even to the smallest matters, and what grand results will flow from such*

行　大　山　功　簣。民　居　世
終　德　九　虧　○　迪　惟　王。
累　爲　仍。十節一　允　茲　保　生　乃　厥

in great matters;—as when, in raising a mound of nine fathoms the
10　work is unfinished for want of one basket *of earth*. If you really
follow this course, the people will preserve their possessions, and
the throne will descend from generation to generation.

a course. 不矜細行,—矜 is used here
much with the same meaning as in the Con.
Ana. XV., xxi., 君子矜而不爭,
Choo He was asked whether the term were not
used in the same way in the two passages, and
replied, 'Much about it. The idea is that of
pitiful consideration, and firm conservation.'
(相似)是個矜惜持守之意
爲山, 云云,—see the Con. Ana.,
IX., xviii. 仍=八尺, 'eight cubits.' I
call it 'a fathom,' as being the nearest approximation to it which we have in our designations of measures. The paraphrase in the
'Daily Explanation' is:—譬如爲山者,
積累工夫之土, 已至九仍, 所少不過
一簣肯加益山岂可乃心之功成也而
缺　　　得而　　　　　　

10. 允迪茲,—comp.
Pt., II., Bk. III., p, 1.　　允迪厥德
　　　　　　　　　生民保厥

居,—生民, 'the living people,' is merely
an equivalent of 庶民. The phrase is found
also in the 孝經. For 保厥居
Medhurst has well—'may protect their hearths.'
惟乃世王=王業可永,
'the imperial inheritance may be perpetuated.'
I append Lin Che-k'e's observations on this:—

凡如矢迪三王事則永者,
後一稽允世世細此天祈之休者,
受慎所謂卜其亦於
氏所孫乎獻以疆
訓以周七一王君
觀見之百年却世大爲社
訓中國以是訓王,厥
既以是訓王,
太保夷所獻,
四太保類者十也,
太之茲卜夫而
命以大爲不在大也。
太四太之茲十也,
蓋不

THE BOOKS OF CHOW.

BOOK VI. THE METAL-BOUND *COFFER*.

金縢

我先王。　未可以戚　○周公曰　爲王穆卜　公曰我其　弗豫○二　年王有疾　既克商二

1　I. Two years after the conquest of the Shang dynasty, the king
2　fell ill, and was quite disconsolate. The two dukes said, "Let us
3　reverently consult the tortoise concerning the king"; but the duke
of Chow said, "You may not so distress our former kings."

THE NAME OF THE BOOK.—金縢, 'The Metal bound.' 縢 is defined by 緘, 'to tie or shut up,' 'to seal or fasten.' A certain chest or coffer, which was fastened with bands of metal, plays an important part among the incidents of the Book. It is called, p. 11, 金縢之匱; and from this the name is taken. The Book is found in both the texts.

CONTENTS. King Woo is very ill, and his death seems imminent. His brother, the duke of Chow, apprehensive of the disasters which such an event would occasion to their infant dynasty, conceives the idea of dying in his stead, and prays to 'the three kings,' their immediate progenitors, that he might be taken and king Woo left. Having done so, and divined that he was heard, he deposits the prayer in the metal-bound coffer, where important archives were kept. The king gets well, and the duke is also spared; but five years after, Woo really dies, and is succeeded by his son, a boy only thirteen years old. Rumours are spread abroad that the duke has designs upon the throne, and he withdraws for a time from the court. At length in the third year of the young king, Heaven interposes. He has occasion to open the metal-bound coffer, and the prayer of the duke is found. His devotion to his brother and the interests of his family is brought to light. The boy monarch weeps because of the unjust suspicions he had harboured, and welcomes the duke back to court, amid unmistakeable demonstrations of the approval of Heaven.

The whole narrative is a very pleasing episode in the history of the times, and is more interesting to the foreign reader than most other portions of the Shoo. It divides itself naturally into two chapters:—the first, parr. 1—11, ending with the depositing the prayer in the coffer; and the second, detailing how it was brought to light, and the duke cleared by means of it from the suspicions which had been cherished of him.

CH. I. Pp. 1—11. THE PRAYER OF THE DUKE OF CHOW; ITS OCCASION; HIS SUBSEQUENT DIVINATION, AND DEPOSITING THE PRAYER IN THE COFFER. 1. *The illness of king Woo.*

既克商二年,—the current chronology refers this to the 14th year of king Woo, the year after the death of Show, B.C. 1,120. K'ang-shing thought that the year of the conquest of Shang should not be included in the two years, and the critics of the present dynasty generally concur with him. Ming-shing says that if the historian had meant to say that the year was that succeeding the change of dynasties, as Gan-kwŏ, Sze-ma Ts'een, and Wang Suh

告 秉 焉 周 方 壇 同 爲 以 公（四節）
太 珪 植 公 北 于 墠 三 爲 乃
王 乃 璧 立 面 南 爲 壇 功 自

4　　He then took the business on himself, and made three altars of earth, on the same cleared space; and having made another altar on the south, facing the north, he there took his own position. The convex symbols were put *on their altars* and he himself held his mace, while he addressed the kings T'ae, Ke, and Wăn.

think, he would have used 惟 and not 旣, and we should have read 惟克商二年. I cannot undertake to settle this trivial point. 弗豫 (so in Sze-ma Ts'een. Kĕang Shing, after the 說文, gives 不愈)＝不悅豫, 'was not happy.' We may suppose that he was distressed, thinking of the troubles that might arise on his death.

The other reading—不愈, 'did not get well,' would give a simpler meaning.

2. *Proposal of the two dukes to divine respecting the issue of the king's illness.* The 二公, 'two dukes,' are understood to be 太公 and 召公. The latter is the duke of Shaou spoken of on p. 1 of the last Book. T'ae-kung,—see on Mencius, IV., Pt. I., xiii. He played a very important part in the establishment of the Chow dynasty, as counsellor to Wăn and Woo, and was invested by Woo with the principality of Ts'e, which his descendants held for nearly 640 years. He is the 尙父 in the apocryphal edition of the 'Great Speech.' 穆卜,—穆 (Ts'een has 繆) is defined by Gan-kwŏ, after the 爾雅, by 敬, 'reverently.' Ts'ae gives its meaning—誠一而和, 'with entire sincerity and in common,' saying that on great emergencies all the officers, great and small, united in the ceremony of divination, so that 穆一卜 is equivalent to 共卜, according to the view of an older interpreter whom he cites. This interpretation would give more emphasis to the 戚 in the next par., but I do not see that we can insist on extending the meaning of the term beyond the 敬 of Gan-kwŏ.　3. *The duke of Chow declines the proposal.* 周公,—this is the first time that we meet in the Shoo with this famous name, though we shall find him hereafter playing a most important part. But for him, indeed, the dynasty of Chow would probably

not have taken root. He was equally mighty in words and in deeds,—a man of counsel and of action. Confucius regarded his memory with reverence, and spoke of it as an evidence of his own failing powers and disappointed hopes, that the duke of Chow no longer appeared to him in his dreams. He was the 4th son of king Wăn, by his queen T'ae-sze. The eldest was Pih-yih-k'aou (伯邑考); the second was king Woo; and the third was Sëen (鮮), the Kwan Shuh (管叔), mentioned in p. 12. There were six other younger brothers, but of all Wăn's sons, only king Woo and the duke of Chow were representatives of their father's virtue and wisdom. Chow was the name of the city where king T'ae fixed the central seat of his House;—see page 281, on the name of this part of the Shoo. It became the appanage of Wăn's 4th son, Tan (旦), and hence, he is known as the 'duke of Chow.'　戚＝憂 'to trouble,' 'to distress.' It would appear that the two dukes proposed to have a solemn service of divination in the ancestral temple of the imperial House, and the duke of Chow negatives their proposal on the ground that there was no necessity for troubling the spirits of the departed kings by so much ado merely to divine the issue of the king's illness. He had himself determined what *he* would do. K'ang-shing says that he negatived their proposal, because he knew that the king would not die at this time. This view is grounded in a passage in the Bk. 文王, 世子, Pt. i., p. 2., of the Le Ke, where king Wăn is made to interpret a dream of his son so as to assure him of a certain number of years. But there is much in that Book which we cannot receive. If the duke knew that his brother would recover, the prayer which follows, and his offer to die in his room, lose all their meaning and value.

P. 4. *The duke's preparations for his prayer.* 公乃自以爲功,-功＝事 'business or duty.' Gan-kwŏ paraphrases :— 周公乃自以請命爲已事. 三壇同墠,-築土曰壇,除地曰墠, 'the rearing up of earth is called 壇; the clearing away of the ground is called

之　有　三　疾　遘　元　曰、乃　王。王
責　丕　王、若　厲　孫　惟　册　○　季
于　子　是　爾　虐　某、爾　祝　史　文
　　　　　　　　　　　　　　五節

5　　The *grand* historian *by his order wrote* on tablets his prayer to
the following effect:—"A. B., your chief descendant, is suffering
from a severe and dangerous sickness;—if you three kings have in
heaven the charge of *watching over* him, *Heaven's* great son, let me

墠：The duke cleared and levelled a space
of ground, and there he built three altars facing
the south, one for each of the kings to whom
he intended to pray,—his father, his grandfather,
and his great-grandfather, by whose wisdom
and virtues the fortunes of their House had culminated in the possession of the empire. On the
same area he raised another altar facing the north,
where he himself took his place. K'ang-shing
says that the altars were at Fung (Bk. III., p. 2.),
and that the area remained to his day. 植

璧秉珪,—璧 and 珪 (＝圭) were two
of the 'five tokens of gem,' mentioned in the
Can. of Shun, p. 7, conferred by the emperor
upon the various princes in connection with
their investitures. There were two *peih*, belonging to the *tsze* and the *nan* respectively, and
three *kwei*, that appropriate to the duke of
Chow being the 桓圭. But we can hardly
understand the terms here of the badges of
nobility, or tokens of imperial appointment.
Gan-kwŏ says the *peih* were brought and laid
upon the altars of the three kings in reverence
to them, and the *kwei* was the duke's proper
hwan kwei, which he held in his hands as the
evidence of his person and rank in appearing
before them. But from p. 8, we should rather
conclude that all the articles were proper to
the worship of the three kings. The 璧 is
described as resting on a square base, while out-
wards it was round like the arch of heaven.

Pp. 5—8. *The prayer.* 5. 史乃册
祝,—史＝太史, 'the grand historiogra-
pher.' His services were called in to record
the prayer. I take 祝 as＝祝詞, 'the
language of the prayer.' Gan-kwŏ explains
the clause:—史為册書祝辭, 'The
historian wrote for him on a tablet (or tablets)
the words of the prayer.' This is the view now
given in the 'Daily Explanation':—周公
告三王之神,命太史書祝
詞于册, 若曰, 云云. This, it
seems to me, must be the meaning of the text.

K'ang-shing, however, says:—策, 周
公所作, 謂簡書也, 祝者讀

此簡書以告三王, 'The tablet,
i.e., the writing, was made by the duke of
Chow; the priest read this writing to inform
the three kings.' In this way the 史 is altogether unaccounted for. Woo Ch'ing would put
a comma at 册, and explains—'The historiographer wrote the tablet, and the priest (祝)
read it.' But who does not get the impression
that the duke of Chow was himself the only
priest on the occasion? 爾元孫某,
—'Your great-grandson, such an one.' The
duke, no doubt, used the name of king Woo.
But in the Chow dynasty, the practice of 'concealing the name,' as it is called (諱名), came
into vogue. K'ang-shing supposes that it was
king Ching, who first dropt the name, and substituted 某 for it, when he found the prayer,
as related in p. 16. 遘＝遇 'to meet
with,' Wang K'ang-t'ang says:—'A sage has
nothing about him which could bring on sickness, but he may happen to meet with evil
malaria in the air:—hence the use of 遘;'—
see a note in the 集傳. We need not lay so
much stress on the character. 若爾
三王至某之身,—this passage has
wonderfully vexed the critics, and the editors
of Yung-ching's Shoo say that no one interpretation of it which has been given should be
pertinaciously held to. The view in the translation is substantially that of Ts'ae, who says:
一武王為天元子,三王當任
其保護之責于天,不可令
其死,如欲其死,則請以旦
代武王之身, 'King Woo is the great
son of Heaven; you three kings ought to have
the charge of protecting him in heaven, and
should not let him die. If you wish that he
should die, pray let me Tan be a substitute for
his person.' Feeling that the 于天 lay loosely
on this view in the sentence, he supposed that
some characters following 天 have been lost.
The interpretations of K'ang-shing and Ying-tă

天、以旦代
某之身。○
予仁若考、
能多材多
藝能事鬼
神乃元孫
不若旦多
材多藝、
能事神鬼。
○乃命于

6 Tan be a substitute for his person. I have been lovingly obedient to my father; I am possessed of many abilities and arts which fit me to serve spiritual beings. Your chief descendant on the other hand has not so many abilities and arts as I, and is not so 7 capable of serving spiritual beings. And moreover he was appointed in the hall of God to extend his aid to the four quarters *of the empire*, so that he might establish your descendants in this lower world.

may be seen in the 後案 and the 註疏. Choo He preferred the view of a Chaou E-taou (晁以道), that 責 = 'to require the service of,' and the meaning is—'If God require the services of your eldest son in heaven, let me be a substitute for him.' Maou K'e-ling prefers the view of a Seu Chung-san (徐中山):—

惟爾元孫某遘疾若此，儼實不
三王以爲大子則旦也，其元孫甚重
天之死，請代耳。

Ts'ae's construction of the sentence is not more objectionable than either of these two. Thus much is plain:—first, that the duke of Chow offered himself to die in the room of his brother king Woo; and second, that he thought his offer might somehow be accepted through the intervention of the great kings, their progenitors, to whom he addressed himself.

P. 6. *Reason why the duke should be taken instead of the king.* 予仁若考，—考 = 父；若 = 順. Gan-kwŏ gives the meaning as 我仁能順父, 'I could affectionately obey my father.' Ts'ae takes the same view, only extending the meaning of 考 to 祖父, 'forefathers' generally. Medhurst translates the clause by—'my benevolence is equal to that of my forefathers,' which the language will admit of. Woo Ch'ing, indeed, gives for it—我之仁德如父. Still the other view is to be preferred. The duke would probably have declined to say that he was more virtuous than king Woo, though he was conscious of possessing certain qualities which might render him the better addition of the two to the spirit-world. Sze-ma Ts'een has only 旦巧能, and on his authority Keang Shing

would cast 仁若 out of the text; but though the 'Historical Records' show us the interpretation which their compiler put upon the Shoo, their authority cannot always be pleaded in favour of this or that reading.

We should be glad if we could ascertain from this paragraph what ideas the duke of Chow had about the other world, but his language is too vague to afford us satisfaction. He says he was better able than his brother to serve spirits;—did he then expect that some such service would have to be performed by him after death? and who was the spirit, or who were the spirits, to whom the service was to have been rendered? These questions are suggested by his words; and yet it may be, that all which he meant to say was that he was more religious,—more acquainted with ceremonies, and fonder of sacrificial services,—and therefore was somehow better fitted for admission to the spirit circle. I suppose he did not know his own meaning very clearly.

Chinese critics are concerned to free the duke of Chow from the charge of boasting which may be fixed on him from the paragraph. Tsëang Te-shǎng (蔣悌生; Ming dyn.) says:— 'The duke of Chow did not boast of his services, but was the humblest of men;—how is it that here he boasts of himself in such a way to the spirits of the three kings? On this occasion, so important to his family and the kingdom, his love for his brother prevailed over every other consideration. He had not leisure to consider whether he was boasting or modest. The case is one of those instances in which the virtue of sagely men moves Heaven. Let it not be lightly thought of or spoken about;'—see the 集說.

P. 7. *Reason why king Woo should be spared.* 乃命于帝庭，—the 帝 here is 上帝 or God. Ma Yung says:—武王受命于天帝之庭，—'king Woo received appointment in the hall of the God of heaven.' Medhurst has translated:—'He has

○乃卜三龜、一習吉、　許我我乃屏璧與珪。　爾之許我、我其以璧　○今我卽命于元龜、　我先王亦永有依歸。　呼、無墜天之降寶命、　方之民罔不祗畏、嗚　定爾子孫于下地、四　帝庭、敷佑四方、用能

The people of the four quarters stand in reverent awe of him. Oh! do not let that precious Heaven-conferred appointment fall to the ground, and *all* our former kings will also have a perpetual

8 reliance and resort. I will now seek for your orders from the great tortoise. If you grant *what I request*, I will take these symbols and this mace, and return and wait for the issue. If you do not grant it, I will put them by."

9 The duke then divined with the three tortoises, and all were favourable. He took a key, opened and looked at the *oracular*

received the decree in the imperial hall,' which is a great weakening of the duke's argument, and without the sanction of any critic. 四方至祗畏,—the critics generally connect this with the preceding clause, and extend the force of the 用能 to it. It seems rather to be a description of the success of Woo's govt.,—exaggerated, indeed, but justifiable in the circumstances. 天之降 寶命＝天所降之寶命,—as in the translation. 我先王,云云,—'our former kings' are all the princes of the House of Chow, from Shun's minister of Agriculture downward. The saying that they would have 'a perpetual reliance and resort' is to the effect that the sacrifices to them would ever be continued.

P. 8. *The duke proposes to divine for the answer of the kings, and tells them what will be the consequence of their refusing his request.* 我卽命＝今我就受三王之命, 'I will now go at once and receive the command—the decision—of you three kings.' 元龜,—see on 大龜, in the 'Tribute of Yu,' Pt. i., 52. The shells of the tortoise employed for imperial divinations were larger than those employed by the princes. 歸 俟爾命,—'will return and wait for your orders,' which would be seen in the recovery of king Woo, and the duke's death. Ma says:— 待爾命,武王當愈,我當死. 屏璧與珪,—屏 (2d tone)＝去 or 藏. The meaning is, that he would put those instruments of worship aside;—the dynasty would fall, and the House of Chow would have no more imperial sacrifices to offer.

Pp. 9, 10. *The divination is favourable, and the duke deposits his prayer in the coffer.* 9.

卜三龜,—'He divined with the three tortoises' I suppose that the divination took place before the altars, and that a different shell was used to ascertain the mind of each king. Choo He says:—或曰三王前各一 龜卜之. Lin Che-k'e, however, says:— 以龜之三兆卜之, 'He divined according to the three prognostics given by the tortoise.' This is in accordance with the language of the Chow Le, Bk. XXIV., p. 1, 太卜 掌三兆之法,一曰玉兆,二 曰瓦兆,三曰原兆, which Biot

中　册　人　攸　惟　子　王　是　啟
王　于　。　俟　永　新　其　吉　籥
翼　金　○　能　終　命　罔　。　見
日　縢　公　念　是　于　害　○　書
乃　之　歸　子　圖　三　予　公　乃
瘳　匱　乃　一　、　王　小　曰　幷
。　　　納　　　茲　、　　　、

10 responses which also were favourable.　He said, "According to the form *of the prognostic*, the king will take no injury.　I, who am but a child, have got his appointment renewed by the three kings, by whom a long futurity has been consulted for.　I have to wait
11 the issue.　They can provide for our one man."　*Having said this*, he returned, and placed the tablets in the metal-bound coffer; and next day the king got better.

translates :—' Grand Augure.　Il est prèposé aux trois methodes pour l'observation des fissures sur l'ecaille de la tortue.　La première est appelée fissure de jade ; la seconde, fissure de poterie ; la troisième, fissure de plaine.' 一 習 吉,—習＝重, or 襲 ; see the 'Great Speech,' Pt. ii., 5.　啟 籥 見 書,— by 書 we are to understand 占 書, 'written oracles.'　The par. of the Chow Le, following that quoted above, is—其 經 兆 之 體, 皆 百 有 二 十,其 頌 皆 千 有 二 百, 'The forms of the regular prognostications were in all 120, the explanations of which amounted to 1,200.'　Those explanations, no doubt, consisting of a few oracular lines ; were the 書 of the text.　They were kept by themselves, and consulted on occasion, according to certain rules which have not come down.　The duke of Chow at this time had recourse to them.　The meaning of 籥 in this place is very uncertain.　Properly speaking, it denotes a kind of flute.　Here it seems to denote a sort of key with which the apartment or chest, or whatever it might be, in which those oracles were kept, was opened.　K'ang-shing, Ma Yung, and Wang Suh define it nearly in the same way, as 開 藏 之 管 ; 藏 卜 兆 書 管 ; and 開 藏 占 兆 書 管.　10. 體＝兆 之 體, 'the form of the prognostic,' appearing on the shell of the tortoise.　惟 永 終 是 圖, —Woo Ch'ing understands this to be spoken by the duke of himself, so that he not only understood from the divination that the king would

not die, but also that he would get better without himself being taken as a substitute.　The words do not convey that impression to my mind.　In the 'Daily Explanation,' they are referred to the three kings as in the translation. 一我 小 子 新 受 命 于 三 王, 惟 以 久 後 子 孫 爲 計, 而 許 我 以 保 佑 元 子 孫 矣　兹 攸 俟, 能 念 子 一 人, —兹 攸 俟＝ the 歸 俟 爾 命 of par. 8, the only difference being that the words here are those of soliloquy, and not addressed to the kings.　The 一 人 is king Woo.　The duke would seem to be resigning himself to the thought of his own death.　He must be taken, but he can confidently leave the king and the dynasty in the care of the three kings.

11. 金 縢 之 匱, —'the metal-bound coffer.'　Ts'ae says that it was this coffer which contained the oracles of divination, the same which is alluded to in p. 9.　It may have been so ; but I should rather suppose it to have been different, —a special chest in which important archives of the dynasty, to be referred to on great emergencies, were kept.　The duke gave orders to all whose services he had employed in the ceremony to say nothing about it (see p. 17), but it was right that the record of the prayer should be preserved in this repository.　He therefore placed it there, not thinking that it would be—hoping that it would not be—brought to light in his time.

[The prayer of the duke of Chow is addressed to the three kings, and I have said above, that it is addressed to them in the character of mediators or intercessors with Heaven or God.

○武
十二
節
王

既
喪
管
及
其

叔
群
弟
乃
其

流
言
於
公

國
曰、
公

將
不
利

於
孺
子。

○周
十三
節
公

12　II. *Afterwards*, upon the death of king Woo, *the duke's* elder brother, he of Kwan, and his younger brothers, spread a baseless rumour through the kingdom, saying, "The duke will do no good to the

The analogy of the circle of religious notions among the Chinese obliges us to adopt this conclusion, and, in par. 7, we have an express reference to the supreme disposing of God in human affairs. Still it must be allowed that the doctrine of the former kings being only intercessors is not indicated in the text so clearly as it might have been. In illustration of this I shall quote the words of Ts'aou Heŏtseuen (曹學佺; Ming dyn). He says: —'The earlier scholars were led, by the words —"I have received a new appointment for him from the three kings," to doubt whether the duke's language (in p. 6)—"I have many abilities and arts which fit me to serve spiritual beings," really referred to Heaven. They rather thought it did not; but we must not thus pertinaciously insist upon particular expressions. Anciently, when sovereigns sacrificed to Heaven and Earth, they associated their ancestors as assessors and sharers at the ceremony; when they prayed for anything to Heaven and Earth, they depended on the efficacious spirituality of their ancestors to present and second their request. Heaven was the most honourable, and they did not dare to approach it abruptly; their ancestors were the nearest to them, and they could, through the kindness between them, make their thoughts known to them. There is no reason why we should not say that the words, "I have received a new appointment from the three kings," are equivalent to "I have received a new appointment for him from Heaven"' (先儒

文
神
拘
以
天
爲
突、
此
必
于
以
唐
情
新
受

疑
事
如
地、
必
天
所
之
靈、
敢
以
即

上
鬼
此
必
于
以
唐
情
新
受

王、
即
服
必
不
祀
有
宗
祖
至
親
于

三
藝
亦
君
其
祖
至
親
于

于
多
言
人
享、
藉
天
至
宗

命
材
天
者
配
必
蓋
祖
新
請

新
多
指
古
考
亦
請
于
天、

因
能
非
泥、
祖
地
之
而
也、
命
于
天、

Ch. II. Pp. 12—19. AFTER THE DEATH OF KING WOO THE DUKE OF CHOW FALLS UNDER SUSPICION OF NOT BEING LOYAL TO THE THRONE. TWO YEARS PASS BY, AND THEN HEAVEN INTERPOSES TO BRING HIS INNOCENCE TO LIGHT; THE PRAYER IN THE COFFER IS DISCOVERED, AND THE YOUNG KING ACKNOWLEDGES WITH HIS TEARS THE INJUSTICE OF HIS THOUGHTS, AND RECEIVES THE DUKE BACK, WHILE HEAVEN ACCORDS EVIDENT TOKENS OF ITS APPROVAL.

12. *The manner in which the duke of Chow was brought into suspicion.* The last par. closes with the statement that the king suddenly recovered the day after the duke's prayer. This opens with a reference to his death. Five years have elapsed. Woo died B.C., 1,115, and was succeeded by his son Sung (誦), whose reign dates from B.C. 1,114, and who is known in history by the title of Ching (成), 'the Completer.' Ching was only 13 years old, and the duke of Chow acted as regent of the empire. It was natural he should do so, for he was the ablest of all the sons of Wăn, and had been devotedly attached to his brother Woo, whose chief adviser he had been, and was without the shadow of disloyal feeling. The accession of dignity and influence which he now received, however, moved his elder brother Sëen, and some of his other brothers to envy, and they had come to be engaged in a treasonable conspiracy against the throne. We have seen how Woo, after the death of the tyrant Show, pardoned his son, generally known by the name of Woo-kăng (武庚), and continued him in Yin to maintain the sacrifices to the kings of his line. To guard against the very probable contingency of his rebellion, however, he placed three of his own brothers in the State along with him, with the title of 'Inspectors' or 'Overseers' (三監), who should overawe both him and the old ministers of Show. Those overseers were Sëen, known as Kwan Shuh, older than the duke of Chow; Too (度), known as Ts'ae Shuh (蔡叔), immediately younger than the duke; and Ch'oo (處), known as Hoh Shuh (霍叔), the eighth of Wăn's sons. Perhaps Sëen thought that on the death of Woo the regency, if not the throne, should have devolved upon himself. Mencius ascribes the appointment of him as overseer of Yin to the duke of Chow (see Men., II., Pt. II., ix.). as, no doubt, it was made by Woo on his advice. This may have exasperated him the more against Tan who had thus *shelved* him, he would think, away from the court. However it was induced. soon after the death of Woo, those three brothers entered into a conspiracy with Woo-kăng to throw off the yoke of the

得。罪 二 公 王。告 我 之 公 乃
〇 人 年、居 〇 我 無 弗 曰、告
于 斯 則 東 周 先 以 辟、我 二

^{十五節} ^{十四節} (these small annotations appear beside the columns)

13 *king's* young son." Upon this the duke of Chow represented to the two dukes, saying, "If I do not take the law *to these men,* I shall not be able to make my report to our former kings."

14   He resided accordingly in the east for two years, when the

new dynasty, and as a preliminary step, they endeavoured, in the manner indicated in the text, to stir up division between the regent and his nephew.

管 叔,—Kwan was the name of a city and territory,—the pres. sub. dep. of Ch'ing (鄭 州), in the dep. of K'ae-fung, Ho-nan. It formed the appanage of Sëen, the third of Wăn's sons. I suppose that 叔 was originally merely indicative of Sëen's place in the line of his brothers (see on Con. Ana., XVIII., xi.); but it has come to be joined with 管, so that Kwăn-shuh is now in effect simply a historical name. 羣弟,—'the younger brothers' were Too and Ch'oo, as has been detailed above. 流言, —'set words flowing,' = spread a baseless ru-mour. 不利於孺子,—'will not be advantageous to the child.' By 孺子, of course, the young emperor is meant. 13. *The resolution of the duke.* 我之弗辟, —ever since the Han dynasty the meaning of 辟 here has been debated. Gan-kwŏ, reading the term *peih,* according to its proper enuncia-tion, defined it by 法, and explained the text by 我不以法法三叔,則我 無以成周道,告我先王,—as in the translation. K'ang-shing, on the other hand read 辟 as 避, and with the meaning of that term, so that the text = 'If I do not get out of the way,—leave my dignities, and retire from court,—I shall not be able,' &c., &c. The editors of Yung-ching's Shoo do not give a decided opinion on either side. Ts'ae has followed K'ang-shing, but his master Choo He wavered between the two views, approving now the one, and now the other. Maou K'e-ling has a long note on the subject, in his 尙書廣聽錄 Bk. III., recanting his early opinion in favour of K'ang-shing's view, and giving eight reasons for adopting in preference that of Gan-kwŏ. Some of them are sufficiently forcible. I have no hesitation in differing on this point from the generally approved interpretation sanctioned by Ts'ae.

The duke of Chow, on being aware of the insinuations circulated against him, resolved to meet them with promptitude. He owed a duty to the former kings and to the dynasty, and whatever the young king might think, he would act at once against the rebellious and the dis-loyal.

14. *Justice done on the criminals.* The different views that are taken of the last paragraph necessarily affect the interpretation of this. Acc. to Gan-kwŏ, the duke spent two years in the east, operating against Woo-kăng and the false brothers, and at the end of that time he had got them into his hands, and dealt with them according to his views of their several guilt. Ying-tă says:—'居東 (this has already been explained by 東征之) 二年,則 罪人於此皆得,謂獲三叔 及諸叛逆者. K'ang-shing on the other hand says:—居東者,出處東國, 待罪以須君之察已, '"He re-sided in the east" means that he left the court and dwelt in an eastern State, allowing the charge of guilt till the king should have examin-ed into it.' The language so far will certainly admit of this interpretation, but what he says on the next clause is too ridiculous. It is:— 罪人周公之屬黨與知居 攝者,周公出皆奔,今二年 盡爲成王所得,謂之罪人,史 書成王意也, 'The criminals are the partizans of the duke of Chow and his acquain-tances while he held the regency. When he withdrew from the court, they fled; but now in the two years they were all apprehended by king Ching. The historian calls them criminals, writing from the king's point of view.' Even Keang Shing does not venture to adopt this interpretation, but supposes the meaning to be that the duke, while in the east, came to know who the criminals were that had slandered him.

I have said that the phrase 居東 will itself admit of the interpretation put on it by K'ang-shing; but Maou K'e-ling has shown, that if we do not understand it as Gan-kwŏ does, of the duke's operating in the east against his rebel-lious brothers, there is no other place in that direction from the court, to which his sojourn-

代武王之說。十七節二公

周公所自以爲功

敢金縢之書乃得

王與大夫盡弁以

木斯拔邦人大恐

電以風禾盡偃大

大熟未穫天大雷

亦未敢誚公○秋十六

王名之曰鴟鴞○王

後公乃爲詩以貽

15 criminals were got *and brought to justice.* Afterwards he made a poem to present to the king, and called it "The Owl." The king on his part did not dare to blame the duke.

16 　In the autumn, when the grain was abundant and ripe, but before it was reaped, Heaven sent a great storm of thunder and lightning, along with wind, by which the grain was all beaten down, and great trees torn up. The people were greatly terrified; and the king and great officers, all in their caps of state, proceeded to open the metal-bound coffer, and examine the writings, when they found the words of the duke of Chow when he took on himself the business of taking

ing for so long a time can be assigned with any degree of probability.　　　15. *The duke sends a poem to the king to clear himself, but is only partially successful.* The poem here referred to is in the She King, Part I., Bk. XV., Ode ii. It begins:—

> 'O owl, O owl,
> You have taken my young ones:
> Do not also destroy my nest.
> I loved them; I laboured for them;
> I nourished them.—How am I to be pitied.'

The received interpretation of it is that it was composed by the duke after he had crushed the insurrectionary movements in Yin, and put to death Woo-kăng and Kwan-shuh. By the 'owl' is intended Woo-kăng; and by the 'nest,' the dynasty of Chow. The writer meant that king Ching should understand by it the devotion which he felt to the imperial House, and the sorrow which the stern justice he had been obliged to execute upon his brother occasioned him. K'ang-shing took a difft. view of it, in accordance with his interpretation of 罪人斯得 in the last par., and supposed that the duke intended by it to expostulate with the king on the persecution of his friends which he had instituted. But we cannot believe that he would have thus addressed the king as an 'Owl.' There is nothing in the poem or ode, which readily suggests the interpretation to be put upon it; but there is perhaps something in what Choo He says, that readers at the time, all excited by the circumstances to which it

had reference, would not find the difficulty in understanding it which we do. 王亦 未敢誚公,—誚 is now superseded by 譙; it means 'to reprove,' 'to blame.' The clause is understood to intimate that though the king now partially understood the motives of the duke's conduct, and could not blame him for the way in which he had dealt with his other uncles, he still looked on him with some degree of suspicion.

Pp. 16—18. *Heaven interposes to bring the duke's innocence to light by means of the prayer in the metal-bound coffer.*　　16. 秋,—we may suppose this was the autumn of the the third year of Ching,—B.C. 1,112. 雷電以 風,—Lin Che-k'e brings out the 以風 by expanding:—天忽雷電大作又 繼之以風, as in the translation. The paraphrase of the 'Daily Explanation' is similar. 王與至之書,—the 弁 was a 'skin cap,' worn in court at audiences. It is generally said that the king was going to divine that he might discover the reason of the unusual storm, and therefore opened the coffer which contained the oracles of divination. But we saw, on p. 11, that it is not certain those oracles were kept in that coffer. Possibly it was a repository of important archives, which

及王乃問諸史與百執事。

對曰信噫公命我勿敢言。

○王執書以泣曰其勿穆十八節

卜昔公勤勞王家惟予沖

人弗及知今天動威以彰

周公之德惟朕小子其新

逆我國家禮亦宜之。○王十九節

出郊天乃雨反風禾則盡

起二公命邦人凡大木所

偃盡起而築之歲則大熟。

17 the place of king Woo. The king and the two dukes asked the *grand* historian and all the other officers about the thing. They replied, "Ah! it was really thus; but the duke charged us that we should

18 not presume to speak about it." The king held the writing, and wept, saying, "We need not *now* go on reverently to divine. Formerly the duke was 'thus earnest for the royal House, but I, being a child, did not know it. Now Heaven has moved its terrors to display the virtue of the duke of Chow. That I meet him a new man, is what the rules of propriety of our empire require."

19 The king then went out to the borders, when Heaven sent down rain; and by virtue of a contrary wind, the grain all rose up. The two dukes gave orders to the people to take up all the large trees which had fallen, and replace them. The year then turned out very fruitful.

were consulted on great emergencies of the State. 17. 史與百執事,—these were all the officers who had assisted the duke when he made his prayer, &c. 信噫云云,—Ying-tă says:—噫,心不平之聲, '噫 is a sound expressive of dissatisfaction of mind.' Gan-kwŏ calls it 恨辭 They were vexed at being thus obliged to tell what the duke had charged them to keep secret. Keang Shing reads 意, which he explains in a similar way. 18. 其勿穆卜=今觀公 書可不必更穆卜矣;—see the 變之所由我君日 知天命邦人臣

予沖人,—see on 'The Pwan-kăng,' Pt. iii., p. 7. Here king Ching was really a youth. 惟朕小子其新逆 —逆=迎, 'to meet.' Ma Yung read 親 instead of 新, so that the meaning is—'That I go out and meet him in person,' &c. This certainly gives a good meaning; and Ts'ae and Këang Shing both adopt it. Gan-kwŏ and K'ang-shing, however, both understand 新 as in the translation. The language of the latter is:—新迎,改先時之心,更自 新以迎周公. This is rather harsh, but it is more difficult to get a tolerable meaning out of many other passages of the Shoo.

P. 19. The duke is received back, and Heaven signifies its approbation. 王出郊,—it is most natural to understand this going forth to the suburbs with reference to the king's purpose indicated in the 朕小子其新 逆郊 of the last par.   Gan-kwŏ, however, takes 郊 of the place, outside the city, where the great sacrifice to Heaven was offered, and thought that the going forth was to offer a sacrifice of thanksgiving to Heaven for his deliverance from the unjust suspicions which he had harboured.

Ts'ae says that after reading this paragraph it is impossible to doubt the doctrine of 'verifications,' laid down in the 'Plan!'

[I may here, in the vacant space of this page, introduce Wang Pih's chapter on the 金縢 in his 'Doubts about the Shoo.' His views are questionable, but the student will be glad to have a complete specimen of the style and manner of his Work.—

此書敘事成始歷有縢不十抑來武事終其一責其中有武事事中金可五折後此武始也未意望代王

武此七力首其字諳先終後小因如我無保同末六筆之詳餘楊大成之而餘者字事間任

體伐征詳啟敘居明然合而敘法諸之責繼若之也商前略書事東於可蓄總東當家責是以曰責

敘東末册其言詳隱盡誓是諳義子之則意子是是始納也流潔情事四縢諸文不望天文不

與一後之此不止曲判於敘征然有竊責願三于面無卻元三篇證新代惟終不也公在我周之息公字能意脫孫卜而三命王永之忘王之公之公事曰者爲後全廷乃謂啟是子身以王代天代而聲征而非於則語帝舉者言乃小以命爲王代天代而聲征而非於天之于復吉之書子欲代但三以亦之代入心恩東義也]。

神命合是者之也,公當我者言死,公以作爲私居一悟鬼乃字幷卜吉者公者待之不從是下以而只牴事如二乃此龜果王則圖所人公不俟只天得之卜不能矣孫此吉以之三瘳是茲一而而當辟公不避穆初不味元於皆參卜于王終計於瘳心則弗以固公二近

THE BOOKS OF CHOW.

BOOK VII. THE GREAT ANNOUNCEMENT.

大誥

一節
王若曰、猷大誥
爾多邦越爾御
事、弗弔天降割
于我家不少延
洪惟我幼沖人、
嗣無疆大歷服、
弗造哲迪民康、
殂曰其有能格

1   I. "The king speaks to the following effect:—'Ho! I make a great announcement to you, *the princes of* the many States, and to you, the managers of my affairs.—Unpitied am I, and Heaven sends down calamities on my House, without exercising the least delay. It greatly occupies my thoughts, that I, so very young. have inherited this illimitable patrimony, with its destinies and domains. I have not displayed wisdom, and led the people to tranquillity, and how much less should I be able to reach the knowledge of the decree of Heaven !

THE NAME OF THE BOOK.—大誥, 'The Great Announcement,' At the commencement of the first paragraph, these two characters,— 大誥,—occur, and they are thence taken and made the name of the Book. Gan-kwŏ, indeed, says that the Book sets forth great doctrines for the information of the empire, and thence it received its name (陳大道以誥天 下、故以名篇). But we look in vain for any 'great doctrines' in the Book. The emergency which called the announcement forth was sufficiently important to justify the duke of Chow in calling it 'great.' We need not look for any higher or deeper meaning in the title. The Book is found in both the texts.

CONTENTS ; DATE ; AND STYLE. The prefatory note says, 'When king Woo had deceased, the three overseers and the wild tribes of the Hwae rebelled. The duke of Chow acted as prime minister to king Ching; and having purposed to make an end of the House of Yin, he made "The Great Announcement."' This sets forth the occasion on which the address was composed, but when we come to look at the contents, we find very little appropriate, according to our views, to the circumstances. The young emperor speaks of the responsibility lying on him to maintain the empire gained by the virtues and prowess of his father, and of the senseless movements of the House of Yin to regain its supremacy ; he complains of the reluctance of many of the princes and high officers to second him in putting down the revolt ; and proclaims with painful reiteration the support and assurances of success which he has received from the divining tortoise-shells. The three overseers are not mentioned, though we may find an allusion or two to them. The whole tone is feeble. I have divided, it will be seen, the 15 paragraphs in which it is now generally edited into five chapters.

The date of the announcement is generally referred to the third year of Ching B.C., 1,112. But such an arrangement of events supposes the duke of Chow's residence in the east, spoken of in the last Book, to have been a voluntary exile, and that this expedition against Yin was undertaken after he returned in the manner described. But I saw reason to understand the sojourning in the east as a description of this very expedition, and that the return mentioned was on its successful termination. On this view the announcement was made in the first or second year of Ching, and the expedition was finished in the third year. On that point,—the date of the extinction of Woo-kăng and his revolt, there is an agreement.

The style of the Book is about as difficult as that of 'the Pwan-kăng.' 'We may doubt,' says Wang Gan-shih, 'whether parts have not been lost, and other parts have not fallen out of their proper place. Our plan is to let alone what we cannot understand, and to explain what we find ourselves able to do.' 'It is difficult,' says Choo He, 'to point the Book. The sentences are very long, and students generally try to break them up into shorter ones, which makes the interpretation more difficult still.'

Ch. I. Pp. 1, 2. NOTWITHSTANDING HIS YOUTH AND INCOMPETENCIES, THE KING FEELS BOUND, BY HIS DUTY TO HIS FATHERS AND TO HEAVEN, TO DO HIS UTMOST TO PUT DOWN THE REVOLT WHICH WAS THREATENING THE RECENTLY ACQUIRED EMPIRE. 1. 王若曰,— these are the words of the duke of Chow, spoken by him as regent of the empire, and in the name of the young king. We are not to suppose indeed that Ching had anything to do with the announcement. Doubting the duke's loyalty, he would not have sent him to attack his other uncles ; but the duke acted as the great duties of his position required him to do, and would not allow the safety of the dynasty to be perilled by weak scruples. At the same time it was right that his address should appear as in the name of the king. There was no other king but Ching, and no other is intended by 王 throughout the Book. K'ang-shing, however, says that by 王 we should understand the duke himself. His words are :—王, 周公也, 周公居攝命大事, 則權稱王, 'The king is the duke of Chow. He was regent of the empire, and in giving charge about such great affairs, in the exigency of the circumstances, he called himself the king.'

Keang-shing, Ming-shing, and other opponents of 'the false K'ung.' adopt this view, and the ingenuity with which they argue for it is amusing ; but it is too absurd to justify our entering into an examination of their arguments. Comp. the 王若曰 in the Pwan-kăng, Pt. i., 16 ; and often in several of the Books of Chow that follow. 猷大誥爾多邦,—猷 appears to have come into use, under the Chow dynasty, as an exclamation, like the 咨 of the 'Canon of Yaou.' I do not see what other meaning can be given to it here, or in the next Bk., p. 1 ; et al. Here Ma Yung and others in the Han dynasty read it after 誥,—大誥猷爾, 云云,—and explained it by 道. Gan-kwŏ even attempted to give it the same meaning in its place at the beginning of the sentence :—周公稱王命, 順大道, 以誥天下, 云云. But this is exceedingly harsh and unnatural. Lin Che-k'e was the first, so far as I have ascertained, who explained the term as an exclamation. It is a pity that this meaning of it does not appear in the dictionary. 爾多邦=爾在外多邦之諸侯. 越爾御事,—see the 'Great Speech,' Pt. i., p. 2. 弗弔,—弔 (read teaou)=恤 'to pity,' as in the She King, Pt. III., Bk. III., Ode x., st. 5. In the 'Pwan-kang,' Pt. iii., 7, it was read teih, with the meaning of 至, 'to come to,' i.e., to reach the mark of goodness ; and so Gan-kwŏ took it, and Keang Shing takes it, but with different relations to the rest of the sentence ;—see the 註疏 and the 尚書集註音疏. Ts'ae expands the phrase as in the translation :—我不為天所恤. 天降割于我家, 不少延,—割=害, 'injuries,' 'calamities.' 'Heaven sends down calamities on my House,'—this has reference especially to the early death of king Woo ; and we may include also the present troubles occasioned by the revolt in Yin. 不少延.—'without a little delay.' Blow was following on blow in quick succession. Gan-kwŏ put a stop at 少, and carried 延 to the next sentence. Of this construction I shall speak on the next clause. K'ang-shing pointed as in the text and interpreted 不少延 as = 'not few and prolonged.' 延 may certainly be thus taken as = 長 ; but the whole phrase 不小延 is more naturally construed as I have done in the translation, following Ts'ae and other Sung critics. 洪惟=大思, 'I greatly think.' Gan-kwŏ, I have just said, began this

于　予　不　人　敷　求　水　子　已　二節　知
天　不　忘　受　賁　朕　子　若　子　　　天
降　敢　大　命　敷　攸　惟　涉　惟　　　命。
威　閉　功　茲　前　濟　往　淵　小　　　○

2　'Yes, I who am but a little child am in the position of one who
has to cross a deep water;—it must be mine to go and seek how to
cross over. *I must* diffuse the elegant institutions of my predecessor, and augment the appointment which he received *from Heaven*;
—so shall I be not forgetful of his great work. Nor shall I dare to
restrain the majesty of Heaven seen in the inflictions it sends down.

clause with 延, and his comment on 延惟
我幼沖人 is—凶害延大,惟
累我幼童人, 成王言其不
可不誅之意, 'The calamities are so protracted and great that they involve me who am
so young;—the king's meaning is that there
was nothing for him but to cut off the criminals.'
This is very far-fetched, and must be rejected.
　　嗣無疆大歷服.—歷 is de-
fined as=數, 'fate,' destiny.' Woo Ch'ing
says:—歷＝天之歷數. 服＝'do-
mains.' Ts'ae says—五服, 'the five domains;' but they were more than 'five' under
the Chow dynasty. Nearly all the critics define
服 by 事, and then expand it into something
like 服王事; but Ts'ae's meaning is much
simpler. 　弗造哲,迪民康,—on
this Gan-kwŏ has—不能爲造智道
以安人, 'I cannot practise the ways of
wisdom to repose the people.' Këang Shing
has—弗遭逢明哲之人以道
于安, 'I have not met with (＝found), intelligent men to lead the people to repose.'
Better than either, Woo Ch'ing read 造 with
an aspirate,＝'to go to,' 'to arrive at;' and
says:—弗能造於明哲以導民
於安, 'I have not attained to wisdom, so as
to conduct the people to tranquillity.' So I take
the words. 　朝日, 云云,—I take 格
here with Gan-kwŏ as＝至. 'to reach to.' I
do not know what the young king, or rather the
duke of Chow, had in view by 天命, 'the
decree or appointment of Heaven,' nor can I
discern the bearing of the whole clause on the

rest of the announcement. Perhaps a glimpse
of light is afforded by Kin Le-ts'ëang, who
says:—此言成王以幼沖嗣位,
流言展轉,而事變如此,未
能上測天意如何,以起下
文求濟卜茲之意, 'This speaks
of how king Ching, inheriting the throne at so
early an age, with the baseless rumours going
about, and such changes of events occurring,
was unable to fathom what might be the mind
of Heaven, in order to introduce what is said
below about his seeking how to cross over his
difficulties, and the intimations afforded by divination;'—see the 集說. 2. 已 is used,
acc. to Ts'ae, as a continuative particle, indicating that though the speaker had come to a pause,
yet he must go on expressing his sentiments
(已, 承上語辭已而有不能
已之意). Our 'Yes' corresponds to it.
　　子惟至攸濟,—'this,' says Gan-
kwŏ, 'expresses the king's awe' (言祇懼).
He might have said—'awe and perplexity.' 敷
賁, 敷前人受命,—the former clause
expresses the young king's apprehensive perplexity; this seems to express what under all
circumstances he felt it incumbent upon him to
do. The language however, is difficult to construe and interpret. Lin Che-k'e says:—'Gan-
kwŏ read 賁 *fun*, as in the "Pwan-kāng," Pt.
iii., 7, and with the same signif. of *great*, and
gave the meaning—'I will spread and practise
great principles, so spreading and displaying
the appointment received by Wǎn and Woo.'
But the text only says 敷賁, and to make
that＝'I will display great principles' is wide
of the mark and forced. Soo and Lin Tsze-
hwuy (林子晦) read the character *pe*, with
the meaning of 'to adorn' (飾; as in the
'Announcement of T'ang,' p. 5). Soo then in-

越 亦 西 于 有 卽 紹 大 王 用。
茲 不 土 西 大 命 天 寶 遺 ○
蠢。 靜。 人。 土。 艱。 曰。 明。 龜 我 寧 三節

3 II. 'The Tranquillizing king left to me the great precious tortoise, to bring into connection with me the intelligence of Heaven. I consulted it, and it told me that there would be great trouble in the region of the west, and that the western people would not be still. Accordingly we have the present senseless movements.

terpreted—"What I diffuse must be to adorn and extend the appointment received by my predecessors, and not forget their merit," while Lin Tsze-hwuy says, "The meaning is—I will cultivate and illustrate the institutions, to impart ornament to the empire." The character 賁 is thus both pronounced and interpreted by them differently from Gan-kwŏ; but the meanings they bring out are as far from being clear as his. Wang Gan-shih says, better than any of them, that the text is maimed, and we need not weary ourselves to fix its meaning. The translation simply follows the view of Ts'ae, which is that of Soo Tung-po. 予不敢, 云云,—in this clause the king intimates how it was his duty to punish Woo-kăng and all aiding him in his revolt. He would let the justice of Heaven take its course; he would not restrain it, but execute it rather against them. 于, following 閟, is rather perplexing; but we have met with it before, similarly following transitive verbs.

Wang Gan-shih put a stop at 威, and read 用 with what follows—寧王, 云云, and Choo He approved of this construction;—see the 附錄. In this point Ts'ae chose to follow the two K'ung, rather than his master. Woo Ch'ing, however, points with Gan-shih, and gives this view of the clause preceding, having closed a paragraph with 大功:— 'When Heaven was sending down its terrors on me, I did not dare to conceal them, but used the tortoise,' &c., &c.

Ch. II. Pp. 3—6. THE DIVINATIONS HAD INFORMED THE KING OF THE COMING TROUBLES, AND THEY NOW ASSURED HIM ON THE PRESENT EXPEDITION. MANY OF THE BEST AND ABLEST OF THE PEOPLE WERE SUPPORTING HIM. THEY MIGHT THEREFORE GO FORWARD WITH CONFIDENCE. 3. 寧王,—'the Tranquillizing king.' Gan-kwŏ says that king Wăn is intended; but the phrase 寧考 in par. 8 determines that we interpret the epithet of king Woo, Ching's father. 紹天明,—紹 =繼, 'to continue and transmit.' At a grand

reception of visitors at court there were the attendants and officers who received them, and went between them and the prince. They and their function were called 介紹. Similarly we are told here that the tortoise-shell was a connecting medium between the mind of man and the mind of Heaven. And this was the belief of the duke of Chow! 卽命 is used like the same phrase in the last Book, p. 8. 曰有大至不靜,—this is to be taken as the reply of the tortoise, or the result obtained from the divination. Gan-kwŏ indeed makes the 曰 commence a new paragraph. 卽命 is with him = 'I have consulted it, and received its instruction;' and then for a time all reference to the tortoise ceases, and 曰 = 'The king also says.' This construction is to me intolerably harsh. 曰 follows immediately on the divination by the tortoise-shell, and introduces the reply which was received. That reply is sufficiently enigmatical. The troubles arose in the east, and the oracle was that the west would be troubled. This difficulty is solved by saying that the troubles arose indeed in the east, but they necessarily went on to trouble the west. The 'Daily Explanation' paraphrases the text as if the oracle had been thus explicit:—龜

卽 命 曰, 異 曰 東 方 諸 俟 起
而 叛 亂, 將 有 大 艱 之 難 之 事 于
于 西 土, 使 西 土 之 人, 疲 于 晏
奔 命 不 得 安 靜, 是 西 土 然
然 之 時, 龜 兆 已 豫 告 矣. This was, it will be seen, a prophecy, rather than the solution of a doubt, and the oracle was like those of the west. We may compare it with the 'Aio te, Æacida, Romanos vincere posse.' 越茲蠢,—these are again the words of the king. 蠢=蟲動, 'insects moving, wriggling about,' in the spring. It is often used in

有　翼　○　鄙　曰　疷　知　敍　誕　○
十　日　今　我　予　民　我　天　敢　殷
夫　民　蠢　周　復　不　國　降　紀　小
予　獻　今　邦。　反　康　有　威　其　腆
　　　　　　　五節　　　　　　　　　　　　　　　　四節

4 'Little as the *present* prosperity of Yin is, *its prince* greatly dares to take in hand its *broken* line. Though Heaven sent down its terrors *on his House*, yet knowing of the evils in our kingdom, and that the people are not tranquil, he says—"I will recover *my patrimony*"; and so *he wishes* to make our State of Chow a border territory again.

5 'One day there was a senseless movement, and the day after, ten men of worth among the people appeared to help me to go forward

the sense of 'silly,' 'impertinent.' 4. *The guilt of Woo-kăng.* 殷小腆,—this 腆 has marvellously vexed the critics. Gan-kwŏ took it as = 小, and K'ang-shing did the same. Ma Yung made it = 至, meaning probably 'Yin, who has but little attained.' Wang Suh made it = 主 so that 殷小腆 = 'this small princelet of Yin.' The 說文 defines it by 多, 'many or much;' and Ming-shing says this justifies the 小 of Kang-shing, like *lucus a non lucendo!* Ts'ae gives 厚, 'prosperous,' 'flourishing' for it, which is no doubt the correct meaning here. Compare 自洗腆致用酒 in the 'Announcement about Wine,' p. 6. Tung-po was the first to bring this meaning of the term to the interpretation of the text. 敍, —'to arrange,' 'to place in order;' then, 'a series' 'a rank.' Here, being under the govt. of 紀, it is taken as = 緒, 'the end of a cocoon, or of a ball of thread;' then 'a thread,' 'a line,' and with the same metaphorical applications as our word 'line.' The clause, as expanded by Ts'ae, is— 乃敢大紀其既亡之緒. All the old interpreters understood 天降威 of the troubles of the imperial House, with special reference to the rumours about the duke of Chow set on float by his brothers, following so quickly on the death of king Woo. The same view is taken also by Woo Ch'ing and Këang Shing. If the 知 had been before the 天 we must have construed in this way. The meaning which appears in the translation is given by Ts'ae, who follows his expansion of the previous clause, quoted

above, by— 是雖天降威于殷, 然亦武庚知我國有三叔疵隙, 民心不安, 故敢, 云云. 予復反鄙我周邦,—we must put a stop at 復, and then supply 而欲, as in the translation. 予 is Woo-kăng himself speaking, but we cannot refer the 我 also to him. 予復 = 我將復殷業. 鄙 is used for 'a border,' 'a border town.' It has here the force of a verb. 5 今蠢至以于,—獻 = 賢 (comp. the 'Yih and Tseih,' p. 7. Këang Shing reads 義, but with the same meaning); 于 = 往, 'to go.' Who the 'ten men of worth' were, we do not know. Gan-kwŏ supposed they belonged to Yin, 'loyal and far-seeing men in the rebellious territory.' This is not likely. I suppose they were men of the imperial domain who had been forward to express their attachment to the dynasty of Chow. The 今蠢, 今翼日, indicate the promptitude with which they had come forward. Ts'ae expands the clause:—今武庚蠢動, 今之明日, 民之賢者十夫, 輔我以往, 云云. 救寧武圖功,—救 = 撫, 'to soothe,' 'to tranquillize;' 救寧 go together, = 撫定商邦, 'to soothe and settle the country of Shang. 武 = 繼, 'to continue.' [武 is used for 'military prowess or achievement,' and also for 迹, 'footsteps,' 'traces,' from which the

越　臣　邦　卜　御　君　肆　六節　休　圖　翼
庶　○　于　予　事　越　予　　　朕　功　以
士　爾　七節　惟　曰　尹　告　　　卜　我　于
御　庶　伐　以　予　氏　我　　　幷　有　敉
事　邦　殷　爾　得　庶　友　　　吉　大　寧
罔　君　逋　庶　吉　士　邦　　　○　事　武
　　　　播

to restore tranquillity and to perpetuate the plans *of my father*. The great business I am engaging in will have a successful issue, *for* I have divined and always got a favourable intimation. 'There-
6 fore I tell you, the princes of my friendly States, and you, the directors of departments, my officers, and the managers of my affairs,—I have obtained a favourable reply to my divinations. I will now go forward with you from all the States, and punish those vagabond and transported ministers of Yin.

7   III. '*And now*, you the princes of the various States, and you the various officers and managers of my affairs, all retort on me, saying,

signification given to it in the text is derived. How the same character comes to have signifi- cations so different is one of the mysteries which a Lexicographer may solve by tracing its his- tory, and showing how forms originally distinct have coalesced in one.] 武圖功＝繼 嗣武王所圖之功. This construc- tion of the clause is given by Ts'ae, and Keang Shing concurs in it. Other views may be seen in the 註疏, and in Woo Ch'ing's commentary.

我有, 云云,＝大事, 'great affair,' referring to the warlike expedition about to be proceeded with. It is said in the 左傳 that 'the "great affairs" of a State are sacrifice and war,' (國之大事, 在祀與戎). 幷吉,—'all together are lucky.' The king had divined; and the 'three men' who had operated with the three shells, or interpreted the threefold intimation of the one shell, all foretold a happy result;—see the 'Great Plan,' p. 24. Ts'ae gives the connection of the two parts of the clause thus:—知我有戎 事休美者, 以朕卜三龜而 幷吉也.   We are not to suppose that this divining was the same as that mentioned in par. 2. That was earlier, before the rebellion had revealed itself; this was with reference to the expedition which was in progress.   6.

肆予至御事,—肆＝故, 'therefore.'

尹氏, 'the governors or directors,'＝庶 官之正, 'the heads of the various magis- terial departments.' Gan-kwŏ says they were the 卿大夫, 'nobles and great officers.' Compare the 百尹 of Bk. XXII., p. 3. We might bring out the meaning of the 氏 by saying—'the directors, of the several surnames.'

予得吉卜, 云云,＝于, as in the last par., ＝往. 逋播臣,—'the ab- sconded scattered ministers.' Woo-kăng and the old adherents of his House, who continued with him, are intended by this contemptuous language. There was enough in the circum- stances of their condition to afford a ground for so describing them.

Ch. III. Pp. 7—9. THE KING COMPLAINS OF THE RELUCTANCE OF THE PRINCES AND OFFICERS TO GO FORWARD WITH HIM TO THE EXPEDITION, AND REPLIES TO THEIR PROPOSAL TO GO CONTRARY TO THE DIVINATIONS.   7. *The proposal of the princes and officers to go contrary to the ora- cles, and abandon the expedition.* 罔不反 —'there is not one who does not retort.' K'ang- shing says—無不反我之意, 'all oppose my views.' Keang Shing would take 反 as simply ＝復, 'to reply.' The two ideas are here combined in the term. All the rest of the par. is to be taken as the language of the mal- contents. Gan-kwŏ, indeed, takes only 艱大

艱于朕身越予　造天役遺大投　蠢鰥寡哀哉子　思艱曰嗚呼允　○肆予沖人永　征王害不違卜。　小子考翼不可　宮邦君室越予　不靜亦惟在王　不反曰艱大民

八節

"The hardships will be great, and that the people are not still has its source really in the king's palace, and in the mansions of those princes of the *troubled* State. We, little ones, and the old reverent men as well, think the expedition ill-advised. Why does your majesty not go contrary to the divination?

8 'I, in my youth, think also continually of the hardships, and say, Alas! these senseless movements will deplorably afflict widowers and widows! But I am the servant of Heaven, which has assigned

'the difficulties will be great,' as their words, and makes out all the rest to be a portion of the king's reply. But, to my mind, the text is altogether unmanageable on this view. The exegesis which I have followed, and which appears in the translation, is not unattended with difficulties; but it gives an interpretation of the passage in harmony with the general tenour of the Announcement, and not harsher, as regards particular expressions, than we are obliged to admit in many other places 民不靜 至君室,—this is an allusion, as plain as the duke of Chow could permit himself to make, to the dissatisfaction of his three brothers charged with the oversight of Yin, the rumours which they had spread against himself, and the suspicions which those had awakened in the king's mind. The 邦君 are Sëen, Too, and Ch'oo. 室, as opposed to 宮, I translate by 'mansion.' 越予小子,考翼,不 可征云云,—this passage presents several difficulties, and no construction of it has been proposed, against which objections cannot be urged. 予小子 is taken by Gan-kwǒ of the king speaking of himself, and this is the one strong point in his construction mentioned above. In the translation the phrase is taken in the plural:—so the princes and officers, opposed to the expedition, describe themselves. 考 is taken as＝老, 'old,' 'fathers.' 翼＝ 敬, 'to be reverent,' *i.e*, in the conduct of business. The character is thus used in the She King, as may be seen in the dict. 考翼＝父

老之敬事者. 害 (read in the 4th tone)＝曷, 'why.' The paraphrase of the whole in the 'Daily Explanation' is:—予等敬之協聽而達之未至于練成人謀卜,小子固無所知識乃老不違,事之父皆以曷不曷遺卜,人龜兆乎憑難可乎

Pp. 8, 9. *How the king replies to the princes and officers, complaining of their want of sympathy with him, and urging again the authority of the oracles.* 8. 允蠢鰥寡,哀哉,— 'indeed the senseless movements; widowers and widows, alas:' Gan-kwǒ brings out the meaning thus:—信蠢動天下,使無妻無夫者受其害,可哀哉. Woo Ch'ing observes that the young and strong would be carried off to the expedition, and so the widowers and widows would be left in their solitude without those whose duty it was to care for them. 予造天役＝予 所爲之事,皆天所役使, 'the things which I do are all services required from me by Heaven.' Keang Shing takes 造＝遭, as in p. 1, which would give here a good enough meaning. 遺大,投大于我身遺 —Heaven is the nominative to the verbs 遺 and 投. The 'Daily Explanation' has:—天

亦惟卜用鳴呼天明

茲命今天其相民矧

寧王惟卜用克綏受

于寧王與我小邦周

不敢替上帝命天休

圖功。○己予惟小子

恤不可不成乃寧考

御事綏予曰無毖于

邦君越爾多士尹氏

沖人不卬自恤義爾

九節

me this great task, and laid this hard duty on my person. I therefore, the young one, do not pity myself, and it would be right in
you, the princes of the States, and in you, the many officers, the
directors of departments, and the managers of my affairs, to soothe
me, saying, "Do not be distressed with sorrow. We shall surely
complete the plans of your Tranquillizing father."

9　'Yes, I, the little one, dare not disregard the charge of God.
Heaven, favourable to the Tranquillizing king, gave such prosperity
to our small State of Chow. The Tranquillizing king divined and
acted accordingly, and so he calmly received his *great* appointment.
Now Heaven is helping the people;—how much more must I follow
the divinations! Oh! the clearly-intimated will of Heaven is to be
feared:—it is to help my great inheritance.'"

實以甚大者遺于吾之身.
甚艱者投于吾之身. 不
卬自恤—卬＝我 or 身, 'I,' 'myself.'
The meaning is that the king would do his duty,
without considering the risks and troubles to
which it would expose him. 義爾至圖
功—義＝以義言之, 'speaking of
the case with reference to what is right.' 毖
＝勞, 'to labour,' 'to distress one's-self.'
(＝毋) 毖于恤＝君毋勞于恤,
'Let not your Majesty distress yourself about
this matter of sorrow.' The princes and officers
are then supposed to say that they would dispose of the revolt for him.—凡 我 臣
者, 不 其 爲 罪
致 可 力 聲 功
討 不 所 之 替
9. 成 圖 替 上
已, 乃 不 寧
,—as in p. 2. 寧 敢 考

帝命.—替＝廢. 'to disregard,' 'to make of
none effect.' 'The charge of God' is that implied
in p. 5, when the divinations were all favourable, and the king was thus instructed to go
forward with the expedition against Woo-kăng
and his associates. 天休至茲命.
—the divinations of king Woo referred to are
those mentioned in 'The Great Speech,' Pt. ii.,
p. 5, 朕夢協朕卜, 襲于休祥.
今天其相民—How was Heaven
now helping the people? Gan-kwŏ replies—
'By the coming forward of the ten men of worth
to support the king.' Possibly the king, or the
duke rather, may have had this in mind.
矧亦惟卜用＝況我亦惟卜
是用. 天明, 云云—the transla-
tion here follows Ts'ae. The 天明, 'intelligence of Heaven,' is that mentioned in p. 3, as
conveyed by the 'great tortoise.' Thus clearly
intimated, it was to be reverenced. Opposition
to it could only entail disaster. How much

于前寧人圖功攸

考我民予曷其不

邦君、天棐忱辭其不

肆予大化誘我友

不極卒寧王圖事、

我成功所子不敢

王若勤哉天閟毖

丕克遠省、爾知寧

王曰、爾惟舊人、爾

十節　畏弼我丕丕基。○

10   IV. "The king says, 'You, who are the old ministers, are fully able to examine the long-distant affairs;—you know how great was the toil of the Tranquillizing king. Now where Heaven shuts up and distresses us is the place where I must accomplish my work;—I dare not but do my utmost to complete the plans of the Tranquillizing king. It is on this account that I use such efforts to remove the doubts and carry forward the inclinations of the princes of my friendly States. Heaven *also* assists me with sincere expressions *of attachment*, which I have ascertained among the people;—how dare I but aim at the completion of the work formerly begun by the

more should they be forward to obey it, when it was to establish the dynasty! Këang Shing takes 畏＝威, and the whole ＝ 'The brilliant majesty of Heaven is aiding me to enlarge this great inheritance.'

Ch. IV. Pp. 10—12. THE KING ADDRESSES HIMSELF MORE PARTICULARLY TO THE OLD MINISTERS OF HIS HOUSE; SETS FORTH HIS OWN WISH TO DO HIS DUTY AS A SON AND A SOVEREIGN, AND COMPLAINS OF THEIR WANT OF SYMPATHY WITH HIM.   10. 王曰,—see on 王若曰, p. 1. It is one of the peculiarities of the Announcements in the Books of Chow, that they are broken up into many parts by the recurrence of these phrases. 爾惟至勤哉,—by 舊人 we are to understand the old ministers of king Woo, (武王之舊臣),—the 考翼 of p. 7, who are there quoted as opposed to the expedition. 遠省,—'to examine the remote,' *i.e.*, the affairs of past days. 天閟至圖事,—this is an instance of what Choo He calls the 'long sentences' of the 'Great Announcement.' 閟者否塞不通之意, '閟 means shut up, without thoroughfare.' 毖者艱難不易之

意, '毖 means difficult and not easy.' These are the definitions given by Ts'ae, who adds— 天之所以否閉艱難國家多難者,乃我成功之所在. The above definition of 閟 is not given in the dictionary, tho' it may be very reasonably derived from the explanation of the term in the 說文 as ＝閉門. The dict. makes it ＝ 慎, after Gan-kwǒ, and with reference to this passage. Këang Shing defines it by 勞, which makes it simply a synonym of 毖. Ts'ae took his definition from Lin Che-k'e. 'The place where king Ching had to accomplish his work,' was the east, where the revolt was going on; but the 所 does not indicate the locality simply, but all the circumstances of the case. 肆予至邦君,—化者,化其固滯 'by 化 is meant dissolving their obstinate obstructions;' 誘者,誘其順從, 'by 誘 is meant inducing them to follow him with accordance.' These again are the definitions of Ts'ae,—very good. 天棐至攸終, —棐 is taken by Gan-kwǒ and most other

父　肯　厎　思　其　○　寧　予　弼　終
薗　堂　法　若　逝　王十一節　人　曷　我　天
厥　矧　厥　考　朕　曰　攸　敢　民　亦
子　肯　子　作　言　若　受　不　若　惟
乃　構　乃　室　艱　昔　休　于　有　用
弗　厥　弗　既　日　朕　畢。　前　疾。　勤

Tranquillizer? Heaven moreover is thus toiling and distressing
my people, so that it is as if they were suffering from disease;—how
dare I allow the appointment which the Tranquillizer, my predecessor, received, to be without its happy fulfilment?'"

11　　"The king says, 'Formerly, at the initiation of this expedition,
I spoke of its difficulties, and revolved them daily. *But* when a
deceased father,*wishing to* build a house, had laid out the plan, if
his son be unwilling to raise up the hall, how much less will he be
willing to complete the roof! Or if the father had broken up the
ground, and his son is unwilling to sow the seed, how much less

critics as = 輔,' 'to aid.' 忱 = 誠 信,
'sincere.' Heaven does not speak;—where were
the 'expressions' of its regard? The ten men
of worth, who had come forward to encourage
the king, might be considered as giving utterance to the 'voice of the people,'=the 'voice of
God.' Choo He was dissatisfied with this interpretation of 棐. He said that 'though all
the elder scholars concurred in it, it made the
passage unintelligible.' He himself, on the
authority chiefly of Yen Sze-koo, made the
character synonymous with 匪, 'not,' so that
the meaning is—'Heaven really does not utter
words, but its mind may be ascertained from
the mind of the people.' This brings out substantially the same meaning as the other view
of 棐.　By 寧人 I understand king Woo.
It is only a variation of the phrase 寧王.
Ts'ae takes it as = 寧臣, 'the tranquillizing
ministers,' meaning those who had co-operated
with king Woo in his great work, and adds that
this description of them would cover with shame
those of them who were dissuading king Ching
from the expedition. See a note from Ch'in Leih
on this point in the 附錄.　天亦云,
云,—here is another consideration, which determined the king's resolution. His father's
object was to give repose and happiness to all
the people. This revolt was distressing them,
—a fever, a serious disease in the State. He
must secure the realization of his father's pur-

pose by putting the revolt down.　　11. *How
his sense of filial duty impelled the king to the expedition.*　若昔日朕其逝 = 初
欲東征之時, 'when I first wished to
undertake this expedition to the east.' So,
Ts'ae and Woo Ch'ing. Then the 言 and 思
of the next clause are to be taken in the past
tense. Woo, indeed, is half disposed to take
言 simply as an expletive or exclamation, but
there is no necessity for having recourse to such
a construction. Thinking of the difficulties
which the expedition was pressed with, the king
might have wished to abandon it; but to prevent
his doing so, there came in the considerations of
his duty to his father which are set forth in the
rest of the paragraph. In this way we get a
consistent meaning from the whole.　　Gan-
kwŏ and Këang Shing, instead of taking 若
昔 as = 昔日, or 昔者, give 若 a full
verbal force, = 順, 'to accord with.' The former then interprets—'In accordance with ancient principles, I must proceed with this
expedition to the east (順古道,我其
往東征矣). I have spoken quite enough
about the difficulties and hardships of the
empire, and I daily think of them.' The latter
says:—'In accordance with the example of the
king my predecessor, I ought to go and punish

肯播矧肯穫
厥考翼其肯
曰予有後弗肯
棄基肆予弗
敢不越邛救
寧王大命。○
若兄考乃有
十二節　友伐厥子民
養其勸弗救。

will he be willing to reap the grain! In such a case will the father, *who had himself* been so reverently attentive *to his objects*, be willing to say, "I have an heir who will not abandon the patrimony?"—How dare I, therefore, but use all my powers to give a happy settlement to the great charge entrusted to the Tranquillizing king?

12　　'If a father have those among his friends who attack his child, will the elders of his people encourage *the attack*, and not *come to the* rescue?'

these revolters (順昔前王之事, 則我其當往征). Of the hardships connected with the expedition I have spoken, and I daily think of them.' The view which I have followed seems to me much preferable to either of these. 若考作室, 既底法. —考 is 'a father deceased.' We must take it so here, king Woo being intended, while Ching is the son on whom it devolves to carry out and finish his father's undertakings. 既底法. —'has settled the plan,' *i.e.*, has laid out the foundation, and defined all the dimensions,—the length, breadth and height. For 堂 Woo Ch'ing says 築基, 'to build up *on* the foundation.' The meaning evidently is to proceed with the building, according to the plan. 構=蓋, 'to cover;' here, ='to construct the roof.'

[Immediately after 構, K'ang-shing read 厥考翼其肯曰予有後弗棄基, which thus occurred with him twice in the paragraph.] 菑,—反土芟草曰菑, 'turning over the earth and removing the grass is called 菑.' It denotes the first steps taken to bring waste land or virgin soil into cultivation. 考翼至棄基.— Are we to take 考翼 in the singular, referring to the 考 and 父 in the preceding clauses, or in the plural, like the same phrase in p. 7? Gan-kwŏ and Ts'ae take it in the singular.

Ts'ae says—'The spirit of king Woo in heaven would not be willing to say that he had a son and successor who would not let his inheritance fall to the ground.' The paraphrase in the 'Daily Explanation' takes the phrase in the plural, =其家敬事之父老, 'the old and reverent elders of the family.' This is the view also of Woo Ch'ing, who has:—其父之輔翼者, 'the assistants of his father.' I must understand the phrase in the singular. 肆子, 云云, —越邛=於我身, 'in my person.' It is a strange and unsatisfactory expression; but all the critics explain it thus.

Q. 12. *The king reproaches the princes and officers who would let the revolt take its course.* A short paragraph, and all but unintelligible. The view which Gan-kwŏ gives may be seen in the 註疏. I cannot make it out, even with the help of Ying-tă. Ts'ae says that he does not understand what is meant by the phrase 民養. He takes it, however, after Soo Tung-po as =人之臣僕, or 民長, as in the translation. 'By 兄考,' he says, 'is intended king Woo; by 友, Woo-kăng and his confederates, the king's uncles: by 子, 'the people; and by 民養. the princes of the States, and the officers.' I would only differ from him in taking 子 not of the people, but of king Ching himself.

不　室　人　戻　敢　越　十　事　爾　○
易　爾　誕　于　易　天　人　爽　庶　王　十
。　亦　鄰　周　法　棐　迪　邦　邦　曰　三
○　不　胥　邦　矧　忱　知　由　君　嗚　節
予　知　伐　惟　今　爾　上　哲　越　呼
十　天　于　大　天　時　帝　亦　爾　肆
四　命　厥　艱　降　罔　命　惟　御　哉
節　　　　　　　　　　　　
永　　　　　　　　　　　　
念　　　　　　　　　　　　
曰　　　　　　　　　　　　

13   V. "The king says, 'Oh! Take heart, ye princes of the various States, and ye managers of my affairs. The enlightening of the country was from the wise, even from the ten men who obeyed and knew the decree of God, and the sincere assistance given by Heaven. At that time none of you presumed to change the *royal* appointments. And now, when Heaven is sending down calamity on the State of Chow, and the authors of these great distresses *appear as if* the inmates of a house were mutually to attack one another, you are without any knowledge that the decree of Heaven is not to be changed!

Ch. V. Pp. 13—15. THE KING CONTRASTS THE PRESENT CONDUCT OF THE PRINCES AND OFFICERS WITH THE PAST, AND TRIES TO STIMULATE THEM TO CARRY OUT THE WISH OF HEAVEN. HE THEN STATES HIS OWN DETERMINATION, AND CONCLUDES BY VINDICATING HIS FOLLOWING THE ORACLES OF DIVINATION.   13. Ts'ae Ch'in, in interpreting this par., struck out a new path for himself, in which I have followed him. The par. mentions 'ten men who obeyed and knew the mind of God.' Were they the 'ten men of worth, mentioned in par. 5, who came forward to support king Ching against the revolt of Yin? All the old interpreters say so, and Woo Ch'ing and Këang Shing, still hold to that view. This is to be said for it, that in the compass of a short Book, we can hardly expect two references to 'ten men,' of the same purport, and yet that they should be difft. men. I would willingly accept Gan-kwŏ's view, if it did not make all attempts to explain the context not only troublesome but to my mind vain. Ts'ae decided that the ten men here were not the ten men of par. 5, but king Woo's 'virtuous men,' his 'ten ministers capable of govt.,' celebrated in 'The Great Speech.' He contends that the predicates of the 'ten men' here are too great for the ten men of the people who came forward to encourage king Ching, and tries to fortify his view by referring to the duke of Chow's language in Bk. XVI., p. 14, where he is speaking of king Wăn's able ministers, as he speaks of the ten men here. The editors of Yungching's Shoo accept his view, but with some misgivings, and think it necessary to preserve the other also. 肆＝放心, 'put your hearts at ease.' 爽邦由哲.—爽＝明, as in 爽厥師, Pt. IV., Bk. II., p. 3. King Woo put an end to the 'dark ways' (昏德) of Show, and displayed the mind of Heaven to the empire, 'by means of the wise men' (由哲), who were his counsellors and helpers,— 'the ten men who walked in (迪) and knew the commands of God.' 越天棐忱. —棐＝輔, as in p. 10. This clause is collateral with 上帝命, and under the regimen of 迪知. 爾時＝爾於是時, 'you at that time.' Among those who followed Woo to the conquest of Shang, there were many of the princes and officers who were now shrinking from the expedition against Woo-kăng. 矧今,云云,—it is difficult to render 矧 here by 'how much more,' in the usual way; yet its force extends to the end of the par., and may be indicated by a point of exclamation. The allusion in 天降戾于周邦 is to the death of king Woo. By 惟大艱人 we

天惟喪殷若穡
夫予曷敢不終
朕畝天亦惟休
于前寧人。○予 十五節
曷其極卜敢弗
于從率寧人有
指疆土矧今卜
羍吉肆朕誕以
爾東征天命不
僭卜陳惟若茲。

14　'I ever think and say, Heaven in destroying Yin is doing husbandman's work;—how dare I but complete the business of my fields! Heaven will thereby show its favour to the former Tranquillizer.

15　'How should I be all for the oracle of divination, and presume not to follow your advice? I am following the Tranquillizer, whose purpose embraced all the limits of the land. How much more must I proceed, when the divinations are all favourable! It is on these accounts that I make this expedition in force to the east. There is no mistake about the decree of Heaven. The indications of the divinations are all to the same effect.'"

are to understand the king's uncles, confederate with Woo-kăng. For 誕鄰胥伐 Ts'ae gives 大近相伐, and the 'Daily Explanation' has 相逼相攻 厥室 is taken by Woo Ch'ing of 其邦君之室, and he supposes the meaning of the whole to be that the rebel-uncles were endeavouring to force others of their brothers in their neighbourhoods to join them in the revolt. The meaning I have given is preferable, though the 誕鄰 is difficult to manage. Gan-kwŏ says that when the king's uncles took arms against him, it was truly like the inmates of one house fighting with each other. If king Woo had been commissioned to destroy Show for his wickedness, much more must it be Heaven's will that this revolt should be suppressed; and yet the princes and officers were telling the king not to proceed with the expedition.

Wang Ts'ëaou traces the course of thought in the par. on Ts'ae's view very clearly:—

通,不不貫脊裴
與天命敢罪此之
天不商如之
心知而時命吉,
知王天協
者也,知
命者真武討卜
帝理能在不夢
上合未也,可周,
知然者不有
迪自易信盈佑

忱又此不在今武庚作
亂可不也,討天亦如此
民亦冀爾朕卜有昔之
裴一又法如此不天人
事而一易然在而昔易
之之而則今人天十征,
武惟之以日考法敢害
則卜惟順惟之則可不
不矣,卜有功不爽言心
可日矣,夫時與之迪
爲知惟日者,者之邦邦者
實同同

P. 14. 穡 is 'a reaper,' but the phrase is here used for a husbandman generally. A husbandman's work is thoroughly to clear his ground of weeds;—he must not let their roots remain. King Woo had spared Show's son, but it was plain that he must now be made an end of. So would king Ching complete the business of his fields. And when hehad done so, the favour of Heaven to king Woo would be more fully displayed;—the empire would be made sure to his posterity.　　15. 子曷其極卜,

敢弗于從，－子何敢盡欲用
卜，而不從爾勿征之言乎.
The answer to this is given in the next clause.
It was not merely a question between the oracles
and the contrary opinions of many of the princes
and officers.　There was the example of king
Woo and his ministers; and there was the duty
of Ching to accomplish the work which his father had begun.　These were potent considerations to go into the scale.　They would determine
in favour of the expedition, even if the oracles
were not so decided.　As the oracles were so
entirely in favour of it, however, there could
be—there ought at least to be—no hesitation in
going forward.　率寧人有指疆土
＝循文王有指意，以安疆土.
This is Gan-kwŏ's explanation of the words, and
I have not met with any other so satisfactory.
His only error is in referring 寧人 to king
Wăn, instead of king Woo.　天命不

僭，—comp. 天命弗僭, in the 'Announcement of T'ang,' p. 5.

[We have thus got to the end of 'The Great
Announcement,' the style of which is at least as
rugged and difficult as that of 'The Pwan-kăng.'
Notwithstanding the uncertainty which attaches
to the interpretation of particular passages,
however, I cannot but believe that the translation gives, with tolerable correctness, the general
meaning of the Book.　In the year B.C. 7, when
Mang, the duke of Han (漢公莽), was
acting as regent of the empire, and designed to
usurp the throne, he published an announcement
modelled upon that of the duke of Chow.　He
incorporated the text of the Show with his own
statements in a very remarkable way.　Kěang
Shing and some others undertake to correct the
text of the Shoo from Mang's Announcement,
which ought not, however, to be appealed to for
that purpose.　It answers very well to show
the general view which Mang and the scholars
about him took of our Book.　Mang's Announcement is preserved in the 前漢書, 第五
十四卷, 翟方進傳.]

THE BOOKS OF CHOW.

BOOK. VIII. THE CHARGE TO THE VISCOUNT OF WEI.

咸休永世無于王家與國其禮物作賓統承先王修古崇德象賢王元子惟稽王若曰猷殷微子之命

窮。○嗚呼乃 咸休永世無 于王家與國 其禮物作賓 統承先王修 古崇德象賢 王元子惟稽 王若曰猷殷 微子之命

1   "The king speaks to the following effect:—"Ho! eldest son of the king of Yin, in accordance with *the statutes of* antiquity, that the honouring of the virtuous belongs to *their descendants* who resemble them in worth, do you continue the line of the kings your ancestors, cultivating their ceremonies and taking care of their various relics. Be a guest *also* in our royal house, enjoying the prosperity of our kingdom, for ever and ever without end.

THE NAME OF THE BOOK.—微子之命, 'The charge to the viscount of Wei.' 微子, —see on the name of the 11th Book of the preceding Part. 命,—see on the name of the 8th Book of the same part.

The prefatory note says:—'King Ching having made an end of the appointment *in favour of the House* of Yin, and put Woo-kăng to death, he appointed K'e, the viscount of Wei, to take the place of the descendants of Yin. Descriptive of this there was made 'The charge to the viscount of Wei.' This no doubt states correctly the time and occasion when the 'Charge' was made. We saw on 'The viscount of Wei,' how K'e was advised by his friends to withdraw from the court of Show and save himself from the destruction which was impending over the tyrant and his House; we saw also the account given by Sze-ma Ts'een of the guise in which

K'e presented himself with the sacrificial vessels of his family before king Woo. Some points in that account may be called in question, but there can be no doubt that K'e was honourably received and treated. When it is said that Woo restored him to his former office, I understand that he confirmed him in his appanage of Wei, so that he continued to be 'the viscount of Wei,' up to the date of this Charge, when he was appointed to be the duke of Sung (宋公), there to continue the sacrifices to T'ang, his ancestor and the founder of the dynasty of Shang.

In the first of the concluding notes to the 'Completion of the War,' I have quoted a passage from the Bk. 樂記 of the Le Ke, in which it is said that king Woo, after his victory over Show, 'when he had descended from his chariot, sent the representative of the House of Yin to Sung.' From this statement, some have contended that K'e's investiture with the dukedom of Sung was from Woo and not from Ching, and was before the revolt which ended in the death of Woo-kăng and not after it. But the editors of Yung-ching's Shoo have given good reasons why the authority of Sze-ma Ts'een, and the preface to the Shoo, should be preferred in this matter to that of the 樂記. If the merits of the men had been the sole ground for Woo's arrangements, he would have at once appointed either of the viscounts of Wei or Ke to continue the sacrifices to T'ang and the other sovereigns of his line, but there were, we can easily conceive, reasons of state, which determined him to make trial, in the first place, of Woo-kăng, as being the son of Show.

The Book is only found in the text of Gan-kwŏ.

CONTENTS. The duke of Chow, as regent of the empire, and in the name of king Ching, tells the viscount that in accordance with the statutes of antiquity, and because of his own worth, he is selected to continue the line of the sovereigns, his ancestors. The virtues of T'ang and of the viscount are then celebrated, and he is charged to go and be prosperous, taking care so to conduct his administration that the new dynasty of Chow might never have occasion to be weary of him. The Book is very short, consisting only of five paragraphs.

P. 1. *The grounds on which the viscount of Wei was called to be the representative of the kings of his line, with some of his duties and privileges.*

王若曰,猷,—see on the last Book, p. 1. 殷王元子,—元子 =首子, or 長子, 'eldest son.' 'The king of Yin' is Te-yih (帝乙), the father both of K'e and Show. How K'e, though older than Show, did not succeed to the throne, has been explained on page 274. Some critics, supposing that 元子 is equivalent to 太子, ='heir-apparent,' and cannot be otherwise applied, have contended on that ground against the authenticity of this Book, but to my mind there is no force in the objection. The 元子 is simply 'the eldest son;'—he may be the heir-apparent, but not necessarily. That idea does not form a part of the significance of the phrase.

稽古崇德象賢,—稽古, see on the 'Canon of Yaou,' p. 1; 崇德謂先聖王之有德者,則尊崇而奉祀之也, '崇德 means that the virtuous of the ancient sage sovereigns were honoured and sacrificed to;' 象賢謂其後子孫,有象先聖王之賢者,則命之以主祀也, '象賢 means that he among the descendants of those ancient sage kings who resembled them in talents and virtue was appointed to preside over the sacrifices to them.' These are the explanations of Ts'ae, similar to those of Gan-kwŏ. He adds:—言古制尊崇成湯之德,以微子象賢而奉其祀

也 The text is very concise, and it takes many characters to bring forth its meaning; but the explanation is, no doubt, correct. To the ancient statutes, which prescribed the honouring and sacrificing to the founders of former dynasties, we have a reference in the Le Ke, Bk. 郊特牲, Pt. i, p. 12, where it is said, 天子存二代之後,猶尊賢也,尊賢不過二代, 'The emperor preserves *representative* descendants of two dynasties, still honouring the worth of their founders. This honouring of *ancient* worth does not go beyond two dynasties.' In what the honouring was displayed, is partly indicated in the remainder of the paragraph. 統承先王,—the empire gathered under one rule is called 一統. Here the sovereigns of Shang are conceived of as all gathered up or collected in the person of K'e, who should henceforth, in himself and his descendants in the dukedom of Sung, stand forth as their representative.

修其禮物,—by 禮 we are to understand 典禮, 'the canons and ceremonies,' the institutions of Shang which had distinguished it from other dynasties; and by 物 we are to understand 文物, 'the literary monuments and other precious relics of the dynasty,'—carriages, flags, dresses, &c. The descendants of K'e held the dukedom of Sung till nearly the end of the Chow dynasty, but by the time of Confucius many of the ceremonies and relics which it was their business to preserve were lost. The sage bewailed this, and said, 'I am able to describe the ceremonies of the Yin dynasty, but Sung cannot sufficiently attest my words. It cannot do so because of the insufficiency of its records and wise men' (Con. Ana., III. ix.). See the introductory note on the 'Praise-songs of Shang,' in the third Part of the She King. 作賓至無窮,—the representatives of the two previous dynasties were distinguished above the other princes of the empire by being denominated 'guests' of the emperor of the dynasty then existing, as meeting him more on a footing of equality. See the She-king, Part III., the 'Praise-songs of Chow,' Bk, III., Song ii., 振鷺于飛,于彼西雝,我客戾止,亦有斯容. See also in the 左傳, 僖二十四年,—宋,先代之後也,於周爲客,天子有事,膰焉,有喪,拜焉. On this part Ts'ae gives some observations of Leu Tsoo-heen, which deserve a place in any commentary:—先王之心,公平廣大,非若後世滅人之國,惟恐苗裔之存爲子孫害,成王命微子,方且撫

德曰篤不忘上
恭神人子嘉乃
聞恪慎克孝肅
修厥猷舊有令
後裔○爾惟踐
功加于時德垂
以寬除其邪虐
誕受厥命撫民
廣淵皇天眷佑
祖成湯克齊聖

2　'Oh! your ancestor, T'ang the Successful, was reverent and sage, vast and deep *in his virtue.* The favour and help of Great Heaven lighted upon him, and he received the great appointment, to soothe the people by his gentleness, and to remove their wicked oppressions. His achievements affected all his age, and his virtue was

3　transmitted to his posterity. And you are the one who pursue and cultivate his plans;—this praise belongs to you of old. Reverently and carefully you discharge your filial duties; gravely and respect-fully you behave to spirits and to men. I admire your virtue, and pronounce it great, and not to be forgotten. God will always

助愛養，欲其與國咸休，永
世無窮，公平廣大氣象，於
此可見，'The minds of the ancient kings were just, generous, and enlarged, not like those of the sovereigns of future times, who on the extinction of a kingdom would extirpate all the members of its royal House, fearing that the preservation of them might be injurious to their own posterity. King Ching not only appoints the viscount of Wei duke of Sung, but goes on to soothe and cherish him, wishing him for ever and ever to share in the prosperity of the empire.—Admirably was the just and enlarged spirit displayed in this.' An objection has been taken to the genuineness of the Bk. on the ground of the phrase 與國咸休, it being supposed that the empire would not be denominated 國 merely; but the objection is as futile as that taken from the use of 元子, which has been already pointed out. Compare the language of the last Bk., p. 4, and of 'The Metal-bound Coffer,' p. 18.

P. 2. *The virtue of T'ang, the founder of the Shang dynasty, which made him worthy to be honoured.* - 齊＝莊 or 肅, 'reverent,' *i.e.,* gravely and reverently attending to all his duties. 皇天眷佑 誕受厥命 —comp. in the 'T'ae-kёă,' Pt. i. p. 2, 天監 厥德 用集大命 撫民以寬,

除其邪虐,—comp. in 'The Instructions of E,' p. 3, 代虐以寬, 兆民允懷. 功加于時,—時＝當時, 'that time,' his own age. 後裔,—'his posterity.' Choo He observes that 裔 properly denotes the bottom of the skirt of a garment (衣裾之末),—the superfluity of it, and from this is applied to express a man's posterity.

P. 3. *The worthiness of K'e, which made him fit to be selected to render the honour due to T'ang.* 踐修厥猷,—猷＝道, 'ways' or 'plans; 踐＝履其後, 'to tread in the steps of T'ang's ways.' 修 expresses the earnestness with which he sought to carry the plans into practice. 令聞,—'a good reputation.' 恪慎至神人,—Lin Che-k'e joins these two clauses together, and supposes that they refer to K'e's taking care of the sacrificial vessels of his House during the overthrow of the dynasty, and his carrying them with him to the army of Chow. It seems more natural to me, however, to take them as in the translation. 篤不忘＝篤厚而不可忘. 上帝時歆,—歆 is 'to enjoy the savour of offer-ings.' K'e, being the representative of the sovereigns of Shang, had the privilege of offering

休無萬毗律以慎夏建帝
無替邦子乃蕃乃○爾時
斁。朕作一有王服欽于歆
○命式世民室命哉上下
嗚。俾世永弘率往公民
呼、我享綏乃由敷尹祗
往有德厥烈典乃茲協
哉周、位、祖、常、訓、東、庸
惟

enjoy your offerings; the people will be reverently harmonious *under your sway.* I raise you, therefore, to the rank of High Duke, to rule this eastern part of our great land.

4   'Be reverent. Go and diffuse abroad your instructions; be carefully observant of your robes and various *other* symbols of your appointment; follow and observe the proper statutes!—so as to prove a bulwark to the royal House. Enlarge *the fame of* your meritorious ancestor; be a law to your people!—so as for ever to preserve your dignity. So also shall you be a help to me the one man; future ages will enjoy *the benefit of* your virtue; all the States will take you for a pattern!—and thus you will make our dynasty of Chow never weary of you.

5   Oh! go, and be prosperous. Do not disregard my charge."

the great solstitial sacrifice to God. It is with reference to this that it is said God would always, or at the appointed season of sacrifice, accept his offerings. 庸=用,—所以, 'therefore,' according to the frequent usage of 用 in the Shoo. 尹茲東夏,—尹=治, 'to rule.' Sung, the pres. dep. of Kwei-tih in Ho-nan, lay east from Fung and Haou, the capitals of Wăn and Woo, which were in the pres. dep. of Se-gan, Shen-se.

[In the 左傳, 僖, 十二年, we have an address to the famous Kwan Chung, evidently modelled on the text of this par. and the next:—王曰, 舅氏, 余嘉乃勳, 應乃懿德, 謂督不忘, 往踐乃職, 無逆朕命.]

Pp. 4, 5. *Charges, Cautions, and Encouragements addressed to K'e.*   4. 慎乃服命,—as a High duke, K'e had the robes and cap, the carriage, flag, &c., appropriate to his rank, and which were the accompaniments of his investiture:—see the Le-ke, Bk. 王制 Pt. ii., p. 7. He is charged to be carefully—cautiously—observant of them, not transgressing the proper statutes. He must not indulge the ambitious thoughts which had brought ruin on Woo-kăng. 以蕃王室,—蕃=屏衞, 'to screen and defend.' 藩 is more common in this sense. 律乃有民,—Gan-kwŏ says:—以法度齊汝所有之民, 'with laws regulate your people.' But this does not give all the emphasis of the text. The 'Daily Explanation' has better:—儀型爾朱之有民, 而作之師. 毗=輔, 'to assist.'   5. 往哉惟休,—Gan-kwŏ and all the critics after him make 惟休=務休美爾政, 'make your government prosperous and good.' I do not see the necessity for this.

[Wang Yen, Chin Tih-sëw, and other scholars remark on the fact that nothing is said in this Book of the wickedness of Show or of Woo-kăng;—how it shows the consideration of the duke of Chow for the feelings of the viscount of Wei, and the estimation in which his worth was held.]

[Here again there is space to introduce another Chapter from Wang Pih:—

士羣蠱以能叛此其其之則義非果身先復果武至之世是必以子詞乃懲有矣

境至敢無不敢於封使庚愚者之修顧豈叛曰矣命後爲也當微之律非而尊

之必孰言則不甚父武知父艾不著必或久公於謬封不命封曰豈綏命之

紂所庚流庚則有其則叛後其也其悔苟叛之知也上惑而始封祀不始也位不之

復勢武非武言未殺也必而殺仁使痛祀於庚後封亦傳之湯而皆詞律厥臣

以叛非叛非之乃非也智者也者叛歛先輕武而於宋封加此之子奉庚書之綏不史

掌之弟之弟非之乃非也智若必保而若者封庚奉周也上禮今非民武告矣

抵庚流庚羣庚周氏子人待說其則則以祀哉智微誅商衙若公命庚加曰庚戒

亂武之武曰蘇其果不此封也也行之也待封庚奉周也上禮今非民武告矣

倡矣弟之發叛故者子子叛曰也人人敉王人不王武以歸說加是也有創此嚴

卷商于道皆財所然而祀夫七於知非位在而武聞微封足邢時右之故沖外可

每然首式箕以粟可聞封之之商子存于年於封者有封庚平付自其謀爾周謀乘

唱政墓於所發不無乃周湯作微也微八乃後庚其子武祀而稍矣所人幼姦以

廢反比訪此散耳寂旣商者六過共家在何後彼未於湯猶宅是左夕之子在謂

不之封復書若奉此君有所王王者之哉德過祀受於當之朝德嗣叔自

嘗王囚而之心悅微之以於之未之賓武子艾晚惡有以受土爲處酒崩管行

未武之旣範之人於忘父大聖孫下作與微其之得可祀武故不遊于王而計

篇昔子閭洪子小獨豈祿有賢子天祀可知庚紂烏則以封之必共酗武政凶

此嘆箕容得君過者王庚未也賢此之誰不武朱染行子可不紂者與惟幸攝而

BOOK. IX.   THE ANNOUNCEMENT TO *THE PRINCE OF* K'ANG.

康
誥

一
節

惟
三
月
哉
生
魄、

周
公
初
基、
作
新

大
邑
于
東
國
洛、

四
方
民
大
和
會、

侯
甸
男
邦
采
衞、

百
工
播
民
和
見、

士
于
周
周
公
咸、

勤、
乃
洪
大
誥
治。

1   [In the third month, when the moon began to wane, the duke of Chow commenced the foundations and proceeded to build the new great city at Lŏ of the eastern States. The people from every quarter assembled in great harmony. From the How, Teen, Nan, Ts'ae, and Wei domains, the various officers stimulated this harmony of the people, and introduced them to the business there was for Chow. The duke of Chow encouraged all to diligence, and made a great announcement about the performance *of the works.*]

THE NAME OF THE BOOK.—康誥, 'The Announcement to *the prince of* K'ang.' Of the ten sons of king Wăn, the ninth was called Fung (封), generally spoken of as K'ang Shuh (康叔). According to the analogy of the titles of the other brothers,—Kwan Shuh, Ts'ae Shuh, &c., we must conclude that K'ang was the name of Fung's appanage, somewhere within the imperial domain. Ma Yung and Wang Suh expressly affirm this. The only ancient scholar who expressed a different opinion was K'angshing, who thought that K'ang was the honorary posthumous title of Fung (康爲號謚). Be this as it may, the Book is the Charge addressed to K'ang, or to the prince of K'ang, on his appointment to the principality of Wei (命爲衞侯), the chief city of which was Chaou-ko, which had been the capital of Show. Wei extended westward from the pres. sub. dep. of K'ae (開州), dep. of Ta-ming in Chih-le, to the borders of the pres. depp. of Wei-hwuy and Hwae-k'ing, in Ho-nan.

That the Book should be called an 'Announcement,' and not a 'Charge' (like the preceding), has occasioned various doubts about it,—and with reason. The title is no doubt taken from the occurrence of the word announcement in the last clause of what stands as the first paragraph (乃洪大誥治); but it will be seen immediately that there are strong grounds for believing that that paragraph is out of its place, and should be removed to the beginning of Bk. XIII., 'The Announcement concerning Lŏ.'

Wang Pih observes that the Book might very well be named 康叔之命, or 孟侯之命 (from the occurrence of 孟侯 in the 2d par). Its name, however, is 康誥, and that has the sanction of Mencius, who makes express reference to it, in Bk. V., Pt. II., iv., 4. We have it even so designated thrice in 'The Great Learning:'—Comm. i., 1; ii., 2; ix., 2. This carries up very nearly to Confucius himself. If we affirm, as I think we must do, the opinion of the scholars of Sung, that the 1st paragraph does not belong to this Book but to Bk. XIII., we must say what they have not done,—what they would not have ventured to say, even if they had seen to what their argument would lead,—that the great sage here made a mistake in compiling and arranging the tablets of the Shoo.

The Book is found in both the texts.

THE DATE OF THE ANNOUNCEMENT; AND ITS AUTHOR. The one of these points depends very much upon the other. The prefatory note says:—'King Ching, having smitten his uncles, the prince of Kwan and the prince of Ts'ae, invested his uncle of K'ang with the rule of the remnant of Yin. *With reference to this*, there were made "The Announcement to K'ang," "The Announcement about Wine," and "The Good Materials." According to this account, then, the appointment of the prince of K'ang, in connection with which this Charge was delivered to him, was made by king Ching, or rather by the duke of Chow, acting in the king's name. And it was not till the time of the Sung dynasty that this view was called in question. Sze-ma Ts'een repeatedly affirms it. He says:—'Tan, the duke of Chow, having received the commands of king Ching, attacked and slew Woo-kăng, and then divided the territory of Yin into two parts, appointing the viscount of Wei to one of them, over the principality of Sung, and the prince of K'ang to the other, over Wei' (周公旦承成王命, 伐誅武庚, 分殷地爲二, 一封微子啟于宋, 一封康叔于微. See Maou K'e-ling, 尙書廣聽錄; and also the 史記, 衞康叔世家, and 宋微子世家). More important still is the testimony given in the 左傳, under the 4th year of duke Ting (定公四年;—B.C. 505), where it is said that after king Woo had overthrown the dynasty of Shang, king Ching settled the empire by means of the regent, the duke of Chow, and that the duke appointed his brother the prince of K'ang over seven of the clans of the domain of Yin, with his seat of government in its capital (封於殷墟).

This view, I have said, was current and uncontradicted for many centuries. Under the dynasty of Sung, Soo Tung-po was the first to throw out the idea that the first paragraph had erroneously found its way into this Book from among the tablets of the 'Announcement about Lŏ.' About the same time, Woo Yih (吳棫; he is also called 才老) and other scholars came to the conclusion that the speaker in the Book was king Woo, and not the duke of Chow. Choo He adopted their views, and was followed by his disciple Ts'ae Ch'in, who sets forth the grounds of them in the following way:—

First, the prince of K'ang was king Ching's uncle (叔父), and could not be called by him 'younger brother,' as is the case in the par. 1. To the reply to this that the duke of Chow was really the speaker, and might so address Fung, he responds that the duke of Chow prefaced all the Charge with 'The king says,' and the words therefore should only be those appropriate to the lips of the king.

Second, if the Charge were given by the duke of Chow, how do we account for the fact that while there are many references in the Book to king Wăn, there is not one to king Woo? And the same question may be asked with reference to the two Books which follow. The words of par. 4,—寡兄勗, have indeed been explained of king Woo, the duke of Chow so speaking of him. But if we suppose that Woo was the speaker, he might very well so describe himself. On the supposition that the duke of Chow was the speaker, the language is contrary to all rule and propriety.

Third, it has been urged that at the time of the overthrow of Shang, Fung was still young, and unfit to be entrusted with an important govt.; and hence that his appointment took place subsequently, under king Ching. But when king Woo obtained the empire, he was about 90 years old. The ten sons of king Wăn, so often referred to, were all by the same mother; Woo was the second of them:—could there be one among them, when Woo was ninety, too young to be entrusted with an important administration? This point is too clear to need to be fortified by other considerations which Ts'ae has adduced.

It cannot be denied that there is much force in the two first of these points. We must assent also to Ts'ae's view of the age of the prince of K'ang. He was no doubt old enough to have received an appointment on the conquest of Shang. But other reasons might have prevented his being invested with a principality which would take him from the imperial court. One such reason, quite sufficient, is suggested in the passage of the 左傳 which has been referred to. It is there said, that, while the duke of Chow was prime minister under the new dynasty, the prince of K'ang was minister of Crime;—and this agrees with the prominent place which the subject of punishments occupies in our Book. The two other points, however, remain;—the general style of the Announcement, and particular expressions in it. For many years, when reading the Shoo without thinking of such critical matters as are now in hand, and without regard to commentators, I got the

越我一二邦　肇造我區夏　威威顯民用　寡庸庸祗祗　○不敢侮鰥　克明德愼罰（四節）　丕顯考文王　子封○惟乃（三節）　侯朕其弟小　○王若曰孟（二節）

2　I. "The king speaks to this effect:—'Head of the princes,
3　my younger brother, little one, Fung.' It was your greatly distinguished father, the king Wăn, who was able to illustrate his
4　virtue and be careful in the use of punishments. He did not dare
to show any contempt to the widower and widows. He employed
the employable, and revered the reverend; he was terrible to those
who needed to be awed:—*so* getting distinction among the people.
It was thus he laid the first beginnings of *the sway of* our small portion
of the Empire, and the one or two *neighbouring* countries were

impression that the speaker in the text must be king Woo;—see the note in 'The Great Learning,' Comm., Ch. i. But I now give in my adhesion to the older view. The authority of the 左傳, as old as the time of Confucius, and of the Preface, is not to be set aside. The 王若曰 at the beginning, and the 王曰 throughout the paragraphs, assimilate the Book closely to the others in which the duke of Chow is undoubtedly the speaker. It will be seen in the notes that some explanation can be given of the most difficult expressions; and it is hardly competent for us to try the language of a man like the duke of Chow by our ideas of the way in which he ought to have spoken. Maou applies here, with considerable force, the saying of Mencius, that 'it is not every ordinary man who can understand the conduct of superior men' (君子所爲，眾人不識).

It still remains to make a remark or two on THE FIRST PARAGRAPH. It speaks of the founding and completion of the city of Lŏ, which was one of the later labours of the duke of Chow, and is commonly referred to the 7th year of king Ching. As the scholars of Sung wished to make out that the Charge to the prince of K‘ang was delivered by king Woo, it was necessary they should remove from it this paragraph;—as was done by Soo Tung-po in the manner which I have related above. But while dissenting from their view of the early origin of the Charge, and not hampered therefore in that respect by the par., I must still maintain the correctness of Shih's decision regarding it.

First, it is appropriate at the commencement of the 'Announcement concerning Lŏ;' while here it is altogether out of place. What had the building of Lŏ to do with the investiture of Fung with the principality of Wei? In the body of the Charge, moreover, there is not a word having reference to Lŏ, or the reasons which had led the duke of Chow to project the establishment of that new city. Second, the appointment of Fung was to Wei, and must have been contemporaneous with the appointment of the viscount of Wei to the government of Sung. It must have taken place in the 3d or 4th year of king Ching, some years before the building of Lŏ.

Gan-kwŏ felt these difficulties, and tried to meet them by supposing that some other noble or nobles had been appointed to rule 'the remnant of Yin,' during the years that elapsed between the suppression of Woo-kăng's rebellion and the building of Lŏ; and that the result having proved unsatisfactory, the prince of K‘ang was then called to the task. This supposition is without any historical ground of support; and Lin Che-k‘e prefers the view of a scholar Wang, (王博士), who supposed that Fung had been appointed to Wei immediately after the suppression of the rebellion, but that the Charge in this Book was not given to him till the time when Lŏ was built. But this solution is to the full as unsatisfactory as that of Gan-kwŏ. The knot cannot be loosed, it seems to me;—why should we hesitate to cut it, by removing the first par. from this Bk. to the 13th? We have seen, indeed, that but for the occurrence of the word 'announcement' in this par., the Book would hardly have been called by its present name; and yet that name was current in the time of Confucius. The sage himself perhaps misplaced the paragraph, or more probably left it, as he found it, in the wrong place. A Chinese critic would not allow this;—a foreign student may say it, when the weight of evidence seems to require him to do so.

CONTENTS. The key-note of the whole Book is in the clause 明德慎罰,—'the illustration of virtue and the careful use of punishments,' in the 3d paragraph. It has been divided into five chapters. The first three parr. (not including par. 1) celebrate the exhibition of those two things, which was given by king Wăn, whereby he laid the foundations of the imperial sway of his House, and afforded an example for all his descendants. Parr. 5—7 inculcate on Fung how he should illustrate *his* virtue, as the basis of his good govt. of the people intrusted to him. Parr. 8—19, inculcate on him how he should be careful in the use of punishments, and set forth the happy effects that would ensue from his being so. Parr. 20—22 insist on the influence of virtue, as being superior in govt. to that of punishments, and how punishments should all be regulated by the ruler's virtue. The last chapter, parr. 23, 24, winds the subject up with a reference to the uncertainty of the appointments of Heaven, and their dependance for permanence on the discharge of the duties they require from those, on whom they have lighted.

P. 1. See on the 'Announcement concerning Lŏ.'

Ch. I. Pp. 2—4. THE DUKE OF CHOW, ADDRESSING FUNG AS HIS YOUNGER BROTHER, SETS FORTH TO HIM THE ADMIRABLE QUALITIES OF THEIR FATHER WĂN. 2. 王若曰, —see on the 1st par. of the 7th Book. The 'king' is king Ching. 孟=長, 'the eldest,' 'the first.' It is here = 'chief;' and 孟侯=諸侯之長, 'Head of the princes.' Acc. to the Le Ke, Bk. 王制, Pt. ii., p. 2, every 州 or province of the empire, embracing 210 國 or States, was under the authority of a chief or 伯. We may conclude therefore that Fung had been invested with that dignity. Fuh-shang has said, indeed, that the son of the emperor when 18 years old, was styled 孟侯 (天子之子,年十八稱孟侯); and K'ang-shing supposes that it is king Ching who is thus addressed in the text. This is one of the extravagances which we are surprised to find men like Këang Shing and Wang Mingshing adopting and defending at the present day. 朕其弟=朕之弟. King Woo might thus have addressed Fung; king Ching could not thus address him. We must believe that, while the duke of Chow spoke as the representative of the young emperor, his nephew, he addressed Fung from the stand-point of his own relation to him. 小子封,—小子 is often used in the Shoo by emperors, whether old or young, in mock humility, as a depreciatory designation of themselves. In the Great Announcement,' p. 7, we found it interpreted of the princes of States. Here it is spoken to Fung and not by him; and we must take it as the language of kindly, brotherly feeling. Fung was younger than either king Woo, or

the duke of Chow; but we cannot suppose that he was under 70 when he was appointed to Wei. 3. 明德慎罰,—these words form the text of the whole Charge. Ts'ae, in illustration of them, quotes from the 左傳 成二年,:—明德慎罰,文王所以造周也,明德務崇之謂也,慎罰,務去之之謂也。 With 克明德 we may compare the 克明俊德, Canon of Yaou, p. 2. The whole tenor of this Book, however, makes it more natural to understand the 德 here of king Wăn's own virtue as seen in his administration of government. 4. 鰥寡,—see 'The Great Announcement,' p. 7; *et al.* 不敢侮鰥寡=the 不虐無告, 'Counsels of Yu,' p. 3. 庸=用, 'to employ.' 祇=敬, 'to reverence.' 庸庸,祇祇,威威=用其所當用,敬其所當敬,威其所當威. 顯民 is a consequence flowing from the virtues just described,=故德著於民; and all that follows, down to 時敘, sets forth the further results of Wăn's conduct thus acknowledged by the people. 肇造我區夏=始造我區域於中夏. 區者小室之名, '區 is the name of a small house.' Here it is employed to denote the original seat of the House of Chow, as but a small territory in the great empire. 惟時怙冒,—the old interpreters put a stop at 怙, and read 冒 along with the clause that follows. I have followed Ts'ae in joining 冒 with 怙. He says:—鑿西土之人,怙之如父,冒之如天, 'the people of all the west relied on him as a father, and looked up to him as to Heaven.' I think the rhythm of the clauses is thus preserved better, and there is no more difficulty in interpreting 冒 than there is if we join it to 聞. It is used for 'a covering for the head;' and generally as = 'to cover.' Wăn's influence was like the gracious overshadowing of the firmament. 聞于上帝,—we must understand the virtue or the fame of Wăn as the subject of the verb 聞. 帝休,—'God approved.' The simple 帝 takes the place of 上帝; and

以修我西土惟
時怙冒聞于上
帝帝休天乃大
命文王殪戎殷
誕受厥命越厥
邦厥民惟時叙
乃寡兄勗肆汝
小子封在茲東
土○王曰嗚呼 五節
封汝念哉今民

brought under his improving influence, until throughout our western regions all placed in him their reliance. The fame of him ascended up to the High God, and God approved. Heaven gave a great charge to king Wǎn, to exterminate the great dynasty of Yin, and receive its great appointment, so that the various States belonging to it and their peoples were brought to an orderly condition. Then your unworthy elder brother exerted himself;—and so it is that you, Fung, the little one, are here in this eastern region.'"

5　II. "The king says, 'Oh! Fung, bear these things in mind. Now *your management of* the people will depend on your reverently

both those names are immediately exchanged for the vague designation of 'Heaven.' 殪=滅, 'to exterminate.' 戎=大, 'great.' 厥邦厥民惟時叙=萬邦萬民, 各得其理, 莫不時叙. It is an exaggeration to speak of Wǎn's influence as having thus extended over all the empire; but we cannot find much fault with it in the circumstances. 乃寡兄勗,—those who understand the speaker to be king Woo find no difficulty in his thus speaking of himself as 寡德之兄, 'your brother of slender virtue.' See the use of 寡人 as a designation of themselves by the princes of States in Mencius, I., Pt. I., iii., 1; *et al.* The language has been a stumblingblock, however, to those who maintain that it is employed of king Woo and not by him. Gan-kwǒ made 寡兄 to=寡有之兄, 'our brother whose match is rarely to be found.' But this is a very unlikely expansion of the phrase, and devised to get over the difficulty so strongly felt by a Chinese. I do not see any serious obstacle to our understanding it as in the translation. Why might not the duke of Chow, once at least in his life, speak thus of one brother to another? He had taken himself 'a great part' in all the exploits of Woo; to speak of him was much the same as to speak of himself. We like him all the better for eschewing the flattering tongue. 在茲東土=在此東方, Wei was not only east from Ching's capital, but it was the eastern part of the territory of which Wookǎng had been permitted to retain the sway.

Ch. II. Pp. 5—7. HOW THE PRINCE OF K'ANG SHOULD CULTIVATE HIS VIRTUE, AND MANIFEST IT IN THE ADMINISTRATION OF HIS GOVERNMENT.　5. *Fung should follow the example of king Wǎn; gather up lessons from the former kings and wise men of Yin; and from the sage monarchs of remote antiquity.* 今民將在祇遹乃文考, 紹聞衣德言,—it will be seen, from the translation, that I understand a 治 before 民, by which 民 is governed. This is after the example of Gankwǒ, Lin Che-k'e, Ts'ae, and others. Then, 遹=述, 'to transmit;' 衣=服, 'to put on,' = 'to carry into practice,'—as in 'The Charge to Yuě,' Pt. ii., p. 12, 誕乃言惟服. The 'Daily Explanation' has:—今汝治民所行之, 可務取而服循勿替. 緒紹繼身遵之, 將敬述文考之. 聞之德言, 被紹. 如衣之遵. 也. Këang Shing takes 民 in the nominative, and supposes that 在 is a verb=視,

乃　弘　哲　別　成　汝　哲　往　考、將
身、于　王　求　人　丕　王　敷　紹　在
不　天、用　聞　宅　遠　用　求　聞　祗
廢　若　康　由　心　惟　保　于　衣　遹
在　德　保　古　知　商　乂　殷　德　乃
王　裕　民、先　訓、耇　民、先　言、文

following your father Wăn;—do you carry out his virtuous words which you have heard, and clothe yourself with them. *Moreover*, where you go, seek out extensively *among the traces* of the former wise kings of Yin what you may use in protecting and regulating their people. *Again*, you must more remotely study the old accomplished men of Shang, that you may establish your heart, and know how to instruct the people. *Further still*, you must seek out besides what is to be learned of the wise kings of antiquity, and employ it in the tranquillizing and protecting of the people. *Finally*, enlarge *your thoughts* to the *comprehension of all* Heavenly *principles*, and virtue will be richly displayed in your person, so that you will not render nugatory the king's charge.'"

'to regard,' 'to look at;'—compare its use in the 'Canon of Shun,' p. 5. He also takes 衣 as =殷, the name of the dynasty. In this way he makes the whole=今 民 將 視 考 汝 之 敬 述 乃 文 考, 紹 文 以 民 所 聞 殷 之 德 言, 汝 當 民 爲 念. This view is certainly no improvement on the other. 往 敷 至 乂 民 —往 =之 國, 'when you go to your State;' 敷 求 =廣 求, 'seek out extensively.' 汝 丕 至 知 訓,—耇 成 人, comp. in the 'Viscount of Wei,' p. 5, 唏 其 耇 長, 舊 有 位 之 人. The course of thought in the paragraph, however, leads us to think of the old accomplished men of a former time, such as E Yin and Foo Yuĕ, by whom the best monarchs of the Shang dynasty had been directed. 惟 is used as a verb, =思, 'to think of,' 'to study.' 宅 心 =處 心, 'to settle your heart,'—to bring it to its proper resting place. 知 訓 =知 所 以 訓 民,—'know how to instruct the people.'

別 求 至 保 民,—Fung is here sent to the earliest sages and monarchs of the empire,—Yaou, Shun, and Yu. 別 求 聞 由,—'you must elsewhere enquire, that you may learn from and follow.' 由 =行. 弘 于 天, 云 云,—it is not easy to say what is the meaning of 弘 于 天. Lin Che-k‘e says:—'To the other injunctions is still subjoined this 弘 于 天. Now 弘 means to widen and enlarge. The critic Sëë says, "Every man has his heavenly nature, which is in him as a fire that has just been kindled, or a spring which is just issuing forth. What is required is the widening and enlarging of it." This explanation is correct. Step by step the prince of K‘ang is carried on to take his rule and pattern from Heaven, after which there is nothing to be added.' I suppose this is the correct view. 'Heaven' is used as the comprehensive designation of all true right principles. The translation has taken its form from the words of Woo Ch‘ing,—又 當 擴 充 其 德 與 天 爲 一, 若 德 足 乎 已, 則 王 之 命 汝 者, 永 不 廢 矣. 6. *With*

命。○王曰、嗚呼小
子封、恫瘝乃身、敬
哉天畏棐忱、民情
大可見、小人難保、
往盡乃心、無康好
逸豫、乃其乂民、我
聞曰、怨不在大、亦
不在小、惠不惠、懋
不懋。○己汝惟小
子、乃服惟弘王、應

六節
七節

6　　"The king says, 'Oh! Fung, the little one, it is as if some disease were in your person; be respectfully careful. Heaven in its awfulness yet helps the sincere. The feelings of the people can for the most part be discerned, but it is difficult to calculate on the *attachment of the* lower classes. Where you go, employ all your heart. Do not seek repose, nor be fond of idleness and pleasure;—so may you regulate the people. I have heard the saying—"Dissatisfaction is caused not so much by great things or by small things, as by *a ruler's* observance of principle or the reverse, and by his energy of conduct or the reverse."'

7　　'Yes, it is yours, O little one,—it is your business to enlarge the royal *influence*, and harmoniously to protect this people of Yin.

what awe and cautious diligence Fung should go about the duties of his government. 恫=痛, 'pain.' 瘝=病, 'sickness.' 恫瘝乃身=疾痛在汝身, 'sickness and pain are in your person.' The meaning is that Fung's appointment was not one of ease, but one of labour, in which he should feel the sufferings of the people as if they were wounds in his own person. 天畏棐忱 is equivalent to 天命不常, 雖甚可畏, 然誠則輔之, 'The appointments of Heaven are not unchanging; and though they are to be thought of with awe, yet it helps the sincere.' 民情大可見, 小民難保=至民情, 好惡, 雖大晷可見, 然小民之心最爲難保, as in the translation. The uncertainty of the will of Heaven, and the changing of the minds of the people,—these are two considerations, which should stimulate Fung to caution and diligence that he might hold fast what he had received. Some would connect 民情

大可見 with what precedes, so that the meaning is—'Heaven in its awfulness yet helps the sincere, and this is greatly seen in the feelings of the people.' But this construction of the text is not so good as the other. 無康=毋自安, 'do not give yourself to repose.' 我聞, 云云,—I have followed in the translation here the interpretation which is given by Ts'ae and in the 'Daily Explanation.' I am not sure, however, but it would have been better to adopt the view of Gan-kwŏ which is to this effect:—'The dissatisfaction of the people may be occasioned by things which are great in themselves, and by things which are small. It shows itself unexpectedly, and it is this which makes the people so difficult to be calculated on. A ruler, therefore, ought always to be bringing his conduct, which may have been defective, into conformity with what is right, and to be acting energetically wherever he may have been remiss.' 7. *The great duties of Fung, and how the happy results of his virtue would appear.* 乃服惟弘王,—服=事; 乃服=汝之事, 'your business.' 弘王,—'enlarge the king.' It would seem that the meaning must be as in the translation.

保殷民、亦惟助王

宅天命、作新民。○

八節王曰、嗚呼、封敬明

乃罰人有小罪非

眚乃惟終自作不

典式爾有厥罪小、

乃不可不殺乃有

大罪非終乃惟眚

災適爾既道極厥

辜時乃不可殺。○

Thus also shall you assist the king, consolidating the appointment of Heaven, and renovating this people.'"

8   III. "The king says, 'Oh! Fung, deal reverently and understandingly in your infliction of punishments. When men commit small crimes, which are not mischances, but purposed, themselves doing what is contrary to the laws, intentionally, though their crimes be but small, you may not but put them to death. But in the case of great crimes, which are not purposed, but from mischance and misfortune, accidental, if the offenders confess unreservedly their guilt, you may not put them to death.'"

應 is explained by 和, 'harmony,' and here used adverbially. This definition does not occur in the dictionary, but it may be deduced from that of 物相應, 'things answering, responding, to one another.' The people of Yin were not in harmonious accord with the dynasty of Chow. It would be the business of Fung to bring them to be so. The view of Gan-kwŏ is different. He says:—汝惟小子, 乃當服行 德政, 惟弘大王道, 上以應 天, 下以安我所受殷之民 衆. 宅＝定, 'to settle,' 'to consolidate.' 作新民,—see on 'The Great Learning,' Comm. ii., 2. The 作 and 新 must be taken, however, both as verbs, blending their meaning together. Perhaps a good version would be—'and make a renovated people.'

Ch. III., Pp. 8—19. How Fung should be careful in the use of punishments.

8. *Modifying circumstances in judging of small and great offences.* 人有小罪, 至 不可不殺.—comp. the 'Canon of Shun,' p. 10, 式爾,—式＝用; 式爾＝用 意如此, 'purposely thus.' The meaning of the phrase is determined by its correlation with 適爾＝偶爾, 'accidentally,' below. 乃有大罪, 云云,—comp. in the 'Canon of Shun,' 眚災肆赦. 既道 極厥辜＝既自稱道, 盡輸 其情, 不敢隱匿, 'When they have themselves confessed, presenting fully all the circumstances, not daring to conceal anything.' This must be the meaning, though Gan-kwŏ supposes Fung himself, or the judge, to be the subject of the clause, explaining it by—汝 盡聽訟之理, 以極其罪, 'after you have employed every resource in hearing the case, so as thoroughly to investigate the offence.'

[Soo Shih contended that the 小罪 and 大罪 here were not to be taken absolutely in the sense of small and great offences, but relatively to each other, as less and greater. The less offence is a capital crime as well as the greater one; but the final decision of the judge might find a way of pardon for what seemed at first unpardonable, and would let the sentence of the law take its course, where there might seem at first to be room for forgiveness. I do not see in the text any ground for this criticism. A small offence, purposed and persevered in, becomes a capital crime;—

或 刑 父 子 棄 疾 勅 明 有 王^{九節}
刑 人 。 惟 咎 惟 懋 服 敘 曰
人 殺 ○ 民 惟 民 和 惟 時 嗚
殺 人 非^{十節} 其 若 其 若 民 乃 呼
人 無 汝 保 保 畢 有 其 大 封
、 、 封 康 赤 、 、 、 、 、

9   "The king says, 'Oh! Fung, there must be the right regulation
in this matter. When you show a great discrimination, subduing
men's hearts, the people will admonish one another, and strive to be
obedient. *Deal with evil,* as if it were a sickness in your person, and
the people will entirely put away their faults. *Deal with them,* as
if you were guarding your infants, and the people will be tranquil
10 and orderly. It is not you, Fung, who inflict a severe punishment
or death upon a man; you may not of yourself so punish a man or

the transgressor is not fit to live. A great
offence, not purposed, repented of, and confessed may be pardoned. This is what the paragraph inculcates.]

9. *The influence of the careful use of punishments in transforming the people and making them
happy.* 有敘＝刑罰有次序,
'in the use of punishments there is an order.'
Këang Shing explains 敘 by 順, and connects
with the preceding.—'If you conform to this method of judging in the case of small and great
crimes,' &c. But the interposition of 王曰,
嗚呼, 封, forbids any such constructive connection between the paragraphs. 時 (＝
是) 乃大明服,—明者明其
罰, '明 refers to the intelligent use of punishments'; 服者服其民, '服 refers
to the subjecting the people thereby.' 民
其勅懋和＝民其戒勅而勉
於和順, 'the people will warn one another, and exert themselves to be harmonious
and obedient.' 若有疾,—this clause is
evidently to be referred to the person of Fung,
like the 若保赤子 below. Let him
deal with the crimes of the people, as he would
with sickness in his own person, not suffering
it, but treating it with tender hand, and the
people would be both awed and won to put
away their faults.   The meaning of 若保
赤子 appears clearly from the use which
Mencius makes of it, III., Pt. I., v., 3. He
says—'If an infant crawling about, is about to

fall into a well, it is no crime in the infant.'
No man would be roused to anger by the sight
of such an infant, and every one would do his
utmost to rescue it. Let Fung thus look upon
the people, to save them from crime as he would
save an infant from falling into a well, and
they would be tranquil and orderly.

[Këang Shing joins 若有疾 with the
previous clause, taking 疾 in the sense of 速,
'quickly.'—'The people will exert themselves
to be harmonious and obedient with the greatest
rapidity.' The structure of the paragraph is
opposed to such a construction, as I have pointed
out above. Shing, however, could plead the
authority of Seun K‘ing, who says in his 富
國篇 三德者誠乎上, 則下
應之如景響, 雖欲無明達,
得乎哉, 書曰, 乃大明服, 惟
民其力懋和而有疾, 此之
謂也. But neither this text nor interpretation
of Seun is correct. The same may be said of
the way in which he quotes and applies the difficult clause—弘于天 of p. 5, which appears in the same 富國篇 as 弘覆
乎天.]

10. *Punishments were to be employed according
to the laws. Fung ought not to allow any feeling
of his own in the use of them.* I have translated
刑 by 'to inflict a severe punishment;' because
刑人殺人 are opposed to 劓人刵
人, the severer punishments to the lighter.
What particular punishment or punishments

于　念　又　殷　時　曰　劓　劓　非
旬　五　日　罰　臬　外　刵　刵　汝
時　六　要　有　司　事　人　人　封
丕　日　囚　倫　師　汝　。○　無　又
蔽　至　服　。○　茲　陳　王　或　曰

put him to death.' Moreover, he says, 'It is not you, Fung,
who cut off a man's nose or ears; you may not of yourself cut off a
man's nose or ears.'"

11   "The king says, 'In things beyond *your immediate jurisdiction*,
have laws set forth which the officers may observe; and those should
be the penal laws of Yin, which were right-ordered.'"

12   "He also says, 'In examining the evidence in criminal cases,
reflect upon it for five or six days, yea for ten days, or three months.
You may then boldly carry your decision into effect in such
cases.'"

are intended by it, it is not easy to see. 'Cutting
off the nose' was one of the regular five punishments, but not 'cutting off the ears,' though
mention is made of this in Bk. XXVII., p. 2.
The 又曰 should probably be before the 非
汝封 which precedes it in the text,—as in
the translation.

11. *In things not falling immediately under his
own jurisdiction, he should let the old laws of Yin
take their course.* The meaning of this par. is
very uncertain. Ts'ae says that he does not
understand what is meant by 外事, 'outside
affairs.' The common view is that it means
有司之事, 'the affairs of the officers,'
matters which it was not necessary the prince
himself should take the management of. Then
臬, anciently 'a small post in front of a gate'
(門橛), marking a limit, is used for laws.
師＝法, 'to follow as the law.' The
'Daily Paraphrase' says:—凡 外 而 有
司 訟 獄 事 必 一 躬
親 綜 理 勢 不 若 不
預 取 法 令 有 昭 示
屬 僚 則 而 所 意 之
入 者 矣 有 詳 一 然
規 列 汝 而 晓 是
確 所 陳 求 以 立
法 也 不 守 必 別 出

條欵也, 但取殷罰以治殷
民可矣, 云云.
Gan-kwŏ adopted a different exegesis, understanding by 外事＝外土諸侯奉王
事. But his interpretation is quite unsatisfactory;—see the 註疏. Ts'ae quotes
the view of one of the critics Leu (呂氏),
that by 外事 are to be understood the affairs
of Wei (衞國事) in opposition to the
affairs which would come under Fung's notice
as the minister of Crime at the imperial court.
But the whole tenor of the Book sufficiently
proves that the charges in it were delivered
with exclusive reference to the govt. of Wei.
Këang Shing gives still a difft. view in the
foll. words:—外事, 聽獄之事也.
聽獄在外朝, 故曰外事.

P. 12. *How Fung should exercise a cautious
deliberation before deciding on criminal cases.*
要囚,—Ts'ae defines this as＝獄辭之
要者, 'the summary of the pleas in criminal
cases.' Medhurst renders it by 'important
criminal cases;' and Gaubil by 'S'il s'agit de
fautes considerables.' They both err by taking
要 in the 3d tone, ＝ 'important,' The dict.
gives one meaning of 囚, with reference to the
text, as 獄辭, 'the evidence in a criminal
case;' and, with the same reference it defines
要 as ＝ 察, 'to examine.' These meanings

心若惟有曰汝義殷陳要
朕汝小遜時封彝時囚
德封子事敘乃用臬。
惟之、未。惟汝其事○
乃心、其○曰盡義罰王
知、朕有已未遜刑蔽曰
。朕汝次汝

(十三節 / 十四 markers as printed)

13   "The king says, 'In setting forth the business of the laws the punishments will be determined by the regular laws of Yin. But you must see that those punishments, as well as the penalty of death, be righteous. And you must not let them be warped to agree with your own inclinations, O Fung. Then shall you be entirely accordant with right, and may say, "These are properly ordered;" yet you must say at the same time, "Perhaps they are

14 not yet entirely accordant with right." Yes, you are the little one;—who has a heart like you, O Fung? My heart and my virtue *also* are known to you.

of the terms are applicable to the phrase when it occurs again in Bk. XV., and I have followed them here. Fung is told that in deciding on evidence, he should do so cautiously, and not hastily. It is supposed to be in a case where guilt would involve death, and when the accused was once executed, there could be no remedying a wrong decision. 服念＝服膺而 念之. 旬＝十日. 時＝三 月. 蔽＝斷, 'to decide.'

P. 13. *Summary of the five preceding paragraphs.* 汝陳時（＝是）臬事,—the difficulty here is with the 事. Ts‘ae connects it with 臬 by means of an 與, ＝'In setting forth these laws and other matters' (敷陳 是法與事). Ying-tă and Kĕang Shing both give it a verbal force. The latter explains: —汝陳是法以從事于罰. Simpler than either of those methods is the construction of Woo Ch‘ing, who makes 事 the object of the verb 陳, and puts 臬 under its regimen; —汝陳列用法之事. 罰蔽 殷彝,—蔽, as in the last par.; 彝＝常, 'what is regular;'—in this case, 'the ordinary laws' of the former dynasty. Still Fung was not blindly to adopt all the laws of Yin. He must be satisfied that they were righteous, —appropriate to the crime, and suited to the

altered times;' 義＝宜. 庸＝用; 勿庸以 次汝封之意. This is plainly the meaning; but the usage of 次 is peculiar. Ts‘ae says that it is the 次 of 次舍, 'a mansion,' 'a dwelling.' 乃汝, 云云,—遜＝順 meaning 'accordant with right.' 時敘＝是有 次敘, having reference to the 有敘 of par. 9. The gist of the whole is, that Fung should never allow a feeling of elation, as if all his affairs were arranged as well as they possibly could be. [Kĕang Shing, following a quotation by Seun K‘ing, in his 致仕篇, of a portion of this paragraph, reduces the whole to—王曰女 陳時臬事, 罰蔽殷彝, 惟刑 誼殺, 勿庸以卽女, 惟曰未 有順事. But only prejudice can, in my opinion, make any of Seun's quotations carry it over the authority of the *textus receptus*. Shing interprets the last clause—'But say, "There are still instances of disobedience among the people."' This is far-fetched.

P. 14. *The confidence and affection subsisting between Fung and the duke of Chow.* See on par. 2. Why these expressions of attachment should be interjected here, it is not easy to understand.

天顯乃弗克恭厥　疾厥子于弟弗念　父不能字厥子乃　事大傷厥考心乃　友子弗祗服厥父　大憝矧惟不孝不　憝。○王曰封元惡　貨暋不畏死罔弗　攘姦宄殺越人于　○凡民自得罪寇

十六節

十五節

15　'All people who of themselves commit crimes, robbing, stealing, practising villainy and treason, and who kill men or violently assault them to take their property, being violent and fearless of death:— those are abhorred by all.'"

16　"The king says, 'Fung, such chief criminals are greatly abhorred, and how much more detestable are the unfilial and unbrotherly!— as the son who does not reverently discharge his duty to his father, but greatly wounds his father's heart; and the father who can no longer love his son, but hates him; and the younger brother who does not think of the manifest will of Heaven, and refuses to respect his elder brother, so that the elder brother does not think of the

Pp. 15—17. *Cases in which severe punishment may be inflicted without hesitation.* 15. *Robbers, murderers, &c.* 自得罪,—'of themselves,' *i.e.*, without being tempted or involved by others, 'offending.' 寇攘姦宄,—comp. the Canon of Shun, p. 26; *et al.* 殺越人于貨,—from this the par. is quoted by Mencius, V. Pt. II., iv. 4, which see. Ts'ae illustrates the meaning of 越 here by a reference to 顚越不恭, in the 'Pwan-kǎng,' Pt. ii., 16; but it is not apt. The character must have in the text the meaning of, 'to throw down,' = 'to assault violently.' 暋=強. 憝=惡, 'to hate,' 'to detest.' Justice executed on such parties would meet with general sympathy and approbation. ·16. *The case of the unfilial and unbrotherly.* 元惡大憝,—this takes up the case of the parties in the last par. The next clause must be completed as in the translation. Ts'ae gives for it:—況不孝不友之人, 而尤爲可惡者. 不孝 is the crime of the son, and 不友 is that of the elder brother. But as the par. goes on to speak of the father's failure in duty as well as

the son's, and of the younger brother's as well as his senior's, we must understand by 不孝 all offences between father and son, and by 不友 all between elder brother and younger. 厥考心,—考 is evidently used of the father when alive. 于父, 至厥子,—this must be, I think, a fresh case, and is not to be connected with the preceding, as if the 于 were equivalent to 以致, 'so that,' which is the paraphrase of the 'Daily Explanation.' We cannot connect 于弟, which immediately follows, with any clause which precedes. 于父 and 于弟 = 'in the case of the father—the younger brother—who,' &c. 字=愛, 'to love;' 疾=惡, 'to hate.' 天顯 is 'the manifest will of Heaven;' requiring that the younger should serve the elder. 不念鞠子哀,— Gan-kwŏ takes 鞠 in the sense of 穉, 'child,' 'junior,' and explains the clause—不念穉子之可哀, 'does not think of the pity he should cherish for his younger brother.' Lin Che-k'e, foll. by Ts'ae, took 鞠=養,

兄、兄亦不念鞠
子哀大不友于
弟、惟弔兹不于
我政人得罪天
惟與我民彝大
泯亂曰乃其速
由文王作罰、刑
兹無赦。○ 不率
大戞、矧惟外庶
子訓人、惟厥正

toil of their parents in bringing them up, and is very unbrotherly
to his junior.   If we who are charged with government do not
treat parties who proceed to such wickedness as offenders, the laws
of our nature given by Heaven to our people will be thrown into
great disorder or destroyed.   You must deal speedily with such
parties according to the penal laws of king Wăn, punishing them
severely and not pardoning.

17   'These, who are disobedient *to natural principles*, are to be thus
severely subjected to the laws ;—how much more the officers
employed in your State as the instructors of the youth, the heads

惟弔兹至泯亂.—all this must be
taken together as one sentence, and interpreted
as in the translation.   The paraphrase of the
'Daily Explanation' is :—夫人較使不勸所滅
倫滅絕天理廢于惡如此至其視人不從天泯
之我加懲與而紊亂乎.   Lin Che-k'e takes
quite a diff't. view of the scope of the passage.
弔 is read by him *teaou*, 'to pity,' and not *teih*,
= 'to come to.' His interpretation is :—'The
criminals I have mentioned above are detested
by all, and to be put to death. But these parties
are to be pitied.   Their offences must be owing
to the failures in duty of us who are charged
with govt.,' &c.   Lin argues ingeniously, but
not satisfactorily, in support of his view. We
feel that he *ought* to be right. Robbers and
murderers must be summarily dealt with for
the preservation of society ; but unkind fathers
and undutiful children, and divided brothers,
cannot be taken cognizance of in the same way
by the law. The duke of Chow, however, makes
them—and here he is correct--in advance of
the others in point of guilt, and goes on to say
that they are to be punished accordingly, without

interposing anything about pitying and teaching
them in the first place.   曰乃云云,
—Woo Ch'ing brings out the force of the
日 very well :—然則如之何哉,
汝其曰速由, 云云. 'What then is
to be done? You must say, "I will quickly
punish them."' What the law of king Wăn
regarding such cases was, we do not know.
There is a difficulty in applying here what is
said about 不孝之刑, and 不弟之
刑, in the Chow Le, Bk. IX., 地官,大
司徒

P. 17. *The case of unworthy and factious
officers.*   不率大戞,—this corresponds
to the first clause of the last par., and must be
construed accordingly.   不率 is descriptive
of the 不孝,不友, and 大戞 of the
punishment which such received. The difficulty
is with the interpretation of 戞. The 爾
雅 defines it by 禮, 'propriety,' which is
taken to = 常法, 'a constant law.' Gan-kwŏ,
adopting this account of the term, makes 不
率大戞 all descriptive of the unfilial and
unbrotherly, as those who do not comply with
the invariable laws of human duty. This is
contrary to the analogy of the last clause, which
I have pointed out, and it must be rejected.

能　惟　義　乃　惟　君　造　節　人、
厥　君　率　其　朕　時　民　乃　越
家　惟　殺　速　憝　乃　大　別　小
人、長、○　由　已　引　譽、播　臣
越　不　亦十八節　茲　汝　惡　弗　敷、諸

of the various official departments, and the petty officers, charged with their several commissions; when they propagate and spread abroad other lessons, seeking the praise of the people, not thinking *of the sovereign* nor using *the rules for their duties*, but distressing him! These lead on to wickedness and are an abomination to me. Shall they be let alone? Do you quickly, according to what is recognized as right, put them to death.

18　'And you are here prince and president;—if you cannot manage your own household, with your petty officers, the instructors, and

---

Ts'ae makes the word = 法, 'laws,' and with verbal force, — 寘之法, 'to subject to the laws.' I have followed this view. Woo Ch'ing gets substantially to the same conclusion by taking it as = 擊, 'to smite,' after the analogy of the 'Yih and Tseih,' p. 9. 外諸子 訓人 = 外諸子以訓人爲職. Medhurst translates the clause by—'the outside princes, whose business it is to instruct the people.' Gaubil has—'Ceux qui, par etat, doivent enseigner les autres;'—more correctly than Medhurst, but he takes no account of the 外. In the Chow Le, Bk. XXXI., p. 16, we have an account of the 諸子, as the various officers charged with the training of the youth of the kingdom, sons of nobles, high officers, and others of the best promise. It is said— 諸子掌國子之倅,掌其戒 令,與其教治,辨其等,正其 位, which Biot translates—'L' attaché aux fils *de dignitaires* est chargé de conduire les suppléants des fils de l' Etat. Il s'occupe de leur règlement special; il dirige-leurs etudes; il distingue leurs rangs, et determine leurs positions *dans les ceremonies.*' This was the function of those officers in the imperial domain, at the court:—there were similar officers in the various states, who as distinguished from these were the 外 諸子. 厥正人 = 庶官之長. 越小臣諸節 —in the 31st Bk. of the Chow Le, referred to above, we have an account of the office of the 小臣 or 'Minor ministers' (petits servi-

teurs;—Biot), parr. 53—55. They were charged with the minor orders of the emperor and, in the States, of the princes, conveying them to the parties to whom they were addressed, and as symbols of their authority they carried the 節, tallies, or credentials appropriate to the mission with which they were charged. 別　至　厥　君 = 乃別爲 頒　布　悅　時　俗　之　意、 譽　之、取　君　任　之　守 體　將　上　委　官　違　道 念　君　并　徒　知 格　念　國　時　(一 = 是) 廢　不　用、 以　病　其　君. 惡、—' these are leaders of wickedness,' *i.e.*, they set an example of wickedness and led others on to it as well. 由茲義,— 'according to this righteousness,' *i.e.*, what is recognized and has been enacted as right to be done in such cases. Gan-kwŏ takes a difft. view of the par. from 乃別播敷, considering it as addressed to Fung himself. Such a construction is most unnatural, and breaks entirely the train of thought.

Pp. 18, 19. *Advice to Fung to be himself an example of what he required in others, and by gentleness make the people rich and happy, and fulfil the hopes which were entertained of him.* Such is the view of these parr. taken by Ts'ae and Woo Ch'ing. Këang Shing supposes that par. 18 speaks of the princes of the various States to which Fung stood in the relation of president (孟侯). The view is ingenious, but it necessitates more wresting and supple-

乃而 教求 要不 全咸 法譽 乃引

惟殷先哲王德用　民迪吉康我時其　懌。○王曰封爽惟（二十節）　有及則子一人以　忌乃裕民曰我惟　裕民惟文王之敬　罔不克敬典乃由　非德用乂。○汝亦（十九節）　惟虐大放王命乃　厥小臣外正惟威

heads of departments, but use only terror and violence, you greatly set aside the royal charge, and try to regulate your State contrary

19　to virtue.　Do you also in every thing reverence the constant statutes, and so proceed to the happy rule of the people.　There are the reverence of king Wăn and his caution;—in proceeding by them to the happy rule of the people, say, "If I can only attain to them."　So will you make me the one man to rejoice.'"

20　IV.　"The king says, 'Fung, when I think clearly of the people, I see they are to be led to happiness and tranquillity.　I think of the virtue of the former wise kings of Yin, whereby they tranquil-

menting of the text than the other. 18. The two preceding parr. had stimulated Fung to be bold in punishing the unfilial and unbrotherly, and refractory officers; but there was a more excellent way,—the way of example. If he could bring all the family virtues into action in his own household, they would flourish also throughout the State. He might so deal with his petty officers, the instructors, and heads of departments also, that they would be glad to perform their duties, instead of having to be punished for the neglect of them. If he could not thus accomplish much by example and influence, his administration would be bad. 小臣外正＝the 外諸子, 正人, and 小臣諸節 of the last par. Choo He took the 惟威惟虐 to be descriptive of the 小臣外正, and supposed the design of the whole to be to warn against being lenient in his government;—see the 集說. I am surprised to find him advocating such an exegesis.　19. 乃由裕民＝由是 求裕民之道, 'by this method seek the proper way of enriching the people,' i.e., of making them good and happy. 'The reverence of king Wăn and his caution' indicate at once his attention to the duties of govt., and the caution of his measures,—particularly those of a penal character. 我惟有及＝我

惟求能及文王之裕民, 斯已矣.

Ch. IV. Pp. 20—22. HOW THE VIRTUE OF THE SOVEREIGN IS THE MOST IMPORTANT THING IN THE GOVERNMENT OF THE PEOPLE, AND RULERS SHOULD SEEK BY VIRTUE TO SUPERSEDE THE NECESSITY OF USING PUNISHMENTS. 20. By the example of the good kings of Yin, and his own wish to copy them, the king seeks to make Fung zealous to govern by virtue. 爽惟民, 迪 吉康,—Gan-kwŏ put a comma at 迪, which character he took in the sense of 道, explaining the whole by 明惟治民之道, 而 善安之. Ying-tă expands this into—'O Fung, a ruler ought clearly to think of the proper way to govern the people, and thereby secure for them a happy tranquillity.' It is much better to put the comma at 民, and take 迪 in the sense of 導, 'to lead,' 'to conduct,' i.e., by means of virtuous influence. We thus bring out the meaning in the translation, 爽 being＝ 明, and 惟＝思. Woo Ch'ing says, clearly and concisely :—明知斯民, 導迪之 則吉康. 我時＝作求,—時

康乂民作求、矧今
民罔迪不適不迪、
則罔政在厥邦。○
廿一節 王曰封子惟不可
不監告汝德之說、
于罰之行今惟民
不靜未戾厥心迪
屢未同爽惟天其
罰殛我我其不怨
惟厥罪無在大亦

lized and regulated the people, and rouse myself to realize it. More-over, the people now are sure to follow a leader. If one do not lead them, he cannot be said to exercise a government in their State.'"

21   "The king says, 'Fung, I cannot dispense with the inspection *of the ancients,* and I make this declaration to you about virtue in the use of punishments. Now the people are not quiet; they have not stilled their minds; notwithstanding my frequent leading of them, they have not come to accord *with my government.* I reflect on Heaven's severe punishments, but I do not murmur. The crimes *of the people* whether they are great or many, *are all*

一是, here equivalent to 是以, 'therefore.' 惟=思. The two characters 作求 have been much disputed. The older scholars and Ts'ae took 求=等, 'a mate,' 'a match,' so that 作求=爲等於商先王, 'to be a mate of, equal to, the former kings of Shang.' It seems to me more natural and simple to take the terms as in the translation, —as Lin Che-k'e and Woo Ch'ing do. 今民罔迪不適,—adhering to the meaning of 迪 as =導, these words are susceptible of two meanings. They may be translated —'The people are sure to follow as they are led'(民無導之而不從者), which is the view of Ts'ae; or—'If the people have none to lead them, they will not go on to *the desired condition*' (民無以迪之,則不能自適於吉康之地), which is the view of Woo Ch'ing. The former interpretation is that which the whole of the paragraph requires. The sentiment is too broadly stated, and the issue did not justify it in the case of the people of Yin; but it is not the correctness of the sentiments that a translator has to do with. 不迪則罔政在厥邦,—this ex-

presses very strongly the feeling of the duke of Chow, that a govt. maintained by force did not deserve to be called a government.

P. 21. *By the failure of his own repeated efforts to secure the good govt. of the people of Yin, the king still further stimulates Fung to strive to realize the sway of virtue.* The mention of the repeated efforts to bring the people of Yin to a state of good order is not appropriate in the mouth of king Woo, supposed to give this charge to the prince of K'ang immediately after the conquest of the dynasty. 予惟不可不監,—we may take the 惟 either as =思 'to think,' or as a particle, = 'indeed.' 告汝德之說于罰之行=告汝以德行罰之說, 'I declare to you this saying, that virtue is to preside over the use of punishments.' 未戾厥心—戾=止, 'to stop.' The people's minds did not acquiesce in the existing state of things, and hence their turbulent movements. 迪屢未同=雖屢經開導究竟同歸于治. 惟厥罪多,—I cannot find any better way of explain-

封,惟　曰,嗚　寧　遠　用　蔽　怨,勿　嗚　顯　無
命　呼,　不　乃　康　時　用　呼,　聞　在
不　肆　汝　猷　乃　忱,　非　封　于　多,
于　汝　瑕　裕　心,　丕　謀　敬　天。○　刄
常,　小　殄。　乃　顧　則　非　哉,　王　曰,
汝　子　　以　乃　敏　彝,　無　曰　其
　　廿　○　民　德。　德。　　作　廿　尚
　　三　王　廿　　　　　三
　　節　　三節　　　　　節

chargeable on me, and how much more shall this be said, when the report of them goes up so manifestly to Heaven!'"

22 "The king says, 'Oh! Fung, be reverent. Do not what will create murmurings; do not use bad counsels, and uncommon ways. Decidedly and with sincerity, give yourself to imitate the active virtue *of the ancients*. Hereby give repose to your mind, examine your virtue, send far forward your plans, and thus by your generous forbearance you will conduct the people to repose *in what is good:* —so shall I not have to blame you or cast you off.'"

23 V. "The king says, 'Oh! you, Fung, the little one, *Heaven's* appointments are not constant. Do you think of this, and do not

ing this than that given in the translation. The 'Daily Explanation' has:—

萬　有
方　罪,
惟　民　無
厥　小　知
罪,　在　亦
不　於　皆
在　大,　其
於　微　尚
多,　至　上
即　纖　
教　所　
失　致　
於　也。
天,—尙=上. The cry of the crimes of the people of Yin ascended, and was clearly heard in heaven;—it was not merely with a few and slight offences that the king had to charge himself.   22. *Various advices to Fung, winding up the chapter.* 無作 怨=汝慎毋作可怨之事, 'Do not do things that will create murmurings.' This is a dissuasive from the use of punishments. They will be followed by the resentment of the people; govt. carried on by them is not on a good plan; punishments may be occasionally resorted to, but they are not the regular method of procedure. 蔽時忱=蔽=斷;時=是; 忱=誠. The clause has an adverbial force, and is carried on to the clauses that follow;= 'with the determination of sincerity.' 丕則,—則 is a verb, —'to imitate.'

顧=‘to have the eyes constantly on,' 'to regard and examine.' 裕乃以民 寧,—this will be the result of obedience to the advice just set forth, = 由是寬裕 相安於至 德化之至 耳. Ch. V. Pp. 23, 24. A CONSIDERATION OF THE UNCERTAINTY OF THE APPOINTMENTS OF HEAVEN SHOULD DEEPEN THE IMPRESSION OF THE WHOLE CHARGE.   23. 肆,—Ts‘ae confesses that he does not know the meaning of 肆 here. There does not seem much difficulty in it. We may take it as=‘therefore,' or 'now.' 命不于常,—命 is of course 天命. For the sentiment, compare 'The Instructions of E,' p. 8; *et al.* See also the expansion of it in 'The Great Learning,' Comm. x. 11. 命 不于常,—'the appointments of Heaven are not in—*i.e.*, are not characterized by—constancy.' 無我殄享=毋 或不 念使自我而殄絶所享之國

念哉無我　殄享明乃　服命高乃　聽用康乂　民○王若〔廿四節〕　曰往哉封　勿替敬典　聽朕告汝　乃以殷民　世享

make me deprive you of your dignity. Reflect clearly on the charges you have received. Think highly of what you have heard, and tranquillize and regulate the people accordingly.'"

24   "The king thus says, 'Go, Fung. Do not disregard the statutes you should reverence; hearken to what I have told you:—so with the people of Yin you will enjoy *your dignity*, and hand it down to your posterity.'"

也. Këang Shing makes the meaning to be —'Do not make me deprive you of the privilege of sacrificing to the spirits within your jurisdiction.' The issue is the same; but this meaning of 享 is far-fetched.   明乃 服命,—comp. 慎乃服命 in the last Bk., p. 4. 服命 may be taken here as there, 服 being 七章之服, and 命 the 七命 of a prince of Fung's rank. So, Këang Shing; but it seems to me better to take the clause as in the translation, = 命汝所

受于我之誥命.   高乃聽, —we must take 高 in the sense of 'to think highly of.' Ts'ae says:—高其聽, 不可卑忽我言.   24. Ts'ae observes that the 世享 here responds to the 殄享 of the last par. It does so, and shows that 享 is to be taken of the enjoyment of the princely dignity. Gan-kwŏ gives for the clause: —即汝乃以殷民世世享國福傳後世.

THE BOOKS OF CHOW.

BOOK X. THE ANNOUNCEMENT ABOUT DRUNKENNESS.

肇我民惟元祀。
兹酒惟天降命、
御事朝夕曰祀、
邦庶士越少正
西土厥誥毖庶
考文王肇國在
于妹邦。○乃穆
王若曰、明大命
酒誥

1   "The king speaks to this effect :—'Do you clearly make known my great commands in the country of Mei.

2   'When your reverent father, the king Wăn, laid the foundations of our kingdom in the western region, he delivered announcements and cautions to *the princes of* the various States, all the *high* officers, with their assistants, and the managers of affairs, saying, morning and evening, "For sacrifices spirits should be employed." When Heaven was sending down its *favouring* decree, and laying the foundations of *the eminence of* our people, *spirits* were used only in

THE NAME OF THE BOOK.—酒誥, 'The Announcement about Drunkenness.' I have spoken of the proper meaning of the term 酒 on Part IV, Bk. VIII., Pt. iii., 2. In the 'Songs of the five Sons,' and the 'Punitive Expedition of Yin,' I was unwilling to depart from the common usage of translators, and rendered 酒 by 'wine;' but there can be no doubt that the term in the ancient Books signifies 'spirits distilled from rice,' = our 'ardent spirits.' The French term 'vin' seems to be capable of a wider application than our 'wine.' Gaubil says: —'Le titre de ce chapitre signifie avis ou ordres sur l'usage du vin. Il s'agit ici du vin de riz, qui fut decouvert, suivant la plûpart des auteurs, du tems de Yu, fondateur de la premiere dynastie. Le raisin n'est à la Chine que depuis les premiers Han.' The title therefore might be correctly translated 'The Announcement about Spirits,' but the cursory reader would most readily suppose that the discourse was about spiritual Beings. I have preferred in consequence to render it by—'The Announcement about Drunkenness.'

The Book is found in both the texts. There are the same questions about the date of it, and the speaker in it, which have been discussed with reference to 'The Announcement to the prince of K'ang;' and it is not necessary to enter on them again here. I suppose the speaker to be the duke of Chow, addressing his brother Fung in the name of the young king Ching.

CONTENTS. The Announcement, as has just been said, is, like the last, addressed to Fung as invested with the govt. of Wei. We have seen how the drunken debauchery of Kĕĕ was the chief cause of the downfal of the Hea dynasty, and how that of Shang was brought to an end mainly by the same vice in Show. The people of Yin had followed the example of their sovereign, and the vice of drunkenness, with its attendant immoralities, extensively characterized the highest and the lowest classes of society. One of Fung's most difficult tasks in his administration would be to correct this evil habit, and he is in this Book summoned to the undertaking. He is instructed on the proper use, and the allowable uses of spirits; the disastrous consequences of drunkenness are strikingly set forth; he is called to roll back the flood of its desolation from his officers and people.

The scholar Woo Ts‘ae-laou, earlier than Choo He, thought that there was in the Book sufficient evidence of its being composed of two announcements originally distinct:—the first, embracing parr. 1—7, being addressed by king Woo—[Ts‘ae-laou is one of the most earnest advocates of the early date of the Book]—directly to the people of Yin; and the second, parr. 8—17, being addressed to Fung. Ts‘ae has examined this hypothesis, in his introductory observations on the Book, and adduced sufficient reasons for rejecting it. The whole, as we now have it, was, no doubt, addressed to Fung; but in the 6th and 7th parr. the king seems to forget that he is speaking to him, and appeals to the people and officers of Yin, for whose sakes the announcement was made. There is nothing unnatural or much out of the way in this.

The criticism of Woo suggests, however, a natural division of the Book into two chapters:—the first preliminary, parr. 1—7, chiefly on the original use and the permissible uses of ardent spirits; the other, addressed directly to Fung, and showing how drunkenness had proved the ruin of the Shang dynasty, and how they of Chow, and particularly Fung in Wei, should turn the lesson to account.

In the 'Complete digest of Commentaries on the Shoo,' the following summary of the contents is given:—The whole is to be looked at from the stand-point of the first par., after which the contents might be divided into 4 chapters. Parr. 2—8 would form the first. The speaker relates the instructions of king Wăn on the subject of spirits, to introduce his own commands to the country of Mei, and concludes by relating how their dynasty of Chow rose by obedience to Wăn's lessons. Parr. 9—12 would form the second. They describe the rise and fall of the Shang dynasty, and how they should look into it as a glass, where they would see their present duty.

The 13th par. strictly charges Fung with the duty of imposing the lessons he received upon his people and officers, and on other princes, and of rendering a personal obedience to them himself. The other parr., 14—17, would form the fourth chapter, and state how obedience to the commands on the use of spirits should be enforced

Ch. I. Pp. 1—7. FUNG IS ORDERED TO MAKE THE KING'S COMMANDS KNOWN THROUGH MEI. THE PRINCIPLES INCULCATED BY KING WAN IN REGARD TO THE USE OF ARDENT SPIRITS ARE STATED; AND THE SPEAKER DECLARES HIS OWN COMMANDS IN HARMONY WITH THEM. 1. In the north of the pres. dis. of K‘e (淇縣), in the dep. of Wei-hwuy, Honan, there is a place called 妹鄉,—a relic of the ancient name of the whole territory. It was in Mei that Show had his capital;—the imperial domain north from Chaou-ko, was all called Mei acc. to Gan-kwŏ. In the She king, Pt. I., Bk.' IV., Ode iv., 'the villages of Mei,' 'the north of it,' and 'the east of it,' are all mentioned. The character in use for the name there is 沬, but the country intended is the same which is here called 妹. Fung's principality of Wei must have embraced the greater part of it.

明大命,—明 is in the imperative mood. The whole＝封, 今汝往治妹地, 當以我誥誡之辭, 敷布于妹邦之臣民.

Pp. 2—6. *The lessons of king Wăn on the use of ardent spirits. 2, 3. Spirits should be used only in sacrifices. So it is in times of prosperity; when calamities come upon a State, the cause will be found to be drunkenness.* 乃穆考,—the old interpreters all took 穆 as simply denoting the place of king Wăn's shrine or spirit-tablet in the temple of ancestors;—see on the 'Doctrine of the Mean,' xix., 4. Many still follow this view, as Kĕang Shing, for instance, who says:—周家世次文王第當穆故稱穆考. I cannot think that this is the meaning, and much prefer to take 穆＝敬, as in the translation,—an epithet descriptive of king Wăn, who is celebrated in the She King as the 穆穆文王. It is observed, by those who understand the character in this way, that king Wăn in the last Bk. p. 13, is called 顯考, because the subject there is the manner in which he displayed his virtue (明德), while here he is called 穆考, being spoken of as instructing and cautioning his people. 肇國在西土,—'founded our kingdom in the western regions.' But Wăn was not the *founder* of the House of Chow, whose fortunes had been gradually growing in the west. We must make allowance for the duke of Chow's language in speaking of his father. See, moreover, the statements of king Woo's about Wăn's receiving the command of Heaven, 'to soothe the regions of the empire,' Bk. III., p. 5; *et al.* 厥誥毖至朝夕曰,—'in his announcements &c., he said.' 毖＝慎＝戒謹, 'to caution,' 'to warn;'—diff. from the meaning of the character in Bk. VII., p. 8. 庶邦 is taken by Lin Che-k‘e as＝諸侯, 'the princes of the various States,' *i.e.*, of the States within his jurisdiction

惟 罔 用 小 惟 罔 喪 用 威　○
辜。非 喪 大 行 非 德 大 我 天　三節
○ 酒 亦 邦 越 酒 亦 亂 民 降

3 the great sacrifices. When Heaven has sent down its terrors, and our people have thereby been greatly disorganized and lost their virtue, this might also be invariably traced to their indulgence in spirits; yea, the ruin of States, small and great, *by these terrors*, may be also traced invariably to their crime in the use of spirits.

as chief of the west' (西伯). This seems the simplest view of the phrase. 庶士, —'all the officers.' These, acc. to Ying-tǎ, were the 朝臣, 'ministers of the court.' It is better to understand them as the 正, or 官 之 長, 'Heads of the various magisterial departments;'—so, the 'Daily Explanation.' Then the 少正 are the assistants of those Heads of departments; and the 御事, all who held any office, however low it might be. 祀兹 酒=惟祭祀，則用此酒, 'only in sacrifices should these ardent spirits be used.' 惟天降命，肇我民，惟元 祀,—Medhurst translates this:—'And Heaven sent down the decree in the first instance to our people (to make it) that they might use it principally in sacrificing.' Gaubil has :—'Cet ordre, ajoûtoit-il, est venu du ciel; quand pour la première fois il donna le vin aux peuples, il voulut que ce ne fut que pour les cérémonies religieuses.' These versions are erroneous or defective in several points, but they agree in the view they give of the general scope of the passage. It is substantially that propounded by Gan-kwŏ, whose commentary is :—惟 天 下 教命，始令我民，知作酒 者，惟爲祭祀. This interpretation has been generally received by the critics. In the 'Daily Explanation' we have :—天令我 民始作此酒者，止爲郊社 宗廟之大祭饗而設，此外 無可用酒之時矣. This construction uses too much freedom with the text, which says nothing about Heaven's having given the command to make wine. 肇我民, standing as the characters do here, must be under the government of 降命, and = 'to found our people.' Woo Ch'ing and Këang Shing do not follow the usual view, but their own explanations are not more admissible. Ch'ing

says :—如今我民作酒，惟用之 於大祭祀，是天以此教人 也, letting the 肇 slip quietly out of sight. Shing says :—惟天之下教命，始 開導我民者，惟始于祀也. Here 肇我民 is better dealt with, but I know not whence he derives the 始 in his last clause (始于祀), and I cannot admit the 命 of 降命 to stand here for 教命. The view of the meaning which appears in the translation does not seem to have occurred to any commentator. I am led to it chiefly by considering the relation in which 天降命 here, and 天降威 at the beginning of the next par. evidently stand to each other. I have had occasion before to translate 命 by 'favouring decree' (See IV., Bk. VII, Pt. i., 4; *et al.*) This indeed is its common signification. Heaven only confers its appointments where its approbation has gone before. Compare also the contrast between 威 and 命 in the 'Conquest of Le,' p. 4, *et al.*, exactly corresponding to what appears here. It does not matter whether we understand the speaker to be king Wǎn, or, as I rather think, king Ching, commenting on Wǎn's 祀兹酒. He goes back to the days of early simplicity and virtue, when that character was being formed in the chiefs and people of Chow, in virtue of which they went on to attain the supremacy of the empire; and then they made no use of spirits excepting at the great sacrifices. In 元祀 the 元=大, and we may take the 'great sacrifices' as those to Heaven, the earth, and ancestors. Sacrifices were not so numerous then as they afterwards became.

In the third par. two causes are assigned for the ruin of virtue and prosperity,—the terrors of Heaven and indulgence in spirits. The 用 expressly asserts the agency of Heaven, and the 亦, as clearly, that of intemperance. We must understand that the terrors of Heaven are its justice manifested in the punishment of men's guilt. Men first wrest spirits from their proper use to feed their own lusts, and there is a natural issue of evil consequences. Then Heaven, seeing men obstinate in their wicked course, righteously accelerates their overthrow and ruin. Ts'ae says:—酒之禍人也, 而以爲天降威者, 禍亂之 成, 是亦天爾. Ts'ae, it will be seen, takes 我民 as simply =人. So, Gan-kwŏ and others. This avoids the necessity of supposing any special references to events in the history of the House of Chow; but the 我民 is special. We cannot take it here otherwise than in the prec. par. The translation I have given involves such references, tho' we cannot say what events they were which the speaker had in his mind. Indeed, we might translate in the future tense, instead of the present complete as I have done; and in the last portion of the par., 越小大, 云云,—the speaker passes from his own people to speak of the subject with relation to all States great and small. 酒 惟行, 酒惟辜,—'intemperance is their conduct, intemperance is their guilt.'

[Choo He gives a view of the meaning of 天 降命 and 天降威, in which I am not able to concur, but it is worthy to be preserved, and made current beyond the sphere of China. He says:—'Nan-heen (張南軒; a critic of the Sung dynasty, contemporary with Choo He), in his treatise upon this Book, has brought out the meaning of the two phrases 天降命, 天降威, much better than any of the critics in the many centuries before him; and here I transcribe the whole of his remarks:—"Strong drink is a thing intended to be used in offering sacrifices and in entertaining guests:—such employment of it is what Heaven has prescribed. But men by their abuse of such drink come to lose their virtue and destroy their persons:— such employment of it is what Heaven has annexed its terrors to. The Buddhists, hating the use of things where Heaven sends down its terrors, put away as well the use of them which Heaven has prescribed. It is not so with us of the Learned (i.e., the Orthodox) school:—we only put away the use of things to which Heaven has annexed its terrors, and the use of them of which it approves remains as a matter of course.

'"For instance, in the use of meats and drinks, there is such a thing as wildly abusing and destroying the creatures of Heaven. The Buddhists, disliking this, confine themselves to a vegetable diet, while we only abjure the wild abuse and destruction. In the use of clothes, again, there is such a thing as wasteful extravagance. The Buddhists, disliking this, will have no clothes but those of a dark and sad colour, while we only condemn the extravagance. They, further, through dislike of criminal connection between the sexes, would abolish the relation between husband and wife, while we only denounce the criminal connection.

'"The Buddhists, disliking the excesses to which the evil desires of men lead, would put away, along with them, the actions which are in accordance with the justice of Heavenly principles, while we, the orthodox, put away the evil desires of men, and what are called Heavenly principles are the more brightly seen. Suppose the case of a stream of water.—The Buddhists, through dislike of its being foul with mud, proceed to dam it up with earth. They do not consider that when the earth has dammed up the stream, the supply of water will all be cut off. It is not so with us, the orthodox. We seek only to cleanse away the mud and sand, so that the pure clear water may be available for use. This is the difference between the Buddhists and the Learned school."'.

軒降不爲此天之命其而至必於窮衣賸絕而天人譬之既不者
酒威及物即之之降者降於欲暴極壞侈夫已理欲如濁窒然可
詰處, 今本天故降威去降命於暴食珍奢色而婦釋之所水而則澄酌
一段, 千載奉降於也, 乃而釋衣至儒本者天釋之水泥儒無其此儒
誠備以之至威者之者著珍蔬而侈之已吾氏公謂焉窒也
天年說祀也德氏與儒服惡儒惡去人之者惡士飲而水釋之分也
命者酒賓人身惡之然者不至必去願併儒然知吾之也
雨夫所之客以即天降去去之至於欲其而願與去矣沙土儒清

Apart from the interpretation of the disputed phrases in the text, the contrast here drawn between Buddhism and Chinese orthodoxy is interesting. It will, perhaps, suggest to the reader the words of the apostle Paul, about 'forbidding to marry, and commanding to abstain from meats, which God hath created to be received with thanksgiving.' It may remind him also of the controversies in the West about the subjects of vegetarianism, and total abstinence from all spirituous liquors.]

文王誥教小
子有正有事、
無彝酒、越庶
國飲惟祀、越德
將無醉。○惟
曰、我民迪小
厥心臧聰聽
祖考之彝訓
越小大德小

四節

五節

4　'King Wăn admonished and instructed the young and all who were charged with office and in employment, that they should not ordinarily use spirits.　Throughout all his States, he required that they should be drunk only on occasion of sacrifices, and then that virtue should preside so that there might be no drunkenness.　He said,

5　"Let my people teach their young men that they are to love only the productions of the ground, for so will their hearts be good.　Let *the youth also* hearken diligently to the constant lessons of their fathers.　Let them look at virtuous actions whether great or small in the same light."

Pp. 4, 5.　*Further instructions of king Wăn on the use of spirits, showing his anxiety especially that the young should be kept from the habit of drinking them, and trained to virtuous industry.*　In par. 2 we have the opinion of Wăn that spirits were intended to be used only at sacrifices, their strong and fragrant odour being acceptable to the spirits worshipped (蓋藉以薦馨香;—see the 日講, *in loc.*); here it would appear that he also permitted the use of them by the worshippers *after the sacrifices*, only requiring that they should not go to excess.

4.　小子, 有正, 有事,—小子= 少子之稱, '小子 is the appellation of young people.'　Ts'ae observes that such are more readily swayed by impulses and led away by strong drink, and therefore king Wăn addressed himself specially to them.　But does this paragraph speak of the young only?　Kăng Shing thinks so, and explains 有正有事 as descriptive of 小子:—'the young who have their superiors and their duties.'　His language is:—正, 長也, 小子有長 上之人, 有服勞之事, 常酒 則必慢上, 而廢事, 故戒令 毋然.　It would simplify this par., if we could consider it all occupied with the duty of the young, but Shing's explanation of 有正, 有事 is too forced, and contrary moreover to the analogy of other passages in the Book;—see particularly 有正 in par. 7.　I must take

有正, therefore, with Ts'ae, as = 有官 可守者, and 有事 as = 有職業 者.　無彝酒 = 毋常於酒, 'that they should not be always (ordinarily) at wine.'　飲惟祀 = 其飲惟於 祭祀之時, 'their drinking should only be at times of sacrificing.'　Compare 祀茲 酒 in par. 2.　The text is a relaxation or extension of the rule in regard to the use of spirits, which would flow from the former statement.　德將無醉,—將 is here = 節, 'to regulate,' 'to keep in order.'　We do not find this meaning of the character in the dictionary.

5.　惟曰,—we must suppose 文王 as the subject of 曰.　Some think differently.　Woo Ch'ing, for instance, says that here king Woo delivers to K'ang-shuh the words which he should go and announce to the people of Mei, = 'When you now proceed to your State, you ought to say,' &c.　(今汝之往, 惟 當言, 曰).　But this is inadmissible.　迪 = 訓導, 'to instruct and lead,' 'to train.'　厥心臧—臧 = 善, 'good.'　Ts'ae says:—'When they toil at their sowing and reaping, and labour on their fields, desiring nothing beyond, then what they keep in their minds will be correct, and their goodness will grow from day to day.'　Wăn's idea was that if the young were trained to industrious habits, they would not be likely

子、其爾典聽朕
有正越庶伯君
致用酒。○庶士
父母慶、自洗腆○七節
孝養厥父母、
車牛遠服賈用
厥考厥長、肇牽
藝黍稷、奔走
嗣爾股肱、純其
子惟一。○妹土、六節

6   '*Ye people of* the land of Mei, if you can employ your limbs, largely cultivating your millet, and hastening about in the service of your fathers and elders; and if with your carts and oxen you traffic to a distance, that you may thereby filially minister to your parents:—then, when your parents are happy, you may set forth your spirits clear and strong, and use them.

7   'Hearken constantly to my instructions, all ye *high* officers, ye assistants, and all ye noble chiefs:—when you have largely done

to fall a prey to intemperance. The fact sung by our children in the words,

> 'Satan finds some mischief still
> For idle hands to do,'

was held in substance by him. 聽 = 'to give a ready ear to.'

小子惟一,=不可以小德大德小子惟 爲一視之可也, 'Let them not look on watchfulness in the use of spirits as a small virtue. The young should look in the same way on what are called great virtues and small virtues, equally observing them.' Gan-kwŏ takes the clause difftly, but not so well. Këang Shing takes it as declarative that the young of king Wăn's States became equally observant of great virtues and small;—but neither can I agree with him.

Pp. 6, 7. *The duke of Chow, in the name of king Ching, addresses the people and officers of Mei directly, and warns them against using spirits excepting in certain specified cases.* P. 6 is addressed to the people. They might drink spirits after having toiled for their parents and done all their duty for them. Both this par. and the next must be taken as addressed directly by the speaker to the people of Mei. Woo Ch'ing and others try to put them into the mouth of Fung, following the 惟曰 of the last par.; but such a construction is forced on the text. 嗣爾股肱,—'connect your arms and legs;' *i.e.*, employ your limbs, one after the other; let none of them be idle. 純至稷—純

=大; 純藝='largely, or diligently, cultivate.' 黍 and 稷 are two species of millet, put by synecdoche for 五穀, 'the five kinds of grain;'—intimating perhaps that millet was cultivated more than the others in Mei. 肇至賈,—肇=敏, 'to be diligent,' 'urgent.' 服=事; 服賈 = 'doing the business of traffic.' The whole='if you are diligent in leading about your carts and oxen, pursuing to a distance the business of traffic.' 厥父母慶,—慶=喜慶, 'to be happy and complacent.' This is better than to take the term, with Gan-kwŏ and others, in the sense of 善, 'to approve,' as if the meaning were—'when your parents approve of your conduct.' 自洗腆致用酒, —洗 (*sëen*) and 腆 are both verbs, intimating operations to be performed upon the spirits, to make them fit for use, the effect of the former being to make them clear; of the latter, to make them strong. The 自=自此 the 'then' of the translation. Gaubil cannot be said to translate the clause at all. Medhurst has for it:—'then you may bathe and enjoy your abundance, and after that make use of wine.' The meaning of the whole par. is—that spirits might be used at family feasts. The 'Daily Explanation' expresses this clearly enough in its paraphrase of this clause:—自此,則洗以致其潔,腆以致其豐,以用

永不忘在王家。
亦惟天若元德，
王正事之臣，
用逸茲乃允惟
饋祀爾乃自介
中德爾尚克羞
克永觀省作稽
醉飽丕惟曰爾
惟君爾乃飲食
教爾大克羞耇

your duty in ministering to your aged and serving your sovereign, you may eat and drink freely and to satiety. And to speak of greater things:—when you can maintain a constant watchful examination of yourselves, and your conduct is in accordance with correct virtue, then may you minister the offerings of sacrifice, and at the same time indulge yourselves in festivity. In such case you will indeed be ministers doing right service to your king, and Heaven likewise will approve your great virtue, so that you shall never be forgotten in the royal House.'"

酒於父母之前，而燕樂於家庭之內，其亦可矣． P. 7 is addressed to the ministers and officers of Mei. I suppose the 庶士，有正 and 庶伯君子 to correspond to the 庶士，少正, and 御事 of par. 2. The 御事 are here styled 庶伯君子 by way of compliment. 爾大克至醉飽，—Gan-kwŏ supposed that this was addressed to Fung himself, and explains it by—汝大爲君之道，則矣，如此，汝乃飲食醉飽之道，先戒羣吏以聽教，次戒康叔以君義 Ming-shing may well set this view aside as 'wide of the mark,' but it is not easy to arrive at the true meaning. The 惟君 is really unmanageable, and Ts'ae honestly confesses that he does not understand it. He explains 羞 by 養 and 羞耇 by 養老, which is a more likely interpretation than any other that I have seen. The translation is after the paraphrase in the 日講：—爾能盡誠致敬，養老奉君之禮，則雖飲食醉飽，亦無非禮節，大修酬之間，日以勸之也．

不爲過矣．—here again Gan-kwŏ strangely supposes that Fung is addressed, and 丕惟曰＝我大惟教汝，曰．Këang Shing supposes that the subject of 曰 is 君;—'when you can 羞耇，惟君, then your prince will say,' &c. This view also is unsatisfactory. I have taken, with Ts'ae, 丕惟曰 as＝以事之大者而言．作稽中德，—稽＝合，'accordant with;' 中德 is 'virtue exactly correct, without inclination or deflection.' 爾尚克羞饋祀，—尚＝庶幾，'perhaps;' but more is meant than meets the ear. The king politely indicates by the character his full conviction that the officers, being such as he described, would be acceptable worshippers. 羞 is here ＝進． 爾乃自介用逸，—介＝助，'to assist.' The sacrifice to the spirits is represented as the great or chief ceremony; the subsequent festive indulgence by those who have taken part in it is a subsidiary ceremony (享神爲正，而我後飲是之也;—this is the very pithy gloss of a 朱養醇, one of the five critics at the end of the long list of authorities quoted in Yung-ching's

至于帝乙、成王畏
德秉哲、自成湯咸
迪畏天顯小民、經
曰、在昔殷先哲王、
○王曰、封、我聞惟
九節
于今克受殷之命。
不腆于酒、故我至
子、尚克用文王教、
棐祖邦君御事小
○王曰、封、我西土
八節

8　II. "The king says, 'O Fung, in our western regions, the princes of States, the managers of affairs, and the youths, who in former days assisted *our ancestor*, were able to obey the lessons of king Wăn, and indulge in no excess of spirits ; and so it is that I have now received the appointment which belonged to Yin.'"

9　"The king says, 'O Fung, I have heard it said that formerly the first wise sovereign of Yin manifested a reverential awe of the bright principles of Heaven, and of the lower people, steadfast in his virtue, and holding fast his wisdom.　From him, T'ang the Successful, down to the emperor Yih, the sovereigns all completed

Shoo, whose age the editors say they have been unable to ascertain). 正事之臣、—Woo Ch'ing takes this as =有正有事之臣, with reference to par. 4 ; but the context makes it more natural to take the phrase as = 'ministers doing right service.'　天若元德、—若=順, 'to accord with,' equivalent to 'to approve.'　The critics all call attention to the various relaxations of Wăn's original rule, that spirits should be used only for sacrifices.　They say that we have in them an instance of prohibition by permission (不禁之禁).　Soo Tung-po says:—'Spirits are what men will not do without.　To prohibit them and secure a total abstinence from them is beyond the power even of the sages.　Here, therefore, we have warnings on the evils of drunkenness in the abuse of them, and the joy that is found in the virtuous use of them is set forth ;—such is the way in which the sages lay their prohibitions upon men' (see the 集說).

Ch. II. Pp. 8—17. THE KING, ADDRESSING FUNG DIRECTLY, SHOWS HIM THE CONSEQUENCES OF TEMPERANCE AND INTEMPERANCE RESPECTIVELY, IN THE FORTUNES OF THEIR OWN HOUSE, AND OF THE DYNASTY OF YIN ; AND REQUIRES HIM TO ILLUSTRATE, INCULCATE, AND ENFORCE HIS LESSONS IN MEI.　8. *How the fortunes*

of Chow had risen by obedience to the lessons of king Wăn. 我西土至小子、—the 棐祖 make this passage very perplexing.　棐 is taken as =輔, 'to assist,' and 徂=往, 'gone by,' 'of the time past.'　The two characters are best joined as descriptive of the parties immediately enumerated,—as in the translation.　Gan-kwŏ and Lin Che-k'e suppose that 文王 is the nominative to 棐, which then governs 邦君, &c.—我文王在西土、輔訓往日國君、云云.　This is very unnatural. 尚=庶幾, as in the last par.　The peculiarity of its use here is that it is all historical.　9, 10. *The example of various virtue, and especially of temperance, afforded in the prosperous times of the Yin dynasty.* 我聞惟曰、—Ying-tă gives for this—我聞於古、所聞惟曰. 迪畏天顯小民、= 'walked in the fear of Heaven and of the people.'　Compare the 'T'ae-këä,' Pt. iii., p. 1. 自成王咸至于帝乙、—咸, as it now stands, =徧, 'throughout.'　Some would place it after 乙, in which position it would = 'all.'　Yih was the father

助成王德顯越尹　惟不敢亦不暇惟　居罔敢湎于酒不　服宗工越百姓里　百僚庶尹惟亞惟　衞邦伯越在內服　越在外服侯甸男　短曰其敢崇飲。○　恭不敢自暇自逸　相惟御事厥棐有

their royal virtues, and revered their chief ministers, so that their managers of affairs respectfully discharged their helping duties, and dared not to allow themselves in idleness and pleasure;—how much

10　less would they dare to indulge in drinking! Moreover, in the exterior domains, the princes of the States of the How, Teen, Nan and Wei, with their chiefs; and in the interior domain, all the various officers, the directors of the several departments, the inferior officers and employés, and the Heads of great Houses, with the men of honoured name living in retirement, all eschewed indulgence in spirits. Not only did they not dare to indulge in them, but they had not leisure, being occupied with helping to complete their king's virtue and make it more distinguished, and helping the directors of affairs reverently to attend to the service of the sovereign.

of the tyrant Show, himself the 27th emperor of the dynasty. We may admit with Mencius, II., Pt. I., i., 8, that between T'ang and Woo-ting, the 20th of the line, there were six or seven good sovereigns;—the statement in the text is a grand exaggeration. 成王畏相＝成就君德,而無隙越之憂,敬畏賢相,而無驕肆之失　厥棐有恭,—'in their helping had reverence.' The 有恭 is best understood by reference to Mencius, IV., i. 13,—責難於君謂之恭　崇飲,—崇＝尙, 'to value,'＝'to indulge in.' 10. 外服,內服,—by the 內服 we are to understand, of course, the 王畿, or 'imperial domain.' It would appear that an arrangement of the 'domains,' akin to that which obtained under the Chow dynasty, had come, during the dynasty of Yin to supersede the older one introduced by Yu;—see the figure on page 149. By 侯,甸,男,衞, we are to understand

the princes of those domains; and by the presidents of those princes (諸侯之長伯). 邦伯＝侯之長伯. 百僚＝百官之僚屬,—'all the officers belonging to the various departments.' 庶尹＝庶官之長 what are elsewhere called the 正 'the Heads of the various departments.' 惟亞,—亞＝次大夫, 'officers of the second degree.' 惟服,—服＝奔走服事之人, 'petty officers who had to run about discharging their duties.' 宗工＝尊官, 'honoured officers.' Woo Ch'ing describes them as 王朝公卿大夫,及王子弟食采邑,爲大宗者. This is probably correct, and I have translated—'Heads of great Houses.' I take 百姓里居 together, and understand 百官 by

克息惟威淫越厥曰人
畏乃荒儀洗怨命在祗
死逸胕民于命岡今辟。
辜厥于罔非不顯後○
在心酒盡彝易于嗣我
商疾不傷用誕民王聞
邑狠惟心燕惟祗酗亦
越不自　喪厥保身惟
　　　　　　縱

11 'I have heard it said likewise, that in these times the last successor of those kings was addicted to drink, so that no charges came
from him brightly before the people, and he was reverently and
unchangingly bent on doing and cherishing what provoked resentment. Greatly abandoned to extraordinary lewdness and dissipation,
for pleasure's sake he ruined all his majesty. The people were all
sorely grieved and wounded in heart, but he gave himself wildly up
to spirits, not thinking of ceasing, but continuing his excess, till his
mind was frenzied, and he had no fear of death. His crimes accumulated in the city of Shang, and though the extinction of the dynasty

百姓. Officers of distinguished name, who had
retired because of age from the public service,
are intended. 助成王德顯＝助
成人君之德, and使之益顯.
The 助 extends also to the next clause, so that
it＝亦助尹人, 使之祗敬君
事, 而不少怠. Other explanations of
this clause have been proposed, but it does not
seem worth while to discuss them. 尹人＝
御事, above.

11. *The drunkennness of Show, and its issues.*
The 在今後嗣王. of course, is Show.
酗 is defined by 樂酒, 'being fond of strong
drink.' It is often used to denote a state short
of gross intoxication, but we are not to think of
that modified signification here. Woo Ch'ing
explains 酗身 by 酗酒於身. We
might translate it literally—'was a drunken
body.' 厥命至不易,—the translation
of this part is after Gan-kwŏ and Ts'ae, the
latter of whom explains:—昏迷於政,

命令不著於民. 其所祗保
者, 惟在於作怨之事, 不肯
悛改. Woo Ch'ing construes difftly, but it
seems to me with more constraint of the text:
—其命令之出, 無能明於民
之當祗保, 及民怨之不易
弭, 'When he issued his commands, he showed
that he did not understand how he ought to reverence and cherish the people, and when they
resented his conduct, he would not change or
stop it.' 誕惟至威儀,—于非
彝＝于非法, our 'extraordinary.' Ts'ae
refers in illustration to 作奇技淫巧,
以悅婦人, in the 'Great Speech,' Pt. iii.,
p. 3;—see the account of Show's debaucheries on
pp. 269,270. 民罔至畏死,—盡
＝痛, 'to be grieved,' 'to feel sad and sore.'
The 惟 in 不惟自息＝思, 'to think
of;' and the 乃, which follows, ＝仍. Keang
Shing says well:—不思自止息, 仍

人無於水監當於
多誥古人有言曰、
曰、封、予不惟若茲
惟民自速辜。○王 十二節
于殷、惟逸、天非虐、
天降喪于殷、罔愛
自酒腥聞在上、故
天、誕惟民怨庶群
德馨香祀登聞于
殷國滅無罹、弗惟

of Yin *was imminent*, this gave him no concern, and he wrought not that any sacrifices of fragrant virtue might ascend to heaven.　The rank odour of the people's resentments, and the drunkenness of his herds of creatures, went loudly up on high, so that Heaven sent down ruin on Yin and showed no love for Yin,—because of such excesses. There is not any cruel oppression of Heaven; people themselves accelerate their guilt, *and its punishment*.'"

12　"The king says, 'O Fung, I have no pleasure in making you this long announcement; but the ancients have said, "Let not men look *only* into water; let them look into the glass of *other* people."

疾
狠 = 'angrily wrangled.' 然淫泆、乃之言仍也. 辜在至于 天,—商邑 probably means the capital of Show, and 殷國 = 'the dynasty of Yin.' 罹 = 憂, 'sorrowful.' In 弗惟, 惟 = 思 —as in 不惟, above. 誕惟 at 在 上,—the 誕惟, like the same characters in the previous part of the par., indicate that what follows was attributable to Show. 自 酒 = 'abandoning themselves to drink.' 惟逸 = 以紂淫泆故, 'because of these excesses of Show.' There is a difficulty with the concluding clauses. All through the par., the speaker has been dilating on the wickedness of Show, and suddenly it seems to be said, at the end, that the ruin of the dynasty was the work of 'the people.' Ts'ae would interpret 民 of Show and his ministers, according to the analogy of 先民 in 'The Instructions of E,' p. 5. Këang Shing takes 民, as = 冥, and says—天降喪亡, 天非虐也, 惟冥冥昏亂, 自 召辜爾. Other methods to lighten the

difficulty have been tried. In the translation, I take 民 as = 人, 'men,' 'people' generally.

12. *How the House of Chow should see its duty in the history of Yin.* The meaning of 子 不惟若此多誥, is probably what appears in the translation. Ts'ae and Këang Shing bring it out by taking 惟 = 徒, 'vainly,' *i.e.*, merely for the sake of talking. The 'Daily Explanation' puts it—予豈好爲是 多誥哉. 古人有言、云云 —in illustration of this saying, Këang Shing quotes, aptly enough, a fragment of the lost Book of Shang which was called 'The Punitive Expeditions of T'ang' (湯征):—湯曰、人 視水見形, 視民知治不. 我其可不大監撫于時.—this is to be understood interrogatively. Gan-kwŏ took 撫 = 撫安, in which he is correctl followed by Ts'ae, whose expansion of the whole is very lucid:—我其可不以殷民 之失爲大監戒、以撫安斯 時乎. This is much better than, with Këang Shing, to take 撫 = 循, 'to follow,' 'to accord

惟　臣　內　徛　獻　曰　于　可　墜　民
爾　百　史　矧　臣　汝　時　不　厥　監
事　宗　友　太　侯　劼　○　大　命　今
服　工　越　史　甸　毖　子　監　我　惟
休　矧　獻　友　男　殷　惟　撫　其　殷
　　　　　　　　　十三節

Now that Yin has lost its appointment, ought we not to look much
to it as our glass, *and learn* how to secure the repose of our time?

13　'I say to you,—Strenuously warn the worthy ministers of Yin, and
the princes in the How, the Teen, the Nan, and Wei domains; and
still more, your friends, the great Recorder and the Recorder of the
interior, and all your worthy ministers, the Heads of great Houses;
and still more, those whom you serve—with whom you calmly
converse, and who carry out your measures; and still more, those

with,' and 時＝是, referring to the good ways
of the sovereigns of Yin before Show. His
words are:—我 其 可 不 監 于 是,
撫 于 是 乎, 監, 紂 也, 撫, 循
也, 謂 循 商 先 王 之 道 也, 時
是 也, 指 謂 殷.

P. 13. *Fung is required to take home to himself
the lessons about temperance, and to enjoin them on
the princes and officers in his jurisdiction.* 汝
劼 至 男 徛,—劼＝用 力, 'strenu-
ously.' 獻 臣＝賢 臣. These were
good ministers of the former dynasty, who were
still retained in their former offices under Fung.
As 孟 侯, or 'Head of the princes,' his authority extended also over the princes of the portions
of the domains that were under his jurisdiction. He should strenuously warn them,—on
the subject, of course, of abstaining from intemperance. 太 史 友. 內 史 友.—the
duties of the 太 史 and 內 史, with other
officers of the same department, are described
in the Chow Le, Bk. XXVI., 春 官, 宗 伯
第 三 之 十. They were very honourable
and extensive, and such as brought them into
frequent contact and consultation with the
太 宰 or prime minister ('grand administra-
teur general.' Biot). It is said in general that
the 太 史 had the management of what Biot
calls 'the six constitutions (六 典), the eight
regulations (八 法), and the eight statutes

(八 則).' Those six constitutions were the
various departments of the administration,—of
rule, of instruction, of ceremonies, of prescripts,
of punishments, and of business; the regulations and statutes embraced all connected with
the working of those departments. The 內
史 again had the management of 'the eight
powers or prerogatives' of the emperor (掌
八 柄 之 法). These duties branched off
into a great variety of minor functions. The 史
kept all the records which were to be appealed
to in connection with them, so that we may
consider them as having been confidential secre-
taries and advisers of the prime minister. Biot
calls the 太 史, 'le grand annaliste,' and 內
史, 'l'annaliste de l'interieur.' I prefer to
call them 'recorders,' as being a more general
term. The various princes had their 'grand
Recorder,' but the 'Recorder of the interior'
belonged, it is maintained, only to the imperial
court; and the individual mentioned in the text
is supposed, therefore, to have been the old
minister of the court of Shang, now superseded
under the new dynasty and living in Wei.
However this may be, it is said that the two
Recorders were 'friends' of Fung. As men of
research and ability and general good character,
he would so cherish them.

獻 (＝賢) 臣, 百 宗 工,—we must
suppose these, in distinction from the 獻 臣
above, to be those appointed under the existing
dynasty. Or, acc. to the view of Woo Ch'ing,
we may suppose that they were good men,
Heads of influential families, who were not in
office, and are called 臣, in the same way as

拘　勿　曰、○　剛　定　若　薄　若　服
以　佚、群　厥　制　辟、保、違　疇　柔、
歸　盡　飲、十四節或　于　矧　宏　農　矧
于　執　汝　誥　酒。汝　矦　矦　矦　惟

who are, as it were, your mates,—your minister of War, who deals with the rebellious, your minister of Agriculture, who is like a protector *to the people*, and your minister of Works, who settles the boundaries; and above all, do you sternly keep yourself from drink.

14　'If you are told that there are companies who drink together, do not fail to apprehend them all, and send them here to Chow, where I may put them to death.

every individual in the empire is supposed to be a 臣 of the sovereign. 爾事、服休、服柔,—the translation here follows the view of Ts'ae. He supports his explanation of 事 by 'to serve,' from the passage of Mencius, V., Pt. II., vii., 4, where Tsze-sze is introduced as saying, 古之人有言曰、事之云乎、豈曰友之云乎, 'The ancients have said, "The scholar (or virtuous officer) should be served;"—how should they have merely said, "He should be made a friend of?"' This view of 事 being adopted, 服休=坐而論道之臣, 'ministers who sit (by their prince) and discourse to him about principles,' and 服柔=起而作事之臣, 'ministers who rise and perform the business (of their prince).' 服休 is 'to serve in *hours of ease*;' 服柔, 'to serve in active business.' I have hesitated between this view, and that given by Woo Ch'ing:—爾事=服事於爾者、大夫也, 'those who serve you,—your great officers;' 服休=職之優閒者, 'those whose offices were comparatively easy, and allowed of leisure;' 服柔=職之繁劇者, 'those whose offices were more bustling and troublesome.' Gan-kwŏ took a difft. view which is quite inadmissible. He says:—汝身事、服行美道、服事治民, making Fung himself, in the discharge of his duties, the subject. This cannot be right. K'ang-shing had still another view, in which he is followed by Këang Shing, acc. to which the whole = 'the employés, —those who are near to you in festivals and leisure, and those who are near at audiences and sacrifices' (汝之執事、服職于燕息、及朝祭之臣.) This diversity of opinion serves to show how uncertain the meaning is. 圻矦, 'the controller of boundaries,'=司馬, 'the minister of War.' This meaning is determined by the 1st ode in the 4th Book of the She King, Part ii., where it is said—祈(=圻)矦、予王之爪牙. This being determined, it follows that 農矦=司徒, 'the minister of Instruction;' and 宏矦=司空, 'the minister of Works.' These were the 'three high nobles' (三卿), belonging to the court of one of the princes. They were the highest in authority, and might be considered as their prince's 'mates' (疇匹). 薄 (read *pŏh*)=迫. 薄違=迫逐違命者. The minister of Instruction is called 若保, 'the harmonious preserver.' The promotion of agriculture, which supplies the staff of life, being within his province, he is thus denominated. The minister of Works is called 定辟, 'the settler of rules,' *i.e.*, the decider of all questions about the settlements and tenements of the people. Këang Shing would take 辟 in the sense of 君, which does not seem at all applicable here. 剛制于酒=剛果用力自制酒.

Pp. 14—16. *By what rules obedience to the king's injunctions against the use of spirits were to be enforced.* 14. 汝勿佚--佚=失, 'to fail.' The punishment here threatened is so far beyond the crime, that the critics fall upon various devices to explain it, or to mitigate the

司、民湎于酒。
典聽朕毖勿辯乃
于殺。○王曰封汝 **十七節**
恤弗蠲乃事、時同
教辭惟我一人弗
斯明享乃不用我
之、姑惟教之。○有 **十六節**
乃湎于酒、勿庸殺
殷之迪諸臣惟工、
周、子其殺。○又惟 **十五節**

15 'As to the ministers and officers of Yin, who have been led to it, and been addicted to drink, it is not necessary to put them to death;

16 —let them be taught for a time. If they keep these *lessons*, I will give them bright distinction. If you disregard my lessons, then I, the one man, will show you no pity. As you cannot cleanse your way, you shall be classed with those who are to be put to death.'"

17 "The king says, 'O Fung, give constant heed to my admonitions. If you do not manage right your officers, the people will continue lost in drink.'"

force of the language. First, the coming together in companies to drink is supposed to carry with it the design of their assembling, as being not merely to drink, but, under the cloak of that, to plot against the govt. Second, the 其 in 子其殺 is taken to indicate uncertainty. The king would examine for himself into their guilt, and according as he found they had treasonable designs would put them to death. If they really only met to drink, he would inflict on them some lighter penalty. I have allowed the second remark by using the '*may*' in the translation. The former remark may also be correct. If it be not so, we cannot account for the difference of spirit between this and the two next paragraphs. 15. 又惟 殷之迪諸臣惟工＝今殷之 諸百工，其素爲商紂導引 爲惡者. Këang Shing says that 惟 in 惟工 is superfluous. We hardly know what to do with it. 16. 有斯明享＝商 之諸臣果能遵我教而享 之辭存揚之 訓我則不忘 心而享之以爵位，—as

in the translation. This is forcing a meaning out of the words. The most that can be said for it is, that it is more likely than any other construction which has been proposed. K'angshing took 斯 as ＝析, which Këang Shing adopts. He has:—又分析其明用 我教者，獻之古者諸侯有 獻士于天子之制 乃不 用，云云,—the king here turns to the officers of Yin who should persist obstinately in their drunkenness and other evil ways, and addresses them directly. 弗蠲乃事, ＝不能潔汝舊染之汙. 時 ＝是 or 於是.

P. 17. *Concluding admonition to Fung.* 勿 ＝不; it is not imperative. 辯＝治, 'to rule.' Fung was specially to direct his efforts to discountenance drunkenness in the officers,— the higher classes. If he could not succeed with them, his efforts with the lower classes would be vain.

THE BOOKS OF CHOW.

BOOK XI. THE TIMBER OF THE TSZE TREE.

惟 臣 家、 臣、 民 以 王一節
邦 達 以 達 暨 厥 曰、   梓
君。 王、 厥 大 厥 庶 封、   材

1 I. "The king says, 'O Fung, to have a good understanding with the multitudes of his people, and his ministers *on the one hand*, and with the great families *on the other*; and *again* to have the same with all the subjects *under his charge* and with the sovereign:—is the part of the prince of a State.

THE NAME OF THE BOOK.—梓材, 'The Timber of the Tsze tree.' Though it does not affect our understanding of the Book, I am sorry that I cannot give the proper botanical name of the Tsze. It is described as allied to the Ts'ew (楸), which has 'the leaves of a cypress and the trunk of a fir' (柏葉、松身). It was esteemed as the most valuable for making articles of furniture, and for the carver's art. The phrase,—'the timber, or materials, of the Tsze,' occurs in par. 4, and was thence assumed to designate the Book, intimating apparently that the administrator of government ought to give himself to his duties skilfully and thoroughly, as the cabinet-maker deals with his materials. The cultivation of a field and the building of a house are spoken of in the same paragraph; and either of these things might have been used as the name instead of the phrase which it pleased the fancy of the compiler to adopt. The Book is found in both the texts.

CONTENTS. The Book is sadly wanting in unity. The 1st par. is directly addressed to Fung, and we may suppose that the three which follow were so also. He is admonished of his duty to promote a good understanding between the various classes in his State, and between them all and the sovereign; and that, in order to this, his rule must be gentle, eschewing the use of punishments. The interpretation, however, is anything but certain. The remaining paragraphs are of a difft. character. They are not the charges of the emperor, insisting with a prince upon his duties, but the admonitions of a minister loyally and affectionately cautioning his sovereign, and praying for the prosperity of his reign. They would be appropriate as addressed to king Ching by the duke of Chow, or the duke of Shaou. We might also suppose them the response of Fung; but the text gives no intimation of a new speaker being introduced. The whole Book is very unsatisfactory, and it is a translator's greatest comfort that it is short.

Ch. I. Pp. 1—4. *How the prince of a State is a connecting link between all the classes of his people, and between his people and the emperor.*

達=通, 'to reach to,' 'to effect an intercommunication.' By 大家 we are to understand what Mencius, IV., Bk. I., vi., calls 巨室, 'the great Houses,' saying that 'the administration of govt. is not difficult, but lies in not offending the great Families, for whom they affect will be affected by all the State.' It is observed in the 'Complete Digest,' that the force of the 達 is to show how the conduct of the ruler draws forth the approval of all parties, so that there is an uninterrupted flow of their good feeling towards him, and we are not to

往　厥　敬　亦　罔　尹　司　師　○
姦　敬　勞　厥　厲　旅　馬　師　汝　二節
宄　勞　肆　君　殺　曰　司　我　若
殺　肆　祖　先　人　子　空　徒　有　恆

2　'If you regularly in giving out your orders say, "My instructors whom I am to follow, my minister of Instruction, my minister of War, and my minister of Works; my Heads of departments, and all ye, my officers, I will on no account with oppressions put men to death;"———. Let the prince also set the example of respecting and encouraging the people, and these will proceed to respect and encourage them. Let him go on in dealing with those who have been traitors and villains, murderers and harbourers of criminals,

take it as intimating that the ruler brings the higher and lower classes into intimacy and good feeling with one another' (達者吾之行事與其情兩相通徹而無暌阻，非使上下相通之謂). The first 厥臣 is descriptive of the ministers and officers of the State, and those not filling the highest offices, which would for the most part be occupied by the Heads or scions of the great families. The second 厥臣 is descriptive of all the people of the State, the official classes and the unofficial, as being equally the subjects of the sovereign (王) or emperor.

Such is the view of the par. that appears to be given by Ts'ae. Lin Che-k'e took the same, only understanding the 達 of bringing the various classes mentioned into good and harmonious relation with one another. Gan-kwŏ's view was different. He paraphrases:—當其小夫大用其民乃言其賢者與卿大用通之言者以通達於國信通者人之達於民言通以通政於王教於民其政教王惟眾教王教於民良王通民家之道 Of this I can make little or nothing. Ch'ing K'ang-shing had still another view which deserves to be noticed only for its singularity. He seems to have read the last clause—以厥臣達王曁邦君; and then by 王 he understood 二王之後, 'the descendants of the emperors of the two previous dynasties;' and by 邦君, the princes of the various States within Fung's jurisdiction, as

孟侯. Adopting this strange view, Kёang Shing says—以臣民達大家，則聯上下之情，以臣達王與邦君，則聯邦交之誼.

P. 2. *The prince of a State must inculcate on his ministers, and exemplify himself, leniency in dealing with criminals.* Ts'ae honestly acknowledges that the most of this par. is unintelligible to him, and he does not attempt any paraphrase of it. In the translation, I have followed the 'Daily Explanation.' The meaning given is more likely than any other which it has been attempted to put upon the text;—this is the most that can be said for it. 汝若至殺人，—越 is taken in the sense of 發 or 發令, 'to give forth orders.' This meaning of the term is given in the Dict. (＝揚), and supported by examples from the 國語. 師師＝相師爲善之意, 'instructors whom I am to make my model:'—comp. the same phrase in Pt. IV., Bk. XI., p. 2; *et al.* The three ministers immediately mentioned are the instructors intended. 尹＝正官之長, 'the Heads of the various official departments;' and 旅＝眾,—that is, 眾士, 'the whole body of officers.' The 曰 which follows is superfluous, and the sentence is left incomplete. The 'Daily Explanation' supplements it by—'and you all ought to cherish the same regard for the lives of the people' (汝咸當仰體吾好生之心). The older interpreters, followed by Kёang Shing and many others, connect 汝若恆越曰我有

婦　寡　虐、胥　為　敢　人　君　肆　人
合　至　至　狀　民　監　宥。事、亦　歷
由　于　于　無　曰　厥　○　狀　見　人
以　屬　敬　胥　無　亂　王〔三節〕敗　厥　宥、

3 to exercise pardon, and these, when they observe the prince's conduct, will likewise pardon those who have assaulted others and injured their property. When sovereigns appointed inspectors, they did so in order to the government of the people, and said to them, "Do not give way to violence or oppression; and go on to show reverence for the weak, and find connexions for *destitute* women. Your protection of the people must proceed in this way to cherish

師 師 with the prec. par., giving it substantially this meaning,—'Do you accord (若＝順) with this regular rule for your duty, and (越＝于是) then say to yourself, "I have this law which I am to observe."' Then commences with them a new par., and 司 徒, &c., form the subject of the second 曰. On this construction the two 曰 are accounted for; but to put 予 罔 厲 殺 人 in the mouths of all the officers is inadmissible. 亦 厥 君 先 敬 勞, 肆 徂 厥 敬 勞,—勞, in the 3d tone, is taken in the sense of 慰, 'to comfort,' 'to encourage.' The 'respecting' the people (we must understand 民 or 其 民 under the govt. of 敬 勞) is to be taken with reference to the ruler's eschewing the use of punishments rather than run the risk of putting any to death unjustly, 'with oppressions.' 肆＝遂, 'then,' 'thereupon.' 徂＝往, 'to go.' The subject of this verb is the ministers and officers above. Gan-kwŏ supposes the 君 to be the subject of 徂, as well as of the previous verbs:—'It is also the way of a ruler to take the initiative in respecting and encouraging the people; do you therefore, in going to rule this people, be careful to respect and encourage them.' Këang Shing takes 亦 as ＝ 袚＝助, 'to assist,' and connects the clause with the preceding, thus:—'The ministers will say, "We will be cautious with you of putting men to death unjustly." Then they will help their prince to reverence and encourage the people as the thing of greatest importance.' 肆 往 姦, 至 末,—the first of these

clauses—肆 往, 云 云,—is descriptive of the ruler; and the second—肆 亦 見, 云 云,—of his ministers. The former of the two 肆 is in the way, indeed, of this construction. The character introducing, immediately above, the subject of the ministers as distinguished from the ruler, and doing the same here in the second instance, we might have expected 亦 往 instead of 肆 往. This is a serious difficulty; but the view upon the whole harmonizes with the general scope of the paragraph, and enables us to explain the 亦 見 君 事, to which both Gan-kwŏ and Këang Shing do great violence. 肆 往 姦 宄 殺 人 歷 人 宥＝遂 與 往 日 為 姦 宄 殺 人 者, 罪 人 所 經 歷 者, 今 皆 寛 宥, 與 之 為 新. Ts'ae explains 歷 人 by 罪 人 所 過, 'those through whom offenders have passed,' meaning individuals who have connived at crime, and more or less aided and abetted it. 狀 敗 人 are individuals guilty of lighter offences than those mentioned above, whose cases should be summarily dealt with by his ministers and officers, without their being appealed to the ruler himself. We cannot suppose that this charge to Fung to pardon offenders—even murderers, was to be taken without qualification. He could only be required to note and act upon all mitigating circumstances in his punishment of crime.

P. 3. *The object of the emperors in delegating authority to princes and officers is the kindly and benevolent rule of the people.* 王 敢 監,—Ts'ae says that 監 has reference to the 'three Inspectors' appointed by king Woo to oversee Woo-kăng in his govt., and that the same title is given to Fung, as being appointed to a portion of the

攸 兹 古 引 以 厥 越 效 容
辟。監 王 恬 引 命 御 邦 王
○ 罔 若 自 養 曷 事、君 其

them." And when the sovereigns gave their injunctions to the princes of States, and their managers of affairs, what was the charge? It was that they should lead *the people* to the enjoyment of plenty and peace. Such was the way of the kings from of old. An inspector is to eschew the use of punishments.'

same territory. It is very strange that he did not perceive that this view was inconsistent with his other view, that the speaker in this and the two preceding Books was king Woo and not the duke of Chow. Woo could not have spoken thus of what he had done himself. It is better, however, to take 監 as a general title, applicable to all princes—the 公、侯、伯、子 and 男.—Such a use of it is found in the Chow Le, Bk. II., p. 94 (天官太宰),—乃施典于邦國,而建其牧,立其監,云云. 厥亂爲民,—亂=治. The whole=其治本爲民而已, 曰無胥至以容,—we must understand all this as the imperial charge to the princes invested with inspection and rule. The 胥=相, indeed, occasions some difficulty, which is best got over by understanding it of those princes and their ministers and people. This is the solution adopted by Lin Chek'e from Wang Gan-shih (胥者謂君臣上下,並爲戕虐之政也). Gankwŏ took the subject of 曰 to be the 'inspectors.'—Appointed for such a purpose, they ought to teach their people saying, 'Do not among yourselves,' &c. This is plainly inadmissible.

敬 寡,—'respect the few,' *i.e.*, those who have few to help them. 屬 (*chuh*) 婦,=婦之窮獨者,當使之有所歸,而聯屬之, 'in the case of women reduced to straits and solitary, you ought to bring it about that they shall have those to whom they may turn, and find connexions for them.' This is forcing a meaning out of the 屬; but I do not see what better can be done while the text stands as it does. We must interpret one clause by the analogy of another, and 敬 being a verb in 敬 寡, 屬 must be one here. The dict., with reference to this

passage, defines 屬 by 恤, 'to pity;'—after Gan-kwŏ, who gives for the clause—存恤妾婦. I do not think, however, that Gankwŏ understood 屬 to mean 'to pity.' The sense in which he took this term appears in 妾婦, 'concubines,' = women attached to the proper wife, and inferior to her. He supplied the 存恤, as necessary to make sense of the clause. The 說文 quotes it as—至于嬾婦,嬾 meaning 妊, 'pregnant.' The critics who adopt this reading suppose that the preceding 敬 ought to be 矜, to which they give the meaning of 鰥, 'widowers;'—but this is mere conjecture. 合由以容,=Ts'ae takes 合 as =保合 and 容 as =容蓄, understanding the whole as in the translation (又推而保合一國之民,率由此道,以相爲容蓄,使各得其所爲). It would be hard to say that this is really the meaning; but it is preferable to Gan-kwŏ's exposition,—和合其教,用大道以容之,無令見冤枉. 王其效至末,—效=責效, 'to give charge to and require service from.' This is akin to the meaning of the character which the dict. defines by 勉. 厥命曷以=其命何以哉. 引養引恬,—this is the answer to the question. Ts'ae expands it by—亦惟欲其引掖斯民於生養安全之地而已. 監罔攸辟=監其無所用乎刑辟, 'an inspector should have nothing to do with the using of punishments.'

惟曰、若稽田、既勤^{四節}

敷菑、惟其陳修、爲

厥疆畎、若作室家、

既勤垣墉、惟其塗

堲茨、若作梓材、既

勤樸斲、惟其塗丹

艧。○今王惟曰、先^{五節}

王既勤用明德、

爲夾庶邦享、作兄

弟方來、亦既用明

4　　"He says moreover, 'As in the management of a field, when the soil has all been laboriously turned up, they must proceed by orderly arrangement to make its boundaries and water-courses; as in building a house, after all the toil on its walls, they have to plaster and thatch it; as in working with the wood of the *tsze*, when the toil of the coarser and finer operations has been performed, they have to apply the paint of red and other colours'":——.

5　　II. "Now let your Majesty say, 'The former kings diligently employed their illustrious virtue, and produced such attachment by their cherishing *of the princes*, that from all the States they brought offerings, and with brotherly affection they came from all quarters, and likewise showed their virtue illustrious.' Do you, O sovereign,

P. 4. *Fung is required to complete the good work which had been begun.* It will be seen that this paragraph is imperfect. We have the protasis of the sentence thrice repeated in various form, the apodosis being left to be supplied, in some such way as—'so must you, O Fung, proceed in raising in your State the superstructure of govt., of which the foundations have been laid.' 惟曰,—we may understand 王 as the subject of 曰. 稽田,—稽 =治, 'to manage,' *i.e.*, to perform all the necessary operations on. 勤敷菑.— comp. Bk. VII., p. 11. 勤敷='toilfully and widely.' 若作室家,—these two characters—室家—are simply equivalent to the 室 in Bk. VII., p. 11, and = our 'house.'

Ma Yung says that 'a low wall is called 垣, and a high one, 墉' (牆卑曰垣、高曰墉). 惟其塗堲茨,—'there have to be the clay, the facing plaster, and the thatch grass.' 梓材,—see on the name of the Book. 樸斲,—the first of these

characters denotes the rough fashioning of the work, and the second the fine finish given to it (具粗曰樸、致巧曰斲). 艧 is a name given to the various colours used in painting articles of furniture. (采色之名). Wang Kăng-yay observes that 塗, 丹, and 艧 are all verbs, and that we are to understand them—塗之, 丹之, and 艧之, as in the case of 塗、堲、茨 above. It would seem that we should construe so, but it is difficult to determine the independent meaning of 塗. See the 讀書管見, *in loc.*

Ch. 5—8. These four paragraphs are evidently addressed not to a subject, but to the sovereign. Gan-kwŏ takes no notice of the difference in style between them and the preceding ones, and Ying-tă says expressly that the king goes on in them to complete his charges to Fung. This view now finds no advocates. The speaker was evidently some loyal minister of Chow. Kĕang Shing thinks that we have here the response of Fung to the various lessons which he had received. Ming-shing says that, having done with Fung, the duke of Chow now

受命。○已若
八節
民用懌先王
和懌先後迷
肆王惟德用、
七節
土于先王。○
國民、越厥疆
皇天既付中
六節
庶邦丕享。○
德后式典集、

use their statutes to attach *the princes*, and all the States will largely
come with offerings.

6 " Great Heaven having given this Middle kingdom with its people
7 and territories to the former kings, do you, our present sovereign,
employ your virtue, effecting a gentle harmony among the deluded
people, leading and urging them on;—so *also* will you please the
former kings, who received the appointment *from Heaven.*

turns to king Shing, and speaks some words of
warning to him. We need not trouble ourselves
with speculation on so uncertain and unimportant a matter.

P. 5. *How Wăn and Woo ruled the princes
by the influence of their virtue, and future sovereigns must imitate their example.* 先
王,—these 'former kings' can only be Wăn
and Woo. What is said of the effects of
their sway is much exaggerated. Had it been
as the speaker says, there would not have been
the troubles which disturbed the reign of king
Ching. 懷爲夾,—for this Gan-kwŏ
gives—懷遠爲近, 'cherished the distant
and made them near.' The meaning seems to
be that by their kindly cherishing of the
princes of States, Wăn and Woo gained them
and made them a strength and defence to their
govt. (以成夾輔之勢). The last
of Confucius' 'nine standard rules' for the
govt. of the empire,—'the king's cherishing
the princes of the States' 懷諸侯),—
is traced to this expression. 作兄弟
方來,—by 兄弟 Gan-kwŏ understood the
princes who were of the imperial House, the
uncles and brothers, &c., of the sovereign,
in contradistinction from the princes of other
surnames. Këang Shing adopts the same view,
and extends it to princes related to the imperial
House by affinity. It seems to me preferable to
take 兄弟 as in the translation, like the 子
來 in the quotation from the She King, Mencius, I., Pt. I., ii., 3. 后式典集,—
后=君. We are to understand by the term

king Ching, as the successor of Wăn and Woo.
式=用, 'to employ.' Another mean-
ing of the term—'to imitate,'—would suit
equally well. 典, 'statutes,' has reference to
the ruling by virtue, whose influence has just
been described. 集, 'to collect,'=to bring
around, to attach.

Pp. 6, 7. *How the sovereign must attach the
people by a mild rule.* These parr. are held to be
the origin of Confucius' sixth standard rule of
government,—'to treat the mass of the people
kindly as children' (子庶民). 6. The
whole of this is one sentence, and Choo He calls
attention to it as an instance of the *long* sentences
of the Shoo. 中國,—compare 中邦,
'Tribute of Yu,' Pt. ii., p. 15. 7. 肆 is
taken as =今, 'now.' In the 附錄 there
is an ingenious note by Ch'in Leih, contending
that its proper meaning in such cases as this,
at the commencement of clauses, is 故, 'therefore,' or 遂, 'and,' 'thereupon,' and not 今.
和懌先後迷民,—迷民,
'the deluded people;' meaning the people of
the imperial domain of Yin chiefly, but also of
other parts of the empire, who were reluctant
to acknowledge the authority of the dynasty of
Chow. 先,—'go before;' 後—'come after.'
The meaning is that Ching should beset the
people 'before and behind' with his virtue and
kindness, so leading and urging them on.
用懌先王受命,—this implies that
Wăn and Woo could take cognizance of the
character and doings of their successor.

保 孫 子 王 年、于 欲 惟 兹

民。永 孫 子 惟 萬 至 曰、監、

8   "Yes! make these things your study.   I can but express my desire that for myriads of years your descendants may be ever the protectors of this people."

P. 8.   *A loyal prayer for the permanency and prosperity of the dynasty.*   若兹監,—the 監 here is different from that in par. 3. Ts'ae conjectures that it was from the occurrence of the characters 若兹監 in that par. and this, that the compiler of this Book, not observing the differences of meaning and connection in the two passages, was led to edit the first and last portions as belonging to the same document.

THE BOOKS OF CHOW.

BOOK XII. THE ANNOUNCEMENT OF *THE DUKE OF* SHAOU.

豊。則 步 未、六 旣 惟一節
○ 至 自 王 日 望、二 召
惟二節 于 周、朝 乙 越 月 誥

I. In the second month, on the day Yih-we, six days after the full moon, the king early in the morning proceeded from Chow, and

THE NAME OF THE BOOK.—召誥, 'The Announcement of *the duke of* Shaou.' Shaou was the name of a place within the imperial domain, corresponding to the present district of Hwan-k'euh (垣 曲), in the small dep. of Kĕang (絳 州), Shan-se. It was the appanage of Shih (奭), one of the ablest of the men who lent their aid to the establishment of the dynasty of Chow. He appears here as the 'Great-guardian' (太保) of king Ching; and we have met with him before in 'The Hounds of Leu,' and 'The Metal-bound Coffer.' He was one of 'the three dukes,' (三公), or highest officers of the dynasty, and is frequently styled 召公, the 'duke of Shaou.' He appears here in connection with one of the most important enterprizes of the duke of Chow, the building of the city of Lŏh (洛邑), as a new and central capital of the empire. King Woo had conceived the idea of such a city, but it was not carried fully into effect till the reign of his son;—see on the second paragraph below. In Lŏh the duke of Shaou composed the 'Announcement' which forms the subject-matter of this Book, and sent it by the hands of the duke of Chow to the young emperor. It might, perhaps, with more than equal propriety, have been styled 'The Instructions of *the duke of* Shaou' (召訓).

According to Sze-ma Ts'een, Shih belonged to the imperial House of Chow, and consequently had the surname Ke (姬). The historian, Hwang-p'oo Meih, says he was a son of king Wăn by a concubine (文王之庶子);—on what authority I cannot tell. King Woo appointed him to the principality of 'The Northern Yen' (北燕), corresponding to the pres. dep. of Shun-t'een (順天), Chih-le, which was held by his descendants fully nine hundred years. He remained himself, however, at the imperial court. We find him often styled the 'Chief of Shaou' (召伯); and Ts'een says that all the country west of Shen (陝) was under him, as all east of it was under the duke of Chow. See the 史記、三十四、燕召公、世家第四. His posthumous title was K'ang (康), and hence he is sometimes referred to as 召康公奭. As to the date of the Announcement, see on par. 1. It is found in both texts.

CONTENTS. The first seven paragraphs are introductory to the body of the Book, which is composed of the Announcement of Shih. They contain various information about the surveying and planning and building of Lŏh. We may consider them as forming a first or preliminary chapter. Parr. 8–22, contain the Announce-

卜　至　太　日　胐　惟　來　宅　周　太
宅　于　保　戊　越　丙　三　越　公　保
厥　洛　朝　申　三　午　月　若　相　先

2 came to Fung.   Thence the Grand-guardian went before the duke of Chow to inspect the localities, and in the third month, on the day Mow-shin, the third day after the first appearance of the new moon on Ping-woo, came in the morning to Lŏ.   He consulted the tortoise about the localities, and having obtained favourable indications, he

ment, which, however, commences properly with par. 9. The 'Complete Digest' says it may be divided into three parts. In the first, parr. 9—12, Shih sets forth the uncertainty of the favour of Heaven, and urges the young king to cultivate 'the virtue of reverence' in order to secure its permanence, concluding with a recommendation to him not to neglect his aged and experienced advisers. The second, parr. 13—18, speaks of the importance and difficulty of the imperial duties, and enforces the same virtue of reverence by reference to the rise and fall of the previous dynasties. In the last part, parr. 19—23, Shih insists on the importance of the king, at this early period of his reign, and on his personal undertaking of the duties of govt., at once setting about the reverence which was required to attach the people to himself and his House, and insure the lasting favour of Heaven. In the last par. the duke of Shaou gives expression to his personal feelings for the king, in the peculiar situation in which he was placed at Lŏ.   The burden of the announcement all turns on 'the virtue of reverence.' Let the king only feel how much depends on his reverently attending to his duties, and govern for the people and not for himself:—let him do this, and all will be well. The people will love and support the dynasty of Chow, and Heaven will smile upon and sustain it.

Ch. I. Pp. 1—7. PROCEEDINGS OF THE KING, THE DUKE OF SHAOU, AND THE DUKE OF CHOW, IN CONNECTION WITH THE BUILDING OF LŎH.   1. 惟二月至乙未,—according to this statement, the day Yih-we must have been the 21st of the second month, and, as Gaubil observes, we may, from the data here supplied, determine the year to which the Announcement of Shaou should be referred. It was, he says correctly, the year B.C. 1,098. 乙未 being the 21st day of the second month, 乙亥 must have been the 1st, and the 1st day of that year of Chow must have been Ping-woo (丙午), the 43d day of the cycle. But that was the day of the new moon preceding the winter solstice, from which under this dynasty they calculated the year, in B.C. 1,098, or 1,097 (not reckoning A.D.). This result is not accordant with the current chronology of king Ching's reign, nor with the date assigned to it from the

'Bamboo Books.' The building of Lŏ is assigned to his 7th year, which was, on the received system, B.C. 1,109 (or 1,108), and acc. to the Bamboo Books B.C. 1038. It is enough to call attention to this point here, without going into further discussion about it. Ch'ing K'ang-shing proposed to change 二月 into 一月, in which case the year would have begun with 乙亥, the 11th cycle day; and he assigned the building of Lŏ, after Fuh-shang, to Ching's 5th year instead of the 7th. Even if we were to follow him in these points, we should be equally unable to reconcile the note of time given in the text with the arrangements of the chronologers. 王步至豐,—comp. Bk. III., p. 1. The temple of king Wăn was in Fung, and we may suppose had been left standing when Woo transferred the capital to Haou. Now when such an important thing as the establishing of a new capital, which should rank with Haou, if it did not supersede it, was in progress, it was proper that the king should solemnly announce it in the temples of his father and grandfather. That he might do so to the spirit of king Wăn, he went from Chow or Haou to Fung.   2. To Shih the Grand-guardian, and to the duke of Chow, was assigned the duty of making all the arrangements for carrying out the plans of king Woo about establishing a new capital at Lŏ. In fact, Woo had himself taken some measures towards the accomplishment of his views. We are told in the 左傳, under the year B.C. 708 (桓公,二年), that 'he removed the nine tripods or vases to the city of Lŏ' (武王克商,遷九鼎於洛邑). Those vases might be considered a sort of regalia of the empire. Originally cast by Yu, they had passed from the Hea dynasty to Shang, and were now the property of the House of Chow. See a detailed account of them in the 左傳, under the year B.C. 605 (宣公,三年). Sze-ma Ts'een also gives, in his 'Records of the Chow dynasty,' and probably from some of the lost Books of the Shoo, a conversation between the duke of Chow and Woo, in which the latter says, 'On the south I look to San-t'oo [there is still the mountain of San-t'oo, to the south-west of the district

既得卜、則經營。○越三[節]日庚戌、太保乃以庶殷、攻位于洛汭、越五日甲寅、位成。

3 set about laying out the plans.   On Kăng-suh, the third day after, he led the people of Yin to prepare the *various* sites on the north of the Lŏ; and this work was completed on the fifth day, Kĕă-yin.

city of Sung (嵩縣)]; on the north I look, and see the towns near the Yŏh [this is supposed to be the T'ae-hang mountain, north of the Ho, on the border between Shan-se and Ho-nan; see the 'Tribute of Yu,' Part ii., par. 1]; when I look round, I see the Ho; and again I behold the Lŏ and the E' (我南望三塗、北望嶽鄙、顧詹有河、粵詹洛伊). Ts'een adds that Woo laid out or built a settlement for Chow on the spot, and went away (營周居於洛邑而後去). These passages make it plain that Woo had fixed on Lŏ, at the time of his conquest of Shang, as the proper capital for his dynasty, and had taken measures to make it so. There was already, it is likely, some settlement at the place, which he enlarged. His locating at it the vases of Yu was a sufficient declaration to all the empire of his purpose. And that purpose had not been forgotten by the duke of Chow. When we bring together all the passages referring to Lŏ, the natural conclusion is that he had been gradually enlarging the place, and had even removed to it the more dangerous among the old adherents of Yin who still continued disaffected to the new rule. Up to the time when the action of this Book commences, however, nothing had been done towards the building of the palace and other structures which were the necessary appendages to it, and the planning of all these was, I think, the special mission entrusted to the duke of Shaou.

In the statistical account of the empire under the present dynasty, it is stated that the remains of the ancient city of Lŏ,—what was called 成周城, 'the capital of the completed or established Chow,' are 30 *le* on the north-east of the pres. city of Lŏh-yang (lat. 34° 43', N.; lon. 4°, W.); and those of the old city of Ho-nan, what was the 'imperial city' (王城) and 'the eastern Capital' of Chow—are 5 *le* on the west of it. The imperial city got the name of Ho-nan (河南) about the year B.C. 509, when the emperor King (敬王) left it, and took up his residence in the 成周城. I may add to these notices of Lŏ, that notwithstanding the wishes of king Woo and his labours, king Ching continued to reside at Haou; it was not till the reign of P'ing (平王) that the court was removed to the east, B.C. 769.

惟太保先周公相宅,—that the Grand-guardian (see Bk. XX., p. 5) was the duke of Shaou is nowhere said in the Book itself, but the title and the prefatory note (see page 10) are sufficient evidence on the point. 先 may be construed in the 1st tone or the 3d. 相=視, 'to survey.' 宅,—Kĕang Shing gives for this, very aptly,—可定居處, 'the places which might be fixed for residence.' The character does not denote so much 'a dwelling,' as the site of a dwelling. 越若至于洛,—Ts'ae takes 越若來 as simply a conjunction (古語辭),—our 'thereupon.' Attempts have been made to translate the characters. Medhurst renders them—'proceeding leisurely on his journey,' which might be taken as a translation of Gan-kwŏ's 於順來, but he wrongly joins them to the preceding clause. Others (see Lin Che-k'e *in loc.*) take them as—'so, in obedience to the charge, he came.' Our best plan is to follow the view of Ts'ae. 朏, formed from 月 and 出, 'the moon come forth,' denotes the third day of the month. As this was Ping-woo, the second month must have been 'small,' consisting only of 29 days; and Mow-shin was the 5th of the 3d month. From Fung to Lŏ was 300 *le.*, so that if Shih commenced his journey, as the critics suppose, on the day Yih-we of the month before, he must have travelled leisurely enough. 卜宅=用龜卜宅都之地, 'he used the tortoise to divine where the capital should be built.' Wang K'ang-t'ang observes on 經營, that we are not to understand those terms of any actual work in building, but only of the determination of the dimensions of the wall, the palace or court, the ancestral temple, &c.;—see the 集說. 3. 越三日庚戌,—it may be observed that in these three days both Kăng-suh and Mow-shin are included. So, in the case of the 'three days' in the last par. 以庶殷、攻位于洛汭,—庶殷=殷之眾民,

豕　邑、　午、　二、　用　越五節　于　于　○
一、　牛、　乃　越　牲　三　新　洛、　若四節
○　一、　社　翼　于　日　邑　則　翼
越六節　羊　于　日　郊　丁　營。　達　日
七　一、　新　戊　牛　巳、　○　觀　乙

4 The day following, being the day Yih-maou, the duke of Chow came in the morning to Lŏ, and thoroughly surveyed the plans for the new **5** city. On Ting-sze, the third day after, he offered two bulls as victims in the suburbs; and on the morrow, Mow-woo, at the altar to the spirit of the land in the new city, he sacrificed a bull, a goat,

'all the people of Yin.' This confirms what I have said above about the population of the imperial domain of Yin having already been in part removed to Lŏ,—the city commenced by king Woo. 攻位 describes the marking out on the ground of the foundations of the various structures from the plans of Shih. 洛汭, —see 'The Songs of the five Sons,' p. 3. 五日甲寅,—the five days include Kăng-suh and Kĕă-yin. The latter was the 11th of the 3d month.

Pp. 4—7. *The measures of the duke of Chow.*

4. 達觀于新邑營,—達 = 徧, 'all over.' The duke made a thorough survey of all the Guardian's plans and arrangements for the building of the new city; and, as we conclude from the next two parr., approved of them. **5.** 用牲于郊牛二, —the disputes about the sacrifice or sacrifices here intended are very warm and lengthy. Ts'ae says that by 郊 are intended the sacrifice or sacrifices to Heaven and Earth (郊祭天 地也). Whether he meant that the duke of Chow offered two sacrifices,—one to Heaven and one to Earth; or only one sacrifice to Heaven and Earth together, offering the two bulls at the same altar, does not appear. Maou K'e-ling, supposing that the latter was his view, shows that to sacrifice to Heaven and Earth together was an uncanonical practice. But I should rather think that Ts'ae meant that two sacrifices were offered, one to Heaven in the southern suburb, and one to Earth in the northern, a single bull being used at each. These sacrifices of course would be on occasion of the marking out the spots for the respective altars. Maou himself thinks that only one sacrifice— that to Heaven—is spoken of, and that two victims are mentioned, because How-tseih (后 稷), as the great ancestor of the House of

Chow, was associated with Heaven at the sacrifices to it. So far he is correct in saying that How-tseih participated in the usual sacrifices under the Chow dynasty to Heaven, and that there was special provision for a victim-bull to him, and one to the supernal Power. This was the view, moreover, of Gan-kwŏ. If the text were that 'the duke of Chow sacrificed, to Heaven, using two bulls,' I should adopt it. As the text stands, however, I prefer the view given above, and which I have said was probably that of Ts'ae. 社于新邑, 牛一, 羊一, 豕一, 一社 = 'he offered the sacrifice at the altar to the spirit of the land.' Maou contends that this was the sacrifice to Earth, corresponding to the previous one to Heaven. But the text shows clearly that he is wrong, This sacrifice was offered 于新邑, 'in—*i.e*, within —the new city,' whereas the sacrifices to Heaven and Earth were both celebrated in the suburbs, outside the city. We are to understand here, beyond doubt, the sacrifice to the spirit of the land, with which there was always associated that to the spirit of the grain. The altars were and still are within the wall of the imperial city. Who the spirits thus sacrificed to were, is a question not easy to determine. It seems to me probable that they were not spirits distinct from God, who was served in the sacrifices to Heaven and Earth. Compare the dictum of Confucius in 'The Doctrine of the Mean,' xix., 6. Whatever opinion may be held on this point, the human worthy associated at the sacrifice to the spirit of the land was Kow-lung (勾龍), minister of Works to the very ancient emperor Chuen-heuh, whose place on the list of Chinese sovereigns is immediately after Hwang-te. The human associate with the spirit of the grain was How-tseih. These same names appear in the ritual of the present dynasty (see the 大清通禮, 卷之七). A long note on this paragraph by the editors of Yung-ching's Shoo is well worth the attention of the student.

日甲子、周公
乃朝用書命
庶殷侯甸男
邦伯。○厥既 七節
命殷庶○庶殷
丕作○太保 八節
乃以庶邦冢
君出取幣、乃
復入錫周公
曰、拜手稽首

6 and a pig. After seven days, on Kĕä-tsze, in the morning, from his written *specifications* he gave their several charges to the people of Yin, and to the chiefs of the States from the How, Teen, and Nan

7 tenures. When the people of Yin had thus received their orders, they arose with vigour to do their work.

8 II. The Great-guardian then went out with the hereditary princes of the various States to bring their offerings; and when he entered again, he gave them to the duke of Chow, saying, "With my head in my hands and bowed to the ground, I present these before the

6. 用書,—I have translated 書 by 'written specifications.' The duke had employed the six days after Ting-sze (that day is not included in the 七日) in writing out the work which was to be done in executing the Guardian's plans, with all the necessary specifications, and especially of the parties to whom the different parts of it should be assigned. The Chiefs of countries (邦伯) in the tenures specified must have been the pastors of the provinces (州牧). They would give their instructions to the princes belonging to their respective jurisdictions, who again would issue the necessary commands to the companies of their people whom they had brought with them to labour on the work in hand. 7. Lin Che-k'e observes on this:—'The duke of Shaou completed all his plans for Lŏ in 7 days, from Mow-shin to Kĕä-yin inclusive; then came the duke of Chow, and in ten days he was ready with all his specifications, and the work was grandly in hand:—so earnest and prompt were they with their measures. All together, from the day Yih-we, when king Ching came to Fung, to the day Kĕä-sze, there elapsed but one month. The foundation of 10,000 years' possession and prosperity was laid in one month! Future ages could not show such an achievement!' The observation must be accepted with due allowance for its grandiloquence.

Ch. II. Pp. 8—23. THE ANNOUNCEMENT.
8. The old interpreters all thought that king Ching was present in Lŏ when this announcement was made. It may be well to give the exposition of Gan-kwŏ. On 太保至復入 he says:—諸侯公卿並觀于王、王與周公俱至、文不見者、王無事也、召公與諸侯出取幣、欲因大會顯周公, 'The various princes, the dukes and high nobles appeared together before the king. The king and the duke of Chow had both come to Lŏ. The text is silent about the king's coming, because there was nothing to be done by him *at that time*. The duke of Shaou and all the princes went out to fetch the ceremonial offerings, wishing to take occasion of the great assembly to glorify the duke of Chow.' On 錫周公至若公 he says:—召公以幣入、成王命、賜周公曰、敢拜手稽首、陳王所宜順周公之事, 'The duke of Shaou then entered with the offerings, and, proclaiming the command of king Ching, gave them to the duke of Chow, saying, "I venture, with my face to my hands and my head to the ground, to set forth the things in which the king ought to act in accordance with the duke of Chow."' On the last clause he says:—召公指戒成王、而以衆殷諸侯於自乃御治事、爲辭謙也、諸侯在故托焉, 'The duke of Shaou's aim was to admonish king Ching, and that he addressed himself to the multitudes of Yin and the princes, down to the managers of affairs [see Ying-tä's paraphrase], was the language of modesty. The princes were present, and he took the opportunity to address himself to the king through them.'

K'ang-shing's view of the passage was substantially the same as that of Gan-kwŏ. That the king was present, and that the design of

曷 疆 疆 惟 大 改 呼、乃 告 旅
其 惟 惟 王 國 厥 皇 御 庶 王
奈 恤 休、王 殷 元 天 事。殷、若
何 嗚 亦 受 之 子、上 ○ 越 公
弗 呼、無 命 命、兹 帝、嗚 自 誥
    無   亦   九節

king and your Grace. Announcements for the instruction of the multitudes of Yin must come from you with whom is the management of affairs.

9   "Oh! God dwelling in the great heavens has changed his decree in favour of his eldest son, and this great dynasty of Yin. Our king has received that decree. Unbounded is the happiness connected with it, and unbounded is the anxiety:—Oh! how can he be other than reverent?

Shih was to glorify the duke of Chow for the services he had performed:—these are assumptions, for which I can find no support in the tenour of the Book itself. That the offerings were presented to the duke of Chow for himself is broadly contrary to the last paragraph. The interpretation, moreover, of 旅王若公, and of 越自乃御事, is intolerably harsh and forced. In the translation I have preferred to follow the views of Ts'ae, who himself followed Choo He. There is a great assembly of the two dukes and the princes who were with them at Lǒ. The duke of Chow is about to return, or at least to send a communication, to king Ching in Haou. The duke of Shaou, revering the king's majesty in the regent, takes the opportunity to send by him the loyal presents of the princes, and his own loyal wishes and advices to the court. And there was the greater propriety in his doing so now, as it was understood that the duke of Chow was about to withdraw from the duties of the regency, and the king might be expected to take the administration of affairs into his own hands. 以 庶 邦 冡 君,—以＝與; see the dict. in voc. 冡君,—comp. Bk I., Pt i., p. 2. 旅王若公,—旅＝陳, 'to set forth,' 'to exhibit;' with reference to the offerings, which would be set down and displayed in the court below the hall where they were assembled. The 若 is very perplexing. We have seen how the old interpreters tried to manage it. Ts'ae takes it as simply ＝與, 'and.' This gives a good enough sense, but I must confess that I cannot think of a similar use of the term elsewhere. 誥告至末,—this is an indirect call to the king to come before the people in his own person, pointing out to them the

course of their duty, and leading in the way of it. The duke delicately avoids any direct mention of the king, but he really intends him as 'the manager of affairs.' In this way we see the force of the 自, which the old interpreters could not manage.

Pp. 9—12. With the favour shown by God to the king there was connected much anxiety. He must reverently cherish the thought of his responsibilities and duties; learn from the experience of the former dynasties; and listen to the advice of his wise and aged ministers. 9. 皇天上帝,—see on 皇上帝, in 'The Announcement of T'ang,' p. 2. 元子,—see on Bk., VIII., p. 1. Here and in par. 13, it is a designation equivalent to 'the emperor.' When he is called Heaven's eldest son, the mind thinks of the favour which must rest upon him, and may well deem his state secure. K'ang-shing says here:—凡人皆云天之子,天子爲之首耳, 'All men may be called the sons of Heaven; the emperor is the head or the eldest of them.' 惟王受命,—'the king here is king Ching,'＝our king, who was now become God's eldest son. 曷其奈何不敬,—this puts the duty of being reverent in the strongest way. On the meaning of this 'being reverent' Ts'ae says, that 'it is being sincere and without guile, the eyes, ears, words, and movements all being accordant with reason; the likings and dislikings, the usings and refusings never contrary to the will of Heaven. When one's virtue thus agrees with that of Heaven, he will surely be able to receive the bright favouring decree of Heaven' (敬則

敬。○天既遞終大
邦殷之命茲殷多
先哲王後在天越厥
後王後民茲服厥
命厥終智藏瘝在
夫知保抱攜持厥
婦子以哀籲天祖
厥亡出執嗚呼天
亦哀于四方民其
眷命用懋王其疾

十節

10　"When Heaven rejected and made an end of the decree in favour of the great State of Yin, there were many of the former intelligent kings of Yin in heaven. The king, however, who had succeeded to them, the last of their race, from the time of his entering into their appointment, proceeded in such a way as at last to keep the wise in obscurity and the vicious in office. The poor people in such a case, carrying their children and leading their wives, made their moan to Heaven. They even fled away, but were apprehended again. Oh! Heaven had compassion on the people of the four quarters; its favouring decree lighted on our earnest founders. Let the king sedulously cultivate the virtue of reverence.

誠實無妄視聽言動一循
乎理好惡用捨不違乎天，
與天同德固能受天明命
也). 10. Much of the language of this paragraph, it is observed by Ts'ae, is difficult of explanation; but there is a general agreement as to the meaning of most of it. King Ching is reminded of the fall of the dyn. of Yin through the misgovernment and wickedness of Show, and how it was because of the earnest virtue of his own predecessors that they had been called to the sovereignty of the empire.—Let it be his to imitate them. 天既至在天，—遞=遠, 'far,' 'distant;' here, as I understand it, = 'to reject.' 終=絕, 'to make an end of.' It is difficult to give the force of the 茲. Perhaps we should join it emphatically to 殷.—'Of this Yin, thus rejected, many of the former kings, &c.' The speaker believed that the good kings were in heaven, and he intimates that it might therefore have been expected that they would have been able to preserve their dynasty; but that could not be. 越厥 至瘝在—越 is here = 'but,' 'however.'

後王後民,—both these phrases seem to be best taken of Show, who is the subject of all this portion. Gan-kwŏ, however, understood 厥後王後民 茲服厥命 of good sovereigns and their people, who worthily continued the sway of their predecessors. It is only at 厥終, 'the last of them,' that the tyrant comes with him upon the stage. 瘝=病, 'to distress.' 瘝在=病民之人在位. 夫知至籲天,—on 夫知 Wang Suh says:—匹夫知欲安其室, 'the ordinary people, who knew enough to wish to secure the comfort of their families.' Compare 匹夫 in Ana., IX., xxv. This is as satisfactory as anything which can be said about the 夫知 here. 夫 should be read in the upper first tone. 祖厥亡出執=往而逃亡, 出見拘執, 無地自容, as in the translation. 其眷命用懋='it looked round and gave its appointment to those who were employing themselves earnestly on virtue.' Comp. 眷命 in 'The Counsels of Yu,' p. 4.

有王雖小元子哉其
能稽謀自天。〇嗚呼
古人之德矧曰其有 十三節
無遺壽耇曰其稽我
厥命。〇今沖子嗣則 十三節
面稽天若今時既墜
今相有殷天迪格保、
天若今時既墜厥命。
夏天迪從子保面稽
敬德。〇相 十一節 古先民有

11　"Examining the men of antiquity, there was *the founder of* the Hea dynasty. Heaven guided his mind, allowed his descendants to succeed him, and protected them. He acquainted himself with Heaven, and was obedient.—But in process of time the decree in his favour fell to the ground. So also when we examine the case of Yin. Heaven guided *its founder*, so that he corrected *the errors of Shang*, and it protected his descendants. He *also* acquainted himself with Heaven, and was obedient.—But now the decree in favour of him has fallen to

12　the ground. Our king has now come to the throne in his youth:— let him not slight the aged and experienced, for it may be said of them that they have studied the virtuous conduct of our ancient worthies, and still more, that they have matured their plans in the light of Heaven.

13　"Oh! although the king is young, yet is he the eldest son of Heaven. Let him but effect a great harmony with the people, and

Ying-tă gives for the clause:—其睿顧天行下、選擇賢聖命用勉力敬者、以爲民主. 11. By 有夏, 'the holder of Hea,' we are to understand Yu, as the founder of the Hea dynasty. So by 有殷 T'ang is meant. 先民=古人, 'the ancients.' To 相古 the 今相 afterwards responds. 天迪從子保=天啟迪之, 又從其子而保佑之, as in the translation. In the case of T'ang, it was not necessary to take notice of the transmission of the throne to his descendants. The hereditary principle had long been established. 面(=鄉)稽天若='he looked 仰考天心, 敬順不違, 'he looked

up and examined the mind of Heaven, reverently obedient and not opposing it.' The first 今時 must be understood as in the translation. 12. 無遺壽耇—無=毋, imperative. 耇,—see Bk. IX., p. 5. The 曰 may be taken as in the translation (and it is better taken so), or we may understand it, with Kĕang Shing, as = 當曰, 'he—our young king—ought to say.' On the 稽古人之德, it is said that they could thus give precedents and authorities in every case they were consulted on, and on the 稽謀自天, that in their advice there would thus be nothing contrary to what was right.

Pp. 13—18. *The importance of the king's position, and duties to which he must address himself, especially now on his personally undertaking the*

成命治民今休。 時中乂王厥有 祀于上下其自 自時配皇天毖 曰其作大邑其 自服于土中旦 ○[十四節]王來紹上帝 用顧畏于民碞。 今休王不敢後。 丕能誠于小民。

that will be the blessing of the present time. Let not the king presume to be remiss in this, but continually regard and stand in awe of the perilousness of the people.

14   "Let the king come here as the vicegerent of God, and undertake himself *the duties of government* in the centre of the land. Tan said, 'Now that this great city has been built, from henceforth he may be the mate of great Heaven; from henceforth he may reverently sacrifice to the upper and lower *spirits*; from henceforth he may in this central spot administer successful government.' Thus shall the king enjoy the favouring regard *of Heaven* all complete, and the government of the people will now be prosperous.

responsibilities of the govt. The whole is enforced by a second reference to the previous dynasties.

13. 元子哉,—see on par. 9. 其丕 能誠于小民,今休,—the 其 is strongly hortative. 誠＝和, 'harmony,' 'to be harmonious.' We had the char. before in 'The Counsels of Yu,' p. 21, where the meaning was different. The 'Daily Explanation' thus paraphrases:—王其大能誠和小 民,使之歡欣鼓舞,……,則小民 情安而天命固,豈不爲今後 日之休美乎. 王不敢後 —'let the king not postpone'—what? His effecting a great harmony with the people. And that was to be accomplished by means of 'the virtue of reverence.' Gan-kwǒ put a comma at 用, and interpreted—當不敢後能 用之士,必任之爲先, 'let the king not leave in the background capable officers, but make employment of them a primary consideration.' This is far-fetched; and so is his explanation of 碞, the erroneousness of which is pointed out in the dict. The character＝ 險, 'precipitous,' 'perilous.' 14. 王來 紹上帝,自服于上中—紹上 帝, 'to continue God.' We often find it said

of emperors, and especially of the founders of dynasties that they 繼天立極, 'carried on *the work of* Heaven, and set up the perfect *model*.' There underlies such language the view that Heaven delegates its sway to the Powers ordained by it. Compare, for the general sentiment, Bk. I., Pt. i., p. 7; and for the use of 紹, Bk. VII., p. 3. 自服于土中 ＝labour himself in the midst of the land. The 'himself' must have reference to the young king, now undertaking the responsibilities of govt. 服＝行事, 'to labour.' Lǒ is said to be 'in the middle of the land' from its central position. It must have been, in the time of Chow, about the central spot of the empire, and was therefore well fitted to be the seat of administration. The commentators speak of it as not only in the middle of the land, but as 'in the centre of heaven and earth,' and they undertake to show how this was determined by means of a dial! See the whole geodesy of the duke of Chow, in the Chow Le, Bk. IX., pp. 26—31. Lin Che-k'e takes these two clauses as historical, and considers them to be decisive on the point of the king's being at this time in Lǒ. It seems to me much more natural to read them in the imperative mood. 旦曰至中 乂,—the duke of Shaou supports his advice by using the similar language of the duke of Chow, whom he names 旦, in accordance with the rule that 'ministers should be called by their

○王先服殷御事，比介于我有周御事，節性，惟日其邁。○王敬作所，不可不敬德。○我不可不監于有夏，亦不可不監于有殷，我不敢知曰，有夏服天命，惟有

(marginal section markers: 十五節, 十六節, 十七節)

15   "Let the king first bring under his influence the managers of affairs of Yin, associating them with the managers of affairs of our dynasty of Chow. This will regulate their *perverted* natures, and they will make daily advancement.

16   "Let the King make reverence the resting-place *of his mind*. He may not but maintain the virtue of reverence.

17   "We should by all means survey the dynasties of Hea and Yin. I do not presume to know and say, 'The dynasty of Hea was to enjoy the favouring decree of Heaven for *so many* years,' nor do I

names in the presence of the emperor.' 配皇天 —see on Pt. IV., Bk. V., Pt. iii., p. 3. 禋祀于上下, —compare 上下神祇 in the 'Announcement of T'ang,' p. 3. On 中乂 Wang Ts'eaou says that it denotes that 'from the centre the king would diffuse his rule throughout the four quarters of the empire'(自中而布治於四方). Here the words of Tan seem to terminate. 成命, —'the completed appointment.' The will of Heaven in favour of the House of Chow would now be put beyond doubt and beyond the risk of being assailed.

Pp. 15, 16. The king would have in the first place to attach to his House the disaffected officers of the previous dynasty; but let him bear in mind that he must always set the example of the virtue of reverence in himself. 15. 服 is here a transitive verb. The 'Daily Explanation' defines it by 化, 'to transform.' 比介于我有周御事 —比=親, 'to be near to.' 介=助, 'to assist,' to co-operate with. This extension of confidence to the officers of Yin would be the way to win their confidence and attachment, and the associating them with the friends of the present dynasty would lead them to change their views. 節性，惟日其邁 —Ts'ae gives for this— 以節其驕淫之性，則日進於善而不已；—as in the translation. Lin Che-k'e contends that by 性 we should not understand the *perverted* nature, but the *good* nature, which was still in the officers of Yin, and had only to be properly directed. His words are:— 節之者，非強其所無也，以其所固有之性，還以治之也。去其不善，而反之善也，有以節之，則臣民將遷善遠罪而不自知，惟日其進於善也. The difference of view is more in words than in reality.

16. After all, the *primum mobile* of govt. must be the personal character and example of the king. 王敬作所＝王當以敬爲居心之所. The 所 is used like 止 in the 知止 of 'The Great Learning.'

Pp. 17, 18. *The lessons to be learned from the two previous dynasties; and the emphasis which they should have now at the commencement of the present dynasty, and of the king's personal entrance on his responsibilities.* 17. Compare p. 11. The 有夏 and 有殷 here, however, are to be extended to all the sovereigns of the two dynasties. Moreover, what was said above had reference more especially to the establishment of those dynasties by the blessing of Heaven; here the subject is their fall, for want of 'the

歷年、我不敢知曰、不其

延、惟不敬厥德、乃早墜

厥命、我不敢知曰、有殷

受天命、惟有歷年、我不

敢知曰、不其延、惟不敬

厥德、乃早墜厥命。○今（十八節）

王嗣受厥命、我亦惟茲

二國命嗣若功、王乃初

服。○嗚呼、若生子、罔不（十九節）

在厥初生、自貽哲命、今

presume to know and say, 'It could not continue longer.' The fact was simply that, for want of the virtue of reverence, the decree in its favour prematurely fell to the ground. *Similarly*, I do not presume to know and say, 'The dynasty of Yin was to enjoy the favouring decree of Heaven for *so many* years,' nor do I presume to say, 'It could not continue longer.' The fact simply was that, for want of the virtue of reverence, the decree in its favour pre-

18 maturely fell to the ground. The king has now inherited the decree,—the same decree, I consider, which belonged to those two dynasties. Let him seek to inherit *the virtues of* their meritorious *sovereigns ;*—especially at this commencement *of* his duties.

19 "Oh! it is as on the birth of a son, when all depends on *the training of* his early life, through which he may secure his wisdom in the future, as if it were decreed to him. Now Heaven may

virtue of reverence' in their rulers. The 'Daily Explanation' says that the first 我 is to be understood of the king, and the others of the duke of Shaou himself. It is much better to take the character always in the plural.

有夏服天命惟有歷年,—服天命 is more than 受天命, which most of the paraphrases give for it. It indicates not only that Hea received the favouring decree of Heaven, but that it was *under* that decree. The guardian will not venture to say that Heaven had only decreed so many years to its rule.

18. 厥命,—the 厥 is to be understood of 天, 'Heaven.' The next clause is in apposition with this, 惟 being＝思. Gan-kwŏ takes it differently, and explains down to 功 where

he ends the paragraph thus:—其夏殷也,繼受其王命,亦惟當以此夏殷長短之命爲監戒,繼順其功德者,而法則之. He overlooks the 我 before 亦惟 嗣若功王乃初服＝當嗣(＝繼)其有功者,況王乃新邑初政,服行教化之始乎. This must be the meaning, but the language is very elliptical

Pp. 19—23. *The great issues depending on the king's now, on his assuming the government, taking the right course; and the Guardian's anxiety that by his virtuous reverence and gentle sway he should lay the foundations of permanent prosperity.*

19. 嗚呼至哲命,—by 初生 we

功。○其惟王位在　殄戮用乂民若有　民淫用非彝亦敢　○其惟王勿以小　德之用、祈天永命。　王其疾敬德王其　服。○宅新邑肆惟　命歷年、知今我初　天其命哲命吉凶、

廿二節　廿一節　二十節

have decreed wisdom *to our king*; it may have decreed good fortune or bad; it may have decreed a *long* course of years:—we only know that now is with him the commencement of his duties.

20　　"Dwelling in the new city, let the king now sedulously cultivate the virtue of reverence. When he is all-devoted to this virtue, he may pray to Heaven for a long-abiding decree in his favour.

21　　"In the position of king, let him not, because of the excesses of the people in violation of the laws, presume also to rule by the violent infliction of death. When the people are regulated gently, the merit of government is seen.

must understand not the infancy, but the early years, when the child becomes the proper subject of education. Then such a foundation of goodness may be laid, that the youth shall 'himself hand down an appointment of wisdom.' He shall appear to be, shall really be, wise through this training, as much as if Heaven had previously decreed him to be so. 命歷年 = 或命歷年長久. After this we must understand 皆不可預知, 'all these things we cannot know beforehand.'

20. The Guardian evidently supposes that the king will make the new city which was founded the seat of his government. The meaning of 今, 'now,' for 肆 seems to suit the connection here better than that of 故 or 遂. The 其 in 王其德之用 gives to the second part of the par. a slightly hortative force. Chin Tih-sew observes upon the sentiment, 'The favour of Heaven is entirely just, and is not to be obtained by praying for it. The text tells the king to pray, because to be all-devoted to the practice of virtue is prayer without praying, (天命至公, 不可以求而得也。曰祈者, 蓋一於用德乃

不祈之祈). Compare with this the words of Confucius about himself, Ana., VII., xxxiv.　21. From 其惟王 to 戮用 is one sentence, and a good instance of the long sentences of the Shoo. Gan-kwŏ and Këang Shing, indeed, break it up into two, and understand the first part as meaning—'Let not the king go to excess in employing the people, beyond the regular periods when he may call them out in the public service.' By doing so, he would, as Mencius phrases it, rob the people of their time, and take them away from their necessary labours in agriculture (see Mencius, page 11). But the introduction of such a topic seems foreign to the style of the Announcement. It involves, moreover, taking the 亦敢 which follow as = 亦勿敢, which is very harsh. The subject of avoiding punishments in the administration in govt. was a favourite one with king Ching and his ministers. See many passages in Bks. IX., and X. 民若有功, —'when the people accord there is merit. They must be ruled,' 'in harmony with their feelings, and the true laws of their nature.' Ts'ae observes that the people may be compared to the water of a stream when it is overflowing and spreading abroad; it is acting contrary to its nature. But if you dam it up, you only make the evil worse. Lead it into its proper course, and you accom-

德元、小民乃惟刑
用于天下、越王顯。廿三節
○上下勤恤其曰
我受天命丕若有
夏歷年、式勿替有
殷歷年、欲王以小
民受天永命。○廿四節拜
手稽首曰子小臣、
敢以王之讎民百
君子、越友民保受

22 "It is for him who is in the position of king to overtop all with his virtue. In this case the people will imitate him throughout the whole empire, and the king will become more illustrious.

23 "Let the king and his ministers labour with a common anxiety, saying, 'We have received the decree of Heaven, and it shall be great as the long-continued years of Hea,—it shall not fail of the long-continued years of Yin.' I wish the king through the inferior people to receive the long-abiding decree of Heaven."

III. *The duke of Shaou* then did obeisance with his head to his hands and bowed to the ground, and said, "I, a small minister, presume with the king's *heretofore* hostile people, with all his officers, and his *loyal* friendly people, to maintain and receive his majesty's dread

plish the purpose. 22. 其惟王位 在德元,—'He being king, his position is at the head of *all* virtue.' It is simpler to take 元 as =首, than to give it the substantial meaning which it has in the first diagram of the Yih King, as that quality in Heaven which corresponds to 仁, 'benevolence,' 'goodness complete' in man. 小民乃惟刑 (=法) 用于天下,—'the inferior people on their part will be found imitating him and employing virtue throughout the empire.' 越王顯,—'and the king will be illustrious,' *i.e.*, the virtue of the king will thereby be more widely and brilliantly displayed.

23. 上下勤恤,—by 上下 we are to understand 君臣, 'the sovereign and his ministers.' 恤,—as in p. 9, =憂, 'to be anxious.' Then the 其 in 其曰 is strongly hortative. 式勿替云云,—both Gan-kwŏ and Ts'ae define 式 by 用, but it is difficult to find a place for any other meaning of it here than as a conjunction = 'and.' The 'Daily Explanation,' after defining it by 用, is obliged in the paraphrase to substitute 又 for it. 勿替='we are determined that it shall not fail of.' At 欲 the duke of Shaou speaks again in his own person. The 'people,' ruled over as he desired, would wish the rule to be perpetual, and the wish of the people would be the wish of Heaven.

Ch. III. Pt. 24. We must understand 召 公 before 拜手稽首. The Guardian here winds up his address. He will do his duty with the people under his charge. It remains for the king to secure the permanence of the dynasty. In the meantime he presents the offerings of the princes, to aid at the sacrifices to be offered, on the inauguration of the new capital. 王之讎民,—these are the people of Yin that had been removed to Lŏ, and could still not be spoken of as other than disaffected and hostile. 百君子,—compare the same phrase in Bk. X., p. 7. It is used here

永　能　用　恭　敢　顯　命　末　明　王
命。祈　供　奉　勤。我　王　有　德　威
　天　王　幣、惟　非　亦　成　王　命

command and brilliant virtue. That the king should finally obtain the decree all complete, and that he should become illustrious,—this I dare not to labour about.   I only respectfully bring these offerings to present to his Majesty, to assist in his prayers to Heaven for its long-abiding decree.'"

as complimentary to the ministers and officers of Yin, in whom loyal feelings might arise when they were thus spoken of. The 'friendly people' are the adherents of the House of Chow. 威命 must be the king's charge for the building of Lŏ. 明德 has more sound than sense. 王末至亦顯,—this describes the king's consolidation of the dynasty,

and transmitting the crown to his descendants. That must be the king's own work. The Guardian would not presume to think that his labours could effect it. 惟恭 云云,—the king would be coming to Lŏ, and by solemn sacrifices inaugurate the new city, and then the offerings would be useful. This is a delicate way of conveying to him those expressions of the princes' fealty.

~~~~~~~~~~~~~~~~~

Wang Pih's 'Doubts' about this Book and the next are the following:—洛誥之篇,

三山林氏說之亦然下蓋葉氏看知而愚曉鼇大破易召殷遷營詞焉王周公

生洛誥疑曰可取參可疑也不體誥未公

之所始朱子不取者又竊謂者統梳理公攻洛焉有祀有周公即辟之詞焉

氏說之所終又召公說洛以是以王缺文敢謂誥固亦雜者相攻之詞焉有武復辟之詞焉此所

先誥釋公不又誥不有人之洛最周有為有之詞以成命以

公於周漸言召此有謂妄語誥此中詞之來宗焉有成王不册以

東萊者誥自何時此與誥尚何者辭一召明中詞之作成文復辟之詞焉

召誥之所作成文王幼周公復歸政謂所何以

觀後之戒德明自看相節明治周歸一於一儒嘗精也成如氏亦愚之所

也召止而不在新政若洛禋於周公中易事咨安然王長伊尹謂所何以

誥是詞而闇為明白洛相節治周公之就程子辭復王有固此公歸政初避而不能

雖成王初新政若卜禮復辟命册而皆未之復位欲得王前周公謂歸政謂所何以

載新政乃以此作頑公止此詞反殺也以來以此嘗嘗王於之害何此無疑也

相政服則兩民成欲是殷雜第諸未誠位政正蘇然此

洛致若疾則作頑公欲止此反義名乎也

○ 明 復 曰 稽 拜 周 洛
王 辟。子 朕 首 手 公 誥

[In the third month when the moon began to wane, the duke of Chow commenced the foundations and proceeded to build the new city at Lŏ of the eastern States. The people from every quarter assembled in great harmony. From the How, Teen, Nan, Ts'ae, and Wei domains the various officers stimulated this harmony of the people, and introduced them to the business there was for Chow. The duke of Chow encouraged them all to diligence, and made a great announcement about the execution *of the works.*]

1   I. The duke of Chow bowed his head to his hands and then to the ground, saying, "Herewith I report the *execution of my commission*

THE NAME OF THE BOOK.—洛 誥, 'The Announcement about Lŏ.' The prefatory note (see page 10) says :—'The duke of Shaou having surveyed the localities, the duke of Chow went to build this capital, called Ching Chow, and sent a messenger to announce the divinations. With reference to this, the ANNOUNCEMENT ABOUT Lŏ was made.' As will be seen from the next note, however, the action of the Book goes many months beyond the report about the survey and divinations; but it all has reference, more or less, to the city of Lŏ. It may well be said to be about Lŏ. The use of the term 'Announcement' has its difficulties, and must be taken more vaguely than in the account of the Announcements of the Shoo which I have given on page 177. The Book is found in both texts.

CONTENTS. Ts'ae says:—'The arrangements for the building of Lŏ having been made, the duke of Chow sent a messenger to inform the king of the result of his divinations. The historian recorded this as the announcement about Lŏ, and at the same time recorded a dialogue between the king and his minister, and how the king charged the duke to remain at Lŏ and conduct the government of it.' He goes on to say more particularly :—'Parr. 1—3 contain the duke's message about his divinations; and par. 4 gives the king's reply. Parr. 5—13 are occupied with instructions from the duke to the king on the measures which he should pursue on taking up his residence at Lŏ. In parr. 14—21, the king charges the duke to remain at Lŏ, and undertake its government. In parr. 22—24, the duke responds, accepting the charge, and dwells on the duties which the king and himself would have to discharge. Parr. 25—28 relate the action of the duke on a certain message and gift from the king, intended for his special honour. In parr. 29—31, the historian relates to sacrifices offered in Lŏ by the king, and the proclamation which he issued, and adds how long the duke continued in his government ;—showing how the duke began the city and completed it, and how king Ching, after offering the sacrifices and inaugurating the government, returned to Haou, and did not after all make his capital at Lŏ.'

The Seven divisions thus indicated, present themselves to any careful student of the Book. Maou K'e-ling, differing widely from Ts'ae in his view of the general tenour, and of particular passages and terms, gives the same, only including parr. 22—28 in one. Many critics make more to do than is necessary about the want of historical order in the Book, and suppose that portions have been lost, and other portions transposed. I have already given my opinion that the first paragraph in 'The Announcement to the Prince of K'ang' should be the first par. here. As to other portions being lost, the Book may be explained without resorting to so violent a supposition. It is not by any means so plain as it might be, but I am inclined to think that it is as plain as it ever was.

The first paragraph from the Announcement to the Prince of K'ang. For the reasons why this par. should be edited here and not as a portion of Bk. IX., see page 383. 三月 哉生魄,—see on Bk. III., pp. 1 and 4. This would be the 16th day of the month. In the last Book, pp. 4—6, we saw that on the 12th day of the 3d month, the duke of Chow arrived at Lŏ; on the 14th and 15th, he sacrificed to Heaven and Earth, and to the spirit of the land, while on the 21st he was ready with specifications of all the works which were to be executed. It would appear from this par. that on the 16th he made a commencement with the foundations of some of the works. 作新大邑 于東國洛,—the 'Daily Explanation' gives for this—作新大邑于成周 之東,洛邑之地,而有王城 下都之建焉, 'he made the new great city on the east of Ching Chow, in the territory of the city of Lŏ, and there was the building both of the imperial city and of the lower capital.' This may be understood by referring to the note on p. 2 of the last Book; but the text does not so clearly indicate that the building of the two cities is spoken of. The 成周城 went also by the name of 下都, 'the lower capital.'

侯, 甸 男邦, 采, 衞,—see the figure of the domains of Chow on p. 149. The five of them which constituted, with the imperial domain, the 'Middle Kingdom' are here enumerated in their proper order, though why the 邦 should be introduced between 男 and 采 I cannot explain. 百工播民和,— 百工=百官, 'all the officers,' including, probably, from the princes downwards; 播民 和=宣揚民心之和,—'spread abroad the harmony of the people.' 見士于周, —士 is taken as=事, 'business,' the work to be done. Ch'in Leih explains 見士 by 朝見而趨事, 'presented themselves as if at court, and hastened to the works.' We do not know well what to make of the phrase. 周公咸勤,—the 'Daily Explana-

tion' takes this as='The duke of Chow himself and all with him laboured diligently.' Gan-kwŏ explains it as in the translation. I understand 誥治 as meaning that the duke now announced in a general way the works which were to be executed, preparatory to the specifications which were issued five days after

Ch. I. Pp. 1—3. THE DUKE'S MESSAGE TO THE KING, INFORMING HIM WHAT HE HAD DONE, AND LAYING BEFORE HIM MAPS, PLANS, AND THE RESULT OF HIS DIVINATIONS. 1. There is a controversy which it is not easy to settle on the meaning of 復 in this par., and the view to be taken of the whole Book depends very much upon it. Gan-kwŏ took 復 as= 還政, 'to restore the government.' He explains the whole par. thus:—周公盡禮致敬,言我 復還明君之政於子,成王, 年二十成人,故必歸政而 退老, 'The duke of Chow, in the most ceremonious way and with the utmost reverence, said, "I return the government of the intelligent sovereign to you, my son." By his son he meant king Ching, who was now 20, and full grown. It was requisite that the duke should return the govt. to him, and withdraw into retirement in his old age.' This interpretation, which is still held by many, was not doubted till the Sung dynasty, when the critic Wang (? Wang Gan-shih) was the first to suggest that 復 should be taken as meaning 'to report,' 'to announce the fulfilment of a commission,' referring to the phrase 反命, which is common in Mencius, and to the use of 復 alone by him, Bk. I., Pt. I., vii., 10,—有復於王 者. The duke, he contended, had never been anything but regent; he could not speak of himself as *restoring* the govt. This view was adopted by Ts'ae, and became current through his commentary.

Maou K'e-ling refers to the 1st words of Pt. IV., Bk. VI.,—伊尹既復政厥辟, as decisive in favour of the older view; but the use of the 政 there after 復 makes the passages by no means parallel, nor was the position of the duke of Chow to king Ching the same as that of E Yin to T'ae-këä. It must be allowed at the same time that Mencius' 復於王 is different from the simple 復子 of the text.

On the whole, I must incline to the view adopted by Ts'ae. In the answer of the king to the duke's message there is not a word about his accepting the restoration or resignation of the govt. It was understood between them, and throughout the empire, that the time was come for the king to undertake the duties of the administration himself, and we shall see hereafter in this Book that the duke expresses his purpose to go into retirement, now that the building of Lŏ was in a state of forwardness;

瀍水西、惟洛　乃卜澗水東、　河朔黎水我　于洛師我卜　惟乙卯朝至　民明辟。○予三節　東土其基作　乃肩保大相　基命定命予　如弗敢及天

2 to my son, my intelligent prince. The king appeared as if he would not presume to determine the founding and the fixing of our appointment by Heaven, whereupon I followed the *Grand*-Guardian, and made a great survey of this eastern region, with a view to found the place where he might become the intelligent sovereign of the people.

3 On the day Yih-maou, in the morning, I came to the city of Lŏ. I *first* divined concerning the *country about the* Le water on the north of the Ho. I then divined concerning the east of the Kĕen water and the west of the Ch'en water, when the *ground near the* Lŏ was

but the most natural interpretation of the text is as in the translation.

The duke's bowing and putting his head to the ground was intended for the king, but performed in the presence of the messenger, who was to carry the report to court. The duke was now in Lŏ, and the king was probably at Haou. The duke calls the king his 'son,' expressing his affection for him, and he calls him his 'intelligent prince,' giving him honour.

P. 2. The view taken of the former par. affects the meaning which is given to this. Gan-kwŏ took 如=往, 'formerly;' 天基命定命=天始命周家安定天下之命, 'Heaven's favouring decree when first it charged our House of Chow to tranquillize and settle the empire;' and 予乃肩保=我乃繼文武安天下之道, 'I therefore continued the ways of Wăn and Woo to tranquillize the empire.' Kĕang Shing, again, taking 復 in the same way, keeps the natural interpretation of 如 as =若, but by 基命 he understands king Wăn, 'the first commissioned,' and by 定命 king Woo 'settler or completer of the commission.' In his view of 肩保 he agrees with Gan-kwŏ, and says that the 基 in 其基=謀, 'to plan.' The advocates of the other interpretation of 復 understand by 基命, 'the laying the foundations of the appoint-

ment to the empire,' and by 成命, 'the securing permanently that appointment'—results which were both to be realized be making Lŏ the capital of the empire.—Then by 保 is intended the duke of Shaou, the 'Grand-guardian' (太保); and 其基作民明辟=其庶幾爲王始作民明辟之地, as in the translation, the 其 having, as often, the signification of 期, 'to expect,' 'to aim at.' In this way the par. has a unity and consistency in itself, which we do not find in the other interpretations. I cannot but understand it thus, and doing so I cannot but take the previous 復 as Ts'ae does.

P. 3. 予惟至洛師,—see the last Book, p. 4. Lŏ is called 師 as being intended to be the capital, where the emperor should reside. See in the dict.—天子所居曰京師. It is needlessly embarrassing the interpretation to make, with Gan-kwŏ and K'ang-shing, 洛師=洛之衆.

卜河朔黎水,—I have been strongly inclined to translate this in the past complete tense,—'I had previously divined,' &c. The Le water was a name given to the united stream of the Wei (衛河) and the K'e (淇河), on its reaching a place which was afterwards called Le-yang (黎陽), in the north-east of the pres. dis. of Seun (濬), dep. of Wei-hwuy. This was not far from the old capital of Show,

伻　休　宅　天　公　拜　及　食　食
來、公　其　之　不　手　獻　伻　我
來　既　作　休　敢　稽　卜。　來、又
視　定　周　來　不　首　○　以　卜
予　宅、匹　相　敬　曰、王　圖　瀍
　　　　　　　　　　四節　　　水東、亦惟洛

indicated. Again I divined concerning the east of the Ch'en water, and the *ground near the* Lŏ was likewise indicated. I *now* send a messenger with a map, and to present the divinations."

4   II. The king bowed his face to his hands and his head to the ground, saying, "The duke has not dared but to acknowledge reverently the favour of Heaven, and has surveyed the locality to find where our Chow may respond to that favour. Having settled the locality, he has sent his messenger to come and show me the divinations,

and the duke would seem to have thought that it might be sufficient to remove the disaffected people of Yin to it, instead of transporting them so far as Lŏ. The text appears to say that he had divined about this site, after reaching Lŏ; but I think it must have been a previous measure, and intended merely to satisfy the people of Yin. The duke himself could never have seriously contemplated settling the capital of the dynasty there. Whensoever and wheresoever he divined about this place, we must understand, that the result was unfavourable. 我乃至洛食,—for the Kĕen and Ch'en rivers, see the 'Tribute of Yu.' Pt. i., p. 55. The east of the Kĕen and west of the Ch'en was the site fixed for the imperial city (王城); and the east of the Ch'en was that of 'the lower capital' (下都), to which the people of Yin were removed. But both sites were near the Lŏ, and the divination was favourable in each case. To understand the phrase 洛食, we must refer to the method of divining by the tortoise shell, described on page 336. If the ink, smeared on the back of the shell, was dried up—eaten, licked up—by the fire, the trial was favourable; if it was not so dried up, the result was considered to be unfavourable. Kĕang Shing, following K'ang-shing, gives another meaning of 食, which I hardly understand. K'ang-shing's words are: —我以乙卯日於洛之眾, 觀召公所卜處皆可長久居民, 使服田相食.   In the last Book nothing is said about the duke of Chow's divining about the sites. This the duke of Shaou had done previous to the arrival of the other. Many say that we are only to

understand from the text that the regent adopted the Guardian's divination. But then he had himself divined about the site near the Le water, nor have we reason to suppose that the duke of Shaou had divined for the site of 'the lower capital.' There is a perplexity here which the scantiness of our information does not enable us to unravel. 伻 (perhaps the character should be 抨) 來以圖及獻卜,—伻=使, 'to send;' 圖=洛之地圖, 'a plan or map of the country about the Lŏ.'

Ch. II. P. 4. Tʜᴇ Kɪɴɢ's ʀᴇᴘʟʏ ᴛᴏ ᴛʜᴇ ᴍᴇssᴀɢᴇ. 王拜手稽首,—see on the 'T'ae-kĕă,' Pt ii., pp. 3 and 4. 公不敢至匹休,—by 天之休 we are to understand 天之休命, 'the favouring decree of Heaven,' calling the House of Chow to the sovereignty of the empire; then 其作周匹 (=配) 休=其意欲所定之宅 爲我周配答天休之地, as in the translation. The passage is obscure, but this seems to be the meaning. 伻來至恆吉,—K'ang-shing thought that by the repetition of 來 it was indicated that two messengers were sent by the duke; but there is no necessity to understand the terms so. 視=示, 'to show to.' 卜休恆吉=卜兆之休美而常吉者. This is better than to take it

于　稱　公　誨　拜　敬　予　貞、　我　卜
新　殷　曰、　言。　手　天　萬　公　二　休
邑、　禮　王　○　稽　之　億　其　人　恆
咸　祀　肇　周五節　首　休、　年　以　共　吉、

favourable and always auspicious.　Let us two sustain *the responsibilities* in common.　The duke has reverently acknowledged the favour of Heaven, making provision for me for myriads and tens of myriads of years.　With my face to my hands and my head to the ground, *I receive* his instructive words."

5　III. The duke of Chow said, "Let the king at first employ the ceremonies of Yin, and sacrifice in the new city, doing everything in

with Gan-kwŏ as＝所卜之美常吉之居, 'the admirable sites which he divined, and which will always be fortunate.'　二人共貞,—by the 'two men' are meant the king and the duke of Chow.　I don't know what to make of the 貞.　Gan-kwŏ has—我與公共正其美, from which I get no meaning apt in the place.　Ma Yung explained the term by 當, 'to bear,' 'to sustain,' which is preferable to the other.　Hea Sëen says:—王欲與公共當此吉卜, 'The king wishes along with the duke to sustain the duties arising from the auspicious divinations.'

公其至之休,—the meaning of this is that as Heaven had shown its favour to the House of Chow in calling it to the sovereignty, so the duke by all his care in founding the new capital had fixed upon a central seat where that sovereignty could be maintained for ever.　Before 誨言 we must understand 以謝, or some words of similar import.　I do not think we are to suppose that the king made a second prostration.

Ch. III. Pp. 5—13.　ADVICES BY THE DUKE ON THE SACRIFICES WHICH THE KING SHOULD OFFER ON COMMENCING HIS ADMINISTRATION IN THE NEW CITY, AND ABOUT HIS SUBSEQUENT GOVERNMENT.　HE ALSO INTIMATES HIS OWN PURPOSE NOW TO RETIRE FROM PUBLIC LIFE.

We must suppose that these advices were given in Haou.　The duke had returned there some time after receiving the king's reply to the message which he sent.　It is most likely that he had left Lŏ immediately after the duke of Shaou had made what is called his announcement, and set forth before him the various offerings which were presented by the princes, to be used, it is said, at the sacrifices which would be offered,—we may suppose on the solemn inauguration by the king in person of the new city as the capital of the empire.　However this may be, it is plain that the duke, in the first instance at least, is speaking to the king in some other place from which he is urging him to go to Lŏ.

P. 5.　*The sacrifices which the king should offer in the first place.*　王肇稱殷禮,—both Gan-kwŏ and K'ang-shing take this clause as in the translation, understanding by 殷禮 'the ceremonies of the Yin dynasty.'　K'ang-shing says that the ceremonies for the services of the present dynasty had not yet been settled, or if settled, had not yet been made publicly known.　That would be done next year, which would be the first of the king's independent reign.　In the meantime he should employ the ceremonies of Yin.　Ying-tă, on the other hand, in his gloss on Gan-kwŏ's commentary, says that the ceremonies had been settled, but from their general agreement with those of the previous dynasty, they are still called here 殷禮.　This remark is very unsatisfactory.　We cannot tell why the duke gave this particular advice, but I do not see that the phrase can be rendered otherwise than I have done.　Ts'ae, indeed, after Wang Gan-shih and Lin Che-k'e, proposes to take 殷 in the sense of 盛, so that the meaning would be—'Let the king employ the fullest ceremonies.'　To justify such a meaning of the term, they refer to an expresion in Kung-yang's commentary on the Ch'un Ts'ew, under the 2d year of duke Wăn (文公二年), where it is said—五年而再殷祭; but 殷 there means 'great,' and not 'full.'　The reference is to the 'great sacrifices,' called 祫 and 禘 (see Ana., III., x.).　As Maou K'e-ling observes, we may speak of 殷祭, but not of 殷禮.　The text is silent on the sacrifice or sacrifices, which the duke wished the king to offer as his first act in the new city.　Gan-shih

汝　祀　以　曰、　今　庶　周　伻　予
受　惟　功　記　王　有　子　從　齊
命　命　作　功　卽　事。○　惟　王　百
篤　曰、　元、　宗、　命　　　曰、　于　工、

秩
無
文。○

6 an orderly way, but without any display. I will marshal all the officers to attend your majesty from Chow, merely saying that probably there will be business to be done.

7   "Let the king instantly give orders, saying, 'Let those distinguished by merit be recorded; the most meritorious shall be the first in the sacrifices.' Let him also command, saying, 'You in whose behalf this order is given must give me your assistance with sincere ear-

supposed it was that mentioned in par. 29;—which is not likely. I should rather suppose it was a series of sacrifices like those offered by Suin on his undertaking the duties of government for Yaou; see the 'Canon of Shun,' p. 6. The occasion was a grand one,—the inauguration of Lŏ as the capital, and of Ching's becoming of age and taking the government in his own hands.

咸 秩 無 文,—秩＝序, 'order,' 'to arrange orderly;' 無 文,—'without ornament.' Simplicity was a characteristic of the ceremonies of Yin as compared with those of Chow;—see Con. Ana., III., xiv. Gan-kwŏ took 無 文 differently, and Ts'ae agrees with him. The latter's exposition of the whole par. is:—王 始 舉 盛 禮 祀 之 于 洛 邑, 皆 序 其 所 當 祭 者, 雖 祀 典 不 載, 而 義 當 祀 者, 亦 序 而 祭 之 也, 'Let the king begin by employing the fullest ceremonies in his sacrifices at Lŏ, offering in order to all the spirits to which he ought to sacrifice. There may be some to which in right he ought to sacrifice that are not contained in the sacrificial canons; let him likewise sacrifice to them, having arranged them in their proper order.'

P. 6. In what way the duke would instruct the officers to attend the king to Lŏ. 齊 百 工 ＝整 齊 百 官; meaning probably nothing more than what appears in the translation, though some of the critics (see the 集 說) dwell on the 齊, as if it included all moral adjustment. 從 王 于 周,—this can only mean—'follow the king from Chow to Lŏ;' as the 'Daily Explanation' has it—從 王 自 周 以 適 洛. 庶 有 事,—this is not so indefinite as Gan-kwŏ has it,—

庶 幾 有 善 政 事, 'probably there will be some business of good government.' Indeed, he appears to have thought it a remark of the duke to himself, ＝ 'I may consider the govt. will now go on well.' From the usage of the phrase 有 事, it would be understood that he intimated that sacrifices were to be offered.

P. 7. How the king should stimulate the officers to loyal exertions by promising them a place in the sacrificial canon according to their merit. Compare 'The Pwan-kăng,' Pt. i, p. 16,—兹 子 大 享 于 先 王, 爾 祖 其 從 與 享 之, and the note where it is said that under the Chow dynasty there was a 'Recorder of Merits,' who entered the names of meritorious ministers among the imperial kindred when alive, and regulated the arrangement of their spirit tablets at the sacrifices in the ancestral temple, when they were dead. It is to this custom, which the dyn. of Chow took from Yin, that the duke refers. 記 功 宗 ＝記 功 之 尊 顯 者, as in the translation. Kĕang Shing, after Gan-kwŏ, makes 宗 a verb.—'Record the meritorious and honour them.' How they should be honoured is shown in the next clause, so that the general meaning is not affected by the way in which we construe 宗.   In the Le Ke, Bk. XXIII., called 祭 法, or 'The Laws of Sacrifice,' p. 9, there is a list given of various services to the state which would entitle their performers to be sacrificed to (夫 聖 王 之 制 祀 也, 法 施 於 民 則 祀 之, 以 勞 定 國 則 祀 之, 死 勤 事 則 祀 之, 以 禦 大 災 則 祀 之, 能 禦 大 災 則 祀 之, 能 捍 大 患 則 祀 之)   惟

惇大成裕汝永有｜卽有僚明作有功、｜周工往新邑伴煥、｜撫事如予惟以在｜其絶。○厥若彝及｜燄燄厥攸灼敘弗｜朋其往無若火始｜獳子其朋獳子其（九節）｜汝其悉自教工。○｜弼。○丕視功載乃（八節）

8 nestness.' Freely display the record of merits, for it is you who must yourself in everything train the officers. My young son, can
9 you indulge partiality? If you do so, the consequences hereafter will be like a fire, which, a spark at first, blazes up, and by-and-by cannot be extinguished.
10 　"Let your observance of the constant rules of right and your soothing measures be like mine. Take only the officers that are in Chow to go to the new city; and make them there join their *old* associates. With intelligent vigour establish your merit, with a generous largeness richly completing *the public manners*:—so shall you obtain an endless fame."

命云云,—this is evidently to be addressed by the king to the officers, = 王又惟勉勵之曰,汝等旣受此襃獎之命,宜感激殊恩厚輔王室 (see the 日講). Gan-kwŏ strangely takes it as addressed to the king.—惟天命我周邦,汝受天命厚矣當輔大天命.

Pp. 8, 9. *Publicity should be given to the record of merits, and entire impartiality maintained in it.* 8. 不視功載,—Gan-kwŏ makes this = 'Observe the services of all the officers, and record the meritorious, omitting none.' It is better to take 視 = 示, as in p.

4. 功載 = 記功之載籍. This record should be displayed where all could see it. The evidences afforded by it of the king's impartiality would powerfully influence the officers to the cultivation of a public spirit. This is the import of the second clause.

9. 朋 = 比 'to be partial;' comp. Ana., II. xiv. 獳子其朋 must be taken inter-rogatively, = 獳子其可少狗比黨之私乎. 其往 = 自是而往, 'from this forward.' 無 (= 毋) 若火, 云云,—'do not be like fire;' &c. It is difficult in translating to keep to the style of the text. 燄燄—the 說文 defines this by 火行微. 敘 = 'by degrees.' Ts'ae says:—將次第延爇不可得而撲滅矣.

P. 10. *How the king should make the duke his model.* 厥若彝 = 其順常道, 'his (= your) following the constant path.' 惟以在周工往新邑 = 惟用見在周官,勿參以私人往新邑,—'use the officers of Chow that now exist, not mixing with them other men of mercenary views, to proceed to the new city.' The meaning is that the king at first should only surround himself with the men whom the duke had tried and proved. 伴煥卽有僚,—Ts'ae put a comma at 煥, and interpret-

辭。○公曰已汝

惟沖子惟終。○^{十一節}

汝其敬識百辟^{十二節}

享亦識其有不

享享多儀儀不

及物惟曰不享、

惟不役志于享、

凡民惟曰不享、

惟事其爽侮。○

11　The duke said, "Yes, young as you are, be it yours to complete
12 *the work of your predecessors.* Cultivate *the spirit of* reverence, and
you will know who among the princes *sincerely* present their offerings to you, and who do not. In those offerings there are
many observances. If the observances are not equal to the articles,
it must be said there is no offering. When there is no service of
the will in the offerings *of the princes,* all the people will then
say, ' We need not *be troubled about* our offerings,' and affairs will
be disturbed by errors and usurpations.

ed 伻嚮 by 使百工知上意嚮,
'cause all the officers to know the views of the
sovereign.' But this is too great a supplement
to the text, nor is there any necessity for it.
嚮 and 卽 may very well be joined
together. The duke tells the king to take the
officers now in Chow to Lŏ, and there make
them join their companions, *i.e.*, labour in their
old departments at their old duties. Lin Che-
k'e has it:—使之向就舊僚以
趨事. It is difficult to say whether we
should understand 明作有功惇大
成裕, as descriptive of the king's measures,
or of the conduct of the officers. I have taken
it with the former reference. 汝永有
辭,—comp. the 'T'ae-kǎ,' Pt. i., p 7. I did
not accept the meaning of ' praise' there, but we
may as well admit it here, where the words are
addressed to the king, and he is not himself the
speaker.

　Pp. 11—13. The counsels here are of a wider
import, and relate to how the king should deal
with the princes of the empire, and attach the
masses of the people to himself. The duke also
plainly intimates his own purpose to retire from
public life. The 公曰 in p. 11 might seem
to intimate that they were delivered at a different
time and place from those which preceded; but

it is better to leave that point as incapable of
any very definite settlement.　　11.　*The*
greatness of the work devolving on the king.
已 indicates that the duke felt constrained to
go on with what he had to say.　惟終＝
終文武之業, 'finish the work of Wǎn
and Woo,' *i.e.*, secure the establishment of the
dynasty of Chow.　　12.　*The importance of*
sincerity in the offerings and in all expressions of
loyalty of the princes; and how the king might know
whether they were sincere or not. Ts'ae puts a
stop at 敬, so that 汝其敬 is equivalent
to the duke of Shaou's repeated admonition that
the king should cultivate the virtue of reverence.
It is supposed that Ching, reverent himself and
sincere, would, as if intuitively, know whether
the princes were sincere or not in their expressions of loyalty.　享多儀,—'in the
presenting of offerings, there are many ceremonial usages.' 禮＝儀. See the use of this
passage made by Mencius, VI., Pt. II., v., 4.
The 'Complete Digest,' on that passage, says
that 多＝厚, and paraphrases—享上貴
厚乎禮意.　惟不役志于
享＝諸侯惟不役志于享, as
in the translation.　惟事其爽侮.
—爽侮＝差爽僭侮.　13. *How*

十三節
乃惟孺子、頒朕
不暇聽朕教汝
于棐民彝汝乃
是不蘉乃時惟
不永哉篤敘乃
正父罔不若予、
不敢廢乃命汝
往敬哉茲予其
明農哉彼裕我
民、無遠用戾。○

13 "Do you, my young son, manifest everywhere my unwearied diligence, and listen to my instructions to you how to help the people to observe the constant rules of right. If you do not bestir yourself in these things, you will not be of long continuance. If you sincerely and fully carry out the course of your correct father, and follow exactly my example, there will be no venturing to disregard your orders. Go and be reverent. Henceforth I will study husbandry. There do you generously rule our people, and there is no distance from which they will not come to you."

the king should address himself generally to the government of the people with diligence and reverence. The duke will withdraw to his fields. 乃惟 孺子, 頒朕不暇,—Ts'ae says he does not understand 頒朕不暇, but thinks the meaning may be—成王當頒布 我汲汲不暇者,—as in the translation. This appears to have been the view likewise of Gan-kwŏ. Këang Shing reads on to 聽 before putting a comma, and takes 頒 (the 說文 quotes the passage with 攽)=分, 'to separate,' 'to divide,' alleging for this the authority of K'ang-shing. He has:—政事 繁多, 孺子分其任, 我有所 不暇聽, 'The business of government is burdensome. Divide, my son, the duties. *Even* I had not time to listen to everything.' 棐民彝=輔民常性之道, 'to help the course of the people's constant nature.' The meaning seems to be what I have given in the translation. If the people be thus ruled,—influenced, not forced,—it may be hoped they will be forward to obey the guidance. 蘉 =勉, 'to use effort,' 'exert one's-self.' There are disputes as to the form of the character, but none as to the meaning. 乃時惟不 永哉=汝是惟不可長哉, 篤敘乃正父,—敘, 'to arrange order-

ly.' Here the meaning is that king Ching's measures should all be ordered after those of his father. We cannot suppose that any other than king Woo is meant by 正父, though Keang Shing explains the phrase by 'those whom your father honoured,' referring to the great captains and ministers who assisted in the overthrow of Show. 予其明農哉, —all the critics understand that the duke of Chow here intimates his purpose to withdraw from public life. Gan-kwŏ, however, would interpret—'I will retire as old, and teach the husbandmen about righteousness;' and in illustration of this, Ying-tă quotes a passage from Fuh-shang's 'Introduction to the Shoo' (尙書 大傳), that it was the rule for retired officers to occupy themselves in the villages with teaching the young (禮, 致仕之臣, 教 於州里, 大夫爲父師, 士爲 少師, 朝夕坐於門塾而教 出入之子弟). But we cannot suppose that the duke of Chow would come under any such rule. 彼裕至末=彼=在 彼, 'there,' *i.e.*, in Lŏ; 戾=至, 'to come.' The whole=汝若于彼洛邑, 果 能盡心教養寬裕其民, 則無 四方愛戴皆往 遠而不至矣 (see the 日講)

下　公　咸　將　民　天　揚　顯　予　王
勤　德　秩　禮　居　命　文　德　沖　若
施　明　無　稱　師　和　武　以　子　曰
于　光　文　秩　。　恆　烈　予　公　公
四　于　。　元　○　四　奉　小　稱　明
方　上　○　祀　惇　方　答　子　丕　保
、　　　　　　十五節　　　　　　　　十四節
　　　　　　　　十六節　宗

14　IV. The king spoke to this effect:—"O duke, you are the enlight-
ener and sustainer of my youth.　You have set forth great and illustrious virtues, that I, notwithstanding my youth, may display a
brilliant merit like that of Wăn and Woo; reverently respond to the
favour of Heaven; harmonize and long preserve the people of all
15　the regions, and settle their multitudes here; and that I may give due
honour to the great ceremony *of recording* the most distinguished,
regulating the order for the first places at the sacrifices, and doing
everything in an orderly manner without display.

16　"But your virtue, O duke, shines brightly above and below, and
is displayed actively throughout the four quarters.　On every

Ch. IV. Pp. 14—21. Tʜᴇ ᴋɪɴɢ, ᴡɪᴛʜ ᴍᴀɴʏ
ᴄᴏᴍᴘʟɪᴍᴇɴᴛꜱ, ʀᴇꜱᴘᴏɴᴅꜱ ᴛᴏ ᴛʜᴇ ᴄᴏᴜɴꜱᴇʟꜱ ᴏꜰ
ᴛʜᴇ ᴅᴜᴋᴇ, ᴀɴᴅ ᴘʀᴏᴍɪꜱᴇꜱ ᴛᴏ ᴀᴄᴛ ᴀᴄᴄᴏʀᴅɪɴɢʟʏ.
Aᴛ ᴛʜᴇ ꜱᴀᴍᴇ ᴛɪᴍᴇ ʜᴇ ɪɴᴛʀᴇᴀᴛꜱ ʜɪᴍ ɴᴏᴛ ᴛᴏ
ᴄᴀʀʀʏ ᴏᴜᴛ ʜɪꜱ ᴘᴜʀᴘᴏꜱᴇ ᴏꜰ ʀᴇᴛɪʀɪɴɢ, ᴀɴᴅ
ᴄʜᴀʀɢᴇꜱ ʜɪᴍ ᴛᴏ ʀᴇᴍᴀɪɴ ᴀᴛ Lǒ. Ch'in Leih
observes that after the 13th par. there ought to
be some mention of the king's having gone with
the duke from Haou to Lǒ, and he supposes
that a portion of the Book is here lost. The
natural inference from parr. 18—21 certainly is
that the king, when he spoke them, was in Lǒ;
but we need not suppose that any tablets were
lost. The Book may never have been longer or
less confused than it now is.

Pp. 14, 15. *The king, with mention of his obligations to the duke for his counsels, promises to take
his advice about the sacrifices to be offered and the
record of merits to be made.*　　14. 公明
保予沖子,—it is much more natural to
construe this historically, in the indicative mood,
than to take it with Gan-kwǒ in the imperative.
He says the meaning is:—'You ought, O duke,
to enlighten and sustain me. You must not
leave me'(言公當明安我童子
不可去之).　　稱=舉 or 揚, 'to
speak of,' 'to display.' The 'great and illustrious virtues' which the duke had celebrated
are those implied in the counsels which he had
just given. If the king could 揚文武烈,
he would display the virtue required in p. 11.

If he could 奉答天命, he would escape
the evil menaced in the 乃時惟不永
of p. 13. If he could 和恆四方民居
師, he would realize the 彼裕我民,無
遠用戾, also of p. 13.　Choo He says that
居師=營洛邑, 定民（=眾民
之）居, 'to build the city of Lǒ, and settle
the dwelling of the people there.'　　15. This
par. must be construed in close connection with
the preceding. It has reference to the counsel
given in p. 7.　惇宗將禮,-將=大,
'great; 宗 is evidently employed from the 記
功之宗; 惇='to deem important,' 'to
give the due importance to.'　　稱秩元
祀,—this also must be interpreted from p. 7.
Of the last clause it is not necessary to treat
again.

P. 16.　*The great services of the duke in the
business of the govt., which left the king nothing to
do but to attend to the sacrifices.* We must
understand all this as said by the king to prepare the way for pressing the request that the
duke would not carry out his purpose of with-
drawing from public life.　旁作穆
穆迓衡,-旁='on every side' as in the

旁　迂　文　予　王　裴　不　王十　小
作　衡　武　冲　十　迪　若　日八　子
穆　不　勤　子　七　篤　時　公節　其
穆　迷　教　夙　節　岡　○　子　退
　　　　　　　日
　　　　　夜
　　　　　毖
　　　　　祀
　　　　　○
　　　　　公
　　　　　功
　　　　　○

hand appears your deep reverence to secure the establishment of order, so that you fail in nothing of the earnest lessons of Wăn and Woo It is for me the youth *only* to attend reverently early and late to the sacrifices."

17 The king said, "Great, O duke, has been your merit in helping and guiding me;—let it ever continue so."

18 The king said, "O duke, it is for me, the little child, to return to my throne in Chow, and I charge you, O duke, to remain behind.

'T'ae-kёa,' Pt. i., p. 5,—旁 求 俊 彦 衡 'a steelyard,' here = 'to balance,' 'to make even.' When it is said 迂 衡, we see the duke calmly and reverently 'meeting' all difficulties and emergencies, and adjusting them with the balance of his wisdom and measures. Gan-kwŏ is evidently wrong, when he takes this clause not as descriptive of the character of the duke's government but of its results, and interprets:—四 方 旁 來, 為 敬 敬 之 道, 以 迎 太 平 之 政 不 迷 文 武 勤 教,—Kёang Shing ingeniously takes this as = 'you make no error; with civil capacity and with military you teach the empire.' I prefer, however, to construe as in the translation. 予 冲 子, 云 云,= 'What have I to do? I should not do so well as you in the administration of affairs. I have only to perform the sacrifices which devolve upon me.'

P. 17. *The king briefly recapitulates the duke's services, and asks him to continue them, and not withdraw from public life.* 迪 = 啟, 'to teach,' 'to direct.' Ts'ae says:—公 之 所 以 輔 我 啟 我 者 厚 矣, 當 常 如 是, 未 可 以 言 去 也. Gan-kwŏ's explanation of 岡 不 若 時, though wrong, is yet amusingly ingenious:—天 下 無 不 順, 而 是 公 之 功, 'the whole empire accords, and affirms by its approval the merit of your services!'

Pp. 18—20. *The king declares his own purpose to return to Haou, and charges the duke to continue in public life, remaining at Lŏ, and completing the measures of government which he had initiated.*

18. On the interpretation of this par.

there is as much diversity of opinion as, on par. 1. The view in the translation is that of Ts'ae, adopted from Lin Che-k'e and other early scholars of the Sung dyn. The old interpreters, followed by many in the present dynasty, understand that the king is here acceding to the duke's request that he would proceed to Lŏ, and promises that he would there appoint the duke's son, Pih-k'in (伯 禽), to the principality of Loo.

Where were the king and the duke when the par. was spoken? The old interpreters say—'In Haou;' and Gan-kwŏ supposes that the king is on his throne, at a solemn audience where the duke has resigned the regency, so that 予 其 退, 即 辟 于 周 = 'I will when I have retired from this audience, go and be king in Lŏ.' I cannot read the Book without getting the impression that the speakers were now in Lŏ. And without referring to any passages, which might require a lengthy and minute discussion of them, the *fact* that king Ching did not take up his residence at Lŏ, and that this city did not till after many reigns become the real capital of Chow, is sufficient to show that the king is not here promising to go to Lŏ, but saying that he will retire from it. On this view 即 辟 于 周 has its natural meaning. Chow is Haou, as in the first par. of last Book. I should say that this clause ought to be decisive on the point of the dialogue's taking place in Lŏ, were it not for the 從 王 于 周 of par. 6. And allowing all the weight we can to the interpretation of 于 周 necessarily adopted there, I must still think that 即 辟 于 周 is strongly confirmatory of the view of the Book taken by the Sung scholars.

With regard to 命 公 後, 'it indicates,' says Kёang Shing, 'the appointment of Pih-k'in. The king's idea was that if he conferred the investiture on his son, he might retain the

卽　工、　監　迪三　救　禮、　未　四　命十　卽
辟　誕　我　將十　公　亦　定　方　公九　辟
于　保　士　其節　功。　未　于　迪節　後。　于
周、　文　師　後、○　　　克　宗　亂、○　　　周、
武　　　　　　　　　　　　　　　　　
受　　　　　　　　　　　　　　　　　
民　　　　　　　　　　　　　　　　　
亂　　　　　　　　　　　　　　　　　

19 Order has been initiated throughout the four quarters of the empire ; but the ceremonies to be honoured *by general observance* have not yet been settled; and I cannot look on your merit as completed.

20 Commence on a great scale what is to be done by your remaining here, being an example to my officers, and greatly preserving the people whom Wăn and Woo received :—by your good government you will prove the help of the whole empire."

duke at court as the prime minister of the govt.' Nothing can be argued conclusively on either side of the question from the words of the text. 命公後 may be taken as in the translation; and when I look at them without reference to the controversy agitated about them, I must understand them thus. They may, however, likewise be taken as Gan-kwŏ and the other early interpreters did.

Referring to Sze-ma Ts'een, he tells us that king Woo, immediately after the overthrow of Show, invested his brother Tan with the principality of Loo, and that Tan did not proceed to take the charge of it, but remained at court to assist the king, (封周公旦於少昊之虛、曲阜、是爲魯公、周公不就封、留佐武王; See the 魯周公、世家第三). He tells us also, that after the death of Woo, when the duke of Chow had resolved, notwithstanding the injurious suspicions afloat about him, to remain as regent of the empire during the minority of Ching, he invested his son Pih-k'in with Loo, and gave him this charge :—'A son of king Wăn, brother of king Woo, and uncle of king Ching, I am not of mean position in the empire. But I have sometimes thrice left my bath unfinished, and thrice left a meal, to receive officers, fearing lest I might fail to secure a man of virtue and ability for the service of the govt. When you go to Loo, be careful lest your being a prince make you arrogant to others.' According to this account, Pih-k'in had been invested with Loo several years before the building of Lǒ. Ts'ae argues the same thing from passages of Bk. XXIX; but I do not insist on them, because Maou K'e-ling has shown that they need not be taken as decisive on the question. Still Ts'een's statements carry in themselves evidence of their correctness. Of all his brothers and adherents, the duke of Chow was the one whom king Woo was bound to reward. No doubt he did confer on him the country of Loo; and as the duke was detained

from it all his reign and during-so many years of his son's reign, there must have been some one to supply his place. I believe that Pih-k'in went to Loo at once, and that subsequently, in the 3d or 4th year of Ching, his father resigned the dukedom entirely to him. This being the case, there is no room left for the understanding the text—命公後—as the old interpreters did.

19, 20. *The king could not look on the duke's work as done, and he calls his attention to various points which were yet to be settled.* 19. 四方迪亂=四方開治, taking it 迪=啟 or 開. Këang Shing takes it=進, and says:—四方雖進於治. The meaning is substantially the same. 未定宗禮,—Ts'ae takes 宗禮 as referring to the 功宗 of p. 8, and 惇宗將禮 of p. 15. It may be so, but I rather understand the king to be speaking here of the ceremonies in general, by which their dyn. was to be distinguished from those which preceded it. Këang Shing says they are called 宗禮, 'being honoured by all the empire' (宗禮者言禮爲天下所宗). 亦未克救公功,—救 has occurred twice before, in Bk. VII., pp. 5 and 11, joined with 寍, and in the sense of 撫 or 安, 'to soothe' 'to settle.' 'It means,' says Woo Ch'ing, 'to honour and reward.' I do not see how to translate the term faithfully, and bring out a meaning appropriate to the contents. 20. 迪將其後 means, acc. to Ts'ae, 啟大其後, as in the translation. Woo Ch'ing takes 迪將 as 'an introductory phrase,' but says he

王命予來承
拜手稽首曰、
世享。○周公[廿二節]
替刑四方其
其康事公勿
哉我惟無斁
祗歡公無困
己公功蕭將無困
曰公定予往
為四輔。○王[廿一節]

21　The king said, "Remain, O duke. I will certainly go. Your meritorious deeds are devoutly acknowledged and reverently rejoiced in. Do not, O duke, occasion me this difficulty. I on my part will not be idle or tired in seeking the tranquillity of the people; and let not the example which you have afforded be intermitted. So shall the whole empire enjoy for generations *the benefits of your virtue*."

22　V. The duke of Chow bowed his face to his hands and his head to the ground, saying, "You have charged me, O king, to come here.

does not understand the meaning of it. The 其後 would certainly seem to have reference to the 命公後 of p. 18. I do not see how Gan-kwŏ makes out of 迪將 his 公留 教道, 將助我. 監我士師 工,—士師工 is equivalent to 百官 Among the officers there were those called 士, and others called 師. 監 may be taken, with Ts'ae,' 'to afford an example to,' or, with Gan-kwŏ, 'to inspect,' 'to oversee.' 亂為 四輔,—I do not think that this means more than—'effecting good government, and being a help to me on every side.' Compare with 四輔 the 四鄰 in the 'Yih and Tseih,' p. 5. Ts'ae takes the phrase as a name of the new city, or the two new cities of 成周 and 王 城, taken in connection with Haou and Fung, as the *points d' appui* of the empire,—which is far-fetched, and intended to strengthen his view of 後 as meaning to remain at Lŏ, sufficiently strong without such support. In a passage in the Le Ke, Bk. VIII., (文王世子), p. 17, mention is made of the appointment of 四輔 and 三公, from which it would appear that 'four' men were denoted by the former phrase. If so, and we are to interpret the text in acc. with that passage, we must suppose that the king wishes the duke alone to be to him all that those four highest and trusted ministers could be.

P. 21. *The king finally announces his determination not to remain himself at Lŏ, and requires the duke to do so.* Of course the old interpreters make 予往已 mean, 'I will go to Lŏ.' Këang Shing puts no comma at 已, but reads on from 予往 to 祗歡, making 往=往 日, 'formerly.' All agree in taking 定= 止, only with the old interpreters and their modern adherents it means, 'remain to assist me as my premier,' while with Ts'ae it = 're-main here' at Lŏ. The 'Daily Explanation' paraphrases from 公功 to 困 哉 (哉 perhaps should be 我) thus:—我公迪 衡迪亂之功, 人皆肅敬而且 奉行之, 無敢違逆于外, 無有拂戾 祗畏而歡悅之, 于中. This is acc. to the views of Ts'ae, and I must think that the other interpretations of this par. are non-natural. 斁=厭, 'to dislike,' 'to turn away from.' 公勿 替刑,=公勿替所以監我士 師工者, taking 刑=儀刑. Këang Shing takes 斁=解, but the meaning comes to the same. He would point the whole differently, however.—我惟無斁其康事公 勿替, 刑四方其世享.

Ch. V. Pp. 22—24. THE DUKE ACCEPTS THE CHARGE LAID UPON HIM; SETS FORTH HOW

保　受　乃　武　恭。　來、　大　獻　四　作
乃　命　光　王、　○　相　惇　民、　方　周
文　民　烈　弘　⊟三節　宅、　典　亂　新　恭
祖　越　考　朕　孺　其　殷　爲　辟、　先、
　　　　　　　　　　子

I undertake *the charge*, and will protect the people whom your grandfather Wăn received by decree, and *whom* your glorious and meritorious father Woo *also so received*. I will enlarge the reverence which I cherish for you.

23　"*But*, my son, come *frequently* and inspect this settlement. Pay great honour to *old* statutes, and to the good and wise men of Yin. Good government here will make you indeed the new chief of the empire, and an example of *royal* respectfulness to all your

HE WILL FULFIL ITS DUTIES; AND TELLS THE CO-OPERATION WHICH HE EXPECTS FROM HIM.

22. 王命子來,—this has reference evidently to the 命公後 of par. 18. Naturally and legitimately we understand 來 of coming to a place; and that place can be no other than Lŏ. The old interpreters holding that the duke only agrees to remain in public life, without any reference to his undertaking the govt. of the new city, say that his returning might have been called a 去 or 'going away,' so his continuing may be called a 來 or 'coming' (see the gloss of Ying-tă *in loc.*). This is very forced. 承保至武王,—this responds to the king's 誕保文武受民 in p. 20. Woo Ch'ing correctly observes that we are to understand 受命民 after 武王, being omitted in the text for the sake of brevity (省文). 越＝及. Gan-kwŏ and Kĕang Shing take it as ＝于, with which I cannot make sense. They also take 承 and all the other verbs as in the infinitive mood under the govt. of 命. But it is much better to suppose that in 承 the duke speaks in his own person. To me the 朕 in the last clause necessitates this construction. 弘朕恭,—'I will enlarge my reverence.' 恭 is to be taken according to the account of it by Mencius, IV., Bk. I., i., 13, 責難於君謂之恭. The duke would do his duty; he will not allow the king to be remiss in performing *his*. Wang Ts'eaou says ingeniously:—王於文王

道,繁重之以所之辭之上一,即所之奉之承事節王,即治洛也.
公言其恭展其下兩成王,以治洛
令周公分見其恭下望之也,即所謂承保也.
欲周所欲展文效一,即所謂
欲其民殺者朕恭在下之弘朕自效.
王其不弘朕意洛之弘事
王安而也,敬治謂

23. 孺子來相宅,—I must translate this in the imperative, according to the view which has been taken of the last. The paraphrase in the 'Complete Digest' is:—王雖歸周,而此洛邑,王當來省視以治之, 'although your majesty is returning, you ought to come and examine and see this city of Lŏ, to govern it.' Though the duke gives up the hope which he had cherished, that the king would take up his residence in the new city, he endeavours to make the best of his disappointment, and hopes that the advantages to be derived from Lŏ will in part at least be secured by frequent and regular visits to it from the king. 典＝典章, 'statutes,' *i.e.*, we may suppose, the rules and principles of govt. approved or established by Wăn and Woo. 殷獻 (＝賢民,) 'the good able people (＝men) of Yin,' are, we may again suppose, men belonging to old official families of Yin, who had kept themselves from the degrading vices which had occasioned the downfall of the dynasty. Both 典 and 民 are governed by 惇, and a conjunction is understood between its two objects. This is forcing a meaning out of the text, but the meaning thus obtained is more likely than any other which

刑、乃單文祖

先考朕昭子

其師作周孚

前人成烈答

子越御事篤

○　予曰以多
廿四節

惟王有成績。

乂、萬邦咸休、

曰、其自時中

successors of Chow." "From this time," said *the duke*, "by the government administered in this central spot, all parts of the empire will be conducted to repose, and this will be the completion of your merit, O king.

24　"I, Tan, with the numerous officers and managers of affairs, will consolidate the achievements of our predecessors, in response to the *hopes of the* people. I will afford an example of sincerity to future ministers of Chow, seeking to render complete the pattern intended for the enlightenment of you, my son, and thus to carry fully out the virtue of your grandfather Wăn."

has been put upon it. Comp. the view of Gan-kwŏ:=大其厚行典常于殷賢人, and that of Kĕang Shing:—其大厚取典于殷之賢民(=治)爲四方新辟,—comp. the 亂民明辟 of par. 2.　作周恭先—Ts'ae expands this by 人君恭以接下,以恭而倡後王, 'as the sovereign shows respectfulness towards your ministers, and by such respectfulness leads the way for future kings.' Gan-kwŏ's view is the same:—爲周家見恭敬之王,後世所推先. Kĕang Shing brings out nearly the same meaning by another construction of the characters:—作立周邦以恭敬爲先務. The 曰 is perplexing. The simplest way is to suppose 公 as the nominative to it. I understand 自時 as in the 'Complete Digest'=今而後. With 中乂 compare the 自服土中, and 自時中乂 in the last Book, p. 14.　24. The duke here speaks fully and bravely of what he himself will do. We have had instances before of his superiority to the mock humility with which Chinese statesmen generally veil appreciation of themselves and their services.　多子越御事,—see on the Con. Ana., I., i.,

for the meaning of 子. 多子 is 'the many gentlemen;' and from the 御事 which follows, we conclude that the gentlemen intended the officers of the superior classes,—as the critics say, 卿大夫.　答其師(=衆)—'in answer to the multitudes.' The meaning must be as in the translation.　作周孚先—孚=信, 'faithfulness,' 'loyalty.' The expression is correlate to the 作周恭君 of the last par.; and they throw light on each other. As the king would show to future kings an example of respectfulness in dealing with his ministers, so the duke would show to future ministers an example of loyal devotedness in serving his sovereign.　考朕昭子刑,—考=成, 'to complete.' Ts'ae takes 昭子 as = the 明辟 of par. 1, so that the meaning of the clause is—'I will render complete the pattern afforded by you, my illustrious son.' The editors of Yung-ching's Show observe that everywhere else he takes 昭 or = 明, 'to enlighten,' and that there is no reason to depart from that signification here; so that the meaning of the whole is as in the translation.　單=盡, 'to complete,' 'to carry fully out.' Everything necessary to consolidate the dynasty might be considered as carrying out—completing—the virtue of king Wăn, its proper founder.

德。○伻來毖殷乃命寧予以秬鬯

　廿五節

寧予以秬

閟二卣曰

明禮拜手

○稽首不敢享。

廿六節

宿則禮于

文王武王。

○惠篤敘

廿七節

25　VI. *Afterwards, the duke of Chow took occasion to say,* " *The king* has sent messengers to admonish *the people of* Yin, and with a soothing charge to me, along with two flagons of the black millet herb-flavoured spirit, saying, 'Here is a pure sacrificial gift, which with my hands to my face and my head to the ground I offer for you to enjoy its excel-

26　lence.' I dare not keep this, and offer it in sacrifice to king Wăn and

27　king Woo." *In doing so, he prayed,* "Let him be obedient to and

Ch. VI. Pp. 25—28. THE CONDUCT OF THE DUKE IN DECLINING SOME EXTRAORDINARY GIFTS FROM THE KING, AND TAKING OCCASION FROM THEM TO OFFER A PRAYER TO WAN AND WOO, EXPRESSIVE OF HIS LOYALTY.

I cannot say that I am satisfied with the meaning of these parr. as it appears in the translation; but no interpretation of them has been proposed which can be fully acquiesced in by a cautious student. I have mainly followed the view of them given by Ts'ae, who himself followed Soo Shih. The action of them is referred to some time subsequent to that in which the previous parr. were spoken. The king is supposed to have returned to Haou, and thence he sends messages and gifts, doing honour to the duke as if he had been a departed spirit, and were continuing in heaven the guardianship of the dynasty which he had so efficiently discharged during his life. This was improper, and may be deemed improbable; but if we remember how the boy had given ear to the rumours that the duke had designs upon the throne, and consider that even now he was not really following his advice, and fixing his residence at Lŏ, we may believe that the young emperor had more awe of the powerful minister than love for him, and that he wished to propitiate him by such an extraordinary offering.

伻來毖殷，乃命寧予—王遣使誥誡殷民，因念周公之功，而來慰寧之，錫以殊典，'The king sent messengers with admonitory lessons for the people of Yin, and being impressed with the merits of the duke, at the same time to soothe his mind, by the gift of an extraordinary mark of his regard.' 秬鬯

二卣，—秬 is a species of black millet, used in the distillation of spirits. 鬯 is a species of fragrant grass employed to flavour the spirits. The two characters are used here as a name of the spirit which was made from them. 卣 is the name of a cup or bowl of medium size, in which such spirit was usually kept. A larger vessel used for that purpose was called 彝, and a smaller, 罍; the size of the 卣 was between the others. 曰明至末，—this is supposed to be the message of the king which accompanied the offering. 明＝潔, 'pure;' 禋＝敬, 'to revere,' 'reverent.' The 'Daily Explanation' gives for this clause:—此秬鬯之酒，所以明潔禋敬，以奉神而格帝者也，我敢拜手稽首，以此美物，而致享于公焉. 26. 予不敢宿，—Ts'ae says that 宿 here has the same meaning as the phrase 三宿 in Bk. XXII., p. 26, where the character is explained by 進爵, 'to advance the cup;' making the meaning to be—'I do not dare to drink this spirit.' But it will be seen on that passage, that if we must so define 宿 there, we cannot admit the signification in this text. And why should there be any difficulty in understanding here as I have done. There is an instance of the same usage, quite in point, in the Ana., X., viii., 8. The duke was so far from using for himself the king's gift, that he could not even allow it to remain by him, but presented it at once in a sacrifice to Wăn and Woo. 27. This par. is to be taken as a prayer for the king, offered when the duke sacrificed to Wăn and Woo with the spirit which

朕　其　敘　殷、　○　乃　乃　年　自　無
子　永　萬　乃　王　引　德　厭　疾、　有
懷　觀　年、　承、　伻　考。　殷　于　萬　遘
廿八節

observant of your course. Let him meet with no evil or sickness. Let him satisfy his descendants for myriads of years with your virtue. Let the people of Yin enjoy protracted prosperity." *He also said to the messengers*, "The king has sent you to Yin, which has received

28 his charges well ordered for myriads of years; but let the people ever have to observe the virtue cherished by my son."

had been sent to himself. 惠篤敘—
惠＝順, 'to accord with,' 'accordingly;' for
篤敘 comp. the 篤敘乃正父 of p.
13. The clause ＝ 願使王順承先
業, 篤之而不遺, 敘之而不
棻, 憲章是守, 無有愆忘, 而
後可焉, (see the 日講). 無(＝毋)
有遘自疾,—'let him not bring on (遘
＝遇, 'to meet with;' but with more of an
active signification) himself any sickness.'
萬年厭于乃德,—厭 is in the 3d tone,
'to be full,' 'satiated.' We must suppose that
the king is prayed for in his descendants for
ten thousand years;—as Ts'ae has it, 子孫
萬年厭飽乃德　殷乃引考,
—Ts'ae takes 引考＝長壽, 'protracted
longevity;' and the 'Daily Explanation' gives
for the passage,—願使殷餘之亡
民, 長享有幹有年之樂, 'make
the poor remnant of Yin long enjoy the happiness
of prosperity and plenty.'　　28.　We are to
suppose that the duke now addresses the messengers who had come from the king, and sends
the counsel here contained to Haou, to the effect
that though he would do his duty to carry out the
admonitions which had been sent to the people
of Yin, yet the government of them could only
be effected by the personal virtue of the king.
I am well aware, in thus interpreting these
four paragraphs, that serious objections may
be taken to the way in which the whole is
supplemented, and many of the clauses explained. All that can be said is that the interpretation
seems to me more likely than any other that has
been proposed. It will suffice if I subjoin here
that proposed by Gan-kwŏ. He first reads
伻來毖殷乃命寧 (putting a stop
at 寧) along with 考朕昭子刑, 乃
單文祖德, interpreting—'"The method
by which I will complete the enlightenment of

you, my son, is to complete the virtue of your
grandfather Wăn." This he says with reference to the ceremonies which he would establish.
"The reason why you must dwell here in the
middle of the land, is that Wăn and Woo have
sent you to come and carefully teach the people
of Yin, recognising their charge, and giving
them repose'" (我所成明子法, 乃
盡文祖之德, 謂典禮也, 所
以居土中, 是文武使已來
慎教殷民, 乃見命而安之)
He then begins a new par. with 子, and on 子
以至休享 says:—'The duke of Chow
had been regent for seven years; and having
produced a happy tranquillity throughout the
empire, he took two bowls of black millet wine,
and with purity and the utmost reverence had
presented it to Wan and Woo that they might
enjoy it, and announced to them the happy state
of the empire. Having done this, he had resigned the government, but king Ching had induced
him to remain as his chief minister. He therefore recounts those things here (周公攝
政七年致太平, 以黑黍酒以
二器, 明潔致敬, 告文武, 成留
美享, 旣告而致政, 王子不
之, 本(?故)說之). On from 至武王
he says:—'The duke says, "Seeing
this happy tranquillity of the empire, I made a
pure announcement to Wăn and Woo not delaying over it'" (言我見天下太平,
則潔告文武, 不經宿). Par. 27
is then taken as addressed to the king, and expounded:—"Do you, in administering the govt.,
observe the regular constitutions, and carry
them fully into execution, with an orderly discrimination. Allow none to follow courses
which would be productive of calamity and
distress. So will the empire for myriads of
years be satiated with your virtue, and *the dynasty of* Yin will for ever become that of Chow"
(汝爲政當順典常厚行之,

册、册、王騂一、王祭新辰、德。
惟逸命牛武騂歲邑王○
告祝作一、王牛文烝在戊 廿九節

29   VII. On the day Mow-shin, the king in the new city performed the annual winter sacrifice, offering a red bull to king Wăn, and the same to king Woo. He then commanded a declaration to be prepared, which was done by Yih in the form of a prayer, and it simply announced the remaining behind of the duke of Chow. The king's

使有次序，無有遇用患疾
之道者，則天下萬年厭於
汝德，殷乃長成為周）．On the
28th par. he says:—'"When the king causes
the people of Yin, high and low, to have such
orderly relations with one another, then will be
seen *the course of govt.* for myriads of years,
and the people will for ever look to our descendants and turn to their virtue." Thus he
stimulates the king to complete the work *begun
by Wăn and Woo*' (王使殷民，上下
相承有次序，則萬年之道，
民其長觀我子孫而歸其
德矣，勉使終之）．

It would be easy to fill pages with smaller
variations of view that have been proposed on
this difficult passage; but the student will probably think that it has been dwelt upon at
sufficient length. I will, however, here subjoin
the version of Gaubil, and a note which he gives
on the character 禋. His version is:—'Vous
avez envoyé un exprès pour faire instruire les
peuples de Yin, et vous lui avez ordonné de me
demander en quel état étoit ma santé; outre
cela vous m'avez envoyé en present deux vases
remplis du vin Ku-tchang, et vous avez ainsi
parlé: il faut avoir le cœur pur et respectueux.
Je me prosterne à terre, et je me sers de ces
deux heureux vases pour marquer mon respect.
'Je n'oserois boire de ce vin; mais je m'en
suis déja servi pour honorer avec respect Ven-
vang. et Vou-vang.
'Je souhaite que le Roi soit exact à imiter
ses ancêtres, qu'il vive long tems sans fâcheux
accident, que jusqu'à dix mille ans il ait des
imitateurs de sa vertu, que les nouveaux sujets
de la dynastie Yin jouissent d'une longue et
heureuse suite d'années.
'Je souhaite que jusqu'à dix mille ans vous
gouvernicz hereusement les peuples de Yin.
Dans tout ce qui les regarde, faites ensorte qu'ils
se plaisent à suivre vos exemples.'
I need not speak of the character of this
version. His note is to the following effect:—
'The characters 秬 鬯 express a wine made
from black millet or 秬, and an odoriferous

herb called 鬯. Acc. to the thought of king
Ching, this required in him who used it a heart
pure and full of respect. It was set apart
therefore for the ceremonies performed to Heaven, or spirits, or to ancestors. It was employed
perhaps in all the three ceremonies. Now the
character which expresses the respect to be
shown in the use of this wine is 禋, which
is composed of three other characters:—示,
meaning *to show to;* 西, *the west;* and 土,
country. Could the ancient Chinese have had in
view, in the use of this character, the country
of the west from which they had come forth?
Do we have in it, applied to these ceremonies,
the vestiges of some ancient ceremony, in which
they regarded the west, when they honoured
Heaven, the Spirits, or their first ancestors?
The Chinese characters are composed of several
other characters, and the whole has regard to
the thing expressed by the composite character;
the several characters are the simple ideas which
make the composite one. The analysis which
I make here of the character 禋 is but a conjecture. I only give it as such, and I do not
care to engage to find proofs of it in the ancient
monuments and traditions of China. I know
that several Europeans have abused the analysis
of Chinese characters; but the Chinese themselves make sometimes such analyses.'
Gaubil was at home when he brought his knowledge of mathematical and astronomical science
to bear on the illustration of Chinese chronology;
but this conjecture about the meaning of the
term 禋 cannot be called happy. 示 suggests the idea of some *religious* meaning, as belonging to the whole character; but the other
half of it—垔—is entirely *phonetic,* and suggests
merely its name or sound. It enters in the same
way into more than 30 other characters. The
character is used in the 'Canon of Shun,' p. 6,
where I do not know that the idea of the objects
sacrificed to being the fathers of the nation
who had their seats in the west ever occurred
to any one.

Ch. VII. Pp. 29—31. HISTORICAL NOTICES
OF THE PUBLIC ANNOUNCEMENT OF THE DUKE'S
APPOINTMENT TO REMAIN AT Lŏ; AND OF HIS
SUBSEQUENT GOVERNMENT.   29. 戊辰.

惟 保 ○ 在 後 ○ 王 賓 周
七 文 惟 十 作 王 八 殺 公
年 武 周 有 册 命 大 禋 其
。 受 公 二 逸 周 室 咸 後
　 命 誕 月 誥 公 祼 格 王
　 、 。 。 。 。

<small>卅一節</small> <small>三十節</small>

guests, on occasion *of* the killing the victims and offering the sacrifice, all made their appearance. The king entered the grand apartment, and poured out the libation.

30　The king charged the duke of Chow to remain, and Yih, the preparer of the document, made the declaration;—*all* in the 12th month.

31　*Then* the duke of Chow greatly sustained the decree which Wăn aud Woo had received, through the space of seven years.

—we may conclude from the next par. that this was in the 12th month. The king was then in Lŏ. We may believe that he had come to it expressly for the service which is here described. Gan-kwŏ supposed that he had arrived on the day Mow-shin; but in that case we should have read 王到新邑, and not 王在新邑. 烝 is the name given to the winter sacrifice in the temple of ancestors. Ts'ae read the three characters 烝祭歲 together, with the meaning which I have given in the translation;—whether correctly or not I cannot undertake to say. The 歲, occurring where it does, is a great difficulty. Këang Shing puts a comma at 烝, and then takes 祭歲 as another sacrifice, offered on the first day of the first month of the next year. This was the view of K'ang Shing, who also supposed that after the usual service of the day there was still the special sacrifice to Wăn and Woo, which follows. Lin Che-k'e says the best plan is to allow that the 歲 is inexplicable, and so pass over it. I believe he is right. 駬,—see Ana., VI., iv. 王命作册,—comp. on Bk. VI., p. 5. 逸祝册,—逸 was the name of the 史, or 'Recorder,' who officiated on the occasion;—see again Bk. VI., p. 5, and also Bk. X., p. 13. Over 惟告周公其後

there is fought again the battle as to the meaning of 後, which has been gone into on par. 18. 王賓殺禋咸格,—'the king's guests' denotes all the princes present and assisting at the ceremonies, and specially those representing the previous dynasties. 殺=殺牲, 'killing the victims.' 禋 is descriptive of the whole service as 'a pure sacrifice presented in the temple of ancestors.' 王入太室祼 =王乃入太室, 祼地以降神, 'the king entered into the great apartment (*i.e.*, the middle hall of the temple), and poured the fragrant spirits on the ground to invite the descent of the spirits.' 30. I understand this par. as a *resumé* of the preceding, with an additional note of time. 31. According to the translation which I have given, the 'seven years' mentioned are to be calculated from the 7th year of king Ching. As Ch'in Sze-k'ae says:— 'The duke of Chow acted as regent for seven years, and then wished to retire from public life; but king Ching detained him in the govt. of Lŏ, where he spent other seven years, making in all fourteen years from the death of king Woo' (see the 集說). This view of course is contrary to the old interpreters and those who adhere to their views. They think that the 'seven years' here are simply the seven years of the duke's regency.

THE BOOKS OF CHOW.

BOOK XIV. THE NUMEROUS OFFICERS.

士。商用邑于公月.惟^一節　　多
○　王告洛.新初周三　　士

1   I. In the third month, at the commencement of *the government of* the duke of Chow in the new city of Lŏ, he announced *the royal will*

THE NAME OF THE BOOK.—多士, 'The numerous Officers.' By the 'numerous officers' are intended the officers of the previous dynasty, who had been removed along with the people to the new city of Lŏ. The phrase occurs several times, and is taken to designate the Book, which indeed was addressed to those officers. It is found in both the texts, and has its place among the 'Announcements' of the Shoo.

The prefatory note about the Book (see page 10) says that when the new city of Ching-chow was completed, the obstinate people of Yin were removed to it; and that it was then that the duke of Chow announced to them the royal will, as it is here set forth. This statement has given rise to some discussion. We have met with various passages in the two last Books, which make it appear that many of the people of Yin had been removed to the country about the Lŏ before the dukes of Shaou and Chow received their mission to proceed thither. The same thing may be argued from passages in this Book itself as well. Hence Ts'ae follows in the wake of Woo Ts'ae-laou, and says we have here an instance of how little the notices in the so-called Confucian preface are to be depended on. Maou K'e-ling has endeavoured to weaken the force of their observations, but with little success.

It is just possible that king Ching, on returning to Haou after the sacrifice described in the end of last Book, ordered another migration of the people of Yin to Lŏ, and on a large scale; and that their arrival at the new settlement gave occasion to this address. This would reconcile the statement in the preface and the intimations which are found of previous removals of the people; but it can be given only as a supposition.

CONTENTS. The object of the announcement is to reconcile the minds of the people of Yin, and especially of the higher classes among them, to their lot. The day of Yin had gone by. The House of Chow was in the ascendant. They had been dealt with kindly and generously. They had better acquiesce in their condition, and by loyalty deserve well of their new masters. If they did not do so, a worse thing would come upon them.

The address or announcement, much broken up, occupies the whole of the Book after the introductory paragraph. It has been divided into four chapters. The first, parr. 2—4, vindicates the justice of the sovereigns of Chow in taking the empire to themselves. The second parr. 5—15, unfolds the causes why the dynasty of Yin had been set aside. The third, parr. 16—23, shows how it had been necessary to remove the people to Lŏ, and with what good intention the new city had been built. The fourth, parr. 24—26, shows that comfort and prosperity are here at Lŏ open to their attainment, while by perseverance in disaffection they will only bring misery and ruin on themselves.

Ch, I. Pp. 1—4. WHEN THE ADDRESS WAS DELIVERED. THE HOUSE OF CHOW HAD OVERTHROWN THE DYNASTY OF YIN, NOT FROM AMBITION, BUT IN EXECUTION OF THE WILL OF GOD.

1. *Introductory.*   惟三月,—this third month is most naturally reckoned from the sacrifice described in the concluding parr. of the last Book. Some call the year the first of Ching's reign, *i.e.*, after he attained his majority. Others call it the first of the duke of Chow's government of Lŏ. Woo Ching

弋　非　○　殷　威　佑　于　遺　王
殷　我　　肆　命　致　命　殷　多　若
命　小　　爾　終　王　將　我　士　曰
惟　國　　多　于　罰　天　有　弗　爾
天　敢　　士　帝　勅　大　周　弔　殷
　　　　　　　　　　　　　明　喪

2 to the officers of the Shang dynasty, *saying*, "The king speaks to this effect :—'Ye numerous officers who remain from the dynasty of Yin, great ruin came down on Yin from the want of pity in compassionate Heaven, and we, the princes of Chow, received its favouring decree. We accordingly felt charged with its bright terrors; carried out the punishments which kings inflict; rightly disposed of the appointment of Yin; and finished *the work* of God.

3 Now, ye numerous officers, it was not that our small country dared to aim at the appointment of Yin. But Heaven was not with

would identify this month, indeed, with the third of the previous year, and the address here with what I have called the 'written specifications' delivered then to the people of Yin and the chiefs of the various States; but it is sufficient to have referred to his view. 初于新邑洛,—始行治洛之事, 'when he commenced discharging the business of the govt. of Lŏ.' 用告商王士,—we might take 用 as simply = 'thereupon.' The critics, however, all complete its meaning as in the translation,—用成王之命. The officers are said to be those of 'the king of Shang,' meaning Show; or perhaps we should take 王 in the plural, and then 商王, = 'the Shang dynasty.'

Pp. 2—4. *Chow only executed justice in overthrowing Yin,—was but the instrument in the hands of God.* 2. 弗弔旻天大降喪于殷,—for the meaning of 弗弔 comp. Bk. VII., p. 1, and XVI., p. 2. On 旻天, see Pt. II., Bk. II., p., 21, and on Men. v., Pt. I., i., 1. In addition to the two explanations of the meaning of 旻 which are cited in the notes on Mencius, I find a third, given here by Ma Yung,—that the autumnal sky is called 旻, because 'the autumn air is killing' (秋氣殺也,); and he argues that what is said immediately after of ruin inflicted by Heaven confirms this acct. of the character. Kĕang Shing approves

this view; but there is more force in the language, when we take 旻 as = 'compassionate.' With sorrow was the ruin sent down, but Yin could not be spared, so great was its wickedness. —'Without pity, pitying Heaven sent down great ruin on Yin.' 我有周佑命 = 我周受眷佑之命, as in the translation. This requires a considerable supplement. Kĕang Shing, without such sup., makes the text = 我周佑助天命, 'our Chow lent its aid to the charge of Heaven ;'—with which the student will probably be still less satisfied. 將天明威,—comp. in 'The Announcement of T'ang,' p. 4, 將天命明威. 致王罰,—in 'The Speech of T'ang,' p. 4, we have 致天之罰, 'carry out the punishment appointed by Heaven.' The 'punishment' here is the same, but described with reference to the agents employed by Heaven to execute it. 勅殷命,—it is not easy to catch the exact force of 勅 here and in p. 14. We must accept the definition of it by 正, 'to correct,' 'to rectify.' But in the rectification of the decree of Yin, there was involved the overthrow of the dynasty. 終于帝 = 終上帝之事, 'to complete the work or business of God.' 3. 弋殷命,—弋 'to shoot at.' See Ana. VII., xxvi. K'ang-shing and Wang Suh read 翼, but they must have written, we may almost say, that

格嚮于時夏、
逸則惟帝降、
逸有夏不適、
聞曰上帝引
天明畏。○我
下民秉爲、惟
帝不畀、惟我
敢求位。○我惟〔四節〕
亂弼我我其
不畀允罔固、〔五節〕

Yin, for indeed it would not strengthen its misrule. It *therefore*
4 helped us;—did we dare to seek the throne of ourselves? God was
not for *Yin*, as appeared from the conduct of our inferior people, in
which there is the brilliant dreadfulness of Heaven.

5 II. 'I have heard the saying—"God leads men to tranquil security;" but the sovereign of Hea would not move to such security,
whereupon God sent down *corrections*, indicating His mind to

character by mistake for 弋. They define it by 取, 'to take,' and by 驅, 'to drive out.'

天不畀,—'Heaven did not give,' *i.e.*, did not any longer give its favour to Yin. Gan-kwǒ read this on with the next clause, and has 天不與信無堅固治者, 'Heaven did not—or does not—give its favour to those who are not sincerely strengthening their govt.' Këang Shing and Ming-shing, pointing in the same way, but dissatisfied with Gan-kwǒ's explanation, take 罔=誣, and change 固 into 怙, on the slenderest ground,—in fact, without any ground at all,—making the whole= 天不與信誣罔而怙亂者, which is to me more unsatisfactory than the view which they condemn. The view given in the translation was first proposed by Soo Shih. 我其敢求位 is to be taken interrogatively. 4. How was the mind of Heaven known to be averted from Yin? This par. supplies the answer:—'By the disaffection of the people.' We have here again the doctrine of *vox populi vox Dei*. 惟帝不畀,—the change of style from the indefinite term 'Heaven' to the personal 'God' is to be remarked. We have met with it before. 惟我下民秉爲=惟我下民之所秉爲, 'was what our people held fast and did.' The expression 秉爲 is peculiar, but this explanation of it is much preferable to that of Gan-kwǒ, who reads 爲 in the 3d tone, and says: 一惟我周家下民秉心爲我, 'the lower people of our House of Chow maintained their *right* hearts, and were for us.' A

peculiar force of the 惟, common in the Shoo, is very marked here. It serves to link the various propositions together, indicating that they form a series, each one being a sequence of what has preceded.

Ch. II. Pp. 5—15. THE REASONS FOR THE OVERTHROW OF YIN; ILLUSTRATED BY REFERENCE TO YIN'S OWN OVERTHROW OF THE DYNASTY OF HEA. 5, 6. *The fall of Hea and rise of Shang.* 5. 上帝至適逸,—the meaning of these clauses has been very variously explained. The whole par. seems to me to speak about Këě, and the ruin of the Hea dynasty brought about by him; and in acc. with this, these two preliminary clauses are best understood as in the translation. 上帝引逸 =上帝引人至於安逸之地, 'God leads men to a condition of tranquil ease.' How does he lead men to this? By the inward satisfaction and outward prosperity which belong to a course marked by obedience to His will. It is added that 'the sovereign of Hea—Këě, that is—would not move to this security.' 有夏不適逸=桀乃不適於逸,自趨於危, 'Këě would not go to security, but hurried himself on to peril' (see 陳大猷 in the 集說). Gan-kwǒ's view makes the passage have reference to Këě, but is more superficial. It is thus paraphrased by Ying-tă:—'The feeling of supreme Heaven is a wish that the people should always enjoy a tranquil happiness; but Këě, the king of Hëä, rebellious to Heaven and injurious to the people, would not allow them to move towards this tranquil happiness.' Këang Shing likewise understood Këě by 有夏, but he takes in 則 as belonging to the second clause. He then says that 引佚 (he reads 佚 for 逸)=引

弗克庸帝、大
淫洪有辭惟
時天罔念聞、
厥惟廢元命、
降致罰。○^{六節}乃
命爾先祖成
湯革夏、俊民
甸四方。○^{七節}自
成湯至于帝
乙、罔不明德

him. *Kĕĕ*, however, would not be warned by God, but proceeded to greater dissoluteness and sloth and excuses for himself. Then Heaven no longer regarded nor heard him, but disallowed his

6 great appointment, and inflicted extreme punishment. Hereupon it charged your founder, T'ang the Successful, to set Hea aside, and by

7 means of able men to rule the empire. From T'ang the Successful down to the emperor Yih, every sovereign sought to make his virtue

進遺佚之賢, 言天欲人君
任賢, 'to lead or bring forward worthies left in obscurity, meaning that Heaven wishes sovereigns to employ the worthy.' The second clause='but Kĕĕ would not conform to this rule of employing the worthy.' Woo Ch'ing struck out a new path for himself, supposing that down to 格 it is the great Yu and other good kings of Hea who are spoken of.—'When sovereigns love idleness and pleasure, God leads and puts them away. But the kings of Hea, like Yu, K'e, and Shaou-k'ăng, by their anxious diligence accorded with this mind of Heaven, and went not on to any idle ways, so that God sent down to them his favour and protection (上帝於
人君之好逸樂者, 引而去若
君之有夏之君, 若禹若啟若
之康, 皆以憂勤合天意而
少適於逸, 則上帝降格眷
不佑之). This variety of opinion shows that the meaning of the text is uncertain; but that which I have given seems to be decidedly the preferable view of it.

則惟帝降格, 嚮于時夏,—here also, both the meaning and the pointing are far from being agreed upon. Woo Ch'ing's view of the whole par., which has been given above, makes him pass after 格 to Kĕĕ, to that 嚮于時夏=向至于是夏桀
'But when it came to this sovereign of Hea, Kĕĕ.' Kĕang Shing, after Ma Yung, puts a comma at 時, and reads 夏 with the next clause. The scope of the whole, however, is pretty clear. In consequence of Kĕĕ's character and course, Heaven sent down various premoni-

tory warnings, to arouse him to a recognition of its will. Ts'ae says:—帝猶未遽絕
也, 乃降格災異, 以示意嚮
於桀. Gan-kwŏ takes the 嚮, 'towards,' as not expressing the *will* of Heaven but its *favour* towards the House of Hea, so that the visitations intimated in 降格 were expressions of its kindly regard, which regard was only extinguished by the subsequent recklessness of Kĕĕ. But this is finding too much in the character. 弗克庸帝命=不能用帝
命 (or 戒), 'could not use the warnings given him by God.' 有辭,—comp. 夏王
有罪矯誣上天, in the 'Announcement of Chung-hwuy,' p. 3. It is better to understand the phrase as I have done, with such a reference, than to take it, with Woo Ch'ing and others, as simply=有可罪之辭.
惟時 may be 'then;' or 'thereupon,'
時=是. 元命=大命, 'great appointment,' *i.e.*, to be sovereign of the empire. This is better than to take 大命=始時
之命, as Kĕang Shing does. 降致
罰,—'sent down and carried punishment to the uttermost.' 6. 俊民甸四方,
—comp. the 'T'ae-kĕă,' Pt. i. 5, 旁求俊
彥. 甸=治 'to rule.' Lin Che-k'e joins 俊民 to the preceding 革夏, which is very unlikely.

Pp. 7—12. *How the dynasty of Yin long continued, and how it finally perished.* 7. Com-

天不畀不明厥德。○

保降若茲大喪。○惟

民祗。○惟時上帝不　十一節

淫厥泆。○罔顧于天顯　十節

聽念于先王勤家、誕

罔顯于天、矧曰其有

澤。○在今後嗣王。誕　九節

敢失帝罔不配天其

保父有殷殷王亦罔

恤祀。○亦惟天丕建、　八節

8 illustrious, and duly attended to the sacrifices.　And thus it was that while Heaven exerted a great establishing influence, preserving and regulating the house of Yin, its sovereigns on their part were humbly careful not to lose the favour of God, and strove to manifest a good-doing corresponding to that of Heaven.　9 But in these times, their successor showed himself greatly ignorant of *the ways of* Heaven, and much less could it be expected of him that he would be regardful of the earnest labours of his fathers for the country.　Greatly abandoned to dissolute idleness, he paid no regard to the bright principles 10 of Heaven, nor the awfulness of the people.　On this account God no longer protected him, but sent down the great ruin which we have 11 witnessed.　Heaven was not with him because he did not seek to illus-

p. Bk. X., p. 9, 成湯咸至于帝乙, 成王畏相,云云.　恤祀—' were anxious about the sacrifices,' *i.e.*, diligently attended to them　The account of T'ang in the 'T'ae-kĕa,' Pt. i., 2, gives a good illustration both of the 明德 and the 恤祀.　8. Observe how the 亦 in the two parts of the par. correspond to each other.　罔敢失帝,—' did not dare to lose God,' *i.e.*, the favour of God.　The critics all say 無敢失上帝之則 or 上帝之意, ' did not dare to neglect the pattern set them by God, or to fail of the wish of God.'　罔不配天其澤＝使德澤之及民者有以配天之廣大, ' caused their virtuous beneficial influence to reach the people in a manner corresponding to the vastness and greatness of Heaven.'　Kĕang Shing most unwarrantably changes and enervates the sentiment, making the text merely ＝ 無不配天,享

其福澤, ' all stood before Heaven and enjoyed its blessing.'　9. 在今後嗣王,—comp. Bk. X., p. 11.　It is Show, of course, who is spoken of.　罔顯于天＝不明於天道, ' unintelligent of the ways of Heaven.'　The meaning given to 罔顯于民 in the par. of the 10th Bk. just referred to might suggest another version of the text; but it will be found that we must take 顯 actively here, whereas it was passive in the other passage.　矧曰,—comp. the same phrase in Bk. X., p. 13; *et al.*　先王勤家＝先王之勤勞於國家, ' the earnest toil of the former kings for the country.'　罔顧,云云,—comp. 迪畏天顯小民, Bk. X., p. 9.　10. 惟時＝惟是之故, ' on this account.'　11. Gan-kwŏ and Kĕang Shing take this par. as one long clause, assigning the reason of the ruin just men-

十二節　凡四方小大邦

十三節　喪、罔非有辭于罰。○王若曰、爾

殷多士、今惟我

周王、丕靈承帝

十四節　事。○有命曰割

殷、告勑于帝。○

十五節　惟我事不貳適、

惟爾王家我適。

12 trate his virtue. *Indeed*, with regard to the overthrow of all States, great and small, throughout the four quarters of the empire, in every case there are reasons to be alleged for their punishment.'"

13 "The king speaks to this effect:—'Ye numerous officers of Yin, the case now is this, that the sovereigns of our Chow, from their

14 great goodness were charged with the work of God. There was the charge to them, "Cut off Yin." *They proceeded to perform it*, and announced the correcting work to God. In our affairs we have followed

15 no double aims:—ye of the royal house *of Yin* must follow us.

tioned.—大喪之所以降、惟天不與不明其德者故也。 It is better to take it as in the translation.—天之所不與紂者、以紂不明其德故耳。　12. A general proposition is here laid down embracing the case of Show. Comp. Bk. X., p. 3.

Pp. 13—15. *The sovereigns of Chow in overthrowing Yin had merely performed the will of God.*　13. 我周王，—'the sovereigns of Chow' were kings Wǎn and Woo. 不靈承帝事，—we must take both 不 and 靈 as adverbs joined to the verb 承. The kings undertook the work, and they did so with a great and almost more than human efficiency. Le-ts'ĕang says:—周之靈承蓋得於不言之表者矣. With 承帝事 comp. 祇承上帝, 以遏亂略, Bk. III., p. 6.　14. 告勑于帝，—we may suppose this announcement to have been made, either while the operations against Show were in progress, as related in Bk. III., pp. 6—8, or after they were completed, as in the same Bk., p. 3.　15. The translation of this par. is after Ts'ae, who succeeds better with it than any other of the critics. He says:—周不貳于帝殷其能貳於

周乎, 'As Chow had not been double to God, dare Yin be double to Chow?'　王家＝商王士, p. 1.　Lin Che-k'e goes round about the passage in a strange way:—我于割殷之事、應天順人、一舉而不使惟殷都也、不待再命所用兵、天之商王之家、遂至于商王之家、既亡至于召我適爾叛、乃復再、乃爾適爾殷都也, 'In the business of cutting off Yin, we were acting in obedience to Heaven and in accordance with men. One movement accomplished the work. We did not need to go twice to the capital of Yin. But you would not discern to whom the favour of Heaven had fallen. After your overthrow you rebelled, and caused us a second time to put our forces in motion. It was you, belonging to the House of the kings of Shang, who called us to go to your capital of Yin.'　As far-fetched is the interpretation of Kĕang Shing, who takes 適＝敵, 'enemies.'—惟我事順天下、不有貳心而爲敵者、惟爾王家叛作難、與我爲敵謂武庚也。

時惟人居士王大亦動洪○
惟天奉西子曰戾念自無予
天德爾惟獻肆天乃度其十
命不非時告不卽邑我曰六
無康我其爾正于○不惟節
違寧一遷多○殷予爾爾

（十八節・十七節・十六節）

16　III. 'May I not say that you were very lawless?　I did not *want*
17　to remove you.　The thing came from your own city.　When I consider also how Heaven has drawn near to Yin with *so* great tribulations, it must be that there was *there* what was not right.'"

18　"The king says, 'Ho! I declare to you, ye numerous officers, it is simply on account of these things that I have removed and settled you in the west;—it was not that I, the one man, considered it a part of my virtue to make you untranquil.　The thing was from

Ch. III. Pp. 16—23. Tʜᴇʏ ʜᴀᴅ ᴏʙʟɪɢᴇᴅ ᴛʜᴇ ᴋɪɴɢ ʙʏ ᴄᴏɴᴛɪɴᴜᴇᴅ ᴅɪsᴀғғᴇᴄᴛɪᴏɴ ᴛᴏ ʀᴇᴍᴏᴠᴇ ᴛʜᴇᴍ ᴛᴏ Lǒ. Hᴇ ʜᴀᴅ ᴅᴇᴀʟᴛ ᴋɪɴᴅʟʏ ᴡɪᴛʜ ᴛʜᴇᴍ, ᴀɴᴅ ᴡᴀs ᴘʀᴇᴘᴀʀᴇᴅ ᴛᴏ ᴅᴏ sᴏ sᴛɪʟʟ ᴍᴏʀᴇ. Tʜᴇɪʀ ʀᴇᴍᴏᴠᴀʟ ᴛᴏ Lǒ ᴡᴀs ɪɴᴛᴇɴᴅᴇᴅ ғᴏʀ ᴛʜᴇɪʀ ɢᴏᴏᴅ. 16, 17. *It was the lawless and continued disaffection of Yin which had necessitated their removal.* 16. 子其曰, 云云,—the emphatic force of the 其 is brought out in English by using the negative interrogation. 無度=無法, 'lawless,' 'unregulated.' The reference is to the rebellion of Woo-kǎng and his people, with the king's uncles who had been set over them. 不爾動,—動, 'to move,' 'to excite;' in this case = 'to remove.' 自乃 邑,—comp. 造攻 自鳴條 in the 'Instructions of E,' p. 2. 17. Here, as in p. 11, I have translated according to the view of Ts'ae, whose exposition of the whole is—子亦 念天就殷邪,屢降大戾 旣死,武庚又死 故邪愿不 正,言當遷徒也. Gan-kwǒ expounds it:—我亦念天,就於殷大 罪而加誅者,故以紂不能 正身念法, 'I also thought of Heaven; and having reference to the great crimes of Yin, inflicted the punishment of death, because Show would not correct himself and think of the laws.' This is absurd enough, but not so much

so as it may at first appear, Gan-kwǒ understanding the 爾洪無度 of the last par. to have reference to Show. Këang Shing takes a view of the par. quite as wide of the mark, making 正=殺, 'to put to death,' and interpreting:—我亦念 武庚之 叛 是 天就于殷而大拂戾之 爾 非 爾多士之由,故不正 而遷 多 釋所以不誅而遷爾 之 士意.

P. 18. *The king reiterates his assertion that in removing them to Lǒ he was merely obeying the will of Heaven. There was no reason why they should murmur against him.* 獻,—see on Bk. VII., p. 1. 惟時=惟是之故, 'on account of these things,' the facts, mentioned in the two prec. parr. 遷居西爾,—'have transferred your dwelling and *wested* you,' *i.e.*, have removed and settled you here in the west. Lǒ lay south and west from Show's old capital, though it was to the east of Haou, Woo's capital. Këang Shing strangely argues for the meaning of 西 as being 止息, 'to give rest to,' so that the meaning is—'I have changed the place of your dwelling in order to give you rest' (遷所 居以西息汝). 非我奉德 不康寧=非我奉持其德 勞動爾,不安寧爾. The expres-

予罪、時惟天命。○

予惟率肆矜爾、非

敢求爾于天邑商、非

人惟聽用德、肆予

有服在百僚、予一

曰夏迪簡在王庭、

革夏命。○今爾又
二十節

先人有册有典、殷

怨。○惟爾知、惟殷
十九節

朕不敢有後、無我

the decree of Heaven; do not resist me; I dare not have any further
19 *change for you.* Do not murmur against me. Ye know that your
fathers of the Yin dynasty had their archives and narratives *showing*
20 how Yin superseded the appointment of Hea. Ye now indeed say
further, "*The officers of* Hea were chosen and promoted to the
imperial court, or had their places among the mass of officers." I,
the one man, listen only to the virtuous and employ them; and
it was with this view that I presumed te seek you out in *your* heavenly city of Shang. I thereby follow the ancient *example*, and have
pity on you. *Your present non-employment* is no fault of mine;
it is by the decree of Heaven.'"

sion 奉德 is here difficult. Këang Shing
gives for the whole—非我所秉之德
性不靜安, 'was not because my disposition is restless.' 時=是. 無違,
朕不敢有後,—I have translated this
after Ts'ae, and Gan-kwŏ took substantially the
same meaning:—汝無違命、我亦
不敢有後誅. The editors of Yung-
ching's Shoo say this interpretation is suitable
enough; but they also mention with approbation
another, proposed by Lin Che-k'e:—'The thing
was from the decree of Heaven. That was not
to be resisted, and I did not dare to make any
delay in obeying it. Do not murmur against
me, as if the transference of you here proceeded
from me.' It is difficult to decide between the
two. On the whole, I think the first is preferable.

Pp. 19, 20. *Yin's overthrow of Hea sufficiently
justified Chow's overthrow of Yin; and if the
officers of Yin were not now treated so well as those
of Hea had been, they had only themselves to blame.*
19. 殷先人=殷之先世,
'the prior—early—ages of Yin.' 有册有
典,—Koo Seih-ch'ow says that by 册 we are

to understand the engraved tablets kept in the
depositories, and by 典, the same circulated
through the empire (藏府曰册、頒行
曰典). 20. 夏迪至百僚,—
迪=進, 'to bring forward;' 簡=拔, 'to
make choice of,' 'to promote.' By 夏 we are
evidently to understand 夏之士, 'the officers of the Hea dynasty.' The officers of Yin
urge that they were not treated as those of Hea
had been. 天邑商,—all agree that the
capital of the Yin dynasty and country about it
are here intended. But why is it called 'the
heavenly city?' K'ang-shing says, 'Because it
had been originally established by Heaven.' Leu
Tsoo-heen and others say, 'Because there the
emperors of Yin—the sons of Heaven—had
dwelt.' Wang Suh says:—'The king means to
say, "Shang, which is now my heavenly city."'
I think it may be spoken ironically—'*your*
heavenly city.' Këang Shing takes the language
from 子一人 to 商 to be spoken of the
appointment of the viscount of Wei.—'I also
had regard to and employed the virtuous, and
I therefore ventured to seek out the descendant
of your kings in the city,' &c. This is amusingly ingenious, but few will be found to adopt the

王曰、多士、昔朕來自奄、予大降爾四國民命、我乃明致天罰、移爾遐逖、比事臣我宗、多遜。○王

21　　"The king says, 'Ye numerous officers, formerly, when I came from Yen, I greatly mitigated the penalty in favour of the lives of the people of your four countries. At the same time I made evident the punishment appointed by Heaven, and removed you to this distant abode, that you might be near the ministers who had served in our honoured *capital, and learn* their much obedience.'"

view. The king is evidently speaking of what he had done to those whom he was addressing. 予惟率肆矜爾＝予惟循商故事，矜恤爾而已. The meaning is that the king hoped their removal to Lŏ would lead them to virtue and loyalty, so that it was really an act of kindness to them. While they were vicious and disaffected, it would be contrary to the will of Heaven to confer dignities and offices on them.

P. 21. *The officers and people of Yin had really been dealt with very leniently.* This par. refers to the time three or four years back, when the rebellion of Woo-kăng, supported by the king's uncles, had been disposed of. The wild tribe of the Yen—a district corresponding to the pres. dis. of K'ëuh-fow, dep. of Yen-chow, Shan-tung—had joined with the insurgents. We hear of them again in Bk. XVIII., as in arms a second time against the new dynasty. The crushing of the Yen had been the last act in the suppression of the rebellion. When that was accomplished, the duke of Chow—for he was the agent, though the thing is here ascribed to the king, after the manner of 'The Great Announcement' —had time to deal with the people of Yin. Our natural conclusion from this par. is certainly that many of the people of Yin were then removed to Lŏ. 降爾四國民命--降 is here used in the sense of 減, 'to diminish,' 'to mitigate.' Their lives were all forfeited; but the king spared their lives, and only banished them. We have not met with this usage of the character before; but it is now quite common in legal language. Gan-kwŏ took 民命 as equivalent to 君. Ying-tă says:—民以君爲命，故民命謂君也, 'The people consider their sovereign to be their life, and hence the sovereign is designated "the life of the people."' The meaning then is—'I made an end of the rulers of your four kingdoms, thereby executing on them the punishment appointed by Heaven.' But this is very far-fetched, and unwarranted. Nor is the view given by Këang Shing more likely.—'I sent down lessons and commands for you, the people of the four kingdoms, and carried clearly out the punishment appointed by Heaven upon their rulers.' By the 'four kingdoms' we are to understand the 'imperial domain of Yin,' which had been portioned out to Woo-kăng, and three of the king's uncles;—see the note on Bk. VI., p. 12.

移爾遐逖＝移爾遠居于洛. Both 遐 and 逖 are defined by 遠 'far,' 'distant.' 比事臣我宗多遜，--宗 is here taken as ＝宗周, 'the honoured Chow,' a name given to Haou, the old capital of Chow, in distinction from the new capital of 成周 at Lŏ. It was in the duke's mind, in prospect of the new capital, that the old trusted ministers of Chow should remove to it, when the influence of their character and principles would affect beneficially the adherents of the old dynasty brought there into contact with them. The translation is after the 'Daily Explanation:'—移爾遠居於洛，使爾得密邇王室，親比臣子，遠離頑梗之俗，漸摩遜順之風. There is little to choose between this and the following ingenious exposition by Choo He:—以親我，事我，臣我，宗法我周，濟濟多遜之盛, 'that ye might be near us, serve us, and be ministers to us, honouring and imitating the rich and full obedience of our Chow.'

曰、告爾殷多士、今予
惟不爾殺、予惟時命
有申、今朕作大邑于
兹洛、予惟四方罔攸
賓、亦惟爾多士攸服
奔走臣我多遜。○
乃尚有爾土、爾乃尚
宅爾宅、○爾克敬、天
惟畀矜爾、爾不克敬
爾不啻不有爾土予

22　"The king says, 'I declare to you, ye numerous officers of Yin, —now I have not put you to death, and therefore I repeat to you my charge again. I have built this great city here in Lŏ, considering that there was no other place in which to receive my guests from the four quarters, and also that you, ye numerous officers, might here with zealous activity, perform the part of ministers to us with
23　much obedience. You have still here I may say your grounds, and here you may still rest in your duties and dwellings.
24　　If you can reverently obey, Heaven will favour and compassionate you. If you cannot reverently obey, you will not only not have

Pp. 22, 23. *The king again repeats his objects in building Lŏ, and impresses on the officers of Yin the kindness with which he was treating them.*
22. 予惟不至有申,—申=重, 'to repeat.' They had received one charge on their first removal; the present address might be considered a repetition of it. 今朕 作大邑于兹洛,—possibly the 'great city' here may be the 王城, or imperial city, in connection with the building of which we have seen that the duke of Shaou was specially despatched. Though 'the lower capital,' where the officers of Yin were located may have been previously built, at least in part, the design intended by it could not be realized, until the other was likewise prepared. 四方罔攸 賓=四方諸侯岡有賓禮之 所. The king's 'guests' were the princes coming to court from all the States. 攸服 奔走,—'where ye might serve, hasting and running.' 23. Gan-kwŏ took this par. as a promise.—'If you learn obedience to us, and

become loyal subjects, then you will still have here your grounds,' &c. But it is better to take the language as historical, and showing how generously they *had been* treated. 尚=庶幾, here = our 'I may say.' 幹=事, 'business,' 'duties.' 止=居, 'dwellings,' 'settlements.'

Ch. IV. Pp. 24—26. Let the officers of Yin acquiesce in their lot, and they may have a happy and prosperous future in Lŏ. If they refuse to do so, they will bring on themselves utter ruin. 24. 爾克敬,—'If you can reverence.' We are not to find in 敬 here all that is denoted by 'the virtue of reverence' in Bk. XIII., but a standing in awe and submission to what had happened to them. 畀矜爾,—each of these verbs 畀 and 矜 has a meaning of its own. We are not to think that they run into each other. As Lin Che-k'e has it, 天 有以畀予之,矜憐之. 必 啻=但, 'only.' 致天之罰于 爾 躬,—compare 致天罰 in p. 21. The

言，爾攸居。　曰，時予乃或　遷。○王曰又　子乃興從爾　于茲洛爾小　厥有幹有年　邑，繼爾居爾　爾惟時宅爾　于爾躬。○今　亦致天之罰

廿六節　廿五節

your lands, but I will also carry to the utmost Heaven's inflictions
25 on your persons. Now you may here dwell in your villages,
and perpetuate your families; you may pursue your occupations
and enjoy your years in this Lǒ; your children also will prosper:
—*all* from your being removed here.'"

26　"The king says,—; and again he says, 'Whatsoever I have
spoken, is all on account of *my anxiety about* your residence *here*.'"

punishment of Heaven there spoken of had only deprived them of their grounds in Yin; this would deprive them of their lives.　25.
今爾惟時 (=是) 宅爾邑,—the 爾, prefixed to 邑, indicates, I think, that we are not to suppose that Lǒ is intended by 邑, —which, however, is the view of Lin Che-k'e. Ts'ae says that we are to understand the 'villages' formed by the families around every four 井, or space of 3,600 *mow*. Every family, in connection with such a settlement, had its five *mow*, for houses and private garden,—2½ in the field, and 2½ in the associate village; see Mencius, I., Pt. I., iii., 4. Taking this view, we must understand that the king is not addressing here the *officers* of Yin merely, but the body of the people who had been removed from their old settlements.　居 will then signify the homes of the several families belonging to each village.　幹,—as in p. 23.　從爾遷, —Gan-kwǒ takes this, as an additional predicate about their descendants, and makes 興從爾遷 = 起從汝化而遷善, 'will arise, and following your transformation also become good.' It is much better to take the clause as I have done,—a view first proposed by Soo Shih.

P. 26.　After the 王曰 there must be something wanting. Compare the two last paragraphs of Book XVIII. There is probably something lost also after the 又曰. We cannot take 時 as meaning 'now;' it must be =是, and would hardly commence a sentence. 爾攸居 is also elliptical. Ts'ae brings out the meaning thus:—時我或有所言, 皆以爾之所居止爲念也. Këang Shing makes the clause hortatory:—今我乃有言告汝, 汝其安所居哉. This is not so likely.

THE BOOKS OF CHOW.

BOOK. XV.   AGAINST LUXURIOUS EASE.

周公曰、嗚呼、君子
公呼所
曰、君其
[一節] [二節]

無逸○先知稼穑之
逸知艱
○稼難、乃逸、

則難稽先無子
知乃之知逸所
小逸、艱稼○其

1   I. The duke of Chow said, "Oh! the superior man rests in this,
2   —that he will have no luxurious ease. He first understands the
painful toil of sowing and reaping, how it conducts to ease, and thus

THE NAME OF THE BOOK.—無逸, 'Avoiding Luxurious Ease.' These words are taken from the first paragraph. They are the keynote to the whole Book, and hence are rightly taken to designate it. Gaubil says the characters mean—'*Il ne faut pas se livrer au plaisir.*' Medhurst entitles the Book—'On avoiding luxurious ease.' 逸 and 佚 are used interchangeably. Their primary signification is that of 'idleness;' compare Mencius, VII., Pt. II., xxiv. 1, and IV., Pt. II., xxx. 2. But as the character is used in the Shoo, it does not denote a mere passive idleness, but one in which, while the proper duties are neglected, improper lusts and gratifications may be eagerly sought; see the 'Counsels of Yu,' p. 14; *et al.* Still the idea of the term here is that of 'luxurious or indulgent ease.' 無 is used as the imperative 毋. The Book is found in both the texts. It comes under the division of 訓 or 'Instructions.'

CONTENTS. The prefatory note is simply to the effect that 'the duke of Chow made the *Woo Yih;*' without a word about the time or occasion of it. The general view, which there is no reason to dispute, is that the duke of Chow addressed it to king Ching, soon after he had resigned the government into his hands. That the minister thought it necessary thus to admonish the young sovereign confirms what I have several times urged, that there was between them a measure of dissatisfaction on the one

side and of suspicion on the other. There are six pauses in the course of the address, which is resumed always with a 周公曰嗚呼, 'The duke of Chow said, "Oh!"' A division into seven chapters is thus suggested.

In parr. 1—3, the duke leads the king to find a rule for himself in the laborious toils which devolve on the husbandman. In parr. 4—7, he refers to the long reigns of three of the sovereigns of the Yin dynasty, and the short reigns of others, as illustrating how the blessing of Heaven rests on the diligent sovereign. In parr. 6—11, the example of their own kings, T'ae, Ke, and Wăn is adduced with the same object. In parr. 12, 13, the duke addresses the king personally, and urges him to follow the example of king Wăn and flee from that of Show. In 14, 15, he stimulates him by reference to ancient precedents to adopt his counsels, and shows the evil effects that will follow if he refuse to do so. In parr. 16—18, he shows him by the examples of the good kings of Yin and of king Wăn how he ought to have regard to the opinions of the common people, and gird himself to diligence. The last par. is a single admonition that the king should lay what had been said to heart.

Ch. I. Pp. 1—3. THE GREAT PRINCIPLE, THAT THERE SHOULD BE NO INDULGENT EASE. IT IS ENFORCED BY A REFERENCE TO THE TOILS OF HUSBANDRY, AND THE FREQUENT DEGENERACY OF THE SONS OF THOSE WHO HAVE TOILED

人之依。○相_{三節}
小人厥父母
勤勞稼穡厥
子乃不知
稽之艱難
逸乃諺
否則侮厥父
母曰昔之人_{四節}
無聞知。○周
公曰嗚呼我

3 he understands *the law of* the support of the inferior people. I have observed among the inferior people, that where the parents have diligently laboured in sowing and reaping, their sons *often* do not understand this painful toil, and abandon themselves to ease, and to village slang, and become quite disorderly. Or where they do not do so, they throw contempt on their parents, saying, 'Those old people have heard nothing and know nothing.'"

4 II. The duke of Chow said, "Oh! I have heard that aforetime the emperor of Yin, Chung-tsung, was grave, humble, reverential, and

HARD. 1. 君子所其無逸.—K'ang-shing thought that 君子 here was spoken simply of the ruler (君子止謂在官長者), without any implication of the virtuous character which is commonly denoted by the expression. He must be wrong. The designation is to be taken of 'the man of virtue,' with an application of it implied to such a man in authority. I take 所 as a verb =止. The usage is akin to that in Bk. XIII., p. 16,—王敬作所. 其無 (=毋) 逸 is then under the govt. of 所. Ts'ae, after Leu Tsoo-hëen, gives for the par.—君子以無逸爲所, which brings out the meaning very well. Ch'ing and Gan-kwŏ both put a comma at 所,—which is very harsh. The former says:—君子處位爲政, 其無自逸豫也; and the latter:—君子之道, 所在念德, 其無逸豫. 2. It is as well to take 君子 as the subject of the two 知 here. The meaning would be substantially the same if we supposed the language directly addressed to king Ching, when 先知 would = 'when you first understand.' The only difficulty is with the characters 乃逸. The characters simply show that ease and plenty are a result of the toils of husbandry. Gan-kwŏ attributed a sort of hortatory force to them, and inter-

preted:—稼穡農夫之艱難事, 先知之乃謀逸豫, 'sowing and reaping are the toilsome business of the husbandman. This must first be known, and then plans for ease may be laid.' Soo Shih objected to this that the object of the duke of Chow was to get the king to put away the thought of ease, and it was not likely he would begin to suggest to him the idea of 'planning for ease.' The criticism is subtle, but correct. 'What the inferior people depend on' is their hard toil in the fields. That is the law of their support. Ease comes from it as a matter of course. Ease finds them; they do not seek it. 3. 相小人,—compare 相古先民, Bk. XII., p. 11. 小人,—as in the last par., = 小民. 乃逸乃諺, 既誕 = 乃縱逸自恣, 乃習俚巷鄙語, 既又誕妄, 無所不至, as in the translation. 誕 is 'a proverb,' 'a saying.' Gan-kwŏ understands by it 'coarse language,' taking it=唁;—see Ana. XI., xvi., 4. Këang Shing reads—乃佚, 乃憲, 既誕不則, 'they become idle, and indulge in pleasure, behave rudely, and are lawless.' I prefer the received text and interpretation. 昔之人=古老之人, as I have translated it; or it may mean—'our predecessors.'

Ch. II. Pp. 4—7. THE ADVANTAGES OF AVOIDING SELF-INDULGENT EASE SHOWN BY THE HISTORY OF SEVERAL OF THE SOVEREIGNS

嘉言陰人時有肆治嚴聞
靖言三作舊五中民恭曰、
殷言年其勞年宗祗寅昔
邦乃不卽于。之懼畏在
至雍言位外○享不天殷
于不其乃爰其國敢命王
小敢惟或暨在七荒自中
大、荒不亮小高十寧、度、宗
　寧、　　　宗　　　

五節

fearful.　He measured himself with reference to the appointment of Heaven, and cherished a reverent apprehension in governing the people, not daring to indulge in useless ease.　It was thus that Chung-tsung enjoyed the throne for seventy and five years.

5　　"If we come to the time of Kaou-tsung, he toiled at first away from the court, and was among the inferior people.　When he came to the throne, it may be said that, while he was in the mourning shed, for three years he did not speak.　*Afterwards* he was *still inclined* not to speak; but when he did speak, his words were full of harmonious *wisdom.*　He did not dare to indulge in useless and easy

OF THE YIN DYNASTY.　　4.　*The case of Chung-tsung.*　昔在殷王中宗—the 在 here and the following parr. = 'in the case of.' 中宗 was the sacrificial title (廟號) of the emperor described.　See the note on T'ae-mow, p. 220.　嚴 and 恭 are said to express the king's reverence as shown externally, while 寅 and 畏 describe his inward feeling of it. 天命自度,—by 天命 Ts'ae and many others understand 天理, 'Heavenly principles,' so that the meaning of the clause is, 'He measured (= defined the rules of life 'for) himself in accordance with heavenly principles.'　But this is needless refining.　The meaning rather is that Kaou-tsung felt that 'the appointment of Heaven,' which placed him upon the throne, brought with it certain duties and responsibilities, on his discharge of which depended his retaining Heaven's favour; he therefore measured himself to know whether his course was what it ought to be.　Woo Ch'ing brings this meaning out very clearly:—天命在躬, 易失難保, 則惟恐不能永保天命也.　I have

said on p. 220 that we might doubt the length of Chung-tsung's reign, if it were not thus guaranteed by the duke of Chow.　Two brothers are said to have preceded him on the throne;—first Yung-ke, who reigned 12 years, and before him Sëaou-këă, who reigned 17 years.　If Chung-tsung were born in the same year that their father died, B.C. 1664, he must have been 30 when he succeeded to the empire.

5.　*The case of Kaou-tsung.*　See Book. VIII., of the last Part.　其在高宗時,—the 時 should evidently be read with the first clause, but it is difficult to explain it, or to account for it.　舊勞于外, 爰暨小人,—comp. 'The Charge to Yuĕ,' Pt. iii., p. 1.　The old interpreters took 舊=久, 'long.'　It is better to take it as = 'at first,' *i.e.,* while his father was alive (當其爲太子之時).　爰=於是; and 暨=與, 'with.'　The text must be supplemented:—於是與小人同其事.　It is perplexing to find 暨 used as a preposition, and not simply a conjunction.　作其卽位,—in order

無時或怨肆高
宗之享國五十
有九年。○其在
祖甲、不義惟王、
舊爲小人作其
卽位、爰知小人
之依、能保惠于
庶民、不敢侮鰥
寡、肆祖甲之享
國三十有三年。

六節

ways, but admirably and tranquilly presided over the empire of Yin, till in all its States, great and small, there was not a single murmur. It was thus that Kaou-tsung enjoyed the throne for fifty and nine years.

6　"In the case of Tsoo-këǎ, he would not unrighteously be emperor, and was at first one of the inferior people. When he came to the throne, he understood *the law of* the support of the inferior people, and was able to exercise a protecting kindness towards their masses, and did not dare to treat with contempt the widower and widows. Thus it was that Tsoo-këǎ enjoyed the throne for thirty and three years.

to bring out the meaning of 作, Woo Ch'ing says:—起自民間，卽天子位, 'He arose from among the people, and ascended the imperial seat.' But in trying to account for the 作, he overlooks the 其 作 has here merely a conjunctive force, 一 及. 乃 或亮陰，三年不言,—see 'The Charge to Yuĕ,' Pt. i., p. 1. I have said there that we are not to suppose that the emperor during the years of mourning maintained a total silence, but only kept from speaking on governmental matters. This is perhaps indicated by the 或. 其惟不言，言乃雍. —I have translated this according to the account which we have in the beginning of 'The Charge to Yue.' K'ang-shing supposed that the duke is still speaking of Kaou-tsung during the time of mourning; but that is very unlikely. The history is evidently being carried on and forward. 嘉靖殷邦,—'he made the States—the empire—of Yin admirable and tranquil,' *i.e.*, he hushed all jarrings, and produced great prosperity.

6. *The case of Tsoo-këǎ.* Tsoo-këǎ was the son of Kaou-tsung. I have mentioned on p. 269 that Sze-ma Ts'een says that Tsoo-këǎ was lewd and disorderly. Similar testimony is found in the 國語. Having respect to these statements, Gan-kwŏ could not admit that the emperor spoken of here was the son of Kaou-tsung, and maintained that we were to find him in T'ae-këǎ, the grandson of T'ang. But from Chung-tsung the duke comes on to Kaou-tsung, approaching to the rise of their own dynasty of Chow;—how unnatural the address would be if he were now to go back to the beginning of the times of Yin! Moreover, the son of Kaou-tsung was styled Tsoo-këǎ, while the grandson of T'ang was called T'ae-këǎ. Nor does the confinement of T'ae-këǎ for a season by E Yin for his misdeeds sufficiently answer the requirements of the text,—不義惟王，舊爲 小人，知小人之依. Gan-kwŏ says:—湯孫太甲，爲王不義 久爲小人之行，伊尹放之 桐, 'Tae-kea, being king, proved unrighteous. He had long displayed the conduct of an unworthy person, and E Yin confined him in T'ung.' But the meaning thus given to 小人, which has already occurred three times in the address, and always with the signification of 'the inferior people,' without any implication of unworthiness, must be rejected. On every ground we must conclude that the sovereign spoken of was not the grandson of T'ang. He was the son of Kaou-tsung. K'ang-shing has a story that Woo-ting wanted to disinherit Tsoo-këǎ's elder brother in favour of him, and that Tsoo-këǎ, thinking such a proceeding would be unrighteous, withdrew and lived for a time among

惟我周太王王季、　周公曰、嗚呼厥亦　六年、或四三年。○　年、或七八年、或五　亦罔或克壽、或十　樂之從、自時厥後、　聞小人之勞、惟耽　知稼穡之艱難、　生則逸、生則逸、不　○自時厥後立王、

七節　八節

7　"The emperors which arose after these all their life-time enjoyed ease. From their birth enjoying ease, they did not understand the painful toil of sowing and reaping, nor hear of the hard labours of the inferior people. They only sought after excessive pleasures, and so not one of them enjoyed the throne for a long period. They continued for ten years, for seven or eight, for five or six, or *perhaps only* for three or four."

8　III. The duke of Chow said, "Oh! there likewise were king T'ae and king Ke of our own Chow, who attained to humility and reverential

the common people (祖甲以爲不義、逃於民間). Ts'ae adduces this as the ground of the language in the text,—不義惟王、舊爲小人. Ying-tă and Maou K'e-ling after him object to this account, that no authority can be adduced for it, and that there is no evidence of Kĕa's elder brother being unworthy, while it is defaming a good king like Woo-ting to say that he wanted to disinherit his eldest son in favour of a younger brother. K'e-ling, therefore, supposes that Tsoo-kĕa, in his youth, had been dissolute, and consorted with unworthy associates (不義惟王、舊爲小人、言祖甲少行不義、爰及非類). But here is the meaning of 小人 to which I have objected above. His explanation is as much an hypothesis as that of K'ang-shing, whom he vehemently condemns. The truth is,—while it is plain that it is the son of Kaou-tsung of whom the duke of Chow speaks, we do not know enough of that emperor to explain all his language. Gan-kwŏ for 保惠于庶民 gives 安順於庶民. It is better to take 惠＝愛, as in the translation.

7. *The other emperors of Yin.* 生則逸、—'being born, they had ease.' The 'Daily

Explanation' says:—身爲帝王之裔、長于宮禁之中、生則止見安逸耳. Kĕang Shing says ingeniously that the repetition of 生則逸 indicates that thus it was with one emperor and another. It is as well, however, to construe as I have done. 惟耽樂之從—another reading for this is 惟湛樂是從; but the meaning is the same. 克壽、—'could come to old age;' but the sequel shows that he is speaking of the occupancy of the throne. A long life and a long reign, however, would generally go together. It is to be observed that the reigns of the other sovereigns of Yin were not so short as this says. There were six emperors after Tsoo-kĕa, of whom one reigned 21 years; a second, 23; and the tyrant Show himself, 28. Between Kaou-tsung and Chung-tsung, again, there were 12 reigns, of which only 2 were under ten years.

Ch. III. Pp. 8—11. THE DUKE DIRECTS THE KING'S ATTENTION TO THE PRINCES OF THEIR OWN DYNASTY,—TO KINGS T'AE AND KE, AND ESPECIALLY TO KING WAN. 8. 厥亦云云、—the 厥 corresponds to the 其 with which pp. 5 and 6 begin. 太王、王季、—see Bk. III., p. 5; and the notes in pp. 268, 269.

邦惟正之供　盤于遊田以庶　民○文王以庶　暇食用咸和萬　于日中昃不遑　鮮鰥寡自朝至　恭懷保小民惠　田功○徽柔懿　王卑服卽康功　克自抑畏○文

十一節

十節

九節

9　awe.　King Wăn dressed meanly, and gave himself to the work of
10　tranquillization, and to that of husbandry. Admirably mild and beautifully humble, he cherished and protected the inferior people, and
showed a fostering kindness to the widower and widows. From
morning to midday, and from midday to sundown, he did not allow
himself time to eat;—thus seeking to secure the happy harmony
11　of the myriads of the people. King Wăn did not dare to go to any
excess in his excursions or his hunting, and from the various States
he received only the correct amount of contribution. He received

克自抑畏,—抑 means 'to press hard,' and 'to repress.' Hence 自抑 = 'to be humble.'　9. 文王卑服,—comp. what Confucius says about Yu, Ana, VIII., xxi. 卽 = 就, 'to approach to;' here == 'to apply to.'　康功 = 安民之功, 'services giving repose to the people.'　田功 = 養民之功, 'services giving nourishment to the people.' See Mencius, I., Pt. II., v., 3. Këang Shing takes 服 = 事, so that the par. would have a very unworthy meaning,—'king Wăn occupied himself with mean affairs,' &c.　10. 徽柔懿恭,—徽 and 懿 are both defined by 美, 'admirable,' 'excellent.' If Wăn's mildness, it is said, had not been 徽, it would have been weakness; and if his respectfulness had not been 懿, it would have been hypocrisy (足恭之恭; see Ana. V., xxi.).　惠鮮鰥寡,—惠鮮 is a difficult expression, and Këang Shing reads 惠于鰥寡, which is much simpler. Ts'ae, adhering to the meaning of 鮮 as 'fresh, with no taint of corruption,' says that 'widowers and widows hang their heads down, all out of spirits; and when you give them an alms, you make them as it were become alive.' This is very

strained. We must take 鮮 = 善, a meaning which it sometimes has. Gan-kwŏ seems to miss the meaning altogether, and construes absurdly.　昃 is the sun declining in the west. 自朝至于日中昃 = 自朝至于日之中, 自中至于日之昃.　不遑暇食,—both 遑 and 暇 signify 'leisure.' Ying-tă observes that in their conjunction we have an instance of the duplicated expressions (複語) of the ancients.

11. 盤于遊田,—we met with 盤遊無度 in Pt. III., Bk. III., p. 1, where 盤 has the sense of 樂, 'pleasure.' Here, followed by 于, however, the meaning of 盤桓不止, 'incessant movement,' is to be preferred. On the 遊 see Mencius, I., Pt. II., iv., 5. There were the proper seasons both for tours of inspection and hunting expeditions. Wăn made them both at those seasons, and did not protract them beyond the regulated length of time.　田 = 畋, 'to hunt.'　以庶邦惟正之供,—Ts'ae, after earlier critics of the Sung dynasty, takes this as = 於常貢正數之外, 無橫斂也, 'beyond the correct amount of the regular tribute, he made no oppressive exactions;' and he adds that if Wăn dealt in

王受命惟中身、厥

享國五十年。○周十二節

公曰鳴呼繼自今、

嗣王則其無淫于

觀于逸于遊于田、

以萬民惟正之供。

○無皇曰今日耽十三節

樂乃非民攸訓、非

天攸若時人丕則

有愆無若殷王受

the appointment *of Heaven* in the middle of his life, and enjoyed the throne for fifty years."

12   IV. The duke of Chow said, "Oh! from this time forward, do you who have succeeded to the throne imitate his avoiding of excess in his sights, his ease, his excursions, his hunting; and from the myriads

13 of the people receive only the correct amount of contribution. Do not allow yourself the leisure to say, 'To-day I will indulge in pleasure.' This is not holding out a lesson to the people, nor the way to secure the favour of Heaven. Men will on the contrary

this way with the States which acknowledged his authority as chief of the West, it is easy to see how gentle was his taxation of his own people. Gan-kwŏ interpreted the clause quite differently:—以眾國所取法則,當以正道供待之, which Ying-tă expounds, 'He considered that it was from him that all the States had to take their pattern, so that his proper business was to regulate himself with a right heart, to minister the treatment to them.' This is hardly intelligible; and Këang Shing would gladly reduce the whole clause to 唯政之恭, 'and reverently attended to the business of the govt.,' from a passage in the 國語, 楚語 上, which even Yuh-tsae says ought not to be credited in the case;—see 段大令古文尙書撰異, *in loc.*

受命惟中身,—Wăn's 'receiving the appointment' here can only be understood of his succeeding to his father as one of the princes of the empire. Gan-kwŏ observes that Wăn died at the age of 97, and as he was 47 when he came to the principality of Chow, the expression 中身, 'middle of his life,' must not be pressed.

Ch. IV. Pp. 12, 13. THE DUKE URGES KING CHING TO MAKE THE MAXIM OF 'NO DAY FOR IDLENESS' THE RULE OF HIS LIFE, AND TO ESCHEW THE EXAMPLE OF SHOW.   12. Gan-

kwŏ points 繼自今嗣王,云云, and understands the duke to have in view all future sovereigns of the House of Chow (繼從今已往嗣世之王,皆戒之), so that the 則 that follows is merely a particle. I prefer, however, the construction of Ts‘ae, which appears in the translation. Acc. to it, the words are addressed to king Ching, though there is of course a lesson in them for future kings as well; 則 is a verb, = 法, 'to imitate,' and the 其 which follows it refers to king Wăn. 觀 = our 'sight-seeing.'   以萬民 takes here the place of 以庶邦, being appropriate to the case of the emperor, whereas the other expression was descriptive of Wăn as the 'Chief of the West,' the Head of a portion of the States.

Këang Shing gives for the par.—鳴呼繼自今嗣王其毋淫于酒,毋佚于游田,維正之共, which appears in one of the chapters of 'The Books of Han,' and was perhaps the reading of Fuh-shang.   13. 皇 must be taken as = the 遑 of par. 10.   非民攸訓 = 非民之所以爲教, 'is not what the people should take as their lesson.   天攸若 =

訓厥張民保猶聞公酒之
之不爲無惠胥曰德迷
乃聽幻或訓古哉亂
變人。○胥教告之。○酗
亂乃此十五節譸誨胥人、嗚于
亂人乃壽誨胥古呼十四節
                      我周

greatly imitate you, and practise evil.   Become not like Show, the
king of Yin, who went quite astray, and was abandoned to the
practice of drunkenness."

14   V. The duke of Chow said, " Oh ! I have heard it said that, in the
case of the ancients, *their ministers discharged their functions* in warning
and admonishing them, in protecting and *loving* them, in teaching
and instructing them; and among their people there was hardly
one who would impose on them by extravagant language or deceiv-
15 ing tricks.   If you will not listen to this *and profit by it*, your
ministers will imitate you, and so the correct laws of the former

天之所順, 'what Heaven will accord
with.'   時＝是, corresponding to the 乃
above.   時人丕則有愆＝是人
大則效之, 斯有愆尤矣.
酗于酒德,—comp. 'The Viscount of
Wei,' p. 1.   It is very evident that 德 may be
spoken of *vice* as well as of *virtue*.

Ch. V. Pp. 14, 15.   THE DUKE URGES THE
KING TO RECEIVE GOOD ADVICE, REFERRING TO
THE CASE OF ANCIENT SOVEREIGNS WHO HAD
DONE SO, AND POINTING OUT THE EVIL CONSE-
QUENCES OF A CONTRARY COURSE.   14. By
古之人 we are probably to understand the
three sovereigns of Yin celebrated in the second
chapter, and king Wăn.   猶胥至教
誨,—we have to understand 其臣, 'their
ministers,' as the subject of the verbs 訓告,
&c.   The force of the 猶, 'still,' is thus brought
out :—'The virtue of those ancient sovereigns
was complete.   It seemed as if they needed no
assistance; but *still* their ministers did not cease
to instruct them,' &c.   胥＝相.   It indicates
the mutual intercourse of sovereigns and ministers, while we must restrict the action of the
verbs to the latter.   民無或, 云云,
—this shows the result throughout the empire,
when those good sovereigns were guided and
supported in such a way by their ministers.
The dict. explains 譸張 together by 誑, 'to

lie,' 'to deceive.'   This is plainly the meaning,
but I do not know that 張 by itself is ever
found with this signification.   幻 is defined by
變名易實以眩觀, 'changing names
and transposing realities, to deceive the sight.'
In Fuh-shang's text this clause appears to have
wanted the commencing 民, and the 胥
after 或.   15.   An application of the statements in the prec. par. is here made to king
Ching.   If he will not listen to them, 人乃
訓之(＝人乃法則之), 'men will
learn of him.'   The 'men' intended are his
ministers.   正刑＝正法, 'correct
laws.'   Ts'ae instances the light punishments and
light taxation, which were the rule with ancient
good sovereigns, and which would be superseded
by severe penalties, and heavy exactions.
至于小大 is to be joined with 正刑.
民否,—'the people disapproving.'   The
disallowing and changing the laws which were
favourable to them will awaken their disaffection and displeasure.   Hostile feelings will be
cherished in their hearts, and turn to curses on
their tongues.   詛祝,—these two terms
together ＝ our 'to curse.'   Ying-tă says that
'to ask the spirits to make miserable is called
詛; and to announce one's thoughts to the
spirits by words is called 祝' (請神加殃
謂之詛, 以言告神謂之祝).
Ts'ae and many others explain the par. in

先王之正刑、至于小
大民否則厥心違怨
否則厥口詛祝。○周 十六節
公曰嗚呼自殷王中
宗及高宗及祖甲、及
我周文王茲四人迪
哲。○厥或告之曰小 十七節
人怨汝詈汝則皇自
敬德厥愆曰朕之愆
允若時不啻不敢含

kings, both small and great, will be changed and disordered. The people blaming you will disobey and rebel in their hearts;—yea, they will curse you with their mouths."

16　VI. The duke of Chow said, "Oh! those kings of Yin, Chung-tsung, Kaou-tsung, and Tsoo-kёa, with king Wăn of our Chow,—these
17　four men carried their knowledge into practice. If it was told them—'The inferior people murmur against you, and revile you,' then they paid great and reverent attention to their conduct; and with reference to the faults imputed to them they said, 'Our faults are really so.' *They acted thus*, not simply not daring to cherish

the way thus exhibited; and I don't think we can do better with it. Woo Ch'ing, taking 此厥 不聽 as Ts'ae does, gives for the rest a construction of his own, and makes the meaning—'If you will not hearken to this and profit by it, then men will persuade you to change and confuse the correct laws of the former kings. Those laws were very favourable to the people; and when they are so changed, the people, small and great, will cherish, some of them, a rebellious resentment in their hearts, while others will proceed to curse you with their mouths.' (成則王于小矣, 此古人…… 不聽信于 道說以先王之 法先變之則怨 變亂甚于心者矣, 王人之正一大或 于乃民或有詛 之變有違祝于口者矣)。 Këang Shing reads 此厥不聖人乃 亂正刑云云,='When the ancient sovereigns were not sage, then men led them away to change,' &c., according to the view of Woo Ch'ing. He is compelled, however, to doubt

the genuineness of the 民; and indeed, if 民 be genuine here (and there is no evidence to the contrary), the same character in the prec. par. cannot be assailed. The reading of 聖, moreover, and consequent making this chapter terminate without any application to king Ching, takes from its connection with the rest of the Book.

Ch. VI. Pp. 16—18. THE DUKE PRESSES ON THE KING THE DUTY OF LISTENING TO ADVICE BY THE EXAMPLE OF THE GOOD SOVE-REIGNS WHOM HE HAS MENTIONED, AND POINTS OUT AGAIN THE EVIL CONSEQUENCES OF A CONTRARY COURSE. 16. 迪哲,—'trod in the way of their knowledge.' Ts'ae says this is what Mencius calls 'the richest fruit of wisdom,—the knowing, and not putting the knowledge away' (智之寶, 知而弗去 是 也; see IV., Pt. I., xxvii. 2.). 17. 皇自 敬德—皇=大, 'great,' 'greatly.' We may take 敬德 as in Bk. XII., or more generally, as I have done in the translation. Ying-tă makes the clause=增修善政, 'they increasingly cultivated good government.'

怒。○此厥不聽人
乃或譸張爲幻曰
小人怨汝詈汝則
信之則若時不永
念厥辟不寬綽厥
心亂罰無罪殺無
辜怨有同是叢于
厥身。○周公曰嗚
呼嗣王其監于茲。

18 anger. If you will not listen to this *and profit by it*, when men with extravagant language and deceptive tricks say to you, 'The inferior people are murmuring against you and reviling you,' you will believe them. Doing this, you will not be always thinking of your princely duties, and will not cultivate a large and generous heart. You will confusedly punish the crimeless, and put the innocent to death. There will be a general murmuring, which will be concentrated upon your person."

19   VII. The duke of Chow said, "Oh! you king, who have succeeded to the throne, make a study of these things."

厥愆＝于其所誣毀之愆, 'in the case of the faults which were wrongly imputed to them.'   18. This is the application of the prec. two parr., as par. 15 was an application of 14. Këang Shing cannot adopt 聖 here in the first clause as in p. 15, not having the precedent which he there had. Still he says we ought to read 聖; but I cannot think so. The duke of Chow would not have put the case that the worthies he celebrated could have behaved themselves so unworthily. At 則若是 the transition is abrupt, but the meaning is plain. 不永念厥 辟＝不能永念其爲君之 道, as in the translation. This is much better than, with Këang Shing, to read 辟 as *p'eih*, and understand the expression as ＝不能 引咎自責也, 'they could not have acknowledged the blame, and reproved themselves.' 怨有同,—'resentments will be the same,' *i.e.*, people may receive injuries of different kinds, but all will agree in the feeling of injury and resentment.

Ch. VII. P. 19. *Concluding exhortation, that the king should think of all that had been said to him, and use the address as a light to guide him to safety and excellence,—as a beacon to warn him from what was evil and dangerous.*

THE BOOKS OF CHOW.

BOOK XVI. PRINCE SHIH.

周 命、旣 于 天 ○ 曰、周 一節
旣 我 墜 殷、降 弗 君 公 君奭
受、有 厥 殷、喪 二節 奭。若 二節
愛、 有 厥 殷、喪 弔、奭。若

1 I. The duke of Chow spake to the following effect, " Prince Shih,
2 Heaven, unpitying, sent down ruin on Yin ; Yin has lost its appointment, and the princes of our Chow have received it.   I do not dare,
however, to say, as if I knew it, 'The foundation will ever truly

THE NAME OF THE BOOK.—君奭, 'Prince
Shih.' With these words the Book begins,
and they are taken to be its designation. Shih
was the name of the duke of Shaou; see on the
title of Book XII. It was to him that the
address or announcement here preserved was
delivered, so that his name is not an inappropriate designation for it. The Book is found
in both the texts.

CONTENTS. Ts'ae says that the duke of
Shaou had announced his purpose to retire
from office on account of his age, when the duke
of Chow persuaded him to remain at his post;
and the reasons which he set before him were
recorded to form this Book. If this was the
design of the duke of Chow, he was a master
of the art of veiling his thoughts with a cloud
of words. There are expressions which may be
taken, indeed, as intimating a wish that the
prince Shih should continue at court, but some
violence has to be put upon them.

The prefatory notice is to the effect that,
when the two dukes were acting as chief ministers to king Ching, the duke of Chow was
'not pleased' (不 悅; see p. 11), and the
duke of Chow made the 'Prince Shih.' This
expression—'not pleased'—has wonderfully
vexed the ingenuity of the critics. It is of no
use adducing their various explanations of it,
for there is nothing in the Book to indicate the
existence of such a feeling in Shih's mind. If

he was really entertaining such a feeling from
any cause, and had in consequence sought leave
to withdraw from public life, the duke of Chow
thought it his best plan to make no open
reference to those delicate points.

The two principal ideas in the address are—
that the favour of Heaven can only be permanently secured for a dynasty by the virtue of
its sovereigns; and that that virtue is secured
mainly by the counsels and help of virtuous
ministers. The ablest sovereigns of Shang are
mentioned, and the ministers by whose aid it
was, in a great measure, that they became what
they were. The cases of Wăn and Woo of
their own dynasty, similarly aided by able men,
are adduced in the same way; and the speaker
adverts to the services which they—the two
dukes—had already rendered to their House
and their sovereign, and insists that they must
go on to the end, and accomplish still greater
things. It may be that he is all the while
combating some suspicion of himself in the
mind of prince Shih, and rebuking some purpose which Shih had formed to abandon his
post at the helm of the State; but this is only
matter of inference, and does not by any means
clearly appear. It will be seen that I have,
for convenience' sake, arranged the three and
twenty paragraphs in four chapters.

Ch. I. Pp. 1—6. CHOW IS FOR THE PRESENT
RAISED BY THE FAVOUR OF HEAVEN TO THE
SOVEREIGNTY OF THE EMPIRE. BUT THAT FA-

尤　天　帝　亦　君　于　敢　天　基　我
違　威　命　不　已　不　知　棐　永　不
惟　越　弗　敢　曰　祥　曰　忱　孚　敢
人　我　敢　寧　時　。　其　我　于　知
在　民　永　于　我　○　終　亦　休　曰
我　罔　遠　上　我　嗚　出　不　若　厥
　　　　念　我　　　呼　　　　　　

三節

abide in prosperity. [If Heaven aid sincerity,—]' Nor do I dare
to say, as if I knew it 'The final end will issue in our misfor-
3 tunes.' Oh! you have said, O prince, 'It depends on ourselves.' I
also do not dare to rest in the favour of God, never forecasting
at a distance the terrors of Heaven in the present time when
there is no murmuring or disobedience among the people;—*the
issue* is with men. Should our present successor to his fathers

YOUR MAY NOT BE PERMANENT. THE DUKE OF
CHOW IS ANXIOUS, AND PRINCE SHIH SHOULD
BE THE SAME, TO SECURE IT BY CULTIVATING THE
VIRTUE OF THE KING. 1. 君奭,—in the
plainness of ancient manners, it is said, when
people were talking together they called each
other by their names. Shih, however, is honoured with the title of 'prince,' which might be
given to him, as he had been invested with the
principality of Yen. See on the name of Bk.
XII. 2. *Chow had superseded Yin in the
possession of the empire, but it could not be known
beforehand how long it would continue.* 弗既
弔,云云,—see Bk. XIV., p. 2. The 既
in the next two clauses has no conjunctive force,
but marks the perfect tense. 我不敢
知至末,—compare Bk. XII., p. 17. That
passage seems to have misled the old interpreters, and still to mislead many of the present
day, as to the meaning of the text. They make
the speaker to have the fate of the past-away
dynasty of Yin before him, and not that of their
existing Chow.—'I do not dare to know and
say, "The House of Yin at its beginning might
have long accorded with prosperous ways,"'
&c. It is plain to me that the speaker has before him the destiny of Chow, which they of
the dynasty must fashion for themselves. Whether it would be long or short must depend on
their conduct. 厥基永孚于休
—'its foundation will for ever be sincerely established in prosperity.' I do not understand
the next clause,—若天棐忱, 'if Heaven
assist the sincere.' Whether we suppose the
speaker to have reference to the past Yin or the
present Chow, these words seem equally out of
place. To say that either dynasty might be

sincerely virtuous, and so be aided by Heaven,
and yet not abide in security, is contrary to
reason, and, to the most strongly cherished
principles of Chinese doctrine. Medhurst read
the words with the next part of the par.—'And
should Heaven aid us in very deed, still I would
not dare positively to affirm that our end would
be entirely the result of misfortune.' But such
a construction is inadmissible. I have put the
clause in the translation as incomplete, and also
within brackets, to intimate that I think it
out of place. 其終出于不祥,
—Këang Shing reads 其崇出于不
詳; but he explains 崇 by 終, and 詳 by
善 (一祥). Another reading, evidently false,
was—道出于不詳.

Pp. 3—5. *The duty of the ministers of Chow
was to do what they could in the present to secure
the permanence of the dynasty.* 3. 嗚呼,
君已曰, 時我,—the simplest way of
explaining these words, is by taking 時我—
是在我而已, 'it—the permanence of
the dyn.—depends on us,' and supposing that
the duke refers to a remark to that effect
made at some former period by Shih. Lin
Che-k'e and others adduce his language in many
parts of his Announcement, e.g. pp. 19, 20, which
they think the duke has in view. This is very
likely. Other methods to try to get a meaning
from the passage are harsh and violent. Gan-
kwŏ, for instance, took the meaning to be—'Oh!
prince, what shall I say? I will say, "You
should approve of my remaining in the govt."'
It is strange that Maou K'e-ling should still
approve of such a construction. Woo Ch'ing

前人恭明
克經歷嗣
其墜命弗
天難諶乃
天命不易
家不知。○
前人光
上下遇佚在
大弗克恭
後嗣子孫

（四節）

prove greatly unable to reverence Heaven and the people, and so bring to an end their glory, could we in our families be ignorant of it?

4 The favour of Heaven is not easily preserved. Heaven is hard to be depended on. Men lose its favouring appointment because they cannot pursue and carry out the reverence and brilliant virtue

takes 君已 in the same way, and then makes 曰時我 = 'But it is my duty to do my utmost to preserve the favour of Heaven.' 我亦至惟人,—the 惟人 with which this part ends corresponds to the 時我 at the beginning, and = 實惟在人而已. 弗永遠念天威越我民罔尤違 is all one clause, and to be read together,—another instance of Choo He's long sentences in the Announcements of the Shoo. Ts'ae explains it by 不永遠念天之威於我民無尤怨督違之時. Këang Shing puts a stop at 威, understanding the duke as giving one reason for his remaining in the govt. that he could not rest in the present favour of Heaven, but must forecast a change in the aspects of Providence. For the same resolution he finds another reason in the words that follow—越我民罔尤違,惟人在 (so he points), = 'That our people may be kept from murmurs and disaffection depends on the right men being there.' To make the language in any way bear this interpretation he is obliged to suppose that 越 is a mistake for 曰. Gan-kwŏ paused at 命, and made 弗永遠念天威越我民罔尤違 an address to Shih, = 'Why do you not think of the terrors of Heaven, and set about affecting and transforming our people, that they may not commit errors and fall into opposition.' Interpretation could hardly be more unlicensed. Nor does he succeed better in what remains of the par. K'e-ling labours in vain to impart some likelihood to his views. 在我後至末—the 在 is used as in the last Book, pp. 5 and 6. By 我後嗣子孫 we must understand king Ching. The

same interpretation must be given of the reading—我嗣事子孫, adopted by Këang Shing from a passage in the 'Books of the Early Han;'—see the 王莽傳上. 恭上下,—Ts'ae understands 'Heaven' to be meant by 上, and 'the people' by 下, so that the expression = 敬天敬民. Others understand 'Heaven and Earth' to be intended. 遇佚前人光 = 過在絕佚墜文武光顯. 在家不知 is to be taken interrogatively, = 可得謂在家不知乎. Ts'ae, holding that the object of the address was to induce the duke of Shaou to abandon his purpose of retirement, takes the question as addressed to him,—'Could you be ignorant of it?' The old interpreters, holding that the speaker is much occupied with vindicating his own remaining in the government, take it in the first person,—'Could I be ignorant.' The best plan seems to be to put it as in the translation. It may thus be applied to either of the dukes; and I believe that the duke of Chow intended it both for himself and his friend. 4, 5. 天命不易,天難諶,—comp. the 'Both possessed Pure Virtue,' p. 2 ; et al. Këang Shing, on the authority mentioned above, reads—命不易,天應棐諶, which may safely be rejected on internal grounds. In interpreting the rest of the par. there is much difference of view. Acc. to that followed in the translation, 前人恭明德 = 前人之恭德與明德, 'the reverent virtue and the brilliant virtue of their forefathers; the former referring to the 恭上下 of the last par., and the latter to the 前人光. This 恭明德 is governed by the

伊尹格于皇天、在

既受命時則有若

奭、我聞在昔成湯

王受命。○公曰、君
（七節）

延、天不庸釋于文

信、我道惟寧王德

子。○又曰、天不可
（六節）

前人光施于我沖

旦、非克有正迪惟

德。○在今子小子
（五節）

5 of their forefathers.　Now I, Tan, being but as a little child, am not able to correct *our king*.　I would simply conduct him to the glory of his forefathers, and make his youth partaker of that."

6　He also said, "Heaven is not to be trusted.　Our course is simply to seek the prolongation of the virtue of the Tranquillizing king, and Heaven will not find occasion to remove its favouring decree which king Wan received."

7　II. The duke said, "Prince Shih, I have heard that of ancient time, when T'ang the Successful had received the favouring decree, he had with him E Yin, making his virtue like that of great Heaven.

verbs 經歷 and 嗣.　Gan-kwǒ, instead of construing the passage thus, put a stop at 歷, and read on the conclusion with the first part of the 5th par.—嗣前人恭明德在今子小子旦 'To continue the reverent and brilliant virtue of our forefathers rests now with me the little child Tan.' Këang Shing has nearly the same punctuation. After all this, no two agree in explaining the former portion—乃其 (K. S. omits this 其) 墜命弗克經歷. It will suffice to mention the view of K'e-ling:—夫天之墜命者,以其不能有經歷人, 'now Heaven lets its favouring decree fall to the ground, because they cannot have men of experience!'　For 非克有正 云, the 'Daily Explanation' gives:—

云真吾以沖治于／有君前子民遏／格也人使知佚／心所光其所前／之孜大上經人／術致德而歷之／可啟付天不光／以迪天而耳／我匡我惟至／之正者我而／非克有正

P. 6.　*The favour of Heaven being so uncertain, the way to secure it is by perpetuating the virtue of king Woo.*　We are to understand king Woo by 'The Tranquillizing king,'—see on Bk. VII., p. 3. Ts'ae expands the text very clearly:—天固不可信,然在我之道,惟以延長武王之德,使天不容捨文王所受之命也.

Ch. II. Pp. 7—10.　WHAT BENEFITS WERE DERIVED DURING THE TIME OF YIN FROM THE GREAT AND ABLE MINISTERS WHO LIVED IN DIFFERENT REIGNS.　IT WAS FOR PRINCE SHIH IN HIS TIME TO SERVE IN THE SAME WAY THE DYNASTY OF CHOW.　7. *The most distinguished ministers of Yin, and the emperors under whom they flourished.*　我聞至皇天,—the 若 prefixed to all the names = 'a man like,' yet not implying any other besides the minister thus pointed out.　伊尹,—see the first introductory note on 'The Instructions of E.'　格于皇天,—see 'The Charge to Yuě,' Pt. iii., p. 10.　在太甲至保衡,—see on 'The T'ae-këa,' Pt. i. p. 1, and 'The Charge to Yuě,' Pt. iii., p. 10.　The duke of Chow here calls E Yin by his name or title, with evident reference to the beginning of the 'T'ae-këa,'　太戊至王家

有殷故殷禮陟　惟茲有陳保父　有若甘盤。○〔八節〕　賢在武丁時則　乙時則有若巫　咸父王家在祖　屜格于上帝巫　則有若伊陟臣　保衡在太戊時　太甲時則有若

T'ae-kĕă, *again*, had Paou-hăng. T'ae-mow had E Chih and Chin Hoo, through whom his virtue was made to affect God; he had *also* Woo Heen, who regulated the royal House. Tsoo-yih had Woo 8 Heen. Woo-ting had Kan Pwan. These *ministers* carried out their principles, and effected their arrangements, preserving and regulating the empire of Yin, so that, while its ceremonies lasted, *those sove-*

—see the notices 22 and 23 in the Confucian preface. We may assume that in this passage the duke of Chow had before him the Books of Shang mentioned in those notices, which are now lost. If we had them, we should find the expression 格于上帝, as we find 格于皇天 in 'The Charge to Yuĕ.' From the 13th notice in the preface we learn that T'ang had a minister called Chin Hoo. He would be an ancestor probably of the Chin Hoo mentioned here in connection with T'ae-mow. 祖乙至巫賢,—if we had the lost Book Tsoo-yih (see Pref., n. 26), we should probably find this Woo Heen mentioned in it. 甘盤,—see 'The Charge to Yuĕ,' Pt. iii., p. 1. We cannot but be surprised that the duke does not make any mention of Foo Yuĕ. Keang Shing throws out the hint that Kan Pwan and Foo Yuĕ may have been the same man,— which is absurd. Gan-shih says that as Pwan was the earliest instructor of Woo-ting, the wisdom which guided that emperor to get Yuĕ for his minister was owing to him; but this does not account for the omission of Yuĕ in the duke's list. Perhaps something like a reason for it is suggested by the next par. 8. *The happy result of the services of those ministers.* 率惟茲有陳,—this must be spoken of the six great ministers just enumerated.—'In accordance with this,'—*i.e.*, their course of action so described—'they had an arrangement.' The meaning is very obscure. The critics, however, all expand it much as Ts'ae does:—六臣循惟此道, 有陳列之功. 殷禮陟配天,—Gan-kwŏ takes 殷禮, 'the ceremonies of Yin,' as = 'the govt. of Yin'

(安上治民之禮), and the whole clause as meaning that the govt. of Yin was so good that its sovereigns were on earth the representatives of God above, and occupied the imperial seat (殷得此安上治民之禮, 能升配上天, 天在人上, 故謂之升, 爲天之子是配也). This is ingenious, but it imposes too great violence on the language. 禮 cannot be taken as the nominative to 陟 and 配. 殷禮 are most naturally taken adverbially, = 'according to the ceremonial usages of Yin,' or as in the translation. Then 陟 and 配天 are predicates of the emperors of Yin, probably of those who are specially mentioned in the preceding par., the former char. describing them as 'deceased' (see 'The Canon of Shun,' p. 28), and 配天 declaring the fact of their being associated with Heaven in the sacrifices to it. In the present dyn. all its departed emperors are so honoured at the great sacrificial services. Under the Chow dyn. only How-tseih and king Wăn enjoyed the distinction. The rule of the Yin dyn. seems to have been to associate the five emperors of whom the duke has been speaking. [We have perhaps in this custom a reason for the omission of Foo Yuĕ iu the prec. par. From the Pwan-kang, Pt. i., 14, we learn that their ministers shared in the sacrifices to the sovereigns of Yin. Each emperor would have one minister as his assessor, and so Woo-ting could not have both Kan Pwan and Foo Yuĕ. Though the latter may have been the greater man of the two, the sacrificial honour was given to the other as having been the earlier instructor of the emperor. The duke, having the emperors

配天、多歷年所。

○天惟純佑命、（九節）

則商實百姓王

人、罔不秉德明

恤、小臣屏侯甸、

矧咸奔走惟茲

惟德稱用乂厥事

辟、故一人有事

于四方若卜筮。（十節）

罔不是孚。○公

reigns though deceased were assessors to Heaven, while it extended over many years. Heaven thus determinately maintained its favouring appointment, and Shang was replenished with men. The various officers, and members of the royal House holding employments, all held fast their virtue, and displayed an anxious solicitude *for the empire.* The smaller officers, and the chiefs in the How and Teen *domains,* hurried about on their services. Thus did they all put forth their virtue, and aid their sovereign, so that whatever affairs he, the one man, had in hand, throughout the four quarters of the empire, an entire sincerity was conceded to them as to the indications of the tortoise or the milfoil."

as sacrificed to in his mind, had no occasion therefore to mention Yuě. This explanation was first suggested by Soo Shih.]

I acquiesce in this view of the text, in preference to that proposed by Gan-kwŏ. It has its difficulties, however, and one of the principal is that we are obliged to find another subject for the verb 歷 in the concluding clause. The use of 所, at the end is peculiar. The 'Daily Explanation' says it is merely 'an expletive' (語辭), which is saying that no account of it can be given. A usage of it apparently analogous to that here is given in the Dict., with the definition—指物之辭, 'a demonstrative.'

P. 9. *The same subject.* 天惟純佑命則商實,—such is the punctuation adopted by Ts'ae, and also by Keang Shing. Gan-kwŏ read on to 百姓, but the meaning which he endeavours to make out for 商實百姓 is inadmissible. Ts'ae supports the explanation of 實 which appears in the translation, by referring to Mencius, Book VII., Pt. II., xii., 1,—不信仁賢, 則國空虛, 'If men of virtue and ability be not trusted, a State will become empty and

void.' The meaning seems to be that Heaven smiled upon the empire sustained by those great ministers, and there was no lack of smaller men to do their duty in their less important spheres with ability and virtue. 百姓王人,—it is not possible to say positively what officers are intended by these designations. Woo Ch'ing takes 百姓 as 'the people of the imperial domain' (王畿之民; comp. the use of the phrase in 'The Canon of Yaou,' p. 2); but it must be used of officers or ministers, and not of the people. I suppose it ＝百官. Perhaps Keang Shing is correct in taking 百姓 as the officers with different surnames from that of the imperial House (異姓之臣), and 王人 as cadets of that House in official employment (王之族人、同姓之臣). 明恤＝明致其恤有憂國之心. The phrase is correlative with 秉德, and is not to be joined with 小臣 below,—as Gan-kwŏ does. 小臣屏侯甸＝爲屏藩于侯甸之服者—'those who acted as screens (＝the prin-

其　申　奭　造　命　殷　汝　格　曰
集　勸　在　邦　厥　嗣　永　保　君
大　寧　昔　。○　亂　天　念　乂　奭
命　王　上　公　明　滅　則　有　天
于　之　帝　曰　我　威　有　殷　壽
厥　德　割　君　新　今　固　有　平

10　　The duke said, "Prince Shih, Heaven gives long life to the just and the intelligent;—it was thus that *those ministers* maintained and regulated the dynasty of Yin. He who at last came to the throne was extinguished by the majesty of Heaven. Think you of the distant future, and we shall have the decree *in favour of Chow* made sure, and its good government will be brilliantly displayed in our new-founded State."

11　　III. The duke said, "Prince Shih, aforetime when God was afflicting Yin, he encouraged anew the virtue of the Tranquillizing king, till at last the great favouring decree was concentrated in his

ces) in the How and Tëen domains.' 矧= 'still more;' or simply = 'likewise.' 惟
兹惟德稱=惟此內外之臣,皆舉稱其德, 'all these ministers, about the court and away from it, throughout the empire, displayed and exerted their virtue.
若卜兹, 罔不是(=是之)孚(=信之)=如龜之卜,如著之兹, 天下無不敬信之

P. 10. *Advice to Shih, grounded on the prec., that he should do for Chow what those ministers had done for Yin.* 天壽平格,— Gan-kwŏ supposes that 平格 is spoken of the sovereigns of Yin, (平至之君. It is better to understand the characters of the ministers who have been spoken of. They are called 平, 'level,' free of all selfishness, and 格, 'intelligent,' all-reaching and embracing. 壽 conveys not only the idea of long life, but also of prosperity,—as in the last Book, p. 7. Show is intended by 有殷嗣 天滅威=天滅之以示威, 永念 —'think of the distant future.' This is better than to take the terms as simply = 'always think of this.' 厥亂明我新造

邦=其治效亦赫然明著於我新造之邦, 'its efficient govt. will be gloriously and brilliantly displayed in our new founded kingdom.' Maou K'e-ling understands Lŏ to be 'the newly founded country;' but the dynasty is what is meant; compare the passage of the She King, quoted in 'The Great Learning,' comm., ii., 3. [It does not appear from this par. that the duke of Shaou had expressed his wish to withdraw from the public service, but the duke of Chow is evidently urging him to continue at his post to the last.]

Ch. III. Pp. 11—17. IT WAS BY THE AID OF THEIR ABLE MINISTERS THAT THE KINGS WAN AND WOO WERE RAISED TO THEIR GRAND DISTINCTION AND THE SOVEREIGNTY OF THE EMPIRE. THE DUKE OF CHOW LOOKS TO SHIH TO COOPERATE WITH HIM IN MAINTAINING THEIR DYNASTY OF CHOW. 11. 上帝割= 'God was cutting,' *i.e.*, was bringing about the overthrow of the dynasty of Yin. Këang Shing, after K'ang-shing, takes 割 for 蓋, a particle of style, the force of which passes into the verbs that follow; but there is no necessity to resort to such a device. Hea Seen observes that 'Heaven encouraged king Wăn, and afterwards encouraged king Woo; hence the language— 申勸;—see the 集說. 申 is 'a term, continuative of what has gone before,' (繼前之辭) In the Le Ke, Bk. 緇衣, p. 24, we find this par. in the form—

知　亦　蔑　來　括　若　夭　有　修　躬
天十　　德　兹　。　泰十　有　若十　和。
威四惟　降　迪　○　顛三若　虢二我○
乃節純　于　彝　又節、散　叔、有節有惟
　佑　國　教、曰　有宜　有　夏、文
惟　　人　　無　若生、若　亦王
時　秉　。　文　能　南、閎　惟尚
昭　德○王　往　宮有　克

12　person.　*But* that king Wăn was able to conciliate and unite the portion of the great empire which we came to possess, was owing to his having such ministers as his brother of Kih, Hwang Yaou, San E-săng, T'ae Teen, and Nan-kung Kwŏ."

13　　He repeated this sentiment, "But for the ability of these men to go and come in his affairs, developing his constant lessons, there would have been no benefits descending from king Wăn on the

14　people.　And it also was from the determinate favour *of Heaven*, that there were these men of firm virtue, and acting according to their knowledge of the dread majesty of Heaven, to give themselves

在昔上帝周田觀文王之德，其集大命于厥躬． This was, no doubt, the reading current in the Han dyn. as from Fuh-shang. 12. *King Wăn and the ministers who aided him.* 惟文有至有夏＝我有夏＝我所有之諸夏, 'the empire, or the portion of the empire, which we had.' The reference is to the two-thirds of the empire which acknowledged the authority of Wăn. 尚＝庶幾, 'perhaps.' Tsow Ching-k'e says that the terms 克尚 intimate the difficulty of Wăn's undertaking, and the greatness of the assistance which he derived from his ministers. 虢叔,—from a passage in the 左傳, 僖五年, we learn that this was a son of king Ke, and a younger brother of Wăn. Kih was the name of his appanage, in the pres. dis. of Paou-ke (寶雞), dep. of Fung-ts'ëang, Shen-se. [This was called the western Kih. There were two other districts called Kih under the Chow dynasty,—the eastern Kih, and the north-ern.] 閎, 散, 泰, and 南宮 are surnames; and 夭, 宜生, 顛, and 括 are

names. So says Gan-kwŏ, and there is no reason to call the thing in question, except in the case of the second, whose surname is said by some to have been 散宜. Of those five ministers we can hardly be said to know more than the sur-names and names. It would be a waste of time to refer to the legendary tales that are circulated about them. If we were surprised that there was no mention in p. 7 of Foo Yŭe, it is no less strange that the greatest of Wăn's ministers, the 太公望, should here be passed over in silence. 13. It is certainly most natural to take 又曰 here as introducing another remark, confirmatory of the preceding, by the duke of Chow. I can by no means accede to the view of Gan-kwŏ, and of Këang Shing and K'e-ling among the moderns, that 又曰無能往來 is an observation of king Wăn, who, though he had those five ministers, still said, 'They are not able (＝enough) to go and come in my affairs.' In order to make the rest of the par. harmonize in any way with this construction, they are obliged to take 蔑德＝'exquisite virtue.' 14. This par. corresponds to par. 9. What E Yin and the others did for the emperors of Yin, that did these five ministers for king Wăn,—and all by the determinate favour of Heaven. The 'Daily Explanation' expands 亦惟純佑秉德 into＝我

文王、迪見冒聞于上
帝惟時受有殷命哉。
○武王惟茲四人尚
迪有祿後暨武王誕
將天威咸劉厥敵惟
茲四人昭武王惟冒、
丕單稱德。○今在予
小子旦若游大川予
往暨汝奭其濟小子
同未在位誕無我責。

to enlighten king Wăn, and lead him forward to his high distinction and universal over-rule, till his fame reached the ears of God, and
15 he received the decree of Yin. There were still four of these men who led on king Woo to the possession of that decree with all its emoluments. Afterwards, along with him, in great reverence of the majesty of Heaven, they slew all his enemies; and *then* these four men made king Woo distinguished all over the empire,
16 till *the people* universally and greatly proclaimed his virtue. Now, with me Tan, who am but a little child, it is as if I were floating on a great stream; let me from this time cross it along with you, O Shih. Our young sovereign is *powerless* as if he had not yet

文王之時,有虢叔等五臣,文故迪
爲王,之輔佐,亦惟天意在之,故迪
王,純一不二,以佑助之人,迪
生此等秉持明德之人.—comp.
知天威,哲 in the last Book,
p. 16. 乃惟時昭文王=乃
惟以是昭文王. Kĕang Shing puts
a stop at 昭, and makes 乃惟時昭 to
be descriptive of the ministers, as becoming
thoroughly enlightened and virtuous. This
construction is not good. 迪見冒=
啟迪其德,使著見於上,覆
冒於下. Comp. Bk. XIV., p. 4. 15.
King Woo and his able ministers. 武王
至有祿,—茲四人, 'four of these
men.' One of them had died,—it is supposed,
the prince of Kih. 有祿,—comp. 'The
Counsels of Yu,' p. 17. King Wăn had the
decree,—the appointment to the possession of

the empire; but Woo came into the possession
itself. 後暨武王,—暨 is used here
as in the last Book, p. 5,=與, a preposition,
'along with.' 劉,—see 'The Pwan-kăng,'
Pt. i., p. 2. 昭武王惟冒=昭
武王,遂覆冒天下. Kĕang Shing
puts a stop at 昭, as in the last par., and reads
睊 for 冒, with which character the passage
is quoted in the 說文. The meaning would
then be—'king Woo looked humbly down on
all beneath.' But the punctuation and reading
are both bad. 16. *The duke of Chow en-
treats Shih to co-operate with him in supporting their
new dynasty. If he will not do so, the consequences
will be disastrous.* We must suppose that all
the four ministers who had aided Woo were now
dead, and the burden of the State was on the
dukes of Chow and Shaou. 游=浮水,
'to float on the water.' 予往暨(=與;
as in the last par.) 汝奭其濟=我
自今以往 與汝奭同心輔

裕我不以後人
惟艱告君乃猷
無疆惟休亦大
監于茲我受命
曰鳴呼君肆其公
其有能格。○
鳴鳥不聞矧曰
造德不降我則
收岡冔不及耇

十七節

ascended the throne. You must by no means lay the whole burden on me; and if we draw ourselves up without an effort to supply his deficiencies, no good will flow to the people from our age and experience. We shall not hear the voices of the singing birds, and much less can it be thought that we shall make his *virtue* equal to Heaven."

17　　The duke said, "Oh! consider well, O prince, these things. We have received the favouring decree *of Heaven,* to which belongs an unlimited amount of what is desirable, but having great difficulties attached to it. What I announce to you are counsels of a generous largeness. I cannot allow the successor of our kings to go astray."

佐, 共濟艱難 可也. 小子
同 未 在 位,—by 小子 here we must
understand king Ching. The duke had, indeed,
resigned the regency, and the govt. was in the
emperor's hands. But Ching was still young,
and unequal to his high duties. 誕無我
責, 收岡冔不及,—Ts'ae thinks there
is something wanting before the former of these
clauses, and says he does not understand the
latter. Gan-kwŏ took 誕無我責 as
=汝大無非責我之留, 'and
you are blaming me for remaining in the
govt.,' which agrees with his view that the
duke of Shaou was dissatisfied, because the
other had not retired upon resigning the regency. The terms will bear the meaning which
I have given in the translation; and it appears
to me more in harmony with the tenor of the
address. As to the meaning of the second
clause, the editors of Yung-ching's Shoo give a
modified approval to the view of Leu Tsoo-heen,
adduced by Yu E-shoo (余芑舒; of the
Yuen dyn.), making the words addressed to the
duke of Shaou:—召公若收斂退藏,
岡冔勉成王之所不逮. I take
the characters much in the same way, but
consider that the duke of Chow is speaking of
himself as well as of prince Shih. I can hardly
tell how Gan-kwŏ interprets here. He uses

many words, but I do not understand them.
Këang Shing points—誕無我責收岡
冔不及,='Do not you by any means
charge me to retire. I will exert myself, and
exertion is never made without success!'
耇造德=耇老成人之德.
鳴鳥,—by 'the singing birds' are meant
the male and female phœnix, fabled to appear at
court in times of great prosperity. See on the
'Yih and Tseih,' p. 9. In the She King, Pt. III.,
Bk. II., Ode viii., st. 9, mention is made of the
phœnixes flying about and screaming on the
hills. The ode is ascribed to the duke of Shaou,
and is supposed to celebrate king Ching and
the happiness of his times. 其有能
格,—this is said with reference to the predicates
in p. 7 about what the ministers of Yin did for
their sovereigns. 17. *The duke urges Shih
to lay to heart what he has said to him.*
肆其監于茲,—comp. the last Book,
p. 19. 肆 is taken =大. 我受至
惟艱,—comp. Bk. XII., p. 9. By 後
人, 'the after man,' we are to understand king
Ching. The 前人 at the beginning of next
par. renders this very probable.

兹誥予惟曰襄我二　天威。○予不允惟若　于殷喪大否肆念我　奭其汝克敬以予監　公曰君告汝朕允保　德丕承無疆之恤。○　宣乘茲大命惟文王　極曰汝明勗偶王在　心乃悉命汝作汝民　迷。○公曰、前人敷乃

18 IV. The duke said, "The former king laid bare his heart, and gave full charge to you, constituting you one of the guides of the people, and saying, 'Do you with intelligence and energy prove a helper to the king; do you with sincerity support and carry on this great decree. Think of the virtue of king Wăn, and enter greatly into his boundless anxieties.'"

19 The duke said, "What I tell you, O prince, are my sincere thoughts. O Shih, the Grand-protector, if you can but reverently survey with me the decay and great disorders of Yin, and thence consider the dread majesty of Heaven *which warns* us!——

20 "Am I not to be believed that I must thus speak? I simply say, 'The establishment of our dynasty rests with us two.' Do you agree

Ch. IV. Pp. 18—23. 18. *The duke of Shaou had received a special charge from king Woo to be a guardian of the young king and of the dynasty.* 前人, 'the former man,' is to be understood of king Woo. On his deathbed he had given the charge, of which a portion is here adduced, to the dukes of Chow and Shaou. 敷乃心,—the 乃 here would seem to＝其, the adj. pronoun of the third person. The phrase, however,＝所敷者乃其心腹. 作汝民極,—this has reference to the appointment of Shih to be the Grand-guardian, in which office he was to be a support and pattern for the people. Lin Che-k'e says:—凡爲大臣者,皆曰以爲民極. 偶王＝輔弼嗣王, 'to help the heir king.' Two, joined in any way, are called 偶. Shih was to prove as a help-meet to the king. In 乘大命, we have the metaphor of a carriage in which the sovereign

appointment was placed and carried on. 惟文王德,—the 惟＝念, 'to think of.' 丕承無疆之恤,＝comp. 無疆惟恤, Bk. XII., p. 9. 19. *The duke of Chow earnestly begs Shih to enter into his anxieties, and learn from the fate of Yin to labour for the establishment of their dynasty.* 其汝克敬,—this is hortatory, and the meaning seems to be best brought out by giving the translation an optative form. 以予 may be taken as＝與予. 大否 (p'ei)＝大亂, 'great disorders,' or 大阢, 'great distresses.' 我天威,—'our Heavenly terrors,' i.e., the terrors of Heaven which were to be dreaded by them, and guarded against through a diligent discharge of their duties. 20. *So much was dependent on the two dukes that they ought to be exerting themselves to the utmost, and especially to be looking out for men who might hereafter supply their places.* 予不允惟若兹誥 is

海　文　至　篤　後　敬　時　人
隅　王　于　棐　人　德　二　汝
出　功　今　時　于　明　人　有
日　于　日　二　丕　我　天　合
罔　不　休　人　時　俊　休　哉
不　怠　我　我　○　民　滋　言
率　丕　咸　式　嗚　在　至　曰
俾　冒　成　克　呼　讓　惟　在

廿一節

with me? Then you *also* will say, 'It rests with us two.' And
the favour of Heaven has come to us so largely:—it should be ours
to feel as if we could not sustain it. If you can but reverently
cultivate your virtue, and bring to light our men of eminence, then
when you resign to some successor in a time of established security,

21   "Oh! it is by the earnest assistance of us two that we have come
to the prosperity of the present day. But we must go on, abjuring
all idleness, to complete the work of king Wǎn, till it has entirely
overspread the empire, and from the corners of the sea and the
sunrising there shall not be one who is disobedient to our rule."

to be taken interrogatively. The 'Daily Explanation' gives for it:—凡我言語,豈是不足取信于人,而如此諄諄告汝乎. 襄我二人,一襄=成. The two men are evidently the duke of Chow himself, and the duke of Shaou. The clause =王業之成在我與汝而已,—as in the translation. Gan-kwŏ took the two men to be Wǎn and Woo, and this idea put him to the greatest straits throughout the par. Even Maou K'e-ling does not venture to defend such as an interpretation. 在時(=是)二人=在我二人. 戡=堪 or 勝, 'to be equal to,' 'to sustain.' I do not know what to make of the 在 in the last clause. The speaker does not complete his meaning. He simply says—'In the fact of yielding to successors in a time of great prosperity,'———. Critics supply what is wanting according to their different opinions as to the main object which the duke of Chow had in view in the address.   21. *The two dukes* *had done much for Chow in the past; it remained for them to complete their work.* 篤棐時(=是)二人=篤於輔君 (or 王室)者是我二人   我式 (=用),—'we thereby.' The 'we' is we of Chow, =our dynasty.   丕冒=使丕徧覆冒于斯民, 'causing it universally to overspread this people.'   罔不率俾=無不循我化, 可臣使也, 'all yield to our transforming influences, and become subjects who may be employed.'

[M. de Guignes observes on this paragraph:—'It is sufficiently singular that a philosopher like Chow-kung inspires here the spirit of conquest; it was then, therefore, the taste of the Chinese, who sought to extend themselves more and more to the east.' See 'Le Chou-king,' p. 237. The duke's words hardly called for such a remark. He is merely seeking the full establishment of their dynasty,—that Chow should enter into all the possessions of Yin.]

治。若茲往敬用　初惟其終祗　亦罔不能厥　惟乃知民德　公曰嗚呼君、　于天越民。○　誥予惟用閔　不惠若茲多　○公曰君子

廿二節
廿三節

22　The duke said, "O prince, am I not speaking in accordance with reason in these many declarations?　I am only influenced by anxiety about *the decree of* Heaven, and about the people."

23　The duke said, "Oh! O prince, you know the ways of the people, how at the beginning they can be *all we could desire*, but it is the end *which is to be thought of.*　Act in careful accordance with this fact.　Go and reverently exercise your government."

P. 22.　*The duke affirms the reasonableness of his remarks, and re-states the grounds of them.* 予不惠若茲多誥 is to be taken interrogatively, like the commencing clause of p. 20. This is sufficient against the view of Këang Shing, who reads it indicatively, and takes 惠＝慧, so that the meaning is—'I in my want of wisdom make these many declarations.' 惠＝順於理, 'accordant with reason.' We have met with it before, having this meaning. 予惟用閔于天越(＝及)民＝予惟用憂天命難以永保, 及生民無所倚賴.

23.　*The uncertainty of the attachment of the people should make ministers careful to retain their good will.*　民德＝'the ways of the people;' now all-attachment to a govt., now disaffected and rebellious.　惟其終＝當思其終.

THE BOOKS OF CHOW.

爲克人七蔡致百惟一蔡
卿庸三乘叔碎工周節仲
士祗年降于管群公之
叔德不霍郭叔叔位命
卒周齒叔鄰于流冢
乃公蔡于以商言宰
命以仲庶車囚乃正

1　When the duke of Chow was in the place of prime minister, and directed all the officers, the *king's* uncles spread abroad an *evil* report, in consequence of which he put to death the prince of Kwan in Shang; confined the prince of Ts'ae in Koh-lin, with an attendance, however, of seven chariots; and reduced the prince of Hǒ to be a private man, causing his name to be erased from the registers for three years. The son of the prince of Ts'ae being able to display a reverent virtue, the duke of Chow made him a high noble, and when his father died, requested a decree from the king, investing him with the country of Ts'ae.

THE NAME OF THE BOOK.—蔡仲之命, 'The Charge to Chung of Ts'ae.' Ts'ae was the name of the small State or district, which formed the appanage of Too, a younger brother of the duke of Chow, on whose history I have slightly touched in the note on p. 12 of Bk. VI. The name still remains in the dis. of Shang-ts'ae (上蔡), dep. of Joo-ning, Honan. Too was deprived of this appanage, but it was subsequently restored to his son, and the Charge preserved in this Book was given to him on the occasion. The name of Too's son was Hoo (胡). He is here called Chung; but that character only denoted his place in the roll of his brothers or cousins. A Chinese scholar has attempted to explain it to me thus.—Too was younger than king Woo, and so, from the standpoint of king Ching, he is called 蔡叔,

'(younger) uncle of Ts'ae.' King Ching and Hoo were cousins,—'brothers,' according to Chinese usage of terms, and Hoo, being the younger of the two, was called 蔡仲, '(second) brother of Ts'ae.'

The Book is only found in the old text, or that of Gan-kwŏ. There is some difference of opinion as to the place which it should occupy in the list of the Books of Chow. Ts'ae thinks it ought to be placed before 'The Announcement about Lŏ.' In the 'Little Preface,' as we have it from Ch'ing, it is placed the 96th in the list of Books, immediately before the 'Speech at Pe.' Ming-shing allows that so it is wrongly placed, which indeed is evident, but says that Ch'ing gave the preface as he found it without venturing any alterations, whereas the author or forger of Gan-kwŏ's commentary took it upon him to remove the notice to where it now stands. Whether Gan-kwŏ's commentary be a forgery or not, the Book occurs in it, I apprehend, in the place which it originally occupied. There is no necessity for supposing with Ts'ae that it should be before Book XIII. We do not know in what year Ts'ae Shuh died. Ts'ae Chung's restoration to his father's honours may not have taken place till after the building of Lŏ, and king Ching had taken the government, upon reaching his majority, into his own hands.

CONTENTS. The first par. is of the nature of a preface, giving the details necessary to explain the appointment of Hoo. The seven paragraphs that follow are the king's Charge, directing him how to conduct himself, so that he might blot out the memory of his father's misdeeds, and win the praise of the emperor.

P. 1. *Prefatory details.* 惟周公至 百工,—comp. 'The Instructions of E.,' p. 1. 羣叔流言,—comp. Bk. VI., p. 12. 致辟,—'carried out the law to the utmost,' = 'put to death.' [This confirms the interpretation given of 我之弗辟, in Bk. VI., p. 13.] 囚蔡叔至七乘,—囚 = 'to confine.' K'ang-shing defined the term by 拘. 郭鄰 was the name of a place; but where it was, we cannot tell. Sze-ma Ts'een, in the 管蔡世家第五, says that Ts'ae Shuh was allowed an attendance of 'ten chariots and 70 footmen.' In the 左傳 定四年, mention is also made of 70 footmen, but the chariots are seven, as in the text. For 以車七乘 the 'Daily Explanation' gives—猶以車七乘隨之   降

霍叔至不齒,—the name of Hoh Shuh was Ch'oo (處). Ch'oo's appanage was Hoh, the name of which remains in Hoh Chow, dep. of P'ing-yang (平陽), Shan-se. 三年 不齒,—'for three years he had not his teeth,' *i.e.*, he was struck off the family roll. The names of all the brothers were entered according to their 'teeth' or ages; hence one of the definitions of 齒 in the dict. is by 年也, 列也. 蔡仲至卿士,—蔡仲, see the note on the 'name of the Book.' Ts'een says that 'when the duke of Chow heard of the good character of Hoo, he raised him to be a noble of Loo' (周公聞之, 而舉胡以爲魯卿士). The opinion of the speaker in the passage of the 左傳 referred to above was the same (蔡仲 改行帥德,周公舉之,以爲 已卿士). Ts'ae on the contrary thinks that the office of 'high noble,' conferred on Hoo, was within the imperial domain, and not in Loo. This view appears to me the more likely; but the text does not enable us to decide the point.

命諸王邦之蔡=請命于 成王,復封其國于蔡使繼 叔之後, 'He requested a decree from king Ching, and again invested Hoo with Ts'ae, that he might continue the line of his father.' Gan-kwŏ thought that the Ts'ae with which Hoo was invested was not the same which had been the appanage of his father, but another on the east, 'between the Hwae and the Joo,' to which the name of Ts'ae was given, to mark the connection between it and the former. This is not likely, nor is it supported by proper historical evidence.

[Shih King (郝敬; of the Ming dynasty) denies the various statements in this par., saying they are legends founded on a misapprehension of the duke of Chow's language in 'The Metal-bound Coffer,'—我之弗辟,我無 以告我先王; and that to suppose that the duke killed one brother and degraded two others, as he is here said to have done, is injurious to his character, and would establish a precedent of most dangerous nature. Having thus settled it that the statements are not true, he goes on to the conclusion, that this Book is a forgery. But this is egregious trifling. The statements of this par. were staple of Chinese history before the burning of the Shoo. The passage of the 左傳 adduced above, and the sequel of which contains a part of par. 3, is sufficient to prove this. The duke of Chow is easily vindicated from any charges brought against his character for the deeds which are related here.]

率　無　乃　之　哉　東　猷　率　若　諸
乃　怠　邁　猷　○　土　肆　德　曰　王
祖　以　迹　惟　爾　往　予　改　小　邦
文　垂　自　忠　尚　即　命　行　子　之
王　憲　身　惟　蓋　乃　爾　克　胡　蔡
之　乃　克　孝　前　封　侯　慎　惟　○
彝　後　勤　爾　人　敬　于　厥　爾　王

2　"The king speaks to this effect, 'My little child, Hoo, you follow the virtue *of our ancestors*, and have changed from the conduct *of your father*; you are able to take heed to your ways;—I therefore appoint you to be a prince *of the empire* in the east. Go to your country. Be reverent!

3　'In order that you may cover the faults of your father, be loyal, be filial. Urge on your steps in your own way, diligent and never idle, and so you will hand down an example to your descendants.

Pp. 2—8. THE CHARGE.　2. *The virtue of Hoo, to which he was entitled for the distinction conferred on him.* 王若曰,—it may seem that this should be translated—'The king spake to the following effect,' rather than as I have done. I apprehend, however, that the charge was delivered by the duke of Chow in the king's name, in the same way as the charge to the Viscount of Wei, Bk. VIII. The 命諸王邦之蔡 in the last par. leads me to this view, nor need it be rejected though Hoo's appointment may have taken place after the building of Lǒ. 率德改行 must = 循祖之德,改父之行,—as in the translation. 東土,—Ts'ae was to the east of Haou, Ching's capital. 往即乃封,—the first definition of 封 in the dict. is 爵諸侯之土, 'the country with which a prince was invested.' The primary meaning of the term, however, was, no doubt, 'a tumulus or mound;' and Sëě Ke-seuen (薛季宣) ingeniously accounts for its being used as the designation of a territory in this way:—天子建侯立國,分以天子之社,使置社於其國,因謂之封, 'The emperor, when appointing a prince over a State, took from the earth of his own altar to the spirit of the land, and gave it to the prince, that he might raise an altar to the spirit of the land in his State, which was thence called by the name of 封. Compare the note on 'The Tribute of Yu,' Pt. i., p. 35.　3. *Hoo must go on as he had begun, covering by his good deeds the evil memory of his father.* 爾尚至惟孝,—the force of the 尚 is partly concessive, and partly hortatory. By 前人 is intended, of course, Hoo's father. Though Hoo was acting contrary to his father's example, yet as his conduct would remove the disgrace that rested on his father's memory, it is characterized as 'filial.' 邁迹自身,—Gan-kwǒ gives for this—行善迹用汝身. There is a reference plainly to the conduct of Hoo's father, who had left no traces of good by which he might direct his steps. Lin Che-k'e says:—汝之行善迹當自汝身而始. The characters, as I understand them, are literally:—'Do you push boldly on (邁即勇往,力行之意), treading on your own person.' The conclusion,—無若爾考之違王命—is quoted in the 左傳, as referred to above.

[Ch'in Foo-lëang says:—'When Shun gave charge to Yu, he made no reference to the misconduct of his father K'wǎn; and the duke

訓、無若爾考之違王命。

○皇天無親惟德是輔、【四節】

民心無常惟惠之懷為惡

善不同同歸于治為惡

不同同歸于亂爾其戒

哉。○慎厥初惟厥終終【五節】

以不困不惟厥終以

困窮。○懋乃攸績睦乃【六節】

四鄰以蕃王室以和兄

Follow the constant lessons of your grandfather, king Wǎn, and be
not like your father disobedient to the royal orders.

4 'Great Heaven has no affections;—it helps only the virtuous.
The people's hearts are not constant;—they cherish only the kind.
Acts of goodness are different, but they contribute in common to
government. Acts of evil are different, but they contribute in
common to disorder. Do you be cautious!

5 'To give heed to the beginning, think of the end:—the end will
then be without distress. If you do not think of the end, it will be
in distress, and that the greatest.

6 'Exert yourself to achieve your proper merit. Seek to be in
harmony with all your neighbours. Be a fence to the royal House.
Live in harmony with your brethren. Tranquillize and help the
inferior people.

of Chow, when giving charge to the viscount
of Wei, made no mention of Woo-kăng. How
is it that he here makes mention so repeatedly
and distinctly of Hoo's father? Hoo's father
was his own brother. It was necessary he
should speak of him, on the principle explained
by Mencius, VI., Pt. ii., iii.;'—see the 集說.]

P. 4. 皇天至之懷,—comp. the
'Tae-kĕă, Pt. iii., p. 1. 皇天無親惟
德是輔 is quoted as from the Books of
Chow, in the 左傳, 僖五年. 5.
慎厥初惟厥終,—Comp. 慎終
于始, in the 'Tae-kĕă,' Pt. iii., p. 6. The
same sentiment is here brought differently out.
惟 is to be taken = 思, as in the same ex-

pression—惟厥終—in the last Bk. p. 23.
In the 左傳, 襄, 二十五年, there
is a quotation from the Shoo, the original of
which is probably in this par.—慎始而
敬終, 終以不困.

P. 6. Rules for Hoo in his relations with others.
懋乃攸績=勉汝所立之
功, 'exert yourself in achieving your proper
merit.' What that merit was is not said. 'It
embraced,' says Tsëaou Hwang (焦竑), 'the
bringing forward the able, the intelligent administration of the government, and the right use of
punishments.' 四鄰='the prince of the
neighbouring States on every side.' 以

弟康濟小民。

○率自中、無〔七節〕

作聰明亂舊

章、詳乃視聽

罔以側言改

厥度則予一

人汝嘉。○王〔八節〕

曰嗚呼小子

胡、汝往哉、無

荒棄朕命。

7　'Follow the course of the Mean, and do not by assuming to be intelligent throw old statutes into confusion. Watch over what you see and hear, and do not for one-sided words deviate from the right rule. Then I, the one man, will praise you.'"

8　"The king says, 'Oh! my little child, Hoo, go, and do not idly throw away my charge.'"

蕃, 以和.—the 以 does not connect the clauses with those which precede 兄弟, 'brethren,' are the princes and nobles of the same surname with himself.　7. *Rules of a more internal character.* 率自中,—Lin Che-k'e observes that this clause is equivalent to the 率性 at the commencement of the 'Doctrine of the Mean.' We need not, however, look for any moral or metaphysical doctrine in the text. 中 is here 'the middle,' 'the proper Mean.'　Emphasis is to be laid on the 作 in the second clause. Wang Ts'ëaou says:—'Intelligence is a Heavenly virtue; assuming to be intelligent is a selfish shrewdness' (聰明, 天德也, 作聰明則私智耳. 詳=審, 'to exercise a discriminating judgment.' 厥度,—厥 might be translated in the second person,—'your,' or even in the first. Ts'ae expands from 審乃 thus:—視聽不審, 惑於一偏之說, 則非中矣, 其能不改吾身之法度乎.

P. 8. *Concluding admonition.*

THE BOOKS OF CHOW.

BOOK XVIII. NUMEROUS REGIONS.

多方

惟一節
五月丁亥、王來

自奄至于宗周。○

周二節
公曰王若曰猷

告爾四國多方、惟

爾殷侯尹民、我惟

大降爾命爾罔不

知。○洪惟圖天之

命弗永寅念于祀。

1 I. In the fifth month, on the day Ting-hae, the king arrived from
2 Yen, and came to the honoured city of Chow. The duke of Chow
said, "The king speaks to the following effect, 'Ho! I make an
announcement for you of the four kingdoms and many *other* regions.
Ye who were the officers and people of the prince of Yin, I have
dealt very leniently as regards your lives, as ye all know. You
3 kept reckoning greatly upon *some* decree of Heaven, and did not
keep with perpetual awe before your thoughts *the preservation of*
your sacrifices.

INTRODUCTORY NOTE. The Preface to the
Shoo contains the names of two Books now
lost, which had their place between 'The Charge
to Chung of Ts'ae' and 'The Numerous Regions.' The one was styled 'The Government
of king Ching,' and was made on occasion of an
expedition of the king to the east, when he
smote the wild tribes of the Hwae, and extinguished the State of Yen (東伐淮
夷遂踐奄). The other had reference
to the king's removal of the chief or ruler of
Yen to the district of P'oo-koo (蒲姑) in

Ts'e, and was styled 將蒲姑, which we
do not know how to translate, being unable,
from the loss of the Book, to say how the
character 將 should be taken. The Book
that now comes under our notice was a sequel
to these two, the prefatory note saying that it
was made on the return of the king to Haou
from Yen (成王歸自奄, 在宗周
誥庶邦, 作多方).
Now, the prefatory note to 'The Great Announcement' says that after king Woo's death,

when Woo-kǎng and the three uncles of Ching, who had been placed as overseers of him in Yin, rebelled, the wild tribes of the Hwae rose at the same time and made common cause with them. In 'The Numerous Officers,' p. 21, again, the king is made to say to the nobles of Yin, that, 'when he came from Yen,' he dealt very leniently with them. The question has been raised whether, in those and other notices, we have intimations of only one expedition against the tribes of the Hwae and Yen, or of successive expeditions. On the lost Book of 'The Govt. of king Ching,' Ch'ing K'ang-shing says that the exploits described in it were those of the duke of Chow when he put down the rebellion of his brothers, and that he did not know how the Book had been arranged in the place assigned to it in the Preface. Këang Shing, Wang Ming-shing, and others, who all but swear to the words of Ch'ing, would arrange all the Books I have mentioned before 'The Numerous Officers.' In the standard chronology, moreover, the 'Numerous Regions' is assigned to the fifth year of king Ching, B.C. 1,110 (or 1,111). On the other hand, Gan-kwǒ maintains that the wild tribes spoken of were not tamed by one visit of the imperial forces. The duke of Chow smote them, he says, and Yen with them, when quelling the rebellion of his brothers and Woo-kǎng, but they rebelled again when the duke had resigned the regency, and the king himself, probably attended by his uncle, took the field against them; and it was on his return from extinguishing the State of Yen, that the announcement contained in the 'Numerous Regions' was made. It is of the operations at this time against the Hwae and other wild tribes, he thinks, that mention is made in 'The speech at Pe.'

I am inclined in this matter to adopt the view of Gan-kwǒ. We may conclude from the arrangement of the Books that this was the opinion of the compiler of the Preface. If we may credit what Mencius says, the records of the Shoo do not tell us a tithe of the wars carried on by the duke of Chow to establish the new dynasty :—'He smote Yen, and after three years put its ruler to death. He drove Fei-leen to a corner by the sea and slew him. The states which he extinguished amounted to fifty' (Mencius, Bk. III., Pt. II., ix., 6). I may conclude this note with the remarks of Shoo Shih on the difficulty with which the dynasty of Chow was established. He says :—' "The Great Announcement," "The Announcement to the prince of K'ang," "The Ann. about Drunkenness," "The timber ofthe Tsze," "The Ann. of the duke of Shaou," "The Ann. about Lǒ," "The Numerous Officers," and "The Numerous Regions,"—these eight pieces, each having its different subject, yet have all a general reference to the fact that the minds of the people of Yin would not submit to Chow. When I have read "The Great Speech," and "The Completion of the War," I have always exclaimed—'How easily did Chow take the empire from Yin!' But when I read these eight Books, I exclaim—'With what difficulty did Chow bring Yin to a quiet submission!' "The Numerous Regions" was addressed not to the off. of Yin only, but also to those of the other regions throughout the empire ;—showing us that it was not the people of Yin only who refused to acknowledge the

new sway. One can understand how deep had been the influence of the six virtuous kings who came after T'ang. Under the tyranny of Show, the people were as if in the midst of flaming fire, and they turned to Chow as water flows downwards, without thinking of the virtue of the former kings. But when the empire was a little settled, they were no longer amid the fires, and their thoughts turned to the seven emperors of Yin, as a child thinks of its parents. Though sages like king Woo and the duke of Chow followed one another with their endeavours to soothe them, their insurrectionary movements could not be repressed. Had the new dynasty not possessed the duke of Chow, it could hardly have been established.—This he knew, and it was this which made him apprehensive, and that he did not dare to withdraw from public life.' See the 集傳.

THE NAME OF THE BOOK.—多方, 'The Numerous Regions.' The phrase occurs in the 2d par., and up and down throughout the greater portion of the Book ; and hence it is used to designate the whole, indicating that it was addressed to the representatives not of one region, but of many. In parr. 24—29, the phrase 多士, 'numerous officers,' takes the place of 多邦, and Woo Ch'ing has removed so much to the former Book ;—for which he is hardly to be blamed. 'The Numerous Regions' is found in both the texts.

CONTENTS. The king has returned to his capital in triumph, having put down rebellion in the east, and specially extinguished the State or tribe of Yen. A great assembly of princes and nobles,—the old officers of Yin, and chiefs from many regions besides,—is gathered on the occasion. They are all supposed to have been secretly, if not openly, in sympathy with the rebellion which has been trampled out, and to grudge to yield submission to the rule of Chow. The king, by the duke of Chow, reasons and expostulates with them. He insists on the leniency with which he had dealt with them in the past ; and whereas they might be saying that Chow's overthrow of the Yin dynasty was a usurpation, he shows that it was from the will of Heaven. The history of the empire is reviewed, and it is made to appear that king Woo had displaced the emperors of Shang, just as T'ang, the founder of Shang, had displaced the emperors of Hea. It was the course of duty for them therefore to submit to Chow. If they did not avail themselves of its leniency, they should be dealt with in another way.

Having thus spoken, the duke turns, at par. 24, and addresses the many officers of the States, and especially those of Yin who had been removed to Lǒ, speaking to them in the style of 'The Numerous Officers.' Finally he reminds them all that it is time for them to begin a new course. If they do well, all will be well with them ; if they continue perverse, they will have themselves to blame for the consequences.

Ch. I. Pp. 1—12. TIME WHEN, AND PARTIES TO WHOM THE ANNOUNCEMENT WAS MADE. A REVIEW OF THE DOWNFALL OF THE HEA

DYNASTY, AND OF THE HISTORY OF THAT OF SHANG;—TO SHOW THE WAY OF HEAVEN IN THE RISE AND FALL OF THE IMPERIAL SWAY.　　1.

See the introductory note. On 奄 and 宗周, see the notes on Bk. XIV., p. 21. Gaubil observes that whereas the most approved history of the empire refers the date of this Book to the 5th year of king Ching, or B.C. 1,111, there really was no day Ting-hae in the 5th month of that year in the calendar of Chow. The correctness of his observation is easily verified, for the Chow year corresponding to B.C. 1,111, must have commenced with the cycle day 辛酉. But we have seen (p. 421) that it was in the year B.C. 1,098 that the duke of Chow resigned the regency. The next year, B.C. 1,097, began, if the calendar was correct, on the 6th cycle day, or 己巳, and the 5th month must have commenced with the day 丁卯 or 戊辰, so that the day Ting-hae would be the 20th or 21st of it. Gan-kwŏ arrived at the same result from his view that the day 戊辰, Bk. XIII., p. 29, was the last day of the year. Let these numerical statements have whatever weight is due to them;—they seem to me to show that this Book follows 'The Announcement about Lŏ,' in chronological order, and that we are right in rejecting the early date assigned to it by K'ang-shing and his followers.

2. 周公曰, 王若曰,—the announcement is thus introduced differently from any that have preceded. 'The Great Announcement' for instance begins with 王若曰, though the king could have had little or nothing to do with it. The language of it, like the expedition which it vindicated, was all from the duke of Chow. The compilers of the Books, however, did not think it necessary to prefix a 周公曰, as they have done here. The only reason for the addition in the text at all satisfactory assumes (what I have inferred on other grounds) that this announcement was made after the duke had resigned the regency. The king might then have been expected to declare his sentiments in his own person. He did not do so on this occasion. There were reasons, no doubt, for his not doing so, though we cannot assign them. The duke of Chow was spokesman as before; and to indicate their different positions we have the prefix—'The duke of Chow said.' 猷, 告爾四國多方,—on 猷告, see upon Bk. VII., p. 1. Woo Ch'ing understands by 四國 'all the States in the four quarters of the empire' (四方諸國), and by 多方, 'the people of all the States' (諸國之民). This is ingenious but not satisfactory. 四國多方 stand collaterally, and indicate different regions. The 'many regions' are more extensive than the 'four States,' and cannot be taken as embraced in them. We must understand the 四國 as in

Bk. XIV., p. 21, of the imperial domain of Shang or Yin, which had been divided into four parts presided over by three of king Woo's brothers, and by Woo-kăng, the son of Show. It seems to me absurd to suppose, with Kĕang Shing, that Yen was one of the States thus classed together.

Then by 多邦 are intended the princes and people of other regions generally. It is probable the people of Yen, in the rising which had been quelled, had raised the standard of the fallen dynasty, and that the issue of their struggle had been eagerly waited for by the people of the old imperial domain, and of other eastern regions. However that may be, the duke of Chow and other friends of the new dynasty thought the time a fitting one to give another and general exposition of the grounds on which they vindicated for it the sovereignty of the empire. 惟爾殷侯尹民, 云云, —by 殷侯, 'the prince of Yin,' is denoted Woo-kăng. Kĕang Shing takes 殷=眾, so that 爾殷侯尹民=爾諸侯治民者, 'ye princes of the empire, governing the people;' but such a meaning of 殷 in this place is very unlikely. Woo Ch'ing retains 殷 in the sense of 'the Yin dynasty,' but takes the clause in the same way as Shing (殷諸侯之尹其民者), saying that whereas the 'people' were addressed in 爾四國多方, the speaker here rises to address their 'rulers' (誥民而因及其君). But there is no such gradation of thought in the text, and Ch'ing's exegesis lies under the additional disadvantage of making 惟=及, 'and.' The duke of Chow, having called the attention of all in the assembly to what he had to say (告爾四國多方), here turns and addresses himself more particularly to the nobles and people who had occupied the imperial domain of Yin. I understand 殷侯尹民 as=殷侯之百官與眾民. The 'Daily Explanation' differently:—爾殷侯所尹正統轄之民　我惟大降爾命,—see on Bk. XIV., p. 21. I understand the language here as in that previous passage, in accordance with the views of Ts'ae. Here, however, he supposes that the king says he is sparing their lives a second time, and 爾罔不知 is with him=爾宜無不知, 'Be ye all aware of this.' But this clause and the former are to me plainly historical, and refer to what is past. Ts'ae's view is fully and clearly expanded in the 'Daily Explanation:'—爾……助奄作叛今奄國既滅皆當以從逆坐

○惟帝降格于夏、有夏誕厥逸、不肯感言于民、乃大淫昏不克終日勸于帝之迪、乃爾攸聞。○ 四節

4 'God sent down correction on Hea, but the sovereign *only* increased his luxury and sloth, and would not speak kindly to the people. He proved himself on the contrary dissolute and dark, and would not yield for a single day to the leading of God;—this

誅、我惟不忍多殺、大降恩赦、宥爾殷民之命、爾等宜無不知之、勿復生二心. 3.

This par. is the key-note to the Book, and it is right to connect it closely with what precedes. The subject of it is 'the officers and people of Yin,' who had deemed the empire belonged to the House of T'ang by a 'divine right' (天之命), and did not consider that what Heaven had given, it might and would take away, if there were not the earnest and virtuous discharge of the duties of government. Ts'ae makes Yen to be the subject of the par. Thus the 'Daily Explanation' follows the passage just quoted with—'And do you know the reason why Yen has perished? The people of Yen presumed greatly on their private views, reckoned on the decree of supreme Heaven, and with evil action rose in rebellion. They used no far-reaching reverent forethought, which would have led them to obey the laws, and rest in their lot, whereby they would have preserved the sacrifices to their ancestors. They have thus suddenly brought destruction on themselves; and do you look to Yen as a beacon, and know that the decree of Heaven is not to be rashly sought or relied on.' But why should we suppose that the speaker has here the State of Yen in view? It is mentioned indeed in the 1st par., but that is an addition by the compiler, and Yen is nowhere referred to in the address. It was too insignificant, moreover, to occupy the place which must be assigned to it, if we suppose that the announcement is thus made to turn upon its history.

No similar objections can be made to the view which I have taken. The sacrifices to the emperors of the Yin dynasty were allowed, in the generous clemency of king Woo, to be continued by their lineal descendant Woo-kăng, the son of the tyrant Show; but no sooner was Woo dead, than he and his adherents rose in rebellion against the new dynasty, and brought down new and heavy punishments, though still tempered with mercy, upon themselves. I am surprised that none of the Chinese critics have thus connected the 2d and 3d parr.

Gan-kwŏ joined the 3d par. with the 4th, and supposed that Kĕĕ, the last emperor of the Hea dyn., was the subject of it. Kĕang Shing deals with it very inanely, saying that it is a general declaration, = 'Should kings reckon on the decree of Heaven, and not reverently consult with long forethought, for their sacrifices' (王者圖度天命、而不長敬念于祭祀乎)? 洪惟、—see on the same characters in Bk. VII., p. 1. Kĕang Shing would make them in both places merely a phrase of introduction or exclamation; but we are not reduced to have recourse to such a device.

Pp. 4—7. *How the sovereignty of the empire passed from the House of Hea to T'ang.* 4. Ts'ae thinks that some paragraphs introductory to this have been lost, his reason being that it is the custom in the Shoo to precede the account of the downfall of a dynasty because of the wickedness of its last emperor with a reference to the virtuous emperors who preceded him. That is the practice certainly, but the duke of Chow may not have observed it here. We are not obliged to suppose any loss of text. 惟帝降格于夏、—comp. Bk. XIV., p. 5. The 'Daily Explanation' here takes 格 =正. 感言于民、—感=憂、'sorrowfully,' 'with sympathy.' 不克終日勸于帝之迪、—終日, in the Analects and Mencius, is used for 'a whole day.' Here the phrase = 'one day,' 'a single day.' Kĕang Shing has for it 一日; and the 'Daily Explanation' gives 終日之暫. 'He could not for a single day be advised by (exert himself on) the leading of God,'—the critics dwell on the phrase—'the leading of God,' and understand by it the unceasing monitions of conscience,—all the ways by which the heart of man is touched in Providence, which may be described as efforts on the part of God to keep him from evil, and lead him into the way of righteousness. 5.

恭洪舒于　丕惟進之　承于旅罔　亂不克靈　因甲于內　崇亂有夏、　乃大降罰、　于民之麗、　命不克開　厥圖帝之　五節

5 is what you have heard. He kept reckoning on the decree of God *in his favour*, and would not promote the means of the people's support. By great inflictions of punishment also, he increased the disorder of the States of Hea. The first cause *of his evil course* was the internal misrule, which made him unfit to deal well with the multitudes. Nor did he seek at all to employ men whom he could

Ts'ae says that most of this par. is not understood by him. He brings out the meaning which appears in the translation, however, and is on the whole more successful in dealing with it than the other critics. The same subject evidently is continued,—the crimes of Këě, which occasioned the overthrow of the Hea dynasty. 厥圖帝之命.—compare the notes on 'The Speech of T'ang,' p. 3. 不克開于民之麗,—the expression 民之麗 has been taken variously. Gan-kwŏ explains 麗 by 施, so that the meaning is—'that which should be bestowed on the people,' viz., good govt. and lessons of instruction; and the whole = he could not begin even to govern and instruct the people as he ought. This is very unsatisfactory. In the Yih King (離卦) it is said— 日月麗乎天,百穀草木麗乎土. Këang Shing, taking 麗 there as = 附, 'to be attached to,' understands the text as = 'he could not do what would make the people attached to him.' Ts'ae defined the character in the Yin by 依, 'to rely on,' and not by 附, from which he deduces the meaning of the text which I have given.—Këě made no provision for the necessaries of life among the people, such as food and clothing. 乃大至有夏,—this continues the description of Këě. He is the subject of 降. Woo Ch'ing on the contrary understands 'Heaven' as the subject of 降, and makes the clauses descriptive of the punishment of Këě. 因甲至于旅,—the critics are all agreed that by 內亂, 'internal disorder,' we are to understand the vile debaucheries of which Këě was guilty in his connection with Me-he (see pp. 170, 171). With Ts'ae, Woo Ch'ing, and others, I take 甲 = 始, 'to begin,' and 因 is equivalent to

a noun, the subject of 甲. K'ang Shing and Wang Suh both took 甲 as = 狃, or 習, but they do not account for the 因. Equally unsatisfactory is the exegesis of Gan-kwŏ, who takes 甲 as if it were 夾. With 靈承于旅 comp. Bk. XIV., p. 13, 我周王丕靈承帝事. Here 旅 is taken, by all the critics except Woo Ch'ing, as = 眾, 'all the multitude of the people.' The only difficulty in so taking it is with 承, which would so be applied to describe the act of the superior to his inferiors,—which is contrary to its common usage. Feeling this, Ch'ing takes 旅 as denoting the sacrifice to God which was so called (see the dict. *in voc.*), who takes the clause as = 'he could not attend well to the sacrifices to God.' But this is so far-fetched that it is better to acquiesce in the other view, even with the difficulty attaching to it. 罔丕至于民,—I have translated here, after the 'Daily Explanation,' which has:— 無能大進賢人而敬用之, 使大布寬舒之澤于其民. There is little to choose between this and the view of Ts'ae and Woo Ch'ing:—'Nor could he make great approaches towards the virtue of reverence in which he might have shown a generous largeness of heart to the people' (不能大進於恭,而大寬裕其民). Gan-kwŏ gave quite a different meaning to the second clause:—'Nor could he greatly advance to the virtue of reverence, but was very indifferent and idle in governing the people' (大舒惰于治民). Keang Shing reads 荼 instead of 舒, and interprets:—'The greatly

不克明保享于民、　惟夏之恭多士大　民不克永于多享、　惟以爾多方之義　○惟天不畀純乃 七節　于成湯、刑殄有夏。　主、乃大降顯休命　邑。○天惟時求民 六節　叨懫日欽、劓割夏　民、亦惟有夏之民、

respect, and who might display a generous kindness to the people, but he daily honoured the covetous and cruel, who were guilty of
6 cruel tortures in the cities of Hea. Heaven on this sought *a true* lord for the people, and made its distinguishing and favouring decree light on T'ang the Successful, who punished and destroyed the
7 sovereign of Hea. Heaven's refusal of its favour *to Hea* was decided, and it was because the righteous men among your many regions were not permitted to continue long in their posts of enjoyment, and the many officers whom Hea respected were quite unable to maintain an intelligent preservation of the people in the enjoyment *of their*

false were employed by him, and put into offices, to the calamity and bitter suffering of the people' 誣罔大者、惟進之任、使供職、大爲患苦于民)。惟有夏至末 — 叨 = 饕, 'to be gluttonous or greedy,' 'to covet;' 懫, *i.q.* 懥, = 忿 'to be angry,' 'resentful.' 劓割夏邑, —comp. in 'The Speech of T'ang,' p. 3, 率割夏邑. 劓, 'to cut off the nose,' is better translated here generally. Këang Shing reads 氏 after 夏, on the authority of the 說文; but the meaning which he gives to the whole is very far-fetched. —'The people also under the rule of Hea, suffering the oppression of greed and cruelty, longed more every day to see the kingdom of Hea cut off.' Only one searching for strange meanings could attempt to draw this from the text.

P. 6. 時 = 是. 天惟時求民主 = 天惟是之故求可爲民主者. 7. 惟天不畀純 = 天之不畀於桀 (=夏) 者大矣, 'Heaven's refusal *of its favour to Këĕ, (or Hea)* was great and decided.' The rest of the par.

explains why Heaven thus withdrew its favour. We have in Bk. XVI., p. 9, an opposite declaration of Heaven's favour to Shang, —天惟純佑命 It is well to take 純 in the same way in both passages, as meaning 'determinate,' 'decided.' 爾多方之義民 —義民, 'righteous people,' = 賢者 'men of virtue and ability.' They are called 'of your many regions,' *i.e.*, the many regions of the empire. We can lay no stress on the 爾, 'your.' 永於多享, —'long in much enjoyment,' = 'long in the enjoyment of their offices.' Këang Shing says:—不能久長多享祿位、言桀不任賢 不克明保享于民, —'could not understand to preserve and secure enjoyment for the people.' The use of 享, and the 于 before 民, render the language obscure, but the meaning seems to be what I have given. The 'Daily Explanation' gives for it—不能明達治體、以保安享有國家之民, 'they could not understand the art of govt. so as to secure their tranquil enjoyment (= possession) of the people of the empire.'

克用勸。○要
囚、
〔十一節〕

不明德慎罰、亦
以至于帝乙、罔
〔十節〕

厥民刑用勸。○
〔九節〕慎厥麗乃勸。○

簡代夏作民主。
湯克以爾多方
克開。○〔八節〕乃惟成

至于百爲、大不
乃胥惟虐于民、

lives, but on the contrary aided one another in oppression, so that of the hundred ways of promoting *prosperity* they could not advance one.

'In the case indeed of T'ang the Successful, it was because he was the choice of your many regions that he superseded Hea and became the lord of the people. He paid careful attention to the essential virtues *of a sovereign*, in order to stimulate the people, and they on their part imitated him, and were stimulated. From him down to the emperor Yih, the sovereigns all made their virtue illustrious, and were cautious in the use of punishments;—thus also exercising a stimulating influence *over the people*. When they, having

Ying-tă quotes the view of Too Yu (杜預) to the same effect, making 胥＝受, 'to receive;'—see the 註疏. Këang Shing defines 胥 by 皆, 'all.' It is equivalent to 'all,' but with the further meaning of 'mutual' co-operation. 至于百爲、大不能開，—Gan-kwǒ connected the former of these clauses with the one preceding.—'They aided one another in oppression, even in a hundred different ways.' The last four characters are then simply an addition to the indictment.—'And they were greatly unable to initiate any plan of good' (大不能開民以善). It is better to connect the clauses together as I have done. The 不克開 leads us back to 不克開于民之麗 in p. 5, and the meaning comes out as in the translation.

Pp. 8—12. *The empire gained by the virtue of T'ang, and maintained by that of his successors, was finally lost by the wickedness and misgovernment of Show.* 8. It is only in the interpretation of the intermediate clause of this par.,—克以爾多方簡, that there is a difference of opinion. We may translate it 'on the ground of being chosen by your many regions;' and the meaning, as stated by Yaou Shun-muh (姚舜

牧), is that 'Heaven, in seeking a lord for the people, simply followed the choice of the many regions' (天求民主，蓋從多方之所簡耳). Gan-kwǒ and Këang Shing translate, however,—'was able among your many regions to choose *the worthy*.' But this is *forcing* a meaning, much more than the other construction, from the characters themselves, nor is the sentiment so suitable to the tenor of the Book. 9. We ought surely to take 麗 here as in p. 5. Ts'ae, however, makes, 厥麗 to be ＝ 'what he depended on,' *i.e.*, the essential virtue of a sovereign, or benevolence. 刑＝法, 'to imitate,' 'to find a pattern.' Gan-kwǒ takes it in the sense of 'punishment.' —'His people, though he might punish them, were stimulated to virtue!' The student will mark the force of the 乃 and the 用 in the two clauses. And yet, such is the peculiar character of the Chinese language, that the critics interpret 用 in the next par. quite differently. 10. 明德慎罰,—see Bk. IX., p. 3. The assertion made here about the sovereigns of the Shang dynasty down to Yih, must be taken with large allowance. 11. 要囚,—see on Bk. XI., p. 11. It is strange to find this specified

殄戮多罪、亦克用勸。

開釋無辜、亦克用勸、

○今至于爾辟、弗克
〔十二節〕

以爾多方享天之命。

○嗚呼王若曰誥告
〔十三節〕

爾多方非天庸釋有

夏、非天庸釋有殷。○

乃惟爾辟以爾多方、
〔十四節〕

大淫圖天之命屑有

辭。○乃惟有夏圖厥
〔十五節〕

examined the evidence in criminal cases, put to death those chargeable with many crimes, they exercised the same influence; they did so

12 also, when they liberated those who were not purposely guilty. But when *the* throne came to your *late* sovereign, he could not with *the good will* of your many regions continue in the enjoyment of the favouring decree of Heaven.'"

13 　II. "Oh! the king speaks to the following effect, 'I announce and declare to you of the many regions, Heaven had no set purpose to do away with the sovereign of Hea, or with the sovereign of Yin.

14 But it was the case that your ruler, being in possession of your many regions, abandoned himself to great excess, and reckoned on the favouring decree of Heaven, making trifling excuses for his

15 conduct. And so in the case of the sovereign of Hea;—his schemes

with reference to the emperors; but so it is in the text. 開釋無辜,—comp, in 'The Counsels of Yu,' p. 12, 與其殺不辜, 寧失不經. 12. By 爾辟, 'your sovereign,' we are to understand Show. 以爾多方 should be interpreted with reference to the 以爾多方簡 of p. 8. The critics have all overlooked this.

　Ch. II. Pp. 13—16. How ᴛʜᴇ sovereignty of the empire, having passed from Hᴇᴀ ᴛᴏ Yɪɴ, by the will of Heaven, passed again from the tyrant Show to the princes of Chow. 13. The critics have much to say on the manner in which this par. begins, —the repetition of 王若曰, and the 嗚呼, which precedes. But what can be said to the purpose, more than that the duke of Chow chose thus to speak? Very strange is the method of Këang Shing, who makes the 嗚呼 an exclamation concluding the previous paragraph. 庸釋,—庸=用, 有心之謂也 (Ts'ae), our 'on purpose,' 'with premeditation;' 釋=去之, 'to put away,' 'to remove.' By 有夏 and 有殷, we are to understand Këë and Show. The removal of them, however, was equivalent to the overthrow of their respective dynasties. 14. 爾辟=爾君, 'your sovereign,' referring to Këë. 以爾多邦,—'by—on the ground of—your many regions.' Këang Shing gives:—'relying on the multitudes of your many regions.' 屑有辭—屑, as in p. 22,=輕, 'lightly,' 'triflingly.' Compare in Bk. XIV., p. 5, 大淫泆有辭. 15. Here the speaker turns again to Këë, the representative of the Hea line (有夏). Lëu Tsoo-heen says that the 集 here is that of 積

子　惟　狂　聖　惟　厥　後　之　降　政
孫　五　克　罔　降　政　王　○　時　不
誕　年　念　念　時　不　逸　乃　喪　集
作　須　作　作　喪　蠲　厥　惟　有　于
民　暇　聖　狂　○　烝　逸　爾　邦　享
主　之　天　惟　十七節　天　圖　商　間　天

of government were not of a tendency to secure his enjoyment *of the empire*, so that Heaven sent down ruin on him, and the chief of

16　your State entered into the line of his succession. *Indeed*, it was the case that the last sovereign of your Shang was luxurious to the extreme of luxury, while his schemes of government showed neither purity nor progress, so that Heaven sent down such ruin on him.

17　'The wise, not thinking, become foolish, and the foolish, by thinking, become wise. Heaven for five years waited kindly, and forbore with the descendant *of T'ang, to see if* he would indeed prove himself the true ruler of the people, but there was nothing

集, meaning 'to—collect,' and the 享 is that of 享國, meaning 'to enjoy the empire.' He adds that 'good governmental measures bring together all means of prosperity' (治世之政, 聚其所以興). This is the easiest way of explaining the characters. Këang Shing, not so well, takes 集=就. Woo Ch'ing is here, as frequently, peculiar. He makes 不集于享 to mean—'the princes were alienated, and he could not bring them together and make them come to court with their offerings' (諸侯離心, 不能合聚之, 使來朝享). 時 (=是) 喪,—'this ruin,'=such a ruin. 有邦間之—by 有邦 is meant T'ang, so called as being then merely one of the princes, 'the holder of a State.' 間之,—'separated—interrupted—it.' Koo Seih-ch'ow says:—'From Yu to Këĕ there had been a continuous succession of 400 years; but from this it was interrupted and broken off' (自禹至桀, 四百年之統, 自此間而斷也). 16. Lin Che-k'e observes on 逸厥逸 that it means 'he carried his 逸—his luxurious in-

dolence to excess.' This is better than to take one of the characters in the sense of 過, 'to go beyond.' 蠲烝,—蠲=潔, 'pure;' 烝=進, 'to advance,' 'progress.' The meaning of the clause 不蠲烝 then comes out as in the translation. Këang Shing, after Ma Yung, takes 烝=升, 'to ascend,' so the whole = 'his measures of govt. did not go up purely to Heaven.' This is far-fetched, but not so much so as Woo Ch'ing's interpretation. He takes 烝, in its sense of 'the winter sacrifice,' and hence for 'sacrifices' in general, so that 不蠲烝 = 'he did not offer his sacrifices with purity!'

P. 17. 惟聖至作聖,—these two sayings have wonderfully exercised the ingenuity of the critics. Confucius has said (Ana. XVII., iii.) that 'the wise of the highest class and the stupid of the lowest class cannot be changed.' Surely he who can be called 聖 belongs to 'the wise of the highest class;'—how can the dictum of the great sage and the sentiment of the duke of Chow in this passage be reconciled? The student is not concerned to reconcile them. What the duke says we know to be accordant with facts. He had not come to the folly and arrogance of the sage and his school exalting the 'sagely man' above the attributes

惟　惟　旅　周　顧　爾　開　方　天　岡
式　典　克　王　之　多　厥　大　惟　十八
教　神　堪　靈　○　方　顧　動　求　節
我　天　用　承　惟　岡　天　以　爾　可
用　天　德　于　我　堪　惟　威　多　念
　　　　　十九　　　　　　　　　　聽
　　　　　節　　　　　　　　　　○

18 in him deserving to be regarded.　Heaven then sought among your
many regions, making a great impression by its terrors to stir up
one who might look *reverently* to it; but in all your regions, there was
19 not one deserving of its regard.　There were, however, our kings of
Chow, who treated well the multitudes of the people, and were able
to sustain the burden of virtuous *government*, and to preside over
all services to spirits and to Heaven.　Heaven thereupon instructed

of humanity, and all created beings.　須＝
待, 'to wait.'　服＝寬限, 'to allow in-
dulgently a longer time.'　The 之 in 之子
孫 occasions a difficulty.　Woo Ch'ing makes
it ＝是, 'this,' as in the expression 之子
于歸, quoted in the 'Great Learning,' Comm.
ix., 6.　It is better to take it as merely giving
emphasis to the active meaning of the verbs 須
and 服.　Show of course is intended,—'the
descendant' of T'ang.　The clause 誕作民
主 ought, I think, to be connected with the
preceding, as appears in the translation.　Gan-
kwŏ, however, and in recent times Këang Shing,
understand it as ＝'But he greatly played the
people's lord, and there was nothing in him,'
&c.　When it is said that Heaven forbore with
Show for five years, giving him the opportunity
of repentance, there must have been something
remarkable in the closing period of his history,
which was known to the duke of Chow and his
hearers, and to which allusion is made.　We,
however, do not know the events of the time
with sufficient minuteness to be able to say
what it was.　See on the 十三年 in the
'Great Speech,' Pt. i., p. 1.　18. 大動以
威,—greatly moving by its terrors.'　Moving
whom?　Gan-kwŏ says—'Show.'　But this is
evidently wrong.　The individuals intended to be
moved were the princes of the various regions;
the terrors employed to move them were the
overthrow of Show, and the troubles generally
of the time.　There is a difficulty in interpreting the expressions 顧天 and 顧之.
Ts'ae gives 以 開 發 其 能 受 眷

顧 之 命 者, 'to influence and bring forth
one who might receive its decree of favour
and regard,' for 開 厥 顧 天.　Then for
岡 堪 顧 之 there is given 皆 不 足
以 堪 眷 顧 之 命, 'all were insuf-
ficient to sustain the favouring decree.'　Woo
Ch'ing explains in the same way.　　But 厥
顧 天 must mean 'their looking to Heaven,'
not 'Heaven's looking to them.'　顧 simply
＝回視, 'to turn round and look at,' commonly with the idea of kindness or favour
attached.　I suppose that the subject of the
former 顧 is 'the princes,' and the object,
Heaven, while of the latter the subject is Heav-
en, and the object, the princes.　　19. 我
周 王—these 'kings' were Wǎn and Woo.
靈 承 于 旅,—see p. 5.　　惟 典
神 天,—典＝主, 'to preside over.'　The
whole ＝主 神 天 之 祀, 'who could
preside over the sacrifices to spirits and to
Heaven.'　The phrase 神 天 has occasioned
some difficulty.　When Dr. Medhurst made
his translation of the Shoo, he supposed that
神 was an adj. qualifying 天, and rendered
the passage by—'Only they could superintend
the worship of the Divine Heaven.'　Subsequently he saw the error of this, and has corrected
it in his 'Theology of the Chinese,' pp. 56, 57,
where he refers to the paraphrase of the 'Daily
Explanation,'—誠 可 典 司 神 天, 爲
上 帝 百 神 之 主 矣.　Gaubil trans-

享　介　方　裕　〇　爾　誥　今　尹　休
天　乂　爾　之　爾　四　我　我　爾　簡
之　我　曷　于　曷　國　惟　曷　多　畀
命　周　不　爾　不　民　大　敢　方　殷
今　王　夾　多　忱　命　降　多　〇　命

them, and increased their excellence, made choice of them, and gave them the decree of Yin, to rule over your many regions.

III. 'Why do I now presume to make *these* many declarations? I have dealt very leniently as regards the lives of you, the people of these four States. Why do you not show sincere and generous obedience in your many regions? Why do you not aid and co-operate with us the kings of Chow to secure the enjoyment of

lated the clause by—'Il (he takes 我周王 as singular) fut en état d'être mis à la tête des affaires qui regardent les esprits;' and observes, in a note, that 典神天 is equivalent to the 作神主 in the 'Both possessed pure Virtue,' p. 3. So far he is correct; but the 天 should not be sunk in a translation. Its use shows very clearly, how, while the ancient Chinese could say of God, whom they intended by 'Heaven,' that He was a *spirit*, just as we do, they did not consider Him as merely one of 'the host of spirits.' No Chinese critic has ever taken 神 here as an adjective. They invariably understand a conjunction between 神 and 天. I need only give further what Ch'in Ta-yew says on the passage:—可爲神與天 之主，山川宗社之得其安，三光寒暑之得其序，皆人君有以主之 If it be still asked why 天, as the more honourable, does not precede 神, we may reply with Dr. Medhurst, that 天神 might have been taken as meaning 'the spirits of heaven;' or (which seems to me more likely, as that usage of 天神 is foreign to the Shoo) that the collocation was chosen to avoid the coming together of the closely allied sounds of 典 and 天. 惟天式教我用 休，—'Heaven therefore (see 式 in Bk. XVI., p. 21) taught us, and thereby was excellence.' By the 我, 'us,' are intended the 我王, at the beginning of the par., and I have therefore kept the third person in the translation.

Ch. III. Pp. 20—23. THE KING COMPLAINS OF THE RELUCTANCE WITH WHICH THE RULE OF CHOW WAS SUBMITTED TO; SHOWS THE FOLLY OF IT, AND DECLARES THAT, IF PERSEVERED IN, IT SHOULD BE DEALT WITH IN ANOTHER STYLE.

20. 曷敢，—'how dare I?' The critics make no remark on the use of 敢, 'to dare,' 'to presume,' here. It is strange from the lips of the king in this connection. He might very well speak of himself as 'presuming,' with reference to Heaven; but it sounds oddly as it stands. 我惟，云云，—see on p. 2. Yaou Shun-muh says:—'At the commencement of the announcement, the king tells them how he had spared their lives, and starts from that to unfold the reasons why Heaven now bestows its favour and now withdraws, that they might be taught to nip the unquiet and insurrectionary tendencies of their hearts in the bud. Here he reminds them a second time of the same thing, wishing to show them the path of self-renovation and improvement, that they might escape the miseries of extreme punishment in which they were going on to involve themselves.' See the 集說. 21. 爾曷不忱 裕之，—I take the 之 here like the same character in 須暇之, p. 17, as giving emphasis to the previous verbs. This usage corresponds to that which is not unfrequent with our English *it*.—'Why do you not sincere it, and liberalize it?' Treated so well by the govt. of Chow, why would they not obey it sincerely and with a largeness of mind like that which had been shown to them. It is not easy to translate the clause. Medhurst misses the meaning; and when Gaubil says 'Pourquoi ne seriez-vous pas desormais fideles et tranquilles dans votre pays,' the '*tranquilles*" by no means brings out sufficiently the meaning of 裕. 夾介

爾尚宅爾宅、畋爾
田爾邑不惠王熙
天之命。○爾乃迪
屢不靜爾心未愛、
爾乃不大宅天命、
爾乃屑播天命爾
乃自作不典圖忱
于正。○我惟時其
教告之、我惟時其
戰要囚之、至于再、

Heaven's favouring decree? You now still dwell in your dwellings, and cultivate your fields;—why do you not obey our kings, and
22 consolidate the decree of Heaven? The paths which you tread are continually those of disquietude;—have you in your hearts no love for yourselves? do you refuse so greatly to acquiesce in the ordinance of Heaven? do you triflingly reject that decree? do you of yourselves pursue unlawful courses, scheming *by your alleged*
23 *reasons* for the approval of upright men? I simply instructed and declared to you; I secured in trembling awe and confined the chief criminals:—I have done so twice and for three times.

=夾輔介助, to assist and 'to aid.' 乂 is best taken as =保, 'to preserve,' 'to maintain.' The kings of Chow had received the favouring decree of Heaven; but that decree had to be made firm or sure by the cheerful acquiescence of the people and princes in their sway. 今爾至爾田,—comp. the closing par. of the 'Numerous Officers.' 惠 =順, 'to accord with,' = 'to obey and have sympathy with.' 熙=廣, 'to make wide,' = 'to strengthen.' 22. The 'Daily Explanation' says that here 'the people of Yin are reproved as to the past, and admonished as to the future.' The first clause is to be supposed narrative; but all the others are best taken interrogatively. 爾乃迪屢不靜 =爾乃屢蹈不靜. This is somewhat harsh, requiring the inversion of 迪屢; but what can we do? Këang Shing takes 迪 in the sense of 道.—'I have sought to guide you repeatedly, but still you are not tranquil.' This construction is more objectionable. Their 'paths of disquietude' were the rebellious movements in which they had repeatedly engaged. 爾心未愛 is taken by Gan-kwŏ and Këang Shing indicatively,=

'you do not yet love our dynasty of Chow.' I prefer, however, to understand it as in the translation. Ts'ae gives:—爾心其未 知所以自愛也. 宅天命,—宅=居 or 安, 'to rest or repose in.' 屑, —see par. 14. 不典=不法, 'lawless ways.' The last clause, 圖忱于正, is a difficult one. Gan-kwŏ and Ying-tă are as enigmatical upon it as the text itself. Këang Shing takes 正=長, 'superiors,' and gives:—謀取信于長上, 'scheming to be believed by your superiors.' But what 'superiors' can we think of in the case? The translation is after the 'Daily Explanation,' which says:—且爾等反覆叛亂,自作 不法之事,爲正人所深惡, 乃猶以義不忘殷,圖見信 于正人乎, 23. *Past leniency would not be continued, if they still continued dissatisfied and gave disturbance.* 我惟至于三 is to be taken as descriptive of the king's past dealings with the rebellious. Kin Le-ts'ëang says:—'教告之 refers to the announcements made before the expedition to the East

我監五祀。○越
士、今爾奔走臣
方多士、暨殷多
嗚呼獻告爾有
自速辜。○王曰
不康寧、乃惟爾
非我有周秉德
乃其大罰殛之、
用我降爾命、我
至于三、乃有不

But if you do not take advantage of the leniency with which I have spared your lives, I will proceed to severe punishments and put you to death. It is not that we, the sovereigns of Chow, hold it virtuous to make you untranquil, but it is you yourselves who accelerate your crimes *and sufferings*.'"

24   IV. "The king says, 'Oh! ho! I tell you, ye many officers of the various regions, and you, ye many officers of Yin, now have ye been hurrying about, doing service to my overseers for five years.

(謂東征之前, 文告之); 戰
要囚之 refers to the captives and prisoners, during that expedition, who however were not put to death' (謂東征之時, 俘囚之, 然不殺)· 惟時＝惟是· We may retain the signification of 惟 as 'only,' 'simply.' We cannot, however, interpret 要囚 as we have done in the previous instances of its occurrence, p. 11, and Bk. IX., p. 12. The 之 here perhaps requires that we interpret the phrase differently. Wang Ts'eaou gives for it 束而囚執之. 非我, 云云, —comp. the two last clauses of Bk. X., p. 11. Compare also Bk. XIV., p. 18, 非我一人奉德不康寧.

Ch. IV. Pp. 24—29. THE KING ADDRESSES MORE PARTICULARLY THE NUMEROUS OFFICERS WHO HAD BEEN REMOVED TO Lŏ, AND URGES THEM TO THE RIGHT DISCHARGE OF THEIR DUTIES. IF THEY DO WELL, THEY WILL HAVE GREAT REWARDS. IF THEY PROVE IDLE AND PERVERSE, THEY WILL BOTH BY HEAVEN AND THE KING, BE MORE HEAVILY PUNISHED THAN THEY HAD YET BEEN. Woo Ch'ing, as I stated in the note on the name of the Book, removes this chapter to the 'Numerous Officers,' with the exception of a part of the 29th par., which he seems to reject altogether. In this measure, he followed the example of the critics Woo and Hoo (probably 吳才老 and 胡明仲). The change of the style of address, from 多方 to

多士, certainly gives countenance to it, though the 有方多士 in par. 24 may be pleaded in favour of the received arrangement. The point, however, is of little importance.

P. 24. Ying-tă explains 爾有方多士 by 汝在此所有四方之多士, 謂四方之諸侯, 'you who are here, the numerous officers of the four quarters. The princes from the four quarters of the empire are thus designated.' I would rather take 有方 as ＝所有之方, equivalent to 'all the quarters of the empire.' 臣我監五祀 (＝年. The Yin term for 'year' is used, perhaps because it is the old officers of that dyn. who are addressed),—acting as ministers to my overseers for five years.' Kёang Shing supposes that the 'overseers' are the three uncles of the king, who had been appointed by his father to oversee Woo-kăng, and finds a reference to the past;—'Ye hurried about, doing service to my overseers for five years.' But this interpretation is quite absurd; and moreover the 今 is inexplicable on it. It is only exceeded in absurdity by the view of Gan-kwŏ, who would interpret:—'Ye run about serving my overseers. If you do so for five years without fault, I will restore you to your original territory!' King Ching's 'overseers' were the ministers of Chow, under whose charge the officers and people of Yin removed to Lŏ were placed. The statement that those officers had served them there for 'five years' should put

乃　亦　尚　克　爾　不　爾　枲　多　惟
位　則　不　勤　邑　睦　惟　○　正　有
克　以　忌　乃　克　爾　和　自　爾　胥
閱　穆　于　事　明　惟　哉　作　罔　伯
于　穆　凶　○　爾　和　爾　不　不　小
乃　在　德　爾 廿七節　惟　哉　室　和　克　大
　　　　　　　廿六節

25　There are among you the employés, the chiefs, with the numerous
directors, small and great :—endeavour to discharge your duties ac-
26　cording to the laws.　It is from yourselves that the want of harmony
arises :—strive to be harmonious.　In your families there is a
want of concord :—strive to be harmonious.　When intelligence
rules in your cities, then will ye be proved attentive to your duties.
27　Do not be afraid, I pray you, of the evil ways *of the people*;
and moreover by occupying your offices with a reverent sedateness,
you will find it possible to select from your cities individuals on

beyond a doubt what I have all along maintained, that the removal of the people to the new
settlement had taken place before the building
of the imperial city of Lŏ.　See the 集傳.

25. 胥, 伯, and 正 are all names
given to various officers.　They were common
designations under the Chow dyn.;—see the note
from Ch'in Sze-k'ae in the 集傳.　But what
胥, what 伯, and what 正 are here intended
we cannot tell, and any very definite translation
of the terms cannot be given.　Ts'ae gives
枲 the meaning of 事, 'affairs,' 'business,'=
'duties.'　The dict. refers to the passage under
the meaning of 法, 'laws,' which we know that
枲 often has.　I have combined the two.　[We
know that Fuh-shang read 越惟有胥賦,
小大多政, which Këang Shing of course
edits; but I cannot find or give any suitable explanation of such a text.]　26. There seems
to be some gradation of thought here, from harmony of mind to harmony of conduct; thence to
social harmony in the families of the people;
and thence again to what we may call a general
political harmony :—all to be secured by the
harmony of the officers addressed.　Wang Ts'ëaou
says that 'the first 和哉 requires serene tranquillity of mind in order to the harmony of the
body or whole character, and the second requires
the harmonious obedience of the whole character
to reason in order to the harmony of the family.'
See the 集說.　This significance of the difft.

clauses, however, is very indistinctly intimated,
and hence Gan-kwŏ gives another interpretation, which it is not worth while to adduce and
animadvert upon.　27, 28.　The former of
these parr. describes certain things to be aimed
at by the numerous officers, if they could succeed in which, there would be the results which
the latter par. sets forth.　It must be allowed
that it requires considerable ingenuity to decide on the meaning which is to be given to
the clauses of the former.　爾尚不忌
于凶德—忌 is to be taken in the sense
of 畏, 'to fear.'　尚 has its force of exhortation or entreaty.　The 凶德, 'evil conduct,'
is to be referred to the people, whose stupidity
and obstinacy (頑民) made them so difficult
of management.　穆穆=和敬貌,
'the appearance of harmony and reverence.'
克閱于乃邑謀助=能簡閱
爾邑之賢者以謀其助, 'can
select the worthy in your cities, thus consulting
to get their assistance.'　Such is the view of
the meaning proposed by Ts'ae, only that he
finds the idea of concession in 尚.　Woo
Ch'ing's interpretation is different.　He says:—

度　幾　無　有　凶　惡　之　德　可　忌
諱　也　亦　且　蕭　敬　在　之　位　
能　臨　視　於　爾　爾　而　者
大　矣. Këang Shing reads the first clause

惟　凡　命　多　在　在　惟　天　洛　邑
逸　民　爾　士　大　王　其　惟　邑　謀
惟　惟　亦　爾　僚　庭　大　畀　尚　介
頗　曰　則　亦　。　、　介　矜　永　。
大　不　惟　不　○　尚　賷　爾　力　○
遠　享　不　克　王　爾　爾　、　畋　爾
王　爾　克　勸　曰　事　、　我　爾　乃
命　乃　享　忱　嗚　、　迪　有　田　自
、　　　、　我　呼　有　簡　周　、　時
　　　　　　　　廿　服
　　　　　　　　九
　　　　　　　　節
廿八節

28　whom you may calculate. You may thus in this city of Lŏ long continue, cultivating your fields. Heaven also will favour and compassionate you; and we, the sovereigns of Chow, will greatly help you and confer rewards, selecting you to stand in our royal court. Only be attentive to your duties, and you may rank among our great officers.'"

29　"The king says, 'Oh! ye numerous officers, if ye cannot exhort one another to pay a sincere regard to my charges, it will further show that you are unable to honour your sovereign, and all the people will *also* say—"We will not honour him." Thus will you be proved slothful and perverse, greatly disobedient to the charges of your sovereign.

along with par. 26, and edits it—爾上不碁于凶德. For 碁 he gives the authority of the 說文; but that is of no importance, as this character is there explained by 忌. But the 說文 quotes the passage with 尚 and not 上, which Shing arbitrarily assumes to have been the original reading. The meaning which he thus finds is:—'You will be proved attentive to your duties, and your superiors will have no occasion to detest your evil ways.' 爾乃至爾田,—自時(=是)洛邑 seems to='from this—on the ground of your behaviour in this—city of Lŏ.' The force of 尚 is sufficiently given by our 'may.' On 畋爾田, Wang Ts'ëaou observes that 'to cultivate a field (田) is called 畋, in the same way as to catch fish (魚) is called 漁.' 畀矜爾=畀字矜憐於爾, 'gift you and compassionate you.' 介賷

爾=介助賷錫於爾, 'aid you and confer bounties on you.' In 尚爾事, the 尚 has its hortative force. Ts'ae gives for the clause—其庶幾勉爾之事. 有服在大僚,—comp. 'The Numerous Officers,' p. 20. It will there be seen how the officers of Yin desired the favours that are here promised them.

P. 29. *If they will not be won by the leniency shown and the favours promised to them, but continue disaffected, and make the people also disaffected, they shall be dealt with summarily and severely.* The critics are here concerned to free the duke of Chow from the charge of speaking, or making the king speak, like one of the chiefs and arbiters among the princes, of whom we read so much in Mencius,—first coaxing and then threatening, subduing men merely by their strength. Leu Tsoo-heen goes into the point at length, and says that here we have the judgment and the infliction of Heaven always preceding the judgment and act of human authority. But we should find the same thing in the speeches of those tyrant-chiefs. The duke said what seemed most likely to him to accomplish his

則惟爾多方
探天之威，我
則致天之罰，
離逖爾土。○
王曰，我不惟
多誥，我惟祗
告爾命。○又
曰，時惟爾初、
不克敬于和、
則無我怨。

Throughout your many regions, you will bring on yourselves the terrors of Heaven, and I also will inflict its punishments, removing you far from your country.'"

30　V. "The king says, 'I do not *wish to* make these many announcements, but in a spirit of awe I lay my commands before you.' He
31　also says, 'Now you may make a *new* beginning. If you cannot reverently realize the harmony *which I enjoin*, do not *hereafter* murmur against me.'"

end. 嗚呼至不享,—comp. Bk. XIII., p. 12. The meaning of 享 is the same in both passages, only the idea of 'offerings' is more here as the expression simply of loyal obedience. 頗=僻, 'depraved,' 'perverse.' 遠王命=違王命; 探=求取 'to seek for and bring on.' 離逖爾 土,—comp. 移爾退逃, Bk. XIV., p. 21. The king would seem to be threatening the refractory with another and more distant banishment. Ts'ae conjectures that 多方 is a mistake for 多士, which, I think, is very likely.

Ch. V. Pp. 30, 31. *The conclusion of the address.* 我不至爾命,—the relation between the two clauses seems to require that the former should be supplemented as in the translation. 時惟爾初=今與爾更始, 'now I grant to you to change and begin *afresh*.' The 時, however, is not=今, but=是.

THE BOOKS OF CHOW.

BOOK XIX. THE ESTABLISHMENT OF GOVERNMENT.

立政　　周公若曰拜　手稽首告嗣　天子王矣用　咸戒于王曰　王左右常伯　常任準人綴　衣虎賁周公　曰嗚呼休兹

一節

1　I. The duke of Chow spoke to the following effect, "With our heads to our hands and then to the ground, we make our declarations to the new emperor, our king." In such manner accordingly all *the other ministers* cautioned the king, saying, "In close attendance on your Majesty there are the regular presidents, the regular *high* officers, and the officers of the laws; the keepers of the robes *also*, and the guards."—The duke of Chow said, "Oh! admirable are these *officers*. Few, however, know to be sufficiently anxious about them."

THE NAME OF THE BOOK.—立政, 'The Establishment of Government.' This phrase occurs four or five times in the course of the Book, and is thence taken to denominate it;—with considerable appropriateness. The subject treated of throughout is, it will be seen, how good government may be established. The Book is found in both the texts.

CONTENTS. The editors of Yung-ching's Shoo give the following summary of the Book from Tung Ting (董鼎), of the Yuen dynasty, which is tolerably complete:—'In imperial govt. there is nothing more important than the use of *proper* men; and when *proper* men are being looked out for, the first care should be for those to occupy the "three *high* positions." When these are properly filled, all the other offices will get their right men, and imperial govt. will be established. The appointment of the officers of business, of pastoral oversight, and of the law (宅事, 牧, 準; p. 2) is the great theme of the whole Book (其綱領), and the words, "Admirable are these! But to know to be sufficiently careful about them," ——, are its pulse [其血脈; *i.e.*, may be felt everywhere, throbbing in all the sentiments]. Parr. 2 and 3 illustrate the subject from the history of the Hea dynasty; parr. 4 and 5 do the same from that of the House of T'ang; and in parr. 9 to 15 it is shown how Wăn and Woo, like the founders of the previous dynasties, knew how to be anxious about the selection of their officers, and so obtained the great inheritance of the empire, initiating the happy state which was then continuing. From par. 16 to the end, the duke earnestly addresses the king on his duty to put away from him men of artful tongues; to employ the good, distinguished by their habits of virtue; to be always well prepared for war; and to be very careful of his conduct in the matter of litigations. His object in all was that the king should learn from the founders of the different dynasties how he should manifest anxiety on the great subject of the Book, and should be warned by the fate of Kĕĕ and Show against allowing himself to be indifferent about it. The whole is an example of loyal affection, which we seem even to the present day to be able to take hold of.'

Lin Che-k'e comments upon it, arranged in three chapters:—parr. 1—5; 6—15; 16—28. The student will find the arrangement in five chapters which I have adopted of more assistance to him.

THE ORDER OF THE PARAGRAPHS; AND DATE. There is no ancient authority for altering the arrangement of the received text; but the reader can hardly fail to be annoyed with the long list of officers of Wăn and Woo in parr. 8—15.— Why should the speaker go at so much length into their appointments, after having touched so briefly on those of Yu and T'ang? The student's attention is distracted by the lengthy enumeration; it could only have diverted the young king's mind from the important lesson which the duke wished to impress upon him. There is, again, the greater portion of par. 2,—from 乃敢 to the end, which has always seemed to me to have no proper connection as it stands. The only Chinese critic, however, whom I have met with, who owns to feeling the same difficulties is Wang Pih. He does not scruple to say that the text as it stands is 'head and tail in disorder, and without connection.' His conception of the occasion when the duke delivered the sentiments of the Book is this:—It was soon after king Ching undertook the responsibilities of the government. At such a time it was proper that all the officers should unite in *lessoning* him, and the duke of Chow accordingly appeared with a host of them, great and small, and when they had expressed their views on the point which seemed most important to them, he took the subject up, and prosecuted it in his own way. Pih would thus remove parr. 8—11, and the part of par. 2 to which I have referred, and make them all one long preliminary paragraph;—周公若曰拜 手稽首,告嗣天子王矣,用 咸戒于王曰,王左右常伯 常任,準人,綴衣,虎賁,趣馬, 小尹,左右攜僕,百司,庶府, 大都小伯,藝人,表臣百司,

大史,庶常吉士,司徒,司馬, 司空,亞旅,夷,微,盧,烝,三亳, 阪尹,乃敢告教厥后曰,拜 手稽首后矣,曰宅乃事,宅 乃牧,宅乃準,茲惟后矣,謀 面用丕訓德,則乃宅人,茲 乃三宅無義民,周公曰,嗚 呼,休兹,知恤鮮哉.

The praise of ingenuity cannot be denied to this arrangement of the text, and if it were proper to decide on such a point simply on internal grounds, I should not hesitate to adopt it.

Wang Pih supposes that this announcement was made after the duke of Chow had resigned the regency. Such was the opinion of all the early scholars; and likewise, we may presume from the order in which the Book stands, of the compiler of 'The Little Preface,' though his note says nothing on the point (see Pref. N. 54). Now, however, in the received chronology, the Book is referred to the 4th year of king Ching. This date was first proposed by Hoo Woo-fung (胡五峰; one of the early Sung writers, author of the 皇王大紀), and is argued for in the 通鑑綱目,—on very insufficient grounds, as will be seen from the notes on various paragraphs.

Ch. I. P. 1. CIRCUMSTANCES ATTENDING THE DELIVERY OF THE ADDRESS; AND ITS TEXT. 周公若曰至王矣,—it will be seen that I have translated 拜手, 云云, in the first person plural, understanding that the duke of Chow appeared before the king with a long train of ministers, and that he here speaks first in their name,—for himself and for them. Then 用咸戒于 王 intimates that the ministers all took up the subject, and began to speak for themselves. As the 'Daily Explanation' has it:—羣臣 用皆進戒于王. They have hardly entered on their admonitions, however, when the duke takes the word from them, and continues the address in his own person,—周公 曰,嗚呼,云云. Gan-kwŏ supposed that the duke of Chow was the speaker in his own person throughout. Hence he understood 拜手,云云 as = 'with my head to my hands, &c., I make an announcement.' For 用咸戒于王曰, he gives—又用 王所立政之事,皆戒于王

曰, 'He also took up the various procedures of the king by which he should establish his govt., and warned him on the subject of them all, saying,'———. But Lin Che-k'e well observes that this is very forced, and apart from the meaning of the text. The interpretation which I have given was first fully developed by Ch'in Shaou-nan (陳少南), who found the germ of it in the comment of Wang Suh,— 于時周公會羣臣, 共戒王, 其言曰, 拜手稽首者, 是周公讚羣臣之辭, 休兹, 此五官美哉. Dr. Medhurst makes 拜手, 云云, to be addressed by the duke to all the ministers.—'The duke of Chow, *addressing his ministers*, spoke to the following effect, Bow down and make obeisance, while you address the new emperor and king.' This construction is to be decidedly rejected, but there can be pleaded for it the authority of Woo Ch'ing, who says:—前周公若曰, 公與羣臣言也, 後周公曰, 公與王言也. 嗣天子王矣,—'the son of Heaven who has inherited (or, who is continuing) the line of succession, the king.' This language, it is said, is more appropriate, if addressed to the young king, a minor, than if addressed to him when of full age. It seems to me, on the contrary, what we should expect, if spoken to Ching now fully seated on the throne of his father. 常伯, 常任, 準人, —'the regular chiefs, the regular holders of office, and the equalizing men.' It is difficult to say what officers are intended by these designations. Leu Tsoo-heen says:—'These are the occupiers of 'the three positions,' mentioned in the 4th par.; but nowhere else in the Books of the three early dynasties do the designations appear. May we not suppose that they were other names for the high nobles and assistants about the imperial court? Different names were given to the occupants of offices, as when the prime minister was called A-hăng (阿衡) and Paou-hăng (保衡), and when the three chief ministers about a prince's court were called K'e-foo (圻父), Nung-foo (農父), and Hwang-foo (宏父). In the same way, the names in the text are to be taken simply as diversified designations of the great ministers who assisted in the govt. during the three dynasties. The two designations of 綴衣 and 虎賁 which follow are the names of two selected from among the various classes of inferior officers, as specimens of the rest. With

those who were in the great offices was lodged the safety or the peril of the throne; by those whose offices brought them into familiar intercourse with the sovereign his character was liable to be affected:—the condition of the empire depended equally on them both.' See the 集說. There can be no doubt these observations give the general meaning of the text, and the reason why the ministers and officers mentioned in it are specified; but how are we to translate the different designations? Gaubil avoids the difficulty by retaining the names, and giving vague accounts of the officers intended by them in his notes. It seems reasonable to take, with Lin Che-k'e, the 常伯 here as = the 宅乃牧 of par. 2; the 常任 as = the 宅乃事; and the 準人 as = the 宅乃準. We may then understand by 常伯 the chiefs or presidents who had a pastoral charge of the people (牧民之長); by 常任, the high ministers of War, Instruction, Works, &c., in the imperial domain; and by 準人, the law officers. 準 = 'level,' 'to level,' 'the instrument to make or determine a level.' 準人 are the officers who guard the laws, the instrument of justice. The officers called 綴衣, 'Connected Robes,' and 虎賁, 'Tiger Braves,' are not known to have existed under these names in the previous dynasties; this Book shows that they were an institution in the times of Wăn and Woo. We do not find the name of 綴衣 in the Chow Le, but there are enumerated the 'master of the furred robes' (司裘), the 'master of robes to the empress' (內司服), the 'tailor' (縫人), and the 'master of robes' (司服) which must have been kindred appointments. See Books VI., VII., and XXI. The 虎賁 are expressly mentioned in Bk. XXXI. They were guards, amounting, acc. to K'ang-shing, to 800 men, generally in attendance on the emperor's person; but might be detailed off to other services. 休兹＝美矣此官, as in the translation. Many critics understand the characters as meaning—'Admirable are these *observations*!' But it would be hard to say what observations have been made. The duke takes the word out of the mouth of the others, and at once gives out the text which he proceeds to illustrate in his own way. 知恤鮮哉＝知以不得人爲憂者殆亦鮮矣. 'those who know to make the not getting the proper men for them a subject of sorrow are few.'

宅稽厥行怕上大有古知
乃首后乃于帝競夏之恤
事后曰敢九迪籲乃人鮮
宅矣拜告德知俊有迪哉
乃曰手教之忱尊室惟　○
　　　　　　忱尊　　　二節

2   II. "Among the ancients who exemplified *this anxiety* there was the founder of the Hea dynasty. When his House was at its strength, he sought for able men to honour God. *His advisers,* when they knew of men thoroughly proved and trustworthy in the practice of the nine virtues, would then presume to inform and instruct their sovereign, saying, 'With our heads to our hands and then to the ground, O sovereign, we would say, Let such an one occupy one of your high offices: Let *such an one* be one of your pastors: Let such an one be one of your law-officers. By such appointments

Ch. II. Pp. 2, 3. THE IMPORTANCE OF THIS PRINCIPLE,—AN ANXIOUS CONCERN TO GET THE OFFICES OF STATE FILLED BY THE RIGHT MEN, ILLUSTRATED IN THE HISTORY OF THE HEA DYNASTY.   2. 古之人迪惟有夏＝古之人君,迪行知恤之道者,惟夏王大禹, 'of the ancients who walked in this course of a wise anxiety there was the great Yu, the Sovereign of Hea.' 迪＝行 or 蹈, 'to walk,' 'to tread.' Gan-kwŏ and Këang Shing take it as＝道; but they bring out the same meaning.   有室 大競＝當王室,大强之時, 'when the imperial House was greatly strong.' Këang Shing, after Gan-kwŏ, by 有室 understands 卿夫大之家, 'the families of the high nobles and officers;'—an interpretation not nearly so good as that which I have followed.   籲(＝呼＝求), 俊尊上帝, —comp., in p. 4, 丕釐上帝之耿命, and, in p. 6, 以敬事上帝. These three passages supply a very striking testimony of the recognition in those times of God as ruling over the nations of the earth. Yu, T'ang, and kings Wăn and Woo, the founders of the three great dynasties which are still celebrated, all considered it their great business to honour and serve God. They were simply His ministers. Whatever were the errors of religious belief and worship into which they fell, they held fast this important principle—that they were called to their high stations by the one Supreme Ruler,

and were bound to occupy in them so as to please Him. 迪知忱怕于九德之行,—this, I think, is spoken of Yu's ministers, the advisers who were about him. Not only did *he* seek out able men to honour God, but *they* also sympathized with him in his views, and co-operated with him, and recommended to him men of whose character and fitness they were assured. As Wăng Ts'ëaou tersely says: 一古之賢臣,以人事君,古之賢君,以人事天, 'The good and able ministers of antiquity served the sovereigns by *recommending the right* men; the good and able sovereigns of antiquity served Heaven by *employing those* men. For 九德之行 see 'The Counsels of Kaou-yaou,' pp. 3, 4. Lin Che-k'e explains 迪知 by 驗之於實迹而知之, 'those whom they knew by examination of their actual conduct.'   宅乃事, 云云,—these three clauses are to be taken not as general advice with regard to putting good men in the positions indicated, but as specific, with reference to the individuals whom they had in view as displaying more or fewer of 'the nine virtues.'   茲惟后矣＝如此而後可以爲君也, 'do this, and so will you prove yourself the sovereign indeed.'   謀面至末,—Gan-kwŏ quite misunderstood the meaning of this part of the par., led away in the first place by interpreting the 三宅 of the 五宅三居, 'three localities assigned to the five banishments,'

用上越暴弗民訓后牧
三帝成德作。德矣宅
有之湯作作○則謀乃
宅耿、陟往桀乃面準、
克命丕任、德宅用兹
即乃釐是惟人、丕惟
　　　　惟　　　
　　陂　亦　乃　
　　　　三節　　　四節

you will discharge your royal duty. If you judge by the face only, and therefrom deem men well schooled in virtue and appoint them, then those three appointments will all be occupied by unrighteous

3　people.'　The way of Këĕ, *however*, was not to observe this precedent. Those whom he employed were cruel men;—and he had no successors.

4　III.　"After him there was T'ang the Successful, who, rising to the throne, greatly administered the bright ordinances of God. He employed to fill the three *high* positions those who were equal to those

mentioned in the 'Canon of Shun,' p. 20. He gives for the whole:—謀所面見之乃乃之國事無疑則能用大順德乃其能居賢人于衆官若宥次能三居無義民大罪之外裔之次九州之外 'Consult on the ground of the things you have seen before your face, and which will not admit of doubt; you can then employ those who are greatly accordant with virtue, and will be able to fill all the offices with men of worth. Thereafter you can locate the unrighteous people in the three places assigned to them:—those whose crimes are heinous, farthest among the four wild tribes; less heinous criminals beyond the nine provinces; and those whose offences are lighter still beyond the boundaries of their several States.' This interpretation of 三宅 is altogether foreign to the scope of the paragraph; but it continued till the Sung dynasty, and even then Soo Tung-po followed it. 謀面 is 'to judge merely from the face, or outward appearance.' 謀面用丕訓德則乃宅人=徒謀之面貌而用以為大順于德乃宅任之. Këang Shing avoids the old interpretation of 三宅, and brings out a meaning something like what I have given, but by hard shifts. He reads 亂 before 謀; takes 面=

向; 丕 for 不; 義 for 儀; and interprets, 'If your counsels are deceived, and you move towards men who are not virtuous, and place them in these offices, then the occupants of these three positions will be able to give no good example to the people.'　3. 桀德—'Këĕ's virtue,' *i.e.*, his evil way, 德 being in a bad sense. 弗作往,—'did not do the past,' *i.e.*, did not imitate the example of Yu in employing the worthy. The language is not clear, but it is better to point and construe as I have done,—after Ts'ae. Gan-kwŏ and Këang Shing have each a different method; but they take the same view of the whole paragraph. 任是惟暴德=所任者乃惟暴德之人.

Ch. III. Pp. 4, 5. THE IMPORTANCE OF THE SAME PRINCIPLE EXEMPLIFIED IN THE HISTORY OF THE SHANG DYNASTY.　4. 亦越 may be taken, with Ts'ae, as a compound conjunction,= our 'again,' 'further.'　陟丕釐上帝之耿命,—'ascended, and greatly regulated the bright appointment of God.'　陟, 'ascended,' seems to be used with reference to T'ang's from being the chief of a second-rate State becoming emperor. Other explanations of the term are given, but it is not worth while to dwell on them. 釐=理 or 治, 'to regulate,' 'to administer.' Gan-kwŏ prefers the meaning of 賜, 'to give;'—but very inappropriately. The

羞　在　德　方　厥　商　宅　丕　克　宅
刑　受　○　用　邑　邑　三　式　卽　曰
暴　德　嗚　丕　其　用　俊　克　俊　三
德　暋　呼　式　在　協　其　用　嚴　有
之　惟　其　見　四　于　在　三　惟　俊

positions; and those who were called possessors of the three grades of
ability could display that ability.   He then studied them severely
and greatly imitated them, making the utmost use of them in their
three positions and with their three grades of ability.   The people in
the cities of Shang were hereby all brought to harmony, and those in
the different quarters of the empire were brought greatly under the
5 influence of the virtue thus displayed.   Oh! when the throne of T'ang
came to Show, his character was all violence.   He preferred men of
severity, princes of States who deemed cruelty a virtue, to share

meaning is, that when T'ang was established
on the throne, his whole system of govt. was in
harmony with the mind of God.   His institutions might be regarded as divine ordinances.
乃用三有宅克卽宅,—this
is clearly paraphrased in the 'Daily Explanation'—乃又能旁求賢才,相助
爲理,所用以居常伯常任
準人之官,爲三有宅者,實
能就是位,而不曠廢其職.
Still more evident here than in the 2d par. is
the blunder of Gan-kwŏ in taking 三宅 of
'the three places of banishment.'   三有
俊,—'the three—or three classes—of possessors of ability, men among a thousand.' Gan-kwŏ
and Këang Shing suppose that men are meant
who possessed the 'three virtues' mentioned in
'The Great Plan,' p. 17; but it is simpler to
understand that by 俊 are intended men who
had talents and virtue which would make
them eligible to the three high positions.   On
such T'ang had his notice fixed, and was
prepared to call them to office at the proper
time.   曰三有俊克卽俊=所
稱三俊,實能就是德而不
浮其名.   嚴惟至三俊,—
Woo Ch'ing may be said to expunge 嚴惟
丕式, for he says that they are 'a form of
introduction' (發語辭).   Gan-kwŏ and
Këang Shing interpret the passage thus:—
'T'ang's majesty became a great example to the

empire because he was able to use the right
men' (湯之嚴威惟能大法
于天下者,以其能用三宅
三俊).   They differ, however, in the meaning which they give to 三宅; but their construction of the text is far inferior to that of
Leu Tsoo-heen and other critics, which I have
followed.   惟 is not the particle, but the verb,
=思, 'to think of,' 'to study;' and 式=
法 or 效, 'to imitate.'   Tsoo-heen says that
T'ang's way with E Yin, first sitting as a learner
at his feet, and then reposing entire confidence
in him as his minister, may illustrate the meaning.   其在商邑,—by 'the cities of
Shang' we are to understand all the territory of
the imperial domain.   用丕式見德,
—'thereby were led to great imitation, and saw
the virtue of their sovereign.'   The 'Daily Explanation' expands it:—其在四方之
遠而自慕者,用以大爲取
法,如親見其君德而無不
順治焉.   5. 其在受,—comp.
the commencement of parr. 5 and 6 in Bk. XV.
暋=强, 'strong,' 'violent.'   Ts'ae explains
羞刑 by 進任刑戮者, 'he advanced
to office those who punished capitally.'   Këang
Shing also gives 進任 for 羞; but I must
take 羞刑 as a description of 暴德之
人, 'men of violent character, like his own, who

上帝立民長伯。○
三有俊心以敬事
知三有宅心灼見
亦越文王武王克
受命、奄甸萬姓。○
乃伻我有夏、式商
于厥政、帝欽罰之、
庶習逸德之人、同
人、同于厥邦、乃惟

with him in the *government of the empire;* and at the same time, the host of his associates, men who counted idleness a virtue, shared the offices of his court. God then sovereignly punished him, and caused us to possess the great empire, enjoy the favouring decree which Shang had *afore* received, and govern all the people in their myriad realms.

6   IV. "Subsequently there were king Wăn and king Woo, who knew well the minds of those whom they put in the three positions, and clearly saw the minds of those who had the three grades of ability. Thus they could employ them reverently to serve God,

advanced (=deemed) punishments as the proper instrument of govt.' Show had pleasure only in those princes of the States who were such. 厥邦, 'his countries,' seems to be opposed to 厥政, 'his govt.,' *i.e.*, the fiefs to the court. I take 欽 in the sense of 'sovereignly.' Anything with the express sanction of imperial authority is so denominated. 伻我有 夏, 式商受命=使我 周有此 諸夏, 用商所受之命. 奄 甸萬姓,—'entirely to rule the myriad surnames.' Compare in Bk. XIV., p. 6, 成 湯革夏, 俊民甸四方. We need not seek for any other meaning to 甸 (as Ts'ae does) than the general one of 治, 'to govern.' 萬姓,—comp. Pt. III., Bk. III., p. 9. I suppose that 萬 is used without any particular reference to the surnames of the people as being so many, or that 萬姓=萬邦之民.

Ch. IV. Pp. 6—15. THE SAME PRINCIPLE OF ANXIETY ABOUT EMPLOYING THE RIGHT MEN EXEMPLIFIED IN THE KINGS WAN AND WOO.

6. Ts'ae observes that when it is said that Wăn and Woo knew *the minds* and saw *the minds* of the 三宅 and 三俊, this is equivalent to the language of the 2d par., 迪知忱恂而非謀面. It certainly indicates that those sovereigns sought to obtain the most thorough knowledge of those whom they placed or would place in the highest offices of trust. Tsoo-heen calls attention to the difference between 知 and 見.—They *knew* what was in the highest servants of their govt.; they *saw* what the men of ability could prove themselves to be, when called to employment. 立民長伯,—those whom Wăn and Woo thus appointed were the 三宅 and 三俊. Ts'ae, arguing from the language of the Bk. 王制 in the Le Ke, makes the 長 to be the governors of a 屬 or five States, and the 伯 to be the Chiefs of a 州 or 210 States. I do not think that we need to seek for such a definite application of the terms. Ch'in Leih says that it was a common practice of antiquity for the princes of States to reside at the imperial court, and there sustain office, while the officers of the court were also sent forth, as princes of

尹　臣　小　庶　右　趣　○　夫　立　七節
伯　百　伯　府。　攜　馬　虎　牧　政　　
庶　司　藝　○　僕　小　賁　作　任　八節
常　太　人　大　百　尹　綴　三　人　　
吉　史　表　都　司　左　衣　事。　準　九節

7　and appointed them as presidents and chiefs of the people. To establish their government, they had the men of office, the officers of law, and the pastors, and these appointments were their three

8　concerns. *They had also* their guards; their officers of the robes; their equerries; their heads of petty officers; their personal attendants;

9　their various overseers; and their treasurers. They had their governors of larger assigned cities and of the smaller; their men of arts; the overseers whose offices were beyond the court; their grand historiographers; and their chiefs of direction :—all, good men of constant virtue.

States. See the 集說. 7. Këang Shing briefly and comprehensively explains this par.— 文武立政, 以任人, 準夫, 牧, 爲三事. 任人 is the 常任 of par. 1; 準夫, the 準人; and 牧, the 常伯.

8. The long enumeration of officers in this and some following paragraphs has no organic connection with the rest of the Book, the argument of which would be improved by the omission of it. I have shown in one of the introductory notes how Wang Pih would dispose of it. All that we can do is to explain the various designations in the best way we can. 趣 (read *ts'ow*) 馬,—'equerries.' These belonged to the department of the 校人 or masters of the imperial stud. Their rank was that of 下士. See the Chow Le, Books XXVIII. and XXXII. 小尹＝小官 之長, 'the heads of small officers.' We cannot define the designation more particularly. 左右攜僕,—Gan-kwŏ understands this phrase as in the translation,—左右攜 持器物之僕. Ts'ae supposes that 攜 has this signification, and that 僕 denotes 'charioteers' (僕御). Woo Ch'ing, again would confine the two characters to this latter meaning. Gan-kwŏ's interpretation seems the preferable. 百司,—'the hundred superintendents or overseers.' The phrase denotes

all the officers who had their special individual charges. Many 司 are mentioned in the Chow Le,—the 司服, 司門, 司市, 司甲, 司弓矢, &c. 庶府,—'all the treasurers.' In the Chow Le, Bk. VI., we have the 大府, or 'Grand Treasurer;' the 玉府, or 'Treasurer of gems, pearls, gold ornaments,' &c.; the 內府, or 'Keeper of the inner treasury;' and the 外府, or 'Keeper of the outer treasury,'—the treasury of disbursements. Other 府 are mentioned in other places. Wang Yen says :—'The 庶府 denote all charged with the management of the imperial wealth' (凡掌財). 9. The 大都 小伯 must be construed, with Ch'in Shaou-nan, 大小都伯, 'the commandants of Too, great and small.' The clause is an instance of what is called 'interlaced style' (互文 見意), and when completed would be 大 都之伯 小都之伯. On the meaning of 都, see the note on Mencius, II., Pt. II., iv., 4. By the 'great *Too*' here we are to understand the cities in the imperial domain assigned for the support of the highest nobles (公之采邑), and by the 'small *Too*' the cities assigned to those of inferior dignity. 藝人,—'men of arts'. This is understood to

以　事、克　厥　文　_{十二節}亳　微、亞　司　士。
克　司　立　宅　王　阪　盧、旅。○　馬、○
俊　牧　兹　心、惟　尹。烝　○　司　司_{十節}
有　人、常、乃　克　○　三　夷_{十一節}空、徒。

10　"*In the various States* there were the minister of Instruction, the minister of War, and the minister of Works; with the many officers subordinate to them.

11　"Among the wild tribes of the Wei, the Loo, and the Ching; in the three Pŏ; and in dangerous places: they had wardens.

12　"King Wăn was able to have in himself the minds of those in the *three high* positions, and so it was that he established those regular officers and superintending pastors, so that they were men of ability

include, according to the language of the Le Ke, Bk. 王制, Pt. iv., p. 10, 'all who employ their arts in the govt.,—priests, historiographers, archers, charioteers, doctors, diviners, and the practisers of the various mechanical arts' (凡執技以事上者，祝、史、射、御、醫、卜、及百工)。 表臣百司,— these 百司 are distinguished from those in the prec. par. by the addition of 表臣, 'outside ministers.' We are to understand officers with special charges, as in the former case, but located away from the court. 大史,— see on Bk. X., p. 13. We are to understand here not only the 'Grand Historiographer,' but all the officers in his department. 尹伯 is defined by Ts'ae 有司之長, 'the heads of the several classes of offices.' He illustrates his meaning by referring to the 庖人 (=庖尹), or 'butcher,' and the 內饔, or 'cook,' whose offices were both subordinate to that of the 膳夫, or 'master cook,' who was their 伯。 庶常吉士,—this is descriptive of the officers enumerated, and of the subordinates employed by them.

P. 10. This par. has reference to the various officers in the States of the princes. See 'The Speech at Muh,' p. 2.

P. 11. This par. would seem to go on to speak of the officers,—overseers or governors,—whom Wăn and Woo appointed among the wild tribes, the 尹 at the close belonging to each of the tribes specified, all included under the commencing 夷. The 三亳, however, occasions a difficulty, for their people were the descend-

ants of T'ang's original subjects, and could not be classed with the 夷, under which term therefore we can only include the 微, the 盧, and the 烝. The two first of these are mentioned in the 2d par. of Bk. II., referred to above, with other wild tribes, who acted with the forces of king Woo in his overthrow of Show. The 烝 are not mentioned there, and there is much difference of opinion as to how that term should be taken. Gan-kwŏ adopts the meaning of 眾, 'the multitudes;' Ming-shing approves that of 君, 'rulers,' which is given to it in the 爾雅; and others suppose it is the name of a wild tribe, like the two preceding terms. The 'three Pŏ' were Mung (蒙) or the 'northern Pŏ,' in the pres. dis. of Shang-k'ew, dep. of Kwei-tih in Ho-nan; the western Pŏ, in the pres. dis. of Yen-sze, dep. of Ho-nan; and the 'southern Pŏ,' which was only a few *le* from the northern. Ts'ae says that he does not understand the meaning of 阪. He supposes however that it may mean 'strong positions' (阪=險) throughout the five domains, where it was deemed proper to locate special officers. K'ang-shing joined it with 三亳, and supposed that it denoted the three strong-holds, where the overseers of the different Pŏ were placed.

Pp. 12—15. *Further exemplification in Wăn and Woo of their anxiety to get right men; and of the confidence which they reposed in them when got.* 12. 文王惟克厥宅心,—we must explain these words from the 克知三有宅心 in par. 6. King Wăn was able to know fully the minds of his officers,

不　王　茲　王　庶　是　有　庶　攸　德
敢　率　。　罔　獄　訓　司　獄　兼　。
替　惟　○　敢　庶　用　之　庶　于　○
厥　敉　亦　知　慎　違　牧　慎　庶　文
義　功　越　于　文　。　夫　惟　言　王
　　　十五節　　　　　　　　　十三節
　　　　　　　　　十四節　　　　　　罔

13 and virtue. He would not himself appear in the various notifications, in litigations, and in precautionary measures of government. There were the officers and pastors *to attend to them*, whom he *simply*
14 required to be obedient and not disobedient. *Yea*, as to litigations and precautionary measures *he would seem as if* he did not presume
15 to know about them. He was followed by king Woo, who carried out his work of settlement, and did not dare to supersede his right-

and to employ them with entire confidence. Gan-kwŏ, indeed, took the language differently:—文王惟其能居心遠惡舉善, 'king Wăn was able to set his mind on this,—the putting far off the bad and elevating the good.' But, as Choo He has observed, if this were the meaning, we should have read 克宅厥心, and not 克厥宅心. Këang Shing reads 文王維厥度心, which he interprets—'King Wăn employed his deliberating mind.' 乃克立茲常事, 司牧人,—by 常事 are intended the 常任 of par. 1, and by 司牧人 the 常伯. The 準人 are not mentioned here, unless the 司牧人 be taken to include them and all the other officers who have been enumerated. 克俊有德＝皆是寔能俊而有德, being a description of the qualifications and virtue of Wăn's officers. 13, 14. These parr. are intended to show how king Wăn, having appointed the right men, left them to the management of their offices, and did not interfere with them in the discharge of their duties. 罔攸兼＝ 無所兼理, 'he in no way interfered with;—did not attend to, along with his own duties.' 庶言＝號令, 'governmental orders and notifications.' This seems to be the only proper meaning of this phrase in the connection. It must run on with the 庶獄

and 庶慎,—all under the govt. of 罔攸兼于. Këang Shing, partly after Gan-kwŏ, would attach 文王罔攸兼于庶言 to the previous par., with the meaning that king Wăn was guided in appointing his officers by the deliberations of his mind, and paid no attention to the praise or censure of individuals by others (庶言＝眾人毀譽之言). 庶獄＝獄訟, 'civil and criminal causes;'—see on Ana. XII., xiii. 庶慎 ＝國之禁戒儲備, 'all things in the State which were to be guarded against and provided for.' 惟有至末,—the 之 is taken as＝及, a particle of connection. 是訓用違,—this is a very difficult clause. I have translated it after Foo Yuen-tsoo (傅元初; Ming dyn.), who says:—文王宅之賢, 無非常德吉士, 任人欲其得有違命者, 推誠訓士, 安駇其命。不欲其違命耳。 14. Litigations and precautionary measures only are mentioned here, because king Wăn could not but know the notifications that went forth in his name. 15. *How King Woo entered into the spirit and work of his father.* 率惟敉功＝率循文王安定天下之功. Comp. 未克敉公功, Bk. XIII., p. 19. By 義德 Ts'ae thinks we

慎　民　乃　克　準　我　子　丕　德　德
時　和　俾　灼　人　其　王　基　以　率
則　我　亂　知　牧　立　矣　○　並　惟
勿　庶　相　厥　夫　政　繼　嗚　受　謀
有　獄　我　若　我　立　自　呼　此　從
間　庶　受　丕　其　事　今　孺　丕　容

十六節

eous and virtuous men ; who entered *also* into his plans, employing
as before his forbearing and virtuous men.　It was thus that they
unitedly received this vast inheritance.

16　V. "Oh ! young son, the king, from this time forth be it ours to
establish the government, appointing the *high* officers, the officers of
the laws, and the pastors ;—be it ours clearly to know what courses
are natural to them, and then greatly to employ them in the government, that they may aid us in the management of the trust of the
people, and harmoniously conduct all litigations and precautionary
measures.　And let us never allow others to come between us and

should understand 義德之人; and
similarly 容德. We get an easier meaning
certainly by taking the expressions in this way,
than if we understand them of king Wăn himself.

Ch. V. Pp. 16—24. THE DUKE ADDRESSES
KING CHING DIRECTLY, AND URGES HIM EVER
TO ACT ON THE PRINCIPLE WHICH HAS BEEN
ILLUSTRATED.　15, 16.　*How the king should
carefully choose, entirely trust, and steadily maintain
his officers.*　孺子, 王,—this language
has been pressed to show that the address was
delivered when the king was a minor.
子, it must be conceded, is properly ＝乳子,
'a sucking child ;' but it is used away from that
signification, whether it was applied to Ching
about his 15th year, or his 20th.　When the duke
of Chow had resigned the regency, he still
continued to think of the king as the boy he had
watched over, and ruled for, and so he calls
him here, when offering these counsels which
are not at all appropriate to him as a minor.
我其至牧夫,—the critics all say
that 我 here (and in other clauses below) refers
to king Ching.　Woo Ch'ing says, 'The six 我
in pp., 15, 16, are all the duke's 我ing king
Ching' (六我皆我成王).　Ch'in Ta-
yew says, 'By the 我 the duke identifies him-

self with the king.　Sovereign and minister
should compose, as it were, one body' (我者
我其君,君臣一體也).　All this
may be correct, but we may as well translate by
the plural of the first personal pronoun.　立政
covers the 立事, 準人, 牧夫, as it does
任人, 準夫, 牧 in p. 7.　It is remark-
able how the order of enumeration, when speaking of the 'three positions, is continually varied.
我其克灼知厥若,—comp.
the language of p. 6.　若 here must be equal
to 心 there.　The critics generally define it by
順, and then understand by 知厥若,
'know that they are accordant with right,'
obedient to heavenly principle.　Ts'ae, much
more happily, goes on to explain 順 by 心之
安, 'that in which the mind reposes,' and then
adduces, to illustrate the meaning, the words of
Confucius (Ana. II., x.) 察其所安,人
焉廋哉, 'Examine in what things a man
rests.　How can he conceal his character !'
丕乃俾亂＝大委任之,使展
布四體以為治.　Këang Shing would
strangely make 丕 here only a particle of introduction.　我受民＝我所受

是　庶　文　矣　言　且　受　德　言　之。○
乂　獄　孫　繼　咸　己　民。　之　我　　　自一話一
之。　庶　其　自　告　受　○　彥　則　　　　十七節
○　慎　勿　今　孺　人　嗚　以　未　　　話一
　　惟　誤　文　子　之　呼　乂　惟　　　　十八節
自　正　于　子　王　徵　予　我　成

17 them. *Yea*, in our every word and speech, let us be thinking of officers of complete virtue, to regulate the people whom we have received.

18　　"Oh! I, Tan, have received these excellent words from others, and tell them all to you, young son, the king. From this time forth, O accomplished son *of Woo*, accomplished grandson *of Wăn*, do not err in regard to the litigations and precautionary measures;—let

之民, 'the people whom we have received,' *i.e.*, who have been entrusted to us by Heaven, and transmitted to us by our ancestors. 時則勿有間之,—時=如是, 'thus,' 'in this condition.' 間之,—'to come between them;' either between them and their work, or between them and us. Këang Shing joins this clause on to the next, and reads 物 instead of 勿, from Wang Ch'ung's 論衡. He labours hard but unsuccessfully to interpret his text.

17. In translating this par. I have followed Ts'ae, who takes 末=終 and 惟=思 自一話一言=一話一言之間, 'during the space of one word or one sentence.' Lin Che-k'e has the same view. Woo Ch'ing would refer 一話一言 to the 庶言 of par. 13. Gan-kwŏ's comment on the whole par. is strangely laboured and absurd:—言政當用一善,善在一言而已,欲其口無擇言,如此我則終惟有成德之美以治我所受之民.

18—21. *The king is repeatedly and variously warned against erring in the matter of litigations and precautionary measures.* There was probably some disposition in the young emperor to interfere with the regular course of these two departments, which made the duke dwell so

pointedly upon them.   18. 徽言=美言 or 善言, 'admirable words' or 'good words.' He refers no doubt to all that he has said in the address. The 'men from whom he received them' were probably the host of ministers and officers, who had commenced to address the king when he took the words out of their mouth. Lin Che-k'e praises the honesty of the duke of Chow in making this acknowledgment, and contrasts him with some other statesmen who used the ideas of others, taking all the credit of them to themselves. 文子,文孫,—'the accomplished son, the accomplished grandson.' King Shing no doubt is intended. 正是乂之,—there is no end of the disputes about how 正 is to be taken. Ts'ae supposes that it=正人, which phrase we have in Bk. IX., p. 17. From the conclusion of p. 21 we must conclude that the 有司之牧夫 are intended. Wang Ts'ëaou makes a good observation on this par.:—'The prec. par. says that the sovereign is not to let other men interrupt the proceedings of his officers; here he is admonished not to throw those proceedings into error by interference of his own' 上言勿間之以人,此言勿誤之以已,大抵人君任賢不專,其弊有是二端,故反覆言之也).   19. 自古商

于　文　勘　勿　在　憸　宅　政　商
庶　孫　相　以　厥　人　之　立　人
獄　孺　我　憸　世　不　克　事　亦
惟　子　國　人　繼　訓　由　牧　越
有　王　家　其　自　于　繹　夫　我
司　矣　。　惟　今　德　之　準　周
之　其　○　吉　立　是　茲　人　文
牧　勿　今　士　政　罔　乃　則　王
夫　誤　文　用　其　顯　俾　克　立
。　　　子　　　　　　　
　　　　　　　　　　父　　
　　　　　　　　　　。　　
　　　　　　　　　　○　　
　　　　　　　　　　國　　
　　　　　　　　　　則　　
　　　　　　　　　　罔　　
　　　　　　　　　　有　　
　　　　　　　　　　立　　
　　　　　　　　　　政　　
　　　　　　　　　　用　　

(二十節) *(廿一節)*

19 the proper officers regulate them. From of old to the founder of
Shang, and downwards to king Wăn of our Chow, in establishing
government, when they appointed *high* officers, pastors, and officers
of the laws, they settled them in their positions and unfolded their
talents. It was thus that they gave the government into their hands.

20 In the empire never has there been the establishment of government in the employment of artful-tongued men;—*with such men,*
unlessoned in virtue, never can *a government* be distinguished in the
world. From this time forth, in establishing government, make
no use of artful-tongued men, but *seek for* good officers, and get
them to use all their powers in aiding the government of our empire.

21 Now, O accomplished son *of Woo,* accomplished grandson *of Wăn,*
young son, the king, do not err in the matter of litigations. There
are the officers and pastors *to attend* to them.

人＝自古及商人. By 'of old,' Yu,
the founder of the Hea dyn., must be intended.
克由繹之—由繹 is explained
by 紬繹 'to unroll a clue,' 'to get hold of
the end, and draw out all the silk.' The high
officers, being put in their positions, were made
to unfold all their talents. We may keep the
proper meaning of 由, however. See the comment of Leu Tsoo-hëen in the 集說:—由
繹 由 其 外 而 繹 其 中 也，由
其 言 而 繹 其 心，云 云. 茲 治
乃 俾 乂＝茲 其 所 以 使 之
事. It is better to understand the clause thus,
than to take it, with Gan-kwŏ, as＝此 乃

使天下治. 20. *Men of artful tongues
should on no account be allowed to get office.*
諞 (K. S. edits 憸) 人＝佞 人, 'specious,'
'talkative,' 'artful men.' Chëong Kew-shing
gives the following account of them:—憸 人
者，傾 巧 辯 給 之 人，詐 是 飾
非，言 足 拒 諫，悅 其 心 則 譽
桀 紂 爲 堯 舜，失 其 意 則 誣
伯 夷 爲 盜 跖　不 訓 于 德，
訓 is commonly defined by 順, but we may
retain its proper signification.　其 惟 吉
士＝其 惟 用 有 常 吉 士. See par.
9. 21. Comp. par. 13.

其惟克用常人。　自今後王立政、　大烈。○嗚呼、繼　光、以揚武王之　以觀文王之耿　海表罔有不服、　方行天下、至于　兵、以陟禹之迹、　○其克詰爾戎　廿二節　廿三節

22　　"Have well arranged also your military accoutrements and weapons, so that you may go forth beyond the steps of Yu, and be able to travel over all beneath heaven, even to beyond the seas, everywhere meeting with submission:—so shall you display the bright glory of king Wăn, and render more illustrious the great achievements of king Woo.

23　　"Oh! from this time forth, may you and your successors, in establishing the government, seek to employ men of constant virtue."

P. 22.　This par. suddenly introduces a subject diff..from those hitherto dwelt upon, and seemingly quite out of place in the Book. At the close of his address to prince Shih, however, we found the duke of Chow all at once break into the same warlike mood. There he would have the dynasty extend its sway, till 'from the corners of the sea to the sunrising there should not be one disobedient to the rule of Chow.' Here his enthusiasm rises higher, and he will have the empire extended beyond its limits in the time of Yu. Many of the critics argue that after the dynasty of Hea began to decline, the wild tribes all round the empire encroached upon it, till the 'nine provinces' of Shang hardly embraced half the territory which those of Yu had done. There is no definite testimony, however, to this effect. If it were so, we can well suppose that the duke of Chow was bent on extending the sway of his House, to recover at least all the ground that had been lost from the time of Yu.　詰爾戎兵,—詰 is defined by 治, 'to have in good order.' The term means 'to interrogate judicially.' Its proper force here is 'to maintain a strict inquiry into.'　戎 and 兵 are used in the dict. to define each other; both signify 'military weapons.' Gan-kwŏ is followed by Ts'ae in distinguishing them, as I have done in the translation (戎服兵器).　陟禹之迹,—'ascend the footsteps of Yu.' But this hardly makes sense. The 'Daily Explanation' defines 陟 by 越而過之, 'to go beyond.' For the 'footsteps of Yu,' the limits of his different progresses, see 'The Tribute of Yu,' Pt. ii., p. 23, and the 'Yih and Tseih,' p. 8. 方行天下,—方＝四方 or 徧.　觀 is used in the sense of 見, ＝ 'to cause to be displayed.' Leu Tsoo-heen tries to argue that the duke of Chow is not inciting the king here to warlike expeditions, but only to be prepared for war as the best security for peace. He lays down this maxim very tersely:—古人治兵,乃所以弭兵,後世銷兵,乃所以召兵. Këang Shing defines 詰 by 謹, 'to be circumspect,' 'to watch against,' so that he brings out the meaning that the king was to have done with war and cultivate the arts of peace, as the means of securing universal submission! For this interpretation there is no more ground than for Tsoo-hëen's reasoning. [I am glad to find that Woo Ch'ing thinks this par. as much out of place as I do. 'It has no connection,' he says, 'with the text before and after. It may be presumed that a portion of the Book has been lost.']

P. 23.　The duke here repeats the burden of his address, extending his wishes from king Ching to his successors. 常人＝常德之人. Comp. 庶常吉士, p. 9, and in 'The Counsels of Kaou-yaou, p. 2, 彰厥有常,吉哉.

○周公若曰、太史、司寇蘇公、式敬爾由獄、以長我王國。兹式有慎、以列用中罰。 廿四節

24 VI. The duke of Chow spake to the following effect, "O grand historiographer, the minister of Crime, the duke of Soo, dealt reverently with all the criminal matters which came before him, thereby to perpetuate the fortunes of our empire. Here was an example of careful anxiety *for other ministers*, to rank with him in the ordering of the appropriate punishments."

Ch. VI. P. 24. I cannot see that this par. has any connection with the rest of the Book. It appears indeed to be more out of place, if possible, than par. 22. It is evidently a fragment of some of the lost Books which has got tacked on here. 司寇蘇公,—'the minister of Crime, the duke of Soo.' From a passage in the 左傳, 成十一年, we learn that the duke of Soo (where Soo was I have not ascertained) was called 忿生, and was minister of Crime to king Woo. 式敬爾由獄,—Gan-kwŏ gives for this—能用法, 敬汝所用之獄, 'could use the laws so as to reverence the criminal cases which you use.' But what meaning can a reader get from this? Këang Shing endeavours in vain to explain it. I take 敬爾 together as an adverb, = 'reverently.' 式=用; different from below, which = 法. 由獄=所斷之獄, 'the criminal causes which he decided,'—which 'passed through' his hands. 兹式, 云云,—the 'Daily Explanation' gives for this:—嗣爲司寇者, 于此取法而加謹焉, 則必能以輕重偏重之條列, 用其中罰, 無偏重之條, 無失入失出之慮, 刑獄清, 而天下無寃民矣. This seems to give the meaning, but I prefer to take 列 as referring to the duke of Soo, and = 'to rank with him.'

BOOK XX. THE OFFICERS OF CHOW.

周　德　辟　民　庭　甸　萬　惟 一節
董　歸　罔　六　綏　四　邦　周　　周
正　于　不　服　厥　征　巡　王　　官
治　宗　承　群　兆　弗　侯　撫

1 I. The king of Chow brought the myriad regions *of the empire* to tranquillity; he made a tour of inspection through the How and Tëen tenures; he punished on all sides the chiefs who had refused to appear at court; thus securing the repose of the millions of the people, and all the *princes of the* six tenures acknowledging his virtue. He then returned to the honoured capital of Chow, and strictly regulated the officers of the administration.

THE NAME OF THE BOOK.—周官, 'The Officers of Chow.' The Book contains a general outline of the official system of the Chow dynasty. It details the names and functions of the principal ministers about the court, to whom various counsels moreover are addressed by king Ching. 'The Officers of Chow' is not an inappropriate name for it. It is found only in the old or Gan-kwŏ's text. Ts'ae assigns it to the class of the Books of the Shoo called 'Instructions' (訓體).

DATE; AND QUESTION OF GENUINENESS. The first par. refers the Book to king Ching, without any mention of the duke of Chow. Its date therefore must be in some year after the duke resigned the regency, and the king took the govt. into his own hands. As the next Book but one (now lost) contained an account of the duke's death, in the 11th year of Ching, we may assign the 'officers of Chow' to the 9th or 10th year of that monarch. I introduce the subject of the date here, because of the strangeness of the prefatory note about it, that the Book was made 'when king Ching

had made an end of the House of Yin, and extinguished the wild tribes of the Hwae' (see page 12). The 'making an end of the House of Yin' carries us back to the death of Woo-kăng in the 2d or 3d year of Ching (see P. N. 41); from which the extinction of the Hwae tribes would bring us down to his 7th or 8th year. The 1st par., which is the proper introduction to the Book, makes no mention of either of those events. I do not think the prefatory notice is entitled to any consideration.

On the question of the GENUINENESS of the Book, it will be sufficient here to give the remarks of Ts'ae, reserving the fuller discussion of the points he mentions for their proper place in the annotations. He says:—'This Book disagrees with the Chow Le, as we now have it, in various points. For instance, the Chow Le does not contain the ministers called here the "three *Kung*," and "the three *Koo*." Some have said that the *Kung* and *Koo* were dignities, enjoyed by other ministers, and were not specific offices; but if we refer to parr. 5 and 6, where it is said that "the three *Kung* discourse of the principles of reason, and adjust the States," and that "the three *Koo* assist the *Kung* to diffuse widely all transforming influences," these are specific duties, belonging to offices to which there can be none superior. Others would identify the 太師 here with the 師氏 of the Chow Le, and the 太保 with the 保氏; but this cannot be, for the 師氏 and 保氏 are only subordinate officers in the department of the minister of Instruction.

'Again, it is said here, p. 14, that "in six years the chiefs of the five tenures attend once at court," whereas in the Chow Le, Bk. XXXVIII., the princes of the six tenures appear at court, from such and such a tenure, every year; from another tenure in two years; and so on;—a quite different arrangement. These discrepancies give rise to doubts; but the Chow Le could only have been made by a sage. Or perhaps, the duke of Chow, when he was making all his arrangements for the officers of the government, had not come to the offices of the 師 and 保. What I mean is this, that he was restrained by some consideration of their greatness from speaking of them. Moreover, the book was not completed when the duke died. The laws and regulations in it had not all come into practice;—This may account for the discrepancies I have pointed out. And still farther:—What must have formed the sixth part of the Chow Le, "The officer of the Winter," is lost. The beginning and end of it are incomplete. It is a work of the duke of Chow, to which alas! he did not put the finishing hand. Let the reader of the Shoo, however, compare it carefully with the classic, and he will be able to judge of the governmental arrangements of the duke of Chow.'

CONTENTS. The Book has a beginning, middle, and end, more distinctly marked than we generally find in the Books of the Shoo. The first par. is introductory, and describes the condition of the empire when the arrangements of the official system of Chow were publicly announced; all the other parr. contain that announcement. The king begins by referring to the arrangements of former dynasties. He then, parr. 5—14, sets forth the principal offices of State, the ministers of which had their residence at court, and goes on to the arrangements for the administration of the provinces. The remaining parr. contain many excellent advices to the ministers and officers, to discharge their duties so that the fortunes of the dynasty might be consolidated, and there be no dissatisfaction among the myriad States. The whole, it will be seen, falls naturally into a division into five Chapters.

Ch. I. THE CONDITION OF THE EMPIRE WHEN THIS ADDRESS TO THE MINISTERS AND OFFICERS WAS PROMULGATED. Rebellion had been quelled; disobedience had been punished; peace had been secured at length within the borders of the empire.—There was now leisure to attend to the right ordering of the system of administration. 惟周王撫萬邦,—'the king of Chow soothed the myriad regions.' This phrase,—'the myriad regions,' as well as the 四征 and 兆民 below, are taken by Ying-tă as vague expressions, it being proper,

when speaking of the movements and measures of the emperor, to do so 'in large terms;' and both Lin Che-k'e and Ts'ae approve of the remark. I have spoken of the five tenures of Yu, and the ten tenures of the Chow dynasty on pp. 148, 149; and the difficulty of reconciling them with one another, and of reconciling the dimensions of even the five tenures with the actual extent of the country. There are other difficulties, however, in the way of taking the 'myriad regions' of the text literally, which may be seen in the note of Ch'in Sze-k'ae *in loc.* He says:—'The empire of Chow was 10,000 *le* square. A space of 1,000 *le* square, giving an area of 1,000,000 square *le*, would contain 100 States, each 100 *le* square; and the whole, 10,000 such States. But the territory of one of the greater princes was 100 *le* square:—it is easy to see how the tenures could contain 10,000 States. At the beginning of the Chow dynasty, however, the princes who assembled at Muh were only 800 (see on p. 298, App. to the Great Declaration). And in the "Imperial Regulations" [see the Le Ke, Bk. 王制] the States of the empire only amount to 1,713. For these reasons Ying-tă said we were not to take the 10,000 in the text literally.' We can indeed only regard the 'myriad States' of the text as a great exaggeration; and we must take in the same way the statement in the 左傳, about the great Yu, that 'when he assembled the princes at mount T'oo, they came with their gems and silks from ten thousand States' (哀公七年;—禹合諸侯於塗山,執玉帛者萬國). 巡侯甸,—see the figure of the tenures of Chow, on p. 149. Those of the How and the Teen were the first and second beyond the imperial domain. The critics seem to think that the king's progresses were not confined to them, but extended at least to the 'six tenures' immediately mentioned. 'These two are mentioned,' says Ying-tă, 'as being nearest to the imp. domain.' But why should we extend the meaning of the text in this way? There may have been good reasons, not recorded, why only the *How* and *Teen* tenures were inspected at this time. 四征弗庭＝四方征討不庭之國. Ying-tă says the king had only smitten the Hwae tribes, and the statement here that his punitive expeditions had extended on every side is an exaggeration like that in 'myriad regions.' Here again our best way is simply to take the text as we find it. 弗庭＝弗來庭者, as in the translation. Gan-kwŏ takes 庭＝直, a meaning which the character has, but which does not seem so appropriate here. 兆人,—comp. Pt. III., Bk. III., p. 5. 六服,—the Chow dyn. had nine *fuh*, or ten, including the imp. domain. By the 'six tenures' here are probably to be understood the How, Tĕen, Nan, Ts'ae, Wei, mentioned in the 1st par. of the 'Announcement about Lŏ,' and the imp. domain. There is much discussion on the point among the critics, however:—see Lin Che-k'e *in loc.*

州　四　內　建　唐　未　亂　制　若　官。
牧　岳　有　官　虞　危。保　治　昔　○
侯　外　百　惟　稽　○邦　于　大　王二節
伯。有　揆　百。古，曰三節于　猷　曰。

2　　II. The king said, " It was the grand method of former times to regulate the government while there was no confusion, and to
3　secure the country while there was no danger." He said, " Yaou and Shun studied antiquity, and established a hundred officers. At court there were the General Regulator, and the *President* of the Four Eminences. Abroad there were the Pastors of the provinces, and the princes of States. Thus the various departments of

犀辟＝諸侯．　　承德＝奉
承周德，'honoured and received (＝acknowledged) the virtue of the House of Chow.'
歸于宗周,—where did the king return from ? This announcement, occurring here, affords some ground for Ying-tă's view, that the king made a progress not only through the How and Teen tenures, but through all the others. By 宗周 it would seem that we should understand Woo's capital of Haou ;—see on Bk. III., p. 1. There king Ching continued to have his residence, notwithstanding the duke of Chow's wish that he should remove to the new city of Lŏ. The prefatory notice, however, says that the king returned to Fung, which had been the capital of Wăn. The various methods by which it has been attempted to harmonize the two statements may be seen in Lin Che-k'e. He himself approves of the view of Ch'in Shaou-nan,—that king Ching first came to Haou, 'the honoured city of Chow' in the text, and there deliberated and determined on the various arrangements for the officers ; and that then, before the public proclamation of them, he went to Fung, to announce the intended measure in the temple of king Wăn.　董正
治官＝督正治事之官, 'strictly managed the rectification of the officers administering the affairs of government.'

Ch. II. Pp. 2—4. FIRST PART OF THE KING'S ADDRESS:—THE PRECEDENTS OF FORMER DYNASTIES, AND HIS OWN ANXIETY TO DISPLAY A SIMILAR WISDOM.　2. 若昔大猷.—Gan-kwŏ gives for this—當順古大道, 'we ought to accord with (＝to follow) the great method of antiquity.' It is better to take 若 with Lin Che-k'e, as an introductory particle, so that 若昔 simply＝在昔, 'anciently.' Ts'ae understands the phrase thus. He is wrong, however, I think, in his interpreta-

tion of 大猷 as＝大道之世, as if it were in apposition with 若昔, and the whole meant—' in ancient times, the age when right principles greatly prevailed.' Gaubil takes the passage thus, and appears to think that some great meaning lies hid in it. He translates:—'Anciently, in the time *de la grande loi*, good government consisted in preventing troubles, and in preserving the kingdom without danger ;' adding in a note, ' We see that the time of *the grand law* is a time of innocence ; the troubles and the dangers of States come not till after this time. I believe that king Ching means to say that innocence of manners and public tranquillity are the basis of good government. The commentaries give here no light on the text.' The text is really sufficiently plain.　若昔
大猷＝'The grand method of former times was this :'—. The next par. illustrates how this method was carried out by Yaou and Shun, and Yu, and T'ang. When they had brought peace about in their distracted empires, they proceeded to secure it by the ordering of their official system. And Ching, having got the empire tranquillized at length, would now go on to imitate their example.

3.　唐虞稽古,—for 唐 and 虞 see on the names of Pt. I., and II. Yaou and Shun are intended, and it seems better to give those well-known names in the translation. Medhurst for 稽古 gives—'examined the records of antiquity.' But a statement so remarkable should not be supplemented. Gaubil observes that ' these two sovereigns, it may be inferred, had certain sources of knowledge, that is to say, some history, of the times anterior to theirs.' The expression may lead us to infer so, but I have not introduced the inference into the version. Gaubil adds:—'The author of the 左傳 speaks of the officers of Hwang-te, and of Shaou-haou, who reigned before Yaou. Confucius, in his commentaries on the Yih King,

厥官。○立太師
前代時若訓迪
夙夜不逮仰惟
小子祗勤于德
惟其人。○今子
立政不惟其官
亦克用乂明王
咸寧夏商官倍
庶政惟和萬國

government went on harmoniously, and the myriad States all enjoyed repose. In the dynasties of Hea and Shang, the number of officers
was doubled, and they continued able to secure good government.
Those intelligent kings, in establishing their government, cared not so
4 much about the number of the offices as about the men.   Now I, who
am a little child, cultivate with reverence my virtue, concerned day
and night about my deficiencies.   I look up to *those* former dynasties,
and seek to conform to them, while I instruct and direct you, *all*
my officers.

speaks of Fuh-he, of Shin-nung, and of Hwang-te,
as of princes of an earlier date.' This subject will
be found touched on in the prolegomena.
內有至侯伯.—for 百揆, see on the
'Canon of Shun,' p. 2.　四岳,—see on
the 'Can. of Yaou,' p. 11; *et al.*　州牧,—see
on the 'Can. of Shun,' p. 16. Ts'ae takes 侯
伯 as = 'the chiefs of the princes of States;'
and Ying-tă identified them with the 五長,
mentioned in the 'Yih and Tseih,' p. 8. Much
preferable to either of those views is that
of Lin Che-k'e, that the 侯 and 伯 are two
of the five orders of feudal princes, among
whom the provinces were divided,—two specified
for the whole 庶政惟和,—comp.
庶績咸熙, 'Can. of Shun,' p. 27.
Medhurst translates 亦克用乂 by 'and
yet they were enabled to maintain order,' as if
it were surprising that they should be able to
do so with two hundred officers instead of one
hundred. We ought not to suppose any adversative force in 亦. Lin Che-k'e appears to
have had an impression of the meaning similar
to that of Dr. Medhurst, for he writes of the officers of Hea and Shang being double the number
of those of Yaou and Shun, and of those of the
Chow dyn. being still more numerous (amounting to 360), because men were more able in the

earlier times. It is strange that it did not occur
to him that, as the population grew with the
lapse of time, the number of officers was necessarily increased.　明王至末,—Gan-
kwŏ joined this to the next par., and understood
it as a general remark about 'intelligent kings,'
with which Ching prefaces the account of his
own arrangements. It is better to understand
the remark as applying to Yaou and Shun, Yu
and T'ang. The gist of it is, that these sovereigns were not anxious to have the show of
many offices, but to get right men. Ts'ae says:
—明王立政,不惟其官之多,
惟其得人而已

4. 祗勤于德.—'reverently sedulous
about my virtue.' 逮=及, 'to reach to.'
夙夜不逮=夙夜常恐有所
不及. We must suppose that he measured
his deficiencies with reference to the standard
of Yaou, and the other 'intelligent monarchs.'
仰惟前代時(=是)若(=順)
=予仰承前代之明王,惟奉
順不違, 'I look up to those intelligent
monarchs of former dynasties, seeking to honour
them and conform to them, and not to act contrary to their example.'　訓迪厥官,
—'to lesson and lead the officers,'

化寅亮天　孤貳公弘　少保曰三　少師少傅　六節
惟其人。○　官不必備　爕理陰陽　論道經邦　兹惟三公　太傅太保

5   III. "I appoint the Grand Tutor, the Grand Assistant, and the Grand Guardian. These are the three *Kung*. They discourse of the principles of reason, and adjust the States; harmonizing *also* and regulating the operations of Heaven and Earth. These offices need not *always* be filled:—there must *first* be the men for them.

6   "*I appoint* the Junior Tutor, the Junior Assistant, and the Junior Guardian. These are called the three *Koo*. They assist

Ch. III. Pp. 5—14. THE SECOND PART OF THE KING'S ADDRESS, GIVING THE PRINCIPAL OFFICIAL AND GOVERNMENTAL ARRANGEMENTS UNDER THE NEW DYNASTY. 5, 6. *The three Kung, and three Koo.* We cannot well translate 公 and 孤 in these parr. Medhurst calls the 三公, 'three dukes,' and the 三孤, 'three conspicuous ones.' But the terms are here as names of office, and not of nobility. We may suppose that the *Kung* were so called with reference to the public spirit and freedom from all selfishness which 公 denotes. The dict. says the *Koo* were so named to show that, though they were assistant to the *Kung*, they were not to be considered as subordinate officers of their departments. Gan-kwŏ's account of the name is somewhat similar:—孤, 特也, 卑於 公, 尊於卿特置此三者. When it is said—'I appoint the Grand Tutor,' &c., (立大師云云), we are not to understand that these names and the offices belonging to them were first constituted by king Ching. From Pt. IV., Book XI., we see that they were in existence in the time of the Shang dyn. King Wăn had 太公 for grand Tutor, and under Woo that office was exercised by the duke of Chow, while the duke of Shaou was Grand Protector or Guardian. The meaning must be, that the offices were now more definitely declared a part of the governmental system of the Chow dynasty. Lin Che-k'e is of opinion that little is to be gained by attempting curiously to define the names 師, 傅, and 保, and distinguish them from one another. Kea K'wei (賈逵) held that 保 had reference to the preservation of the person; 傅, to aiding in virtue and righteousness; and 師, to the guidance of instructions. Gan-kwŏ said that 'the 師 was the

emperor's pattern; the 傅, his helper; and the 保, his sustainer in virtue and righteousness.' The renderings in the translation cannot be far from the exact meaning. The business of the three *Kung* was 論道經邦, 爕理陰陽. By 道 we are to understand all principles of reason and truth,—all the *courses or ways*, which it was proper for the emperor to pursue. The effect of the *Kungs*' discoursing on these with him would be seen in the States of the empire, in the govt. of which there would be no disorder. It would be seen also in the harmony of all the elements of nature, and the material prosperity which was dependent on them. This seems to be what is intended by 'harmonizing and regulating the *Yin* and *Yung*.' On the two characters 陰 and 陽, which occur with their mystical application nowhere else in the Shoo, it may be sufficient here to give the note of Gaubil:—'Chinese books are filled with these two characters. In their natural sense 陽 signifies "clear," "light," and 陰, "obscure," "darkness." In Chinese Physics 陽 is "movement," or the principle of movement; and 陰 is "repose," or the principle of repose. The moral and metaphorical applications of the terms are infinite, and extend to whatever is susceptible of them more or less, whether in Physics or in Morals. The sense of this paragraph is that all goes well in the empire; that the laws are in vigour; that commerce flourishes; that there are no public calamities; that the seasons are not deranged.' I believe that the meaning is not more than what Gaubil says. The remarks of Wang Kăng-yan are quite express on the point:—爕理陰陽, 別無他道, 惟區處人事, 各得其宜, 則 天地之氣自順, 故堯舜在 上, 而天災滅熄 [This is a sad mis-

海。均 百 治 掌 冢七予 地
〇 四 官 統 邦 宰節〇 一 弼
　人。　　　　　　〇

the *Kung* to diffuse widely all transforming influences; they with reverence display brightly *the powers of* heaven and earth :—assisting me, the one man.

7　"*I appoint* the prime minister, who presides over the ruling of the empire, has the general management of all other officers, and secures

representation], 庶 政 太 和, 在 夏 戀 德, 而 岡 容 有 天 災, 考 其 所 爲 不 過 任 庶 政, 使 四 岳 九 官, 十 二 牧, 分 而 已, 初 未 嘗 特 設 變 其 理 性 而 已, 初 未 嘗 特 設 變 理 陰 陽 之 官, 亦 未 聞 別 有 變 理 陰 陽 之 政, 云 云. See my remarks on 'The Doctrine of the Mean,' i. 5; *et al.*

官 不 必 備, 惟 其 人,—the meaning of this is briefly and clearly given by one of the brothers Ch'ing.—不 得 其 人 而 居 之, 不 若 闕 之 之 愈 也, 'If the right men cannot be got to put in these positions, it is better to leave them unoccupied.'

貳 公 弘 化, 寅 亮 天 地,—貳 公, 'seconding (= helping) the *Kung*.'

天 地 correspond to 陰 陽 in the former par. Tsoo-hëen says that 'Heaven and Earth are used with regard to the visible forms of those bodies or powers, and 陰 and 陽 with regard to their 氣, or operating energy.' Gaubil is wrong when he would understand 'religion' by 'Heaven' and 'government' by 'Earth.'

[I have stated, in the introductory note from Ts'ae, the objection taken against the genuineness of this Book, from the Chow Le's saying nothing about the duties of the three *Kung* and three *Koo*. But the existence and exalted dignity of these offices are referred to repeatedly in the Chow Le. For instance, Bk. XXI., p. 3, commences—王 之 三 公 八 命, 其 卿 六 命, which declares the existence of the *Kung*, and intimates their superiority in rank to the executive ministers of the government. Par. 32 of Book XXXVI, again, gives the *Koo* likewise precedence of those ministers.

—左 九 棘, 孤, 卿, 大 夫 位 焉, 羣 士 在 其 後, 右 九 棘, 公, 侯, 伯, 子, 男 位 焉, 羣 吏 在 其 後, 面 三 槐, 三 公 位 焉, 州 長, 眾

庶 在 其 後. The Chow Le therefore is not silent on these great ministers, as we might suppose from what Ts'ae says. It only does not treat of them separately, defining their duties, and enumerating the officers in their departments. But they were not the heads of departments. They composed the emperor's cabinet or privy council. Biot calls them happily—'les conseillers auliques,' and 'les vice-conseillers.' They were the prototypes of the 內 閣, or 'Inner Council' of the present day. It did not belong to the plan of the Chow Le to speak of them more fully than it does.

But if we could not thus account for the little that is said about them in that Work, the inference would be against it, and not against this Book. There can be no doubt as to the genuineness of the first half of par. 5. If all the rest of the Book be forged, so much—立 太 師, 太 傅, 太 保, 茲 惟 三 公—has come to us with the guarantee of Ch'ing Heuen; and even Këang Shing edits it as a veritable fragment of 'The Officers of Chow.']

Pp. 7—12. *The six chief ministers of the executive.* Only the minister is mentioned, but in every case we are to understand that he was the head of a department with many subordinate officers. There is a close correspondence between those six departments of Chow, and the 'six Boards' (六 部) by which the govt. of the empire is now administered. 7. 冢 (= 大) 宰,—'the great or prime governor.' The name was as old as the Shang dynasty, for we find it applied to E Yin, Pt. IV., Bk. IV., p. 1. This was the office of the duke of Chow (see Bk. XVII., p. 1.), who united with it the dignity of 'Grand Tutor.' The 冢 宰 is 'the officer of Heaven' (天 官) of the Chow Le, and is represented now by the 'Board of Civil Office' (吏 部). He was superior to all the other great ministers, and was called 'their Head' (六 卿 之 首). This difference between him and them is intimated, I think, by the 統 百 官, 'has the general management of all the officers.' This is probably what is intended by the difficult clause in Pt. IV., Bk. IV., p. 1, 百 官 總 已 以 聽 冢 宰.

司_八　教、　宗_九　禮　司_十　政　平_{十一}　司
徒_節　敷　擾_節　治　馬_節　統　邦_節　寇
掌　五　兆　神　掌　六　國。　掌
邦　典、　民。　人、　邦　師、　○　邦

8 an uniformity throughout all within the four seas: the minister of
Instruction, who presides over the education of the empire, inculcates the duties attaching to the five relations of society, and trains
9 to obedience the people: the minister of Religion, who presides over
the ceremonies of the empire, attends to the service of the spirits
10 and manes, and makes a harmony between high and low; the
minister of War, who presides over the *military* administration of
the empire, commands the six hosts, and secures the tranquillity
11 of all the States: the minister of Crime, who presides over the
prohibitions of the empire, searches out the villainous and secretly

must understand 立, from p. 5, at the commencement of this and the other parr. The
邦 in them is also to be taken as = 邦國,
'the empire.'　　8. 司徒,—'the superintendent of the multitudes,' perhaps with a
reference to the meaning of 徒 as 'disciples.'
This officer was as old as the time of Shun;—see
the 'Can. of Shun,' p. 19. He is the 'officer of
Earth' (地官) of the Chow Le. His department seems to merge in that of the present
'Board of Rites,' for we can hardly identify it
with the 'Board of Revenue' (戶部).

敷五典,—comp. 敬敷五教, 'Can.
of Shun,' p. 19.　　擾 = 安, 'to tranquillize.'
Ts'ae for 擾兆民 gives 馴擾兆民
之不順者, 而使之順.　　9.
宗伯,—this office was also as old as the time
of Shun. See 'Can. of Shun,' p. 23; which
supplies an explanation of the name 宗伯,
as = 宗廟官長, 'chief officer of the ancestral temple.' Otherwise, we might translate
it by—'The reverend,' 'The very reverend.' He
was the 'officer of the Spring' (春官) of the
Chow Le; and his department now is that of
the Board of Rites (禮部), which also absorbs
in a great measure the functions of the 'minister of Instruction,' as I have observed.　　治
神人 = the 掌建邦之天神地
祇人鬼之禮, 'manages the ceremonies to
be paid to the spirits of Heaven, of Earth, and of

Men,' of the Chow Le. Gaubil says:—'Il s'agit
des ceremonies religieuses pour les esprits, et
des civiles pour les hommes morts.' One cannot
restrain a smile at the distinction which he
introduces between the ceremonies, as here
'religious,' and there only 'civil!' 和上下,
—all festive, funeral, and other ceremonies, as
well as those of sacrifice, came under the 宗
伯, who had therefore to define the order of
rank, precedence, &c. This is what is intended
by the 'high and low' of the text.　　10.
司馬,—Ts'ae says that 'no arm of warlike
measures is more important than the cavalry,
and hence the minister of War was called
"master of the Horse"' (軍政莫急於
馬, 故以司馬名官). This minister
does not appear among the officers of Shun. He
is the 'officer of Summer' (夏官) of the
Chow Le, and appears in the 'Board of War'
(兵部) of the present day.　　掌邦政,
—'handles the govt. of the empire.' But the
same might be said of every other minister;—
why is the name of 'government' used only in
connection with the minister of War? Ts'ae
says:—'Military measures are used to punish
and to smite,—to correct the evil-doers; they are
the greatest of the measures of imperial govt.'
(戎政用以征伐而正彼之
不正, 王政之大者). 六師,—
see on 'The Punitive Expedition of Yin,' p. 1.
　　11. 司寇,—'manager of banditti' (羣
行攻刧曰寇). Kaou-yaou was Shun's
minister of Crime, though he was only called
士; see the 'Can. of Shun,' p. 20. There is

禁詰姦慝刑暴亂。○_{十二節}司空掌邦土居四民時地利。○_{十三節}六卿分職各率其屬以倡九牧阜成兆民。○_{十四節}六年五服一朝又六

wicked, and punishes oppressors and disturbers of the peace : *and* the
12 minister of Works, who presides over the land of the empire, settles the four classes of the people, and regulates the seasons for obtaining the advantages of the ground.

13 "These six ministers, with their different duties, lead on their subordinates, and set an example to the nine pastors of the provinces, enriching and perfecting the condition of the millions of the people.

14 In six years the chiefs of the five tenures attend once at court. When this has been done a second six years, the king makes his tours of

now the 'Board of Punishments' (刑部); but the text says that the minister of Crime 'handled the *prohibitions* of the empire.' 'He is so described,' observes Ch'in King, 'to show the benevolent purpose of punishments, as instituted to *deter* men from doing evil.' This minister was 'the officer of Autumn' (秋官) of the Chow Le. 12. 司空,—'the minister of Works.' He was the 'officer of Winter' (冬官), of the Chow Le, the portion of which relating to his department was unfortunately lost, though the scholars of the Han dynasty have endeavoured to supply it. The present 'Board of Works' (工部) corresponds to this minister, and his functions. In the 'Canon of Shun' we have the name of 司空, and also of 共工, which appears to have been the more ancient designation ;—see the 'Can. of Yaou,' p. 10. 司空 may be translated—'overseer of the unoccupied,' suggesting to us that the earliest duties of this minister must have been to assign unoccupied lands. Kin Le-ts'ëang says :—'The 司空 was the minister who managed unoccupied grounds (空土), dividing and defining them in preparation for the investiture of ministers ; for dotations to officers ; for assignment as fields to husbandmen, shops to mechanics, and stances to traffickers. All the ground unapportioned was under his management ; once apportioned, the minister of War, and the minister of Instruction had then to do with it.' See the 集說. 居四民,—'settles the four *classes of the people,' i.e.,* arranges that scholars or officers, farmers, workers, and merchants

shall all live in the places best adapted for them. 時地利,—'times the advantages of the earth.' This would seem to imply that different operations might be required at different times, and that changes and removals of settlements might come to be desirable ;—all to be done by the advice and authority of the minister of Works.

Pp. 13, 14. *Relation of the six ministers to the pastors of the provinces ; and rule for imperial progresses, and appearances of the various princes at court.* 13. 各率其屬,—'each one leads on those belonging to his department.' The subordinates of each department amounted, in theory, to sixty. As the Chow Le exists, however, the dept. of the prime minister has 63 officers ; that of the minister of Instruction, 76 ; that of the minister of Religion, 69 ; that of the minister of War, 69 ; and that of the minister of Crime, 65. The excess in each, it is supposed, belonged originally to the officers of the dept. of the minister of Works, the account of which is commonly believed to be lost. See the work of Ch'in Sze-k'ae *in loc.* 以倡九牧,—'to go before—be an example to—the nine pastors.' We do not learn from the Shoo how communications were maintained between the six ministers at the imperial court and the pastors of provinces. 14. 六年至又六年,—in the Chow Le, Bk. XXXVIII., it is said that the princes of the How tenure appeared at court every year ; those of the Teen, every two years ; of the Nan, every three years ; of the Ts'ae, every four years ; of the Wei, every five years ; and of the Yaou, every six years. This seems a different arrangement from that described in the text. The text mentions five

年、王乃時巡考制
度于四岳諸侯各
陟○朝于方岳大明黜
○王曰、嗚呼、凡　十五節
我有官君子、欽乃
攸司、慎乃出令、令
出惟行弗惟反以
公滅私民其允懷。
○學古入官議事　十六節
以制政乃不迷其

inspection in the four seasons, and examines the regulations and measures at the four mountains. The princes attend on him, each at the mountain of his quarter, and promotions and degradations are awarded with great intelligence."

15　IV. The king said, "Oh! all ye men of virtue, my occupiers of office, pay reverent attention to your charges, and be careful of the commands you issue; for, once issued, they must be carried into effect and not be retracted. By your public feeling extinguish all selfish aims, and the people will have confidence in you, and be gladly obedient.

16　Study antiquity in order to enter on your offices. In deliberating on affairs, determine by help *of such study*, and your arts of government

tenures and not six;—perhaps the Yaou tenure was too distant, and too little reduced to the order of the nearer domains, to be made much account of in king Ching's time. The text of the Shoo and of the Chow Le so far agree, that in six years the princes from *all* the tenures had appeared at court. They differ in this, that the text would appear to make the princes to appear there only once, whereas, acc. to the other authority, all but those of the Yaou tenure would have appeared repeatedly. The interpretation must be strained either in the one case or the other, to make the two accounts agree. 王乃時巡以下,—Compare parr, 8, 9. Shun's progresses were made every five years, and the nobles all appeared during the intermediate ones. As the empire and its population grew, it was found necessary to separate the progresses by a longer interval.

Ch. IV. Pp. 15-20. THIRD PART OF THE ADDRESS :—VARIOUS EXHORTATIONS TO THE MINISTERS AND OFFICERS AS TO THE WAY IN WHICH THEY SHOULD DISCHARGE THEIR DUTIES.
15. *How they should attend to their offices, especially in the matter of issuing orders, and in putting away all selfishness.* 君子 is best taken here as 有德之稱; the king thus shows his respect for his officers. 欽乃

攸司=敬汝所主之職. 慎乃出令,—what commands are we to understand by 令 here? Most critics take them as 'governmental notifications' (國家政令), but I cannot think so. Such orders would go forth as from the sovereign himself. I understand the commands here, with Leu Tsoo-hëen, as orders to be issued by superior officers to their subordinates; to which I would add notices by any of them to the people under their jurisdiction. 令出惟行, 弗惟反,—反=回還, 'to return,' 'to come back.' It is here nearly equal to our 'to retract.' The difficulty is with the 惟, especially in 弗惟反. Ts'ae gives 欲 for it in both cases. —令出欲其行,不欲其壅逆而不行. There seems no better way of dealing with it. 民其允懷=民莫不敬信懷服. 16. *The necessity of study—of acquainting themselves with the past and the present—in order to their discharge of their duties.* 學古至不迷,—學古

驕　後　惟　惟　戒　面　忽　官　無　爾
祿　艱　克　志　爾　澨　荒　蓄　以　典
不　○　果　業　卿　事　政　疑　利　常
期　位　斷　廣　士　惟　不　敗　口　作
侈　不　乃　惟　功　煩　學　謀　亂　之
恭　期　罔　勤　崇　○　牆　怠　厥　師

will be free from error. Make the regular statutes *of our* dynasty your rule, and do not with artful speeches introduce disorder into your offices. To accumulate doubts is the way to ruin your plans; to be idle and indifferent is the way to ruin your government. Without study, you stand facing a wall, and your management of affairs will be full of trouble.

17   I caution you, my high nobles, exalted merit depends on the *high* aim, and a patrimony is enlarged only by diligence. It is by means of bold decision that future difficulties are avoided.

18 With rank, pride comes unperceived, and extravagance in the

而入官; it is, no doubt, to these words that Tsze-ch'an, the minister of Ch'ing, refers in the 左傳, 襄二十一年, when he says—僑聞學而後入政, 未聞以政學者也. In illustration of the advice, comp. Bk. IX., p. 5. The clause 議事以制 seems also to be quoted in the 左傳, 昭六年, in connection with the same Tsze-ch'an. 其爾至厥官, —by 典常 we are to understand the statutes of the existing dynasty. The 'Daily Explanation' expands 其爾典常作之師 clearly, though rather lengthily:—然天下宜于古, 而未即宜爲經畫, 皆庶遵事有者, 宜于今又當本之公也, 爾典常, 今我當宜文武之典, 尤宜于先王當官, 率由以代之, 奉爲師法. We may compare with the sentiment that in 'The Charge to the viscount of Wei,' p. 4, 率由典常. 利口, —Ts'ae thinks the 'sharp mouths' are those of the officers themselves; Wang Käng-

yay thinks they are those of others to whose suggestions the officers listen. What is said in 'The Charge to Chung of Ts'ae,' p. 7, may be pleaded to determine in favour of either view, —無作聰明亂舊章, 罔以側言改厥度. 不學牆面,—compare Con. Ana., XVII., x. 17. *The necessity of a high aim, of diligence, and of decision.* This advice (and we may suppose, with Ts'ae, the others that follow also) is addressed to the 卿士, 'the chief ministers and officers;' but we need not confine its application to them. Gan-kwŏ says:—此戒凡有官位, 但言卿士, 舉其掌事者. 功崇惟志,—this may be expressed by 功之以志崇, or 崇功在志, or 功之所以崇乃志, &c. I call attention to this to illustrate the use of the 惟, which may be called the particle *par eminence* of the Shoo. Choo He illustrates the sentiment by 斷以不疑, 鬼神避之, 需者事之賊也. This last expression is from the 左傳. We say—'Procrastination is the thief of time;' the Chinese say—'Procrastination is the thief of business.' 18. *Against pride and extravagance.* 位不期驕,—see, for the

儉惟德無載爾偽、
作德心逸日休、作
偽心勞日拙。○居 十九節
寵思危罔不惟畏、
弗畏入畏。○推 二十節 賢
讓能庶官乃和、不
和政厖舉能其官、
惟爾之能稱匪其
人、惟爾不任。○王 廿一節

same way with emolument. Let reverence and economy be *real* virtues, and do not show them in your affairs with hypocrisy. Practise them as virtues, and your minds will be at ease, and you will daily become more admirable. Practise them in hypocrisy, and your minds will be toiled, and you will daily become more stupid.

19 In the enjoyment of favour think of peril, and never be without a cautious apprehension. He who is without such apprehension

20 finds himself amidst what is to be feared. Push forward the worthy, and give place to the able, and harmony will prevail among all your officers. When they are not harmonious, the government becomes a tangled confusion. If those whom you advance are able for their offices, the ability is yours. If you advance improper men, then you are not equal to your duty."

meaning of 期, on 期于予治, in 'The Counsels of Yu,' p. 11. The cure for pride is 'reverence' (恭), akin to what we call 'self-respect.' If a man feel that he is in himself above his rank he will not be lifted up by it. Similarly, the cure for extravagance is 'economy' (儉). But this reverence and economy must be real, and not assumed,—true virtues. This is the meaning of 恭儉惟德、無載 爾偽, 'Reverence (the cure for pride) and economy (the cure for extravagance) must be *truly* virtuous, and not *merely* conveyances (=carriages to convey) for your hypocrisy.' I cannot do anything better than this with the 載. Mencius probably had this passage in view, when he wrote 恭儉豈可以聲音 笑貌為哉, (IV. Pt. I., xvi).

19. *In prosperity think of adversity.* 居寵 思危,—comp. in 'The Tʻae-kĕă, Pt. iii., p. 5, 無安厥位、惟危 We find the text quoted in the 左傳 襄十一年, with 安 for 寵. We may take the 惟 in 惟畏 as =思, according to the construction of the Tʻae-kĕă, *l. c.* 弗畏入畏=不 知祇畏, 則入于可畏之中 Shin She-hing observes that 'the first two 畏 intend the apprehension of the mind, while the last indicates the calamity of overthrow and disgrace.' 20. *How it would be for their own good and the public advantage to advance the meritorious.* The first four characters— 推賢讓能, are found in Seun Kʻing, 仲 尼篇 讓能,—'yield—show complaisance—to the able.' 政厖,—the 說文 defines 厖 by 石大貌, 'the appearance of a great rock.' The meaning of 亂, 'confusion,' is commonly given to it here. 舉 能其官=所舉者能修其官.

無　萬　康　乃　政　亂　爾　大　三　曰、
斁。　邦　兆　辟、　以　爾　有　夫、　事、　嗚
　　　惟　民、　永　佑　有　官、　敬　暨　呼、

21　　V. The king said, "Oh! ye *charged with* the threefold business *of government*, and ye great officers, reverently attend to your departments, and conduct well your affairs of government, so as to assist your sovereign, and secure the lasting happiness of the millions of the people :—so shall there be no dissatisfaction among the myriad States."

Ch. V. P. 21. THE END OF THE ADDRESS:—THE HAPPY AND PERMANENT RESULTS OF THE MINISTERS AND OFFICERS ACTING AS THEY WERE EXHORTED. 三事,—see last Book, p. 7. The 'six ministers are intended by the phrase; but how to classify them as the 任人, 準夫, and 牧 respectively, I do not know. By 大夫 are intended all the subordinate officers of the six departments. 爾有政,—亂 is evidently = 治. Wang

Kǎng-yay says that the last clause, 萬邦惟無斁 is inexplicable. The 無斁, as describing the feeling of the people to the officers, is inadmissible, he thinks, and he cannot construe the 惟. But there are many more difficult passages in the Shoo. I do not think the meaning is that the States would never be wearied of the officers, but that they would never be weary of the dynasty sustained by them in such a way.

THE BOOKS OF CHOW.

BOOK XXI. KEUN-CH'IN.

哉、兹政、弟孝德陳王一節
○東命克友惟若君陳
昔二郊汝施于爾曰、
周敬尹有兄惟令君
　　　　　兄恭爾君

1　I. The king spake to the following effect, "Keun-ch'in, it is you who are possessed of excellent virtue, filial and respectful. Being filial, and friendly with your brethren, you can display those qualities in the exercise of government. I appoint you to rule this eastern frontier. Be reverent!

INTRODUCTORY NOTE. Keun-ch'in was the successor, in 'the eastern capital,' of the duke of Chow, who henceforth passes off the stage of the Shoo, which he has occupied so long. Between the 'Officers of Chow' and the 'Keun-ch'in' there were two Books, which are both lost. The loss of the second we must much deplore, for it contained an account of the death of the duke of Chow, and an announcement made by king Ching at his bier. The duke died in Fung, the capital of his father Wăn, and, dying, signified his wish to be buried at Ching-chow, which he had built and watched over. The place was dear to him; but his wishes in regard to it were always to be disappointed. He had sought to make it the capital of the dynasty, but king Ching would not leave Haou. He now wished that his dust should rest in its soil, but the king chose rather to have him buried in Peih, the cemetery of their House (in the pres. district of Han-yang, dep. of Se-ngan). The object, according to Sze-ma Ts'een, was to honour him. He says that 'the king buried him in Peih, near by king Wăn, to show that he did not presume to look on the duke as a minister.'

The duke of Chow was undoubtedly one of the greatest men whom China has produced, and I do not know the statesman of any nation with whom his countrymen need shrink from comparing him. But this is not the place for writing either his history or his eulogium; I only wish, before passing on with the translation of the Shoo, to consider the claim which has been advanced for him to the invention of the mariner's compass. Gaubil held that he was versed both in astronomy and geometry, and says expressly that the use of the compass was known to him;—see 'Le Chou-king,' p. 214, note 4. The common opinion of the Chinese is that not only was the use of the instrument known to him, but that he discovered it. In the chapter on 'Inventions' (制作), in the 幼學故事尋源, or 'Inquiries into ancient things for the use of Learners,' it is said —'The duke of Chow made the south-pointing chariot, which has come down to us in the form of the mariner's compass' (周公作指南車, 羅盤是其遺制).

The circumstances under which he is said to have made this instrument may be given first in the narrative of P. De Mailla, in his 'Histoire Generale de la Chine,' pp. 316—318. When I subjoin the sources of his narrative, the reader will see how the history has been compiled, and whether we can put faith in the things related. P. De Mailla says:—'This same sixth year of his reign, king Ching, after having established his different officers, received the news that the ambassadors of a foreign kingdom, called Yŭĕ-tchang-tchi (越裳氏), were come to bring him presents and do him homage. This kingdom, situated to the south of the country of Kiao-tchi (交趾) or Cochin-china, had never sent anybody to China. The emperor gave orders that the ambassadors should be conducted to the court, and that great honours should everywhere be paid to them. This prince (? the king, or the duke of Chow) received them very well, treated them with distinction, and accepted their presents, among which was a white pheasant,—a species heretofore unknown; after which he made the inquiry be put to them on what business they had come. They replied by interpreters, that the elders of their country said loudly, that for three years they had had neither winds nor tempest, no unseasonable rains nor great waves of the sea, and that there must be some special cause for such favour of Heaven; that apparently the throne of China was occupied by a sage emperor, who had procured for them these benefits.

'After that, the duke conducted them to the ancestral temple of the reigning family, where he caused to be displayed on the one side the presents which they had brought, and on the other those which king Ching was sending to their prince. Among these were five chariots of a new invention. They accommodated the travellers, and indicated at the same time the route which they kept, by means of a small box, made in the form of a pavilion or dome, suspended from the roof, in which was a hand that always pointed to the south, to whatever side the chariots might turn. It was on this account that they were called Tchi-nan-tshe (指南車), or chariot of the south. This machine was very useful to the envoys of Yue-tchang-tchi, for when they were arrived at the kingdom of Fou-nan-lin, on the borders of the sea, they took to some barques, and by means of this compass they needed only one year to return to their own kingdom.'

Now, the Shoo does not contain, and never contained, any account of this embassy from Cochin-china, and I have searched in vain for any mention of it in Sze-ma Ts'een. The earliest mention of it is in Fuh-shang's 'Introduction to the Shoo' (尚書大傳). His account is the following:—

年裳澤政人曰久
六越雉政人曰久
攝平獻日其請曰
天九譯公不君使喬
下譯公不君之黃
居和而公饗不其
公重歸君子則黃
作樂象以爲施賜
禮三以焉君此國
制以王加不也賜
以成不何君吾國
　不令受命此吾

'In the sixth year of the duke of Chow's regency, he framed the ceremonial and official statutes of the dynasty, and made its music. The whole empire became harmonious and tranquil. At that time, ambassadors came from Yŭĕ-chang, with three elephants, and interpreters speaking nine languages, and presented a white pheasant. King Ching put them in the hands of the duke of Chow, who said, "Where the benefits of his virtue have not been experienced, the superior man declines to receive gifts; and a sovereign does not acknowledge as his subjects those to whom he has not issued the orders of his govt.;—on what ground is it that this offering comes to us?" The ambassadors begged to say, "We come by the command of the elders of our kingdom. They said, 'For a long time there have been no unusual winds nor unseasonable rains in the sky. Is it not likely that there is a sagely man in the middle kingdom? Why should you not go and pay homage at his court?'" On this the duke of Chow presented them in the ancestral temple.'

It will be observed that in this account no mention is made of the 'south-pointing chariots.'

We come to Han Ying, not much later than Fuh-shang. In his 'Introduction to the She King' (韓詩外傳), composed about the middle of the second century B.C., we have substantially the same account of the embassy from Yŭĕ-chang, but with certain marvels which preceded it. He says:—

時禾
成王之秀王
三王同生幾為一成公
苗同充而何成周下
貫幾物長秀年天越
桑滿周意此及獻果雉
車周三三一而山白幽
日苗至比悠也川重
同氏遠譯未何故見
一周達路達國以黃
重恐吾之日迅風疾
公而命公受三年於
苗使也不吾有聖人
三來矣殆溢也人
大譯不來國
問入著也於乎
日海之是
始意譯於中
裳往入國
於此海中國
深盡矣意有
譯賜往盡聖
髮雨天往人
　　　朝乎
　　　周公
　　　乃薦
　　　於宗
　　　廟

'In the time of king Ching, three stalks of grain grew through a mulberry tree and came out in one flowering head, which was almost large enough to fill a cart, and long enough to fill the box of it. The king said to the duke of Chow, "What is this thing?" The duke replied, "Three stalks growing into one head probably betoken that the empire is now at length becoming one." Sure enough, three years after, the ruler of Yŭĕ-chang sent an embassy with interpreters speaking nine different languages, which presented a white pheasant to the duke of Chow. The interpreters were necessary, because the distance was very great, with dark and deep mountains and rivers, so that the ambassadors might not be understood. The duke of Chow asked to what they were indebted for the offerings, when the interpreters said, "We received the command from the grey-haired men of our kingdom, who said, 'For long, even for three years, we have had neither violent winds nor disastrous rains, nor storms on the sea. We may believe that there is a sage in the middle kingdom;—why not go and present yourselves at his court?' This is the reason we are come.'"

I do not find this account in the Introduction of Han Ying, as it is now generally edited; but it is quoted continually in illustration of the embassy from Yuĕ-chang;—see the 四書人名考, on the 'Life of the duke of Chow.' There seems to be no reason to doubt its having come from Han Ying; but it will be seen that neither does he make any mention of the 'south-pointing chariots.'

The earliest authority that I have found for connecting the duke of Chow and the embassy from Cochin-china with these chariots is the 中華古今注, a Work of the Tsin dynasty, the writer of which, after giving his opinion that the invention was due to Hwang-te, about 1,500 years anterior to the Chow dynasty! adds that Hang Kĕĕn of the 'After Han,' attributed it to the duke of Chow. We read:—'The duke having produced by his govt. a state of great tranquillity, the people of Yuĕ-chang came with interpreters speaking different languages, and presented one white pheasant, two black pheasants, and the tusk of an elephant. The ambassadors being astray as to their road back, the duke gave them two pieces of ornamented and embroidered silk, and five light carriages, all made on the pattern of pointing to the south. The ambassadors were conveyed in these to the south, as far as the city Lin [probably the pres. Kwei-lin, metrop. of Kwangse] of Foo-nan near the sea, so that in a year they reached their own country, &c.' (後漢
書, art. 大駕指南車).

My readers will probably be disposed with me to set down the embassy from Yuĕ-chang as a mere legend, and the claim of the duke of Chow to be the inventor of the 'south pointing chariot' as nothing better.

It is attributed to him under different circumstances in a fragment of the Works of 鬼谷子, 'The hero of Demon valley,' a Taouist charlatan, somewhat later than Mencius, towards the end of the Chow dynasty. What he says, is that 'the prince of Suh-shin presented a white pheasant to king Wăn. There being a fear lest he should lose his way on his return home, the duke of Chow made the south-pointing chariot to conduct him safely' (蕭愼氏獻白雉於文王, 還恐迷路, 周公因作指南車以送之;—see the 太平御覽, 卷第七百七十五, art. I.). Now, the Book of the Shoo which immediately followed the 'Officers of Chow' was about the chief of Suh-shin; but the presumption from the prefatory notice is that it did not contain anything about the duke of Chow. It related, moreover, to a visit from that chief to king Ching, and not to king Wăn.

Allusion has been made to the account which carries back the making of the south-pointing chariot to Hwang-te, more than 2,600 years before Christ. This is given by Sze-ma Ts'een.—Hwang-te was operating to put down a rebellious chief, called Ch'e-yew, who frustrated his measures for a time by enveloping the armies in clouds of mist, so that the emperor's men could not tell their position. Against this magical contrivance, Hwang-te made the chariots in question, and succeeded in taking the rebel alive. Later narrators ascribe the chariots to Hwang-te's empress; and there have been those who, forgetting the claims both of Hwang-te and the duke of Chow, have ascribed them to Kwan Chung, the chief counsellor of the duke Hwan of Ts'e, in the 7th cent. B.C.;—see the 事物紀原, 卷第二.

The general opinion among the Chinese, therefore, that the duke of Chow made the 'south-pointing chariot,' cannot be received as resting on a historical foundation. The 'south-pointing chariot' altogether may be called in question. The accounts of its construction as being drawn by four horses, with the wooden figure of a genius (木仙人) on the roof, are all fabulous;—see the 太平御覽, l. c. It would be hard to say that the mariner's compass was the child of this chariot. The truth, I imagine, is this, that the Chinese got some knowledge of the compass—found it out themselves, or learned it from India—not long before the Christian era, and that then the fables about the making of south-pointing chariots in more ancient times were invented.

THE NAME OF THE BOOK.—君陳, 'Keun-ch'in.' Ts'ae says that this was the name of the minister; and as the Book contains the charge given to him, it is called after him. Others would translate the characters—'Prince Ch'in,' as we translate the title of Bk. XVI., by 'Prince Shih.' Thus Hea Seen says:—'He must have been invested with some principality as its ruler, on which account he is called 君,

民 之 昭 厥 司 往 懷 萬 公
其 訓 周 常 茲 慎 其 民 師
父。惟 公 懋 率 乃 德 民 保

2   II. "Formerly, the duke of Chow acted as teacher and guardian of the myriads of the people, who cherish *the remembrance of* his virtue. Go you, and with sedulous care undertake his charge; act in accordance with his regular ways, and exert yourself to illus-

Prince' (必封國爲君, 故稱君). But as we know nothing of any principality with which this Keun-ch'in had anything to do, it is better to abide by the view of Ts'ae, in which he followed Gan-kwŏ.

K'ang-shing supposed that Keun-ch'in was a son of the duke of Chow, a younger brother of Pih-k'in, but the evidence seems conclusive that this was not the case. The charge could hardly have been delivered without containing some reference to such a relation between Keun-ch'in and his predecessor. See in Lin Che-k'e, on the point. The Book is found only in the text of Gan-kwŏ.

CONTENTS. I take the summary of these which is given in the 'Complete Digest of Commentaries on the Shoo.'—'The whole Book may be divided into three parts. The first, which is also the first par., contains the words of Keun-ch'in's appointment to the charge of the eastern capital. The concluding words,—"Be reverent," are specially emphatic, and give the key-note to all that follows. The second part contains parr. 2—6, and enjoins on Keun-ch'in to exert himself to illustrate the lessons of the duke of Chow, and thereby transform the people of Yin. The third part, parr. 7—14, further enjoins on him to give full development to those lessons, and adduces various particulars in which his doing so would appear,—all illustrative of the command at the commencement, that he should be reverent.'

Ch. I. P. 1. THE CHARGE TO KEUN-CH'IN; AND THE GROUND OF IT IN HIS PERSONAL EXCELLENCE. 惟爾至有政,—the 'filial piety and respectfulness' (孝恭) are the attributes which compose the 'excellent virtue' attributed to Keun-ch'in. Gan-kwŏ interprets 恭 wrongly of 'self-respect' (行已以恭). It is expanded, however, in the next clause into 友于兄弟, and is thus made to embrace both the respectfulness of the younger brother and the kindness of the elder. 克施有政,—'can be displayed *in* the possession (or *by* the possessor) of govt.' This sequel does not commend itself so readily to a foreigner as it does to the Chinese. A man, it seems to us, may be a good son and a good brother, and yet be but poorly fitted for the

duties of an administrator, while it is true that a bad son and a bad brother cannot be trusted to discharge the duties of any other relation. The doctrine of king Ching, however, is that of all Chinese authorities, ancient and modern;—compare 'The Great Learning,' Comm., ch. ix.

[This portion of the Keun-ch'in is quoted by Confucius, Ana. II., xxi.; but not to the letter. It would be absurd, however, to conclude from that that the text here is not genuine.]

By the 東郊, 'eastern border or frontier,' we are evidently to understand Ching-chow, 'the lower capital,' to which the people of Yin had been removed. Gaubil is quite wrong, when he would understand by 郊 here the sacrifice offered to Heaven, or the place of it. Ch'in Sze-k'ae gives the following statements: —'The imperial city formed a square of nine *le*. Outside the city was called the 郊. Fifty *le* off was called the "near 郊, or frontier," and a hundred *le* off was called the "remote frontier." Ching-chow would be in the "near frontier."'

Ch. II. Pp. 2—6. KEUN-CH'IN MUST FOLLOW THE EXAMPLE AND LESSONS OF THE DUKE OF CHOW; MUST FEEL THE DIFFICULTY OF HIS DUTIES; SEEK THE COUNSEL OF OTHERS, BUT USE HIS OWN JUDGMENT; EVER ASCRIBING HIS MERIT AND SUCCESS TO THE EMPEROR. 2. 師保萬民,—'tutored and preserved the myriads of the people.' The myriads of the people were those of Yin who had been removed to Lŏ. —This is a very clear instance of the way in which such high-sounding phrases as 萬民 are employed. 往慎乃司,—from the 厥常 which follows, we must interpret 乃司 of the duke of Chow,=其所司之職, 'that which he was charged with.' Medhurst takes 乃 as =汝, 'you,' which it often is; but its usage in the Shoo permits us also to take the 乃司 as I propose. Ts'ae also takes it thus. 惟民其乂=則民

民惟草。○圖厥政、
其戒哉爾惟風下
聖亦不克由聖爾
聖若不克見旣見
逸豫。○凡人未見
訓惟日孜孜無敢
尚式時周公之獻
非馨明德惟馨爾
香、感于神明、黍稷
○我聞曰、至治馨

3 trate his lessons:—so shall the people be regulated. I have heard
that he said, 'Perfect government is like piercing fragrance, and
influences the spiritual Intelligences. It is not the millet which
has the piercing fragrance; it is bright virtue.' Do you make
this lesson of the duke of Chow your motto, being diligent
from day to day, and not presuming to indulge in luxurious ease.

4 Ordinary men, while they have not seen a sage, *are full of desire*,
as if they could not get a sight of him; but after they have seen
him, they are still unable to follow him. Be cautioned by this.
You are the wind; the inferior people are the grass.

其治矣. 　　3. 我聞曰至惟
馨,—that the king is here quoting words which
he had heard, directly or indirectly, from the
duke of Chow, appears clear from the 式時
周公之獻訓. Gan-kwŏ only heard in
them the voice of some ancient worthy. 馨
=香遠聞, 'fragrance smelt at a distance'
黍稷,—these two kinds of millet, used in
sacrifice, represent all the articles of sacrifice,
—grain, flesh, fruits, spirits, &c. The clauses
黍稷非馨, 明德惟馨, are found
quoted from the Books of Chow, in the 左
傳, 僖五年. The general sentiment is
the same as that which we find so often in the
prophets of Holy Scripture,—the worthlessness
of sacrifice without an earnest moral purpose
in the offerer. 爾尚式(=法)時
(=是)周公之獻訓=爾尚取
此周公發明夫道理之訓,
而大法之. So says the 'Daily Explanation,' taking 獻 as an adj., qualifying 訓.
This may be done, but it is not necessary.
4. 凡人至由聖,—this is quoted as

from 'The Keun-ch'in' in the Le Ke, Bk.
緇衣, par. 15. It might be thus with the
凡人, 'the common people;' but the king
tells Keun-ch'in it ought not to be so with him.
He must set an example to the multitude of
obedience to the sage's lessons, remembering
that they would take their cue from him.
爾惟風, 下民惟草,—comp. the
Ana. XII., xix., 君子之德風小人
之德草草上之風必偃. The
student will not be sorry to have the following
illustration of the comparison by Soo Tung-po:
—天地之化育, 有可以指者, 而日知其所以自天得蕩化
言者, 有不可以求而得暖而皆知其所以布所以搖之
皆知其所以潤以爲雷電皆悠知其故求舞之君子
其所以爲震, 雪霜風不入可鼓然於地之至於其有於物, 至
而出地者, 蓋不物知所以

若　德　斯　之　后　繹　師　有　莫
時　鳴　猷　于　猷　○　虞　與　或
惟　呼　惟　外　則　六節　庶　出　不
良　臣　我　曰　入　爾　言　入　艱
顯　人　后　斯　告　有　同　自　有
哉　咸　之　謀　爾　嘉　則　爾　廢

5 "In revolving the plans of your government, never hesitate to
acknowledge the difficulty of the subject. Some things have to
be abolished, and some to be adopted:—going out and coming
in, seek the judgment of your people about them; and when
there is a general agreement, exert your own powers of reflection.

6 When you have any good plans or counsels, enter and lay
them before your sovereign in his palace. Thereafter, when
you are acting abroad in accordance with them, say, 'This plan or
this view is all due to our sovereign.' Oh! if all ministers were
to act thus, how excellent would they be, and how distinguished!"

民, 似 之 云云.　5. 圖 厥 政,
—'planning your govt.' The 爾, lower down,
shows that we are to take 厥 in the second
person. Compare the same expression in Bk.
XVIII., pp. 15, 16.　莫 或 不 艱 may
be taken imperatively, as in the translation, or
indicatively,—'there will perhaps always be
difficulties.'　出 入 自 爾 師 虞,—
the 出 入 seem to trouble the critics considerably. Ying Yung (應鏞) says on them:—
出 上 之 意 以 達 之 下, 入 下
之 言, 以 達 之 上, 'giving out the
views of the sovereign to make them known to
the people; bringing in the words of the people
to make them known to the sovereign;' comp.
on the 'Can. of Shun,' p. 25. Ch'in Ta-yew
says—出 謀 之 國 人, 入 謀 之 左
右, 'going out, consider the matters with
the people; coming in, consider them with your
associates.' But we may very well translate
the terms literally, and consider the meaning
as = 'always and everywhere.'　師 = 衆,
'all,' 'the multitude of the people.'　虞 =
度, 'to calculate,' 'to consider.'
同 則 繹,—'when their words agree, then
unroll the matter,' i.e., come to your own deci

sion. Compare 克 由 繹 之, Bk, XIX.,
p. 19. Gan-kwŏ gives for 繹 here—陳 而
布 之;—not so well.

[In the Le ke, Bk. 緇衣, p. 19, we find the
words quoted from 'The Keun-ch'in,'—出
入 自 爾 師 虞, 庶 言 同, the concluding 則 繹 being omitted.]

6. 謀 is defined by Ts'ae as 言 切 於 事,
'words important to business;' and 猷 as 言
合 於 道, 'words agreeing with reason.' The
'plans' and 'counsels' of the translation seem
to correspond to the characters.　Of 良 顯
it is said—良 以 德 言, 顯 以 名
言, '良 has reference to virtue; 顯 to fame.'
The critics take different views of king
Ching's requirement in this par., that he should
himself have all the credit of Keun-ch'in's
wisdom and successes. Some, like a 葛 氏,
quoted by Ts'ae, see in it a disclosure of the
king's weakness and vanity. Others would
make the king be speaking of Keun-ch'in's
ways in the past.—'When you had good plans
and counsels, you entered,' &c. This construction is not natural; and besides it would not
much lighten the conclusion as to the king's
unjust vanity. Many critics endeavour to

弗　宥　予　曰　○　有　倚　無　惟　○
若　惟　曰　辟　八節　制　法　依　弘　王
于　厥　宥　爾　殷　從　以　勢　周　曰
汝　中。　爾　惟　民　容　削　作　公　君
政　○　惟　勿　在　以　以　威　丕　陳
弗　有　勿　辟、　辟、　和。　寬　無　訓、　爾
　九節　　　　　予　　　而　　七節

7　　III. The king said, "Keun-ch'in, do you give their full development to the great lessons of the duke of Chow. Do not rely on your power to exercise oppression; do not rely on the laws to practise extortion. Be gentle, but with strictness of rule. Promote harmony by the display of an easy forbearance.

8　　"When any of the people of Yin are amenable to the laws, if I say 'Punish,' do not you therefore punish; and if I say 'Spare,'

9　do not you therefore spare. Seek the due course. Those who are disobedient to your government, and uninfluenced by your instruc-

make it out that the king is only laying down what ministers should do, with a lofty superiority to the imputation of vanity to which it might subject himself! The truth is, king Ching was but a very ordinary man.

[The whole of this par. is found, quoted from 'The Keun-ch'in,' in the Le Ke, Bk. 坊記, p. 15.]

Ch. III. Pp. 7—14. That Keun-ch'in's grand object should be to carry out the plans of the duke of Chow, with the spirit and measures in which he should do this.
7. It is observed by Hea Sëen that this paragraph describes the way in which Keun-ch'in should carry out the plans of his predecessor among the people of Yin who did not violate the laws. There must be an absence of all oppression, but generosity must at the same time be accompanied with firmness. 作威 = 'to play the awe-inspiring.' 無 (=毋) 倚法以削, — 削 = 'to cut,' 'to pare.' Its application here is to the practice of extortion. Keun-ch'in it is observed by Lin Che-k'e, was not likely to do either of the things against which he is here warned, but it was right for the king to speak to him as he does, as it was right for Shun's counsellors to warn him against vices from which as a sage he was far removed. 從容以和, — 'be easy and tolerating to harmonize.' The meaning seems to be that Keun-ch'in should carry himself easily and forbearingly, and so effect a harmony between the people and himself and

his measures. Ts'ae explains the clause — 和 不可一於和, 必從容以和 之, 而後可以和厥中, which Kăng-yay says he does not understand. Ts'ae has a trick of poising his sentences, with more reference to their sound than their sense.

Pp. 8—10. These parr. regard how Keun-ch'in should deal with the people who were transgressors of the laws. He should have respect to the decisions of the law, and to the end of all law; and to nothing else. 8. 在 辟, — 辟 = 法, 'the laws,' meaning the punishments assigned by them. The 'Daily Explanation,' for 殷民在辟, gives — 凡 此殷民, 苟有犯法而入于 刑辟之內者. 惟厥中 = 惟 當審其輕重之中, 'you ought simply to judge according to the due medium of lightness and severity.' The case which the emperor puts here is a very remarkable one, — that of himself seeking to interfere with the operation of the laws, and yet telling Keun-ch'in not to pay regard to him. There are both weakness and goodness in what he says. 9. 若 = 順. 辟以止辟乃辟 — this would seem to say that even in such cases, where punishment was inevitable, it should be modified by a consideration of the end of all punishment. But the idea of *a modification* of the punishment is out of place; and therefore Gaubil has probably given the real meaning of the passage by translating — 'vous devez les

化于汝訓辟以
止辟乃辟。○〔十節〕
于姦宄敗常亂 狃〔十一節〕
俗三細不宥。○〔十二節〕
爾無忿疾于頑
無求備于一夫。○〔十三節〕
必有忍其乃
有濟有容德修亦
大。○簡厥修。〔十三節〕
簡其或不修進

tions, you will punish, remembering that the end of punishment
10　is to make an end of punishing. Those who are inured to villainy
and treachery, those who violate the constant duties of society,
and those who introduce disorder into the public manners:—those
three classes you will not spare, though their particular offences
be but small.

11　"Be not passionate with the obstinate, and dislike them. Seek
12　not every quality in one individual. You must have patience
13　and you will be successful; have forbearance and your virtue will
be great. Mark those who manage their affairs well, and also

punir séverement, afin d'empêcher que les autres ne tombent dans les mêmes fautes.' 10. 狃=習, 'practised,' 'habitually given to.' 敗常,—comp. 反道敗德, 'Counsels of Yu,' p. 20; and 欲敗度，縱敗禮, 'T'ae-këa,' Pt. ii., p. 3. Wang Ts'ëaou refers, pertinently enough, to Bk. IX., p. 15, for instances of the crimes which are thus described. P. 16 may also illustrate the 亂俗 三細不宥=人犯此三者，雖小罪，亦不可宥. Sun Ke-yew (孫繼有) observes:—三細非以三者為細也，三事中所犯自有大小，舉小以該大

Pp. 11—13. *How Keun-ch'in should show patience and generous forbearance in dealing with the people.* 11. 無(=毋)忿疾,—'do not burst out into anger, and cherish dislike against.' 疾 is the abiding of the 忿;—comp. 身有所忿懥, 云云, 'Great Learning,' Comm., vii. 1. By 頑 are intended the 'stupidly obstinate' people of Yin, who should continue opposed to the sway of Chow. They would give occasion for the 'patience,' immediately spoken of. 無求備于一夫,—comp. Ana. XVIII., x., 無求備于一人

This regards the people of Yin, who might be prepared to submit cordially, and who would give occasion for a 'generous forbearance.'

12. 若有忍其乃有濟,—this appears in the 國語, as from the Shoo, but slightly varied,—必有忍也若能有濟也. Comp. Ana., XV., xxxvi. 有容德乃大,—'have forbearance, and the virtue is great.'—Ts'ae says:—'*Patience* is associated with *the issues of* business; *forbearance*, with virtue. The king's discourse distinguishes these two things, as the one is more deep, and the other more shallow.' *Forbearance* then is superior to *patience*. Kang-yay condemns this reading of the text; but something of the sort seems to be implied. 13. 簡,—'to select;' meaning here 'to mark,' 'to take distinguishing notice of,' whether in the way of approval or the contrary. On 簡厥修 the 'Daily Explanation' gives—

至有者，其表殊別，無不修
有業修者，無不修而
職能修其職，能簡其不涍而
其不簡使混自奮
能修開爾亦不
居好當里將
安遊者宅井疆
有業宅井將
修田安遊職厥則
不力亦職

有辭于永世。　福其爾之休終　予一人膺受多　允升于大猷惟　德時乃罔不變　好爾克敬典在　上所命從厥攸　厚因物有遷違　不良。○惟民生十四節　厥良以率其或

mark those who do not do so. Advance the good to induce those who may not be so to follow *their example.*

14   "The people are born good, and are changed by *external* things, so that they resist what their superiors command, and follow what they *themselves* love. Do you but reverently observe all the statutes, and they will become virtuous; they will thus all be changed, and truly advance to a great degree of excellence. Then shall I, the one man, enjoy much happiness, and your excellent *services* will be famous through long ages!"

者亦知愧矣.　On　進厥艮,　親五品不遷者有之,　蓋因
云云　Ts'ae says:—進行義之艮　物有遷耳,是以違上所好,　命
者以率其不艮,則人勵行　教令有所不行,從厥攸好,　厥
　　　　　　　　　　　　　　　　　　而放,僻邪侈,無所不爲,　已
P. 14. *The radical goodness of human nature*　者,其也,指民而言自狗好者,
always makes it capable of being reformed. What　所好耳,以爲從上所好者,　非
happy effects would follow from Keun-ch'in's con-　非也.　爾克敬典在德一
ducting his govt. to this issue.　Ts'ae makes this—'If you can reverently
厚,—compare Ana., VI., xvii.,　惟民生　observe all the duties of society, and that with
也直.　Ts'ae considers that　人之生　a real virtue,' influenced no doubt by his view of
命,從厥所好 mean—'They resist what　違上所命,從厥所好.　Our safer
their rulers *only* command, *not exemplifying the*　plan is to take 敬典 accord. to its use in the
same themselves, and follow what they love:'　'Ann. to the prince of K'an,' where it twice
according to the teaching in the 'Great Learn-　occurs;—in parr. 19 and 24. 在德 will then
ing,' Comm., ix. 4. On this view the statement　be descriptive of the conduct of the people thus
is that of another fact in the ways of men　ruled over. So, Lin Che-k'e:—爾能敬典
additional to what is said in the two previous　以導之,其所行惟在於德,
clauses; and may be considered as the founda-　則無有不變. 'If you can reverence
tion of the 在德 in the admonition to Keun-　the constant statutes, and so lead them on, what
ch'in which follows. Another view, which I have　they do will be in *the way of* virtue, and so all
followed, is ingeniously suggested by Wăng　will be changed.' 允升于大猷=
Kăng-yay. Acc. to it 違上所命,從厥　信其能升進於大道. 其
(=其)所好 is merely an expansion or　爾,云云,—all this belongs to Keun-ch'in.
illustration of 因物有遷 The whole of　Ts'ae is wrong in making 終有辭于永
Kăng-yay's annotation on the passage is with　世, belong both to him and the king.
reading:=孩提之童,皆知愛親
及長皆知敬兄,民生本厚
也,知誘物化,然後百姓不

THE BOOKS OF CHOW.

BOOK XXII. THE TESTAMENTARY CHARGE.

憑 被 纇 王 ○ 王 哉 惟一節
玉 冕 水 乃 甲二節 不 生 四 顧
几。服。相 洮 子。懌。魄。月、命

1　I. In the fourth month, when the moon began to wane, the king
2　was indisposed.　On the day Kĕă-tsze, he washed his hands and
face, his attendants put on him his cap and robes, and *he sat up*, lean-

INTRODUCTORY NOTE. This Book brings us
to the closing act of the reign and life of king
Ching. His reign, according to the current chronology, lasted 37 years, ending B.C. 1,079. The
thing, however, is by no means certain. Nothing
can be gathered on the point from the Shoo or
from Sze-ma Ts'een. Between the appointment
of Keun-ch'in, moreover, as related in the last
ʼook, and Ching's death, the history is almost
ʼank. The only events chronicled, and which
e the authority of Ts'een, are a coinage of
nd money, with a square hole in the centre,
he prototypes of the modern cash; and an
.actment that the manufactures of cloth and
ılk should be two cubits two inches wide, in
ᴗieces of forty-four cubits long.

THE NAME OF THE BOOK.—顧 命, 'The
Testamentary Charge.' Dr. Medhurst has most
unfortunately rendered these characters by
'Retrospective Decree.' 顧＝還 視, 'to
turn round and look;' and 顧 命 is 'The
charge given, when turning round and looking.'
K'ang-shing says:—囬首曰顧, 臨死
囬顧而發命. 'To turn round the
head is called 顧. *The king*, when about to
die, turned round and looked *at his ministers*,
and so issued his charge.' The phrase is now
generally employed for a 'testament,' or 'dying
charge,' such application being derived from its

use here in the Shoo. The Book is found in
both the texts.

CONTENTS. King Ching, feeling that his end
is near, calls his six principal ministers and
other officers around his couch, and commits
his son Ch'aou to their care and guidance. The
record of all the circumstances and the dying
charge form a chapter ending at par. 10 with
the announcement of the king's death. The
rest of the Book is occupied with a detailed
account of the ceremonies connected with the
publication of the charge, and the accession of
Ch'aou to the throne. It is an interesting
monument of the ways of that distant time on
such occasions. M. De Guignes tells us that
Father Gaubil said that if all the other Books
of the Shoo had been filled with the names of instruments, dresses, arms, &c., like this, he would
not have undertaken to translate the Work.
The difficulties which it presents of this nature,
however, are not greater than we had to en-
counter in translating 'The Establishment of
Government.'

Ch. I. Pp. 1—10. THE SICKNESS; TESTA-
MENTARY CHARGE; AND DEATH OF KING CHING.

1. 哉生魄,—'at the beginning of
the growth of darkness,'＝when the moon began
to wane, the 16th day of the month. See on
the 'Completion of the War,' pp. 1, 2, and 4.

不懌,—'was not pleased.' The phrase
＝不豫 in VI, p. 1,—an euphemism, instead

事。百 氏、毛 公、彤 奭、召 ○三節
○ 尹 虎 公、衛 伯 芮 太 乃
王四節御 臣、師 侯、畢 伯、保 同

3 ing on the gem-adorned bench. He then called for the Grand-
protector Shih, the baron of Juy, the baron of T'ung, the duke of
Peih, the prince of Wei, the duke of Maou, Sze, the master of the
warders, the master of the guards, the Heads of the officers,—*all*
the superintendents of affairs.

of saying directly that the emperor was unwell.
Woo Ch'ing observes that 'the emperor's being
ill is expressed by 不懌 and 不豫, and
his decease by 登遐 and 宴駕, because
his ministers could not bear to name such things
directly.' 2. 甲子,—'on the day Kĕä-
tsze.' But what day of the month this was
cannot be determined. Hëa Sëen observes that
'the historians of Han conclude that it was the
same day intended by 哉生魄 in the 1st
par., but it is to be presumed they are wrong.
In the "Completion of the War," p. 1, we read—
惟 一 月 壬 辰 旁 死 魄, 越 翼
日 癸 巳, where the day intended by 旁
死 魄 is determined by its calendaric name
preceding. In the text here there is no such
name given, and we cannot say what day
甲子 was.' See the 集 說. On the conclusion of the historians of Han, and the year
of king Ching's death, Gaubil says :—'Lew Hin,
who lived some years B.C., and Pan Koo (班
固), the historian, who flourished 70 or 80
years after Christ, place the year of the death
of king Ching in 1,079, B.C., and make him to
have reigned 37 years ; and they are followed in
these points by the standard History (通鑑
綱目). They add that, on this year of
Ching's death, the day 庚戌, the 47th of the
cycle, was new moon of the 4th month of the
calendar of Chow, and that 甲子 was the
day of full moon ;—citing the text of this par.
On the year B.C., 1,079, the day 庚戌 was
the 28th February of the Julian year, but new
moon was several days after ; the day 甲子
was the 14th of March, and the full moon was
not till several days after. Those two authors
therefore make a false calculation, founded on
their false principles of the motion of the sun and
moon, and of the return of the period of seventy-
six years. The year 1,068 (or 1,069) B.C. was
the year of the death of king Ching ; the 16th
of March was the day 甲子, and also the day

of full moon in the morning for China. The
place of the sun shows that it was the 4th month
of the calendar of Chow, because the equinox
happened in the course of it.' The argument of
Gaubil here agrees with that which I have
presented on Bk. XII., p. 1 ; but the data are
less sure, as we cannot be certain that 甲子
in the text should be connected with the date in
the 1st par., as the reasoning supposes. I receive
the impression that it should not be so connected. 王乃洮頮水＝王乃用
水盥手洗面. The meaning of 頮
(＝靧), 'to wash the face,' is sufficiently established ; and hence Ying-tă says it remains that
洮 be taken for 'to wash the hands.' Ma Yung
made it ＝ 'to wash the hair.' The 說文 has
沬 for 頮.   相被冕服,—it is not
worth while to try and settle the question of
what particular cap or crown and robes the king
wore on this occasion. His 冕 or crowns were
six, and for each there was the appropriate occasion. See on the duties of the 司服 in the
Chow Le, Bk. XXI. The present was an extraordinary occasion, and no doubt his attendants
settled on their principle of court etiquette the
proper habit in which he should receive his
ministers. The text determining nothing, however, on the point, critics are left to decide
the questions which they raise, according to
their several views. See Lin Che-k'e and
Këang Shing, *in loc.* We must leave in the
same way the question undetermined of who
the 相 was or were. The 太僕 and
officers of his dept. are probably intended. See
the Chow Le, Bk. XXXI., *in* 太僕. Ts'ae
would take the term more generally as ＝
扶相者, 'the supporters and assistants.'
被冕服＝以冕服被(＝加
在)王身. Lin Che-k'e ingeniously refers
to the practice of Confucius, Ana. X., xiii. 3,—
'When he was sick, and the prince came to
visit him, he had his head placed to the east,
made his court robes be placed over him, and
drew his girdle across them.' The sage would

命　予　言　不　彌　日　惟　疾　曰、
汝。審　嗣　獲　留　臻　幾　大　嗚
○　訓　兹　誓　恐　既　病　漸、呼、

4　　The king said, "Oh! my illness has greatly increased, and it will soon be over with me. The malady comes on daily with more violence and without interruption. I am afraid I may not find another opportunity to declare my wishes about my successor, and therefore I now lay my charge on you with special instructions.

not receive a visit from his prince in his undress, even though he was sick; and in the same spirit king Ching would be properly arrayed on the occasion in the text. 憑玉几—we are to conceive of the king seated on a mat, and leaning forward in his weakness on the bench or stool before him. The benches used at various imperial ceremonies were of five kinds, of which the 'gem-adorned' was the most honourable. See the Chow Le, Bk. XX., on the duties of the 司几筵. Difft. accounts are given of their size. They were all, acc. to Ma Yung, 3 feet long. Yuen Ch'in (阮諶) says they were '5 feet long, and 2 feet high.' 3. The duke of Shaou, and the other five ministers mentioned, were no doubt the six *K'ing* of Bk. XX. On the death of the duke of Chow, the duke of Shaou had succeeded him as 冢宰, or prime minister, retaining also his dignity of 'Grand-Guardian.'

A baron of Juy is mentioned in the prefatory notice to one of the lost Books, as having made the Ch'aou Ming (巢命), by order of king Woo. The one in the text may be the same, or a son of his. Juy is referred to the pres. dis. of Chaou-yih (朝邑), dep. of Se-ngan, Shen-se. The baron of Juy was minister of Instruction. The baron of T'ung was probably the minister of Religion. His principality of T'ung was in the sub. dep. of Hwa (華州), dep. of T'ung-chow. 'The duke of Peih,'—see Bk. XXIV. Ch'in Sze-k'ae says that he succeeded the duke of Chow as chief of all the princes of the east, and in the office of Grand-Tutor. He was minister of War. 'The prince of Wei,'—see on the name of Bk. IX. He or his son was now the minister of Crime. 'The duke of Maou must have been the minister of Works. He is supposed to be called *Kung* or 'duke' here from having been appointed Grand-Assistant. Where Maou was is not certainly known. 師氏,—see on Bk. II., p. 2. By 虎臣 we are to understand the 虎賁 of Bk. XIX., p. 1,—the 虎賁氏 of the Chow Le, Bk. XXXI. 百尹＝百官之長,

'the heads or chiefs of the various departments of officers;'—as frequently.

We may take 御事, with Woo Ch'ing, as a general designation of all the ministers and officers mentioned. It is said that the king sent 'a common summons' for them all to come to his presence (同召). On common occasions the order to repair to the imperial presence was given to the 'six K'ing,' who would 'lead on the officers belonging to their several departments' (see Bk. XX, p. 13); but on the present extraordinary occasion the order was sent directly to all, of whatever rank. Such at least is the explanation given of the phrase 同召.

Pp. 4—9. *The king's charge.* 4. *The severity and dangerousness of his illness, rendering it necessary for him to take that opportunity of making his wishes known to them.* 疾大漸惟幾,—疾 is the general name for sickness or disease. When the sickness is severe, the term 病 is used. 漸＝進, 'to advance,' 'to grow.' 幾 is defined by 殆 or 危, 'perilous.' The 'Daily Explanation,' however, for 惟幾, gives 但幾希不絕耳, 'it wants only a little to the extinction of my breath.' 臻＝至, 'to come on.' 彌＝益, 'to increase,' or it may be construed with 留, in the sense of 終, 'to continue.' 恐不獲誓言嗣,—'I am afraid I shall not find *the opportunity* to speak solemnly and publicly about the succession.' This is the simplest way of construing this clause, and is that adopted by Woo Ch'ing and Këang Shing. Gan-kwǒ's method, followed by Ts'ae, is over ingenious:— 恐遂死,不得誓言以嗣續我志, 'I am afraid I shall forthwith die, and not be able to make a public declaration to develop continuously what I have in my mind.' 審訓＝詳審發訓, 'with careful exercise of thought I issue instructions.' 5.

昔
君
文
王
武

王
宣
重
光
奠

麗
陳
教
則
肄

肄
不
違
用
克

達
殷
集
大
命。

○
在
後
之
侗

敬
迓
天
威
嗣

守
文
武
大
訓

無
敢
昏
逾。
○

5 The former sovereigns, king Wăn and king Woo, displayed in succession their equal glory, making sure provision for the support of the people, and setting forth their instructions. *The people* accorded a practical submission; they did so without any opposition, so that their influence extended to Yin, and the great

6 appointment *of Heaven* was secured. After them, I, the stupid one, received with reverence the dread *decree* of Heaven, and continued to keep the great instructions of Wăn and Woo, not daring blindly to transgress them.

The brilliant and successful rule of Wăn and Woo. 昔君＝先王, 'the former kings.' 昔 is used as an adj. 宣重光,—'published—manifested—their doubled light,'＝相繼而能明其德, as Ch'in Ya-yen expresses it, 'continued one the other, and could make their virtue illustrious.' This is much better than to understand, with Ma Yung and Këang Shing, that 重光 is the light of the heavenly bodies combined together, and that 宣重光 is merely a figurative description of the virtue of Wăn and Woo, as like the brightness of the sun and moon. 奠(＝定)麗,—comp. Bk. XVIII., p. 5. I take 麗 in the same way as there. The various views of its meaning taken by the critics all re-appear on this passage. 則肄肄不違,—肄 is found with the meanings of 習, 'to practise,' and of 勞, 'to toil.' Gan-kwŏ takes the latter meaning, and understands the characters of Wăn and Woo, ＝'thus they toiled; and though they toiled, they did nothing contrary to what was right' (文武勤勞, 雖勞而不違道). So, Lin Che-k'e, as far as regards the meaning of 肄. The other meaning, however, is preferable. It was approved by Choo He, and adopted by Ts'ae. Acc. to it, 民, 'the people,' is understood as the subject of 肄.

There is no difficulty in this way with 不違. Këang Shing also takes this view, and attributes the repetition of 肄 to the gasping utterance of the dying king. This is not necessary. The repetition of the character gives emphasis to its meaning. I put no comma after the 1st 肄, as is generally done. 用克達殷,—'thereby they could reach to all Yin,' *i.e.*, the whole empire came under their influence.

6. *How king Ching had endeavoured to discharge his kingly duties.* 在後之侗,—'The stupid one who was after *them*.' So Ching designates himself. Gan-kwŏ and Woo Ch'ing find in 侗 the idea of 'youth' as well as of 'stupidity' (侗幼而未有知也); but there is no such idea in the term in Ana., VIII., xvi. Këang Shing, on the authority of the 說文, and partly also of Ma Yung, edits—在夏后之詷, from which he endeavours to force out the meaning of 承文武之業, 在中夏爲諸侯之共主, 'receiving the possession of Wăn and Woo, and being in the Central Great Land the common lord of all the princes!' 敬迓天威,—'I reverently met (＝set myself to receive) *the* dread *decree* of Heaven.' By 天威 is meant, no doubt, the 大命 of last par.,—the appointment to the empire, enforced by the dread requirements of Heaven

以釗冒貢于非
亂于威儀爾無
邦○思夫人自
邇安勸小大庶
艱難○柔遠能
元子釗弘濟于
時朕言用敬保
興弗悟爾尚明
今天降疾殆弗

7　"Now Heaven has laid affliction on me, and it seems as if I should not again rise or be myself. Do you take clear note of my words, and in accordance with them watch reverently over my eldest son, Ch'aou, and greatly assist him in the difficulties of his

8　position. Be kind to those who are far off, and help those who are near. Promote the tranquillity of the States, small and great, and encourage them *to well-doing*.

9　"I think how a man has to govern himself in dignity and with decorum :—do not you allow Ch'aou to proceed heedlessly on the impulse of improper motives."

from those who held it.　　7, 8. *The general duties which the ministers would have to perform for his son and successor.* 今天至弗悟,—Ts'ae puts a comma at 疾, and joins 殆 with the words that follow, as an adverb, = 'probably,' 'it is to be feared that.' Gan-kwǒ and Kёang Shing put the comma after 殆, and make it an adj., descriptive of the sickness. I prefer the former construction. 弗悟;—'will not awake,' *i.e.*, to a conscious ability for my duties. 元子釗,—Ching thus declares his eldest son as his successor. Ch'aou was the son's name. He is known in history by his honorary title of K'ang (康). I have not been able to ascertain how old he was at his accession. 弘濟于艱難,—no particular hardships and difficulties are meant, in which the new emperor might be involved, but those of his position generally. As the 'Daily Explanation' has it:—以宗社之重,基業之大,付之一人,可謂艱難矣. 柔遠能邇安—see the 'Can. of Shun,' p. 16.　　On 勸 云云, Ying-tă says—又當安

勸小大眾國,安之,使國得安存,勸之,使相勸爲善, 'tranquillize them, making the States feel in a condition of tranquil safety ; encourage them, making them emulate one another in well-doing.' 遠邇 and 大小庶邦 are composite designations for the whole empire.　　9. *Special charge to them to watch over the character of his son.* 思夫人,—夫人, 'this man,' = 'men' generally, or 'any man.' 自亂 (=治) 于威儀,—for 威儀 see on 'The Doctrine of the Mean,' xxvii., 3. 貢=進, 'to advance.' 非幾,—'improper springs,' *i.e.*, of action. Choo He was asked the meaning of this phrase by one of his disciples, who said that most critics took 幾 in the sense of 危, 'perilous,' but that he thought it should be taken as simply = 事, and 非幾=非所當爲之事, 'things which ought not to be done.' The master answered that 幾 meant 事之微, 'the small *beginnings or springs* of things.' Ching had in view, no doubt, the mind of his son, as the spring and regulator of all his conduct.

恤　之　逆　干　齊　桓　崩　越　還　幾
宅　外　子　戈　侯　南　○　翼　出　○
宗　延　釗　虎　呂　宮　太　日　綴　茲
○　入　於　賁　毛　保　乙　衣　旣
丁　翼　南　百　伋　俾　命　丑　于　受
卯　室　門　人　以　爰　仲　王　庭　命

10　Immediately on receiving this charge, the officers retired. The tent was then carried out into the court; and on the next day, *being* Yih-ch'ow, the king died.

11　II. The Grand-protector then ordered Chung Hwan and Nan-keung Maou to instruct Leu Keih, the prince of Ts'e, with two shield-and-spearmen and a hundred guards, to meet the prince Ch'aou outside the south gate, and conduct him to *one of* the wing apartments *near to that where the king lay*, there to be as chief mourner.

10.　*The king's death.*　茲旣受命

還 (read *seuen*),—茲 is to be taken adverbially,—是時, 'then.' We must understand 羣臣, 'all the ministers,' as the subject of 受命.　還=退, 'retired,' *i.e.*, from the apartment where they had received the charge. Gan-kwŏ, as amplified by Ying-tă, makes the meaning to be that they retired from around the king to the ceremonial places in the apartment appropriate to their different ranks. In this way the interpreter only gives himself trouble. I prefer the simpler view.

出綴衣于庭,—we are obliged to seek a meaning for 綴衣 here quite difft. from that assigned to it in Bk. XIX., p. 1, where it denotes—'the keeper of the robes.' K'ang-shing would make the 衣 to mean the 'grave clothes,' and 綴衣 = 'they made the grave clothes' (連綴小殮大殮之衣). But this view, though defended by Ming-shing, may safely be pronounced absurd. If it were to be admitted, we should have to find a third meaning for the phrase on its recurrence in p. 14. Ts'ae is right in defining it here, after Gan-kwŏ, by 幄帳, a kind of 'tent,' or curtains and canopy, set up over the emperor, when he held audiences. This had been prepared when he sent for his ministers to give them his last charge; and that ceremony over, it was now carried out into the court. Into what court? This question will be best answered, and the student prepared to understand the next chapter, if I refer to the form of the imperial palace in the time of Chow. It will easily be conceived by any one who has studied the architecture of the courts of the high officers throughout the empire at the present day.

The palace was much more long or deep than wide, consisting of five series of buildings, continued one after another, so that, if it had been according to etiquette, and all the gates had been thrown open, one might have walked in a direct line from the first gate to the last. The difft. buildings were separated by courts partially open and embracing a large space of ground. The gates of the different divisions, had their particular names. The first or outer gate, fronting the south, was called 臯門; the second was called 雉門; the third, 庫門; the fourth, 應門; and the fifth 路門, called also 畢門 and 虎門. Outside the second gate—the 雉門—was held the 'outer levee,' (外朝) when the sovereign received the princes and officers generally. Outside the 5th gate—the 路門—was held the 'audience of government' (治朝), when the king met his ministers, to consult with them on the business of the State. Inside this gate were the buildings which formed the private apartments, called

路寢, in the hall of which was held 'the inner audience' (內朝), and where the sovereign on occasions feasted those whom he designed specially to honour.

[Such is the general view of the palace given by Choo He. Acc. to K'ang-shing, the second gate was the 庫門, and the 雉門 was the third. Into a discussion of this point we need not enter. The gates were only gates according to our idea, in name, and included a large space, covered by a roof supported on pillars.]

The place where Ching delivered his testamentary charge was probably the hall in front of his bed-chamber, a sort of throne with curtains and canopy—the 綴衣,—being provided for the occasion. When he had finished, either before or after the retirement of the ministers, he was removed back to his chamber, and the tent—so to name it—was carried out into the court within the 路門. Medhurst mistook the meaning, and translated 出綴衣于庭, with reference to the ministers,—'going out, they set up their tents in the courtyard.' Gaubil saw that 綴衣 should be referred to the king; but he translated the clause by—'On detendit les rideaux, et on les remporta,' taking no notice of the 于庭.

Ch. II. Pp. 11—29. PUBLIC DECLARATION OF THE KING'S CHARGE TO HIS SUCCESSOR, WITH THE VARIOUS CEREMONIES OBSERVED ON THE OCCASION.　11. *Immediate measure to recognize Ch'aou as the successor to the throne.* 太保至呂伋,—the Grand-Guardian being also the 冢宰, or 'prime minister,' the regulation of all matters fell to him.　Of Chung Hwan and Nan-keung Maou, we know nothing more than is here related. They were, no doubt, officers of trust and distinction about the court. 俾爰齊侯 simply = 使齊侯, 'to cause,' or 'to instruct the prince of Ts'e.' 俾爰 = 俾於, but the 爰 has little independent meaning. Kёang Shing would define it by 引, 'to lead,' after the 說文; but what then becomes of the 俾, to which 爰 is merely supplementary.　The prince of Ts'e was the son of 太公, the friend and minister of king Wăn, who had been enfeoffed by Woo with the principality of Ts'e, the capital of which was Ying-k'ew (營邱), in the pres. dis. of Lin-tsze, dep. of Ts'ing-chow, Shan-tung.　Keih is known in history as duke

Ting (丁公 or 玎公).　His place at court, say all the critics, was that of 虎賁氏, or master of the guards. If it was so, it shows the dignity of that office, that it should be held by one of the chief princes of the empire.　以二干戈虎賁百人,—Gan-kwŏ supposed that 'the two shield-and-spearmen' were Hwan and Maou themselves, and that the meaning is that these officers were sent to the prince of Ts'e to get from him a hundred of the guards under his command, whom they preceded with spear and shield, to meet the prince. But the text, as it stands, will not bear this interpretation. It does seem strange, indeed, that only two men thus armed should have been selected; but so the record says. Medhurst, by mistake, took 干 for 千 and has rendered—'two thousand spearmen.' The style might have suggested to him that he was in error.

逆子釗於南門之外,—逆 = 迎, 'to meet.' Ts'ae and most of the other critics suppose the 5th or the 路 gate to be that intended. They think also that Ch'aou had been by his father's side at the time of his death, and that he went out purposely from the buildings in the rear, that he might be met thus publicly, and conducted back to be near the corpse as chief mourner. I cannot help thinking that by the 'south gate' we are to understand the first or outer gate of all,—the 臯門. This is the view of Kёang Shing, who thinks further that the prince had been absent on some expedition, and that he was now returning, just in the nick of time. This last supposition appears to me unlikely. The prince may have been absent from the palace, tho' not far off, when his father died, or he may have purposely gone outside, that his entrance in such a style, which was a public declaration that he had been appointed successor to the throne, might be seen by all.　延入翼室,恤宅宗,—翼室, 'a wing apartment.' On each side of the hall, immediately in front of the private apartments, called the 後堂, there was a 夾室, side chamber, or wing, only not spread out, as in our idea of the wings of a house. That to which the prince was conducted was the 東夾室, 'side chamber on the east.'　恤宅宗 = 爲憂居之宗主, 'to be the lord of the mournful dwelling.' The 'mourning shed' called 梁闇 was not yet erected. At the present stage the apartment indicated in the text was the proper one for the prince to occupy.

命作冊度。○越十三節
七日癸酉、伯相
命士須材。○狄十四節
設黼扆綴衣。○
十五節牖間南嚮、敷重
篾席、黼純、華玉
仍几。○十六節西序東
嚮、敷重底席、綴
純、文貝仍几。○

12 On the day Ting-maou (*two days after the king's death*), he
ordered a record to be made *of the charge*, and the ceremonies *to be*
13 *observed in publishing it.* On Kwei-yew, the seventh day after, as
chief *of the west* and premier, he ordered the *proper* officers to
provide the wood for *all* the requirements *of the funeral.*
14 The salvage men set out the screens ornamented with figures
15 of axes, and the tents. Between the window *and the door*, facing
the south, they placed the different mats of bamboo basket-work,
with their striped borders of white and black silk; and the usual

12. *The writing of the charge, and of the ceremonies to be observed.* The order here given is to be understood as from the Grand-Guardian. It would be given to the 內史, or 'Recorder of the Interior,' who was charged with the writing of the appointments of the emperor (內史掌書王命;—see the Chow Le, Bk. XXVI.). 作冊度=爲冊書法度, 'to make the writing on a tablet (or tablets), and the regulations.' For what was thus written see par. 24. The 'regulations' are all the ceremonies connected with conveying the appointment of Ching to his son. Few, if any, students, I apprehend, will be found to adopt Këang Shing's notion, that by 度 is intended 冊長短之數, 'the measure of the length of the tablets.' 13. *An order to prepare wood.* 伯相,—no doubt the Grand-guardian is still intended. In the 1st par, of the next Bk. he is introduced as 'leading forward all the princes of the western regions,' and we have seen before that he and the duke of Chow were 'the two chiefs,' the one having under his jurisdiction the east of the empire, and the other the west. Shih is here designated accordingly, as uniting the dignities of Chief and Premier, though it is difficult to assign a reason why the compiler of the Bk. should vary his style in so perplexing a manner. Ts'ae defines 須 by 取, 'to take,' 'to procure;' but this meaning of the character is not found in the dict., nor is it necessary. We may take it as an adj., ='requisite,' 'necessary,' and 命士須材 will='required *from* the *proper* officers the necessary materials,' those materials being probably of wood, though that is not necessarily implied in the term. So Gan-kwŏ:—命士致材木須待以供喪用. Acc. to the usual custom, the deceased monarch had been shrouded and coffined on the day 壬申, the seventh after the day of his death. The duties to him, therefore, were so far forward, that they might proceed to the announcement of his testamentary charge. There were only the shell or outer coffin (槨), and what were called the 明器, to be further provided; and it was with reference to them, I suppose, that the order in this par. was given. On those 明器, see the Le Ke, Bk. 檀弓下, Pt. i., p. 44, *et al.* It is not easy, however, to say definitely all that we are to understand here by 材. Ming-shing goes more at length into an examination of the point than any other of the critics whom I have seen.

Pp. 14—18. *At four points, where the emperor had been wont to receive his guests, the arrangements are made as if he were still alive.* 14. 狄設,—in the Le Ke, Bk. 祭統, p. 22, we find—翟者,樂吏之賤者; and assuming that 翟 and 狄 are interchangeable, the 狄 here are commonly described as 'the attendants on the musicians.' In the 大喪記, Pt. i., p. 3, again, we find 狄人設階, which is more to the point, showing that certain 狄 or 狄人 were employed in performing the more servile offices at the ceremonies of funerals and mourning. I suppose they were natives of some of the wild *Teih* tribes; and we know that some of the 虎賁, or 'guards' were taken from those people. I have ventured to translate the character by our old term 'salvage,' which seems to convey a less intense meaning than savage. 黼扆綴衣,—we have seen the meaning of 綴衣 on p. 10. What was called 黼扆 is represented as a screen, with axe-heads figured on it, which was placed under the canopy that overshadowed the emperor, and behind him. As to the meaning of the terms, the 爾雅, Bk. II., sect. 釋宮, says that 'the space, east and west, between the window and the door, was called 扆(牖戶之間謂之扆,注云,牖東戶西也). Here the screen in question was placed; and we may believe, with many of the critics, that from its place it took its name. [The only difficulty in the way of this is that in the 爾雅 the character is in the 1st tone; whereas in combination with 黼 it is pronounced in the 2d.] Anything painted or embroidered black and white alternately is said to be 黼. The 爾雅, sect. 釋器 says that 'an axe is called 黼, the wooden handle being black as compared with the glittering head and edge.' However this be, the screen about which we are concerned is called indifferently 斧扆 and 黼扆, the axe-heads on it being understood to be emblematic of the decision of the imperial determinations. We are to understand that four such screens and tents were arranged in the four positions immediately indicated. Gaubil is wrong in translating both 狄 and 黼扆, in the singular.—'L'officier appelle Tie eut soin de mettre en état l'ecran, sur lequel etoient représentées des haches.' We are to understand also that all these and other arrangements were made by the direction of the Grand-Guardian. The 命 of the preceding paragraphs is to be conceived to be constantly repeated.

15. The first tent and screen were placed in front of the 'rear hall' belonging to the private apartments, of course directly fronting the south. There the king was in the habit of giving audience to his ministers and to the princes (此平時見羣臣,覲諸侯之坐). 牖間 would seem, to mean 'between the windows;' but from the account of 扆, given above from the 爾雅,

we must take 牖 as an abbreviation for 牖戶之間;—as in the translation. 敷重篾席.—敷=設, or 鋪, 'to spread out.' On these mats the king sat; there were three of them, one over the other; and the text would lead us to suppose that all those mentioned here were made of bamboo splints woven together, having the edges bound with silk stripes of black and white alternating (黼 is explained above; 純 [read *chun*, 2d tone]=緣, 'a border].' Ying-tă, however, quotes a passage of the Chow Le, Bk. XX., on the duties of the 司几筵, which, while it throws considerable light on the text, states that the three mats were each of a difft. material, and that each had its peculiar border.—凡大朝覲,大饗射,凡封國命諸侯,王位設黼依,依前南鄉,設莞筵紛純,加繅席畫純,加次席黼純,左右玉几. This passage, as translated (not quite accurately, but sufficiently so for my purpose) by Biot, is:—'En général, dans les grands réunions du printemps et de l'automne, dans les grands banquets, dans les cérémonies où l'on tire de l'arc, où un royaume est concédé en fief, où un grand dignitaire est nommé, il dispose le paravent brodé en noir et blanc, à la place que doit occuper l'empereur. Le devant du paravent fait face au midi. Il place la matte en joncs fins à bordure variée. Il ajoute la natte à lisière qui a une bordure peinte. Il ajoute la natte à rangées qui a une bordure mélangée de noir et de blanc. A gauche et à droite sont les petits bancs en jade pour s'appuyer.' Gan-kwŏ thinks that 篾 [this character is disputed] 席 is the 次席 of the above passage, the topmost of the three mats, the historian not thinking it necessary to describe the others particularly. Possibly it may be so; but the point is really not of much importance. 華玉仍几.—華玉=彩色之玉, 'gems of variegated colours.' The bench was adorned with such. 仍 is used as an adj., = 'usual,' 'ordinary;' intimating that the bench was the same which was used in such position by the living emperor (仍,因也,因生時所設). Woo Ch'ing, however, explains the term differently, but by no means in so satisfactory a manner. He says:—仍几謂雖飾之漆之,尚仍其質,其文不皆滅質也,吉事尚文,凶事尚質故爾, 'The benches are called 仍几, because, though they were ornamented and lacquered, their proper material could still be distinguished, its substance not all concealed by the ornamenting. The reason of this was

仍 紛 筍 繢、西十 仍 純 豐 繢、東十
几 純 席、敷 夾八 几 雕 席、敷 序七
○ 漆 玄 重 南節 ○ 玉 畫 重 西節

16 bench and adorned with different-coloured gems.　In the side space
on the west, facing the east, they placed the different rush mats, with
their variegated border; and the usual bench adorned with veined

17 tortoise-shell.　In the side space on the east, facing the west, they
put the different mats of fine grass, with their border of painted

18 silk; and the usual bench carved and adorned with gems.　Before the
western side-chamber, facing the south, they placed the different
mats of fine bamboo, with their dark mixed border; and the usual
lacquered bench.

that in festive matters the ornamental takes the prominence; but on occasions of mourning and sorrow, the simple and substantial. Perhaps we ought to translate 几 in the plural, acc. to the pass. of the Chow Le just referred to.

16. 西序東繢.—it is difficult without a picture to get for one's-self or to give the reader an idea of the 序. They were on the front hall (前堂) of the private apartments. The wall which was the boundary of this portion of the 'hall' did not extend all the way across, and from the extremity of it short walls were built towards the south, coming forward to about a line with the pillars that supported the roof. These walls were originally called the 序, acc. to the 爾雅;—東西牆謂 之序. They were so called, as 'fencing or differencing between the inside and out' (所以序別內外). The screen and tent here spoken of were placed, I believe, in the side space between the 序 and outer wall of the hall. The 東繢 is descriptive of the position of this space, and is not to be understood of the aspect of the screen and mats, which must always have been 'towards the south.' Gaubil translates 西序 by 'devant l'appartement occidental,' and Medhurst by 'in the western ante-chamber;' but both are wrong. The space was not an 'apartment,' but a portion of the hall with its own designation. Here the emperor, morning and evening, took his seat to listen to affairs of business (此旦夕聽 事之坐也).　底席.—'bottom mats.' Ma Yung, Wang Suh, and Gan-kwŏ, all say that these mats (or at least the bottom one of them) were made of 青蒲, 'green rushes or reeds:' and I have so translated.

K'ang-shing thinks that bamboo mats, the splints very fine, were intended (底、致也、篾纖 致席也).　It is really all guess work. 綴 is supposed to have the sense of 雜彩, 'variegated.'　　17. 東序西繢,—comp. on last par.　At this point the emp. feasted his ministers and the elders of the king- dom (此養國老、饗羣臣之坐).　豐席.—'great or superior mats.' Mats made of a kind of grass called 莞 (hwan) are probably meant;—why they were named 豐 席 I cannot tell. The 集傳 calls them 筍席, by mistake apparently for 莞席. 畫=彩色, i.e., silk painted in various col- ours.　　18. 西夾南繢,—this appears to have been the 西夾室, 'western side apartment,' i.e., of the 'rear hall,' responding to that on the east, which was the 'wing apart- ment' (翼室), occupied for the time by prince Ch'aou as the place of mourning. Here the emperor had his private meals (此私燕 之坐).　筍席,—筍 is commonly used for 'the young and edible shoots of bamboo;' here it is read yun, and means a soft, flexible species of bamboo, of which mats were made. 玄紛純.—'dark mixed border.' How it was mixed, I don't know. Perhaps the silk edging was all dark, but of different shades. The 'Daily Explanation' says:—其席之 緣、則以黑色之繪雜爲之. The reason, it is said, for preparing all these places, as if king Ching had been still alive, was to afford so many resting places for his spirit, which it was presumed would be present

越玉五重　陳寶赤刀　大訓弘璧　琬琰玉夷　序大玉　圖在東序河　胐之舞衣　大貝鼖鼓　在西房兌　十九節

19   They *set forth* also the five kinds of gems, and the precious things
of display.   There were the red knife, the great lessons, the large
convex symbol of gem, and the rounded and pointed maces,—
all in the side space on the west; the large gem, the gems from
the wild tribes of the east, the heavenly sounding stone, and the
river plan,—all in the side-chamber on the east; the dancing
habits of Yin, the large tortoise-shell, and the large drum,—all

at the ceremony of communicating his dying
charge to his son. They could not tell at what
particular spot it would choose to be, and therefore would enable it to have a choice. As Ts'ae
expresses it, 將傳先王顧命, 知神
之在此乎, 在彼乎, 故兼設
平生之坐.

P. 19. *Display of various precious relics.*
越玉五重陳寶,—this clause covers
the rest of the par., which gives in detail the
gems and precious relics, with the places in
which they were set forth. Ying-tă has noticed
this construction of the par.:—此經爲
下總目,下復分別言之. I
take 陳 passively, and understand a 列 before 玉, governing both it and 寶.   赤
刀,—'the red knife.' This was, no doubt, a
knife which had been distinguished at some
time in the history of the empire. It would be
of no use wearying ourselves, as the critics have
done in vain, to discover what knife it was.
Concerning 'the great lessons' Gaubil enquires:
—'Was this the history of the empire, or some
Book of religion or morals? or the one and the
other?' We might put such questions indefinitely. Wang Suh thought we were to understand the Canons and Counsels of Parts I. and
II. Ts'ae would go farther back, to the 'Books
of the three 皇 and five 帝,' mentioned by
Gan-kwŏ in his Introduction to the Shoo; but
he thinks the lessons of Wăn and Woo may also
be included! 弘 (=大) 璧,—see on Bk.
VI., p. 4, where also the duke of Chow is represented as holding a mace (珪) in his hand.
To the imperial 珪, 'maces,' or 'sceptres,' belonged the 琬琰. From the text we should
naturally have concluded that one article was in-

tended by those terms; but from the Chow Le,
Bk. XX., on the duties of the 典瑞, we learn
that there was one 'gem-token' called 琬, and
another called 琰.   They were each 9 inches
long:—the former rounded, expressive of good
will; the other pointed, expressive of sharp
severity against evil. All these articles were
exhibited in 'the western side-space,' behind
the screen, &c., of p. 16.   大玉至東
序,—大玉, 'great gem-*stone*;' but said by
K'ang-shing to be from mount Hwa. 夷玉,
'gem-*stones* contributed by the E, or wild tribes
of the east.' Ts'ae would take 夷 as = 常,
'common,' which does not seem at all so likely
a meaning.   天球,—see for the meaning
of 球, on the 'Yih and Tseih,' p. 9. Gaubil
thinks that 天球 means 'the heavenly sphere,
a celestial globe, or something else, to represent the movement of the stars.' But the use
of the character 球 for 'a globe' is quite
modern.   河圖,—this was some scheme
to represent the first suggestions of the eight
diagrams of Fuh-he. The fable was, that a
dragon-horse came forth from the waters of the
Ho, having marks or signs on his back, from
which that emperor got his idea. See what is
said on the 'Book of Lŏ,' p. 321.   胐之
至西房,—胐, see on the name of Pt. III.,
Bk. IV.   大貝,—'great tortoise-shell.'
Among the gifts by which the friends of king
Wăn propitiated the tyrant Show, when he had
confined the rising chief in prison, mention is
made of a tortoise-shell curved as the pole of a
carriage.   There was a drum under the Chow
dyn., called 鼖鼓, made 8 feet long. That in
the text, however, would probably be a similar

之戈和之
弓垂之竹
矢在東房。
○大輅
二十節
賓階面綴
輅在阼階
面、先輅在
左塾之前、
次輅在右
塾之前。○

in the western apartment; and the spear of Tuy, the bow of Ho, and the bamboo arrows of Suy,—all in the eastern apartment.

20　　The grand carriage was by the guests' steps, facing the south. The next carriage was by the eastern steps, facing the south. The foremost carriage was in the front of the left lobby; and the next carriage was in the front of the right lobby.

instrument transmitted from former times. By the western and eastern apartments we are to understand two rooms, east and west of the 路寢, forming part therefore of the private apartments. They were behind the 夾室 of the 'rear hall,' and of larger dimensions.

兌之至東房,—Tuy, Ho, and Suy were, no doubt, famous artificers of antiquity, and distinguished respectively for the making of the several articles here mentioned. That is all we can be said to know of Tuy and Ho, but Suy is supposed to be the same with Shun's minister of Works.

Ts'ae suggests that the various articles here enumerated were set forth not merely as relics of the empire, but as having been favourites with king Ching;—to keep up the illusion of everything appearing as if he were there alive. He gives also a good remark from Yang She (楊時, 中庸傳):—宗器, 於祭陳之, 示能守也, 於顧命陳之, 示能傳也, 'The articles of honour were set forth at the sacrifices, to show that the emperor could preserve them; they were set forth at the ceremonies of announcing a testamentary charge, to show that he could transmit them.'

P. 20. *Display of imperial carriages.* In the Chow Le, Bk. XXVII., on the duties of the 巾車, we have a full account of the imperial carriages, which were of five kinds,—玉, 金, 象, 革, and 木:—*i.e.*, the grand carriage ornamented with gems; the second, ornamented with metal (gold, we may suppose); the third, ornamented with ivory; the fourth with leather and lacquered; the fifth, a wooden carriage, lacquered. Ts'ae supposes that all the five carriages are included in the text, the grand carriage being the 玉輅 (or 路, which is the more common designation); 綴輅, 'the connected carriage,' being the 金輅; 先輅,

'the front carriage' the 木輅; and 次輅 'the next carriage (or carriages) in order,' both the 象輅 and the 革路. In this view he differs from all the old commentators. Gan-kwŏ, Ma Yung, and Wang Suh took the carriages in the par. to be those of the Chow Le in the order of their rank, the fourth, or leather carriage—the chariot of war—being omitted, as inappropriate to the occasion. K'ang-shing had a view of his own. The 大輅 was with him, as the others, the 玉路, but the 綴輅 was also a 玉路 No. 2, while the 先輅 and the 次輅 were the 象路 and a 象路 No. 2 (玉路之貳, 象路之貳). I should prefer to adopt the view of Gan-kwŏ and those who agree with him. There can be no satisfactory explanation given of the names 綴, 先, and 次, and our course is simply to translate them as we best can. The carriages were all arranged inside the Loo (路) gate; and this gives us some idea of the dimensions of the palace, or the ground which it inclosed, as two carriages could stand opposite to each other (and not close together, we may suppose) between the gate and the steps by which the hall was ascended. On the west of the hall were the guests' steps, those by which visitors ascended; on the east were those appropriate to the host, the 主階, called here 阼階. The front of those steps was of course towards the south. The 爾雅 says—門側之堂謂之塾, 'Halls by the side of the gate were called 塾.' We may translate 塾 by 'lobby.' Ts'ae observes that the carriages were thus displayed, as in the case of the screens, tents, and relics, that everything might be done as when the king was alive. The student will ask where they were brought from, and how they were brought inside the Loo gate. Of course

廿一節
二人雀弁執
惠立于畢門
之內四人綦
弁執戈上刃
夾兩階戺一
人冕執劉立
于東堂一人
冕執鉞立于
西堂一人冕
執戣立于東

21 Two men in brownish leather caps, and holding three-cornered halberds, stood inside the gate leading to the private *apartments:* Four men in caps of spotted deer-skin, holding spears with up-turned blades, stood one on each side of the steps east and west, and near to the platform of the hall. One man in a great officer's cap, and holding an axe, stood in the hall *near the front* at the east *end.* One man in a great officer's cap, and holding a *somewhat different* axe, stood in the hall, near the front at the west *end.* One man in a great officer's cap, and holding a lance, stood at the

they were brought, by the officer called 典路, from their usual houses or repositories. How they were brought inside the Loo gate cannot be explained so clearly. Ming-shing says that from the Loo to the Kaou or outer gate there was a level way. This is not the case now in the structure of the large public buildings from which I have endeavoured to give a general idea of king Ching's palace.

P. 21. *Arrangement of guards about the gate and hall.* 二人至之內,—弁 is sometimes used as a general designation for all coverings of the head used in ancient times. Here it denotes a leathern cap worn by guards, and which is figured something like a 冕, having the surmounting cover, but no pendents attached. 雀弁,—'sparrow cap,' *i.e.,* acc. to K'ang-shing, with reference to the colour, which was like a male sparrow's head. The 惠 was a species of 矛, a kind of spear or lance, sharp-pointed, with hooks bending downwards (凡矛上銳而旁勾,象物之芒旁勾,所以象物之生). Gan-kwŏ says the 惠 was 三隅矛, 'a three-cornered *maou.*' I suppose the point above the 'hooks' was fashioned in this way, which would make it more a halberd than a spear. We have seen that 畢門 is another name for 路門. These two men stood, each on one side, inside the fifth gate, within which everything yet described had been transacted.

四人至階戺,—the 綦弁 was different in form from the 雀弁, in being without the surmounting cover. It was made of the skin of a spotted deer, probably the *axis.* The 戈 spear had a blade with upturned edge, projecting on one side from the base of the point.

堂廉曰戺, 'The side of the platform of the hall was called 戺.' 'The two stairs' are mentioned in the last par. We are to conceive of a guard accoutred as described, standing near the platform of the hall on each side of the steps by which it was ascended.

一人至西堂,—the 冕 here was of the same form as that worn by the emperor, but distinguished from it by the number of the pendents and the nature of the gems strung upon them. The critics are probably right in determining that the 冕 here was that worn by a 大夫 or 'great officer,' having 'five pendents with black gems.' 鉞 is the common name for 'a battle-axe.' The 劉 was a weapon of the same kind, but with some peculiarity of form, which it is difficult to ascertain. By 西堂 and 東堂 we are to understand the portion of the 'front hall' or platform east and west, in front of the two 序 described on par. 19. K'ang-shing says:—序內半堂西堂而立瞿, 以前曰堂, 此立於東近階而者當在東西廂, 一人至西垂,—戣 and 也

太宗皆麻冕　○太保太史、　蟻裳入卽位。　士邦君麻冕　由賓階隮、　王麻冕黼裳、　立于側階。○　一人冕執銳　瞿立于西垂、　垂、一人冕執

front and eastern end of the hall.   One man, in a great officer's cap, and holding a *somewhat different* lance, stood at the front and western end of the hall.   One man in a great officer's cap, and holding a pointed weapon, stood by the steps on the north.

22 The king, in a hempen cap and a variously adorned skirt, ascended by the guests' steps, followed by the nobles aud princes of States, in hempen caps and black ant-coloured skirts.   Having
23 entered, they all took their places.   The Grand-protector, the Grand-historiographer, and the minister of Religion were all in hempen

are described as being varieties of the 戟, 'a spear or lance with three points.' I do not think that their exact form can be determined. See the figures in Ch'ing Yaou-teen's (程瑤田) 考工創物小言, in the 皇清經解,卷五百三十七. The dict. defines 垂 by 堂之盡處,近階者, 'the extremities of the hall, near the steps.' These men stood east and west respectively from the bearers of the 劉 and the 鉞. See Yaou-teen's 釋宮小記,經解卷五百三十五. 一人至側階, —Ts'ae says that 銳 ought to be 鈗, after Ying-tă, and on the authority of the 說文, which, however, only defines the character as 'a weapon grasped by the imperial attendants' (侍臣所執兵). 側階, —'the side steps;' but both Ts'ae and Këang Shing agree in saying that the steps on the north of the hall, of which there was only one flight are to be understood. Shing says :—側階,北下階也,在北堂之下,側之言特,北堂惟一階,故曰側階. So, also Ying-tă, who observes further, that 'of the seven weapons mentioned in this par. it is only the 戈 of which we have any particular account. Of the rest we have no description. The names and forms of ancient and modern weapons being different, we cannot

arrive at any certain knowledge about the various arms here mentioned. Wang Suh contented himself with saying that the characters were names of ancient weapons.'

Pp. 22—24. *The announcement of the testamentary charge; and the manner of it.* All was now ready for the grand ceremony and all the performers, in their appropriate array, take their places in the hall. 22. 麻冕— see Ana., IX., iii. 黼裳,—the skirt of the emperor's dress on sacrificial occasions was variously adorned. See the 'Yih and Tseih,' p. 4. The 'axe' (黼) was one of the figures upon it, and Ying-tă supposes it is mentioned here, by synecdoche, for all the others. It may be so; but I take 黼, as in p. 15. Ch'aou is here for the first time called 'king;' but still he goes up by 'the guests' steps,' not presuming to ascend by the others, while his father's corpse was in the hall. 隮=升. 蟻裳,— 'ant skirts;' meaning dark, like the colour of ants. 'They all entered and took their places;' *i.e.*, the places proper to them, according to their various ranks. 23. 太保至彤裳, —we can easily see how the three dignitaries here mentioned should take the prominent part in the ceremony which they did. Their skirts were of a pale red colour (彤=纁),—the proper colour of their sacrificial dress. 介圭, —'the grand mace' (介=大), a cubit and 2 inches long, called also 鎮圭. See the Chow Le, Bk. XIII., on the duties of the 玉

下用，答揚文武
循大卞，燮和天
訓臨君周邦，率
揚末命，命汝嗣
皇后憑玉几道，
御王册命。○曰廿四
秉書由賓階，太史
由阼階隮、
圭，上宗奉同瑁、
彤裳，太保承介

caps and red skirts. The Grand-protector bore the great mace. The minister of Religion bore the cup, and the mace-cover. These two ascended by the eastern steps. The Grand-historiographer bore the testamentary charge. He ascended by the guests' steps, and advanced to the king with the record of the charge, saying,

24 "Our great lord, leaning on the gem-adorned bench, declared his last charge, and commanded you to continue the observance of the lessons, and to take the rule of the empire of Chow, complying with the great laws, and securing the harmony of the empire, so as to respond to and display the bright instructions of Wăn and Woo."

人. It belonged to the emperor, and was one of the emblems of his sovereignty. 上宗 —this was, no doubt, the minister of Religion, the 宗伯 of Bk. XX., p. 9. In the Chow Le he is called 大宗伯, and immediately subordinate in his department were the two 小宗伯. 'Thus,' says K'ang-shing, 'there were three 宗伯. By 上宗 here are intended the 大宗伯 and one of the 小宗伯, one of them carrying the 同, and the other the 瑁.' This view may be rejected without hesitation. 上宗 is the 宗伯 *par eminence*, so denominated probably as superior to the two 小宗伯. 同 is defined—爵名, 'the name of a cup.' It must have been some particular cup which the emperor only had the right to employ in sacrificing. 瑁,—see on the 'Can. of Shun,' p. 7. This was what I have called there 'a sort of frame by which the genuineness of the gem-tokens conferred on the difft. princes was tested.' We see here that it was itself made of gem. We can easily understand how the other tokens or maces could be tested by it; but it is not explained how it was applied to the 璧圭. The Grand-guardian

and the minister of Religion ascended by the east or emperor's steps, because the authority of king Ching was, as it were, in their persons, to be conveyed in the present ceremony to his son. 書 is the testamentary charge which the historiographer had written or graved on tablets by the guardian's order;—see par. 12. He ascended by the guests' steps, being only an employé in the premier's department. Other reasons for his doing so have been assigned;—unsatisfactorily. 御 here is best defined by 進, and 御王册命＝以册命進於王. 曰,—'saying.' Some make 命 the nominative to this, as if what follows were what had been written. But this is not to be supposed. What was written was what the king had spoken, as recorded in parr. 4—9. In presenting the record the historiographer made the brief speech which is here given. 末命道揚命＝宣揚臨終之命. 命汝嗣訓＝命汝嗣守文武之大訓, 'charged you to continue to keep the great lessons of Wăn and Woo.' 臨君周邦,—'to descend and be sovereign over the country (＝empire) of Chow.' 大卞＝大法, 'the great laws.' This clause seems to declare that the emperor was not

祭 王 乃 廿六節 忌 四 其 予 答 王 廿五節 之
三 三 受 天 方 能 末 曰 再 光
咤 宿 同 威 以 而 小 眇 拜 訓c
上 三 瑁 ○ 敬 亂 子 眇 興 ○

25 The king twice bowed *low*, and then arose, and said, "I am utterly insignificant and but a child; how can I be able to govern the four quarters *of the empire* with such a reverent awe of
26 the dread majesty of Heaven?" He then received the cup and the mace-cover. Thrice he advanced with a cup *of spirits;* thrice he sacrificed; and thrice he put the cup down. The minister of Religion said, "It is accepted."

absolute, but subject to certain constitutional laws. Sëĕ Ke-seuen, however, would make 'the great law' to be that delivered by Shun to Yu in Pt. II., Bk II., p. 15.

Pp. 25, 26. *Ch'aou's acceptance of the sovereignty.* 眇, derived from the *eye* and *small,* has the sense of 'little,' 'insignificant.' The repetition of it expresses that idea strongly. The whole expression—眇眇予末小子 is a very humble designation of himself by the new emperor. 而亂,—亂 is in the sense of 治. The critics nearly all take 而 =如, and complete the meaning—其能如父祖治四方, 'can I govern the four quarters of the empire as my ancestors did?' This does not seem to be necessary. 其能而亂四方=其何能而治四方, according to a common usage of 而. 敬忌天威,—comp. 敬迓天威 in par. 6. 敬忌 occurred in Bk. IX., p. 19. 26. 乃受同瑁,—the king received these things from the minister of Religion, who had taken them up to the hall. 'He received them,' says K'ang-shing, 'one with each hand;' but we do not know the manner of the action. Nothing is said of his receiving 'the great mace,' which the guardian had borne up. No doubt he had received it, and disposed of it somehow. 三宿,三祭, 三咤—Ts'ae after Gan-kwŏ defines 宿 by 進爵, 'advanced the cup.' K'ang-shing says:—宿, 肅也, 徐行前曰肅, '宿 i. q. 肅, meaning to go gently forward.' The two definitions, it will be seen, may admit of a similar interpretation. When the king received the record of the charge he was standing at the top of the western steps a little eastwards, with his face to the north. The historiographer stood by king Ching's coffin, on the south west of it with his face to the east. There he read the charge, after which the king bowed twice, and the minister of Religion, on the south west of the king with his face to the north, presented the cup and mace-cover. The king took them, and having given the cover in charge to an attendant, advanced with the cup to the place between the pillars where the sacrificial spirits were placed. Having filled a cup, he advanced to the east of the coffin, and stood with his face to the west; then going to the spot where his father's spirit was supposed to be, he sacrificed, pouring out the spirits on the ground after which he put the cup on a bench appropriated for it. This he repeated three times. Such is the account of the ceremony given by Ying-tă, which must be nearly correct, if it be not so in every particular. He says three different cups were used, while we should rather suppose that the sacrifices were all made with one,—the 同 which is mentioned. The account in this point, however, agrees better with the 三咤, 咤 being taken in the sense of 奠爵, 'to set down a cup.' There is a difference of opinion both as to the form and meaning of this character. On these points Ch'in Leih has said:—'There are two explanations of 咤. Gan-kwŏ defined it as meaning 奠爵, "to put down a cup;" and most scholars have concurred in his view. Soo Shih, however, considered that it meant "to raise to the teeth without drinking," like 嚌, in the par. below. At first I was inclined to agree with Soo, principally because of the 'mouth' (口) at the side of the character. Subsequent examination altered this view. 咤 is a mistake for 宅, with which the 說文 quotes the passage. Gan-kwŏ's explanation ought not to be altered. If 咤 and 嚌 were the

宗曰饗。○太保
受同、降盥以異
同秉璋以酢授
宗人同拜、王答
拜。○太保受同、
祭嚌宅授宗人
同拜、王答拜。○
太保降、收諸侯
出廟門俟。

27　The Grand-protector received the cup, descended the steps, and washed his hands. He then took another cup, and in his hand a half mace, in order to make the responsive sacrifice. Having given the cup to an attending officer, he did obeisance. The king
28 returned the obeisance. The Grand-protector then took back the cup, and sacrificed with it. He then just tasted the sacrificial spirits, returned to his place, gave the cup to the attendant, and did obeisance. The king returned the obeisance.

29　The Grand-protector descended from the hall, when the various articles were removed, and the princes all went out from the temple gate and waited.

same in meaning, why should we not find one or the other of them in the two contiguous paragraphs?' See the 集說. 上宗曰饗,—both Gan-kwǒ and Wang Suh explain this—'The minister of Religion said to the king, "Drink now;"' referring to the custom for the offerer to drink some of the sacrificial wine, and so receive blessing from the spirit or spirits sacrificed to. I prefer to take the meaning as in the translation. The 'Daily Explanation' says:—宗伯乃傳神命而言曰、先王已饗之矣.

Pp. 27—29. *How the Grand-protector concluded the ceremony*. 27. 太保受同,—the 同 here must be that which the king had used. If we are to suppose with Gan-kwǒ that a difft. cup was employed for each libation, I should think that the 同 may have been used to fill them. 降盥,—'descended—*i.e.*, went down the steps, putting the cup back into a basket (下堂反于篚)—and washed his hands.' It was customary to wash the hands before offering sacrifice. The 璋 is described as a 'half mace carried by ministers' (半圭曰璋臣所奉). Its make is called 邸剡, in the Chow Le, Bk. XX., 典瑞.

With the new cup and this mace the guardian again ascended the steps—以酢=以報祭, 'to return the sacrifice;' here, it seems to me = 'to repeat the sacrifice,' 'to offer a second sacrifice.' The young king had in his sacrifice acknowledged to the spirit of his father that he had received his testamentary charge; it now belonged to the Grand-guardian to inform the same spirit that he had communicated that charge. 授宗人同拜=以授宗人而拜. By 宗人 we are to understand one of the employés in the dept. of the minister of Religion. The 'bowing' was to the spirit of the departed king, represented probably by a tablet, where it was supposed to rest. The guardian could not bow, and carry the cup and mace at the same time; he therefore handed them to the attendant. 王答拜,—the king returned the obeisance as for his father.

28. 嚌,—see on 咤 in the last par. 宅=居. The 'Daily Explanation' expands it into—退居其所立之位. 拜, 王答拜,—as in the last par. Many critics, however, say that the bows were made to the new king, and returned by him for himself. I do not think this is unlikely. The critics have not borne sufficiently in mind that the service described in this Book was one of an extraordinary character. 29. 收=有

司收撤器用, 'the proper officers removed the apparatus of the service.' 廟門,—this is the Loo gate, The private apartments had for the time, through the presence of the coffin and by the sacrifices, been converted into a sort of ancestral temple.

俟,—'waited;' *i.e.*, they waited to have an audience of the new sovereign.

~~~~~~~~~~~~~~~~~~~~

I append here the remarks of Wang Pih on this Book and the next. The difficult point on which he dwells will be found treated of on the last par. of the Announcement of king K'ang:—

嫌正豈蠱成非出公外議而之評宜而以後今已
起至也豈隙乎豈故召內可矣卒議權變權免古而
肯公者門變有變乎使之密倉之變處之不乎人
不大忌俟大未之計施髮者於世處猶然謂猶用一
而以顧覦一所履之設一室儀後曰論乃變易尹
肉之所孽此古身患其無王禮免雖法是處可伊
骨行無餘倡命臣定定不哉常經公權者
待念而宄心慮前危未之綏考終畏以其召議權
心之然姦人之創防張大以暇而可易失公之用
之疑洞料惑王懲此恢小所不開吁未不周世善

當正多大之服足天聖制公擁鎮公不人
只一不之氏成誠公之事周宰宜周而聖
書始之詞終蘇既言召下處盡冢謂安下以
二其之始也喪此公天以未位下之天亦
誥正誥家可之也周以所之也天山待防
之一命國事也室髮崩臨泰心之
康一中紀之釋萬聖輔無王以下人嫌
王篇開載敍三非世賢王亳之君如之疑
顧命爲終是謂以暫爲之夾當武主天聖爲
合其全典論而以下賢義當幼定以肯

THE BOOKS OF CHOW.

BOOK. XXIII. THE ANNOUNCEMENT OF KING K'ANG.

康王之誥

皆再拜稽首王義　二臣衛敢執壤奠一　稱奉圭兼幣曰一　右皆布乘黃朱賓　東方諸侯入應門　入應門左畢公率　太保率西方諸侯　王出在應門之內、一節

I. The king came forth and stood *in the space* within the fourth gate of the palace, when the Grand-guardian led in all the princes of the western regions by the left *half* of the gate, and the duke of Peih those of the eastern regions by the right *half*. They then caused their teams of light bay horses, with red manes and tails, to be exhibited; and the princes, raising aloft their secptres and *other* presents, said, "We, your servants, defenders *of the throne*, venture to bring here the productions of our territories and set them forth." With these words, they did obeisance twice, bowing their heads to the earth. The king, righteously continuing the virtue *of his pre-decessors*, returned their obeisance.

THE NAME OF THE BOOK.—康王之 誥, 'The Announcement of king K'ang.' We have seen, on par. 7 of the last Book, that K'ang was the honorary posthumous title con- ferred on Ch'aou, the successor of Ching, and third sovereign of the dynasty of Chow. In the dict. we find three explanations of the character, used with such an application. It may denote that the individual so denominated was 'an abyss, a fountain, sending forth its waters' (淵源流通曰康); or that 'he was gentle and mild, fond of happiness' (溫柔好樂曰康); or that 'he caus- ed the people to be tranquil and happy' (令 民安樂曰康). Immediately on K'ang's accession, he made the Announcement which is here recorded.   The Book is found in both the texts; but something more must be said on this point.

THE CONNECTION BETWEEN THIS BOOK AND THE LAST. The Book is found in both the texts. In Fuh-shang's Shoo, however, this Book and the last formed only one Book. Yet the 'little preface' shows us that there were in Confucius' Shoo two Books, one called 'The Testamentary Charge,' and one, 'The Announcement of king K'ang.' We cannot but believe also that Fuh-shang's one Book contained the whole of them both. The only question is as to where the division of them should take place. Choo He says, 'Take away the prefatory notices, and we should not think of making any division. The one part runs naturally, by the connection of the style, into the other, (除 却 序 文 讀 著, 則 文 勢 自 相 接 連). All the old interpreters, excepting Gan-kwŏ,—K'ang-shing, Ma Yung, and Wang Suh,—extended the Testamentary Charge to par. 3 of the Announcement, and made the latter very brief indeed. Much more natural is the division as it stands in the *textus receptus*, and which I here assume was made by Gan-kwŏ, whether he acted merely on his own sense of fitness, or had special authority for the arrangement in the recovered tablets which were submitted to him. As the Books now stand, the first is complete, and the second. The portion which precedes the Announcement is a proper introduction to it, while it is out of place as an appendix to the Testamentary charge.

Tae Tung-yuen, of the present dynasty, pronounces both divisions wrong, but his own view, if he can be said to have one on the point in hand, is very unsatisfactory. Accepting Fuh-shang's arrangement of the whole in one Book, he would divide it into three parts:—the first, parr. 1—13, relating to the Testamentary Charge; the second, parr. 14—29, describing the accession of king K'ang, *the year after his father's death;* and the third, being all comprehended in the Announcement, relating all that took place at the first public audience or levee by the new monarch, immediately after the accession. Granting all this, he still divides the two Books at the same point as Gan-kwŏ. Of his view, that from p. 14 of the Charge the things described all belonged to the year after Ching's death, I shall speak on par. 1. See 戴 東 原 集 卷 一.

CONTENTS. The action of the Book follows immediately that of the last. A great assembly of princes do homage after their fashion to the new king, and caution and advise him on the discharge of the great duties to which he is called. He responds with the declaration which has given name to the Book, referring to his predecessors, and asking the assistance of all his hearers that his reign might be a not unworthy sequel of theirs. With this the proceedings terminate, and the king resumes his mourning dress which he had put off for the occasion. It will be seen that I have arranged the paragraphs in three chapters.

Ch. I. Pp. 1—3. FIRST AUDIENCE OF THE PRINCES AND MINISTERS HELD BY KING K'ANG. THEIR OFFERINGS; AND ADVICE.   1. 王 出 在 應 門 之 內 = 王 乃 出 路 (= 廟) 門, 立 于 應 門 之 內, 'The king went out from the Loo gate, and stood in the space between it and the Ying gate.' The 應 gate, we have seen, was the 4th of the palace gates. It took its name, according to Ch'in Sze-k'ae, from a drum near it which was called the 應 鼓. Between it and the 5th gate was held the 治 朝 or 'audience of govt.,' at which king K'ang on this occasion received the homage of all the princes, showing himself to them for the first time, as 'the son of Heaven.'

[Ts'ae, by mistake, calls this the 內 朝. It would not be correct, however, to call it, with Sze-k'ae, the 外 朝.]

On the Guardian and the duke of Peih's leading the princes of the west and the east respectively, see on the last Bk., p. 3. The princes of the west entered by the left or eastern side of the gate, and those of the east by the right or western side, and took their places accordingly. This appears to have been all according to rule. The Le Ke, Bk. 曲 禮, 上, Pt. ii., p. 29, says, 'The host enters on the right of the gate, and proceeds to the eastern steps; the guest enters on the left, and proceeds to the western steps.' From west to east and from east to west, therefore, was the rule. See Lin Che-k'e, *in loc.* 皆 布 (= 陳) 乘 黃 朱,—a team of four horses (馬 四 匹) was called 乘. Those horses were 黃 朱, 'yellow and red.' The former character expresses the general colour of the animals. But 'yellow' in Chinese is applied to many shades; that intended here being, I apprehend, a 'light bay.' 朱 is understood to denote that their tails and manes were dyed this colour. This is inferred from a passage in the 左 傳, 定 十 年, which describes such an operation:—宋 公 子 地, 有 白 馬 四, 公 嬖 向 魋 取 而 朱 其 尾 鬣 以 與 之. Ts'ae mentions that some interpret the 黃 朱 of 'baskets of yellow and red silks,' such as are mentioned in 'The Tribute of Yu;' but such an interpretation is very unlikely in this passage.

賓 稱 奉 圭 兼 幣 = 諸 侯 乃 舉 所 奉 之 守 圭 及 幣 帛, 'The princes raised aloft the several maces which they kept, and their *other* presents.' 賓 = 諸 侯;—see the Chow Le, Bk. XXXVIII., p. 1,—大 行 人 掌 大 賓 之 禮, where by 大 賓 is meant all the princes from the

嗣德答拜。○太保暨芮伯，咸進相揖，皆再拜稽首曰，敢敬告天子，皇天改大邦殷之命，惟周文武誕受羑

2　The Grand-guardian and the chief of Juy, with all the rest, then advanced and bowed to each other, after which they did obeisance twice, bowing their heads to the ground, and said, 'O Son of Heaven, we venture respectfully to declare our sentiments. Great Heaven altered its decree in favour of the great empire of Yin, and Wăn and Woo of our Chow greatly received the same, and carried it out,

---

Yaou domain inwards. 奉圭,—these are the maces or gem-tokens conferred on them by the emp., and which they brought with them when they appeared at court. Ying-tă thought that by 幣 we were to understand the horses already exhibited—or a portion of them at least—in the courtyard; but I cannot believe so. A passage in the Book of the Chow Le just quoted, on the duties of the 小行人, beginning 合六幣, may be consulted. Other offerings, referred to in the address below, are no doubt intended. The princes, indeed, could not be raising them aloft themselves; but they had attendants with them who did so. 一二臣,—'we, one or two ministers.' Comp. the use of 二三 in the Ana., III., xxiv., *et al.* 執壤奠= 執壤地所出之贄奠之. We are to suppose that one of the princes spoke in the name of all the others. 王義嗣德答拜,—the words 義嗣德 seem introduced by the recorder of the Book to explain how it was that the young king returned the obeisance of the princes. Lin Che-k'e observes that, as a rule, the sovereign does not return the 拜 of his ministers, yet K'ang was on this occasion ·the *host* and the princes all were his *guests*, and such an interchange of courtesies was according to etiquette. Ts'ae, Woo Ch'ing, and Këang Shing, all find a deeper meaning in the language. K'ang, they say, was now the declared successor to the throne, but until the year of his father's death was elapsed, his reign could not chronologically commence. His returning the obeisance, therefore, was a recognition by himself and all the princes that he and no other was to be their sovereign;—it was done 'in righteousness,' though not perhaps in rule.' Ts'ae says:—答拜既正其爲後,且知其以喪見 Shing's comment is:—誼 (so he reads) 德者,明

王當喪，未嗣位，特以繼先王之體，誼當嗣先王之德，以諸侯之朝，故答拜，此之謂禮以誼起. If this criticism of Ts'ae &c. be correct, as I believe it is, it disposes of the view of Tae Tung-yuen, that all the ceremonies from par. 14 of the last Book took place in the year after Ching's death. There remains, indeed, the difficulty on which he insists.—How was it that the princes of the various domains happened to be at court with their offerings, &c., as if in readiness for the old king's death, and the accession of the new? The difficulty must be acknowledged; but perhaps it would disappear if we had fuller information about the time. To my mind it is not so great as that of supposing that the action is suddenly carried over many months, between parr. 13 and 14 of the last Book, without the slightest note of time in the text:—to say nothing of the conclusion of Ts'ae and others from these words -王義嗣德.

Pp. 2, 3. *The advice given by all the princes to the young king.* 太保暨芮伯,—the princes advanced in the last par. to present their offerings under the leading of the Guardian and the duke of Peih, as the Chiefs of the east and west respectively. Now the duke of Peih gives place to the baron of Juy, the minister of Instruction, and ranking among the six *K'ing* next to the prime minister. 咸進相揖,— it seems the simplest construction to take 咸 =the 皆, which immediately follows, meaning all the rest of the princes and ministers, who then 相揖, 'moved their left or right arms to one other,' as they took their several places in the order required by the court etiquette. See the account of Confucius' movements in the court of Loo, Ana., X., iii., 2. Ying-tă would confine 咸進 to the Guardian and the baron of Juy.— 'These two made all the others advance, motion-

高祖寡命。
師無壞我
哉張皇六
今王敬之
遺後人用
厥功用敷
賞罰戡定
陟王畢協
土。○惟新
若克恤西

3 manifesting their kindly government in the western regions. His recently ascended Majesty, rewarding and punishing exactly in accordance with what was right, fully established their achievements, and transmitted this happy state to his successors. Do you, O king, now be reverent in your position. Maintain your armies in great order, and do not allow the rarely equalled appointment of our high ancestors to come to harm."

ing to them with their arms to take their proper places, to which motion the ¡princes responded.' Woo Ch'ing has still a difft. view, taking 相 as 相＝擯相之人; but this only complicates the construction.   曰,—the Guardian was no doubt spokesman for all the others.   惟 周至羑若,—the difficulty here is with 羑若, which Ts'ae acknowledges that he does not understand. He mentions the view of Soo Shih, that somehow there is an allusion to the confinement of king Wăn by the tyrant Show in 羑里; but I do not see how this is to be brought out of the text. He mentions also the conjecture of some that 羑若 is the same as 厥若 in p. 6, 羑 being an error of the text for 厥. Gan-kwŏ took 羑 as meaning 道. Ma Yung and Wang Suh did the same. Ying-tă observes that 羑 and 猷 are allied in sound, and that therefore we may explain 羑 by 道. I have translated accordingly (文武大受天道而順之), though I rather suspect that the text is corrupted. Kĕang Shing makes 羑＝進, and says:—天改殷之命, 惟文武大受, 而進順之. There is no authority for such an interpretation of the char.   克恤西土,—the patrimony of the chiefs of Chow was in the west. It was in that part of the empire that their virtue was first recognized, and the foundations of their influence laid.   惟新陟王,—'the newly ascended king.' Ching was not yet buried, and had not received his honorary title. He could only be thus spoken of.   畢協至人休,—by the 'rewards and

punishments,' which king Ching is said to have 'finished harmonizing,' i.e., administering according to what was right, we are to understand probably the investitures of many princes, and the suppression of rebellions, with the punishment of the rebels, in which the duke of Chow played so conspicuous a part. These are all, allowably, attributed to the king himself; and by these he completed the work begun by Wăn and Woo, and the dynasty might be considered established in the possession of the empire. 戡＝克, 'he succeeded in.' 敷遺後人休,—休 may be considered as in the objective gov. by 遺. 後人 is under the govt. of the preposition 於 understood. Woo Ch'ing gives the meaning of the whole very clearly:—賞當功, 罰當罪, 盡 合其宜, 克勝其任, 安定文 武之功, 用能延及于今後 人, 有此休美.   張皇六師, —'Keep your six armies like a bent bow, and magnify them.' The duke of Shaou would seem to have in mind the counsel given to himself by the duke of Chow, Bk. XVI., p. 21, and also what was said by that duke to king Ching, Bk. XIX., p. 22.   無 (一毋) 壞我高祖寡命,—寡命 is defined by Ts'ae—艱難寡得之基 命, 'the appointment difficult to be got, and such as is seldom to be got.'   Kĕang Shing gives Wang Suh's account of 寡:—美文 王少有及之, 故曰寡命. The speaker, in 我高祖, 'our high ancestor (or ancestors),' identifies himself with the imperial House. This gives some support to what is said, on p. 420, of the duke of Shaou's having been the son of king Wăn by a concubine.

○王若曰、庶^{四節}邦侯甸男衞、惟子一人釗、報誥。○昔君^{五節}文武丕平富、不務咎底至齊信用昭明于天下、則亦有能羆之士、不二心之臣、

4　II. The king spoke thus:—"Ye princes of the various States, chiefs of the How, Teen, Nan, and Wei domains, I, Ch'aou, the one 5 man, make an announcement in return *for your advice*. The former sovereigns, Wăn and Woo, were greatly just, and enriched *the people*. They did not occupy themselves with people's crimes. Pushing to the utmost and maintaining an entire impartiality and sincerity, they became gloriously illustrious throughout the empire. Then they had officers brave as bears and grisly bears, and ministers of no

Ch. II. Pp. 4—6. REPLY OF THE KING TO THE PRECEDING ADDRESS; CALLED HIS ANNOUNCEMENT. 4. The *princes* do not appear as parties in the preceding address, nor are the *ministers* (羣臣) mentioned here. But we must suppose that the address emanated from the princes as well as the ministers, and that the reply was made to them equally. No mention is made of the domain which was between the Nan and the Wei; no doubt the chiefs from it were present, and they may have been present also from beyond the Wei, though the text says nothing about them. 子一人釗,—the emperor called himself—'I, the one man,' and did not add his name. It was the rule, however, for the successor to the throne to do so, while the period of mourning for the deceased sovereign lasted.—See the case of the young emperor 猛, mentioned in the 左傳, 昭二十二年. 報誥,—Lin Che-k'e expands this:—諸侯戒我, 故我以誥報之. 5. *The merits of Wăn and Woo; and how they were supported by their ministers and officers.* 昔君,—as in the last Bk., p. 5. 不平富,—'were greatly just and rich.' The critics are probably correct in interpreting the language of the govt. of Wăn and Woo,—that it was just, carefully guarding the rights of the people, and that it was liberal, making taxation light, so that the people had plenty for all their wants. The paraphrase of the 'Daily Explanation' is:—文武之爲君也,有溥博均平之德,輕徭役,薄賦斂,使天下家給人足,莫不富厚有

餘,以豐民之財. Wang Suh's comment is brief and satisfactory:—文武道大,天下以平,萬民以富,是也. 不務咎,—'they did not bend their minds on—address their efforts to—the faults *of the people*.' The meaning seems to be that they were not on the watch to find out crime and punish it. To quote again from the Daily Explanation:—人或有罪,不得已而用刑,則輕省而不務深刻,謹慎而不致錯誤,審出,毋失入,不專意求人之罪惡而務置之于法. I can by no means accept Kĕang Shing's definitions of 務=趣, and 咎=災. He says:—文武大平,富天下之民,使不趣于咎災,言爲民除害. 底至齊信,—底至=推行而底其至, 'they pushed the practice and carried it to the utmost.' The question arises of what it was that they carried to the utmost? Was it the virtues indicated in the two previous parr., so that 齊 and 信 are merely adjectives? or are we to take those two characters as nouns, denoting other virtues, having a substantial meaning of their own? Lin Che-k'e, Ts'ae, and the Sung critics generally take the former view. Ts'ae says:—齊信者,兼盡而極其誠也,文武務德,不務罰之心,推行而底其至,兼盡

服　綏　伯　之　侯　四　用　命　保
于　爾　父　人　樹　方　訓　于　父
先　先　尚　今　屏　。　厥　上　王
王　公　胥　予　在　○　道　帝　家
雖　之　暨　一　我　乃　付　皇　用
爾　臣　顧　二　後　命　畀　天　端
　　　　　　　　　　六
　　　　　　　　　　節
　　　　　　　　　　建　界

double heart, who *helped them to* maintain and regulate the royal House.　　Thus *did they receive* the true favouring decree from God; and thus did great Heaven approve of their ways, and give them 6 the four quarters *of the empire.*　　Then they appointed and set up principalities, and established bulwarks *to the throne*, with a view to us their successors.　　Now do ye, my uncles, I pray you, consider with one another, and carry out the service which the dukes, your predecessors, rendered to my predecessors.　　Though your persons be

而極其誠, 內外充實. Gan-kwŏ took the latter view, making 齊＝中. He gives—致行至中信之道; and I have translated accordingly. Ma Yung likewise took 齊＝中; but he put a stop there, and joined 信 as an adverb with the clause that follows, in which construction Këang Shing has followed him. 熊羆之士,—see Bk. II., p. 9. 用端命于上帝,—用 ＝ 'thus,' 'thereby.' 端＝正直, 'correct.' We seem to be obliged to understand a 受 after 用:—'they thus received the right favouring decree from God.'　Këang Shing is the only one who construes differently, saying—用能端直其命于上帝, 言正命以待天也. What follows, 皇天, 云云, is an expansion of this clause, a more accurate description of the 'favouring decree.' 訓 ＝ 順, 'to accord with,'—'to approve.' 6. *He appeals to the great princes to assist him as their fathers had assisted Wăn and Woo, and in accordance with the intention of their appointments.* 命建侯樹屏,—the subject of 命 is Wăn and Woo, as founders of the dynasty, so that the force of the term merges in that of 建 and 樹. This is much better than, with Këang Shing, to suppose the par. to begin at

皇天 above, and make 天 the nominative to 命.—乃命之建侯, 云云. The 'planting of defences or screens' (樹屏) is nothing different from the 'setting up of princes' (建侯). 在我後之人,—在 must be taken as ＝'with reference to,' 'for the sake of.' 一二伯父,—一二, as in par. 1. Ying-tă observes that when the emperor was addressing princes of large States who bore the same surname with himself, he called them 伯父; and if their principalities were small, he called them 叔父. The princes of a different surname were addressed by him as 伯舅 and 叔舅. Here Cha‘ou speaks more particularly to the great princes of his own surname. 尚胥至先王,—胥＝相; 暨＝與: 胥暨＝'with one another.' 顧＝顧念而不忘, 'to think of and not forget.' 綏＝安. According as we take this to mean 'to soothe,' 'to tranquillize,' or 'to pursue quietly and steadily,' we get two views of the passage.　Lin Che-k‘e, after Soo Shih, adopts the latter view, and compares the sentiment with that in the 'Pwankăng,' Pt. i., p. 14, and Pt. ii., p. 14.—使諸侯能盡忠於王室, 如其先公之於先王, 則爾先公在天之靈於是安矣. If you, princes,

服。釋揖皆○遺恤王心身
　冕趨聽　鞠厥室罔在
　反出命群公子若用不外
　喪王相既羞。無奉在乃

distant, let your hearts be in the royal house. Thus enter into my anxieties and act in accordance with them, so that I, the little child, may not be put to shame."

7　　III. All the dukes, having heard this charge, bowed to one another and hastily withdrew. The king put off his cap, and assumed again his mourning dress.

can discharge all loyal service to the royal House, as your predecessors did to mine, then their souls will have repose in heaven.' I was at first inclined to this view, but a closer inspection of the text makes me prefer the former, which is that given by Ts'ae after Gan-kwŏ. 用奉恤厥若 may be taken as in the translation, after Ts'ae and Gan-kwŏ. The 'Daily Explanation' has:—用以此心，仰奉在上之憂勤，而順承毋達. Or we may translate—'Be thus reverently anxious to act in accordance with the requirements of your duty,' which is the view taken by Lin Che-k'e.—汝諸侯其職所當順者，當奉恤之，而不敢忽忘. 鞠子＝稚子, 'a child,' one who has not yet left his mother's arms.'

Ch. III. P. 7. The audience closes, and the king resumes his mourning. The use of 相揖 here confirms the interpretation of the phrase which I have adopted in p. 2. The concluding statement, showing that the king and all the officers only assumed their mourning dress at the conclusion of this Announcement, has, since the time of Soo Shih, given rise to a controversy, which will probably be among Chinese critics interminable. According to Shih, everything about the publication of the Testamentary Charge and the subsequent proceedings ought to have been transacted in mourning garb; and the neglect of this was a melancholy violation of *propriety*. If the duke of Chow had been alive, Shih thinks that he would not have allowed it, and he wonders why Confucius selected the documents recording it to form a portion of the Shoo. In point of fact, it cannot be proved positively that any violation of the proprieties established by the duke of Chow was committed, for the ceremonies to be observed on various occasions in the imperial court have not been transmitted. But to a student from the west the controversy appears trivial. We are glad to have the ceremonies actually observed at so distant a date brought before our eyes so graphically as is done in 'The Testamentary Charge,' and 'The Announcement of king K'ang.'

BOOK XXIV. THE CHARGE TO *THE DUKE OF* PEIH.

畢命

一節
惟十有二年、
六月庚午朏、
越三日壬申、
王朝步自宗
周、至于豐以
成周之衆命
畢公保釐東
郊。○王若曰

二節

1 I. In the sixth month of his twelfth year, the day of the new moon's appearance was Kăng-woo, and on Jin-shin, the third day after, the king walked in the morning from the honoured city of Chow to Fung, and there, with reference to the multitudes of Ching-chow, gave charge to the duke of Peih to protect and regulate the eastern frontier.

INTRODUCTORY NOTE. If that reign must have been happy which, extending over a considerable number of years, has yet left few or no memorials in history, that of king K'ang may be so characterized. It extended over twenty-six years, but no other event of it, after the Announcement of the last Book, is alluded to in the Shoo or by Sze-ma Ts'een, but that appointment of the duke of Peih, to which we have now arrived. Ts'een, indeed, tells us that 'during the time of kings Ching and K'ang, the empire was in a state of profound tranquillity, so that punishments were laid aside, and not used for more than forty years' (成康之際,天下安寧,刑錯四十餘年不用). Happy China!

THE NAME OF THE BOOK.—畢命, 'The Charge to *the duke of* Peih.' The territory of Peih was in the pres. dis. of Ch'ang-ngan (長安), dep. of Se-ngan. It was not a large principality, whose ruler was entitled to be styled duke or *Kung*. That title is employed here as a denomination of dignity or office, the chief of Peih having succeeded to the duke of Chow as Grand-Tutor;—see on Bk. XXII., p. 3. He was a scion of the House of Chow. This and his being Grand-Tutor may both be inferred from the manner in which king K'ang addresses him as 父師. Ch'in Sze-k'ae says that his name was Kaou (高). He must have been well advanced in years, when the 'Charge' recorded here was addressed to him, for, acc. to p. 5, he had played his part in the fortunes of his House from the time of king Wăn. The Book was not in the Shoo of Fuh-shang.

CONTENTS. 'King K'ang,' says Ts'ae, 'considering *the condition of* the multitudes of Ching-chow, appointed the duke of Peih to protect and regulate *that district and its people.* This Book contains the charge to him as it was recorded on tablets.'

Keun-ch'in, who had succeeded to the duke of Chow in charge of Ching-chow, has followed him to the grave. By the labours of those two great ministers, a considerable change had been effected in the character of the people of Yin who had been transferred to that district. King K'ang appoints the duke of Peih to enter into and complete their work, adopting such measures as the altered character of the people, and altered circumstances of the time, called for. The charge occupies all the Book after an introductory paragraph, and may be divided into three chapters, each introduced by the words—'The king said.'

The first, parr. 2—5, speaks of what had been accomplished in Ching-chow, and the admirable qualities of Kaou which fitted him to accomplish what remained to be done. The second, parr. 6—11, speaks of the special measures which were called for by the original character and by the altered character of the people. The third, parr. 12—15, dwells on the importance of the charge, and stimulates the duke, by various motives, to address himself to fulfil it effectually.

Ch, I. P. 1. THE TIME; PLACE; AND GENERAL NATURE OF THE CHARGE. 惟十 至壬申,－朏, see on Bk. XII., p. 2. As it denotes the third day of the moon, we are again enabled to bring the commonly received chronology to the test of calculation. Here I will give the note of Gaubil, as on par. 2 of 'The Testamentary Charge:'—'It is agreed that the day 庚午 here is the third day of the sixth moon of the calendar of Chow. Lew Hin and Pan Koo pretend that this was the year corresponding to B.C. 1,067, to which year they refer the twelfth year of king K'ang; and this chronology is followed in the 通鑑綱 目. In the year B.C. 1,067, the 16th of May was, indeed, the day 庚午, or the 7th of the cycle, but the 14th of May was not the first day of the moon which did not happen till several days after; and that year therefore was not the 12th of K'ang's reign. Laying down the principle avowed by Pan Koo and Lew Hin about the third day of the moon, the cycle names in the text agree with the year B.C. 1,056. The 16th of May was the day of new moon in China; the 18th, the third day of the moon, was 庚午; and this month was the sixth in the calendar of Chow, since during it the sun entered the sign of the Twins. From "The Announcement of Shaou," " The Announcement about Lŏ," and this Book, we see that the Chinese astronomers

of those times counted the day when the sun and moon were veritably in conjunction to be the first day of the moon. The time of a lunation was divided into the time of brightness and the time of obscurity; the passage from the obscure to the bright time was described as "the death of the obscure," and the passage from the bright to the obscure time as " the birth of the obscure;"—see "The Testamentary Charge." The standard History gives 26 as the years of K'ang's reign; if that be correct, his death took place B.C. 1,042, since we have found that B.C. 1,056 was his 12th year; and B.C. 1,067 was the first year of his reign.

'This year, B.C. 1,067, should be marked by the cycle characters 庚戌, the 11th year of the cycle. Now, the "Bamboo Books" do mark his first year so; but the year which they denote is that B.C. 1,007, differing from the true year, which appears to have been demonstrated, exactly an entire cycle of 60 years.'

[As the cycle names of the days here afford ground for such important conclusions, in which Gaubil, I may state, was anticipated by Chang Yih-hing (the Buddhist priest mentioned on page 19), under the T'ang dynasty, it becomes desirable to establish the genuineness of the par., which may be hastily thrown aside with the remark that it only occurs in one of the controverted Books. Now this we are able to do, so far as the year, month, and days are concerned, from a passage in the 漢律歷志 第一下, being that referred to by Gaubil, and which is to this effect:—康王十二年,六月 戊辰朔,三日庚午,故畢命 豐刑日,惟十有二年六月 庚午,朏,王命作策豐刑. We do not know what to make of 豐刑 here; but it is plain that Lew Hin had seen a copy of the 'Charge to Peih,' in this par. substantially the same with what we have in the text before us.]

王朝至于豐,－朝步, see on Bk. III., p. 1. 宗周,—see on Bk. XX., p. 1. We are to understand Haou. 'The king went to Fung,' says Ts'ae, 'to give the charge in the temple of king Wăn, because the duke of Peih had been minister to him.' 成周,—this was what was called 下都, 'the lower capital,' See on Bk. XXI., p. 1., where also 東郊, 'the eastern frontier,' is explained. 保＝ 安; 釐＝理. The time had come to adopt a difft. method with the people of Yin from those pursued by their former overseers, the duke of Chow and Keun-ch'in;—as is explained below.

既　王　遷　厥　左　殷　于　王　嗚
歷　室　于　家　右　命　天　武　呼
三　式　洛　毖　先　。○　下　王　父
紀　化　邑　殷　王　惟　用　敷　師
世　厥　密　頑　綏　周　克　大　惟
變　訓　邇　民　定　公　受　德　文

三節

2　　II. The king spoke thus:—Oh! Grand-tutor, it was when king
Wăn and king Woo had diffused their great virtue through the
empire that they were able to receive the appointment which Yin
3　had enjoyed.　The duke of Chow acted as assistant to my royal
predecessors, and tranquillized and established their empire.　Cautiously did he deal with the refractory people of Yin, and removed
them to the city of Lŏ, that they might be quietly near the royal
house, and thus be transformed by its lessons.　Six and thirty years
have elapsed, the generation has been changed, and manners

Ch. II.　Pp. 2—5.　Fɪʀsᴛ ᴘᴀʀᴛ ᴏғ ᴛʜᴇ
Cʜᴀʀɢᴇ.　Hᴏᴡ ᴛʜᴇ ᴇᴍᴘɪʀᴇ ʜᴀᴅ ʙᴇᴇɴ ɢᴏᴛ ʙʏ
Wᴀɴ ᴀɴᴅ Wᴏᴏ, ᴀssɪsᴛᴇᴅ ʙʏ ᴛʜᴇ ᴅᴜᴋᴇ ᴏғ
Cʜᴏᴡ; ᴡʜᴀᴛ ᴛʜᴇ ᴅᴜᴋᴇ ʜᴀᴅ ᴅᴏɴᴇ ᴡɪᴛʜ ᴛʜᴇ
ᴘᴇᴏᴘʟᴇ ᴏғ Yɪɴ.　Nᴇᴡ ᴍᴇᴀsᴜʀᴇs ᴡᴇʀᴇ ɴᴏᴡ
ᴄᴀʟʟᴇᴅ ғᴏʀ; ᴀɴᴅ ᴛʜᴇ ᴄʜᴀʀᴀᴄᴛᴇʀ ᴏғ ᴛʜᴇ ᴅᴜᴋᴇ
ᴏғ Pᴇɪʜ, ᴡʜɪᴄʜ ᴍᴀʀᴋᴇᴅ ʜɪᴍ ᴏᴜᴛ ᴀs ᴛʜᴇ ᴍᴀɴ
ғᴏʀ ᴛʜᴇ ᴏᴄᴄᴀsɪᴏɴ.　2. 父師,—acc. to
what was said on 一二伯父 in par. 6 of
the last Book, we might translate this by 'Uncle
and Tutor.' Lin Che-k'e, moreover, says that the
duke of Peih was 'a son of king Wăn, a younger
brother of king Woo and the duke of Chow,
and an uncle of king Ching (文王之子,
武王周公之弟,成王之叔
父); but I do not know his authority for such
a statement.　Sze-ma Ts'een has given the
names of Wăn's ten sons by his queen T'ae-sze,
and this duke is not among them.　I believe he
was a scion of the House of Chow; but we may
take 父師 here in the same way as in Pt.
IV., Bk. XI., p. 1, as = 太師. If he had
really been a brother of the duke of Chow, we
might have expected some reference to the fact
in the course of the Charge.　　3. 惟周
公左右先王,—the critics generally
understand by 先王 all K'ang's predecessors,
—Wăn, Woo, and Ching.　Lin Che-k'e contends
with much force that the phrase should in this
place be restricted to king Ching.　It is hardly
necessary to depart from the more common

view. Ching must certainly be included. Gaubil
gives—'le roi, mon pere;' Medhurst erroneously,—'these former kings.'　厥家 = 厥
國家, 'their (or his) empire.' 毖殷 至
厥訓,—comp. Bk. XIV., pp. 18—21. 密
邇王室,—comp. 密邇先王, Pt. IV.,
Bk. V., Pt. i., p. 9.　The 王城 or 'imperial
city' of Lŏ was the place where the 'nine
vases' of the empire were deposited, and where
it was intended that the emperor should give
audience to all the princes.　The people of Yin
in Ching-chow and the country about might very
well be said to be near the 'royal house.'　The
'Daily Explanation' expands 式化厥訓
into 日聞我周之仁聲善政,日
親我周之仁人君子,由是潛
消其悍暴之習,而漸化于
德義之訓.　　既歷三紀,—
'there have elapsed—been gone through—three
Ke, or periods of twelve years.' A period of
twelve years was denominated a 紀, acc. to
Ying-tă, because in that period the planet
Jupiter completed a revolution in his orbit, and
the cycle characters of the 地支, or 'earthly
branches,' had also run their round.　We do not
know exactly from what year we are to reckon
these 36 years. If, as is commonly believed,
the reign of Ching lasted 37 years, and we add
12 years of K'ang's reign to them, we obtain
four duodenary periods, and not three.　Even

風移、四方無
虞子一人以　四節
寧。○道有升
降政由俗革、
不臧厥臧民　五節
罔攸勸。○惟
公懋德克四
小物弼亮四
世正色率下、
罔不祗師言、

have altered. Through the four quarters of the empire there is no occasion for anxiety, and I, the one man, enjoy repose.

4　　The prevailing ways now tend to advancement and now to degeneracy, and measures of government must be varied according to the manners *of the time.* If you do not manifest your approval of what is good, the people will not be led to stimulate themselves

5　in it. But your virtue, O duke, is strenuous, and you are cautiously attentive to small things. You have been helpful to and brightened four reigns, with deportment all-correct, leading on the inferior officers, so that there is not one who does not reverently take your words as a law. Your admirable merits were that of many in the

---

if we reckon from the date of the 'Announcement about Lŏ,' we have more than 40 years. A supposition of Gaubil, that king K'ang intends the time which had elapsed from the death of the duke of Chow, seems to me very likely. 世變,—our word 'generation' answers to 世 Ts'ae says;—父子曰世, 'Father and son are called a 世.'— 'One generation passeth away, and another cometh.' 四方無虞,—see the use of 無虞 in Pt. II., Bk. IV., p. 6.

P. 4. *Govt. must be varied according to the character of the people; the time was come for discriminative measures.* 道有升降, —it would be hard to say how Gan-kwŏ understood this clause. His comment on it is— 天道有上下交接之義, which Ying-tă only makes more dark by his expansion of it. I have followed Ts'ae who observes that 有升＝有隆, 'generous,' 'affluent,' 'good;' and 有降＝有汙, 'foul,' 'impure;' and then illustrates this clause and the next by saying that, when the duke of Chow took charge of Ching-chow, the character of the people, with their evil habits all-unchanged, rendered a firm and cautious dealing with them necessary. When Keun-ch'in took charge, the people were considerably improved, and hence he was enjoined to be forbearing with them, and promote harmonizing measures. 不

臧云云,—the people, we are to suppose, were now in that state, that the good of many of them deserved to be acknowledged, and that acknowledgement would act as the best stimulus to others. The paraphrase of the 'Daily Explanation' is:—至于今日,善者固多,而不善者亦容與起其不善益多之,務善者,且懲治其為慕者,庶幾殷民有所畏相勸而化耳. 臧＝善. In the first case it is a verb; in the second, a noun in the concrete. 5. *The great virtue of the duke of Peih.* 克勤小物,—小物, 'little things,'＝'small matters' (細行).

By 四世, 'four generations,' we are to understand the reigns of Wăn, Woo, Ching, and the existing reign of K'ang. Ying-tă refers to a passage in the 國語,晉語 四 (near the end), about king Wăn, how he 詢於八虞,而次於二虢……而訪於辛尹,重之以周召, 畢,榮, which shows that in the 8th cent. B.C., it was the current belief that the duke of Peih had been a minister of king Wăn. 正色率下,—'with correct countenance

樹　里　淑　往　以　今　曰　拱　王　嘉
之　彰　慝　哉　周　予　嗚　仰　予　績
風　善　表　○　公　祗　呼　成　小　多
聲　癉　厥　旌　之　命　父　○　子　于
弗　惡　宅　別　事　公　師　王　垂　先

times of the former kings; I, the little child, have but to let my
robes hang down, and fold my hands while I look up for the complete effect *of your measures.*"

6　　III. The king spoke, "Oh! Grand-tutor, I now reverently
7　charge you with the duties of the duke of Chow.—Go! Signalize the
good, separating the bad from them; give tokens of your approbation
to their neighbourhoods, distinguishing the good so as to make it ill
for the evil, *thus* establishing the influence and reputation *of their
virtue.* Where the people will not obey your lessons and statutes,

leading on those below you.' But by 色
we are to understand all the deportment. Lin
Che-k'e refers, aptly enough, to the words of
Confucius about the man in authority, Ana.
XX., ii., 2,—君子正其衣冠尊
其瞻視儼然人望而畏之,
不亦威而不猛乎. 祗師
言＝祗敬而師法公言. The
師 is a verb,＝'to imitate,' 'to take as a
model.' 嘉績多于先王,—this
clause is in a measure opposed to the next.—
'Even under my predecessors your admirable
merits have been many; how much more must
I be indebted to you!' 子小子,云
云,—we must not understand 'the robes let
down and the hands folded' as expressive of
idleness and indifference. The king figures
himself in the ancestral temple, in his robes
and attitudes of reverent ceremony, happy in
the thought that he had so able a minister on
whom he might entirely depend. Compare the
same language in the conclusion of Bk. III., p.
10.

The king certainly is not sparing in his laud-
ation of the minister.

Ch. III. Pp. 6—11. SECOND PART OF THE
CHARGE:—THE SPECIAL DUTIES WHICH THE
DUKE WAS TO DISCHARGE; THE DIFFICULTIES
WITH WHICH HE WOULD HAVE TO CONTEND; AND
THE METHOD BY WHICH HE MIGHT BE SUCCESS-
FUL. 6. 祗命,—'reverently charge.'
The charge being so great, being communicated
in the temple of king Wăn, having respect to
the completion of the work of the duke of Chow,

king K'ang could not but have a feeling of reverence in delivering it. The work that Keun-
ch'in had done is not mentioned, but he appears
in p. 13.　7. Many of the people of Yin
had profited so much by the labours of the duke
of Chow and Keun-ch'in with them, that they
might be pronounced reformed, and should receive marks of favour, while those who continued obstinately bad should be made to feel that
they were marked. 旌別 (low. 4th
tone) 至風聲,—these clauses show how
the good should be dealt with. 旌 is the name
of a peculiar kind of flag, used among other
purposes to mark out places or paths; as a verb
here, it＝our 'to signalize.' 旌別淑
(＝善) 慝(＝惡)＝旌善別惡, with
the meaning in the translation. 表厥宅
里＝表異善人之居里. 表,
—'a signal,' 'to set up a signal;'—akin to 旌.
彰善癉惡＝彰顯其善以
病其爲惡者. The two parts of the
clause are connected as in the first clause.
樹之風聲,—with 樹之 comp. the
expression 死之, Ana., XIV., xvi. The whole
＝'planting—setting up—for them, *i.e.*, the good,
their influence and reputation.' The 'Daily
Explanation' gives for it—善者之風
聲,使之卓然樹立,顯于當
時,傳于後世. 弗率至畏
慕,—these three clauses describe how the bad

率訓典、殊厥
井疆、俾克畏
慕申畫郊圻、以
慎固封守、○八節
康四海。○政
貴有恆辭尚
體要不惟好
異商俗靡靡
利口惟賢、餘
風未殄公其

mark off the boundaries of their hamlets, making them fear *to do evil* and desire *to do good*. Define anew the borders and frontiers, and be careful to strengthen the guardposts through the territory, in order to secure the tranquillity of the whole empire.

8   "In measures of government to be consistent and constant, and in proclamations a combination of completeness and brevity, are valuable. There should not be the love of what is extraordinary. Among the customs of Shang was the flattery of superiors. Sharp-tonguedness was the sign of worth. The remains of these manners are not yet obliterated. Do you, O duke, bear this in mind.

should be dealt with. 殊厥井疆＝殊別其井居疆界 井.—'the wells,' about which their farms were distributed. It may be translated here by 'hamlets.' We see how the people—the peasantry—of Yin were distributed over the country of which Ching-chow might be considered the centre. 申畫郊圻,—Ts'ae says that 圻 and 畿 are the same; but the meaning of 界, given for 圻 in the dict., answers very well. Wang Ts'eaou says :—'The city of Lǒ and the honoured capital of Chow were the two centres of the imperial domain. The honoured capital of Haou might be considered to have a square of 800 *le*, or 64 squares of 100 *le* each, attached to it; and Lǒ or Ching-chow to have a square of 600 *le*, or 36 squares of 100 *le* each. The extent from east to west was greater than from north to south, but altogether there was as much as a square of 1,000 *le*. Thus the borders of Lǒ were also the borders of Haou.' See the 集說. 固封守, 'strengthen the *places of* ward within the boundaries over which you are appointed.'—封域之內, 高深險阻已設守禦者,益謹飭之. Wang Ch'ung-yun observes that, while the separation of the good from the bad was calculated to have a beneficial moral effect upon the people, these latter measures were a safeguard against any attempts at insurrection.

Pp. 8—11. *The difficulties the duke would have to contend with; and how to contend with them.* 8. 恆 is defined as the opposite of 暫 or 'what is brief.' 辭＝辭令, 'proclamations,' 'govt. orders.' 體要＝理完言簡, 'complete in principle, and compendious in expression.' We may take 貴 and 尚 as synonyms. 靡靡 is taken as having the meaning of 隨順, 'ready acquiescence,' *i.e.*, of inferiors with their superiors. Ying-tă shows that this was the meaning given to the phrase in the time of Confucius, by quoting the remarks of Han K'e (韓起), a statesman of Tsin, contemporary with the sage :—韓宣子稱紂使師延作靡靡之樂, 靡靡者, 相隨順之意. [I have tried without success to verify this reference. Han K'e appears repeatedly in the 左傳, 昭公, but I have not met with the remark attributed to him. Ying-tă has probably confounded 韓宣子 with the scholar 韓非子, in the 3d Bk. of whose Works (十過第十) mention is made of 師延, who 與紂爲靡靡之樂.] The sharp-tonguedness of the times of Yin is indicated in Pt. IV., Bk. V., Pt. iii., p. 9, and Bk. VII., Pt.

終、淫矜侉將由惡
雖收放心閑

義服美于人、驕

寵惟舊怙侈滅

○茲殷庶士、席十節

奢麗萬世同流。

實悖天道、敝化

由禮以蕩陵德、

世祿之家、鮮克

念哉。○我聞曰、九節

9 I have heard the saying—'Families which have for generations enjoyed places of emolument seldom observe the rules of propriety. They become dissolute and do violence to virtue, setting themselves in positive opposition to the way of Heaven. They ruin the formative principles of good; encourage extravagance and display;

10 and tend to carry all *future* ages on the same stream with them.' Now the officers of Yin had long relied on the favour which they enjoyed. In the confidence of their prideful extravagance they extinguished their *sense of* righteousness. They displayed before men the beauty of their robes, proud, licentious, arrogant, and boastful;—the natural issue was that they should have ended in being thoroughly bad. Although their lost minds have been *in a measure*

i., p. 17.   9. On the general lesson of this par., comp. various passages of Bk. XV. 由 禮＝從禮, 'to pursue the course of propriety.' 陵＝犯, 'to violate,' or 侵, 'to invade,' 'encroach upon.' 敝化— 'they injured transforming changes,' *i.e.*, they corrupt the public manners, acc. to which the characters of individuals are moulded. 敝＝ 壞. 10. 席寵惟舊,—席, is used in the sense of 因 or 藉, 'to depend on.' Their 'favour' had been to them the mat on which they rested. The dict. gives on the character a note of Yen Sze-koo:—席猶因也, 言 若人之坐於席也. For the 'Daily Explanation' gives—怙恃其 驕侈. 侈 is 'extravagance' taking its rise from pride. 服美于人,—Lin Che-k'e understands this as meaning—'They tried to surpass other men in the beauty of their dress' (美于他人); but it is better to take the 于 after the adj. as in p. 5,—嘉績 多于先王   Luh Këen (陸鍵;

Ming dyn.) defines 驕 as＝心肆, 'the dissoluteness of the mind;' 淫＝心佚, 'the voluptuousness of the mind;' 矜＝心傲, 'the arrogance of the mind;' 侉＝心浮, 'the froth of the mind.' 將由惡終,—the 將 shows the natural issue of the various ways and attributes which have been described, and attributed to the officers of Yin. It would be wrong to translate it as an historical future. We find a portion of this par., without any note of quotation, in the 左傳, where 必 appears instead of 將.—襄 二十七年, 叔 孫曰, 服美于人, 必以惡終. 雖收 云云,—it is here that the phrase, 放心, 'the lost mind,' to which so much importance was subsequently attached by Mencius, occurs for the first time in the classics. 閑之,—'to bar them.' 'The root of evil,' says Ch'in King, 'might still be present; and though the lost mind has been recovered, it may be carried off again on the occurrence of temptation.'   11. 資 (＝貨財, 'goods,' 'pro-

之惟艱。○資富能訓

惟以永年、惟德惟義、

時乃大訓、不由古訓、

于何其訓。○王曰嗚

呼父師邦之安危惟

茲殷士不剛不柔厥

德允修。○惟周公克

慎厥始惟君陳克和

厥中惟公克成厥終、

三后協心同底于道、

11 recovered, it is difficult to keep them under proper restraint. If with their property and wealth they can be brought under the influence of instruction, they may enjoy lengthened years. Virtue and righteousness!—these are the great lessons. If you do not follow with them *these* lessons of antiquity, wherein will you instruct them?"

12 IV. The king said, "Oh! Grand-tutor, the security or the danger of the empire depends on these officers of Yin. If you are not *too* stern with them nor *too* mild, their virtue will be truly cultivated.

13 The duke of Chow was able to exercise the necessary caution at the beginning *of the undertaking;* Keun-ch'in displayed the harmony proper to the middle of it; and you, O duke, can bring it at last to a successful issue. You three princes will have been one in aim, and have equally arrived at the proper way. The penetrating power of your principles, and the good character of your

perty.') 富能訓, 惟以永年,—it is difficult to say whether we should understand 資富能訓 as meaning, 'Having property and wealth, if they can also be instructed,' or 'Notwithstanding their property and wealth, if they can be instructed.' I think the former view is preferable, as Ch'in King says:—既富以養其身, 又訓以養其心, 全正性, 所以順正命, 此所以永年也. 時乃大訓,—時=是. 'The lessons of antiquity' can only mean those of 'virtue and righteousness.' The crowding of difft. subjects into one short paragraph is annoying and perplexing.

Ch. IV. Pp. 12—15. THE CONCLUSION OF THE CHARGE:—IMPORTANCE OF THE WORK ENTRUSTED TO THE DUKE; AND MOTIVES TO MAKE HIM EXERT HIMSELF. 12. 邦之安危,—by 邦 here we must understand the whole empire. The king had said in par. 3 that he had no occasion for anxiety about anything in the empire. His language here is different. 'It shows,' says Ts'ae, 'that he was one who could not rest easily in small achievements.' He would make assurance doubly sure.

不剛不柔,—this is the rule of conduct for the duke of Peih. He was to pursue the right medium in dealing with the officers of Yin. 13. 惟周公至厥終,—comp. Bk. XXI., p. 7. 三后協心, 同底于道,—Wang Ts'eaou says:—三后之政, 前後以相濟爲之宜, 適因革之宜, 是曰同底; 三后之心, 是曰協心, 各行其所當然, 是曰同底

成烈以休于前政。
惟慎厥事欽若先王
惟既厥心罔曰民寡、
乂。○嗚呼罔曰弗克、
聞子孫訓其成式惟
窮之基亦有無窮之
公其惟時成周建無
予小子永膺多福。○
四夷左袵罔不咸賴、
道洽政治澤潤生民、

measures of government, will exert an enriching influence on the people, so that the wild tribes, with their coats buttoning on the left, will all seek their dependence on them, and I, the little child,

14 will long enjoy much happiness. Thus, O duke, here in Ching-chow will you establish for ever the imperial possession *of Chow*, and you will have an inexhaustible fame. Your descendants will follow your perfect pattern, governing accordingly.

15 "Oh! do not say, 'I am unequal to this;' but exert your mind to the utmost. Do not say, 'The people are few;' but attend carefully to your business. Reverently follow the accomplished achievements of the former kings, and complete the excellence of the government of your predecessors."

于道, 'The govt. of the three princes differing as this earlier and that later, yet each aiding the others, is what is called 協心; their measures, different as the change of manners and times required, yet always right in their own circumstances, is what is called 同底于道. 道洽,—comp. 洽於天下, Mencius, II., Pt. I., i., 7. 道洽 and 政治 are one thing, or the course and the issue of the rule of Ching-chow.

生民,—see Bk. V., p. 12. 左袵 see Ana., XIV., xviii., 2. 予膺多福—see Bk. XXI., p. 14. 14. 公其周之基,—Gan-kwŏ expounds this—惟以是成周之沿無窮其成式惟公之子孫為子孫訓乂,—the 'Daily Explanation' gives for this:—有治民之責者亦遵守成

法論矣。以致治安、譽流奕世、謀詒後昆、皆于公今日之盡矣。 15. 惟既厥心,—既=竭盡, 'to exert to the utmost.' The duke ought not to shrink from his duty, because it was arduous. 罔曰至厥事,—neither might he trifle with his work, thinking it easy.

欽若,—comp. in the 'Can. of Yaou,' p. 3. By 'the former kings' we are to understand Wăn, Woo, and Ching. 以休于前政,—the 'former government' is that of the duke of Chow and Keun-ch'in. The clause will bear to be translated,—'that you may realize an excellence superior to the govt. of your predecessors;' but we have two instances of 于 after an adj. in this Book, and not indicating comparison. I prefer to consider 休 as an active verb, and the whole = 以休美周公君陳之政.

○惟_{二節}予小　紀于太常。　厥有成績　服勞王家、　世篤忠貞、　乃祖乃父、　呼君牙惟　王若曰、嗚　君牙_{一節}

1 The king spoke thus:—"Oh! Keun-ya, your grandfather and your father, one after the other, with a true loyalty and honesty, laboured in the service of the royal House, accomplishing a merit

INTRODUCTORY NOTE. In the note at the commencement of the last Book, I have said that the annals of king K'ang are peculiarly barren. No other event of his reign is commemorated but the appointment of the duke of Peih to the govt. of Ching-chow. During his time, however, several worthies of whom we have had occasion to speak passed off the stage. In Loo, Pih-k'in, the son of the duke of Chow, died B.C. 1,062 (or 1,063), and was succeeded by his son Ts'ew (酋), or duke K'aou (考公), who gave place in the king's 20th year to duke Yang (煬公). Yang died in the last year of the reign, and was followed by his son Tsae (宰), or duke Yew (幽公). To the same year is assigned the death of Shih, the duke of Shaou, the co-worker with the duke of Chow in the establishment of the dynasty.

The viscount of Wei, the prince of K'ang, and Chung of Ts'ae have all likewise their deaths chronicled in this reign.

King K'ang was succeeded by his son Hëa (瑕), known as king Ch'aou (昭王), to whom the standard History assigns a very long reign of 51 years. The Shoo, however, is silent about him. The appointment of Keun-ya to be minister of Instruction, in the Book to which we have now arrived, was made by king Muh (穆), Ch'aou's son and successor, the first year of whose reign is commonly placed in B.C. 1,000 (or 1,001). The brief notices of Ch'aou and his reign which we find in Sze-ma Ts'een and other authors are unfavourable to him. The first symptoms of decay in the dynasty date, indeed, from his time. In B.C. 1,038 the duke of Loo was murdered by a younger brother, who established himself in his room, while the king could do nothing to avenge so great an outrage.

Ch'aou died in a hunting expedition to the south, according to most accounts, being drowned in the river Han, which he was crossing in a boat, whose planks were only glued together! This account is no doubt fabulous.

THE NAME OF THE BOOK.—君牙, 'Keun-ya.' The name is taken from that of the person whose appointment to be minister of Instruction forms the subject of the Book. Keun-ya's surname is not known. His father and grandfather, it appears, had been in the same office before him; and hence it is conjectured that he may have been the grandson of the Chief of Juy, who was minister of Instruction at the commencement of king K'ang's reign. This is possible; but we cannot say more, for, acc. to the received chronology, the commencement of Muh's reign was separated from that of K'ang by nearly 80 years.

The Book was not in Fuh-shang's Shoo.

CONTENTS. The Book is short, containing only seven paragraphs. The 1th and 5th parr.

冰。○ 尾、 危、 方、 左、 王 緒、 武 子、
○ 涉 若 心 右 之 亦 成 嗣
三節 于 蹈 之 亂 臣、 惟 康 守
今 春 虎 憂 四 克 先 遺 文
命

2 which was recorded on the grand banner. I, who am but a little child, have inherited the charge of the line of government transmitted from Wăn and Woo, from Ching and from K'ang, and keep also thinking of their ministers who were able to aid them in the good government of the four quarters *of the empire;*—the trembling anxiety of my mind makes me feel as if I were treading

speak of the duties of the minister of Instruction. The other paragraphs stimulate Keun-ya to the discharge of them by motives drawn from the merits of his forefathers, and the services which he would render to the empire, making his sovereign no unworthy descendant of Wăn and Woo.

Pp. 1—3. *The king speaks of the merits of Keun-ya's grandfather and father; of his own anxiety to get ministers equal to those of his ancestors; and of his hope that Keun-ya would render him services which should prove that he was the worthy scion of a good stock.* 1. 世篤 至 王 家,—Ma San (馬森; Ming dyn.) gives the following definitions of 忠 and 貞: 一盡心之謂忠，無一念之不 實也，守道之謂貞，無一事 之不正也, 'The putting forth one's whole mind is called 忠; there is not in it the insincerity of a single thought: holding firm the way of principle is called 貞; there is not in it the incorrectness of a single action.' We must understand a preposition, 於 or 爲, between 勞 and 王. 紀於太常, —太常 is the name of the grand imperial banner. The Chow Le, Bk. XXVII., makes mention of the 司常, or 'superintendent of banners,' who had charge of all the 'nine flags or banners' (九旗). 常, therefore, is in that passage used apparently as synonymous with 旗. Commonly, however, we find it used with reference to the grand standard, on which were figures of the sun and moon, with figures of dragons, lying along its breadth, one over the other head above tail. The sun and moon,

however, were the distinctive figures of the grand banner. It was borne aloft when the emperor went to sacrifice;—see the same Bk. of the Chow Le, on the duties of the 巾車, p. 2. The names of meritorious ministers, moreover, were inscribed on it during their life time, preparatory to their sharing in the sacrifices of the ancestral temple after their death;—see the Chow Le, Bk. XXX., on the duties of the 司勳, p. 3. 2. 惟予至遺緒, —it is inferred, and with reason, from the language of this clause, that the king had lately succeeded to the throne, and that this Charge to Keun-ya was delivered in the early part of his reign. Chronologists generally refer it to his 3d year. But how is it that while speaking of the line or clue of govt., as being transmitted to him from Wăn and Woo, Ching and K'ang, he makes no mention of K'ang's successor, his own father? The prefatory note expressly assigns the charge to king Muh. 亦惟 至四方,—the meaning of this is, that while the king felt that he himself could not follow his predecessors *passibus æquis*, he thought also how they, so superior to him, had yet been assisted by very able ministers. What cause was there then for anxiety to him! 惟＝ 思. In the edition of the 'Thirteen *King*,' for 先王之臣 we have 先正之臣 But Gan-kwŏ's comment—亦惟父祖 之臣—shows that he must have read 先 王. 先正 probably crept into the text from Bk. XXVIII., p. 1, *q. v.* 亂四方, —see 'The Testamentary Charge,' p. 25. 蹈 虎尾,—this representation of perilousness is also found in the Yih King, under the diagram

爾子翼作股
肱心膂纘乃祖
舊服無忝祖考。○_{四節}弘敷五
典式和民則。
爾身克正正
敢弗正民心
罔中惟爾之
中。○_{五節}夏暑雨，
小民惟曰怨

3 on a tiger's tail, or walking upon spring ice. I now give you charge to assist me; be as my limbs to me, as my heart and back-bone. Continue their old service, and do not disgrace your grandfather and father.

4 　"Diffuse widely *the knowledge of* the five invariable relations *of society*, and reverently seek to produce a harmonious observance of the duties belonging to them among the people. If you can be correct in your own person, none will dare to be but correct. The minds of the people cannot attain to the right Mean *of*

5 *duty*;—they must be guided by your attaining it. In the heat and rains of summer, the inferior people may be described as murmuring

履. 3. 今命至心膂, comp. the various ways in which Kaou-tsung spoke of Yuĕ's relations to him, IV., Bk. VIII., Pt. i., pp. 5—8; and also par. 11 of the 'Yih and Tseih.' 舊服=先公之舊職, 'the old office of your fathers.' The only difficulty is with the 乃. It would seem to be = 汝, and then 乃舊服, is 'the old duties which would almost seem hereditary in your family.' Ying-tă ingeniously says—繼汝先世舊所服行. This par. and the next show that Keun-ya's father and grandfather had been the ministers of Instruction.

P. 4. *The special duties of Keun-ya, and the importance of his exemplifying himself the lessons which he taught.* 弘敷五典,—comp. Shun's charge to Sëĕ, his minister of Instruction,—敬敷五教. 五教 embraces what are here called 五典 and 則. 典 denotes the social relations, with their obligations, as so many *canons* or unchanging rules of life; 則 denotes those obligations recognised and obeyed as practical duties or laws of conduct. 式=敬, 'reverently.' 爾身, 云云, —comp. Ana. XII., xvii., 子帥以正, 孰敢不正. The paraphrase of the 'Daily Explanation' is interesting:—至于立教

典身矣，景必正，則心之導之
心，爾難于求清，自典民疚化民
與偏正之，而之先乎，然無爲望
身無之表曲流能者，悖粹以而
之而民猶表期身，正不純中
爾正求下也，而爾不于中
則其自上之，源事敢至
本欲先上之直，之民其能
之則不蓋源之無而欲不地
爾中也

在爾正至于流濁矣，有中
即爾有之不，卽爾心微得乎

5. *How sympathy for the hardships of the people should move Keun-ya to labour for their good.* 小民惟曰怨 咨,—'the inferior people may be described as murmuring and sighing.' 惟曰 is to be taken as in Bk. XIII., p. 12,—儀不及物 惟曰不享. 祁=大, 'great.' 厥 惟艱哉,—'theirs indeed are hardships!' As the 'Daily Explanation' says, 小民終 歲勤動，求溫飽而不 可得，何其 饑寒切身，怨咨無告

乃　罔　我　哉　哉　寧　以　惟　咨
訓　缺　後　武　文　。　圖　艱　冬
用　爾　人　王　王　○　其　哉　祁
奉　惟　咸　烈　謨　嗚　易　思　寒
若　敬　以　啟　丕　呼　民　其　小
于　明　正　佑　承　丕　乃　艱　民
　　　　　　　　　　　　顯　　亦
　　　　　　　　　　六節　　　惟
　　　　　　　　　　　　　　　日
　　　　　　　　　　　　　　　怨
　　　　　　　　　　　　　　　咨
　　　　　　　　　　　　　　　厥

and sighing.　And so it is with them in the great cold of winter.
How great are their hardships!　Think of their hardships in order
to seek to promote their ease, and the people will be tranquil.
6 Oh! how great and splendid were the plans of king Wăn!　How
greatly were they carried out by the energy of king Woo.　They
are for the help and guidance of us their descendants;—all in
principle correct and deficient in nothing!　Do you with reverence
illustrate your instructions, and enable me to honour and follow

生理之艱哉.　　思其,云云,
—the advice here given to Keun-ya is substantially the same with that given to T'ae-kĕä
by E Yin,—無輕民事惟難. The
student will say, 'But Keun-ya was the minister
of Instruction, whose province was the minds
of the people, whose business was their moral
training:—how is it that he is here directed to
think of the difficulties of their lot, and to
provide for their material well-being?'　In answer to this, there may be quoted first the remarks of Chang Urh-kĕa (張爾嘉; Ming
dyn.):—'When the nourishment of the people
is provided for, their moral training may be
carried on with advantage.　While they are
groaning amid their sufferings from hunger and
cold, it is vain to require from them to pursue
the Mean, and discharge all the duties belonging to their various relations.'　See the 集說
Next we may refer to the exposition of the duties
of the minister of Instruction in the 9th Bk. of
the Chow Le, from many parts of which we might
suppose that he was the minister of Agriculture,
and charged with the care of the material well-
being of the people, rather than with what is
commonly understood as the business of their
education.　That poverty tends to crime, and
competency to virtue is a maxim recognised in
China from its earliest history.　These remarks
seem to explain sufficiently anything that might
seem incongruous in this par.　There is no

necessity to suppose with Lin Che-k'e that it is
spoken to Keun-ya, not as minister of Instruction merely, bnt as uniting with that office
the dignity of one of the Kung, and so charged
with 'the harmonizing and regulating of the
operations of Heaven and Earth' (Bk. XX., p.
5), able somehow therefore, and bound, to moderate the heats of summer and the cold of
winter.

[In the Le Ke, Bk. 緇衣, p. 17, we have
most of this par., with some trifling variations:
—君雅曰,夏日暑雨,小民
惟日怨資,冬祁寒,小民亦
惟日怨.]

P. 6.　*The king mentions the achievements of
the dynasty in the past, and hopes not to come short
of his predecessors by the help of Keun-ya, who
likewise will thus be shown no unworthy son of
his fathers.*　丕　顯　至　罔　缺,—see
all this quoted by Mencius, III., Pt. VI., ix., 6.
用　奉　若　于　先　王,—by 先
王 we are probably to understand kings Ching
and K'ang.　若＝順.　The whole＝使予
得奉順成康之舊.　　對揚
文武之光命,—compare 答揚
文武之光訓, Bk. XXII., p. 4.予楊文訓,
however, indicates what issued from Wăn and

先王、對揚文
武之光命、追
配于前人。○
王若曰君牙、 七節
乃惟由先正
舊典時式民
之治亂在茲、
率乃祖考之
攸行、昭乃辟
之有乂。

the example of my *immediate* predecessors, to respond to and display the bright decree conferred on Wăn and Woo:—so shall you be the mate of your by-gone fathers."

7   The king spoke thus:—"Keun-ya, do you take for your rule the lessons afforded by the former courses of your excellent fathers. The good order or the bad of the people depends on this. You will thus follow the practice of your grandfather and father, and make the good government of your prince illustrious."

Woo; 命, what was conferred on them. 追 配于前人,—this clause must have reference to Keun-ya, and not, as Gan-kwǒ supposed, both to the king and the ministers. 前人 are the grandfather and father of Keun-ya, already referred to. Literally the clause is— 'Going back, you will match your former men.'

P. 7. *The king finally urges Keun-ya to follow the example of his father and grandfather in the same office.* 君牙至時 (=是) 式 (=法),—先正, comp. the same phrase in IV., Bk. VIII., Pt. iii., p. 16. There, however, it denotes 'the former premier,' or chief of the administration of Shang, while here we can only understand it of Keun-ya's father and grandfather. 在茲,—'on this;' *i.e.*, your thus following your fathers. 率乃云云,—the 'Daily Explanation' has for this:— 爾亦惟率由乃祖考之行事以正民之德厚民之生俾安養遂教化行以顯乃辟政治之美不亦休哉.

[The whole of this Charge appears forced and exaggerated.]

THE BOOKS OF CHOW.

BOOK XXVI. THE CHARGE TO KEUNG.

冏命

慈。與厲后先克冏王^{一節}
○思中人于惟若
昔^{二節}免夜宅德子曰，
在厥以丕嗣弗伯

1 The king spoke thus:—"Pih-keung, I come short in virtue, and have now succeeded to the former kings, to occupy the great throne. I am fearful and conscious of the peril *of my position*. I rise at midnight, and think how I can avoid falling into faults.

THE NAME OF THE BOOK; AND DATE.—冏命, 'The Charge to Keung.' The prefatory note says that 'king Muh appointed Pih-keung to be the 太僕正, and thereupon was made the 'Charge to Keung.' From par. 1 we learn that Pih-keung (伯冏) was the name of the individual to whom the charge was given; the title therefore might have been 伯冏之命, or simply 伯冏, after the analogy of the title of the last Book. No reason can be given for the form of the name as we have it, but that it was the fancy of the compiler to call it so. As Lin Che-k'e says, 此篇與君牙篇而官史伯冏各去其命之命體君牙則亦是命名其字皆是命以其字牙則加但以命以其一時之意也.

As to the office which Pih-keung was appointed to fill, there are two opinions. In the preface it is called 太僕正; and in the Book, p. 4,

太僕正. He is no doubt included among the 正 of p. 6, and we must admit, therefore, the designation in the preface as correct. Now 僕 is used first for 'servant,' without reference to the nature of the service. The dict. gives the definition of the 說文,—給事者, 'one who renders services,' and illustrates this by a passage from the Le Ke, 禮運,—仕于公曰臣, 仕于家曰僕, 'a public officer is called 臣; an officer in the family is called 僕.' But the character also means 'a charioteer' (御車曰僕). The difft. views depend on whether the general meaning or the special be supposed to predominate in the case before us.

When we refer to the Chow Le, we find many officers in the dept. of the minister of War denominated as 僕. In Bk. XXXI., we have the 太僕, 祭僕, 御僕, and 隸僕; and in Bk. XXXII., we have the 太馭 (馭 is taken here to=僕), 戎僕, 齊僕, 道

從, 御 其 忠 咸 之 小 齊 聰 文
罔 僕 侍 良, 懷 臣, 大 聖, 明 武,

2 Formerly, Wǎn and Woo were endowed with all intelligence, august and sage, while their ministers, small and great, all cherished loyalty and goodness. Their servants, charioteers, attendanst,

僕, and 田僕. The student naturally, and I think correctly, supposes that he has in the 太僕 of Bk. XXXI. the office of Pih-keung; but Gan-kwŏ and Ying-tă, whose views Lin Che-k'e approved of, were of opinion rather that he should be identified with the 太馭 of Bk. XXXII. The duties of the 太僕 are described in many parr. He, or they—for there were two officers so denominated—regulated the dress of the emperor on diff't. occasions, and the positions where he should stand or sit. He received the great commands of the emperor, and delivered them to those for whom they were intended; and conveyed on the other hand to the emperor memorials from without. He went before the emp. to and from audiences. These details are sufficient to show how close were his relations with the emperor, and how intimate were the services which he rendered.

The 太馭, under whom (though this point is not so clear) appear to have been the 戎僕, &c., mentioned above, had charge of the grand carriage of the emperor, and drove him in it to sacrifices. So far they were close enough together, but their relations were by no means so numerous and intimate as those of the emp. and the 太僕. Why should we suppose that Pih-keung was appointed 太馭 and not 太僕?

The only reason is that the 太馭 were great officers of the second degree (中大夫) while the 太僕 were only of the third (下大夫). There would be force in this, if the one office had been under the other. But there is no evidence to show that this was the case. The two K'ungs erroneously supposed it was, and hence they were led to a wrong conclusion about the office of Pih-keung.

There were two 太僕, under whom were 4 petty servants (小臣), 6 servants for sacrifices (祭僕), 12 special servants (御僕), 2 treasurers (府), 4 clerks (史), 2 helps (胥), 20 waiters (徒), with perhaps others. Pih-keung must have been the senior or chief of the two. Biot translates the term by, 'Grand Domestique.' 'High Chamberlain' is the nearest I can come to it in English.

[This long investigation of the office of Pih-keung may be wearisome to some readers. I thought it worth while to enter on it, because many Chinese critics have professed themselves unable to determine the point. M. de Guignes, who had certainly read the Shoo with care, at least in Gaubil's version, strangely says, in his summary of the Book, that 'Keung was one of the great officers of king Muh. He is named Pih-keung (伯冏), because he was chief of several vassal princes!' So difficult is it, without prolonged and close study, to interpret correctly documents in this language.]

The Book is only found in the 'old text.'

CONTENTS. King Muh represents himself as conscious of his own incompetencies, and oppressed with a sense of the important duties devolving on him. His predecessors, much superior to himself, were yet greatly indebted to the aid of the officers about them;—how much more must this be the case with himself!

He proceeds to appoint Keung to be the High Chamberlain, that he may guide correctly all the other servants about the imperial person, and so promote his virtue; telling him the manner of men whom he should employ, and the care which he should exercise in the selection of them.

Pp. 1—3. *Preliminary to the appointment.* 1. *The king's great anxiety in the thought of his own incompetency and his high position.* 子弗克于德,—'I am not competent in the point of virtue.' Compare Kaou-tsung's 台恐德弗類 in 'The Charge to Yue,' Pt. i., p. 2. 嗣先人宅丕后,—宅=居; 丕=大. Ts'ae gives for the whole. 繼前人居大君之位. 怵惕—see Mencius, II., Pt., I., vi. 3. Ying-tă says here, that the phrase denotes 'the commotion of the heart (心動之名. 厲=危, 'perilousness.' 中夜以興,—以 perhaps has an adverbial force, = 'thereupon.' 2. *Wǎn and Woo, sage as they were, were yet greatly aided by the servants about them.* 齊=莊, or 肅, 'grave,' 'august.' 侍御僕從—侍=給侍左右, 'those who were about them, on the right and left, min-

汝　克　愆　位　良　咸　不　不　厥　匪
作　紹　糾　之　實　休　臧　欽　辟　正
大　先　謬　士　賴　。　下　發　出　人
正　烈　格　匡　左　○　民　號　入　以
正　。　其　其　右　惟　祗　施　起　旦
于　○　非　不　前　予　若　令　居　夕
群　今　心　及　後　一　萬　罔　罔　承
僕　予　俾　繩　有　人　邦　有　有　弼

and followers, were all men of correctness, morning and evening waiting on their sovereign's wishes or supplying his deficiencies. *Those kings*, going out and coming in, rising up and sitting
down, were thus made reverent. Their every warning and command
was good. The people yielded a reverent obedience, and the
3 myriad regions were all happy. But I, the one man, am destitute
of goodness, and really depend on the officers who have places
about me to help my deficiencies, applying the line to my faults,
and exhibiting my errors, thus correcting my bad heart, and
enabling me to be the successor of my meritorious predecessors.

4   "Now I appoint you to be High Chamberlain, to see that all belonging to your department and my personal attendants are correct,

istering and waiting; 御＝御車者, 'charioteers;' 僕＝太僕羣僕, 'the chamber-
lains and all their subordinates;' 從＝凡
從王者, 'all in close attendance on the
sovereign's person.' Choo He remarks that anciently and in the Han dyn., 'all who were even
in mean offices about the sovereign were officers
of some rank' (士, 大夫). 承＝順,
'to accord with,' 'to obey.' 弼＝匡正,
'to support and correct.' 出入至不
欽,—this is to be understood of the sovereigns.
發 號 施 令,—Wang Gan-shih
observes that 'intimations of the imperial will
to serve as warnings were called 號, while
such as were to have the force of laws were
令' (發之以爲警戒之謂號、
施之以爲法守之謂令).

3. *The king declares how much more he must be
dependent on the good services of those about him.*

繩愆糾謬.—繩 is the 'line' by
which things are made straight. We naturally
look for a corresponding figure in 糾, but we
do not have it. It is taken here by Gan-kwŏ,
as ＝舉, 'to raise up,' 'to exhibit.' Lin Che-
k'e understands by 繩, the 'thread which is
used in mending rents;' and he takes 糾 in the
sense of 察, 'to examine.' 先烈, 'the
former ardent and meritorious ones' are Wăn
and Woo.

Pp. 4—8. *The appointment of Pih-keung.—
His duties, and rules for their discharge.*   4.
大正＝太僕正;—see the note on the
name of the Book. 正于至之臣,
—the 于 need not be translated. It merely
carries on the action of 正 to 臣. 羣
僕侍御 are all the officers of the High
Chamberlain's department mentioned in the said
note. Ts'ae taking 大正 as ＝太僕,

侍御之臣、懋乃后
德交修不逮。○愼五節
簡乃僚無以巧言
令色便辟側媚、其
惟吉士。○僕臣六節
厥后克正、僕臣諛、
厥后自聖后德
臣不德惟臣。○爾七節
無昵于憸人充耳
目之官迪上以非

that you may strive to promote the virtue of your sovereign, and
5 together supply my deficiencies. Be careful in choosing your
officers. Do not employ men of artful speech and insinuating
looks, men whose likes and dislikes are ruled by mine, one-sided
6 men and flatterers; but employ good men. When these household
officers are correct, their sovereign will be correct; when they are
flatterers, the sovereign will consider himself a sage. The sovereign's virtue and his want of it depend equally on those officers.
7 Cultivate no intimacy with flatterers, nor get them to fill the
offices of my ears and eyes;—they will lead their sovereign to

would yet include among them the various officers of the carriages who were under the
太馭, which, I said, we saw to be wrong.
The 御 here can have nothing to do with the
carriages. I have my doubts, indeed, whether
it should be translated 'charioteers' in p. 2.
変修,—'cultivate together.' 変 is used as
in 上下変征利, Mencius, I., Pt. I., i.,
3. Wang Ts'ëaou says on it:—言左右
前後非一人、変以修君之
所不逮爲事也. 5. *How Keung
should be careful in selecting his officers.* 愼
簡乃僚,—僚＝朋, 'friends,' 'compan-
ions,' 'brother officers.' But we must take the
term here as meaning the subordinate officers
of the Chamberlain's dept. It would appear
from this that, under the Chow dyn., it was the
business of every head of a dept. to select all
the members of it. There were, no doubt,
general principles for his guidance, but it was
his to choose the men. 巧言令色,—
see 'The Counsels of Kaou-yaou,' p. 2. 便
辟,—see Ana., XVI., iv. Ts'ac defines them

here:—便者, 順人之所欲, 辟
者, 避人之所惡. 吉士,—as
in Bk. XIX., p. 9,＝善士 or 君子.
其惟吉士＝所用者惟吉士
而已. 6. *The importance of having correct
men about the sovereign.* 僕臣, we may
translate this here by 'household officers.'
后德惟臣, 不德惟臣,—Gan-kwǒ
says for this:—君之有德, 惟臣成
之, 君之無德, 惟臣誤之, 言
君所行善惡, 專在左右.
自聖,—'sages himself,'＝自以爲聖.
7. *The king warns Keung again against
having anything to do with flatterers.* 昵,—
see Pt. IV., Bk. VIII., Pt. ii., 5. 憸人,
—see Bk. XIX., p. 20. 充耳目之
官,—'to get them to fill the offices of the ears
and eyes.' The king must in a great measure
hear with the ears and see with the eyes of those
about him. See the phrase 耳目之官

先王之典。○

非〔八節〕人其吉惟

貨其吉若時、

瘝厥官惟爾

大弗克祗厥

辟惟予汝辜。

○〔九節〕王曰嗚呼

欽哉永弼乃

后于彝憲。

8 disregard the statutes of the former kings. If you choose your men not for the goodness of their personal qualities, but for the sake of their bribes, the offices will thus be all made of no effect. Your great want of reverence for your sovereign will be apparent, and to you I will impute the blame."

9 　 The king said, "Oh! be reverent! Ever help your sovereign to follow the regular laws of duty *which he should exemplify*."

in Men., VI., Pt. I., xv., 2. 　　8. *Let Keung choose his officers on the ground of what they are, and not for what they have or can give him.*
貨 is here = 賂, 'to bribe,' 'a bribe.' 非人其吉, 惟貨其吉,—this is addressed directly to Pih-keung.—'If it be not the man in whom is the excellence, but it is the bribe in which *you see* the excellence.' Gan-kwŏ missed the point and terseness of the language:—若非其人實吉良, 惟以貨財配其吉良, 以求入于僕侍之中, 　若時 = 如是, 'thus.' 瘝 = 曠, 'to make void,' 'to leave as it were empty.' This is difft. from its use in Bk. IX., pp. 6, 17. Perhaps 瘝在, Bk. XII., p. 10,

should be explained in accordance with this text.

P. 9. 　*The conclusion.* 　彝憲 = 常法, 'the regular or constant laws of conduct,' which the sovereign should observe.

CONCLUDING NOTE. The character of king Muh does not stand high with Chinese historians. Towards the end of his long reign, for 55 years are assigned to him, he took it into his head that he should travel, without any definite purpose of usefulness, all over the empire, wherever he could go. He did not prove the man that the critics say might have been expected from the language of his Charges to Keun-ya and Pih-keung. Lin Che-k‘e thinks his fallings off have been exaggerated. To my mind these two addresses betray a tendency to exaggeration, and betoken a feebleness of mind,

THE BOOKS OF CHOW.

詰 刑、度 耄、百 享 命、惟 呂
四 以 作 荒 年 國 王 呂 刑

1   I. In reference to the charge to *the prince of* Leu :—When the king had enjoyed the throne till he was the age of a hundred years, he gave great consideration to the appointment of punishments, in order to restrain *the people of* all quarters.

INTRODUCTORY NOTE. The two last Books, there was reason to believe, were to be referred to the commencement of king Muh's reign ; this, we learn from the Book itself, was the work of its close, when the king was not less than a century old. During the half century that he occupied the throne, the House of Chow went on to decline. Acc. to Sze-ma Ts'een, the king would engage in hostilities with the wild tribes round about, contrary to the counsels of his advisers, losing consequently the former reverence with which they had regarded the sovereigns of Chow, and the good-will also of many of the princes. As to the character of his enactments about punishments, which were the work of his hundredth year, opinions are greatly divided, some critics condemning it so much that they cannot understand why Confucius gave the Book a place in the Shoo. I will reserve the expression of a judgment in the case till we have considered its different parts in detail.

THE NAME OF THE BOOK.— 呂 刑, '*The prince of* Leu upon Punishments,' or 'The Punishments *of the prince* of Leu.' The Prefatory note says that 'Leu received the orders of king Muh to set forth the lessons of Hea on the redemption of punishments, and there was made LEU ON PUNISHMENTS' (see page. 13., n. 64). We can hardly say that any of this appears in the Book, for Leu, or the prince of Leu, is mentioned only once. The king is the speaker throughout. Nothing is said of Hea. We may accept the tradition, however, that Leu was Muh's minister of Crime, and that the regula-

tions which the king announces had in the first place been digested by him.

呂 is to be taken as = 呂 侯, 'The prince of Leu,' being itself the name of a principality, the place of which cannot be clearly ascertained. The Book is quoted in the Le Ke several times, and in other works, by the name of 甫 刑, 'The Punishments *of the prince* of Foo.' Indeed this was the prevailing name of it during the Han dynasty. The truth seems to be, that the descendants of the prince of Leu were appointed to the principality of Foo, and their territorial title was transferred to him and to this Book. The Houses of Ts'e (齊), Shin (申), Heu (許), and Foo (甫), all traced their descent to Yaou's president of the Four Eminences, surnamed Keang (姜 氏). He or his son was to the great Yu 'a minister who served the purpose of his heart and backbone' (心 呂 之 臣). In this way the surname of 呂 arose among his descendants, and was retained by the princes of Ts'e, the most distinguished family of them. Possibly the prince of Leu, with whom we have here to do, may have had the same title from his importance to king Muh. However this may be, 呂 刑 was the older and the proper title of this Book. Mih Teih quotes it by that name. It was found in both the texts.

CONTENTS. I confine myself for the present to the account of these given in the 'Complete Digest.'—'Par. 1 is the historiographer's account of the circumstances in which these lessons on punishments were made. Parr. 2—12 relate the lessons of antiquity for the information of the judges and princes, being a historical resumé which it was important for them to be acquainted with. Par. 13 is addressed specially to the princes, admonishing them of the diligence and carefulness to be employed in the use of punishments. Parr. 14—20 tell them how they should proceed in that use so as to make punishments a blessing. Par. 21 insists again on the reverence with which punishments should be employed. The last par. is addressed to future generations, and directs them to the ancient models, that punishments may never be but a blessing to the empire. Throughout the Book, "virtue" and "exact adaptation" are the terms which carry the weight of the meaning. *Virtue* must underlie the use of punishments, and *exact adaptation* will be the manifestation of it' (通 篇 以 德 與 中 爲 主, 德 其 本 也, 中 其 用 也).

It will be seen that I have divided the king's address into six chapters, each of which commences with the words—'The king said.' This differs only in one trifling point from the arrangement of the 'Complete Digest.'

Ch. I. P. 1. INTRODUCTION :—The TIME AND OBJECT FOR WHICH THE ANNOUNCEMENT ABOUT PUNISHMENTS WAS MADE. 惟 呂 命,— this clause has no syntactical connection with the rest of the par. Ts'ae says that the characters are used in the same way as 惟 說 命 in 'The Charge to Yuĕ,' Pt. ii., p. 1; but the student will perceive that the cases are not at all analogous. 惟 說 命 is an integral part of the par. where it stands, and supplies the nominative to the first verb in the par. which follows. We may suppose that the prince of Leu had received charge to digest the subject of punishments in acc. with his own views and those of king Muh; that he had done so; and that the king published the result as is subsequently narrated. In this way we may give 惟 呂 命 the meaning which appears in the translation.

It is not certain how the rest of the par. ought to be pointed. Should 耄 and 荒 be joined together and stand intermediately between what precedes and what follows, qualifying more especially what follows? or should we put a stop at 耄, joining it to 享 國 百 年, and make 荒 an adv., qualifying 度? Gan-kwŏ took the former method, in which he is followed by Ts'ae, who says that 耄 is the designation of one who is old, with the weakness and mental disorders of age (老 而 亂 之 稱). 荒 he defines, after Gan-kwŏ, by 忽, 'sudden,' 'neglectful,' and

subjoins Mencius' account of it,—從 獸 無 厭 謂 之 荒, 'Pursuing the chase without satiety is what I call being wild;'—see Men. I., Pt. II., iv. 7. On this construction, the two characters are strongly condemnatory of the king's character, and would go to show that the enactments about punishment which the Book relates were stigmatised by the historiographer as made by him in his dotage, and the licentiousness of his reign. Leu Tsoo-hëen and Ch'in Leih, whose opinions are appended in Yung-ching's Shoo, construing 耄 and 荒 together like Ts'ae, yet endeavour to make them have a difft. bearing on the statement 度 作 刑 which follows;—but unsuccessfully.

Soo Shih adopted the second method of pointing which I have indicated. He put a stop at 耄, and joined 荒 to the verb 度 as an adv., signifying 'greatly;'—referring, in support both of the construction and of that meaning of 荒, to the words of Yu in the 'Yih and Tseih,' p. 8, 惟 荒 度 土 功, 'I kept planning with all my might my labour on the land.' I have followed this view in the translation. Ts'ae admits that it is ingenious and admissible (亦 通), saying, however, that 'the character 耄 alone is one of condemnation' (耄 亦 貶 之 之 辭). But in this latter criticism he is incorrect. We have the character used by Shun of himself in 'The Counsels of Yu,' p. 9, where it simply expresses the fact of his great age, and I do not think that we are to seek for any other meaning for it in the text.

The general rhythm of the par. also satisfies me that Shih's construction is to be preferred, unless indeed we should introduce a 詳 before 刑, as Këang Shing does, but on insufficient authority. Thus taken, the historiogaprher in this par. indicates neither censure nor approbation of king Muh's labours on the subject of punishments; and this is a recommendation of the view.

It still remains to direct attention to the peculiarity of the language—享 國 百 年 耄, which, on the analogy of Bk. XV., p. 4, *et al.*, and most naturally too, would be understood as saying that king Muh occupied the throne for a hundred years. Such a view has its supporters. Wang Ch'ung, for instance, maintains it, in his 論 衡 卷 一, 氣 壽 篇, adding that Muh lived altogether to the age of about 140. This cannot be admitted. Sze-ma Ts'een says he was 50 when he succeeded to the throne, and that he reigned 55 years. 詰 has a meaning here intermediate between that in Bk. XX., p, p. 22, and that in XX., p. 11, = 禁.

奪 義 寇 民、及 作 尤 有 曰、方。
攘 姦 賊 罔 于 亂 惟 訓、若 ○
矯 宄 鴟 不 平 延 始 蚩 古 王 二節

2   II. The king said, "According to the teachings of ancient times, Ch'e-yew was the first to produce disorder, which spread among the common people, till all became robbers and murderers, owl-like in their conduct, traitors and villains, snatching and filching, dissemblers and oppressors.

CH. II. PP. 2—11. THE FIRST PART OF THE KING'S ADDRESS;—INTRODUCTORY. THE FIRST RISE OF DISORDER IN THE EMPIRE; THE CASE OF THE PEOPLE OF MEAOU; HOW SHUN DEALT WITH THEM; AND HOW HE WENT ON TO LABOUR BY HIS MINISTERS FOR THE PEOPLE, ENDING WITH THE SUBJECT OF PUNISHMENTS. 2. *Ch'e-yew, the first author of disorder in the empire.*

若古有訓,—this clause is equivalent to the 曰若稽古, with which the Canons of Yaou and Shun commence. 若 may be taken with Woo Ch'ing, as 'an introductory particle.' Then 古有訓='From of old there are the lessons.' Gaubil translates—'*Selon les anciens documents.*' But that is more than the text says. He adds in a note,—'These ancient documents are without doubt some books of history which subsisted in the time of king Muh.' Possibly so; but then we know nothing about them, their author, or their authority. There has been no allusion hitherto in the Shoo, if we except the words of Shun in the 'Yih and Tseih,' p. 4, to anything anterior to the time of Yaou; and here all at once king Muh carries us, as will be seen, three centuries farther back, even to before the year 1 of the calendared history of the empire. 始作 亂,—'first produced disorder.' 亂 indicates that the 'disorder' was 'rebellion,' resistance to the Powers that were of the time. 平 民,='the quiet orderly people.' 寇賊 姦宄,—see the 'Can. of Shun,' p. 20. 鴟義,—'the 鴟 (probably the owl) watches its opportunity,' says Ch'ing, 'to dart on its prey. So vividly are the ways of those robbers and murderers represented.' 矯=詐, 'dissemblers.' 虔 has several meanings in the dict., one or two of which would suit the connection here, while others are of an antagonistic meaning. Ts'ae and Woo Ch'ing accept that of 劉=殺, 'murderers,' which I have modified to distinguish it from 賊.

Ch'e-yew, to whom the bad eminence of being the first rebel is here assigned, can hardly be considered a historical personage. The two characters of the name may be translated—'The Stupid and Extraordinary.' According to Sze-ma Ts'een, when the power of the descendants of Shin-nung, the second of the five *Tes*, with whom he commences his history, was declining, great confusion prevailed, and the princes all turned their arms against one another. Then the star of Hwang-te began to rise, and the well inclined gathered around him as their leader. Of all the princes Ch'e-yew was the most violent and oppressive. He attempted to seize the imperial power, when Hwang-te took the field against him, and put him to death after three engagements, and himself superseded the House of Shin-nung. Many fables about dragons, mists, and the invention of the compass, have been mixed up by subsequent writers with the struggle between Hwang-te and Ch'e-yew.

One tradition, indeed, makes Ch'e-yew later than Hwang-te. Gan-kwŏ says he was 'the ruler of Kew-le' (九黎之君); and in the 國語, 楚語, 下, we read that 'Kew-le became disorderly and vicious during the decay of Shaou-haou' (及少皥氏之 衰也,九黎亂德). Now Shaou-haou was the son of Hwang-te. It is true that Gan-kwŏ says, on the next par., that 'Ch'e-yew was destroyed by Hwang-te;' but the impression which we get from the 國語 is that the speaker conceived of the first interruption of good order and vritue as having taken place in the time of Shaou-haou.

The authority of Confucius again is pleaded for making Ch'e-yew a common man, and the greediest of all men (蚩尤庶人之 貪者). See Wang Ming-shing, *in loc.* See also the 16th chapter of Premare's preliminary discourse, prefixed to Gaubil's Shoo-king, where he has given all the information that Lo Peih (羅泌) has collected about Ch'e-yew in his 路史.

I pass on from this par. to the next with two remarks.—First, It is not clear for what purpose king Muh commences his discourse of punishments with this mention of Ch'e-yew.

罔 麗 椓 淫 無 曰 五 以 弗 虡。
差 刑 黥 爲 辜 法 虐 刑 用 ○
有 并 越 劓 爰 殺 之 惟 靈 苗民
辭。 制 茲 刵 始 戮 刑 作 制 民

3 "Among the people of Meaou, they did not use the power of good, but the restraint of punishments. They made the five punishments engines of oppression, calling them the laws. They slaughtered the innocent, and were the first also to go to excess in cutting off the nose, cutting off the ears, castration, and branding. All who became liable to those punishments were dealt with without distinction, no difference being made in favour of

Perhaps he meant to indicate, as the 'Daily Explanation' says, that it was this rebel who first gave occasion for the use of punishment at all. (言古人制刑之由). Second, It is plain that at the commencement of human history Chinese tradition placed a period of innocence, a season when order and virtue ruled in men's affairs.

Pp. 3, 4. *The wickedness of the people of Meaou; and the excessive use of punishments among them.* The king appears to pass over a period of three or four hundred years; and from the time of Ch'e-yew, anterior, acc. to the prevailing accounts, to the invention of the cycle by Hwang-te, he comes down to the time of Shun. So, it will be seen, we must understand these and the following paragraphs. 苗民,—I do not see how we can take these characters otherwise than in the translation. K'ang-shing says that they mean 'the ruler of Kew-le.' 'The prince so denominated,' he says, 'giving trouble in the days of Shaou-haou, was dealt with by Chüen-heuh (顓頊),—afterwards the successor to the throne,—who put Kew-le to death, and removed a portion of his family to the outskirts of the empire on the west. There they reappeared as the chiefs of San-mëaou, and in the reign of his successor Kaou-sin (高辛氏) or the emperor Kuh (帝嚳), B.C. 2,431, displayed their hereditary wickedness, when it devolved finally on Yaou to take them in hand. (苗民謂

于 效 苗 頊 子 至 惡
九 黎 之 君 也, 九 黎 君 之 道, 九 黎 之 弃 善 變 九 黎 後 流 三 苗 之
少 昊 尤 者 少 而 必 苗 九 誅 者 又 復 九
當 民 代 孫 高 辛 之 氏 重 刑 有 昊 居 于 之 衰 裔

堯 典 又 誅 之). This pedigree of the chiefs of the Meaou is ingenious, but I can only regard it as a fancy of the learned scholar. Equally fanciful is his explanation of the character 民 as applied to the ruler of the Meaou, that it is indicative of contempt, and stigmatises him as no better than one of the common herd. Gan-kwŏ, who is followed by Woo Ch'ing, for 苗民 gives 三苗之君, 'the ruler of San-meaou.' As I said above, I do not see how this can be allowed. Of course it is the ruler or rulers who are spoken of, and this can be indicated, as I have done, by using the indefinite *they* as the subject of 用. 弗用靈, 制以刑,—the meaning of this seems to be that given by Gan-kwŏ,—不用善化民, 而制以重刑, 'they did not use what was good to transform the people, but restrained them by heavy punishments.' 惟作五虐之刑.—we cannot be surprised that some of the critics should argue from this that the invention of 'the five punishments' is here attributed to the chiefs of the Meaou. But the conclusion is not warranted by the language, nor by history. 'The five punishments'—cutting off the nose, and the ear, castration, branding, and death—are all recognised by Shun (Can. of Shun, p. 11). They used those same punishments in Meaou, but excessively and more barbarously. The use of 虐 and 淫 sufficiently show this to be all that is taught in this par. See the remarks of Ch'in Leih in the 集說. 曰法=名之曰法; or, as Woo Ch'ing gives it, 非法而爲之法也 殺戮 ('they killed and slaughtered') 無辜,—this was the way in which they abused the heaviest punishment, that of death.

矜　腥　德　民　于　詛　中　○
庶　。　刑　罔　上　盟　于　民
戮　○　發　有　上　虐　信　與
之　皇　聞　馨　帝　威　以　胥
不　帝　惟　香　監　庶　覆　漸　四節
　　哀　　　　　戮　　　五節
　　　　　　　　方
　　　　　　　　告
　　　　　　　　無
　　　　　　　　辜

泯
泯
棼
棼
罔

4 those who could offer some excuse. The mass of the people were gradually affected by this state of things, and became dark and disorderly. Their hearts were no more set on good faith, but they violated their oaths and covenants. The multitudes who suffered from the oppressive terrors, and were *in danger of* being murdered, declared their innocence to Heaven. God surveyed the people, and there was no fragrance of virtue arising from them, but the rank odour of their *cruel* punishments.

5 "The great emperor compassionated the innocent multitudes who were *in danger of being* murdered, and made the oppressors feel the

椓＝去陰之刑, 'castration.' The char. was originally written 斀. 越茲, 云云,—this was the way in which they abused the four punishments just mentioned. K'ang-shing takes 麗 here＝施,—于此施刑并制; but I prefer to retain the meaning of 附, as in the translation. 民與胥漸,—on the extent of 民 here, see on the next par. 漸 (read *tsëen*, 1st tone)＝漸染, 'were soaked and dyed.' The 胥,＝相, shows how the influence was communicated from one to another. 泯泯＝昏. 棼棼 (Shing edits 紛紛)＝亂. 罔中于信,—中 is here ＝心, 'the heart;' the centre of the man. Ch'in King says:—罔中于信，無中心出於誠信者，信不由中也. 以覆詛盟,—覆, 'to turn upside down,' governs 詛 and 盟. I hardly know how to construe Ts'ae's 相與反覆詛盟而已. Shing quotes, in illustration of the sentiment, from the 左傳, 隱三年, these words,—信不由中，質無益也. 虐威庶戮＝其

被虐威而陷于刑戮之眾. 罔有, 云云,—Comp. Bk. X., p. 11. On the meaning of 馨, see XXI., p. 3. 刑發聞惟腥,—'what the punishments sent forth to be smelt was only a rank odour.' Ts'ee says:—而刑戮發聞，莫非腥穢.

[For the first part of par. 3, we find in Mih's 尚同中 呂刑之道曰，苗民否用練折則刑，惟作五殺之刑曰法. The critics say that 練 and 靈, 弗 and 否, 折 and 制 were all sounded like each other. Even if we should admit this, how do we have 則 for 以, and 殺 for 虐?

The same pass. appears in the Le Ke, Bk. 緇衣, p. 3, in a form which is somewhat different still:—甫刑曰，苗民匪用命，制以刑，惟作五虐之刑曰法.]

Pp. 5—11. *How the Meaouites were dealt with; the evils produced by them remedied; and the system of punishments in the empire put into a satisfactory state.* 5 The important question in connection with this paragraph is as to the emperor whom we are to understand by 皇帝. K'ang-shing, followed of course by

辜報虐以威過
絕苗民無世在
下。〇乃命重黎
六節
絕地天通罔有
降格群后之逮
在下明明棐常、
鯀寡無蓋。〇皇
七節
帝清問下民、鯀
寡有辭于苗德
威惟畏德明惟

terrors of his majesty. He restrained and *finally* extinguished the people of Meaou, so that they should not continue to future generations.

6 Then he commissioned Ch'ung and Le to make an end of the communications between earth and heaven, and the descents *of spirits* ceased. From the princes down to the inferior officers, all helped with clear intelligence *the spread of* the regular principles of duty,

7 and the solitary and widows were no more disregarded. The great emperor with an unprejudiced mind carried his inquiries low down among the people, and the solitary and widows laid before him their complaints against the Meaou. He sought to awe *the people* by his virtue, and all were filled with dread; he proceeded *also* to

Këang Shing and Wang Ming-shing thought that in this par. and the next it was Chuenheuh who was the subject, after which the discourse turns to Yaou. Gan-kwŏ, who is foll. by Woo Ch'ing, makes the emperor to be Yaou all through. Neither view is admissible. The things spoken of in parr. 8, 9, can only be ascribed to Shun. 乃命 at the beginning of p. 8, connects it so closely with p. 7, that we can only understand Shun to be the 皇帝. And as there is no intimation of that 皇帝 being difft. from the person indicated by the same title in par. 5, we must believe that Shun who is the principal subject in all the rest of this chapter is there intended. This is the view of Ts'ae, after Lin Che-k'e.

We get from what is said of the Meaou in these parr. a higher idea of them and their prince than is commonly entertained. From king Muh's language I judge that Shun had in him a powerful rival, and that the struggle which lasted through the reigns of Yaou, Shun, and Yu was of a dynastic nature. The chief of San-meaou was more than the head of a barbarous horde. He was a dangerous rival for the throne. The 'people' mentioned in p. 4, were probably the people of the empire generally. 皇帝至不辜,—we must take 庶戮 here as in the last par. 過絕, 云云,—the measures referred to in the 'Can. of Shun,' pp. 12 and 27, are thus described. The

'Daily Explanation' gives:—竄其君于
三危,分北其黨,以遏其繼世焉.
苗之民,而不使其百姓之害.
下國,以貽

6. 乃命至降格,—this par. seems to interpose a difficulty in the way of the view which I have adopted above, that it is Shun who is to be understood as 'the emperor' in all this chapter. We read nothing in the Shoo of his appointing any ministers to do the work here spoken of. No Ch'ung and Le were officers of his. Nor do they appear among the ministers of Yaou, though it is attempted to identify Ch'ung with He (羲) and Le with Ho (和).

The passage formed the subject of a conversation in the lifetime of Confucius, between king Ch'aou (昭王; B.C. 514—488) of Tsoo and one of his ministers, called Kwan Yih-foo (觀射父). 'What is meant,' asked the king, 'by what is said in one of the Books of Chow about Ch'ung and Le, that they really brought it about that there was no intercourse between heaven and earth? If they had not done so, would people have been able to ascend to heaven?' (周書所謂重黎實使天地不通者何也,若無然,民將能登天乎). The minister replied that that was not the meaning of the language at all, and he proceeded to give his own view of it at great length, and to the following effect:—Anciently, the people attended to the discharge of their duties to one another, and left the worship of spiritual beings—seeking intercourse with them, and invoking and effecting their descent on earth—to the officers who were appointed for that purpose. In this way things proceeded with great regularity. The people minded their own affairs, and the spirits minded theirs. Tranquillity and prosperity were the consequence. But in the time of Shaou-haou, through the lawlessness of Kew-le, a change took place. The people intruded into the functions of the regulators of the spirits and their worship. They left their duties to their fellow-men, and tried to bring down spirits from above. The spirits themselves, no longer kept in check and subjected to rule, made their appearance all irregularly and disastrously. All was confusion and calamity, when Chuen-heuh took the case in hand. He appointed Ch'ung, the minister of the South, to the superintendency of heavenly things, to prescribe the rules for the spirits, and Le, the minister of Fire (or of the North), to the superintendency of earthly things, to prescribe the rules for the people. (命南正重司天以屬神,命火正(=北正)黎司地以屬民). In this way both spirits and people were brought back to their former regular courses, and there was no unhallowed interference of the one with the other. This was the work described in the text,—'the bringing to an end the communication between earth and heaven.' Subsequently, the chief of San-meaou showed himself a Kew-le *redivivus*, till Yaou called forth the descendants of Ch'ung and Le who had not forgotten the virtue and function of their fathers, and made them take the case in hand again.

From the details of this strange passage of which I have given a summary, it would appear that the speaker considered that the Ch'ung and Le of the text were ministers of Yaou, descended from those of Chuen-heuh; and this has given rise to the opinion which I have alluded to on p. 3. of 'The Canon of Yaou,' that this was the ancestry of the minister He and Ho who are mentioned there.

That opinion is without a tittle of satisfactory evidence. Acc. to Yih-foo's statements, Ch'ung's function was that of the minister of Religion, and Le's that of the minister of Instruction, while He and Ho were simply ministers of astronomy, and their descendants continue to appear as such in the reign of Ch'ung-k'ang, the grandson of Yu, long after we know that men of other families were appointed to the two important ministries in question. Gaubil's speculations about the employment of the astronomer in the time of Yaou, not only to calculate and observe the motions of the heavenly bodies, but also to do away with conjurors, false worship, &c., fall to the ground;—see 'Le Chou-king,' p. 292, n. 1. He says also, that as Chung and Le are the same as He and Ho, if we suppose that Shun is the emperor spoken of here, we must assume that he gave those officers a new commission. But if we were to allow that it is Yaou who is spoken of, which I have shown on the last par. to be inadmissible, we should have the same difficulty with the statement of which I began this note. Ch'ung and Le are nowhere in the previous parts of the Shoo, or in any other reliable documents of history, mentioned as officers of his, any more than of Shun. I do not see that any light can be thrown on the passage. The statements of Kwan Yih-foo in the 國語 are entitled to little or no consideration.

羣后之逮在下,—I have translated this and the rest of the par. after Ts'ae. The 'Daily Explanation' gives for it:—當其時有土之諸侯,及在下之百官,皆精白其心,輔助常道,民之順是道者,則嘉與之,悖是道者則匡正之,以慶賞刑威之典,爲輔助常道之具,其時好惡明,賞罰當,雖鰥寡之無告,爲善則必蒙福,亦未有蔽而不得伸者. The meaning is, that through the reforms introduced by Ch'ung and Le, a general reformation among all the higher classes was produced. Princes and inferior officers co-operated with those ministers, and the way was opened for the poorest and most helpless of the people to make their complaints and distresses known to the emperor. A foundation is thus laid for the 皇帝清問下民, with which the next par. commences. It will be observed how all this agrees with the view of little less than a dynastic struggle between Shun and the Meaou.

[Këang Shing follows 罔有降格 with 皇帝清問, and edits to the end of p. 8 on a very unsatisfactory authority, that of Mih Teih, in whose 尙賢,中, we read;—呂刑道之曰,皇帝清問下民,有辭有苗,曰羣后之肆在下,明明不常,鰥寡不蓋,德威維威,德明維明,乃名三后,恤功於民,伯夷降典,哲民維刑,禹平水土,主名山川,稷隆播種,農殖嘉穀,三后成功,維假於民.]

P. 7. *How Shun proceeded to remedy and remove the evils inflicted by the Meaou.* 清心,—'with a clear mind.' Ts'ae gives 虛心 for it,—'with an unprejudiced mind.' 辭 is here=訟辭, 'pleas,' 'accusations.' 德威云云,—this is understood to be a de-

明。○乃八節命
三后恤功
于民伯夷
降典折民
惟刑禹平
水土主名
山川稷降
播種農殖
嘉穀三后
成功惟殷

8 enlighten them by his virtue, and all were enlightened. And he charged the three chiefs to labour with compassionate anxiety in the people's behalf. The baron E delivered the statutes *of ceremony*, to prevent the people from rendering themselves obnoxious to punishment. Yu reduced to order the water and the land, distinguishing by name the hills and rivers. Tseih spread abroad a knowledge of husbandry, so that *the people* could largely cultivate the admirable grains. When the three chiefs had accomplished their

scription of Shun's method of governing the people, in opposition to the wicked ways of the Meaou. Ts'ae says:—苗以虐爲威, 以察爲明,帝反其道.以德 威而天下無不畏,以德明 而天下無不明. These clauses are quoted in the Le Ke, Bk. 表記, p. 34, where it is added 非虞帝其孰能 如此乎. Ch'in Sze-k'ae remarks that this is a clear testimony that Shun is the emperor spoken of. It certainly shows that that opinion has the 表記 on its side, whatever weight may be attached to it.

P. 8. *How Shun proceeded in the work of government by means of his ministers.* The 'three 后,' princes or chiefs, are those immediately mentioned. 恤功于民=致憂 民之功, 'to carry out their merits in painful anxiety for the people.' This is Ts'ae's explanation of the phrase, and is better than Woo Ch'ing's, who says:—恤功,以民事 爲憂也. 伯夷至惟刑,— 伯夷, see 'The Can. of Shun,' p. 23. The 'statutes' which E delivered were of course those of what are there called 'the three ceremonies,'—all the canons of religious worship. I am not able to construe 折民惟刑. Gankwŏ defines 折 by 斷, 'to decide,' and gives for the whole:—伯夷下典禮教民, 而斷以法, understanding 刑 to mean 'the laws' of propriety or ceremony. But such a meaning of 刑 may be at once rejected in

this place. Soo Shih, Wang Kang-chin (王 綱振), and a host of critics, go about in vain to defend it by trying to show that rules of propriety and penal laws are essentially the same thing; —see the 集傳 and the 集說. Ma Yung and K'ang Shing seem to have read 㧗(=哲) 'wise,' 'knowing.' Taking that term here as a verb, we get the meaning—'and made the people wise on the subject of punishments;' in which interpretation few will acquiesce. Wang Mingshing, defending this reading, says:—智民 者,民愚無知,今道之以禮 是智其民. But he thus avoids saying anything on 惟刑. Ts'ae gives for the clause—以折民之邪妄, 'to cut off the perversity of the people,' in the same way eschewing the most perplexing characters. The 'Daily Explanation,' however, after extending his words just quoted, adds—使不入于 刑辟. Woo Ch'ing comes nearest to an admissible construction of the passage:—伯 夷教民以禮,民入于禮而 不入于刑,折絕斯民入刑 之路, 'The baron E taught the people the rules of ceremony, so that they were observers of propriety, and did not pursue punishable ways, thus shutting up the path by which the people, entering on it, would have been led to punishment.' The translation follows this interpretation. 主名山川,—'superintended the naming of the mountains and rivers.' Këang Shing gives a more specific meaning to 主, making it = 立山川之 主, 'he appointed the spirits who should preside

于民。○<small>九節</small>士制
百姓于刑之
中以教祗德。
○<small>十節</small>穆穆在上、
明明在下、灼
于四方、罔不
惟德之勤、故
乃明于刑之
中、率乂于民

9 work, it was abundantly well with the people. The minister of Crime
exercised among the people the restraint of punishments, in exact
10 adaptation to each offence, to teach them to reverence virtue. The
greatest gravity and harmony in the sovereign, and the greatest intelligence in those below him, thus shining forth to all quarters *of the
empire*, all were rendered diligent in cultivating their virtue. Hence,
if anything more were wanted, the clear adjudication of punishments
effected the regulation of the people, and helped them to observe the

over the mountains and rivers, and arranged their sacrifices.' This is not necessary. Ying-tă observes that the hills and rivers being as old as heaven and earth themselves, they ought to have had names before this; but Yu's regulation of the waters constituted a new era. Old things were passed away, and the names of those objects were perhaps lost, so that Yu named them anew! Certainly, the oldest names of the mountains and streams of a country are those given by the first inhabitants; as the Chinese believe that their hills and rivers got their names from Yu, this is to us a strong evidence that the country was first peopled, or began to be occupied, in his time. On the work of Tseih, see 'Can. of Shun,' p. 18. His appointment there has precedence of that of the baron E, and so has that of Kaou-yaou as the minister of crime. This is a not unimportant point of dif-ference between the more ancient document and these statements of king Muh. 降,—'sent down;' here = 'taught the knowledge of.' 農 is taken = 厚, as in 'The Great Plan.' 殖＝生. 惟殷于民,—殷 ＝盛, 'affluent,' 'abundant,' or, as a noun, 'affluence,' 'prosperity.' The 'Daily Explana-tion' says:—殷 富庶之意也.

P. 9. *The appointment of the minister of Crime, and the object of it.* The minister of Crime was Kaou-yaou. In the 'Can. of Shun,' p. 20, as here, he is simply called 士. [Under the Han dynasty, however, the passage appears with 爰 instead of 士.] 制百姓于刑之中,—'restrained—regulated—the peo-ple in the midst of punishments;' *i.e.*, surround-ed them with punishments. This was done, however, not with the design of punishing them,

but, as is subjoined, 'to teach them to rever-ence virtue,' so that punishments should be unnecessary. Keang Shing edits 東; and he and others make the word emphatic, meaning 'punishments exactly adapted to the degree of the offence' (不輕不重之謂·輕重適中之誼). This is refining; but it may be admitted.

From king Muh's thus separating Kaou-yaou from the 'three princes' in the last par., both emperors and people have at difft. times been led to place the minister of Crime on a lower level than the other great ministers of State. Kaou-yaou was certainly no inferior man with Shun. Nor was he so in the estimation of Muh. He is mentioned by him last, as it was his object to make all his previous statements converge to the subject of punishments.

P. 10. *The happy results of this govt. of Shun.* 穆穆在上 is descriptive of Shun; 明明在下, of his ministers. These two clauses are the subjects of the next— 灼于四方; and the effects on all the people are told in 罔不惟德之勤. Notwithstanding all this happy influence on the people, there was yet room for the warning use of punishments, as intimated in 故乃明,云云. This is the common interpreta-tion of the paragraph. The 刑之中 here is more favourable to the pregnant mean-ing of the 中, on which I have spoken in the last par. The only critic of note who takes a difft. view of the several clauses is Woo Ch'ing. He takes them all after 明明在下, as

元　德　惟　言　罔　富　惟　訖　典　裴
命　自　克　在　有　敬　訖　于　獄
配　作　天　身　擇　忌　于　威　非　彝。

〇

11 regular duties of life.　In examining criminal cases, the officers executed the law not only against the powerful, but also against the
wealthy.　They were all reverence and caution.　They had no occasion to make choice of words in reference to their conduct.　The
virtue of Heaven was attained to by them; from them was the
determination of so great a matter as the lives of men.　In their low
sphere they yet corresponded to *Heaven*, and enjoyed its favour."

descriptive of the ministers and princes:—
四方諸侯皆惟德之勸故
能明于皋陶制刑之中導
民爲善禁民爲惡民之裴
彝者皆順法而刑不用. This
is ingenious; but the ordinary view is to be
preferred.

P. 11.　*The impartiality of the administration
of justice under Shun.*　典獄=典獄
之官, 'the officers presiding over criminal
causes,' under Kaou-yaou.　非訖(=盡)
于威惟訖于富=非惟得盡
法於權勢之家,亦惟得盡
法於賄賂之人,言不爲威
屈,不爲利誘. 'they not only carried out
the law against the powerful, but also against
those who offered bribes, *i.e.*, they were neither
bent by terrors nor seduced by gain.' This
seems to be the meaning, tho' the language has
been variously interpreted. Lin Che-k'e, for
instance, makes it an indignant expression of
contempt against minions of justice, especially among the Meaou, who gratified their own
spleen and pride by the terrors with which their
office invested them, or sought to enrich themselves by taking bribes.— 凡典獄之吏,
非欲誅殺以立威則欲納所
賄以致富者,若訖于貨謂貨
謂庶貨威者託于威也威
奪者,此皆獄吏之常態也.
罔有擇言在身=在躬無
一不可以告人,有不必擇
而後言者, 'in their persons—conduct
—there was nothing which they could not tell,
nothing about which it was necessary first to

make choice of words, and then to speak.'
惟克,云云,—it would seem necessary to
explain these clauses of the officers in criminal
causes.　Gan-kwǒ did so, and expounds:— 凡
明於刑之中,無擇言在身,
必是 (it will be seen he does not interpret
the par. historically) 惟能天德,自
爲大命,配享天意在於天
下. This is not very perspicuous, but by the
help of Ying-tă's paraphrase and glosses we
can see that the pass. was supposed to say 'that
all judges, with the reverence and caution mentioned, being just and impartial like Heaven,
made for themselves a great decree, securing
long life and other prosperity, responding to
(享=當) the mind of Heaven, throughout
the empire.' This is very vague and unsatisfactory.　　Ts'ae interprets of the 典獄
之官, after Gan-kwǒ, but confines himself,
as is too much his wont, to vague and general
phrases, so that we cannot tell what he understood by 大命, and 配享在下. I
have translated after the 'Daily Explanation,'
which may be supposed to give the more definite
expression of Ts'ae's views. Its language is:—
夫天德無私,能制人死生
之大命,今克典獄者亦無私,人
則之爲大命,德天德而死而在我作,則
矣.命,乃天德在於我可配享于
雖自我命豈不天哉. Wang Ch'ung-yun has called this interpretation in question, and instead of referring
the clauses to 典獄, would refer them to
Shun as the emperor who appointed Kaou-yaou,
and whose careful provision for the administration of justice, was to be rewarded by the

享在下。○王曰

嗟四方司政典

獄非爾惟作天

牧今爾何監非

時伯夷播刑之

迪其今爾何懲

惟時苗民匪察

于獄之麗罔擇

吉人觀于五刑

之中惟時庶威

12　III. The king said, "Ah! you who superintend the government and preside over criminal cases throughout the empire, are you not constituted the shepherds of Heaven? Whom ought you now to survey as your model? Is it not Pih-e, spreading among the people his lessons to avert punishments? And from whom ought you now to take warning? Is it not from the people of Meaou, who would not examine into the circumstances of criminal cases, and did not make choice of good officers who should see to the right apportioning of the five pnnishments, but chose the violent and bribe-snatch-

possession of the empire long continued, and the favour of Heaven. He supports his explanation of 元命 as = 國, by 厥惟廢 元命, in Bk. XIV., p. 5., and that of 配享在下 by 克配上帝 in 'The T'ae-kёă,' Pt. iii., p 3, and by 配天其澤 in Bk. XIV., p. 8. The editors of Yung-ching's Shoo mention his view with approbation, but do not positively decide in favour of it. His interpretation of 元命 is better supported than that in the translation; but I cannot bring myself to admit that king Muh turns here to speak, either historically or by way of admonition, of sovereigns generally.

Ch. III. P. 12. THE KING ADDRESSES THE PRINCES AND OFFICERS OF JUSTICE ON THE GROUND OF THE STATEMENTS WHICH HE HAS MADE, AND URGES THEM TO TAKE THE BARON E AS THEIR MODEL, AND TO LOOK TO THE MEAOU AS A BEACON. 四方司政典獄,—from Gan-kwŏ downwards, the critics all take this as a designation of the 諸侯, or 'princes,' so that the king is addressing not them and their officers of justice, but them only. The view is to my mind very questionable. It is grounded on the appellation of 'shepherds of Heaven,' which follows. That is often given, no doubt, to the princes who rule,—to the sovereign *par eminence*, and to all who hold appointments under him; but why may we not suppose that it is here extended to judges also, whose decisions should always be according to the truth,—according to the mind of God? 監＝監法 'to

consider and imitate.' This determines the meaning of 懲, which is in opposition to it, as = 懲戒, 'to condemn and beware of,' 'to take as a warning.' 非時(＝是)伯夷 播刑之迪,—there is here the same difficulty which we found in trying to explain the 折民惟刑 of par. 8. Perhaps the 迪, in the sense of 'leadings' (開導), is appropriate to the functions of E, whose rules of ceremony and propriety might be considered as designed to avert men from punishments and punishments from them. So, it will be seen, I have translated 刑之迪. This is putting some stress on the characters, but it gives a more satisfactory explanation of the text than any of the constructions proposed by the critics. Gan-kwŏ takes 迪＝道, and gives for the whole:—言當視是伯夷布刑 之道而法之. So, Kёang Shing:— 非是伯夷施刑之道乎. The 'Daily Explanation' seems to get, by a round-about process, to the same conclusion with myself:—惟時伯夷制爲禮典 折民之入于刑而所導播之苗 者不至是克謂刑民 迪者此克作爾時(＝是) 當監也牧惟時所

勤今聽季哉○辭降亂奪
爾爾朕弟伯王降咎無貨
罔罔言幼父曰咎于辜斷
不或庶子伯嗚于苗上制
由戒有童兄呼罰苗帝五
慰不格孫仲念乃民不刑
日勤命皆叔之絶無蠲以
　　　　　　。厥　　、
　　　　　　　世

ers, who determined and administered them so as to oppress the innocent, until God could not hold them guiltless, and sent down calamity on Meaou, when the people had no plea to urge in mitigation of punishment, and their name was cut off from the world?"

13   IV. The king said, "Oh! lay it to heart. My senior uncles, and all ye my brethren and cousins, my sons and my grandsons, listen all of you to my words, in which, it may be, you will receive a most important charge. You will tread the path of satisfaction only by being daily diligent;—do not have occasion to beware of the want of diligence. Heaven, in its wish to regulate the people, allows us for a day to make use of punish-

—I have translated interrogatively here, in response to the previous question. 匪 察于獄之麗,—this has reference to the 越兹麗刑并制 of p. 3. Literally the characters mean—'they did not examine into the obnoxiousness of criminal cases,' i.e., they did not seek to find out either the real criminals or the degree of guilt. From this to the end of the par., we have a striking instance of the long sentences of the Shoo. 罔擇 至無辜,—Keang Shing's comment on this is brief and clear:—不選擇善人,使眾 觀于五刑之中,惟正人任之,使斷上 恃威奪五刑貨以罰亂無辜. 乃絶 制五刑帝不蠲—蠲＝潔, 'clean;' as a verb, 'to consider clean,' 'to acquit.' 厥世,—this has reference to the 遏絶 苗民,無世在下, of p. 5. What was there ascribed to Shun is here ascribed to God; 'showing,' says Sun Ke-yew, 'that Shun was only the minister of Heaven's justice.'

Ch. IV. P. 13. THE KING ADDRESSES HIMSELF TO THE PRINCES OF THE SAME SURNAME WITH HIMSELF, AND CALLS THEM TO CO-OPERATE WITH HIM IN THE DILIGENT AND CAREFUL ADMINISTRATION OF PUNISHMENTS. 伯父,—see on Bk. XXIII., p. 6. 伯兄,仲叔季弟 —these were all the king's cousins, his 兄 弟. Brothers may also be included. On 伯,仲,叔, and 季, see Con. Ana., XVIII., xi. Both Gaubil and Medhurst are wrong in taking 仲叔 together, as meaning 'junior uncles,' 'mes oncles paternels cadets.' 幼 子童孫,—when we consider that king Muh was now a hundred years old, he may very well have had grand-children who were high in office or rulers of States. [Këang Shing reads 僮 and not 童, arguing that 童 was properly the designation of 'a menial' or 'servant,' and 僮 that of 'a young person.' There is a note in the dict., under 僮, to the same effect, where it is added that in the lapse of time, through inadvertence and error, the characters have changed meaning.] 庶有格命,

兆 德 五 休 雖 以 尙 惟 我 天
民 一 刑 勿 畏 奉 敬 終 一 齊
賴 人 以 休 勿 我 逆 在 日 于
之 有 成 惟 畏 一 天 人 非 民
其 慶 三 敬 雖 人 命 爾 終 俾

ments. Whether crimes have been premeditated, or are unpremeditated, depends on the parties concerned;—do *you deal with them so as* reverently to accord with the mind of Heaven, and serve me, the one man. Though I would put them to death, do not you therefore put them to death; though I would spare them, do not you therefore spare them. Reverently apportion the five punishments, so as to complete the three virtues. Then shall I, the one man, enjoy felicity; the people will look to you as their sure dependence; the repose of such a state will be perpetual."

—Ts'ae, after Gan-kwŏ, defines 格 by 至,= 至善 or 至當; and I have translated accordingly. Këang Shing, after K'ang-shing, defines 格 by 登, so that 格命=壽考, 'longevity.' This view may be rejected without hesitation. Nor does another advocated by Soo Shih and Sëë Ke-seuen, to which the editors of Yung-ching's Shoo are not disinclined, seem worthy of much more attention. According to it, the 命=天命, and 庶有格命= 庶幾可以格于上帝, as in Bk. XVI., p. 7. Ts'ae explains 爾罔不由 慰日勤 by 爾所用以自慰者 無不以日勤, 'Let the method which you employ to find satisfaction—ease of mind—to yourselves be only that of daily diligence.' The 'diligence' must be understood with reference to the investigation of criminal cases and the administration of punishments; and hence it is added—爾罔或戒不勤. When punishment was once wrongly inflicted from a want of carefulness, the evil was done; regret and repentance would be of little avail. Lin Che-k'e interpreted 由 and 慰 differently, but not, I think, so well. He says:—爾當 無不由朕之言, 相慰勉而 日愈勤, 'you should stimulate one another from my words, and be daily more diligent.' [Gan-kwŏ read 日勤, which Këang Shing still edits. See Ying-tă's explanation of this text.] 天齊至在人,—these clauses

have been variously pointed and interpreted. 天齊于民 is spoken of the design of Heaven in the use of punishments. It is to bring the people to a state of adjustment and good order. So far, all agree; but here agreement ends. I have put a comma with Ts'ae after 日, and 俾我一日=俾我爲 一日之用耳, as in the translation. Then 非終 and 惟終 are interpreted after the analogy of the same expressions in Bk. IX., p. 8; and it is very natural to do so, because the discourse there is all on the subject of the administration of the penal laws; and the meaning thus obtained well suits the general tenor of the paragraph. Gan-kwŏ pointed—天齊于民,俾我,一日非 終,惟終在人; but his explanation of this is hardly intelligible:—天整齊 於下民使我爲之,一日所 行,非爲天所終,惟爲天所 終,在人所行. Of all who have adopted this pointing, Ch'in King may be said to have succeeded best; and the editors of Yung-ching's Shoo commend his interpretation, which is given in the 附錄, and is to this effect:—'Heaven would by punishments regulate the people, and not being able to do so itself, entrusts the work to me. But Heaven's heart of love for the people is inexhaustible, and I also cannot in one day complete the thing. For associates to complete it, I must look to others, and depend on them.' On other attempts to give a consistent meaning to the

敬 非 姓、爾 刑、告 邦 吁、○ 寧
非 人、何 安 在 爾 有 來、王十惟
刑、何 擇 百 今 祥 土、有 曰、永。

14   V. The king said,   "Ho! come, ye rulers of States and territories,
I will tell you how to make punishments a blessing.   Now it is
yours to give repose to the people:—what should you be most concerned about the choosing of?   Should it not be proper men?   What
should you deal with the most reverently?   Should it not be punishments?   What should you calculate the most?   Should it not be
to whom they should reach?

passage on this construction, I need not dwell.
Ts'ae has here outstript all the other commentators.   敬 逆 天 命,—'reverently
anticipate—meet—what Heaven has appointed;'
i.e., do you seek simply to do justice This
will be to fulfil the mind of Heaven, and also
the best service you can render to me.
雖 畏 勿 畏, 雖 休 勿 休,—the
advice here is the same with that given by king
Ching to Keun-ch'in, Bk. XIX., p. 8; 畏
taken as = 威, and then as = 辟, 'punishment,' being the putting forth of the terrors of
rule.   It is here again—'many men, many
minds.'   Most critics do not admit any reference in the words to the king's own wishes;
and take the meaning to be substantially as
Ch'in King gives it:—'In using punishments,
although people seem to give a dread submission, do not you think that realized; though
they praise you, do not you think what you
have done worthy of praise.   Never be weary
or satisfied, and so your way and mind will be
in accord with the inexhaustible heart of love
belonging to the sovereign and to Heaven.'
Këang Shing edits 祇 事 不 怠 after 勿
宥, and would exclude 惟 敬 五 刑;—
on very poor authority.   以 成 三 德
—the 'three virtues' are those of 'The Great
Plan,' p. 17,—the virtues of 'correctness and
straightforwardness,' of 'strong government,'
and of 'mild government.'

As Wang Yen says in the 集 說:—'Punishments being light when they ought to be
light, this would be "mild govt.," and the
mildness would not be weak indulgence. Being
severe when they ought to be severe, this would
be "strong govt.," and the strength would not
be oppression.   Being intermediate between
light and heavy, this would be "correct and
straightforward govt.," and the correctness and
straightforwardness would not degenerate to
one-sidedness' (刑 當 輕 而 輕 以
成 柔 德 而 柔 不 至 於 縱 弛

當 重 而 重, 以 成 剛 德, 而 剛
不 至 於 苛 暴 介 輕 重 之 間,
以 成 正 直, 而 正 直 不 至 於
偏 倚).   The three concluding clauses
all show the happy result of the princes' listening to the king's advice.   Gan-kwŏ is wrong
in taking 一 人 有 慶 = 天 子 有
善, and then making the other two clauses
dependent on this.

Ch. V. Pp. 14—20. THE KING SHOWS ALL
HIS PRINCES AND CHIEFS HOW THEY SHOULD
PROCEED IN THE ADMINISTRATION OF JUSTICE SO
AS TO MAKE PUNISHMENTS A BLESSING.   This
chapter must be considered the most important
of the Book.   Its contents are what is intended
by the 荒 度 作 刑 of par. 1.   I suppose
that the various things here announced in a
general way by the king were all drawn out,
and had been published, with the necessary
details and explanations, by the prince of Leu.

P. 14.   Preliminary address to all the princes.
吁 來 有 邦 有 士,—吁 is called
in the dict. 疑 怪 之 辭, 'a particle of doubt
and surprise.'   We have had it seven times
already in the Shoo, where our 'alas!' was
always suitable.   But that expression of feeling
is not what we should expect here.   Lin Che-k'e
makes the term on the contrary here expressive
of joyful alacrity (吁 來 者 歡 而 呼
之 使 前 也).   We have the different
readings of 于 and 於 (woo).   有 邦
(another reading is 國) 有 士 may be considered as descriptive of the princes of the
empire generally,—of the imperial surname and
of others.   Këang Shing says that 有 國
(so he reads) indicates the princes outside the
imperial domain, and 有 士, those having
appanages within it; but I do not think we
can thus discriminate the phrases.   告 爾

五 簡、五 于 簡 辭、師 造 及、何
罰、正 刑 孚 五 聽 其 〇 度
五 于 不 刑 正 辭 五 備、兩 十五節非

15 "When both parties are present, *with their documents and witnesses* all complete, let all the judges listen to the five-fold statements which may be made. When they have examined and fully made up their minds on those, let them adjust the case to one of the five punishments. If the five punishments do not meet it, let them adjust it to one of the five redemption-fines; and if these

祥 刑,—祥 = 'felicitous'; here, as a verb, 'to make felicitous.' 'Punishments,' says Ch'in Ya-yen, 'used not to distress or oppress the people, but to give them repose, are called 祥 刑.' K'ang-shing read 詳, and interpreted it by 審察之, 'discriminating examination.' The two characters, 祥 and 詳, might very easily be confounded. [Mih Teih quotes the passage with 訟刑, which is evidently an error.] 何 擇 云 云,—we have here three questions, with the answers to them, given also interrogatively, as in the translation. To quote again from Ya-yen,—三 言 何 者, 設 爲 問 辭 以 致 其 疑 三 言 非 者,設 爲 答 辭 以 致 其 決. 何 度 非 及 = 當 何 所 謀 度 乎,豈 非 刑 之 所 當 逮 及 者 乎, 'what ought you to deliberate about and calculate? Should it not be as to those to whom punishments should reach?'

[Këang Shing, professing to follow the text of Mih Teih, reads—在 今 而 安 百 姓, 何 擇 非 人,何 敬 非 刑,何 度 不 及. But Mih has—女 何 擇 言 人, 何 敬 不 刑,何 度 不 及. Ming-shing says that Mih's writings are too full of erroneous characters to allow his text to be relied on, and that 非 刑,非 及 is no doubt the true reading. That Mih did read the last clause—何 度 不 及, however, is plain from the comment which he subjoins,— 能 擇 人 而 敬 爲 刑,堯、舜、禹、 湯、文、武 之 道 可 及 也. 何 度 不 及 would mean—'what can you plan which you may not reach?' This shows clearly

one of the differences between the usages of 非 and 及.]

P. 15. *The manner of proceeding in hearing cases, and adjudicating upon them.* 兩 造 具 備,—造 = 至, 'to come,' 'to appear;' and 兩 造 = 'the two parties interested—the plaintiff and defendant—having both appeared.' 具 = 俱 = 'all,' 'completely;' 具 備,— 'being fully provided,' i.e., having set forth all the particulars of their several cases. Ts'ae says:—具 備 = 詞 證 皆 在, '具 備 means that the representations and witnesses are all there.' 師 聽 五 辭, —師 is defined in the 集 傳 by 眾, 'all.' Këang Shing defines it by 士 師, 'judges,' of whom there were four, mentioned in the Chow Le, Bk. XXXIV., and who rank immediately after the 'assistant minister of Crime.' Gan-kwŏ for 師 聽 gives 眾 獄 官 共 聽, 'let all the judges hear in common.' The proper construction seems to be to take 師 in the meaning of 'judge,' but in the plural. Chang Kew-shing says:—'The parties concerned should not be one-sided in their representations, and the judges should not be one-sided in listening to the case. If only one listened to it, his intelligence might be unequal to it, and his deliberations might be inadequate, and therefore the rule was made that all the judges should hear the case in common.' See the 集 說.

五 辭,—'the five pleadings,' i.e., the statements, with the evidence, on both sides, whether incriminating or exculpating. They are called 'five,' as the penalty might be one or other of the 'five punishments.' It is important to bear in mind that it is of cases of a serious nature, and punishable with these penalties that the king is speaking. Ts'ae says: —五 辭 麗 於 五 刑 之 辭 也. 五 辭 簡 孚,—簡 = 核 其 實, 'being

審 惟 來、惟 反、惟 過 過。正 罰
克 均、其 貨、惟 官、之 ○ 于 不
之。其 罪 惟 內、惟 疵 五十六 五 服、
節

again are not sufficient for it, let them reckon it among the five
cases of error.

16   "In *settling* the five cases of error there are evils *to be guarded
against*;—being warped by the influence of power, or by private
grudge, or by female solicitation, or by bribes, or by applications.
Where such things are, the offence becomes equal to the crime
before the judges. Do you carefully examine, and prove yourselves
equal *to every difficulty*.

searched out to the very truth of them;' 孚＝
無可疑 'with no room for doubt.'   正
于五刑―正, 'to lay down straight,' here
＝'to determine or adjust correctly,' *i.e.*, with reference to the penalty with which the particular
crime should be visited. Fan Sze-lin observes
that this does not intimate the ordering of the
punishment to be inflicted forthwith, but the
registering of the sentence in a book (非
便用五刑, 只以此情辭
質正于刑, 書當於何等刑
加之也).   五刑不簡,—the
meaning is, no doubt, what appears in the translation; but the exact force of the 簡 does
not readily appear. Këang Shing, defines it,
both here and above, by 誠, 'sincere,' 'true,'
and explains here by 所犯非其誠,
無惡意, 而所爲惡也, 'the
crime was not really intended. There was the
criminal act, but not the evil intention.' The
text, however, does not say anything so specific;
and such a case, we may judge, should at
once be referred to the 'five cases of error.'
Literally we may translate the clause—'If the
five punishments be not examined out;' meaning—if the result of investigation do not show
that one of those punishments should be employed.   五 罰,—'the five fines,'—the
five redeemable cases. These are detailed below. The king speaks evidently of a system
that had been established. We cannot infer
from the text that it had been established by
himself, though it may have been so. This point
will be considered by and by.   五 罰
不 服,—'if the five fines will not produce
submission;' *i.e.*, if such a sentence will not be
acquiesced in as just.   五 過,—'the five
classes of error,' *i.e.*, the various cases of inad-

vertence. What should ensue on the adjudication of any charge to be so ranked, does not
appear. Ts'ae, after Gan-kwŏ, says the result
would be pardon and dismissal (質于過
而 宥免之). Such was the rule prescribed to Kaou-yaou by Shun. See 'The Counsels of Yu,' p. 12,—宥過無大, 'you
pardon inadvertent faults however great.' The
rule of the Chow dynasty seems to have been
more stringent. Wang Gan-shih, as quoted in
the 集說, says that various penalties mentioned in the Chow Le, such as the stocks,
exposure on a public stone, labouring on public
works, were the punishments for crimes of error,
which were not freely pardoned. Some degree
of criminality must have been supposed to attach
to the cases which were thus punished.

P. 16.   *Caution to the judges against being
warped in their decisions.* The text speaks only
of offences that might be committed in the last
of the proceedings described in the prec. par.;
but the same influences might work their evil
effect in the other measures as well. The judges
might reduce crimes from any one grade to that
beneath, or raise them, making them out greater
than they really were, from the same improper
motives. The warning is given with reference
to the classing offences as cases of error merely;
but it was intended to be understood with a
general application.   五 過 之 疵,―
'the maladies of the five cases of error.' Evidently what is intended are the evil influences by
which offences that were not cases of error were
yet determined and registered as such. Gaubil
mistook the meaning entirely, and rendered—
'Ces cinq sortes de fautes sont occasionnées,
1°, parcequ'on craint un homme en place,' &c.
惟官至惟來,—the 'maladies' are
here stated so concisely that it does not seem
possible to give anything like a literal translation of the text. The nearest I can come to it
would be—'The maladies that may affect *the
determining of* the five cases of error are *the
influence of* authority, revenge, closet *influence,*

○五刑之
疑有赦、五
罰之疑有
赦、其審克
之、簡孚有
眾、惟貌不
稽無簡不
聽其嚴天
威。○墨辟

十七節
十八節

17　"When there are doubts as to the infliction of any of the five punishments, that infliction should be forborne. When there are doubts as to the infliction of any of the five fines, it should be forborne. Do you examine carefully, and overcome every difficulty. When you have examined, and many things are clear, yet form a judgment from studying the appearance of the parties. If you find nothing on examination, do not listen to the case any more. In everything stand in awe of the dread majesty of Heaven.

bribes, and solicitations.' The 'Daily Explanation' for 官 gives—畏他人之權勢已 而不敢爭怨而謁女之門，不能謝絕 之聽貨賄請囑均＝其罪與犯人同, 'the offence of this is to be classed with that of the criminal in connection with whom it is shown.' 其 審克之,—'do you distinguish and overcome it ;' i.e., judge carefully, and so that your judgments shall be correct, superior to all difficulties and temptations. Woo Ch'ing says:— 審克謂審之而能得其審 也.

for 反報不公平; for 貨廣干來凡 有其罪惟

P. 17. The care which should be exercised in coming to a conclusion in doubtful cases. 五 刑之疑有赦,—if we give to 赦 here its full meaning, as Woo Ch'ing and some other critics do, and say that where it was doubtful whether a crime should be adjudicated to one of the five punishments, it was to be absolutely pardoned, and the charge dismissed, we go against the rule in p. 15, 五刑不簡，正 于五罰, and the direction moreover would be against all reason. With Gan-kwŏ, Lin Che-k'e, Ts'ae, and the host of commentators, therefore, I adopt a lighter meaning of 赦, as in the translation. Lin says:—五刑之疑 尚不免於罰，而謂之赦者，

蓋雖以金自贖，而幸其不 至殘潰其肌體，是亦赦也. 簡孚有眾,—'the points on which certainty has been attained by investigation may be many.' This construction seems preferable to that adopted by Gan-kwŏ,—簡核 誠信有合眾心, 'the investigations, conducting to an assured faith, may agree with the views of the multitude.' Notwithstanding this result, the king would still have the judges carefully study the countenance and demeanour of the accused. Those may convey an impression of innocence, which will outweigh contrary appearances and presumptions. 無簡不聽—'if there be no *result from* examination, there should be no more listening to the case.' As Ts'ae puts it 然聽獄以簡核爲本苟 無情實，在所不聽 [Këang Shing, on the authority of the 說文, instead of 貌 reads 緢, which he makes out to mean 'carefully,' 'minutely' (微細). This leads him to construe the clauses 其審克之、 簡孚有眾, and 惟緢有稽 無簡不聽 But 其審克之 is more suitable as the termination of a par. or sentence, than at the commencement.] 其 嚴天威—具＝俱, 'all,' 'in all.' 嚴 ＝敬, 'to revere.' Chang Kew-shing says: —具，俱也，謂上所言，皆敬 天威.

鍰、辟、鍰、疑閱疑閱疑閱疑
閱疑閱實赦、實赦、實赦、
實赦、實其其其其其其
其其其罪、罰罪、罰罪、罰罰
罪、罰罪、六宮倍荆倍劓百
墨千大百辟、差、辟、倍、辟、鍰、

18   "When in a doubtful case the infliction of branding is forborne, the fine laid on instead must be 600 ounces *of copper;* but you must first have satisfied yourselves as to the crime. When the case has reference to the cutting off the nose, the fine must be double this, the same care having been taken to determine the crime. Where the penalty would be cutting off the feet, the fine must be 3,000 ounces;—with the same careful determination of the crime. Where the penalty would be castration, the fine must be 3,000 ounces;—with the same careful determination of the crime. Where the punishment would be death, the fine must be 6,000 ounces;—with the same careful determination of the crime.   Of crimes that

P. 18.   *The law of the redemption of punishments.* 其罰百鍰—'the fine is a hundred *hwan.*' The *hwan* was equal to six *leang, i.e.,* six Chinese ounces. Some uncertainty attaches, however, to this estimate. Këang Shing inclines to the view that 100 *hwan* were equal only to 3 *kin,* or Chinese pounds. The coins or metal in which this and all the other fines were paid is called by Gan-kwŏ 黃鐵, 'yellow iron.' Ying-tă observes that 'anciently, gold, silver, copper, and iron, all went by the general name of *kin* (金). Gan-kwŏ calls the metal spoken of here 黃鐵, and that intended in 'The Can. of Shun,' p. 11, 黃金; but in either case he means copper' (銅). It was that metal which was required anciently in all redemption payments. Medhurst makes the metal to be '*silver,*' for which he has no authority. Gaubil says he knows nothing about whether the fine was paid in copper or in some other metal. There has never been but one opinion on the subject, so far as I am aware, among the Chinese themselves. 其法惟倍—倍='double,'—1,200 ounces. 荆=刖足, 'cutting off the feet.' This was the third of the five punishments, and not 劓, or 'cutting off the ear,' as we might perhaps infer from p. 3, if there be no error of the text there. Cutting off the ear

would not be a greater penalty than cutting off the nose. 倍差=倍而又差. But the amount is not at all certain. Ts'ae says it is 500 *hwan,*—double the previous fine, and a degree (次) more.   Ma Yung makes it 533 *hwan* and one third of a *hwan* (倍者倍二百爲四百,差又加四百之三分一,凡五百三十三鍰,三分鍰一也). Këang Shing thinks this estimate excessive, and reduces it to 333 *hwan* and a third (倍差者于倍百鍰爲二百之外又差出二百之三分二,凡三百三十三鍰三分鍰之一). The truth is, we do not know certainly the proportion denoted by 差.   I apprehend that 倍蓰 in Men., VI., Pt., I., xi., 7, is another form of the 倍差 here, and therefore agree with Ts'ae.   宮辟 is called the 淫刑, 'punishment of illicit intercourse.' It was inflicted on the male by castration, and on the female by close confinement (男子割勢, 婦人幽閉).   五刑之屬三千,—'pertaining to the five punishments

罰之屬千、劓罰之

屬千、剕罰之

屬千、荆罰之屬五

百、宮罰之罰之屬三百、

大辟之罰其屬二

百、五刑之屬三千、

上下比罪、無僭亂

辭、勿用不行、惟察

惟法、其審克之。○

上刑適輕下服、下

十九節

may be redeemed by the fine in lieu of branding there are 1,000, and the same number of those that would otherwise incur cutting off the nose. The fine in lieu of cutting off the feet extends to 500 cases; that in lieu of castration to 300; and that in lieu of death to 200. Altogether, set against the five punishments there are 3,000 crimes. *In the case of others not exactly defined*, you must class them with the *next* higher or *next* lower offences, not admitting assumptive and disorderly pleadings, and not using obsolete laws. Examine; act lawfully:—judging carefully, and proving yourselves equal to every difficulty.

19　"Where the crime should incur one of the higher punishments, but there are mitigating circumstances, apply to it the *next*

there are 3,000 crimes.' Acc. to the Chow Le, Bk. XXXVI., on the duties of the 司刑, the crimes to be visited with the five punishments are stated to be 2,500, 500 being assigned to each penalty. By king Muh's enactments the total number of crimes was increased, but at the same time a larger number were classed as liable to the lighter penalties and fines, and a smaller number as liable to the heavier punishments. Thus the Chow Le makes 500 offences punishable with death; king Muh, only 200; against the 500 of the former, punishable with branding or cutting off the feet, he assigned in each case 1,000. 上下比罪,—'above and below compare the offence.' This is understood to be spoken with reference to offences which did not come exactly under any statutory definitions. Their proper place must be sought by comparison with other recognised offences of a heavier and a lighter character. The 'Daily Explanation' says:—法之所定有限, 其有犯而則 犯無窮則 人之所律者, 罪無以上罪疑 而正附其罪比之, 罪疑 無比 以上刑比之

以下刑比之. In such cases special caution was necessary, and therefore it is added 無僭亂辭, 勿用不行. Ts'ae says he does not understand these clauses, but they will admit the interpretation which appears in the translation. 不行＝已革之 法, 'annulled laws' (舊有是法而 今不行者). 惟察云云, Even Këang Shing reads 其審克之 as the concluding clause of the paragraph, thereby admitting the force of the remark which I made on his mode of pointing par. 17.

P. 19. *General principles affecting the determination of crimes and the adjudication of the punishment due to them* 上刑至有 權—上刑 denotes a crime, which, on a first and superficial view, would seem to require to be dealt with by one of 'the higher penalties;' but there are circumstances discovered on examination which 適輕, 'tend to a lighter *consideration of it*.' It must then 下服, 'be adjudicated to the penalty for offences of the next lower class.' The 'Daily Explanation'

中、折　佞　人　○　齊、世　權　輕　刑
察　獄　折　極　罰　有　重　刑　重　適
辭　罔　獄　于　懲　倫　刑　罰　諸　重
于　非　惟　病、非　有　惟　世　罰　上
差. 在　良　非　死、要。齊　輕　有　服、

lower. Where it should incur one of the lower punishments, but there are aggravating circumstances, apply to it the *next* higher. The light and heavy fines are to be apportioned *in the same way* by the balance of circumstances. Punishments and fines should *also* be light in one age and heavy in another. To secure uniformity in this *seeming* irregularity, there are certain relations of things *to be considered*, and the essential principle *to be observed*.

20   "The chastisement of fines is short of death, yet it will produce extreme distress. They are not *therefore* persons of artful tongue who should determine criminal cases, but really good persons, whose awards will hit the right mean. Examine carefully where there are any discrepancies in the statements; the view which you were

defines 服 by 受刑, 'to receive punishment.' 權 denotes properly 'the weight of a steelyard,' moved backwards and forwards along the arm as the thing weighed is light or heavy. This original meaning of the char. appears clearly in 輕重諸罰有權. Këang Shing's exposition of the meaning is here terse and perspicuous:—本在上刑之科 而情適輕, 則減一等治之, 本在下刑之科, 而情適重, 則加一等治之, 宜輕宜重, 有權焉, 不可執一也. 刑罰 世輕世重,—the different circumstances of different times form the weights to be employed in determining the penalties to be adjudicated to crimes committed in them. The adjudicating minds, however, will be found to come to different conclusions. Thus Ying-tă quotes from the Chow Le, Bk. XXXV., near the beginning, that 'in a new country—*i.e.*, immediately after a revolution—the punishments should be light; in a well-ordered country, moderate; and in a rebellious country, heavy' (刑, 新國, 用輕典, 平國, 用中 典; 亂國, 用重典). Këang Shing, again, quotes from Seun K'ing, 正論篇, that 'when a State is well governed, the punishments should be severe, and light when it is in disorder' (治則刑重, 亂則刑輕). This will always be; but an approximation to uniformity may be obtained by what is said in conclusion,—惟齊非齊, 有倫有 要. Wang Gan-shih, correctly and ingeniously, defines 倫 by 先後之序, 'the order of precedence and sequence,' and 要 by 眾 體所會, 'that in which all the different members meet.'

P. 20. *General observations on the character of the men who should act as judges, and on points to which they should specially direct their attentions.* 罰懲至在中,—艮, as opposed to 佞, evidently denotes what we mean by 'good and honest.' 罔非在中 may be understood either of the awards of such men (輕重出入, 不失乎中), or of their character in judging (公正不偏, 無不在中). Këang Shing takes the latter view, but the former is to be preferred. 察 辭于差,—'examine pleas in difference;' *i.e.*, where a prisoner or a witness is making false statements, he will probably not be long or perfectly consistent with himself. Let the judge mark any discrepancy, and follow up from it his quest of the truth. 非從

備　孚　而　克　其　中　胥　明　哀　非
有　其　孚　之　罰　正　占　啟　敬　從
幷　刑　輸　獄　其　其　咸　刑　折　惟
兩　土　而　成　審　刑　庶　書　獄　從

determined not to follow you may see occasion to follow; with compassion and reverence settle the cases; examine clearly the penal code and deliberate with all your assessors, that your decisions may be all likely to hit the proper mean and be correct:—whether it be the infliction of a punishment or a fine, examining carefully, and mastering every difficulty. When the case is thus concluded, all parties will acknowledge the justice of the sentence; and when it is reported, the sovereign will do the same. In sending up reports of cases, they must be full and complete. *If a man have been tried on* two counts, his two punishments *must be recorded*."

惟從,—非從 may be considered as governed by 從. A judge should ever be open to the evidence, and not allow the impressions which he receives to be affected by foregone conclusions in his own mind. Gan-kwǒ connected this clause closely with the preceding, as does Këang Shing:—'Follow up the inquiry from the point where discrepancy of statement has arrested your attention, and find out the truth. Having got the truth, do not follow the statement, but follow the truth' (既得其情, 非從其辭, 惟從其情) This view has nothing to recommend it. 明啟刑書胥占,—'clearly open—(*i.e.*, lay open, unfold. The literal signification is not that intended)—the book (or books) of punishment, and mutually deliberate.' 占 = 度, 'to deliberate,'—as if they were considering the oracles of divination.' 獄成而孚 = 若是則獄成於下, 而民信之, 'in this way the case will be concluded below, and the people will believe—have confidence in—the judgment.' 輸(= 奏, 'to report, send up a statement of the case') 而孚 = 獄輸於上而君信之, 'when the case is reported, the sovereign will believe—have confidence in—the judgment.' Këang Shing, after Gan-kwǒ, takes the second 而 as = 汝, and interprets the whole:—獄成而信矣乃輸汝信于上, 'when the case is thus concluded,

and you have got to the truth of it, then present a memorial of your assured conclusion to the sovereign.' This is very harsh and unnatural.

其刑上備, 有幷兩刑,—the 'Daily Explanation' expounds this:—獄辭須犯而將見又不可遺漏當其上奏而擬亦上裁方自取自謹慎之意. 備載其情辭或一人問擬 雖從重開列取自謹慎之意. 輕罪詳慎精.

[In this chapter there are many good advices concerning the care and the methods with which justice should be administered. The principal thing, however, on which the king dwells is the redemption of punishments, and I fear he must be left with the obloquy generally attaching with Chinese writers to his memory, as having been the first to introduce, at least on an extensive scale, the system of accepting money as a compensation for the most heinous offences. He says, indeed, that the fine was to be exacted only where there was some doubt as to the justice of inflicting the punishment itself. China certainly, within the range of its history, was never the country where a government would, openly and without some glossing of the fact, take money as a satisfaction for transgressions of the law; but it is easy to see how grossly the regulations of king Muh were sure to be abused. I cannot conceive the scheme here set forth to have emanated save from a weak and needy monarch. The prefatory note says that this Book developes and explains the laws of the Hea dynasty for the redemption of punishment; but there is no intimation in the Book itself of such a thing, nor is the statement supported by any other authority. The student meets with

刑。○王曰、嗚
呼、敬之哉、官
伯、族姓、朕言
多懼、朕敬于
刑、有德惟刑、
今天相民、作
配在下、明清
于單辭民之
亂罔不中聽
獄之兩辭無

廿一節

21   VI. The king said, "Oh! let there be a feeling of reverence. Ye judges and chiefs, and all ye who my relatives are of the royal House, *know all* that I speak in much fear. I think with reverence of the subject of punishment, for the end of it is to promote virtue. Now Heaven, wishing to help the people, has made us its representatives here below. Be intelligent and pure in *hearing* one side of a case. The right ordering of the people depends on the impartial hearing of the pleas on both sides;—do not seek for private

the assertion continually; but there is really no evidence for it whatever;—it rests merely on the dictum of that note, for which moreover it would not be difficult to find another explanation.

The Book grounds itself in the history of Shun, and especially on his establishment of penal laws and the administration of them. Now, the redemption of punishments is mentioned by him. The notice is very brief. We are told that 'he gave delineations of the statutory punishments, and enacted banishment as a mitigation of the five great inflictions; with the whip to be employed for short-coming officers, and the stick for offending teachers, and money to be received for redeemable offences.' (See 'The Can. of Shun,' p. 11.) Whatever the offences were that might be redeemed with Shun, those deserving or seeming to deserve any of the five punishments were not among them. Nor does the Chow Le contain anything to indicate that prior to Muh the redemption of punishments was recognised by the emperors of the dynasty. To him belongs the bad distinction of this legislation.

Once introduced into China, however, the redemption of punishments has entered into the penal code of every subsequent dynasty. Two tables will be found in the preliminary matter to Sir George Staunton's translation of the Penal Code of the present Mwan-chow rulers of the empire, pp. 72, 73, giving the scale, first, of the pecuniary redemption of necessary redeemable offences, and second, of the redemption of others not necessarily redeemable, but made so on petition. According to the latter, the punishment of death may be compounded for on a graduated scale, according to the rank of the offender, rising from 1,200 ounces of silver for a private individual to 12,000 for an officer above the 4th rank. The scale for redemption from perpetual banishment is between 720 and 7,200 ounces. And that for temporary banish-

ment and blows with the bamboo is between 480 and 4,800 ounces. Great official corruption and depravation of the general morality must connect with such a code.]

Ch. VI. P. 21. THE KING AGAIN ADDRESSES THE PRINCES AND JUDGES GENERALLY, AND EXHORTS THEM TO REVERENCE, IMPARTIALITY, AND PURITY, IN THE ADMINISTRATION OF JUSTICE.

官、伯、族、姓,—by 官 and 伯 we may understand the 典獄 and 司政 of p. 12. Ying-tă endeavours to show that 族姓 are to be taken, the former as meaning the princes who were cadets of the royal House, and the latter as those who were of other surnames. He says:—襄、十二年、左傳、哭諸侯之例云、異姓臨于外、同族于禰廟、是相對、則族爲同姓、姓爲異姓. But the *whole* of the passage will not support his inference. It is—凡諸侯之喪、異姓臨於外、同姓於宗廟、同宗於祖廟、同族禰廟. There is thus no opposition in the passage between 姓 and 族. By 族姓 we are to understand the 伯父、伯兄、仲、叔、季弟、幼子、童孫, of p. 13. The passage in the 左傳 itself bears out this view. 有德惟刑,—the 'Daily Explanation' paraphrases this by—刑爲不得已而用、先王所以教民祗德者、是有德惟刑、而不當

或私家于獄
之兩辭獄貨
非寶惟府辜
功報以庶尤
永畏惟罰非
天不中惟人
在命天罰不
極庶民罔有
令政在于天

advantage to yourselves by means of those pleas. Gain got by the decision of cases is no precious acquisition; it is an accumulation of guilt, and will be recompensed with many evils:—you should ever stand in awe of the punishment of Heaven. It is not Heaven that does not deal impartially with men, but men ruin themselves. If the punishment of Heaven were not so extreme, the people would have no good government all under heaven."

以刑視刑也 I think this is probably the meaning; but the critics are far from being agreed in it. Gan-kwŏ, for instance, interprets from 朕言,—'My words are mostly those of warning. I feel reverently about punishments, and ought to employ none but the virtuous to preside in their administration.' 今天至在下,—Ts'ae understands this as meaning that 'Heaven would by punishments aid the people, and you, who are in the office of judges, may be said to correspond to it below' (天以刑相治斯民,汝實任責,作配在下). The meaning which I have given requires less of supplement, and equally lays a foundation for the advices that follow. See Wang Kăng-yay, in loc. 單辭 is supposed by Ts'ae to mean 'statements unsupported by witnesses' (無證之辭). The words are literally—'single pleas.' They seem clearly to be opposed to the 兩辭 which follows, and = 'one side of a case,' such as that which will first come before a magistrate. 亂 is to be taken in the sense of 治, 'to govern,' 'to order rightly.' 兩辭=兩造者之辭 'the cases of both the parties.' 無或至惟罰,—this must all be construed as if it were one sentence. 獄貨 is the result of 私家于獄之兩辭 府 is defined by 聚, 'to collect,' 'to accumulate,' and 功 by 事, 'deeds.' 惟府辜功,—'but it is forming a treasury of deeds of guilt.' 尤=殃, 'judgments,' 'miseries.' Literally 庶尤 is 'numerous extraordinary evils.' 惟人在命,—from the relation of this clause to that which precedes,—非天不中, we can easily determine its meaning; but it is not easy to see clearly the force of 在命. We may at once dismiss the view of Gan-kwŏ and Këang Shing, that 命=教命, 'instructions and commands.' The paraphrase of the latter is:—夫天之罰人,非天道不中也,惟人自取之在其教命不中耳. 命 has very much the meaning of 'fate,' and 惟人在命=人自造命,而有以致之, 'man makes his own fate, and brings the punishment of Heaven on him.' So says Kăng-yay, but he throws no light on 在. Woo Ch'ing tries to do this, saying 人之爲人于在有生之命, 'man is man in having the fate of his life;' i.e., men bring punishment on themselves, because it is their prerogative to be by their conduct the arbiters of their own fate. After all, the meaning must be taken a good deal on trust; the language cannot be satisfactorily explained. 天法至末,—the simplest way is to take these two clauses as an admonition to the princes and judges, that if they do not do what they can to insure good govt. for the people, Heaven's punishments will surely overtake them. Gan-kwŏ, Këang Shing and others, take 極 as =中, 'the perfect mean, and highest excellence,' referring to

下。○王曰嗚
呼嗣孫今往
何監非德于
民之中尚明
聽之哉哲之人
惟刑無疆之
辭屬于五極
咸中有慶受
王嘉師監于
兹祥刑。監于

廿二節

22   VII. The king said, "Oh! ye who shall hereafter inherit *the dignities and offices* of the present time, to whom are ye to go for your models? Must it not be to those who maintained and promoted the virtue belonging to the unbiassed nature of the people. I pray you give attention to my words. The wise men *of antiquity* by their use of punishments have obtained boundless fame. Everything relating to the five punishments exactly hit with them the due mean, and hence came their excellence. Receiving from your sovereigns the good multitudes, behold in the case of those men punishments made felicitous."

皇極 in 'The Great Plan,' but I cannot construe the last clause on that view.

Ch. VII. P. 22. Conclusion;—the king wishes to impress his lessons on the judges and princes of future ages. It seems most natural to understand 嗣孫, of the descendants of those whom the king was addressing. Indeed I do not see how the 孫 or the 今往 can be taken in any other way. 非德于民之中,—it is difficult to tell exactly what Gan-kwŏ understood by this. He says:—非當立德於民,爲之中正乎. He then connects 尚明聽之哉 with this.—'If you do so, you will perhaps listen to my words.' Këang Shing connects the clauses similarly, but takes the 聽 in the sense of 聽獄, 'to listen to criminal cases.' The 哉 indicates to me that 尚明聽之 is spoken by the king without any syntactical relation to what precedes. Moreover, after 監 we expect that individuals will be spoken of as models to those who are addressed. I therefore take 非德于民之中, with Ts'ae, as = 非用刑于民之中者德而能全民所受之中德乎. 哲人至有慶,—acc. to the translation, 哲人 are those referred to as models,—the baron E and others mentioned in the first part of the king's address. Ts'ae explains the whole:—明哲之人,用刑而有無窮之譽,蓋由五刑咸得其中,所以有慶也. He takes 極 as simply = 刑, 'punishments,' but it must denote more than that,—'punishments rightly inflicted and duly apportioned' (五刑之施,皆中正之極也). The editors of Yung Ching's Shoo, without condemning Ts'ae's view, direct attention to a construction proposed by Seu K'ëaou (徐僑) and some other critics, who understand 無疆之辭 of 'the numberless pleas, false and true, that might be advanced on any question before the judges.' The wise men spoken of could carry the light of principle and a clear understanding into all this confusion, and referring every point to the laws, bring out an issue exactly accordant with right.—徐僑曰情辭雖難窮,惟智哲人而無窮以辭係法,各協其極,有慶矣. 則用刑雖有疆界,而以辭以理其極自然有見,以來辭之理哲紛燭之自然. 嘉師,—'the good multitudes.' This is a designation for the people, as naturally possessing the 'unbiassed nature,' which is denominated 民之中 above.

CONCLUDING NOTE. The student, after this careful examination of 'Leu on Punishments,' will not wonder that many of the Chinese critics themselves should have been puzzled to account for its finding a place among the documents of the Shoo. They ask, 'Did Confucius mean that it should meet with approval or disapproval?' Ts'ae thinks he admitted it into his compilation by way of warning, and because in the kindly feeling of compassion for the people that breathes in it, it shows that the generous spirit of former times was not yet extinct. It is of no use speculating in this way. I suppose Confucius admitted the Book, because it was the best of the times that he could find. It is a pity that he did not accompany it with some exposition of his own views on the historical allusions in it, and on Muh's scheme for the redemption of punishments.

Wang Pih's 'Doubts' about this Book are:

有不亂極殺報報戒人，乃忍之是盡刑制言謂辭姦意惻人之典聽刑巡末切言與凡而不謂死者者一下不殺者之五之斯愚之本矜聖存於世贖王其一斯者贖往而可必死死生於天人好殺義為人也哉吏獄之哀風變察後其穆至此財情可所得約者者為為忍於聖毫不至以聖虐義法典刑四遺之精為以謂勞為民本如無之人特也也忍也一可之首是之於也乎制凡之法能以非予民乃刑者下章殺非戒立不生有不仁書則苗害書察人語代變其可戒朱匱計以之賞天三而死者人下小好豈於為之苗有大律精聖之三之以尚之也財為術辟之人世矣必生一天者為心至以刑有師不者能識克有世亦姦刑取度以之得大鐵殺後簡而為為忍以之刑之刑徒不審猶其書之用可無無宜以刑千可哉其人也法法而所人意乃也而其恒以於獄訟之遊年權足

BOOK XXVIII. THE CHARGE TO PRINCE WAN.

文侯之命

一節
王若曰父義和丕
顯文武克愼明德
昭升于上敷聞在
下惟時上帝集厥
命于文王亦惟先
正克左右昭事厥
辟越小大謀猷罔
不率從肆先祖懷

1   The king spoke to the following effect :—" Uncle E-ho, how illustrious were Wăn and Woo! Carefully did they illustrate their virtue, till it rose brightly on high, and the fame of it was widely diffused here below. Therefore did God cause his favouring decree to light upon king Wăn. *Thereafter* there were ministers who aided and illustriously served their sovereigns, following and carrying out their plans and counsels great and small, so that my fathers sat tranquilly upon the throne.

INTRODUCTORY HISTORICAL NOTE. The Book of the Shoo at which we have now arrived is separated from the last by an interval of two hundred years. Between king P'ing who gave the Charge to the prince Wăn and king Muh there had reigned seven sovereigns of the House of Chow ; and it is remarkable that not a single document of the reign of any of them was incorporated by Confucius with this volume. Of such monuments there must have been many. No Books have here been lost. Those two hundred years in the dynasty to which he himself belonged were left by the sage a blank. This fact is sufficient to prove that Confucius did not compile the Shoo as a history of his country, or even intend that it should afford materials for such a history. His design, we may rather judge, was to bring together such pieces as might show the wonderful virtue and intelligence of ancient sovereigns and statesmen, who should be models to those of future ages. But in all the space of time of which I am writing, there was neither sovereign nor statesman to whom it could give him pleasure to refer. Indeed, king Woo, the first of the sovereigns of Chow, had no successor equal to himself. But for his brother, the duke of Chow, the dynasty would have come to an early end. There was a constant degeneracy after king K'ang. Its progress was now and then temporarily, but feebly, arrested. Power and influence passed with a steady progress from the imperial court to one feudatory and another, till in the time of Confucius himself the successors of Woo were hardly more than 'shadows of an empty name.' According to my plan I introduce here the names of the sovereigns between Muh and P'ing, and a few particulars of their reigns.

[i.] E-hoo (繄扈), the son of Muh, and known as king Kung (共王), or 'The Reverent' (諡法, 既過能改日共), succeeded to the throne B.C. 945, and reigned for 12 years, acc. to the common chronology. The only incident of his reign of which we find mention is given by Sze-ma Ts'een from the 國語, 周語上, and is to the effect that the king was on one occasion rambling near the river King, in the pres. dep. of P'ing-leang (平凉), Kan-suh, attended by the duke K'ang of Meih (密康公), a small principality in that part of the country, when three young ladies introduced themselves into their company. Duke K'ang's mother advised him to leave them to the emperor, but he appropriated them to himself. Within a year the king made an end of him and his principality, indignant, we are to suppose, at the duke's conduct in the matter of the three ladies. I do not know that this story, as I have given it, is entitled to much faith. None is due to the romantic account of it, which is found in the history of P. de Mailla.

[ii.] King Kung was succeeded, B.C. 933, by his son Këen (囏), known as king E (懿王), or 'The Mild' (諡法, 溫柔賢善日懿), who reigned 25 years. All that Ts'een says of him is that in his time 'the royal House went on to decay, and poets made him an object of their satire.' He removed the capital to Hwae-le (槐里), a place in the pres. dis. of Hing-p'ing (興平), dep. of Se-gan. This seems, however, to have been merely a temporary measure. The 'Bamboo Books' speak of several irruptions of barbarous tribes in this reign.

[iii.] A brother of king E, by name Peih-fang (辟方), succeeded him, and is known as king Heaou (孝王), or 'The Filial' (諡法, 慈惠愛親日孝). Ts'een says nothing more of him than that he came to the throne and died. His reign, however, lasted from B.C 908 to 894. During this period, the chiefs of the House destined to supersede that of Chow begin to make their appearance on the stage of affairs. They traced their lineage up to the baron Yih (益, often called 翳), the Forester of Shun. One of them, named Fei-tsze (非子), had made himself famous at this time by his skill in rearing horses, and was taken into the king's service to superintend

his studs in the plains near the rivers K'ëen and Wei (汧渭之間), and was finally invested with a small territory of which the chief city was Ts'in, still the name of an inferior department of Kan-suh. The king appointed him there to continue the sacrifices to Yih, as the head of the Ying clan or family (號日秦嬴), which thenceforth begins to make a great figure in the empire.

[iv.] On the death of king Heaou, the princes raised a son of his brother and predecessor, of the name of Sëe (燮), to the throne, which he occupied for 16 years, till B.C. 878. He is known as king E (夷王), or 'The Peaceable' (諡法, 安心好靜日夷). He proved a weak sovereign, and was in bondage to the princes to whom he owed the empire. It is objected to him that, when he gave audience to them, he descended from the dais to meet them, as if he were their equal merely. The chief of the State of Tsoo extended the possessions of his House during this reign, and assumed the right of investing his sons with his conquests without reference to the court. He arrogated to himself, moreover, the title of king. The imperial authority was evidently but little cared for.

[v.] King E was succeeded by his son Hoo (胡), known as king Le (厲王), or 'The Cruel' (諡法, 殺戮無辜日厲). A long reign of 51 years is assigned to him, but during the last thirteen years he was a fugitive, and the govt. was administered by two of the nobles. In B.C. 841, the people rose in rebellion, their patience exhausted by the various oppressions, engendered by the avarice, suspicions, and cruelty of the sovereign. The king made his escape, and fled to Che (彘), in the pres. sub. dep. of Hoh (霍州), dep. of P'ing-yang, Shanse, where he found a refuge. Disappointed by the escape of the tyrant, the people sought to wreak their fury on his eldest son, by name Tsing (靖), quite a youth, who had hidden himself in the house of the duke of Shaou, a descendant of Shih so famous in the early reigns of the dynasty. The loyalty of the ancestor had descended to the present Head of the family. As a minister, he had remonstrated, though in vain, with king Le, on his evil courses; he now sacrificed his own son to save the heir to the crown. The people surrounded the house, and insisted on Tsing being delivered to them that they might satiate their fury by tearing him in pieces. The duke gave his own son, of the same age as the prince, into their hands, and on him they worked their pleasure. Subsequently, the dukes of Shaou and Chow carried on the govt. for the prince until Le's death, which took place in Che in B.C. 827.

[vi.] Prince Tsing commenced a long reign of 46 years in B.C. 826. He is known as king Seuen (宣王), or 'The Distinguished' (諡法, 聖善周聞日宣). He had learned wisdom in the school of adversity, and from the statesmen who had protected his youth. Most of the princes returned in a measure to their allegiance, but the empire was distracted by irruptions of the barbarous tribes on every side. In B.C. 821, there was a great drought, and the misery of the people was extreme. The virtue of the king seems to have experienced a decay. In B.C. 815, he neglected, notwithstanding the remonstrances of his ministers, the custom of putting his own hand to the plough, and turning up a furrow in a field enclosed for the purpose, as an acknowledgment of the dependance of the empire on agriculture, and an example to all its husbandmen. He was proceeding to resign himself to idle habits, when the queen divested herself of her ornaments, and accused herself of seducing the king to self-indulgence, and to lie long in bed. This roused him to resume his early ways. In his 39th year, B.C. 788, he took the field against one of the western tribes, known by the name of the Keang (羌), as if they were sprung from the same stock as the princes of Ts‘e, and sustained a great defeat at a place called Ts‘een-mow (千畝), or 'The Thousand Acres.' From the chagrin of this he never recovered. A few years after, he was proceeding 'to number the people,' like king David of Israel, with a view to collect an immense force, and wipe out the disgrace he had incurred. His ministers succeeded in averting his purpose, but he became melancholy and capricious, put to death some of his most faithful advisers, and died in a fit of moody insanity, as we may judge, in B.C. 779.

[vii.] Seuen was succeeded by his son Nëe (湟), known as king Yew (幽), or 'The Dark' (諡法動靜亂常曰幽), who was slain by a tribe of barbarian invaders called 'The Dog Jung' (犬戎) after an inglorious reign of 11 years. In the sixth year of his reign, on the 29th of August (new style), B.C. 775, occurred an eclipse of the sun. It is commemorated in the She King, Pt. II., Bk. IV., Ode iii., as 'an announcement of evils by the sun and moon.' Other symptomatic aberrations, as they appeared to be, in the order of nature are mentioned by the poet along with it:—

'The thunder roars, the lightning flashes;—
There is a want of repose, a want of good.
All the streams are overflowing;
The tops and crags of the mountains fall.
High hills become valleys;
Deep valleys become hills.
Alas! that this man
Will not correct himself.'

This eclipse gives us a point of chronological certainty for the history of this reign. It is the first of the long list of eclipses, by the mention of which Chinese history from the 8th century before Christ acquires more certainty than belongs to that of the earlier ages. The ruin and death of king Yew were brought about by the ascendancy which a female favourite, called Paou-sze (褒姒), gained over him. He had married and established as queen a daughter of the prince of Shin (申. This principality was in the pres. sub. dep. of Tang [鄧州], dep. of Nan-yang, Ho-nan); and his son by her, called E-k‘ew (宜臼), was recognised as heir-apparent of the throne. The rise of Paou-sze was followed by the degradation of the prince and his mother. E-k‘ew was sent, as a preliminary measure, to the court of Shin, 'to learn good manners.' His mother was then reduced to a second place, and Paou-sze was declared queen in her room, and an infant son by her took the place and dignity of heir-apparent. Scenes were enacted like those of Këe and Me-he, or of Show and Tă-ke. To please Paou-sze the king made game of all the nobles. The prince of Shin called in the assistance of the Dog Jung, and attacked the capital. He did not intend the death of the king, but only that of the intruding favourite and her son, and the restoration of his daughter and grandson to their rights. His barbarian auxiliaries, however, could not be controlled; the king flying from Haou was pursued by them and put to death, while Paou-sze became the captive of their chief.

Thus ended the sway of what is called 'the Western Chow.' The victorious nobles having expelled the Jung from the capital with some difficulty, brought back E-k‘ew from Shin, and hailed him as king. He is known as king P‘ing (平王), or 'The Tranquillizer' (諡法執事有制曰平). His first measure was to transfer the capital eastwards to Lŏ-yang, fulfilling at length, but under disastrous circumstances, the wishes of the duke of Chow; and from this time, B.C. 769, dates the history of 'the Eastern Chow.'

The Name of the Book.—文侯之命. 'The Charge to prince Wăn.' I have related in the above note how the Jung who had been called in by the prince of Shin to punish king Yew went far beyond his wishes, killing the king, and wishing to keep possession of the capital. To get rid of them he obtained the assistance of the princes of Tsin (晉), Ts‘in (秦), Wei (衞), and Ch‘ing (鄭), who in the first place drove out the barbarians, and then sent for Yew's son from Shin to take possession of the vacant throne. Among his earliest measures was the rewarding of the princes who had come in this way to the relief of the royal House; and this Book is said to contain the appointment of the prince of Tsin to be president or chief of several of the other princes (以文侯爲方伯).

The princes of Tsin were descended from king Woo's son, called Yu, and generally styled, from the name of his appanage, the prince of T‘ang (唐叔虞). His son removed from T‘ang to Tsin; and in course of time the principality came, though not without a struggle with a usurping uncle, to Ch‘ow (仇), in B.C. 780, and was held by him for 35 years. He received after death the title of Wăn, or 'The Accomplished;'—it was he to whom the Charge in this Book was given. See in the dictionary

下 澤 畛 丕 造 予 予 呼 ○ 在
民 于 資 愆 天 嗣 小 閔 _{二節} 位。

2   "Oh! an object of pity am I, who am but a little child.   Just
as I have succeeded to the throne, Heaven has severely chastised
me, and cut off our resources of bounty to the inferior people;

no fewer than six different descriptions of character, any one of which might be considered to
be expressed by the title Wăn.

In this account of the time and occasion of this
Charge, I have followed the authority of the prefatory note, supported by Gan-kwŏ, K'ang-shing,
and Wang Suh. The Book itself, however, it will
be perceived, does not mention the name of the
king, and the name of E-ho, by which the
receiver of the Charge is called, is only, as will
be seen on par. 1, an occasion of perplexity.
There was a tradition during the Han dynasty
that the Book belonged to a later period, and in
Sze-ma Ts'een's history the Charge appears as
given, B.C. 631, by king Sëang (襄王) to duke
Wăn of Tsin, who was then the leading prince
of the empire. Ma Yung also, we may infer from
his explanation of the characters 義和, held
this view. There is nothing in the matter of
the Charge itself absolutely decisive in favour
of either hypothesis. It seems, perhaps, to suit
better the relations between king P'ing and the
prince (=marquis) Wăn than those between
Sëang and duke Wăn.

The Book is found in both the texts.

CONTENTS. The Book is short, containing
only four paragraphs, which are divided into
three and one by the usual mark of change of
subject in the 'Announcements' and 'Charges'
of the Shoo,—the compiler's statement of 'The
king said.'

The king begins by celebrating the virtue
and happy condition of Wăn and Woo, and the
services rendered to the State by the worthy
ministers of subsequent reigns. He contrasts
with this the misery and distraction of his own
times, deploring especially his want of wise
counsellors and helpers, and praising prince
Wăn for the services which he had rendered.
The Book then concludes with the special Charge
by which the king would reward the prince's
merit in the past, and stimulate him to greater
exertions in the future.

P. 1.   *The king celebrates the virtue of Wăn
and Woo who founded their dynasty, and the happiness of their successors who were assisted by
able ministers.* 父義和,—'Uncle E-ho.'
The princes of Tsin, we have seen, were a
branch of the imperial House; and hence
the king addresses Wăn as his 'uncle;'—see
on Book XXIII., p. 6. But Wăn's name, as
has been mentioned, was Ch'ow (仇), so that
we are brought to the conclusion that he is
here called by his 'style' (字) or marriage
designation. Such is the view of Gan-kwŏ.

Other explanations of the characters were attempted by K'ang-shing, and Ma Yung, which
may be seen in the 後案.   惟時
(=是,=是之故)上帝集厥命
于文王,—this is the common way of
speaking about the origin of the Chow dynasty,
—that the divine appointment lighted on king
Wăn. But as king Woo has just been mentioned along with him, as equally virtuous and
distinguished, it seems strange that he should
be dropt in this important declaration. The
truth is that father and son in the persons of
Wăn and Woo were blended together as *one*
founder of the dynasty of Chow. If the appointment of Heaven lighted on Wăn, it would also
have dropt from him to the ground but for the
character of Woo.   In interpreting the rest of
the par. we may begin with the last clause, where
the king must intend by 先祖, 'my forefathers,'
not Wăn and Woo, but those who succeeded them.
The 'Daily Explanation' would limit them to
Ching and K'ang, with whom the line of powerful
monarchs of Chow may be said to have ceased.
But king P'ing might not have been willing to
acknowledge this, and we may suppose that he
speaks of his predecessors generally, as having
fallen on better times than himself. Explaining
先祖 thus of the sovereigns subsequent to
Woo, the same individuals are probably intended by 厥辟; and the phrase 先正
denotes 'their ministers;'—also generally, without any special application, Wăn's own ancestor, 'the prince of T'ang,' being included among
them. Comp. the 2d par. of the 'Keun-ya.'

謀猷,—see on Bk. XXI., p. 6.   懷
=安, 'to be tranquil.' 先祖懷在
位=我先祖得安在位.

P. 2.   *The king deplores the unhappiness of his
own position, himself young and feeble, and the
empire chastised by Heaven and torn by barbarian
invaders, while he could expect little assistance from
his ministers.* 嗣造至下民,—Gan-
kwŏ, Wang Suh, and Këang Shing, all take
造 as =遭, 'to meet with,' so that it governs
天丕愆. This is quite allowable; but when
we carry on the regimen of 造 to the next
clause,—畛資, 云云, the construction
becomes too forced. I therefore adopt the
view of Ts'ae, that 造=始, and 嗣造=

侵戎我國家
純，即我御事、
罔或耇壽俊
在厥服子則
罔克曰惟祖
惟父其伊恤
朕躬嗚呼有
績子一人永
綏在位。○父 三節

and the invading barbarous tribes of the west have greatly injured our empire. Moreover, among the managers of my affairs, there are none of age and experience, and distinguished ability, in their offices. I am *thus* unequal to the difficulties of my position, and say to myself, 'My grand-uncles and uncles, you ought to compassionate my case. Oh! if there were those who could establish their merit in behalf of me, the one man, I might long enjoy repose upon the throne.'

方嗣位之初, 'just as I have succeeded to the throne.' 天 is then the nominative to 愆 and 殄. 愆, meaning 'a fault,' 'a crime,' is here used as a verb, = 'to deal with as a criminal,' 'to chastise.' The 'Daily Explanation' for 天不愆 gives 為天所大譴 貸澤于下民, 'the necessaries descending like moistening rain upon the lower people,' mean the favours and help which ought to flow from the throne to the people, but which were now cut off. The king is probably referring to his own troubles and the troubles of the people, occasioned by the removal of the capital from Haou to Lŏ-yang. 侵戎我國 家純,—the 戎 here naturally leads our thoughts to the western barbarians, and especially to the 'Dog Jung,' who had killed king Yew, and kept possession of Haou. Gan-kwŏ, however, takes the term in the sense of 兵, 'weapons.' But whether we take it in that meaning, or as a name, we have to understand a verb like 傷, 'to injure,' carrying on the action of 侵戎 to 國家. 純=大, 'great,' or 'greatly.' 即我至厥服,—者 壽 go together, signifying 'aged,' 'men of years and experience.' I do not see how we can discriminate these terms, and hence the 俊,= 'talented,' stands awkwardly by itself. 服=官 or 職, as in Bk. V., p. 3. Këang Shing adopts here a reading current in the Han dynasty, and edits:—即我御事, 罔

或耇壽咎在厥躬（一躬）, 'among the managers of my affairs, there are none of age and experience. The evils are on my person.' This is not liable to the difficulty which 俊 presents in the common reading; but the sentiment does not seem appropriate to the place. 子則罔克.—'I then am not adequate;' *i.e.*, feeble, unsupported; in the midst of calamities, the king felt unequal to the difficulties he had to cope with. 曰惟至 末,—the 曰 indicates that the king thus spoke to himself. As Ying-tă says, 私為 言. 惟祖惟父 is an appeal to the princes of the same surname with himself. As 父, we have seen, denotes 'uncles,' 祖 will be 'grand-uncles.' The 'Daily Explanation' gives for it—爾諸侯有在我祖 父之列者. Medhurst has missed the meaning, and renders—'Of those who have stood before my grandfather and father.' Gaubil has missed it in a different way:—'Quel est donc celui qui pourra me tenir lieu de grandpere et de pere?' 伊 is here a particle,= 惟. We have to suppose a second 子一 人 as the nominative to 綏. The end of this par. thus corresponds to that of the preceding. Chang Kew-shing observes that the weakness of king P'ing's character is here apparent. He shows no self-reliance. He has no higher aim than to live quietly and have tranquillity in his time.

義和汝克昭乃
顯祖汝肇刑文
武用會紹乃辟、
追孝于前文人、
汝多修扞我于
艱若汝予嘉。○
王曰父義和其
歸視爾師宷爾
邦用賚爾秬鬯
一卣彤弓一彤

四節

3 "Uncle E-ho, you render still more glorious your illustrious ancestor. You were the first to imitate the example of Wăn and Woo, collecting *the scattered powers*, and continuing *the all-but-broken line of* your sovereign. Your filial piety goes back to your accomplished ancestor, *and is equal to his*. You have done much to repair my *losses*, and defend me in my difficulties, and of you, being such, I am full of admiration."

4 The king said, "Uncle E-ho, return home, survey your multitudes, and tranquillize your State. I reward you with a jar of spirits, made from the black millet, mixed with odoriferous herbs; with

P. 3. *The king acknowledges the services which prince Wăn had rendered, and praises him.* By 乃顯祖, 'your distinguished ancestor,' we are to understand the prince of T'ang. He also is intended by the 前文人 below. 汝肇刑文武,—whether we define 肇 by 始, as in the translation, or by 敏, 'earnestly,' as Këang Shing does, it seems very extravagant to be comparing prince Wăn to the kings Wăn and Woo. Ts'ae observes that the principles of Wăn and Woo might be said to be extinct, when the ministers about the court were only such as are described in the last par., but now prince Wăn had begun to lead the way to their revival, (後罔或耆壽俊在厥服,則刑文武之道絕矣,今刑文武自文侯始,故曰肇刑文武). 用會紹乃辟,—會=合, 'to unite;' 紹=繼, 'to continue.' But 'to unite and continue your sovereign' is not very intelligible. The meaning is as I have given it. P'ing was a fugitive, and his claim to the throne disallowed, when his father was killed. Then the Jung held possession of the capital. It was owing, he means to say, principally to prince Wăn, that the forces of several princes—which the king might call his forces—were collected, the Jung driven out, and he himself brought back to the throne. 追孝于

前文人,—'with your filial piety you pursue after the former accomplished man.' The meaning is much the same as that of the former clause, 汝克昭乃顯祖. 汝多修扞我于艱, 'you have done much to repair and to guard me in difficulties.' Wang Ts'eaou says:—修,完於殘破之後,扞,禦於侵侮之時.

P. 4. *The Charge.* 其歸視爾師,—師=衆, 'multitudes,' 'people.' The sending the prince home might be considered a favour, as his attendance on the king in the removal from Haou to Lŏ must have been a service of no little difficulty and fatigue. 用賚爾秬鬯一卣,—to explain the 用,='therefore,' the 'Daily Explanation' introduces in its paraphrase—予嘉汝功, 'I admire your merit.' We must suppose some thought in the king's mind, which is not expressed in the text. On 秬鬯一卣, comp. the explan. of 秬鬯二卣 in Bk. XIII., p. 21. The spirits thus presented to him would be employed by prince Wăn in sacrificing to his ancestor, the prince of T'ang, and announcing to his spirit the favour conferred on him by the king. 彤=赤, 'red;' 盧=黑, 'black.' The conferring on a

顯　都　宁　小　能　往　馬　一　矢
德。用　簡　民　邇　哉　四　盧　百
　　成　恤　無　惠　柔　匹　矢　盧
　　爾　爾　荒　康　遠　　　百　弓
　　　　　　　　　　父

one red bow and a hundred red arrows ; with one black bow, and a hundred black arrows ; and with four horses.   Go, my uncle !   Show kindness to those who are afar off, and help those who are near at hand ; cherish and secure the repose of the inferior people ; do not idly seek your ease ; inspect and compassionate *all in* your capital, *and other cities*—thus completing your illustrious virtue."

prince of a bow and arrows was understood to invest him with the power of punishing all within his jurisdiction who were refractory to the imperial commands, but not of taking life without first reporting to the court.   See in the Le Ke, Bk. 王 制, Pt. ii., p. 19,—賜 弓 矢,然 後 征,賜 鈇 鉞,然 後 殺. Whether anything special was denoted by sending to Wăn two bows of different colours, and two sets of arrows, I do not know.   柔 遠 能 邇,—see Bk. XXII., p. 8 ; *et al.*

簡 恤 爾 都.—都 here is most probably to be understood as used not for the chief city only, but for all the other cities of the State. Ts'ae, after Gan-kwŏ, makes it = 國 之 都 鄙, 'from the capital to the borders.' Soo Shih made the 簡 refer to 'the officers' (簡 閱 其 士), over whom the prince should keep a watchful eye, and 恤 to the people, for whom he should exercise a compassionate care (惠 恤 其 民).   It is by no means clear to me that this Charge is the appointment of Wăn to be a 方 伯, 'chief of a region.' That opinion probably arose from the view to which I have referred, that it was duke Wăn to whom the Charge was given.

CONCLUDING HISTORICAL NOTE.   In the 51st or last year of P'ing's reign, occurred an eclipse of the sun, Feb. 14, B.C. 719. He is the last of the emperors of the Chow dynasty, with whom the Shoo has anything to do ; but the 'Spring and Autumn' commences in B.C. 721, with the first year of duke Yin (隱 公) of Loo, and continues the history for about two centuries and a half longer.

It may be well here to give a list of the rest of the sovereigns of Chow. P'ing was the 13th.

[xiv.]   King Hwan, (桓 王), or 'The Laborious' (克 敬 勤 民 曰 桓), grandson of P'ing. B.C. 718—696.

[xv.]   King Chwang (莊 王), or 'The Unsuccessful' (武 而 不 遂 曰 莊), son of Hwan. B.C. 695—681.

[xvi.]   King He (僖 王 ; also written 釐 王), or 'The Essayer' (有 伐 而 還 曰 釐), son of Chwang. B.C. 680—676.

[xvii.]   King Hwuy (惠 王), or 'The Kind' (柔 質 慈 民 曰 惠), son of He. B.C. 675—651.

[xviii.]   King Sëang (襄 王), or 'The Virtuous Enlarger' (辟 地 有 德 曰 襄), son of Hwuy. B.C. 650—618.

[xix.]   King K'ing (頃 王), or 'The Trembling' (甄 心 動 懼 曰 頃), son of Sëang. B.C. 617—612.

[xx.]   King Kwang (匡 王), or 'The Corrector' (貞 心 大 度 曰 匡), son of K'ing. B.C. 611—606.

[xxi.]   King Ting (定 王), or 'The Establisher, (安 民 法 古 曰 定), son of Kwang. B.C. 605—585

[xxii.]   King Këen (簡 王), or 'The Easy-minded' (平 易 不 訾 曰 簡), son of Ting. B.C. 584—571.

[xxiii.]   King Ling (靈 王), or 'The Uninjuring' (亂 而 不 損 曰 靈), son of Këen. B.C. 570—544.

[xxiv.]   King King (景 王), or 'The

Righteously-successful' (由義而濟曰景), son of Ling. B.C. 543-519.

[xxv.] King King (敬王), or 'The Respectful' (善合法典曰敬), son of King. B.C. 518-476. King King (景) died in the beginning of summer, when his son Măng (猛), known as king Taou (悼王), was declared his successor; but he died before the year was out, and does not enter into the list of emperors.

[xxvi.] King Yuen (元王), or 'The Popular' (行義悅民曰元), son of King (敬). B.C. 474-466.

[xxvii.] King Ching-ting (貞定王), or 'The Pure and Correct' (清白守節曰貞, 純行不爽曰定), son of Yuen. B.C. 465-440.

[xxviii.] King K'aou (考王), son of Ching-ting. B.C. 439-425. In the spring of B.C. 446, Ching-ting died, and was immediately succeeded by his eldest son,—king Gae (哀王),—who was shortly killed by a brother, who seized the throne, and is called king Sze (思王). He again was killed before the end of the year by another brother, who held the throne, and became king K'aou.

[xxix.] King Wei-lĕĕ (威烈王), or 'The Majestic and Resolute' (彊毅執正曰威, 秉德尊義曰烈), son of K'aou. B.C. 424-401.

[xxx.] King Gan (安王), or 'The Tranquil' (好和不爭曰安), son of Wei-lĕĕ. B.C. 400-375.

[xxxi.] King Lĕĕ (烈王), or 'The Resolute' (秉德尊義曰烈), son of king Gan. B.C. 374-368.

[xxxii.] King Hëen (顯王), or 'The Illustrious (?),' younger brother of Lĕĕ. B.C. 367-320.

[xxxiii.] King Shin-tsing (慎靚王), son of Hëen. B.C. 319-314.

[xxxiv.] King Nan (赧王), or 'The Ruined and Sad' (喪國忝恤曰赧), son of Shin-tsing. B.C. 313-255.

Nan surrendered the empire to the chief of Ts'in, but the supremacy of that State was not fully acknowledged till B.C. 221.

THE BOOKS OF CHOW.

BOOK. XXIX. THE SPEECH AT PE.

竝 徐 淮 徂 聽 無 嗟 公 一節 費
興。戎 夷 茲 命 譁 人 曰 誓

1   The duke said, "Ah! ye men, make no noise, but listen to my commands. We are *now* going *to punish* those wild tribes of the Hwae and of Seu, who have risen up together.

THE NAME OF THE BOOK.—費誓, 'The speech at Pe.' This Book carries us back from the times of P'ing to those of Ching, the second of the emperors of Chow. The speech recorded in it is attributed in the Preface to the Shoo to Pih-k'in the son of the duke of Chow; and there is a general acquiescence of tradition and critics in this view. We may account for its position out of the chronological order from its being a record not of any imperial doings, but of the sentiments of the prince of a State. K'ang-shing and others placed it before 'Leu on Punishments,' which arrangement, still leaving it out of the order of time, would deprive us of the explanation just given. The speech has reference to some military operations against the tribes on the Hwae and other wild hordes of the province of Seu or T'seu; but we saw that they were in insurrection many times during the reign of Ching, and we cannot tell to what year the Book should be referred. Pih-k'in presided over his principality for the long period of 53 years, and died B.C. 1,062. The speech was made at Pe (費;—see Ming-shing on what he says was the older form of the name). On the situation of this place I give the note of Ch'in Sze-k'ae:—'Pih-k'in had his capital in the pres. dis. of K'euh-fow (曲阜), dep. of Yen-chow, and Pe was in the dis. still so called, in the dep. of E-chow (沂州). Now, acc. to the 寰宇記, E is east from Yen-chow 385 *le*; Pe is 95 *le* to the north-west of E; K'euh-fow is east from Yen-chow 30 *le*; and thus from K'euh-fow to Pe was 280 *le* or

thereabouts. At the commencement of the "Spring and Autumn," Pe was an independent principality, for in the first year of duke Yin (B.C. 721) we read in the 左傳 that 'the baron of Pe led a force to fortify Lang' (費伯帥師城郎). Afterwards, it became the chief city of the Ke family of Loo, as we read again, in the first year of duke He (B.C. 658), that 'he granted to Ke Yew the fields on the south of the Wăn, and Pe' (公賜季友汶陽之田及費). In the Analects also Min Tsze-k'een appears as asked to be governor of Pe (Ana. VI., vii.). We may conclude, therefore, that, in the time of Pih-k'in, Pe did not belong to Loo. But it was in his jurisdiction as the chief or ruling prince of the regions of the east (東方伯). Gan-kwŏ is wrong when he says that Pe was a place in the eastern border of Loo, and Ying-tă when he says that Pih-k'in did not go beyond the territory of Loo. Pih-k'in's speech was like that of K'e at Kan, or of T'ang at Ming-t'eaou, or of king Woo at Muh; *i.e.*, it was made like those when the army approached the territory of the enemy.'

The Book is in both the texts.

CONTENTS. Pih-k'in appears at the head of his host proceeding against the tribes of the Hwae and the wild people of Ts'eu. Having commanded silence, he issues his orders, first, that the soldiers all have their arms in good order; next, that the people of the country take

乃 ○
善 二節
敕

弓 ○
矢, 善
鍛 二節
乃 敕

無 敵 乃
備 敢 甲
乃 乃 冑,
鋒 不 干,

礪 乃
乃 戈,
戈, 鋒,
矛,

刃、 無
無 乃
善。 敢
○

不
善。
○
敢

2   " Have in good repair your coats of mail and helmets ; have the laces of your shields well secured :—presume not to have any of these but in perfect order.   Prepare your bows and arrows ; temper your lances and spears ; sharpen your pointed and edged weapons :—presume not to have any of these but in good condition.

care of the oxen and horses of the army ; further, that the troops on no account leave their ranks or go astray ; and finally, he appoints the day when he will commence operations against the enemy, and commands that all the requisite preparations be made.

P. 1.   *Opening of the speech.   Occasion of the expedition.*   By ' men ' we are to understand all in the host, his own subjects of Loo, and the troops of States whom he had called to aid in the expedition,—officers and common men.   徂 茲, 云云,—there is a difficulty here with the interpretation of 徂茲.   Ts'ae, after Soo Shih, takes the characters as = 往者, ' formerly,' so that the meaning of the clause is—' Formerly, the wild tribes of the Hwae and the Ts'eu rose in insurrection together.'   But why refer to what they had done in former times ? We must understand, on this construction, something like—' And now again, they take advantage of our present circumstances, and give fresh trouble, so that we have to take the field against them.'   This is the way in which the ' Daily Explanation ' brings out the meaning :—往者淮夷叛亂, 爲王室之患, 今又乘我始就國封, 軍旅未習, 乃脅徐方之戎 一時並起.   Gan-kwŏ's view was different.   He took 徂 indeed as = 往,—not adverbially, however, but as a verb, meaning ' to go,'—' we are going,' or ' let us go.'   The 茲 is = 此, ' this,' or ' these.'—' We are going to those tribes of the Hwae and of Seu, who have risen up together ;' *i.e.,* we are going to chastise them.   This construction is followed by Lin Che-k'e and Këang Shing, the latter of whom expounds the clause :—言往征此淮徐戎, 並起爲寇者.   I have translated according to this view.   ' The wild tribes about the Hwae ' are mentioned so far back as the time of Yu ;—see ' The Tribute of Yu,' Pt. i, p. 35.   They belonged to the province of Ts'eu, and why there should be mentioned in addition to them another tribe, called the ' Jung

of Ts'eu ' is a question which cannot be fully answered.   戎 was properly the name of the wild people on the west of the Middle kingdom.   Possibly, a tribe of them had forced their way to the eastern coasts, and settled in one or more places of Ts'eu, continuing to retain their original designation.   Wang Kăng-yay [often mentioned likewise as Wang Ch'ung-yun (王 充耘)] has an instructive and suggestive note on the passage :—' 徂 means " to go."   The passage is best taken with K'ung Gan-kwŏ as meaning—" We are now going to smite those E and Jung."   K'ung says that the various tribes of wild people were simply bridled by the emperors of the early dynasties and allowed to dwell in different places within the different provinces ; but I venture to think that the true state of the case concerning them was this :—Anciently, when the country was first peopled, it was not possible for the principles of propriety and righteousness to penetrate everywhere with a transforming power.   All who were unaffected by those principles were classed as E or Jung, and all who recognised them and came under their influence were said to be Hwa and Hea (輒謂爲華夏).   We are not to suppose that it was necessary to be living outside the nine provinces, in what are called " the four seas," in order to be Jung and E.   In the account of Yu's five domains, indeed, the Man and the E are said to have been in the domain of Restraint and the Wild domain ; but when we examine the state of the empire of Chow, we find " the white Teih " (白狄) in T'ae-yuen [in Shan-se], the E of the Hwae and the Jung of Ts'eu in the province of Ts'eu, the Lae E in Ts'e (齊有萊夷), and the Jung of Luh-wun about the E river (伊川有陸渾之戎).   Even such great States as Woo and Tsoo had to drive out the E and Teih.   It is plain that these tribes were not confined to the two domains to which we have referred.   Shun told Kaou-yaou to restrain by punishments the Man and E who were disturbing the empire, which simply means that he was to punish those who denied the principles of propriety and righteousness, and violated them.   The critics, not examining the case sufficiently,

越　逋　其　刑　汝　穽　乃　牿　今_{三節}
逐　逃　風　○　則　牿　擾　牛　惟
祗　無　臣_{四節}　馬　牿　敏　馬　淫
復　敢　妾　牛　有　之　敢　杜　舍
　　　　常　傷　傷

3　"We must now largely let the oxen and horses loose, and not keep them as usual in enclosures :—do you shut up your traps, and fill up your pitfalls, and do not presume to injure any of the animals let loose. If any of them be injured, you shall be dealt with according to the regular punishments.

4　"When the horses and cattle are seeking one another, or when your followers, male or female, abscond, presume not to leave the

have rashly said that Kaou-yaou took weapons of war to deal with those people. They have not considered that the Man and E were dwelling with the mass of the ordinary population of the Middle Kingdom. There was no occasion for military operations against them. It is absurd to think of such measures as those of after ages,—the despatch of a great general to punish and smite the various tribes of barbarians.'

P. 2. *The soldiers must have their weapons all in good order.* 敹 is defined in the 說文 by 擇, 'to select,' and the 玉篇 similarly gives 簡 for it. Ts'ae explains it by 縫完, 'to stitch and make whole,' and K'ang-shing by 穿徹, which comes to the same thing. The meaning evidently is that in the translation, whatever may be the specific force of this term. The 'coats of mail and helmets' were made of leather, which may have been studded or fenced with more or less of metal. 敿 means properly 'the strings attached to a shield.' The soldiers are required to see that they were in good order. 無不弔 (*teih*),—'in perfect condition.' 弔＝至. Ts'ae defines 鍛 by 淬, 'to put in the fire and then in water,'＝'to temper.' The character denotes the 'forging' of metals generally. 鋒刃,—'sharp points and edges,'—*i.e.*, weapons for thrust and cut.

P. 3. *The people must look after the ground in the line of march, so that the cattle of the army should not be injured.* The charge here must be taken as addressed to the people, though that is not mentioned in the text. 淫舍牿牛馬,—牿 is defined in the 說文 as 牛馬牢, 'an enclosure or stable for oxen

and horses.' K'ang-shing endeavours to explain it from 梏, 'manacles,' *i.e.*, hobbles attached to the feet; but this is to be rejected. As they marched through the country, the soldiers would have, especially at night, to let loose (舍＝放) their cattle, to rest them and let them seek pasture, instead of keeping them in stables or enclosures. They would have to do this 淫, 'extensively and carelessly' often. The critics all define 淫 here by 大, 'greatly;' but the other meaning which I have indicated must not be omitted. Below, in 傷牿 and 牿之傷, 牿 is used simply to indicate the cattle. Ying-tă says:—既言牛馬在牿遂以牿爲牛馬之名,下云傷牿,牿之傷,謂牛馬也. What is intimated about the character of the country shows how thinly it must have then been peopled. With 擾 and 穽 comp. 擾 and 阱 in 'The Doctrine of the Mean,' Ch. vi. 敏＝塞, 'to fill up.' None of the commentators touch on 'the regular punishments' for the offences here indicated, nor do I know what they were.

P. 4. *The soldiers must on no account leave their entrenchments or ranks; and the people must carefully return strayed animals and absconded followers.* 馬牛其風,—the dict. explains 風, with reference to this passage, by 佚, 'to stray;' but usage shows that such straying is like that 'when the wild ass snuffeth up the wind;'—牝牡相誘謂之風. 臣妾逋逃,—the 臣妾 are cam

魯人三郊三遂　逮汝則有大刑　乃糗糧無敢不　我惟征徐戎峙　有常刑。○甲戌　牛誘臣妾汝則　攘踰垣牆竊馬　有常刑無敢寇　越逐不復汝則　之我商賚汝乃

五節

ranks to pursue them. But let them be carefully returned. I will reward you who return them according to their value. But if you leave your places, to pursue them, or if you who find them do not return them, you shall be dealt with according to the regular punishments. And let none of you *people* presume to rob or detain *vagrant animals or followers*, or to jump over enclosures and walls to steal away horses or oxen, or to decoy away servants and female attendants. If you do so, you shall be dealt with according to the regular punishments.

5　"On the day Keă-suh I will punish the tribes of Seu;—prepare roasted grain and other provisions, and presume not to have any deficiency. If you do, you shall suffer the severest punishment. Ye men of Loo, from the three environing territories, and the three tracts beyond, prepare your posts and planks. On Keă-suh I will commence

followers who had to gather fuel, cook, &c. Kin Le-ts'ëang tells us that 'to every chariot there were attached three men in mail, and 70 foot soldiers, with other 25 followers, who are those intended here by 臣妾.' 越逐,—越 means 'getting over' the entrenchments. 祗復之,—this must be understood as addressed to the country-people who should fall in with such animals and camp-followers. Both they, and soldiers who should themselves pursue after the vagrants, are addressed in 乃越逐 不復,汝則有常刑; but the rest of the par. regards only the people who should thus offend. Gan-kwŏ, indeed, supposes that 無 敢,云云, is addressed to the soldiers, against stealing from the people, and Woo Ch'ing that it is forbidding them to steal one from another; but the view which I have proposed seems much more likely. 我商賚汝,—'I will deliberate and reward you;'—the meaning is as I have expressed it in the translation. The peculiar force of 攘, 'to appropriate on temptation of occasion offered,' should be expressed in a translation.

P. 5. *The time is fixed for direct operations, and everything required to be in readiness.* We are to suppose that the marching would be over by the day Këa-suh, and that they would be then in front of the enemy. 峙＝儲備, 'to have collected and prepared.' 魯人 三郊三遂,—the country beyond the capital to a certain extent was called 郊, and beyond this again it was denominated 遂. Gaubil observes that 'it is difficult at the present day to get correct ideas of what was really intended by these designations of the frontiers; and that it is difficult to account for the mention of three *kĕaou* and three *suy*.' Wang Suh thinks that the troops from the *këaou and suy* on the east were left to guard the country, and hence, as only those from the other three went forth on the expedition, only they are mentioned. This was the view also of Gan-kwŏ. Ying-tă, however, puts forward another view, which is inconsistent with this, though he does not seem to be aware of the inconsistency.—In the imperial domain, to a distance of 100 *le* was called 郊, and beyond that was the 遂. In the 郊 were the six *hëang* (六鄉), which furnished the 'six hosts' (六軍), while the

則　敢　乃　郊　殺　無　供　築　甲　峙
有　不　芻　三　魯　餘　汝　無　戌　乃
大　多　茭　遂　人　刑　則　敢　我　楨
刑。汝　無　峙　三　非　有　不　惟　榦、

my entrenchments;—dare not but be provided with a supply of these. *If you be not so provided*, you shall be subjected to various punishments, only short of death. Ye men of Loo, from the three environing territories, and the three tracts beyond, prepare the forage, and do not dare to let it be other than in abundance. *If you do*, you shall suffer the severest punishment."

---

suy extending 200 *le* beyond, furnished, if need were, six subsidiary hosts. In a large State of 100 *le* square, the *keuou* extended 20 *le* from the capital; and as it was supposed to furnish only 'three hosts,' and, if need were, three auxiliary hosts, it is inferred that these might all be called 三郊三遂之人. The language in the text, therefore, is simply equivalent to 'the army of Loo,' and we do not need to inquire further about a 4th *keuou* and a 4th *suy*.

楨榦 are 'the posts and planks' for the framework in which walls are raised in China by pounding earth and lime together (題曰楨, 旁曰榦). From the mention of the 'men of Loo,' it is inferred that there were men of other States also in the army, while they were required to provide the planks and posts, and forage, such labour being easier

to them, as they were nearer than the others to the seat of war. 無餘刑,—'punishments without remainder.' It is difficult to say what punishments are meant. The addition of 非殺 shows that they were short of death. Gan-kwŏ simply says—'various punishments.' K'ang-shing and Wang Suh agree in saying that the punishments were such as would involve the parents and children of the offender, so that none should be exempt from them.

We have in this par. and the last the 'regular punishments' (常刑), which were well defined and known; the 大刑, 'great punishment' or death; and these 無餘刑. 芻茭 are distinguished as 'new-mown grass and hay.'

THE BOOKS OF CHOW.

BOOK XXX. THE SPEECH OF *THE DUKE OF* TS‘IN.

之群告予無士嗟公一秦
首。言汝誓譁聽我曰節誓

1   The duke said, "Ah! my officers, listen to me without any noise. I solemnly announce to you the most important of all sayings. *It is this which* the ancients have said, 'Thus it is with all people,

NAME OF THE BOOK.—秦誓, 'The Speech of *the duke of* Ts‘in.' At the time when this speech was made, the States of Tsin (晉) and Ts‘in (秦) were among the most powerful of the empire. In B.C. 630, they were engaged together in the siege of the capital of Ch‘ing (鄭), and would have extinguished that principality, but the duke of Ts‘in was suddenly induced to withdraw his forces, leaving three of his officers in friendly relations with the court of Ch‘ing, and under engagement to defend the country from aggression. These men, however, were entirely in the interest of their own prince, and one of them, called Ke-tsze (杞子), sent word, in B.C. 627, to Ts‘in, that he was in charge of one of the gates of the capital, and if an army were sent to take the place by surprise, Ch‘ing might be added to the territories of Ts‘in. The duke—duke Muh (穆公)—laid the matter before his counsellors. The most experienced of them—the famous Pih-le He (百里奚) and Këen-shuh 蹇叔)—were against taking advantage of the proposed treachery. The duke, however, listened rather to the promptings of his own ambition, and the next year sent a large force, under his three ablest commanders, hoping to fall upon Ch‘ing all unexpected. The attempt failed. Ch‘ing was warned of the approaching danger; and the commanders, vexed and disappointed, were leading the army back, when it was attacked by the troops of Tsin among the passes of the Heaou mountain (殽山), in the pres. dep. of Ho-nan, and sustained a terrible defeat. The troops were nearly all cut to pieces, and the three commanders were taken prisoners.

The duke of Tsin was intending to put these captives to death, when he was persuaded by his mother to send them back to Ts‘in, that duke Muh might himself sacrifice them to his anger for their want of success. Muh, however, did no such thing. He went out from the capital to meet his defeated officers, and comforted them, saying that the blame of the defeat was his own, who had refused to listen to the advice of his wise counsellors. Then it is said he made the speech here recorded, for the benefit of all his ministers.

That the speech was made on the occasion thus described rests on the authority of the preface to the Shoo, which has generally been followed by the critics. The 左傳, however, while it relates how Muh met his commanders and comforted them, says nothing of the speech. And Sze-me Ts‘een places it three years later, and on a different occasion. After some unsuccessful attempts to wipe out the disgrace at the Heaou hills, Ts‘in made a great raid on its neighbour in B.C. 624, when Tsin did not dare to meet the enemy in the field. Then duke Muh crossed the Ho, and had the bones of his slaughtered host collected, and interred in one place, making great sacrifices and mourning on the occasion, and delivering this speech, to acknowledge and transmit the memory of the fault he had committed.

二節　○古人有言曰、民訖自若是多盤、責人斯無難、惟受責俾如流○三節　是惟艱哉。○心之憂日月逾邁若弗云來。○四節　惟古之謀人、則曰未就予忌惟今之謀人、姑將

2 —they mostly love their ease. In reproving others there is no difficulty, but to receive reproof, and allow it to have a free course,
3 this is difficult!' The sorrow of my heart is this, that the days and months pass away, as if they would not come again.
4 "There were my old counsellors,—I said, 'They will not accommodate themselves to me,' and I hated them. There were my new counsellors, and I would for a time give my confidence to them.

I do not know whether we should accept the testimony of the preface or that of Ts'een on this point. But the thing is of little moment. They agree in making the speech refer to the defeat which had been incurred by the duke's refusal to listen to wise counsel.

The Book is found in both the texts.

Contents. The general nature of these may be gathered from the preceding note; but what is really said is more vague and less to the point of the occasion than we might have expected. The 'Complete Digest' says that parr. 2, 3 declare the fact of the duke's repentance; parr. 4, 5, the grounds of it; and parr. 6—8, the sincerity or emphasis of it.

P. 1. *The duke seeks to engage the attention of his officers.* 我士,—'my officers.' All his ministers are so denominated. 誓告 ='solemnly tell.' 羣言之首,—'the head (= the most important, the chief) of all words.' The duke means the ancient saying which he proceeds to state, and which seemed to him, in the mood of mind in which he was, to be so important. Ying-tǎ gives for the clause—我告汝以言中之最要者.

P. 2. *The saying of the ancients, that it is easy to give and difficult to receive reproof.* 民訖(=盡)自若是多盤,—'people all are naturally thus,—*they are most for pleasure*.' Choo He said he thought that 'this clause simply meant that it is the disposition of most men to love ease' (想只是說人情要安逸之意). This is probably

all that is intended; but I do not see the appropriateness of the sentiment as an introduction to what follows. 受責俾如流,—'to receive reproof, and cause—allow—it to be like flowing water.' The meaning is that the reproof is not resisted, but flows on freely. Gaubil mistook the sense, and has translated —'recevoir les avis et les reprimandes des autres, sans les laisser couler comme l'eau, c'est là la difficultè.'

P. 3. *The duke deplores the swift passing away of time.* 逾 and 邁 are to be taken as synonyms, =過 or 往, 'to move on,' 'to proceed.' From Ying-tǎ's notes on Gan-kwŏ's commentary, we see that he read 員, and not 云. But those terms were anciently interchanged. Whichever we read here, it is to be taken in the sense of 旋 or 運, 'to return,' 'come round.' The duke is conscious that he has done wrong; what he deplores is that the wrong cannot be undone. The day is past, and it will not come again, that he might do differently on it.

P. 4. *He acknowledges his error in rejecting the advice of his aged counsellors and following that of new men, and declares he will not do so again.* By 古之謀人, 'ancient counsellors,' the duke intends Pih-le He and Këen-shuh, who advised him against attempting to surprise Ch'ing; and by 今之謀人, 'modern or recent counsellors,' he means Ke-tsze and the other officers who seduced him to the undertaking. 曰 = 'I said to myself.' 未就予

皇俾惟不仡既番髮然以
多君截違仡愆番則尚為
有子截我愆番良罔猷親
之易善尚我良士所詢雖
。辭諞不尚士旅愆茲則
○我言欲勇旅力。黃云
昧　　　夫力○

Although it may be so *with old men and new*, hereafter I will take advice from the men of yellow hair, and then I shall be free from

5 error. That good old officer!—all his strength is exhausted, but may I still have him! That dashing brave officer!—his shooting and charioteering are faultless, but I had rather not wish him! As to men of quibbles, skilful at cunning words, and able to make the superior man change his purposes, what have I to do with making much use of them?

忌＝其不就我意,乃忌疾之. See other explanations of this in Woo Ch'ing and Këang Shing, the latter of whom adopts a different reading,—as usual. Both their constructions are intolerably harsh. 姑將以為親＝姑且將以為可親而與之謀, 'for a time I thought they might have my confidence, and be counselled with.' 雖則云然 converts the cases of those counsellors into general characteristics of old and new men.

P. 5. *Old counsellors; martial counsellors; and crafty counsellors.* 番番良士,—番 (read *po*) 番 is best taken as＝老貌, 'the appearance of age.' The 仡仡＝勇貌, 'the appearance of boldness;' and 截截＝辯給貌, 'the appearance of disputatiousness.' Gan-kwǒ, indeed, makes 番番＝勇武, 'brave and martial.' The phrase has this meaning in the She King, but we cannot admit it here. It is inappropriate to the old counsellors. See Ming-shing, *in loc.* 番 is here equal to the later 皤, 'old.' 旅力既愆,—Gan-kwǒ makes 旅力＝眾力, meaning 'the strength of all the members.' It is better to take 旅＝呂 or 膂, 'the backbone,' and understand 旅力 as simply equivalent to 'strength.' 既愆＝'has failed.' But 愆 has always a moral sense,＝'a failure,' 'an error,' 'a sin.' We can understand our moral meaning of 'failure' arising from the primary material meaning of the term, but we are called to suppose a reverse process in regard to the usage of the Chinese character. Of all the critics Ts'ae appears to be the only one who felt the pinch of this difficulty, and he supposes that the duke is referring to an incident which occurred on the setting forth of the ill-fated expedition. The three commanders were the sons of the two aged ministers who were opposed to it; and when the troops were leaving the capital, the old men wept bitterly. This led to some strong language about them from the duke, and Ts'ae would make the language＝'There is that good old officer, whom I blamed for his want of strength!' But this is much forced, and after all the idea of the *want* or *failure* of strength must somehow be introduced into the version. Moreover, the duke is here speaking of different classes of counsellors, in consequence of what had occurred to himself indeed, but generally, and without particular reference to the men who had advised, or blamed, or sanctioned the expedition to surprise Ch'ing. 射御不違＝善射善御不違於法者. This officer violates in nothing *the rules of his art.* 諞言＝巧言, 'artful speech.' 易辭＝'to change his words;' such change of course growing out of a change of purpose. 皇＝遑, 'leisure.' The duke says he had no leisure—he had something better to do than—to attend to such men.

昧我思之如有一
介臣斷斷猗無他
技其心休休焉其
如有容人之有技
若己有之人之彥
聖其心好之不啻
如自其口出是能
容之以保我子孫
黎民亦職有利哉。

6   "I have deeply thought and concluded;—Let me have but one resolute minister, plain and sincere, without other abilities, but having a simple complacent mind, and possessed of generosity, regarding the talents of others, as if he himself possessed them; and when he finds accomplished and sage-like men, loving them in his heart more than his mouth expresses, really showing himself able to bear them:—such a minister would be able to preserve my descendants and my people, and would indeed be a giver of benefits.

P. 6. *The duke's conception of a thoroughly good and valuable minister.* 昧昧我思之.—Gan-kwǒ joined this to the preceding par., and for 我皇多有之, 昧昧我思之 gives = 我前多有之, 以我昧昧思之而不明故也. 'Formerly I had many such, because I thought darkly of it, and was not intelligent.' But the balancing of the sentences in par. 5 shows that we ought to stop at 有之, and that 昧昧我思之 must belong to another subject. 昧昧=深潛, 'deeply.'

From 如有 to the end of par. 7 is quoted in the 'Great Learning,' Comm. x. 14, with some trifling variations in particular characters. Këang Shing edits the text here, now retaining the characters in the *textus receptus*, and now giving those of the 'Great Learning;'—but on no critical principle that I can see. 一介臣,—in the 'Great Learning' we have 一个臣, 'a single minister.' 介 gives us the idea of 'resolute.' Ma Yung explains it by 耿介 一心端愨者. 斷斷=誠一之貌, 'the appearance of sincere simplicity.'

For 猗 the 'Great Learning' has 兮.

Both the one and the other = 然, to be construed with 斷斷. 休休=易直好善, 'easy, straightforward, and loving good.' K‘ang-shing defines it by 寬容貌, 'the appearance of generous forbearance.' 不啻謂心之所好甚于口之所言也, '不啻 means that the love in his heart is greater than the language in his mouth expresses' (Woo Ch‘ing).

For 是 in 是能容之, the 'Great Learning' gives 寔, which is an emphatic 是. 以保我子孫黎民=以故能保安我子孫眾民,='on these accounts (*i.e.*, with these qualities, thus endowed) he is able to protect,' &c. For 亦職有利哉 the 'Great Learning' gives 亦尚有利哉, which is easier to construe. Ts‘ae defines 職 by 主 'to preside over,' the idea being that from such a man benefits, and only benefits, would come. His 'office, that over which he presided, would be, as it were the making of the people prosperous and happy.'

之　榮　曰　哉　孫　以　不　彥　疾　○
慶　懷　由　。　黎　不　達　聖　以　人　七
。　亦　一　○　民　能　是　而　惡　之　節
　　尚　人　八　亦　保　不　違　之　有
　　一　、　節　曰　我　能　之　人　技
　　人　邦　邦　殆　子　容　俾　之　冒
　　　　之　之
　　　　　　杌
　　　　　　隉、

7　"But if *the minister*, when he finds men of ability, be jealous and hates them; if, when he finds accomplished and sage-like men, he oppose them and do not allow their advancement, showing himself really not able to bear them;—such a man will not be able to protect my descendants and people; and will there not indeed be dangers from him?

8　"The prosperity and unsettledness of a State may arise from one man. The glory and tranquillity of a State also may perhaps arise from the excellence of one man."

P. 7. *A thoroughly bad and dangerous minister.* For 冒, 'to cover over,' the 'Great Learning' has 娼, synonymous nearly with 疾. For 不達 it has 不通, but that variation does not affect the meaning at all.

P. 8. *A summary statement of the consequences flowing from the good and bad minister respectively.* The general meaning of the terms 杌隉 is sufficiently determined by their opposition to 榮懷. The critics generally content themselves with saying that they = 不安, 'unrest.' But that is the idea conveyed by 隉 alone, as its opposite 懷 = 安, or 'tranquillity.' Now in the dict. the first definition of 杌 is 木無枝, 'a tree without branches,' which gives us the idea of 'sterility.' The opposite idea is conveyed by 榮, 'a plant in the glory of its leaves and flowers.' 隉 is formed from 阜 and 毀 abbreviated, and = 'a mound falling to pieces.'

By the 'one man' to whom such consequences are attributed, either of good or evil, we are to understand the good minister of par. 6 or the bad one of par. 7. This is the opinion of Ts'ae, after Gan-kwǒ, and of the commentators generally. The editors of Yun-ching's Shoo, however, call attention to the opinion of Leu Tsoo-hëen and some others, that the duke intends himself as '*the* one man' of the State. This does not seem at all likely.

INDEXES.

INDEX I.

OF SUBJECTS.

Parts of the whole Book are indicated by I., II., &c.; *separate Books by* i., ii. &c.;
Parts of Books by Pt. i., Pt. ii., &c.; *and Paragraphs by* 1, 2, &c.

T

Y

INDEX II.

INDEX OF PROPER NAMES.

INDEX III.

OF CHINESE CHARACTERS AND PHRASES;

INTENDED ALSO TO HELP TOWARDS THE FORMATION OF A DICTIONARY AND CONCORDANCE

FOR THE CLASSICS.

THE 1st RADICAL. 一.

一 *yth* / *yi*

(1) One. II. i. 8: V. xxx. 6; *et alibi sæpe.* = anyone; but never used simply as our article *a.* III. iii. 5, 6; *et al.* = the first. III. iii. 4: V. iv. 4, 5, 6, 7; *et al.* (2) One and undivided, all-one, pure. II. ii. 15: IV. vi. 3, 4, 5; *et al.* = one and the same, unchanging. IV. vi. 6. = agreeing. V. vi. 9. (3) ? The uniform decision of the mind. IV. vi. 8. (4) To make one, to unite. II. ii. 20. = to consider as one and the same. V. x. 5. = to be of one mind. IV. vii. Pt. ii. 8. (5) Once. II. i. 9: V. xx. 14. (6.) 一二, one or two, = a few. V. ix. 4. = we. V. xxiii. 1. = you. V. xxiii. 6. (7) 一人, the one man. = the emperor. *Sæpissime.* V. xxx. 8, is doubtful.

丁 *ting*

The fourth of the calendaric stem-characters. IV. xxii. 12; *et al.* 武丁, one of the kings of the Shang dynasty. V. xvi. 7.

七 *ts'eih* / *ch'i*

Seven. I. i. 12; *et sæpe.* = the seventh. V. iv. 4, 7, 20. 七政, the seven Directors, *i.e.*, the sun, moon, and five planets. II. i. 5.

三 *san*

(1) Three. I. i. 8; *et sæpe.* = the third. III. iii. 7; *et al.* = three classes. V. xxi. 10. (2) Thrice. V. xviii. 23; *et al.* = repeatedly. III. iii. 5. (3) 三苗, the country of the Meaou. II. i; *et al.* 三危, the name of a country. II. i. 12; *et al.* (4) 三帛, II. i. 8. 三就 and 三居, II. i. 20. 三禮, II. i. 23. 三考, II. i. 27. 三事, the three businesses. II. ii. 8. The same phrase is used differently in V. xix. 7, and xx. 21. 三德, II. iii. 4. The phrase has a different and more specific meaning in V. iv. 17, and xxvii. 18. 三品, III. i. Pt. i. 44, 32. 三錯, III. i. Pt. i. 68. 三壤, III. i. Pt. ii. 15. 三正, the three months on which the year might be made to commence; but the meaning is doubtful. III., ii. 3. 三風, IV. iv. 7. 三王, king Wăn, his father, and grandfather. V. vi. 5. 三宅 and 三俊, V. xix. 4, 6. 三毫, V. xix. 11. 三公 and 三孤, the highest ministers under the Chow dynasty. V. xx. 5, 6. 三紀, V. xxiv. 3. 三后, the duke of Chow, Keun-ch'in, and the duke of Peih. V. xxiv. 13. Other persons are intended by the phrase in xxvii. 8. 三郊三遂, V. xxix. 5. 三江, III. i. Pt. i. 40. 三澨, the three great dykes. III. i. Pt. ii. 8. (4) 二三, now two, now three, unstable. IV. vi. 5.

上 *shang* / *chang*

Above. that which is above;—used of place, time, and rank. Used for Heaven, the supreme Power. IV. vii. Pt. ii. 7, 12; *et al.* In the 12th par., however, and not a few other places, the idea is not so much of Heaven as the Power, but as the place whence the power comes forth. Used for the sovereign, and superiors generally. IX. vi. 7: V. xxi. 14: *et al.* Used for early ages. IV. xi. 1. The highest in quality or class. III. i. Pt. i. 8, 25, 34; *et al. sæpe.* 上公, a *kung* of the highest class. V. viii. 3. 上宗 V. xxii. 23, 26. 上天, the supreme Heaven, IV. ii. 3; but compare IV. iii. 4. 上帝, God;—see 帝. 上日, the first day. II. i. 4. 上下 constantly appear as correlates, = high and low; heaven and earth; Heaven and the people; the sovereign and the people; the sovereign and his ministers; mountains and marshes. Observe 在上, IV. x. 6; also V. xxii. 21.

The usage of 上 as a preposition, with 在 or 於 preceding, is unknown in the Shoo.

土
shang
chang

Up. 2d tone. To ascend; upwards. V. iv. 5. To send up. V. xxvi. 20.

下
hëa
hsia

(1) Beneath, that which is below;— used of place, time, and rank. It stands often for the people, or inferiors generally; but the phrase 下民, the inferior people, is very common, as in I. i. 11: II. i. 2: V. xxvi. 2; &c. The lowest in quality or class. III. i. Pt. i. 18, 25; *et al.* Spoken of after times, or later ages. IV. xi. 1: V. xxvii. 5. Used often for ministers. II. ii. 12: V. xxiv. 5; *et al.* 天之下, all under heaven. II. iv. 7. 天下, as a designation of the empire, is common. 下土, the low grounds. III. i. Pt. i. 58. 下地, this lower world, in app. to 帝庭, the court of God. V. vi. 7. 下國, the States of the empire. V. i. Pt. ii. 4. (2) As a verb. To keep under, to down-tread. III. iii. 4. (3) 上下, as correlates. See on 上.

To descend, = downwards. V. iv. 5.

下
hëa
hsia

不
puh
pu

Not. *Passim.* With other negatives, —罔, 莫, 無, conveying a strong affirmation. Observe also 不無, IV. x. 7. It is itself repeated with the same effect, having another character between,— 不可不, 不敢不, 不睯不. Observe how, like other negatives, it attracts the object of the verb to itself in V. ix. 22: xiv. 22.

The second of the calendaric branch-characters. IV. iv. 1: V. xxii. 10.

丑
ch'ow
ch'ou

丕
p'ei
p'i

Great; greatly. The adverbial use is the more frequent. II. ii. 14: iv. 2: III. i. Pt. i. 78; *et al. sæpe.* It is repeated,— 丕丕, = vast. V. vii. 9: xiv. 15. 丕子, the great son *of Heaven,* = the emperor. V. vi. 5. 丕時, a time of great prosperity. V. xvi. 20.

世
she
shih

(1) An age, a generation; ages. II. ii. 8, 12: IV. ii. 1; *et al.* Adverbially, = for ages, from age to age. IV. vii. Pt. i. 14: V. i. Pt. iii. 4; *et al.* So, 世世 V. viii. 4. 世輕世重, in one generation and in another, &c. V. xxvii. 19. 厥世, his age, all his life. IV. v. Pt. ii. 9. Obs. 七世之廟, IV. vi. 4. (2) = hereditary possession, a hold on successive ages; the hereditary principle. II. iv. 8: V. i. Pt. i. 5: xxvii. 5, 12.

The third of the calendaric stem-characters. V. xi. 2.

丙
ping

A hillock; a height. III. i. Pt. i. 16, 陶丘, the hill of T'aou. III. i. Pt. ii. 10.

丘
k'ew
ch'iu

I. q. 竝, together. See 竝.

並
ping

THE 2D RADICAL. |.

中
chung

The middle, that which is in the middle —used of place, time, quality, and rank. III. i. Pt. i., 8, 18, 25; &c. The Mean; to hold the course of the Mean. II. ii. 15: IV. ii. 8: V. xvii. 7: xxv. 4: xxi. 8: xxvii. 4. = impartially. V. xxvii. 22. Used absolutely, = in the middle, with ref. to time IV. ix. 3; with ref. to place, V. xiii. 23. 于......中, 于......之中, used both of place and metaphorically. V. vi. 11: xiii. 14: xxvii. 9, 10, 12. 在中 xxvii. 20. 日中, 宵中. I. i. 4, 6, where 中 = of the medium length. But 日中, V. xv. 10, — midday, and 中夜, V. xxvi. 1, — midnight. 中身, V. xv. 11, — the middle of life. 中邦, the middle region or regions. III. i. Pt. ii. 15. 中國. V. xi. 1. 中江, a part of the Këang. III. Pt. ii. 9. 中宗, one of the kings of the Shang dynasty. V. xv. 4, 16.

That which hits, appropriate. V. xiv. 24. It is very doubtful whether we should acknowledge two tones of 上, 下, and 中, in the Shoo.

中
chung

THE 3D RADICAL. ﹑.

丹 *tan*

(1) Cinnabar. III. i. Pt. i. 52. (2) To paint with vermilion. V. xi. 4. (3) The name of the appanage of Yaou's son, Choo. II. iv. 8.

主 *choo* chu

(1) A lord or ruler. III. ii. 2. The emperor is 民主, III. vi. 11 : V. xviii. 6, 8, 18; and 神主, IV. vi. 3. (2) To regard—be regarded—as the chief thing. II. vi. 8. To preside over. V. xxvii. 8.

THE 4TH RADICAL. 丿.

乂 *e* ai

(1) To regulate, to correct; to be regulated, brought to order. I. i. 11, 12 : II. ii. 2 : IV. ii. 2 : *et al. sæpe.* Sometimes the meaning simply = to aid. V. xiv. 9 : xviii. 21 ; *et al.* It is often found with 保, V. xvi. 8, 10 : *et al.* Used adverbially. V. iv. 4. = orderliness. V. iv. 6, 34. (2) Men of eminence, of a hundred. II. iii. 4 : IV. viii. Pt. iii. 7.

乃 *nae* nai

Passim. Two usages are met with everywhere. (1) As a particle, at the beginning of paragraphs, and after the subject of a clause. The idea of connection which it expresses is very various, = thereupon. so, however, &c. I. i. 3, 11 : II. i. 1, 7, 8, 13, 28; *et al.* (2) As a possessive pronoun, = your. Once, in II. 13, it is used for you in the objective; but it is seldom if ever, used in the nominative. I. i. 3 : ii. 8, 11, 14, 17, 20 ; *et al.* It is also used (3) as the copula; but this is less common. II. ii. 21 : IV. vi. 6 : V. xxvii. 10. Sometimes, however, we are in doubt whether to take it as a particle or as the copula. Often likewise we might resolve cases of the second usage into its verbal force. This appears especially where we have to translate it in the third person, as in V. xvi. 18 : xxi. 2. *Obs.* also 由乃在位, IV. vii. Pt. i. 5.

之 *che* chih

(1) Of. The sign of the possessive case. The regent follows the 之, and the regimen precedes it. They may be respectively a noun, a phrase, or a larger clause. (2) Him, her, it, them. The antecedent, however, has often to be gathered from the context; as in II. ii. 7 : iii. 2 : iv. 6 : *et al.* (3) We have 之 and another objective, as in 邦之蔡, V. xvii. 1, and other places. Some of these instances are peculiar. *E. G.* III. iii. 9 ; *et al.* (4) The idiom 之謂 occurs only once. V. iv. 6. 有之, has it, = says, also occurs only once. III. iii. 6. So also 若之何. IV. xi. 3. Such cases as 惟刑之恤 may be re-

duced to (1), V. xvii. 4, 惟德是輔, 惟惠之懷, shows clearly how they are to be understood. Observe 侵于之彊, V. i. Pt. ii. 8, where the text is probably imperfect. 之 occurs everywhere, but not so frequently as in the Four Books. (5) In V. xix. 13, 21 之 = 及, and.

乎 *hoo* hu

This only occurs four times in the Shoo (1) A part. of interrogation. I. i. 9. (2) A preposition. II. iii. 2. (3) An exclamation. III. iii. 5, 9.

乘 *shing* ch'êng

To mount on, to sail in. II. iv. 1 : IV. vii. Pt. ii. 6. To support, maintain. V. xvi. 18.

乘 *shing* ch'êng

3d tone. (1) The numeral for carriages. V. xvii. 1. (2) A team of four horses. V. xxiii. 1.

THE 5TH RADICAL. 乙.

乙 *yih* yi

The second calendaric stem-character IV. iv. 1 : V. xii. 1 ; *et al.* 祖乙 and 帝乙, two kings of the Shang dynasty. V. xvi. 7, and V. x. 9 : xiv. 7 · xviii. 10.

九 *kew* chiu

Nine. *Sæpe.* The ninth. V. iv. 4, 39. 九州, the nine provinces into which Yu divided the empire. III. i. Pt. ii. 14. 九有, the empire, as consisting of those provinces. IV. vi. 2, 3. 九山, 九川, 九澤, the hills, &c., in those provinces. III. i. Pt. ii. 14. We have also 九族, the nine classes of kindred. I. i. 2 ; *et al.* 九功, 九歌, II. ii. 7. 九德, II. iii. 4 : *et al.* 九成, II. iv. 9. 九河. III. i. Pt. i. 13 : *et al.* 九江. III. i. Pt. i. 48 ; *et al.* 九疇, V. iv. 3. 九夷. V. v. 1. 九牧, V. xx. 13.

亂 *lwan* luan

(1) To govern, to bring into good order ; a state of good order. II. iii. 3 : IV. vii. Pt. ii. 14 ; Pt. iii. 6 : *et sæpe.* (2) To throw into disorder, disorderly ; rebellion. III. iii. 7 : iv. 4 : IV. i. 1 : ii. 2, 7 ; *et sæpe.* (3) To ferry across. III. i. Pt. i. 70.

THE 6TH RADICAL. 亅

予

I, me; my. *Passim.* The phrases 予一人 and 予小子, are constantly used by the emperors in speaking of themselves. 予沖人, and some others, are also found. In V. vi. 10, 予

一人 =our emperor. It is also plural. We, us; our. III. iii. 9 : IV. i. 3 : ii. 6 : *et al.*

事
sze
shih

(1) An affair; business; the course and conduct of business. II. i. 3 : III. iv. 3 : IV. 1, 2 : V. xxiv. 6, 15; *et sæpe.* 事事, all affairs. IV. viii. Pt. ii. 8. 三事, see 三. 五事, V. iv. 4, 9. 六事, III. ii. 2. 御事 and 執事 are common. See 御 and 執. The use of 事, 宅事, and 立事, in V. xix. is peculiar. (2) As a verb. To be engaged, have business to do. II. iii. 4. To serve,—God, man, spirits. IV. vi. 11 : viii. Pt. ii. 11 : V. i. Pt. 1. 6 : xviii. 1 ; *et al.*

THE 7TH RADICAL. 二.

二
urh

Two, *Sæpe.* The second. II. i. 8 : III. iii. 6 : V. iv. 4, 5, 7, 8 ; *et al.* 一二, see 一. 二三, see 三. 二生, two living animals. II. i. 8.

于
yu
yü

(1) A preposition, following both transitive and intransitive verbs. Its proper meaning is *in, on ;* but it may be translated very variously,—to, at, in the case of, from, against, &c. *Passim.* (2) Than. Forming the comparative degree. IV. vii. Pt. iii. 4 : V. i. Pt. ii. 5, 8 ; *et al.* (3) To proceed, to go forward. V. iii. 1 : vii. 5, 6 : and perhaps elsewhere.

云
yun
yün

(1) To speak. IV. xi. 8 : V. xxx. 4. (2) To come round, return. V. xxx. 3.

五
woo
wu

Five. The fifth. III. 9 : V. iv. 4. 5, 39, 40 : *et al.* We have 五品, II. i. 19 : 五典, II. i. 1, 9 : V. xv. 14 ; xxv. 4 ; *et al.;* 五教, II. i. 19 ; *et al.;* and 五常, V. i. Pt. iii. 2 ;—all connected in signification. 五瑞, II. i. 7 ; and 五玉, II. i. 8 ;—also connected. 五禮, II. i. 8 ; *et al.* 五刑, II. i. 11 ; *et al.,* *sæpe.* 五服, II. i. 20 ; with a difft. meaning, II. iii. 6 ; with a third meaning, II. iv. 8. 五流 and 五宅, II. i. 20. 五辰, II. iii. 4. 五章; 五色; 五采; 五聲; 五言 ; II. iv. 4. 五行, III. ii. 3 : V. iv. 3, 4. 五事, see 事.

井
tsing
ching

A well, = hamlets. V. xxiv. 7.

亞
ya

Secondary. = officers of inferior rank. V. ii. 2 : x. 10 : xix. 10.

THE 8TH RADICAL. 亠.

亡
wang

(1) To perish, come to ruin. II. iii. 6, 7 ; *et al.* To be going on to ruin. IV. ii. 7. (2) To flee away, to escape. V. xii. 10.

变
këaou
chiao

Together, one with another. III. i. Pt. ii. 15 : V. xxvi. 4. Obs. IV. viii. Pt. iii. 2.

亦
yih
yi

Also, and moreover : even. *Passim.* It is often followed by other particles,— 亦惟, 亦越, 亦則,—in a way which we do not find in the Four Books; but it always indicates the *addition* of some circumstance or consideration. II. iii. 1. is peculiar, and there perhaps it = altogether.

亥
hae
hai

The last of the calendaric branch characters. V. iii. 8 : xviii. 1.

享
hëang
hsiang

(1) To present offerings. V. xi. 5 : xiii. 12 : xviii. 29. To offer sacrifice. IV. vii. Pt. i. 14 : V. i. Pt. iii. 25. (2) To confer dignities. V. x. 16. The dignity conferred. V. ix. 23, 24. (3) To enjoy. V. viii. 4 : xiii. 21. With the object expressed, as 國, 命. V. xv. 4, 5, 6, 11 : xxviii. 1, 11 ; *et al.* = to accept a sacrifice. IV. v. Pt. iii. 1. = to satisfy. IV. vi. 3. (4) 南变, the name of a place. I. i. 5.

亮
leang
liang

(1) To aid. II. i. 17, 26. (2) Brilliant; to display brilliantly. II. iii. 4 : V. xx. 6 : xxiv. 5.

亮
lëang
liang

Low. 1st tone. In the phrase 亮陰, the emperor's mourning shed. IV. viii. Pt. i. 1 : V. xv. 5.

亳
pŏ
po

The name of T'ang's capital. IV. iii. 1 : iv. 2 : v. Pt. ii. 1 : viii. Pt. iii. 1. There were three places of this name,— 三亳. V. xix. 11.

亶
tan

Sincere. V. i. Pt. i. 3. Sincerity. V. xvi. 18. To make sincere. IV. vii. Pt. ii. 1.

THE 9TH RADICAL. 人.

人
jin
jên

A man, men ; man = humanity ; = inhabitants. *Passim* = others, opp. to one's self. II. ii. 3 ; *et al.* = every man. IV. xi. 9. 罪人, criminals, IV. iii. 5 : V. vi. 14. Similarly, with characters and phrases, it everywhere forms concrete nouns We may notice 一人, see 一; 遒人, III. iv. 3 ; 冲人, V. vii. 10, *et al.;* 格人, IV. x. 2 ; 庶人, all the people, V. iv. 25 : 小人 the inferior people, V. xv. 18, *et al.;* and sometimes = mean men, II. ii. 20 ; 王人, members of the imperial House, V. xvi. 9 : 準人,

V. xix. 1, 12, 16, 19; 藝人, V. xix. 9; 宗人, V. xxi. 27, 28; 臣人, — great officers, III. iv. 2 : V. xxi. 4, 6.

仁
jin
jĕn

Benevolence : benevolent. IV. ii. 5 : v. Pt. iii. 1. 仁人, benevolent or virtuous men. V. i. Pt. ii. 6 : iii. 6. = lovingly. V. vi. 4. This character only occurs these five times.

仇
k'ew
ch'ou

To be hostile to. III. iii. 9 : IV. ii. 6. 作仇, to contract mutual animosities. V. i. Pt. ii. 3.

今
kin
chin

Now. *Passim.* 今日, to-day, the present time. V. xv. 13 : xvi. 21. Observe 今...今翼日, V. vii. 5; 繼自今, V. xviii. 18; *et al.;* 今其有 今罔後, IV. vii. Pt. ii. 7.

介
kĕae
chieh

(1) To aid, co-operate with. V. x. 7 : xii. 15 : xviii. 21, 27, 28. (2) Great. V. xxii. 23. (3) Resolute. V. xxx. 6.

仍
jing
jĕng

= usual, ordinary. V. xxii. 15, 16, 17, 18.

他
t'a
ta

Other. V. xxx. 6.

付
foo
fu

To give. V. xi. 6 : xxiii. 5.

仞
jin
jĕn

A measure of eight cubits. We may call it a fathom. V. v. 9.

仡
yih
yi

仡仡. Bold, martial-like. V. xxx. 5.

代
tae
tai

(1) Instead of ; to supersede. II. iii. 5 : IV. iv. 3 : viii. Pt. i. 2 : V. vi. 5, 16 : xviii. 8. (2) A dynasty. V. xx. 4.

令
ling
lĕng

(1) An order, commands. IV. viii. Pt. i. 1 : V. xx. 15 : xxvi. 2. (2) Good, excellent. IV. v. Pt. iii. 3 : V. viii. 3 : xxi. 1 : xxvii. 21. = insinuating. II. iii. 2 : V. xxvi. 5.

以
e
i

Passim. Several usages are marked distinctly enough. (1) At the beginning of sentences or clauses, being followed by a noun or substantive clause, after which comes the predicate of the sentence, it = to take, to use. *E. g.* I. i. 12 : II. i. 20 : iv. 4 : IV. iii. 1 : *et sæpe.* Sometimes the predicate and object are expressed by a single verb, and we have cases, such as are mentioned in Index III. to Mencius' Works, where it has been supposed that 以 is merely a sign of the accusative. *E. g.* IV. vii. Pt. ii. 1, 6. (2) Following the principal verb of the sentence, and followed by a noun, it = a preposition, and may be variously translated,—by, with, on the ground of, &c. I. i. 12 : II. i. 1, 9, 11 ; *et sæpe.* In sentences of four characters, such as 以宜制事, we see how this usage and the last may

run into each other. (3) Where it stands singly between the subject and predicate of the sentence, it = thereby. *E. g.* II. i. 24 : IV. v. Pt. i. 7 ; Pt. iii. 8 ; *et sæpe.* (4) Its most common usage, perhaps, is as our *to,* the sign of the infinitive mood, when we might often translate it by— and thereby. *E. g.* I. i. 2, 4, 5, 6, 7, 8 ; *et sæpissime.* (5) To use, employ. V. xv. 20 ; *et al.* Most instances of its occurrence can be reduced to the above usages ; but there are not a few passages, in which we hardly know how to construe the character, even though the general meaning may be plain enough. *E. g.* III. iii. 8 ; IV. viii. Pt. ii. 2 ; xi. 6 ; V. iv. 38 ; vi. 16 ; ix. 12 ; xi. 3 : xiii. 3 : xv. 12 ; xxvi. 1 ; *et al.*

仰
yang

To look up to. IV. viii. Pt. iii. 8 : V. xx. 4 : xxiv. 5.

仲
chung

(1) = 中, mid ; the middle of. I. i. 4, 5, 6, 7. (2) The second of brothers. V. xxvii. 13. Such is its meaning in 羲仲, 和仲, I. i. 4, 6 ; and in 蔡仲, V. xvii. 1 ; 仲康, III. iv. 1 ; and 仲虺, IV. ii. 2. In 仲桓, V. xxii. 11, 仲 is probably the surname.

任
jin
jĕn

(1) To employ, put in office. II. ii. 6 : IV. vi. 2 : vii. Pt. i. 7 : V. xix. 3. (2) 常任 and 任人, V. xix. 1, 7, denote certain high officers. (3) To be equal to one's office. V. xx. 20.

任
jin
jĕn

Artful. II. i. 16. 遲任, IV. vii. Pt. i. 13, a man's name.

伊
e
i

(1) The name of a river. III. i. Pt. i. 55 ; Pt. ii. 13. (2) A particle, = 惟. V. xxviii. 2. (3) A surname. 伊尹, IV. iv. 1 ; *et al., sæpe.* 伊陟, V. xvi. 7. (4) 祖伊, the name of a minister of the tyrant Show. IV. x. 1, 6.

伏
fuh
fu

To lie hidden. II. ii. 3. To suppress, make to lie hidden. IV. vii. Pt. i. 5. To be made to lie hidden, to be subjected. IV. iii. 5.

伐
fă
fa

(1) To smite, to punish. II. ii. 20 : V. iii. 1. Obs. 伐厥死, IV. vii. Pt. i. 16. Punishing. V. i. Pt. ii. 8. (2) To strike, to attack. V. vii. 12, 13. = blows. V. ii. 8. (3) To boast. II. ii. 14.

伋
k'eih
ch'i

A name. 呂伋. V. xxii. 11.

休
hew
hsiu

(1) Excellent ; excellence. II. ii. 13 : IV. v. Pt. ii. 7 : viii. Pt. i. 11 ; Pt. ii. 4 ; Pt. iii. 11 : V. xix. 1 ; *et al.* (2) Blessing, prosperity ; favourable, prosperous ; to bless. II. iv. 1 : IV. iii. 7 : V. iii. 7, 9 : iv. 34 : vii. 5, 9 ; *et sæpe.* (3) To be gentle, to spare ; gentleness. V. xxvii. 13 : II. ii. 7. (4) 休休, simple and upright,

loving good. V. xxx. 6. 服休, V. x. 13, is peculiar.

伯
pih
pi

(1) A father's elder brother, an uncle. 伯叔, IV. vii. Pt. iii. 8. 伯父, V. xxiii. 6 : xxvii. 13. (2) The eldest of brothers. 伯兄, elder brothers or cousins. V. xxvii. 13. (3) The third title of nobility, which is often translated *baron*. 芮伯 and 彤伯, V. xxii. 3. 葛伯, IV. ii. 6. But the term was used for the chief or superintendent of many princes of all ranks, as in 西伯, IV. x. 1. So also in V. xxii. 13; and perhaps elsewhere. It sometimes, however, denotes the princes or chiefs generally, and officers likewise not so high in rank. IV. vii. Pt. iii. 8 : V. x. 72: xii. 6 : *et al.* 常伯, V. xix. 1, must denote princes of highest rank about court. Yu is styled 伯禹. II. i. 17; E, 伯夷. II. i. 23 : V. xxvii. 8. We have also 伯與, II. i. 21, 伯囧 V. xxvi. 1, where the two characters are probably the designation. The minister of Religion is styled 宗伯 V. xx. 9.

To make to, to send, to send to. V. xiii. 3, 4, 10, 25, 28 : xxix. 5.

伻
p'ăng
p'êng

A position, place. Applied (1) to sites of buildings. V. xii. 3. (2) Places or seats of ceremony. II. iv. 9 : IV. vii. Pt. iii. 1 : V. xxii. 22. (3) Places of office or rank. II. ii. xx.; *et sæpe.* (4) The throne or imperial seat. I. i. 12; *et sæpe.*

位
wei

To aid, to favour. IV. ii. 7 : iii. 5 : *et al.* 眷佑. IV. v. Pt. ii. 2. V. viii. 2.

佑
yew
yu

What; whom; how. II. i. 17 : iii. 2, 3 : iv. 1; *et al.* 如何, as how. I. i. 12 : II. iii. 1. 若之何. IV. xi 3. 奈何. III. iii. 5 : V. xii. 9.

何
ho

To err, to fail. IV. vii. Pt. i. 16 : V. x. 14. In V. xvi. 3, 遏佚前人光, it seems to = to end, to overthrow.

佚
yih
yi

Glib-tongued. V. xxvii. 20.

佞
ning

作
tsŏh
tso

Passim. (1) Its prevailing use is in the sense of to make, to do; with the same extensive application which those terms have in English. Actively, to do, to make, to build, to constitute. Neuter, to be, to become; to act. 東作, the labours of the spring. I. i. 4. = active operations. V. iv. 31. It forms what we call the emphatic present tense. V. iv. 14; *et al.* (2) To arise. II. vii. Pt. ii. 1; where the idea of active operation is probably present. (3) In III. i. Pt. i. 9,

18, 26, 50; and. IV. vii. Pt. ii. 11, it is used with reference to the cultivation of the ground. It is often difficult to construe it. *E. g.* V. ix. 20; xv. 5, 6 : xix. 3·

伾
p'e'i
使
sze
chih
來
lae
lai

大伾. The name of a hill. III. i. Pt. ii. 7.

(1) To cause, to make to. II. i. 17 : V. iv. 13. (2) To employ, to command. IV. vi. 11 : V. ii. 6.

To come. II. ii. 6, 14 ; *et sæpe.* Coming, = future. IV. ii. 1. = solicitations, people coming to ask favours. V. xxvii. 16. 越若來, V. xii. 2, is a conjunction. Obs. 往來, V. xvi. 13.

侈
ch'e
ch'ih

Extravagance. V. xx. 13 : xxiv. 10. Obs. 侈服, V. i. Pt. i. 5.

侉
kwa
kua

Ostentatious, boastful. V. xxiv. 10.

侍
she
shih

To be in attendance on ; attendants. V. xxvi. 2, 4.

侗
t'ung

Stupid. King Ching denominates himself—在後之侗 V. xxii. 6.

供
kung

To present to; to contribute. V. xii. 24 : xv. 11, 12 : xxix. 5.

依
e
i

(1) To depend, rely on. II. ii. 10 : III. iii. 9 : V. vi. 7 : xv. 2, 6 : xxi. 7. (2) To be in accordance with. II. ii. 18. Obs. II. i. 24.

侮
woo
wu

To contemn, treat with contempt; contemptuousness. II. ii. 20 : V. i. Pt. i. 6 ; Pt. iii. 2 ; *et sæpe.* = to pay no regard to, deal summarily with. IV. ii. 7. Obs. 威侮, III. ii. 3.

侯
how
hou

(1) The second of the five orders of nobility. V. xvii. 2 : xx. 3. It often follows the name of the principality. *E. g.* 殷侯, V. xviii. 2; 衞侯, xxii. 3. (2) A noble or prince generally. So, in the phrase 諸侯, V. xxii. 29 : xxiii. 1; *et al.* 侯服, the domain of the nobles. III. i. Pt. ii. 19. This, indicating often the princes of the domain, is the most common usage of 侯. V. iii. 3 : ix. 1 ; *et al.* = principalities. V. xxiii. 6. Observe 孟侯, V. ix. 2. (3) A target. II. iv. 6.

侵
ts'in
ch'in

To invade ; invading. V. xxviii. 2 : i. Pt. ii. 8.

便
p'ëen
p'ien

Adulatory, cringing. V. xxvi. 5.

俊
tseun
tsun

Men of distinguished ability, men among a thousand ; their superior ability. V. v. 36, 37; *et al.* We have 俊乂, II. iii. 4; 俊彦, V. i. Pt. i. 5. Obs.

三有俊, V. xix. 4. To give distinction to. I. i. 2.

Manners, the prevailing customs of a time or state. III. iv. 6 : V. xxi. 10 : xxiv. 4, 8.

俗
suh
su

(1) To protect, maintain, secure II ii. 20 : IV. ii. 9 ; *et sæpe.* We have 定保, IV. iv. 2 ; 保乂, V. xvi. 8, 10 ; *et al.*; 保惠, V. xv. 6, 10 ; 保釐, V. xxiv. 1. — to secure, to reckon on. V. ix. 6. (2) 太保 and 少保, the names of the highest officers under the Chow dyn. V. xx. 5, 6. 太保, occurs often. 保 alone is used in the same way, as in, V. xvi. 19 : xiii. 2. Obs. the cases of 師保, IV. v. Pt. ii. 3 ; V. i. Pt. iii. 3 ; xxi. 2. 保衡, the name, or *title* of office, of E Yin. V. xvi. 7.

保
paou
pao

To wait for. V. iii. 8 : vi. 8, 10 : xxii. 29.

俟
sze
szû

To believe, put confidence in. IV. i. 4 : V. i. Pt. iii. 3 ; *et al.* To be believed in ; sincerity. IV. vii. Pt. i. 7 : V. iii. 9 ; xxiii. 5. Good faith. V. xxvii. 4. True. V. vi. 17.

信
shin
shên

To cultivate ; to regulate, put in order : to be cultivated. II. i. 8 : ii. 7, 17 ; *et al.* 身修, self-cultivation. II. iii. 1. Compare with this, IV. v. Pt. ii. 4 : viii. Pt. iii. 5 : V. ix. 4. To repair. III. i. Pt. i. 4 ; *et al.* It is variously applied according to the things spoken of. Obs. III. iv. 2 ; IV. vii. Pt. i. 7 ; V. i. Pt. iii. 3 ; xvi. 12.

修
sew
hsiu

Together. III. iv. 6.

俱
keu
chü

To begin, to be the first to...... III. iv. 4.

倣
shuh
shu

To double ; to be doubled. V. xx. 3 : xxvii. 18.

倍
pei
pei

To give, grant to, to allow, to make or cause. II. ii. 7, 8 ; *et sæpe.* Followed directly by a pronoun,—俾汝,— to act to. IV. vii. Pt. ii. 4. Observe 俾乂 and 俾亂, I. i. 11 ; V. xix. 16, 19. — to submit, preceded by 率. V. iii. 6 ; xvi. 21. We find it preceding 率 with its ordinary signification.

俾
pe
pei

To invert, turn upside down. V. iii. 8.

倒
taou
tao

To bend on one side. IV. vii. Pt. ii. 8 : V. xxi. 7.

倚
e
i

To lead on, be an example to. V. xx. 13.

倡
ch'ang

To be wearied. II. ii. 9.

倦
keuen
chüan

The determined order or degree between things. II. i. 24 : V. ix. 11 : xxvii. 19. In the phrase 彝倫, V. iv. 2, 3, it means the orders or relations of human society.

To make to lie down, to hush. V. iii. 2. To be prostrated. V. vi. 16, 19.

倫
lun

偃
yen

(1) To borrow. IV. iv. 2. (2) Great. 自假 = self-elated. II. ii. 14.

假
këa
chia

Deflected. V. iv. 14.

偏
p'ëen
p'ien

(1) On the side. V. xxii. 21. (2) One-sided. V. iv. 14, 19 : xvii. 7 : xxvi. 5. (3) Low and undistinguished. I. i. 12.

側
tsih
tsê

To assist, be a helpmate to. V. xvi. 18.

偶
gow
ou

太傅, the Grand-helper, and 少傅, the Assistant-helper, were great officers under the Chow dyn. V. xx. 5, 6. 傅巖, the place where Foo-yuě was found. IV. viii. Pt. i. 3.

傅
foo
fu

西傾, the name of a mountain. III. i. Pt. i. 70 ; Pt. ii. 2.

傾
k'ing
ch'ing

(1) To prepare ; preparations. V. xxix. 2 : IV. viii. Pt. ii. 8. (2) Complete. V. iv. 32, 33 : xxvii. 15, 20. — all talents. IV. iv. 5. — all filled up. V. xx. 5.

Arrogant. I. i. 12 : II. i. 24 : iv. 8 : IV. vii. Pt. i. 6.

備
pei

傲
gaou
ao

To wound ; to be wounded. IV. viii. Pt. i. 8 : V. ix. 16 : x. 11 : xxix. 3. 無傷, does no injury, — does not matter. V. i. Pt. ii. 5.

All. I. i. 11 : II. i. 17, 21, 22, 23 : ii. 18.

傷
shang

僉
ts'ëen
ch'ien

A servant. We have 臣僕, a subject. IV. xi. 8. 攜僕, personal attendants. V. xix. 8. In V. xxvi. 2, 4, 6, it denotes the subordinate officers of the dept. of 太僕, or high-chamberlain.

Associate officers or ministers. II. iii. 4 : IV. viii. Pt. i. 9 ; V. 10 : xiv. 20 : xviii. 28 : xxvi. 5. 百僚, occurs often, — 百官, the various officers, the body or mass of them.

To see displayed. I. i. 10.

僕
puh
p'o

僚
lëaou
liao

僝
chan

偽
wei

Deceitful, deceitfully. V. xx. 18.

僭
tsëen
chien

To be in error. IV. iii. 5 : vi. 5 : V. vii. 15. = to assume ; assumptive. V. iv. 19, 34 : xxvii. 18.

僻
peih
p'i

Perverse. V. iv. 19.

儀
e
i

Usages, observances. V. xiii. 12. Demeanour, manners. 威儀, dignity, majestic manners. V. x. 11 : xxii. 9. = measured gambolings. II. iv. 9.

億
yih
yi

A hundred thousand. V. i. Pt. i. 8 ; Pt. ii. 6 : xiii. 4.

儆
king
ching

To warn, to be warned. II. ii. 6, 14 : IV. iv. 7.

儉
këen
chien

To be economical ; economy. II. ii. 14 : V. xx. 18. 儉德, self-restraint. IV. v. Pt. i. 6.

THE 10TH RADICAL. 儿.

允
yun
Jun

Sincerely, truly ; really ; in accordance with the truth of a case. I. i. 1, 8 : II. ii. 3, 8, 10, 15, 21 ; *et sœpe.* Sincere, to be believed. V. xvi. 20. Observe 允塞 II. i. 1. To believe, put confidence in. II. i. 16 : IV. viii. Pt. ii. 4. Sincerity. V. xvi. 19. Obs. 成允 II. ii. 14. Observe also 克允, II. i. 20 ; and 惟允, II. i. 25.

元
yuen
yüan

(1) The first. II. i. 14 : IV. iv. 1. (2) = the eldest. V. viii. 1 : xii. 9, 13 : xxii. 7. (3) Great. V. ix. 16 : x. 2, 7 ; *et al.* We have 元后 for the sovereign, II. ii. 14, 17 ; *et al.;* 元龜, II. ii. 18 : *et al.;* 元孫, great-grandson, V. v. 5. 6 : 元祀, V. xiii. 7, 15, means the first place at sacrifices. 元命, V. xxvii. 11, is peculiar. (4) The head. But 元首, II. iv. 11, probably = the great head,—the sovereign. 在德元, in the head-*place* of virtue, = surpassing others. V. xii. 22. (5) Good. II. i. 16. 元良, the greatly good. IV. v. Pt. iii. 8.

兄
heung
hsiung

An elder brother. V. ix. 4, 16 : xxi. 1. It is singularly joined with 考 in V. vii. 12. 兄弟, brothers ; cousins of the same surname. V. xvii. 6 : xxvii. 13. = as brothers, in a brotherly way. V. xi. 5.

充
ch'ung

To fill. V. xxvi. 7.

兆
chaou
chao

A million, millions. V. i. Pt. ii. 6. 兆民, the millions of the people, = the people. III. iii. 5 : IV. ii. 5 : iii. 5 ; *et sœpe.*

先
sëen
hsien

First ; formerly. II. ii. 18 : IV. ix. 1 : V. xi. 2 ; *et al.* As an adj., former, we find everywhere the combination 先王; also 先后; 先民; 先人; 先正; 先祖; 先輅; 先公; 先烈. = ancestors, forefathers. IV. v. ｜ t. ii. 7 : V. i. Pt. i. 6.

先
sëen
psien

3rd tone. To go before, setting an example. III. i. Pt. ii. 17 : IV. vii. Pt. i. 12 : V. xi. 7. So also we should tone, perhaps, in V. xiii. 23, 24 ; and in xii. 2.

光
kwang
kuang

To shine, to enlighten. II. v. 7 : V. i. Pt. iii. 5 ; *et al.* = glory. I. i. 1 : V. i. Pt. ii. 8 ; *et sœpe.* = bright, glorious. V. xiii. 22 : xxii. 24 : xxv. 6.

克
k'th
k'o

Passim. (1) Its most common use is before a verb, when it is equal to our anxiliary *can, to be able to* ; often, however, giving emphasis simply to the verb which follows. *E. g.* I. i. 1, 2, 12. Not unfrequently it stands alone, at the end of brief sentences, giving the idea of *competency* with reference to what has been spoken of, or is in the mind. *E. g.* II. ii. 3, 4 : V. xxviii. 2. It is followed also by a noun or pronoun, and = to be able for, to attain to. *E. g.* IV. iii. 9 : vi. 3, 8 : V. xxvii. 11, 16, 17, 18, 20. Once, we have a preposition between it and the noun. V. xxvi. 1. (2) As an active verb, to be able for, and more, to subdue, prevail against. IV. iv. 7 : V. v. 1 : vi. 1 ; *et al.* = subduing. V. iv. 17. (3) Crossing. V. iv. 21. A man's name. V. xxii. 19.

兌
tuy
tui

To avoid. V. xxvi. 1. To dispense or have done with. IV. viii. Pt. i. 1.

免
mëen
mien

充
yen

兗州, one of Yu's nine provinces. III. i. Pt. i. 12.

兜
tow
tou

驩兜, a minister of Yaou, dealt with as a criminal by Shun. I. i. 10 : II. i. 12 : iii. 2.

兢
king
ching

兢兢, to be wary. II. iii. 5.

THE 11TH RADICAL. 入.

入
juh
ju

To enter. *Sœpe.* It is almost always followed by 于, as in. II. i. 入官, to enter on office. V. xx. 16. 入畏, V. xx. 19. 出入, going out and coming in, = always and everywhere. V. xxi. 2.

內
nuy
nei

The inside, that which is within. Its prepositional use hardly appears in the Shoo; but obs. IV. viii. Pt. iii. 8 : xxii. 21 : xxviii. 1. We have 于內 V. xxi. 6. = in the palace; in the court. III. iii. 6 : V. xx. 3. Internal. V. xviii. 5. Interior. V. x. 10. 作內, internal operations. V. iv. 30. = female solicitation. V. xxvi. 16. It is generally found in correlation with 外. 內方, the name of a mountain. III. i. Pt. ii. 3. 內史, the Recorder of the interior. V. x. 13.

兩
lëang
liang

Two,—always with definite reference, = the two, the pair. II. ii. 21 : V. xxii. 21 : xxvii. 15, 20, 21.

兪
yu
yü

Yes. I. i. 12 : II. i. 17, 21, 22, 23 ; *et al.* It is not found, excepting in the first two Parts.

THE 12TH RADICAL. 八.

八
pa
pa

Eight. = the eighth. II. i. 8 : *et al.* We have 八音, the different kinds of musical instruments, formed of eight difft. materials. II. i. 13, 24 ; *et al.*; 八政, the eight objects of government. V. iv. 4, 7 ; 八蠻, the eight *man* or savage tribes. V. v. 1.

公
kung

(1) Public feeling. V. xx. 15. (2) The highest *title* or dignity under the Chow dynasty. V. xx. 5, 6 ; *et al.* (3) The *title* of the highest princely rank. Found *passim* in the fifth Part ; but only once in the Parts preceding, viz. IV. viii. Pt. ii. 2. The name of the principality often precedes, as in 周公, 毛公, 畢公. Observe 上公, V. viii. 3 ; and 公劉 V. iii. 5.

六
luh
liu

Six. = the sixth. V. iv. 4 ; *et al.* We have 六宗, whose meaning is not well ascertained, II. i. 6 ; 六府, the six magazines, II. ii. 8 : III. i. Pt. ii. 15 ; 六德, six of the nine virtues ; II. iii. 4 ; 六律, the six pitch-tubes ; II. iv. 4 ; *et al.*; 六卿, the leaders of the imperial hosts, III. iv. 1 ; but in V. xx. 13, 六卿 = the six ministers of the executive under Chow ; 六事, III. ii. 2 ; 六師, the imperial armies. V. i. Pt. iii. 1 ; *et al.*; 六極, V. iv. 40 ; 六服, V. xx. 1.

共
kuug

Together with, in common, all together. II. iv. 7 : IV. vii. Pt. ii. 13 ; Pt. iii. 3 ; V. iv. 31 : xiii. 4. To share in common. IV. vii. Pt. i. 7 ; Pt. ii. 4.

共
kung

1st tone. 共工, the title of an ancient officer, minister of Works. I. i. 10 : II. i. 12, 21.

兵
ping

Weapons of war. 戎兵, V. xiii. 22.

其
k'e
ch'i

The third personal pronoun, singular and plural. The possessive pronoun of the third person. As a demonstrative, the, that, this, these, those. It is found everywhere, and with peculiar usage. Very often it comes between the nominative and the verb, making the nominative emphatic, as in I. i. 11. But the nominative preceding may be a pronoun of any person, or a noun in any person, and the person of the 其 varies accordingly. *E. g.* IV. i. 3. 4. Often, again, 其 gives to the sentence or clause where it occurs a hortatory or imperative force. The clause is often terminated by a 哉, as in I. i. 12, but often not ; *E. g.* V. xxvii. 16, 17, 20. 惟 often follows the 其 with this force. *E. g.* V. xix. 23. Sometimes the demonstrative force = then, in such a case ; in the case of. *E. g.* II. ii. 20 : IV. iii. 8. In many instances, such as 其訓, IV. v. Pt ii. 9 ; 非人其吉, V. xxvi. 8, where the meaning may be plain enough, it is difficult to bring the usage under any general rule. A concluding particle. IV. xi. 3.

其
ke
chi

All, in every thing. IV. iv. 7 : V. xxvii. 15, 17. = to amass. IV. vii. Pt. ii. 14.

具
keu
chü

典
tëen
tien

(1) Written books. V. xiv. 19. (2) Canons, statutes, regular rules and ways. III. iii. 8 : iv. 4 : IV. ii. 2 ; *et sæpe.* 五典, the five relations of society and the virtues belonging to them. II. i. 2 ; *et al.* 典常 are found together. V. viii. 4 : xx. 16. 不典, unlawful ways. V. ix. 8 : xviii. 22. = statutory. II. i. 11. = constantly. V. x. 7, 17. (3) To direct, superintend. II. i. 23. 24 : V. xxvii. 11, 12. To be directed to, bent on. IV. viii. Pt. iii. 5. To consider, care for. V. ix. 3, 5.

兼
këen
chien

Together with, and. V. xxiii. 1. To comprehend. = to absorb. IV. ii. 7. To embrace along with other duties. V. xix. 13.

冀
k'e
ch'i

冀州, one of Yu's nine provinces. III. i. Pt. i. 1. So, 冀方, III. iii. 7.

THE 13TH RADICAL. 冂.

冊
ts'ih
ts'ĕ

A tablet, or tablets with writing on them. V. vi. 11 : xiii. 29, 30 : xxii. 12. = records. V. xi. 19. To prepare such a tablet. V. vi. 5 : xiii. 29.

再
tsae
tsai

Twice. V. xviii. 23 : xxii. 25 : xxiii. 1, 2. To do twice, to repeat. II. ii. 17.

冒
maou
mao

(1) To pursue blindly or heedlessly. V. i. Pt. i. 5 : xxii. 9. (2) To overspread. V. xvi. 14, 15, 21. To be overspread by. V. ix. 4. (3) Used for 媢, to be jealous of. V. xxx. 7.

冕
mëen
mien

A cap of ceremony ;—of various form and materials, acc. to the rank and circumstances of the wearer. IV. v. Pt. ii. 1 : V. xxii. 2, 21, 22, 23 : xxiii. 7.

THE 14TH RADICAL. 冖.

冢
ch'ung

(1) Great, highest. 冢君 = hereditary princes. V. i. Pt. i. 2, 6 ; *et al.* 冢土, the great earth, or the altar to the spirit of the earth. V. i. Pt. i. 10. 冢宰, prime minister. The title was used in both the dynasties of Shang and Chow. IV. iv. 1 : V. xvii. 1 : xx. 17. (2) 幡冢, the name of a mountain. III. i. Pt. ii. 3, 8.

THE 15TH RADICAL. 冫.

冬
tung
冰
ping
凝
ying

Winter, in the winter. I. i. 7 : V. iv. 38 : xxv. 5.

Ice. V. xxv. 2.

To be accomplished. II. iii. 4.

THE 16TH RADICAL. 几.

几
ke
chi

A bench or long stool. V. xxii. 2, 15, 16, 17, 18, 24.

凡
fan

All. IV. iii. 7 : vii. Pt. i. 17 : xi. 2 : V. iv. 10, 11, 13, 16, 23 ; *et al.*

凰
hwang
huang

The male of the phœnix. II. iv. 9.

THE 17TH RADICAL. 凵.

凶
hëung
hsiung

(1) Bad fortune ; unfortunate. II. ii. 5 : IV. vi. 5 : V. iv. 30, 31, 33, 40 ; *et al.* 凶德, evil, suffering, condition. IV. vii. Pt. iii. 4. (2) Cruel, injurious ; wicked. IV. iii. 3 : V. i. Pt. i. 6 ; Pt. iii. 3, 8 ; *et al.*

出
ch'uh
ch'u

(1) To go or come forth. II. ii. 10 : III. i. Pt. ii. 10 : V. xxx. 6 ; *et al.* 出于, to issue in. V. xvi. 2. 出入, see 入.

出日, the rising sun. I. i. 4 : V. xvi. 21. Obs. V. xii. 10. (2) To put or send forth. II. i. 25 : ii. 17 : IV. vii. Pt. i. 1, 15 ; *et al.* Obs. V. xi. 3.

THE 18TH RADICAL. 刀.

刀
taou
tao

A knife. V. xxiii. 19.

刃
jin
jên

A sharp blade, attached to a spear. V. xxii. 21. Edged weapons. V. xxix. 2.

分
fun
fên

To divide ; to separate ; to share ; to distribute. V. iii. 9 : II. i. 27 : IV. vii. Pt. ii. 15 : V. v. 3. Separate. V. xx. 13. Separately. I. i. 4, 6.

刊
k'an

To hew down. II. iv. 1 : III. i. Pt. i. 1 ; Pt. ii. 14.

列
lëë
lieh

To arrange ; to be arranged. IV. viii. Pt. iii. 7 : V. iii. 10 : xix. 24.

刑
hing
hsing

(1) Punishments. *Sæpe.* 五刑, the five punishments. II. i. 11, 20 : ii. 11 : V. xxvii. 13 ; *et al.* To punish. II. iii. 6 : V. ix. 16 ; *et al.* As an adjective. V. xxvii. 20 ; *et al.* (2) Laws generally. V. xv. 15. A pattern ; behaviour. V. xiii. 21, 24 : I. i. 12. To imitate. V. xxviii. 3 ; *et al.*

初
ch'oo
ch'u

The beginning or commencement ; in the beginning, at first. II. i. 8 : ii. 19, 21 : *et sæpe.* 初一, the first. V. iv. 4. 初生, early days. V. xii. 18. To commence. V. ix. 1 : xiv. 1.

別
pëë
pieh

(1) To separate. III. i. Pt. ii. 9. To distinguish. V. xxiv. 7. = besides. V. ix. 5, 17. (2) 大別, the name of a mountain. III. i. Pt. ii. 3, 8.

利
le
li

(1) Gain, money. IV. ii. 5 : v. Pt. iii. 9. Advantage. IV. vii. Pt. ii. 4 : V. xxx. 6. 地利, V. xx. 12. Advantageous. V. vi. 12. 利用, conveniences. II. ii. 7. (2) 利口, sharpness of tongue. V. xx. 16 : xxiv. 8.

剖
k'oo
k'u

To cut open. V. i. Pt. i. 5.

刵
e
i

To cut off the ears. V. ix. 10 : xxvii. 3.

制
che
chih

To order, regulate, define. IV. ii. 8 : vii. Pt. i. 12 ; *et al.* = strictness of regulation. V. xxi. 2. Regulations. II. xx. 14. 制于, to restrain one's self from. V. x. 13.

刻
k'ih
k'o

To injure. IV. xi. 8.

則
tsih
tsê

(1) Then; denoting either a logical sequence or a sequence of time. We must often leave it untranslated in English. *Passim.* (2) Rules. III. iii. 8 : V. xxv. 4, (used in connection with 典). A model. IV. viii. Pt. i. 1. (3) To take as a law or pattern, to imitate. III. i. Pt. ii. 15 : V. vi. 22 ; *et al.*

前
ts‘een
ch‘ien

(1) The front. 在...之前 = before. V. xxii. 20. In front. V. iii. 8 : xxvi. 3. (2) Former, as an adj. *Sæpe.* 前人, father, predecessor, forefathers, is very common. *E. g.* V. vii. 2, 10, 14.

創
sëŏ
hsiao

To pare. = to practise extortion. V. xxi. 7.

剔
te‘ih
t‘i

To cut open, rip up. V. i. Pt. i. 5.

荆
fei

To cut off the feet. V. xxvii. 18.

剖
p‘ow
p‘ou

To cut out. V. i. Pt. iii. 3.

剛
kang

Strong; stern. II. i. 24 : V. iv. 17 : xxiv. 12. Vigour. II. iii. 3. Sternly. V. x. 13.

剝
pŏ
po

To tear off, = to degrade. V. i. Pt. ii. 5.

割
kŏ
ko

To cut off; to injure, to afflict. I. i. 11 : IV. i. 2, 3 : V. xiv. 14 : xvi. 11 : xviii. 5. Sometimes the object is not expressed. = afflictions, calamities. V. vii. 1.

創
ch‘wang
ch‘uang

To take warning. II. iv. 8.

剿
tsëaou
chiao

To cut off. 剿絕, III. ii. 3.

劉
lew
liu

(1) To slay. V. xvi. 15. = to wish others to die. IV. vii. Pt. i. 2. (2) A kind of battle axe. V. xxii. 21. (3) 公劉. One of the ancestors of the Chow family. V. iii. 5.

劓
e
i

To cut off the nose. IV. viii. Pt. ii. 16 : V. ix. 10 : xxvii. 3, 18. 劓害, V. xviii. 5, must be translated generally,— to injure.

THE 19TH RADICAL. 力.

力
leih
li

Strength. II. ii. 20 : V. i. Pt. i. 8 ; *et al.* = influence. II. iv. 4. Strongly. IV. i. 3 : V. i. Pt. ii. 3 : xviii. 28.

功
kung

Work done, or to be done; achievement, services, merits. I. i. 10 : II. i. 9, 26 ; *et sæpe.* Meritorious. II. ii. 18. 九功, the nine services. II. ii. 7. 辜功以自, deeds of guilt. V. xxvii. 21.

為功, made it his own work. V. vi. 4, 16. 恤功于民, to labour compassionately for the people. V. xxvii. 8.

加
këa
chia

To add, or be added, to ;—to affect. V. viii. 2.

劫
k‘ëä
ch‘ia

Strenuously. V. x. 13.

助
tsoo
chu

To help, assist. V. ix. 7 : v. 10.

勅
ch‘ih

Written also, 勑 and 飭. To receive warning, admonish one's self. V. ix. 9. To have it in charge ; to give in charge. II. iii. 6 : iv. 11. With the idea superadded, that the charge is a work of correction. V. xiv. 2. = the execution of such a charge. V. xiv. 14.

勇
yung

Valour ; brave. IV. ii. 2 : V. xxx. 5.

勉
mëen
mien

To urge, exert one's self. IV. vii. Pt. i. 15.

動
tung

To move, to put in action; to take action. IV. vi. 14 : viii. Pt. ii. 6 : V. x. 14. 16 : xviii. 18. = movements. II. iv. 2 : IV. vi. 5. To move, to excite, to affect. II. i. 13, 21 : vii. Pt. i. 12 ; Pt. ii. 1 : Pt. ii. 5 : V. iii. 7. = to remove. V. vi. 18.

勗
heŭh
hsü

To exert one's self. To act earnestly for. V. i. Pt. ii. 9 : ii. 7, 8, 9 : ix. 4 : xvi. 16, 18.

務
moo
niu

To bend the mind to, to strive after. IV. viii. Pt. iii. 4 : V. i. Pt. iii. 4 : xxiii. 5.

勝
shing
shêng

To surpass. III. iii. 5.

勞
laou
lao

To toil, to be toiled ; to toil for; toil. IV. vii. Pt. 1. 11, 14 ; Pt. ii. 10, 13 : V. vi. 18 : xv. 3, 5, 7 : xx. 18 : xxv. 1.

勞
laou
lao

3d tone. To encourage, to reward. V. xi. 2.

勢
she
shih

Power, influence. V. xxi. 7. = the powerful. IV. ii. 4.

勤
k‘in
ch‘in

To be laborious or diligent ; to toil for, be laborious about. It is sometimes followed by 于. II. ii. 9, 14 : IV. vii. Pt. i. 14 : V. iii. 5 : *et sæpe.* = laboriously. V. xi. 4, 5 ; *et al.* = to encourage to diligence. V. ix. i.

勳
heun
hsün

(1) Merit; important service to the empire. II. ii. 20 : V. i. Pt. i. 5 : iii. 5. (2) 放勳, the name of the emperor Yaou. I. i. 1.

勵
mae
mai

To exert one's strength. V. xix. 20.

勵
le
li

To exert one's-self. II. iii. 1.

勸
k'euen
ch'üan

To advise, to encourage, to stimulate. II. ii. 7 : IV. vii. Pt. ii. 7 : V. vii. 12 : xvi. 11 : xxvi. 8. To be stimulated, to come under the influence of. V. xviii. 4, 9, 10, 11. To encourage, advise, one another. V. xviii. 29 : xxiv. 4.

THE 20TH RADICAL. 勹

勿
wuh
wu

Do not;—prohibitive. *Sæpe.* Sometimes the prohibition is indirect. *E. g.* II. ii. 6 : V. vi. 17.

包
paou
pao

(1) Bundles; things wrapped up. III. i. Pt. i. 44, 52 (N.B.) (2) Bushy. III. i. Pt. i. 33.

THE 21ST RADICAL. 匕

化
hwa
hua

To change, to exercise a transforming influence. V. xx. 6. Transforming influences. V. xxiv. 9. = to exchange. II. iv. 1. = to dissolve doubts. V. vii. 4. = to be influenced, transformed, by. V. i. Pt. ii. 3 : xxi. 9 : xxiv. 3.

北
pih
pei

(1) The north; on the north; northwards; northern. III. i. Pt. ii. 7, 8, 9, 10, 13 : IV. ii. 6 : V. vi. 4. 北岳, a mountain. II. i. 8. (2) To be defeated and flee. V. iii. 8.

北
pei

3d tone. To be separated. II. i. 27.

THE 22D RADICAL. 匚

匡
k'wang
k'uang

To correct. To assist. IV. iv. 7 : v. Pt. ii. 2, 3 : vii. Pt. i. 2 : viii. Pt. i. 9 : V. xxvi. 3.

匪
fei

Not. IV. iii. 7 : viii. Pt. iii. 3 : V. xx. 20 : xxvi. 2 : xxvii. 12.

匭
kwei
kuei

A box or case. III. i. Pt. i. 52.

匯
hwuy
hui

The whirling turbulent waters of the Han and Keang near their junction. III. i. Pt. ii. 8, 9.

匱
kwei
kuei

A coffer or chest. V. vi. 11.

THE 23D RADICAL. 匸

匹
p'eih
p'i

(1) 匹夫匹婦, any ordinary man or woman. IV. vi. 11. (2) Responsive. V. xiii. 4. (3) A denominator of horses. V. xxviii. 4.

匿
neih
ni

To conceal. IV. vi. Pt. i. 7.

區
k'eu
ch'ü

區夏, a small portion of the empire. V. ix. 4.

THE 24TH RADICAL. 十.

十
shih

Ten. *Sæpe.* 十愆, the ten evil ways. IV. iv. 7. It is generally found in the Shoo in combination with other numerals, both cardinal and ordinal.

千
ts'een
ch'ien

A thousand. II. iv. 8 : V. i. Pt. i. 8 : ii. 2 : xxvii. 18.

午
woo
wu

The seventh of the calendaric branch characters. V. i. Pt. ii. 1 : iii. 8 : xii. 2, 5 : xxiv. 1.

升
shing
shêng

To ascend, to rise. II. i. 1 : IV. v. Pt. iii. 4 : V. xxi. 14 : xxviii. 1. 升降 advancement and degeneracy. V. xxiv. 4. Grass,—all kinds of grasses, III. i. Pt. i. 44.

卉
hwuy
hui

半
pwan
pan

The half. IV. viii. Pt. iii. 5.

卑
pei

Mean. V. xv. 9.

協
heĕ
hsieh

To agree, to be united, in. II. i. 1 : IV. vi. 8; *et al.* = both together. II. ii. 18. To agree with. V. i. Pt. ii. 5. 協比, to form parties. IV. vii. Pt. iii. 3. To harmonize with what is right. V. xxiii. 3. To be brought to harmony with the right. II. ii. 1 : V. iv. 11 : viii. 3 : xix. 4. To bring to harmony. I. i. 2 : II. i. 8 : IV. v. Pt. ii. 4 : V. iv. 2. = harmoniously. V. iv. 4. = to help. IV. i. 3.

卒
tsuh
tsu

(1) To die. V. xvii. 1. (2) To complete. V. vii. 16. (3) Then; when all was over. II. i. 8.

南
nan

The south. III. i. Pt. ii. 23 : V. xxii. 15 18. 南訛, = the transformations of the summer. I. i. 5. Southwards; on the south. II. i. 8 : III. i. Pt. ii. 7, 8 : IV. ii. 6. Southern. III. i. Pt. ii. 6 : V. vi. 4 : xxii. 1. 南河, the southern part of the Ho. III. i. Pt. i. 53. 終南, the name of a mountain. III. i. Pt. i. 76. 南交, a place on the borders of Cochin China. I. i. 5. 南巢, the place where Këĕ was confined. IV. ii. 1. 南岳, the name of a mountain. II. i. 8. 南宮, a double surname. V. xvi. 12 : xxii. 11.

THE 25TH RADICAL. 卜

卜
puh
pu

To divine by means of the tortoise-shell; divination. II. ii. 18 : IV. vii. Pt. i. 2; Pt. ii. 7 : V. iv. 20, 23, 24, 25 ; *et sæpe.* 卜龜 is to divine with the tortoise-shell. V. vi. 9. 卜宅 is to divine about the locality. V. xii. 2.

卞 *yëen* pien — A law, a rule. V. xxii. 24.

占 *chen* chan — (1) To determine the answers on divination, to examine the prognostics. V. iv. 24. 官占, the officer charged with this work. II. ii. 18. Used for 筮. V. iv. 23. (2) To deliberate. V. xxvii. 20.

卣 *yew* yu — A wine-jar or bottle, of medium size. V. xiii. 25 : xxviii. 4.

THE 26TH RADICAL. 卩.

卬 *gang* ang — I, the speaker's own person. V. vii. 8, 11.

卯 *maou* mao — The 4th of the calendaric branch-characters. V. xii. 4 : xiii. 3 : xxii. 12.

危 *wei* — (1) Unstable and insecure. II. ii. 15. Perilousness. IV. v. Pt. iii. 5 : V. xx. 2, 19 : xxiv. 12. To have a feeling of danger. 危懼, IV. iii. 6. 憂危, V. xxv. 2. (2) 三危, the name of a place. II. i. 12 : III. i. Pt. i. 78 ; Pt. ii. 6.

即 *tseih* chi — (1) To go, approach, to. II. iv. 8 : III. i. Pt. i. 83 : *et sæpe.* Foll. by 于. V. xiv. 17. Observe 即命, V. vi. 8 : vii. 3; 克即宅, 即俊, xiv. 17; and 殷之即喪, IV. x. 7. = to apply one's-self to. V. xv. 9. (2) As a particle. = as to, even. V. xxviii. 2 ; instantly, V. xiii. 7.

卿 *k'ing* ch'ing — A high noble and officer. 六卿, the six leaders of the imperial armies. III. ii. 1. But in V. xx. 13, the same phrase indicates the six chief ministers under the Chow dynasty. 卿 is found everywhere else with 士 following;— IV. iv. 7 : xi. 2 : *et sæpe.* In V. xvii. 1, 卿士 is merely a compound designation of one individual; and in all the other places they should probably go together, as indicating one class of officers.

THE 27TH RADICAL. 厂.

厎 *che* chih — (1) To come to, to cause to come to; to be able to be brought to. II. i. 3 : iii. 3 : III. i. Pt. i. 6, 32, 41, 66, 77 : *et passim.* It is used with other verbs—厎貢, III. i. Pt. i. 52; Pt. ii. 15; 厎綏, IV. vii. Pt. i. 4. = to execute. V. i. Pt. i. 10. Obs. 自厎 IV. Pt. ii. 3; 厎遂, IV. xi. 1; 厎商之罪, V. iii. 6. (2) To settle. V. vii. 11. (3) 厎柱, the name of a hill. III. i. Pt. ii. 1, 7. In many copies of the Shoo 厎 is printed 底, and few Chinese teachers are aware of the error. In reality the character 底 occurs only once,— in V. xxii. 16.

厖 *mang* — V. xx. 20. Should probably be 庬, confused.

厚 *how* hou — Thick. III. iii. 9. = great, rich. V. i. Pt. iii. 4. In 民生厚, V. xxi. 14, 厚 = good; but 厚生, II. ii. 7, = making the means of living abundant.

原 *yuen* yüan — A plain. III. i. Pt. i. 77 : IV. vii. Pt. i. 12. 太原, 東原, and 敷淺原 are all the names of plains. III. i. Pt. i. 5. 32; Pt. ii. 4.

厥 *heuĕ* chüeh — A personal and possessive pronoun, used everywhere; and much in the same way as 其. It is properly of the third person, and, as a personal pronoun, it is only so found. As a possessive, however, it is often = my, our, your. *E. g.* IV. viii. Pt. ii. 10 : V. i. Pt. i. 7, 9 : iv. 2 : xxvi. 1, 8. It is frequently used also as a demonstrative, = the, that, those. *E. g.* I. i. 4, 5, 6, 7 : IV. viii. Pt. iii. 1 : V. iii. 2. Still more common than in the case of 其, however, there are instances, where it is difficult to construe the character with reference to its more common usages, *E. g.* V. i. Pt. iii. 1 : II. iii. 3 : V. xv. 8, 15, 17, 18.

厭 *yen* — To be satiated. V. xiii. 27.

厲 *le* li — (1) Severe, dangerous. V. vi. 5. (2) Oppressively. V. xi. 2. (3) To be conscious of peril. V. xxvi. 1.

THE 28TH RADICAL. 厶.

去 *k'eu* ch'ü — 2d tone. To put away. II. ii. 6.

參 *ts'an* ch'an — To be arranged in order. IV. x. 6.

THE 29TH RADICAL 又.

又 *yew* yu — Further, also, again,—continuing a narrative by the addition of further particulars. II. iv. 11 : III. i. Pt. ii. 7, 8, 9, 10, 12, 13; *et sæpe.*

及 *k'eih* ch'i — To come to, to reach, to attain to. IV. vii. Pt. i. 12, 14, 17; *et sæpe.* 不及 is frequent, meaning deficiencies, to be unequal to, not to be up to, &c. = to come to the knowledge of, to determine.

V. xiii. 2. It very often simply = and. *E. g.* III. i. Pt. i. 4, 28, 46; Pt. ii. 1.
= with. V. iv. 25.   = to. V. xxvii. 2.

友
yew
yu

A friend, friends. IV. vii. Pt. i. 10: V. vii. 12: x. 13. Friendly. V. i. Pt. i. 2, 6; *et sæpe.* To be friendly. V. ix. 16. Foll. by 于, xii. 24. 弗友, not friendly, = disobedient. V. iv. 17.

反
fan

(1) To return. III. iii. 9: IV. x. 6. (2) To take back, = to resume. V. xxiii. 7. To retract. xx. 15. To retort. vii. 7. 復反, to recover. vii. 4. 反風, to bring a contrary wind. vi. 19. (3) To go contrary to. II. ii. 20. = perversity. V. iv. 14. To overthrow. iii. 8. = in revenge, for private grudge. V. xxvii. 16.

叔
shuh
shu

(1) The third of brothers. I. i. 5, 7. So also in V. xxvii. 13, where it includes cousins. (2) A father's younger brother. = uncles. V. xvii. 1. So, 伯叔, V. v. 3. 霍叔, 蔡叔, 管叔, were brothers of king Woo, and uncles of Ching. V. xvii. 1: vi. 12. 虢叔, a brother of king Wăn, and uncle of the duke of Chow. V. xvi. 12.

取
ts'eu
ch'ü

To take. V. xii. 8. = to capture. V. i. Pt. ii. 8. = to take in hand, to make an end of. IV. ii. 7.

受
show
shou

(1) To receive. *Passim.* Especially in the phrases,—受命, 受天命. Obs. 受終, II. i. 4; 受其敗, IV. xi. 8. To receive to employment. II. iii. 4. 受上帝, to receive gifts from God. II. iv. 2. (2) The name of the tyrant, the last emperor of the Shang dynasty. V. i. Pt. i. 4, 6, 8; *et sæpe.* He is in other books commonly mentioned by his epithet of 紂.

叢
ts'ung
ts'êng

Crowded together. V. xv. 18. 叢脞, II. iv. 11, = vexatious. See 脞.

THE 30TH RADICAL. 口.

口
k'ow
k'ou

(1) The mouth. II. ii. 17: IV. vii. Pt. i. 18: viii. Pt. ii. 4: V. xv. 15: xx. 6. 利口, see 利. 逸口, an exceeding mouth, = extravagant talk IV. vii. Pt. i. 12. 口實, that which fills the mouth, = matter for remark. IV. ii. 1. (2) 壺口, the name of a hill. III. i. Pt. i. 3; Pt. ii. 1.

古
koo
ku

Antiquity; the ancients; ancient. I. i. 1: IV. viii. Pt. iii. 3: V. ix. 5: *et sæpe.* We have 古人, 古之人, 古先民, generally referring to the ancient sovereigns. Anciently, of old. IV. iv. 2: vii. Pt. i. 7, 14; *et al.* Observe 自古商人, V. xix. 19; and 若古, V. xxvii. 2.

叨
ta'ou
t'ao

To be covetous, greedy. V. xviii. 5.

召
chaou
chao

To call for, to summon. III. ii. 1: V. xxii. 3. To call forth, to provoke. IV. xi. 7.

召
shauou
shao

In the *title* of V. xii.; the name of the appanage of Shih, the Grand-protector in king Ching's reign.

可
k'o

May, might; can, could. Like *may* in English, 可 may represent possibility, liberty, duty. It occurs frequently, but not so often as in the Four Books. 可以 occurs only once. V. xvi. 10. 可 standing alone, = to do, to be competent. I. i. 9, 11.

台
e
i

The first personal pronoun. Used also as a possessive. III. i. Pt. ii. 17: IV. i. 1, 3; *et sæpe.* It does not occur in the 5th Part.

史
she
shih

A recorder, historiographer. V. vi. 5, 17. 內史, see 內. 太史, the Grand-recorder. V. x. 13: xix. 9, 24: xxii. 23.

右
yew
yu

The right side; on the right side. II. ii. 4. V. ii. 1; *et al.* As an adj., the right. V. xxii. 20. 左右 go frequently together, with reference to the officers immediately about the sovereign. IV. vi. 7: viii. Pt. i. 4: V. xix. 1, 8; *et al.* The same characters, used as a verb, but with changed tones (左右), = to assist. II. iv. 4; *et al.* Observe 夾右, III. i. Pt. i. 11.

司
sze
szû

To preside over, to superintend; that which one presides over, his proper business. We are puzzled sometimes, whether to construe the character as a noun or a verb. III. iv. 4: IV. ix. 5: V. xx. 15: xxi. 2: xxvii. 12. Officers. V. ix. 11: x. 17. So, 百司, V. xix. 8, 9; and 有司, II. ii. 12: V. xix. 13, 21. Obs. 司牧人, V. xix. 12; 司馬, the minister of War, V. ii. 2: xi. 2: xix. 10: xx. 10; 司空, the minister of Works. II. i. 17: V. ii. 2: iv. 7: xi. 2: xix. 10: xx. 12; 司寇 the minister of Crime, V. iv. 7: xix. 24: xx. 11; 司徒, the minister of Instruction. II. i. 19: V. ii. 2: iv. 7. xi. 2: xix. 10: xx. 8.

吁
yu
yü

Alas. I. i. 9, 10, 11: II. ii. 6: iii. 2: iv. 1, 3. We should perhaps translate in the same way in V. xxvii. 14.

各
kŏ
ko

Each, every one. II. iv. 8: IV. iii. 7: V. iv. 32; *et al.* Obs. IV. vii. Pt. iii. 7.

合
hŏ
ho

To agree. IV. xi. 7: V. xvi. 20. To unite, make to blend. II. iv. 9. To preserve in harmony. V. xi. 3. 合黎, the name of a hill. III. i. Pt. ii. 5.

吉
keih
chi

(1) Good. IV. vii. Pt. i. 12; Pt. ii. 16: V. xxv. 5, 8: xxvii. 12; *et al.* (2) Fortunate, lucky. II. ii. 5: IV. vi. 5; *et al.* Often used with reference to the favourable indications obtained by divination. II. iii. 3: V. iv. 26, 27, 28, 29, 30, 31; *et al.*

同
t'ung

(1) To unite; to bring—to be brought—to the same order or rule; together; the same. II. i. 8: ii. 18: iii. 6: iv. 7: III. i. Pt. i. 15, 18, 75; Pt. ii. 7, 14: iv. 5; *et sæpe.* = to share in. IV. vii. Pt. ii. 14: V. xix. 5. 大同, a great agreement. V. iv. 26. = the same as. V. xvi. 16. (2) The name of a cup. V. xxii. 23, 26, 27, 28. (3) Forms part of the name of a hill. III. i. Pt. ii. 12.

名
ming

(1) To name. II. ii. 10: V. vi. 15: xxvii. 8. (2) Famous, the best. V. iii. 6: III. i. Pt. i. 52.

后
how
hou

(1) A sovereign, the sovereign. II. ii. 2: III. iv. 2: V. iii. 2; *et sæpe.* 元后, the great sovereign. II. ii. 14, 17; *et al.* So, 丕后. V. xxvi. 1. We have 后王, IV. viii. Pt. ii. 2; and 王后, V. xxii. 24. God is called 上天神后, IV. iii. 4. But Pwan-kăng calls his ancestors—我先神后, IV. vii. Pt. ii. 10. 后土, V. iii. 6. (2) A prince, one of the feudal chiefs of the empire. II. i. 8. The phrase 羣后, in this sense, is frequent. We have 三后;—see 三; 后夔, III. iii. 2; 后稷, II. i. 17, 18: vi. V. xxvii. 8.

吏
le
li

An officer. 天吏. III. iv. 6.

吝
lin

Sparing, slow. IV. ii. 5.

君
keun
chün

(1) To rule over. IV. viii. 1: V. xxii. 24. As a noun, a sovereign, a ruler. Applied to the emperor. II. ii. 4, 17: V. xxii. 5: xxiii. 5; *et sæpe.* Applied to princes, rulers of States. V. i. Pt. i. 2, 6; *et sæpe.* See especially in Bk. xvi., addressed to 君奭. The phrase 君子, = princely, superior man, occurs, but not so frequently as in the Four Books. It has hardly assumed as yet its technical meaning. II. ii. 20: V. i. Pt. iii. 2: v. 4: x. 7: xii. 24: xv. 1: xx. 15: xxx. 5. (2) In 君陳, V. xxi., and 君牙, xxv., 君 appears to be a part of the name.

否
fow
fou

(1) Not, not to have. I. i. 12. If not, with reference to something going before. II. iv. 6: IV. v. Pt. iii. 2: V. xv. 3. (2) To disapprove, disallow. IV. vii. Pt. iii. 11: V. xv. 15.

否
p'ei

Distresses. ? disorders. V. xv. 17.

吾
woo
wu

I. V. i. Pt. i. 6. = our. IV. xi. 3.

含
han

To hold in the mouth. = to conceal (?). IV. vii. Pt. i. 8. To cherish. V. xv. 17.

呂
leu
lü

(1) = 呂侯, the prince of Leu. V. xxvii. 1. (2) The surname of the princes of Ts'e. V. xxii. 11.

告
kaou
kao

To tell to, announce, declare to. *Passim.* It is sometimes followed by 于, but not often. To announce or appeal to Heaven. IV. iii. 3: V. xxvii. 4. 無告, the helpless, those who have none to appeal to. II. ii. 3.

周
chow
chou

In IV. v. Pt. i. 3, it should probably be 君. Throughout the 5th Part, the character occurs everywhere as the name of the ancient seat of the princes of the Chow dynasty, which is its meaning always in the name—'the duke of Chow;' and as the name of the dynasty itself. Frequently it denotes the capital, Haou, as in xii. 1: xiii. 6, 10, 18, which is also called 宗周. See xviii. 1; *et al.* We have also 成周 for the name of the new capital at Lŏ, xxiv. 1, 4.

呱
koo
ku

呱呱, the wail of an infant. II. iv. 8.

呼
hoo

In the exclamation 嗚呼, Oh! *Passim.*

命
ming

Passim. (1) As a verb. To charge, command, appoint. The subject may be the emperor, any leader or chief, Heaven or God. As a noun. Commands, order, requirements, charge. Those may be from man, as in the titles of several of the Books, or from Heaven or God. In this latter sense its common reference is to the favour or decree of God in dealing with the appointment to the sovereignty of the empire. We have 元命, = the great appointment, *i.e.*, to the throne, V. xiv. 5; but the same phrase in V. xxvii. 11, means the power of life and death. As a verb, also in the passive. II. i. 1: V. vi. 7. To request authority. V. xvii. 1. To consult, ask the will of. II. ii. 18. In V. viii. 4, it means the symbols of investiture. (2) Life. The idea sometimes approaches that of fate, destiny. IV. vii. Pt. i. 4, 12; Pt. ii. 9; Pt. iii. 2, 6: V. xviii. 2; *et al.* Obs. 惟人在命 V. xxvii. 21; 自敗哲命, V. xii. 19; 惟命, V. xxvii. 1. (3) 文命. Perhaps the name of Yu. II. ii. 1.

咈
fuh
fo

To oppose, to do despite to. II. ii. 6: IV. iv. 5: xi. 5. Perhaps it should have the same meaning in I. i. 11, though I have translated there after Ts'ae.

和
ho

(1) To harmonize; to cultivate harmony with; to be harmonious. I. i. 2: II. i. 24: ii. 7; *et sæpe.* = to unite. V. xvi. 12. = to be obedient. V. ix. 9. Harmonious, harmony. IV. vii. Pt. i. 12: V. xviii. 24: ix. 1: *et al.* Spoken of soup.

IV. viii. Pt. iii. 2. (2) A surname. I. i. 3, 6, 7, 8 : II. iv. 1, 9. So also probably in V. xxii. 19. (3) The name of a river. III. i. Pt. i. 66. (4) Part of a designation,—義 和. V. xxviii. 1, 3, 4.

咎
kew
chiu
(1) Calamity. II. ii. 20 : V. xxvii. 12. (2) Crime, the fault. IV. vii. Pt. i. 12 : Pt. ii. 4 : V. iv. 11 ; *et al*. As an adj., = evil, criminal. V. iv. 13. (3) Unfavourable. V. iv. 34.

咤
too
tu
To set down a cup. V. xxii. 26.

咨
tsze
tszû
(1) To consult with ; to inquire and find. I. i. 9, 10 : II. i. 16. (2) An exclamation, = Ah ! I. i. 8, 11, 12 : II. i. 17, 21, 22, 23, 26 : ii. 20.

咨
tsze
tszû
3d tone. 怨 咨, to murmur and sigh. V. xxv. 5.

咸
heën
hsien
(1) All. It stands very often at the beginning of clauses of sentences, and collects in one all the subjects of the verb which follows. Those subjects sometimes are only two. V. xix. 1 : xxiii. 2. are peculiar, 咸 being equivalent to—they and all the rest. In Part V., however, standing in the same way at the beginning of clauses, it is often used adverbially, and = entirely, in every thing. *E. g.* viii. 1 : ix. 1 : x. 9 : xiii. 5, 15. (2) A name. 巫 咸. V. xvi. 7.

哀
gae
ai
To compassionate. V. xxvii. 5. Compassionately, with sorrow. V. xxii. 10 : xxvii. 20. Sorrow, painful labour. V. ix. 16. 哀 哉, an exclamation, = Alas. Placed at the end of the sentence. V. vii. 8.

品
p'in
A rank, a sort. 五 品, the five relationships of society. II. i. 19. 金 三 品, gold, silver, and copper. III. i. Pt. i. 44. 52.

哉
tsae
tsai
(1) A particle of exclamation. It occurs everywhere, but is not complicated with other particles as in the Four Books. Our point of exclamation—! is generally sufficient for it. (2) To begin. IV. iv. 2 : V. iii. 2 : ix. 1 : xxii. 1.

哲
chĕ
chê
Wise ; wisdom. II. i. 1 : iii. 2 : IV. iv. 6 : viii. Pt. i. 1 : V. iv. 6, 34 : vii. 1, 13 : ix. 5, 20 : x. 9 : xii. 10, 19 : xv. 16 : xxvii. 22.

唐
t'ang
The name of a principality where Yaou once ruled. The word is used to indicate him. V. xx. 3. With the addition of 陶. III. iii. 7.

問
wun
wên
To ask, to inquire. IV. ii. 8 : V. vi. 17 : xxvii. 7.

商
shang
(1) To deliberate. V. xxix. 4. (2) Everywhere as the name of the dynasty so called. Sometimes the character denotes its original seat ; sometimes, in Pt. V., what had formed its imperial domain ; and sometimes its capital. Obs. 天 邑

商, V. xiv. 20, which is different from 商 邑, x. 11. On the phrase 有 商, see 有. (3) A surname. V. iii. 9.

啓
k'e
ch'i
(1) To open. IV. viii. Pt. i. 7 : V. vi. 9, 16. = to open up, commence. V. iii. 5. 啓 寵, to open the way to favourites. IV. viii. Pt. ii. 9. To institute. V. xi. 3. 啓 明, to develope intelligence. I. i. 9. (2) To instruct. We have 啓 迪, IV. v. Pt. i. 6 : vi. 2 ; and 啓 佑, V. xxv. 6. (3) The name of Yu's son. II. iv. 8.

寴
ch'e
ch'i
Only. 不 寴, V. xiv. 24 : xv. 17 : xxx. 6.

善
shen
(1) What is good ; the good ; good. II. ii. 7 : IV. iii. 3, 8 : iv. 8 ; *et sæpe*. To have in good condition. V. xxix. 2. (2) Skilful, to be skilful. V. xxx. 5.

喜
he
hsi
To rejoice, joyful. II. iv. 11 : IV. vii. Pt. ii. 4.

喪
sang
To mourn ; mourning ; the observances of funeral ceremonies. II. i. 13 : IV. viii. Pt. i. 1 : V. iii. 9 : xxiii. 7.

喪
sang
3d tone. Active and neuter. To die, perish, go to ruin. To ruin ; to lose. As a noun, ruin. IV. i. 3 : iv. 7 : viii. Pt. ii. 7 : x. 4, 7 : xi. 2. 8 : V. i. Pt. ii. 5, (= to degrade) ; Pt. iii. 3 : v. 6 : vi. 12 : vii. 14 : x. 3, 11 : xiv. 2, 10, 12 : xvi. 2, 19 : xviii. 15, 16.

喬
k'ëaou
ch'iao
High ; tall. III. i. Pt. i. 42.

單
an
(1) To complete. V. xiii. 24. (2) Greatly. V. xvi. 15. (3) Single. 單 辭, one side of a case. V. xxvii. 21.

嗇
sih
sê
嗇 夫, certain inferior officers. III. iv. 4.

嗚
woo
wu
Passim. In combination with 呼, as an exclamation, = Oh !

嗜
she
shih
To delight in, lust after. III. iii. 6.

嗟
tseay
chieh
An exclamation. Ah ! III. ii. 2 : iv. 2 : IV. iii. 2 : V. i. Pt. i. 2 ; *et al.*

嗣
tsze
tszû
(1) To inherit ; inheriting ; to succeed to. *Passim.* The expression 嗣 王, inheriting (= new) king, is frequent. Obs. 嗣 造, V. xxviii. 2. Heirs, successors. II. ii. 12 : IV. iv. 6 : V. xvi. 10. The successor, or heir. V. xxii. 4. (2) To employ or labour with. V. 6.

嘉
këa
chia
As an adj., good, admirable. II. ii. 3 : IV. iv. 8 : V. xxi. 6 ; *et al.* As a verb, to deem or pronounce admirable, to admire. II. ii. 14 : V. viii. 3. Obs. IV. vii. Pt. iii.

器
k'e
ch'i

4, and V. xv. 5, where it = to display admirable ——— .

Vessels, utensils. IV. vii. Pt. i. 13 : V. v. 2. 玉器, the five tokens of gem. II. i. 8.

噫
e
i

An exclamation of dissatisfaction. V. vi. 17.

嚌
tse
chi

To taste, or merely raise to the lips. V. xxii. 28.

囂
yin

Insincere. I. i. 9, 12.

嚮
hëung
hsiang

Over against, towards. V. xxii. 15, 16, 17, 18. 嚮邇, to be approached. IV. vii. Pt. i. 12.   = to approach, to draw near to. V. xiii. 10.   = to show one's mind to. xiv. 5.   = encouragingly, attractively. IV. iv. 4.

嚴
yen

To revere, stand in awe of. V. xxvii. 17. Severe, dignified. V. xv. 4. Severely. II. iii. 4 : V. xix. 4.

THE 31ST RADICAL. 囗.

囚
ts'ew
ch'iu

(1) To confine, imprison. V. xvii. 1; and perhaps. xviii. 23. Imprisonment. V. iii. 8. (2) The pleas in criminal cases. 要囚 = to examine the evidence in criminal cases. V. ix. 12.

四
sze
szê

Passim. Four. The fourth. 四方, the four quarters, occurs everywhere, mostly as a designation of the empire. 四征, to proceed against on every side. V. xx. 1. 四夷, the wild tribes all around. II. ii. 6 ; *et al.* 四海, as a designation of the empire, is very common. 四海之內 occurs only once. IV. viii. Pt. iii. 8. 四民, the four classes of the people. V. xx. 12. We have many other phrases.—四國, V. xviii. 2, 20 ; *et al.*; 四隣, xvii. 6. (II. iv. 5 is different); 四輔, xiii. 20; 四隩, III. i. Pt. ii. 14; 四載, II. iv. 1; 四岳, I. i. 12, *et al.*; 四門, 四目, 四聰, II. i. 1, 15; 四時 I. i. 8; 四表, I. i. 1.

回
hwuy
huy

The crooked; bad. V. i. Pt. iii. 3.

因
yin

As a noun, the cause. V. xviii. 5. As a preposition, by means of, on account of. III. iii. 2 : V. xxi. 14. Along. III. i. Pt. i. 70. As a verb, to go on to more of what has been spoken of. I. i. 5.

困
k'wăn
k'wên

Distress, to be in distress. V. xvii. 5. 困窮, the distressed and poor. II. ii. 17 ; *et al.,* with a different shade of meaning. To distress. (act.). V. xiii. 21. To be distressed about. IV. vii. Pt. ii. 6.

囧
këung
chiung

The proper form of the name 冏, in V. xxvi. 1.

固
koo
ku

Sure, from; to be sure. III. iii. 4 : V. xvi. 10. Firmly. II. ii. 18. To strengthen, make sure. IV. ii. 7 : V. xiv. 3 : xxiv. 7.

國
kwŏ
kuo

A kingdom, a State. Spoken of the States of the empire. IV. iv. 7 : V. i. Pt. ii. 4 : iv. 19 ; *et sæpe.* 萬國 = the empire. V. xx. 3. So, 國家, V. xxviii. 2 ; *et al.* Also, 邦國. V. xx. 10. Spoken of the empire. V. xv. 5, 6, 7 : *et sæpe.* May sometimes be translated by—dynasty. V. xii. 8, 18 ; *et al.* 中國, V. xi. 6. 國人, the people. V. xvi. 13.

圉
yu
yü

朱圉 the name of a mountain, III. i. Pt. ii. 2.

圖
too
tu

(1) To plan, to aim at. III. iii. 5 : IV. v. Pt. ii. 3 : vii. Pt. i. 7 : V. vi. 10 ; *et sæpe.* Plans, objects. IV. v. Pt. i. 6. To reckon on. V. xviii. 3, 5, 14. (2) A plan or map. V. xiii. 3 : xxii. 19.

THE 32D RADICAL. 土.

土
t'oo
t'u

(1) Earth. One of the five elements. II. ii. 7 : V. iv. 5. The land, as opposed to water. II. i. 17 : V. xxvii. 8. The ground or soil. III. i. Pt. i. 7, 16, 17, 24 ; *et al., sæpe.* (2) Territory, regions; grounds. III. i. Pt. ii. 16 : V. xxvii. 14 : xxiii. 2 : xx. 12 : xiv. 23, 24 ; *et al., sæpe.* (3) The earth, personified and deified, is called 后土. V. iii. 6. Comp. 冢土, I. i. Pt. i. 10.

在
tsae
tsai

Passim. (1) As a preposition, and neuter verb. Its radical meaning is—in, to be in. But we must render it variously in translating,—in, on, in the case of, with reference to ; to depend on, rest on, lie in, &c. Once standing alone, it = to be present. IV. iv. 1. It often precedes what we should call adverbs of place or time,—昔, 今, 上, 下, 後, 中, &c. Obs. such usages as 在寬, II. i. 19. (2) To examine. I. i. 7 : II. i. 5.

圭
kwei
kuei

A gem-stone. III. i. Pt. ii. 23. Tokens of gem, given by the emperor to the nobles. V. xxii. 23 : xxiii. 1.

圮
p'e
p'i

To injure, subvert. I. i. 11.

地
te
ti

The earth, in correlation with Heaven. II. ii. 8 *(n. b.)* V. xx. 6 *(n. b.)*: xxvii. 6. *(n. b.)*. The ground. IV. viii. Pt. i. 8: V. xx. 12. 天地, Heaven and Earth, = the supreme Power. V. i. Pt. i. 3. 永地, a lasting settlement. IV. vii. Pt. i. 6.

圻
k'e
ch'i

(1) Frontiers. 郊圻, V. xxiv. 7. (2) 圻父, a designation of the minister of War. V. x. 13.

均
keun
chün

To equalize. V. xx. 17. To be equal. V. xxvii. 16.

坐
tso

To sit. IV. v. Pt. i. 5.

垂
ch'uy
ch'ui

(1) To hand down, transmit; to be transmitted. IV. ii. 8: V. viii. 2: xvii. 3: (2) To let hang down. In the phrase 垂拱, V. iii. 9: xxiv. 2. (3) The edge of a raised hall or platform. V. xxii. 21.

垂
shwuy
shue

The name of Shun's minister of Works, and of a famous mechanician (probably the same). II. i. 21: V. xxii. 19.

垣
yuen
yüan

A wall or enclosure. Specifically, a low wall. 垣墉. V. xi. 4. 垣牆, V. xxix. 4.

城
ch'ing
ch'êng

析城, the name of a mountain. III. i. Pt. ii. 1.

埴
chih

Clayey. III. i. Pt. i. 33.

執
chih

To hold, grasp; to seize. V. iii. 3: vi. 17: xxii. 21; *et al.* = to bring and show. V. xxiii. 1. To be laid hold of. V. xii. 10. To look upon, to hold as—. V. i. Pt. ii. 9. 執事 and 執事之人 = officers. V. vi. 17: IV. vii. Pt. iii. 8. 執藝事, to be engaged in mechanical affairs. III. iv. 3. 執中, to hold fast the Mean. II. ii. 15.

基
ke
chi

A foundation. V. iii. 5. 初基, to lay the foundations. V. ix. 1. 基命, the founding decree. V. xiii. 2. The character, however, is generally used for the superstructure raised on the foundation, and = patrimony, possession, inheritance. IV. v. Pt. i. 2: V. vii. 9, 11: xvi. 2: xix. 15: xx. 14.

堂
t'ang

The hall, or outer apartment,—a raised platform. V. xxvii. 21. To build the hall, *i.e.*, to complete the building. V. vii. 11.

堪
k'au

To sustain; to be fit or worthy. V. xviii. 18, 19.

堯
yaou
yao

The emperor Yaou. I. 1: IV. viii. Pt. iii. 10.

報
paou
pao

To recompense, reward. V. iii. 10: xxvii. 5. To be recompensed. V. xxvii. 21. = in reply to. V. xxiii. 4.

壑
tseih
chi

To detest. II. i. 25.

塗
t'oo
t'u

(1) Miry; mire. III. i. Pt. i. 42, 51: IV. ii. 2. To plaster. V. xi. 4 *(n. b.)*. (2) 塗山, the name of a principality. II. iv. 8.

塞
sih
sae

Sincere. II. i. 1: iii. 3.

塾
shuh
shu

An apartment by the side of a gate. V. xxii. 20.

墉
yung

A wall. Specifically, a high wall. V. xi. 4.

墊
tëen
tien

To be flooded, merged in the water. II. iv. 1.

墍
k'e
ch'i

To overlay with fine plaster. V. xi. 4.

墓
moo
mu

A grave. V. iii. 8.

墜
chuy
chui

To fall down among. IV. ii. 2. To let fall, to drop, to lose. III. iii. 8: IV. iv. 8: V. vi. 7: x. 12: xii. 11, 17: xvi. 2, 4.

墠
shen
shan

A levelled space, a small terrace. V. vi. 4.

墨
mip
mo

To brand, branding. IV. iv. 7: V. xxvii. 18.

隳
to

To fall to ruin. II. iv. 11.

墳
fun
fên

? rich. Spoken of soil. III. i. Pt. i. 17, 24, 33, 58.

壇
t'an

An altar. V. vi. 4.

壚
loo
lu

Dark and thin. Spoken of soil. III. i. Pt. i. 58.

壞
hwae
huai

To be spoiled, or ruined. II. ii. 7: V. xxiii. 3.

壤
jang

(1) 三壤, three qualities of the soil. III. i. Pt. ii. 15. (2) Mellow. Spoken of the soil. III. i. Pt. i. 7, 58, 59. (3) The productions of different States. V. xxiii. 1.

THE 33D RADICAL. 士

士 *sze* shih — *Passim.* (1) It is the general designation for officers. The idea of *scholar* does not appear in the Shoo. The combinations of 卿士 (see 卿), 庶士, 多士 are frequent. (2) Specially, the minister of Crime. II. i. 20 : ii. 11 : V. xxvii. 9. (3) In II. i. 20 : III. iv. 5, 7, and some parr. of V. i., 士 probably = warriors, gallant men. (4) In V. iii. 7, 士女 = men and women.

壬 *jin* jên — (1) The 9th of the calendaric stem-characters. II. iv. 8 : V. iii. 1 : xxiv. 1. (2) Artful. II. iii. 2.

壺 *hoo* hu — See 口.

壽 *show* shou — Long life. V. iv. 36. 耆壽 V. xxviii. 2, and 壽耆, xii. 12, = men of age and experience. = a long reign. V. xv. 7. As a verb, to grant long life to. V. xvi. 10.

THE 35TH RADICAL. 夊.

夏 *hea* hsia — (1) Summer. I. i. 5 : V. iv. 28 : xxv. 5. (2) The dynasty so called. *Passim.* On 有夏, see 有. (3) A name for the empire. II. i. 20 : V. iii. 5 : viii. 3 : ix. 4 : xix. 5. So, 華夏 V. iii. 6. (4) Variegated. III. i. Pt. i. 35. (5) 雷夏, the name of a marsh. III. i. Pt. i. 14.

夔 *kwei* kuei — (1) Grave, reverential-looking. II. ii. 21. (2) The name of Shun's director of music. II. i. 24.

THE 36TH RADICAL. 夕

夕 *seih* hsi — The evening. 朝夕, IV. viii. Pt. i. 5. V. x. 2. 旦夕. V. xxvi. 2.

外 *wae* wai — (1) The outside; outside, external. Generally, as correlate with 內. III. iii. 6 : 6 : V. iv. 30 : xx. 3 : xxi. 6. away from court. V. x. 11 : xv. 5 : xxiii. 6. 外諸子 and 小臣外正, certain officers so named. V. ix. 17, 18. In the regions beyond. II. iv. 8. 於…之外, V. xxii. 11. (2) 外方, the name of a mountain. III. i. Pt. ii. 2.

夙 *suh* su — Early in the morning. 夙夜, early and late. II. i. 23, 25 : iii. 4 : V. i. Pt. i. 10 : v. 9 : xiii. 16 : xx. 4.

多 *to* — Many, numerous; much; mostly. *Passim.*

夜 *yay* yeh — The night. Generally combined with 夙. See 夙. 晝夜, II. iv. 8. 中夜, midnight. V. xxvi. 1.

夢 *mung* mêng — (1) To dream ; a. dream. IV. viii. Pt. i. 2 : V. i. Pt. i. 5. (2) The name of a marsh. III. i. Pt. i. 50.

THE 37TH RADICAL. 大.

大 *ta* — (1) To be great ; great ; greatly. *Passim.* We have 大龜, the great tortoise. III. i. Pt. i. 52 ; *et al.*; 大家, the great Families, V. xi. 1 ; 大輅, the grand chariot of the emperor. V., xxii. 20 ; 大正, the high chamberlain, xxvi. 3 ; 大辟, the punishment of death., V. xxvii. 18 ; &c., &c. (2) Applied to Yu, = Yu the Great. II. ii. 1, 5 : III. iii. 3. (3) 大夫. See 夫. (4) 大川, perhaps the Yellow River. V. iii. 6. (5) 大陸, the name of a tract of flat ground. III. i. Pt. i. 9 ; and of a place in it, Pt. ii. 7. 大野, the name of a lake. III. i. Pt. i. 31. 大別, see 別. 大伾 ; see 伾.

太 *t'ae* t'ai — Great. 太康, the third emperor of the Hea dyn. III. iii. 1. 太甲 and 太戊, emperors of the Shang dyn. V. xvi. 7 ; *et al.* 太王, king T'ae, the grandfather of king Wăn. V. iii. 5 : vi. 4 : xv. 8. 太保, 太傅, 太師 ; see 保, 傅, 師. 太史 ; see 史. 太宗, the minister of Religion. V. xxii. 23. 太室, the grand apartment of a temple. V. xiii. 28. 太常, name of the grand banner. xxix. 1. 太原 ; see 原. 太岳, 太行, 太華, names of mountains. III. i. Pt. ii. 1, 2.

天 *t'ëen* t'ien — (1) The visible heavens, the sky. I. i. 10, 11 : II. iv. 1. 昊天, the firmament in which the heavenly bodies move. I. 3. 天下, II. i. 12 : ii. 4, 14 ; *et sæpe* ; used for 天之下, belong to this meaning. To this also should be reduced, probably, II. ii. 8 : V. xx. 6. (2) It is once used for the place where God and happy spirits dwell. V. vi. 5. (3) Its most common use is for the supreme governing Power, understood to be omniscient, omnipotent, and righteous. In this sense it is constantly interchanged with the names God, and supreme God. It is employed in this way more than 150 times. It has sometimes the adjunct of 上, supreme. IV. ii. 3: iii. 5, and more often that of 皇, great. II. ii. 4: III. iv. 2; *et al.* (4) 天地 occurs once, where we might expect 天 alone, for the governing Power. V. i. Pt. i. 3. (5) 天子, a designation of the emperor. III. iv. 5: IV. viii. Pt. i. 1: V. iv. 16; *et al.* (6) Heavenly. V. xix. 20: xxii. 19; *et al.* Obs. V. ix. 5: xxvii: 6.

夫 *foo fu*

An individual, a man. IV. viii. Pt. iii. 10: V. ii. 2: vii. 5: xxi. 11. 匹夫匹婦, V. vi. 11, and 愚夫愚婦, III. iii. 5, = any ordinary man or woman. 獨夫, a solitary man, with some degree of contempt. V. i. Pt. iii. 4. 夫 alone in. V. xii. 10, = the ordinary people. We find it added to other words, making them = concrete nouns.—勇夫, V. xxx. 5; 牧夫, xix. 13, 16, 19, 21; 準夫, xix. 7; 稽夫, vii. 14; 嗇夫, III. iv. 4. The usage in 萬夫之長, IV. vi. 10, is peculiar. 大夫, a designation of officers generally, below those of the highest rank. IV. viii. Pt. ii. 2: V. ii. 6: vi. 16: xx. 21. 夫子 = heroes, a complimentary designation. V. i. Pt. i. 9: ii. 7, 8, 9.

夫 *foo fu*

Low. 1st tone. It is found with this tone only once, as a demonstrative. 夫人 = this man, any man. V. xxii. 9.

夭 *yaou yao*

Up. 1st tone. (1) Long and thin. Spoken of grass. III. i. Pt. i. 42. (2) 閎夭, a man's name. V. xvi. 12.

夭 *yaou yao*

To cut life short. IV. ix. 3

失 *shih*

To lose. V. i. Pt. i. 11. To lose the favour of. V. xiv. 8. To err. III. iii. 5: IV. vii. Pt. ii. 11. To fail in paying attention, to disregard. II. ii. 6: III. iii. 7: IV. vii. Pt. ii. 2.

夷 *e i*

(1) To squat on the heels. V. i. Pt. i. 6. (2) Ordinary. V. i. Pt. ii. 6. (3) To feel comfortable, at ease. I. 6. (4) A name given to the barbarous tribes in and around the middle kingdom. It is specially appropriate to those on the east, but we find those on the west expressly so designated in IV. ii. 6; and the term is often used for such tribes generally, as in III. i. Pt. ii. 21; V. xix. 11: xxii. 19. Such is the force of 四夷, II. ii. 6;

et al. 蠻夷 is also so used. II. i. 16, 20; and 九夷八蠻, V. v. 1. We have of specific tribes—the 淮夷, III. i. Pt. i 35. *et al.*; the 萊夷, 26; the 和夷, 66; and the 鳥夷, 10, 44. See also V. xix. 11. (5) 嵎夷, the place in the extreme east to which Yaou sent his astronomers. I. 4: III. i. Pt. i. 22. (6) 伯夷, Shun's minister of Religion. II. i. 23.

夾 *keă chia*

(1) To keep—be—near to. III. i. Pt. i. 11: V. xxii. 21. (2) To aid. V. xviii. 21. To this meaning we should probably refer V. xi. 6. (3) Applied to a side apartment of the palace. V. xxii. 18.

奄 *yen yen*

(1) Suddenly. II. ii. 4. (2) Entirely. V. xix. 5. (3) The name of a country. V. xviii. 1; *et al.*

奇 *k'e ch'i*

Wonderful, strange. V. i. Pt. iii. 3: v. 8.

奈 *nae nai*

Also written with 柰 instead of 奈. In combination with 何, = how. III. iii. 5: V. xii. 9 *(n. b.)*

奉 *fung*

To bear or carry with both hands. V. xii. 24: xxii. 23. 奉圭, the sceptres which they bore. xxiii. 1. = to escort. IV. ii. 1: v. Pt. ii. 1. = to receive. 奉辭, to carry orders. II. ii. 20. To serve,—the sovereign, ancestors, Heaven. IV. v. Pt. ii. 7: V. i. Pt. ii. 4; Pt. iii. 1: xxvii. 13. Before other verbs, = reverently. We have 奉恤, 奉答, 奉若, 奉畜, 奉將, V. xxiii. 1: xiii. 14: IV. viii. Pt. ii. 2: vii. Pt. ii. 9: ii. 2: III. iv. 5. 奉德, V. xiv. 18; and 奉其恫, IV. vii. Pt. i. 12, are peculiar.

奏 *tsow tsou*

(1) To report to the emperor. II. i. 9. To advance, go forward to. II. iv. 7. (N.B.). To bring forward, introduce. II. iv. 1. (2) Spoken of music. = to beat. III. iv. 4.

契 *seĕ hsieh*

Shun's minister of instruction. II. i. 17, 19.

奔 *pun*

To hurry away, to run. IV. x. 1. To flee to, in submission. V. 11. 9. 奔走 to hurry about. V. iii. 3: x. 6: xiv. 22: xvi. 9: xviii. 24.

奚 *he hsi*

Why. IV. ii. 6.

奠 *tëen tien*

(1) To fix or settle, to determine. III, i. Pt. i. 1: IV. vii Pt. iii. 1: V. xxii. 5. (2) To set down, and to display. V. xxiii. 1.

奢 *ch'ay ch'e*

Extravagant. V. xxiv. 9.

奪
t'o
t'o

蠹
shih

奮
fun
fên

To take away from, to snatch. II. i. 4. (*N. B.*): V. xxvii. 2, 12.

The name of the Grand-protector in king Ching's reign. V. xvi. 1, 7, 10 ; *et al.*

To display energy in—. II. i. 17 : III. i. Pt. ii. 20.

THE 38TH RADICAL. 女.

女
neu
nü

A daughter. I. i. 12. A female. V. iii. 7.

奼
neu
nü

Low. 3d tone. To wive, to give one's daughter to another in marriage. I. i. 12.

奴
noo
nu

To enslave. V. i. Pt. iii. 3.

好
hawo
hao

That which is good. = peace. II. ii. 17.

好
haon
hao

3d tone. To love, to be fond of. II. ii. 12 : iv. 8 : IV. ii. 8 ; *et sæpe.*

如
joo
ju

As; to be as. II. i. 8 : V. i. Pt. ii. 9 : xiii. 10 : xxx. 11. = to be as if ; if. II. i. 13 : V. xiii. 2 : xxx. 6. 如何, see 何. In Pt. IV. i. 3 : vii. Pt. i. 2 : ix. 4 : x. 4, we have 其如台, = what is that to us ? that does not concern us.

姚
pe
pi

A deceased mother. 考妣, a parent deceased. I. 13.

The name of a district of country, in the imperial domain of Shang. V. x. 1, 6.

妹
mei
mei

Female camp-followers. V. xxix. 4.

妾
ts'ëĕ
ch'ich

始
ch'e
shih

To begin, make a beginning : to be the first to—. II. iv. 4 : V. xxvii. 2, 3. The beginning ; in the beginning, at first. IV. ii. 9 : v. Pt. iii. 2, 6 : vi. 6 : viii. Pt. iii. 5 : V. xiii. 9 : xxiv. 13.
For a time ;—an expression of leniency and laxity. V. x. 15 : xxx. 4.

姑
koo
ku

姓
sing
hsing

A surname, surnames. II. i. Pt. ii. 16 : V. v. 3. 百姓, the hundred surnames, is a designation of the people. I. 2 : II. i. 13, 19 : ii. 6 : III. iii. 3 : vii. Pt. i. 12 ; Pt. iii. 3 : V. i. Pt. ii. 7, 9 : ii. 6 : xxvii. 9, 14. 萬姓, the myriad surnames, is used in the same way. In one case we have 爾萬方百姓, but 萬姓 need not always be so resolved. In V. x. 10 : xvi. 9. 百姓=百官, or officers of

distinguished name. 族姓, V. xxvii. 21.

姦
këen
chien

Selfish and open-wickedness. I. 12. Villainous, openly wicked. V. i. Pt. iii. 3 : xx. 11. In all other passages it is combined with 宄, the phrase = villains and traitors, or to play the part of such. II. i. 20 : IV. vii. Pt. i. 12 ; Pt. ii. 16 : xi. 2 : V. ii. 6 : ix. 15 : xi. 2 : xxi. 10 : xxvii. 2.

威
wei

Majesty, terrors. Used in this sense very often with reference to Heaven's dread purposes, and the manifestation of them. II. ii. 7 : iii. 7 : V. xvi. 3, 10, 14, 15, 19 ; *et al.* 作威, to display terrors, to play the tyrant. IV. iii. 3 : V. i. Pt. iii. 3, 4 : iv. 18, 19 ; *et al.* To be violent ; the violent. V. ix. 18 : xxvii. 12. 威儀, dignity of demeanour, majesty. V. x. 11 : xxii. 9. To awe ; to overawe. V. xxvii. 7. 威威, to awe those who should be awed. V. ix. 4. Dread, majestic. III. iv. 5 ; *et al.* 威用, to use in an awing manner. V. iv. 4. 威侮五行, to waste and despise the five elements. III. ii. 3.

娶
ts'eu
ch'ü

To marry. II. iv. 8.

婚
hwăn
huên

Relatives. IV. vii. Pt. i. 10.

婦
foo
fu

A married woman. 婦子, wives and children. V. xii. 10. 婦人, a woman, used in contempt. V. i. Pt. i. 5. So 婦 alone, ii. 6. 匹婦, 愚婦, see 夫.

媚
mei
mei

Flatterers. V. xxvi. 5.

嬀
kwei
kuei

The name of a stream. I. 12.

嬪
pin

To be—do the duty of—wife to. I. 12.

THE 39TH RADICAL. 子.

子
tsze
tzŭ

Passim. (1) A son. IV. iii. 3 : V. vii. 11. 12 ; *et sæpe.* = descendants. V. xii. 11. 子孫, sons and grand-sons, = descendants is very common. We have also 幼子童孫, V. xxvii. 13, and 子子孫孫, xi. 18. 胄子, II. i. 24, in the same sense. 婦子, see 婦. 小子, 鞠子, 孺子, 沖子, 元子, 天子, 丕子, are all appellations given to the emperor, or used by him of himself. (2) As a verb, to treat as a son. II. iv. 8, (n. b.): IV. v. Pt. ii. 5. (3) An officer, officers. V. xiii. 24. Applied to certain specified officers,— 庶子訓人, V. ix. 17. Observe IV. xi. 8, where we translate it by—*you*. 夫子 and 君子, see 夫 and 君 (4) The first of the calendaric branch-characters. V. ii. 1 : iii. 8 : xii. 6 : xxii. 2. (5) A title of nobility, viscount. We have 微子, II. xi. 1; and 箕子, V. iii. 8 : iv. 1, 2, 3.

孔 *k'ung*
Great. II. iii. 2. Greatly. III. i. Pt. i. 48; Pt. ii. 15 : IV. iv. 8.

孕 *ying*
Pregnant. V. i. Pt. i. 5.

字 *tsze* tzu
To love, to cherish. V. ix. 16.

存 *ts'un*
To be in a state of preservation or flourishing. IV. ii. 7.

孚 *foo* fu
To believe, repose confidence in. V. xvi. 9 : xxvii. 20. Sincerity, faithfulness. V. xiii. 24. What is certain or fully proved. xxvii. 15, 17. To be fully established in. IV. v. Pt. iii. 9 : V. xvi. 2. Sincerely, truly. IV. iii. 5 : ix. 5.

孜 *tsze* tzŭ
孜孜, to be diligent, untiring. II. iv. 1 : V. i. Pt. iii. 3 : xxi. 3.

孝 *hëaou* hsiao
To be filial; filial piety. I. 12 : IV. v. Pt. ii. 7 : V. viii. 3 : ix. 16 : x. 6 : xvii. 3. xxi. 1 : xxvii. 3.

孟 *măng* mêng
(1) Chief or head. 孟侯. V. ix. 2. (2) First, the beginning. 孟春, the first month of spring. III. iv. 3. (3) 孟豬, the name of a marsh. III. i. Pt. i. 57. 孟津, the name of a ford, and a place. III. i. Pt. ii. 7 : V. i. Pt. i. 1 : iii. 8.

季 *ke* chi
(1) The youngest of brothers or cousins. V. xxvii. 13. (2) The last month of a season. III. iv. 4. (3) 王季, the father of king Wăn. V. iii. 5 : vi. 4 : xv. 8.

孤 *koo* ku
(1) Solitary, standing alone. III. i. Pt. i. 35. = helpless. IV. vii. Pt. i. 15. (2) 三孤, the three ministers, second in dignity at the court of Chow. V. xx. 6. Children. Used adverbially, = along with your children. III. ii. 5 : IV. i. 4.

孥 *noo* nu
A grandson. V. xix. 18, 21. 子孫 is very common for descendants. In V. xviii. 17, it is singular. 孫 alone is used for descendants, and descendant. IV. vii. Pt. ii. 14 : v. xxvii. 22. We have 幼孫, IV. vii. Pt. ii. 12 : 元孫, V. vi. 6; and 曾孫, V. iii. 6.

孫 *sun*

孳 *tsze* tzû
To breed. I. 4.

學 *hëŏ* hsio
To learn; learning. IV. viii. Pt. iii. 1, 3, 4, 5 : V. xx. 16.

孺 *yu* yü
A suckling; but 孺子 = young son. Used in reference to king Ching, in speaking of him or to him. V. vi. 12 : xiii. 9, 13, 28 : xix. 16, 18, 21.

孽 *nëĕ* nieh
Calamities. IV. v. Pt. ii. 3. It appears in the text as 孼, which is not so correct as the form in the margin.

THE 40TH RADICAL. ⼧.

宄 *kwei* kuei
Traitorous, to play the part of a traitor. Found always in connection with 姦,— see 姦.

宅 *tsih* chai
(1) To reside in. Spoken of place. I. 4, 5, 6, 7; *et sæpe*. Obs. V. xxii. 28. To be made habitable. III. i. Pt. i. 78; Pt. ii. 14. A site or locality; dwellings; neighbourhood. V. xii. 2 : xiii. 4, 23. 五宅, II. i. 20. 宅里, V. xxiv. 7. (2) Spoken of office,—to occupy. II. i. 17 : ii. 9; *et al*. Of a special service. IV. viii. Pt. i. 1 : V. xxii. 1. To put into office. V. xix. 2, 12, 19. 有宅, office-able. xix. 2, 4. 宅, the office occupied. xix. 4. (3) To settle, consolidate. IV. v. Pt. i. 2 : V. ix. 5, 7 : xviii. 22.

宇 *yu* yü
Sides of a roof, = roofs. IV. iii. 6.

守 *show* shou
To keep, guard, have the charge of. II. ii. 17 : IV. iii. 7 : V. xxii. 6 : xxv. 2. = guard-posts. V. xxiv. 7. 有守, men who keep themselves in the right way. V. iv. 11.

守 *show* shou
Low. 3d tone. In the phrase 巡守, to make a tour of inspection. II. i. 8, 9.

安 *gan* an
A condition of tranquil security. V. xxiv. 12. To rest, repose in. II. iv. 2 : IV. v. Pt. iii. 5 : vii. Pt. i. 11 (*a. b.*): V. v. 8. To tranquillize, give repose to. II. iii. 2 : IV. vii. Pt. ii. 6 : V. xxii. 8 : xxvii. 14. 安安 = naturally, without effort. I. 1.

宏 *hwang* huang
(1) To enlarge. IV. vii. Pt. iii. 7. (2) 宏父 = the minister of Works. V. x. 13.

宗 *tsung*
(1) Belonging to one's ancestors. 宗廟, and 宗 alone, the temple of ancestors. III. iii. 8 : IV. iv. 8 : V. Pt. i. 2 : V. i. Pt. i. 6; Pt. iii. 3. Connected with this is the name of the minister of Religion, as 秩宗, II. i. 23. 宗伯,

V. xx. 9. 太宗, and 上宗, xxii. 23, 26. Officers in his department are called 宗人, xxii. 27, 28. 宅宗, to occupy the place of chief mourner, V. xxii. 4. A cup used in sacrifices is called 宗彝, II. iv. 4. 神宗, Shun's ancestral temple. II. ii. 19. (2) To honour; honourable. 六宗, II. i. 6. The capital of the Chow dynasty is called 宗周 and 宗 alone. V. xiv. 21 : xviii. 1 : xx. 1 : xxiv. 1. 高宗 and 中宗 are the temple titles of two of the emperors of the Shang dynasty. IV. ix. 1 : V. xv. 4, 5, 16. 工宗, the most meritorious. xiii. 7. So 宗 alone, p. 15. 宗禮, honourable ceremonies,—ceremonies which all should observe, p. 19. 宗工, V. x. 11. 13. (3) To appear at court,—applied to the waters of the Këang flowing to the sea. III. i. Pt. i. 47. (4) 代宗, a mountain. II. i. 8.

官
kwan
kuan

An officer of government; an office. Either of these meanings will suit most of the passages where the characters occur. 百官, all the officers. II. ii. 19 : III. iv. 2 : V. iv. 1 ; *et al.* We have 官, when we should expect a more definite term, the officer intended being understood. V. xxvii. 21. To put into office. II. iii. 2 : V. i. 5. To preside over, —in the phrase 官占. II. ii. 18. = the influence of power. V. xxvii. 16.

定
ting

(1) To establish, to settle; to be settled. I. 8 : II. ii. 18 : III. i. Pt. i. 41 : iv. 2 ; *et sæpe.* (2) = to remain, to stop. V. xiii. 21.

宜
i

(1) To approve of or require as right. V. vi. 8. (2) The name of a sacrifice to the earth. V. i. Pt. i. 10. (3) In a name. 宜生, V. xvi. 12.

宣
seuen
hsüan

To spread, extend. II. iv. 4. To manifest, to display. II. iii. 4 : IV. vii. Pt. ii. 6 : V. xxii. 5.

室
shih

A house. V. vii. 11, 13. 室家, a house and its chambers. V. xi. 4 : IV. ii. 6. An apartment. V. xxii. 11. So 太室, xiii. 29. A mansion, as opposed to 宮. V. vii. 11. So in xviii. 26. But we have 宮室 together as belonging to the emperor, V. Pt. i. 5, while they are together as belonging to the nobles, IV. iv. 12. The most common use of 室, however, is for the Royal House, 王室. III. iv. 5 : V. viii. 4 : xvii. 6 : xxiii. 6 : xxiv. 3. So, 有室, in xix. 2.

宥
yew
yu

To forgive; to show leniency to. II. i. 11 : ii. 12 : V. xi. 2 : xxi. 8, 10.

宮
kung

(1) A palace, V. vii. 7. Joined with 室, a palace or mansion. IV. iv. 7 : V. i. Pt. i. 5. (2) 宮辟, the punishment of castration. IV. xxvii. 18. (3) In the double surname 南宮, V. xvi. 12 : xxii. 11.

In the phrase 冢宰, prime minister. IV. iv. 1 : V. xvii. 1 : xx. 7.

宰
tsae
tsai

To injure, be injurious. V. i. Pt. i. 5 : iii. 6 : iv. 19 : v. 8. To receive injury. V. vi. 10. 凶害, cruel injuries. IV. iii. 3.

害
hae
hai

Why. IV. vii. 7.

害
hŏ
ho

The night. I. 6.

宵
sëaou
hsiao

(1) A house, a family,—generally. II. ii. 14 : iv. 8 : IV. vii. 17 : V. ii. 5 : iv. 36, 37 ; 家人, a household. V. ix. 18. 室家, see 室. (2) A Family, a clan. II. iii. 4 : IV. iii. 6 : iv. 4, 7 : V. iv. 13, 19 ; *et sæpe.* Connected with this is the use of 國家 for the empire. V. vi. 18 : xxviii. 2 : *et sæpe.* 家 alone has also this meaning. IV. vii. Pt. ii. 6 : V. xiv. 9 ; *et al.* (3) 王家, and sometimes 家 alone, = the Royal House. V. vii. 1 : viii. 1 : x. 7 ; *et al.* (4) Obs. 私家, to seek one's own advantage, V. xxvii. 21 ; and 朋家, V. Pt. ii. 3, to form parties.

家
këa
chia

(1) To bear with, show forbearance IV. xi. 6 : V. xxx. 6, 7. The forbearing. xix. 15, = to nourish. V. xi. 3. 從容, an easy forbearing manner. (2) A name. V. iii. 8.

容
yung

(1) To keep, to allow to remain. V. xiii. 26. (2) To advance with the cup, —in sacrifice. V. xxii. 26.

宿
suh
hsü

(1) To revere, show reverence. II. i. 23 : iii. 6. Before other verbs, = reverently, respectfully. I. 4, 6 : V. xv. 4 : xviii. xx. 6. (2) The third of the calendaric branch characters. V. xii. 3.

寅
yin

(1) To hush. 遏密, I. i. 13. (2) = secretly, quietly. 密邇, IV. v. Pt. i. 9 : V. xxiv. 3.

密
meih
mie

To rob, play the robber. 寇賊, II. i. 20, V. xxvii. 2. 寇攘, V. ix. 15 : xxiv. 4. 司寇, the minister of Crime. V xv. 7 : xix. 24 : xx. 11.

寇
k'ow
k'aw

富
foo
fu

Riches. V. iv. 39. To be rich. iv. 13 : xxiv. 11 : xxvii. 11. To enrich. V. xxiii. 5.

寒
han

Cold ; to be cold. V. iv. 32, 34 : xxv. 5.

察
ch'ă
ch'a

To examine. V. xxvii. 12, 18, 20.

寡
kaw

(1) To be few. V. xxiv. 15. (2 A widow. In the phrase 鰥寡 V. vii. 8 : ix. 14 : xv. 6, 10 ; *et al.* = the weak. V. xi. 3. (3) 寡命, the rarely equalled decree. V. xxiii. 3. 寡兄, your unworthy brother. vii. 5.

實
shih

(1) To be filled. V. xvi. 9. 口實, that which fills the mouth, matter for remark. IV. ii. 1. (2) To be real ; real. IV. viii. Pt. i. 1 : vii. Pt. 1. 10. Really ; positively, exactly. IV. ii. 4 : v. Pt. ii. 2 : V. xxiv. 9 : xxvi. 3 : xxvii. 18.

寧
ning

To be in a state of repose, and tranquillity. III. iii. 4 : IV. iv. 2 : V. v. 7 : xxiv. 3 ; *et sæpe*. To give repose or tranquillity to ; to soothe. IV. iii. 6 : V. xiii. 25 : xiv. 18 ; *et sæpe.* 寧王寧人, and 寧考 are all designations of king Woo. V. vii. 3, 8, 9, 10, 11, 14, 15 ; *et al.* A state of tranquillity : serenity of mind. V. iv. 36 : xxvii. 13. (2) It is better to. V. i. Pt. ii. 9. The comparison is completed in II. ii. 12.

審
shin
shĕn

To examine carefully, to judge. V. xxvii, 16, 17, 18, 20. To describe minutely. IV. viii. Pt. i. 3. Discriminatingly. V. xxii. 4.

寬
hwan
hwan

To be gentle. II. i. 24 : iii. 3 (*n. b.*) : V. ii. 5 : xxi. 7. 在寬, be gentle, or the course to pursue is gentleness. II. i. 19. To make gentle. V. xv. 18. Gentleness. II. ii. 12 : IV. iv. 3 : V. viii. 2.

寶
paou
pao

Precious. V. vi. 7 : vii. 3 : xxvii. 21. Precious things. IV. vii. Pt. iii. 12 : V. v. 3 : xxii. 19. To consider precious. V. v. 8.

寵
ch'ung

Favour. IV. v. Pt. iii. 9 : V. xx. 19 : xxiv. 10. To confer favours (寵綏). V. i. Pt. i. 7. 啟寵, to open the way to favourites. IV. viii. Pt. ii. 9.

THE 41st RADICAL. 寸

封
fung
fêng

(1) Boundaries. V. xxiv. 7. (2) A territory over which a prince is appointed. V. xvii. 2. (3) To raise a tumulus ;— over a grave, V. iii. 9 ; for an altar, II. i. 10. (4) The name of Wăn's ninth son, the prince of K'ang. V. ix : x., xi., *sæpe.*

射
shay

To shoot with bow and arrows. IV. vii. Pt. i. 15 (*n. b.*) : V. xxx. 5.

將
tsëang
chiang

(1) Shall, will, about to. It expresses a purpose, or a likely result. III. iii. 9 : IV. iii. 6 : vi. 1 : vii. Pt. ii. 6, 17 ; Pt. iii. 4 (*n. b.*), 6 : xi. 6 (?) : V. iii. 6 : vi. 12 :

xxiv. 10 : xxx. 4 (*u. b.*). (2) To take, = to be charged with. III. iv. 5 : IV. iii. 4 : V. i. Pt. i. 5 : xiv. 2 : xvi. 15. (3) ? To regulate. V. x. 4. (4) Great. V. xiii. 15. (5) ? To acknowledge. V. xiii. 21. 迪將其後 in p. 20 is about inexplicable. To engross, to do alone. IV. viii. Pt. iii. 10.

專
chuen
chuan

To honour. V. xix. 2.

尊
tsun

To respond to. IV. viii. Pt. iii. 11 : V. xxv. 6. To reply. V. vi. 17.

對
tuy
tui

To lead ;—actually. III. i. Pt. i. 57. mentally = to survey and lay down the course of. Pt. ii. 1, 3—13.

導
taou
tao

THE 42d RADICAL. 小.

小
sëaou
hsiao

Small. *Passim.* Often used with 大. To become small IV ii. 8. Of phrases we have 小子, used by the emperor, and to him and others, but only by the ministers E Yin and the duke of Chow ; 小尹, V. xix. 8 ; 小伯, p. 9 ; 小臣, V. ix. 17, 18, *et al.* ; 小民, the inferior people. V. xii. 13, 21, 22, 23 ; *et sæpe* 小人 is also used of the lower people. V. xv. 2, 3, 5, 6, 7, 17, 18. Only once, II. ii. 20, does it denote the mean in opposition to the superior man.

A little. V. vii. 1.

少
shaou
shao

少
shaou
shao

3d tone. Junior, assistant. V. x. 2. The 少保, 少傅, 少師, were the three ministers second in dignity at the court of Chow. V. xx. 6. The 少師 appears before under the dyn. of Shang. IV. xi. 1, 3.

尚
shang

(1) Pray, may it be that. II. ii 20 : III. iv. 5 ; *et passim.* This is the prevailing usage of the character in the Shoo. The exhortation and entreaty are not so evident indeed in all cases, and the meaning approaches to a reflective *perhaps,* as in V. xxx. 8. (2) To ascend. V. ix. 21. (3) Still, in both the meanings of—in addition to, and notwithstanding. V. x. 7, 8 : xiv. 23 : xvi. 12, 15 : *et al.* (4) To esteem, be reckoned valuable. V. xxiv. 8.

THE 43d RADICAL. 尤.

尤
yew
yu

(1) Evils, = judgments, calamities. V. xxvii. 21. (2) To murmur, to grudge. V. xvi. 2. (3) 蚩尤, the name of the first rebel. V. xxvii. 2.

就
tsew
chiu

三就, three places to be repaired to. II. i. 20. To accommodate one's-self to. V. xxx. 4.

THE 44TH RADICAL. 尸.

尸
she
shih

To occupy in a sham way, like a personator of the dead. III. iii. 1: iv. 4.

尹
yin

(1) To direct, to rule. V. viii. 3: xviii. 19: xxi. 1. (2) Directors,—the heads of other officers, or official departments. V. xi. 2: xviii. 2. They are called 尹 氏, vii. 6; 庶尹, II. iv. 10: V. x. 10; 師尹, V. iv. 35; 尹伯, xix. 9; 百 尹, xxii. 3. The 小尹 are different. V. xix. 8; and perhaps 尹 in p. 11. (3) The designation of T'ang's prime minister E Yin. IV. iv. 1; *et sæpe*. He speaks of himself in the style 尹躬, IV. v. Pt. i. 2, 3: vi. 3.

尾
wei

(1) The tail V. xxv. 2. (2) 孳尾, to pair and copulate. I. 4. (3) 部尾, a mountain. III. i. Pt. ii. 2.

居
keu
chü

(1) To abide, reside in;—properly spoken with reference to place, but used also with ref. to office and condition. III. i. Pt. i. 39: IV. iv. 5: v. Pt. i. 9: viii. Pt. ii. 10: V. vi. 14; *et al.* Dwellings, homes, families. II. i. 20: IV. vii. Pt. iii. 5, 10: V. xiv. 18, 25; *et al.* (2) To settle, to locate. V. xiii. 14: xx. 12. (3) To abide sitting: V. i. Pt. i. 6: xxvi. 2. (4) The virtues appropriate to the several circumstances of life and condition. V. iv. 2. (5) Accumulated stores of grain. II. iv. 1.

届
këae
chieh

To reach to. II. ii. 21.

屋
uh
wu

王屋, a mountain. III. i. Pt. ii. 1.

屑
sëĕ
hsieh

Lightly, triflingly. V. xviii. 14, 22.

展
chen
chan

To develope. V. v. 3.

屏
ping

A screen or defence. V. xxiii. 6. To act as defences in, or to make defences of. V. xvi. 9.

屏
ping

3d tone. To put aside. V. i. Pt. iii. 3: vi. 8.

屢
leu
lü

Frequently. II. iv. 11: V. ix. 21: xviii. 22.

屬
shuh
shu

To pertain or belong to. V. xx. 13: xxvii. 18, 22.

屬
chuh
chu

To be connected with. III. i. Pt. i. 73: IV. vii. Pt. ii. 6. 屬婦, to find connections for destitute women. V. x. i. 3.

THE 46TH RADICAL. 山.

山
shan

A mountain, a hill. *Sæpe.* A mound. V. v. 9. A hill-site. IV. vii. Pt. iii. 4. The emblematic mountain on the emperor's robe. II. iv. 4. 九山, the hills of the nine provinces. III. i. Pt. ii. 14. 名山, mount Hwa. V. iii. 6. 山 often follows the names of mountains. Those into whose names the character itself does not enter, and which will be found in their proper places, are 衡, 恆, 歷, 塗, 羽, 刑, and perhaps some others.

岐
k'e
ch'i

The name of a mountain. III. i. Pt. i. 4, 76; Pt. ii. 1.

岡
kang

The ridge of a mountain. III. iv. 6.

岱
tea
tai

A mountain, forming one of the boundaries of Ts'ing-chow, and Seu-chow. III. i. Pt. i. 21, 26, 28. In II. i. 8, it is also called 岱宗.

岳
yŏ
yü

(1) A mountain so called, and also 太岳. III. i. Pt. i. 4; Pt. ii. 1. There were also the four mountains, called 四岳, V. xx. 14,—the northern, the southern, the eastern, and the western, all referred to in II. i. 8. (2) The second if not the first minister, about the courts of Yaou and Shun, was styled 四岳. I. 11, 12: II. i. 7, 15, 17, 23: V. xx. 3.

岷
min

A mountain in Lëang-chow. III. i. Pt. i. 63.

岍
k'ÿen
ch'ien

A mountain in Yung-chow. III. i. Pt. ii. 1.

峙
che
chih

To provide, have collected and prepared. V. xxix. 5.

島
taou
tao

An island. 島夷, III. i. P. i. 10, 44.

峻
tseun
tsun

Lofty. III. iii. 6.

崇
ts'ung
ch'ung

(1) To honour. IV. ii. 9: V. i. Pt. iii. 3: ii. 6: iii. 10; *et al.* = to indulge in. V. x. 9. (2) To be exalted, made great. V. xx. 17. (3) Greatly. IV. vii. Pt. ii. 11, 14: V. xviii. 5. (4) The name of a mountain in the present Hoo-nan. II. i. 12.

崑
kwăn
kuên

The name of a mountain in the west of the Ko-ko-nor. III. iv. 6. It probably is the same with the 崑崙 in III. i. Pt. i. 83.

崙
lun

See 崑 above.

崩
păng
pêng

(1) To die,—spoken of an emperor. V. xxii. 10. (2) To let fall, or drop off. V. i. Pt. ii. 9.

嵎
yu
yü

嵎夷, the most eastern point of Yaou's empire. I. 4 : III. i. Pt. i. 23.

嶓
po

Called also 嶓冢, a mountain in Lëang-chow. III. i. Pt. i. 63 ; Pt. ii. 3, 8. A mountain in Ts'eu-chow. III. i. Pt. i. 35.

嶧
yih
yi

巖
yen

傅巖, the name of a place in the present Shan-se. IV. viii. Pt. i. 3.

THE 47TH RADICAL. 巛.

川
ch'uen
ch'uan

A river, a stream. *Sæpe.* 九川, the rivers and streams in the nine provinces. II. iv. 1 : III. i. Pt. ii. 14. 大川, V. iii. 6, probably, denotes the Ho.

州
chow
chou

The name of a great division of the empire,—a province. Yu divided the empire into nine. See III. i., *passim* : II. iv. 8. Shun divided these into twelve. II. i. 10.

巡
seun
hsüu

To go round and survey. V. i. Pt. iii. 1. Used of an imperial tour of inspection. V. xx. 1, 14. See 守.

巢
ch'aou
ch'ao

南巢, the place where Këë was kept in confinement. IV. ii. 1.

THE 48TH RADICAL. 工.

工
kung

(1) Work. II. iii. 5. (2) Workmen. II. i. 21. (3) Service, duty. II. iv. 8. (4) Officers. III. iv. 3 : V. iii. 4 ; *et al.* 百工, all the officers. I. 8 : III. iv. 3 : V. xiii. 6 ; *et al.* 宗工, honoured officers, Heads of clans. V. x. 10, 13. = masters of music. II. iv. 6. Obs. 士師工, V. xiii. 20. (5) 共工, the ancient name for the minister of Works. I. 10 : II. i. 12. 21.

左
tso

The left (adj. and noun); on and in the left hand. IV. ii. 4 : V. ii. 1 : xxii. 20 : xxiv. 13. On 左右 and 左右, see 右.

巧
k'ëaou
ch'iao

Artful, artfulness. II. iii. 2 : V. i. Pt iii 3 : xxvi. 5.

巨
keu
chü

Great. IV. viii. Pt. i. 6.

巫
woo
wu

(1) 巫風, sorcerers' fashion. IV. iv. 7. (2) A surname. V. xvi. 7.

差
ts'ze
tz'û

To make a distinction in. V. xxvii. 3. Discrepancies. p. 20. 倍差, two and a half times. p. 18.

THE 49TH RADICAL. 己.

己
ke
chi

One's-self. In the Shoo of the 2d and 3d persons. II. ii. 3, 6 : IV. ii. 5, 8 : V. i. Pt. ii. 5 : xxx. 6. Observe. 總己, IV. iv. 1.

已
e
i

(1) Have, indicating the present complete tense. V. xvi. 3 : xix. 18. (2) To stop, rest, have done with. I. i. 11 : V. ix. 17 : xiii. 21 (*n. b.*). (3) = yes. The speaker assents to or approves of what has been said, and goes on to add something more. V. vii. 2, 9 : ix. 7, 14 : xi. 8 : xiii. 11.

巳
sze
szû

The sixth of the calendaric branch-characters. V. iii. 1 : xii. 5.

巽
sun

To resign. I. 12.

THE 50TH RADICAL. 巾.

市
she
shih

A market-place. IV. viii. Pt. iii. 10.

布
poo
pu

(1) To display. IV. iv. 3 : V. xxiii. 1. (2) To spread abroad. IV. ii. 3.

希
he
hsi

To become thin. Spoken of the feathers of birds and hair of animals. I. 5.

帛
pih
pai

Pieces of silk. 三帛, I. 8.

帝
te
ti

(1) God. The name is continually interchanged with 上帝, supreme God. II. i. 6 : iv. 2 : IV. i. 2 : ii. 3 : iii. 2 (皇天上帝), 8 : iv. 8 : v. Pt. iii. 3 : vii. Pt. iii. 6 : viii. Pt. i. 2 : V. i. Pt. i. 6, 7, 10 ; Pt. iii. 3 : viii. 6 : iv. 3, 15 : vi. 7 : viii. 9, 13 : viii. 3 : ix. 4 : xi. 2 : xii. 9, (皇上帝) 14 : xiv. 2, 4, 5, 8, 9, 13, 14 : xvi. 3, 7, 11, 14 : xviii. 4, 5 : xix. 2, 4, 5, 6 : xxiii. 5 : xxvii. 5, 12 : xxviii. 1. (2) The title of the ancient emperors Yaou and Shun *Passim* in the first two Parts. Also in. IV. viii. Pt. iii. 10 : V. xxvii. 5, 7 (皇帝). (3) 帝乙, one of the emperors

of the Shang dynasty. V. x. 9: xiv. 7: xviii. 10. The 帝 is wrongly translated —should not be translated—in these passages.

師 *sze szü*

(1) The multitudes, the people; all. I. 12: II. i. 25: ii. 9. 1V. ii. 3: V. xiii. 14, 24; *et al.* (2) A capital city. V. xiii. 3. (3) An army, a host. II. ii. 20, 21: V. i. Pt. ii. 1; *et al.* 六師, the imperial army. III. iv. 1: V. i. Pt. iii. 1; *et al.* (4) Instructors. IV. ii. 8: V. i. Pt. ii. 7; *et al.* 師師, the instructors whom I am to follow. V. xi. 2. (5) Applied to various officers:—to the high dignitaries, 太師 and 少師, V. xx. 5, 6; *et al.*; 炎師 =太師, IV. xi. 1, 3, 4: V. xxiv. 2, 5, 12; 師保 together, applied to E Yin. IV. v. Pt. ii. 3, and to the duke of Chow, V. xxi. 2; the same characters appear to be plural, V. i. Pt. iii. 3; 師氏, the captain of the warders, V. ii. 2: xxii. 3; officers generally, V. xiii. 20; 師尹, V. iv. 35; 師長, IV. vii. Pt. iii. 8: viii. Pt. ii. 2; tutors, a high office appointed by Yu, II. iv. 8; judges, V. xxvii. 15. (6) A model; to take as a model. IV. vi. 8: II. iii. 4: viii. Pt. iii. 3: V. xx. 16; *et al.* 師師, to imitate one another. II. iii. 4: IV. xi. 2.

席 *seih hsi*

(1) A mat. V. xxii. 15, 16, 17, 18. (2) = to rely on. V. xxiv. 10.

常 *chang*

(1) Regular, constant, unchanging; constancy; constantly. II. iii. 3: III. iv. 2, 3: IV. iv. 8: v. Pt. iii. 1: V. xxix. 3, 4; *et al.* Obs. 常伯, 常任, 常事, V. xix. 1, 12. Constant in virtue, V. xix. 9, 23. The regular principles of duty. V. xxi. 10: xx. vii. 6. Regular ways. V. xxi. 2. 五常, the five regular virtues of society. V. i. Pt. iii. 2. 典常. V. viii. 4; xx. 16. (2) 太常, name of the Grand-banner. V. xxv. 1.

幣 *'pe pi*

Offerings,—presents to the emperor,— of various kinds. V. xii. 8, 24: xxiii. 1.

THE 51st RADICAL. 干.

干 *kan*

(1) A shield, shields. IV. viii. Pt. ii. 4: V. ii. 14: xxix. 1. 二干戈, two shield-and-spearmen. V. xxii. 11. (2) To seek for; to expose one's-self to. II. ii. 6, 11: III. iv. 4. (3) 比干, a relative of the tyrant Show, who cut out his heart. V. iii. 5.

平 *p'ing*

(1) To reduce to order, to adjust, to tranquillize; to be reduced to order. I. 2, 4, 5, 6, 7; III. i. Pt. i. 32, 65: *et sæpe.* The

work of Yu is spoken of as 平水土, II. i. 17: V. xxvii. 8. 平康, a condition of peace and tranquillity. V. iv. 17, 36. (2) Just. V. xxiii. 5. (3) Common, ordinary. V. xxvii. 2.

平 *p'ëen p'een*

平平, level and easy. V. iv. 14.

年 *nëen nien*

A year, years. IV. ix. 3: V. i. Pt. i. 1: *et sæpe.*

并 *ping*

All together, in common. V. vi. 9: vii. 5, 15: xxvii. 3, 20.

幹 *kan*

Business, occupations, duties. V. xiv. 23, 25.

THE 52d RADICAL. 幺.

幻 *hwan huan*

Deceiving, deceit. 爲幻, the practice of deception, deceiving tricks. V. xv. 14, 18.

幼 *yew yu*

Young. IV. vii. Pt. i. 15; Pt. ii. 12: V. vii. 1: xxvii. 13.

幽 *yew yu*

(1) Dark, = ignorant, *i.e.*, the idle and undeserving. II. i. 27. (2) 幽都, the extreme north of Yaou's empire. I. 7. 幽洲, an island where Shun confined the minister of Works. II. i. 12.

幾 *ke chi*

Up. 1st tone. The small beginnings or springs of things. II. iii. 5. = motives. V. xxvii. 9. 惟幾 = to attend to the slightest particulars. II. iv. 2, 11. But in V. xxvii. 4, the same phrase = there is but a little between me and death.

THE 53d RADICAL. 广.

序 *seu hsü*

Short walls, running north and south, in the hall in front of the private apartments of the imperial palace. V. xxii. 16, 17, 19.

底 *te ti*

Bottom, that which is underneath. V. xxii. 16. See 底.

庚 *kăng kêng*

(1) The 7th of the calendaric stem-characters. V. iii. 3: xii. 3: xxiv. 1. (2) 盤庚, one of the emperors of the Shang dynasty. IV. vii.

府 *foo fu*

A treasury. III. iii. 18. Treasurers. V. xix. 8. 六府, the six magazines or treasuries of nature. II. ii. 8: III. i. Pt. ii. 15. To form a treasury, to accumulate. V. xxvii. 21.

度 *too tu*

(1) Measures of length. II. i. 8: V. xx. 4. (2) Measures generally, = rules, regulations, laws. Often joined with 法. II. ii. 4: III. iii. 1: IV. v. Pt. i. 7: Pt. ii. 3; *et al.* 無度, lawless. V. i. Pt. ii. 3: xiv. 16. Compare 非度, IV. xi. 2.

百度, all measures, all the conduct. V. v. 5. As a verb, to bring under rule. IV. vii. Pt. i. 17.

To measure or calculate; to deliberate. II. iv. 8: V. i. Pt. i. 8: xv. 4: xxvii. 1, 14.

度
tŏ
to

庬
mung

See 厖.

庭
t'ing

The court of a palace. V. xxii. 10. It is found generally as = the court or place of audience of the sovereign. IV. vii. Pt. i. 5; Pt. ii. 1: V. xiv. 20: xviii. 28. To appear at court. V. xx. 1. 帝庭, the court of God. V. vi. 7.

庶
shoo
shu

Passim. It is one of the words, whose frequency is characteristic of the Shoo. As an adjective, numerous, all; the various, all comprehended in a class. II. iv. 11 will show how it is employed like the indefinite 百. 庶民, V. iv. 9, 10, 11, 16, 25—30; *et al.,* = the common people, the masses. 庶人, III. iv. 5: V. xvii. 1, = the common people, or one of the common people, in distinction from men of rank. It is used also as a noun = the multitudes. II. ii. 11: iv. 1: IV. i 1. = the several classes. II. iv. 7. See 庶殷殷庶, V. xii. 7, where the usages as subst. and adj. come together. 庶羣, the herd of creatures. V. x. 11. (2) It may be, the result will probably be. V. xiii. 6: xxvii. 13.

康
k'ang

(1) To tranquillize, to secure the repose of. IV. viii. Pt. i. 9: V. xvii. 6; *et sæpe.* We find it along with other verbs, 惠康, 康寧, 康乂, 康保. Obs. 惟康, study stability. II. iv. 2. To be brought to repose; a condition of ease and tranquillity. II. iv. 11: IV. vii. Pt. i. 6; Pt. ii. 4: V. vii. 1, 4. We have 康彊, V. iv. 26; 平康, p. 17; *et al.* We may take it adverbially in IV. x. 3, and V. ix. 6. Obs. 而康而色, V. iv. 11. (2) 太康, and 仲康, two of the emperors of the Shang dynasty. III. iii. 1, and iv. 1. 康 was also the posthumous title of the son of king Ching, and he appears among the emperors of the Chow dyn. as king K'ang. V. xxv. 2.

庸
yung

(1) To use,—either to display, or to employ. I. 9, 12: II. ii. 16: IV. vi. 3; *et al.* = to have occasion to, on purpose, therefore, thereon. II. iv. 11: IV. v. Pt. i. 4: viii. Pt. i. 2: V. v. 3: viii. 3: x. 15: xvi. 6: xviii. 13. 庸庸, to employ the employ-able. V. ix. 4. 徵庸, to be called to be employed. II. i. 27. Opp. to 靜, and = when employed. I. 10. Obs. 庸帝命, V. xiv. 5. (2) Merit, services.

II. i. 9, 17. 自庸, to seek one's merit in. (3) The name of a wild tribe. V. ii. 3.

廉
lëen
lien

To be discriminating; discrimination. II. iii. 3.

廟
mëaou
miao

An ancestral temple. Either alone, or with 宗. IV. v. Pt. i. 2: vi. 10: V. i. Pt. i. 6; Pt. iii. 3: iii. 3. An apartment of the palace is so called on occasion. V. xxii. 29.

廡
woo
wu

Luxuriant. V. iv. 32.

廢
fei

To abolish or set aside; to disregard; to render nugatory. II. ii. 3: III. iv. 1: IV. vii. Pt. iii. 7: V. ix. 5: xiii. 13: xiv. 5: xxi. 5.

廣
kwang
kuang

To be enlarged; vast, wide. II. ii. 4: III. i. Pt. i. 24: IV. vi. 11: V. viii. 2: xx. 17.

THE 54TH RADICAL. 廴.

延
yen

(1) To conduct. V. xxii. 11. (2) To extend to. V. xxvii. 2. To be prolonged. II. ii. 13: V. xii. 17: xvi. 6. = to delay. V. vii. 1.

建
këen
chien

To establish or set up, to appoint, II. iv. 8: IV. ii. 8; *et sæpe.* Without any object, = to exert an establishing influence. V. xiv. 8. Used adverbially. V. iv. 4.

THE 55TH RADICAL. 廾.

弁
pëen
pien

A skin or fur cap. There were different kinds of it. V. vi. 16: xxii. 21.

異
e
i

異哉, well but. I. 11. The meaning is uncertain.

THE 56TH RADICAL. 弋.

弋
yih
yi

To aim at. V. xiv. 3.

式
shih

(1) A model, a law. V. viii. 4: xx. 14. To take as a model, to imitate. V. xix. 4: xxi. 3: xxv. 7. To give an example of. V. xix. 24. (2) To reverence; reverently. IV. viii. Pt. i. 2: vii. Pt. iii. 13: V. xxv. 4. To bow to the cross-bar of a carriage, in token of reverence. V. iii. 9. (3) Explained by 用, and = to employ, to use; to cause; thereby, thereon. IV. ii. 3: viii. Pt. iii. 7: V. xi. 5: xvi. 21: xviii. 19: xix. 5, 24: xxiv. 3. 式爾, purposely. V. ix. 8. = and. V. xii. 23.

THE 57TH RADICAL. 弓.

弓
kung
A bow. V. xxii. 19 : xxviii. 4 : xxix. 2.

弔
teaou
tiao
Always in the phrase 弗弔, which appears to mean—unpitying. V. vii. 1 : xiv. 2 : xvi. 2.

弔
teih
ti
To come or proceed to. IV. vii. Pt. iii. 7 : V. ix. 16. That which has come to the extreme ; in perfect order. V. xxix. 2.

引
yin
To lead, to lead on to. V. ix. 17 : xi. 3 : xiv. 5. 引慝, to take crime to one's-self. II. ii. 21. 引考 = to enjoy long prosperity. V. xiii. 27.

弗
fuh
fu
Not. *Passim.* The frequency of its use is characteristic of the Shoo. = do not. V. ii. 9.

弘
hwang
huang
Large ; to enlarge, give full development to ; largely. V. viii. 4 : xiii. 22 : xx. 6 : xxi. 7 : xxii. 7, 19 : xxv. 4. Observe 弘于天, and 弘王, V. ix. 5, 7.

弟
te
ti
A younger brother or cousin. III. iii. 3 : V. vi. 12 ; *et al.* 兄弟, brethren or cousins. V. xvii. 6 : xxi. 2. 父母弟 = paternal and maternal relatives. V. ii. 6. 作兄弟, with brotherly affection. V. xi. 5.

弱
jŏ
jao
(1) Weak ; weakness. IV. ii. 7 : V. iv. 40. = to despise. IV. vii. Pt. i. 15. (2) 弱水, the name of a stream. III. i. Pt. i. 72 ; Pt. ii. 5.

張
chang
To be displayed. V. i. Pt. i. 8. To be adjusted. IV. v. Pt. i. 7. 張皇, maintain in great display. V. xxiii. 3. 譸張, extravagant talk. V. xv. 14, 18.

弼
peih
pi
To help ;—sometimes = to correct. II. ii. 11 : iv. 5, 8 : V. i. Pt. i. 11 ; *et sæpe.* An assistant, helpers. II. iii. 1 : iv. 2 : IV. viii. Pt. i. 2.

彊
k'ëang
ch'iang
Valour, strength. II. iii. 3. 康彊, sound and strong in body. V. iv. 26. In p. 17, 彊 = violence, or the violent.

彌
me
mi
Still more. V. xxii. 4.

THE 58TH RADICAL. 彐.

彝
e
i
(1) A cup. 宗彝, a cup used in the ancestral temple, and a figure of which was embroidered on the lower garment of the emperor, which he wore on great occasions. II. iv. 4. (2) The nature of man, with its sense of the duties belonging to its various relations. V. iv. 2, 3 : ix. 16. (3) A rule, a law. IV. iii. 7 : V. ix. 13, 22 ; *et sæpe.* (4) Constant, regular ; to be constant, addicted to. V. x. 4, 5 : xvi. 13 : xvii. 3 ; *et al.*

THE 59TH RADICAL. 彡.

形
hing
hsing
The figure, appearance. IV. viii. Pt. i. 3.

彤
t'ung
(1) Red, painted with vermilion. V. xxii. 23 : xxviii. 4. (2) The name of a certain supplementary sacrifice. IV. ix. 1. (3) The name of a principality. V. xxii. 8.

彥
yen
Men admirable and accomplished. IV. v. Pt. i. 5 : V. xix. 17. : xxx. 6, 7.

彫
tëaou
tiao
Carved. III. iii. 6.

彭
p'ăng
p'êng
彭蠡, the name of a lake,—the present Po-yang. III. i. Pt. i. 38 ; Pt. ii. 8. 彭 was also the name of a wild tribe. V. ii. 3.

彰
chang
To display, give distinction to. V. xi. 18 : xxiv. 7 : IV. vii. Pt. i. 6. To make—be made—manifest ; plainly. II. iii. 3 : iv. 4 : IV. iii. 3 : iv. 8 : V. i. Pt. ii. 3 ; Pt. iii. 2. Observe. IV. ii. 5.

影
ying
A shadow. II. ii. 5.

THE 60TH RADICAL. 彳.

役
yih
yi
To serve ; to make to serve. V. ii. 9 : v. 5 : vii. 8 : xiii. 12.

彼
pe
pi
That, those. III. iii. 7 : V. i. Pt. ii. 5, 8. = there. V. xiii. 13.

往
wang
(1) To go, to go to. *Passim.* The phrase 往哉 is very common. (2) The past. 既往, IV. v. Pt. ii. 3. So, perhaps, V. xix. 3. The future. 其往, henceforward. V. xiii. 9.

征
ching
chêng
To punish, to execute imperial justice. II. ii. 20 : III. iv. 1 : IV. ii. 6 : V. iii. 1, 7 : vii. 7 (*n. b.*) ; *et al.*

徂
tsoo
tsu
(1) To go, to go to. II. ii. 20 ; *et sæpe.* It is much used along with 征. (2) Like the 2d use of 往, = the past. V. x. 8.

待
tae
tai
To wait for. IV. v. Pt. i. 5.

徇
seun
hsün
To go along or round. III. iv. 3. = to review. V. i. Pt. ii. 1.

很
hĕn
hen
疾很 = to be frenzied. Spoken of the mind. V. x. 11.

律
leuh
lü
(1) Standard tubes, used as pitch pipes in music, and for other purposes. II. i. 8, 24. 六律. II. iv. 4. (2) To be a law to. V. viii. 4.

後
how
hou

That which is after. (1) **As a noun.** A future;—afterwards. IV. v. Pt. i. 3 : vii. Pt. ii. 7 ; V. vi. 15 ; *et al.* An heir, successors. V. vii. 11 : xvii. 3 : xix. 3. Those behind. V. iii. 9. Obs. V. xxii. 6. (2) **As an adj.** Future, after. We have 後人, 後王, 後嗣, 後昆, 後裔, 後日, 後言, and perhaps other phrases. IV. ii. 8 : iv. 6 : v. Pt. i. 5 : x. 11 : V. viii. 2 ; *et al.* 前後之人, xxvi. 3. (3) **As a verb.** To put last, postpone. IV. ii. 6. To be remiss in. To remain. V. xii. 13, xiii. 13, 20, 29, 30. 先後, V. xi. 7, need not be toned.

徐
seu
hsü

徐州, one of Yu's provinces. III. i. Pt. i. 28. 徐戎, certain wild tribes. V. xxix. 1, 5.

徒
t'oo
t'u

(1) Followers. IV. ii. 14. Soldiers. V. iii. 9. (2) 司徒, the minister of Instruction. II. i. 19 : V. ii. 2 : iv. 7 : xi. 2 : xix. 10 : xx. 8.

得
tih
tê

To get, to be got. IV. ii. 8 : V. vi. 14 : vii. 6 : xii. 2 (= to get successfully.) 得罪, to commit crime, offend. V. ix. 15, 16.

從
ts'ung

To follow ; to act in accordance or compliance with. II. ii. 3, 5, 6, 13, 18 ; *et passim.* = to employ as before. V. xix. 15. 從子保, to allow the son to succeed, and to protect him. V. xii. 11. 月之從星, the moon's following (= course among) the stars. V. iv. 38. = accordance with reason. V. iv. 6. To be made to follow,—to a certain place. III. i. Pt. i. 74 ;—their natural channels, p. 9. To be observed. II. i. 2. From ;—as a sequence of. Adverbially, = consequently. V. xiv. 27 : IV. viii. Pt. ii. 3 : vii. Pt. i. 14.

從
sung

從容, to show an easy forbearance. V. xxi. 7.

從
tsung

Low, 3d tone. Followers, immediate attendants. V. xxvi. 2.

御
yu
yü

(1) To drive a carriage. III. ii. 4 : V. xxx. 5. (2) To wait on, be in attendance on. III. iii. 3. 侍御, V. xxvi. 4. (3) To advance—present—to. xxii. 23. (4) To manage, superintend. In the phrase 御事, managers of affairs, which was a favourite description of managers and officers under the Chow dyn. V. i. Pt. i. 2 : II. ii. ; *et sœpe.* (5) To condescend to. Spoken of the emperor's demeanour to his ministers. II. ii. 12.

偏
p'ëen
p'ien

All round. To extend one's proceedings all round. II. i. 6.

復
fuh
fu

To return, give back. II. i. 8 : IV. vi. 1 : vii. Pt. iii. 6 : V. xxix. 4. To report the execution of a commission. V. xiii. 1. To recover. V. vii. 4. To reply to. IV.

viii. Pt. i. 11. 紹復, to continue. IV. vii. Pt. i. 4.

Again. V. xii. 8.

復
fow
fou

循
seun
hsün

To comply with. 率循, V. xxii. 24.

微
we
wei

(1) Small. II. ii. 15. To be reduced to obscurity. V. iv. 37. (2) The seat of a wild tribe. V. ii. 3 : xix. 11. (3) A principality so called. IV. xi. 1. To wait for. II. iv. 2 : III. iii. 3 : IV. ii. 6 : v. Pt. ii. 5.

徯
he
hsi

徵
ching
chĕng

(1) To be called. II. i. 28. (2) To be verified, III. iv. 2. Verifications. V. iv. 4, 32, 34.

德
tih
tê

Virtue, virtuous deeds ; virtuous ; virtuously. *Passim.* 九德, II. iii. 3. 一德, IV. vi. 3, 4. 三德, V. iv. 4, 13. 奉德, V. xiv. 18, and 秉德, xviii. 23, = to hold as a virtue. The term is also used of conduct, or a course, which is not virtuous, but indifferent or positively evil ; as in IV. i. 3 : vii. Pt. iii. 4 ·(*n. b.*) : viii. Pt. ii. 5 : V. i. Pt. ii. 3 : iv. 10 : xv. 13 : x. 23 : xviii. 27 ; *et al.* Excellent ; excellently. V. xv. 10 : xix. 18. To set forth the excellence of. II. i. 2.

徽
hwuy
hui

THE 61st RADICAL. 心.

心
sin
hsin

The heart ; the heart, the mind, denoting the mental constitution generally. Observe 心腹腎腸, IV. vii. Pt. iii. 3 ; and 股肱心膂, V. xxv. 3 ; 天心, the mind of Heaven, and 上帝之心, the mind of God. IV. iii. 8, and vi. 3. 宅心, V. ix. 5, to settle, establish, the heart ; but the same phrase is different in xix. 6, 12. Must, as an auxiliary. IV. i. 3 : iv. 8 : v. Pt. iii. 4, 7 : V. i. Pt. i. 11 ; Pt. ii. 5, 7 : xx. 5 : xxi. 12.

必
peih
pi

忌
ke
chi

(1) To fear. V. xviii. 27. To be apprehensive, cautious. 敬忌, V. ix. 19 : xxii. 25 : xxvii. 11. (2) To hate. V. xxx. 4.

忍
jin
jĕn

To bear, to endure. 弗忍, to be unable to endure. III. iii. 2 : IV. iii. 3. Patience. V. xxi. 12.

忒
t'ih
t'ĕ

Errors. V. iv. 19, 23.

忘
wang

To forget, to be forgotten. V. vii. 2 : viii. 3 : x. 7.

志
che
chih

The will, the aims. *Sæpe.* 百志, all one's purposes. II. ii. 6. = earnest thought. II. i. 24. 役志, to make the will to serve, service of the will. V. xiii. 12.
To disgrace. I. 12: IV. v. Pt. i. 3: V. xxv. 3.

黍
t'een
t'ien

忠
chung

To be loyal; loyalty. To give one's whole heart to. IV. ii. 7: iv. 5, 7: V. i. Pt. i. 5: xvii. 3: xxv. 1: xxvi. 2.

忱
shin
ch'ên

To be sincere; sincerity. IV. iii. 9: vii. Pt. ii. 6: V. vii. 10, 13: ix. 6, 22: xvi. 2: xix. 2. To regard sincerely. xviii. 29. To be believed. xviii. 21. Observe. 忱 裕之, xviii. 21. To believe sincerely. IV. viii. Pt. ii. 13.

念
neen
nien

To think; to think of, to regard, thoughts. II. ii. 7, 10; *et sæpe.* 服念, to reflect on. V. ix. 12. Thoughtfully. V. iv. 4.

忸
nuh
nu

忸怩, to blush, to be ashamed. III. iii. 9.

忽
hwuh
hu

To slight, to show indifference. V. xx. 16. Defects of govt. II. iv. 4; but this passage is uncertain.

忿
fun
fên

To be angry. V. xxi. 11.

怒
noo
nu

To be angry; anger. IV. vii. Pt. iii. 3: V. i. Pt. i. 5: iv. 3: xv. 17. 自怒, to anger one's-self. V. vii. Pt. ii. 6.

怙
hoo
hu

To rely on. It occurs in three combinations, each of which requires study. 怙終, II. i. 11: 怙冒, V. ix. 4; 怙侈, V. xxiv. 10.

思
sze
szû

To think, to think of. II. iii. 1: iv. 1: IV. v. Pt. ii. 7: *et sæpe.* Thinking. V. iv. 6. To wish. II. iii. 8. The character is marked in the third tone in I. 1, to be thoughtful.

怠
tae
tai

To be idle. II. ii. 6, 9: *et sæpe.* = to cease, IV. xi. 7. To grow weary. IV. i. 3. Idly. III. ii. 3.

急
keih
chi

Haste. V. iv. 24.

性
sing
hsing

The nature. Used with ref. to man. IV. v. Pt. i. 9: V. xii. 15. 天性, the Heavenly nature. IV. x. 3. 恆性, the nature invariably right. IV. iii. 2. Used with ref. to animals. V. v. 8 (*n. b.*)

怨
yuen
yüan

To murmur, to murmur against. III. iii. 3: IV. ii. 6: V. ix. 21; *et sæpe.* What provokes resentment. V. ix. 22: x. 11. = dissatisfaction. III. iii. 5: V. ix. 6. = enmity. V. i. Pt. iii. 2.

怩
ne
ni
nieh

忸怩, to blush, to be ashamed. III. iii. 9.

怪
kwae
kuai

Strange. III. i. Pt. i. 26.

怵
ch'uh
ch'u

怵惕, to be alarmed. V. xxvi. 1.

恂
seun
hsün

To be sincere. 忱恂, V. xix. 2.

恆
hăng
hêng

(1) Constant; constancy; constantly. IV. iii. 2 (see 性): iv. 7: xi. 3: V. iv. 34: xi. 2: xiii. 4: xxiv. 8. To make constant, to preserve long. V. xiii. 14. (2) 恆山, the name of a mountain. III. i. Pt. ii. 1. The name of a river. III. i. Pt. i. 9.

恐
k'ung

To fear, be afraid. IV. ii. 1: vii. Pt. ii. 8: viii. Pt. i. 2: x. 1: V. vi. 16: xxii. 4. = to frighten. IV. v. Pt. i. 12.

恤
seuh
hsio

To pity, compassionate. II. i. 11: IV. i. 2: V. vii. 8; *et al.* 恤宅, the house of mourning. V. xxii. 11. To be anxious about. V. xii. 23: xiv. 7: xvi. 9: xix. 1. Anxieties. IV. vii. Pt. ii. 15: V. xii. 9: xvi. 18. 奉恤, to enter into anxieties. V. xxiii. 6. 恤功, to labour anxiously. xxvii. 8.
To be ashamed, to be ashamed of. IV. viii. Pt. ii. 9; Pt. iii. 10.

恥
ch'e
ch'ih

恪
k'ŏ
k'o

To respect. Reverently. 恪謹, IV. viii. Pt. i 3. 恪慎, V. viii. 3.

恫
t'ung

To be pained. 奉其恫, to feel the smart. IV. vii. Pt. ii. 12. 恫瘝, sickness and pain. V. ix. 6.

恬
t'een
t'ien

To be peaceful, at ease. 引恬, to lead to the enjoyment of ease. V. xi. 3.

恭
kung

To respect or revere; to obey reverently, attend reverently to; respectfulness, reverence. I. 10: II. i. 1: ii. 20: iii. 3, 6: IV. vii. Pt. i. 17: V. iii. 7: *et sæpe.* = courteous, humble. I. 1: V. xv. 4, 10. Before other verbs, its force is adverbial and = reverently. III i. 3: IV. vii. Pt. iii. 5, 10: V. i. Pt. iii. 3; *et sæpe.* Obs. V. xviii. 5, 17, where the meaning = respected (past participle).

息
seih
hsi

To stop, cease. V. x. 11.

悅
yuĕ
yueh

To be pleased. IV. v. Pt. ii. 5: V. iii. 9. To please, give pleasure to. V. i. Pt. iii. 3.

悉
seih
hsi

All; altogether, fully. IV. i. 1: vii. Pt. i. 5: V. xvi. 18. In everything. V. xiii. 8.

悔
hœny
hui

To repent. III. iii. 9: IV. vii. Pt. i. 12, 17. Repentance. V. iv. 22.

悖
pei
To oppose, act contrary to. V. xxiv. 9.

悛
tseuen
chüan
To repent and alter. i. 悛心, a penitent heart. V. i. Pt. i. 7.

悟
woo
wu
To awake. = to recover. V. xxii. 7.

患
hwan
huan
Calamity, disaster. IV. viii. Pt. ii. 8.

悲
pe
pei
To be sad. III. iii. 9.

情
ts'ing
ch'ing
The feelings. V. ix. 6. ·

惇
tun
(1) To give honour to. II. i. 16 : V. xiii. 15, 23. = in a large and generous way. II. iii. 1 : V. xiii. 10. To prove the solidity of. V. iii. 9. Observe 五惇哉, II. iii. 6. (2) 惇物, the name of a mountain. III. i. Pt. i. 76.
To stand in awe of. IV. vii. Pt. i. 6.

惕
t'eih
t'i
怵惕, see 怵.

惟
wei
No other character occurs so frequently in the Shoo as this. I have counted more than 350 instances of its use. We find it constantly at the beginning of Books and paragraphs, where it is hardly susceptible of translation, and we may content ourselves with saying that it is an initial particle. Here we may call it, *now*; there it is simply as the note which a man gives when he clears his throat preparatory to speaking. We find it again as frequently in the middle of sentences, coming after the subject, and acting as the *copula* to connect it and the predicate. · For this usage of it the student may refer especially to. III. i., where it occurs nearly 30 times. Again, it is sometimes treated as a verb, and defined by 思, to think of, to care for. *E. g.* II. iv. 3 : IV. v. Pt. iii. 5 : V. i. Pt. i. 5 ; Pt. iii. 4. Lastly, it is used constantly as a conjunction, connecting sentences and clauses together, and must be variously translated—*and, but, and so, namely,* &c. It often = *only*, half adverbial, half conjunctive. *E. g.* II. ii. 3, 20 : IV. vii. Pt. ii. 4, 6 : V. iv. 18. Its use along with 哉, as in II. i. 11, 16, 17, 20, 23, 25, 26 ; and after 亦, 其 and 洪, as in IV. vii. Pt. i. 7 ; Pt. ii. 5 : V. i. Pt. i. 4, is to be observed.

惠
hwuy
hui
(1) To be kind to ; to love. V. i. Pt. ii. 4 : xv. 10. We have 惠康, xxvii. 4 ; 保惠, xv. 6, 14 ; 子惠, IV. v. Pt. ii. 5. To be kind ; the kind. II. iii. 2 : V. xvii. 4. (2) To accord with, to obey. II. i. 17 : ii. 5 : IV. i. Pt. i. 1 : V. xiii. 27 : xviii.

21. To be accordant, accordingly, with reason. II. iv. 8 : V. ix. 6 : xvi. 22. (3) A kind of three-cornered halberd. V. xxii. 21.

惡
yŏ
o
Evil, wickedness ; the evil. V. i. Pt. iii. 4 : iv. 40 : xxiv. 7 ; *et al.* 爲惡, deeds of evil. V. xvii. 4. 元惡, chief criminals. V. ix. 16. 惡德, men of wicked practices. IV. viii. Pt. ii. 5. 先惡, to set an example of wickedness. IV. vii. Pt. i. 12.

惡
woo
wu
To hate. V. xxx. 7. 作惡, manifestations of selfish disliking. V. iv. 14.

惰
to
To be idle ; to be idle at. II. iv. 11 : IV. vii. Pt. i. 11.

愆
k'een
ch'ien
To go beyond. V. ii. 7, 8. To be in error ; faults. II. ii. 12 : IV. viii. Pt. iii. 6 : V. xv. 13, 17 ; *et sæpe.* 十愆, the ten evil ways. IV. iv. 7. = to chastise. V. xxviii. 2. ? = to be exhausted. V. xxx. v.

愚
yu
yü
Simple. 愚夫愚婦, III. iii. 5.

愛
gae
ai
To love, to be loved. V. x. 5, 11. (foll. by 于) : II. ii. 17. Love. IV. iv. 4. Compassion. III. iv. 7. To love one's-self. V. xviii. 22.

感
kan
To influence. II. ii. 21 : V. xxxi. 3 (foll. by 于).

愧
kwei
k'uei
To be ashamed. 愧恥, IV. viii. Pt. iii. 10.

慎
shin
shên
To be careful to—, to attend carefully to ; carefully. II. i. 2 : ii. 17 : iii. 1 : iv. 2, 11 : III. i. Pt. ii. 15 : *et sæpissime.* To be cautious in. V. ix. 3 : xviii. 10. = careful anxiety. xix. 24. 庶慎, precautionary measures. xix. 13, 14, 16, 18. 恪慎. V. viii. 3.
To be honest and blunt ; bluntness. II. iii. 3.

願
yuen
yüan

慄
leih
li
慄慄, to be apprehensive. IV. iii. 6.

慆
t'aou
t'ao
Excessive, insolent. IV. iii. 7.

慕
moo
mo
To desire *to do good.* V. xxiv. 7.

慙
ts'an
To be ashamed of, a feeling of shame for. IV. ii. 1.

慝
neih
ni
The wicked, secretly wicked. V. xx. 11 : xxiv. 7. 引慝, to take the wickedness or guilt to one's-self. II. ii. 21.

慢
man

慮
leu
lü

慰
wei

To contemn, be insolent. II. ii. 20 : V. vi. 3, 慢遊, idle dissipation. II. iv. 8.
To think anxiously ; to think anxiously about. IV. v. Pt. iii. 8 : viii. Pt. ii. 6.

To soothe. 由慰, to tread the path of satisfaction, the way to soothe one's-self. V. xxvii. 13.

慶
k'ing
ch'ing

(1) Excellence. V. xxvii. 22 : xxx. 8. (2) To be happy ; happiness. V. x. 6 : xxvii. 13. (3) To congratulate ; cause for congratulation. IV. ii. 6 : iv. 8.

慽
ts'eih
ch'i

To be sorrowful. IV. vii. Pt. i. 1. To sympathize with ; sympathizingly. IV. vii. Pt. ii. 3 : V. xviii. 4.

憂
yew
yu

To be sorrowful ; sorrow. II. iii. 2 : V. iv. 40 : xxx. 3. 憂危, V. xxv. 2. 居憂 and 宅憂, to occupy the place of sorrow and mourning. IV. v. Pt. i. 10 : viii. Pt. i. 1. To sympathize with. IV. vii. Pt. ii. 6. Obs. 勸憂, IV. vii. Pt. ii. 7.

憑
p'ăng
p'êng

To lean upon. V. xxii. 2, 24.

憝
tuy
tui

To be abhorred. V. ix. 15, 16, 17.

憲
hëen
hsien

Laws, rules ; a pattern. II. iv. 11 : III. iv. 2 : IV. viii. Pt. iii. 6 : V. xvii. 3 : xxvi. 9. To take as a pattern. IV. viii. 1 t. ii. 3.

憸
seen
hsëen

憸人, flatterers. V. xix. 20 : xxvi. 7. 憸民, the poor people. IV. vii. Pt. i. 12.

應
ying

(1) To respond, be responded, to. II. iv. 2, 7. = harmoniously. V. ix. 7. (2) The name of the fourth gate of the palace. V. xxiii. 1.

懋
mow
mou

(1) To exert one's-self, to be energetic ; to labour strenuously for. II. i 17 : ii. 11 : iii. 6 : iv. 1 : IV. iv. 2 : V. Pt. ii. 6 ; Pt. iii. 3 : *et sæpe*. (2) To be great. IV. ii. 5. To make great. IV. ii. 5. To acknowledge the greatness of. II. ii. 14.

懌
yih
yi

To please. V. xi. 7. To be pleased. IV. v. Pt. i. 7 : V. ix. 19. 不懌, to be indisposed, sick. V. xxii. 1.

懍
lin

懍懍, and 懍乎, to be full of trembling awe. V. i. Pt. ii. 9 : III. iii. 5.

懫
che
chih

To be resentful. = Cruel. V. xviii. 5.

懲
ch'ing

To correct. V. i. Pt. i. 6. To correct one's-self, to take warning. V. xxvii. 12. To punish ; punishment. V. xxvii. 20.

懿
e
i

Admirably. V. xv. 10.

懷
hwae
huai

(1) To embrace, surround. I. 11 : II. iv. 1. (2) To cherish,—either to love and be grateful to, or to love and protect. II.

ii. 10 : iii. 2 : III. iii. 9 ; *et sæpe.* 懷保, V. xv. 10. Foll. by 于. IV. v. Pt. iii. 1 : viii. Pt. iii. 4. To cling to,—as a place. IV. vii. Pt. ii. 4. = to obey gladly. IV. iv. 3 : V. xx. 15. (3) To be tranquil ; tranquillity. V. xxviii. 1 : xxx. 8. (4). 覃懷, the name of a tract of country. II. i. Pt. i. 6.

懼
keu
chü

To fear. IV. ii. 4 : V. xxvii. 21. 祇懼, to be reverently afraid. V. i. Pt. i. 10 : xv. 4. 危懼, to be tremblingly afraid. IV. iii. 6.

THE 62D RADICAL. 戈.

戈
ko

A spear or lance. V. ii. 4 : iii. 8 : xxii. 19, 21. = a spearman. xxii. 11. 干戈, IV. viii. Pt. ii. 4. 戈矛, V. xxix. 2.

戊
mow
mou

The fifth of the calendaric stem-characters. V. i. Pt. ii. 1 : iii. 8 : xii. 2, 5 : xiii. 29. 太戊, one of the emperors of the Shang dynasty. V. xvi. 7.

戌
seŭh
hsü

The eleventh of the calendaric branch-characters. V. iii. 3 : xii. 3 : xxix. 5.

戎
jung

(1) A weapon of war. 戎兵, V. xix. 22. 興戎 and 起戎 = to raise war. II. ii. 17 : IV. viii. Pt. ii. 4. 戎衣, to don arms. V. iii. 8. = to attack. V. i. Pt. ii. 5. (2) Great. IV. vii. Pt. i. 11 : V. ix. 4. (3) The name of the wild tribes of the west. III. i. Pt. i. 83 : V. xxviii. 2. But we find *jung* in the east. V. xxix. 1, 5.

成
ching
chêng

(1) To complete, to perfect, to establish. I. 8 : II. ii. 6 : IV. 8, 11 ; *et passim.* 成民, to perfect the condition of the people. V. xx. 13. Obs. 成裕, xiii. 10 ; 成允, II. ii. 14. To be completed. I. 11 : V. xxvii. 20 ; *et al.* Observe 天成, II. ii. 8 ; 性成, IV. v. Pt. i. 9. 九成, is spoken of music, II. iv. 9. Completed ; complete, perfect. III. i. Pt. ii. 23 : IV. viii. Pt. ii. 13 ; Pt. iii. 6 : V. iii. 3 : v. 8 ; *et sæpe.* 成人, complete men, thoroughly accomplished. V. ix. 5 ; *et al.* 成命 = the determinate counsel. V. iii. 7. 成功 = an office whose work is done. IV. v. Pt. iii. 9. But the same phrase often occurs, = to complete one's work, completed work. 西成, the realizations of the autumn. I. 6. 成

alone = completion. V. xxiv. 5. (2) The posthumous title of the 2d emp. of the Chow dyn. V. x. 9, 10 : xxv. 2. 成湯, T'ang the Successful. IV. ii. 1 : vi. 3 ; *et sæpe.* 成周, the capital at Lŏ, to which the people of Yin were removed. V. xxiv. 1, 14.

我
go
wo
The first personal pronoun ; also possessive. I, me, my, we, us, our. *Passim.*

戒
këae
chieh
To caution ; cautions, warnings. II. ii. 7 : III. iii. 3 : iv. 2 : IV. vi. 1 : V. xix. 1 : xx. 17. To beware of. IV. viii. Pt. ii. 4 : V. xxvii. 13. 戒哉, be cautious, take care. II. ii. 6 : III. iv. 7 : IV. v. Pt. i. 3 : V. xvii. 4 : xxi. 4.

牂
ts'ëang
ch'iang
To do violence, to assault. V. xi. 2, 3. To be injurious. IV. vii. Pt. ii. 13.

或
hwo
huo
Perhaps. V. xiv. 26 : xv. 18 : xxi. 13. It most frequently occurs after negative adverbs, as 罔, II. ii. 11. *et sæpe* ; 無, IV. vii. Pt. i. 5, *et sæpe* : 莫, V. xxi. 5 ; 不, IV, vii. Pt. ii. 6 : 弗, IV. xi. 1 ; and 未, III. iii. 6 ; when its force is to put the assertion with some reservation, or to make the command with some modification. Sonetimes it makes the sentence hypothetical,—if, should it be that. V. x. 14 : xv. 17 : III. iv. 3. Observe V. xv. 5.

戚
ts'eih
ch'i
To distress. V. vi. 3.

憂
këă
chia
To tap, to strike gently. II. iv. 9. Read *k'ëă,* = to subject to the laws. V. ix. 17.

戡
k'an
(1) To subdue. IV. x. 1. (2) To sustain, be equal to. V. xvi. 20. = fully. xxiii. 3.

戣
kwei
kuei
A kind of lance. V. xxi. 21.

截
tsëĕ
chieh
截截 = quibbling. V. xxx. 5.

戮
luh
lu
(1) To put—be put—to death. V. ii. 10. 殄戮. V. xii. 21 : xviii. 11. Obs. 孥戮, III. ii. 5 : IV. i. 4. To murder, to slaughter. V. i. Pt. iii. 1 : xxvii. 3. = in danger of being murdered. xxvii. 4. 5. To ruin. IV. x. 7 (foll. by 于). (2) ? disgrace. V. i. Pt. iii. 4. (3) Used for 勠, to exert. IV. iii. 4.

戰
chen
chan
(1) To fight. 大戰, they fought a great battle. III. ii. 1. (2) To fear, be full of awe. V. xxviii. 23. 戰戰, IV. ii. 4.

戲
he
hsi
To sport, to play. IV. vii. Pt. iii. 2 : x. 2.

戴
tae
tai
To carry on the head. = to support, to honour, II. ii. 17 : IV. ii. 6.

THE 63D RADICAL. 戶.

The projecting edge of a raised hall or platform. V. xxii. 21.

戹
sze
szŭ
(1) Tribulations, calamity. IV. v. Pt. ii. 3 : V. vii. 13 : xiv. 17. (2) 獲戾, to commit transgression, to offend. IV. iii. 6. (3) To come to. V. xiii. 13. (4) To stop or still. V. ix. 21.

戾
le
li
A place. V. vii. 10. (2) To rest in ; a resting place. V. xv. 1 : xiv. 16. (3) That which ; which. IV. vii. Pt. i. 7 : V. Pt. i, 11 : ii. 10 (= wherein) : iii. 6 : v. 8 : vi. 16, 19 : xxi. 14 : xxx. 4 (罔所). (4) At the end of a sentence,—an expletive. V. xvi. 8.

所
so
(1) An apartment. V. xxii. 19. (2) The name of a constellation,—a part of Scorpio. III. iv. 4.

房
fang
(1) The name of a principality. III. ii. 3. (2) The name of a minister of T'ae-mow. V. xvi. 7.

扈
hoo
hu
繡扆, a screen ornamented with figures of axes. V. xxii. 14.

扆
e
i

THE 64TH RADICAL. 手.

手
show
shou
The hands. It is used—but with one exception—always in the phrase 拜手稽首, to do obeisance with the hands to the face and the head to the ground. II. iv. 11 : IV. v. Pt. ii. 3, 4 : V. xii. 8, 24 ; *et al.* The other instance is 假手于, to borrow a hand from, to make use of. IV. iv. 2.

扑
p'uh
p'u
To beat with a stick, or with twigs. II. i. 11.

扞
han
To defend. V. xxviii. 3.

承
ch'ing
ch'êng
To receive. II. iv. 6 : III. iv. 1 : IV. iii. 7 ; *et al.* To take and carry. V. xxii. 23. To receive, = to wait on one's wishes. IV. viii. Pt. i. 1 ; Pt. iii. 7 : V. xxvi. 2 ; *et al.* To receive, = to carry out one's plans or work ; to receive and undertake the charge of. III. iv. 5 : IV. v. Pt. ii. 7 : vii. Pt. ii. 3, 4 ; Pt. iii. 5 : V. iii. 5 ; *et sæpe.* = to acknowledge. V. xx. 1. = to anticipate. IV. viii. Pt. i. 11. 祇承上帝, reverently to obey the will of God. V. iii. 6. So, 承上下神祇. IV.

v. Pt. i. 2. 承于 = to treat, to deal with. V. xviii. 5; but IV. vii. Pt. i. 3, is different. 承以, following up with. IV. viii. Pt. ii 2. 統承, V viii. 1.

技
ke
chi
Abilities. V. xxx. 6, 7. 奇技, wonderful contrivances. V. i. Pt. iii. 3.

抑
yih
yi
To repress. 自抑, to attain humility, V. xv. 8.

投
t'ow
t'ou
To throw, to lay. 投于, to lay on. V. vii. 8.

折
chě
chê
(1) To break off. 短折 = shortening of life. V. iv. 40. (2) To determine, to settle. V. xxvii. 30. The meaning of 折民惟刑, in p. 8, is hardly determined.

抱
paou
pao
To carry in the arms. V. xxii. 10.

拊
foo
fu
To tap, or touch gently. Spoken of the handling of musical instruments. II. i. 24 : iv. 9, 10.

援
pă
pa
To be pulled or torn up. V. vi. 16.

拘
keu
chü
To hold fast. 執拘, to apprehend. V. x. 14.

拙
chuě
chuch
To be stupid; stupid. IV. vii. Pt. i. 8 : V. xx. 18.

招
chaou
chao
To call out. IV. viii. Pt. iii. 7.   = to bring on. II. ii. 21.

拜
pae
pai
To do obeisance. The ministers bow to the emperor, and he returns the obeisance. V. xxii. 26, 27, 28; *et al.* The fullest expression of homage is 拜手稽首;—see 手. The form—拜稽首 is also frequent. II. i. 17, 21, 22, 23 : ii. 18; *et al.* We have 拜昌言, to do reverence for the excellent words. II. ii. 21; iii. 1.

括
kwŏ
kuo
(1) The end of an arrow applied to the string. IV. v. I t. i. 7. (2) A name. V. xvi. 12.

拱
kung
To fold the hands, *i. e.* to bring them together in the style of ceremony. In the phrase 垂拱, V. iii. 9 : xxiv. 5.

持
ch'e
ch'ih
To hold. In the phrase 攜持, V. xii. 10.

指
che
chih
To point to, to indicate. IV. vii. Pt. i. 7 : = referring to, as to. IV. x. 8. 有指, what he aimed at. V. vii. 15.

振
chin
chên
In the phrase 振旅, II. ii. 21. ? to withdraw.

授
show
shou
To deliver, give to. I. 3 : V. xxii. 27, 28.

掌
chang
To take charge of, to handle, to direct. III. iv. 1 : V. xx. 7—12.

探
t'an
To bring on. V. xviii. 29.

接
tsěě
chieh
To receive; to be received. IV. v. Pt. ii. 7 : V. v. 7.

推
t'uy
t'ui
To push and overthrow. IV. ii. 7. To push forward, advance. V. xx. 20.

掩
yen
To cover, conceal. IV. vii. Pt. i. 14.

揆
k'wei
k'uei
To calculate.   = to study. III. i. Pt. ii. 20. 百揆, the name of the highest minister under Yaou and Shun. II. i. 2, 17 : V. xx. 3.

揖
yih
yi
To bow,—in salutation. V. xxiii. 2, 7.

揚
yang
(1) To be displayed. IV. viii. Pt. iii. 11 : V. i. Pt. ii. 8 : xiii. 14 : xiv. 22 : xxv. 6. = to point out, bring to the light. I. 12. 道揚, to declare. V. xxii. 24. (2) 揚州, one of Yu's nine provinces. III. i. Pt. i. 37.

搜
sow
sou
Appears in the text in the from 搜. 渠搜, the name of a mountain and wild people, in the west. III. i. Pt. i. 83.

損
sun
Loss, damage. II. ii. 21.

搏
pŏ
po
To strike forcibly,—as the strings in playing a lute. II. iv. 9.

摯
che
chih
To come, to arrive. IV. x. 4.

撫
foo
fu
(1) To soothe; to bring to tranquillity. V. i. Pt. iii. 4 : iii. 5 : viii. 2 : xiii. 10 (foll. by 于): xx. 1. 撫綏, IV. v. Pt. i. 2. (2) To accord with, be observant of. 撫于……II. iii. 4.

播
po
(1) To spread abroad ; to propagate, diffuse. IV. vii. Pt. i. 7 : V. ix. 17 : xxvii. 8, 12. Applied to the sowing of seed, in which application some read it in the 2d tone. II. i. 18 : iv. 1 : V. vii. 11.   = to encourage. V. ix. 1. (2) To be separated. III. i. Pt. ii. 7.   = transported. V. vii. 6. (3) To reject. V. i. Pt. ii. 3 : xviii. 22. (4) 播 and 播家, the name of a mountain. III. i. Pt. i. 1. 4 : Pt. ii. 8.

樸
pŏ
p'u

撻
t'ă
t'a

擇
tsih
chai

擊
keih
chi

攉
hwa
hua

擾
jaou
jao

攘
jang

攜
hwuy
hui

To strike. 樸滅, to extinguish. IV. vii. Pt. i. 12.

To flog. = the scourge. II. iv. 6. To be beaten. IV. viii. Pt. iii. 10.

To choose, to select. V. iv. 20; xxvii. 11, 12, 14.

To tap,—as in playing the sounding-stone. II. i. 24: iv. 9, 10.

3d tone. A trap. V. xxix. 3.

(1) Docility. II. iii. 3. To train to obedience. V. xx. 8. (2) To throw into confusion. III. iv. 4.

To steal upon occasion offered. 寇攘, V. ix. 15: xxix. 4. 奪攘, V. xxvii. 2. 攘竊, IV. xi. 6.

(1) To lead by the hand. 攜持, V. xix. 8. (2) To carry. 左右攜僕, personal attendants. xii. 10.

THE 65TH RADICAL. 支.

支
che
chih

析支, the name of a mountain in the west and of the wild tribes about it. III. i. Pt. i. 83.

THE 66TH RADICAL. 支.

收
show
shou

攸
yew
yu

改
kæ
kaí

攻
kung

放
fang

(1) To recover. V. xxiv. 10. = to take and remove. xxii. 29. (2) = to keep back, to draw ons's-self up from effort. V. xvi. 16.

It is for the most part identical in meaning and use with 所. (1) A place. III. i. Pt. i. 75. The place where. V. xiv. 22, 26; *et al.* (2) That which, that whereby. IV. ii. 6: Pt. i. 7: vii. Pt. i. 5; Pt. ii. 4, 6; *et sæpissime.* 罔攸 is frequent. II. ii. 3: IV. viii. Pt. i. 1: V. xi. 3: *et al.* In one place we have 罔有攸. IV. i. 4. Obs. V. xiii. 19. (3) Serves the purpose of the copula. III. i. Pt. ii. 14.

To change, to alter. IV. ii. 5: V. xii. 9: xvii. 2, 7: xxiii. 2.

To attack. III. ii. 4: V. iii. 8. = to punish. IV. ii. 7. = to work upon. V. xii. 3.

To let go, to send away. V. iii. 2. = to banish. II. i. 12: IV. iii. 1. To dismiss. V. i. Pt. iii. 3. (2) To neglect, to disobey. V. ix. 18. 放心, the lost heart.

xxiv. 10. (3) 放勳, the name of Yaou. I. 1. Many comm. read 放 here, and explain differently. So with the character in 放齊, the name of one of Yaou's ministers. I. 9.

政
ching
chêng

Government; the measures and rules of government. *Passim.* 八政, the eight objects of govt. V. iv. 4, 7. 七政, the sun, moon, and five planets; but the meaning is doubtful. II. i. 5. 庶政, the various departments of govt. V. xx. 3. 政人, parties charged with the administration of govt. V. ix. 16. 立政 is the name of the 19th Book, Pt. V., where the phrase often occurs. 同于厥政, to share in the offices of govt. xix. 5.

故
koo
ku

(1) Therefore. IV. x. 3: V. x. 8, 11: xvi. 8, 9: xxvii. 10. (2) As a preposition, coming after its regimen, on account of. IV. vii. Pt. ii. 5: viii. Pt. i. 2. (3) What is purposed. II. ii. 12.

效
hĕaou
hsiao

To require, as a charge. V. xi. 3.

敉
mei

To settle, to establish. V. xix. 15. 敉寧. V. vii. 5, 11. ? to consider as completed. xiii. 19.

敘
seu
hsü

To arrange orderly. II. iii. 1: V. ix. 9; *et al.* To be arranged. II. i. 2: ii. 7: iv. 8: III. i. Pt. i. 7, 8: V. iv. 2, 3; *et al.* Arrangements. II. ii. 7 (九敘): iii. 6: III. i. Pt. i. 83: *et al.* Observe. 篤敘, V. viii. 13, 27. An order, a series; = a line. V. vii. x. 4. By degrees. V. xiii. 9. = to employ according to qualifications. IV. vii. Pt. iii. 10.

教
kĕaou
chiao

To teach. II. i. 29: iii. 5; *et sæpe.* We have 告教, V. xix. 2; 教告, xviii. 23; 教誨, xv. 14; and 誥教, x. 4. Teaching, instructions, lessons. V. xiii. 13, 16. = education. xx. 8. 教辟, x. 16. 文教. III. i. Pt. ii. 20. 五教, the duties belonging to the five relations of society. II. i. 19: ii. 11: V. iii. 9. 教刑, the punishment in schools. II. i. 11. = influence. III. i. Pt. ii. 23.

敏
min

To be active or earnest; to be active in; active. II. ii. 2: IV. viii. Pt. iii. 4: V. ix. 22.

救
kew
'chiu

To save, to rescue. IV. v. Pt. ii. 3: vii. Pt. ii. 13: V. vii. 12.

敔
yu
yü

An instrument, to give the signal of stopping the other instruments of music. II. iv. 9.

敗
pae
pai

To ruin; to violate. II. ii. 20 : IV. v. Pt. ii. 3 : xi. 1 : V. xx. 16 : xxi. 10. Obs. 戕敗人, V. xi. 2.   = destroyers. IV. vii. Pt. i. 12. Ruin. IV. xi. 8.

歛
něĕ
nieh

To fill up. V. xxix. 3.

做
pe
·pi

To ruin. V. xxiv. 9.

敢
kan

To venture, presume, dare. *Passim.* In one passage, = daringly, vigorously. IV. vii. Pt. iii. 10.

散
san

(1) To disperse. V. iii. 9. (2) A surname. V. xvi. 12.

敬
king

Passim. To respect, to revere. It is used as an active verb, to respect, to attend respectfully to, the action so described being determined by the object which follows, as in 敬致, I. 5; 敬德 V. xii. 10, 20, *et sæpe*, (comp. 敬厥德 IV. v. Pt. iii. 3); *et al*; 敬刑, V. xxvii. 13; 敬罰, V. ix. 8. Very often no object follows, or only a 之, especially in the phrases 敬哉 and 敬之哉, when the verb = to be reverent. Reverence, respectfulness. II. iii. 3. Observe especially 敬作所, V. xii. 16. It occurs frequently before other verbs, when its force of course is adverbial, = reverently, respectfully. *E. g.* I. 3 : II. i. 19 : iv. 7 : V. xvi. 23.

敵
teih
ti

Enemies, opponents. V. xvi. 15. 敵讎, IV. xi. 2, 7. To oppose, resist. V. iii. 9 (foll. by 于). To be resisted. V. i. Pt. ii. 9.

敷
foo
fu

(1) To spread, lay out,—as mats. V. xxii. 15, 16, 17, 18. (2) To divide and arrange. Spoken of Yu's work. III. i. Pt. i. 1. So, foll. by 于, and without an object. II. ii. 1. (3) To spread abroad; to set forth, to publish. II. i. 19 : ii. 21 : IV. iii. 3 : V. iv. 9 ; *et sæpe*. To lay bare the heart. IV. vii. Pt. iii. 3 : V. xvi. 18. Obs. 敷遺, V. xxiii. 3 : 敷佑, V. ix. 8 ; 敷菑, V. xvi. 20 ; and 敷施, II. iii. 4. Observe also 敷納 (奏) 以言, II. iv. 7 : i. 9. = extensively. V. vi. 5 : IV. iv. 6. 敷言 = amplification. V. iv. 15, 16. To be spread abroad. V. xxviii. 1. (4) 敷淺, the name of a plain. III. i. Pt. i. 4.

數
soo
shu

Numbers, calculations. In the phrase 曆數 II. ii. 14 : V. iv. 8.

敹
lĕaou
liao

To have in repair. V. xxix. 2.

敽
kĕaou
chiao

To secure the laces of a shield. V. xxix. 2.

斁
yih
yi

To be satiated with, to dislike. IV. v. Pt. ii. 7 : V. viii. 4 : xx. 21.   = to be tired of and intermit. V. xiii. 21.

斁
too
tu

To go to ruin. V. iv. 3.

斂
lĕen
lien

To concentrate, collect. V. iv. 9. Exactions. IV. xi. 7. It is read both in the 2nd and 3d tones.

斅
heaou
hsiao

To teach. IV. vii. Pt. i. 5 (foll. by 于): vii ; Pt. iii. 5.

THE 67TH RADICAL. 文.

文
wăn
wên

(1) Veined, ornamented. V. xxii. 16. = ornamented fabrics. III. i. Pt. i. 16. = display. V. xiii. 5, 15. (2) Learning, accomplishments. 文教, III. i. Pt. ii. 15. 文德, II. ii. 21. = the occupations of peace. V. iii. 2. Accomplished. I. i : II. i. 1 : V. xix. 18, 21 : xxviii. 3. (3) 文命, perhaps the name of Yu. II. ii. 1. The honorary title of king Wăn. It is found *passim* in the phrases 文王, 文祖, 文考, 文武. In II. i. 4, 14, however, 文祖 denotes the ancestor of Yaou. In the title of V. xxviii., 文 is likewise an honorary name.

THE 69TH RADICAL. 斤.

斥
ch'ih

Salt land. III. i. Pt. i. 24.

斨
ts'ëang
ch'iang

The name of an officer about Shun's court. II. i. 21.

斮
tsŏ
tso

To cut through. V. i. Pt. iii. 3.

斯
sze
szû

This, these. V. x. 16 : xxi. 6. Making, with the preceding subject, an emphatic nominative. V. vi. 16 : xxx. 2. (2) As a conjunction, forthwith, thereon. V. iv. 11, 13 : vi. 14.

新
sin
hsin

New. IV. vii. Pt. i. 4, 13 ; Pt. ii. 5, 16 : Pt. iii. 6 ; *et sæpe*. To be new or renewed. IV. ii. 18. To renovate one's-self. III. iv. 6. Newly, recently. IV. vi. 6 : V. vi. 10 ; *et al.* 作新, to make new. V. ix. 7. Obs. V. vi. 18.

斷
chŏ
cho

斷
twan
tuan

斷
twan
tuan

To carve; to do fine work on wood. V. xi. 4.

(1) To determine. V. xxvii. 12. 果斷, a bold decision. V. xx. 17. (2) 斷斷, plain and sincere. V. xxx. 6.

2d tone. To cut off; to make an end of. IV. vii. Pt. i. 3; Pt. ii. 13.

THE 70TH RADICAL. 方.

方
fang

(1) A region, a quarter. Used of the cardinal points. V. vi. 4. Of the regions of the empire. III. iii. 7: V. xviii. 2, 7, 8; *et sæpe.* The phrase 四方, the four quarters, is everywhere used for the empire. 萬方, the myriad regions, is also used in the same way. IV. iii. 1, 2, 3, 8: v. Pt. i. 2. As an adverb, 方 = on all sides, from all quarters, everywhere. IV. xi. 2: V. xi. 5: xix. 22; *et al.* Obs. 方夏, V. iii. 5. (2) As a conjunction, then, now. II. iv. 8: IV. iv. 3: xi. 4: V. iv. 13. In II. i. 28, 方 is inexplicable. (3) To disobey. I. 11. (4) 外方 and 內方 are the names of mountains. III. i. Pt. 11. 2, 3.

In. V. vi. 12: x. 12: xviii. 7: xxii. 11.

於
yu
yü

旅
woo
wu

施
she
shih

旁
pang

旄
maou
mao

旅
leu
lü

An exclamation. Oh! I. 2 (*n. b.*), 11: II. i. 24: ii. 7: iv. 10.

To give; to display, to be displayed. II. iv. 4, 8: IV. vii. Pt. i. 10: V. xiii. 16: xvi. 5: xxi. 1. To give out (act.) V. xxvi. 2. = to use, to employ in office. II. iii. 4.

(1) On every side. IV. v. Pt. i. 5: viii. Pt. i. 3; Pt. iii. 7: V. xiii. 16. (2) To be by the side of, = near to, immediately following. V. iii. 1.

A kind of ensign, formed of ox-tails. V. ii. 1.

(1) Properly a body of 500 men. = hosts. II. ii. 21: V. iii. 9. (2) The multitudes,—spoken of the people. V. xviii. 5-19. (3) Numerous officers. We have 亞旅, V. ii. 2: xix. 10; and 尹旅, xi. 2. (4) 旅力, strength. V. xxx. 5. (5) To set forth, display, to. V. xii. 8. (6) The term used for sacrificing to mountains. III. i. Pt. i. 65, 76; Pt. ii. 14. (7) The name of a western tribe. V. v. 1.

旌
tsing
ching

To signalize. V. xxiv. 7.

族
tsuh
tsu

Relatives,—the different branches of a family or clan. V. i. Pt. i. 5. So, 族姓, V. xxvii. 21. 九族, the nine classes of kindred. I. 2: II. iii. 1: IV. ii. 8. ? 圯族, I. 11.

THE 71ST RADICAL. 无.

旡
ke
chi

(1) A particle of past time, denoting what is spoken of as done, completed. *Passim.* Observe 旡月, II. i. 7; 旡往, IV. v. Pt. ii. 3; 旡 alone, IV. viii. Pt. iii. 1. (2) It very often serves as a conjunction, = when; or leads us to construe the clause where it occurs in the nominative absolute. (3) To be consumed. V. i. Pt. i. 6. (4) To exert to the utmost. V. xxiv. 15.

THE 72D RADICAL. 日.

日
jih

(1) The sun. I. 3: II. iv. 4; *et al.* 出日, the rising sun. I, 4. 納日, the setting sun. I. 6. (2) A day, days. *Passim.* We have 上日 and 元日 for the first day of the month, II. i. 4, 14; 今日, to-day, V. xvi. 21, *et al.*; 翼日, the day following, V. xxii. 10, *et al.* (observe 今翼日, V. vii. 5); 日中, midday, V. xv. 10; but the meaning is difft. in I. 4. The character is also used often adverbially, = daily. *E. g.* II. ii. 11: IV. ii. 8: vi. 6: V. xxi. 3.

旦
tan

(1) The morning. II. ii. 19: IV. v. Pt. i 5. 旦夕, morning and evening. V. xxvi. 2. (2) The name of the duke of Chow. V. vi. 5, 6: xii. 14; *et al.*

旨
che
chih

Good, excellent. IV. viii. Pt. ii. 12.

早
tsaou
tsao

Early, prematurely. V. xii. 17.

旬
seun
hsün

A decade of days. I. 8: II. ii. 21: III. iii. 1: V. ix. 12.

旱
han

Drought. IV. viii. Pt. i. 6.

昊
haou
hao

Vast, wide. 昊天 is the appearance of the firmament in summer. I. 3.

旻
min

旻天 is the appearance of the firmament in autumn. The phrase is generally taken as = the pitying heavens. II. ii. 20: V. xiv. 2.

昃
ts'ih
chai

The sun declining to the west, the afternoon. V. xv. 10.

昆
kwăn
kuên

Afterwards. II. ii. 18. Futurity. IV. ii. 8.

昌
ch'ang

Good, admirable. 昌言, admirable words. II. ii. 21: iii. 1: iv. 1. To be prosperous or flourishing. IV. ii. 7: V. iv. 13.

明
ming

Passim. (1) To be clear, bright; and metaphorically, to be intelligent. Clear, brilliant; intelligent. I. 1, 9: II. i. 1: ii. 11: V. xxvi. 2; *et sæpe.* Clearness,—spoken of seeing. IV. v. Pt. ii. 7: V. iv. 6; *et al.* Intelligence. V. vii. 3, 9. 神 明, spiritual intelligences. V. xxi. 3. = pure. V. xiii. 25. In the sense of intelligent it is often associated with 聰. It is doubled to heighten the idea. V. xxvii. 6, 10: III. iii. 8; but 明明 in I. 12 is different. (2) To illustrate; to make illustrious; to enlighten; to be enlightened; to be illustrious. V. xx. 14: xxiii. 5: xxvii. 7: xxviii. 2: xvi. 20; *et sæpe.* To understand clearly. V. xxii. 7; *et al.* To study. V. xiii. 13. To adjust clearly. II. iv. 4. To distinguish. II. iv. 7; *et al.* Obs. II. i. 15, 27: III. iii. 5.

昏
hwăn
huên

To be dark; dark, used metaphorically, morally dark, blinded. V. iv. 37: xviii. 4; *et al.* To be bewildered. II. iv. 1. 昏德, dark as to virtue, = blindly vicious. IV. ii. 2. Blindly. V. xxii. 6; *et al.*

易
yih
yi

To change, (both act. and neuter). IV. vii. Pt. ii. 15: V. iv. 36, 37: vii. 13: x. 11: xxx. 5. 易種, to perpetuate seed. IV. vii. Pt. ii. 16. 朔易, changes of the winter. I. 7.

易
e
i

3d tone. What is easy; agreeable. V. xxv. 5. To be easy, = easily preserved. V. xvi. 4. To take easily, make little account of. V. v. 3.

昔
seih
hsi

Formerly. IV. viii. Pt. iii. 10: V. vi. 18; *et sæpe.* 在昔. V. iv. 3: x. 9: xvi. 7, 11. 若昔. V. vii. 11: xx. 2. As a noun, 昔之人. V. xv. 3.

星
sing
hsing

A star, the stars. I. 3, 4, 5, 6, 7: II. iv. 4: V. iv. 8, 38.

春
ch'un

Spring. I. 4: V. xxv. 2. In the spring. III. iv. 3: V. i. Pt. i. 1.

昧
mei

(1) Dark, sombre. 昧谷, the sombre valley. I. 6. 昧爽, the early dawn, between the dark and light. IV. v. Pt. i. 5: V. ii. 1: iii. 8. The wilfully dark or blind. IV. ii. 7. (2) 昧昧 = deeply. V. xxx. 6.

昬
hwăn
huên

(1) Used for 昏, blindly. V. ii. 6. (2) Used for 暋, to be strong, energetic. IV. vii. Pt. i. 11.

昭
chaou
ch'ao

To display; to make illustrious or glorious. IV. ii. 8. iv. 3: V. iii. 7: v. 3; *et al.* To be illustrious. V. xxiii. 5. To enlighten. V. xiii. 24: xvi. 14. Brightly. I. 2: II. iv. 2: IV. iii. 4.

是
she
shih

(1) This, these. V. iv. 26: xix. 3. = on this. III. i. Pt. i. 16. 若是, thus. V. xxx. 2. = really. V. xxx. 6, 7. (2) To be. II. iv. 8: III. i. Pt. i. 70: iii. 5: V. ii. 6: *et al.* This is the most common use of the term, and it is generally followed by a verb, which may be construed as in the participial mood.

昴
maou
mao

The name of a star. I. 7.

昵
neih
ni

To be near to, familiar with. V. i. Pt. ii. 3 (昵比): xxvi. 7 (foll. by 于). = familiars, favourites. IV. viii. Pt. ii. 5. Low. 2d tone. The shrine appropriate to the spirit-tablet of a father. IV. ix. 5.

昵
ne
ni

時
she
shih

Passim. (1) A time, the time; the seasons, a season or period of three months. I. 3, 8, 9: II. i. 8, 16: IV. v. Pt. ii. 6: vii. Pt. ii. 3: viii. Pt. ii. 6: V. i. Pt. i. 11; Pt. iii. 1: ix. 12; *et sæpe.* Always. IV. v. Pt. iii. 3: viii. Pt. iii. 4; *et al.* Then. II. iv. 7: V. ix. 9; *et al.* Seasonable; seasonableness; seasonably. II. i. 2: V. iv. 32, 34, 37; *et al.* 自時, henceforth. V. xii. 14: xiii. 23: xv. 7; *et al.* To time, to regulate the seasons with a view to— . V. xx. 12. (2) Used as a synonym of 是, this, these; to be. The frequency of this usage is characteristic of the Shoo. I. 12: II. i. 17, 18: III. iv. 4: IV. iii. 9: iv. 7: V. xxii. 7: xxiv. 11, 14: ix. 4, 11, 13: xiv. 22, 25; *et sæpe.* 時 alone, and 若時, thus. I. 2: II. iii. 2: IV. vi. 6: V. xiii. 17; *et sæpe.* What is right II. iv. 6. Obs. 惟時, II. iii. 4: iv. 11: V. xiv. 10, 18; *et al.*

晝
chow
chou

Day, by day. 晝夜, II. iv. 8.

晨
shin
ch'ên

The morning. = to announce the morning, to crow. V. ii. 5.

智
che
chih

Wisdom; the wise. IV. ii. 2; V. xii. 10.

暇
hea
hsia

Leisure. V. x. 10: xiii. 13. 遑暇, xv. 10. 自暇, to give one's-self leisure. V. x. 9. 須暇, to wait and forbear. V. xviii. 17.

暑
shoo
shu

To be hot, summer heat. V. xxv. 5.

暘
yang

Sunshine. V. iv. 32, 34. 暘谷, the valley of sunshine,—a place in the extreme east of Yaou's empire, probably in Corea. I. 4.

瞀
min

暫
tsan
chan

To be violent. V. ix. 15 : xix. 5.

A brief time, for a brief time. IV. vii. Pt. ii. 16.

暴
paou
pao

Violence, oppression. V. i. Pt. i. 5 ; Pt. ii. 5 : ii. 6. Oppressors. V. xx. 11. So, 暴德 and 暴德之人, V. xix. 3, 5. Oppressive to one's-self, wantonly indifferent to virtue. IV. ii. 9. To oppress, be injurious to. V. iii. 6.

曁
ke
chi

(1) A conjunction. And. I. 8 : II. i. 17, 21 : III. i. Pt. i. 35 : IV. iv. 2 : vi. 3 : V. iii. 4 ; *et sæpe.* With, along with. II. iv. 1 : IV. vii. Pt. ii. 12 : V. xv. 5 ; *et al.* Observe. 胥曁. V. xxiii. 6. (2) To be come to, = the uttermost ends of. III. i. Pt. ii. 23. 曁 does not occur in the Four Books.

曆

To calculate. I. 3. 曆數, the calendaric calculations. V. iv. 8. 天之曆數 = the determinate appointment of Heaven. II. ii. 14.

曠
k'wang
k'uang

To make vacant. II. iii. 5.

THE 73D RADICAL. 曰.

曰
yuĕ
yüeh

To speak, to say, saying. *Passim.* Commonly the nominative is expressed. It is used in soliloquy, and = to say to one's-self. *E. g.* V. xx. viii. 2. It is sometimes passive, and = to be called, to be : may be said to be, may be pronounced. *E. g.* V. iv. *Passim:* xxx. 7 : 8. Next to 惟, 曰 is probably the character of most frequent occurrence in the Shoo.

曲
k'euh
ch'ü

To be bent or crooked. V. iv. 5.

曷
hŏ
ho

Why ; how. IV. vii. Pt. i. 12 ; Pt. ii. 4, 6, 11, 12 ; Pt. iii. 5 : V. i. Pt. i. 7 : *et sæpe.* = when. IV. i. 3. = whither. III. iii. 9.

書
choo
shu

A writing, written document. IV. v. Pt. i. 2 ; Pt. ii. 2 : viii. Pt. i. 2 : V. vi. 16, 18 : xxii. 23. Written specifications. V. xii. 6. A record, a book of record. II. iv. 6 : V. xxvii. 20. Written oracular responses. V. vi. 9.

曾
tsăng
tsêng

曾孫, a great grandson, but used = descendant. V. iii. 6.

替
t'e
t'i

(1) To disregard. V. v. 3 : vii. 9 : viii. 5 : ix. 24. (2) To intermit. V. xiii. 21. = to fail of. xii. 23. (3) To supersede. V. xix. 15.

會
hwuy
hui

(1) To assemble (both act. and neuter). II. ii. 20 : V. i. Pt. i. 1 ; Pt. ii. 1 : iii. 8 : ix. 1. To meet with. V. iv. 14. To meet. Spoken of waters. III. i. Pt. ii. 9, 10, 11, 12, 13. Observe 會同, III. i. Pt. i. 15 ; Pt. ii. 14. To unite. V. xxviii. 3. (2) Used for 繪, to depict. II. iv. 4.

THE 74TH RADICAL. 月.

月
yuĕ
yüeh

The moon. I. 3 : II. iv. 4 : V. i. Pt. iii. 5. A month, months. *Passim.*

有
yew
yu

Lower. 3d tone. And. I. 8 : II. i. 8, 10, 13, 16, 26 ; *et sæpe.* It is always used in enumeration of numbers, and follows 十.

有
yew
yu

(1) The impersonal substantive verb, —there is, there was, there will be. I. 11, 12 ; *et passim.* (2) To have, to possess. Also *passim.* It is often auxiliary merely to the verb that follows. The student must observe that 有 before the names of principalities, dynasties, = the holder or holders, the sovereign or sovereigns, of such. *E. g.* II. ii. 20, 21 : iii. 2, 5, 7 : IV. viii. Pt. iii. 10 : V. i. Pt. ii. 4. The name of the principality may be followed by 氏, as in III. ii. 3. 有 must be construed in the same way before many other nouns. *E. g.* IV. ii. 9 : V. Pt. iii. 1 : The term must often be construed as if it were preceded by a 所, *E. g.* II. ii. 17 : iv. 4 : IV. ii. 4 : V. i. Pt. iii. 5. Observe particularly the phrase 有眾, which may generally be thus resolved. III. iv. 2, 5 : IV. i. 2, 3 : V. i. Pt. i. 10 ; *et al.* So, 有司. II. ii. 12. It is difficult, however, sometimes to account for the 有. *E. g.* III. iii. 1 : V. iii. 8 : xii. 13. To be conscious of having, to have boastingly. IV. viii. Pt. ii. 7 ; *et al.* 九有, the nine provinces. IV. vi. 2.

朋
p'ang
p'êng

To form selfish friendships or associations. II. iv. 8 : V. i. Pt. ii. 3 : iv. 10 : xiii. 9.

服
fuh
fu

(1) To wear ; dress,—robes, garments. II. iv. 4, 7 : III. i. Pt. i. 10, 44 : IV. v. Pt. ii. 1 : V. xxii. 2 : xxiv. 10 ; *et al.* (2) A great variety of meanings may here be classed together. To undergo. V. xxv. 1. To serve ; service ; business ; to perform duties. IV. vii. Pt. i. 3 : V. i. Pt. i. 5 : ix. 16 : xii. 14, 18, 19 : xiv. 22 : xxv. 3 ; *et al.* = to enjoy, especially with 命, IV. vi. 6 : V. ix. 23 : xii. 10, 17 ; *et al.*; but 服命 in V. viii. 4, and perhaps some other places, is different. = offices. V. xviii. 28 : xxviii. 2 : x. 13 (*n. b.*). To work on the fields. IV. vii. Pt. i. 9, 11. 服言, to carry out one's words.

IV. viii. Pt. ii. 12. (3) To submit. II.
i. 12, 16; IV. v. Pt. ii. 5: V. iii. 8; *et al.*
To produce submission. V. xxvii. 15:
To subject animals to the yoke. V. iii. 2.
To be subjected to. V. xxvii. 19. (4) 服
念, to cherish and think of. V. ix. 12.
(5) A tenure or domain, domains. II iv.
8 (五 服): III. i. Pt. ii. 18—22: V.
xx. 1 (六 服); *et al.*

胐
fei

The moon re-appearing. The 3d day
of the month. V. xii. 2 : xxiv. 1.

朔
sŏ
so

(1) The first day of the moon. II. ii.
19: III. iv. 4: IV. v. Pt. ii. 1. (2) The
north; northern; northwards. I. 7: II. 1.
8: III. i. Pt. ii. 23: V. i. Pt. ii. 1: xiii. 3.
朔 易, the changes of the winter. I. 7.

朕
ch'in
sh'ên

I, me, my, we, our. *Passim.* The character is used most frequently by the emperors in speaking of themselves, but with
no special emphasis, being constantly interchanged with 我, 予, and other terms.
It is used also by ministers in speaking
of themselves. *E. g.* II. ii. 10, 20 : iii. 8 :
III. i. Pt. ii. 17 : V. xiii. 1, 13, 22, 24, 28 ;
et al. It had not yet become the imperial
We.

望
wang

(1) To be full moon, the 15th day of
the month. V. xii. 1. (2) The name of
a sacrifice offered by the emperor to the
mountains and rivers. II. i. 6, 8 : V. iii. 3.

朝
chaou
chao

Morning, in the morning. V. i. Pt. i.
3 : ii. 1 : iii. 1 : xii. 1, 2, 4, 6 : xiii. 3 : xv.
10 : xxiv. 1. 朝 夕, morning and even-
ing. IV. viii. Pt. i. 5 : V. x. 2.

朝
ch'aou
ch'ao

To appear at court or before the emper-
or. II. i. 9 : V. xx. 14. Spoken of the
waters of the Han and Keang hurrying
to the Sea. III. i. Pt. i. 47.

碁
ke
chi

A round year of 366 days. I. 8.

期
k'e
ch'i

(1) To expect, to anticipate. 不 期,
unexpected, unperceived. V. xx. 18. With
a view to. II. ii. 11. (2) A hundred
years old. 耄 期, between ninety and
a hundred. II. ii. 11.

THE 75TH RADICAL. 木.

木
muh
mu

(1) A tree, trees. II. i. 22: III. i. Pt.
i. 17, 33, 42 : IV. iii. 5 ; *et al.* = timber.
III. i. Pt. i. 44. = woods. II. iv. 1 : III.
i. Pt. i. 1. (2) Wood, one of the elements. V. iv. 5. One of the six magazines
of nature. II. ii. 7. Wood, generally. IV.
viii. Pt. i. 11. Wooden-tongued. III.
iv. 3.

未
we
wei

(1) Not yet; not, but the force of the
yet can generally be detected. II. iii. 8 :
IV. iii. 5 ; *et sœpe.* Has sometimes to be
translated by—there never was......III.
iii. 6 : V. ix. 13, 14. (2) The eighth of
the calendaric stem-characters. V. iii. 3 :
xii. 1.

末
mŏ
mo

(1) Final, last. V. xxii. 24. **Finally.**
xii. 24. (2) Ever, always. V. xix. 17.
(3) Trivial, insignificant. V. xxii. 25.

本
pun
pên

The root. III. iii. 4 : V. i. Pt. iii. 4.

朱
choo
chu

(1) Red. Spoken of the manes and
tails of horses. V. xxiii. 1. (2) The
name of an officer about the court of
Shun. II. i. 22. The name of Yaou's son.
I. 9 : II. iv. 8. 朱 圉, the name of a
mountain. III. i. Pt. ii. 2.

朽
hew
hsiu

Rotten. III. iii. 5.

杵
ch'oo
ch'u

A wooden pestle, pestles. V. iii. 8.

杌
wuh
wu

A tree without branches, = a want of
prosperity. V. xxx. 8.

材
ts'ae
ts'ai

(1) Materials of wood. V. xxii. 13.
Timber. V. xi. 4. (2) *I. q.* 才, abilities. V. vi. 6. = men of ability. IV. vi. 7.

杖
chang

To hold or grasp. V. ii. 1.

杜
too
tu

To shut or fill up. V. xxix. 3.

東
tung

(1) The east. V. xxii. 6. In the east.
V. xi. 14. Eastwards, on the east. II. i. 8 :
III. i. Pt. ii. 7—13, 23 : IV. ii. 6 : V. iii.
7 : vii. 15. Eastern. V. viii. 3 : ix. 1, 4 ;
et sæpe. 東 作, the labours of the
spring. I. 4. (2) 東 陵, the name of
a mountain. III. i. Pt. ii. 9. 東 原, a
tract of country. III. i. Pt. i. 32.

杶
ch'un

The name of a tree. III. i. Pt. i. 52.

松
sung

The pine tree. III. i. Pt. i. 26.

析
seih
hsi

(1) To disperse, to be separated. I. 4 :
IV. vii. Pt. iii. 5. (2) 析 支 and 析
城 are names of mountains. III. i. Pt.
i. 83 ; Pt. ii. 1.

林
lin

(1) A forest. V. iii. 8. (2) 桃 林,
the name of a tract of country. V. iii. 2.

枚
mei

One by one. II. ii. 18.

果
kwo
kuo

Bold, determined. 果 毅, V. i. Pt.
iii. 4. 果 斷, V. xx. 17.

枲
se
hsi

Hemp. III. i. Pt. i. 26, 60.

柏
pih
pai

(1) The cypress tree. III. i. Pt. i. 52.
(2) 桐 柏, the name of a hill. III. i.
Pt. ii. 2, 11.

某
mow
mou

Such an one. V. vi. 5.

染
jěn
jan

To be dyed or stained with. III. iv. 6.

柔
jow
jou

To be gentle with, to show kindness to; mild; mildness. II. i. 16: iii. 3: V. iv. 17: xv. 10: xxii. 8: xxiv. 12: xxviii. 4.

柱
ch'oo
ch'u

底柱, the name of a hill. III. i. Pt. ii. 1, 7.

柚
yew
yu

The pummelo fruit. III. i. Pt. i. 44.

柴
ch'ae
ch'ai

To offer a burnt-offering to Heaven. II. i. 8: V. iii. 3.

柷
chuh
chu

A musical instrument, a kind of rattle, giving notice to the instruments of a band to strike up. II. iv. 9.

栗
leih
li

To be majestic and dignified. II. i. 24: iii. 3. In many editions of the Shoo, 栗 appears in II. ii. 21, instead of 慄, to be fearful.

栝
kwŏ
kuo

? the cedar tree. III. i. Pt. i. 52.

格
kih
ko

(1) To come or go to,—used both of place and conduct. I. 8: II. i. 2, 3, 14: ii. 9, 21: iv. 9: IV. i. 1: vii. Pt. i. 6: V. v. 8: xxvi. 6. To reach to. I. 1: IV. viii. Pt. iii. 10: V. vii. 1: xvi. 16. To make to reach to. V. xvi. 7. (2) To correct; correction. IV. ix. 2: V. xii. 11: xiv. 5: xviii. 4: xxvi. 3. To be corrected, become reformed. II. iv. 6. (3) Most excellent; intelligent. IV. x. 2: V. xxvii. 13.

桃
t'aou
t'ao

See 林.

桀
kěě
chieh

The name of the tyrant, the last emperor of the Hea dynasty. IV. ii. 1: V. i. Pt. ii. 4, 5: xix. 3.

桐
t'ung

(1) The dryandra, III. i. Pt. i. 35. (2) 桐柏, see 柏. The name of the place where T'ang's grave was. IV. v. Pt. i. 9, 10,

桑
sang

The mulberry tree. Used as an adj., III. i. Pt. i. 16.

桓
hwan
huan

(1) The name of a river. III. i. Pt. i. 70. (2) 桓桓 a martial bearing. V. ii. 9. (3) A name. V. xxii. 11.

梁
lëang
liang

(1) The name of a hill. III. i. Pt. i. 4. (2) 梁州, one of Yu's nine provinces. III. i. Pt. i. 62.

梅
mei

Plums or prunes. IV. viii. Pt. iii. 2.

梓
tsze
tszŭ

The name of a tree, the wood of which was much used by the cabinet-maker and the carver. V. xi. 4.

條
t'eaou
t'iao

(1) Orderly divisions. IV. vii. Pt. i. 9. (2) High, tall. III. i. Pt. i. 17. (3) 鳴條, the name of a palace of Këě. IV. iv. 2.

棄
k'e
ch'i

(1) To throw away, to abandon. II. ii. 20: III. ii. 3: iv. 4: IV. vii. Pt. ii. 13: viii. Pt. iii. 2: x. 3: V. i. Pt. ii. 3; Pt. iii. 3: ii. 6: vii. 11: xvii. 18. To put away, —spoken of one's faults. V. ix. 9. (2) The name of Shun's minister of Agriculture, the ancestor of the House of Chow. II. i. 18.

棐
fei

To assist, help. V. vii. 10, 13: ix. 6: x. 8, 9: xiii. 13, 17: xvi. 2, 21: xxvii. 6, 10.

棼
fun
fěn

棼棼, to be in confusion, disorderly. V. xxvii. 4.

椓
chŏ
cho

To castrate, castration. V. xxvii. 3.

植
chih

To place, to set up. V. vi. 4.

楛
hoo
hu

The name of a tree, the wood of which was used for making arrows. III. i. Pt. i. 52.

楨
ching
chĕng

The posts of the framework used in rearing walls of earth and lime pounded together. 楨榦, V. xxix. 5.

楫
tsëě
chieh

Oars. IV. viii. Pt. i. 6.

業
yě
yeh

(1) A patrimony, possessions. IV. vii. Pt. i. 4: V. xx. 17. (2) 業業, to be fearful. II. iii. 5.

極
keih
chi

(1) A support and pattern. V. xvi. 18. (2) That which is extreme. Applied to the idea of perfection or the highest excellence. V. iv. 4, 9, 10, 11, 14, 15, 16. Applied to the extremity of misery. 六極, V. iv. 4, 40. Applied to punishments. 五極. V. xxvii. 22. Extreme. xxvii. 21. To be extremely affected by; to be extremely for. V. xxvii. 20: vii. 15. Fully; to the utmost. V. iv. 33: ix. 8. A place of rest. IV. vii. Pt. iii. 5.

榦
yan

(1) The name of a tree whose wood was used for bows. III. i. Pt. i. 52. (2) The planks used for the sides of building frames. See 楨.

榮
kung
jung

Glory, flourishing condition. V. xxx. 8.

榭
seay
shě

A high terrace with buildings on it. V. i. Pt. i. 5.

構
kow
kou

To cover over, to construct the roof. V. vii. 11.

樂
yoh
yo

Music. II. i. 24.

樂
loh
lo

Pleasure. II. ii. 6 : V. xv. 7, 13.

樸
p'ŏ
p'o

To fashion rudely in wood. V. xi. 4.

樹
shoo
shu

To plant, to set up. IV. viii. Pt. ii. 2 : V. i. Pt. iii. 4 : xxiii. 6 : xxiv. 7.

橋
k'eaou
ch'iao

鉅橋, a place where the tyrant Show had collected great stores of grain. V. iii. 9.

橘
keŭh
chü

Small oranges. III. i. Pt. i. 44.

機
ke
chi

A spring, the centre of motion in any contrivance or implement. IV. v. Pt. i. 7.

檢
k'een
chien

To regulate. 檢身, IV. iv. 5.

檿
yen

A sort of wild mountain mulberry tree. III. i. Pt. i. 26.

櫱
nee
nieh

Shoots from a felled tree. IV. vii. Pt. i. 4.

權
k'euen
ch'üan

(1) The weight of a steelyard, = the balance of circumstances. V, xxvii. 16. (2) Power. V. i. Pt. ii. 3.

THE 76TH RADICAL. 欠.

次
ts'ze
tz'û

(1) Next in order. V. iv. 4 : xxii. 20. (2) A position, a post. III. iv. 4. To halt, to take up a position. V. i. Pt. ii. 1. (3) To suit, to accord with. V. ix. 13.

欲
yŭh
yü

To wish, to desire. II. iv. 4, 6 : x. 4 : V. i. Pt. i. 11 : xi. 8 : xii. 23 : xxx. 5. Desires, —in a good or bad sense. II. ii. 6, 13 : IV. ii. 2 : v. Pt. ii. 3.   = dissoluteness. II. iii. 5.

欽
k'in
ch'in

To respect, to be reverent. I. i. 11, 12 : II. i. 11, 23, 26 : V. viii. 1 : xviii. 5 ; *et sæpe.* Reverently. III. iv. 5 : IV. viii. Pt. iii. 7. Obs. 欽若, to accord reverently with. I. 3 : IV. viii. Pt. ii. 3 : V. xxiv. 15. 欽厥止, reverently determine your end. IV. v. Pt. i. 7. Sovereignly. V. xix. 5.

歆
hin
yin

To accept or enjoy a sacrificial offering. V. viii. 3.

歌
ko

To sing, singing. II. i. 24 : IV. iv. 7. A song, songs. II. ii. 7 : iv. 11 : III. iii. 3.

歡
hwan
huan

To rejoice. V. xiii. 21.

THE 77TH RADICAL. 止.

止
che
chih

(1) To stop, to halt. II. iv. 9 : V. ii. 7, 8. To make to stop, make an end of. V. xxi. 9. (2) = dwellings. V. xiv. 23. One's resting place, the end or aim. II. iv. 2 : IV. v. Pt. i. 7.

正
ching
chêng

(1) To correct, adjust, regulate ; to be correct, exact ; correctness. I. 5, 7 : II. ii. 7 : III. i. Pt. ii. 15 : IV. ii. 2 : vii. Pt. iii. 1 : V. i. Pt. iii. 3 : iv. 13, 14, 17 : xiii. 3 : xv. 11, 12, 15 : xxvi. 6 : xxvii. 20 ; *et al.*   = to punish ; punishments ; a righting. II. ii. 11 : IV. i. 2 : ix. 4.   = correct men. V. xviii. 22. (2) It is used of ministers generally. V. xix. 18 : xxviii. 1. And of particular ministers ; we have 外正, V. ix. 18 ; 正人, ix. 17 ; 少正, x. 2 ; 大正, xxvi. 4 ; *et al.,* as in x. 4, 7 : xviii. 25. 先正, IV. viii. Pt. iii. 8, = the former premier, but in V. xxv. 7, the same phrase = your correct father. (3) The month or months with which the year commenced in difft. dynasties. III. ii. 3 : IV. vi. 3. The first month of the year. II. i. 4, 14 : ii. 19.

此
ts'ze
tz'û

This, these. III. iii. 6, 7 : V. xv. 15, 18 : xix. 15.

步
poo
pu

A pace, a step. V. ii. 7. To travel. V. iii. 1 : xii. 1 : xxiv. 1.

武
woo
wu

(1) To be martial ; prowess. IV. iv. 3 : V. i. Pt. ii. 8 ; Pt. iii. 6.   = awe-inspiring. II. ii. 4. Warlike measures or ways. III. i. Pt. ii. 20 : V. iii. 2, 3. (2) The posthumous title of the first king of the Chow dynasty. V. vii. 5. 武王, V. vi. 12, 16 ; *et sæpe.* The combination of this title and that of his father—文武—is very frequent. (3) 武丁, one of the emperors of the Shang dynasty. V. xvi. 7.

歲
suy
sui

A year, a round year. I. i. 8 : II. i. 8 : III. iv. 3 : IV. viii. Pt. i. 6 : V. iv. 8, 35—37 : vi. 19. 烝祭歲, to offer the annual winter sacrifice. V. xiii. 29 ; but the meaning is doubtful.

歷
leih
li

(1) To pass through. V. xvi. 8 : xxiv. 3. Obs. 有夏歷年, &c., V. xii. 17, 19, 22. 經歷, to pass through and carry out. V. xvi. 4. 歷人, harbourers of criminals. V. xi. 2.   = destinies, as if it were 曆數, V. vii. 1. (2) Fully, repeatedly. IV. vii. Pt. iii. 3. (3) 歷山, the name of a mountain near which Shun once lived. II. ii. 21.

歸
kwei
kuei

(1) To return. II. i. 8 : IV. iii. 1 : v. Pt. ii. 1 : V. vi. 8, 11 : xx. 1.   = to send. V. iii. 2 : x. 14. To retire ; retirement. IV. vi. 1. (2) To turn to. III. iii.

9: IV. vi. 4 : V. iv. 14 : xvii. 4. 依歸, dependence and resort. V. vi. 7.

THE 78TH RADICAL. 歹

死
sze
szŭ

To die; death. II. i. 28: IV. vii. Pt. ii. 13: V. ix. 15; x. 11: xxvii. 20. Observe 殛死 and 伐厥死, IV. vii. Pt. i. 16: V. iv. 3. 一死, one dead animal. II. i. 8. 死魄, the dead dark disk, — new moon. V. iii. 1.

殂
tsoo
tsu

殂落 = to decease. II. i. 13.

殃
yang

Evils, miseries. IV. iv. 8.

殄
t'een
t'ien

To cut off; to cast of. II. i. 25: iv. 8: V. ix. 22, 23 : xviii. 6: xxviii. 2. We find it with other verbs :—殄戮, V. xii. 21: xviii. 11; 殄礪, V. i. Pt. iii. 4: 暴殄, V. iii. 6; 殄滅. IV. vii. Pt. ii. 16. To be cut off. V. xxiv. 8.

殆
t'ae
t'ai

(1) Perilous. V. xxx. 7. (2) A particle, = I apprehend, it seems to be that. V. xxii. 7.

殉
seun
hsün

To desire, to seek for. IV. iv. 7.

殊
shoo
shu

To mark off, show to be different. V. xxiv. 7.

殖
chih

To plant, to cultivate. V. xxvii. 8. (2) To revive and prosper. IV. x. 5. To make to prosper. IV. ii. 9. (3) To accumulate. IV. ii. 5.

殘
ts'an

To injure, to oppress. 殘害, V. i. Pt. i. 5. 凶殘, the cruel oppressor. V. i. Pt. ii. 8.

殛
keih
chi

(1) To keep prisoner to death. II. i. 12 : V. iv. 3. (2) To destroy. IV. i. 1. We have 罰殛 in V. ix. 21, and xviii. 23, = to punish and destroy, or perhaps only = to punish severely.

殪
e
i

To destroy, to exterminate. V. ix. 4.

殲
ts'een
chien

To destroy utterly. III. iv. 6: V. i. Pt. iii. 4.

THE 79TH RADICAL. 殳.

殳
shoo
shu

The name of an officer about the court of Shun. II. i. 21.

殷
yin

(1) To determine exactly, to regulate; to be regulated. I. 4. 6: III. i. Pt. i. 48. (2) Affluent, abundant, — to be well

with. V. xxvii. 8. (2) The name of the capital to which Pwan-kăng removed the govt. of the Shang dynasty. IV. vii. Pt. i. 1. From the time of this removal, the dynasty was called either Yin or Shang, and in Pt. V. the character occurs everywhere in this application. After the rise of the Chow dyn., however, in Bks. vii.—xxiv., we are to understand very often by the term, not the dynasty, as over the empire, but the imperial domain of it, or even, more restrictedly, that portion of the domain which was for a time possessed by Woo-kăng, the son of Show. On the phrase 有殷, the sovereign of Yin, the House of Yin, V. xii. 11 : xviii. 13 ; et al., see 有.

殺
shă
sha

To kill, to put to death; the penalty of death. II. ii. 12 : III. iv. 4 : V. ix. 8, 10, 13, 15, 17; et sæpe. 殺戮, V. i. Pt. iii 3 : xxvii. 3. 同于殺, to be classed with those who should be put to death. V. x. 16.

毅
e
i

To be bold and resolute; boldness. II. iii. 3. 果毅, V. i. Pt. iii. 4.

THE 80TH RADICAL. 毋.

毋
moo
mu

Do not. II. ii. 18.

毋
moo
mu

A mother. I. 12: III. iii. 3. 父母, parents. II. ii. 21 : V. x. 6: xv. 3. The emperor is spoken of as the parent of the people, V. iv. 16; and Heaven and Earth as the parent of all things, V. i. Pt. i. 3.

每
mei

Every. III. iv. 3.

毒
tuh
tu

Poison, venom. 荼毒, wormwood and poison. IV. iii. 3. Painful smart. 生毒, IV. vii. Pt. i. 12. Painful. IV. vii. Pt. i. 11. Painful or poisonous injury. V. i. Pt. ii. 4. To poison, V. i. Pt. iii. 3. In anger, in hate. IV. xi.

THE 81ST RADICAL. 比.

比
pe
pi

(1) To compare. V. xxvii. 18. (2) 比干, a relative of the tyrant Show, put to death by him. V. iii. 9. 3d tone. (1) To be—keep—near to. IV. iv. 6: V. xii. 15: xiv. 21. So, 昵比, to cultivate intimacies with. V. i. Pt. ii. 3. 比德, = selfish confederations. V. iv. 10. To agree. IV. vii. Pt. iii. 3. So, vii. Pt. ii. 12. To join (act.). V. ii. 4.

比
pe
pi

(1) To attend carefully to. V. xii. 14 : xiii. 16. (2) To admonish; admonitions. V. x. 2, 13, 17: xiii. 25: xxiv. 3. (3) To distress; to be distressed. V. vii. 8. 10.

毗
pe
pi

To assist, help. V. viii. 4.

THE 82D RADICAL. 毛.

毛
maou
mao

(1) The hair,—of animals. III. i. Pt. i. 44, 52. Applied also to the down and feathers of birds. I. 6, 7. (2) The name of a principality. The duke of Maou was a high minister in the time of king Ching of the Chow dynasty. V. xxii. 3 (3) A name. V. xxii. 11.

毨
sëen
hsien

To be sleek or glossy. 毛毨, I. 6.

氄
jung

To be downy. To be full of feathers. 氄毛, I. 7.

THE 83D RADICAL. 氏.

氏
she
shih

It follows the names of principalities and dynasties, denoting the rulers or sovereigns of them, and is used as we sometimes use *the* in English,—*The* O'Donoghue, &c. 師氏 an officer of the Chow dynasty, the master of the imperial warders. V. ii. 2: xxii. 3. 尹氏 seems to = all the 尹, the heads of departments. V. vii. 6.

民
min

The people. *Passim.* It is used also as we use *people*, without reference to rank, = men generally; *E.g.* V. xxx. 2. Of phrases we have 黎民, all the people, or the black-haired people, I. 2 : II. i. 18 : ii. 2 : V. xxx. 6, 7; *et al.*; 小民, the inferior people. V. xi. 2 : xxv. 4; *et sæpe;* 下民, also meaning the inferior people. V. xxi. 4 : xxv. 5 : xxvi. 2; *et sæpe;* though sometimes 下 seems to be opposed simply to Heaven above, and the phrase = mankind, as in V. iv. 2: and in I. 11, and II. iv. 2, we may perhaps say that 下民 means the people living in low places; 生民, simply = the people, V. v. 10 : xxiv. 13; 庶民, the masses or multitudes of the people, V. iv. 9—16, 26—30, *et sæpe;* so, 烝民, V. iii. 6; 萬民, the myriads of the people, and 兆民, the millions, III. iii. 5 : IV. iv. 3 : vii. Pt. ii. 12 : V. xv. 12; *et sæpe;* 四民, the four classes of the people, scholars or officers, farmers, mechanics, and merchants, V. xx. 12; 俊民, men of eminent ability, heroic men, V. xiv. 6 : xvi. 20; *et al.*; 獻民, wise men, V. xiii. 23; 先民 spoken with reference

to the emperors of former dynasties, V. xii. 11, and in p. 10, 後民 is used with ref. to the last emperor of the Shang dynasty.

THE 85TH RADICAL. 水.

水
shwuy
shui

Water, waters. II. iv. 8 : III. i. Pt. ii. 8 : IV. xi. 2; *et al.* One of the elements. V. iv. 5. One of the six magazines of nature. II. ii. 7. 洪水, the inundation. I. 11 : II. iv. 1 : V. iv. 3. So, 滛水, II. ii. 4. = with water. V. xxii. 2. Yu's work is described as 平水土, II. i. 17 : V. xxvii. 8. 水 is added constantly to the names of streams, or forms part of those names, like *water* in our *Blackwater.*

永
yung

Long, long-continued, perpetual. IV. v. Pt. i. 6 : V. vi. 10 : xii. 20, 23, 24; *et sæpe.* Far-reaching. II. iii. 1; *et al.* 永念, think of what is long distant. V. xvi. 10. 永世, long ages. IV. viii. Pt. iii. 3; *et al.* 永世無暨, for ever and ever without end. V. viii. 1. To continue long. V. xviii. 7. To prolong, to perpetuate; prolongation. II. i. 24, (some read in 3d tone): IV. vii. Pt. i. 4 : V. xviii. 28; *et al.* 日永, the day is at its longest. I. 5. = length of years. IV. ix. 3. Ever, for ever, perpetually. II. ii. 8, 17 : IV. ii. 9 ; *et passim.*

求
k'ew
ch'iu

To seek, to seek for. IV. iii. 4 : iv. 5, 6 ; *et sæpe,* in the 4th and 5th Parts. To seek allegiance. IV. vi. 4. Obs. 作求, V. ix. 20.

汙
woo
wu

Filthy. III. iv. 6.

汝
joo
ju

You (nom. and obj.), your. *Passim.*

江
keang
chiang

(1) The Këang, one of the two great rivers of China, now called the Yang-tsze. III. i. Pt i. 45, 47, 53 : Pt. ii. 8, 9. A part of its course is called 北江, Pt. ii. 8; and a part 中江, Pt. ii. 9. (2) 三江, three rivers in Yang-chow, which do not seem to have been identified with certainty. III. i. Pt. i. 40. (3) 九江, the nine streams, generally supposed to be a name for the T'ung-t'ing lake. III. i. Pt. i. 48, 52 : Pt. ii. 4, 9.

池
ch'e
ch'ih

A pond, ponds. V. i. Pt. i. 5.

汩
kw'uh
ku

To throw into disorder. V. iv. 3.

汭
juy
jui

The north of a stream. Or perhaps, the place of junction between two streams. I. 12 : III. i. Pt. i. 73, 82 : Pt. ii. 7 : iii. 3 : V. xii. 3.

汶
wăn
wên

The name of a stream, now lost in the great Canal. III. i. Pt. i. 27 ; Pt. ii. 10.

决
keuĕ
chüeh

To open a passage for a stream. II. iv. 1.

沂
e
i

The name of a river in Shan-tung and Keang-soo. III. i. Pt. i. 29 ; Pt. ii. 11.

沃
yuh
yü

To irrigate, to enrich. IV. viii. Pt. i. 7.

沇
yen

The name of a stream, subsequently known as the Tse (濟), and flowing into the Ho. III. i. Pt. ii. 10.

沈
ch‘in
ch‘ên

To be sunk ; to sink (act. and neuter). III. iv. 4 : IV. vii. Pt. i. 12 : xi. 1, 4. 沈湎, to be sunk in drunkenness. V. i. Pt. i. 5. 沈潛, the reserved and retiring. V. iv. 17.

沔
mĕen
mien

The name of a stream. III. i. Pt. i. 70.

冲
ch‘ung

Young, small. The phrases 冲子 冲人, a youth, the youth, are used to the emperors, and by them of themselves. IV. vii. Pt. ii. 7 : V. vi. 18 : vii. 1, 8 : xii. 12 : xiii. 11, 14, 16 : xvi. 5.

沙
sha

流沙, the moving sands, the pres. desert of Gobi. III. i. Pt. ii. 5. 23.

沮
tseu
chü

(1) The name of a stream in Yen-chow, whose waters flowed into the marsh of Luy-hea. III. i. Pt i. 15. (2) The name of another stream in Yung-chow, an affluent of the Wei. III. i. Pt. i. 74 ; Pt. ii. 12.

沱
t‘o

A branch of the Keang. There were one or more streams of this name in King-chow, III. i. Pt i. 49 ; and also in Lëang-chow, III. Pt. i. 53, 64 ; Pt. ii. 9.

河
ho

The Yellow River, though its channel in the latter part of its course was different from what it is now. III. i. Pt. i. 11, 20, 36, &c.; Pt. ii. 1, 7, 10, 12, 13 ; iii. 2 : IV. vii. Pt. ii. 1 : viii. Pt. iii. 1 : V. i. Pt. ii. 1 : xiii. 3. 九河, nine channels, forming a delta in the northern part of Yen-chow, by which a portion of the waters of the Ho were through Yu's skill discharged into the sea. III. i. Pt. i. 13. 西河, the western Ho, that portion of it which runs from north to south betweee Shen-se and Shan-se. III. i. Pt. i. 71, 82. 南河, the most southern part of the Ho. III. i. Pt. i. 53. 河圖, the river plan,—the scheme on a dragon's back, which is fabled to have emerged from the Ho, and supplied Fuh-he with the idea of his diagrams. V. xxii. 19.

治
ch‘e
che
chih

To manage, to regulate. III. i. Pt. i. 4 : V. xii. 14 : xv. 4 : xvi. 23 : xx. 1, 7, 9. = to punish. III. iv. 6. = the performance of works. V. ix. 1.
3d tone. To be well regulated ; where management and regulation take effect, —good government. II. ii. 8, 11, 13 : iv. 4 : IV. v. Pt. iii. 2 : viii. Pt. ii. 5 : V. iii. 9 : xvii. 4 : xx. 2 : xxi. 3 : xxiv. 13 : xxv. 7.—There is some uncertainty in determining in several instances to what tone we shall assign this character.

沿
yüen
yüan

To follow the course of a stream or shore. III. i. l t. i. 45.

泆
yih
yi

To be dissipated ; dissipation. V. x. 11 : xiv. 4, 9.

法
fă
fa

(1) Laws. V. xxi. 7 : xxvii. 3. 法度, II. ii. 6 : IV. vii. Pt. i. 5. = imperial appointments, or way of procedure. V. vii. 13. To act according to the laws. V. xxvii. 18. (2) A plan,—as of a house. V. vii. 11.

泗
sze
szŭ

The name of a stream, which is now one of the feeders of the great Canal, but which anciently flowed into the Hwae. III. i. Pt. i. 35, 36, 45 : Pt. ii. 11.

波
po

(1) 滎波, the name of a marsh in Yu-chow. III. i. Pt. i. 56. (2) = waters. III. i. Pt. ii. 5.

泣
k‘eih
ch‘i

To weep, to shed tears. II. ii. 21 : iv. 8 : V. vi. 18.

泥
ne
ni

Miry. 塗泥, III. i. Pt. i. 42, 51.

泰
t‘ae
t‘ai

A surname. 泰顚, a minister of king Wăn. V. xvi. 12.

泯
min

To be exhausted or destroyed. V. ix. 16. 泯泯, to become dark or blinded. V. xxvii. 4.

洋
yang

洋洋, vast, = of vast significance. IV. iv. 8.

洗
sëen
hsien

To clarify spirits. V. x. 6.

浲
keang
ching

(1) Waters overflowing. 浲水, the flood of Yaou's time. II. ii. 14. (2) The name of a stream, an affluent of the main stream of the Ho. III. i. Pt. ii. 7.

洛
lŏ
lo

(1) The name of a river in Ho-nan, one of the principal tributaries of the Ho. III. i. Pt. i. 53, 55, 60 ; Pt. ii. 7, 13 ; *et al.* (2) 洛 alone, and 洛邑, occur often as the name of the 'capital of the completed Chow,' to which the people and officers of a part of the imperial domain of Yin were removed. V. ix. 1 : xii. 2, 3, 4 : xiv. 1, 22, 25 ; *et al.*

津
tsin
chin

(1) A ford. IV. xi. 2. (2) 孟津, the name of a ford over the Ho, and of the country about it. III. i. Pt. iii. 7 : V. i. Pt. i. 1 : iii. 8.

洪
hung

(1) Water overflowing. 洪水, Yaou's flood. I. 11 : II. iv. 1. (2) Great. 洪範, the Great Plan. V. iv. 3. Greatly. V. xiv. 16 : xviii. 5. 洪大, V. ix. 1 洪惟 = I greatly think. V. xiv. 16 : xviii. 5 ; but ? i. Pt. iii. 4.

洮
t'aou
t'ao

To wash the hands. V. xxii. 2.

洲
chow
chou

An island. 幽洲, II. i. 12.

洽
hĕă
hsia

To penetrate, to permeate. II. ii. 12 (foll. by 于). V. xxiv. 13.

流
lew
liu

(1) To flow along ; to flow away. III. i. Pt. ii. 7, 10 : V. iii. 8 : xxiv. 9 : xxx. 2. To make to flow. V. i. Pt. ii. 4. 流言, flowing words, a rumour. V. vi. 12 : xvii. 1. (2) To banish. II. i. 12. Banishment generally. 五流, II. i. 11, 20. The most distant banishment. III. i. Pt. ii. 22. (3) 流沙, see 沙. = to regulate. II. iii. 4.

浚
seun
hsün

浩
haou
hao

浩浩, of vast extent, the appearance of Yaou's flood. I. 11 : II. iv. 1.

浮
fow
fou

(1) To float. Foll. by 于, meaning generally to float along or on, but sometimes to float to. III. i. i t. i. 20, 27, 36, 82 ; *et al.* 浮磬, sounding-stones, lying on the banks, or seeming to float near them. III. i. t. i. 35. (2) To exceed. V. i. Pt. ii. 5 (foll. by 于).

海
hae
hai

The sea, seas. It generally denotes the sea on the east of China. II. iv. 7 : III. i. Pt. i. 21, 24, 28 ; Pt. ii. 1, 7, 8, 9, 10, 11 ; *et al.* 南海, the southern sea. III. i. Pt. ii. 6. 四海, II. i. 13 : ii. 1, 4, 17 : iv. 1, 8 : III. i. t. ii. 14, 23 : iv. 1 : IV. iv. 4 : viii. Pt. iii. 8 : V. i. Pt. i. 11, Pt. iii. 3 : iii. 8. See 四. Marine. III. i. Pt. i. 26. 海隅 and 海表, see 隅 and 表.

浪
lang

滄浪, the name of the Han in a portion of its course. III. i. Pt. ii. 8.

涇
king
ching

A river of Yung-chow, which joins the Wei. III. i. Pt. i. 73 ; Pt. ii. 12.

涉
shĕ
shê

To cross over—go through—a stream. IV. vii. Pt. ii. 1 : xi. 2 : V. i. Pt. iii. 3 : vii. 2. = to tread on. V. xxv. 2.

涯
yae
yai

The bank of a river. IV. xi. 2.

淄
tsze
tzŭ

A river in Ts'ing-chow. III. i. Pt. i. 23.

淑
shuh
shu

The good, virtuous. V. xxiv. 7.

淪
lun

To sink. 淪喪, to sink in ruin. IV. xi. 2. 8.

淫
yin

To go to excess,—with a bad meaning ; excess, dissoluteness. II. ii. 6 : IV. iii. 7 : x. 2 : V. i. Pt. ii. 3 : x. 11 : xii. 21 : xiv. 5, 9 : xv. 12 : *et al.* The bad. IV. iii. 3. 淫朋, lawless confederacies. V. iv. 10 Compare 朋淫, II. iv. 8. 淫風, the fashion of dissipation. IV. iv. 7. Extraordinary. V. i. t. iii. 3. Excessively. V. xxvii. 3. Extensively and carelessly. V. xxix. 3.

淺
ts'ĕen
ch'ien

敷淺, the name of a plain. III. i. Pt. ii. 4.

淮
hwae
huai

A river which rises in Ho-nan, and afterwards joins the Ho, but which in Yu's time held its own course to the sea. III. i. Pt. i. 28, 29 ; *et al.* 淮夷, wild tribes about the Hwae. III. i. Pt. i. 35 : V. xxix. 1.

深
shin
shen

Deep. IV. iii. 6.

淵
yuen
yüan

Deep. V. vii. 2 : viii. 2. Deep waters. V. iii. 6. An abyss. IV. iii. 6.

清
tsing
ch'ing

To be pure. II. i. 23 : V. xxvii. 21. With an unprejudiced mind. V. xxvii. 7. To cleanse. V. i. Pt. i. 11.

渠
k'eu
ch'ü

(1) Great, principal. III. iv. 6. (2) 渠搜, the name of a mountain. III. i. Pt. i. 83.

溫
wăn
wên

To be mild ; mildness, gentleness. II. i. 1, 24 : iii. 3.

渭
wei

A river, which rises in the pres. Kan-suh, and flows into the Ho, near the end of its course from north to south. III. i. Pt. 70, 73, 82 ; Pt. ii. 12.

游
yew
yu

To float on or across. V. xvi. 16.

湎
mĕen
mien

To be sunk in wine or intemperance. 沈湎, V. i. Pt. i. 5. 湎于酒, V. x. 10, 15, 17.

湯
shang

湯湯, the appearance of a flood. I. 11.

湯
t'ang

Commonly spoken of as 成湯, T'ang the Successful, the founder of the Shang dynasty. IV. ii. 1 : vi. 3 : V. i. Pt. ii. 4, 8 : viii. 2 : x. 9 ; *et al.*

源
yuen
yüan

The source of a river. III. i. Pt. ii. 14.

準
chun

準, 準人, and 準夫, in V. xix. 1, 2, 7, 16, 19, are names for the officers or guardians of the laws.

溢
yih
yi

To overflow, to flow out. III. i. Pt. ii. 10.

滄
ts'ang

滄浪, see 浪.

滅
mëë
mieh

To extinguish, extinguishing ; to be extinguished. III. iii. 1 : IV. iii. 3 : V. i. Pt ii. 3 : x. ii. xvi. 10 : xxiv. 10. 殄滅, IV. vii. Pt. ii. 16. 樸滅, IV. vii. Pt. i. 12. 滅亡, extinction and ruin. III. iii. 7.

滋
tsze
tzŭ

To be abundant. V. i. Pt. iii. 4. Abundantly. V. xvi. 20.

滌
teih
ti

To clear. III. i. Pt. ii. 14.

滎
jung

滎波 and 滎, the name of a marsh. III. i. t. i. 56 ; t. ii. 10.

滔
t'aou
t'ao

To insult, = to assail. Always in the phrase 滔天. I. 10, 11 : II. iv. 1.

滿
mwan
man

= pride, the fulness of one's-self. II. ii. 21. 自滿, to be full of one's-self. II. ii. 14 ; IV. ii. 8.

漂
p'eaou
p'iao

To float. 流漂, to float away. IV. iii. 8.

漆
ts'eih
ch'i

(1) Varnish. III. i. Pt. i. 19, 60. Varnished. V. xxii. 18. (2) The name of a stream, a tributary of the Wei. III. i. Pt. i. 74 : Pt. ii. 12.

漢
han

A large stream, flowing into the Këang. III. i. Pt. i. 47, 53 ; Pt. ii. 8.

漳
chang

A stream, flowing from east to west, and in Yu's time joining the Ho in the pres. dis. of Fow-shing. 衡漳, III. i. Pt. i. 6.

漸
tseen
chien

To advance by degrees ; more and more. III. i. Pt. i. 33 : V. xxii. 4.

漸
tseen
chien

1st tone. To permeate ; to be affected. III. i. t. ii. 23 : V. xxvii. 4.

瀁
yang

The name of the Han in the early part of its course. III. i. Pt. ii. 8.

潛
ts'een
ch'ien

(1) To dive,—to lie hid. 沈潛, the reserved and retiring. V. iv. 17. (2) The name of streams flowing from the Han

and rejoining it again. III. i. Pt. i. 53, 64, 70.
An affluent of the Ho. III. i. Pt. i. 55 ; Pt. ii. 13 : V. xiii. 3.

澗
këen
chien

潤
jun

To soak. V. iv. 5. 澤潤 to exert an enriching influence on. V. xxiv. 13.

澤
tsih
tsê

(1) A marsh. We have 震澤, III. i. Pt. i. 41 ; and 菏澤, p. 52. To become a marsh. III. i. Pt. ii. 8. To be formed into a marsh. Pt. i. 14. 九澤, the marshes of the nine provinces, Pt. ii. 14. (2) = favours, bounties. V. xiv. 8. 資澤, xxviii. 13. 潤澤, see above.

澧
le
li

The name probably of a stream, flowing into the Këang. III. i. t. ii. 9.

滋
she
shih

三滋, probably three dykes on the Han. III. i. Pt. ii. 8.

澮
kwae
kuai

A field ditch or channel. II. iv. 1.

濟
tse
chi

2d tone. (1) 濟濟, numerous. II. ii. 20. (2) The name of a stream. ? flows now into the sea as the 小清 III. i. Pt. i. 20, 27 ; Pt. ii. 10.
3d tone. (1) To cross over a stream. IV. vii. Pt. ii. 6 : viii. Pt. i. 6 : V. vii. 2 : xvi. 16. (2) To help. V. iii. 8 : xvii. 6 : xxii. 7. (3) To be successful. III. iv. 7 : V. xxi. 12.

濬
tse
ch'i

濬
seun
hsün

(1) Deep, profound,—spoken of Shun. II. i. 1. (2) To deepen the channel of a river. II. i. 10 : iv. 1.

濮
puh
pu

Name of the country of a wild tribe, in the present Hoo-pih, one of those which assisted king Woo against the tyrant Show. V. ii. 3.

濰
wei

A river of Ts'ing-chow. III. i. Pt. i. 23.

濱
pin

The shore of the sea, or bank of a river. III. i. Pt. i. 24, 35.

瀍
ch'an

The name of a stream, an affluent of the Lŏ. III. i. Pt. i. 55 ; Pt. ii. 13 : V. xiii. 3.

灃
fung

The name of a river, an affluent of the Wei. III. i. Pt. i. 75 ; Pt. ii. 12.

灉
yung

The name of a river in Yen-chow. III. i. Pt. i. 15.

THE 86TH RADICAL. 火.

火
ho

(1) Fire. II. iv. 4 : III. iv. 6 : IV. vii. Pt. i. 8, 12 : V. xiii. 9. One of the five elements. V. iv. 5. One of the six magazines of nature. II. ii. 7. (2) The name of a star. I. 5.

灼
chŏ
cho

(1) To burn or blaze. V. xiii. 9. To shine forth. V. xxvii. 10. Clearly. V. xix. 6, 16.

災
tsae

(1) Calamities, judgments. IV. iii. 3: iv. 2: vi. 5: vii. Pt. ii. 7: xi. 4, 8: V. i. Pt. i. 4. = punishment. IV. xi. 6. 作災, to inflict suffering. IV. vii. Pt. i. 14. 自炎, to cause suffering one's-self. IV. vii. Pt. i. 12. (2) Offences by mishap. II. i. 11: V. ix. 8.

炎
yen

To blaze; to blaze over. V. iv. 5: III. iv. 6.

炙
chih

To roast. 焚炙, V. i. Pt. i. 5.

炭
t'an

Charcoal. 塗炭, IV. ii. 2.

烈
lëĕ
lieh

(1) Violent, fierce,—spoken of natural phenomena. II. i. 2: III. iv. 6 (烈于 fiercer than). = energy. V. xxv. 6. (2) Merit, achievement; merit-achieving, meritorious. IV. iv. 1: v. Pt. ii. 6: vii. Pt. i. 3: viii. Pt. iii. 10: V. viii. 4: xiii. 14. 22, 24: xix. 22: xxiv. 5. Observe 前烈, V. iii. 5, and 先烈, xxvi. 3.

烝
ching
chêng

(1) All, the multitudes of. 烝民, II. iv. 1: IV. vi. 9: V. iii. 6. (2) To advance, make progress. V. xviii. 16. Under this meaning comes. 烝烝, denoting probably *gradually*. I. 12. (3) Name of the winter sacrifice in the temple of ancestors. V. xiii. 29. (4) Name of a wild tribe subject to the House of Chow. V. xix. 11. But the meaning is doubtful.

焉
yen

A final particle, used at the end of sentences to round them. It only occurs four times in the Shoo. V. ii. 7, 8: vi. 4: xxx. 6.

焚
fun
fên

To burn; to be burned. V. i. Pt. i. 5: III. iv. 6.

無
woo
wu

Not, do not, to be without. *Passim.* 無 is the opposite of 有, both in its personal and impersonal forms, = not to have, to be without; and there is—was—not, there will not be, there not being. Obs. 有無, II. iv. 1, and 有罪無罪, V. i. Pt. i. 7. Its imperative usage, in the sense of 毋, is very frequent. Observe also 無大, 無小, however great, however small. II. ii. 11.

So. It only occurs twice. IV. vii. Pt. ii. 10: V. xxx. 4.

然
jen
jan

(1) To be bright,—intelligent. II. ii. 6. (2) To be fully discharged. I. 8: II. i. 17, 27: iv. 11. (3) To enlarge, to consolidate. V. xviii. 21.

熒
k'ëung
ch'iung

The friendless. V. iv. 12.

照
chëaou
chiao

To shine. V. i. Pt. i. 5.

煩
fan

To be burdensome, full of trouble. IV. viii. Pt. ii. 11: V. xx. 16.

熊
heung
hsiung

(1) A bear, bears. III i. Pt. 1. 79: V. ii. 9. 熊羆之士, soldiers brave as bears and grisly bears. V. xxiii. 5. (2) The name of an officer about the court of Shun. II. i. 22. (3) 熊耳, the name of a mountain at which Yu began his survey of the Lŏ. III. i. Pt. ii. 2, 13. To be ripe. V. vi. 16. To be fruitful. V. vi. 19.

熟
shuh
shu

燄
yen

燄燄, fire slowly and gradually spreading, the first beginnings of a fire. V. xiii. 9.

燎
lëaou
liao

To burn, to blaze. IV. vii. Pt. i. 12.

燕
yen

Easy, unoccupied. 用燕, for pleasure and idlenesss' sake. V. x. 11.

營
ying

To build. IV. v. Pt. i. 9. Plans for building. V. xii. 2, (經營), 4.

燠
yuh
yü

To be warm. V. iv. 32, 34.

燮
sëĕ
hsieh

To harmonize. 燮和, V. xxii. 24. 燮理, V. xx. 5. = in a state of harmony. V. iv. 17.

THE 87TH RADICAL. 爪.

爭
tsäng
tsêng

To contest. II. ii. 14.

爰
yüen
yüan

(1) A particle at the beginning of sentences and clauses, = on this, and so. IV. vi. 3: viii. Pt. i. 4: V. xv. 5, 6: xxvii 3. (2) It follows the verb, like 于, carrying it on to its object. IV. vii. Pt. iii. 1: V. xxii. 11. After the noun, as a verb itself, = to be seen in, to consist in. V. iv. 5. Obs. 既爰, and thereupon, IV. vii. Pt. i. 2.

爲
wei

Passim. (1) To be, to be in the place of; sometimes, to make to be. III. iii. 5: IV. iv. 5: V. iii. 6: xi. 5; *et sæpe.* 以爲, to consider to be. IV. ii. 1; but more frequently 以爲 = to take to be, to undertake, to employ. V. ii. 6: vi. 4, 16: xvii. 1. In. V. iv. 16, 以爲 = and so becomes. (2) To become. III. i. Pt.

ii. 7—10. (3) To do, to act, to make. II. iv. 4 *(n. b.)*: IV. v. Pt. iii. 8: V. i. Pt. ii. 3: v. 9: vi. 15: xi. 4; *et al.* 有爲, to have conduct, administrative power. V. iv. 11, 13. 秉爲, to hold fast and do, = practice. V. xiv. 4. 百爲, all the ways of good action in govt. V. xviii. 7. 爲幻, the practice of deceiving tricks. V. xv. 14. 爲善, the practice of good. V. xvii. 4.

爲
wei
爵
tsёŏ
chio

3d tone. To act on behalf of; in relation to. IV. vi. 7: V. vi. 2: xi. 3.

Dignities, degrees of nobility. IV. v. Pt. ii. 5: V. iii. 10.

THE 88TH RADICAL. 父.

父
foo
fu

A father, fathers. I. 12: IV. vii. Pt. i. 14; Pt. ii. 13, 14: V. vii. 11: ix. 16: xxv. 1. 父母, parents, parent. II. ii. 21: V. x. 6: xiii. 13: xv. 3. Spoken of the emperor. V. iv. 16. Spoken of Heaven and Earth. V. i. Pt. i. 3. 父母弟, paternal and maternal relatives. V. ii. 6. 伯父, senior uncle, uncles. V. xxiii. 6: xxvii. 13. So, 父 alone. xxviii. 1, 2, 3, 4. 師父 = Grand-tutor. IV. xi. 1, 3, 4: V. xxiv. 2, 5, 12. ? ought 父 here to be in the 2d tone.

父
foo
fu

2d tone. An honourable designation, — minister or officer. We have 圻父, 宏父, and 農父, the three great ministers at the court of a prince of the empire. V. x. 13.

THE 89TH RADICAL. 爻.

爽
shwang
shuang

(1) To enlighten. IV. ii. 3: V. vii. 13. 爽惟, to think clearly. V. ix. 20, 21. (2) Light. 昧爽, between the dark and light, in the early dawn. IV. v. Pt. i. 5: V. ii. 1: iii. 9. (3) = to lose, to forfeit. IV. vii. Pt. ii. 12. Errors. V. xiii. 12.

爾
urh

(1) You, your. *Passim.* (2) An adverb, = our *ly.* 式爾, purposely; 適爾, accidentally. V. ix. 8; *et al.*

THE 90TH RADICAL. 爿.

牆
ts'ёang
ch'iang

A wall, walls. III. iii. 6: V. xx. 16: xxix. 4 (垣牆).

THE 91ST RADICAL. 片.

牖
yew
yu

A window. 牖間 = between the window and the door. V. xxii. 15.

THE 92D RADICAL. 牙.

牙
ya

君牙, the minister of Instruction under king Muh. V. xxv. 1, 7.

THE 93D RADICAL. 牛.

牛
new
niu

A bull, oxen. V. iii. 2: x. 6: xii. 5: xiii. 29: xxix. 3. 4.

牝
p'in

Female. 牝鷄, a hen. V. ii. 5.

牡
mow
mou

The male of animals. = a victim. IV. iii. 4.

牧
muh
mu

(1) A pastor or shepherd. Applied to the governors of provinces. II. i. 7, 16: V. xx. 3, 13. They are called 天牧, the shepherds of Heaven. V. xxvii. 12. The same is the application probably of 牧, 牧夫 and 牧人, in V. xix. 2, 7, 12, 13, 16, 19, 21. (2) To learn to live by pasturage. III. i. Pt. i. 26. (3) 牧野, the wilderness of Muh, the place, in the pres. Ho-nan, not far from the capital of Show, where the struggle between him and king Woo was determined. V. ii. 1: iii. 9.

物
wuh
wu

(1) Things, articles. III. i. Pt. 26: V. v. 3, 6, 8; *et al.* 土物, productions of the ground. V. x. 5. 方物, productions of difft. regions, V. v. 2. 天物, creatures of Heaven. V. iii. 6. 萬物, all things. V. i. Pt. i. 3. = relics. V. viii. 1. = matters. V. xxiv. 5. (2) 敦物, the name of a mountain. III. i. Pt. i. 76.

牲
shăny
shêng

An animal used for sacrifice,—a victim, victims. IV. xi. 6 (犧牷牲): V. i. Pt. i. 6 (犧牲): xii. 5.

牷
ts'euen
ch'üan

A complete victim, without blemish. IV. xi. 6.

特
t'ih
t'ê

A single ox or victim. II. i. 8.

牽
k'ёen
ch'ien

To lead forward. V. x. 6.

牿
kuh
ku

An enclosure for oxen and horses. Used also for the cattle enclosed. V. xxix. 3.

犁
le
li

犁老, old men, time-worn sires. V. i. Pt. ii. 3.

犠
he
hsi

A victim, uniform in colour. IV. xi. 6: V. i. Pt. i. 6.　See 牲.

THE 94TH RADICAL. 犬.

犬
k'euen
ch'üan

The dog, dogs. V. v. 8.

犯
fan

To offend against, expose one's-self to be punished. II. ii. 12.

狂
k'wang
k'uang

Wildness. V. iv. 34. 發出狂, to manifest insanity. IV. xi. 3. Foolish. V. xviii. 17.

狃
new
niu

To be practised, accustomed. V. xxi. 16.

狄
teih
ti

(1) The common name for the wild tribes on the North. IV. ii. 6. (2) Barbarians employed in menial offices about the imperial court. V. xxii. 14.

狎
hëǎ
hsia

To be near to. IV. v. Pt. i. 9. To be familiar with,—used adverbially in the phrase 狎侮, to treat with contemptuous ease or familiarity. V. i. Pt. iii. 2: v. 4.

狐
hoo
hu

The fox. III. i. Pt. i. 69.

狹
hëǎ
hsia

To consider and treat as narrow and mean. IV. vi. 11.

猗
e
i

I. q. 兮, a particle, following adjectives, and = our *ly*. 斷斷猗, V. xxx. 6.
Fierce, raging,—spoken of fire. III. iv. 6.

猶
yew
yu

Still, notwithstanding. IV. v. Pt. ii. 3: vii. I't. i. 12: V. xv. 14. Still more, especially. IV. vii. Pt. i. 3.

猷
yew
yu

(1) To plan, deliberate. IV. vii. Pt. i. 6. 猷詢 to consult with. V. xxx. 4. Plans, counsels. IV. vii. I't. i. 15; Pt. ii. 12, 15: V. viii. 3; *et al.* 謀猷 V. xxi. 6: xxviii. 1. 猷訓, lessons. V. xxi. 3. 有猷 to have counsel, to be wise in counsel. V. iv. 11. (2) The course. the way,—as indicated by wise counsel. IV. iii. 2: V. xvii. 2: xx. 2: xxi. 14. (3) An exclamation,—Ho! V. vii. 1: viii. 1: xiv. 18: xviii. 2, 24.

猾
ywǎ
hua

To disturb. II. i. 20.

獄
yuh
yü

A case or cases of litigation,—either civil or criminal. V. ix. 13, 14, 16, 18, 21, 24: xxvii. 11, 12, 20, 21.

獒
gaou
aou

A species of large dog. V. v. 1.

獨
tuh
tu

Solitary, single. V. i. Pt. iii. 4. = the childless. V. iv. 12. Only. IV. ii. 6.

獲
hwǒ
huo

To get, to find. What is got is to be ascertained from the contcxt. To get success. IV. v. Pt. iii. 8: viii. Pt. iii. 3. To obtain the help of. V. iii. 6. To find opportunity. V. xxii. 4. 獲戾, to offend. IV. iii. 6. To apprehend,—spoken of criminals. IV. xi. 2. To get,—generally. IV. vi. 11: viii. Pt. iii. 10 (*n. b.*).

獸
show
shou

Animals, beasts. V. v. 8. 鳥獸, birds and beasts. I. 4—7: II. i. 22; *et al.* 百獸, all animals. II. i. 24; iv. 10.

獻
heen
hsien

(1) To present, to offer. IV. xi. 9: V. v. 2: xiii. 3. (2) = 賢, the wise, worthy II. iv. 7: V. vii. 5: x. 13: xiii. 23.

THE 95TH RADICAL. 玄.

玄
heuen
hsüan

(1) Dark-coloured, III. i. Pt. ii. 23: IV. iii. 4: V. xxii. 18. = dark-coloured, deep azure silks. III. i. Pt. i. 35, 52: V. iii. 7. (2) Mysterious, deep. II. i. 1.

率
suh
hsü

(1) To lead, lead on; to have the presidency of. II. ii. 19: V. iii. 1: xx. 3: xxiii. 1: xxiv. 1. 率作 = to take the initiative. II. iv. 11. Foll. by another verb, 率 often = to lead one another. II. i. 16, 24: iv. 10; *et al.* (2) To follow, to obey, act in accordance with. IV. ii. 2: iv. 2: v. t. i. 7: V. vii. 13; *et sæpe.* 弗率, the disobedient. II. ii. 20: IV. vii. Pt. ii. 1. In. IV. x. 3, 率典 probably means the statutes which should be followed, the regular statutes. We have the phrases 率由, V. viii. 4; 率俾, V. iii. 6: xvi. 21; 率從, V. xxviii. 1; 率循, xxii. 24. (3) As an adverb,—in everything, universally. IV. i. 3 (*ter*): V. xxvii. 10. ? on this, therefore. IV. vii. Pt. i. 1.

THE 96TH RADICAL. 玉.

玉
yuh
yü

A gem, gems. III. iv. 6: IV. vii. Pt. ii. 14: V. 3. 大玉, the great gem,—some particular gem. V. xxii. 19. 五玉, the five sceptres of investiture, given to the nobles. II. i. 8. Gem-adorned. II. i. 5: xxii. 2, 15, 17, 24. 玉食 = the revenues of the empire. V. iv. 19, 19. *Passim.* (1) The title of the sovereigns of China, during the Hea, Shang, and Chow dynasties, = king, kings. Often used as an adjective,—royal, imperial.

王 *wang*

王人, members of the royal house. V. xvi. 9. 先王, the former king or kings. *Passim.* 三王, the three kings, meaning king Wăn, his father, and grandfather. V. vi. 10. In V. v. 12, it means—to possess the throne. (2) To acknowledge the imperial sovereignty,— spoken of the feudal princes coming to court. II. ii. 6. (3) 王屋, the name of a mountain. III. i. Pt. ii. 1.—— In Pt. v. 文王 and 武王 are very common. We have also 成王, x. 9, 10; 王秀, king Ke, iii. 5: vi. 4: xv. 8; and 太王, in the same passages. The character hardly occurs in the 3d tone, which we find so often in Mencius. Perhaps there may be two or three instances of it in the Shoo.

玕 *kan* 琅玕, the name of a precious stone III. i. Pt. i. 81.

玩 *wan* To play or trifle with. V. v. 6.

珍 *chĭn chên* As an adj. = fine, rare. V. v. 8.

珠 *choo chu* Pearls. III. i. Pt. i. 35.

珪 *kwei kuei* Some kind of gem-stones fashioned, used by the duke of Chow in worshipping his ancestors. V. vi. 4, 8.

班 *pan* (1) To distribute, = to return. II. i. 7. (2) = to withdraw and retire. II. ii. 21.

球 *këw ch'iu* A sounding stone. IV. ii. 9. 天球, V. xxii. 19. The gem-stone suitable for the manufacture of sounding stones. III. i. Pt. i. 81.

琅 *lang* 琅玕, see 玕.

理 *le li* To regulate. 爕理, V. xx. 5.

珶 *kwăn kuen* Some kind of precious stone, III. i. Pt. i. 44.

琬 *yuen yüan* A rounded mace. V. xxii. 19.

琰 *yen* A pointed mace. V. xxii. 19.

琳 *lin* Some kind of precious stone. III. i. Pt. i. 81.

琴 *k'in ch'in* A lute. 琴瑟, II. iv. 9.

瑁 *maou mao* A sceptre-cover,—an instrument of gem, used by the emperor to test the different sceptres of the princes. V. xxii. 23, 26.

瑕 *hëa hsia* To blame. V. ix. 22.

瑞 *suy jui* 五瑞, the five gem tokens of investiture, conferred on the princes. II. i. 7.

瑟 *sih shê* A lute. See 琴.

瑤 *yaou yao* A kind of precious stone. III. i. Pt. i. 44.

璆 *k'ëw ch'iu* Probably gem-stones for the manufacture of sounding stones. III. i. Pt. i. 69.

璋 *chang* A half mace, carried by ministers. V. xxii. 27.

璣 *ke chi* (1) Pearls not quite round. III. i. Pt. i. 52. (2) 璿璣, some kind of astronomical instrument used by Shun. II. i. 5. But the meaning is doubtful.

璧 *peih pi* An instrument of gem, with a square base, and convex above,—one of the tokens of investiture. Used by the duke of Chow in worship. V. vi. 4, 8. 弘璧, V. xxii. 19.

璿 *seuen hsün* Revolving. 璿璣, see 璣.

THE 99TH RADICAL. 甘.

甘 *kan* (1) Sweet; sweetness. V. iv. 5. To esteem to be sweet, to delight in. III. iii. 6. (2) The place of a great battle in ancient times,—in the present Shen-se. III. ii. 1. (3) A surname. IV. viii. Pt. iii. 1: V. xvi. 7.

THE 100TH RADICAL. 生.

生 *shăng shêng* (1) To produce. IV. ii. 2: vii. Pt. i. 12. To beget, or to give birth to. V. xii. 19. To be born; to live; life. II. i. 28: iv. 6: IV. v. Pt. ii. 2: vi. 9: vii. Pt. i. 2; Pt. ii. 7: x. 5: V. xv. 7: xxi. 14. Life,—all living things. II. ii. 12. 二生, two living animals. II. i. 8. 厚生 = abundant means of sustentation. II. ii. 7. 生民 simply = the people. V. v. 10: xxiv. 13. Elsewhere 生民 = produced the people. 生魄 means the 16th day of the moon, V. iii. 4 : ix. 1 ; and 生明 the third day, iii. 2. 生生 = to foster life, IV. vii. Pt. iii. 10, 12 ; and = to increase and multiply. Pt. ii. 12, 17. 蒼生 = grassy shores. II. iv. 7. (2) In a name. 宜生, V. xvi. 12.

THE 101st RADICAL. 用.

用
yung

Passim. The frequency of this character is a peculiarity of the Shoo. The same also may be said of the way in which it is employed,—corresponding very much to the usages of 以. (1) To use, to employ. II. i. 8 : iii. 6 : IV. ii. 5, 8 : V. xix. 1, 4, 20, 23, 24 ; *et sœpe.* = to obey. III. ii. 5. 用罪, 用德, the criminal and the well-doer. IV. vii. Pt. i. 16. 用 alone is explained as meaning the use of virtue in V. xii. 22. Useful. V. v. 8, 利用, gainful for use, = conveniences of life. II. ii. 7. 器用, vessels for use. V. v. 2. 績用 = work that should have been done. I. 11. (2) Like 以, it is very often used like the sign of the infinitive,—to, so as to ; or may be resolved by thereby, and thereby. IV. vii. Pt. ii. 4, 9 : Pt. iii. 4, 5, 6 : viii. Pt. i. 8 : x. 2 : V. i. Pt. ii. 8 : ii. 7 : xxiii. 3, 5, 6 ; *et sœpe.* Connected with this is a usage, where 用 seems to merge in the verb that follows it. *E. g.* III. iv. 2 : IV. xi. 1, 7 : V. iv. 9 : xvi. 9, 22, 23. (3) = therefore. II. iv. 8 ; *et al.* Obs. 兹用 = 所以, II. ii. 12. Thereon. V. xix. 1. —There are not a few passages, however, where it is hardly possible to construe the character. *E. g.* IV. xi. 6 : V. vii. 2 : xiii. 13 : xix. 13.

THE 102d RADICAL. 田.

田
t'een
tien

(1) Cultivable fields. II. ii. 21 : III. i. Pt. i. 8, 18, 25 ; *et sœpe.* 田畝, fields and acres. IV. vii. Pt. i. 11. 田功, the work of agriculture. V. xi. 4. (2) To hunt,—used for 畋. V. xv. 11, 12.

由
yew
yu

(1) From,—to proceed from ; to use, to follow. IV. vii. Pt. i. 5 : Pt. iii. 7 : V. iii. 8 : vii, 13 : viii. 4 (率由) : ix. 5, 16, 17, 19. = by ; with, V. xxii. 22, 23 : xxiv. 10. It is sometimes difficult to construe 由. *E. g.* V. ix. 19 (see 繇), 24 : xxvii. 13. (2) Sprouts from a felled tree. IV. vii. Pt. i. 4.

甲
kĕă
chia

(1) A coat of mail. 甲胄 = armour of defence. IV. viii. Pt. ii. 4 : V. xxix. 2. (2) The first of the calendaric stem-characters. 甲子, V. ii. 1 : iii. 8 : xii. 6 : xxii. 2 ; 甲寅, xii. 3 : 甲戌, xxix. 5. = to begin. V. xviii. 5. (3) 太甲, the grandson of T'ang, V. xvi. 7. The name also of the 5th Book, Pt. IV. 祖甲, a later emperor of the dynasty of Shang. V. xvi. 6, 16.

申
shin
shĕn

(1) To repeat ; again, further. I. 5, 7 : II. iv. 2 : V. xiv. 22 : xvi. 11 : xxiv. 7. (2) The 9th of the calendaric branch-characters. V. xii. 2 : xxiv. 1.

男
nan

A part of the 2d domain of Yü, and the fourth of the domains of the Chow dynasty. III. i. Pt. ii. 19 : V. ix. 1 : x. 10, 13 : xii. 6 : xxiii. 4.

甸
teen
tien

(1) To rule, to govern. V. xiv. 6 : xix. 5. (2) The imperial domain of Yu, and the third of the domains of the Chow dynasty. III. i. Pt. ii. 18 : IV. iv. 1 : V. iii. 3 : ix. i : x. 10, 13 ; *et al.* To give. V. iv. 3 : xviii. 7, 19 : xxiii. 5.

畀
pe
pi

(付畀). = to be for, to favour. V. xiv. 3, 4, 24 : xviii. 28.

畋
t'een
t'ien

(1) To hunt. III. iii. 1 : IV. iv. 7. (2) To cultivate. V. xviii. 21, 28.

甽
k'euen
ch'üan

(1) Small channels in a field, for the purpose of irrigation. II. iv. 1. (2) A valley, where a stream runs. III. i. Pt. i. 26, 35.

畏
wei

(1) To fear ; to stand in awe, be apprehensive ; to be feared, dreadfulness, awfulness. II. ii. 17 : iii. 2 : IV. i. 2 : vii. Pt. i. 11 : V. i. Pt. ii. 9 : iii. 5 : vii. 9 : ix. 6 : xiv. 4 ; *et al.* Both the active and passive meanings appear in 畏畏, IV. xi. 5, and 弗畏 入畏, V. xx. 19. In V. xxvi. 13, 畏 alone = to fear to do evil. (2) To awe. II. iii. 7. = to put to death. V. xxvii. 13.

To violate. III. iv. 4.

畔
pwan
pan

To continue, to remain. V. xxii. 4. The more correct form of the character is 留.

留
lew
liu

To keep, to feed. Applied to animals. V. v. 8. To nourish. Applied to the people. IV. vii. Pt. ii. 9, 13.

畜
ch'uh
ch'u

畝
mow
mu

The Chinese acre,—acres, = fields. IV. vii. Pt. i. 11 (田畝) : V. vii. 11.

畢
peih
pi

(1) All. V. i. Pt. ii. 1 : v. 2. Entirely. V. ix. 9 : xxiii. 3. (2) To be finished, to be completed. V. vii. 10. (3) A name for the 5th gate of the imperial palace. V. xxii. 21. (4) The name of a principality. V. xxii. 3 : xxiii. 1 : xxiv. 1.

略
lëŏ
lio

(1) To be defined, marked out. III. i. Pt. i. 22. (2) A course, ways of proceeding, V. iii. 6.

番
po

番番, the appearance of being old. V. xxx. 5.

畫
hwă
hua

To define, as in the line out. V. xxiv. 6. Figured. V. xxii. 17. Thus *figured* is better here than *painted* as in the translation.

異
e
i

Different. V. v. 5: xxii. 27. Strange V. v. 8. What is strange or extraordinary. V. xxiv. 8.

當
tang

Ought. V. x. 12. Ought to be considered as belonging to,—to be in, to rest on. IV. iii. 8.

疆
kĕang
chiang

A limit, boundaries. V. i. Pt. iii. 8: xi. 4: xxiv. 7. 疆土, territory. V. vii. 15: xi. 6. In the phrase 無疆, unlimited, boundless. IV. v. Pt. ii. 2: V. vii. 11: xii. 9: xvi. 17, 18: xxvii. 22.

疇
ch'ow
ch'ou

(1) Who? whom? I. 9, 10: II. i. 21, 22: III. iii. 9: IV. viii, Pt. i. 11. (2) A class, divisions. II. i. 17: V. iv. 3. (3) A mate, mates. V. x. 13.

THE 103D RADICAL. 疋.

疑
e
i

To doubt, hesitate; doubtful; doubts. II. ii. 6, 12: V. iv. 4, 20, 25: xx. 16. = as being doubtful. V. xxvii. 17, 18.

THE 104TH RADICAL. 疒.

疵
ts'ze
tz'ŭ

A malady, an evil.—Used of moral and social evils. V. vii. 4: xxvii. 16.

疾
tseih
chi

(1) Sickness, affliction, IV. viii. Pt. i. 8: V. iv. 40: vi. 1, 5: vii. 10; *et sæpe.* 罪疾, affliction—punishment—for crime. IV. vii. Pt. ii. 11, 12. 疾狼 = to be frenzied. V. x. 11. (2) To dislike, to hate. V. xxi. 1: xxx. 7 (冒疾). (3) Sedulously. V. xii. 10, 20.
Severe sickness. V. xxii. 4. Distress. xxvii. 20.

病
ping

To make ill or sick. V. i. Pt. iii. 3.

痛
fŏo
fu

瘝
kwan
kuan

(1) To distress. V. ix. 6 (恫瘝乃身 = the pain distresses you), 17; 瘝在, the distressers (= oppressors) are in office. V. xii. 10. (2) To make void, render useless. V. xxvi. 8.
To be thin, = to be starving, IV. xi. 7.

瘳
tseih
chi
ch'ow
ch'ou

To cure, to be cured. IV. vii. Pt. ii. 6: viii. Pt. i. 8: V. vi. 11.

癉
tan

3d tone. To afflict, to distress,—make it evil with. V. xxiv. 7.

THE 105TH RADICAL. 癶.

癸
kwei
kuei

The last of the calendaric stem-characters. II. iv. 8. 癸巳, V. iii. 1. 癸亥, V. iii. 8. 癸酉, V. xxii. 13.

登
tăng
têng

To ascend. V. iii. 8. To raise, to make to ascend. I. 9. = to call up. IV. vii. Pt. ii. 1. = to complete, to sustain. V. i. Pt. iii. 4.

發
fă
fa

(1) To send forth. V. xxvi. 4: xxvi. 2 (發施). = to distribute. V. iii. 8. 發出, to manifest. IV. xi. 3. = to begin. IV. vii. Pt. i. 12. (2) The name of king Woo. V. i. Pt. i. 6: ii. 7.

THE 106TH RADICAL. 白.

白
pih
pai

White. V. ii. 1. Whitish,—applied to the colour of soil. III. i. Pt. i. 7, 24.

百
pih
pai

A hundred, I. i. 8: V. xxvii. 1, 18; *et al.* 百夫長, captains of hundreds. V. ii. 3. It is used as a round number, denoting all of the class who are spoken of or spoken to. We have 百官, II. ii. 19; *et al.*; 百工, V. ix. 1; *et al.*; 百宗工, V. x. 13; 百獸, II. i. 24; *et al.*; 百僚, V. xiv. 20; *et al.*; 百志, II. ii. 6; 百穀, V. iv. 36, 37; *et al.*; 百揆, II. i. 2; *et al.*; 百執事, IV. vii. Pt. iii. 8; *et al.*; 百祥, 百殃, IV. iv. 8; 百辟, V. xiii. 12; 百君子, V. xii. 24; 百度, V. v. 5; 百為, V. xviii. 7; 百司, V. xix. 8, 9; 百尹, V. xxii. 3. 百姓, see 姓.

皆
keae
chieh

All. At the commencement of clauses, summing up what has preceded. IV. i. 3: vii. 8: V. xxii. 23: xxiii. 1, 2, 7: xxvii. 13.

皇
hwang
huang

(1) Great. We have 皇祖, the great ancestor, III. iii. 4; 皇帝, the great ruler, the emperor, xxvii. 5, 6; 皇上帝, the great supreme ruler, or God. IV. iii. 2; and 皇天, great Heaven, II. ii. 4: IV. iv. 2: v. Pt. ii. 2: viii. Pt. iii. 10: V. i. Pt. i. 5: iii. 6 (皇天后土): viii. 2: xi. 6: xii. 9 (皇天上帝), 14: xvi. 7: xvii. 4: xxiii. 2, 5. Greatly. V. xv. 17. So, in 張皇, xxiii. 3; or we may take 皇

there as a *hiphil* verb. (2) The sovereign; royal. V. iv. 4, 9, 10, 11, 15. (3) *l. q.* 遑, leisure, to be at leisure. V. xv. 13 : xxx. 5.

THE 107TH RADICAL. 皮.

皮
p'e
p'i

The skins of animals—with the hair on. III. i. Pt. i. 5, 69, 83.

THE 108TH RADICAL. 皿.

盈
ying

To be full. 貫盈, V. i. Pt. i. 9.

益
yih
yi

(1) To advantage; that which is advantageous; advantage. II. ii. 21 : V. i. Pt. ii. 5 : v. 8. (2) The baron Yih was forester to Shun, and assistant to Yu in his labours caused by the inundation. II. i. 22 : ii. 4, 6, 21 : V. iv. 1.

盛
sh'ing
shêng

To be complete. v. 4.

盛
shing
shêng

= vesselful. V. i. Pt. i. 6.

盜
taou
tao

Robbers. V. i. Pt. i. 6.

盟
măng
mêng

A covenant. 詛盟, V. xxvii. 4.

盡
tsin
chin

To exert to the utmost. V. ix. 6. To call forth all—. V. v. 4. 自盡, to develop one's-self fully. IV. vi. 11. Entirely, all. IV. vii. Pt. i. 2 : V. xi. 16, 19 : ix. 13 : x. 14.

監
këen
chien

To survey, to inspect. Spoken of Heaven or God. V. v. Pt. iii. 2 : ix. 3 : V. xxvii. 4. To survey, inspect; to look to, —look to and study, either as a pattern or a warning. IV. v. Pt. iii. 3 : vi. 3 : viii. Pt. iii. 6 : xi. 7 : V. ix. 21 : x. 12 (*n. b.*); xii. 17 : xv. 19 : xvi. 17, 19 : xxvii. 12, 22. ? to afford an example to. V. xiii. 20. Overseers. V. xii. 3 : xviii. 24. 監, in V. xii. 3, is marked in the 1st tone, but wrongly. In the sense there, the character is said to be in the 3d tone, and also in x. 12, and the meaning to be to take warning generally. The other applications of the character may be read either in the 1st tone or the third. See the 經韻集字析解.

盤
pwan
pan

(1) To pursue pleasure, III. iii. 1 : V. xxx. 2. (2) To go to excess. V. xv. 11 (foll. by 于). (3) A name. IV. viii. Pt. iii. 1 : V. xvi. 7. 盤庚 one of the emperors of the Shang dynasty. IV. vii.

盥
kwan
kuan

To wash the hands. V. xxii. 27.

盧
loo
lu

(1) Black. V. xxviii. 4. (2) The name of one of the wild tribes confederate with Chow against Shang. V. ii. 3 : xix. 11.

THE 109TH RADICAL. 目

目
muh
mu

The eyes. V. ⟨⟩. 5 : xxvi. 7 (*n. b.*). 四目, the eyes of the four quarters,—the eyes of all. II. i. 15. Ministers are called 股肱耳目. IV. iv. 4.

直
chih

To be straight. V. iv. 5, 14. Upright, straightforward; the upright; straightforwardness. II. i. 23, 24 : iii. 3 : iv. 2 : IV. iv. 7 : V. iv. 17.

眇
meaou
miao

眇眇, insignificant. V. xxii. 25.

相
sëang
hsiang

Mutually, one another, II. i. 24 : IV. ii. 6 : xi. 2 : V. i. Pt. ii. 3 : xxiii. 2, 7. Sometimes the action of the verb following 相 passes not on parties indicated in the text, but on the speaker, or the person or parties in his mind. III. iv. 3 : IV. vii. Pt. ii. 15.

相
sëang
hsiang

3d tone. (1) To aid, assist. IV. x. 2 : V. i. Pt. i. 7 : iii. 8 : iv. 2 ; *et sæpe.* (2) To lead. IV. vii. Pt. iii. 9. (3) Used for premier. IV. viii. Pt. i. 4 : V. xxii. 13 ; for ministers generally. IV. v. Pt. i. 3 : V. x. 9 ; for attendants. V. xxii. 2. (4) To look at; to inspect, examine. IV. vii. Pt. i. 12 : V. xii. 2, 11 : xiii. 2, 4, 23 ; *et al.*

省
sing
hsing

To examine. II. iv. 11 : IV. v. Pt. i. 7 : viii. Pt. ii. 4 : V. iv. 35 : vii. 10 : x. 7 (觀省, see and examine yourselves).

眚
săng
shêng

Inadvertent offences. II. i. 11 : V. ix. 8.

眩
heuen
hsüan

To be made confused or dizzy. 瞑眩, see 瞑.

睦
muh
mu

To be harmonious. I. 2 : V. xxviii. 26. To cultivate harmony with. V. xvii. 6.

衆
chung

All. It is found often,—before nouns, after pronouns, and alone : in the same way as our *all.* III. iv. 2, 7 ; *et sæpe.* It often = multitudes, the people. II. ii. 3, 12, 17 ; *et al.*

眷
keuen
chüan

To regard, look on,—favourably. We can in the Shoo always construe it as an adverb,—fondly, graciously, II. ii. 4 : IV. v. Pt. ii. 2 : vi. 3 : V. viii. 2 : xii. 10.

睿
yui
jui

To be perspicacious,—penetrating to what is minute; perspicaciousness. V. iv. 6.

瞍
tsow
sou

瞽瞍 the name of Shun's father. II. ii. 21.

瞑 眩
mëen
nien

瞑眩, used of medicine distressing the patient, but salutary. IV. viii. Pt. i. 8.

瞿
k'eu
ch'ü

A kind of lance. V. xxii. 21

瞽
koo
ku

(1) Blind. A blind man. II. i. 12. Blind musicians. III. iv. 4. (2) 瞽

瞍, see 瞍.

THE 110TH RADICAL. 矛.

矛
maou
mao

A spear, spears, V. ii. 4 : xxix. 2.

矜
king
ching

(1) To pity, compassionate. V. i. Pt. i. 11 (foll. by 于) : xiv. 20, 24 : xviii 28 (畀矜) : xxvii. 5 (哀矜). (2) To attend earnestly or jealously to. V. v. 9. (3) To be elated with one's self, boastful. II. ii. 14 : IV. viii. Pt. ii. 7 : V. xxiv. 10.

THE 111TH RADICAL. 矢.

矢
she
shih

(1) Arrows. V. xxii. 19 : xxviii. 4 : xxi. x. 2. (2) *I. q.* 誓, solemn, of the nature of protestation. IV. vii. Pt. i. 1.

矣
e
i

A final particle. It does not occur often in the Shoo, and only after an adjective or a short clause, where its force is both decisive and exclamatory, V. ii. 1 : xix. 1, 2, 16, 18, 21. See Index III. to Mencius on the character.

知
che
chih

To know. *Passim.* Observe 夫知, V. xii. 10, which can hardly be construed.

矧
shin
shên

Still more; how much more! The nature of the sentence sometimes makes the meaning—still less; how much less, I. ii. 21 : IV. ii. 14 : vii. Pt. i. 12 : V. vii. 9, 13, 15 ; *et sæpe.* The 矧 is often followed by 曰. IV. vii. Pt. i. 3 : V. vii. 1 : ix. 21 (*n. b.*) : xii. 12 : xiv. 9.

短
twan
tuan

Short. IV. vii. Pt. i. 12 : V. iv. 40. The shortest. I. 7.

矯
këaou
chiao

To pretend, to falsify. 矯誣, IV. ii. 3. = dissemblers. V. xxvii. 2.

THE 112TH RADICAL. 石.

石
shih

(1) Stones. III. i. Pt. i. 26 (怪石) : IV. iv. 6. The stone,—a measure of weight. III. iii. 8. Used for the sounding or musical stone. II. i. 24 : iv. 4. (2) 碣石, the rocks of Këĕ, a famous landmark in the time of Yu, somewhere on the north of the present gulf of Pih-chih-le. II. i. Pt. i. 11 ; Pt. ii. 1. (3) 積石, the name of a mountain in the west, where Yu began his survey of the Ho. III. i. Pt. i. 82 ; Pt. ii. 7.

砥
che
chih

Whetstones. III. i. Pt. i. 52.

砮
uoo
nu

Stones for arrowheads. III. i. Pt. i. 52, 69.

碞
yan
an

To be precipitous. 民碞, the perilousness (= changeableness) of the people. V. xii. 13.

碣
k'ĕĕ
chiêh

碣石, see 石.

磬
k'ing
ch'ing

Sounding stones, or stones for their manufacture. III. i. Pt. i. 60, 69.

礪
le
li

Grindstones. III. i. Pt. i. 52 : IV. viii. Pt. i. 6. To grind, to sharpen. V. xxix. 2.

THE 113TH RADICAL. 示.

示
she
shih

To show, to intimate to. V. iii. 2.

祁
k'e
ch'i

Great, greatly. V. xv. 5.

社
shay
shè

The spirit-tablets or altars of the spirits of the land. III. ii. 5. 社稷 = the spirits of the land and of the grain. IV. v. Pt. i. 2. 郊社 = the sacrifices to Heaven and Earth. V. i. Pt. iii. 3 (?). To sacrifice to the spirits of the land. V. xii. 5.

祀
sze
szû

(1) To sacrifice. V. iii. 3 : xiii. 5. A sacrifice, sacrifices. III. iii. 8 : IV. viii. Pt. ii. 11 (祭祀) : ix. 1 : V. i. Pt. i. 6 : *et sæpe.* 元祀, see 元. (2) A year. 祀 was the term specially used in this meaning in the Shang dynasty. IV. iv. 1 : v. Pt. ii. 1 : viii. Pt. i. 1 : V. iv. 1 : xviii. 24.

祈
k'e
ch'i

To pray,—to and for. V. xii. 20. 24.

祖
tsoo
tsu

A grandfather. III. iii. 4, 8 : IV. v. Pt. i. 3, 7 : Pt. ii. 6 : V. xiii. 22, 24, *et al.* But in other passages, we must adopt the general meaning of ancestor. *E. g.* IV. vii. Pt. ii. 13, 14 : viii. Pt. iii. 10 : xi. 1. This appears especially where we find 高祖, as in IV. vii. Pt. iii. 6, and sometimes 先祖, as in V. xiv. 6. Sometimes by 祖 we must understand

—the spirit-tablets of ancestors, as in III. ii. 5: IV. iv. 1 (sing. and 祖 = grandfather,). So, 文祖, the temple or spirit-tablet of Yaou's ancestor; and 藝祖, II. i. 4, 8, 14. 祖考 = the spirits of ancestors, II. iv. 3: but = grandfather and father, in V. x. 5 : xxv. 1, 3, 7. 　　 = grand-uncle. V. xxviii. 2.

(2) 祖甲 and 祖乙 were emperors of the Shang dynasty. V. xv. 6, 16: xvi. 7. (3) 祖巳 and 祖伊 were ministers of the Shang dynasty. IV. ix. 2 : x. 1, 6.

祇
k'e
ch'i

The spirit or spirits of the earth. Always found in connection with 神. IV. iii. 3 : v. Pt. i. 2 (上下神祇): xi. 6 : V. i. Pt. i. 6 (上帝, 神祇, 社稷, &c.).

祇
che
chih

To reverence, to respect; to attend reverently, or respectfully to. II. iv. 8: III. i. Pt. ii. 17 : V. iv. 8 (n. b.): v. Pt. i. 3 : V. x. 10 : xxvi. 2 : xxvi. 9. Reverent. V. xvii. 1. 祇祗, to revere the reverend. V. ix. 4. 民祇, the awfulness of the people. V. xiv. 9. Used adverbially before other verbs,—reverently, respectfully. II. ii. 1, 21 : IV. iv. 1 : V. i. Pt. i. 10 : iii. 6 : vi. 7 : viii. 3 ; *et sæpe.*

祝
chuh
chu

A prayer. 冊祝, V. vi. 5. To write a prayer. 祝册, V. xiii. 29. 　 = with a curse. V. i. Pt. iii. 3.

祝
chow
chou

詛祝, to curse, to utter maledictions. V. xv. 15.

神
shin
shèn

Spirits, spiritual beings. They may be the spirits of the departed, and spirits generally, real or imaginary. II. ii. 19, 21 : IV. viii. Pt. ii. 11 : V. iii. 8. So, 鬼神, II. ii. 18 : III. iv. 2 : IV. v. Pt. iii. 1 : V. vi. 6. In this last instance we have also 神鬼, but with no difference of meaning. 神人, spirits and men. II. i. 24 : V. viii. 3 : xx. 9. 神主, lord of the spirits, is a designation of the emperor. IV. vi. 3. Specifically, 神 denotes the spirit or spirits of heaven,—in the phrase 神祇. IV. iii. 3 : V. Pt. i. 2 : xi. 6 : V. i. Pt. i. 6. See the note on this last passage, where it appears that 上帝 is to be discriminated from 神. He is so discriminated in II. i. 6, from 羣神, the host or herd of the spirits. 神 also is to be discriminated from 天, in V. xviii. 19. Spiritual.

神明, spiritual intelligences. Spiritual, = mysterious, or active and invisible. II. ii. 4. 神宗 = the temple or shrine of Shun. II. ii. 19. 神后, ancestors now in the spirit world. IV. vii. Pt. ii. 10; but 神后 is a denomination of 上帝, in IV. iii. 4.

To sacrifice. IV. iv. 1.

祠
tsze
tzû

To sacrifice. V. xxii. 26, 28. Sacrifices, a sacrifice. V. i. Pt. ii. 5 : iii. 9. 祭祀,

祭
tse
chi

IV. viii. Pt. ii. 11. 烝祭, V. xiii. 29. To be felicitous, happiness. IV. iv. 8:

祥
ts'eang
ch'iang

vi. 5 : vii. Pt. ii. 14. 休祥, V. i. Pt. ii. 5. To make felicitous ; made a blessing. V. xxvii. 14, 22.

To pour out a libation. V. xiii. 29.

祼
kwan
kuan

Revenues, emolument. IV. vi. 9 *(n. b.)*: V. xvi. 5 : xx. 18 : xxiv. 9. 天祿, Heaven-conferred revenues, = the possession of the empire. II. ii. 17.

祿
luh
lu

Prohibitions. V. xx. 11.

禁
kin
chin

The name of a sacrifice, offered with purity and reverence. II. i. 6 : V. xiii. 25, 26, 29.

禋
yin

Calamity. 　　 = causers of calamity. IV. iii. 3. To send down calamities on, —to punish. IV. vii. Pt. i. 12.

禍
ho
huo

Happiness ; happinesses. IV. vii. Pt. i. 14 : V. xxi. 14 : xxiv. 13. 五福, the five happinesses. V. iv. 4, 39. 　 = favours. 作福, to confer—be the source of—favours. V. iv. 11, 13, 18, 19. To bless. IV. iii. 3.

福
fuh
fu

Ceremonies ; rules of propriety ; propriety. II. i. 8 : IV. ii. 8, 9 : v. Pt. ii. 3 : viii. Pt. ii. 11 : V. vi. 18 : viii. 1 : xiii. 5, 15, 19 : xvi. 8 : xx. 9 : xxiv. 9. 五禮, religious, mourning, festive, military, and State ceremonies. So perhaps 五禮. in II. iii. 6. 三禮, three religious ceremonies, the worships of the spirits of Heaven, of Earth, and of men. II. i. 23.

禮
le
li

THE 114TH RADICAL. 内.

禹
yu
yü

Baron Yu, afterwards the great Yu, the remover of the deluge, and founder of the Hea dynasty. II. i. 17 : ii. 1, 5, 7, 9, 10, 14, 18, 20, 21 ; *et sæpe.*

禽
k'in
ch'in

Birds. V. v. 8. Includes *beasts*, and = hunting. III. iii. 6.

THE 115TH RADICAL. 禾.

禾
ho
huo

Grain growing. V. vi. 16, 9.

私
sze
szû

Private, selfish. 私昵, favourites. IV. v. Pt. ii. 5. 私家, to be selfish, follow one's own prejudices. V. xxvi. 21. Selfish aims. V. xx. 15. To favour partially. IV. vi. 4.

秉
ping

To grasp, to hold. V. ii. 1: vi. 1: xxii. 23, 27. 秉德, to maintain virtue. V. xvi. 9, 14; the same phrase, in xviii. 23, = to consider it a virtue. 秉爲 = the decided conduct. V. xiv. 4. 秉哲, to maintain wisdom. V. x. 9.

秋
ts‘ëw
ch‘iu

The autumn; in the autumn. I. 6 (仲秋): III. iv. 4: V. vi. 16. = the harvest. IV. vii. I't. i. 9.

秕
pe
pi

Empty or blasted grain. IV. ii. 4.

秩
chih

To arrange in order. I. 4, 5, 6. 秩宗, arranger of the ancestral temple, = minister of Religion. II. i. 23. In order, in an orderly manner. II. i. 8: V. xiii. 5, 15. = social distinctions. II. iii. 6.

秬
k‘eu
ch‘ü

Black millet. Spirits distilled from black millet. V. xiii. 25: xxviii. 4.

秸
këĕ
chieh

The stalk of grain without the ears. III. i. I't. ii. 18.

移
e
i

To remove. V. xiv. 21. To be altered. V. xxiv. 3.

稟
pin

To receive orders. IV. viii. Pt. i. 1

種
chung

To sow. II. ii. 10.

種
chung

2d tone. Seed. V. xxvii. 8. = descendants. IV. vii. Pt. ii. 16.

稱
ch‘ing
ch‘êng

(1) To lift up. V. ii. 4: xxviii. 1. To undertake. IV. i. 1. To employ. V. xiii. 5, 15: xvi. 9: xx. 20. To display. V. xiii. 14. (2) To proclaim. V. xvi. 15.

稷
tseih
chi

(1) A kind of millet, said to be the best of all grains. IV. vii. Pt. i. 11. 黍稷, V. x. 6: xxi. 3. (2) The tablets or altars of the spirits presiding over the grain or agriculture of a country. 社稷, IV. v. Pt. i. 2. (3) 后稷, prince Tseih, the high ancestor of the House of Chow, was Shun's minister of agriculture. II. i. 17, 18: iv. 1: V. xxvii. 8.

稼
këa
chia

To sow. 稼穡, to sow and reap, sowing and reaping. V. iv. 5: xv. 2, 3, 7.

稽
k‘e
ch‘i

2d tone. To bow the head to the ground. Always in the formulas 稽首 and 拜手稽首. II. i. 17, 21, 22, 23: ii. 18: iv. 11: IV. v. Pt. ii. 3, 4: viii. Pt. ii. 13; Pt. iii. 11: V. xii. 8, 20: xiii. 1, 4, 22, 25: xix. 1, 2: xxiii. 1, 2.

稽
k‘e
ch‘i

1st tone. (1) To examine, to study. I. 1: II. i. 1: ii. 1, 3 (foll. by 于), 16: iii. 1: IV. vii. Pt. ii. 6: V. iv. 4, 20: viii. 1: xii. 11, 12: xx. 3: xxvii. 17. 卜稽, to examine by divination. IV. vii. Pt. i. 2. (2) To manage, to cultivate. 稽田, V. xi. 4. (3) To agree with. V. x. 11.

穀
kuh
ku

(1) Grain. V. xxvii. 8. One of the six magazines of nature. II. ii. 7. 百穀, all kinds of grain. II. i. 18; V. iv. 36, 37. (2) To be good. V. iv. 13.

穆
muh
mu

Reverent; profound and grave. V. x. 2. 穆穆, to be profoundly reverent; to be submissive. II. i. 2: V. xiii. 16: xviii. 27; xxvii. 10. Reverently. V. vi. 2, 18.

積
tseih
chi

(1) To accumulate. IV. viii. Pt. iii. 4. Accumulated. IV. vii. Pt. i. 10. (2) 積石, the name of a mountain. See 積石.

穡
sih
shê

To reap, gather in the harvest. IV. vii. Pt. i. 9. 稼穡 see 稼. 穡事, the business of harvesting. 穡夫, a reaper, a husbandman. V. vii. 14.

穢
wei
hwŏ
huo

Filthiness. = wickedness. IV. vii. Pt. ii. 8. Rank odour. V. i. Pt. ii. 3.

穫
hwŏ
huo

To cut down the grain, to reap. V. vi. 18: vii. 11.

THE 116TH RADICAL. 穴.

空
k‘ung

司空, the minister of Works. II. i. 17: V. ii. 2: iv. 7: xi. 2: xix. 10: xx. 12.

穽
tsing
ching

I. q. 阱. Pitfalls. V. xxix. 3.

窮
k‘eung
ch‘iung

(1) To exhaust. 無窮, inexhaustible, unending. V. viii. 1: xxiv. 14. To be exhausted, brought to distress. In the phrase 困窮. II. ii. 17: V. xvii. 5. The same phrase = the distressed and poor. II. ii. 3: IV. v. Pt. ii. 5. (2) The name of a principality, held by E, the rebellious opponent of T‘ae-k‘ang. III. iii. 2.

窴
ts'wan
ts'uan

To drive to and confine in till death. II. i. 12.

竊
ts'ĕĕ
ch'ieh

To steal, V. xxix. 4. 攘竊, IV. xi. 6. 草竊, to commit highway robbery. IV. xi. 2.

THE 117TH RADICAL. 立.

立
leih
li

To stand erect; to be set up. V. vi. 4: xv. 7: xxii. 21. = firmness. II. iii. 3. = firmly. V. i. Pt. ii. 9. To establish, to set up, to appoint. IV. iv. 4: viii. Pt. i. 4: V. ii. 4: iv. 20, 24: xix. 6, 7, 12, 16, 19, 20, 23: xx. 3, 5.

竝
ping

I. q. 並. Together, unitedly. II. iv. 1: IV. iii. 3: V. xix. 15: xxix. 1. = even. IV. v. Pt. ii. 5.

章
chang

(1) To polish, to decorate. I. 2 (平章). To be decorated. V. iv. 36. 五章 the five decorations,—emblematic figures on robes. III. iii. 6. (2) = statutes. institutes. V. xvii. 7.

童
t'ung

Boys, youths. IV. iv. 7. 童孫, young grandsons. V. xxvii. 13.

端
twan
tuan

Correct, = favourable. V. xxiii. 5.

競
king
ching

To be strong. V. xix. 2.

THE 118TH RADICAL. 竹.

竹
chuh
chu

The bamboo. 竹矢, bamboo arrows. V. xxii. 19.

笥
sze
szŭ

A sort of chest for containing rice or clothes. IV. viii. Pt. ii. 4.

笙
săng
shĕng

A kind of organ; the calabash-organ. II. iv. 9.

筍
yun
yün

A kind of soft, flexible bamboo, that can be made into mats. V. xxii. 18.

答
tă
ta

To respond to,—in conduct. V. xiii. 4, 24: xxii. 24. To respond in acknowledgment of favours. V. ii. 6. In response. V. xxii. 27, 28: xxiii. 1. In reply. V. xxii. 25.

筮
she
shih

To divine by means of the stalks of the milfoil. II. ii. 18: V. iv. 20, 24. 31: xvi. 9.

箘
k'wăn
k'uĕn

A kind of bamboo, good for making arrows. III. i. Pt. i. 52.

箕
ke
chi

The name of a principality, held by the relative of the tyrant Show, known as 箕子, the viscount of Ke. V. iii. 9: iv. 1, 2, 3.

管
kwan
kuan

(1) A musical instrument,—a kind of flute. II. iv. 9. (2) The name of the appanage of the third son of king Wăn, known as 管叔. V. vi. 12: xvii. 1.

箴
chin
chên

To remonstrate,—a kind of moral puncturing. IV. vii. Pt. i. 12. 箴言, in p. 5, words of remonstrance.

節
tsĕĕ
chieh

(1) Tallies, tokens of authority. In the phrase 小臣諸節, V. ix. 17. (2) To regulate. V. xii. 15.

範
fan

A plan, a pattern. 洪範, V. iv. 3.

築
chuh
chu

(1) To pound,—as in raising mud walls, = to build. = who was a builder. IV. viii. Pt. i. 3. To raise entrenchments. V. xxix. 5. (2) To raise and set up. V. xvi. 19.

篚
fei

Baskets,—round, of bamboo, in which articles of tribute were brought to court. III. i. Pt. i. 19, 26, 35, 44, 52, 60. To basket,—to bring in baskets. V. iii. 7.

篠
seaou
hsiao

A species of slender bamboo. III. i. Pt. i. 42, 44.

篤
tuh
tu

(1) Sincere, earnest. V. xxvi. 1. = the sincere. IV. vii. Pt. iii. 6. To follow sincerely. IV. xiii. 13, 27. Sincerely, earnestly. V. xiii. 7: xvi. 21. (2) To consolidate. V. iii. 5: V. xiii. 24. To be great. V. iii. 5: xiii. 17.

篾
mĕĕ
mieh

Bamboo splints, fit for basket-work, made into mats. V. xxii. 15.

簣
kwei
kuei

A basket. 一簣 = one basketful. V. v. 9.

簜
t'ang

A species of large bamboo. III. i. Pt. i. 42, 44.

簡
kĕen
chien

(1) To be hasty, impetuous. II. i. 24. (2) To be easy, indifferent to many things. II. iii. 3. A generous ease. II. ii. 12. (3) To choose, select. IV. vii. Pt. iii. 9: V. xiv. 20: xviii. 8, 19, 28. (4) To examine, to mark. IV. iii. 8: V. xxi. 13: xxvii. 15 (簡孚), 17: xxviii. 4. In xxvii. 15, we have also 五刑不簡, where 不簡 = do not meet the case.

簫
seaou
hsiao

An instrument of music. But 簫韶 is used for the music of Shun. II. iv. 9.

簵
loo
lu

A species of bamboo, good for making arrows. III. i. Pt. i. 52.

籥
yŏ
yo

I. q. 鑰. A kind of key for opening the case where oracular responses were kept. V. vi. 9. The meaning is doubtful.

籩
pĕen
pien

豆籩, sacrificial vessels. V. iii. 3.

籲
yu
yü

To cry to, to appeal to. IV. vii. Pt i. 1 ; Pt. ii. 5.   Foll. by Heaven or God. V. i. Pt. ii. 3 : xii. 10 : xix. 2. The character should be without the 竹.

THE 119TH RADICAL. 米.

米
me
mi

Rice hulled. III. i. Pt. ii. 18. 粉米, the emblematic flour of rice represented on the lower robe of the emperor. II. iv. 4.

粉
fun
fĕn

To grind, or reduce to powder or flour. 粉米,—see above.

粒
leih
li

Grains of rice. = to have rice (or grain generally) to eat. II. iv. 1.

粟
suh
hsü

Rice in the husk. III. i. Pt. ii. 18 : IV. ii. 4. In V. iii. 8, we may understand perhaps grain generally.

粢
tsze
tzŭ

A kind of millet. 粢盛, V. i. Pt. i. 6.

精
tsing
ching

To be discriminating. II. ii. 15. i. 6.

糗
ch'ow
ch'ou

Parched grain. V. xxix. 5.

糧
lëang
liang

Provisions of grain. V. xxix. 5.

糱
nëĕ
nieh

Malt. IV. viii. Pt. iii. 3.

THE 120TH RADICAL. 系.

糾
këw
chiu

To raise up, to exhibit. V. xxvi. 3.

紀
ke
chi

(1) To arrange different threads of silk. Hence to arrange, to regulate generally ; and what is arranged, or arranges. 紀綱, rules and laws. III. iii. 7. 人紀, human distinctions or relationships. IV. iv. 5. 天紀, the heavenly arrangers or arrangements. III. iv. 4. These are called the five arrangers, 五紀, in V. iv. 4, 8. To be chronicled. V. xxv. 1. 紀其叙 = to take in hand—arrange—its *disturbed* order or *broken* line. V. vii. 4. (2) A period of twelve years. V. xxiv. 3.

紊
wăn
wên

To be confused, confusion. IV. vii. Pt. i. 9.

納
nă
na

To receive,—to take in. IV. viii. Pt. ii. 9 : II. iv. 4, 6, 7. 納言 = the minister of Communication. II. i. 25. To present,— to send in, as in payment of tribute. III. i. Pt. i. 52 : Pt. ii. 18 : IV. viii. Pt. i. 5. To place or put. V. vi. 11. To be appointed. II. i. 2. 納日 = the setting sun. I. 6.

純
shun
ch'un

(1) To be decided ; determinate ; determinately. V. xvi. 9, 14 : xviii. 7. (2) To enlarge ; great. V. x. 6 ; xxviii. 2.

純
shun
chun

2d tone. A border,—as of a mat. V. xxii. 15—18.

紛
fun
fên

Mixed. V. xxii. 18.

索
sŏ
so

(1) A rope. = reins. III. iii. 5. (2) = ruin, dissolution. V. ii. 5.

累
luy
lêi

To involve,—to go on to affect. V. v. 9.

細
se
hsi

Small. V. v. 9 : xxi. 10.

紵
ch'oo
ch'u

A coarse kind of hemp, or the cloth made from it. III. i. Pt. i. 60.

紹
shaou
shao

To connect, continue. IV. vii. Pt. i. 4 : viii. Pt. iii. 11 : V. ix. 5 : xxvi. 3. 紹上帝 = to be the vicegerent of God. V. xii. 14. 紹天明, to bring in connection with the intelligence of Heaven. V. vii. 3. 會紹乃辟 = connecting *the all but broken line of* your sovereign. V. xxviii. 3.

組
tsoo
tsu

璣組, strings of pearls. III. i. Pt. i. 52.

終
chung

(1) The end ; the result. Often in connection with 始. IV. ii. 9 : iv. 4 : v. Pt. iii. 2, 6 : vi. 6 : viii. Pt. iii. 1, 5 : V. xvi. 2, 23 : xvii. 5. = a successful issue, expecially in the phrase 有終. IV. iii. 9 : V. Pt. i. 3 ; Pt. ii. 3 : viii. Pt. i. 10 : V. xxiv. 13. = retirement,—the resignation of Yaou. II. i. 4. = futurity. V. vi. 10. As an adverb,—eventually, finally, in the end. II. ii. 14 : V. v. 9 : xxi. 14. As a verb,—to end (neut. and act.), II. i. 17 : V. iv. 39 : xxv. 10. To make an end of. V. xii. 10. To finish. V. vii. 10, 14 : xiii. 11 : xiv. 2 (終于上帝, finished the work of God). 終允德, IV. v. Pt. i. 10, and 終

厥德, Pt. ii. 2, = in the end he was virtuous. To be repeated, = repeatedly, purposely. II. i. 11 : V. ix. 8 : xxvii. 13.

終日, a single day. V. xviii. 4. (2) 終南, the name of a mountain. III. i. Pt. i. 76.

結 *kĕĕ* chieh

To tie. 結怨, to contract enmity. V. i. Pt. iii. 2.

絕 *tscuĕ* chüeh

To cut short; to extinguish. III. ii. 3 (勦絕): iii. 8 : IV. ix. 3 : V. xxvii. 5, 6, 12. To be extinguished. V. xiii. 9. 自絕, to extinguish—bring premature ruin on—one's-self. IV. x. 2. But the same phrase, foll. by 于, in V. i. Pt. iii. 2, = to cut one's-self off from. So, in IV. vii. Pt. ii. 15, 胥絕 = mutually alienated.

統 *t'ung*

To gather together in one,—used adverbially. V. viii. 1. 大統, the great connected whole, = the empire. V. iii. 5. To command in chief. V. xx. 7, 10.

絲 *sze* szŭ

Raw silk. III. i. Pt. i. 19, 26.

絺 *he* hsi

(1) Fine grass-cloth. III. i. Pt. i. 26, 60. (2) 絺繡 seem used together, = to embroider. II. iv. 4.

綏 *suy* sui

(1) To soothe, to make tranquil and happy. IV. v. Pt. i. 2 (撫綏): vi. 9 : vii. Pt. i. 4 ; Pt. ii. 13 ; Pt. iii. 11 : V. i. Pt. i. 7 (寵綏): iii. 7 ; *et al.* Observe 綏厥猷, IV. iii. 2. Tranquilly. V. vii. 9. = to carry out. V. xxiii. 6. To be secure. V. xxviii. 2. (2) The name of the fourth of Yu's domains. III. i. Pt. ii. 20.

經 *king* ching

(1) What is regular, and according to the standard. II. ii. 21. 經德, regular —stedfast—in virtue. V. x. 9. (2) To go through. 經歷, V. xvi. 4. (3) To plan, to define. 經營, V. xii. 2. To adjust. V. xx. 5.

綦 *k'e* ch'i

綦弁, a cap made of the skin of the spotted deer. V. xxii. 21.

綱 *kang*

The large rope of a net, round which it is netted, and by which it is drawn. IV. vii. Pt. i. 9. = laws. 紀綱, III. iii. 7.

網 *wang*

A net. IV. vii. Pt. i. 9.

綴 *chuy* chui

(1) 綴輅, the connected—next—carriage,—one of the emperor's carriages. V. xxii. 20. (2) Variegated. V. xxii. 6. (3) 綴衣, the name of a kind of tent set up over the emperor, when he gave

audiences. V. xxii. 10, 14. But the same phrase in xix. 1, 8, denotes the keepers of the robes.

綽 *ch'ŏ* ch'o

Liberal, generous. 寬綽厥心, to cultivate a large and generous heart. V. xv. 18.

緒 *seu* hsü

Properly the end or point of silk in a cocoon. Used for a line or clue of inheritance. III. iii. 8 : IV. v. Pt. iii. 3 : V. xxv. 2. 基緒 = the inheritance or possession. IV. v. Pt. i. 2.

縞 *kaou* kao

Plain white silks. III. i. Pt. i. 35.

縢 *t'ăng* t'êng

To bind or fasten. 金縢 = the metal-bound *coffer.* V. vi. 11, 18.

縱 *tsung*

To yield one's-self remissly to. V. x. 1. Self-indulgence. IV. v. Pt. ii. 3.

總 *tsung*

(1) To gather together under one,—to take the leading of. II. ii. 9 : IV. viii. Pt. ii. 1. To accumulate. IV. vii. Pt. iii. 12. I do not know the meaning of 總己, IV. iv. 1. (2) The whole of the plant of grain. III. i. Pt. ii. 18.

績 *tseih* chi

(1) Duties, services. I. 8, 11 : II. iii. 1. Achievements. II. ii. 14 : V. xiii. 23 : xxiv. 5 : xxv. 1. (2) To be achieved, carried out successfully. II. i. 3 : iii. 8. To be operated on successfully. III. i. Pt. i. 6, 66, 77. To achieve good. IV. vii. Pt. iii. 4 : V. xvii. 6. To achieve for. V. xxviii. 2.

繁 *fan*

Numerous. IV. ii. 4.

繇 *yaou* yao

Luxuriant. III. i. Pt. i. 17.

織 *chih*

Woven fabrics. Of silk, we have 織文 and 織貝, III. i. Pt. i. 19, 44. Of hair, pp. 69, 83.

繡 *sew* shiu

絺繡 embroidered. II. iv. 4.

繩 *shing* shêng

A string,—with reference to the carpenter's line. IV. viii. Pt. iii. 11. To apply the string to,—to correct. V. xxvi. 3.

繹 *yih* yi

To draw out or unroll a clue. To unfold,—by reflection. V. xxi. 5. 由繹 = to unfold and make use of the powers of others. V. xix. 19.

繼 *ke* chi

To continue, to perpetuate, V. xiv. 25. 繼自今, on from this time. V. xv. 12 : xix. 16, 18, 20, 23.

纁 *heun* hsün

Purple silks. III. i. Pt. i. 52.

纊 *k'wang* k'uang

Fine floss silk. III. i. Pt. i. 60.

續
suh
hsu

To connect, = to prolong. IV. vii. Pt. ii. 9.

纖
s'en
hsien

Fine chequered silks. III. i. Pt. i. 35, 60.

纘
tswan
tsuan

To continue. IV. ii. 2 : V. xxv. 3.

THE 121st RADICAL. 缶.

缺
k'eue
ch'üeh

To be deficient, wanting. V. xxv. 6.

THE 122d RADICAL. 网.

罔
wang

A negative adverb. It occurs nearly as often as 無 or 不 and its frequent use is characteristic of the Shoo. It is, as nearly as possible, synonymous with 無 in all its usages, = no, not ; do not ; to be without ; and there is not, there was not, &c. Especially it is found before other negatives, 罔不, 罔非, &c., and before 所, 攸 and 或. We have, in IV. iv. 8, a 罔大罔小, corresponding to the 無大無小, which I have called attention to under 無.

罪
tsuy
tsui

A crime, an offence. II. ii. 12, 20, 21 : V. xxvii. 16, 18 ; *et sæpe.* 罪 alone, II. i. 12 ; 罪人, V. vi. 14 ; *et al.*; 有罪, II. iii. 6 ; *et al.*; and 用罪, IV. vii. Pt. i. 16 ; all = the criminal or criminals. 罪疾, the pain—punishment—of crime. To treat—deal with—as criminal. IV. iii. 4 : vii. Pt. iii. 2 : V. i. Pt. i. 5 : ix. 16.

置
che
chih

To place, to set. IV. viii. Pt. i. 4.

罰
fă
fa

Punishment, generally. II. ii. 12 : III. ii. 3 : iv. 5 : IV. i. 4 : V. ix. 3, 8, 11, 13, 16, 21 ; *et sæpe.* Specifically, the punishment of fine. Thus it is used in V. xxvii. 18, 19, 20 ; and in p. 17, we have the phrase 五罰, the five fines. We meet often with 天罰 and 天之罰, the punishment appointed by Heaven. *E. g.* V. i. Pt. i. 10 ; Pt. iii. 3 : ii. 6. 王罰, the punishment inflicted by kings. V. xiv. 2. To punish. IV. vii. Pt. ii. 12 : V. xv. 18 ; *et al.*

罹
le
li

(1) To be sorrowful ; to suffer distress from. V. x. 11 : IV. iii. 3. (2) To be involved. V. iv. 11.

罷
pe
pi

(1) A large species of bear. III. i. Pt. i. 69. Used to describe and stimulate soldiers. V. ii. 9 : xxiii. 5. (2) Name of an officer at the court of Shun. II. i. 22.

THE 123d RADICAL. 羊.

羊
yang

The sheep or goat. V. xii. 5.

羌
këang
chiang

The name of a pastoral tribe in the north-west, confederate with Chow against Shang. V. ii. 3.

美
mei

Admirable, beautiful. To beautify, = to do good service to. IV. viii. Pt. ii. 10. 服美, to wear fine robes. V. xxiii. 10.

羑
yew
yu

羑若, to pursue the same course. V. xxiii. 2. But the meaning is uncertain.

羞
sew
hsiu

(1) To feel ashamed ; shame : IV. viii. Pt. ii. 4 : V. iii. 8 : xxiii. 6. (2) To nourish. IV. vii. Pt. ii. 10 : V. x. 7. (3) To bring forward, to advance. This signification assumes various modifications, being here = to cultivate, and there = to employ. IV. vii. Pt. iii. 11 : V. iv. 13 : x. 7 : xix. 5.

羣
k'eun
ch'ün

A flock or herd ; a company. It is used to denote all of a class. Alone it = companies. V. x. 14. 羣庶 = herds of creatures. V. x. 11. We have 羣后, II. i. 9 : *et sæpe* ; 羣牧, II. i. 7 ; 羣神, II. i. 6 : 羣臣, IV. viii. Pt. i. 1 ; 羣弟, V. vi. 12 ; 羣叔, xvii. 1 : 羣辟, xx. 1 : 羣公, xxiii. 7 : 羣僕, xxvi. 4 ; 羣言, xxx. 1.

義
e
i

(1) To be righteous ; righteous ; righteousness, what is right. III. iii. 3 : IV. ii. 8 : v. Pt. i. 9 : ix. 3 : V. i. Pt. i. 8 : iii. 9 : iv. 14 : ix. 13, 17 ; *et al.* 不義惟王, deemed it not righteous to be king. V xv. 6. Righteous men. V. ix. 15. 鴟義, owl-like ways. V. xxvii. 2. (2) 義和, the designation of prince Wan. xxviii. 1, 3, 4.

羲
he
hsi

The name of one of the families, which had the care of astronomy, &c., in Yaou's time, and subsequently. I. 3, 4, 5, 8 : III. iv. 1, 4.

羹
käng
kêng

Soup. IV. viii. Pt. iii. 2.

THE 124th RADICAL. 羽.

羽
yu
yü

(1) Feathers. II. ii. 21 : III. i. Pt. i. 44, 52. (2) The name of a mountain in the east, where Shun confined K'wän. II. i. 12. It is queried whether this was the

弈
*e
i*

same mountain mentioned in III. Pt. i. 30, 35.

A famous archer of antiquity, the prince of K'eung, and opponent of T'ae-k'ang. III. iii. 2.

習
seih
hsi

(1) To practise; practice. IV. v. Pt. i. 9. (2) To repeat; repeatedly. II. ii. 18: V. vi. 9. Observe 庶習逸德 之人, V. xix. 5.

翕
heih
hei

Altogether. 翕受, to receive all. II. iii. 4.

翟
teih
ti

A long-tailed pheasant. Probably'= the feathers of this bird. III. i. Pt. i. 35.

翼
yih
yi

(1) Wings. 翼室, a wing apartment. V. xxii. 11. To act as wings to,— to assist. II. ii. 1: iv. 4: V. xxii. 10: xxv. 3. (2) 翼日, next day. V. iii. 1: vi. 11: vii. 5: xii. 4, 5. (3) To be reverent,—in the phrase 考翼 V. vii. 7, 11.

THE 125TH RADICAL. 老.

老
laou
lao

Old. the old. IV. vii. Pt. i. 15: V. i. Pt. ii. 3 (黎老).

考
k'aou
k'ao

(1) A deceased father. II. i. 13: V. i. Pt. i. 5, 10: III. 5; *et al.* But we find it also, where the father or fathers must be living. V. ix. 16: x. 6; and perhaps in other passages. 祖考, grandfather and father; progenitors generally. II. iv. 9: V. x. 5: xxv. 3, 7 (2) Longevity. V. iv. 39: xiii. 27 (*n. b.* 引考). (3) To examine. II. i. 3: V. vii. 7, 8, 10, 12. (4) To complete. V. xiii. 24.

耄
maou
mao

90 years old. 耄期, between 90 and 100, II. ii. 9. But it is used in connection with 百年 or 100 years. V. xxvii. 1. Old venerable men. IV. xi. 3. Old: the aged. IV. iv. 7: V. xxviii. 2 (耆壽).

耆
k'e
ch'i

者
chay
chê

(1) He or they who,—at the end of a phrase or clause, which contains a predicate to the who. III. iii. 5: iv.: IV. ii. 8. (2) After a numeral. 五者, these five. V. iv. 32.

耇
kow
kou

Old. IV. xi. 5: V. ix. 5: x, 7: xii. 12 (耇壽). 耇造德, benefits from age and experience. V. xvi. 16.

THE 126TH RADICAL. 而.

而
urh

(1) And, and then; and yet, sometimes = but. II. i. 12, 16, 24: iii. 2, 3: iv. 6, 8: IV. i. 2: vii. Pt. i. 9, 12: V. i. Pt. ii. 1: iii. 8, 9: iv. 12: vi. 19: xxi. 7: xxii.

25: xxx. 7. (2) = they; their. V. iv. 11, 13, 19. The meaning here, however, is uncertain. It will be seen that 而 is comparatively infrequent in the Shoo.

THE 128TH RADICAL. 耳.

耳
urh

(1) The ears. V. v. 5. 耳目, eyes and ears, is spoken of ministers as being such to their sovereign. II. iv. 4: and perhaps V. xxvi. 7. (2) 熊耳, the name of a mountain. See 熊.

耽
tan

耽樂, excessive pleasure. V. xv. 7. To be addicted to pleasure, xv. 13.

耿
kăng
kêng

Bright. V. xix. 4, 22.

聒
kwŏ
kuo

聒聒, to keep clamouring. IV. vii. Pt. i. 7.

聖
shing
shêng

To be sage; sage, sagely. IV. iv. 3, 7, 8: viii. Pt. i. 11: V. viii. 2: xxi. 2: xxx. 6, 7. The sage, a sage,—with particular reference. II. ii. 4: IV. iv. 2: IV. viii. Pt. ii. 3; Pt. iii. 9: V. xxi. 4. Sageness. V. iv. 6, 34. 自聖, to think himself sage. V. xvii. 7.——聖 has not yet in the Shoo assumed its technical meaning of a sage, sage, as the highest type of humanity and a particular order of men. In V. xviii. 17, it can mean nothing more than *the wise.*

聞
wăn
wên

To hear; to hear of. II. i. 12: II. iv. 4: III. iv. 5 (聞知, also in xv. 3): IV. i. 2: ii. 8: vii. Pt. ii. 4 (*n. b.*): viii. Pt. ii. 12 (foll. by 于): V. i. Pt. ii. 3: iv. 3: ix. 5: xiv. 5. (念聞); *et sæpe.* To be heard. II. i. 1: IV. ii. 4 (聽聞): V. ix. 21: xxviii. 1. To be smelt. V. x. 11: xxvii. 4.

聞
wăn
wên

3d tone. Reputation, fame. V. viii. 3: xxiv. 4. Some other passages, V. ix. 4: xvi. 14, are also marked, in many editions of the Shoo, in this tone, but they are simply passives. If they should be marked, the passages indicated above as having the passive meaning should also be so.

聰
ts'ung

To be acute of hearing. IV. v. Pt. ii. 7. = distinctness. IV. iv. 6. = acutely. V. x. 5. 達四聰 = to hear with the ears of all, II. i. 15. It is generally found in combination with 明, which phrase = to hear and see, in II. iii. 7; = to be intelligent, in V. xvii. 7: xxvi. 2; = the intelligent, in IV. ii. 2: V. i. Pt. 3.

聲
shing
shêng

(1) The notes in music. II. i. 24. 五聲, the five notes. II. iv. 4. (2) Music,—meaning dissolute music, in the phrase 聲色, IV. ii. 5. (3) Fame III. i, Pt. ii. 23; V. xxiv. 7.

職
chih

聽
t'ing

(1) Office, the duties of office. III. iv. 1: V. xx. 13. (2) To preside over, to secure a certain effect. V. xxx. 6.

To hear, to listen to. II. ii. 16, 20: iv. 1: V. i. Pt. i. 2; I't. ii. 2, 7: iv. 6 (= hearing); *et sæpe*. Often the idea of obedience enters into the term. *E. g.* IV. iv. 1: V. ix. 24: xv. 15, 18. 聽罪, to acknowledge one's offences. IV. ix. 4. To be listened to. IV. ii. 4; *et al.* 高乃聽, think highly of what you have heard. V. ix. 23.

THE 129TH RADICAL. 聿.

聿
yuh
yü

Then, thereon. IV. iii. 4.

肄
e
i

To practise. 肄肄 = with earnest practice or submission. V. xxii. 5.

肅
suh
su

To be grave; to venerate. 祇肅 IV. v. P. i. 2. Gravity. V. iv. 6, 34. Gravely. V. viii. 3. So, probably, in the difficult phrase 肅將, V. i. Pt. i. 5: xiii. 21.

肆
sze
szû

(1) An introductory particle or conjunction. It most commonly = therefore. *E. g.* II. ii. 20: IV. iii. 4: v. Pt. i. 2: V. i. Pt. i. 6; Pt. iii. 4; *et sæpe*. Other meanings suit better, however, in many cases, as thereafter, thereon, in II. i. 6, 8; but, in IV. vii. Pt. iii. 4, 7; *et al.*; now, in V. xi. 7: xii. 20: xiii. 3; *et al.* It occurs twice in V. xi. 2, one of the instances being hardly explicable. In xiv. 20, 予惟率肆矜爾, 肆 is always read along with 率, but a new meaning must then be coined to suit the case. We should put a comma at 率, and read 肆 with 矜; but I believe the text to be corrupt. (2) To let go. 肆赦, II. i. 11. (3) To be at ease, to take heart. V. vii. 13. (4) To be reckless. V. i. Pt. iii. 3. (5) To set forth, to offer. 肆祀, V. ii. 6. (6) Greatly, V. xvi. 17, 19.

肇
chaou
chao

(1) To institute. II. i. 10. To lay the foundations of. V. iii. 5: x. 2. Obs. 肇位, to come to the throne, to begin a reign. III. iv. 1. Before other verbs, it = to begin. IV. iv. 5: V. ix. 4: ? xxviii. 3. = from the first, IV. ii. 4; at first, V. xiii. 5. (2) To be earnest or diligent. V. x. 6; ? xxviii. 3.

THE 130TH RADICAL. 肉.

肖
heaou
hsiao

To be like, to resemble. IV. viii. Pt. iii. 3.

肜
yung

The name of a supplementary sacrifice, offered the day after the regular sacrifice. IV. ix. 1.—This meaning is erroneously introduced in p. 674, under the character 彤.

股
koo
ku

The thigh, the upper part of the leg. We find it always in connection with 肱. IV. viii. Pt. iii. 9: V. x. 6. The phrase is used metaphorically of ministers. II. iv. 4, 11: V. xxv. 3.

肩
këen
chien

The shoulders. = to employ, to sustain IV. vii. Pt. iii. 10. = to maintain, in p. 13.

肱
kwang
kuang

The upper arm. See 股.

肯
kăng
kêng

To be willing. V. vii. 11: xviii. 4.

育
yuh
yü

To nourish, to keep. V. v. 8. 遺育, to leave those who may be brought up. IV. vii. Pt. ii. 16. Here it = children.

胄
chow

胄子, sons. II. i. 24.—Of the same sound as this character, and hardly distinguishable from it in form, is 冑, a helmet, which is found in the phrase 甲冑, in IV. viii. Pt. ii. 4: V. xxix. 2. It belongs to the 13th Radical 冂, and the character should have been entered on p. 655.

背
p'ei

To turn the back on, to disregard or disobey. IV. v. Pt. ii. 3.

胡
hoo
hu

(1) What. IV. v. Pt. iii. 8. (2) The name of a nephew of the duke of Chow, prince Chung of Ts'ae. V. xvii. 2, 8.

胤
yiu

(1) To inherit. = heirs. IV. ix. 5. 胤子, heir-son. I. 9. To follow after. V. xiii. 2. (2) The name of a state. III. iv. 1: V. xxii. 19.

胥
seu
hsü

(1) Mutually, together. IV. vii. Pt. i. 2, 12, 14; Pt. ii. 3, 6, 15: V. vii. 13: xviii. 7: xxiii. 6: xxvii. 4, 20. 胥 is thus synonymous with 相, though its construction is in most cases more difficult. We find it used in the same way as 相, when one of the parties whose action is intended is not directly expressed :— as in IV. v. Pt. ii. 2: V. xi. 3: xv. 14. (2) Employés.—certain officers who are thus denominated. V. xviii. 25.

能
năng
nêng

To be able, can. It is used everywhere before verbs like our auxiliary. In one case we find the idiomatic use of 而 between it and the verb,—V. xxii. 25.

As an active verb,—to cultivate the ability of, to help. V. xvi. 3 : xxii. 8 : xxviii. 4. To be able to manage, *to can.* V. ix. 18 : xvi. 23. Ability. II. ii. 14 : IV. viii. Pt. ii. 7 : V. iv. 13 (obs. 有能). = men of ability. IV. viii. Pt. ii. 5 : V. iii. 9 : xx. 20.

脅
hëĕ
hsieh

To be pressed, forced. III. iv. 6. To force with. V. i. Pt. ii. 3.

脛
hing
hsing

The leg-bone. V. i. Pt. iii. 3.

脞
ts'o

To cut up meat small. 叢脞 seems to mean a collection of things small and trifling, = vexatious. II. iv. 11.

腆
t'ïen
t'ien

(1) To be prosperous. V. vii. 4. (2) To make strong,—spoken of spirits. V. x. 6. (3) To go to excess,—foll. by 于. x. 8. 11.

腎
shǐn
shên

The kidneys. IV. vii. Pt. iii. 3 (n. b.)

腥
sing
hsing

Rank odour. V. x. 11 : xxvii. 4.

腸
ch'ang

The bowels. IV. vii. Pt. iii. 3.

腹
fuh
fu

The belly. IV. vii. Pt. iii. 3.

膂
leu
lü

The back-bone. V. xxv. 3.

膚
foo
fu

The skin. = shallow—skin-deep—speeches. IV. vii. Pt. i. 7. But the meaning here may be different, and = puncturing, irritating, speeches. Compare. Ana. XII. vi.

膺
ying

= to receive. V. iii. 5 : xxi. 14 : xxiv. 13.

THE 131st RADICAL. 臣.

臣
ch'in
ch'ên

A minister, the correlate of 君. *Passim.* We have 臣人, III. iv. 2 : V. xxi. 6 ; and 臣下, V. i. Pt. ii. 3, both denoting ministers. But 臣庶, II. ii. 11, = ministers and multitudes. Ministry, the duties of being minister. II. ii. 2. To act the part of ministers to,—to serve. V. iv. 21 *(n. b.)*, 22 : xviii. 24.——臣 is generally to be taken of the great ministers of a government ; when it is otherwise, this is indicated. 臣僕 is spoken of himself by a great minister, IV. xi. 8 ; but 僕臣, V. xxvi. 6 (comp. pp. 2, 4) is different. 小臣, V. ix. 17, 18,

means petty officers, but in 予小臣, V. xii. 24, the phrase is merely used in the self-depreciating style of conversation. 臣妾, V. xxix. 4, = camp-followers, male and female. 虎臣, the master of the guards. V. xxii. 3. 表臣, ministers away from court. V. xix. 9.

臧
tsang

To be good, admirable. V. x. 5 : xxvi. 2. Good condition, = prosperity. IV. vii. Pt. i. 16. To approve, declare to be good. IV. ii. 3. 臧厥臧, to show approval of what is good. V. xxiv. 4.

臨
lin

To present one's-self to, and deal with, in the character of the sovereign. II. ii. 12 : III. iii. 5 ; V. xxii. 24. It is spoken of the sun, as seeing and visiting all with his light. 日之照臨, V. i. Pt. iii. 5.

THE 132D RADICAL. 自.

自
tsze
tzŭ

(1) As a preposition, from,—used with reference to time, place, and person. *Passim.* = according as. II. iii. 7 : V. i. Pt. ii. 7 ; *et al.* (2) Self, of all persons,—myself, yourself, himself. Of one's-self. V. ix. 8 ; *et al.* The meaning sometimes approaches to—then, as *a matter of course.* E. g. V. x. 6, 7 : xxx. 2. Its most frequent use in this signification is as joined to verbs in a reflex sense. We have 自賢, to count one's-self possessed of talents and worth ; 自滿 假 ; 自靖 ; 自絕 ; 自庸 ; 自臭 ; 自酒 ; 自鞠 自苦 ; 自安, 自廣, 自厎, 自覆, 自抑畏, 自度, 自疾, 自恤, 自聖, 自亂, (=治.)

臬
nëĕ
nieh

Laws V. ix. 11, 13. 克臬, to be able to observe the laws. V. xviii. 25.

臭
ch'ow
ch'ou

A fetid odour. Used as a verb. = to make one's-self abominable, to ruin. IV. vii. Pt. ii. 6, 8.

皋
kaou
kao.

皋陶, Shun's minister of Crime. II. i. 17, 20 : ii. 10, 11, 12 : iii. 1, 2, 3, 8 : iv. 1, 8, 11. The dict. gives 臯, from 白, as the more correct form of the character.

THE 133D RADICAL. 至.

至
che
chih

(1) To come, to arrive. V. xvi. 20. It is everywhere followed by 于, and 至于 = to come to, to reach to. See everywhere in the 'Tribute of Yu,' *et al.* Generally the point of departure is indicated ; but sometimes it is not, and has

to be gathered from the context. *E. g.*
V. x. 8 : xi. 3, 6 : xv. 5 : xviii. 7, 12, 23.
(2) The most, perfect, entire,—that
which has reached the utmost degree. II.
ii. 21 : V. xxi. 3. 底至, to push to
the utmost extent. V. xxiii. 5.

致
che
chih

To carry out fully. IV. i. 4 : V. xiv. 2,
21, 24 : xviii. 29. It is thus used for the
most part with reference to the infliction
of punishment. Before verbs it indicates
the doing to the utmost what the verb
intimates. IV. vii. Pt. i. 17 : V. x. 6. 致
辟 = to put to death. V. xvii. 1 ; but
致 罰, V. xiv. 5, = extreme punishment. 德之致, the things produced
by virtue. V. v. 3. In I. 5, 致 is understood to mean the extreme limit of the
sun's shadow.

臺
t'ae
t'ai

Towers. V. i. Pt. i. 5. 鹿臺, the
Stag tower, a structure of the tyrant
Show. V. iii. 9.

臻
tsin
chin

To arrive, to come on. V. xxii. 4.

THE 134TH RADICAL. 臼.

與
yu
yü

(1) With, along with. II. ii. 19 : IV.
v. Pt. iii. 2 : V. viii. 1. *And* sometimes
answers better in translation than *with*.
V. vi. 8, 16, 17. The with is sometimes
nearly = for. II. ii. 17 : IV. vi. 1. For,
on behalf of. IV. iii. 4. (2) To give to.
V. ix. 16. So, in IV. vii. Pt. ii. 12, which
is peculiar. To grant, or concede to.
III. iv. 6 : IV. iv. 5 (*n. b.*) (3) Than,
forming a comparative with 寧. II. ii.
12. (4) ? = 而. IV. v. Pt. i. 9.

與
yu
yü

3d tone. To be present at, to share in.
IV. vii. Pt. i. 14.

與
yu
yü

1st tone. 伯與, an officer at the
court of Shun. II. i. 21.

興
hing
hsing

To arise, rise or get up,—with varied
application, = to get better, to rise from
bed, &c. IV. xi. 2, 8 : V. iv. 3 : xxii. 7,
25 : xxvi. 1 : xxix. 1. In xxvii. 4, the
meaning of 興 is no more than *thereon.*
To rise, = to flourish. IV. v. Pt. iii. 2 :
V. xiv. 25. To make to rise or prosper. V. vii. 9. Obs. 有廢有興,
V. xxi. 5. To give rise to, to originate.
II. ii. 17 : iv. 11 : V. xi. 4.

舉
keu
chü

To lift up, = to advance to office. II.
iv. 7 : V. xx. 20.

舊
kew
chiü

What is old ; old. IV. ii. 2, 6 : V. Pt.
iii. 9 : vii. Pt. i. 5, 13 : V. xvii. 6 : xxv. 3,
7. 舊人 = men of old families, in

IV. vii. Pt. i. 7 ; but = the old ministers,
in V. viii. 10. 舊 alone = the old
course, in V. iii. 8. It is often abverbial,
= of old, at first. III. iv. 6 : IV. viii. Pt.
ii. 1 : xi. 5, 8 : V. viii. 3 : xv. 5, 6. =
for long. V. xxiv. 10.

THE 135TH RADICAL. 舌.

舍
shay
shê

(1) To neglect, to abandon. II. ii. 3
(舍己, to give up one's own views
and wishes) : IV. 1. 2. (2) To let loose,
—spoken of cattle. V. xxix. 3.

舒
shoo
shu

To deal gently or kindly with. V xviii.
5 (foll. by 于).

THE 136TH RADICAL. 舛.

舜
shun

The ancient emperor, so denominated.
虞舜, I. 12. 帝舜, II. i. 1, 3, 14,
17, 18 : IV. viii. Pt. iii. 10.

舞
woo
wu

To make postures. Spoken of birds
and beasts = to gambol in a regular way.
II. i. 24 : iv. 10. = to dance. II. ii. 21 :
IV. iv. 7. 舞衣, dancing habits. V.
xxii. 19.

THE 137TH RADICAL. 舟.

舟
chow
chou

A boat. II. iv. 8 : IV. vii. Pt. ii. 6 : viii.
Pt. i. 6.

THE 138TH RADICAL. 艮.

良
lëang
liang

To be good ; good ; the good. II. iv. 11 :
IV. ii. 7 : viii. Pt. i. 2 ; Pt. iii. 9 : V. Pt.
i. 5 ; Pt. iii. 6 : xxi. 13 : xxvi. 3. Excellent, skilful. IV. Pt. ii. 12 : V. xxi. 6.
元良, greatly good. IV. v. Pt. iii. 8 :
V. i. Pt. ii. 5. = goodness. V. xxv. 2.

艱
këen
chien

To be difficult or toilsome ; difficulty,
hardships. IV. iv. 5 : v. Pt. iii. 1 ; Pt. ii.
13 : V. vii. 3, 7, 8, 11 : xvi. 17 : xxiv. 10 :
xxv. 5 : xxviii. 3 : xxx. 3. 艱難, painful toil. V. xv. 2, 3, 7 : xxii. 7. 艱
食, food of toil,—that procured by agriculture. II. iv. 1. To realize the difficulty
or pain of. II. ii. 2 : V. xxi. 5.

THE 139TH RADICAL. 色.

色
sih
sê

(1) The countenance, the looks ; the
deportment. II. iii. 2 : V. xxiv. 5 : xxvi.
5. Observe 而康而色. V. iv.
11. (2) Colours, III. i. Pt. i. 35. 五
色, the five colours. II. iv. 4. (3)

Licentious pleasure. III. iii. 6 : IV. ii. 5 (聲色): iv. 7 : V. i. Pt. i. 5.

THE 140TH RADICAL. 艸.

芮
juy
jui

The name of a principality, the chief of which was minister of Instruction to king Ching. V. xxii. 3 : xxiii. 2.

芻
ts'oo
ch'u

Grass. 芻茭 = forage. V. xxix. 5.

苗
mëaou
miao

(1) Growing grain. IV. ii. 4. (2) 三苗, the name of the original seat of the Meaou, a tribe which occasioned much trouble in the times of Yaou, Shun, and Yu. They are called 三苗, 苗 and 苗民. II. i. 19, 27 : ii. 20, 21 : iii. 2 : iv. 8 : III. i. Pt. i. 78 : V. xxvii. 3, 5, 7, 12.

若
jŏ
jo

(1) To be as; as, as if; if. I. 1, 9, 10 : II. i. 1, 21, 22 : ii. 1, 19, 21 : iii. 1 : iv. 6, 8 ; *et passim.* From *to be as* comes the signification of—to conform to, to follow, to act in accordance with. We have other verbs associated with 若 in this usage; 一欽若, I. 3 ; *et al.* ; 奉若, IV. ii. 2 ; *et al.* ; 祗若, IV. viii. Pt. i. 11 ; 嗣若, V. xii. 18. To cause to conform to. IV. iii. 2.   To be as should be, in accordance with the natural condition. IV. iv. 2 ; *et al.* To be regulated gently. V. xii. 21.   When, in the case that. IV. vii. Pt. i. 9 ; Pt. ii. 5 ; *et al.* 若 occurs before phrases, and adverbs of time, when we cannot translate it. V. vii. 4 : xii. 4 : xx. 2 : xxvii. 2.   To approve. V. x. 7 : xv. 13 ; *et al.* Observe especially 若否, in IV. vii. Pt. iii. 11.   Such as,—in enumerations of famous men, but not always. V. xvi. 7, 12 : xxviii 3 (若汝). In the frequently recurring phrases 若時, 若茲, 若是, the 若 simply = as. Comp. 若之何, IV. xi. 3 ; and 若勤哉, V. vii. 10.   Thus, nearly to this effect,—in the formulas 王 or 公若曰, IV. vii. Pt. i. 6 : xi. 1, 4 : V. viii. 5 ; *et sæpe.* After adjectives = our like or ly. V. iv. 34.—Observe 旅王若公, V. xii. 8 ; 越若來, V. xii. 2 ; 厥若, V. xix. 16 : xxiii. 6 ; 時若, xx. 4 ; 羑若, xxiii. 2.

苦
k'oo
k'u

Bitter. V. iv. 5.   To embitter. 自苦, IV. vii. Pt. ii. 6.

茅
maou
mao

菁茅, a kind of three-ribbed rush, used in straining the spirits for the imperial sacrifices. III. i. 52.

茭
keaou
chiao

Dried grass. 茭芻, forage. V. xxix. 5.

茨
tsze
tzŭ

To thatch. V. xi. 4.

茲
tsze
tzŭ

This, these. *Passim.* It stands sometimes, especially at the beginning of clauses, with adverbial force, and = here ; now ; thus ; therefore. *E. g.* IV. ii. 2 : vii. Pt. i. 3, 14 ; Pt. ii. 14 : V. vii. 2 : x. 7 : xvi. 9, 13 : xix. 19 : xxii. 4.

荊
king
ching

(1) 荊州, one of Yu's nine provinces. (2) There are two mountains called King, mentioned in the Shoo ;—the southern King, one of the boundaries of King-chow, III. i. Pt. i. 46, 54 ; Pt. ii. 3 ; and the northern, in Yung-chow, Pt. i. 76 ; Pt. ii. 1.

草
ts'aou
ts'ao

Grass.—vegetation generally, distinct from trees. II. i. 22 : III. i. Pt. i. 17, 23, 42 : IV. iii. 5 : V. iv. 32 (庶草): xxi. 4. 草竊, to steal among the grass, probably = to commit highway robbery. IV. xi. 3.

荒
hwang
huang

(1) Uncultivated, overgrown with grass and weeds. 荒野, IV. viii. i. Pt. iii. 1. So 荒 alone, in xi. 3, = the wilds. (2) The name of the last of Yu's domains. III. i. Pt. ii. 22. (3) After nouns, it = to be wildly addicted to. We have 酒荒, III. iv. 1 ; 色荒, 禽荒, iii. 6. Perhaps it may be construed in these cases as a noun. (4) As a verb,—to neglect, IV. vii. Pt. i. 8 ; to waste, to ruin. IV. xi. 4 : V. xx. 16. (3) Used adverbially,—wildly ; neglectfully. III. iii. 8 : IV. vii. Pt. ii. 2 : V. i. Pt. iii. 2 : x. 11 : xv. 4, 5 : xviii. 4. Greatly. II. iv. 8 : V. xxvii. 1.

茶
t'oo
tu

A bitter herb. Used metaphorically, as we use wormwood. IV. iii. 3.

莅
le
li

Nearly synonymous with 臨. = to manage, the management of. V. xx. 16.

莠
yew
yu

A useless plant, resembling growing corn in the statk and leaf. IV. ii. 4.

莫
mŏ
mo

Not ; not to be ; do not. II. ii. 24 : IV. iv. 2 (莫不): II. 8 (莫已若者): V. xxi. 5.

萊
lae
lai

Probably the name of a mountain in the present Tăng-chow, Shan-tung. 萊夷, III. i. Pt. i. 26.

菁
tsing
ching

菁茅, see 茅.

蕾
tszě
tz'ĭ

To turn up the ground,—take the first steps in cultivating a field. V. vii. 11: xi. 4.

菏
ko

The name of a marsh. III. i. Pt. i. 57; Pt. ii. 10.

華
hwa
hua

1st tone. Variegated, of different colours. V. xxii. 16. 華蟲, the variegated bird,—the emblematic pheasant embroidered on the upper robe of the emperor. II. iv. 4. 華夏, flowery and great, a name of the empire. V. iii. 6. 重華, perhaps the name of Shun. II. i. 1.

華
hwa
hua

3d tone. The name of a mountain;—the western mountain of Shun's progresses. III. i. Pt. i. 62 ; Pt. iv. ii. 3 (called 太華), 7: V. iii. 2.

萃
ts'uy
ts'ui

To collect, to be assembled. V. iii. 6 (observe the construction, which is intricate).

萬
wan

Ten thousand, a myriad, myriads. It is used generally in a vague manner, and = all of what is spoken of. We have 萬姓, the myriad surnames, == the people, III. iii. 9 : IV. vi. 9 : V. i. Pt. i. 5 : iii. 8 : xix. 5 ; 萬邦, the myriad countries, == the empire, I. 3 : II. ii. 3 : V. xxvi. 2 ; *et sæpe*; 萬事, all matters, II. iv. 11 ; 萬幾, II. iii. 5 ; 萬世, myriad ages, for ever, and 萬年, II. ii. 8 : IV. v. Pt. i. 7 ; Pt. ii. 2 : V. xiii. 4, 27, 28 ; *et al.* ; 萬民, IV. vii. Pt. ii. 12 ; Pt. iii. 5 ; *et al.* ; 萬夫 seems to == the myriad heads of families, another name for the people, in IV. vi. 10 ; 萬方, the myriad regions, IV. ii. 2, 8 : iii. 1, 2, 3, 8 : *et sæpe* ; 萬物, all things, V. i. Pt. i. 3 ; 萬國 occurs only once, —in V. xx. 3.

落
lŏ
lo

In the phrase 俎落, to decease. II. i. 13.

葛
kŏ
ko

The name of a State, not far from the original seat of T'ang, who punished its chief. V. ii. 6.

董
tung

To correct. II. ii. 7. Before another verb, = strictly. V. xx. 1

蒙
mŭng
mêng

(1) Young, youthful. 蒙士, IV. iv. 7. (2) Stupidity. IV. iv. 34. Cloudiness. IV. iv. 29. (3) Two mountains were thus named,—one in Ts'eu-chow, III. i. Pt. i. 30 ; the other in Lëang-chow, p. 65.

蒼
ts'ang

Grass-green. 蒼生, II. iv. 7.

蓄
ch'uh
ch'u

To accumulate. V. xx. 16.

蓋
kae
kai

To cover. V. xvii. 3. To be covered, = to be disregarded. V. xxvii. 6.

蔑
mëě
mieh

Not, to be without. V. xvi. 13.

蔡
ts'ae
ts'ai

(1) Criminals undergoing a lesser banishment. III. i. Pt. ii. 21. It is queried whether we should not read the character *shă* in this meaning. (2) The name of a mountain, which is not well ascertained. III. i. Pt. i. 65. (3) The name of the appanage, in the present Ho-nan, of Too, known as 蔡叔, a younger brother of the duke of Chow. V. xvii. 1. His son is 蔡仲,—in the same par.

蔽
pe
pi

(1) To determine, decide firmly ; to be determined. II. ii. 18 : V. ix. 12. (obs. 不蔽), 13, 22. (2) To conceal. IV. iii. 8.

蕃
fan

(1) To be luxuriant. 蕃廡, V. iv. 32. (2) *I. q.* 藩, to be a fence or bulwark to. V. viii. 4 : xvii. 6.

蕩
t'ang

(1) 蕩蕩, vast. I. 11.   == broad and long. V. iv. 14. (2) To be scattered. 蕩析, IV. vii. Pt. iii. 5. (3) To be dissolute. V. xxiv. 9.

薄
pŏ
po

(1) To reach to, extend over. II. iv. 8. (2) To press on, == to deal sternly with. V. x. 13.——Ought we not to read the character in the first of these meanings—*p'ŏ* ?

藏
ts'ang

To be hidden, kept in obscurity. V. xii. 10.

藝
e
f

(1) An art, arts. V. vi. 6. 藝事, III. iv. 3. 藝人, in V. xix. 9, are certain officers so denominated. (2) *I. q.* 蓺, to cultivate, to bring under cultivation. III. i. Pt. i. 30, 63 : V. x. 1.

藥
yŏ
yo

Medicine. IV. viii. Pt. i. 8.

藪
sow
sou

A large jungly marsh, to which beasts will resort. V. iii. 6.

藻
tsaou
tsao

A kind of water-plant,—duckweed, one of the emblematic figures on the lower sacrificial robe of the emperor. II. iv. 4.

蘇
soo
su

(1) To revive. IV. ii. 6. (2) Apparently the name of a principality or State. V. xix. 24.

蘉
mang

To exert one's-self. V. xiii. 13.

THE 141ST RADICAL. 虍

虎
hoo
hu

A tiger, tigers. V. ii. 9 (comp. for soldiers): xxv. ii. (2) 虎賁, life-guards. V. xxii. 11. The officer commanding them is called 虎臣, in p. 3. He and other officers under him are called 虎賁, in xix. 1, 8. (3) The name of an officer in the court of Shun. II. i. 22.

虐
neŏ
yao

To oppress, tyrannize over. II. 1, 24 : ii. 3 : IV. vi. 3 ; *et sæpe.* Foll. by 于, in V. ii. 6 : xviii. 6. Oppressive, dangerous, —used of sickness. V. vi. 5. Oppression ; sometimes = oppressors. II. iv. 8 : IV. iii. 3 : iv. 3 : V. i. Pt. i. 5 : *et sæpe.* = calamities. IV. vii. Pt. ii. 4. Observe 五 虐之刑, V. xxvii. 3.

To kill, = oppressors. V. xxvii. 2.

虔
k'ëen
ch'ien

The name of a star. I. 6.

虛
hen
hsü

虞
yu
yü

(1) To consider, think about. V. x. 3 : xxi. 5. 無虞, nothing to think about, a time of freedom from all anxiety. II. ii. 6 : V. xxiv. 3. (2) A forester, the designation of the warden of woods and forests under Shun. II. i. 22. = a forester, generally. IV. v. Pt. i. 7. (3) The name of the principality which had belonged to the family of Shun, who is thence called 虞舜, I. 12 ; and 虞 alone, V. xx. 3. Obs. 虞賓, II. iv. 9.

號
haou
hao

1st tone. To cry out. 號泣, II. ii. 21.

號
haou
hao

A warning order or command. V. xxvi. 2.

虢
kih
ko

Name of the appanage of a younger brother of king Wăn, called 虢叔, V. xvi. 12.

虧
k'wei
k'uei

To be wanting. V. v. 9.—— The dictionary gives this character under 虍, —but incorrectly. In the 說文 we find it under 亏, the appearance of the breath slowly ascending and stopped. 虖 is the phonetic element in the character, and 亏 the ideographic ; and it ought to have its place in the dict. under the latter. But 亏 is no longer used for lexical purposes, being thrown out to reduce the number of radicals (as they are termed) as much as possible. This practice has given rise to not a few anomalies in the arrangement of characters.

THE 142D RADICAL. 虫.

虺
hwuy
hui

仲虺, one of the principal ministers of T'ang. IV. ii. 2.

蚩
ch'e
ch'i

蚩尤 appears in V. xxvii. 2, as the first troubler of the empire, a wicked and seditious prince of the most ancient times.

蜀
shuh
shu

A tribe, whose seat was in the pres. dep. of Shing-too, Sze-ch'uen, confederate with Chow against Shang. V. ii. 3.

蟲
ch'ung

An insect ;—but used for animals generally. 華蟲, the emblematic pheasant depicted on the emperor's robe. II. iv. 6.

蟻
e
i

An ant. = ant-coloured. V. xxii. 22.

蠙
pin

蠙珠, pearls. III. i. Pt. i. 35.—The dict. says that this character is 'the name of a kind of pearl.' This is a mistake, I apprehend. It should rather be taken as the *oyster*, in which pearls are found.

蠡
le
li

彭蠡, the name of a lake, the modern Po-yang. III. i. Pt. i. 38.

蠢
ch'un

Insects moving about.—Used for to be stupid, II. ii. 20 ; and for stupid, senseless, agitation. V. vii. 3, 5, 8.

蠲
keuen
chüan

To be clean or pure. V. xviii. 16. To make clean, to cleanse. x. 16. To hold to be clean or guiltless. xxvii. 12.

蠻
man

The wild tribes of the south. But we find it used, where it must mean such wild tribes generally. III. i. Pt. ii. 22. As distinct from the tribes of other quarters, they are spoken of as the 八蠻, V. v. 1. We have 蠻夷, in II. i. 16, 20 ; and 蠻貊, in V. iii. 6.

蠶
ts'an

The silk worm. = to be made fit for silkworms. III. i. Pt. i. 16.

THE 143D RADICAL. 血.

血
heuĕ
hsieh

Blood. V. iii. 9.

衋
heih
? hei

To be pained, to feel the pain of. V. x. 11.

THE 144TH RADICAL. 行.

行
hing
hsing

(1) To go, to travel over. V. xix. 22. To make to go. II. iv. 8. Used of the course of the sun and moon. V. iv. 38. 行遯, to go away and escape. IV. xi.

9. (2) To do; to carry—be carried—into practice; to execute; practice, execution. II. iii. 8: IV. i. 1: v. Pt. i. 7: viii. Pt. ii. 12, 13: Pt. ii. 3, 5: V. i. Pt. i. 5; Pt. iii. 3: ii. 7: iv. 16: ix. 21: xxv. 6. 不行 = obsolete laws. V. xxvii. 18. (3) 五行, the five elements. III. ii. 3: V. iv. 3, 4, 5.

3d tone. Actions, conduct. II. i. 25: iii. 3: III. i. Pt. ii. 17: V. iv. 13: v. 9 (細行): x. 3 (酒惟行): xvii. 2: xix. 2.

太行, the name of a mountain. III. i. Pt. ii. 1.

行 *hing hsing*

衍 *hǎng hêng*

衍 *yen*

衡 *hâng hêng*

= to push out, to infer. V. iv. 23.

(1) The beam of a balance, or steelyard. II. i. 8. 玉衡, the gem-adorned transverse, a part, apparently, of an astronomical instrument used by Shun. II. i. 5. To weigh, to adjust. V. xiii. 16. (2) 阿衡, the name, or a title, of T'ang's minister, E Yin. IV. v. Pt. i. 1; Pt. iii. 10. He is also called 保衡, V. xvi. 7. (3) The name of a mountain, the southern boundary of King-chow. III. i. Pt. i. 46; Pt. ii. 4. It is the southern mountain of Shun's progresses. II. i. 8. (4) 衡漳, the name of a river, an affluent of the Ho. III. i. Pt. i. 6.

衞 *wei*

(1) To defend. = defence. III. i. Pt. ii. 20. 臣衞, we, defenders of the throne. V. xxiii. 1. (2) Name of the 5th of the domains of Chow. V. iii. 3: ix. 1: x. 10, 13: xxiii. 4. (3) Name of a principality which occupied part of the pres. provinces of Chih-le and Ho-nan. V. xxii. 3. (4) The name of a river. III. i. Pt. i. 9.

THE 145TH RADICAL. 衣.

衣 *i*

Clothes, robes. Specifically, the upper garments. 衣裳. IV. viii. Pt. ii. 4. 戎衣, a martial garb. V. iii. 8. 舞衣, dancing habits. V. xxii. 19. The phrase 綴衣 is used in two senses;—as the name of an officer or officers, keepers of the robes, xix. 1, 8; as the name of a sort of tent used in audiences, xxii. 10, 14.

3d tone. To put on, = to carry into practice. V. ix. 5.

衣 *i*

表 *peaou piao*

(1) That which is outside, the outside; beyond. III. iii. 1 (在洛之表). 表臣, outside ministers,—officers be-

yond the court. V. xix. 9. 海表, beyond the seat. V. xix. 22. 四表, the four outsides, the utmost limits, north, south, east, and west. I. i. (2) To serve as a mark to. IV. ii. 2. To set up a mark for,—to signalise. V. xxiv. 3.

Man's good moral nature. II. iii. 6: IV. iii. 2.

衷 *chung*

衽 *jin jên*

The lappel in front of a coat or jacket, buttoning, according to Chinese usage, on the right side. 左衽, V. xxiv. 13.—It is also written 袵.

3d tone. To reach to. I. 1: III. i. Pt. i. 52; Pt. ii. 23.

被 *p'ei p'i*

被 *p'e p'i*

1st tone. To put on one, to dress one with. V. xxii. 2.

裔 *e i*

The lower edge of a garment. 後裔, descendants. V. viii. 2.

裕 *yu yü*

To be generous, enlarged in mind and act; what is generous. V. ix. 22: xiii. 10: xvi. 17. Obs. in IV. ii. 8, 垂裕, to transmit a generous example, and 裕 alone, = to become enlarged. To make generous. V. ix. 5. Obs. 忧裕之, xviii. 21. To rule generously. V. ix. 19: xiii. 13.

裳 *shang*

The lower robe or garment. IV. viii. Pt. ii. 4: V. xxii. 22, 23.

褻 *seĕ hsieh*

Undress, = to take liberties, to allow one's self. IV. vii. Pt. ii. 6.

襄 *seang hsiang*

(1) To overtop. I. 1: II. iv. 1. (2) To complete, to perfect; perfection. II. xvi. 20: II. iii. 8.

襲 *sih hsi*

A double garment, = to be repeated. V. i. Pt. ii. 5.

THE 146TH RADICAL. 西.

西 *se hsi*

The west. V. xxii. 17. On the west, (adv. and prep.); westwards; at the west. II. i. 8: III. i. Pt. ii. 23: I. 6: V. xiii. 3. Western. V. xxii. 16, 18, 19, 21: xxiii. 1; *et. al.* Ch'ang and Fă, afterwards king Wăn and king Woo, were 西伯, chiefs of the west, IV. x. 2; and 西土 appears often as a denomination of the western portion of the empire, subject to, or acknowledging the supremacy of, the House of Chow. V. i. Pt. ii. 2; Pt. ii. 2, 5: ii. 1, 9: vii. 3; *et al.* We have 西戎 in III i. Pt. i. 83, which is acc. to rule; but 西夷, in IV. ii. 6, shows how promiscuously the term 夷 may be used. 西岳, the western mountain, II. i. 8, is mount Hwa (see 華). 西傾, III. i. Pt. i. 70; Pt. ii. 2, is a mountain far to the west, commonly thought to be in the Koko-nor. 西河, III. i. Pt. i. 70, 72, 82, is the Ho, in its course from north to south. As a verb, 西爾 = wested you, settled you in the west. V. xiv. 8.

要
yaou
yao

1st tone. (1) To restrain. V. xviii. 23—(?). 要服, the domain of restraint,—the 4th of Yu's tenures. III. i. Pt. ii. 21. (2) In the phrase 要囚, to examine the evidence in criminal cases. V. ix. 12: xviii. 11.—This is a perplexing phrase, especially as we have to interpret it differently in xviii. 23.

要
yaou
yao

That which is important, the essential principle, V. xxvii. 19. 體要, in V xxiv. 8, is probably the completeness of a govt. measure.

覃
t'an

覃懷. a tract in the pres. dist. of Hwae-k'ing, Ho-nan, operated on by Yu. III. i. Pt. i. 6.

覆
fuh
fu

To subvert, overthrow. III. iii. 8: iv. 4 (顛覆); IV. ii. 9: v. Pt. i. 5: V. xxvii. 4.

THE 147TH RADICAL. 見.

見
k'een
chien

To see, to observe; to be seen, IV. v. Pt. i. 3: V. vi. 9: ix. 6: xi. 2: xix. 4, 6 (灼見): xxi. 4.

見
heen
hsien

(1) To appear before. II. ii. 21: IV. iv. 1. (2) To appear, to present one's-self, be seen. III. iii. 5: V. xvi. 14.—It is hardly possible to make anything of 見士于周, V. ix. 1.

To admonish, III. iv. 3 (n. b.).

規
k'wei
k'uei

To see, V. i. Pt. ii. 7: iv. 6 (= seeing). To look at, to consider, III. iii. 5: IV. v. Pt. ii. 7: viii. Pt. i. 8: xvii. 1: xxviii. 4. To have a regard to. IV. v. Pt. ii. 6: vii. Pt. ii. 4. *I. q.* 示, to display. V. xiii. 8.

視
she
shih

親
ts'in
ch'in

(1) To love; to show affection to. I. 2: IV. v. Pt. iii. 1 (天無親). V. xvii. 4 (*i. d.*): v. 3. To love mutually. II. i. 19. To love relations, IV. iv. 4. (2) Relatives. V. i. Pt. ii. 6. (3) To approach, place one's-self near to. 以爲親, V. xxx. 4.

觀
kin
chin

(1) To give audience to. II. i. 7, 8.—In the index to Mencius, I have said that this char. means—'to wait upon a superior,' 'to appear at court.' Such is its usage in his Works, and so the dict. defines

it, making special reference to the first instance of its occurrence in the Shoo, where it is not the appearance of the inferior, but the action of the superior, which we are led to think of. The common idea is that of—*a case of audience*. It is only used in one other instance in the Shoo,—V. xix. 22, where I have rendered it *to display*, bringing that meaning out of 見, by which interpreters explain it.

覺
keŏ
chiao

To apprehend, to perceive. 無覺, unperceived. IV. viii. Pt. iii. 5.

觀
kwan
kuan

To see, to contemplate. I. 12: II. iv. 4: IV. vii. Pt. i. 8: V. i. Pt. i. 6: x. 11 (觀省): xii. 4: xiii. 28: xxvii. 12 (foll. by 于). = to prove, to evidence. IV. vi. 10. This idea may be traced also in I. 12; *et al.* = seeing, sights. V. xv. 12.

THE 148TH RADICAL. 角.

角
keŏ
chiao

A horn, horns. V. i. Pt. ii. 9.

THE 149TH RADICAL. 言

言
yen

To say, to speak; to speak about. II. i. 24: ii. 10: iii. 3: IV. iv. 1: viii. Pt. i. 1, 2; Pt. ii. 12: V. xiv. 26: xv. 5; *et sæpe*. 讒言, to defame. IV. viii. Pt. iii. 3. To talk, used contemptuouly, I. 10. We have often 言曰, to speak, saying, and the formula 有言曰. *E. g.* IV. v. Pt. i. 5: vii. Pt. i. 13; V. i. Pt. iii. 4: iv. 2, 3: x. 12. Words. II. ii. 3, 16, 17, 21. = reports. II. i. 9: iv. 7. = compositions. II. iv. 5. 納言, the designation of Shun's minister of communication. II. i. 25. 五言 seems to = 五聲, the five notes of music, in II. iv. 4. 庶言 = notifications, in V. xix. 13. 言 alone, in V. iv. 6, = speech; and in xix. 17, 一言 = a speech, or a single remark. Of phrases with 言, we have 昌言, II. iv. 1; *et al.*; 食言, to eat one's words, be false to them, IV. i. 4; 聖言, IV. iv. 7; 辯言, v. Pt. iii. 9; 矢言, vii. Pt. i. 1; 逸言, vii. Pt. i. 7, and 箴言 and 浮言, both in p. 10; 敷言, V. iv. 15, 16; 流言, to set words flowing, to raise a rumour, V. 7 : xviii. 1; 德言, ix. 5; 誨言, xiii. 4; 側言, xvii. 7; 徽言, xix. 17; 謅言, xxx. 5.

討
t'aou
t'ao

To punish. II. iii. 6.

訓
hsun
hsün

(1) To instruct, to admonish, to lesson. It is generally foll. by 于. E. g. IV. iv. 1, 7 : viii. Pt. iii. 2 : V. v. 1. But not always,—as in V. ix. 5 : xv. 14 (訓告), 15. To be instructed in. V. iv. 16 : xix. 20. Obs. 諸子訓人, V. ix. 17 : 非民攸訓, xv. 13; 審訓, xxii. 4. A lesson, instructions. III. iii. 4, 6 : iv. 2 : IV. v. Pt. i. 9 (n. b.); Pt. ii. 3 : vii. Pt. i. 6 : V. iv. 15 (n. b.) : viii. 4; et sæpe. 大訓, the great lesson, was some relic of antiquity. V. xxii. 19.. (2) To follow. V. xxiv. 14. So, in 嗣訓, xxii. 24. This meaning may be derived from the passive use of the character above. (3) To approve. V. xxiii. 5.

訖
keih
chi

(1) All, entirely. V. xiii. 2. To reach to entirely. xxviii. 11 (n. b.) : III. i. Pt. ii. 23 (foll. by 于). (2) To extinguish, IV. x. 2.

記
ke
chi

(1) To record. V. xiii. 7. (2) To make remember. II. iv. 6.

訛
go
o

To transform. 南訛, transformations of the summer. I. 6.

訟
sung

To be wrangling or quarrelsome. I. 9. To wrangle about. IV. vii. Pt. i. 7.

訪
fang

To consult, to inquire of. V. iv. 1 (foll. by 于).

設
shě
shê

To set up ; to establish. IV. vii. Pt. ii. 2 (設中) : viii. Pt. ii. 22 : V. xxii. 14.

許
heu
hsü

To grant, to concede to. V. vi. 8.

詈
le
li

To rail at, to revile. V. xv. 17, 18.

詔
chaou
chao

To announce to, to tell, = to advise. IV. xi. 7. 無詔, p. 8, = with none to appeal to.

詛
tsoo
tsu

To curse. 詛祝, V. xv. 15. 詛盟, oaths and covenants. V. xxvii. 4.

詠
yung

To make music,—as an accompaniment to the voice. II. iv. 9.

詢
seun
hsün

To consult with ; to consult on. II. i. 3, 15 (foll. by 于) : ii. 16, 18 (弗詢之謀) V. xxx. 4 (猷詢)

試
she
shih

To try ; to test ; to make the experiment. I. 11, 12 : II. i. 9 : IV. vii. Pt. ii. 6, 17.

詩
she
shih

Poetry. II. i. 24. A piece of poetry, a poem. V. vi. 15.

詰
k'ëĕ
ch'ieh

(1) To punish. V. xx. 11. (2) To keep in good condition or order. xix. 22. (3) To restrain. xxvii. 1.

話
hwa
hua

To address,—with a kindly feeling, IV. vii. Pt. ii. 1. 一話, one word, = every word. V. xix. 17.

詳
ts'ëang
hs'iang

To pay attention to, watch over. V. xvii. 7.

誅
choo
chu

To cut off, to destroy. V. i. Pt. i. 9. Used as a noun in III. iv. 4,—先王之誅, the death appointed by the former kings.

誓
she
shih

To make a speech or solemn declaration to, to address. II. ii. 20 : V. i. Pt. i. 2; Pt. ii. 1; Pt. iii. 4. A speech. V. xxx. 1. 誓言, IV. i. 4. = solemnly. III. ii. 2 : xxii. 4.

誘
yew
yu

To lead on. V. vii. 10. In a bad sense, = to decoy. V. xxx. 4.

誕
tan

(1) To make great, to increase. V. xviii. 4. The term is often used adverbially, = greatly. E. g. II. ii. 21 : IV. iii. 1 : vii. Pt. ii. 1, 7 : V. i. Pt. iii. 4, 5 : iii. 5 : vii. 4, 13, 15. Obs. 誕惟, V. x. 11, which some would make to be merely an initial phrase. (2) To be disorderly or dissolute. V. xv. 2.

誚
ts'ëaou
ch'iao

To blame. V. vi. 15.

誠
ching
ch'eng

To be sincere. 克誠 = the sincere. IV. v. Pt. iii. 1.

誣
woo
wu

To make false pretensions to. 矯誣, IV. ii. 3.

誤
woe
wu

To err. V. xix. 18, 21.

誥
kaou
kao

To announce to, to make an announcement. IV. v. Pt. iii. 1 (foll. by 于) : viii. Pt. i. 2 : V. vii. 1 : ix. 1 : x. 2 (誥毖), 4 (誥教), 12, 14 : xii. 8 (誥告) ; xiii. 30 ; xvi. 20, 22 : xviii. 13 (誥告), 20, 30 : xxiii. 4. An announcement. IV. ii. 2 : iii. 2 : and in the titles of several Books.

誨
hwuy
hui

To teach. 教誨, V. xv. 14. Instructions. IV. viii. Pt. i. 5. 誨言, instructive words. V. xiii. 4.

說
shwŏ
shuo

To speak. 讒說, slanderous talkers, II. i. 25 : iv. 6.   = words. V. vi. 16. 德之說, words or discourse about virtue. V. ix. 21.
The prime minister of Woo-ting, of the Shang dynasty. Everywhere in IV. viii.

說
yuĕ
yüeh

誰
shwuy
shui

Who? II. iv. 7.

請
ts'ing
ch'ing

To request, beg leave. IV. iii. 4.

論
lun

(1) To discourse of. V. xx. 5. (2) Orderly relation, the order of antecedence and sequence. V. xxvii. 19.

諛
yu
yü

To flatter, be a flatterer. V. xxvi. 6.

諞
p'ëen
p'ien

諞言, artful sayings. V. xxx. 5.

諟
she
shih

To judge, consider. 顧諟, IV. v. Pt. i. 2.

諧
heae
hsieh

To be harmonious. I. 12 : II. i. 24 : iii. 1 : iv. 10 (perhaps = to be made harmonious). To make harmonious, to manage harmoniously, or suitably to the requirements of the case. II. i. 21, 22 : ii. 18.

諫
këen
chien

To remonstrate. IV. iv. 3 : IV. viii. Pt. i. 1 (foll. by 于 = with). Remonstrance, reproof. IV. iv. 3 : viii. Pt. i. 11. 諫輔 = the reprover and helper. V. i. Pt. ii. 5.

諴
han

(1) Sincerity. II. ii. 21. (2) To make harmonious (foll. by 于). V. xii. 13.

諶
shin
shĕn

To trust, to rely on. IV. vi. 2 : V. xvi. 4.

諸
choo
chu

(1) A preposition,—by, in, of, from. IV. v. Pt. iii. 7 : viii. Pt. i. 4 : V. vi. 17 : xvii. 1. (2) All, various ;—little more than a sign of the plural. V. ix. 17 : x. 15 : xxvii. 19. (3) In the phrase 諸侯, the various feudal princes of the empire. IV. i. Pt. ii. 19 : V. xx. 14 : xxii. 29 : xxiii. 1.
Village slang. To become addicted to such. V. xv. 3.

諺
yen

謀
mow
mou

To consult ; to consult with. II. i. 18 (詢謀) : V. iv. 25 (foll. by 及). 謀面, to judge by the face. V. xix. 2. To plan, to consult for. IV. vii. Pt. ii. 7 ; Pt. iii. 10 : V. xviii. 17.   = deliberation. V. iv. 6, 34. 謀人, counsellors. V. xxx. 6. Plans. II. ii. 6, 16 : IV. vii. Pt. i. 8 ; Pt. iii. 7 : V. ix. 22 (非謀, bad plans):

xii. 12 : xix. 15 : xx. 16 : xxi. 6 : xxviii. 1 (猷謀).

謂
wei

To say. IV. vii. Pt. iii. 5 : V. i. Pt. ii. 5. To be called. IV. ii. 8 : iv. 7 : viii. Pt. ii. 11. The idiomatic use of 之謂, = to be called, occurs only once ;—in V. iv. 26 ; and it may there be easily resolved, so as to give 之 its proper signification of *of*.

謙
k'ëen
ch'ien

Humility. II. ii. 21.

謨
moo
mu

Counsels. II. iii. 1 : IV. iv. 8 : V. xxv. 6 ; and in the titles of some Books. 謨訓, well-counselled instructions. IV. iv. 2.

謬
mew
miu

Errors. 糾謬, V. xxvi. 3.

謹
kin
chin

To give careful attention to. III. iv. 2 : IV. vii. Pt. i. 3.

譁
hwa
hua

To make a noise. V. xxviii. 1 : xxx. 1.

識
shih

To know, understand. V. xiii. 12.

識
che
chih

To remember, to keep a remembrance of. II. iv. 6.

議
e
i

To deliberate on. V. xx. 6.

譸
chow
chou

To deceive, impose on. 譸張, V. xv. 14, 18.

譽
yu
yü

Praise. II. ii. 6 : V. ix. 17.

變
pëen
pien

To change (act. and neut.); to be changed. I. 2 : IV. v. Pt. i. 8 : vii. Pt. i. 7 : V. xv. 15 : xxi. 14 : xxiv. 3.

讎
ch'ow
ch'ou

To be an enemy. V. i. Pt. iii. 4 : IV. xi. 2 (敵讎). Hostile. V. xii. 24. = hateful. IV. xi. 7.

讒
ch'an

To calumniate. 讒說, slanderous talkers. II. i. 25 : iv. 6. 讒言, to defame. IV. vii. Pt. iii. 2.

讓
jang

To yield ; to yield to, or in behalf of. I. 1 (*n. b.*) : II. i. 3, 17, 21, 22. 23 (foll. by 于) : iv. 2 (= to be humble), 9 : V. xvi. 20 : xx. 20.

THE 150TH RADICAL. 谷.

谷
kuh
ku

A valley. 暘谷, the Bright valley, somewhere in the remotest east. I. 4. 昧谷, the Dark valley, somewhere in the remotest north. I. 6.

THE 151st RADICAL. 豆.

豆
tow
tou

A vessel for containing flesh. 豆
籩, sacrificial vessels. V. iii. 3.

嘗
k'e
ch'i

How ? III. iii. 5 : IV. vii. Pt. ii. 9.

豐
fung

(1) To be abundant, excessive. IV. ix.
5. Superior,—in quality. V. xxiv. 1.
(2) The name of king Wǎn's capital. V.
iii. 2 : xxii. 17.

THE 152d RADICAL. 豕.

豕
ch'e
ch'ih

A pig. V. xii. 5.

象
sëany
hsiang

(1) To resemble, have the appearance
of. I. 10 : V. viii. 1. To delineate, represent. I. 3 (歷象) : II. i. 11 : iv. 8.
A likeness delineated. IV. viii. Pt. i. 3.
The emblematic figures on the emperor's
robes. II. iv. 4. 天象, heavenly
figures. III. iv. 4. (2) Shun's half brother. II. i. 12.

豬
choo
chu

I. q. 豬, a lake, a receptacle of waters.
(1) To *inlake*,—to form into a lake. III.
i. Pt. i. 30, 38, 56. (2) 孟豬, Pt. i.
57, and 豬野, p. 77, are the names of
lakes.

豫
yu
yü

(1) To allow one's-self in pleasure or
idle dissipation. IV. v. Pt. ii. 6 : V. xxi. 3.
Pleasure, dissipation. III. iii. 1 : IV. viii.
Pt. ii. 2 : V. ix. 6. Indolence. V. iv. 34.
(2) To be comfortable,—used in reference to a state of sickness. V. vi. 1. (3)
豫州, one of Yu's provinces. III. i. Pt.
i. 54.

THE 153d RADICAL. 豸.

貊
mih
mai

I. q. 貉. The rude tribes of the north.
蠻貊, V. iii. 6.

貌
maou
mao

The appearance, demeanour. V. iv. 6 :
xxvii. 17.

貍
le
li

Probably the jackal. III. i. Pt. i. 69.

貔
pe
pi

A kind of leopard or panther. Soldiers
are exhorted to be such. V. ii. 9.

THE 154th RADICAL. 貝.

貝
pei

(1) Creatures of the sea, with beautiful shells. Used for those shells.   =
tortoise-shell. V. xxii. 16 (文貝), 19.

= cowries. IV. vii. Pt. ii. 14.   (2)
Variegated silks. III. i. Pt. i. 44. But
the meaning is uncertain. I should
almost be inclined to interpret the character of cowries.

貞
ching
chĕng

(1) To be—to become—correct and
firm. IV. v. Pt. iii. 8 : V. v. 5 : xxv. 1. To
be of the correct amount. III. i. Pt. 18.
Solidity. V. iv. 22. (2) To sustain duties
or responsibility. V. xiii. 4.

負
hoo
hu

To bear on the back. 負罪, to
bear—assume to one's-self—the burden of
guilt. II. ii. 21.

財
ts'ae
ts'ai

Treasures, wealth. V. iii. 9. In 財
賦, III. i. Pt. ii. 15, 財 seems to mean
the material wealth or resources.

貢
kung

(1) To present as tribute,—the contribution of an inferior to a superior. V.
v. 1. Articles of tribute. III. i. Pt. i.
i. 19, *et passim.* (2) To advance, to go
forward. V. xxii. 9 (foll. by 于).

貧
p'in

Poverty. V. iv. 40.

貨
ho
huo

Goods, property; wealth. IV. ii. 5 (貨
利) : iv. 7 : vii. Pt. iii. 10, 12 (貨寶) :
V. iv. 7 ; ix. 15.   = bribes. V. xxvi. 8 :
xxvii. 12, 16, 21 (獄貨).

貫
kwan
kuan

To be strung together. 貫盈, to
be full. V. i. l't. i. 9.

責
tsih
tsò

(1) To reprove. V. xxx. 2. (2) To
give in charge ; to lay a charge on. IV.
x. 6 ; V. xvi. 16. A charge. V. vi. 5.

貳
urh

(1) To be double-minded. III. iii. 1.
貳適, V. xiv. 15. (2) To assist,—
act as seconds to. V. xx. 6.

貴
kwei
kuei

To value, count valuable. V. v. 8 :
xxiv. 8.

貽
e
i

To transmit.   = to hand down. III.
iii. 8 : V. xii. 19.   = to send to. V. vi.
15.

賁
pun
pên

虎賁, life-guards. V. xxii. 11. The
officer or officers commanding are also
thus denominated. xix. 1, 8.

賁
fun
fên

Great. 玆賁 = this great inheritance. IV. vii. Pt. iii. 7.

賁
pe
pi

To be ornamented.   = elegant institutions. V. vii. 2.   = brilliantly. IV. iii. 5.

資
tsze
tzŭ

To have property. V. xxiv. 1. 資
澤 = resources of bounty. V. xxviii. 2.

賈
koo
ku

To traffic. 服賈, to pursue the
business of traffic.—In Index III. to
Mencius, this character is defined—'a
stationary trafficker or merchant.' Such
is the account given of it in the dict., in
distinction from 商 ; but this instance

in the Shoo rather points to the idea of travelling about and trafficking.

賊 *tsih* tsei

To injure,—probably to death. **寇賊**, II. i. 20: V. xxvii. 2. **賊虐**, V. i. Pt. ii. 15. **賊刑**, to punish capitally. II. i. 11.

賓 *pin*

(1) To receive guests. II. i. 2 (*n. b.*): V. xiv. 22. = the entertainment of guests. V. iv. 7. To receive as a guest, —respectfully. I. 4. A guest, guests. II. iv. 9 : V. viii. 1 : xiii. 29. **賓階**, the guests' steps,—the steps on the western side of a hall or platform. V. xxii. 20, 22, 23. The term is used for the princes all appearing at court. V. xxiii. 1. This idea is likewise in II i. 2. (2) To come and acknowledge subjection. V. v. 2.

賚 *lae* lai

To confer to; to bestow gifts,—sometimes nearly = to reward. IV. i. 4 : viii. Pt. i. 2 : V. iii. 8 : xvii. 23 : xxviii. 4 : xxix. 4.

賞 *shang*

To reward; rewards. II. ii. 12 : III. ii. 5 : IV. ii. 5 : V. i. Pt. iii. 4 : xxiii. 3.

賡 *kĕng*

To continue. Obs. **賡歌**, II. iv. 11.

賢 *hĕen* hsien

(1) To be possessed of superior virtue and talents. Used generally for men of worth. II. ii. 3, 6 : IV. ii. 6, 7 : V. iii. 9; *et sæpe.* In V. i. Pt. iii. 3, we have the phrase **賢人**. Obs. **惟賢**, in V. xxiv. 8. (2) To be superior to—surpass —others. II. ii. 14. So, **自賢**, p. 20. (3) In a name,—**巫賢**, a minister of the Shang dynasty. V. xvi. 7.

賤 *tsëen* chien

To contemn, consider vile. V. v. 8.

賦 *foo* fu

Revenue, contribution of revenue. III. i. Pt. i. 8; *et passim.* Obs. **財賦**, Pt. ii. 18.

賴 *lae* lai

To depend on. II. ii. 8 : IV. v. Pt. ii. 3 : V. xxiv. 13 : xxvi. 3 : xxvii. 13.

贄 *che* chih

Articles of introduction,—gifts to prepare the way for an audience. II. i. 8.

贊 *tsan*

To assist. II. ii. 21. **贊贊**, to be assiduously assisting. II. iii. 8.

贖 *shuh* shu

To redeem. **贖刑**, II. i. 11.

THE 155TH RADICAL. **赤**.

赤 *ch'ih*

(1) To be red ; red. III. i. Pt. i. 33 : V. xxii. 19. (2) **赤子**, an infant. V. ix. 9.

赦 *shay* shĕ

To forgive. II. i. 11 : IV. i. 4 : iii. 14. 8. **無赦**, without mercy. III. iv. 4 : V. ix. 16. To remit a certain amount of penalty or punishment. V. xxvii. 17, 18.

THE 156TH RADICAL. **走**.

走 *tsow* tsou

To run. III. iv. 4. **奔走**, to hurry about,—generally on service. V. iii. 3 : x. 6 : xiv. 22 : xvi. 9 : xviii. 24.

起 *k'e* ch'i

To rise. V. vi. 19. **起居**, rising up and sitting down. V. xxvi. 2. To rise flourishingly. II. iv. 1. As an active verb,—to raise up; to produce; to give occasion to. IV. vii. Pt. i. 7 ; Pt. ii. 8 : viii. Pt. ii. 4.

越 *yuĕ* yüeh

(1) To pass over. This = to transgress. IV. vii. Pt. ii. 16 (**顛越**): V. Pt. i. 7 (*n. b.* **越厥志**). = to frustrate. IV. v. Pt. i. 5. = to leave one's place. V. xxix. 4. (2) The idea of *passing over* takes various forms, in which the character is used as a conjunction, such as—*moreover, further.* V. x. 3, 10: xviii. 25 : xxii. 19 ; and with these should be classed the instances of **亦越**, V. xix. 4, 6, 15 :—*reaching on to,* = *and,* V. i. Pt. i. 2 : vii. 1, 6, 7, 8, 13 : ix. 17, 18 ; *et sæpissime ;—thereon, so that,* IV. vii. Pt. i. 11 ; *et al. ;—after, in phrases of time,* V. iii. 1, 3 : xii. 1, 3, 5, 6 ;—*in the case of.* V. x. 5, 11 : xxvii. 3 : xxviii. 1 ; *et al. ;—* after active verbs, carrying them on to their object. IV. vii. Pt. iii. 6. (3) To give out orders. V. xi. 2. (4) To throw down, to assault violently. V. ix. 15.— There are not a few instances, in which we hardly know how to translate this character, which is of very frequent occurrence. *E. g.* IV. ix. 1 : xi. 2 : V. vii. 11 (**越印**): xii. 2 (**越若來**), 8.

趣 *ts'ow* ts'ou

趣馬, equerries. V. xix. 8.

趨 *ts'en* ch'ü

To go quickly. **趨出**, hastily withdrew. V. xxiii. 7.

THE 157TH RADICAL. **足**.

足 *tsuh* tsu

(1) The foot. IV. viii. Pt. i. 8. (2) To be sufficient. IV. ii. 4 : V. i. Pt. ii. 3, 5. To be sufficient for one's requirements. V. v. 8.

距 *k'eu* ch'ü

(1) To reach to. II. iv. 1. (1) To oppose, withstand. III. i. Pt. ii. 17 : iii. 2.

跣 *sëen* hsien

To walk barefoot. IV. viii. Pt. i. 8.

路 *loo* lu

A path, a way. III. iv. 3 : V. iv. 14.

踐
tsëen
ch'ien   To tread in, to pursue. V. viii. 3.

蹂
yu
yü   To pass—jump—over. V. xxix. 4.

蹈
ta'ou
t'ao   To tread on. V. xxv. 2.

蹌
ts'ëang
ch'iang   蹌蹌, to fall moving. II. iv. 9.

THE 158TH RADICAL. 身.

身
shin
shĕn   (1) The body. V. xxiii. 6. But the material body is seldom what is expressed by the character. It rather = one's person, one's self. II. iii. 1 : IV. iv. 7, 8 : v. Pt. ii. 4 : vii. Pt. i. 12, 17 : V. iv. 26 : vi. 5 ; *et sæpe.* 修身, self-cultivation, occurs more than once. We also have 檢身, to govern one's person, V. iv. 5. Obs 酣身, V. x. 11 ; and 在身, V. xxvii. 11.

躬
kung   This is synonymous with the last, and used commonly for one's person. *E. g.* II. ii. 14 : IV. vi. 3 : viii. Pt. ii. 4 ; Pt. iii. 4 : V. ii. 10. 尹躬, I, Yin. IV. v. Pt. i. 2, 3. 朕躬 = me, my case. V. xxviii. 2.

THE 159TH RADICAL. 車.

車
keu
chü   A carriage, a cart. II. i. 9 : iv. 7 : V. x. 6 : xvii. 1.

輅
loo
lu   An imperial carriage. V. xxii. 20.

載
tsae
tsai   (1) To do ; to complete. II. iii. 3 ; iv. 2 (nearly unintelligible). To do service to. II. ii. 21. To perform service on. III. i. Pt. i. 3. Undertakings. II. i. 17. (2) To convey, transport ; to contain. V. xx. 8 (載爾僞). That which is conveyed or contained : = a cargo. IV. vii. Pt. ii. 6 ; = a record. V. xiii. 8.

載
tsae
tsai   2d tone. A year, years. I. 11, 12 : II. i. 3, 9, '13, 27, 28 : ii. 9 : iv. 1 : III. i. Pt. i. 18.

輔
foo
fu   To assist. III. iv. 2 : IV. i. 4 : V. i. Pt. ii. 5 : *et al.* 四輔, V. xiii. 20, means to help the empire,—the four quarters, on every side.

輕
k'ing
ch'ing   (1) Light, = that which is lighter. V. xxvii. 19. (2) To slight. IV. v. Pt. ii. 5. To deal lightly with. II. ii. 12.

輯
ts'eih
ch'i   (1) To collect. II. i. 7. (2) To harmonize. IV. iii. 6 (輯寧).

輸
hoo
hu   To report,—to a higher authority. V. xxvii. 20.

THE 160TH RADICAL. 辛.

辛
sin
hsin   (1) Acrid. V. iv 5. (2) The 8th of the calendaric stem-characters. Used alone in II. iv. 8.

辜
koo
ku   A transgression, guilt ; guilty. V. x. 3 (酒惟辜), 11. The character generally occurs with negative adverbs, 不, 非, 無, the phrase meaning guiltless and guiltlessness. II. ii. 12 : IV. ii. 4 : iii. 3 : viii. Pt. iii. 10 : xi. 12 : V. ix. 8 ; *et al.* To proceed to guilt. V. iv. 3. To hold to be guilty. V. xxvi. 8.

辟
peih
pi   (1) A sovereign, a prince. It is generally used in application to the emperor, as in IV. v. Pt. i. 2 : vi. 1 : V. iv. 18, &c. ; but it is used of all the princes of the empire in 百辟, V. xiii. 12, and 羣辟, xx. 1. To play the sovereign, to rule over ; sovereignship. IV. v. Pt. i. 3 (辟不辟) ; Pt. ii. 2 : V. xiii. 18 : xv. 18. (2) Rules, laws,—used in the phrase 定辟, settler of the rules or boundaries. V. x. 13. To this use the character in V. vi. 13 may also be reduced, making it = 'to take the law to.'

辟
p'eih
p'i   (1) To punish ; punishments. V. xi. 3. 致辟, to carry punishment to the extreme, = to put to death. xvii. 1. 宮辟, castration, and 大辟, death : xxvii. 18. Obs. 在辟, in xxi. 8, and 辟以止辟乃辟, p. 9. (2) 便辟 mean persons who are guided in the advice they give by the likes and dislikes of those they advise. V. xxvi. 4.

辭
ts'ze
tz'û   (1) Words. = instructions, orders. II. ii. 20 : V. vii. 10 (沈辭, hardly intelligible) : x. 16 (教辭) : xxiv. 8. = purposes. V. xxx. 5. (2) Pleas, statements and arguments in a case at law. V. xxvii. 15 (obs. 五辭), 18, 20, 21. Akin to this is its signification when foll. by 于, of complaints, xxvii. 7, 12 ; and that of excuses, apologies. V. xiii. 10 : xiv. 5, 12 : xxvii. 3. (3) Fame. V. xxi. 14 : xxvii. 22 ; and perhaps IV. v. Pt. i. 7. (4) *I. q* 辤, to decline. II. ii. 18.

辯
piēn
pien

(1) To dispute. 辯言, IV. v. Pt. iii. 9. (2) To rule, to manage right. V. x. 17.

THE 161st RADICAL. 辰.

辰
shin
ch'ên

(1) The heavenly bodies. The three 辰 are the sun, moon, and stars; and though we have not the phrase 二辰 in the Shoo, it seems the simplest way to take 辰 thus in the important passage, III. iv. 4, of the sun and moon. (2) The zodiacal spaces, within which occur the conjunctions of the sun and moon;—in the phrase 星辰, I. 3: V. iv. 8. In II. iv. 2, the phrase is perhaps simply = the stars. (3) 五辰 = the seasons, as associated with the five elements. II. iii. 4. (4) The fifth of the calendaric branch-characters. V. iii. 1: xiii. 29.

農
nung
nêng

(1) Husbandry. IV. vii. Pt. i. 9, 11: V. xiii. 13. 農炎, the minister of agriculture. V. x. 13. (2) = largely; earnestly. V. iv. 4: xxvii. 8.

THE 162d RADICAL. 辵.

迂
yu
yü

To make crooked, to pervert. IV. vii. Pt. ii. 8.

近
kin
chin

To approach to. V. iv. 16. = to cherish. III. iii. 4.

迓
ya

To meet. = to receive. V. xxii. 6. To go to meet: = to anticipate, IV. vii. Pt. ii. 9: = to rush on, V. ii. 9: = to hasten to accomplish, V. xiii. 16.

迤
e
i

To proceed in a winding way. III. i. Pt. ii. 9.

迪
tёih
ti

(1) The *right* path. II. ii. 5. To pursue the right path. II. iv. 8. To pursue the path of, tread in the steps of. II. iii. 1: IV. viii. Pt. i. 9: x. 3: V. i. Pt. i. 10; *et al.* It is used adverbially, with this meaning, before 知, V. vii. 13: xvi. 19; bef. 哲, xv. 16; bef. 畏, x. 9. Observe 不迪 = unprincipled men,—men who do not pursue the right path. IV. vii. Pt. ii. 16; 汝罔能迪, p. 12; and 出迪, IV. xi. 5. (2) To direct, to lead forward; to develope. IV. v. Pt. i. 5. (啓迪): vi. 3 (*id.*): V. vii. 1: ix. 20, 21: x. 4; *et sæpe.* = to intimate to. IV. vii. Pt. ii. 14. Obs. 殷之迪諸臣, the officers of Yin who have been

led to it. V. x. 15. (3) To advance, to bring forward. We have 迪簡, in V. xiv. 20: xviii. 28. Perhaps the simplest way of taking 不迪 in V. ii. 6, is with this meaning.—迪 is one of the characteristic words of the Shoo, and there is no other perhaps with which a translator has so little satisfaction.

To narrate, relate. III. iii. 3.

逃
shuh
shu

To be erring; to go astray. II. i. 2: ii. 20: III. iv. 4: IV. v. Pt. i. 9: V. xv. 13 (迷亂): xvi. 17: xx. 16. 迷民, the deluded people. V. xi. 7. To err in the matter of, to come short of. 迷于, V. xiii. 16.

迷
me
mi

Footsteps, traces. V. iii. 5 (王迹, the traces of imperial sway): xix. 22. Obs. 邁迹自身 = to pursue vigorously one's own path.

迹
tseih
chi

To pursue,—to take in the past. III. iii. 9. Used adverbially, and with the same reference to the past. V. xxv. 6: xxviii. 3.

追
chuy
chui

To retire, withdraw. II. iv. 5: V. xiii. 18.

退
t'uy
t'ui

Always in combination with 逋. To run away, to abscond. V. xxix. 4. = runaways, vagabonds. V. ii. 6: iii. 6.

逃
t'aou
t'ao

(1) To rebel against, to oppose. II. ii. 21: IV. 7. To be contrary to. IV. v. Pt. iii. 7 (foll. by 于). = rebelliousness, evil. II. ii. 8. To oppose,—in deliberation, or divination. V. iv. 27–30. (2) To meet. V. vi. 18: xxii. 11. = to accord with. xxvii. 13. (3) 逆河, the meeting Ho,—a name given to the Ho, where it entered the sea. III. i. Pt. ii. 7.

逆
yih
yi

To abscond. See 逃. 逋臣, vagabond ministers. V. vii. 6.

逋
poo
pu

To pursue. V. xxix. 4.

逐
chuh
chu

Far. V. ii. 1: xiv. 1 (退逖): xviii. 29 (離逖).

逖
tёih
ti

To carry through. 通道, to open roads. V. v. 1. Intercommunication. 地天通, the communication between earth and Heaven. V. xxvii. 6.

通
t'ung

To go, to put in motion. V. vii. 11 (*n. b.*).

逝
she
shih

To accelerate, to hasten. IV. v. Pt. ii. 3: V. x. 11: xviii. 23. Speedily. V. ix. 16, 17.

速
suh
su

造
tsaou
tsao

(1) To begin. IV. iv. 2. This is the meaning, probably, in 凡我造邦, IV. iii. 7; 新造邦, in V. xvi. 10; and 嗣造, V. xxviii. 2. Obs. 肇造, V. ix. 4. (2) To do; doings. V. vii. 1, 8. Perhaps we may bring under this 耉造德, in V. xvi. 16. (3) To seek for, with reference to. V. ix. 17.

造
ts'aou
ts'ao

To arrive. to come. IV. vii. Pt. ii. 1. The plaintiff and defendant in a suit are called 兩造, the two comparing parties. V. xxvii. 15.

逢
fung
fung

To meet with. V. iv. 26.

遧
hwan
huan

To escape. IV. v. Pt. ii. 3.

逮
tae
tai

To come to. V. xxvii. 6. 不逮, to be deficient; deficiencies. V. xx. 4: xxvi. 4: xxix. 5.

進
tsin
chin

To advance, to enter. IV. viii. Pt. ii. 1 (foll. by 于): V. xxiii. 2. Actively, to advance, to bring forward. IV. vii. Pt. ii. 2 (登進): V. xviii. 5: xxi. 13.

逸
yih
yi

(1) To exceed, to go to excess; to go to excess in,—generally with a bad meaning so that the term often = idleness, dissipation. II. ii. 6: iv. 16: V. x. 7, 9, 11: xv. 1, 3, 12: xviii. 4, 16, 29: *et al.* We have 逸言 and 逸口 = extravagant talk. IV. vii. Pt. i. 7, 12. The combination 逸豫, idleness and pleasure, is frequent. III. iii. 1: IV. viii. Pt. ii. 2: V. ix. 1; *et al.* 逸欲, idleness and lusts. II. iii. 5. = errors. IV. vii. Pt. ii. 8. Sometimes 逸 is used as = to enjoy ease,—in a good sense. IV. vii. Pt. i. 14: V. xiv. 5: xv. 2: xx. 18. The sense is indifferent in V. xv. 7. Obs. V. xix. 5, and 逸厥逸, carried his luxurious ease to the utmost, in xviii. 16. (2) The name of a Recorder. V. xiii. 29, 30.

逾
yü
yü

(1) To cross. V. iii. 19: in III. i. Pt. i. 53, 70; Pt. ii. 1, where it is foll. by 于, in two of the instances at least, it must mean to cross the country to. (2) To transgress. V. xxii. 6. (3) 逾邁, to pass away,—spoken of time. V. xxx. 2.

遂
suy
sui

(1) To accomplish. 底遂 = great deeds. IV. xi. 1. (2) To give free course to. IV. ii. 7. (3) Thereon, and so. IV. xi. 2: V. v. 1. (4) Name of the country to a certain extent beyond the 郊 of a state. 三郊三遂, V. xxix. 5.

遇
yu
yü

To meet with. It occurs only once, —in IV. vii. Pt. ii. 16, in a passage which is hardly intelligible.

遊
yew
yu

To wander about,—generally in a bad sense, thus wasting the time and neglecting duties. We have 慢遊, II. iv. 8; 盤遊, III. iii. 1: and 遊畋, IV. iv. 7. To make excursions. V. xv. 11, 12. Obs. 遊于逸, II. ii. 6.

運
yun
yün

To go round, = to act incessantly. II. ii. 4.

過
kwo
kuo

1st tone. To pass by. III. i. Pt. ii. 4, 7, 8, 9, 12: V. iii. 6.

過
kwo
kuo

3d tone. To go beyond. An error, a fault,—the idea of inadvertence is generally in the term. II. ii. 12: IV. ii. 5; viii. Pt. ii. 9: V. i. Pt. ii. 7. 五過, the five cases of error. V. xxvii. 15, 16.

遏
gŏ
o

To stop. IV. iii. 6. We have 遏密, II. i. 13; 遏佚, V. xvi. 3; 遏絶, xxvii. 5, 率遏 = to exhaust. IV. i. 3.

遐
hëa
hsia

Far. IV. v. Pt. iii. 4. 遐棄, to reject and put far off. III. iv. 4. 遐終, to put far away and make an end of. V. xii. 10. 遐逖, V. xiv 21. To have leisure. V. xv. 10.

遑
hwang
huang

道
ts'ëw
ch'iu

遒人 = a herald. III. iv. 3.

道
taou
tao

(1) A road, a path. V. v. 1. In V. iv. 14, it also means a path or way, and is synonymous with 路. It is there, however, used metaphorically, and we may pass from it to the use of it in the sense of ways or courses of life and conduct. III. iii. 7: V. xvi. 6: xxiii. 5: xxiv. 9. It is used often with reference to Heaven, —the way it follows and the way it approves. II. ii. 21: IV. ii. 9: iii. 3: viii. Pt. ii. 2: V. i. Pt. iii. 2: xxiv. 9. Then 道 means the way which is right, in acc. with Heaven's will, and the path of duty for man. II. ii. 6, 20: IV. v. Pt. iii. 2, 7: viii. Pt. i. 2: V. v. 7: xxiv. 3. Obs. 道心, the affinity of the mind for the right. II. ii. 15. 有道, the right-acting, or the principled. V. viii. 6. I have translated 道 by *principles* in xx. 5, but the idea is rather—courses of govt., the right underlying them. (2) To conduct by their proper courses. III. i. Pt. i. 13, 23, 49, 64. (3) To speak. 道極 =

to confess unreservedly. V. ix. 8. 道
揚, xxii. 24.

達
tă
ta

(1) To reach to. Gen. foll. by 于, II.
iii. 7 (*n. b.*): III. i. Pt. i. 20, 27, 36, 45, 61:
V. xi. 1 (*n. b.*): xxii. 5. 達四聰=
to hear with the ears of all. II. i. 15.
=everywhere. V. xii. 4. (2) To get
forward. V. xxx. 7.

違
wei

(1) To oppose, to go contrary to. II.
ii. 6: IV. vii. Pt. iii. 7: V. iv. 31 (foll.
by 于): vii. 7: xvii. 3: xxi. 14: xxx. 7.
= to be disobedient to, the object
being understood from the context. I. 10:
II. iv. 5: V. xiv. 18: xv. 15: xvi. 3: xix.
13: xxii. 5: xxx. 5. = rebellion, or the
rebellious. V. x. 13. (2) To avoid. IV.
v. Pt. ii. 3.

遘
kow
kou

To meet with. In reference to sickness.—V. vi. 5: xiii. 27.

遜
sun
shün

(1) To accord with. IV. v. Pt. iii. 7
(foll. by 于). Obedience. V. xiv. 21,
22. To observe—to be observed—docilely. II. i. 19. = humble. IV viii. Pt.
iii. 4. (2) To be withdrawn, to be lying
hid. IV. xi. 3.

遠
yuen
yüan

To be distant; what is distant; the
distant. V. i. Pt. ii. 5: v. 8 (遠物=
foreign things): xxii. 8: xxviii. 4: II.
i. 16: *et al.* 無遠, without respect
to distance. II. ii. 21: IV. vii. Pt. i. 16:
V. v. 2: xiii. 13. 遠省, to examine
what is long past. V. vii. 10. 胥遠,
to become distant— alienated—from one
another. IV. vii. Pt. ii. 15. 遠猷,
to send one's plans far forward. V. ix.
22. = to put far away V. xviii. 29.
= to a distance. V. x. 6. = at a
distance. V. ix. 5.

遠
yuen
yüan

3d tone. To keep one's-self at a distance from. IV. iv. 7.

適
shih

(1) To proceed to. IV. vii. Pt. iii. 4
(foll. by 于): V. ix. 20: xiv. 5. Obs.
適輕 and 適重, in V. xxxvii. 19.
貳適 = two aims. V. xiv. 15. (2)
適爾, accidentally. V. ix. 8.
To lie concealed. IV. viii. Pt. iii. 1.
行適, to make one's escape. IV. xi. 9.

遯
tun
t'un

To follow, to walk in. IV. iv. 14.

遵
tsun

遷
ts'een
ch'ien

(1) To remove,—both act. and neut.
II. iii. 2: IV. vii. Pt. i. 1 (foll. by 于);
Pt. ii. 1, 4, 6, 17; Pt. iii. 1, 5: V. xiv.
18, 25: xxiv. 3. (2) To exchange. II.
iv. 2. (3) To be changed. V. xxi. 14.

選
seuen
hsüan

To select, = to approve of. IV. vii. Pt.
i. 14.

遹
yuh
yü

To transmit the ways of, to follow the
example of. V. ix. 5.

遺
wei
e
i

(1) To be left, to be remaining. V. ii.
6: xiv. 2: xxv. 2. (2) To leave neglected. II. ii. 3: V. i. Pt. i. 6: xii. 12. Obs.
遺育, to leave seed or posterity to
one. IV. vii. Pt. ii. 16.
3d tone. To leave to, to assign to. V.
vii. 3, 8. To this tone and meaning. V.
xxiii. 3, 6, should probably be referred.

遺
e
i

邁
mae
mai

(1) Vigorously. II. ii. 10: V. xvii. 3.
(2) To move forward,—= to attain, to
practise. IV. viii. Pt. ii. 2: V. xii. 15. To
be passing on,—spoken of the movement
of time. V. xxx. 3.

還
seuen
hsüan

= to retire. V. xxii. 10.

邇
urh

To be near to. IV. v. Pt. i. 9: V.
xxiv. 3. To approach to. IV. ii. 5. 嚮
邇, to be approached. IV. vii. Pt. i. 12.
What is near, the near. II. i. 16: iii. 1:
IV. v. Pt. iii. 4; *et al.* 邇人, people
at hand. V. v. 8.

THE 163D RADICAL. 邑.

邑
yih
yi

A city or town, cities. Used of the
capital,—IV. v. Pt. i. 3: vii. Pt. i. 3, 4;
Pt. ii. 5, 16; *et sæpe.* Used of other cities,
—III. iv. 1: IV. i. 3; *et sæpe.* = villages.
V. xiv. 25. = a State (?). V. iii. 7.

邦
pang

A State, a country. *Passim.* 有邦,
the possessors or princes of States. II. iii.
5: IV. v. Pt. ii. 5: V. xxvii. 14; *et al.*
萬邦, I. 2: II. iv. 1; *et al., sæpe,* is
used as a designation for the empire.
中邦, the middle region. III. i. Pt. ii.
15, probably denotes the empire proper,
the three interior domains of Yu. 邦
alone is sometimes = empire or dynasty,
as in V. xvi. 10: xx. 7—12; *et al.* In V.
iii. 3, 邦 must denote specially the
imperial domain. In V. ix. 1, we cannot
account for the character. 五邦 in
IV. vii. Pt. i. 3, is better understood as
five different regions, than *five States*. 家
and 邦, the Clan or Family and the
State, are often in contrast, as in IV. iii.
6, 7; *et al.* It is used as a verb, = to
invest with a country. V. xvii. 1.

邪
seay
hsieh

Wicked, depraved. V. viii. 2. That
which is evil. II. ii. 6.

郊
kĕaou
chiao

A certain extent of country, outside and around the capital city; borders, frontiers. V. ii. 1, 9: iii. 8: vi. 19: xxi. 1: xxiv. 1, 7. Observe 三 郊, V. xxix. 5. Used for the place of the sacrifices to Heaven and Earth in the suburbs. V. xii. 5. Used for those sacrifices. V. i. Pt. iii. 3.

郭
kŏ
kuo

郭 鄰, the name of a place. V. xvii. 1.

都
too
tu

(1) Used in Part II. as an exclamation. Oh! II. ii. 4: iii. 1, 2, 3: iv. 1, 2. (2) A capital. IV. viii. Pt. ii. 2: V. xxviii. 4. In V. xix. 9, it denotes the cities of the high nobles in the imperial domain. Obs. 幽 都, I. 7.

鄙
p'ei
p'i

To reduce to the condition of a border territory. V. vii. 4.

鄰
lin

(1) A neighbour, neighbours. IV. v. Pt. ii. 5: V. vii. 13. 四 鄰, the neighbouring States, all round. V. xvii. 6. The same phrase is applied to the emperor's ministers, II. iv. 5; and 鄰 alone, in p. 3. (2) 郭 鄰, see 郭.

THE 164TH RADICAL. 酉.

酉
yew
yu

The tenth of the calendaric branch-characters. V. xxii. 13.

配
p'ei

(1) To be the mate of; to correspond to. IV. v. Pt. iii. 3: V. xii. 14: xiv. 8: xxv. 6: xxvii. 11, 21. (2) To be assessors with,—in sacrifice. V. xvi. 8.

酒
tsew
chiu

Distilled spirits. III. iii. 6: iv. 1, 4: IV. viii. Pt. iii. 2 (酒 醴): xi. 1, 4: V. x. 2, 3, 4, 6, 8, 10, 13, 15, 17: xv. 13. 自 酒, to abandon one's-self to drink. V. x. 11.

酗
hen
hsü

To be furiously inebriated. Foll. by 于. IV. xi. 1, 4: V. i. Pt. ii. 3: xv. 13.

酢
ts'ŏ
ts'o

To offer a responsive (? repeated) sacrifice. V. xxii. 27.

酖
han

To be drunken. IV. iv. 7. Obs. 酖 身, V. x. 11.

酸
swan
suan

Sour. V. iv. 5.

醇
shun

Unadulterated spirits.　＝pure and clear. IV. viii. Pt. ii. 10.

醉
tsuy
tsui

To drink to excess. V. x. 4. In p. 7, it ＝ to drink freely.

醴
le
li

Sweet spirits,—the liquor in the state of fermentation. IV. viii. Pt. iii. 2.

THE 165TH RADICAL. 采.

采
tsae
tsai

(1) Affairs; to conduct affairs. I. 10: II. i. 17: III. 4. Observe 載 采 采, II. iii. 3; and 服 采, V. x. 13. (2) Colours. 五 采, II. iv. 4. (3) The cities and lands assigned to the ministers of the emperor in the domain of the nobles. III. i. Pt. ii. 19. (4) The 5th of the domains of the Chow dynasty. V. ix. 1.

釋
shih

To let go,—send from one's thoughts. II. ii. 10. To let go,—in shooting with a bow. IV. v. Pt. i. 7. ＝ to liberate. V. iii. 8: xviii. 1. To put off,—spoken with ref. to a cap. V. xxiii. 7. To remove, do away with. V. xvi. 6 (foll. by 于): xviii. 13.

THE 166TH RADICAL. 里.

里
le
li

(1) A place of residence. 宅 里, a neighbourhood. V. xxix. 7. 里 居, to be living in villages (＝ in retirement, V. x. 10.) (2) A measure of length. At present it is a little more than one third of an English mile. III. i. Pt. ii. 18—22.

重
chung

Heavy,—what is aggravated. V. xxvii. 19. As a verb, ＝ to attach importance to, IV. vii. Pt. i. 2: V. iii. 9; ＝ to deal severely with. II. ii. 12.

重
ch'ung

Aspirated, and 1st tone. (1) Repeated, more than one of the same kind. V. xxii. 5, 15—19. (2) 重 華, in II. i. 1, is probably the name of Shun. (3) An ancient minister, apparently of the time of Shun. V. xxvii. 6.

野
yay
yeh

Wild country, wilds. IV. viii. Pt. i. 3; Pt. iii. 1: V. iii. 2. The country,—away from court. II. ii. 3. 在 野 ＝ to be in obscurity. II. ii. 20. (2) 牧 野, the scene of the battle between king Woo and Show. V. iii. 9. 大 野, a lake, III. i. Pt. i. 31; so, 豬 野, p. 77.

量
leang
liang

Measures of capacity. II. i. 8.

釐
le
li

To regulate. I. 8: V. xix. 4: xxiv. 1. Obs. 釐 降 in I. 12.

THE 167TH RADICAL. 金.

金
kin
chin

Metal. The 4th of the five elements. V. iv. 5. One of the six magazines of nature. II. ii. 7. ＝ money. II. i. 11. ＝ a weapon of steel. IV. viii. Pt. i. 6.

金三品, gold, silver, and copper. III. i. Pt. i. 44, 52.　= with metal,—adverbial. V. vi. 11, 16.

　　The name of king K'ang of the Chow dynasty. V. xxii. 7, 9, 11 : xxiii. 4.

釗
chaou
chao

鈞
keun
chün

　　(1) A weight of 30 catties, the quarter of a stone. III. iii. 8.　(2) *I. q.* 均, equal, as great. V. i. Pt. i. 9.

鉛
yuen
yüan

　　Lead. III. i. Pt. l. 26.

鉞
yuĕ
yüch

　　A kind of battle-axe. V. ii. 1 : xxii. 21.

鉅
k'eu
ch'ü

鉅橋, a place where the tyrant Show had collected great stores of grain. V. iii. 9.

銀
yin
yin

　　Silver. III. i. Pt. i. 69.

鋌
chih
chih

　　The ears of grain with a small portion of the stalk. III. i. Pt. ii. 18.

銳
juy
jui

　　Some kind of sharp-pointed weapon. V. xxii. 21.

鋒
fung
fung

　　The point of a weapon. V. xxix. 2.

錫
seih
hsi

　　To give, to confer. III. i. Pt. ii. 16. It generally = to give to, being followed by two objectives, the thing given, and the party to whom it is so. IV. ii. 2 : V. iv. 3, 9, 11, 13 : xxii. 8. To present,—as tribute or offering. III. i. Pt. ii. 23. Obs. 錫貢 and 納錫, III. i. Pt. i. 44, 52, 60.

錯
ts'ŏ
ts'o

　　(1) Stones for polishing sounding stones. III. i. Pt. i. 60.　(2) To be mixed,—as revenue made up of various proportions, and kinds of impost. III. i. Pt. i. 8, 26, 43, 59 (*n. b.*), 68.
　　To temper. V. xxix. 2.

鍛
twan
tuan

鋑
hwan
huan

　　A weight, commonly said to be of six *lëang* or ounces; but the exact amount is rather uncertain. V. xxvii. 18.

鏞
yung
yung

　　A large bell. II. iv. 9.

鏤
low
lou

　　Steel. III. i. Pt. i. 69.

鐵
t'ëĕ
t'ieh

　　Iron. III. i. Pt. i. 69.

鐸
toh
tio

　　A bell with a wooden clapper. III. iv. 3.

鑑
këen
chien

　　A mirror,—whatever reflects objects. = a case for inspection or warning. V. i. Pt. ii. 5.

THE 168TH RADICAL. 長.

長
ch'ang

　　Long. 短長, short or long. IV. vii. Pt. i. 12. What is long off, far-distant. Pt. ii. 7. As a verb,—to prolong, V. xix. 24 ; to seek to be long continuing, IV. vii. Pt. i. 15.

長
chang

　　2d tone.　(1) An elder, elders. IV. iv. 4 : xi. 5 (耆長): V. x. 6. As a verb,—to treat as an elder, to exalt. V. ii. 6.　(2) A president, presidents. II. iv. 8 : IV. vi. 10 (萬夫之長, chief of the myriad families): vii. Pt. iii. 8, and viii. Pt. ii. 2 (師長, heads of departments): V. ii. 2 (千夫長, 百夫長, captains of thousands, and captains of hundreds): xix. 6 (長伯).

THE 169TH RADICAL. 門.

門
mun

　　(1) A door, a gate. V. xxii. 11, 21, 29 : xxiii. 1. 四門, all the roads or channels of communication between the court and the empire. II. i. 2, 15.　(2) 龍門, an important pass of the Ho, near which Yu began his labours. III. i. Pt. i. 82 ; Pt. ii. 7.
　　To shut.　= to restrain. V. vii. 2.

閉
pe
pi

開
k'ae
k'ai

　　To open.　= to initiate, to bring forward. V. xviii. 5, 7 : = to stir up. p. 18. 開釋, to liberate. p. 11.

閏
jun

　　Intercalary. I. 8.

閑
heen
hsien

　　To bar.　= to keep under restraint. V. xxiv. 10.

閎
hung
hêng

　　A surname. V. xvi. 12.

間
këen
chien

　　A space between.　= to separate, to come between. V. xviii. 15 : xix. 16.　= to fill up the intervals. II. iv. 9. 牖間, between the window and the door. V. xxii. 15. Some read the character in this passage *hëen*, and in the 1st tone.
　　To think with anxiety about. V. xvi. 22. To be an object of pity. xxviii. 2.

閔
min

閟
pe
pi

　　To shut up. 閟毖, to shut up and distress. V. vii. 10.

閭
leu
lü

　　The gate of a village. V. iii. 3.

閱 *yuĕ* yüeh

(1) To examine. V. xxvii. 18. (2) To select on examination. xviii. 27.

關 *kwan* kuan

What is current or standard. III. iii. 8.

闢 *p'eih* p'i

To throw open. II. i. 15.

THE 170TH RADICAL. 阜.

阜 *fow* fou

Greatly. 阜成, V. xx. 13.

阪 *fan*

Precipitous, dangerous situations. V. xix. 11. The meaning is not well ascertained.

阻 *tsoo* chu

To be in difficulties; to suffer from. 阻飢, II. i. 18.

阼 *tsoo* tsu

The steps leading up to the hall on the east, appropriate to the host. V. xxii. 20, 23.

陂 *pe* pi

Embanked ponds. V. i. Pt. i. 5. To be banked up. III. i. Pt. ii. 14.

陂 *p'o*

To be uneven. V. iv. 14. It will be seen, however, that this was not the original reading here; and the character is commonly read p'e.

阿 *o*

阿衡, the name, or the title, of E Yin. IV. v. Pt. i. 1 : viii. Pt. iii. 10. To be attached—join one's self to. IV. ii. 4 : V. iii. 7.

附 *foo* fu

陋 *low* lou

To be in a mean condition. 側陋, I. 12.

降 *këang* chiang

(1) To send down. I. 12 : II. ii. 20 : IV. iii. 2, 3 : iv. 2, 8 : V. i. Pt. 4 ; Pt. iii. 3 : vi. 7 ; *et sæpe.* It may be variously translated,—to confer, to inflict, to deliver, &c. 降黜 = to make an end of. V. i. Pt. ii. 4. In IV. vii. Pt. iii. 4, it = to remove. (2) To descend. II. ii. 10 : III. i. Pt. i. 16 ; *et sæpe.* 降格, to descend and approach. V. xxvii. 6. = to degenerate. V. xxiv. 4. (3) To spare, to deal leniently with in respect of. V. xviii. 2, 20, 23.

陟 *chih*

(1) To ascend :— with ref. to the throne. II. i. 3 : ii. 14 : V. xix. 4 ; with ref. to death. II. i. 28 : V. xvi. 18 : xxiii. 3. (2) To travel to. IV. v. Pt. iii. 4 : xix. 22. (3) To promote. II. i. 27 : xx. 14. (4) 伊陟, son probably of E Yin, a minister of the Shang dynasty. V. xvi. 7.

除 *ch'oo* ch'u

To remove, to take away. V. i. Pt. iii. 4 : viii. 2.

陰 *yin*

Dark, obscure. 陰陽, the operations of Heaven and Earth. V. xx. 5. = secretly, by an unseen influence. V. iv. 2. = the north side of a mountain. III. i. Pt. iii. 7.

陰 *gan* an

亮陰, probably the shed where the emperor spends his time of mourning. IV. viii. Pt. i. 1 : V. xv. 5.

陪 *pei*

陪尾, the name of a mountain in the pres. Shan-tung. III. i. Pt. ii. 2.

陳 *ch'in* ch'ên

(1) To set forth ; to display. IV. vi. 1 : V. ix. 11, 13 : xxii. 5, 19. Obs. 卜 陳, V. vii. 15 ; 陳修, xi. 4 ; 有陳, xvi. 8. To be displayed. IV. xi. 1. To be marshalled, drawn up. V. iii. 8. (2) To continue long. IV. vii. Pt. ii. 11. (3) 君陳, the name of a minister, the successor of the duke of Chow in Lŏ. V. xxi. 1 ; *et al.*

陸 *luh* lu

大陸, a tract of marshy ground in K'e-chow. III. i. Pt. i. 9 ; Pt. ii. 7.

陵 *ling*

(1) A high mound, a height. I. 11 : II. iv. 1. (2) To do violence to. V. xiv. 9. (3) 東陵, the name of a place, corresponding to the pres. Pa-ling, chief city of the dep. of Yŏ-chow. III. i. Pt. ii. 9.

陶 *t'aou* t'ao

(1) In the phrase 鬱陶, anxieties, to be thinking anxiously. III. iii. 9. (2) The name of the principality over which Yaou first ruled, so that he is sometimes named from it. III. iii. 7. (3) The name of a small hill in the pres. dis. of Ting-t'aou, dep. of Yen-chow, Shan-tung. III. i. Pt. ii. 10.

陶 *yaou* yao

皋陶, the name of Shun's minister of Crime. II. i. 17, 20 : ii. 10, 11, 12 : iii. 1, 2, 3, 8 : iv. 1, 8, 11. To dam up. V. iv. 3.

陻 *yin*

陽 *yang*

(1) The sun. 陽鳥, sun binds, = wild geese. III. i. Pt. i. 39. (2) = the south side of a mountain. III. i. Pt. i. 5, 35, 46, 62 ; Pt. ii. 4. (3) 陰陽, see 陰.

隅 *yu* yü

A corner. 海隅, the corners of the seas. II. iv. 7 : V. xvi. 21.

陒 *nëĕ* nieh

A mound falling to pieces. = unsettledness. V. xx. 8.

階 *këae* chieh

Steps or stairs, leading up to a hall. II. ii. 21 : V. xxii. 20—23.

隕 *yun* yün

To fall down into. IV. iii. 6.

隨
suy
sui

隩
yuh
yü

險
hëen
hsien

隮
tse
chi

隰
seih
hsi

隱
yin

To follow, to accord with. 隨山, following the line of—all along—the hills. II. iv. 1 : III. i. Pt. i. 1.

(1) The inside, inner apartments. = to keep within the house. I. 7. (2.) Habitable ground by the water's edge) 四隩. III. i. Pt. ii. 14.

Precipitous. = alarming. IV. vii. Pt. i. 7.

(1) To fall into a ditch. 顛隮, to be going to ruin, IV. xi. 3, 8. (2) To ascend, to go up. V. xxii. 22, 23.

Low, damp ground. Swamps. III. i. Pt. i. 77.

To feel sympathy. IV. vii. Pt. iii. 8.

THE 172D RADICAL. 隹.

雀
tsëŏ
ch'iao
ch'io

集
tsieh
chi

雉
che
chih

雊
kow
kou

雍
yung

雕
teaou
tiao

雖
suy
sai

雘
hwŏ
huo

A sparrow. As an adj., describing the colour of a cap, = brown. V. xxii. 21.

To collect. Spoken of the sun and moon in an eclipse, = to meet harmoniously. III. iv. 4. Spoken with reference to the decree of Heaven conferring the empire, = to cause to light on. IV. v. Pt. i. 2 : V. xvi. 11 : xxii. 5 : xxviii. 1. = to attach, to bring together to one's-self. V. xi. 5. Foll. by 于, = to go to, to tend to. V. xviii. 15. To be collected. V. iii. 5. = to be completed. V. i. Pt. i. 5.

A pheasant. IV. ix. 1.

To crow,—as a pheasant. IV. ix. 1.

(1) To be harmonious. I. 2 : V. xv. 5. (2) 雍州, one of Yu's nine provinces. III. i. Pt. i. 10.
To carve. Carved. V. xxii. 17.

Though. III. iii. 9 : V. i. Pt. ii. 6 : iv. 13 : xii. 13 ; *et al.*

To paint with vermilion and other colours. V. xi. 4.—This character is given in the dict. under 隹, but such arrangement is evidently wrong. 隹 is merely part of the phonetic element 蒦. The true radical or element of meaning is 丹. This is another instance of the perplexity introduced into Chinese lexi-

cography by the attempt to simplify the subject through reducing the number of the radicals.

A fowl. V. ii. 5.

雞
ke
chi

離
le
li

難
nan

難
nan

To go away from, to leave. III. iv. 4 : IV. ii. 8 : vii. Pt. iii. 5. To be divided. V. i. Pt. ii. 6. 離逖, V. xviii. 29.

To be difficult. IV. vi. 2, 7 : viii. Pt. ii. 11 : V. ix. 6 : xvi. 4 : xxx. ii. To feel the difficulty of. II. iii. 2. Difficulties. IV. v. Pt. iii. 5 : vii. Pt. i. 15. 艱難, hardships and difficulties. V. xv. 2, 3, 7 : xxii. 7.

3d tone. To make it difficult for. = to discourage. II. i. 16.

THE 173D RADICAL. 雨.

雨
yu
yü

雨
yu
yü

雲
yun
yün

雷
luy
lëi

電
tëen
tien

震
chin
chên

霍
hŏ
ho

霖
lin

霽
tse
chi

靈
ling

Rain. II. i. 2 : IV. viii. Pt. i. 6 (霖雨) : V. iv. 21, 32, 33, 38 : xxv. 5.

3d tone. To rain. V. vi. 19. Perhaps the examples in V. iv., might be thus toned.

The name of a marsh. III. i. Pt. i. 50.

(1) Thunder. II. i. 2 : V. vi. 16. (2) 雷夏, the name of a marsh in Yen-chow. III. i. Pt. i. 14. (3) 雷首, the name of a mountain in K'e-chow. III. i. Pt. ii. 1.

Lightning. V. vi. 16.

(1) To move, to agitate. 震驚, II. i. 25. 震動, IV. vii. Pt. iii. 5 : V. iii. 7. 震怒, to be roused to anger. V. i. Pt. i. 5 : iv. 3. (2) 震澤, the name of a marsh. III. i. Pt. i. 41.

The name of the appanage of Ch'oo, one of king Woo's brothers, who is known as 霍叔. V. xvii. 1.

Rain continuing more than three days. 霖雨, copious rain. IV. viii. Pt. i. 6.

Rain stopping, fair weather. V. iv. 21.

What is good. IV. vii. Pt. iii. 7 : V. xxvii. 3. Intelligent. V. i. Pt. i. 3. The phrase 靈承 in V. xiv. 13, = to be charged with, on account of one's goodness ; in xviii. 5, 19, it appears to = to treat or manage well.

THE 174TH RADICAL. 青.

青
ts'ing
ch'ing

Green. III. i. Pt. i. 67.

靖
tsing
ching

Tranquillity. 不靖, dispeace. IV.
vii. Pt. i. 12. 自靖, to make one's-
self tranquil. IV. xi. 9. To tranquillize.
V. xv. 5.

靜
tsing
ching

Quiescence,—the opposite of action. V.
iv. 31. = in stillness, when employed. I. 10. To be quiet, tranquil. V. vii.
3, 7: ix. 21: xviii. 22.

THE 175TH RADICAL. 非.

非
fei

Passim. Not. It very often = it
is not, it is not that, standing commonly, but not always, at the commencement of the clause, and the clause
which follows frequently beginning with
惟 or 乃惟. *E. g.* IV. i. 1: iv.
Pt. i. 7, 12; Pt. ii. 4: V. xii. 24: xiv.
3, 18, 20. It has sometimes a hypothetical force, = if not, without. II. ii. 17:
IV. v. Pt. ii. 2: vi. 11; *et al.* Its signification is sometimes nearly that of an
adjective, = that which is not, improper.
IV. ii. 4: v. Pt. iii. 7: V. xii. 21; *et al.* =
that which is really wrong, a crime. IV.
viii. Pt. ii. 9. As a verb,—to do what is
contrary to, to transgress. III. ii. 4: IV.
xi. 2: V. xxvi. 7. Makes with 罔 an
affirmative. V. x. 3; *et al.*

靡
me
mi

(1) Not. IV. vi. 2. (2) 靡靡,
ready acquiescence, to be flatteringly
obsequious. V. xxiv. 8.

THE 176TH RADICAL. 面.

面
mëen
mien

The face. 面從, to follow to one's
face. II. iv. 5. 謀面, to judge by
the face. V. xix. 2. 北面, facing the
north. V. vi. 4. So 牆面, xx. 16. 面
alone, xxii. 20, means facing the south.
面稽天, looking up to Heaven, to
ascertain its will. xii. 11.

THE 177TH RADICAL. 革.

革
kih
ko

(1) Hides. III. i. Pt. i. 44, 52. (2)
To change, to remove or supersede. IV.
vi. 3: V. iv. 5: xiv. 6, 19. Spoken of
animals changing ther feathers and hair.
I. 5. To be changed. V. xxiv. 4.

鞠
këüh
chü

(1) To exhaust. 自鞠, IV. vii.
Pt. ii. 6. (2) To nourish. IV. vii. Pt.
iii. 10: V. ix. 16.—The meaning in these
passages is doubtful. (3) 鞠子, a
little child. V. xxiii. 6.

鞭
pëen
pien

A whip. II. i. 11.

THE 180TH RADICAL. 音.

音
yin

Musical sounds. 八音, the eight
kinds of musical instruments, = all music.
II. i. 13, 24: iv. 4. 音 alone = music.
III. iii. 6.

韶
shaou
shao

The music of Shun. 簫韶, II.
iv. 9.

響
heang
hsiang

An echo. II. ii. 4.

THE 181ST RADICAL. 頁.

順
shun

To follow, to act in accordance with.
V. i. Pt. i. 9: xxi. 6. To be obedient.
IV. v. Pt. i. 9. = to allow, to indulge.
V. i. Pt. iii. 3.

須
seu
hsü

(1) To wait. 暇須, V. xviii. 17.
(2) Necessary, requisite. V. xxii. 13.—
The meaning here may also be brought
under (1)

頑
wan

To be refractory, obstinately unprincipled. I. 12: II. iv. 6, 8: V. xxiv. 3. 頑
童, IV. iv. 7. The refractory. V. xxi. 1.

頒
pan

To manifest, distribute everywhere.
V. xiii. 13.

頗
p'o

One-sided, perverse. V. iv. 19: xviii.
29.

頷
gih
ê

頷頷, the appearance of unceasingness. II. iv. 8.

頮
hwuy
hui

To wash the face. IV. xxii. 2.

顏
yen

The face, the countenance. III. iii. 9.

願
yuen
yüan

To desire. 可願, what is desirable. II. ii. 17.

顛
tëen
tien

(1) To overthrow. 顛覆, III. iv.
4. 顛越, IV. vii. Pt. ii. 16. To
be overthrown, = felled. IV. vii. Pt. i.
4. 顛隮, to be going to ruin. V. xi.
3, 8. (2) 泰顛, one of king Wǎn's
ministers. V. xvi. 12.

類
luy
lêi

(1) A class, sorts. = the different
characters or classes. V. i. Pt. iii. 3. Of
a class. 不類, not equal to, not so
good as. IV. viii. Pt. i. 2. 自底不
類, to make one's-self unworthy. IV.

顧
koo
ku

v. Pt. ii. 3. (2) To offer a special sacrifice to God. II. i. 6 : V. i. Pt. i. 10.

To regard, to think of IV. v. P. i. 2 : xi. 9 : V. xii. 13 : xiv. 9. = to consult. IV. vii. Pt. i. 12 : V. xxiii. 6. = to examine. V. ix. 22. Observe 開厥 顧天, V. xviii. 18.

顯
hëen
hsien

(1) To be or become illustrious. V. i. Pt. iii. 2, 4, 5 : ix. 3, 4 : xiii. 14 : xxv. 6 : xxviii. 1, 3, 4. 天顯, bright principles of Heaven. V. ix. 16 : x. 5 ; *et al.* Obs. 顯民, to be illustrious with the people. V. ix. 1. = manifestly. V. ix. 21. (2) To be enlightened. IV. v. Pt. i. 5 (*n. b.*) : viii. Pt. iii. 1 : V. xiv. 9. (3) To distinguish, make illustrious. IV. ii. 7 : V. xviii. 6.

THE 182D RADICAL. 風.

風
fung
fêng

(1) The wind. II. i. 2 : V. iv. 32, 34, 38 : vi. 16, 19. 風動, to be moved as by the wind. II. ii. 13. (2) Influence. IV. viii. Pt. iii. 8 : V. xxiv. 7 (風聲 ; but this may mean—the fame of their manners). (3) Manners, fashion. IV. iv. 7 : V. xxi. 4 : xxiv. 8. (4) To feel the sexual appetite,—used of animals. V. xxix. 4.

颺
yang

(1) To speak loudly and rapidly. II. iv. 7. (2) To rewrite and publish. p. 6.

THE 184TH RADICAL. 食.

食
shih

To eat. IV. xi. 6 : V. xv. 10. Spoken of the fire licking up the ink on the tortoise-shell in divination. V. xiii. 3. 食言, to eat one's words, to be false to what he has said. IV. i. 4. To accept support. IV. viii. Pt. iii. 11. Food. II. i. 16 : iv. 1 : IV. x. 3 : V. iii. 9 : iv. 8 : v. 2. 玉食 = the revenues of the empire. V. iv. 18, 19.

飢
ke
chi

To be hungry. 阻飢, to suffer from want. II. i. 18.

飲
yin

To drink. V. x. 4, 7, 9 (崇飲), 14.

飽
paou
pao

To be full. = to satiety. V. x. 7.

餉
hëang
hsiang

To carry provisions to the labourers in the fields ; = provision-carriers. IV. ii. 6.

養
yang

To nourish. II. ii. 7. 民養, V. vii. 12, is hardly intelligble. Obs. 引養, V. xi. 3.

養
yang

3d tone. To support,—spoken with ref. to the support of one's parents. V. x. 6.

餘
yu
yü

That which is over, remaining. III. i. Pt. ii. 5 : V. xxiv. 8. 無餘刑 = all kinds of—no end of—punishments. V. xxix. 5.

餞
tseen
chien

To convoy. I. 6.

饋
kwei
kuei

To present offerings,—specially of food. 饋祀, offerings of sacrifice. V. x. 7.

鄕
hëang
hsiang

To accept,—as the wine of sacrifice. (?). V. xxii. 26.

THE 185TH RADICAL. 首.

首
show
shou

(1) The head. II. iv. 1. In the phrase 稽首, II. i. 17, 21, 22, 23 ; *et sæpe.* (2) The chief, the most important. V. xxx. 1. (3) 雷首, the name of a mountain. III. i. Pt. ii. 1.

THE 186TH RADICAL. 香.

香
hëang
hsiang

That which is fragrant. Always in connection with 馨, and spoken of virtue. V. x. 11 : xxii. 3 : xxvii. 4.

馨
hing
ch'ing

Odours smelt at a distance. 馨香, see above.

THE 187TH RADICAL. 馬.

馬
ma

(1) A horse, horses. III. ii. 4 : iii. 5. V. iii. 2 ; *et sæpe.* 趣馬, equerries. V. xix. 8. (2) 司馬, the minister of War. V. ii. 2 : xi. 2 : xix. 10 : xx. 10.

馭
yu
yü

To drive,—in a carriage. III. iii. 5.

馳
ch'e
ch'ih

To bustle and hurry about. III. iv. 4.

駿
tseun
tsun

= rapidly, hurriedly. V. iii. 3.

騂
sing
hsing

Red. V. xiii. 29.

隲
chih

To make, to constitute. V. iv. 2.

驕
këaou
chiao

To be proud. V. xxiv. 10.

驚
king
ching

To alarm. II. i. 25.

驛
yih
yi

The appearance of a want of connection. Used of one of the indications in divination. V. iv. 21.

驩
hwan
huan

驩兜, a bad minister of Yaou, punished by Shun. I. 10 : II. i. 12 : iii. 2.

THE 188TH RADICAL. 骨.

體
t'e
t'i

Form, appearance. Used of the form of a prognostic in divination. V. vi. 10. Completeness. Used of the character of a proclamation. V. xxiv. 8.

THE 189TH RADICAL. 高.

高
kaou
kao

(1) High. III. i. Pt. i. 1 : IV. v. Pt. iii. 4. The high and lofty. V. iv. 12, 17. The founder of a House, or one's remote ancestor, is described by 高. 高后, IV. vii. Pt. ii. 12, 14 : viii. Pt. i. 9. 高祖, IV. vii. Pt. iii. 6 : V. xxiii. 3. To think highly of. V. ix. 23. (2) 高宗, the sacrificial title of Woo-ting, one of the sovereigns of the Shang dynasty. IV. ix. 1 : V. xv. 5.

THE 190TH RADICAL. 髟.

髮
fă
fa

The hair. V. xxx. 4.

髳
mow
mou

The name of one of the wild tribes, confederate with king Woo against Shang. V. ii. 3.

THE 192D RADICAL. 鬯.

鬯
ch'ang

A kind of fragrant grass, used to flavour spirits. 秬鬯. flavoured spirits distilled from the black millet. V. xiii. 25 : xxviii. 4.

鬱
yuh
yü

In the phrase 鬱陶, III. iii. 9, the thoughts working anxiously and confusedly.

THE 194TH RADICAL. 鬼

鬼
kwei
kuei

In the phrase 鬼神 Spirits, spiritual beings. II. ii. 18 ; IV. iv. 2 : Pt. iii. 1 : V. vi. 6.

魁
k'wei
k'uei

Chief, the principal. 渠魁 = the chief criminals. III. iv. 6.

魄
p'ih
p'o

The disc of the moon, from the time it begins to wane to new moon. 哉生魄 is the 15th day of the moon. V. ix. 1 : xxii. 1. 既生魄, V. iii. 4, is —after the moon began to wane ; 死魄, p. 1, is the last day of the old moon.

THE 195TH RADICAL. 魚.

魚
yu
yü

Fish. III. i. Pt. i. 35 : IV. iv. 2.

魯
loo
lu

The State so called. V. xxix. 5.

鮮
seen
hsien

Fresh fish or meat. 鮮食, flesh to eat. II. iv. 1.

鮮
seen
hsien

2d tone. (1) Few ; rarely, seldom. IV. vii. Pt. ii. 3 : V. xix. 1 : xxiv. 9. (2) 惠鮮, to show a fostering kindness to. V. xv. 10.

鯀
kwăn
kuên

The father of Yu, punished by Shun. I. 11 : II. i. 12 : V. iv. 3.

鰥
kwan
kuan

An unmarried man. I. 12. In all other cases, it appears along with 寡, and probably means widowers. V. vii. 8 : ix. 4 : xv. 6, 10 : xxvii. 6, 7.

THE 196TH RADICAL. 鳥.

鳥
neaou
niao

(1) Birds. Generally in combination with 獸. I. 4, 5, 6, 7 : II. i. 22 : iv. 9 : III. i. Pt. i. 39 : IV. iv. 2 : V. xvi. 16. (2) 鳥鼠 and 鳥鼠同穴, the name of a mountain. III. i. Pt. i. 76 ; Pt. ii. 2, 12.
To collect, accumulate. I. 10.—The passage is hardly intelligible.

鳩
kew
chiu

鳴
ming

(1) The sound of a bird ; anything that emits sound is so called. 鳴鳥, V. xvi. 16, denotes the male and female phœnix. 鳴球 is the sounding-stone. II. iv. 9. (2) 鳴條 was a place near the capital of Këĕ. IV. iv. 2.
The male phœnix. II. iv. 9.

鳳
fung
fêng

鴟
ch'e
ch'ih

An owl. 鴟鴞 is the name of an ode. V. vi. 15. 鴟義, of owl-like conduct. V. xxvii. 2.

鴞
heaou
hsiao

鴞鴞, a species of owl. See above.

THE 197TH RADICAL. 鹵.

鹹
hëen
hsien

Salt (adj.). V. iv. 5.

鹽
yen

Salt (subst.) III. i. Pt. i. 26: IV. viii. Pt. iii. 2.

THE 198TH RADICAL. 鹿.

鹿
luh
lu

The deer. 鹿臺 the name of a tower where Show had accumulated his treasures. V. iii. 9.

麗
le
li

(1) To be fond of display. V. xxiv. 9. (2) To depend on ; to be connected with. 民之麗, what the people depend on for support, V. xviii. 5. 厥麗, p. 9, should, probably, be taken in the same way. 刑之麗, V. xxvii. 12, = the circumstances of penal cases ; but 麗刑, p. 8, = to be exposed to punishment.

麓
luh
lu

The foot of a mountain, II. i. 2.

THE 199TH RADICAL. 麥.

麴
k'euh
ch'ü

Leaven, yeast. IV. viii, Pt. iii. 2.

THE 200TH RADICAL. 麻.

麻
ma

Hempen, V. xxii. 22, 23.

麾
hwuy
hui

To brandish. V. ii. 1.

THE 201ST RADICAL. 黃.

黃
hwang
huang

Yellow. The colour of soil. III. i. Pt. i, 79. Yellow with gold. V. ii. 1. Light bay,—used of horses. V. xxiii. 1. The colour of hair in old men. V. xxx. 4. = yellow silks. V. iii. 7.

THE 202D RADICAL. 黍.

黍
shoo
shu

Millet ;—a kind of glutinous grain. We always find 黍稷 together. IV. vii. Pt. i. 11 : V. x. 6 : xxi. 3.

黎
le
li

(1) Black. It occurs in the phrase 黎民, meaning the black-haired people. I. 2 : II. i. 18 : ii. 2, 10 : iii. 2 : III. iii. 1 : IV. x. 1 : V. xxx. 6, 7. Some critics explain it in all these passages by 眾, all, the multitudinous. (2) All. II. iv. 7. (3) Light, spoken of soil. III. i. Pt. i. 67. (4) The name of an ancient minister. V. xxvii. 6. (5) The name of a river. V. xiii. 3. (6) 合黎, the name of a hill. III. i. Pt. iii. 5.

THE 203D RADICAL. 黑.

黑
hih
hê

(1) Black,—spoken of the colour of soil. III. i. Pt. i. 17. (2) 黑水, the Blackwater. Two rivers are mentioned of this name ; one, the southern boundary of Lëang-chow, III. i. Pt. i. 62 : one, the western boundary of Yung-chow, p. 71 ; and Pt. ii. 6.

默
mih
mo

In silence. IV. viii. Pt. i. 2.

黜
ch'uh
ch'u

(1) To degrade ; to be degraded. II. i. 27 : IV. iii. 5 : V. xx. 14. 放黜, to drive away degraded. V. i. Pt. iii. 3. 降黜 = to make an end of. V. i. Pt. ii. 4. (2) To put away. IV. vii. Pt. i. 6, 10.

黨
tang

Partiality, partizanship. V. iv. 14.

黥
k'ing
ch'ing

To brand. V. xxvii. 3.

黷
tuh
tu

To blacken, to dirty. = irreverence. IV. viii. Pt. ii. 11.

THE 204TH RADICAL. 黹

黻
fuh
fu

One of the symbols,—called that of distinguishing, from its form of two 已 placed in opposition to each other,— embroidered on the lower of the emperor's sacrificial robes. II. iv. 4.

黼
foo
fu

The figure of a hatchet,—also one of the symbols on the emperor's lower robe. II. iv. 4. 黼扆, a screen used at audiences, adorned with figures of axes. V. xxii. 14, 15, 22.

THE 205TH RADICAL. 黽.

鼈
pee
pieh

Tortoises. II. iv. 2.

THE 207TH RADICAL. 鼓.

鼓
koo
ku

A drum. II. iv. 9: III. iv. 4: V. xxii. 19 (鼖鼓).

鼗
t'aou
t'ao

A small hand-drum or rattle. II. iv. 9.

鼖
fun
fen

鼖鼓, a large drum. V. xxii. 19.

THE 208TH RADICAL. 鼠.

鼠
shoo
shu

鳥鼠, the name of a mountain. See 鳥.

THE 210TH RADICAL. 齊.

齊
ts'e
ch'i

(1) To regulate, to adjust uniformly. II. i. 5: IV. vii. Pt. i. 17: V. ii. 7, 8 (= to adjust the ranks of a fighting host): xiii. 6 (= to marshal): xxvii. 13 (foll. by 于), 19 (齊非齊). (2) Reverent, grave. V. viii. 2: xxvi. 2. (3) Impartiality,—where all is perfectly adjusted. V. xxiii. 5. (4) The State so named. V. xxii. 11. (5) 方齊, one of Yaou's ministers. I. 9.

齊
chae
chai

齊栗, the appearance of reverent dread. II. ii. 21.

THE 211TH RADICAL. 齒.

齒
ch'e
ch'ih

(1) Teeth. = elephant's teeth, ivory. III. i. Pt. i. 44, 52. (2) To be arranged according to age, to have one's place in the family roll. V. xvii. 1.

THE 212TH RADICAL. 龍.

龍
lung

(1) A dragon. One of the symbols on the upper sacrificial robe of the emperor. II. iv. 4. (2) An officer in the court of Shun, his minister of Communication. II. i. 23, 25. (3) 龍門, the name of a mountain on the western bank of the Ho, near where Yu began his labours. III. i. Pt. i. 82; Pt. ii. 7.

THE 213TH RADICAL. 龜.

龜
kwei
kuei

The tortoise, whose shell was so much used in divination. V. iv. 26—31. 元龜, the great tortoise, specially good for divination, and proper for imperial use. II. ii. 18: III. i. Pt. i. 52: IV. x. 2: V. vi. 8. So, 大寶龜. V. vii. 3. 三龜, V. vi. 9.

OMISSIONS.

Page 649. Under 变 add—(2) 南变, a place far south, supposed to be in the borders of Cochin-China. I. 5.

Page 666. Beneath 嬪 insert—*pin*.

Page 671. Under 已 add—(2) 祖已, a minister of Woo-ting. IV. ix. 2.

Page 685. Beneath 曆 insert—*leih.* li.

Page 703. Above 窒 insert—穴, *heuĕ* hsüeh. A hole. 鳥鼠同穴, the name of a mountain. III. i. Pt. ii. 12.

Page 710. Under 臣 add—(2) 臣扈, a minister of T'ae-mow. V. xvi. 7.

Page 724. After 遯 insert 遲, *ch'e* ch'ih. A surname. 遲任, IV. vii. Pt. i. 13.

ERRORS.

Page 646. Under 一, for *yth* read *yih*.

„ 651. „ 伾, „ *p'ei* „ *p'ei*.

„ 652. Art. 傅, for 嚴 and where read 嚴 and where.

Page 653. Under 僻, for *peih* read *p'eih*.

„ „ „ 克, „ *k'th* „ *k'ih*.

„ „ For 充 read 兗 (*bis*).

Page 655. Art. 凰, for male read female.

„ „ For 勱 read 勖.

„ 658. Under 厥, „ *heuĕ* „ *keuĕ*.

„ 659. „ 叨, „ *ta'ou* „ *t'aou*.

„ 661. Transfer—(2), &c., from 咎 to 咨.

„ 661. Under 單, for *an* read *tan*.

„ 662. For 囷, read 囮.

Page 663. Under 垂, for shue read shui.

„ „ „ 堪, „ k'au „ k'an.

„ „ „ 墨, „ mip „ mih.

„ 666. „ 好, „ hauo „ haou.

„ 668. Art. 宗, „ 代宗 read 岱宗.

Page 669. For the first 實, read 寒.

„ „ Under 寡, for kaw read kwa and kua.

Page 670. Art. 屏, for 3d read 2d.

„ „ Under 岱, „ tea „ tae.

„ 677. „ 惡, „ yǒ „ gǒ.

„ „ „ 愧, „ kwei „ k'wei.

„ 679. „ 惑, „ hwo „ hwǒ.

„ 681. „ 攺, „ kœ „ kae.

„ 684. „ 昭, „ chaou read ch'aou.

„ 685. „ 書, „ choo „ shoo.

„ 686. Art. 未, „ stem „ branch.

„ 687. Under 龡, „ yan „ kan.

Page 687. Under 榮, for kung read yung.

„ 689. For the radical 毋, and the one immediately following, read 毋.

Page 690. For 汗, read 汗.

„ 695. Art. 爻, for 師爻 read 爻師.

Page 695. For 父 爻 read 爻.

„ 696. Under 猾, for ywǎ read hwǎ.

„ 697. Art. 王, „ 秀 „ 季.

„ „ Under 球, „ kěw „ k'ěw.

„ 700. „ 盛, „ sh'ing „ shing.

„ 705. „ the 2d 純, for shun read chun.

„ 717. „ 誤, for woe read woo.

„ 719. „ 象, „ seany read seang.

„ 720. „ 趨, „ tsen „ tseu.

„ 721. „ 蹈, „ ta'ou „ t'aou.

„ „ „ 輸, „ hoo and hu read shoo and shu.

Page 726. Under 鐸, „ tio read to.

NOTE. Since the publication of my second volume, I have met with three Works, which supply, to a considerable extent, the place of dictionaries to the Classics. The Sinologue, who shall undertake such a dictionary, will find in them a fund of most extensive and precious materials.

[1]. The first and handiest of the three is called 經韻集字析解, 'All the Characters in the Classics and Thesaurus Discriminated and Explained.' It was published at T'een-tsin, in 1822, by an officer, called Heung Show-k'een (熊守謙), who was assisted by a son, a nephew, and a friend, in the compilation. Altogether it contains about 10,000 characters, arranged under the Radicals by the number of strokes, as in K'ang-he's dictionary, and in the order in which they occur in that Work. It gives, moreover, simply the meanings there assigned to them; but wherever a passage of the three oldest classics is quoted with a various reading in any of the more recent ones, that is pointed out. The author estimates the number of characters in 'the thirteen Classics' at rather more than 6,500; but he does not count a character more than once, though difference of name and of tone would seem to require him to do so. The Book is in two volumes, making together only 247 Chinese pages, so that the student finds it very convenient for use. [The 'Thesaurus' mentioned in the title is, of course, the 佩文韻府, or 'Treasury of Tones and Rhymes, compiled in the apartment P'ei-wăn,'—one of the great literary Works undertaken by the order of K'ang-he, and which contains nearly 9,000 characters, with their names and tones defined, and their meaning and usage fully exhibited.]

[2]. The second Work is more voluminous, and consists of two Parts :—the 四書字詁, or 'The Explanation of the Characters in the Four Books,' in 78 chapters; and 羣經字詁, 'The Explanation of the Characters in the various King,' in 72 chapters. It was originally left in manuscript by a scholar named Twan Gŏ-t'ing (段諤廷), of the district of K'een-yang (黔陽) in Hoo-nan, and was afterwards revised, re-arranged, and published, under the auspices of a Hwang Pun-k'e (黃本驥), in 1857.

The arrangement of the characters is perplexing for the student. Taking the 'Great Learning' first, the book gives a table of the different characters in it, chapter by chapter; in the same way it follows with the 'Doctrine of the Mean,' the 'Analects,' and the 'Works of Mencius.' In the second Part, we have the Yih, the Shoo, the She, the Ch'un Ts'ew, the Le Ke, the Chow Le, the three Chuen of Tso-k'ew, of Kung-yang, and of Kuh-leang, the Heaou King, and the Urh Ya, similarly dissected, no account being taken of the characters that have already occurred in the Four Books. The lexical portion follows the dissection in each Part, and the characters are taken in the order in which they have occurred in the Books. There is no arrangement of them with reference to the Radicals or to their sounds. This is troublesome to the learner; and though there is a preliminary chapter exhibiting the characters in each Book under their Radicals, much time and labour are still required to find the place of any term under examination. For the lexical portion itself, it is ample and satisfactory. The oldest definitions of the characters are given, and numerous examples of their use are adduced.

It is said, in a summary, that in the Great Learning there are 394 difft. characters; in the Doctrine of the Mean, 398 additional; in the Analects, other 616; and in the Works of Mencius, 776;—making in the Four Books not quite 2,200 characters. It is to be observed, however, that the same character is not counted twice, though it may be variously toned and enunciated.

In the Yih, again, there are 296 new characters; and in the Shoo, 456. The Index which I have compiled shows in the Shoo King altogether 1,998 different characters, counting a character for each variation of name and tone.

[3]. The third Work is of a different character and of higher pretensions than either of the above. It is called 經籍纂詁, 'A Digest of the Meanings in the Classical Books,' in 106 chapters. It was prepared, by the labours of many eminent scholars, under the superintendence of Yuen Yuen (阮元), to whom I have said, in vol. I., proleg., p. 133, we owe the grand collection of the 'Explanations of the Classics under the Ts'ing dynasty.' In an introductory chapter we have a memorial in which Yuen Yuen, then superintendent of the Transport Service on the grand canal, presents, in obedience to an order, his Work to the Emperor. It is dated in the 17th year of Kea-k'ing, or our 1812. In this digest the arrangement of characters adopted in the Thesaurus is followed.

END OF VOL. III.

DATE DUE

PL 1 10-59-50M